TABLE OF CONTENT

TECHNICAL PROGRAM

Wednesday, November 1

9:00 am - 10:30 am   **Opening Plenary and Keynote 1**

Welcome
Shahram Ghandeharizadeh and Shih-Fu Chang

10:30 am - 11:00 am   **Coffee Break**

11:00 am - 12:30 pm   **Session W2a (Systems): Web Access**

Session W2b (Content Processing): Image Processing

12:30 pm - 2:00 pm   **Lunch Break**

Los An ... er 4, 2000

Sponsored by the ACM Special Interest Groups

SIGMM, SIGGRAPH, and SIGCOMM

...In proceedings of the ACM Multimedia 2000 (Marina del Rey, CA, USA, Oct. 30 – Nov. 4, 2000) ACM, New York, 2000 pp. 23-35.

Ordering Information

Nonmembers: Nonmember orders placed within the U.S. should be directed to:

Addison Wesley Longman
Order Department
One Jacob Way
Reading, MA 01867
Tel: +1 800 447 2226

Addison Wesley Longman will pay postage and handling on orders accompanied by check. Credit card orders may be placed by mail or by calling the AWL Order Department at the number above. Follow-up inquiries should be directed to the Customer Service Department at the same number. Please include the AWL ISBN number with your order:

AWL ISBN 0-201-48566-4

Nonmember orders from outside the U.S. should be addressed as noted below:

Europe/Middle East
Addison Wesley Longman B.V.
Concertgebouwplein 25
NL-1071 LM Amsterdam
The Netherlands
Tel: +31 20 5755800
Fax: +31 20 6645334

Germany/Austria/Switzerland
Addison Wesley Longman
Verlag GmbH
Wachsbleiche 7-12
D-53111 Bonn
Germany
Tel: +49 228 98 515 0
Fax: +49 228 98 515 99

UK/Ireland/Africa
Addison Wesley Longman Ltd.
Edinburgh Gate
Harlow, Essex CM20 2JE
United Kingdom
Tel: +44 1279 623623
Fax: +44 1279 431059

Asia
Addison Wesley Longman
Singapore Pte. Ltd.
25 First Lok Yang Road
Singapore 629734
Tel: +65 264 1740
Fax: +65 266 6016

Japan
Addison Wesley Longman Japan
1-13-19 Gyukuroen Building
Sekiguchi
Bukyu-ku, Tokyo 112-0014
Japan
Tel: +81 33 266 0459
Fax: +81 33 266 0326

Australia
Addison Wesley Longman
Australia Pty. Ltd.
95 Coventry Street
South Melbourne, VIC 3205
Australia
Tel: +61 3 9697 0666
Fax: +61 3 9699 2041

New Zealand
Addison Wesley Longman
New Zealand Ltd.
46 Hillside Road
Glenfield
Auckland 10
New Zealand
Tel: +64 9 444 4968
Fax: +64 9 444 4957

Latin America
Addison Wesley Longman de Mexico
Boulevard de las Cataratas #3
Col. Jardines del Pedregal
CP-01900
Mexico D. F.
Tel: +52 5 652 2343
Fax: +52 5 568 3176

Canada
Addison Wesley Longman Ltd.
26 Prince Andrew Place
P.O. Box 580
Don Mills, Ontario M3C 2T8
Canada
Tel: +416 447 5101
Fax: +416 443 0948

ACM Members
A limited number of copies are available at the ACM member discount. Send order with payment in US dollars

ACM Order Department
P.O. Box 11405
New York, N.Y. 10286-1405

Credit card orders from U.S.A. and Canada: +1 800 342 6626
New York Metropolitan Area and outside of the U.S.: +1 212 626 0500
Fax +1 212 944 1318
Email:orders@acm.org

Please include your ACM member number and the ACM Order number with your order.

ACM Order Number: 433001
ACM ISBN: 1-58113-198-4

Notice to Past Authors of ACM-Published Articles: ACM intends to create a complete electronic archive of all articles and/or other material previously published by ACM. If you have written a work that has been previously published by ACM in any journal or conference proceedings prior to 1978, or any SIG Newsletter at any time, and you do NOT want this work to appear in the ACM Digital Library, please inform permissions@acm.org, stating the title of the work, the author(s), and where and when published.

Thursday, November 2

9:00 am - 10:30 am   **Session Th1: Keynote 2**

10:30 am - 11:00 am   **Coffee Break**

11:00 am - 12:30 pm   **Session Th2a (Systems): Resource Management**

Session Th2b (Content Processing): Image Retrieval

12:30 pm - 2:00 pm   **Lunch Break**

2:00 pm - 3:30 pm   **Session Th3a (Applications): User-Centered Multimedia Technology**

Session Th3b (Content Processing): Video Processing

3:30 pm - 4:00 pm   **Coffee Break**

4:00 pm - 5:30 pm   **Session Th4a (Systems): Multimedia Networking**

Session Th4b (Applications): Empirical and Experimental

Session Th4c (Content Processing): Object Segmentation

11:00 am - 5:00 pm   **Demonstrations**

Friday, November 3

9:00 am - 10:30 am   **Session F1: Highlight Papers**

10:30 am - 11:00 am   **Coffee Break**

11:00 am - 12:30 pm   **Session F2: Panel 2**

1:30 pm - 6:00 pm   **Doctoral Symposium**

ACM MULTIMEDIA 2000 CONFERENCE COMMITTEE

GENERAL CO-CHAIRS:
Shahram Ghandeharizadeh, University of Southern California
Shih-Fu Chang, Columbia University

PROGRAM CHAIRS:
Stephan Fischer, GMD-IPSI
Joseph Konstan, University of Minnesota
Klara Nahrstedt, University of Illinois at Urbana-Champaign

TECHINICAL DEMONSTRATION CHAIR:
Gérard G. Medioni, University of Southern California

DOCTORAL SYMPOSIUM CHAIR:
Ketan Mayer-Patel, University of North Carolina

TUTORIALS CHAIR:
Kevin Almeroth, University of California at Santa Barbara

WORKSHOP CHAIR:
Nevenka Dimitrova, Philips

PANELS CHAIR:
Richard R. Muntz, UCLA

POSTERS CHAIR:
Forouzan Golshani, Arizona State University

WEB MASTER
Roger Zimmermann, University of Southern California

PRINT PROCEEDINGS CHAIR:
Wei-Ying Ma, Hewlett-Packard Laboratories

ELECTRONIC PROCEEDINGS CHAIR:
Roger Price, University of Massachusetts Lowell

PUBLICITY CHAIR:
Michael Vernick, Bell Labs

SOCIAL COORDINATOR:
Cyrus Shahabi, University of Southern California

TREASURER:
Aidong Zhang, SUNY Buffalo

TECHNICAL COORDINATION CHAIR:
Andy Qin, University of Southern California

ASIA LIAISON:
Ming-Syan Chen, National Taiwan University
Desai Narasimhalu, KRDL, Singapore

ACM MULTIMEDIA 2000 TECHNICAL PROGRAM COMMITTEE

CO-CHAIRS
Stephan Fischer, GMD-IPSI
Joseph Konstan, University of Minnesota
Klara Nahrstedt, University of Illinois at Urbana-
Champaign

PROGRAM COMMITTEE
Brian P. Bailey, University of Minnesota
Meera M. Blattner, Community Vision, Inc.
Dave Boyer, Lucent
Nevenka Dimitrova, Phillips Research
Wolfgang Effelsberg, Univ. of Mannheim
Bob Ensor, Bell Labs/Lucent Technologies
Pete Faraday, Microsoft
Jonathan Foote, FX Palo Alto Research
Anoop Gupta, Microsoft
Muriel Jourdan, Unite de Recherche INRIA
Rhone-Alpes
Rainer Lienhart, Intel Corp.
Tom B.C. Little, Boston University
Ketan Mayer-Patel, University of North Carolina
John Nicol, InfoLibria Incorporated
Thomas Plageman, Unik Norway
B. Prabhakaran, National University of Singapore
Raj Rajkumar, Carnegie Mellon University
Lloyd Rutledge, CWI, Amsterdam
James A. Schnepf, College of St Benedict/St
John's University
William Tezlaff, IBM T.J. Watson Research
Nalini Venkatasubramanian, University of
California at Irvine
Harick Vin, University of Texas, Austin
Lars Wolf, University of Karlsruhe
Heather Yu, Panasonic Research
Aidong Zhang, SUNY at Buffalo
HongJiang Zhang, Microsoft Research China

REVIEWERS
Gregory Abowd, Georgia Tech
Joergen Ahlberg, University of Linkoeping
Wasfi Al-Khatib, Purdue University
Ralph Algazi, University of California at Davis
Ali Akoglu, Arizona State University
A. Asbun, Purdue University, USA
Gwendal Auffret, Institut National de
l'Audiovisuel (INA)
Norman I. Badler, University of Pennsylvania
Peter Bajcsy, Scientific Applications International
Corp. (SAIC)
Cagatay Basdogan, California Institute of
Technology
Reinhold Behringer, Rockwell Science Center
Ana Belen Benitez, Columbia
Nicole Berier, GMD IPSI Darmstadt

Jayank Bhalud, Arizona State University
Gordon Blair, Lancaster University
Susanne Boll, University of Ulm
Jill Boyce, Bell Labs/Lucent Technologies
Stephene Bressan, National University of
Singapore
Stephen Brewster, University of Glasgow
Hector Briceno, MIT
John Buford, GTE Laboratories
Dick Bulterman, ORATRiX Development BV
John Byers, Boston University
Kasim Selcuk Candan, Arizona State University
R. Chandramouli, Iowa State University
Eric Chang, Microsoft Research, China
Xiangrong Chen, Microsoft Research, China
W. Chou, Lucent Bell Labs
Hao-hua Chu, Intel
Teh Hung Chuan, National University of
Singapore
Mark Claypool, Worcester Polytechnic Institute
Sam Clements, Microsoft
Michael F. Cohen, Microsoft Research
Phil Cohen, Oregon Graduate Institute
Mauricio Cortes, Lucent Technologies
Geoff Coulson, Lancaster University
Roger B. Dannenberg, Carnegie Mellon
University
Arvind Dasu, Arizona State University
Nigel Davies, Lancaster University
J.F. Delaigle, Universit Catholique de Louvain,
Belgium
Olivier Delerue, Sony CSL, France
Matthias Denecke, Carnegie Mellon University
Yining Deng, HP Labs
Stef Desmet, University of Leuven
Jayanta Dey, GTE Laboratories
Jana Dittmann, GMD-IPSI
John Eakins, Institute for Image Data Research,
University of Northumbria
Gerhard Eckel, German National Research Center
for Information Technology (GMD)
Denise Ecklund, University of Oslo
Frank Eliassen, University of Oslo
Gamal Fahmy, Arizona State University
Wu-Chi Feng, Ohio State University
Edward A. Fox, Virginia Tech
Adrian Freed, CNMAT, University of Berkeley
Robert Gaglianello, Lucent Technologies
Ullas Gargi, HP Laboratories
Simon Gibbs, Sony Electronics
Allen Ginsberg, Lucent Technologies
Andreas Girgensohn, FX Palo Alto Laboratory
Ephraim P. Glinert, National Science Foundation
and Rensselaer Polytechnic University

ACM MULTIMEDIA 2000 CORPORATE SUPPORTERS

ACM Multimedia 2000 is kindly supported by:

GLOBIT GmbH	GLOBIT - Global Information Technology GmbH
Hewlett-Packard	HEWLETT PACKARD
Informix	Informix
Lucent Technologies	Lucent Technologies Bell Labs Innovations
NCR	NCR
Philips	PHILIPS

FROM GENERAL CHAIRS AND TECHNICAL PROGRAM CHAIRS

Welcome to the eighth ACM Multimedia Conference, held November 1-4, 2000 in Marina del Rey, California. The conference location is a part of the greater Los Angeles area which has been the capital of the entertainment and movie industry for several decades. During the past few years, this area has witnessed spectacular growth in the multimedia industry with many successful companies delivering multimedia applications and providing multimedia content and systems expertise. The conference complemented this setting by presenting and exploring technological and artistic advancements in multimedia. Technical issues, theory and practice, and artistic and consumer innovations brought together researchers, artists, developers, educators, performers, and practitioners of multimedia. This conference is sponsored by the Association for Computing Machinery (ACM) and its special interest groups SIGMM, SIGGRAPH, and SIGCOMM in collaboration with the SIGCHI, SIGIR, SIGMIS, and SIGOPS.

The conference would not have been a success without help from so many people who have our special thanks. We thank the members of the Technical Program Committee; each one spent countless hours finding experts to review submitted papers, reviewing papers themselves, and helping us select the very best papers. We also thank the paper reviewers who generously spent many hours reviewing papers and providing valuable feedback to the authors. We received 214 paper submissions and accepted only 36 of them--an acceptance rate of approximately 17%.

We also thank Forouzan Golshani and all reviewers of the poster paper program who did an excellent job in selecting 36 short papers from 108 submissions presented during the conference reception as part of a focus on research-in-progress. Gerard Medioni assembled a set of exciting demonstrations of Multimedia technology.

Nevenka Dimitrova did a tremendous job of organizing four outstanding workshops on emerging topics. She went out of her way to accommodate a late change on the scheduled workshop date. Kevin Almeroth brought together a very interesting tutorial program, and Richard Muntz organized two timely panels on topics that have raised nation wide debate. Ketan Mayer-Patel did a wonderful job of organizing this year's doctoral symposium.

A number of people deserve special thanks for helping with the logistics of the conference. Roger Zimmermann acted as webmaster and ensured that all information pertaining to the conference was available in a timely manner. Wei-Ying Ma oversaw the logistics of printing this proceedings, and Roger Price took responsibility for the electronic proceedings. Aidong Zhang served as Finance Chair and oversaw the conference budget. Michael Vernick spent much effort in promoting the conference as Publicity Chair. Ulrich Neumann served as Local Arrangements Chair and ensured a smooth conference operation. Cyrus Shahabi organized a wonderful banquet on a luxury yacht to bring the conference participants together. Lisette Burgos of ACM played multiple roles from providing assistance with the hotel negotiations to registration.

Lastly, Larry Rowe, the ACM SIGMM Chair, has provided so much valuable assistance with the planning and operation stages of the conference. We are very much in debt to his guidance and leadership for this conference.

General Co-Chairs
Shahram Ghandeharizadeh, USC
Shih-Fu Chang, Columbia University

Technical Program Chairs
Stephan Fischer, GMD-IPSI
Joseph A. Konstan, University of Minnesota
Klara Nahrstedt, University of Illinois at Urbana-Champaign

Keynote 1:
The Computer Revolution Hasn't Happened Yet

Alan C. Kay
Disney Fellow and Vice President of Research and Development
The Walt Disney Company

The printing press was invented in the middle of the 15th century, yet it took 100 years before a book was considered dangerous enough to be banned. 150 years before science was invented, almost 200 years before a new kind of political essay was invented, and more than 300 hundred years before a country with an invented political system (the US) could be argued into existence via the press and a citizenry that could understand the arguments. Schooling and general literacy were also fruits of the press, and also took many centuries to become established. The commercial computer is now about 50 years old and is still imitating the paper culture that came before it, just as the printing press did with the manuscript culture it gradually replaced. No media revolution can be said to have happened without a general establishment of "literacy": fluent "reading" and "writing" at the highest level of ideas that the medium can represent. With computers, we are so far from that fluent literacy -- or even understanding what that literacy should resemble -- that we could claim that the computer revolution hasn't even started. This talk will try to put a shape to the real computer revolution to come.

Dr. Alan Kay, Disney Fellow and Vice President of Research and Development, The Walt Disney Company, is best known for the ideas of personal computing and the intimate laptop computer, the inventions of the now ubiquitous overlapping-window interface and modern object-oriented programming. His deep interests in children and education were the catalysts for these ideas, and they continue to be a source of inspiration to him.

Kay, one of the founders of the Xerox Palo Alto Research Center, led one of the several groups that together developed modern workstations (and the forerunners of the Macintosh), Smalltalk, the overlapping window interface, Desktop Publishing, the Ethernet, Laser printing, and network "client-servers."

Prior to his work at Xerox, Dr. Kay was a member of the University of Utah ARPA research team that developed 3-D graphics. There he earned a doctorate (with distinction) in 1969 for the development of the first graphical object-oriented personal computer. He holds undergraduate degrees in mathematics and molecular biology from the University of Colorado. Kay also participated in the original design of the ARPANet, which later became the Internet.

Dr. Kay has received numerous honors, including the ACM Software Systems Award and the J-D Warnier Prix D'Informatique. He has been elected a Fellow of the American Academy of Arts and Sciences, the National Academy of Engineering, the Royal Society of Arts, and the Computer Museum History Center.

A former professional jazz guitarist, composer, and theatrical designer, he is now an amateur classical pipe organist.

Keynote 2:
Enabling Next Generation Streaming Media Networks

Eric A. Brewer
Co-Founder and Chief Scientist, Inktomi Corporation

The proliferation of broadband access, enhancements in production and encoding technologies and increasing consumer demand for rich, high bandwidth content are fueling the need for reliable and cost-effective streaming media delivery networks that ensure a high quality end-user experience. These networks provide a scalable infrastructure for both live and on-demand streaming media. In his keynote, Dr. Brewer will address specific IP infrastructure needs for streaming media delivery; the importance of caching, multicast and bandwidth provisioning; enhancing media delivery with network edge services; and putting it all together to create a high-performance, reliable streaming media delivery network.

Eric A. Brewer, Chief Scientist and Co-founder of Inktomi Corporation, focuses on long-term strategy and technology. Additionally, he is a tenured Associate Professor of Computer Science at U.C. Berkeley where he leads research into next-generation Internet systems, mobile computing and security. Dr. Brewer was recently featured in Forbes as a member of the "E-gang: The New Digital Entrepreneurs," Upside as one of the top 100 most influential people in the digital world in the "Elite 100," and Vanity Fair as part of the "e-Establishment 50." Dr. Brewer received Masters and Doctorate degrees in Computer Science from the Massachusetts Institute of Technology and holds a Bachelor of Science degree from U.C. Berkeley in Electrical Engineering and Computer Science. Dr. Brewer is an Alfred P. Sloan Research Fellow and is an Okawa Fellow.

A Prediction System for Multimedia Pre-fetching in Internet

Zhong Su*
Department of Computer Science
Tsinghua University
Beijing P.R.China 10084

suzhong_bj@hotmail.com

Qiang Yang *
School of Computing Science
Simon Fraser University
Burnaby BC V5A. 1S6 Canada

qyang@cs.sfu.ca

Hong-Jiang Zhang
Microsoft Research China
5F,Beijing Sigma Center Beijing
P.R.China

hjzhang@microsoft.com

ABSTRACT

The rapid development of Internet has resulted in more and more multimedia in Web content. However, due to the limitation in the bandwidth and huge size of the multimedia data, users always suffer from long time waiting. On the other hand, if we can predict the web object or page that the user most likely will view next while the user is viewing the current page, and pre-fetch the content, then the perceived network latency can be significantly reduced. In this paper, we present an n-gram based model to utilize path profiles of users from very large web log to predict the users' future requests. Our model is based on a simple extension of existing point-based models for such predictions, but our results show that by sacrificing the applicability somewhat one can gain a great deal in prediction precision. Also we present an efficient method to compress the prediction model size so that it can be fitted into the main memory. Our result can potentially be applied to a wide range of applications on the web, including pre-fetching, enhancement of recommendation systems as well as web caching policies. The experiments based on three realistic web logs have proved the effectiveness of the proposed scheme.

Keywords

Web prediction, Markov decision processes, pre-fetching, multimedia.

1. INTRODUCTION

Internet is a global distributed, dynamic information repository that contains vast amount of digitized information, and more and more such information now available in multimedia forms. However, the colossal amount of information also poses great challenge for many
Internet users struggling to access useful information in a timely manner with limited access bandwidth. An effective way to reduce such burden, or at least reduce the perceived latency in browsing or down loading is to pre-fetch or catching the requested multimedia data to the client end while the user is view the current web page or object. To achieve this, we need a

scheme to accurately predict a user's future requests. Fortunately, such prediction is increasingly feasible as more and more browsing information becomes available in web logs. This paper present an effective scheme we proposed to predict users' actions in Web browsing based on information from web logs.

Due to the increasing need for pre-fetching web documents, there has been an increasing amount of work on prediction models on the web. One popular way is to predict next URL based only on present URL. This can be regarded as a Markov model in the graph. Given the current node, what is the probability to access another nodes in the list of known URLs? This may require the knowledge of the context of the web page. Examples are the WebWatcher[6] system and Letzia[10] system. Pre-sending systems go a step further --- they focus on making use of the predictions to send documents ahead of time. Accurate prediction can potentially shorten the users' access times and reduce network traffic when pre-sending is handled correctly.

Prediction models can be either point based or path based. Point-based draw on relatively small amount of information from each session and therefore the prediction can potentially be rather inaccurate. For examples, the best model [1][16] predicts, for a confidence measure of over 50%, future documents with an accuracy of only around 30%. There has been relatively little work on path-based models in the past. These models are built based on the user's previous path data, and can potentially be more accurate. But the general belief is that they may suffer from much lower applicability because sequences with long length are rare. The aim of this paper is to dispel this myth and show that with large enough web access logs one can build an accurate enough prediction models that also come with high applicability.

In web prediction, each URL is a symbol, not numerical values. Therefore, the prediction work based on URL is the task of string symbol prediction, that is to say, predicting the next symbol given past history of symbol appearance in a given string. In this paper, we present a probabilistic path-based prediction model that is inspired by n-gram prediction models commonly used in speech-processing communities [9]. We have found that when using 3-gram and above the prediction accuracy is increased substantially whereas there is only a moderate decrease in applicability. We present a combined approach where multiple high-order n-gram models are organized in a step-wise manner. Experiments show

---

* This work was performed while the author was visiting Microsoft Research China in Beijing.

that this approach achieves a reasonable balance between precision and applicability. We also provide an efficient method to reduce our model size. Our work assumes no knowledge of user profiles as the ones required by Syskill and Webert [12], and no knowledge about linkage structures of web sites as required by WebWatcher. It's only requirement is that user sessions in web access can be logged successfully -- a requirement realistic enough to apply to a wide range of multimedia applications.

This paper is organized as follows. Section 2 relates a list of previous works to our work. Section 3 presents an algorithm for construction of the path-based model, followed by detailed presentation on the proposed prediction algorithms. Section 5 evaluates the performance of the proposed algorithm, and Section 6 presents our method of pre-sending Web document based on our predicate result. Finally the last section provides a summary of this work.

2. RELATED WORK

Prediction has been a topic of interest in traditional computer systems research. Curewitz et al [4] were the first to examine the use of compression modeling techniques to track events and pre-fetch items. They prove that such techniques converge to an optimal online algorithm. They go on to test this work for memory access patterns in an object oriented database and a CAD system. Kroeger et al [7] adapts "Prediction by Partial Match" in a different manner. The problem domain they examine was the file systems access patterns. The hit ratio of 4M caches using PPM is even higher than 90M caches using LRU.

The availability of the web related information has inspired an increasing amount of work in user action prediction. Much work has been done in recommendation systems, which provide suggestions for user's future visits on the web based on machine learning or data mining algorithms. An example is the WebWatcher system [6], which makes recommendations on the future hyperlinks that the user might like to visit based on a model obtained through reinforcement learning. Other recommendation systems include the Letizia system that anticipates a user's browsing actions by making forward explorations and the Syskill & Webert system that learns to rate pages on the World Wide Web. Compared to these systems, our path-based prediction model is obtained by building sequences of user requests of long enough length from all user actions in a user log and predicts the actions which may happens in the next m requests (m >= 1) based on statistical analysis of sequence information.

Due to bandwidth limitations, users on the Internet are experiencing increasing delays in obtaining the desired documents. In response, many researchers have designed pro-active systems that make use of predictions from a learned model to pre-fetch or pre-send documents. The work by Zukerman et al. and Albrecht et al. belong to this class. In this work, a Markov model is learned through training on a web server log based on both time interval information and document sequence information. The predicted documents are then sent to a cache of a certain size on the client side ahead of time. Similarly, Lau and Horvitz [5] have classified user queries and built a Bayesian model to predict users' next query goal or intention based on previous queries and time interval. Our work is also related to that of [11] who studied users' complete web search sequences and the work of Silverstein [13] who provided a detailed statistical analysis of log data. Compared to these systems, our algorithm only makes prediction on users' actions when it gathers enough information regarding the users' actions on a long enough sequence of such requests. When the users are observed to make short sequence visits, we do not make any predictions since such users may be making random visits on the web, and thus the next action may not be predictable. Also, two closely related works are that of [14] [15], who presented path-based prediction models. However, they did not compare the power of different n-gram models nor did they offer a hybrid n-gram model such as we do in this paper.

Our work is also related that of the collaborative filtering evaluation work of [3]. However, their work is based on point rather than sequence models. In addition, their correlation model may require too much computational resource to be applied in real time for web prediction. As noted above, our system is also different from many recommendation systems for it does not require the knowledge of web site link structure. Horvitz [5] presented decision-theoretic policies for guiding the pre-fetching decisions web contents in situations of limited or costly bandwidth. He also studied bi-gram models and found that it is useful in prediction.

3. PATH BASED MODEL

Our path-based model is built on a web-server log file L. We consider L to be preprocessed into a collection of user sessions, such that each session is indexed by a unique user id and starting time. Each session is a sequence of requests where each request corresponds to a visit to a web page (an URL). For brevity, we represent each request as an alphabet. The log L then consists of a set of sessions.

Our algorithm builds an n-gram prediction model based on the occurrence frequency. Each sub-string of length n is an n-gram. These sub-strings serve as the indices of a count table T. During its operation, the algorithm scans through all sub-strings exactly once, recording occurrence frequencies of documents' requests of the next m clicks after the sub-string in all sessions. The maximum occurred request (conditional probability $> \varepsilon$) is used as the prediction of next m steps for the sub-string. The algorithm for building a path-based model on sub-strings is described below.

In our experiment, the filtering step on a web log is according to the following steps:
1) We remove data generated by search engines from the server and import them into a database system.
2) Extract sessions from the data. For any two adjacent page visits, if the time interval between the visits is greater than a time threshold T, then these visits are considered to belong to two different sessions. Here one user session is considered as a sequence of URL requests by a single user. We find it reasonable to set the threshold T to be two hours for NASA data that we present later and 24 hours for MSN data.
3) Removes all requests with low visiting frequency according to a certain threshold θ.

All URLs whose access count is below the θ threshold is removed from the log. Based on our empirical tests to be discussed in Section 4, it is reasonable to set θ to 10 times or less in our web server logs. And we can also show that with such filtering process the precision is raised very much and the applicability is dropped not very much. In our experiments we set θ to 5.

Algorithm **PathModelConstruction**(n: *length of n-gram;* **m**: *predictive steps;* **L**: *log file*)
Begin
Filter the log file L then extract all the sessions from the L.
Initialize the hash table T that stores the occurrence of the document in m steps after n-grams.
Initialize the hash table H that stores results of this model
   For I = 1 to Total Session number
     For J =1 to Current Session Length
      If (J > n) Then
       S = previous n requests from the current position
       C = Set of distinct pages that are the next m requests
   after the current position
       For each item C' of C, Do
        T [P, C']++;
        Update H_{n_m} (P) so that it gives the C' that has
       highest T[P,C'] value $> \varepsilon$;
       End For
      End If
     End For
   End For
Return H_{n_m}
End

As a very simple example, consider a log file L consisting of the following request paths:

A,B,C,D,E
A,B,C,E,F
A,B,C,E,F
B,C,D,K,A
B,C,D,K,B
B,C,D,F,L

If we were to construct a 3-gram model and set m to two, our algorithm returns the following hash table.

Table 1: Hash table of 3-gram model

N-Gram	Prediction
A,B,C	E(100%)
B,C,D	K(66%)
...	...

4. PREDICTION ALGORITHM

Based on the n-gram prediction model constructed out of the log data, we can then make predictions on a user's clicks in real time. Let H_{n_m} be the prediction model built on n-gram model of predicting which are the most probable requests in next m steps. Our algorithm is as follows:

Algorithm **m- step n-gram+** (**P**: *user's current clicking sequence;* **n**: *minimal path length*)
  Begin
    If Length of P < m
      Then return ("No Prediction");
    Else
      Begin
       For I= max (Length (P), max Length of prediction model) downto n do
        If P is an index in hash table H_{I_m} then
         Prediction = H_{I_m} [P];
         Return (Prediction);
        End If
       End For
       Return ("No Prediction");
      End
    End If
  End

For comparison purposes, in our experiment we also test individual n-gram algorithms as defined below:

Algorithm **m- step n-gram** (**P**: *user's current clicking sequence*)
  Begin
    If Length (P) >= n and sub_string(P,Length(P)-n+1,n) is an index of H_{n_m} Then
      Prediction = H_{n_m} [P];
      Return (Prediction);
    End If
    Return ("No Prediction");
  End

As an example, assume that we have built up 1-step 3-gram and 1-step 2-gram models as H_{3_1} and H_{2_1} in the last section. Suppose that we observe that the current clicking sequence consists of only one click "DBC". In this case, the prediction algorithm checks H_{3_1} first to see if an index "DBC" exists. It finds out that the index does not exist. Therefore, it checks the 1-step 2-gram model H_{2_1} for the index "BC", which exists, thus the predicted next click is "D", according to H_{2_1}.

In the evaluation of the algorithm, we use the following measures. Let $S(m)=\{S_1, S_2,...,S_n\}$ be the set of sessions in a log file that have sequence length greater than m. We build models on a subset of these sequences, known as the training sequences, which are separated from the remaining or the testing sequences. When applying the trained model on the testing sequences, let P^+ be the correct predictions and P^- be the incorrect predictions. Because we remove the infrequent requests, the union of P^+ and P^- is a subset of S(m). Let $|R|$ be the set of all requests. We define the following measures for each learned prediction model H_{n_m}:

$$precision = \frac{P^+}{\left(P^+ + P^-\right)} \qquad (1)$$

$$applicability = \frac{P^+ + P^-}{|R|} \qquad (2)$$

In the above equations, *precision* has its similar meaning as often used in information retrieval literature, whereas *applicability* is a new measure that is different from *recall*. In particular, the notion of applicability is measures, out of all requests in the original log, the number of requests can be predicted (correctly or wrongly) by our model.

5. DOMAIN ANALYSIS AND EVALUATION
We first analyze the data set under consideration. This is the data set used in Zukerman et al.'s work on predicting user's requests [Zukerman et al. 1999 and Albrecht et al., 1998]. It consists of server log data collected during a 50-day period of time. It includes 525,378 total user requests of 6727 unique URL's (clicks) by 52,455 different IP's, consisting of 268,125 sessions.

One important piece of information about the server data is revealed in Figure 2. In this figure, the horizontal axis shows integer in log scale, designating the number of user visits (to pages). There are two curves in the figure. The upper curve "Page Ratio" depicts, for each value X on the X-axis, the percentage of pages that are visited X times or less by all users. For the same X value, the lower curve "Request Ratio" depicts, shows the percentage of accumulated visits out of all visits in the log on the pages which are visited X times or less.

$$PageRatio(X) = \frac{\sum_{i=1}^{x}|S_i|}{|S|} \qquad (3)$$

$$RequestRatio(X) = \frac{\sum_{i=1}^{x}(|S_i|*i)}{\sum_{i=1}^{\infty}(|S_i|*i)} \qquad (4)$$

Thus, for example, X=10 represents a visit count of ten times. The upper curve for X=10 shows that around 60% of pages are each visited 10 times or less, and the total number of such visits represents around 15% of all visits there are.

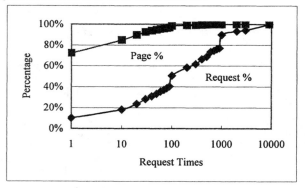

Figure 2. Page vs. request percentage for Monash University data set

We have also repeated the page vs. request ratio for one more data sets, NASA data sets, as shown in Figures 3. The NASA data set contains two months worth of all HTTP requests to the NASA Kennedy Space Center WWW server in Florida[1]. The log was collected from 00:00:00 August 1, 1995 through 23:59:59 August 31, 1995. In this period there were 1,569,898 requests. Timestamps have 1-second resolution. There are a total of 18,688 unique IP's requesting pages, having a total of 171,529 sessions. A total of 15,429 unique pages are requested. MSN data sets, as shown in Figures 4. The MSN.com log is obtained from the server log of **msn.com**, with all identity of users stripped away. It consists of data collected from Jan 27, 1999 to Mar 26, 1999, with a total of 417,783 user requests. This log contains 722 unique IP's requesting 14,048 unique pages. The MSN.com log is unique in that some requests are from groups of users submitted by Proxies or ISP's. Therefore the lengths of some sessions are long. For example, the long sessions range from 8,384 consecutive requests to 166,073 requests.

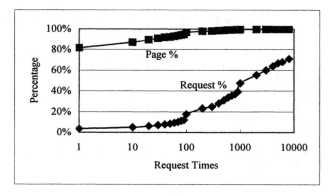

Figure 3. Page vs. request percentage for NASA data set

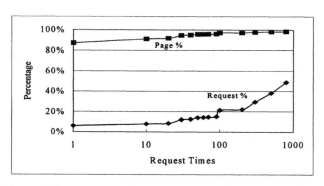

Figure 4. Page vs. request percentage for MSN.com data set

Figures 5 and 6 present the session-length distribution charts for Monash University and NASA data sets. They show, for each session length, the statistical distribution of the sessions having that many consecutive requests on a server. These charts tell us that a significant number of sessions are for one or two requests in a row. However, there are still a sizable number of requests for sessions with lengths greater than three. In fact, our prediction algorithms are aimed at just these sessions. There are several

[1]See http://ita.ee.lbl.gov/html/contrib/NASA-HTTP.html.

reasons for this choice. We hypothesize that for sessions with lengths less than or equal to three it is difficult to make any predictions with significant accuracy based purely on the statistical information. This hypothesis is supported by our individual n-gram precision experiments in all three domains, as shown in Figures 6, 8 and 10, respectively. It can be seen that for all three domains, the prediction errors are reduced significantly when one predicts based on 3-gram sequences as compared to 1-gram data.

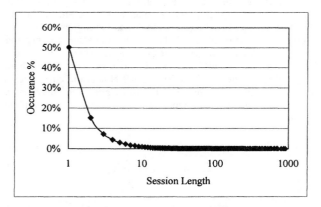

Figure 5. Session length distribution for Monash University data

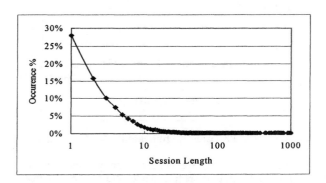

Figure 6. Session length distribution for NASA data

As can be seen from both figures, the data in all three domains follow the same pattern: a large proportion of web pages corresponds to low access ones (less than10 visits per page in the entire log), and together these visits count for a small percentage of total requests as well. Therefore removing them from training set will only decrease precision by a small amount. With the filtering process we can reduce the prediction model to 30% of its original size.

In Figure 7 we show that with the filtering process the precision is raised in high-order n-grams. In our experiments we set θ to 5 (a path must be repeat more than 4 times before it is indexed). It further justifies our filtering operation in the first step of the **PathModelConstruction** algorithm. After applying the model construction algorithm, we have built different hash tables for storing the learned models. For we have compressed the model by eliminating the infrequently occurred patterns these models can be stored in memory. To give an indication of their sizes, for

the Monash University log our **n-gram(1)** table sizes are shown in Table 2. The model size is just about 30% of its original size.

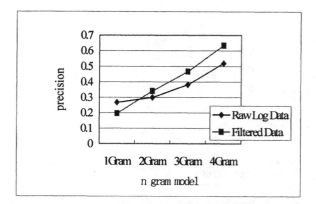

Figure 7. Comparing precision of using raw data and filtered data of different n-gram models for NASA Data

Table 2. Hash table sizes for implementing 1-step n-gram models

Hash Table	1 gram	2 gram	3 gram	4 gram
Table Size	17,434	23.763	22,804	20,958

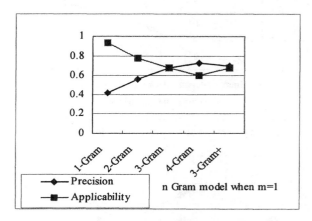

Figure 8. Precision and Applicability as a function of session lengths for Monarsh University data log.1-step n-grams (n=1, 2, 3, 4) represent precision as recorded for sessions having length greater than n.

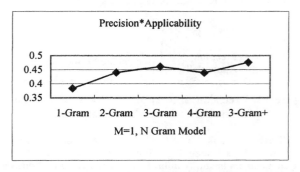

Figure 9. Precision * Applicability for Mosnarsh University data

7

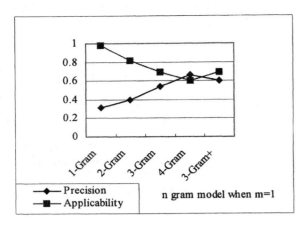

Figure 10. Precision and Applicability as a function of session lengths for NASA data log

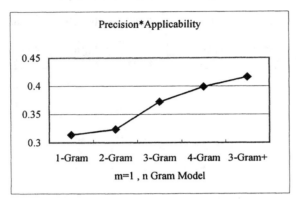

Figure 11. Precision * Applicability for NASA data

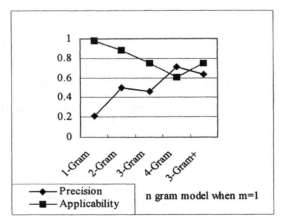

Figure 12. Precision and Applicability as a function of session lengths for MSN data log

For all data, we took 4/5 of the log as training data set and the remaining 1/5 as testing log. For each test, we recorded the precision and applicability information as described by Equations (1) and (2). We have recorded the prediction precision as a function of n where n is the path length of the sequence used for n-gram prediction. Figure 8 and 9 show the precision, the applicability and their product for the Monash University on the same scale. In these and subsequent figures, the x-axes are marked with the length of n-grams (n=1, 2, 3, 4), and the corresponding y-axes represent precision obtained when applying algorithm **n-gram** (1). The remaining mark on x-axes is "3-gram+", which represent experiments on data consisting of sessions having length greater than or equal to three for both training and testing (that is, using **n-gram+(3)** algorithm). As can be seen, our prediction using the combined 3 and 4-gram models achieved a much higher precision than using 1-gram prediction only. Also we can find that "3-gram+" has the highest predictive ability from figure 6. We have also applied the same training and testing to NASA and MSN logs data as shown in Figure 10,11,12,13. The results confirm similar conclusions. For there are too many proxies' visiting logs in MSN data the curve seems a little different. At the place of the three-gram the curve has a sudden drop. However the tendency of the curve is still confirm our conclusions.

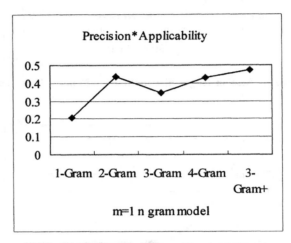

Figure 13. Precision * Applicability for MSN data

In Figures 14 and 15, we compare the precision with the prediction window size m set to 1 and 2. We can observe that the precision increases with larger window sizes.

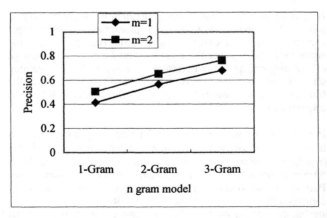

Figure 14. Comparing precision of different window sizes for Monarsh University data

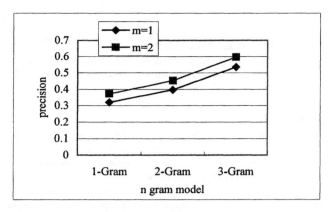

Figure 15. Comparing precision of different window sizes for the NASA data

6. PRE-SENDING DOCUMENTS

Our algorithm predicts, for a given observed path P, the likely documents that are requested by the user within the next window size m. Let the predicted documents that occur within that window be D; D is the set of documents that our n-gram models predict will most likely be accessed. To help the user increase the accessing performance, we can allocate a buffer on the client side, and pre-send these documents to the user via this buffer. Suppose that the buffer has a size of B, and is filled with the top-ranking subset of D. What we are interested in now is how many of the pre-sent documents are actually useful within the next window of size m. This can be measured by the traditional measure of *recall,* defined as the percentage of relevant documents R that are pre-sent and stored in the buffer out of all relevant documents there are.

More precisely, recall that m is the number of documents that actually occurred after a path P of documents is accessed. Let R^+ be the subset of predicted documents D that actually are requested by the user within the next window. Then recall is defined as:

$$recall = \frac{R^+}{m} \qquad (5)$$

Similarly, we can extend our earlier definition of precision by taking into account that, out of *B* documents that we predict will be accessed, R^+ of them are actually accessed. Thus, we have

$$precision = \frac{R^+}{B} \qquad (6)$$

As all other IR systems, we expect precision and recall to complement each other when the buffer size increases.

We have run experiments on the NASA data, as shown in Figures 16. In this experiment, we set the window size to 2 (that is, we predict the next document and the one after next), and increase the buffer size from one to 11. As we can see, as the buffer size increases, the precision decreases while the recall value increases

dramatically. We can also observe that for buffer size = 2, the 3-gram model makes the best combination of precision and recall. As the n in n-gram model decreases, the precision and recall all correspondingly decrease. This further strengthens the importance of our new concept of *applicability,* which as we learned from the last section has the lowest value for 3-gram models as compared with 1- and 2-gram models. For pre-sending systems, one needs to measure their performance using all three measures of applicability, precision and recall.

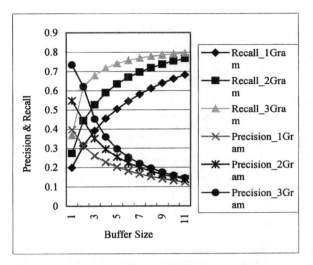

Figure 16. Precision and Recall in the NASA data set for window size two

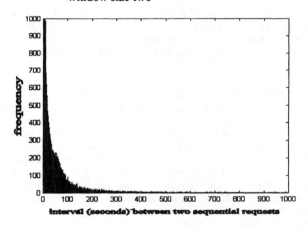

Figure 17. The distribution of users' Requests interval in the NASA's log

Figure 17 shows the distribution of users' requests interval in NASA's log. The horizontal axis is the interval (seconds) between two sequential requests and vertical axis is the frequency of that interval appears in the log. According to NASA's log the average interval between two requests is 95.37865 seconds, which is more than one minute. It will be great helpful if we do pre-fetching during the intervals, especially when user visits page that contains big sized components like image, audio and video data.

We have done a pre-fetching simulation on NASA's data by using 3-Gram+ as the prediction algorithm. We set the buffer size to one in this experiment. Our per-fetching strategy is as follows: once user's requested documents are transferred completely and the next request has not received at the server side we will pre-fetch one document by using our algorithm. The pre-fetching process will be cancelled if the next request from this user is different from our prediction result and the true request has been received at the server side.

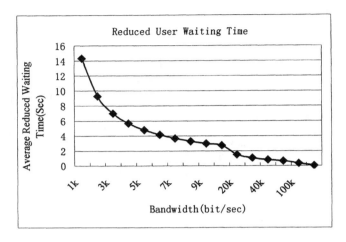

Figure 18. Reduced user requests waiting time under different bandwidth condition by using 3-Gram+ algorithm on NASA's log.

Our experiments test that how much time is saved using pre-fetching this way. Results are shown in Fig 18 as a function of network bandwidth. It can be seen that users' waiting time is reduced by pre-fetching documents using our algorithm, and such reduction increases with bandwidth decreasing.

7. CONCLUSIONS AND FUTURE WORK

In this paper, we have presented an n-gram based model to utilize path profiles of users from very large web log to predict the users' future requests. Our work is aimed at reducing perceived latency when a user is browsing Web content, especially when there are many multimedia objects in a give Web page. Our algorithm is based on the idea that n-gram models for n greater than two will result in significant gain in prediction accuracy while maintaining reasonable applicability. Our experiment results show that for n-gram based prediction when n is greater than 3 gives a precision gain on the order of 10% or more for the two realistic web logs. Our combined algorithm **n-gram+(3)** shows a higher precision than individual 3-gram model and slightly lower than 4-gram model, while at the same time having applicability equal to that of the 3-gram model and higher than that of the 4-gram model. This shows that the **n-gram+(3)** algorithm applies to a significant portion of the web logs for it to be useful. Our results also show that both the training and prediction algorithms can be applied in a real time setting. Our algorithm has immediate applications in web server caching, pre-sending and recommendation systems.

This work is one of several core components of the undergoing framework of adaptive content delivery. To further improve the applicability of the proposed predication algorithm, an important

feature work is to develop schemes for integrating the predication algorithm with cost models for catching and pre-fetching of multimedia content.

8. ACKNOWLEDGMENTS

We thank Steven Johnson of MSR Web Support Group and David Abrecht and Ingrid Zukerman from Monash University for sharing their web log data with us.

9. REFERENCES

[1] Albrecht, D. W., Zukerman, I., and Nicholson, A. E. 1999. Pre-sending documents on the WWW: A comparative study. *IJCAI99 – Proceedings of the Sixteenth International Joint Conference on Artificial Intelligence.*

[2] Balabanovic, M. 1998. Exploring versus exploiting when learning user models for text recommendation. *User Modeling and User-adapted Interaction* 8(1-2):71-102.

[3] Breese J., Heckerman D. and Kadie C. 1998. Empirical Analysis of Predictive Algorithms for Collaborative Filtering. *Proceedings of the Fourteenth Conference on Uncertainty in Artificial Intelligence, Madison, WI, July, 1998.*

[4] Curewitz K M, Krishnan. P and Vitter. J. S. 1993. Practical Prefetching via Data Compression. *SIGMOD Record,22(2):257-266 . ACM, Jun. 1993*

[5] Horvitz, E. 1998 Continual Computation Policies for Utility-Directed Prefetching. *Proceedings of the Seventh ACM Conference on Information and Knowledge Management, November 1998.*

[6] Joachims, T., Freitag, D., and Mitchell, T. 1997 WebWatch: A tour guild for the World Wide Web. *IJCAI 97 – Proceedings of the Fifteenth International Joint Conference on Artificial Intelligence,* 770-775.

[7] Kroeger T M and Darrell D.E. 1996 Predicting Future file-System Actions From Prior Events. *Proceedings of the USENIX 1996 Annual Technical Conference. Jan 1996*

[8] Lau T., and Horvitz, E., 1999 Patterns of search: analyzing and modeling web query refinement. *User Modeling '99,* pp119-128.

[9] Lee, K. F. and Mahajan, S. 1989. Automatic Speech Recognition: The Development of the SPHINX System. *Kluwer,* Dordrecht, The Netherlands.

[10] Lieberman, H., 1995. Letizia: An agent that assists web browsing. *IJCAI95 – Proceedings of the Fourteenth International Joint Conference on Artificial Intelligence,* 924-929.

[11] Maglio, P. P., and Barrett, R. 1997 How to build modeling agents to support web searchers. *User Modeling: Proceedings of the Sixth International Conference,* UM97, 5-16.

[12] Pazzini, M., Muramatsu, J., Billsus, D., 1996. Syskill and Webert: Identifying Interesting web Sites. *Proceedings of the AAAI 1996.,* Portland, OR., pp54-62.

[13] Silverstein, C., Henzinger, M., Marais, H., and Moricz, M. 1998. Analysis of a very large AltaVista query log. *Technical Report 1998-014,* Digital Systems Research center, Palo Alto, CA.

[14] Pitkow J. and Pirolli P. 1999 Mining Longest Repeating Subsequences to Predict WWW Surfing. *Proceedings of the 1999 USENIX Annual Technical Conference.*

[15] Schechter, S., Krishnan, M., and Smith, M.D. 1998, Using path profiles to predict HTTP requests. *Proceedings of the*

Seventh International World Wide Web Conference Brisbane, Australia.

[16] Zukerman, I., Albrecht. W., and Nicholson, A., 1999. Predicting user's request on the WWW. *UM99 – Proceedings of the Seventh International Conference on User Modeling.*

A Caching and Streaming Framework for Multimedia

Shantanu Paknikar
Wipro Technologies
72, Electronic City,
Bangalore 560001
+91-80-3464851

shantanu.paknikar
@wipro.com

Mohan Kankanhalli
School of Computing
National University of
Singapore
Kent Ridge,
Singapore
(65) 874-6597

mohan@comp.nus.
edu.sg

K.R.Ramakrishnan
Department of
Electrical
Engineering
Indian Institute of
Science, Bangalore
+91-80-3092441
krr@ee.iisc.ernet.in

S.H.Srinivasan
Department of
Computer Science
University of
California,
San Diego
shs@cs.ucsd.edu

Lek Heng Ngoh
Kent Ridge Digital
Labs
21 Heng Mui Keng
Terrace
Singapore 119613
lhn@krdl.org.sg

ABSTRACT

In this paper, we explore the convergence of the *caching* and *streaming* technologies for Internet multimedia. The paper describes a design for a streaming and caching architecture to be deployed on broadband networks. The basis of the work is the proposed Internet standard, Real Time Streaming Protocol (RTSP), likely to be the *de-facto* standard for web-based A/V caching and streaming, in the near future. The proxies are all managed by an 'Intelligent Agent' or 'Broker' - this has been designed as an *enhanced RTSP proxy server* that maintains the state information that is so essential in streaming of media data. In addition, all the caching algorithms run on the broker. Having an intelligent agent or broker ensures that the 'simple' caching servers can be easily embedded into the network. However, RTSP does not have the right model for doing broker based streaming/caching architecture. The work reported here is an attempt to contribute towards that end.

Keywords
Caching, Streaming, Proxies, Broker, Layered coding, Replacement Policy, Hit Ratio, Quality Hit Ratio.

1. INTRODUCTION
High-speed local area networks (LANs) are now being widely deployed all over the world. Users on such LANs usually access the Internet (the web) through a proxy server, which also caches, or stores a copy of, popular objects on the local disk(s). The advantages of web caching have been discussed in a number of papers; these have been listed in [1]. If a media file is being retrieved, the download delay can be minimized by means of the *streaming* paradigm, in which *a media file is played out while it is being received over the network.* For an introduction to streaming, refer [1].

We envisage the future of the World-Wide-Web as one involving a large number of streaming transfers of A/V content. Most such transfers would take place with the streaming data passing through one or more of the transparent proxy servers caching the streaming data as it passes through. Effective Web caching techniques will be critical for the successful deployment of streaming multimedia services over the World-Wide-Web. This should be obvious, because of the huge latencies involved, and the requirements of real time play out. However, existing web proxy caching systems have been designed for web pages (HTML documents). Such systems need to be modified for retrieval of streaming A/V data.

In this paper, we describe the design of a media caching framework in which the local broadband network has a number of co-operating caching servers for A/V content, all managed by an 'Intelligent Agent' or 'Broker'. We believe that such a system will use the proposed Internet Standard, Real Time Streaming Protocol (RTSP) in place of the Hypertext Transfer Protocol (HTTP), to implement the streaming of the media data. Thus, not only the server and clients, but the caching proxy servers too, will all 'talk' RTSP. Information on RTSP is available in [2]. This paper describes a framework for the working of such a distributed caching and streaming system. Earlier web caching concepts and algorithms have been modified for the proposed framework. Several novel issues have been identified, and new approaches to tackle them have been proposed.

2. PROPOSED ARCHITECTURE[1]
The architecture consists of a high-speed local network, which contains a number of caching proxy servers. One of these functions as the broker or central controlling agent and the others act as sibling caching proxies. The broker is an *enhanced RTSP proxy server*, and performs the standard caching functions as well as handling the streaming issues. All client requests are transparently routed through the broker. The broker maintains the state information that is so important in all the RTSP sessions. Having an intelligent agent or broker ensures that we can embed the 'simple' caching servers into the network. Another new feature of the proposed architecture is that a server

---

[1] This architecture has been earlier described in [7]. The work reported here is a collaborative effort with the author of [7], and is to be incorporated into that framework.

is allowed to source the content into the caches ahead of any client requests. Thus, the source may not be on-line all the time but its *content* can always be assumed available and hosted in one or more of the caching proxy servers. Besides being used for the obvious purpose of load balancing, the sibling caching proxy servers are individual RTSP proxies in their own right. This enables the broker to transfer control to them efficiently whenever needed. For example, in case of a sibling 'hit', the broker can send an RTSP REDIRECT control command to the client with a pointer to the appropriate caching proxy, which has the clip. The streaming would then take place in an RTSP session from the caching proxy to the client. The sibling proxies do not communicate with each other, it is the broker which manages all the interactions.

As a representative case of caching of multimedia objects, we consider video object caching. We also show how our system can be optimized for the caching of scalably encoded or *layered* video objects. Such objects will have a 'base' layer containing essential information, and one or more 'enhanced' layers containing higher level information. We believe that the framework described in this paper will take advantage of layered coding when the number of layers is between 5 and 10. Such coding schemes have already been proposed [3], [10]. We use RTSP as the basis of our work here as we believe that it is likely to be the de-facto standard for web-based A/V streaming. However, RTSP does not have the right model for doing broker based streaming/caching architecture. Our work is an attempt to contribute towards that end. Additionally, our work is probably applicable to the manipulation of non-live video clips only.

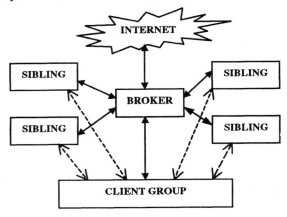

Figure 1. The proposed caching and streaming architecture. The initial interaction is always through the broker. The broker may transfer control to the siblings. The dashed lines indicate that a regular RTSP session can exist between a sibling and a member of the client group.

3. PROPOSALS
3.1 The Auxiliary Cache
As described by the architecture in section 2, the media caching system will be distributed over the broker and it's siblings. The main cache will be a single logical entity physically spread over the disks of the broker and it's siblings. The broker will need to carry out the indexing and retrieval of the information distributed across the proxy servers in an efficient manner. To aid the broker in this task, we use a data structure containing only the *information* related to the cached objects. We call this the 'auxiliary cache', and it is located on the broker (in memory). The idea is adapted from [6]. The auxiliary cache aids the broker in indexing the entries, and allows it to locate the required A/V clip easily. Its use ensures that the broker needs to access the disk caches only for the actual data writing tasks.

3.2 Replacement Policies
The 'weight' of the clip is a measure of its relative importance as compared to the other clips. Thus, higher the weight, lower should be the probability of the clip being replaced. The standard replacement policies are Least Recently Used (LRU) and Least Frequently Used (LFU) policies. In LRU, the weight is inversely proportional to the time since the last access of the object. In LFU, the weight is directly proportional to the number of times the object is accessed. We also have policy based on the size of the objects (SIZE), in which the weight is proportional to the size of the clip raised to some exponent. The value of the exponent determines whether the policy is biased towards smaller or larger objects, as explained in the last portion of this section. In addition, we have a policy called LFU_admin, which is the LFU policy combined with an admission control policy. [Section 3.4] Finally, we experiment with a hybrid policy (HYBRID) proposed in [9], and compare the results with the standard policies. In the hybrid policy, the weight w is computed as

$$w = F^f S^s R^r$$

where F is the number of times the clip is accessed (frequency), S is the size of the clip (size) and R is the time since the last access for the clip (recency). The three exponents f, r, and s are chosen by trial and error. The value for f should be a positive number, meaning that more frequently accessed objects are more likely to be cached. The value of r should be a negative number, such that more recent objects (i.e. those with a smaller value of R) are more likely to be cached. The value of s can be either positive or negative. A positive value would favor caching large objects over small ones. If recency is determined to be more important than frequency, the absolute value of the exponent r should be greater than that of the exponent f.

3.3 New Replacement Policies
The framework proposed takes advantage of clips that are scalably encoded into layers to provide a better Quality-of-Service (QOS) to the clients. The typical number of layers could be between five and ten. Layers higher up (upper enhancement layers) in general, will contain less important information as compared to the lower layers, including the base layer. For the replacement policy, we propose a new *layered* approach: The system caches clip layers as separate objects. These are sorted according to their weights, as computed below:

$$w_l = w\left(\frac{1}{n}\right)$$

where w_l is the weight of the layer, w is the weight of the clip, and n is the number of the layer (for the base layer, $n = 1$). The layers are then successively deleted in decreasing order of their weights until enough space is created for the incoming object. Thus, the highest (least significant) layer of the lowest weight object is deleted first. This policy ensures that the caching system is very robust to transients in the workload, because clips will be deleted from the cache gradually rather than at once. This will increase the chances of at least the base layer of clips being present on the caching system. Clips could also be admitted into the cache one layer at a time, however our experiments [5.2] show that the best results are obtained when the entire incoming object is cached.

3.4 Admission Control

The idea of having admission control is that a clip should be cached only provided it can offset the loss of the clip(s) it replaces. This will make the caching scheme less sensitive to transients in the workload. The outcome of the admission control is either positive or negative. We use the algorithm proposed in [6]. This algorithm checks whether the incoming clip has greater weight than the least weight clip already cached, and has size less than the least weight clip. The result is positive if both conditions are satisfied. A detailed explanation may be found in [1].

3.5 A novel Performance Metric

The system uses the standard performance metrics of 'Hit Ratio' and 'Byte Hit Ratio', defined in several papers [1]. In addition, we now propose a new performance metric, which we call the *Quality hit Ratio*.

3.5.1 Quality Hit Ratio

The proposed proxy caching system is designed to handle layered video clips in addition to standard non-layered ones. Therefore, we cannot do with performance metrics as simple as Hit Ratio and Byte Hit Ratio, because they do not reflect on the *quality* of the video clip that is being returned to the client. In general, more the number of layers of a clip present on the cache, better the quality. Whenever a request for an object is received, the broker converts it to a request for the necessary layer(s) and forwards the request to the source. Whenever a new object (layer) comes into the cache, older objects must be purged from it. We have proposed in section 3.3 that the purging of unnecessary objects be done on a layer by layer basis. Thus, at equilibrium, the system is made up of a number of stored objects, which may or may not have all of their layers present. A cache 'hit' for such a system would occur whenever at least one layer of the requested object is present on the cache.

The system performance will then be reflected not only by a high Hit Ratio; but also by the *quality* of the objects being returned to the clients; that is the quality of the hits. A *high quality hit* implies that almost all layers of that object are present, because a larger number of layers ensure better quality for users. Thus, we state that:

"Not only should any such system maximize the probability of a Hit, but it should also simultaneously maximize the probability of the Hit being of as high quality as possible".

We therefore introduce the twin concepts of *quality hit* and *quality hit ratio*. We define the *quality hit* as a number between 0 and 1 indicating how many out of the total number of layers of that object, are present on the cache. A quality hit of 1 implies that all layers of that object are present. Correspondingly, a quality hit of 0 implies a cache 'miss'. (That is, not even the base layer is present).

Ensuring that at least the base layers of the most popular objects are stored on the system maximizes the hit ratio. Now, if as many layers of the cached objects as possible are stored, the quality of these hits is maximized. Finally, we define the *Quality Hit Ratio* as

$$Q_h = \frac{\sum_{i=1}^{H} \frac{n_i}{L}}{H}$$

where H is the total number of hits, L is the total number of layers for each object, and n_i is the number of layers present for object I.

3.6 Simultaneous Request Policy

Standard caching proxies deal with small[2] objects. For any object, the session between the proxy and the client lasts for a very short time. Thus, staggered requests for the same object can be easily dealt with. By staggered requests we mean that a new client requests an object while that is being served to another client from the source. In this case, the proxy can either ask the client to wait until the present object is cached, or start a separate session with the source for the new client.

However, the above approach will be highly inefficient when the proxy is streaming A/V content to the client. This is because each session in this case will last for a much longer time, and the cost associated with setting up a new connection to the source would be quite high. We propose a new approach, which we call the *simultaneous request policy*, for the case of clients requesting the same clip at staggered intervals. In particular, the proposed scheme takes advantage of the bandwidth mismatch between the local network and the external link to give each successive client (after the first) a slightly better Quality of Service. The bandwidth mismatch is such that the bandwidth between the broker and the client B_{bc} is greater than or less than the bandwidth between the broker and the source, B_{sb}. Thus
$$B_{bc} = k(B_{sb})$$
Where k is any positive real number. For campus networks and corporate intranets, $k > 1$ as the local network is much faster than the external link. In this case, consider the case when a client is being streamed a clip from the external link, through the broker. The bit rate available to the client is limited by the bit rate on the external link, B_{sb}. Let the file size of the clip be denoted by *FILE_SIZE*. Also, the broker caches the clip as it passes through to the client – this is the 'cut-through' caching concept explained in the RTSP draft. Let the portion of the clip cached at time t be denoted by *AVAIL_VIDEO*. Now, if at this time t, another client requests the same clip, it is possible to

---

[2] 'Standard' web objects include html files, small inline images, etc. which have sizes of the order of a few KB.

serve the clip to him at a speed $k(B_{sb})$. The value for k can be shown to be [1]

$$k < \frac{FILE\_SIZE}{(FILE\_SIZE - AVAIL\_VIDEO)}$$

The second client can thus avail of a higher bit rate and a better QOS.

4. IMPLEMENTATION DETAILS

The caching algorithms have been simulated using C. The simulation is driven by a 'trace file', a log file of an actual proxy cache showing the access pattern of requests for some period. *What we really need is a trace file showing the RTSP requests, however such a trace file is not yet available anywhere.* Instead, we use trace files of HTTP requests taken from two proxy servers in IISc. A justification for using these traces is given in the next section. All the experiments are performed in some 'window size.' This is essentially how far back into the trace files to look. For a particular cache size, after the cache is full, the algorithms will stabilize (in terms of hit ratio or any other performance metric) after some time. For the cache sizes and clip sizes that we have used in our experiments, we have found that a window size of 30,000 to 40,000 requests is enough to study the cache behavior.

4.1 Justification of the traces used

The trace-driven simulation approach is the standard one in web caching experiments. For media clips, trace files of this nature are not yet available anywhere, as a proxy caching system exclusively for streaming of A/V clips has not yet been implemented, to the best of our knowledge. Given this situation, we use HTTP traces as the inputs to our simulation. We believe that to some extent, the HTTP traces will reflect user access patterns for media clips too, provided the local network is a broadband one. A justification for this is presented below.

The broker receives requests for A/V clips from a number of clients. For our problem, these A/V clips will invariably be embedded objects in web pages. Even if they are independent presentations, the user will invariably be 'led' to them through a link from some web page. The justifications are:

- RTSP has been designed for the web and is a proposed *Internet* standard.
- It is likely that web pages of the near future might have tags, which point to an RTSP URL instead of an HTTP URL.
- RTSP will not replace HTTP totally. In fact, they will *coexist*. HTTP servers will continue to serve web pages as always. If the web page has a link to a media resource, the client request for that resource is transferred by the HTTP server to the RTSP (media) server. From that point onwards, the client interacts with the RTSP server.

We therefore believe that an overwhelming majority of requests to RTSP servers will be a result of 'transfer of control' from HTTP servers, and a negligible number of requests will be direct requests. Thus, there will be a 'mapping' of HTTP requests to RTSP requests. Thus, if a web page is very popular, then it is quite likely that a clip(s) to which there is a link on that page is

also very popular. This is valid considering the three points mentioned above.

The above means that the request *distributions* for RTSP, that is the user access patterns should be similar to those for HTTP. The differences will be in the mean object size, the standard deviation, and the minimum and maximum object size. In any case, these factors do not influence the performance of the newly proposed layered caching policies [5.2] – they only help determine the maximum cache size necessary for the system to reach equilibrium.

Generating the access patterns has the difficulty that we still do not know what will be the request distribution. In the absence of such data, it appears that using the HTTP patterns is the best option available. An important point is that the only condition for the newly proposed caching algorithms to work well is that the accesses follow a zipf – like distribution[3]. It is well known that HTTP trace files follow a zipf-like distribution [8].

4.2 Analysis of the input trace file

It is important to know the nature of the trace data (the access patterns) used for the simulation. We plot the user access patterns as a rank v/s frequency diagram (the zipf distribution) where the most popular or most frequently accessed document has rank 1. The frequency versus rank plot for the trace file under consideration is shown below.

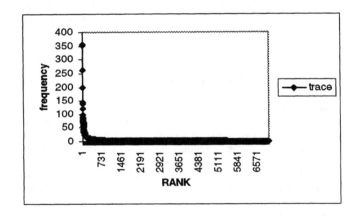

Figure 2. Frequency versus Rank plot for the trace file, indicating object popularity

Similar plots have been obtained for other trace files[4]. The plots confirm the general observations that a few objects are accessed extremely often, while a large number of objects are accessed relatively infrequently.

---

[3] Video-On-Demand literature such as [11] suggests that the popularity of video objects can be modeled using the well-known *zipf distribution*.

[4] These have not been included because of space constraints.

5. RESULTS

5.1 Modified Replacement Policies

The standard caching policies that have been compared are Least Recently Used (LRU), Least Frequently Used (LFU), Size (SIZE), LFU with admission control (LFU_adm) and a hybrid policy (HYBRID) based on LFU, LRU and SIZE [1], [9]. The comparisons are made on the basis of hit ratio and byte hit ratio. In all cases except LFU_adm, the incoming object is always cached. This is to take into account the recency factor, as the incoming object is the most recent. The results are shown in figure 3.

It is interesting to note that the LFU policy outperforms the LRU policy in all the tests, suggesting that for proxy caching, frequency is of greater significance than recency. Also, the importance of the clip size cannot be discounted. Possibly, the best algorithm would be one that would take into account all three factors. The HYBRID policy serves this purpose, and outperforms the others as shown below.

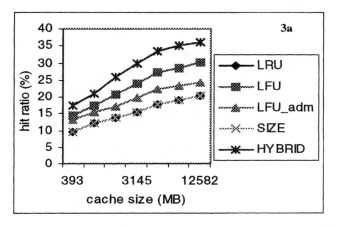

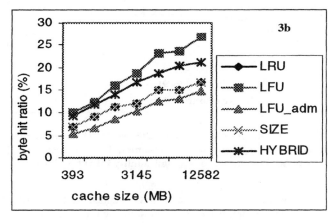

Figure 3. Performance comparison of modified replacement policies with a) hit ratio and b) byte hit ratio plotted against cache size

Our experiments show that the optimum values of the parameters of the HYBRID policy are r = 0, f = 2 and s = -1.5. Thus, the r exponent must be set to 0 for best results. We thus conclude that frequency and size are major factors that determine which objects should be purged from the cache. The incoming object is always cached, and it is here that the temporal locality or recency of requests comes into play. Thus, the object that is admitted into the cache is the incoming one (since there is a high probability that it will be requested again soon). However, the object(s) that is (are) purged from the cache are those with the least weight as determined by the respective replacement policy. Another observation is that byte hit ratio is usually smaller than standard hit ratio. We speculate that this is so because the most profitably cached objects are small ones[5]. We also see that the admission control does not improve the performance. The possible reason is this. The incoming object is the most recent object. If the admission control result is negative, this object is prevented from coming into the cache. Thus, if the traces exhibit the property of recency, then the system performance could deteriorate. Since this is the case in our experiments, it is likely that the traces have some degree of recency.

An important observation from the results is if hit ratio is the performance metric to be maximized, then the HYBRID policy is the best, as shown in the first plot. However, as can be seen from the second plot, the byte-hit ratio is maximized for the LFU policy.

5.2 Layered Replacement Policies

Based on the layered replacement approach mentioned earlier [3.3], we introduce two new layered caching policies: Object-In-Layer-Out (OILO), and Layer-In-Layer-Out (LILO). We compare these with the standard approach used in web caching, which we call Object-In-Object-Out (OIOO). These three policies are then combined with the standard ones [5.1], to give new policies.

Table 1. Layered Replacement Policies

Policy	Incoming Object	Outgoing Object
OIOO	FULL CLIP	FULL CLIP
OILO	FULL CLIP	LAYER
LILO	LAYER	LAYER

In general, whenever the broker in our layered caching system receives a request for a video clip, either a full or partial HIT (or a full or partial MISS) may occur. Here, a 'full' hit implies that all layers are present. In case of a partial HIT, the broker translates the request into one for the 'missing' layer(s) and forwards it up to the source. Now, in a non-layered caching system, the objects stored are complete clips. However, in our type of a layered video caching system, the objects stored by the broker are *layers* of the clips, not the clips themselves.

---

[5] A frequency versus size plot confirms this for HTTP traces. Whether this is true for RTSP traces remains to be seen.

This point is important because, in the first case, for a given cache size, the system's maximum capacity will be to store some N objects. However, in the second case, for the *same* cache size, the system's maximum capacity will be to store $k*N$ objects, where $(1/k)*clip\_size$ is the size of the base layer. Thus, we would expect that for a layered video caching system, the hit ratio for a given cache size would be higher, but the quality hit ratio would be lower. (A 'non–layered' caching system would have a quality-hit ratio of 1).

The implications of the new and simple concept of 'Quality hit ratio' that we have proposed, are worthy of notice. Assuming that clips are available in layered form, a simple paradigm shift in the manner of their retrieval, storage, and removal from the caching system results in the following distinct benefits.

Retrieving one layer at each object request results in an implicit form of admission control. Initially, only one layer is retrieved, the other layers are successively retrieved provided the clip is requested often enough. The layered retrieval increases the probability of providing streaming access to the clip, since the individual layers will require a lower bit-rate as compared with the full clip. Another point to be noted is that retrieving one layer at a time instead of the whole clip results in better load balancing of the external Bsb link – a larger number of requests can simultaneously handled.

Secondly, the hit ratio goes up. This is because, it is possible to tune the system to result in a Quality hit ratio of close to 100% while showing a significant improvement in hit ratio. Again, this is possible mainly because of the fact that some clips are much more likely to be accessed than other ones. It would then be possible to select a 'popularity' threshold above which clips are cached at full quality (all layers) and below which the quality degrades with decreasing clip popularity. (Fewer and fewer layers of the clip are stored). In our simulated system, no such 'threshold' is selected – the system dynamically purges the least significant layers of the least weight objects until enough space is created for the incoming layer.

The plots in figure 4 show the results obtained with the LRU policy. We see that for the hit ratio and byte hit ratio, the LILO scheme outperforms the other two, while having a mean Quality Hit ratio of 89%. Future work would involve minimizing this tradeoff between lowering of the Quality hit ratio and raising of the hit ratio and byte hit ratio.

The plots in figure 5 show the results for the LFU policy. As far as the hit ratio is concerned, the two layered schemes give a much better performance than the OIOO non-layered one. A comparison of the two layered schemes indicates that the hit ratios are roughly the same for both. However, the byte hit ratio in case of LILO is much more than that in case of OILO. In addition, the Quality hit ratio is much higher in case of OILO than in case of LILO. This suggests that a choice between the two layered schemes can be made in the following way. For the LFU policy, to maximize the byte hit ratio; we must use the LILO policy whereas to maximize the Quality hit ratio we must use the OILO policy.

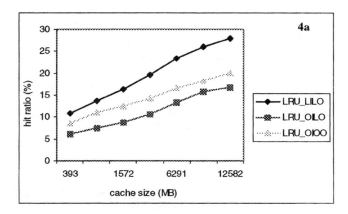

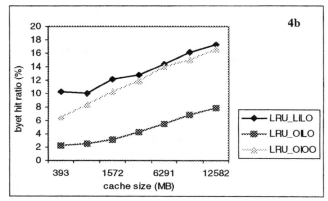

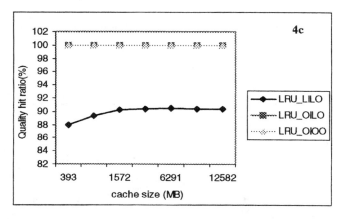

Figure 4. The plots above show the results obtained for the LRU based layered caching schemes, for the metrics hit ratio (4a), byte hit ratio (4b) and quality hit ratio (4c).

The plots in figure 6 show the results obtained for the HYBRID policy. The general behavior is similar to the previous two plots.

Across the four sets of plots, the highest hit ratio is 38.8%, for the HYBRID_LILO scheme. The highest byte hit ratio is 24.6% for the LFU_OIOO scheme. Between the two layered schemes, the highest byte hit ratio is 21.6% for the LFU_LILO scheme.

If only hit ratio was the criterion, then HYBRID_OILO appears to be the best scheme overall, with hit ratios almost the same as LILO and with a Quality hit ratio of almost 100%. However, if byte hit ratio is the criterion, then the LFU_OIOO scheme is the best.

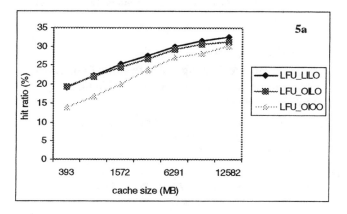

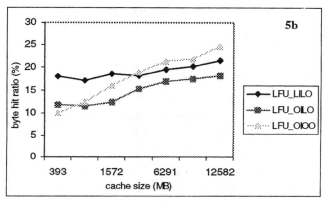

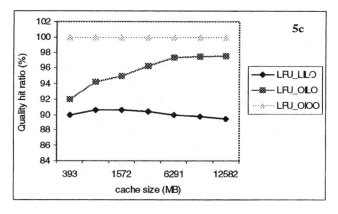

Figure 5. The plots above show the results obtained for the LFU based layered caching schemes, for the metrics hit ratio (5a), byte hit ratio (5b) and quality hit ratio (5c).

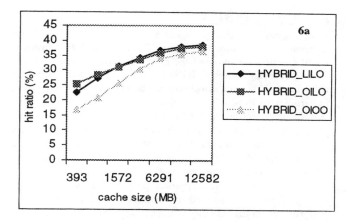

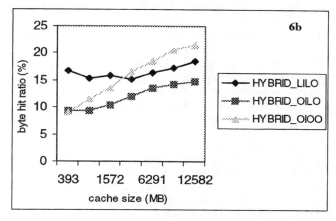

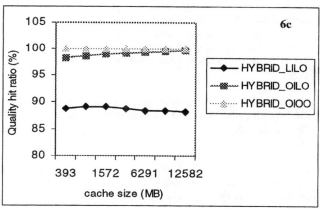

Figure 6. The plots above show the results obtained for the HYBRID based layered caching schemes, for the metrics hit ratio (6a), byte hit ratio (6b) and quality hit ratio (6c).

6. CONCLUSIONS

In this paper, we have proposed a new caching and streaming framework for multimedia objects. The framework has a broker-based architecture and uses the proposed Internet Standard Real Time Streaming Protocol (RTSP). The problem and the area of research itself being a novel one, we hope that the work reported in here proves to be of great value in the near future. It is hoped that the proposed design of a broker based caching and streaming architecture for multimedia will serve as a generic framework. Among the important conclusions drawn through the experiments is that a hybrid caching policy based on frequency, size and recency usually gives the best results. We have also seen that the novel layered replacement approach proposed gives better results than standard object-based replacement schemes. The novel performance metric, Quality Hit Ratio appears to be adequate as a measure for the evaluation of the new layered caching policies.

It appears that caching and streaming are henceforth going to be the major factors influencing the successful deployment of Internet Multimedia systems. However, the convergence of these two technologies is a recent development and has thrown up a number of new challenges. Our work here addresses some of the issues. However, many remain unresolved, and thus open a large number of areas for future work.

The design of the caching and streaming architecture is already in place. The system performance has also been verified through simulation. Therefore, the next logical step in this direction is the implementation of the proposed architecture in an actual network scenario. Also, the integration of the proposed framework into a multicast scenario is extremely important, as multicast is one of the essential technologies of Internet Multimedia. A 'layered multicast' approach needs to be investigated. Stream control issues, particularly related to layered video and RTSP, must be looked into. It is important to add functionality to RTSP to implement 'trick modes' such as FF, REW, etc.

As the Quality hit ratio goes closer and closer to 1, the hit ratio and byte hit ratio drop. This tradeoff between the raising of the Quality hit ratio and lowering of the hit ratio and byte hit ratio needs to be minimized.

Since we are dealing with streaming media, a thorough investigation into QOS related issues, is necessary. This problem involves 3 party QOS negotiation with three cases possible. One, the broker simply 'relays' the requested QOS parameters upward to the source. Two, the broker 'maps' the requested QOS parameters to a new set based on the external resources available. Three, the broker acts as the source itself (this is in case of a cache 'hit') and responds to the request.

Among other issues that require further research, is the generation of the 'sum_clip'. The broker must be able to combine the layers already present with the incoming layer(s) without introducing additional latency. The layered encoding scheme being used will have to provide for this. Secondly, an investigation into the feasibility and advantages, if any, of video interpolation and transcoding schemes is also required. These are possible additional functions of the broker. Thirdly, a performance comparison between a single broker-based architecture and a multiple broker-based architecture is needed. Finally, if possible, a trace file of accesses to a *media server* (audio or video) should be used instead of the HTTP file. This will make the results of the trace driven simulation much more realistic.

7. REFERENCES

[1] S. Paknikar. "A Caching and Streaming Framework for Multimedia". *Masters thesis,* IISc, Bangalore, December 1999.

[2] H. Schulzrinne, et al. "Real Time Streaming Protocol (RTSP)." *Proposed Internet Standard*, RFC 2326, April 1998.

[3] S. McCanne. "Scalable Compression and Transmission of Internet Multicast Video." *Ph.D. Thesis*, University of California, Berkeley, December 1996

[4] M. Abrams, et al. "Caching Proxies: Limitations and Potentials." *Fourth International World Wide Web Conference*, Boston, 1995.

[5] S. Williams, et al. "Removal Policies in Network Caches for World Wide Web Documents." Proceedings of the ACM SIGCOMM, 1996.

[6] Aggarwal, et al. "On Caching Policies for Web Objects." *IBM research report* RC 20619 11/08/96

[7] L.H.Ngoh, et al. "A Multicast Connection Management Solution for Wired and Wireless ATM Networks", *IEEE Communications Magazine*, Vol. 35, No. 11, pp. 52-59, Nov 1997.

[8] P. Cao, et al. "Web Caching and Zipf-like Distributions: Evidence and Implications." *IEEE Infocom*, 1999.

[9] D. Wessels. "Intelligent Caching of World-Wide-Web Objects." *MS Thesis,* University of Colorado, 1995.

[10] A. Swan, S. Mccane and L. Rowe, "Layered Transmission and Caching for the Multicast Session Directory Service", Proc. Sixth ACM Multimedia Conference, Bristol, Sep 1998.

[11] S. Carter and D. long, "Improving Bandwidth Efficiency of Video-On-Demand Servers", Computer Networks 31 (1999) 111-123.

A Reliable Multicast Webcast Protocol
for Multimedia Collaboration and Caching *

L. Kristin Wright
University of Utah
kwright@cs.utah.edu

Steven McCanne†
University of California, Berkeley
mccanne@cs.berkeley.edu

Jay Lepreau
University of Utah
lepreau@cs.utah.edu

Abstract

Large-scale, multi-point, multimedia conferencing applications designed to facilitate long-distance collaboration are enjoying growing popularity. Usually composed of real-time audio, video and shared-drawing applications, these collaborative environments help render the geographical location of collaborators irrelevant. To complement these existing collaborative applications, it would be useful to have the ability to distribute documents synchronously over the World Wide Web (WWW). One model for synchronized information dissemination within the Web is *webcasting* in which data are simultaneously distributed to multiple destinations. The WWW's traditional unicast client/server communication model suffers, however, when applied to webcasting; solutions which require many clients to simultaneously fetch data from the origin server using the client/server model will likely cause server and link overload.

A number of webcasting solutions have been proposed. Many have limited scalability because they are based on unicast while others use multicast for more scalable data delivery but require server modification or have rigid architectures. We believe that successful webcasting solutions will provide scalable, reliable delivery yet still be compatible with the existing Web infrastructure.

In this paper we describe a webcast design that improves upon previous designs by leveraging application level framing (ALF) design methodology. We build upon the Scalable Reliable Multicast (SRM) framework, which is based upon ALF, to create a custom protocol to meet webcast's scalability needs. We employ the protocol in an architecture consisting of two reusable components: a webcache component and a browser control component. We have implemented our design using the MASH multimedia application toolkit and a SRM protocol module called *libsrm*. We present the results of a simple performance evaluation and report on lessons learned while using MASH and *libsrm*.

1 Introduction

Online multimedia environments designed to facilitate long-distance collaboration are enjoying growing popularity: as modern information technology becomes ubiquitous, telecommuting has become increasingly popular; some large universities, faced with growing student

---

*This research was supported by DARPA contract N66001-96-C-8508 and by the State of California under the MICRO program.
†Now at FastForward Networks, Inc. (*mccanne@ffnet.com*).

populations, are exploring distance-learning as an alternative to high-cost bricks-and-mortar expansion; technical conferences are sometimes broadcast as a convenience to those who cannot attend physically. Usually composed of real-time audio, video, and shared drawing applications, collaborative environments are widely deployed [15, 10, 7, 13, 20, 9, 8, 21].

In addition to video, audio, and whiteboard applications, it would be useful to have the ability to distribute documents over the World Wide Web (WWW). For example, a speaker might display slides directly on remote listeners' desktop web browsers. Or perhaps a group of geographically remote colleagues would like to explore a common destination online and would like their individual web browsers synchronized such that the browsers display the same pages simultaneously. There are a number of slightly differing models, each requiring the synchonized distribution of web documents and their embedded objects to multiple sites. A common name for this type of collaborative session is *webcasting* [1, 4, 16, 12].

A simple webcast design might require each remote node, or session *participant*, to individually fetch the required document from the *origin server*, the web server on which the document resides. In this scenario, one participant might send a Uniform Resource Locator (URL), the unique name used to locate a document within the WWW, to the other participants. Upon receipt of the URL, each participant would fetch the corresponding page from the server. The problem with this simple solution is that the aggregate requests, or *server hits*, can lead to *implosion*—a pathology where a resource is unable to keep up with an incoming stream of messages [17]. Servers are constrained by built-in resource limitations in current operating systems such as the number of open sockets, buffer size limits, etc.. As session memberships increase to thousands, protocols which allow even a small percentage of duplicate hits could easily overload a server. Even if the server was able to keep up with a large number of incoming requests, the outgoing replies would likely cause network congestion.

1.1 Webcasting with multicast

To achieve scalability, neither the network traffic nor the number of server hits generated by a collaborative session can be allowed to significantly increase with session membership. A more efficient approach than the simple design described in the introduction would be to use IP multicast to achieve greater scalability. In [5], Deering and Cheriton describe network-layer multicast, a forwarding service that offers more efficient multidestination delivery of packets than either unicast or broadcast. Rather than send out one packet per participant, as in unicast, or replicate a single packet across every link in the network, as in broadcast, multicast protocols send packets across only those links that lead to a receiver in the multicast group. This reduces sender overhead, network traffic, and can reduce end-to-end latency.

One way to leverage multicast to improve scalability would be to modify the browser such that it multicasts data in response to requests from collaborative program participants. This is the general approach taken by [4] and [1]. While this is a more scalable approach than the naive solution suggested in the introduction, modifying the web server limits the usefulness of the resulting webcast application because server modification is only feasible when the server is within the local administrative domain. Requiring web server modifications also introduces a deployment barrier.

A second multicast approach is to build a client-side web proxy to intercept participant's browser requests, fetch the data from the origin server, and then multicast the data to session participants. This approach capitalizes on multicast's scalability without requiring server modification. [12] and [16] both use this approach. They further improve scalability by caching data locally so that any browser requests that can be satisfied using previously cached data need not be forwarded to the server. This approach capitalizes on multicast's scalability without requiring server modification but fails to prevent server implosion common in collaborative situations, e.g., when several students listening to a remote lecture simultaneously fetch a web document referenced by the lecturer.

1.2 Our approach

Our approach borrows quite freely from [12] and [16], but we improve upon existing work by leveraging the Scalable Reliable Multicast (SRM) framework [6] to build a custom protocol to address the server implosion problem mentioned above. SRM embodies a design principle called Application Level Framing (ALF) [3] that applications can leverage to build a protocol that will suit their unique needs. Although unicast protocols generally require ordered, reliable delivery, multicast applications can have widely varying delivery requirements. For example, different applications may require different flow control, rate control or error recovery mechanisms. The insight behind ALF is simply that applications know their requirements better than generic communication protocols. The protocols, then, should implement only the minimum necessary to provide the promised network service but allow applications to express their own semantics in the network protocol. Accordingly, SRM provides reliable multicast service but allows the application to determine its own semantics. We use SRM's flexibility to create a custom protocol that maximizes scalability. We present that protocol herein.

In addition to our custom protocol, we present our webcasting architecture. The architecture is comprised of two components, 1) a *multicast web cache* component maintained using SRM and 2) a webcasting control component. These components can be cleanly decoupled for reuse. The control component multicasts URLs to peer control components and instructs the browser as to what URL it should display. The subsequent browser request is intercepted by the caching component which either satisfies the request from within its multicast web cache or fetches the data from the origin server and multicasts the data to peer caching components. We have implemented

our webcast design in an application called MASHCast using the multimedia application toolkit MASH [14] and a SRM protocol module called *libsrm* which features the SNAP scalable data naming protocol [18].

The remainder of this paper is structured as follows. We first describe our architecture, then SRM's basic reliability mechanisms and our extensions to them. We next present our implementation and initial performance characteristics. Lastly, we report on lessons learned during implementation and the future work those lessons motivate. This paper's contributions are that (i) we bridge a gap in the set of online, collaborative tools by providing a scalable webcast application, (ii) we exploit SRM's flexibility to create a new protocol that maximizes webcast scalability by minimizing origin requests and network traffic, (iii) we embody our protocol in a novel webcast architecture and implementation called MASHCast that features several reusable components, browser independence, and compatibility with existing Web infrastructure, (iv) we present initial performance characteristics, and (v) we report on lessons learned while using the MASH multimedia toolkit and *libsrm*.

2 Dual component architecture

Our webcast architecture consists of a control component called the Casting Director and a multicast caching component called the Web Cache. The Web Cache consists of two subcomponents: a Web Server, which receives requests from the browser, and the Multicache, the multicast web page cache maintained using SRM. Figure 1 shows the components that comprise our architecture.

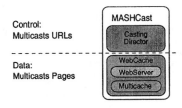

Figure 1: The MASHCast dual-component architecture features decomposable control and data modules.

The Casting Director provides control over a webcast session by synchronously multicasting URLs to peer Casting Directors and forwarding received URLs to the browsers. A sender webcasts a page by specifying the page's URL to the Casting Director via a built-in GUI.[1]

The Web Server subcomponent of the Web Cache provides an interface through which browser requests are received and satisfied. The Web Server forwards browser requests to the Multicache subcomponent of the Web Cache. If the local Multicache cannot satisfy the request from its own cache, it requests the data from peer Multicaches. If no Multicache in the session has the data, a single Multicache is selected in a distributed fashion to fetch the data from the origin server and then multicast the data to the group. To differentiate between the two types of requests, we call a request to the Multicache a *local request* and a request to the origin server an *origin request*. Selection

---

[1]URLs can actually be passed to the Casting Directors using any mechanism which multicasts the URL to the Casting Directors' multicast address. The GUI is a convenience for the user, not a necessity of the design.

and other aspects of our custom protocol employed by the Multicache are discussed in detail in section 4.

While we believe that our architecture's main contribution comes when used as a collaborative webcast application such as MASHCast, our architecture is novel because, in addition to being compatible with existing WWW infrastructure and addressing all sources of server implosion, its components can be cleanly decoupled for reuse. For example, though the Web Cache is not a suitable replacement for existing hierarchical web caching proxies, it can be used apart from the Casting Director as a passive multicast web cache in groups where a caching proxy server is not already in place. Members of a common research group will likely be browsing the same research related web pages. The group members could experience faster browser response times by starting a Web Server process on each machine in the group and specifying the Web Server as their web browsers' HTTP proxy. When a user requests a URL, the request would be intercepted by the local Web Server process.

The Multicache subcomponent can be used alone to cache any type of data in a distributed, scalable, reliable manner. Within MASHCast, the Multicache stores web pages and their embedded objects, but the data type is not specified in Multicache's design.

The Casting Director could be used without the Web Cache component to provide a simple webcasting service. Its use alone lacks scalability, however, because without the Web Cache's custom protocol to suppress duplicate origin requests, each session participant generates a request for each page webcasted leading to implosion.

When used together in MASHCast, the Casting Director and the Web Cache run in different processes on the same machine as the web browser. They use separate multicast addresses to communicate with peer components in the same MASHCast session across the IP Multicast Backbone (MBONE) [2]. For example, all Casting Directors in the same session might use the address 224.4.4.5 to communicate with each other and all Web Caches in the same session might use 224.4.4.10 to communicate with each other. The MASHCast application sits between the web browser and the network. MASHCast's custom protocol minimizes interactions with web servers but, when contact is necessary, data is fetched from the origin server via unicast HTTP. To participate in a MASHCast session, the user need only start the MASHCast application and a web browser on the same machine (we will call this machine the *local* machine) and fetch a special MASHCast bootstrap page into the browser. MASHCast requires configuration of a MASH browser plugin, but once this plugin is configured, no web server modification or browser proxy specification is required.

Once MASHCast is started, a sender webcasts a page by specifiying the page's URL to the Casting Director. Peer Casting Directors listen for URLs and, upon receipt, prepend the request with the URL of the local instance of MASHCast. The resulting *mangled* URL is then forwarded to the Remote Controller. Figure 2 shows how the Casting Director forwards URLs to the browser and other Casting Directors. In the figure, the URL www.cs.berkeley.edu is multicast among the Casting Directors. Upon receipt, the Casting Directors mangle the URL by prepending the local MASHCast Web Server address (localhost:3123/) onto the URL. After the URL is mangled, the Casting Director forwards the mangled URL to the Remote Controller. Because of our mangling scheme, there is no need to configure the browser's HTTP

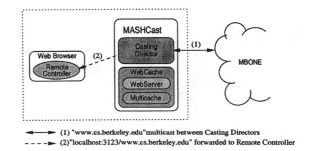

→ (1) "www.cs.berkeley.edu"multicast between Casting Directors
- - → (2)"localhost:3123/www.cs.berkeley.edu" forwarded to Remote Controller

Figure 2: the URL www.cs.berkeley.edu is multicast among the Casting Directors. Upon receipt, the Casting Directors prepend the lcoal Web Server's address onto the URL and forward the mangled URL to the Remote Controller.

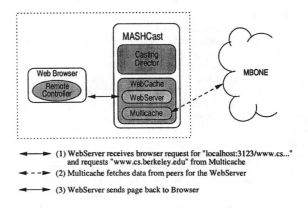

→ (1) WebServer receives browser request for "localhost:3123/www.cs..."
and requests "www.cs.berkeley.edu" from Multicache
- - → (2) Multicache fetches data from peers for the WebServer
→ (3) WebServer sends page back to Browser

Figure 3: If the requested data are not in the local Multicache, the local Multicache requests the data from peer Multicaches.

Proxy; MASHCast can coexist with any caching web proxy the user may have already configured and can also be configured to use such a proxy itself.

When the Remote Controller, a Java applet, receives a URL from the Casting Director, it instructs the browser to fetch the URL. Because the local Web Server's URL has been prepended to the original URL, the request is actually directed back to the local instance of MASHCast. The Web Server subcomponent of the Web Cache receives the browser's page request and attempts to satisfy the request from the Multicache. If the local Multicache does not have the requested page, the Multicache requests the data from peers. Figure 3 shows the Web Cache satisfying the browser's request from the MultiCache. In the figure, the requested data is not in the local Multicache so the Multicache requests the data from peer Multicaches.

As an optimization, the Casting Director could pass the requested URL not only to the Remote Controller but also to the Web Cache. This would serve to prime the cache for the subsequent browser request Web Caches can also be primed before the start of a MASHCast session using scripts read by the Web Cache in *batch mode*; this would optimize response times during forthcoming lectures, for example.

3 SRM background

In this section we describe SRM's reliable service mechanisms. In the next section, we describe how we specialize

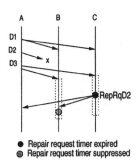

● Repair request timer expired
◉ Repair request timer suppressed

Figure 4: SRM suppresses duplicate requests by delaying requests for random periods.

the SRM framework to create a custom webcast protocol.

Web data are usually either HTML documents or images embedded within an HTML document. The browser can faithfully render these types of data only if they are received in whole. Thus, our application's semantics require reliably delivered data.

A novelty of the SRM framework is its scalable multicast retransmission scheme which relies upon *repair-requests* for loss recovery. Group members are responsible for detecting loss and requesting retransmission. Repair-requests are satisfied with a *repair* message. Repair-requests and repairs are sent to the entire multicast group.

In order to prevent the implosion of repair-request or repair packets sent from receivers to the group, SRM must suppress duplicate repair-requests and repairs. For example, when a data packet is lost near the source, many receivers experience the loss at roughly the same time. Were all of the receivers to send out repair-requests as soon as the loss was detected, the implosion of duplicate repair-requests would likely cause link overload.

Similarly, if many receivers in the group had the requested data and could, therefore, respond to the request, link overload might occur again when the replies were sent.

To avoid implosion, SRM employs a randomized and distributed damping mechanism. In this scheme, repair-requests and repairs are sent only after a randomly chosen delay. All session participants "listen" to all repair-requests and repairs and cancel any duplicates that they may have scheduled so as to prevent implosion.

Figure 4 shows how SRM's randomized suppression can suppress duplicate requests. In the figure and in similar figures to follow, the vertical lines represent increasing time on each of three nodes: A, B and C. Node A sends out a data packet named D1 which nodes B and C successfully receive. Next, node A sends out data packet D2 which is lost before reaching either node B or C. Nodes B and C detect that D2 has been lost upon the receipt of packet D3. Rather than both nodes sending out a repair-request immediately upon loss detection, they instead set request timers with delays that are chosen randomly. The timer intervals are represented in the picture with dashed brackets; timer expiration is represented with the shaded circles. In this example, node C's request timer expires first so node C sends a repair-request for D2. Node B receives this request before its own repair timer expires and suppresses it. The same randomized suppression technique is used for suppressing duplicate repairs.

All participants can cache old data and any participant with a copy of the data can send a repair message. SRM sources periodically send *session messages* reporting

their current state. Participants check their state against session messages to detect tail losses.

3.1 Backoff and cancellation policy

For expository purposes, we made a simplification above that, if true, would result in SRM not being reliable under certain circumstances. One can imagine a scenario in SRM where a repair request is sent out and, according to the suppression algorithm described above, all nodes with duplicate requests scheduled cancel those requests. If, due to network congestion or some other network pathology, the request never reaches a node that can reply, the repair will never be transmitted because all other requests have been cancelled.

To ensure reliability, repair-requests are not cancelled because a single request is not always sufficient for reliability. Rather, SRM uses *exponential backoff*. That is, if a receiver sees a request with the same information as a scheduled request, then it reschedules its request with a delay, on average, double the current delay. Repair-requests are only *cancelled* when the requested data has been received.

Repairs, on the other hand, can be cancelled safely. Suppose a repair that suppressed all other repairs at potentially replying nodes never reaches the node that requested the data. We are assured that another repair-request will soon be issued by the node missing the data because repair-requests are only backed off, not cancelled. When the repair-request is resent, the repair cycle will repeat.

4 SRM extensions

The basic reliability mechanisms we have described would alone meet our reliability requirement. However, without specialization, the protocol would not yield the scalability that we desire. In this section, we describe the customizations that we made to the SRM framework to achieve our scalability goals.

4.1 Leveraging peers' caches

As described in previous sections, scalability is one of our key goals. Towards scalability, our protocol must minimize the number of origin requests. When a URL is webcast, ideally only a single Multicache fetches the data from the origin server and multicasts it to the group. This could be accomplished by designating the multicache where the request originated as the multicache that sends the origin request as in [12] and [16]. In other words, if participant A would like to send the document with URL http://www.cs.berkeley.edu, participant A would fetch the data from the server and multicast it to the session. Without additional changes in the protocol, however, this simple policy could fail to prevent server implosion in common collaborative situations. Consider a remote lecture program where the speaker is webcasting slides which contain hyperlinks to sites relevant to the lecture. It is likely that some of the students will want to immediately visit those sites causing a number of synchronized fetches, i.e., implosion at the origin server.

In an effort to avoid server implosion, we attempt to satisfy browser requests first from our local multicast web cache and, second, from a peer's multicast web cache. The origin server is contacted only if no one in the group has the requested data. Because the CastingDirector mangles the request before forwarding it to the Remote Controller so that it points to MASHCast's Web Server, MASHCast intercepts any page requests. If the data is present in the local multicast cache, the request is satisfied. If the data is not present locally, then a repair-request is multicast to peer Multicaches. Any session participants that have the data in their cache already can respond to the repair-request by scheduling a repair. Eventually, some participant's timer expires and a repair is sent. Satisfying requests from a peer's Multicache can eliminate server hits in several scenarios. Consider the example remote lecture program above. Imagine that one remote student joins the session late and requests a previously seen slide. Using previous solutions' policy where the requesting node sends an origin request and multicasts the resulting data prohibits the late student from leveraging other participant's caches. Enabling the student to benefit from others' caches leads to fewer origin requests and, if other members were within shorter round-trip times than the server, better response times. This scenario is the motivation behind using the MultiCache component alone in groups likely to browse the same pages.

4.2 Injecting data into the Web Cache

In the previous section, we explained how we can reduce server load with an SRM-based web cache. But what happens when no one has the requested data? The reliability model described in [6] assumes that all data is published into the multicast session explicitly by some source. Within the context of a webcache, however, desired data might not yet exist in the session and there must be some mechanism in place to retrieve the data from the origin server and inject it into the multicast cache. Previous solutions solve the problem by sending an origin request if the page doesn't exist locally. As explained above, this can lead to server implosion.

One solution is to have each Web Cache set a repair timer regardless of whether or not they have the data. Should a participant that does not have the data set a repair timer that expires before other repairs are received, that member sends an origin request when their timer expires rather than a repair. Although this solution works, it can lead to duplicate server hits because during the interim period when the data is being retrieved from the origin server, other participants' timers may have expired thereby triggering more origin requests.

4.2.1 Reply-pending messages

To solve this problem, we leverage SRM's flexibility by defining a new message called a *reply-pending* message which notifies other participants that an origin request has commenced and thereby suppresses duplicate origin requests. Upon receipt of a repair-request message, all nodes that do not have the requested data set a reply-pending message timer rather than a repair timer. If a node's reply-pending timer expires, that node sends a reply-pending message to the group *and* fetches the data from the origin server. All session participants listen for reply-pending messages and refrain from sending duplicate web server requests by suppressing their outstanding reply-pending timers.

Figure 5 illustrates how a reply-pending message can suppress duplicate origin requests. When node B's repair timer expires, it not only initiates an origin request but also multicasts a reply-pending message to the group.

Upon receipt of the reply-pending message, Node C surpresses it's reply-pending message.

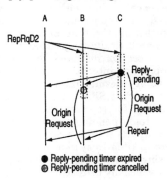

Figure 5: MASHCast reply-pending messages suppress duplicate origin requests by informing peers that an origin request in in-progress.

As was done in [6] for SRM repair-request and repair messages, we must decide between a cancellation or backoff policy for reply pending messages. Figure 6 illustrates what might happen if we implemented exponential backoff of reply-pending messages. Node A sends a repair-request and nodes B and C respond by setting reply-pending timers. Node C's timer expires so Node C multicasts a reply-pending message. Node B responds by backing off it's reply-pending timer. Recall that a timer is scaled back by first cancelling the currently scheduled timer and then setting a new timer with, on average, double the delay. Backoff is represented in the figure with a lighter-colored circle and a second, longer bracket denoting the new, longer timer delay. Despite the fact that the timer has been scaled back, due to a lengthy web server response time the timer still expires before the desired data has been multicast. Once the timer expires, an unnecessary origin request is sent. In fact, since this is more likely to happen as web server response times grow longer, unnecessary origin requests are more likely to be sent when the servers are overloaded thus exacerbating the problem—exactly the behavior we want to avoid.

For this reason, we chose a cancellation policy for reply-pending timers rather than exponential backoff. Al-

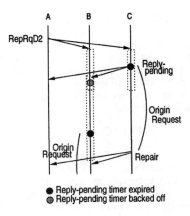

Figure 6: A Reply-pending backoff policy could cause duplicate origin requests. The better policy choice is cancellation.

though it is still possible that duplicate origin requests could be generated despite a reply-pending cancellation policy, the difference is that with a cancellation policy, the repair-request and reply-pending timer intervals can be configured such that the time between any generated duplicates is probabilistically longer than that of a backoff policy. (The next section discusses the relationships between timer suppression intervals in more detail.) We can still ensure reliability despite reply-pending cancellation for the same reason that SRM ensures reliability despite a cancellation policy for repairs: should the participant that sends out a reply-pending timer fail to successfully fetch the requested data from the origin server and multicast it to the group (due to system failure, for example), those nodes missing the data still have outstanding repair-request timers. Eventually those timers will expire, repair-requests will be sent out, and new reply-pending messages will be scheduled.

The techniques presented in Sections 4.1 and 4.2 together have the novel effect of applying SRM's slotting and damping technique to origin server requests. In this manner, origin requests are minimized—something we believe is vital for scalability that previous solutions have not addressed.

4.3 Defining the suppression intervals

This section discusses how we can schedule the repair-request, repair, and reply-pending delay timers to minimize server load and network traffic.

In SRM, repair-request and repair timers are delayed for a random amount of time to avoid implosion. The *suppression interval* over which the repair-request delay is chosen is a function of the participant's estimated distance from the data source. Distances to remote nodes are estimated using timestamps sent in SRM session messages.

Equation 1 shows how SRM defines the request interval when Node A detects a loss of data sent from Node S. C_1 and C_2 are configurable parameters and $d_{S,A}$ is Node A's estimated distance to Node S.

$$[C_1 d_{S,A}, (C_1 + C_2)d_{S,A}] \qquad (1)$$

Equation 2 shows how the repair interval is defined when Node B receives a request from Node A. D_1 and D_2 are configurable parameters, as in equation 1, and $d_{A,B}$ is Node B's estimated distance to Node A.

$$[D_1 d_{A,B}, (D_1 + D_2)d_{A,B}] \qquad (2)$$

The addition of reply-pending messages presents a new interval definition challenge. The challenge is to define the repair and reply-pending suppression intervals such that repair-requests are satisfied by the multicast web cache before the origin server when possible. Equation 3 describes our reply-pending interval:

$$[E_1 d, (E_1 + E_2)d] \qquad (3)$$

How we configure E_1 and E_2 and how we define d in relation to D_1, D_2, and $d_{A,B}$ determines whether the repair and reply-pending intervals are the same, overlapping or distinct. We might need adaptation beyond just the distances between SRM session participants. For example, in determining the value of d in equation 3, it might be useful to be able to factor estimated distance and throughputs between receivers and origin servers.

Figure 7 shows two alternative interval configurations.

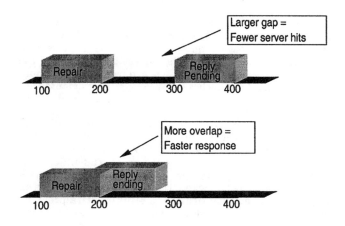

Figure 7: The addition of reply-pending messages presents a tradeoff between response time and origin server load.

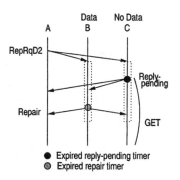

Figure 8: Unaware that node B has the requested data, Node C sends an unnecessary origin request before node B is able to send a repair.

On the upper line, the two intervals are distinct. The repair interval is between 100 and 200 milliseconds and the reply-pending interval is between 300 and 400 milliseconds. By eliminating overlap, we lessen the chance of unnecessary server hits by maximizing the chance that a participant with the requested data will send a repair before other participants' reply-pending timers expire. The tradeoff for minimizing server hits in this way is increase in the required time to inject new pages into the multicast cache when no participant has the data. In this example, 300 milliseconds must elapse before the earliest possible reply-pending timer expires. Alternatively, the lower line in figure 7 shows overlapping intervals which could improve response time but increase the likelihood of unnecessary origin requests.

Figure 8 shows what might happen if the intervals are the same. Node A sends a request. In response, Node B sets a repair timer (denoted by the R) because it has the requested data. Node C sets a reply-pending timer (denoted by the P) because it does not have the requested data. Node C happens to have randomly chosen a shorter delay than Node B and it's reply-pending timer expires before node B is able to fulfill the request. The result is that Node C unnecessarily sends an origin request. This illustrates not only that the repair and reply-pending intervals should not be the same but that, to avoid contacting the origin server when some SRM participant has the data, the repair timer interval should precede the reply-pending timer interval. With such a configuration, the delays for repair timers should precede in time the reply-pending timer delays.

To explore the parameter space, we ran experiments in which we varied the repair and reply-pending intervals and observed any changes in response times and bandwidth usage. The details of this experiment are omitted here due to length but can be found in [22]. The experiments showed that, for most documents, the protocol behaves as expected as the intervals are varied. We discuss exceptions in section 6.

5 Implementation

To verify the efficacy of our design and provide a useful tool for online collaboration, we have implemented a prototype of the MASHCast components—the Casting Director, Remote Controller, and Web Cache—using the MASH multimedia toolkit [14]. We discuss lessons learned while using MASH in section 6.

5.1 Behavior

To get an idea of the behavior of our initial implementation, we performed a simple study. We selected three web sites in geographically distinct areas. Table 1 lists the documents comprising the three web sites, their sizes, and the corresponding round-trip times from the experimental machines to the respective origin servers. Because some of the document names are lengthy, we include in the table monikers for each document which we will use for the remainder of the paper rather than the lengthy names.

Initially, we ran four experiments for each site. Each experiment measured the time taken by the Web Cache to obtain each document. To increase our control over each experiment, we instrumented the web cache to "play" requests at predetermined times from a list of requests in a file "recorded" previously using a web browser and a live user to request the documents. Using such a recording eliminates the variance introduced when using live users to trigger document requests in experiments. In this playback mode, the Web Server and Casting Director components are not needed and were not run.

The four experiments are described below:

1. **Direct.** As a baseline measurement, we instrumented MASHCast to bypass the cache and fetch the requested page immediately. By bypassing the cache, we approximate the amount of time that it would take a browser to fetch a page directly over the Internet with no help from MASHCast.

2. **Miss.** For this experiment, we started a single MASHCast application. We requested the documents and measured the time to fetch the page. This measures the overhead to inject a page into the Multicache. Because of the necessity of an origin request in addition to the overhead of the per-request reply-pending delay, we expected this experiment to yield the longest load time.

3. **Peer Hit.** For this experiment, we started a MASH-Cast application on one machine and primed its cache with the appropriate pages. We then started a second MASHCast participant on a second machine .25ms and requested the page a second time. Because the first participant had the page in its multicache, we

expected it to respond to the second MASHCast's request for data. This experiment measured the time saved by taking advantage of data in a peer's multi-cache. We expected this to be the second fastest load time after a Hit (described below).

4. **Hit.** For this experiment, we measured the time to load a page from the participant's local multicache. We expected this time to be the fastest since no network communication is necessary.

Each experiment was repeated thirty times and the results were averaged. Figure 9 shows the load times by site for each experiment. Note the logarithmic y-axis rendered necessary by the orders of magnitude difference between Peer Hit and Hit times and Direct and Miss times.

As we expected, the load times for both Hit and Peer Hit were faster than either the Direct or Miss. We were surprised, however, that the Peer Hit and Hit times were so similar. The Peer Hit time should have shown document transmission time that the Hit case didn't require. Upon investigation, we found that, based on SRM session messages multicast by the first node, the SRM recovery mechanism at the newly started node was detecting the missing documents and recovering them before the web cache layer requested them. Our experiment was set up such that the first document was requested 9.8 seconds after the application was started. Within that 9.8 seconds, the local node was easily able to detect missing previously sent data, request the data from the session, and recover the data. The effect was that each request resulted in a Hit rather than a Peer Hit.

Rather than try to beat *libsrm*'s efficient recovery mechanisms, we introduced a new recovery policy and a fifth test case. SRM detects and informs the application of data losses but only recovers those losses if the *application* explicitly requests SRM to do so. Our default *aggressive-recovery* policy specifies that lost data is always recovered. We used SRM's *selective reliability* capabilities to implement a second recovery policies for MASH-Cast: our *lazy-recovery* policy specifies that the SRM layer only recover data that the browser has explicitly requested. We expected that lazy-recovery would yield slower response times than those of aggressive-recovery due to the overhead of retrieving data from a peer's cache rather than from one's own cache at the time of request. However, lazy-recovery could save cache space and reduce network traffic to achieve greater scalability in many circumstances—for example, when late joiners in a collaborative session aren't interested in seeing previously webcast data or when the Web Cache is being used as a passive cache.

Our additional test case is described below:

5. **Peer Hit w/Lazy Recovery.** This experiment is identical to the Peer Hit experiment except that the lazy-recovery policy is enabled so that the application will only request recovery of a missing document if the user has requested that document.

Discussion. The advantage gained by using another participant's cache is represented by the difference between the Peer Hit bar and the Direct bar or, if lazy-recovery is desired and enabled, the advantage gained is represented by the difference between the Peer Hit w/Lazy Recovery bar and the Direct bar. Similarly, the advantage gained by using the local cache is represented by the difference between the Hit bar and the Direct bar. These experiments

27

No.	Document	Moniker	RTT in ms	kB
1	www.cs.berkeley.edu/	berk	38.00	9.2
2	www.lcs.mit.edu/	mit	61.00	5.2
3	www.lcs.mit.edu/lcs_style.css	mit-style	61.00	.6
4	www.lcs.mit.edu/images/nav.gif	mit-nav	61.00	12.8
5	www.lcs.mit.edu/images/banner.gif	mit-banner	61.00	12.4
6	www.lcs.mit.edu/images/divider.gif	mit-divider	61.00	.3
7	www.lcs.mit.edu/images/mld.jpg	mit-mld	61.00	8.5
8	www.lcs.mit.edu/images/w3c.gif	mit-w3c	61.00	1.4
9	www.lcs.mit.edu/images/jupiter.gif	mit-jup	61.00	7.0
10	www.lcs.mit.edu/images/cilklogo.gif	mit-cilklogo	61.00	4.2
11	www.lcs.mit.edu/images/bluepix1.jpg	mit-bluepix	61.00	1.9
12	www.cs.utah.edu/	utah	0.85	4038
13	www.cs.utah.edu/mountains3.jpg	utah-mts	0.85	77.7
14	www.cs.utah.edu/banner_title.gif	utah-banner	0.85	1.6

Table 1: Documents requested in experiments.

do not show the scalability gained by fewer net server hits and fewer data transmissions resulting from suppressed duplicate origin requests. These gains are measured on a small scale in [22] and are also the subject of future work discussed in section 6.

We would expect that the difference between the Miss and Direct response times would include the following items:

I On average, half of the repair-request interval plus the minimum delay (150ms).

II On average, half of the reply-pending interval plus the minimum reply-pending delay (175ms).

III Overhead of our cache software.

Given the above, we would expect to see an average of at least 325ms (the sum of first two items above) difference between the Miss and Direct response times. Accordingly, if a horizontal line is drawn across the graph at 325ms, we see that that is indeed a lower bound in the graph.

From individual document response times, we can approximate the minimum and maximum overhead experienced. mit-mld shows the smallest difference between Miss and Direct response times, 359ms of overhead, and mit-nav shows the largest overhead, 620ms. By subtracting the 325ms lower bound found above, we estimate a minimum overhead of 35ms and a maximum overhead of 295ms for our dataset.

Peer Hit w/Lazy Recovery response time is comprised of

I On average, half the repair request delay interval (150ms).

II On average, half the repair delay interval (100ms).

III The transmit overhead to and from the peer.

IV At least the minimum amount of overhead (35ms).

This yields a lower bound of only 285ms. In fact, we experienced much higher load times than expected. Upon investigation, we found that a combination of implementation choices accounted for the poor Peer Hit w/Lazy Recovery performance. Our reply-pending parameter configuration did not allow enough time for the peer cache to satisfy our request so that, in the meantime, a spurious origin request was sent and satisfied. Coupling this with the fact that the MASHCast components are optimized not for performance but for ease of implementation and

policy change (for example, the Web Cache is all interpreted Tcl), and a mismatch in our data naming scheme accounts for the poor performance. Section 6 covers the mismatch in our data naming scheme in more detail.

Though the Peer Hit requests were satisfied via the disk, they uniformly took just slightly longer than Hit requests, which were also via the local disk. At this time, we don't know why this is but believe that analysis of the two code paths will reveal the difference.

In general, the MASHCast components are optimized not for performance but for ease of implementation and policy change. For example, the Web Cache is all interpreted Tcl. *libsrm* implemented in C++ and, at the time of experimentation, was also largely unoptimized.

6 Lessons learned and future work

The MASH multimedia toolkit provides a low barrier-to-entry, multimedia research platform. We believe that our implementation experience with MASH is relevant to the broader multimedia research community looking for such a platform. In this section, we report on lessons learned during implementation and the future work and our observations defined.

The MASH software model is an object-oriented architecture in which objects' methods can be implemented in either C++ or the MIT Object Tcl system (OTcl) [14]. This split object model was especially conducive to our research because it enabled backend mechanisms to be implemented using efficient C++ code while policy could be implemented using TCL for ease of policy modification. We found that this ease of policy change facilitated the experiments discussed in [22] and section 5. In addition to allowing policy modification ease, implementing within the MASH environment allowed us to leverage existing, well-tested MASH components to lessen the implementation effort. Specifically, we used MASH's Announce Listen Manager, HTTP Server and Adaptive Timers. MASH offers many more multimedia components including standard audio and video transmission protocols.

libsrm is an instantiation of the framework presented in [6]. In addition to the SRM reliability mechanisms, *libsrm* incorporates the SNAP hierarchical, scalable naming protocol [18]. *libsrm* is available as a standalone library and as a MASH component. In general, we found *libsrm* simple to use. All of the SRM extensions described in section 4 were implemented in approximately 1200 lines

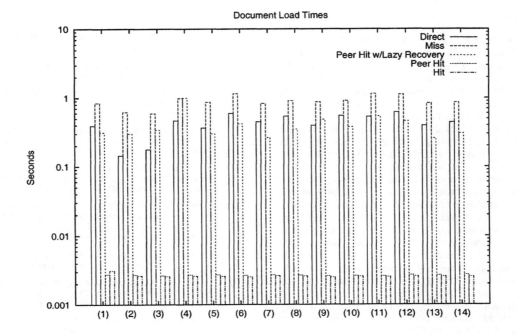

Figure 9: Page load times for each of the five experiments by site. The numbers across the x-axis reference the document numbers in Table 1.

of Tcl code. Lazy recovery was implemented simply by adding a one-line check to see if the URL had been explicitly requested in the application's implementation of the *libsrm* upcall invoked when a loss is detected.

We found that, while we gained critical namespace scalability from SNAP our application didn't conform naturally to SNAP's naming convention. One assumption central to both SNAP and SRM is that data are source-specific. Accordingly, a source is associated with each data name. While this association is desirable for the vast majority of multimedia applications, it is not optimal for a webcast application. Associating an SRM source with Web documents can falsely differentiate the same document. For example, node A might obtain and source `www.cs.berkeley.edu`, naming it `[A,www.cs.berkeley.edu]`. Simultaneously, node B gets the same URL but names it `[B,www.cs.berkeley.edu]`. Fortunately, duplicates can be easily detected at the application level where, in accordance with ALF principles, caching and recovery are managed so that duplicate cache entries are avoided. However, duplicate transmissions do sometimes occur (see below). A non-source-specific naming option would be desirable for transmitting web data. Currently, SNAP maintains namespace trees per source. By adding a new *universal source* with a well-known source-id, we enable SRM to detect non-source specific, duplicate data. This alone does not solve the problem, however, because all applications would have to agree on the same container ID and application data unit (ADU), the two components in a SNAP data name, for like data. We intend to investigate solutions to make SNAP more amenable to applications which do not have source-specific data.

Secondly, we learned that the natural choice for a Web ADU is not optimal. At the outset, the single document or image corresponding to a URL seemed natural. However,

this proved to be too coarse-grained for large documents. Since the SRM layer doesn't notify the application layer that an ADU has arrived until after the entire ADU is received, we occasionally observed the application, unaware that a document was already partially received and would shortly be fully received, spuriously request the document a second time. Compounded with the naming mismatch described above, this led to a transient state in which different SRM names existed for duplicate URLs and duplicate data were multicast. Depending on the document's size, the transmission of duplicates could account for significant amounts of unnecessary data. In hindsight, we would break documents into large fragments so that the application would be notified in a more timely manner of incoming documents. We implemented an earlier version of MASHCast designed for a non-fragmenting SRM library that *did* perform fragmentation and reordering. We should be able to merge this code into the current version with little change other than to expand the fragmentation granularity from 1K to 10K. This size avoids duplicating SRM's underlying 1K fragmentation efforts and avoids fragmenting in the common case of small documents.

Finally, though our small-scale experimentation is adequate to demonstrate MASHCast's performance gains, they are not sufficient to demonstrate proven scalability. Because we have built upon two protocols whose scalability has already been proven in the literature, SRM and SNAP we are reasonably confident that our design is also scalable. Nonetheless, we plan additional experimentation within the year aimed at stressing MASHCast's tolerance to scale within an emulated WAN environment using a large-scale testbed we are building in a local but orthogonal project.

7 Related work

Webcast [1] uses NCSA Common Client Interface to communicate with the Mosaic web browser via TCP/IP to fetch URLS, request Mosaic to report URLs selected by the user, and pull in data from web to local program space. They utilize RMP (Reliable Multicast Protocol) which provides ordered, reliable multicast delivery. RMP uses a token-ring based algorithm to ensure delivery which requires an explicit list of receivers. A per-receiver list precludes them from targeting large groups as we do. A second difference between MASHCast and Webcast is that Webcast is specific to the Mosaic browser.

mMosaic [4] uses a modified Mosaic browser to send documents out via multicast. Reliability is achieved via an announce/listen protocol [19]: documents are sent every four seconds and receivers listen to and store the multicast data. Once a document has been fully constructed it is displayed. When losses occur, they may not be repaired for four seconds. The potential four-second delay to repair losses coupled with the time to download the data can add up poor response time. Lastly, mMosaic is specific to the Mosaic web browser.

mWeb's [16] solution is similar to ours in that they use SRM for reliable distribution. However, they do not take advantage of SRM's flexibility as we do to to further improve scalability by minimizing origin requests.

WebCanal [12] also has a design that is similar to MASHCast's. WebCanal uses a modified version of SRM called Light-weight Reliable Multicast Protocol (LRMP) to multicast documents reliably. Like mMosaic, there is no solution offered for server implosion that can result from many nearly-simultaneous origin requests. Also, LRMP uses a constant for suppression rather than the random, adaptive suppression algorithms found in SRM. We have found that a non-adaptive algorithm can cause pathologies in certain circumstances [11].

8 Conclusions

Large-scale multimedia conferencing applications are enjoying growing popularity. To complement existing audio, video and drawing applications, we have designed a novel webcast architecture which features (i) reusable components and (ii) a custom protocol built upon the SRM framework that maximizes scalability. Our proposal improves upon existing work by leveraging SRM to tailor a custom protocol to satisfy webcasting's unique needs. We have implemented our design in a useful collaborative application that is freely available for download with the MASH multimedia toolkit. Through simple experimentation, we have verified the efficacy of our design, demonstrated the power of ALF to enable applications to tailor protocols to meet their unique needs, and reported on the lessons learned using the MASH multimedia toolkit and *libsrm*.

Acknowledgements

We thank Suchitra Raman, Tina Wong and Yatin Chawathe for the implementation of *libsrm* and significantly improving MASHCast. Yatin also conceived the URL mangling scheme which frees the MASHCast user from having to configure a browser's HTTP proxy.

References

[1] E. Burns et al. Webcast – Collaborative Document Sharing via the MBone. Information online at http://www.ncsa.uiuc.edu/.

[2] S. Casner. Frequently asked questions (FAQ) on the multicast backbone (MBone), Aug. 1994.

[3] D. Clark and D. Tennenhouse. Architectural considerations for a new generation of protocols. In *ACM SIGCOMM '90*, September 1990.

[4] G. Dauphin. mMosaic: Yet Another Tool Bringing Multicast to the Web. In *Workshop on Real Time Multimedia and the WWW*, October 1996.

[5] S. Deering and D. Cheriton. Multicast Routing in Datagram Internetworks and Extended LANs. *ACM Transactions on Computer Systems*, 8(2):85–110, May 1990.

[6] S. Floyd, V. Jacobson, S. McCanne, C.-G. Liu, and L. Zhang. A Reliable Multicast Framework for Light-weight Sessions and Application Level Framing. In *Proceedings of the 1995 ACM SIGCOMM Conference*, August 1995.

[7] R. Frederick. Network video (nv). Xerox Palo Alto Research Center, ftp://ftp.parc.xerox.com/net-research.

[8] T. Frivold, R. Lang, and M. Fong. Extending WWW for Synchronous Collaboration. In *Proceedings of the 2nd International WWW Conference*, Chicago, Oct. 1994.

[9] M. Handley and J. Crowcroft. Network Text Editor (NTE): A scalable shared text editor for the MBone. In *Proceedings of SIGCOMM '97*, Cannes, France, Sept. 1998.

[10] V. Jacobson and S. McCanne. Visual audio tool. Software online at ftp://ftp.ee.lbl.gov/conferencing/vat.

[11] M. Kornacker and K. Wright. Experimental evaluation of a reliable multicast application. U.C. Berkeley CS268 Computer Networks term project and paper. Unpublished report., May 1997.

[12] T. Liao. Webcanal: a Multicast Web Application. In *6th International WWW Conference*, Santa Clara, CA, April 1997.

[13] S. McCanne. A distributed whiteboard for network conferencing. U.C. Berkeley CS268 Computer Networks term project and paper, May 1992.

[14] S. McCanne et al. Toward a Common Infrastructure for Multimedia-Networking Middleware. In *Workshop on Network and OS Support for Audio and Video '97*, 1997.

[15] S. McCanne and V. Jacobson. vic: a Flexible Framework for Packet Video. In *ACM Multimedia '95*, San Diego, CA, November 1995.

[16] P. Parnes et al. mWeb: a framework for distributed presentations using the WWW and the MBone. In *W3C Workshop: Real Time Multimedia and the Web*, Sophia Antipolis, France, October 1996.

[17] S. Pingali, D. Towsley, and J. F. Kurose. A Comparison of Sender-Initiated and Receiver-Initiated Reliable Multicast Protocols. In *Proceedings of ACM Sigmetrics '94*, Santa Clara, CA, 1994.

[18] S. Raman and S. McCanne. Scalable data naming for application level framing in reliable multicast. In *ACM Multimedia '98*, Bristol, UK, September 1998.

[19] E. M. Schooler. A Multicast User Directory Service for Synchronous Rendezvous. Computer Science Department, California Institute of Technology, Sept 1996.

[20] G. Sidler, A. Scott, and H. Wolf. Collaborative Browsing in the World Wide Web. In *Proceedings of the 8th Joint European Networking Conference*, Edinburgh, May 1997.

[21] T. Turletti. INRIA Video Conferencing System (ivs). Institut National de Recherche en Informatique et an Automatique. Software available at http://www.inria.fr/rodeo/ivs.html.

[22] K. Wright. Using *libsrm* for Caching and Collaboration. Technical Report UUCS-99-04, University of Utah, Mar. 1998. http://www.cs.utah.edu/.

A Unified Framework for Semantics and Feature Based Relevance Feedback in Image Retrieval Systems

Ye Lu[1*], Chunhui Hu[2], Xingquan Zhu[3*], HongJiang Zhang[2], Qiang Yang[1*]

1 School of Computing Science	2 Microsoft Research China	3 Department of Computer Science
Simon Fraser University	5F, Beijing Sigma Center	Fudan University
Burnaby, B.C., Canada, V5A1S6	Beijing 100080, China	Shanghai 200433, China
{yel,qyang}@cs.sfu.ca	{i-chhu,hjzhang}@microsoft.com	980015@fudan.edu.cn

ABSTRACT

The relevance feedback approach to image retrieval is a powerful technique and has been an active research direction for the past few years. Various ad hoc parameter estimation techniques have been proposed for relevance feedback. In addition, methods that perform optimization on multi-level image content model have been formulated. However, these methods only perform relevance feedback on the low-level image features and fail to address the images' semantic content. In this paper, we propose a relevance feedback technique, *iFind*, to take advantage of the semantic contents of the images in addition to the low-level features. By forming a semantic network on top of the keyword association on the images, we are able to accurately deduce and utilize the images' semantic contents for retrieval purposes. The accuracy and effectiveness of our method is demonstrated with experimental results on real-world image collections.

Keywords

relevance feedback, image semantics, image retrieval, multimedia database.

1. INTRODUCTION

With the increasing availability of digital images, automatic image retrieval tools provide an efficient means for users to navigate through them. Even though traditional methods allow the user to post queries and obtain results, the retrieval accuracy is severely limited because of the inherent complexity of the images for users' to describe exactly. The more recent relevance feedback approach, on the other hand, reduces the needs for a user to provide accurate initial queries by estimating the user's ideal query using the positive and negative examples given by the user.

The current relevance feedback based systems estimate the ideal query parameters on only the low-level image features

such as color, texture, and shape. These systems work well if the feature vectors can capture the essence of the query. For example, if the user is searching for an image with complex textures having a particular combination of colors, this query would be extremely difficult to describe but can be reasonably represented by a combination of color and texture features. Therefore, with a few positive and negative examples, the relevance feedback system will be able to return reasonably accurate results. On the other hand, if the user is searching for a specific object that cannot be sufficiently represented by combinations of available feature vectors, these relevance feedback systems will not return many relevant results even with a large number of user feedbacks.

To address the limitations of the current relevance feedback systems, we propose a framework that performs relevance feedback on both the images' semantic contents represented by keywords and the low-level feature vectors such as color, texture, and shape. The contribution of our work is twofold. First, it introduces a method to construct a semantic network on top of an image database and uses a simple machine learning technique to learn from user queries and feedbacks to further improve this semantic network. In addition, we propose a framework in which semantic and low-level feature based relevance feedback can be seamlessly integrated.

This paper is organized as follows. In Section 2, we will provide an overview of the current state of the art relevance feedback systems. In Section 3, we will present the details of our work. Section 4 will describe the *iFind* image retrieval system that we have implemented based on the proposed method and provide experimental evaluations showing its effectiveness in image retrieval. Concluding remarks will be given in Section 5.

2. RELATED WORK

One of the most popular models used in information retrieval is the vector model [1, 8, 9]. Various effective retrieval techniques have been developed for this model and among them is the method of relevance feedback. Most of the previous relevance feedback research can be classified into two approaches: query point movement and re-weighting [3].

The query point movement method essentially tries to improve the estimate of the "ideal query point" by moving it towards good examples point and away from bad example points. The frequently used technique to iteratively improve this estimation is the Rocchio's formula given below for sets of

---

* This work was performed at Microsoft Research China.

relevant documents D'_R and non-relevant documents D'_N given by the user.

$$Q' = \alpha Q + \beta \left(\frac{1}{N_{R'}} \sum_{i \in D'_R} D_i \right) - \gamma \left(\frac{1}{N_{N'}} \sum_{i \in D'_N} D_i \right) \qquad (1)$$

where α, β, and γ are suitable constants; $N_{R'}$ and $N_{N'}$ are the number of documents in D'_R and D'_N respectively. This technique is implemented in the MARS system [6]. Experiments show that the retrieval performance can be improved considerably by using relevance feedback [1, 8, 9].

The central idea behind the re-weighting method is very simple and intuitive. The MARS system mentioned above implements a slight refinement to the re-weighting method call the standard deviation method [6]. Since each image is represented by an N dimensional feature vector, we can view it as a point in an N dimensional space. Therefore, if the variance of the good examples is high along a principle axis j, then we can deduce that the values on this axis is not very relevant to the input query so that we assign a low weight w_j on it. Therefore, the inverse of the standard deviation of the jth feature values in the feature matrix is used as the basic idea to update the weight w_j.

Recently, more computationally robust methods that perform global optimization have been proposed. The MindReader retrieval system designed by Ishikawa et al. [3] formulates a minimization problem on the parameter estimating process. Unlike traditional retrieval systems whose distance function can be represented by ellipses aligned with the coordinate axis, the MindReader system proposed a distance function that is not necessarily aligned with the coordinate axis. Therefore, it allows for correlations between attributes in addition to different weights on each component. A further improvement over this approach is given by Rui and Huang [7]. In their CBIR system, it not only formulates the optimization problem but also takes into account the multi-level image model.

All the approaches described above perform relevance feedback at the low-level feature vector level, but failed to take into account the actual semantics for the images themselves. The inherent problem with these approaches is that the low-level features are often not as powerful in representing complete semantic content of images as keywords in representing text documents. In other words, applying the relevance feedback approaches used in text information retrieval technologies to low-level feature based image retrieval will not be as successful as in text document retrieval. In viewing this, there have been efforts on incorporating semantics in relevance feedback for image retrieval. The framework proposed in [4] attempted to embed semantic information into a low-level feature based image retrieval process using a correlation matrix. In this effective framework, semantic relevance between image clusters is learnt from user's feedback and used to improve the retrieval performance. As we shall show later, our proposed method integrates both semantics and low-level features into the relevance feedback process in a new way. Only when the semantic information is not available, our method is reduced to one of the previously described low-level feedback approaches as a special case.

3. THE PROPOSED METHOD
There are two different modes of user interactions involved in typical retrieval systems. In one case, the user types in a list of

keywords representing the semantic contents of the desired images. In the other case, the user provides a set of examples images as the input and the retrieval system will try to retrieve other similar images. In most image retrieval systems, these two modes of interaction are mutually exclusive. We argue that combining these two approaches and allow them to benefit from each other yields a great deal of advantage in terms of both retrieval accuracy and ease of use of the system.

In this section, we describe a method to construct a semantic network from an image database and present a simple machine learning algorithm to iteratively improve the system's performance over time. In addition, we describe a framework in which the previously constructed semantic network can be seamlessly integrated with low-level feature vector based relevance feedback.

3.1 Semantic Network
The semantic network is represented by a set of keywords having links to the images in the database. Weights are assigned to each individual link. This representation is shown pictorially as follows.

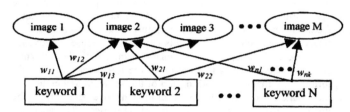

Figure 1: Semantic network

The links between the keywords and images provide structure for the network. The degree of relevance of the keywords to the associated images' semantic content is represented as the weight on each link. It is clear that an image can be associated with multiple keywords, each of which with a different degree of relevance. Keyword associations may not be available at the beginning. There are several ways to obtain keyword associations. The first method is to simply manually label images. This method may be expensive and time consuming. To reduce the cost of manual labeling, we utilize the Internet and its countless number of users. One possible way to do that may be to implement a crawler to go to different websites to download images. We store the information such as the file name and the ALT tag string within the IMAGE tags of the HTML files as keywords associated with the downloaded image. Also, the link string and the title of the page may be somewhat related to the image. We assign weights to these keyword links according to their relevance. Heuristically, we list this information in the order of descending relevance: the link string, the ALT tag string, the file name, and the title of the page. Another approach to incorporate additional keywords into the system would be to utilize the user's input queries. Whenever the user feeds back a set of image being relevant to the current query, we add the input keywords into the system and link them with these images. In addition, since the user tells us that these images are relevant, we can confidently assign a large weight on each of the newly created links. This effectively suggests a very simple voting scheme for updating the semantic network in which the keywords with a majority of user consensus will emerge as the dominant representation of the semantic content of their associated images.

3.2 Semantic Based Relevance Feedback

Semantic based relevance feedback can be performed relatively easily compared to its low-level feature counterpart. The basic idea behind it is a simple voting scheme to update the weights w_{ij} associated with each link shown in Figure 1 without any user intervention. The weight updating process is described below.

1. Initialize all weight w_{ij} to 1. That is, every keyword has the same importance.

2. Collect the user query and the positive and negative feedback examples.

3. For each keyword in the input query, check to see if any of them is not in the keyword database. If so, add them into the database without creating any links.

4. For each positive example, check to see if any query keyword is not linked to it. If so, create a link with weight 1 from each missing keyword to this image. For all other keywords that are already linked to this image, increment the weight by 1.

5. For each negative example, check to see if any query keyword is linked with it. If so, set the new weight $w_{ij}'=w_{ij}/4$. If the weight w_{ij} on any link is less than 1, delete that link.

It can be easily seen that as more queries are inputted into the system, the system is able to expand its vocabulary. Also, through this voting process, the keywords that represent the actual semantic content of each image will receive a large weight.

The weight w_{ij} associated on each link of a keyword represents the degree of relevance in which this keyword describes the linked image's semantic content. For retrieval purposes, we need to consider another aspect. The importance of keywords that have links spreading over a large number of images in the database should be penalized. Therefore, we suggest the relevance factor r_k of the kth keyword association be computed as follows.

$$r_k = w_k (\log_2 \frac{M}{d_i} + 1) \qquad (2)$$

where M is the total number of images in the database, $w_k = w_{mn}$ if $m = i$ and 0 otherwise, and d_i is the number of links i^{th} keyword has.

3.3 Integration with Low-Level Feature Based Relevance Feedback

Since [7] summarized a general framework in which all the other low-level feature based relevance feedback methods discussed in Section 2 can be viewed as its special cases, in this section, we show how the semantic relevance feedback method can be seamlessly integrated with it.

To expand the framework summarized in [7] to include semantic feedback, notice that the inputs to it are a query vector q_i associated with the ith feature, an N element vector $\pi=[\pi_1,...\pi_N]$ that represents the degree of relevance for each of the N input

training samples, and a set of N training vectors x_{ni} for each feature i. As shown in [7], the ideal query vector q_i* for feature i is the weighted average of the training samples for feature i given by

$$q_i^{T*} = \frac{\pi^T X_i}{\sum_{n=1}^{N} \pi_n} \qquad (3)$$

where X_i is the $N \times K_i$ training sample matrix for feature i, obtained by stacking the N training vectors x_{ni} into a matrix. The optimal weight matrix W_i* is given by

$$W_i* = (\det(C_i))^{\frac{1}{K_i}} C_i^{-1} \qquad (4)$$

where C_i is the weighted covariance matrix of X_i. That is

$$C_{i_{rs}} = \frac{\sum_{n=1}^{N} \pi_n (x_{nir} - q_{ir})(x_{nis} - q_{is})}{\sum_{n=1}^{N} \pi_n} \qquad r,s = 1,...K_i \qquad (5)$$

We can see from the above equations that the critical inputs into the system are x_{ni} and π. Initially, the user inputs these data to the system. However, we can eliminate this first step by automatically providing the system with this initial data. This is done by searching the semantic network for keywords that appear in the input query. From these keywords, we can follow the links to obtain the set of training images (duplicate images are removed). The vectors x_{ni} can be computed easily from the training set. To compute the degree of relevance vector π, we can use the following formula.

$$\pi_i = \alpha^M \sum_{j=1}^{M} r_{ij} \qquad (6)$$

where M is the number of query keywords linked to the training image i, r_{jk} is the relevance factor of the jth keyword associated with image i, and $\alpha > 1$ is a suitable constant. We can see that the degree of relevance of the ith image increases exponentially with the number of query keywords linked to it. In the current implementation of our system, we have experimentally determined that setting α to 2.5 gives the best result.

To incorporate the low-level feature based feedback and ranking results into high-level semantic feedback and ranking, we define a unified distance metric function G_j to measure the relevance of any image j within the image database in terms of both semantic and low-level feature content. The function G_j is defined using a modified form of the Rocchio's formula as follows.

$$G_j = \log(1+\pi_j)D_j + \beta \left\{ \frac{1}{N_R} \sum_{k \in N_R} \left[\left(1+\frac{I_1}{A_1}\right) S_{jk} \right] \right\} -$$

$$\gamma \left\{ \frac{1}{N_N} \sum_{k \in N_N} \left[\left(1+\frac{I_2}{A_2}\right) S_{jk} \right] \right\} \qquad (7)$$

where D_j is the distance score computed by the low-level feedback in [7], N_R and N_N are the number of positive and negative feedbacks respectively, I_1 is the number of distinct keywords in common between the image j and all the positive feedback images, I_2 is the number of distinct keywords in common between the image j and all the negative feedback images, A_1 and A_2 are the total number of distinct keywords associated with all the positive and negative feedback images respectively, and finally S_{ij} is simply the Euclidean distance of the low-level features between the images i and j. We have replaced the first parameter α in Rocchio's formula with the logarithm of the degree of relevance of the jth image. The other two parameters β and γ are assigned a value of 1.0 in our current implementation of the system for the sack of simplicity. However, other values can be given to emphasize the weighting difference between the last two terms.

Using the method described above, we can perform the combined relevance feedback as follows.

1. Collect the user query keywords

2. Use the above method to compute x_{ni} and π and input them into the low-level feature relevance feedback component to obtain the initial query results.

3. Collect positive and negative feedbacks from the user

4. Update the semantic network with the method given in section 3.2

5. Update the weights of the low-level feature based component using the methods discussed in [7]

6. Compute the new x_{ni} and π and input into the low-level feedback component

7. Compute the ranking score for each image using equation 7 and sort the results.

8. Show new results and go to step 3

Usually the values of x_{ni} are computed beforehand in a pre-processing step. We can see that using this approach, our system learns from the user's feedback both semantically and in a feature based manner. In addition, it can be easily seen that our method degenerates into the method of Rui and Huang [7] when no semantic information is available. We will show in the next section how our system deals with input queries that have no associated images from the semantic network. Also, next section will present some experimental results to confirm the effectiveness of this approach.

3.4 New Image Registration

Adding new images into the database is a very common operation under many circumstances. For retrieval systems that entirely rely on low-level image features, adding new images simply involves extracting various feature vectors for the set of new images. However, since our system utilizes keywords to represent the images' semantic contents, the semantic contents of the new images have to be labeled either manually or automatically. In this section, we present a technique to perform automatic labeling of new images.

In paper [5], a method was presented which automatically classify images into only two categories, indoor and outdoor, based on both text information and low-level feature. There is currently no algorithm available to automatically determine the semantic content of arbitrary images accurately. We implemented a scheme to automatically label the new images by guessing their semantic contents using low-level features. The following is a simple algorithm to achieve this goal.

1. For each category in the database, compute the representative feature vectors by determining the centroid of all images within this category.

2. For each category in the database, find the set of representative keywords by examining the keyword association of each image in this category. The top N keywords with largest weight whose combined weight does not exceed a previously determined threshold τ are selected and added into the list the representative keywords. The value of the threshold τ is set of 40% of the total weight as discussed in section 4.

3. For each new image, compare its low-level feature vectors against the representative feature vectors of each category. The images are labeled with the set of representative keywords from the closest matching category with an initial weight of 1.0 on each keyword.

Because the low-level features are not enough to present the images' semantics, some or even all of the automatically labeled keywords will inevitably be inaccurate. However, through user queries and feedbacks, semantically accurate keywords labels will emerge.

Anther problem related to automatic labeling of new images is the automatic classification of these images into predefined categories. We solve this problem with the following algorithm.

1. Put the automatically labeled new images into a special "unknown" category.

2. At regular intervals, check every image in this category to see if any keyword association has received a weight greater than a threshold ξ. If so, extract the top N keywords whose combined weight does not exceed the threshold τ.

3. For each image with extracted keywords, compare the extracted keywords with the list of representative keywords from each category. Assigned each image to the closest matching category. If none of the available categories result in a meaningful match, leave this image in the "unknown" category.

The keyword list comparison function used in step 3 of the above algorithm can take several forms. The ideal function would take into account the semantic relationship of keywords in one list with those of the other list. However, for the sake of simplicity, our system only checks for the existence of keywords from the extracted keyword list in the list of representative keywords.

4. EXPERIMENTAL RESULTS

We have presented a framework in which semantic and low-level feature based feedback can work together to achieve greater retrieval accuracy. In this section, we will describe the image retrieval system *iFind* that we have implemented using this framework and show some experimental results.

4.1 The *iFind* Retrieval System

The *iFind* image retrieval system implements the framework discussed in this paper. It is a web based retrieval system in which multiple users can perform retrieval tasks simultaneously at any given time.

The *iFind* system supports three modes of interaction: keyword based search, search by example images, as well as browsing the entire image database using a pre-defined category hierarchy. The main user interface is shown in Figure 2.

When the user enters a keyword-based query, the system invokes the combined relevance feedback mechanism discussed in Section 3.3. The result page is shown in Figure 3.

Figure 2: Main user interface.

Figure 3: The query result page

The user is able to select multiple images from this page and click on the "Feedback" button to give positive and negative feedback to our system. The images with blue background indicate a positive feedback while images with a red background indicate a negative feedback. Images with gradient background are not considered in the relevance feedback process. The system presents 240 images for each query. The first 100 images are actually retrieved using the algorithm outlined in Section 3. The next 120 images are randomly selected from each category. The final 20 images are randomly selected regardless of categories. The purpose of presenting the randomly selected images would be to give the user a new starting point if none of the images actually retrieved by our system can be considered relevant. New search results will be presented to the user as soon as the "Feedback" button is pressed. At any point during the retrieval process, the user can click on the "View" link to view a particular image in its original size, or click on the "Similar" link to perform an example based query. One point of detail to note is that if the user enters a set of query keywords that cannot be found in the semantic network, the system will simply output the images in the database one page at a time to let the user browse through and select the relevant images to feedback into the system.

4.2 Results

Here are some experimental results that we have gathered from our system to validate some simple assumptions and demonstrate its effectiveness. Because we are interested in examining how the semantic network evolves with an increasing number of user feedbacks, we select a very clean but roughly labeled image set as our starting point. The dataset that we have chosen is from the Corel Image Gallery. We have selected 12,000 images and manually classified them into 60 categories.

One assumption we have made in the design of the system is that a significant portion of the total weight of all the keyword associations with an image is concentrated on a subset of keywords that are relevant to the semantic content of the image. This relationship is shown in Figure 4 with the x axis being the number of keywords associated with the image and the y axis being the average percentage of the total weight that are assigned to relevant keywords.

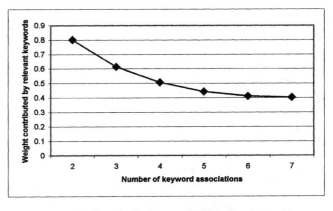

Figure 4: Keyword relevance VS keyword count.

To obtain the graph shown in Figure 4, we have asked human subjects to examine the keyword association on the images having 2 to 7 keywords associated and pick out the relevant keywords. These keyword associations are obtained from the user query using the method described in Section 3. We have also verified that the keywords with large weights are indeed the relevant keywords selected by the users. From the plot of Figure 4, we can see that as the number of keyword associations increase, the percentage of the weight contributed by the relevant keywords levels off to approximately 40%. We therefore conjecture that if we rank the keywords in descending order of their associated weight and select the top few that contribute no more than 40% of the total weight, the selected keywords will be an accurate representation of the semantic meaning of the image. The verification of this conjecture is currently on the list of our future works.

Figure 5 shows the performance of our system in terms of precision and recall. We performed eight random queries on our system. We ensured that none of the query keywords are labeled on any of the images and that there are exactly 100 images with the correct semantic content in our image database. Since we have used exactly 100 images as our ground truth for each query and that we only actually retrieve 100 images, the value of precision and recall is the same. Therefore, we have used the term "Accuracy" to refer to both in our plot.

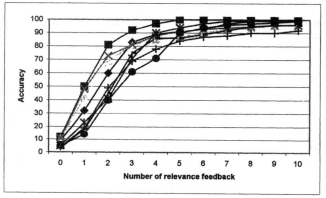

Figure 5: System performance.

As we can see from the results, our system achieves on average 80% retrieval accuracy after just 4 user feedback iterations and over 95% after 8 iterations for any given query. In addition, we can clearly see that more relevant images are being retrieved as the number of user feedbacks increase. Unlike some earlier methods where more user feedback may even lead to lower retrieval accuracy, our method proves to be more stable.

In addition to verifying the effectiveness of our system through the performance measure shown in Figure 5, we have also compared it against other state of the art image retrieval systems. We have chosen to compare our method with the retrieval technique used in the CBIR system [7]. The comparison is made through 8 sets of random queries with 10 feedback iterations for each set of query and the number of correctly retrieved images is counted after each user feedback. The average accuracy is then plotted against the number of user feedbacks. The result is shown in Figure 6.

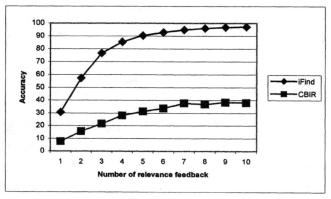

Figure 6: Performance comparison.

It is easily seen from the above result that by combining semantic level feedback with low-level feature feedback, the retrieval accuracy is improved substantially.

5. CONCLUSION

In this paper, we have presented a new framework in which semantics and low-level feature based relevance feedbacks are combined to help each other in achieving higher retrieval accuracy with lesser number of feedback iterations required from the user. The novel feature that distinguished the proposed framework from the existing feedback approaches in image database is twofold. First, it introduces a method to construct a semantic network on top of an image database and uses a simple machine learning technique to learn from user queries and feedbacks to further improve this semantic network. In addition, a scheme is introduced in which semantic and low-level feature based relevance feedback is seamlessly integrated. Experimental evaluations of the proposed framework have shown that it is effective and robust and improves the retrieval performance of CBIR systems significantly.

We have chosen to use the approach summarized in [7] as our low-level feature based feedback component. However, it can be easily demonstrated that this framework is general enough to allow any low-level feedback method to be incorporated. As a future work, we will study the possibility to incorporate the approaches proposed in [2, 4] to further improve the performance of the *iFind* system.

6. REFERENCES

[1] Buckley, C., and Salton, G. "Optimization of Relevance Feedback Weights," in Proc of SIGIR'95.

[2] Cox, I.J., Miller, M.L., Minka, T.P., Papathornas, T.V., Yianilos, P.N. "The Bayesian Image Retrieval System, PicHunter: Theory, Implementation, and Psychophysical Experiments" IEEE Tran. On Image Processing, Volume 9, Issue 1, pp. 20-37, Jan. 2000.

[3] Ishikawa, Y., Subramanya R., and Faloutsos, C., "Mindreader: Query Databases Through Multiple Examples," In Proc. of the 24th VLDB Conference, (New York), 1998.

[4] Lee, C., Ma, W. Y., and Zhang, H. J. "Information Embedding Based on user's relevance Feedback for Image Retrieval," Technical Report HP Labs, 1998.

[5] Paek S., Sable C.L., Hatzivassiloglou V., Jaimes A.,Schiffman B.H., Chang S. F., Mckeown K.R, "Integration of Visual and Text-Based Approaches for the Content Labeling and Classification of Photographs", SIGIR'99.

[6] Rui, Y., Huang, T. S., and Mehrotra, S. "Content-Based Image Retrieval with Relevance Feedback in MARS," in Proc. IEEE Int. Conf. on Image proc., 1997.

[7] Rui, Y., Huang, T. S. "A Novel Relevance Feedback Technique in Image Retrieval," ACM Multimedia, 1999.

[8] Salton, G., and McGill, M. J. "Introduction to Modern Information Retrieval," McGraw-Hill Book Company, 1983.

[9] Shaw, W. M. "Term-Relevance Computation and Perfect Retrieval Performance" Information processing and Management.

Giving Meanings to WWW Images

Heng Tao Shen   Beng Chin Ooi   Kian-Lee Tan

Department of Computer Science
National University of Singapore
3 Science Drive 2, Singapore 117543

ABSTRACT

Images are increasingly being embedded in HTML documents on the WWW. Such documents over the WWW essentially provides a rich source of image collection from which users can query. Interestingly, the semantics of these images are typically described by their surrounding text. Unfortunately, most WWW image search engines fail to exploit these image semantics and give rise to poor recall and precision performance. In this paper, we propose a novel image representation model called *Weight ChainNet*. Weight ChainNet is based on *lexical chain* that represents the semantics of an image from its nearby text. A new formula, called *list space model,* for computing semantic similarities is also introduced. To further improve the retrieval effectiveness, we also propose two relevance feedback mechanisms. We conducted an extensive performance study on a collection of 5000 images obtained from documents identified by more than 2000 URLs. Our results show that our models and methods outperform existing technique. Moreover, the relevant feedback mechanisms can lead to significantly better retrieval effectiveness.

Keywords:

WWW, semantic similarity, image retrieval, relevance feedback, image representation.

1. INTRODUCTION

With the increase in Internet bandwidth and CPU processing speed, the use of images in WWW pages has become very prevalent. Images are used to enhance description of content, to capture attention of readers and to reduce the textual content of a page. Images have become an indispensable component of WWW pages today. This pool of WWW images becomes a very rich source from which users can obtain interesting images. However, managing such images to facilitate their retrieval is an interesting research topic that has not received much attention. In particular, to be able to search for relevant images among such a large collection of images calls for novel mechanisms that exploit the semantics of the images.

Traditional image retrieval systems are not adequate to deal with the problem. Text-based systems [1, 2, 3] use keywords or free text description of images supplied by the authors as the basis for retrieval. These systems can be adopted for WWW images since the textual content of the HTML page in which the image is embedded provides the free text description. However, the entirety of the textual content does not represent the semantics of the image adequately for them to be useful in retrieving the images. In other words, while the textual content may contain information that captures the semantics of the embedded image, it also contains other description that are not relevant to the image. These "noises" lead to poor retrieval performance.

On the other hand, content-based image retrieval systems [4, 5, 6, 7, 8, 10] capture the visual content of an image (such as color, texture and shape) as its semantics and use these features as the basis for similarity matching. Unfortunately, retrieval by content is still far from perfect. First, their effectiveness depends on how precise the user specifies the query. Second, they cannot capture the more useful image semantics, like object, event, and relationship. Finally, they do not scale well. More recently, integrated systems that combine the various features (color, texture and shape) has led to better effectiveness. But, they remain unsatisfactory as different features tend to have different degrees of importance for different classes of queries.

In this paper, we adopt a different approach to identify the semantics of an image within a HTML document. This is based on the observation that an image in a Web page is typically *semantically* related to its surrounding texts, with the exception of *functional* images (such as *new* symbol and *under construction* symbol). These surrounding texts are used to illustrate some particular semantics of the image content, i.e. what objects are in the image, what is happening and where the place is. In particular, in a HTML document, certain components are expected to provide more semantic information than other portion of the text. These include the caption of the image, its title and the title of the document. We propose a novel image representation model called *weight ChainNet*. Weight ChainNet is based on *lexical chain* obtained from an image's nearby text. A new formula, called *list space model,* for computing semantic similarities is also introduced. To further improve the retrieval effectiveness, we also propose two relevance feedback mechanisms. We conducted an extensive performance study on a collection of 5000 images obtained from documents identified by more than 2000 URLs. Our results show that our models and methods outperform existing technique. Moreover, the relevant feedback mechanisms can lead to significantly better retrieval effectiveness.

The rest of this paper is organized as follows. In the next section, we briefly review some related works. In Sections 3 and 4, we present our image semantic representation model and the similarity measure respectively. Section 5 presents the relevance feedback approaches to refine queries for further retrieval. In Section 6, we describe an experimental study and report our findings, and finally, we conclude in Section 7.

2. RELATED WORKS

As discussed in the introduction, traditional text-based and content-based retrieval mechanisms are no longer effective for managing images obtained from the WWW. There have also been several approaches that combine hypertext in WWW pages with information retrieval (IR) engines [10, 11, 12, 13, 14, 16]. These techniques, however, do not apply well to images in WWW for the same reasons.

Recently, [15] extended [16, 18] to work with WWW-based image collections. In [15], an image's content is given by the combined content of the text *nodes*. An image's set of text nodes include textural content (e.g., caption) obtained from the document in which it is embedded, as well as those obtained from its neighboring pages (those pages that are reached by a single hyperlink from the embedded page). This model was further extended to take into account not only the textual content of the immediate neighbors of an image, but also all nodes that can be reached from the image by following at most two hyperlinks (a *two-step link*), thus considering more information about an image node. However, there are no explicit image/query semantics considered. The inner semantic relationship within a text node was lost based on this model. Moreover, while keeping more information is desirable, the approach extracted too much unrelated information. For example, an image's own caption usually describes its content, but its neighboring pages' image captions do not reflect the same content. In addition, the similarity measure did not take into account any semantic structure. Such a similarity measure may not be good enough to show the *real* semantic similarity between an image and a query.

Relevance feedback (RF) is a very important way to improve the accuracy. System refines the query by using feedback information from users to improve subsequent retrieval. The use of relevance feedback using multiple attributes of color has been investigated in [9]. Their results showed significant improvement in retrieval effectiveness by applying RF mechanisms.

3. IMAGE REPRESENTATION MODEL

Two key issues must be addressed in designing an image retrieval system to support WWW images:
- Determine a representation for a WWW image and the query semantics.
- Determine a similarity measure between an image and a query based on their representations.

In this section, we shall address the first issue, and defer the second issue to the next section. Before that, we have identified several desirable properties of a query/image representation:
- *Exactness.* For a representation to be effective, it has to capture the essential image/query semantic meanings.
- *Space efficiency.* The representation should not consume too much storage; otherwise, besides large storage cost, the

database structure will not be effective in reducing much I/O cost.
- *Computationally inexpensive similarity matching.* It should be fast to compute the similarity between the representations.
- *Preservation of the similarity between the image/query semantic meanings.*
- *Automatic extraction.* The representation should be automatically extracted, rather than manually generated.
- *Insensitivity to noise, distortion, rotation.* Any noise or distortion should not affect the representation drastically.

3.1 Semantics of an Embedded Image

To understand the relationship between an image embedded in a HTML document and its surrounding text, we conducted a preliminary study on a collection of images obtained from HTML documents. Based on our findings, we have identified four parts of the textual content that are well related to the embedded image. These are
- Image title. Image file title (simply image title) is a single word that basically indicates the main object that the image is concerned with.
- Image ALT (alternate text). The image ALT tag in HTML document is a phrase that usually represents an abstract of the image semantics.
- Image caption. The image caption usually provides the most semantics about an image. It is the image's surrounding text in the HTML document. It can range from one sentence to a paragraph of text that contains many sentences.
- Page title. Since images are used for enhancing the Web page's content, page title is most probably related to the image's semantics. It is usually a short sentence that summarizes the Web page's content.

There are also some other parts which may provide some information about the image, such as other HTML meta data, However, they contain too much unrelated information. We have also excluded the textual content of the whole HTML document as part of the image's semantics for the same reason, i.e., that some information may be completely unrelated to the image content, and indexing the whole HTML document for each image in a very large database is not expected to provide an efficient solution. Therefore, we just use these four parts to represent image content. We note that all these four parts -- image title, image ALT, page title and image caption -- can be automatically extracted from the HTML document based on hypertext structures.

3.2 Weight ChainNet Model

To represent the image semantics more adequately, we propose the Weight ChainNet model that is based on the concept of *lexical chain* [17]. Figure 1 illustrates an example. A lexical chain (LC) is a sequence of semantically related words in a text. Here, we define it as one sentence that carries certain semantics by its words. As an image title is just a single word, we say it's a trivial lexical chain - *Title Lexical Chain (TLC)*. The text obtained from the ALT tag is referred to as the *Alt Lexical Chain (ALC)*. The page title is represented as a LC too - *Page Lexical Chain (PLC)*. Finally, since a caption comprises multiple sentences, we represent it as three types of lexical chains. Type one is called *sentence lexical chain (SLC)*, which represents one single sentence in an image caption. In Figure 1, each sentence is shown as one column in the caption component, i.e., each column is a SLC. Type two is called *reconstructed sentence lexical chain (RSLC)*, and it represents one new sentence reconstructed from related sentences. Two sentences are *related* if both share one or more words. One common word in two SLCs splits each SLC into two. Based on the first common word, the second SLC's second half is connected to the first SLC's first half to form a RSLC. In Figure 1, a RSLC exists if there is an arrow from one column to another column. The last type is called *caption lexical chain (CLC)*, which represents the whole image caption. A CLC is formed by connecting SLC one after another. In Figure 1, the connections are made by dotted arrows. To illustrate, the followings are some examples from Figure 1.

$$SLC\ (1 \rightarrow 2 \rightarrow 3 \rightarrow 4 \rightarrow 5),$$
$$RSLC\ (1 \rightarrow 2 \rightarrow 8 \rightarrow 9),$$
$$CLC\ (1 \rightarrow 2 \rightarrow ... \rightarrow 13 \rightarrow 14).$$

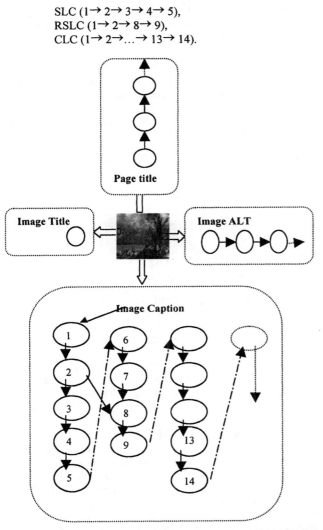

Figure 1: Image Semantic Representation - *Weight ChaiNet*

The ChainNet model is built by these 6 types of lexical chains. Each chain captures a portion of the semantic structure of the image. A TLC indicates the main subject of an image. An ALC provides short description about an image. A PLC shows part of its content. An SLC captures the semantics of a single sentence in the image caption. An RSLC captures related sentences'

semantics, and a CLC keeps the image's overall semantics. That's why we call it ChainNet, which is basically made of a chain of LCs.

However, the ChainNet treats each type of LC as of equal importance, Now, simply representing an image in this way without capturing the relative importance of the various components is not expected to lead to good performance. For example, the image title, ALT, page title and image caption play different roles in representing an image's semantics. The reason we have divided the entire image caption into three types of lexical chains is that we want to differentiate the importance of each type of sentences due to their positions and inner relationship within an image caption. The three types of lexical chains in an image caption are not equally important. The importance order from high to low is expected to be like this: SLC > RSLC > CLC. If all the same words in a query appear in an SLC, an RSLC and a CLC respectively, the SLC possesses the most semantic meanings among the three, followed by RSLC and finally CLC. For example, if a query matches an SLC in the first image, only matches an RSLC in the second image, and only matches a CLC in the third image, it's most likely the case that the first image is most relevant to the query, followed by the second image and then the third image, because an SLC is more semantically structured than an RSLC, which is more semantically structured than a CLC.

To capture the relative importance of the various types of LCs, we assign weights to the various LCs such that LCs that are deem to be more representative of the image content are assigned larger weight values. We shall see how these weights come into play in the similarity measure to be discussed in the next section. We note that for the caption, one word in the caption may have up to three different weights with respect to the lexical chains it belongs to. Of course, each word has at least two weights: a SLC weight and a CLC weight. If the word belongs to one RSLC, it will have three weights. One image caption may have several SLCs and several RSLCs, but only one CLC.

The resultant Weight ChainNet model uses a well-structured notion of image's content to capture the semantic relationship between an image and its nearby text. Such a model can be seen as a semantic representation of the content of an image. This model has the properties of exactness, since it captures an image's essential semantic meanings by an image title, ALT, page title and caption. It is space efficient because it does not keep too many words for image representation. The content can be automatically extracted. It is insensitive to noise since all words are stemmed and no stop words exist. Finally, similarity matching is computationally inexpensive using the proposed *list space model* which we shall introduce in the next section.

For a user query, it's usually a free sentence that describes the image content. Naturally, we represent it as a *Query Lexical Chain - QLC*.

4. SEMANTIC MEASURE MODEL
In this section, we will present our similarity measure model between two lexical chains, and between an image and a query respectively.

4.1 Similarity between two Lexical Chains

We have presented the model for representing image/query semantics. To calculate the semantic similarity between a query and an image, we start from determining the similarity between two basic components in an image ChainNet - LC. In our implementation, we store terms of each LC as a list. All the lists belonging to an image are connected to the image root as shown by the ChainNet model (see Figure 1). We propose a *list space formula* to compute the similarity between two LCs as follows:

$$Similarity_{list1,list2} \equiv \frac{\sum_{i=0}^{list1.size()} \sum_{j=0}^{list2.size()} e_i.weight * e_j.weight}{\sqrt{list1.size()} * \sqrt{list2.size()}} * MatchScale$$

where e_i and e_j are matched words in list 1 and list 2 respectively. Two words are *matched* if they are the same word. We note that we have removed stop words and performed stemming from the various LCs.

In the formula, one important parameter is considered: *MatchScale*. Match scale is defined as the closeness of two lists from the view of match order. For example, one LC is " *US president Clinton and wife visited China in 1997*", and the other one is: " *China president Jiang Zemin welcomed Clinton and wife in Tian'an square*". For these two LCs, there are four matching words. For the first LC, the matched words are in order of "*president Clinton wife China*", and in the other, they are "*china president Clinton wife*". We treat each one as a child LC of its original LC. Therefore, the orders of matched words in the two original LCs are not the same. Obviously, the closer the matched order of two children LCs are, the closer the semantics of the original two LCs are. Inspired from the formula for the *angle between two nonzero vectors in 2d-space*, we define the match scale as below:

$$MatchScale_{v1,v2} \equiv \frac{v1 \bullet v2}{\| v1 \| * \| v2 \|}$$

where v1 and v2 represent the child LC of the first and second original LCs respectively. The element value is the position in their respective LC. But the *dot product* between two LCs is redefined as the following:

$$v1 \bullet v2 \equiv \sum_{i=1}^{v1.size()} v1_i * v2_j$$

Where $v2_j$ is the matched word in $v2$ for $v1_i$ in $v1$. As mentioned, two words are matched as long as they are the same.

The above measure determines the similarity between two LCs. However, the two LCs may not be semantically related. For example, consider the query "Singapore Map". An image about Singapore Food, say I1, that contains several occurrences of "Singapore" in CLC may result in a high similarity value even though the images are not semantically related. On the other hand, another image about Singapore Map, say I2, contains only one occurrence of "Singapore" in CLC may result in a lower similarity value despite the fact that it is a desired image. To ensure that two LCs are *semantically related*, we need another parameter called: *Match Level*. Match Level is the number of the *distinct* matched words by a LC and a QLC, denoted as: **LCMatchLevel (LC, QLC)**. The *match level threshold* is the minimum match level for a LC to keep its original semantics. We say one LC is semantically related to a QLC, if and only if the LC's match level is equal to or greater than QLC's match level threshold. Therefore, in our semantic measure model, *semantic similarity* for a LC with respect to a QLC is indicated by the similarity calculated by list space formula in its *match level*. The match level determines *if* the LC is semantically related to the QLC. And the similarity calculated by list space model shows how *well* it is semantically related to the QLC.

4.2 Similarity between ChainNet and LC

Now it is time to calculate the semantic similarity between an image and a query. From the discussion above, we know that an image is represented by a Weight ChainNet, and a query is in the form of a lexical chain. To calculate their similarity, we use the following formula:

$$imageSimilarity_{image,query} \equiv S(TLC,QLC) + S(ALC,QLC) + S(PLC,QLC)$$

$$+ \sum_{i=1}^{SLC \; number} S(SLC_i,QLC) + \sum_{i=1}^{RSLC \; number} S(RSLC_i,QLC) + S(CLC,QLC)$$

where S is the similarity between two LCs. The image match level is defined as:

ImageMatchLevel (ChainNet, QLC) =
MAX (TLC.weight * LCMatchLevel(TLC, QLC),
         ALC.weight * LCMatchLevel(ALC, QLC),
         PLC.weight * LCMatchLevel(PLC, QLC),
         SLC.weight * LCMatchLevel(SLC, QLC),
         RSLC.weight * LCMatchLevel(RSLC, QLC),
         CLC.weight * LCMatchLevel(CLC, QLC)   )

We say one image is semantically related to a query if and only if its match level is equal to or greater than the query's match level threshold. It has the similarity calculated by the above formula with the query in its match level.

5. RELEVANCE FEEDBACK

Because of the large image collection and the impreciseness of a query, it is important to provide mechanisms to help users in specifying their queries more accurately. One such mechanism is to exploit feedback from users based on resultant images returned from the initial query. By allowing users to indicate the relevant (and irrelevant) images, the original query can be refined to further improve the retrieval effectiveness. For this purpose, we develop two techniques: *semantic accumulation* and *semantic integration and differentiation*.

5.1 Semantic Accumulation

The first method, called *semantic accumulation*, allows the user to pick the most relevant image (from the user's subjective judgement) from the result of previous retrieval as the feedback image. The method accumulates all the previous feedback images' semantics to construct a new query for the next retrieval. The resultant query is represented as a kind of ChainNet called Weight F/Q ChainNet (Feedback/Query ChainNet) since it is constructed by the query and the feedback image's ChainNet. This kind of new query is represented in Figure 2.

Obviously, the combination of every entire ChainNet from each previous feedback images is tedious if the user searches again and again. More seriously, more noise will be added into the new query. Therefore, rather than a whole image ChainNet, we use just one single lexical chain which is most semantically related to the original query in the previous feedback image's ChainNet. This is calculated by the list space model. The steps for this method are:

1. Perform search using the F/Q Weight ChainNet (or Weight ChainNet for first attempt)
2. User selects the current feedback image
3. Construct the feedback image's Weight ChainNet
4. Extract the closest lexical chain to the original query from the feedback image by list space model
5. Use the QLC and the weight ChainNet to construct F/Q ChainNet
6. Use that extraced LC and old QLC to construct new QLC
7. Go to step 1

In this algorithm, the semantic is accumulated by adding one most related LC from every previous ChainNet to QLC to form a new QLC. Therefore, the QLC carries richer and richer semantics as users provide more feedback.

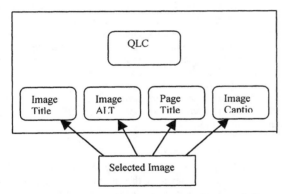

Figure2: F/Q ChainNet in Semantic Accumulation

5.2 Semantic Integration and Differentiation

In the semantic accumulation feedback approach, users can only select one image at a time as the feedback information. To save time and to filter more unrelated images, we introduce another technique: semantic integration and differentiation. In this method, users can select several relevant and irrelevant images simultaneously. By relevant, we mean images that are semantically related to the query as judged by the user and hence should be retrieved. On the other hand irrelevant images are those that the user considers to be unrelated and should not have been retrieved. The system *integrates* the related semantics obtained from the relevant feedback images to construct a new query for the next try. After that, the system combines the semantics from irrelevant images to *differentiate* the irrelevant images from the

returned results. The new query is also represented by a F/Q Weight ChainNet as shown in Figure 3.

The steps for this method are:

1. User selects a number of relevant and irrelevant images.
2. Extract the most semantically related LC from each relevant image's ChainNet to form a new F/Q ChainNet with QLC as a new query.
3. Extract the most un-semantically related LC from each irrelevant image's ChainNet to form a ChainNet for bad images
4. Submit the query
5. From each returned image, remove it from results if it's more related to the bad images' ChainNet.
6. Go to step 1

The semantic similarity formula between two ChainNets can be easily extended from the formula for measuring the similarity between an image and a query.

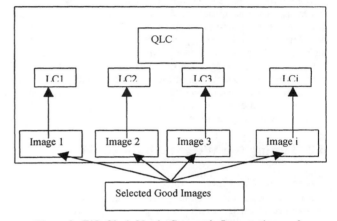

Figure3: F/Q ChainNet in Semantic Integration and Differentitaion

6. EXPERIMENTS

To study the effectiveness of the proposed method, we implemented the proposed model in an image retrieval system and conducted an extensive performance study. This section reports our study and findings.

6.1 Experimental Setup

For purpose of testing the model, we "centralized" the image collection (instead of simply extracting the image at runtime from the various Web sites/pages in the form of a search engine). This is achieved through the design of a Web crawler that automatically searches the WWW for documents with embedded images. The crawler also extracts the image title, image ALT, page URL, page title and image caption from the HTML documents as the images' semantic content. In total, we collected 5232 images from over 2000 different URLs. These images are general, random and diverse enough for us to test on any query. We used 12 text descriptions, as shown in the following table, as our queries for our experiments.

Table 1. Test queries.

Query	Query Description
Q1	Singapore map
Q2	Travel in Spain
Q3	Valentine flower
Q4	Island in the sky
Q5	California beach girl
Q6	England football league
Q7	Green lizard on a red leaf
Q8	Husband is kissing his wife
Q9	National University of Singapore
Q10	Hollywood superstar Jennifer Lopez
Q11	Elephant in the beautiful national park
Q12	Celebrations for new millennium of 2000

Given that we have over 5000 images, it is not practical to scan all images to obtain the relevant images for each query. To determine the set of relevant images for the queries, we adopt the following realistic approach. For each query, we expand the query terms to include terms that are related. This is done using the WordNet [19]. For example, the term girl may be expanded to include the term woman. Each term is then used as a query to extract the list of images whose semantics (or rather the LCs) contain that term. The union of the results from each term form a candidate set of relevant images. We then manually examine the candidate set to eliminate those that are not semantically related to the query to get final set of relevant images.

6.2 Tuning the Weight ChainNet Model

Tuning the Weights
Weight ChainNet model calls for some tuning to be performed. As mentioned earlier, there are 6 types of LCs and different LC types may have different significance in identifying the image semantics. In the first experiment, we evaluate the performance of each type of LCs exclusively to study their different impact on retrieval effectiveness. Figure 4 shows the results.

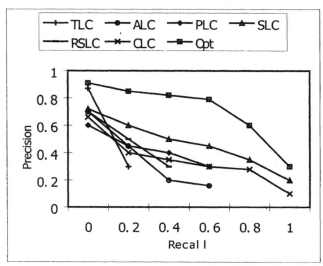

Figure 4: Utility by each Type LC alone to Represent Image

From Figure 4, we can see that for TLC, it cannot achieve >20% recall, although it has high precision. This is due to the lack of information in TLC. For similar reasons, PLC and ALC are not very effective also. For RSLC, since quite a number of images do not have RSLC, it cannot achieve high recall. Only CLC and SLC can result in high recall, but the precision is not satisfactory. TLC, ALC, PLC and RSLC can be used to improve the precision a lot. On the other hand, SLC and CLC can improve the recall. From this result, we have a rough picture of the relative importance of each type of LCs. Clearly, SLC is the most important, followed by TLC, RSLC, ALC or PLC, and finally, it is CLC.

To determine the weights to be assigned to the proposed model that combines all the LCs, we tested different weight combinations from values in 0, 0.2, 0.4, 0.5, 0.6, 0.8 and 1 for each type of LCs. However, we narrowed the search space based on the result from Figure 4 by adopting some simple heuristics. For example, since SLC is the most important, we fixed its weight at 1.0. Moreover, for a LC that is more important, the weights assigned to the other less important LCs cannot be more than its weight. In total, we tested 22 combinations and obtained the following weight assignment for the various LCs: TLC (0.8), ALC(0.6), PLC(0.6), SLC(1), RSLC(0.5), CLC(0.2). In this experiment, we have fixed the scale parameter *coef* of the match level to be 0.6 (see Tuning the Match Level). We shall refer to this scheme as OPT. We also presented the result of OPT in Figure 4. As shown, we can get more than 80% precision with recall of 60%.

Though this experiment is meant to tune the proposed method, we note that it is also a comparative study among the different schemes. Clearly, the results show that using a single LC exclusively cannot provide the best performance, even though such an approach is clearly simple. Moreover, it shows that proper combinations of the various LCs can lead to very effective retrieval results. We also note that the exclusive CLC scheme can be viewed as a form of traditional text-based system without any semantic structure involved. Thus, we expect OPT to outperform existing schemes too.

Tuning the Match Level
There is another parameter that we have to tune, the match level. Recall that the match level is the number of common terms shared by two lexical chains. It determines whether two LCs are semantically related, and then derives if two images are semantically related. In our evaluation system, only those semantically related images are returned.

One single word cannot reflect the semantic meaning of a whole query. If the match level threshold is too small, too many images may be returned to the users. On the contrary, too few images are displayed if the match level threshold is too high. Therefore, it is necessary to choose the best match level thresholds. Since the length of a query is a random variable, a fixed value for match level is not applicable to various queries. We thus define the match level as a linear function of query length:

$$MatchLevel\ Threshold = coef * query.length() + constant$$

where the *coef* is the scale parameter we need to explore in order to get the best results in a reasonable volume. And the *constant* is just an adjustable value.

We tested those 12 queries in Table 1 in order to select the best *coef*. Figures 5a and 5b shows the relationship between precision and *coef* and recall and *coef* respectively.

From Figure 5a, when *coef* is > 0.6, the precision will be greater than 85%. From Figure 5b, we can see that when *coef* is < 0.6, the recall is greater than 60% which is very satisfactory to a large image database. Therefore, observing the combined effect, we select 0.6 as the optimal value of *coef*.

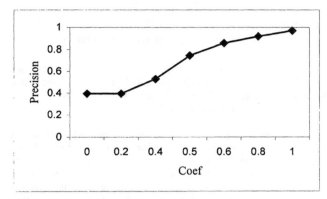

Figiure 5a: Precision Vs. Coef

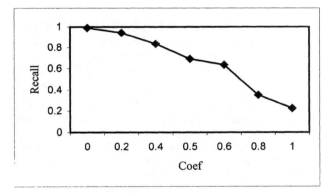

Figure 5b: Recall Vs. Coef

Impact of Match Scale
Match scale explores the importance of match order in the lexical chain. It has the effects in terms of image ranking during presentation of the returned images. Images with higher similarity measures will be returned to users ahead of images with lower similarity values. Figure 6 shows a sample results obtained from Q1. As shown, by considering the match scale, we can get more relevant images being displayed earlier, i.e., ranked higher.

6.3 On Feedback Mechanisms
In this experiment, we study the effectiveness of the two proposed feedback mechanisms: *semantic accumulation* and *semantic integration and differentiantion*. Figure 7 shows the improvement by the two methods respectively. *Opt* is the basic

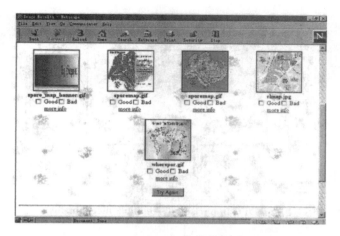

(A) Q1 results before Applying Match Scale

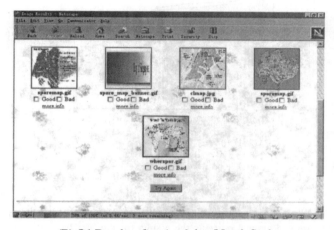

(B) Q1 Results after Applying Match Scale.

Figure 6: Image Results for Q1

Weight ChainNet model without feedback. *Accu* denotes the semantic accumulation method. And *I&D* represents the semantic integration and differentiation method. We note that Accu and I&D represents one application of the feedback loop after Opt returns its resultant images.

From Figure 7, we can see that both methods have improved the precision very much, especially for semantic I&D. We also observe that semantic I&D outperforms Accu. Two reasons account for this. First, in Accu, the whole feedback image ChainNet is used for refining the query. Some noise may be introduced. Second, Accu did not remove those unrelated image from the results. Furthermore, semantic I&D integrates the most relevant LCs in each ChainNet. These LCs do not carry much noise at all. We would like the reader to bear in mind that the comparison is baised against Accu in the sense that Accu employs only one feedback image, while I&D employs several.

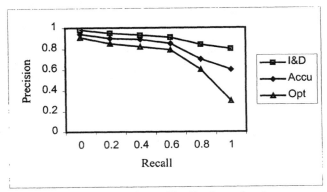

Figure 7: Comparison of feedback mechanisms

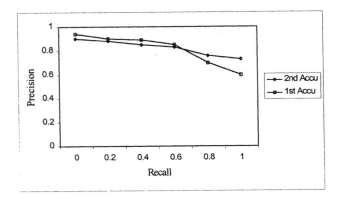

Figure 8: 1st and 2nd try by Semantic Accumulation

To clearly see the effect of the noise that semantic accumulation brought, Figure 8 presents the results for the first feedback and second feedback by semantic accumulation. We can see that the second try on the feedback actually has a bit lower precision, but with relatively higher reacall. But semantic accumulation method has the advantage that the returned image are more semantically related to the specific image selected by user - the feedback image.

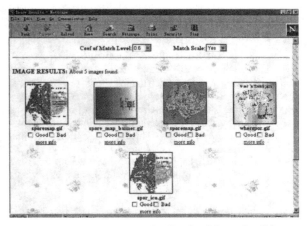

Figure 9: One-step feedback of Accu for Q1.

Figure 10: One-step feedback of I&D for Q1.

Figure 9 shows a sample feedback run of the Accu method for Q1. Compared to the results generated from OPT (the basic Weight ChainNet model without feedback), we see that the set of images retrieved are more relevant.

Figure 10 shows a sample feedback run of the I&D method for Q1.From earlier results without feedback mechanism (see Figure 6), we have identified two relevant and one irrelevant image. As shown in Figure 10, the resultant images are not only more relevant than OPT and Accu approaches, the irrelevant image has also been pruned. In addition, more relevant images have been retrieved.

7. CONCLUSIONS AND FUTURE WORK

In this paper, we have presented a new model to represent the content of images embedded in WWW pages. The proposed Weight ChainNet model combines different types of lexical chains obtained from the surrounding text of an image. Our experimental study showed that the approach can be used as an effective means to represent image semantics. We also proposed two novel feedback mechanisms. In particular, the semantic integration and differentiation method returned more accurate results than semantic accumulation with higher recall. We plan to extend this work in the following ways. First, since we are mainly concerned with the object and event, it may be helpful to guess the lexical chain meaning by applying AI techniques. We are currently looking into some of these techniques. Second, the proposed approach is essentially an Information Retrieval (text-based) approach. We plan to integrate with content-based retrieval methods that capture the visual content of the images. Finally, we are exploring the use of query expansion mechanism [20,21] to enrich the content of the image, i.e., each LC is also expanded using WordNet.

8. ACKNOWLEDGMENTS

This work is part of the VIPER (Visual Property-based Search Engine for image Retrieval) project developed at the National Unviersity of Singapore (see http://unicorn.comp.nus.edu.sg). Discussions with and comments from members of the project team have been helpful.

9. REFERENCE

[1] S.Al-Hawamdeh, B.C. Ooi, R.Price, T.H.Tng, Y.H.Ang, and L.Hi, Nearest neighbor searching in a picture archival system. In *Proceedings of ACM International Conference on Multimedia and Information System*, Pages 17-34, 1991

[2] A.E. Cawkell, Imaging systems and picture collection management: a review. *Information Service & Use*, 12:301-325, 1992

[3] R.Price, T.S Chua, and S.Al-Hawamdeh, Applying relevance feedback on a photo archival system. *Journal of Information Science*, 18:203-215, 1992

[4] J.R. Smith and S.F. Chang. Image indexing and retrieval based on color histograms. In *Proceedings of ACM Multimedia '96*, Pages 87-98

[5] T.S. Chua and W.C. Low. Image retrieval using multiple features and domain knowledge. In *proceeding of International Symposium on Multimedia Information Processing*, Dec, 1997, Pages 543-548

[6] W.Niblack, R.Barber, and W.Equitz. the qbib project: querying images by content using color, texture, and shape. *Technical report, IBM* RJ 9203(81511), Feb, 1993

[7] Greg Pass, Ramin Zabin, and Justin Miller. Computing images using color coherence vectors. In *the Fourth ACM Internaltional Multimedia Conference*, 1996, pages 65-73.

[8] Michael J. Swain and Dana H. Ballard. Color indexing. *International Journal of Computer Vision*, 7(1): 11-32, 1991

[9] T.S. Chua and W.C. Low, and Ch.X. Chu, relevance feedback techniques for color-based image retrieval. In *Proceeding of Multimedia Modelling'98, IEEE Computer Society*, Oct, 1998.

[10] Frisse M.E, (1988). Searching for information in a hypertext medical handbook. *Communications of the ACM*, 3 I(7), pp.880-886.

[11] Frei H.P, and Stieger D. (1992). Making use of hypertext links when retrieving information. *Proceedings ACM-ECHT'92*, Milan, Italy, pp. 102-111.

[12] Croft W.B., and Tutle H.R. (1993). Retrieval strategies for hypertext. *Information Processing & Management*,29(3), pp. 313-324.

[13] Dunlop MD, and Van Rijsbergen C.J,"Hypermedia and free text retrieval", *Information Processing & Management*, 29(3), 1993, Page. 287-298.

[14] Agosti M., and Smeaton A, (1996). Information Retrieval and Hypertext, *Kluwer Academic Publishers*, The Nether-lands.

[15] Harmandas, M. Sanderson and M. D. Dunlop, Image retrieval by hypertext links, *Proceedings of the 20th annual international ACM SIGIR conference on Research and development in information retrieval*, 1997, Pages 296 - 303

[16] Dunlop M.D. (1991). Multimedia Information Retrieval, Ph.D. Thesis. *Computing Science Department, University of Glasgow, Report* 1991/R21.

[17] J.Morris and G.Hirst, Lexical Cohesion Computed by Thesaural Relation and an Indicator of the Structure of Text, *Computational Linguistics*, vol.17, no.1, 1991, Page 22-48.

[18] Shih-Fu Chang, William Chen, and Hari Sundaram, Semantic Visual Template - Linking Visual Fetures to Semantics. *IEEE Intern Conference on Image Processing, Chicago IL*, Oct 1998

[19] G.A. Miller, R. Beckwith, C. Felbaum, D. Gross and K. Miller, Introduction to WordNet: An On-line Lexical Database. Revised Version 1993.

[20] Ellen M. Voorhees and Yuan-Wang Hou, "Vector Expansion in a Large Collection", First Text REtrieval Conference (TREC-1), 1993.

[21] E.M.Voorhees, "Query Expansion using Lexical-Semantic Relations.",ACM-SIGIR,1994.

[22] K.L. Tan, B.C. Ooi and C.Y. Yee, "An Evaluation of Color-Spatial Retrieval Techniques for Large Image Databases", Multimedia Tools and Applications, accepted for publication.

[23] B.C. Ooi, K.L. Tan, T.S. Chua and W. Hsu, "Fast Image Retrieval Using Color-Spatial Information", VLDB Journal, Vol. 7, No. 2, 115-128, May 1998.

A Robust Blind Watermarking Scheme based on Distributed Source Coding Principles *

Jim Chou
University of California - Berkeley
319 Cory Hall
Berkeley, CA 94708

Sandeep Pradhan
University of California - Berkeley
319 Cory Hall
Berkeley, CA 94708

Kannan Ramchandran
University of California - Berkeley
269 Cory Hall
Berkeley, CA 94708

ABSTRACT
We propose a powerful new solution to the multimedia watermarking problem by exploiting its duality with another problem for which we have recently made pioneering constructive contributions. This latter problem is that of distributed source coding, or compression of correlated sources that are distributed. We show how these two seemingly unrelated problems are actually duals of each other. We exploit this duality by transforming our recently introduced powerful constructive framework for the distributed compression problem in [13] to a corresponding dual framework for the watermarking problem. Simulations expose the significant performance gains attained by our proposed watermarking approach and reveal its exciting potential for next-generation watermarking techniques. This can be accredited to the exploitation of the dual roles played by source codes and channel codes in the two problems.

Categories and Subject Descriptors
1 [Multimedia Processing and Coding]: Multimedia Security

General Terms
Digital Watermarking, Data Hiding

1. INTRODUCTION
In the wake of the current Information Technology revolution and the resulting proliferation of digital media content, it is difficult to overstate the importance of multimedia security and copyright protection. Not surprisingly therefore, the field of digital watermarking has generated explosive interest recently. The basic idea behind digital watermarking is to seamlessly insert some information (the digital watermark) into the medium or host signal of interest (e.g., MP3

*Sponsored in part by: NSF MIP 97-03181 (CAREER).

audio, MPEG video, JPEG image, etc.) such that (a) the watermark distorts the host signal minimally (i.e., its presence in the medium is not noticeable), and (b) the watermark can be reliably recovered even if the medium undergoes a certain amount of degradation as a result of both desirable (e.g. compression, signal processing) and undesirable (e.g. malicious attack) reasons. The motivation behind embedding information into the host medium is that if the embedded information can be reliably recovered, then this information can specify the affiliation between the host and its original owner; thus the information must be embedded in a manner that will preclude others from destroying it easily.

Methods for embedding watermarks are wide and varied; popular methods range from modulating the information onto the least significant bits [1] to using the information as a key for indexing pseudo-random noise sequences which are additively combined with the signal (so-called spread-spectrum based methods [7]). Irrespective of the method, the main goal that each method has in common is to embed the maximum amount of information possible given a fixed distortion constraint between the original and watermarked signals (which characterizes the maximum amount of power in the inserted watermark), while allowing for reliable recovery of the embedded information subject to a fixed-distortion attack. However, until recently, the watermarking problem has for the most part been tackled based more on clever tricks and heuristics than on any fundamental theoretical underpinnings (surprisingly, even the popular "spread-spectrum" based watermarking methods turn out to be highly suboptimal [2]).

Fortunately, a recent thread of inspiring research on the field [2, 11, 10] has exposed the fundamental limitations of earlier approaches, and targeted the theoretical foundations for the problem. Inspired by this, practical systems that are grounded on these principles have very recently been proposed [2, 3] which attain significant improvements in the data hiding capacity over previous (and still popular!) classes such as those based on spread spectrum techniques. Our approach to the data hiding problem is in this class of theoretically-inspired next-generation techniques. Our motivation however is unique even in this class, and is inspired by the insight that the watermarking problem is closely connected with, and in fact a dual to, the problem of distributed compression, for which we have recently proposed a powerful constructive framework in [13]. This latter problem is that of source coding with side information (about the source) available only at the receiver. The watermarking problem turns out to be a dual in the sense that it is equivalent to a channel coding problem with side information about the channel available only at the transmitter [11].

This paper is motivated by the goal of exploiting this duality and leveraging our recent insights on a *constructive* framework for the distributed source coding problem [13] to formulate a dual solution to the watermarking problem. It is important to note that our approaches to both problems are rooted in fundamentally sound information-theoretic principles, but unlike information-theoretic results that are non-constructive and asymptotic in nature, our goal is to formulate practical constructions that can lay the foundations for real-world systems.

At the same time, in the context of the watermarking problem, it is important to understand the limitations of our proposed approach related to the assumed distortion metrics for both the watermarking system and the attack channel. In this work, we confine ourselves to Euclidean-space distortions. Our reasons are pragmatic: useful perceptual metrics for media like images and video are severely lacking, while tractable ways of combating more sophisticated attack channels (such as geometric distortion attacks as in the Stirmark freeware package [12]) are difficult to formalize. Nevertheless, we are confident that "good" code constructions which target Euclidean distortion metrics can be leveraged in the construction of "good" codes that target geometric distortions as well, which we propose to do as part of future work.

This paper's primary motivation is to bridge the large existing gap between current watermarking technology and the theoretical limits for watermark transmission for Euclidean distortion metrics. We will show that codes that achieve rate-distortion bounds for distributed source coding can be used to design codes that achieve capacity for digital watermarking. Furthermore, we will provide experimental results based on Gaussian sources and real images with additive white Gaussian noise (AWGN) attacks to unveil the power of this approach.

This paper is organized as follows: In the first section we introduce both the distributed source coding problem and the digital watermarking problem, providing illuminating "toy" examples to illustrate the dualities between the two. In the following section, we generalize the duality between distributed source coding and digital watermarking to the case where the signals are real and Gaussian distributed. In section 4, we use the duality between the two problems to demonstrate how "good" codebooks can be constructed for the digital watermarking problem based on codebooks used for the distributed source coding problem and vice versa. In the final two sections we provide simulation results to demonstrate the power of our approach and to provide some concluding remarks on future work.

2. DUALITY OF DISTRIBUTED SOURCE CODING AND WATERMARKING

In this section we explore the duality between the distributed source coding problem and the watermarking problem.

2.1 Distributed source coding

Source coding with side information is shown schematically in Fig. 1. In this problem, a discrete source X is to be encoded and transmitted to a receiver which has access to some discrete side information Y. Even though the encoder does not have access to Y, using the joint statistics of X and Y, the encoder can compress at the same efficiency as the case when both the encoder and decoder have access to Y. A non-constructive proof of this result was provided by Slepian and Wolf [14]. Pradhan et. al. [13] later provided a constructive algorithm for realizing the results suggested by the proof. To understand how this remarkable result might be realized in practice, we provide the following illustrative example. More detailed constructions can be found in [13]

Example 1: Discrete Case: Consider X and Y to be equiprobable 3-bit data sets which are correlated in the following way: $d_H(X, Y) \leq 1$, where $d_H(.,.)$ denotes Hamming distance. When Y is known both at the encoder and decoder, we can compress X to 2 bits, conveying the information about the uncertainty of X given Y (i.e., the modulo-two sum of X and Y given by: (000),(001),(010) and (100)). Now if Y is known only at the decoder, we can surprisingly still compress X to 2 bits. The method of construction stems from the following argument: if the decoder knows that X=000 or X=111, then it is wasteful to spend any bits to differentiate between the two. In fact, we can group X=000 and X=111 into one coset (it is exactly the principal coset of the length-3 repetition code). In a similar fashion, we can partition the remaining space of 3-bit binary codewords into 3 different cosets with each coset containing the original codewords offset by a unique and correctable error pattern. Since there are 4 cosets, we only need to spend 2 bits to specify the coset in which X belongs. The four cosets are given as

$$\text{coset-1} = (000, 111), \quad \text{coset-2} = (001, 110),$$
$$\text{coset-3} = (010, 101), \quad \text{coset-4} = (011, 110)$$

The decoder can recover X perfectly by decoding Y to the closest (in hamming distance) codeword in the coset specified by the encoder. Thus the encoder does not need to know Y for optimum encoding.

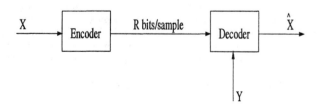

Figure 1: Distributed source coding: only decoder has access to the side information Y.

The above concepts can be generalized to other cases including the encoding/decoding of continuous-valued random variables, where the decoder uses Y to reconstruct the source based on a minimum fidelity criterion. Wyner and Ziv gave a non-constructive proof of the fact that the minimum rate of encoding [15] for a given fidelity criterion D, is

$$R(D) = min_{\hat{X}=f(U,Y),p(U|X)}[I(U;X) - I(U;Y)] \quad (1)$$

where U is the set of codewords representing X, $I(U;X)$ is the Shannon mutual information [6], and the minimization is carried out over all conditional probability density functions $p(U|X)$ and a function $f(U;Y)$ such that $E(X - \hat{X})^2 \leq D$. Pradhan et. al [13] later provided a constructive algorithm for achieving the rates suggessted by Wyner and Ziv's proof. The main idea of encoding is as follows: (1) build a source code to represent X using nearly $2^{nI(U;X)}$ codewords, (2) partition this set into $2^{nR(D)}$ cosets with each coset containing $2^{nI(U;Y)}$ codewords (the set of codewords act as a channel code for the fictitious channel between U and Y), and (3) find the optimal reconstruction, which is obtained as a function $f(U,Y)$.

To elucidate the encoding construction, consider the case where X is an independent identically distributed (*i.i.d.*) Gaussian random variable with side information Y given by $Y = X + N$ (N is an *i.i.d.* Gaussian random variable independent of X). The side information is therefore a noisy version of X and as in the discrete case, it has been shown [15] that an encoder can be designed to represent X as well as the case where the encoder also has access to Y. The practical method proposed in [13] is to design a source code and partition it into a bank of cosets of channel codes. The source code is designed for the optimal representation of X, and is partitioned into cosets which have good distance properties. The source X is quantized to a codeword (referred to as the active codeword) and the index of the coset containing this codeword is sent to the decoder. With the help of Y, the decoder finds the active codeword in the coset whose index is given by the encoder. A practical example is as follows:

Example 2: Continuous Case: Consider an 8-level fixed-length scalar quantizer as the source coder (see Fig. 2), with the rate of transmission fixed at 1 bit/source sample. To

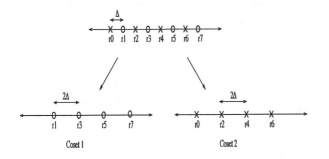

Figure 2: An 8-level quantizer partitioned into 2 cosets containing 4 levels each.

partition the source code, we partition the reconstruction levels into two cosets. The reconstruction levels in coset 1 are denoted as (r_0, r_2, r_4, r_6) and the reconstruction levels in coset 2 are (r_1, r_3, r_5, r_7) (see Fig. 2). The partition is constructed in such a way that the cosets are symmetric and the minimum distance between any two elements within a

coset is kept as large as possible. Upon encoding, X is quantized to a codeword in the composite 8-level quantizer and the index of the coset containing this codeword is sent to the decoder. The decoder finds this codeword in the coset whose index is sent by the encoder, as the one which is closest (in the appropriate distance measure) to Y. In doing so, the decoder can reconstruct the value of X to a codeword which is "close" in terms of squared-error distortion.

In the above example, a simple 8-level scalar quantizer was considered for the sake of simplicity. Encoding constructions, however, can be generalized to more sophisticated source coders. For example, the partition can be done in higher-dimensional spaces using trellis codes. This was proposed in [13] where the n-dimensional product space of scalar quantized reconstruction levels is partitioned into cosets of trellis coded quantizer codebooks.

2.2 Watermarking problem

The digital watermarking problem can be formulated as follows. The encoder has access to two signals; the information (an index set), M, to be embedded, and the signal (host) that the information is to be embedded in. The output of the encoder is the watermarked signal. The attacker will attempt to degrade the signal so that the decoder (who wants to authenticate the watermarked signal) will fail to decode the watermark. The attacker has a distortion constraint on the amount of degradation that he can inflict on the signal. The encoder has to be designed such that the attacker needs to inflict an amount of distortion (to destroy the watermark) that will render the signal to be useless. Mathematically, the goal is to solve the following constrained minimization problem:

$$min_{||W-S||^2 \leq D_1, ||Y-W||^2 \leq D_2} P_e(\hat{M}) \quad (2)$$

where $P_e(\hat{M})$ represents the probability of decoding error.

It was shown in [2, 11] that this problem can be viewed as channel coding with side information (about the channel) at the encoder (see fig. 3). We will consider the case when the

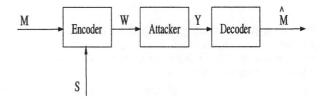

Figure 3: The watermarking problem: the encoder has access to a signal S. M represents the information to be embedded and W represents the watermarked signal.

side information is jointly Gaussian with the noise source. In this case, the attacker is considered to be optimal with respect to his own interests [11] (up to a scaling factor) and the problem becomes the regular AWGN communications problem if both the encoder and decoder have access to the side information Surprisingly, in the case when only the encoder has access to the side information, it has been shown that this system can *perform as well as when both the encoder and decoder have access to the side information [5]*. In fact, this is the key insight which motivates our analysis for the digital watermarking system through exploitation of its dual nature with the distributed source coding problem. Before formulating the details for constructing an encoder/decoder for the watermarking problem, we present an example of channel coding with side-information at the encoder to illustrate key concepts. For this we turn to the problem of writing on defective memories [9], which, like watermarking, can be viewed as channel coding with side-information at the encoder. In this problem the encoder attempts to write data onto faulty registers with one of the registers always being "stuck-at" 0 or 1. The encoder, however, has full knowledge of which register is always "stuck". If the decoder also has this knowledge, then $n-1$ bits can be stored reliably in n registers with one "stuck-at" fault. It was shown in [9] that the encoder can be designed to perform as well as the case when both the encoder and the decoder have access to the "stuck-at" position. We illustrate the method for constructing such an encoder in the following example (which is the dual to Example 1)[1].

Example3: Faulty Registers: Consider a 3-bit memory device, which has one "stuck-at" in any position with a uniform probability of the "stuck-at" being either a one or a zero. When both the encoder and the decoder know the value and the position of the "stuck-at", the encoder can write 2 bits reliably. Now consider the case when only the encoder has access to the "stuck-at". Let $\mathcal{A}$ denote the the set of binary three tuples: $\{0,1\}^3$. We partition $\mathcal{A}$ into cosets of codewords which are compatible with any type of "stuck-at". This partition is the same as the one considered in Example 1. If the encoder wants to write the first message, he chooses a codeword from the first coset which is compatible with the "stuck-at". If the first bit has a "stuck-at" fault of 1, then he chooses [1 1 1] as the codeword to be written on the memory. In this fashion, we can again reliably write two bits (corresponding to the index of the coset), even though the decoder does not have access to the "stuck-at".

The above problem can be generalized into the problem of channel coding with side information, for which the capacity can be calculated. The information-theoretic capacity [9, 8, 5] of such systems is given by

$$C = max_{p(U,S|X)}[I(U;Y) - I(U;S)] \qquad (3)$$

where the maximization is over all conditional probability density functions $p(U, X|S)$. The signal S is the side information about the channel and U represents the codeword space. The main steps for encoding are as follows: (1) build a channel code over the space of U, with the number of codewords being nearly equal to $2^{nI(U;Y)}$ (where n is the block length of encoding), (2) partition this channel codeword space into cosets of source codes with each coset containing nearly $2^{nI(U;S)}$ codewords, and (3) choose a codeword, U, to represent S from the coset which has an index

---

[1] We use the term "stuck-at" loosely to refer to a faulty memory register which is constrained to always be a 1 or a 0.

equal to the message. The size of the index set should be nearly equal to 2^{nC}, where C is given in (3). The signal, X, which is transmitted over the channel is a function $f(U, S)$.

Returning to the watermarking problem, we consider the case where the channel is AWGN (see Fig. 3) and the signal (side information, S) is *i.i.d.* Gaussian. In this case, it was shown by [5] that the capacity (3) is given as

$$C = \frac{1}{2}log\left\{\frac{P}{N} + 1\right\} \qquad (4)$$

where P and N represent the transmitter power constraint and the variance of the channel noise respectively. To achieve capacity, Costa [5] showed that the space of codewords must be of the form $U = X + \alpha S$, where $\alpha = \frac{P}{P+N}$ and N is the variance of the attacker's noise. The codeword U should be chosen in a way that will ensure that the projection of U along the direction orthogonal to S has power P.

The watermarking problem can be posed as a version of the above problem, where the signal (i.e., image, audio, etc.) is given by S, the attack is AWGN (with a distortion constraint of N) and the distortion constraint between the signal and the watermarked signal is given as P. In doing so, the above procedure is reinterpreted as follows: the codeword U is chosen to be a quantized representation of some scaled version of S such that the quantization noise is orthogonal to U (see Fig. 4). This scaling factor can be obtained by the geometrical visualization of the encoding process suggested by [5]. Using geometry, the scaling factor is solved to be

$$\beta S = U + V \qquad (5)$$

where V denotes the quantization noise and β is such that U is the "ideal" rate-distortion-quantized version of βS with $\beta = \frac{P+\alpha^2 Q}{\alpha Q}$. As a result, we have a constructive approach for encoding watermarks into a given signal. The encoding process is summarized as follows: (1) pick a channel code over the space of U, (2) partition the channel code into cosets of source codewords with each codeword representing a quantized version of βS and (3) choose the index of the coset in which the signal is to be quantized based on the watermark that is to be encoded into the signal.

Upon decoding, the decoder finds a codeword, γU in the composite channel code (containing nearly $2^{nI(U;Y)}$) which is closest to the received vector (in some sense) where $\gamma = \frac{P+\alpha Q}{P+\alpha^2 Q}$. The coset containing the decoded codeword is declared as the decoded watermark message. It can be shown [5] that the scaling which is done at the encoder provides the required distance property to tolerate the attacker's noise at the decoder.

3. SUMMARY OF DUALITY

The duality between distributed source coding with side information at the decoder and channel coding with side information at the encoder is best illustrated by a set of diagrams. For a more rigorous treatment of the duality and achievable rates, the reader is referred to [4].

In distributed source coding, the set of possible messages to be encoded will roughly lie on a hyper-sphere of L dimensions for L large. The encoding operation then entails

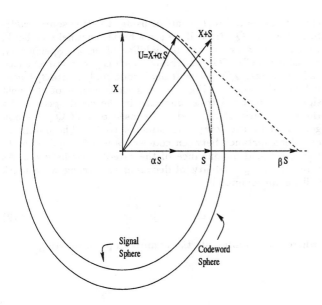

Figure 4: Geometric interpretation of the optimal encoding: U and S denote the codeword chosen for encoding and the signal to be watermarked respectively. This can also be interpreted as choosing that U which is the quantized version of βS as shown. The watermark added onto the signal S is X.

finding a codeword on the codeword sphere (see Fig. 5) that is within the expected distortion to the message point. The selected codeword will belong to one of R cosets, where R is the achievable rate, and the index of the coset will be the encoded message. One will easily notice that the encoding operation for distributed source coding with side-information at the decoder can also be viewed as the decoding operation for channel coding with side-information at the encoder. Using Fig. 5, we see that the message sphere can be viewed as the received signal sphere in the case of channel coding with side information at the encoder. The decoder will then find the codeword on the codeword sphere which is closest (in some sense) to the received signal point. The coset to which the decoded codeword belongs will represent the received message (in the watermarking context, the received message will represent the watermark).

The decoding operation for distributed source coding can be understood with the aid of Fig. 6. The decoder will have both the side-information and the index of the coset available to it. The side-information will roughly lie on a hypersphere given that the dimension is large. To reconstruct the encoded message, the decoder will search through the set of codewords in the coset specified by the encoder, and find the nearest codeword (in some sense). Upon finding the "correct" codeword, the message can be reconstructed as a linear combination of the decoded codeword and the side-information [4]. As to be expected, the encoding operation for channel coding with side information at the encoder parallels the decoding operation for distributed source coding with side-information at the decoder. In the channel coding case, the encoder has both the side-information and the index of the coset (message to be sent) available to it. Again,

the side-information will roughly lie on a hyper-sphere and the encoder will find the codeword in the coset specified by the message that is nearest to the side-information (in some sense) (see also Fig. 4). The encoder will then transmit a linear combination of the codeword and the side-information to the decoder.

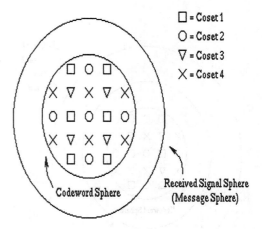

Figure 5: Geometric interpretation of the decoding (encoding) operation for data hiding (distributed source coding) with side information at the encoder (decoder).

The purpose of the above discussion was to illustrate the duality between distributed source coding with side-information at the decoder and channel coding with side-information at the encoder, so that key concepts could be illustrated to inspire "good" codebook constructions. As a result, there is not much rigor in the above discussion. A more rigorous proof of the duality between distributed source coding with side-information at the decoder and channel coding with side-information at the encoder can be found in [4].

4. DESIGN AND CONSTRUCTION
Inspired by the previous section and our earlier work in [13], we can now construct practical solutions to the watermarking problem. We will look at several different codebook constructions to illustrate the necessities in designing a codebook that introduces minimal distortion to the host signal but is robust to the attacker's "noise".

4.1 Codebook design
As mentioned above, the encoding entails taking a channel code and partitioning it into cosets of source codes. Thus, in order to design a good codebook, one needs to use a "good" channel code which can be partitioned into "good" source codes. To illustrate, we will consider three different codebook constructions. The first codebook construction uses Pulse Amplitude Modulation (PAM) as the composite channel code, and partitions the channel code into source code-

words given by a scalar quantizer (SQ); we will refer to this method as PAM-SQ. The next construction uses PAM as the composite channel code, and partitions the channel code into codewords given by a trellis-coded quantizer (TCQ); we refer to this method as PAM-TCQ. And in the final construction we use TCM as the composite channel code, but partition the channel code into source codewords given by a trellis-coded-quantizer; we refer to this method as TCM-TCQ.

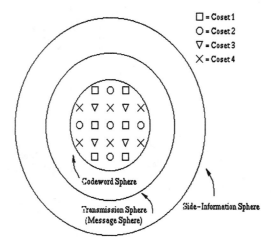

Figure 6: Geometric interpretation of the encoding (decoding) operation for data hiding (distributed source coding) with side information at the encoder (decoder).

The PAM-SQ codebook can be constructed as the product space of 1-dimensional scalar quantizers. The cosets are divided as in Example 2. In this scenario, we can easily calculate the average distortion per sample to be:

$$D = \frac{(2\Delta)^2}{12} = \frac{4\Delta^2}{12} \qquad (6)$$

where Δ represents the step-size of the scalar-quantizer. The minimum distance between codewords will be $d_{min} = \Delta$ and the probability of error per dimension is approximately

$$p = Q(\sqrt{\frac{\Delta^2}{2N_o}}) \qquad (7)$$

Thus, the probability of decoding a wrong watermark is:

$$P_e = 1 - (1-p)^L \qquad (8)$$

where L is the number of watermark bits and assuming that the quantization error is uniformly distributed across each quantization bin and that the attack channel can be modeled as additive white Gaussian noise with variance $N_o/2$. Next, using PAM-TCQ, we can introduce less distortion to the host signal while maintaining the same probability of

error. This is a direct result of using a better source codebook (i.e., TCQ). Now, if we use a better channel codebook, we can also decrease the probability of error. Specifically, consider a TCM-TCQ codebook which is generated as a cascade of a rate-2/3 convolutional code and a rate-3/4 convolutional code (see Fig. 7). A scaled version of the host signal is quantized to a codeword in the coset specified by the watermark. Each coset will consist of a TCQ codebook generated by the composite rate-2/4 trellis. The minimum euclidean distance between codewords will be equivalent to the free euclidean distance of the rate-3/4 trellis code. As a result, the probability of decoding the wrong watermark will be approximately:

$$P_e = N_{free}Q(\sqrt{\frac{d_{free}^2}{2N_o}}) \qquad (9)$$

where N_{free} represents the number of paths starting at one

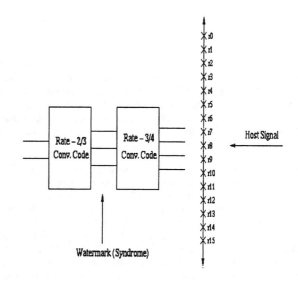

Figure 7: A method for constructing the TCM-TCQ codebook for encoding digital watermarks.

node and ending at the same node with distance d_{free}. The probability of error achieved by TCM-TCQ will in general be lower than either PAM-SQ or PAM-TCQ for a given distortion to the host signal.

From the above analysis, we can see that by choosing good source codebooks, we can limit the distortion introduced to the host signal. On the other hand, by choosing good channel codebooks, we can make the watermark more resistant to attacks. Hence, to design a good watermarking scheme requires a careful choice of source and channel codebooks. In general there are two methods of improving the codebook. The first method involves a direct application of Forward Error Correction (FEC) codes to the watermark message. In general, this has the effect of increasing the euclidean distance between codewords, but has the disadvantage of decreasing the watermark throughput. The other method of improving the codebook is to design a better code in the euclidean space. This will also decrease the probability of error, but has the advantage of maintaining the watermark throughput.

4.2 Algormithm

We now have a means to formulate a practical digital watermarking algorithm. The steps for encoding are as follows:

(1) Design an appropriate codebook (see Section 4.1)
(2) Scale the host signal by β (see Section 2.2)
(3) Determine the codeword, U, in the coset indexed by the watermark message which is closest to the scaled host signal
(4) Transmit a linear combination of the codeword and host signal.

Similarly, the decoding operation can be enumerated as follows:

(1) Scale the received signal by γ (see Section 2.2)
(2) Find the closest codeword, U, to the scaled received signal
(3) Declare the coset that the codeword lies in as the decoded watermark message.

5. PERFORMANCE

To test our watermarking constructions, we have run simulations on the PAM-TCQ and TCM-TCQ cases. The first set of simulations that we conducted, assumed that the signal was Gaussian and that the attack was AWGN. We fixed the probability of decoding error to be less than 10^{-5} and determined the amount of distortion that was necessary to ensure this probability of error given a fixed-distortion attack. The performance curves representing the signal-to-distortion (i.e., signal power vs. watermark power) ratio vs. signal-to-noise (i.e., signal power vs. noise power) at $P_e(\hat{M}) = 10^{-5}$ and a rate of 1 embedded-bit/sample is given in Fig. 8. It can be seen from the figure that TCM-TCQ outperforms PAM-TCQ significantly. The reason for this performance discrepancy is that TCM-TCQ uses a better channel code than PAM-TCQ.

The next simulation that we conducted is of a more practical use. We consider the case where S is the 'McKinley' image and the attack is confined to JPEG compression. We again tested both PAM-TCQ and TCM-TCQ. At an embedding rate of $\frac{1}{64}$ bits/sample, PAM-TCQ incurred a Peak-Signal-to-Distortion-Ratio (PSDR) of 43.48dB in order to withstand a JPEG compression factor of 75%. On the other hand, TCM-TCQ incurred a PSDR of 44.12dB in order to withstand a JPEG compression quality factor of 55%. Again TCM-TCQ outperforms PAM-TCQ. The above experiments were performed assuming that large amounts of data needed (1 bit/64 samples) to be hidden in the host signal. In various watermarking applications, however, often only a few bits need to be hidden in a given image. To alter our proposed solution to operate at lower embedding rates, we can use an outer channel code to code the syndrome. In the interest of demonstrating the power of our approach, we tried the extreme case of using a length 4096 trivial repetition code, to reduce the embedding rate to 1 bit/ image (512x512). For such a case, both the PAM-TCQ and the TCM-TCQ solutions were able to admit JPEG attacks of (1%) and still recover the one-bit watermark successfully. In Fig. 9 we show the watermarked McKinley image, and in

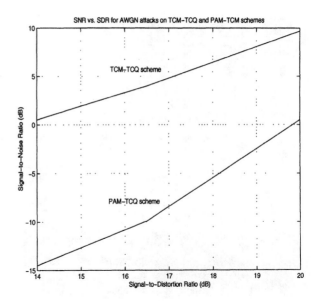

Figure 8: **Performance curves of PAM-TCQ and TCM-TCQ given fixed distortion attacks.**

Fig. 10 we show the attacked McKinley (Q=1%) image, in which we were able to successfully recover the watermarked bit.

Figure 9: **Watermarked McKinley image.**

For the above experiments we used relatively simple source and channel codes to achieve our performance. We can use more sophisticated source and channel codes in our framework to attain even better performance. For example, we can use turbo-coded modulation to improve our channel coding performance, and we can go to higher dimensional channel codes (coded QAM, coded n-dimensional simplex signals, etc.) to lower our rates. Furthermore, we can use

Figure 10: Degraded McKinley image (JPEG compressed, Q=1%). The watermarked bit was successfully recovered.

vector quantization to improve our source codebook.

6. CONCLUSION

In conclusion, we have shown that the watermarking problem and the distributed source coding problem can be viewed as duals of each other, where the former is channel coding with side information at the transmitter and the latter is source coding with side information at the receiver. In the first case, the channel code is partitioned into a bank of cosets of source codes, while in the latter the source code is partitioned into a bank of cosets of channel codes. The two 3-bit binary data examples clearly illustrate the dual nature of the two problems. Through simulation results, it can be seen that with better source and channel codes, our proposed solution will push towards capacity. Furthermore, our solution is easily amenable to codes built for higher-dimensions [13].

As stated in the beginning, all of the results in this paper, targeted Euclidean-space attacks. Current work is in progress to integrate our approach with other methods to address geometric attacks to provide for a more complete watermarking solution.

7. REFERENCES

[1] J. M. Barton. Method and apparatus for embedding authentication information within digital data. *United States Patent #5,646,997*, Issued July 8 1997.
[2] B. Chen and G. W. Wornell. Preprocessed and postprocessed quantization index modulation methods for digital watermarking. *Proc. SPIE Security and Watermarking Multimedia Contents*, 3971, Jan 2000.
[3] J. Chou, S. Pradhan, L. El Ghaoui, and K. Ramchandran. A robust optimization solution to the data hiding problem based on distributed source coding principles. *Proc. of SPIE*, January 2000.
[4] J. Chou, S. S. Pradhan, and K. Ramchandran. On the duality between distributed source coding and data hiding. *preprint*, June 2000.
[5] M. Costa. Writing on dirty paper. *IEEE Trans. on Information Theory*, 29:439–441, May 1983.
[6] T. M. Cover and J. A. Thomas. *Elements of Information theory*. Wiley, New York, 1991.
[7] I. Cox, J. Killian, T. Leighton, and T. Shamoon. Secure spread spectrum watermarking for multimedia. *IEEE Trans. on Image Processing*, 6(12):1673–1687, December 1997.
[8] S. Gel'fand and M. Pinsker. Coding for channel with random parameters. *Problems of Control and Information Theory*, 9:19–31, 1980.
[9] C. Heegard and A. El Gamal. On the capacity of computer memory with defects. *IEEE Trans. on Information Theory*, 29:731–739, September 1983.
[10] P. Moulin. The role of information theory in watermarking and its application to image watermarking. *Preprint*, Mar 2000.
[11] P. Moulin and J. O'Sullivan. Information-theoretic analysis of information hiding. *Preprint*, Mar 2000.
[12] F. Petitcolas and M. Kuhn. Stirmark software.
[13] S. S. Pradhan and K. Ramchandran. Distributed source coding using syndromes: Design and construction. *Proceedings of the Data Comression Conference (DCC)*, March 1999.
[14] D. Slepian and J. K. Wolf. Noiseless encoding of correlated information sources. *IEEE Trans. on Inform. Theory*, IT-19:471–480, July 1973.
[15] A. D. Wyner and J. Ziv. The rate-distortion function for source coding with side information at the decoder. *IEEE Trans. on Inform. Theory*, IT-22:1–10, January 1976.

Automatic recording agent for digital video server

Atsuyoshi Nakamura   Naoki Abe
NEC C& C Media Research Laboratories
4-1-1 Miyazaki, Miyamae-ku
Kawasaki 216-8555 JAPAN

{atsu,abe}@ccm.cl.nec.co.jp

Hiroshi Matoba   Katsuhiro Ochiai
NEC Human Media Research Laboratories
4-1-1 Miyazaki, Miyamae-ku
Kawasaki 216-8555 JAPAN

{matoba,ochiai}@hml.cl.nec.co.jp

ABSTRACT

We propose and evaluate the performance of a number of methods for automatic recording of TV programs for digital video servers, which estimate the user's preference over TV programs based on her/his past viewing behavior and automatically record a selected number of TV programs believed to be of interest to the user. Our methods combine the so-called content-based filtering and social (or collaborative) filtering methods and are based on a certain class of on-line learning algorithms known as the 'specialist' algorithms, recently developed in the field of computational learning theory. We empirically evaluated the performance of content-based part of the proposed methods using preference data on TV programs consisting of scores given by people on actual TV programs. The results are largely encouraging and indicate in particular that our methods are practical in terms of both the precision in predicting the user's preference and computational complexity.

1. INTRODUCTION

The ever falling price of hard disks has made the home use of a digital storage device as a means of recording and storing TV programs a reality. This opens up a host of new applications such as a video-on-demand like function at home. Another important development in TV broadcasting is the introduction of digital broadcasting which has resulted in a dramatic increase in the number of programs available for home viewing. This is the TV version of the information chaos which has been brought about by the Internet and the need for navigation techniques that can help locate the information each user wants has become acute. Such navigation functions for TV programs have become possible now that extra information on TV programs, such as electronic program guide (EPG) and information regarding other users' viewing behavior, is becoming increasingly available, either by integration into the broadcasting itself or via the Internet.

In the present paper, we propose and evaluate the perfor-

mance of a number of methods for automatic recording of TV programs for digital video home servers, which estimate the user's preference over TV programs based on her/his past viewing behavior and automatically record a selected number of TV programs believed to be of interest to the user. Our methods combine the so-called content-based filtering [8] and social (or collaborative) filtering methods [9, 11, 12], and are based on a certain class of on-line learning algorithms known as the 'specialist' algorithms, recently developed in the field of computational learning theory [4]. These are theoretically well-founded methodologies of learning that provide a unified learning framework which bases its predictions on information provided by a variety of sources, such as content-features and other users' preferences.

The automatic recording task for TV programs is distinguished from other typical applications of filtering methods, such as applications to filtering home pages and internet news (e.g. [8, 7]), in at least two important aspects: the storage requirement and the real-time nature of TV broadcasting. The heavy requirement on the storage space by digital video implies a correspondingly severe requirement on the precision of the filtering method employed, and motivates the introduction of a new performance criterion in terms of storage optimization, which is absent in most other filtering problems. The real-time nature of TV poses challenge in at least two ways: one is the fact that the recording method need look ahead in the near future if it hopes to globally optimize its scheduling, and the other is the way collaborative filtering is only effective on the past TV programs which have already been broadcast. Together the TV recording scheduling problem can be formulated as a temporally extended version of the well-known 'knapsack problem' [5].

The methods we propose address all of the issues discussed above in an integrated fashion. Our scheduling methods are based on an efficient dynamic programming algorithm for the original knapsack problem, modified to reflect the peculiarities of the current problem such as the temporal extension and the so-called exploration-exploitation trade-off. (See Section 2 for detailed explanations.) They are then combined with the aforementioned estimation method for the user's preference based on the specialist algorithm, providing a well-founded framework for automatic TV-recording agents. It is these technical developments of the proposed methods that distinguish them from other existing approaches to the problem of personalizing TV-guides (c.f. [2, 1]).

We empirically evaluated the performance of the proposed methods using preference data on TV programs consisting of scores given by people on actual TV programs. In our preliminary experiments, we tested the content-based filtering part only. The results are largely encouraging and indicate that our methods are practical in terms of both the precision in predicting the user's preference and computational complexity.

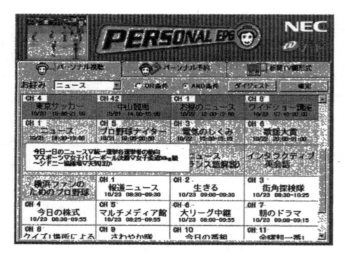

Figure 1: An example user interface of @randomTV. The different shadings indicate four different groups of available programs: (1) manually recorded by the user, (2) recorded by the automatic recording agent, and (3) currently broadcast on tuner.

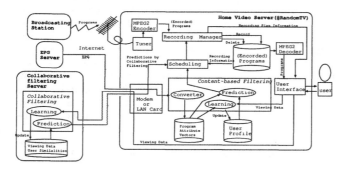

Figure 2: The basic architecture of @RandomTV. This paper proposes methods for collaborative filtering, content-based filtering, and scheduling.

Our recording methods are implemented on a PC-based digital video home server called '@RandomTV' [10] equipped with various functions such as random and user friendly access to the recorded programs. The basic architecture of @RandomTV is shown in Figure 2. The methods proposed in this paper comprise the automatic recording function of @RandomTV, and can be operated with the kind of user interface shown in Figure 1. (See Section 7 for details concerning these figures.) The user is allowed to allocate an arbitrary portion of the hard disk to the automatic recording agent, and the rest for manual recording. The system is also

equipped with connection to the Internet, and we hope to conduct performance evaluation experiments involving both content-based and collaborative filtering in the near future.

2. AUTOMATIC TV RECORDING PROBLEM

We formulate the automatic digital video recording problem as follows. At any time, the recording agent is given a set of candidate programs to record, which consists of the past programs which are currently stored in the hard disk and all programs which are about to be broadcast within some future time window. A limit on the total length of programs that can be recorded is imposed by the storage capacity of the server on which the recording agent is realized. For each program, the probability with which it will be viewed by a particular user can be estimated using the user's past viewing behavior. The goal of the recording agent then is to set its recording schedule for some time window so that the expected viewing time is maximized[1] on the condition that the total storage required by the schedule is never to exceed the given storage capacity. Ideally, this optimization should be carried out over a long enough time window so that a decision to record a program at any point will take into account how this decision will fare in the future, when more programs become available for recording, but a larger time window would require larger computation time, presenting us with a kind of trade-off. Note also that the expected viewing time is dependent on the viewing habits of the users, such as whether they watch TV once a day at a relatively regular time or at random times of the day. The problem we have therefore is a version of the so-called knapsack problem, which is temporally extended in a number of ways.

The estimation of the viewing probability mentioned above is in and of itself a challenging problem. Here we propose to do this estimation by combining the results of both content-based and social (collaborative) filtering methods. In the content-based estimation, we first transform the text description for each TV program in an EPG(electronic program guide) to a vector of 0,1-valued attributes, each standing for the occurrence (or non-occurrence) of a word, as is customary in the field of information retrieval. We then treat each attribute as a 'specialist,' that predicts the probability that the TV program will be viewed, provided the corresponding word occurs in the EPG text for that program. The final estimation is done by weighted average of their predictions. Note here that a 'specialist' is a predictor that makes a prediction only on instances that are in its 'speciality.' In our current scenario, a word predicts only when it occurs in a text.[2] Similarly, in the collaborative filtering/estimation, we treat each of the other users as a 'specialist,' who only votes for those programs on which they have an opinion.

---

[1]We are actually interested in maximizing the user's satisfaction. In the absence of explicit preference information on the programs given by the user, however, this is difficult to quantify. Furthermore, it is reasonable to suppose that, in the long run, the viewed hours will be a good indication of the user's degree of satisfaction.

[2]On-line prediction algorithms based on specialists have been applied to the problem of text categorization, for example by Cohen et al [3].

There is a challenging issue regarding the relationship between the scheduling and estimation, which is known as the 'exploration-exploitation trade-off.' This is the trade-off between recording those programs that are estimated to be highly preferred by the user, and those that the system has little information about and would benefit from obtaining more information. We resolve this issue by in effect maximizing the sum of the expected viewing time and the standard deviation of the estimation, rather than the viewing time itself.

3. THE SCHEDULING ALGORITHMS
3.1 The Temporally Extended Knapsack Problem

As first approximation, the automatic recording problem can be formulated as the so-called knapsack problem, as described below. Let r be a bound on the storage capacity of the hard disk on which the programs are to be stored. Let $1, ..., n$ be the candidate programs currently considered for recording. Usually, these consist of those programs currently stored in the hard disk and those that are about to be broadcast in some time window. Let l_i be the length (say in minutes) of program i and p_i be its currently estimated probability of being viewed. Let x_i be a 0,1-valued (random) variable indicating whether or not program i is to be recorded (1 if it is to be recorded and 0 otherwise.) We then wish to maximize the total expected viewing time

$$\sum_{i=1}^{n} p_i l_i x_i \qquad (1)$$

subject to the constraint that

$$\sum_{i=1}^{n} l_i x_i \leq r. \qquad (2)$$

It is easy to see that this is an instance of the classical knapsack problem.

In the TV recording problem, rather than maximizing the expected viewing time at a fixed future time, we wish to maximize the expected viewing time over some time window. Formally, we wish to maximize

$$\sum_{t} v_t \sum_{i=1}^{n} p_i l_i x'_{i,t} \qquad (3)$$

subject to the constraint that

$$\forall t \sum_{i=1}^{n} l_i x_{i,t} \leq r \qquad (4)$$

where $x_{i,t}$ is a time-dependent variable which is 1 if program i *requires* free space on the hard disk at time t and 0 otherwise, $x'_{i,t}$ is 1 if program i is stored in the hard disk at time t and 0 otherwise, and v_t is the probability that the user watches them at time t. More specifically, $x'_{i,t}$ is 1 for t in the rage of $b'_i \leq t \leq e_i$ and 0 otherwise, where b'_i and e_i respectively stand for the ending time of program i's broadcasting and the time of its deletion from the hard disk. Similarly, $x_{i,t}$ is 1 for $b_i \leq t \leq e_i$ and 0 otherwise, where b_i stands for the starting time of program i's broadcasting. Note that we define $e_i = b_i$ when program i is not selected to be recorded. If the probability distribution v_t is assumed to be uniform, then the above objective function is simplified as follows:

$$\sum_{i=1}^{n} p_i l_i s_i \qquad (5)$$

where s_i stands for the 'survival time' for program i, namely $s_i = \max\{e_i - b'_i, 0\}$. For those programs that are not deleted in the current scheduling, e_i is unknown, so we set $e_i = T + D$, where T stands for the ending time of the current time window, and D is the default survival time after the current window. (In our experiments, D was set to be 240 hours.)

As can be seen in the above formulation, our problem is critically dependent on the user's viewing habits, such as whether they regularly watch the recorded TV programs at night (presumably when they return from work) or they do so at random times of the day, which defines the viewing probabilities v_t in the above formulation. When the user's viewing pattern is regular, say always at 10 p.m., then the problem reduces to the original knapsack problem with a 24 hour time window, whereas for users with random viewing patterns, the temporally extended formulation is more appropriate.

Another important issue has to do with the fact that the values of p_i are estimated from data. When the data size is small and the estimates are relatively unreliable, the objective function may be accordingly unreliable and thus trusting it too much may lead all subsequent actions astray. Those programs that are estimated to have much lower viewing probabilities than their true values may never be selected again and their inaccurate estimates may be left forever uncorrected. This is a case of the so-called exploration-exploitation trade-off. In order to address this issue, we propose a modification to the above basic formulation. In particular, we add a term corresponding to the standard deviation of the estimate to the objective function, resulting in the following modification,

$$\sum_{i=1}^{n} (p_i + \lambda d_i) l_i s_i. \qquad (6)$$

Here d_i is the standard deviation of estimating p_i, and λ is a real-valued parameter controlling the degree to which we take into account the uncertainty of estimation. (In the sequel, we generally abbreviate $p_i + \lambda d_i$ as p_i.)

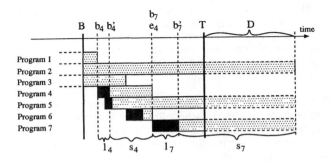

Figure 3: Example recording schedule

Figure 3 shows an example recording schedule. In this example, the time window is between B and T. Programs 1, 2 and 3 are already stored in the hard disk at B, and programs 4, 5, 6 and 7 are about to be broadcast between B and T. A black bar indicates that the program is broadcast during the specified time interval, and a dotted bar indicates that the program is stored in the hard disk. For example, program 4 begins at b_4, ends at b'_4 and is scheduled to be deleted at e_4. Programs 2, 5 and 7 are scheduled to remain in the hard disk at T and, for the purpose of calculating their survival time, are supposed to be deleted at $T + D$.

3.2 Approximate Solutions Using Dynamic Programming

It is well-known that the knapsack problem is NP-complete [5], but this is with respect to the bit-representation of the capacity upper bound r, and in fact there is an efficient algorithm that solves it in time polynomial in r itself, rather than $\log r$, i.e. the knapsack problem is not *strongly* NP-complete. We briefly review this method below. Write the optimal value of the objective function (the expected viewing time) f for the first k programs and capacity upper bound m as $f_k(m)$, then the following recurrence holds.

$$f_1(m) = \begin{cases} p_1 l_1 s_1 & \text{if } l_1 \leq m \\ 0 & \text{otherwise} \end{cases}$$

$$f_k(m) = \begin{cases} f_{k-1}(m) & \text{if } m < l_k \\ \max \left\{ \begin{array}{l} f_{k-1}(m) \\ f_{k-1}(m - l_k) + p_k l_k s_k \end{array} \right\} & \text{otherwise} \end{cases}$$

Thus, we can solve for the optimal value of f by dynamic programming with loops that make sure that the values of f for smaller values of k, m have already been computed at each step.

A solution provided by the above algorithm for the knapsack problem provides a satisfactory solution when viewing is known to take place exactly at the end of the time window being considered. Otherwise it does not provide a satisfactory solution since the hard disk will be full only at the end of the time window and a big part of the disk space will be left unused at early stages. As a next approximation to the temporally extended version of the knapsack problem, we propose to fill in the unused part of the disk space by greedily selecting those with the highest scores per unit disk space and unit length of time, among the programs that were not scheduled to be recorded in the first round. The details of this scheduling method, which we refer to as the 'Optimal-Greedy' method, are shown in Figure 4. Note in the algorithm descriptions that B and T are the beginning and ending times of current time window, and D is the default survival time after the current time window. We use in general $\pi_i(L)$ to denote the list of projections of elements of L to the i-th coordinate.

For comparison, we also use a simpler scheduling algorithm which does both static scheduling and filling-in by greedy heuristics. We call this algorithm 'Greedy-Greedy' and show the details in Figure 4 for completeness. Also for comparison, we consider two variants of Optimal-Greedy, which do not greedily pack the unused part of the schedule output by the optimal (knapsack) algorithm. These are Optimal-Leave and Optimal-Delete and work in the following way. In

Procedure: Optimal-Greedy
/* Use Knapsack algorithm for static schedule */
Input
  r : recording capacity (minutes)
  n : number of programs
  $\{(p_i, b_i, b'_i) : i = 1, ..., n\}$: program information
    (estimeted viewing probability, start time, end time)
  T : end time of time window

For $m = 1$ to r
$$f_1(m) = \begin{cases} 0 & \text{if } m < l_1 \\ p_1 l_1 (T + D - b'_1) & \text{otherwise} \end{cases}$$
For $k = 2$ to n
  For $m = 1$ to r
    $f_k(m) =$
$$\begin{cases} f_{k-1}(m) & \text{if } m < l_k \\ \max \left\{ \begin{array}{l} f_{k-1}(m) \\ f_{k-1}(m - l_k) + p_k l_k (T + D - b'_k) \end{array} \right\} & \text{otherwise} \end{cases}$$
  End
End
$m = r$, List = $\langle \rangle$, Rest = $\{1, ..., n\}$
For $k = n$ to 2
  If $f_k(m) \neq f_{k-1}(m)$ Then
    List= $append$(List, $(k, T + D)$), Rest=Rest$\setminus\{k\}$
    $m = m - l_k$
End
If $f_1(m) > 0$ Then List= $append$(List, $(1, T + D)$)
Fill-Greedy(List,Rest)
Output List

Procedure: Greedy-Greedy
/* Use Greedy heuristic to obtain static schedule */
Input (the same as Optimal-Greedy)

List = $\langle \rangle$, Rest = $\{1, ..., n\}$
Repeat
  C = $\{(i, T + D) : i \in \text{Rest and} \sum_{j \in \pi_1(\text{List}) \cup \{i\}} l_j x_{j,T} \leq r\}$
  If C is empty Then Exit
  $(k, T + D) = \arg \max_{(i, T+D) \in C} \dfrac{p_i (T + D - b'_i)}{T + D - b'_i + l_i}$
  List = $append$(List, $(k, T + D)$), Rest = Rest $\setminus \{k\}$
End
Fill-Greedy(List,Rest)
Output List

Subprocedure: Fill-Greedy
/* Greedily fill in unused part to get final schedule */
Input
  List : set of pairs of program and its planned delete time
  Rest : set of available programs

Repeat
  C = $\{(i, e_i) : i \in \text{Rest and}$
    $\forall t = B, .., T \sum_{j \in \pi_1(\text{List}) \cup \{i\}} l_j x_{j,t} \leq r\}$
  If C is empty Then Exit
  $(k, e_k) = \arg \max_{(i, e_i) \in C} \dfrac{p_i (e_i - b'_i)}{e_i - b'_i + l_i}$
  List = $append$(List, (k, e_k)), Rest = Rest $\setminus \{k\}$
End

Figure 4: The 'optimal-greedy' and 'greedy-greedy' scheduling algorithms.

Optimal-Leave, the optimal knapsack algorithm is used to obtain a static schedule for the next time window, but the programs already stored in the hard disk from the previous schedule are deleted only as it becomes necessary. That is, when the schedule specifies a program to be recorded, a program with the least score among those in the hard disk that are at least as long as the scheduled program is chosen and deleted. Optimal-Delete simply uses the optimal (knapsack) algorithm with no filling of the unused part performed and at each scheduling interval resets the previous schedule, although the programs in the hard disk are included in the candidates for next scheduling.

4. ESTIMATION OF THE VIEWING PROBABILITIES

Typical applications of filtering methods, including both content-based and social (or collaborative) filtering methods, are based on the assumption that scores of some form (either binary, multi-valued, or continuous valued) are available which indicate the degree to which users like the contents. In the problem setting we have here, we base our estimates solely on reinforcement signals of whether a user actually watched a program that was available for viewing. In this regard, the methods we propose here are to be distinguished from usual content-based and social filtering methods [9, 11, 12], since our methods involve the *estimation* of probabilities based on 0,1-valued reinforcement data. We thus use the terms 'content-based estimation' and 'collaborative estimation.' Incidentally, we assume that the information of whether a user watched a program or not is available for those programs that were stored by the automatic recording agent, as well as those *not* recorded by the agent but watched by the user, assuming that such information is available from the user's viewing record on real-time broadcasts and manual recording of TV programs. These are reasonable assumptions to make in practical applications.

4.1 Content-based Estimation

The content-based filtering/estimation method makes use of the text information included in an electronic program guide (EPG). Our estimation method is based on 'SBayes,' which is a variant of the Bayes prediction method for the specialist setting [4]. The original Bayes method makes its prediction (or estimation) using weighted average over the predictions made by a large pool of 'experts' with respect to the Bayesian posterior distribution. The specialist variant is designed to deal with the case in which some of the experts only make predictions for instances in their own speciality (hence the term 'specialists'.)

As mentioned before, the EPG text for each program is transformed into a vector of 0,1-valued attributes, each representing the occurrence/non-occurrence of a word. We then allocate a specialist for each attribute. Each specialist predicts only when it is on, namely when it appears in text, and it predicts the probability that the program in question is to be viewed by the user given that the attribute is on. Now, letting E_c denote the set of specialists whose attribute values are 1, w_i denote the weight of specialist i, and q_i denote the (Laplace) estimate[3] of the conditional viewing

---

[3]That is, the probability estimate is given by $q_i = \frac{V_i + 0.5}{N_i + 1}$, where V_i is the number of times attribute i is on and N_i is the number of times the user watched given that attribute i is on.

probability for attribute i, the viewing probability is to be predicted as

$$p_c = \frac{\sum_{i \in E_c} w_i q_i}{\sum_{i \in E_c} w_i}.$$

After obtaining the reinforcement (1 if the program is actually viewed, 0 otherwise), the specialists' weights are updated. Here only the weights of specialists in E_c are updated, according to the following formulas.

$$w_i \leftarrow \begin{cases} w_i q_i / p_c & \text{if viewed} \\ w_i (1 - q_i)/(1 - p_c) & \text{if not viewed} \end{cases}$$

4.2 Collaborative (Social) Estimation

In order to enhance the prediction accuracy of the content-based estimation method, we propose to make use of information about the viewing behavior of users who have had a chance to watch the same program using their automatic TV recording agents. Our collaborative estimation method estimates the viewing probability of a program stored in the hard disk by a particular user based on the information of whether or not other people have chosen to watch them. Our method is again based on SBayes [4]. Here, we allocate a specialist for each pair of users (u, v). Each specialist (u, v), which incidentally is identical to (v, u), has weight $w_{u,v}$ associated with it. Suppose we wish to make a prediction for the viewing probability of a user u on a particular program. We let E_s denote the set of users on which the information of whether they have chosen to watch that program or not is available. Now let x_v be a 0,1-valued variable standing for whether or not user v has watched that program (1 if she/he watched and 0 otherwise), and let $r_{u,v}$ be the estimate of the probability that $x_u = x_v$. Define $q_{u,v}$ as follows:

$$q_{u,v} = \begin{cases} r_{u,v} & \text{if } x_v = 1 \\ 1 - r_{u,v} & \text{if } x_v = 0 . \end{cases}$$

Then, the viewing probability of user u on that program p_s is estimated as follows.

$$p_s = \frac{\sum_{v \in E_s} w_{u,v} q_{u,v}}{\sum_{v \in E_s} w_{u,v}}$$

As before, after receiving the reinforcement of whether the user actually watched the program or not, the weights are updated for the specialists (u, v) such that $v \in E_s$ holds, according to the following update rule.

$$w_{u,v} \leftarrow \begin{cases} w_{u,v} q_{u,v} / p_s & \text{if viewed} \\ w_{u,v} (1 - q_{u,v})/(1 - p_s) & \text{if not viewed} \end{cases}$$

4.3 Combining the Respective Estimates

Now we combine the predictions made by the content-based and collaborative estimation methods. The final probability estimate p_i (for program i and user u) is obtained as follows:

$$p_i = \frac{\sum_{j \in E_c} w_j q_j + \sum_{v \in E_s} w_{u,v} q_{u,v}}{\sum_{j \in E_c} w_j + \sum_{v \in E_s} w_{u,v}}.$$

Here the standard deviation d_i of the estimation is calculated as follows:

$$d_i = \sqrt{\frac{\sum_{j \in E_c} w_j (q_j - p_i)^2 + \sum_{v \in E_s} w_{u,v} (q_{u,v} - p_i)^2}{\sum_{j \in E_c} w_j + \sum_{v \in E_s} w_{u,v}}}.$$

One can elect to use either one of the two estimates (the content-based and collaborative estimates) independently, or combine them. When we do combine the two estimates for the final estimation, the weight update rules for both content-based estimation and collaborative estimation should be modified by replacing the respective estimates p_c and p_s by p_i in them. In this way, our specialist approach provides a unified framework for both types of estimates.

5. EMPIRICAL EVALUATION

We conducted preliminary experiments in order to evaluate the performance of the proposed methods. Of the multiple methods proposed for estimating the viewing probabilities, we used only the content-based estimation method, since conducting large-scale real-time experiments on the Internet is not yet possible.

The set-up of our experiments was as follows. First, ten people of various age, sex and backgrounds were arbitrarily picked and asked to complete a questionnaire on their preference on TV programs. They were given program guide descriptions for actual TV programs broadcast in Japan, and were asked to mark those programs that they *might watch if they are recorded by an automatic recording agent provided they have sufficient time*. The wording of the question was chosen so that they did not just mark those programs they currently watch daily, which may tend to exhibit regular and predictable patterns. They were asked to do so for all TV programs on the 7 major (non-satellite) Japanese channels, broadcast for 11 weeks in the period of December 1998 till February 1999. There were on the average 216 programs to choose from each day, and 16,595 programs in the entire 77-day period. On the average, each person marked roughly 5 programs per day.

We used the content-based estimation method described in Subsection 4.1 to estimate the viewing probabilities, and used the scheduling methods described in Subsection 3.2 to schedule the recording. The reinforcement information was provided on all the programs the scheduler chose to record and all the programs the user might watch according to the above questionnaires. The obtained schedules were evaluated using the criterion of the total length of the recorded programs that were viewed. We also used the usual criteria of 'precision' and 'recall,' except the duration of the programs were taken into account in their calculations. That is, we define the (time sensitive) precision P as $P = V/C$ where V is the total length (in minutes) of viewed programs and C is the hard disk capacity (in minutes), and recall R as $R = V/M$, where M is the total length of the programs marked by the user, broadcast during the time window in question. We also introduced an additional measure of 'corrected recall' Q, which is defined as $Q = V/\min\{C, M\}$. We introduced this measure because, during the course of successive schedulings, sometimes the capacity of the hard disk is not enough to capture all of the preferred programs and the recall measure seems too stringent, and other times the hard disk capacity far exceeds the total length of the preferred programs and the precision measure seems unfair.

The viewing time of each user was decided according to two different models. In the first model, which we call the random-regular model, the viewing time was set to be once a day at night, with exact time picked uniformly at random from 19,20,21,22 and 23-th hour of each day. In the other model, the viewing interval was picked uniformly at random from 1 to 48 hours. As noted before, when using our scheduling algorithm, it is necessary to decide how often the scheduling algorithm is to be run (scheduling interval) and also to specify the time window for which to optimize the scheduling (scheduling window). In our experiments, we set the scheduling interval and window to be always equal, and we tried using two different values - one hour and 24 hours. We refer to the first method as the 'on-line' method, and the second method as the 'batch' method. The default survival time after current time window D was set to be 240 hours in all experiments. Finally, all the results presented are averaged results over the ten subjects.

6. EXPERIMENTAL RESULTS

We have run experiments to test the proposed methods from a number of different view points. These view points include: (1) Optimal-Greedy v.s. Greedy-Greedy: To see the effect of using a solution for the Knapsack problem. (2) Optimal-Greedy v.s. Optimal-Leave v.s. Optimal-Delete: To see the effect of filling in the unused part of the scheduling output by the optimal (knapsack) algorithm. (3) The Effect of Storage Size: To see how the performance of various methods varies as a function of the storage capacity of the hard disk. (4) On-line v.s. batch methods: To see the relative performance of the two methods on different viewing patterns. (5) The exploration-exploitation trade-off: To see the effect of explicit consideration of the trade-off in terms of the standard deviation of estimation.

6.1 Optimal-Greedy v.s. Greedy-Greedy

Optimal-Greedy seemed to outperform Greedy-Greedy by a small margin, but the difference does not seem significant. These results are shown in the graphs in Figure 5 and Figure 6. In the figure, the graphs show from left to right the total viewed hours of the programs recorded in the hard disk, the corrected recall, recall and precision, The graphs on the top row show 'cumulative' figures, that is, the performance averaged (totaled for the viewed hours) over the entire past, whereas the graphs on the bottom show 'instantaneous' quantities, that is the average quantity for each week.

6.2 Optimal-Greedy v.s. Optimal-Leave v.s. Optimal-Delete

The results for this comparison were as expected: Optimal-Greedy did the best, Optimal-Leave did next best and Optimal-Delete was the poorest. These results with random-interval model are shown in Figure 7.

6.3 The Effect of Storage Size

In order to see the effect of storage capacity on the performance of Optimal-Greedy method we show in Figure 8 plots for this method for three different storage capacities, 5 hours, 10 hours and 15 hours. As expected, larger storage capacity allowed us to obtain a significant gain on the recall at the cost of compromising some what on the precision. Incidentally, note that the instantaneous recall reaches more than 80 per cent, for the random-regular model, when given 15 hours of storage capacity. This figure seems to be high enough to render this method practical in terms of its predictive capability.

6.4 On-line v.s. Batch Methods

Figure 9 exhibits the cumulative performance of on-line and batch versions of Optimal-Greedy with the random-interval model. The results show that the on-line method, which resets its schedule every hour with window size of an hour, is comparable to the batch method, which resets its schedule once a day with one day look-ahead.

6.5 The Exploration-Exploitation Trade-off

In order to assess the effect of the modification to the objective function in terms of standard deviation proposed in Subsection 3.1, we tried a few different values of the controlling parameter λ: 0, 0.2, 0.4, 0.6, 0.8 and 1.0. The results of this experimentation are shown in Figure 10, and shows that the best performance is obtained with $\lambda = 0.2$, namely when the objective function is modified by an additive term of 0.2 times the standard deviation of estimating the viewing probability. We note that the method we propose here is related to a reinforcement learning method due to Kaelbling[6], in which an action such that the highest potential expected reward is chosen, which coincides formally with picking the option that has the largest sum of the expected reward and the standard deviation of its estimate.

7. IMPLEMENTATION AND DISCUSSION

The proposed scheduling methods comprise an essential part of an automatic TV recording agent, which is implemented as a function of a personalized digital video server called '@Random TV,' which integrates TV broadcasting with the Internet. @randomTV is realized on a personal computer equipped with a tuner card for the reception of conventional (analogue) terrestrial TV broadcast, an MPEG2 encoder card and a hard disk drive (HDD) of 64 GByte capacity connected via SCSI3, and runs on the WindowsNT operating system. The capacity of the HDD allows storing approximately 20 hours of TV programs with the usual MPEG2. The user can allocate an arbitrary portion of the HDD for automatic recording by the automatic recording agent, and save the rest for manual recording. For example, supposing that the user has allocated 15GB of this storage to the automatic recording agent, it translates roughly to 5 hours of recording time. Although the capacity of hard disk typically available at households is expected to grow, the number of available channels is expected to grow drastically as well (especially when digital satellite broadcasting is integrated to the system), so we expect that the need for intelligent allocation/scheduling of recording will persist.

We briefly explain the basic architecture of @randomTV, enhanced by the automatic recording agent, as is shown in Figure 2. The methods proposed in this paper comprise the three functions, collaborative filtering, content-based filtering and scheduling functions. The content-based filtering engine obtains viewing data about the user via the user interface, and learn their preference based on these data and predict the viewing probabilities, updating the user's profile in so doing. Here the filtering engine makes use of the EPG data obtained from the EPG server. The home server is connected via a modem or LAN card to the collaborative filtering server, to which presumably a large number of similar home servers are connected via the Internet. The collaborative filtering engine outputs predictions on the viewing probabilities of the user based on viewing data of other users and

this is sent via the modem or LAN to the scheduling engine. The scheduler makes use of these predictions in addition to those predictions output by the content-based filtering engine in making its calculating the recording schedule. The recording schedule it obtains is then relayed to the recording manager, which then manages the actual operations on TV programs, such as recording and deleting. Here the the video signals for TV programs received by the tuner are transformed to digital data by the MPEG2 encoder, which are then stored in the HDD. When viewing, these data are decoded either by a decoder card or by an MPEG2 decoding software and displayed.

Figure 1 shows a snapshot of the user interface of this system. What is shown in the figure is the 'personal EPG' interface, which presents the user with (a filtered set of) programs that can be currently viewed, grouped in the following three categories: Those manually recorded by the user, those recorded by the automatic recording agent, and the programs that are currently broadcast. In the figure, these three groups are indicated with different shadings. The user can click on any of the programs shown in the EPG and start viewing it. They can also move the cursor on the EPG and view the text information for a program of their choice, as is indicated on the left side of the figure. We note that it is this type of short texts describing the content of programs that are used in our content-based filtering/estimation method.

Some of the issues that need to be dealt with when putting the proposed methods into practice are: (1) The number of tuners: Currently our algorithms place no restriction on the number of programs that can be recorded at the same time. Realistically a bound need be placed; (2) What to do with programs when they become old – for example news programs will be worthless after a while, but movies may survive; (3) What to do with programs that have been viewed – currently our methods delete them as soon as they are watched, but we should give the user an option to save them; (4) How to make use of the social information – when viewing information on a large number of users becomes available, say via the Internet, social filtering will be a realistic possibility. But there are other attractive middlegrounds, such as providing the user with the option of using social-filtering with a small but selected number of 'opinion leaders' which can be made available via various means.

Acknowledgement

We thank Dr. K. Maeno, Dr. Y. Koseki, Dr. S. Doi, and Dr. S. Goto of NEC C & C Media Res. Labs., Dr. S. Sakata of NEC Human Media Res. Labs. and Dr. Y. Hara of C & C Res. Labs., NEC USA, for discussions and encouragement on this research.

8. REFERENCES

[1] Tivo: Introducing the new face of television. http://www.tivo.com/.

[2] P. Baudisch. Tv-online: An adaptive tv-program guide on the world wide web. In *Proceedings of the ABIS'96 Workshop*, pages D5.1–D5.4, 1996.

[3] W. Cohen and Y. Singer. Context-sensitive learning methods for text categorization. In *Proceedings of SIGIR'96*, pages 307–315, 1996.

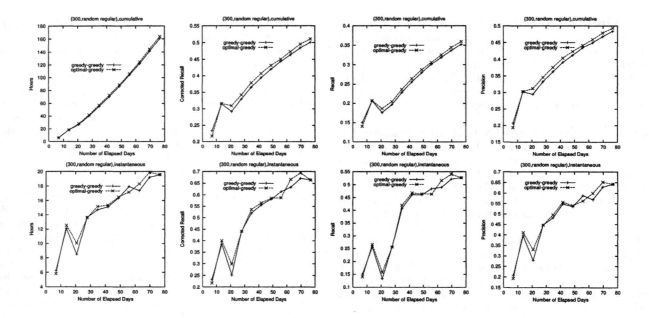

Figure 5: Viewed hours, corrected recall, recall and precision for Optimal-Greedy and Greedy-Greedy with random-regular model and 5 hour storage capacity. Top: cumulative, Bottom: instantaneous.

[4] Y. Freund, R. Schapire, Y. Singer, and M. Warmuth. Using and combining predictors that specialize. In *Proceedings of the Twenty-Ninth Annual ACM Symposium on the Theory of Computing*, pages 334–343, 1997.

[5] M. R. Garey and D. S. Johnson. *Computers and Intractability – A guide to the theory of NP-completeness*. W. H. Freeman and Company, New York, N.Y., 1979.

[6] L. Kaelbling. *Learning in Embedded Systems*. PhD thesis, Stanford University, 1990.

[7] T. Kamba, H. Sakagami, and Y. Koseki. Anatagonomy: a personalized newspaper on the world wide web ? *International Journal on Human-Computer Studies*, June 1997.

[8] K. Lang. Newsweeder: Learning to filter netnews. In *Proceedings of the 12th International Conference on Machine Learning*, pages 331–339, 1995.

[9] A. Nakamura and N. Abe. Collaborative filtering using weighted majority prediction algorithms. In *Proceedings of The 15th International Conference on Machine Learning*, pages 395–403, 1998.

[10] K. Ochiai, H. Matoba, and K. Maeno. @randomtv: A following generation tv program-viewing system using a random access device. In *56th Annual Conference Proceedings of Information Processing Society of Japan*. in Japanese.

[11] P. Resnick, N. Iacovou, M. Suchak, P. Bergstom, and J. Riedl. Grouplens: An open architecture for collaborative filtering of netnews. In *Proc. of CSCW*, pages 175–186, 1994.

[12] U. Shardanand and P. Maes. Social information filtering: Algorithms and automating "word of mouth". In *Proc. of CHI95*, pages 210–217, 1995.

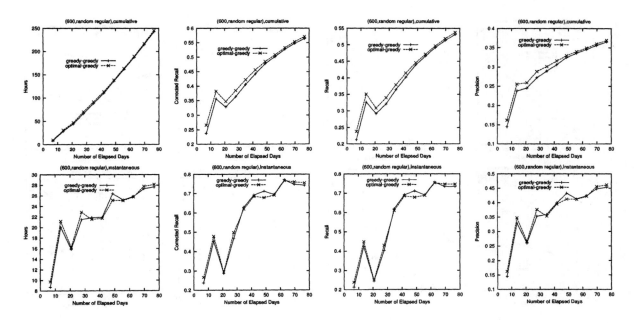

Figure 6: The performance of Optimal-Greedy and Greedy-Greedy with random-regular model and 10 hour storage capacity. Top: cumulative, Bottom: instantaneous.

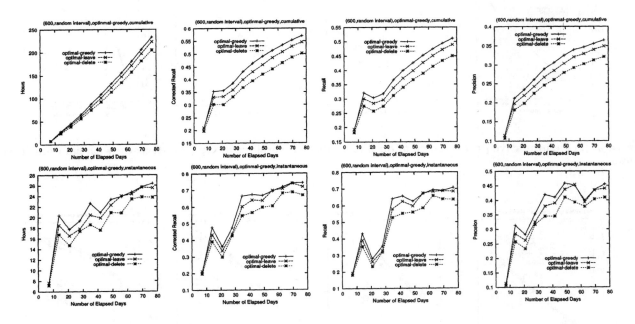

Figure 7: The cumulative performance of Optimal-Greedy, Optimal-Leave, and Optimal-Delete with random-interval model and 10 hour storage capacity. Top: cumulative, Bottom: instantaneous.

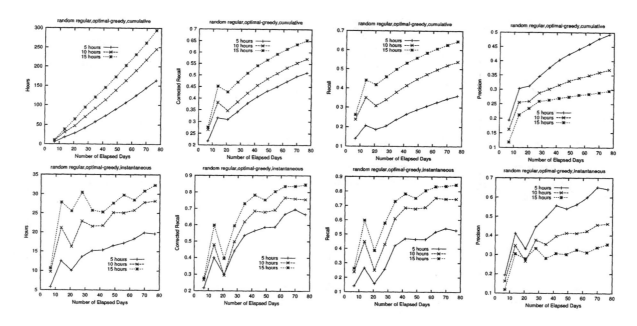

Figure 8: The performance of Optimal-Greedy with random-regular model for various storage sizes. Top: cumulative, Bottom: instantaneous.

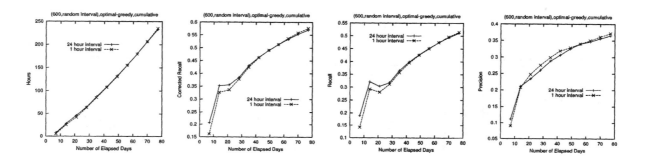

Figure 9: The cumulative performance of on-line and batch versions of Optimal-Greedy with random-interval model.

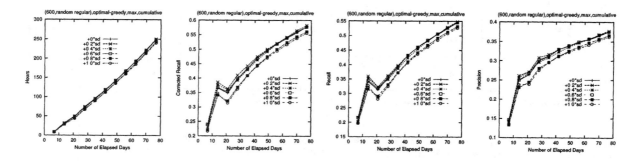

Figure 10: The cumulative performance of Optimal-Greedy with correction with standard deviation and without: with random-regular model.

Temporal Links: Recording and Replaying Virtual Environments

Chris Greenhalgh, Jim Purbrick, Steve Benford, Mike Craven, Adam Drozd, Ian Taylor
School of Computer Science and Information Technology
The University of Nottingham, Jubilee Campus, Nottingham, NG8 1BB, UK
+44 115 9514221   {cmg, jcp, sdb, mpc, asd, imt}@cs.nott.ac.uk

ABSTRACT

Virtual reality (VR) currently lacks the kinds of sophisticated production technologies that are commonly available for established media such as video and audio. This paper introduces the idea of temporal links, which provide a flexible mechanism for replaying past or recent recordings of virtual environments within other real-time virtual environments. Their flexibility arises from a combination of temporal, spatial and presentational properties. Temporal properties determine the relationship between time in a live environment and time in a recording, including the apparent speed and direction of replay. Spatial properties determine the spatial relationship between the environment and the recording. Presentational properties determine the appearance of the recording within the environment. These properties may be fixed, dynamically varied by an application, or directly controlled in real-time by users. Consequently, temporal links have a wide variety of potential uses, including supporting post-production tools for virtual environments, post-exercise debriefing in training simulators, and asynchronous communication such as VR email, as well as providing new forms of content for virtual worlds that refer to past activity. We define temporal links and their properties and describe their implementation in the MASSIVE-3 Collaborative Virtual Environment (CVE) system, focusing on the underlying record and replay mechanisms. We also demonstrate applications for adding new content to an existing virtual world, and a VR post-production editor.

Keywords

Collaborative virtual environments, temporal properties, recording and editing techniques, post-production technologies.

1. INTRODUCTION

Virtual reality (VR) is rapidly emerging as an entertainment medium in areas such as games, theme park rides, and on-line communities. There are also opportunities for convergence with other media such as film, video and television. At one level, virtual reality provides a production tool to support these other media. For example, motion-capture techniques use virtual reality technology to record actors' movements in real-time as part of the process of creating computer animations for films, videos and games [1]. At another level, content originally developed for films and TV shows may find its way into virtual

reality and vice versa. It is now commonplace to spin-off real-time games and rides from films, and more recently films from games. Finally, virtual reality may be directly combined with other media. For example, inhabited television involves staging television shows within on-line virtual worlds, so that the public can directly participate by taking control of virtual characters [2].

However, whereas established media such as video and audio are supported by a wide variety of production and post-production tools for editing, manipulating and assembling content, virtual reality generally is not. There are only a few examples of capturing and editing action within virtual environments so that it may be included in other virtual environments or be transferred into other media (see below).

This paper defines and demonstrates a flexible mechanism for recording activity in virtual environments, manipulating such recordings, and then accessing them as new content within other live virtual environments. This includes the ability to access recordings within recordings. These facilities are made available as a generic system mechanism whose properties may be configured to support a range of potential applications. We anticipate that such a mechanism will be an essential component of future VR production and post-production tools. Our discussion focuses on collaborative virtual environments (CVEs) – distributed virtual environments that support communication among potentially many users over a computer network. The heart of our mechanism is a technique for capturing all activities within a CVE, including the environment itself, multiple users' movements, speech, and interactions with virtual objects, in such a way that this action can be faithfully recreated at a later time. This record and replay technique is made available through the more general mechanism of a 'temporal link'. This allows application developers and end-users to program or directly manipulate the temporal, spatial and presentational relationships between the live environment and the recording. Action within the live environment can take place around and within the display of the recorded activity, and the composition of the two can itself generate further recordings.

Several existing CVEs support some form of record and replay facility. In the CAVERNsoft system [3], recording of an avatar's movements and audio is possible as part of general support for persistent virtual environments. This facility has been used to create the Vmail system [4], a form of VR email, and to create guided tours within tele-immersion applications. As part of the COVEN project, the DIVE system was extended with event logging facilities that could completely record an entire virtual environment and the activity within it [5]. Although initially implemented to support the statistical analysis of patterns of user activity in relation to network traffic, this recording facility was subsequently extended with a replay facility to allow a previous session to be recreated (although not within another live virtual environment). The dVS system supports a similar facility for recording and then replaying a virtual environment. Multi-player 3D games also record and replay techniques to show highlights of previous game-play, examples of which include FIFA soccer from Electronic Arts and the automobile game Driver from GT Interactive Software, the latter allowing players to edit together their own movies from recordings of their own actions. In a related area, recent work on 'virtualized reality' has developed techniques for capturing live action within a physical environment by synthesizing recordings from multiple video cameras to produce a 3D graphical simulation [6]. Furthermore, a script language VRML History has been proposed to facilitate time navigation in WWW browser-based 3D-worlds [7].

Examples of related work which refers to temporal properties in multimedia applications, but not specifically to VR, include the Media Editor Toolkit (MET++) application framework which has methods for manipulation of temporal relations in multimedia presentations [8], the Command Stream Model (and associated TclStream implementation) which introduces a media stream of code fragments that is synchronised to conventional media streams or device controllers, allowing presentation with VCR-type playback [9], and the spatio-temporal model of Vazirgiannis et al. which provides a framework for composition and indexing of multimedia objects [10]. The Where We Were (W3) system is being developed to allow recently recorded video, and 2D sketches, to be incorporated into real-time activities such as brainstorming meetings [11], and the Virtual Meeting-room Service (VMS) presents visual representions of recorded histories from distributed collaborations [12]. The CHIMP framework considers collaborative authoring and editing of multimedia documents, which includes temporal specification of objects [13].

2. DEFINING TEMPORAL LINKS

This section presents a general (i.e., system independent) description of the mechanism of temporal links. An implementation and demonstrations in the MASSIVE-3 CVE system [14] are presented in sections 3 and 4 respectively.

Our departure point is an established idea, that of being able to link together multiple spatial regions to create a virtual environment. In what is perhaps the most flexible scheme proposed to date, an environment is composed of multiple 'locales' that may be linked together to form a larger structure [15]. Each locale defines a local co-ordinate system and can be linked to a number of other locales or even to itself. Each such link specifies a spatial transformation that determines how the other locale is spatially related to the current locale, including the offset of its origin and a scale factor. In this way, locales may be placed adjacent to one another, may be overlaid, may be nested or may even be linked back to themselves to form mirrors and infinite corridors.

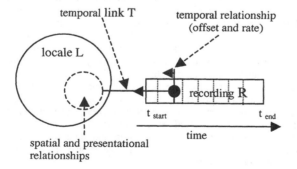

Figure 1. A temporal link

Our mechanism of temporal links extends this approach by allowing a locale to be linked to a recording of past activity from another locale (or indeed, from itself). The recording can be replayed and viewed from within the live locale via the temporal link. In addition to specifying the spatial relationship between a locale and a recording through its spatial properties, a temporal link can also specify temporal and presentational properties. The temporal properties determine the relationship between time in the live locale and time in the recording, including a current position in recorded time and a speed and direction (forwards or backwards) of replay. The presentational properties specify how the appearance of the recording is transformed when it is viewed from within the locale. For example, the recorded activity may be seen in 'black and white' or may be dimmed in order to distinguish it from the live activity.

Figure 1 summarizes the key properties of a temporal link. It shows a temporal link, T that allows a recording of a locale, R to be replayed within a live locale, L. One end of the link indicates its temporal relationship to R in terms of a current position in recorded time and a speed and direction of replay. The other end indicates its current spatial and presentational relationship to L. It should be noted that with a temporal link, a recording is always accessed through a live locale, although the live locale may have no additional content or purpose, and so may appear to be invisible for all intents and purposes.

The live activity within a locale that is linked to a recording may itself be recorded. The resulting new recording will contain both the live action and the temporal link which fully describes how the original recording is related to (and situated within) the new recording. Replaying the new recording will use this temporal link to access and replay the old recording within it in an appropriately synchronized manner. Figure 2 presents a more general scenario in which a locale is linked to multiple recordings, each associated with different spatial, temporal and presentational properties. One of these recordings is itself being generated by current activities within the locale.

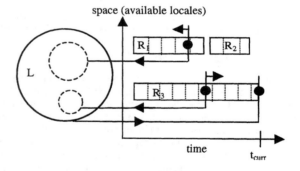

Figure 2. Linking to multiple recordings

The remainder of this section explores the definition of temporal links in greater depth, including the nature of temporal, spatial and presentational properties.

2.1 Temporal properties

As noted above, one aspect of a temporal link specifies the timing of the replay of a recording in terms of a current position in time within the recording, and the direction and speed of replay. This requires a mechanism to translate between 'live time' and 'recorded time'. Live time in the locale progresses according to the local system clock. Recorded time is determined by the system clock of the computer that ran the recording process that recorded and time-stamped events. The temporal link provides a function to map between these two timescales. Specifically, this function allows a value of recorded time to be calculated for each value of live time. The parameters of this function provide the means by which application developers or end users can control the temporal properties of the replay.

Assuming a linear function for the time being (the basis of our implementation as described below), a value of live time is multiplied by a rate and then an offset is added in order to arrive at the corresponding value of recorded time. The offset establishes an initial mapping from a chosen point in live time to a corresponding point in recorded time. The rate determines both the apparent speed and direction of the replay of the recording as live time advances. A rate of 0 will result in recorded time being frozen. A rate of 1 will result in recorded time advancing at the same rate as live time. A negative rate will cause recorded time to run backwards as live time advances.

The rate and offset may be fixed when the link is created, establishing a constant relationship between live and recorded time. Alternatively, they may be manipulated in real-time, for example to enable users in the locale to browse through the recording.

This linear function is just on example of the wide range of functions that might be chosen to map live time onto recorded time. Non-linear functions might be used to create interesting effects. A simple non-continuous function could be used to create a looped replay. A sinusoidal function would result in an continually repeated replay that oscillated forwards and backwards through recorded time. An inverse exponential function would result in a replay that edged ever closer to a moment in recorded time (perhaps a critical event in a story), the longer you watched it. Alternatively, a random function could be used to replay random moments from the past.

2.2 Spatial properties

The spatial properties of a temporal link control the relationship between the spatial frame of reference of the live locale and that of the recording. This relationship is specified by a homogeneous 3D matrix that allows the spatial frame of the recording to be translated, rotated, scaled and sheared relative to that of the live locale. The two spatial frames can be directly matched and overlaid so that the live action takes place around the recorded action and conversely, the recording appears to be a normal part of the live action. Alternatively, the recording can be situated as a separate locale (e.g., as an adjacent locale, a window or mirror onto the past, or as a 'world in miniature').

It may also be useful to be able to locate the recording within an enclosing object (for example making it appear to be playing back inside a virtual television set). This requires additional support for clipping the recorded material as it is replayed so that it does not spill outside of the containing object.

As with temporal properties, the spatial properties may be fixed when the link is created, or may vary dynamically. For example, the recording can appear to move around, rotate, expand and shrink, within the locale.

2.3 Presentational properties

Presentational properties can be used to systematically modify the appearance of the recording so that it can or cannot be distinguished from live action within the live locale according to the requirements of a particular application. This includes modifying graphical attributes such as brightness and color (e.g., dimming the replay or playing it back in 'black and white'), but may also include modifying audio information, for example playing it back quietly or with appropriate effects.

3. IMPLEMENTATION IN MASSIVE-3

This section describes how temporal links are implemented in the MASSIVE-3 CVE system [14]. We begin by considering mechanisms for recording virtual activity, followed by replaying, and finally control (i.e. the temporal links themselves). However, first we need to describe elements of MASSIVE-3's basic operation.

A MASSIVE-3 virtual world is comprised of one or more "locales", each of which is a distinct region of virtual space (as already described). Each locale is implemented as a distributed database (called an "Environment"). This database completely describes the locale and all of its contents, including scenery, buildings, users' avatars and any virtual objects in the locale; this is primarily a shared scene graph. Each process which joins a particular locale contacts a master process for that locale and obtains (over the network) an initial "snapshot" or checkpoint of the locale's current state. Any process that has joined a locale can change it, e.g. by adding, changing or deleting elements of the scene graph. As shown in the left-hand side of Figure 3, each change requested by application code is not performed directly; instead an event object is created which describes the requested change. This event object is then forwarded to the other processes that have joined the locale (not shown), as well as being used to update the local copy of the database.

3.1 Recording

The left-hand side of Figure 3 shows how MASSIVE-3 allows a virtual environment and the activity that occurs within it to be recorded for subsequent recreation. First, we create a checkpoint at the start of a recording, as an initial reference point. Then the rest of the recording consists of the sequence of events that are applied to the locale, each one being time-stamped and written to the file as it is performed. This allows us to record the complete state of a locale and everything that happens to it, including the avatars' movements and interactions with objects. In addition, other media must also be recorded. MASSIVE-3 currently records all audio streams within the locale, writing the audio packets to a second time-stamped log file.

3.2 Replay

The right hand side of Figure 3 shows how a recording can then be used to recreate past locales and activity. We consider this in a number of incremental stages.

3.2.1 Basic Replay

The replay process creates a new replay-only locale over which it has complete control. The initial state of the locale is taken from the first checkpoint in the recording, which is often empty (before any data was placed in the locale). The recorded events can then be read in turn from the recording, and, at the correct moment, injected into the new locale, recreating the activities which occurred in the original locale. The replay application also replays recorded audio streams, synchronized to the replay locale.

Note that the original locale may still exist, and the same recording may be used to create several concurrent replays (each

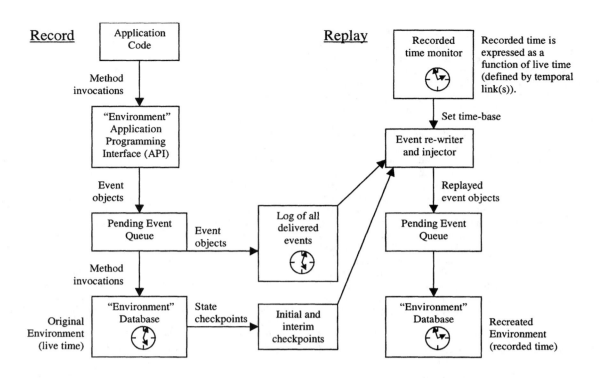

Figure 3. Record and replay in MASSIVE-3

at a different moment in recorded time). Consequently the internal identifiers for the recreated locale and its constituent data items must be changed to ensure that each replay locale is clearly distinguishable. The database annotations that describe audio streams must also be updated to correspond to the appropriate replay streams.

3.2.2 Replay Time

Not all changes in a locale are represented by explicit events. In particular, deterministic processes, such as movement with a known velocity or frame-by-frame interpolation between known positions, are not represented as recorded events. These are implied by the passage of time, and are independently evaluated frame-by-frame for each distributed copy of the locale. Consequently, a replayed locale must explicitly control its own definition of time so that these deterministic processes will reflect recorded time rather than current time.

Each locale has its own, potentially independent, definition of time. For current locales this is normally taken directly from the host computer's real-time clock. However, for replayed locales, time is the moment in history currently being replayed (i.e., recorded time). The replay application uses a specialized event ("SetTimebase") to set the replay locale's definition of time to correspond to that of the recording. Time in a locale is currently defined as a linear function of the current host time, as described (for temporal links) in section 2.1. Changing the recorded time rate (and the rate at which events are re-introduced) allows the replay application to stop the recording, or play it faster or slower than real-time.

Note that deterministic behaviors in the replay locale can be re-evaluated for any moment in recorded time, irrespective of whether this corresponded to a frame time or other key moment in the recording. This gives almost infinite temporal resolution

for these elements of the recording (subject the precision of the behaviors and their evaluation). Consequently, states can be recreated that were never actually observed in the live action. It is also possible to replay the recorded action in a perfected form. For example, network delays may cause glitches in the performance of a virtual environment that could be removed when the action is subsequently replayed.

3.2.3 Reversing Time

MASSIVE-3 also allows recordings to be played backwards, reversing recorded time. Deterministic behaviors are trivially reversed by defining the replay locale's time so that it decreases as live time progresses; the frame-by-frame evaluation of these behaviors will naturally regress.

However, forward-time events cannot be used when moving backwards in a recording. For example, the reverse time version of adding a node in the scene graph is to *delete* that node, and the reverse time version of updating a node's value is to set it back to its old value. MASSIVE-3 allows recordings to be played backwards by constructing "anti-events" during normal (forward) playing of a recording: an anti-event completely reverses the effects of the corresponding forward-time event, as in the above examples. The replay application uses these anti-events when time is moving backwards.

3.3 Control

The last two sections have described the technical mechanisms by which activity in a locale can be recorded and subsequently replayed. This section explains how this is controlled, i.e. how temporal links operate in MASSIVE-3. However, first we must outline the implementation of normal (non-temporal) inter-locale links.

An inter-locale link (called a "boundary") is one of the standard data-types supported by the MASSIVE-3 locale database. As well as the spatial and presentational properties of the link it also gives the name of the environment at the far end of the link. A process that wants to join the linked (far-end) locale looks up the locale's given name using a specialized naming service that is part of MASSIVE-3's run-time system. For a normal locale, the naming system will return the system identifier of the far-end locale and the network address of the locale's current master process, which can then be contacted in order to join the locale (see also the start of section 3). The naming service can also start a locale master process on demand (when a named locale is requested) if one is not already running.

3.3.1 Temporal Links

The key difference between a normal inter-locale link and a temporal link is the form of name given for the far-end locale. For a normal link this is just the name of the far-end locale, but for a temporal link it has the form:

```
original-locale-name@temporal-property-id
```

The "temporal-property-id" is the system identifier of a data item that defines the temporal properties of the link, i.e. the rate and offset to be used to relate live (near-end) and recorded (far-end) time. The '@' symbol may be read as "at the time specified by". This temporal property is normally but not necessarily in the near-end locale.

When the naming service receives a new request for a name of this form it starts a new replay application with the given name. The new replay application locates the event and audio log files created from the original locale (e.g. using a standard file-naming convention). It also finds and joins the locale that contains the link's temporal property data (using the *temporal-property-id*). The replay application then continuously monitors the link's temporal properties and the time in the near-end locale. It combines these to dynamically determine the overall time rate and offset for the replay, which is used as in described in section 3.2.

In summary, to create a temporal link a process creates a data item to contain the link's temporal properties, and then creates the link itself using the correct name (including the identifier of the link's temporal property data item). The replay application will be started automatically as soon as any process requires it. Whenever the temporal property is changed the replay application observes this and adjusts the replay accordingly (e.g. stopping, running faster, slower or backwards).

3.3.2 Replaying Links

A link (temporal or otherwise) is recorded in the same way as anything else in a locale. If the locale is recreated then the link will also be recreated. However, the link must be modified when it is replayed in order to preserve the correct temporal relationships between locales and recordings. Specifically, the destination name of a replayed link must have the replay's temporal properties appended to it. This ensures that the far-end of any replayed link is also historically appropriate.

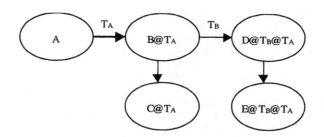

Figure 4. Example multi-locale environment with replay

Consider the example environment shown in Figure 4. This has one current locale, A, which includes a temporal link to a recording of locale B, which it accesses as "$B@T_A$", i.e. B at the time specified by temporal property T_A. When recorded, B had a normal inter-locale link to locale C. When B is replayed this must be rewritten to point to "$C@T_A$", so that (viewed from A) a corresponding recording of C is observed via the recording of B.

Similarly, B had its own temporal link to D that was originally viewed from B as "$D@T_B$". Now, viewed from A, this becomes "$D@T_B@T_A$", i.e. D at the time specified by temporal property T_A (which determines the time in $B@T_A$) combined with temporal property T_B (which is part of the recording).

4. DEMONSTRATING TEMPORAL LINKS

This section presents two demonstrations of temporal links in MASSIVE-3. Both are inspired by on-going experiments in inhabited television, the staging of television shows within CVEs [2]. Members of the public may either watch a broadcast of the show from the virtual environment as if it were television, or may metaphorically 'step through the screen' in order to enter the virtual environment and take control of a virtual character.

The basis of the demonstrators is an experiment called The Ages of Avatar, the latest in a series of public experiments with inhabited television [16]. Its goal was to explore whether entertaining broadcast material can be created by drawing on the characters, settings, and stories of a virtual community. The virtual community in this case was established around an existing television channel, Sky Television's [.tv] (pronounced "Dot TV"). The Ages of Avatar consisted of a series of virtual worlds, loosely based around the theme of The Ages of Man, which was initially implemented using Microsoft's VWorlds system.

To produce our demonstrators we have recreated the worlds in MASSIVE-3, with the aim of aim of showing how temporal links can enhance applications such as inhabited TV. The first demonstrator involves creating new content for an existing world that exploits the ability to refer to the past using temporal links. The second uses temporal links to create an editor tool for the post-production of broadcast material from recordings made in the virtual world.

4.1 Creating new world content

We have extended the content of a world called Behaviour Shift within The Ages of Avatar with new features that exploit the mechanism of temporal links. The theme of Behavior Shift is adolescence; it is a world of distorted perspectives, confused identities and changing behaviors. In keeping with this theme, our extensions allow participants to see their own actions in various, distorted and shifting, ways.

Our first extension has been to create 'shadows' that follow participants around the virtual environment, replaying their recent actions with a delay. These are not shadows in the conventional sense. Rather, they are objects created by replaying a recording in a suitably distorted way. A temporal link is established with an offset of ten seconds into the past and a rate of 1. The spatial properties of the link scale the Y axis to 0 and shear it to the X axis in order to create an approximation of a shadow on the floor. The presentational properties of the link are set to darken the replayed action, making it appear more shadow-like. The resulting shadows show where each participant was located within the environment ten seconds ago, including any interactions with objects at that time. An example of a shadow can be seen in the camera view window of Figure 7 (see later). In this case, the shadow is of a user's avatar interacting with a virtual ball.

Our second extension is a distorting mirror. From a user's point of view, the mirror appears to reflect the region of space directly in front of it, but with various temporal distortions that change their nature over time. Specifically, the replayed action is delayed in time so that the mirror shows action from the recent past. For two thirds of the time the action is shown at half speed and for the remaining third at double speed. Audio is also replayed at the appropriate speed. The net result is that the user sees their own gestures replayed at a mixture of speeds. Figure 5 shows a participant standing in front of the distorting mirror.

Our third extension is a 'Holovid', a device that enables participants to browse through past activity. The Holovid consists of a miniature view of the whole environment at (virtual) table-top size, combined with a series of controls for browsing the recording. Pressing 'play' runs the recording forward at normal speed (ratio of 1) from its current position. Repeatedly pressing play skips forward to the next recorded event. Pressing 'slow forward' plays forwards through the recording at half speed. Pressing 'rewind' plays backwards through the recording at normal speed. Pressing 'stop' halts the recording at its current position. Figure 6 shows a view of the Holovid, with the whole of Behavior Shift world being displayed in miniature. The figure on the left is the avatar of another user who is currently controlling the Holovid.

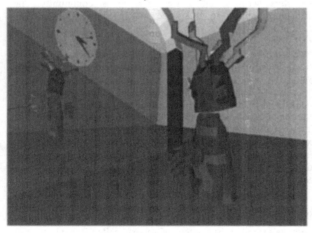

Figure 5. An avatar standing in front of the mirror

Between them, our three examples demonstrate a variety of configurations of temporal links. Temporal and spatial properties can be fixed (as in the shadow), can vary in a pre-programmed manner (the mirror) or can be under direct end-user control (the Holovid). Spatial and presentational properties are also used to situate the recorded material within the live locale in different ways.

Figure 6. The 'Holovid', located inside a room, with user

4.2   A VR post-production editor

Our second demonstration, the VR editor, is a tool for the post-production of broadcast material from recordings made within virtual environments. The editor initially places the user in a live locale. This can be an empty locale that merely acts as a placeholder for recordings, or can contain some scenery, avatars and other objects that are to be overlaid on the recording when the final broadcast is produced.

The user can then create a temporal link, in effect loading an identified recording into this live locale. Once loaded they can browse through this recording at will, marking key moments in time in a list. They can then jump directly to these marked moments and run the recording from that point, forwards or backwards at whatever speed they specify. As the recording runs within the locale they can control the viewpoint of a virtual camera so as to view the replay from any desired perspective or sequence of viewpoints – effectively editing the camera work. Finally, the editor can be instructed to output the results of these manipulations in a number of ways. It can output a series of JPEG frames, with the user specifying how many frames are to be generated and the number of fast-forward, rewind and fast-rewind. A slider can be used to set the speed of these controls. Fast-forward and fast-rewind operate at twice this speed. The current recorded time is shown. At any time the user can use the store button to mark the current time, adding it to a visible list of marked times. Two further buttons can be used to jump to a particular time in this list or to remove an entry from it.

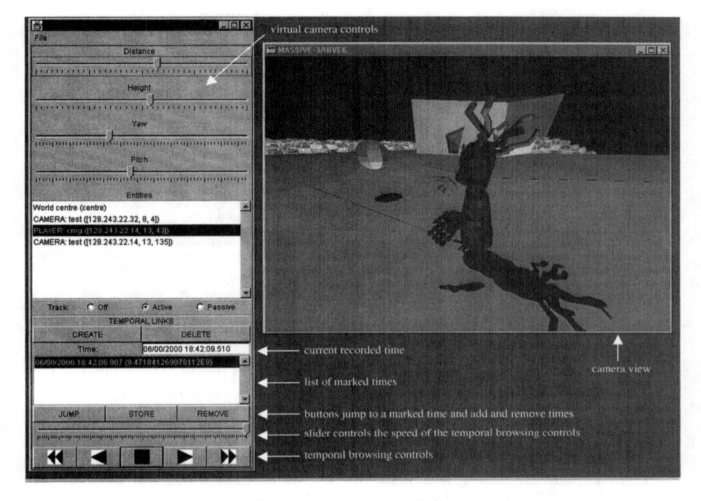

Figure 7. Graphical interface to the post-production

4.3 Other applications

There are many other potential uses of temporal links within CVEs. We conclude this section by briefly discussing two of them.

A key use might be in supporting the post-analysis and discussion of events within virtual environments. On-line debriefings can be carried out within virtual environments that are used for training and simulation, so that participants and experts can discuss and analyze their own performances in depth (e.g., viewing slow motion replays). They might also replay the performances of others to compare them with their own. A variation on this theme is supporting sociologists in analyzing social interaction within CVEs, using techniques such as ethnography and conversation analysis in order to evaluate their effectiveness. These techniques are already used for evaluating CVEs, but currently rely on studying video material captured from a virtual environment, often involving comparing multiple simultaneous recordings showing different participants' perspectives.

Temporal links might also be used to support asynchronous communication in CVEs. Recordings can be sent to other participants as a form of VR email that can then be replayed within a virtual environment (see [4]). The ability to build up layered recordings can support conversational threads in VR bulletin boards. They can also allow interviewers and interviewees to carry out asynchronous interviews. These kinds of techniques might be particularly useful for supporting low-bandwidth users of CVEs, for example where the CVEs use audio for communication, but where some participants are using dial-up modems that can only handle very limited real-time audio data.

5. SUMMARY

We have introduced the mechanism of temporal links as a way of replaying recordings of virtual environments within other virtual environments. The key feature of this mechanism is its generality – through a combination of temporal, spatial and presentational properties temporal links can establish a wide variety of relationships between the recorded material and the live action. Temporal properties control the timing of the recording relative to the live action, including speed and direction of replay. Spatial properties control the positioning of the recorded material within the live action, including scale, orientation and relative location. Presentational properties control the appearance of the recorded material relative to the live action so that it may be distinguished from it if appropriate. These various properties may be fixed, may be varied by the application or may be under the dynamic control of end-users.

We have described the implementation of temporal links within the MASSIVE-3 system, including a number of techniques that were required to make them effective, efficient and suitably flexible. The recording mechanism must capture all events within a locale, including avatars' movements and interactions with objects. The replay mechanism can infer the state of deterministic process at any given moment in recorded time, to give an almost infinite temporal resolution. The ability to reverse time and run the recording backwards is supported by the introduction of anti-events that effectively undo the effects of normal-events. Replaying a recording from a locale that contained links (spatial or temporal), requires that these links are also replayed appropriately to ensure historically accurate representations of the recorded locale's nested recordings and neighboring locales. Finally, we presented a number of demonstrations of temporal links based around an on-going public experiment in inhabited television called The Ages of Avatar. These included creating new content for virtual environments and also a VR editor for the post-production of broadcast material from live recordings in a virtual world.

Our future work will involve developing a broader range of applications of temporal links, especially extending our current post-production editor to become a fully functional VR editing suite that supports the creation of computer animations from action that has captured from real-time virtual environments. Indeed, we see this as being a key long-term benefit of temporal links – enabling non-real-time media such as computer animation to directly exploit live performances and improvised social interaction that take place within real-time collaborative virtual environments. In a sense, CVEs can act as a kind of social motion capture system, recording the dynamics of human social activity for subsequent use in film and video. However, we also propose that mechanisms such as temporal links are essential to the future development of virtual reality as a medium in its own right, one that like other media, needs to be supported by a rich set of production and post-production tools and techniques.

6. ACKNOWLEDGEMENTS

We acknowledge the support of the British EPSRC for the Multimedia Networking for Inhabited Television project under the Multimedia Networking Applications programme, and the European Community for the eRENA project under the ESPRIT IV Intelligent Information Interfaces (I3) programme. We would also like to thank our collaborators at Illuminations Television, British Telecom and BSkyB for their work on The Ages of Avatar that provided the content for our demonstration.

7. REFERENCES

[1] Gliecher, M., Retargetting motion to new characters, *Proc. ACM Computer Graphics* (SIGGRAPH'98), Orlando, USA, July 1998, pp. 33-43.

[2] Greenhalgh, C., Benford, S., Taylor, I., Bowers, J., Walker, G. and Wyver, J., Creating a live broadcast from a virtual environment, *Proc. ACM Computer Graphics* (SIGGRAPH'99), Los Angeles, USA, August 1999, pp. 375-384.

[3] Leigh, J., Johnson, A., DeFanti, T., Brown, M., et al., A review of tele-immersive applications in the CAVE research network, *Proc. IEEE Virtual Reality* (VR'99), Houston, USA, March 1999, pp. 180-187.

[4] Imai, T., Johnson, A., and DeFanti, T., The virtual mail system, *Proc. IEEE Virtual Reality* (VR'99), Houston, USA, March 1999, p. 78.

[5] Frécon, E., Greenhalgh, C. and Stenius, M., The DIVE-BONE – an application-level network architecture for Internet-based CVEs, *Proc. ACM Virtual Reality Software and Technonology* (VRST'99), London, UK, December 1999, pp. 58-85.

[6] Kanade, T., Rander, P., Vedula, S. and Saito, H., Virtualized reality: digitizing a 3D time varying event as is and in real time, in Ohta, Y. and Tamura, H. (eds.), *Mixed Reality, Merging Real and Virtual Worlds*, Springer-Verlag, 1999, pp. 41-57.

[7] Luttermann, H. and Grauer, M., VRML History: Storing And Browsing Temporal 3D-Worlds, *Proc. ACM Virtual Reality Modeling Language Symposium* (VRML'99), Paderborn, Germany, February 1999, pp. 153-181.

[8] Ackermann, P., Direct manipulation of temporal structures in a multimedia application framework, *Proc. ACM Multimedia* (MM'94), November 1994, pp. 51-58.

[9] Herlocker, J.L. and Konstan, J.A., Commands as Media: Design and Implementation of a Command Stream, *Proc. ACM Multimedia* (MM'95), November 1995, San Francisco, USA, p. 155-165.

[10] Vazirgiannis M., Theodoridis Y. and Sellis T., Spatio-temporal composition and indexing for large multimedia applications, *Multimedia Systems*, 6(4), 1998, pp. 284-298.

[11] Minneman, S.L., Harrison, S.R., Where were we: making and using near-synchronous pre-narrative video, *Proc. ACM Multimedia* (MM'93), August 1993, Anaheim, USA, pp. 207-214.

[12] Ginsberg, A., Ahuja, S., Automating envisionment of virtual meeting room histories, *Proc. ACM Multimedia* (MM'95), San Francisco, USA, November 1995, pp. 65-75.

[13] Candan, K.S., Prabhakaran, B., Subrahmanian, V.S., CHIMP: A framework for supporting distributed multimedia document authoring and presentation, *Proc. ACM Multimedia* (MM'96), Boston, USA, November 1996, pp. 329-340.

[14] University of Nottingham, Communications Research Group, MASSIVE-3 / HIVEK, http://www.crg.cs.nott.ac.uk/research/systems/MASSIVE-3

[15] Barrus, J.W., Waters, R.C. and Anderson, D.B., Locales: Supporting Large Multiuser Virtual Environments, *IEEE Computer Graphics and Applications*, 16(6), November 1996, pp. 50-57.

[16] Craven, M., Benford, S., Greenhalgh, C., Wyver, J., Brazier, C.-J., Oldroyd, A. and Regan, T., Ages of Avatar: Community Building for Inhabited Television, to be published *Proc. ACM Collaborative Virtual Environments* (CVE'2000), San Francisco, USA, September 2000.

A Video-Based Rendering Acceleration Algorithm for Interactive Walkthroughs

Andrew Wilson, Ming C. Lin,
Dinesh Manocha
Department of Computer Science
CB 3175, Sitterson Hall
University of North Carolina at Chapel Hill
Chapel Hill, NC 27599
{awilson,lin,dm}@cs.unc.edu

Boon-Lock Yeo, Minerva Yeung
Intel Corporation
Microcomputer Research Labs
2200 Mission College Blvd.
Santa Clara, CA 95052
minerva.yeung@intel.com

http://www.cs.unc.edu/~geom/Video

Abstract

We present a new approach for faster rendering of large synthetic environments using video-based representations. We decompose the large environment into cells and pre-compute *video based impostors* using MPEG compression to represent sets of objects that are far from each cell. At runtime, we decode the MPEG streams and use rendering algorithms that provide nearly constant-time random access to any frame. The resulting system has been implemented and used for an interactive walkthrough of a model of a house with 260,000 polygons and realistic lighting and textures. It is able to render this model at 16 frames per second (an eightfold improvement over simpler algorithms) on average on a Pentium II PC with an off-the-shelf graphics card.

Keywords

Massive models, architectural walkthrough, MPEG video compression, virtual cells, video-based impostors

1 Introduction

One of the fundamental problems in computer graphics and virtual environments is interactive display of complex environments on current graphics systems. Large environments composed of tens of millions of primitives are frequently used in computer-aided design, scientific visualization, 3D audio-visual and other sensory exploration of remote places, tele-presence applications, visualization of medical datasets, etc. The set of primitives in such environments includes geometric primitives like polygonal models or spline surfaces, samples of real-world objects acquired using cameras or scanners, volumetric datasets, etc. It is a major challenge to render these complex

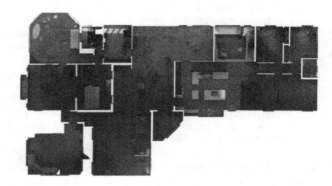

Figure 1: CAD database of a house with realistic lighting and texture. The model has over 260,000 polygons and 19 megabytes of high-resolution texture maps. This model is too large to be naively rendered at interactive rates.

environments at interactive rates, i.e. 30 frames a second, on current graphics systems. Furthermore, the sizes of these data sets appear to be increasing at a faster rate than the performance of graphics systems.

One of the driving applications for interactive display of large datasets is *interactive walkthroughs*. The main goal is to create an interactive computer graphics system that enables a viewer to experience a virtual environment by simulating a.walkthrough of the model. Possible applications of such a system include design evaluation of architectural models [Brooks86,Funkhouser93], simulation-based design of large CAD datasets [Aliaga99], virtual museums and places [Mannoni97], etc. The development of a complete walkthrough system involves providing different kinds of feedback to a user, including visual, haptic, proprioceptive and auditory feedback, at interactive rates [Brooks86]. Real-time feedback as the user moves is perhaps the most important component of a satisfying walkthrough system. This faithful response to user spontaneity is what distinguishes a synthetic environment from precomputed images or frames, which can take minutes or even hours per frame to calculate, and from pre-recorded video. In this paper, we focus on the problem of generating visual updates at interactive rates for complex environments.

There is considerable research on rendering acceleration algorithms to display large datasets at interactive frame rates on current graphics system. These algorithms can be classified into three major categories: visibility culling, multi-resolution modeling, and image-based representations. However, no single algorithm or approach can successfully display large datasets at interactive rates from all viewpoints. Some hybrid approaches that have been investigated use image-based representations to render "far" objects [Maciel95,Shade96,Aliaga96,Aliaga99] and geometric representations for "near" objects [Cohen97,Erikson99,Garland97,Hoppe96]. Commonly used image-based representations include texture maps, textured depth meshes, layered depth images [Aliaga99] etc. However, in terms of application to large models, these image-based representations have the following drawbacks:

- *Sampling:* Most of the algorithms take a few finite samples of a large data set. No good algorithms are known for automatic generation of samples for a large environment.
- *Reconstruction:* Different reconstruction techniques have been proposed to reconstruct an image from a new viewpoint. While some of them do not result in high fidelity images, others require special purpose hardware for interactive updates.
- *Representation and Storage:* A large set of samples takes considerable storage. No good algorithms are known for automatic management of host and texture memory devoted to these samples.

1.1   Main Contribution

In this paper, we present a method for accelerating the rendering of large synthetic environments using video-based representations. Video-based techniques have been widely used for capture, representation and display of real-world datasets. We propose the use of *video based impostors* for representing synthetic environments and rendering these scenes at interactive rates on current high-end and low-end graphics systems. We use a cell-based decomposition of a synthetic environment and associate a *far field* representation with each cell. For each cell, we generate a sequence of far-field images and MPEG compress them using offline encoding. At runtime, we decode the MPEG streams and utilize algorithms that provide nearly constant time random access to any frame, for displaying them. The frames are selected as a function of the viewpoint. We address a number of issues in cell generation and the use of encoding and decoding algorithms, then demonstrate how to combine these algorithms with multi-resolution representation and visibility culling for interactive display. The resulting system has been implemented and used for an interactive walkthrough of a model of a house with realistic lighting and textures. We have tested our system on a PC using off-the-shelf graphics hardware and achieve an average update rate of 16 frames per second in a 260,000-polygon model of a house 31 meters wide by 18 meters deep and 5 meters tall. This update rate represents a significant improvement over simpler rendering algorithms.

Organization: The rest of the paper is organized in the following manner. We survey related work in Section 2 and present our approach in Section 3. Section 4 highlights a number of implementation issues. We describe our system's

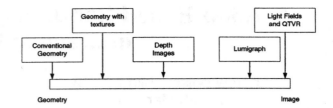

Figure 2: Continuum of representations of an environment, from purely geometric to purely image-based [Lastra99]

performance in Section 5. Finally, we highlight areas for future work in Section 6.

2   Related Work

In this section, we briefly survey related work on rendering acceleration techniques and the use of image-based and video-based representations for rendering real and synthetic environments.

2.1   Interactive Display of Large Datasets

There are two basic types of models commonly used for rendering large data sets: geometric representations (based on a description of the surfaces in the model) and image-based representations. Many hybrid combinations have also been proposed. Based on these representations, different rendering acceleration techniques have been proposed; examples include multi-resolution modeling, visibility culling, and use of image-based representations.

2.1.1   Geometric Models

By far the most common class of model representations is geometric, where *surfaces* in the model are described using polygons or curved primitives. This representation is used for CAD, visual simulation, and most scientific applications. The basic geometric representation, as it is commonly used, stores each surface only once. There is no notion of appropriate resolution, except for textures, which are commonly pre-filtered. More advanced representations keep several levels of detail for objects and select the correct level at run time [Funkhouser93]. Originally, these levels of detail were created manually. In recent years, the problem of automatic generation of levels-of-detail has received considerable attention in computer graphics, vision, and computational geometry. [Cohen97, Erikson99, Garland97, Hoppe96].

2.1.2   Image-Based Representations

There has also been work on the use of images to represent complex, but distant, portions of models at an appropriate resolution [Maciel95,Shade96,Aliaga96]. These algorithms use a surface-centric representation and use image-based impostors for distant geometry. These images have been used for rendering acceleration. However, the use of images introduces a sampling problem: how many samples are needed for high-fidelity rendering? Other image-based representations include camera-centric forms [Chen93,McMillan95,Gortler96,Levoy96]. In

Figure 2, we show these on an axis representing how much geometric information is used in these representations.

The image-based representations store a measure of the amount of light arriving at a point in space, with perhaps some information about the surface. The commercial Quicktime VR representation [Chen95] relies on panoramic images. A user cannot move freely around the space, but can only rotate. The Light Field representation [Levoy96] stores images in a four dimensional data structure representing rays between two finite planes. The Lumigraph [Gortler96] is similar to the Light Field, but can use some geometric information. Images with per-pixel depth [Chen93,McMillan95] organize information as images, but locate the samples in 3D space.

2.1.4 Visibility Culling

Besides multi-resolution models and image-based representations, other rendering acceleration algorithms are based on visibility culling. A particularly fruitful case has been in the architectural model domain because of the partitioning of space into rooms and doors (referred to in the literature as *cells and portals*) [Airey90,Teller91]. For general environments, [Greene93,Zhang97] have presented algorithms that use a combination of object space and image space hierarchies. [Aliaga99] have presented an approach that combines image-based representations, levels of detail, and occlusion culling for large geometric environments.

2.2 Combining Graphics with Video

In addition to the use of image-based representations, many researchers have proposed techniques to use video for rendering real and synthetic environments. There is considerable work on techniques using interpolations among images to create visual continuity during motion or other changes within three-dimensional virtual spaces [Chen93,Boyd98]. Other combinations of graphics and video include virtual sets, where live actors can move within computer-generated settings [Katkere97]. Carraro et al. [Carraro98] have highlighted techniques to incorporate video displays into virtual environments in the context of a multi-user simulator. The MPEG-4 proposal [MPEG4] allows specification of data displays as compositions of video and graphical objects.

2.3 Video for Multimedia Applications

There is extensive work on the use of video for multimedia applications. These include video conferencing, video-on-demand systems, internet video [Patel98], visual effects [Millerson90], etc. Most of these applications involve capturing videos of real-world scenes, then storing and organizing them efficiently using a combination of encoding and decoding algorithms [MPEG2, Kender97, Zhang93, Shen95, Yeung97, MPEG4].

3 Overview

In this section we give a brief overview of our approach. We describe an algorithm for rendering acceleration using virtual cells, which allows us to guarantee a minimum frame rate for an interactive walkthrough by rendering nearby objects as

geometry and replacing distant ones with a simple video-based impostor. Finally, we explain the application of MPEG compression to these impostors.

3.1 Cell-Based Walkthrough

Architectural models of complex environments such as power plants, naval vessels, aircraft, and high-rise buildings are typically too large to render naively at interactive rates on current graphics hardware. Such models often contain anywhere from a few hundred thousand to a few hundred million polygons, divided into objects numbering in the hundreds or thousands (at least). We must reduce the number of primitives rendered at each frame in order to bring a system's performance up to an interactive frame rate of between 20 and 30 frames per second. In complex environments with large open spaces, the rendering acceleration techniques highlighted in Section 2 are not sufficient. We perform interactive walkthroughs of such environments by partitioning the model into regions that contain a bounded number of primitives, then rendering only those primitives contained in the user's current region at runtime. These regions are called *cells* within the model. Cell-based walkthrough originated with the method of cells and portals in architectural models and was generalized to *virtual cells* by [Aliaga99].

3.2 Cells and Portals

Architectural models often exhibit an intrinsic spatial subdivision: individual rooms (*cells*) connected by doorways or windows (*portals*) in otherwise opaque walls. Many architectural environments contain large, crowded spaces where the potentially visible set within a single cell is larger than the rendering budget. In these environments as well as outdoor scenes, we can apply the method of *virtual cells* to achieve rendering acceleration.

3.3 Virtual Cells

We generalize the concept of cells and portals to yield *virtual cells*. The space within an environment where the user might wish to travel is partitioned into cells using some convenient subdivision (regular grid, octree, etc.). Each cell is assigned a large *cull box* which is concentric with the cell itself. The purpose of the cull box is to divide the model into a *near field*, whose contents will not exceed the per-frame rendering budget, and a *far field* consisting of the rest of the model. The walls of the cull box correspond loosely to the walls of a room in traditional cells-and-portals. Thus, the potentially visible set for a particular cell consists of only those objects that intersect the cull box. We replace the far field with an inexpensive *video-based impostor* created as part of an offline process of cell generation. By varying the sizes of the cull boxes for different cells, we can enforce an upper bound on the number of primitives that must be rendered for any viewpoint in any cell.

Virtual cells are generated by first determining which parts of the environment will be explored by the user, choosing sample points within that region of exploration, and finally constructing a rectangular cell around each sample point. Increasing the sampling density generally yields increased fidelity at runtime at the expense of increased storage requirements and preprocessing time. The "volume of interest" is computed by subdividing regions indicated by the user. Another possible approach is to

```
for each cell:
    place viewpoint at center of cell
    set field of view so view frustum intersects cell edges
    for each direction (up, down, north, south, east, west):
        set view dir = $direction
        clip away portions of model in front of cull-box wall
        render remaining geometry
        read back frame buffer and save as image
    end
end
```

Figure 3: Algorithm for generating far-field images once cells have been generated. The resulting images are MPEG-compressed for fast runtime access.

use a Delaunay triangulation of the free space and use it to generate the virtual cells. Figure 4 shows the relationship between a cell and a cull box in our system.

3.4   Video-Based Impostors

To avoid having to render geometry for more than one cell at a time, we replace the far field with an opaque, image-based impostor at runtime. This impostor should have the following properties:

- It should be easy and fast to create.
- It should have a compact representation.
- It should closely approximate the appearance of the replaced objects.
- It should be inexpensive to render.

Several different kinds of impostors have been explored, including flat, textured quadrilaterals, textured depth meshes, layered depth images, and light fields [Aliaga99]. Each has its own tradeoffs in terms of fidelity vs. storage space and the cost of reconstruction. For simplicity, we can use flat, textured quadrilaterals. While they exhibit undesirable perspective artifacts when a piece of geometry may cross between the near and far field, they are easy to generate and impose little rendering or reconstruction load on the system at runtime.

The fidelity of the impostor to the geometry being replaced is similar to the problem of sampling and reconstruction in the context of image-based representations. The algorithm takes a finite number of samples of the environment from locations fixed during preprocessing. At runtime, these samples are used to reconstruct the appearance of the portion of the model captured by impostors. The performance of the algorithm varies considerably as a choice of these samples.

3.4.1   Creating Impostors

Image-based impostors are constructed as an offline preprocess. Once cells have been generated for a particular model, we employ the algorithm in Figure 3 to acquire six images of the far field for each cell. These images will be used at runtime as texture maps for the faces of the cull box. The OpenGL near clipping plane is used to remove portions of the model that fall inside the cull box. A typical resolution for the far-field images is 512x512 in 24-bit color, which requires 4.5 megabytes of storage for each cell during preprocessing. Since a typical environment will have hundreds or thousands of cells, these images must be compressed as part of preprocessing and decompressed on demand at runtime. We apply MPEG

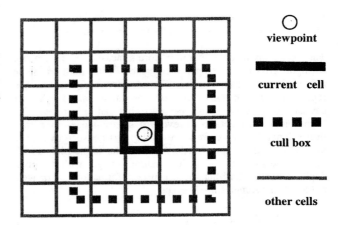

Figure 4: A sample cell grid. The cull box for the cell containing the viewpoint is shown. At runtime, all objects outside the cull box will be replaced with video impostors.

compression to exploit coherence between the far field images for adjacent cells.

3.4.2   Video Compression of Impostors

The images used to compute impostors exhibit considerable coherence from cell to cell. By arranging the 3-dimensional cell structure into a one-dimensional list, we can impose an ordering on the cells and arrange their far-field images into a linear stream. This stream is amenable to compression using video techniques. As an example, consider a path through the model as shown in Figure 10. If the impostors from the north face of each cull box are arranged in a stream, they depict a constant-velocity pan through the environment. Furthermore, all of the objects represented in each image are some minimum distance away from the camera (typically a few meters in models between 20 and 80 meters on a side) due to the size of the cull box. This ensures that object motion due to depth parallax is small enough to be easily handled with motion prediction.

3.5   Offline encoding

Once all the images of the far field are available, we arrange them into linear streams for encoding using video techniques. The result of this encoding is the video-based representations we use to replace distant portions of the model at runtime.

3.5.1   Mapping Cells to Streams

There are many possible ways to arrange a 3-dimensional array as a 1-dimensional list. To maximize the benefits of video compression, we choose a mapping with the following properties:

- Consecutive entries in the list exhibit coherence.
- Changes from one image to the next can be accurately estimated using motion prediction.
- Adjacent cells in space often map to adjacent entries in the list.

In our initial implementation, we have chosen to treat our cell grid as an array. Rows of cells are aligned with the X axis in the model's space, and columns with the Y axis. We map between our cell structure and a 1D stream by arranging the two-dimensional array of cells in row-major order. Each of the six faces of the cull box is used to generate a separate stream of images.

3.5.2 Choice of Encoding Algorithm

In order to achieve maximum efficiency from our video impostors, we chose an encoding scheme that exploits the temporal coherence present in its input stream and is easily and cheaply accessible at runtime. We have chosen MPEG-2 compression, as it provides a satisfactory balance between these constraints. Moreover, hardware and software tools for fast access and manipulation are easily available.

3.5.3 Encoding Parameters

There are three parameters in the MPEG encoding process that govern the performance of the algorithm [MSSG]. First, the encoder allows us to request a particular bit rate for the encoded stream. Since the data is retrieved from a disk at runtime, we set this parameter to be no greater than the bandwidth available from disk to host memory. Secondly, we can constrain the search space for motion vectors in adjacent frames. Since the source images are of a static environment, the only motion is due to camera parallax. Third, we choose the structure of a group of pictures so that the discontinuities when the 1D stream "wraps around" the 2D model are encoded as intra frames. This same technique could be applied to other discontinuities, such as when the 1D stream passes through a wall inside the model.

4 Implementation

In this section, we describe an implementation of our algorithm. Our system assumes that the environment is given as a collection of (possibly texture-mapped) polygons, and that the user has specified a method for constructing cells. We divide our system into two phases: preprocessing, during which cells are created and video-based impostors are generated and compressed, and runtime, during which the user is allowed to walk through the environment. At runtime, MPEG manipulation tools are used to decompress the impostors on demand.

We use a model of a house with realistic lighting and texture for our architectural environment. The house model was constructed from the blueprints of a real house in Chapel Hill, contains some 260,000 polygons, and uses approximately 19 megabytes of textures acquired from the real house using a digital camera. Our system is implemented in C++, uses OpenGL for rendering, and runs under Windows NT.

4.1 Tools for MPEG manipulation

In this section, we give a brief overview of tools used for encoding and decoding.

4.1.1 Offline encoding

We use the freely available MPEG Software Systems Group encoder [MSSG] to generate MPEG-2 streams from the source images of each cell's far field. The encoding parameters are modified according to the cell structure we impose upon the model. In particular, we attempt to place intra frames wherever the viewpoint moves through a wall or "wraps around" to the other side of the model as a result of the 2D-to-1D cell mapping.

4.1.2 Runtime decoding

To decode the MPEG streams containing far-field images at runtime, we use MPL (MPEG Processing Library), a software library developed at Intel Microcomputer Research Labs [Yeo00]. It provides general-purpose, high performance software APIs for MPEG decoding and processing. It is targeted at applications beyond standard decoding and display. MPL offers convenient random access to different levels of an MPEG bitstream, from bits and motion vectors to full frames.

MPL supports both MPEG-1 and MPEG-2 at resolutions up to HDTV (1920x1280) and is optimized with MMX™ and SSE™ technology. Some of its advanced features include random access to any frames with near constant-time access, fast extraction of encoded frames, simultaneous decoding of multiple MPEG sequences, flexible input plug-ins, SMP support and access via callbacks to non-frame-level information in the MPEG bitstream (e.g. raw bits, blocks, macroblocks, GOP and slice, etc.). We used MPL due to its high-speed random-access capability and its ability to handle multiple streams simultaneously.

MPL's random access and backward playback capabilities are enabled by the use of index tables. After a video is created, an index table is created that maps out the frame dependencies and byte offsets of the I, P, and B frames. For instance, to access frame number N, the index table is used to identify the closest I-frame numbered N or smaller; thereafter, MPL decodes from that I-frame to retrieve frame N. The size of the index table is typically less than 1% of the entire MPEG file size. Backward playback is handled as a special case of random access.

Table 1 shows the forward, backward and random access decoding speed on a low-cost Pentium® III 400 MHz PC. As shown in the table, backward decode and random access speed of MPEG1 video at 352x240 resolutions and bit rate of 1.5 Mbps is at about 60 frames/sec, which is more than sufficient for displaying video typically captured at 30 frames/sec.

Table 1: Performance of MPL on a PIII 400MHz PC. Playback rates are given in frames per second.

Video Type	Width	Height	Forward	Backward	Random Access
MPEG1 1.5 Mbps	352	240	272.9	58.6	57.2
MPEG2 5.0 Mbps	704	480	53.7	11.8	11.7
MPEG2 10 Mbps	1280	720	22.0	4.9	4.8

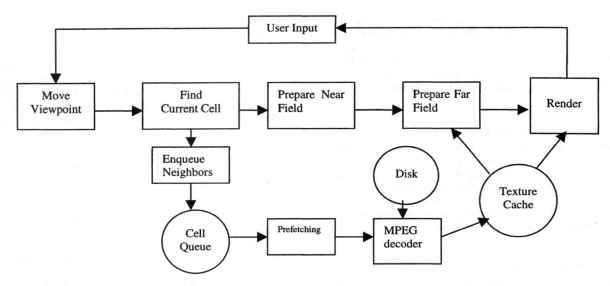

Figure 6: Runtime architecture for interactive walkthrough system. The view-management task communicates with the prefetch task through the cell queue and the texture cache.

Using MPL, we are able to support the following interactions: stop (at any frame), start or resume (from any frame), constant-speed backward playing, constant-speed forward playing and jump to any other video stream at any specified frame.

4.3 Cell structure

We construct a cell grid for the house environment by dividing its two-dimensional bounding box into squares 1 meter on a side. Each of these squares corresponds to a single cell extending from the floor of the model up through the ceiling. The cull box for these cells is 3 meters on a side. This implementation uses only a single layer of cells. However, there is nothing in our method or our system preventing us from using a truly 3-dimensional cell structure. Figure 9 shows an overhead view of the house model with cell boundaries drawn in red. The house model is 31 meters by 18 meters and is 5 meters tall. Rows of cells are aligned with the X axis in model space, and columns with the Y axis. The cell grid contains 558 cells arranged in 18 rows of 31 cells each.

4.4 Preprocessing

Our preprocessing phase, shown in Figure 5, consists of cell generation, far-field rendering, and creation of the MPEG streams that contain the compressed impostor textures. We render and store the video impostors at a resolution of 512x512 in 24-bit color. After all of the impostors have been generated, we compress them as MPEG streams, as described in sections 3.4.2 and 3.5. One stream is generated for each of the six faces of the cull box. Each video stream contains 558 frames (one for each cell in the model).

4.5 System Pipeline

The architecture of the runtime portion of our system is shown in figure 6. We have divided the system's function into two separate tasks, view management and prefetching. View management consists of the actual rendering as well as user

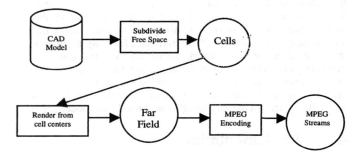

Figure 5: Preprocessing pipeline for generating cells and video streams from a CAD model.

interaction and object and texture preparation. The prefetching task is responsible for decompressing the video impostors for nearby cells. We describe each of these tasks in more detail below.

4.5.1 View Management Task

The view management task, implemented as a single thread, is responsible for generating the image the user sees each frame. It performs four functions:

- Manage user input, including rendering state, navigation mode, and motion of the viewpoint through the model.
- Request far-field textures for nearby cells from the prefetching task.
- Retrieve texture data from the prefetching task and bind it to OpenGL texture memory for rendering.
- Render the model from the user's viewpoint, including the far-field impostors.

The user can switch at will between four navigation modes: trackball (rotate the entire model), drive (move forward and backward, turn left and right), translate (move up and down and side-to-side), and look (remain stationary and change the view direction). Navigation input is collected and applied at the beginning of each frame to minimize latency between user input and program response.

The view management task is also responsible for informing the prefetching task of nearby cells that the user might visit soon. This is accomplished by updating a nearby-cell queue whenever the user crosses a cell boundary. When this happens, the identifiers of the four cells that share a face with the (new) current cell are placed into the queue.

We have implemented the view management task within a single thread in order to avoid costly OpenGL context switches and maintain synchronization with user input. If the far-field textures for the current cell are not yet available when the view management task is ready to render a frame, it pauses and places requests for those textures at the head of the prefetching queue. The alternative, which some users may prefer, is to render a frame with an incomplete far field.

4.5.2 Prefetching Task

The prefetching task is responsible for making sure that the video impostors for both the current and nearby cells are available in memory. We implement it as a free-running process that takes as its input the cell identifiers in the nearby-cells queue. As each cell identifier is dequeued, it is checked against the texture cache. If the video impostors for that cell are already resident, no further work needs to be performed. If not, the relevant frames are decoded from each of the six MPEG streams and placed into the texture cache. The prefetching task does not actually bind these textures in OpenGL. Since this is a time-consuming operation, it is not performed as part of prediction. The view management task is left to bind textures on demand. We have implemented the prefetching task as a single thread on a uniprocessor machine, and multiple threads (to permit multiple MPEG frames to be decoded simultaneously) on multiprocessor machines.

4.6 Memory Management

When working with massive models, host memory is often a scarce resource. It is quite common for the model itself to occupy anywhere from tens of megabytes to tens of gigabytes of storage space, and for the image-based representation to be several times that size. The problem is even worse when the video-based impostor incorporates texture maps, as texture memory on current PC graphics cards is often limited in size and slow to access.

We address this problem by treating the different storage areas as caches for model and texture data. Main memory is divided into two areas: one for the model geometry and associated texture maps, and one for the decompressed far-field representations. We manage the texture cache using a least-recently-used (LRU) replacement policy. OpenGL texture memory is handled in a similar fashion, but is a much more limited resource: a typical PC graphics card may have 32MB of texture memory, more than half of which is occupied by the texture data for the model itself. It is possible to lower this memory requirement by separating textured objects from the rest

of the model and binding the appropriate texture maps only when those objects are present in nearby cells.

5   Performance and Results

In this section, we describe the performance of an architectural walkthrough system implementing our algorithms. We have tested our system on a PC running Windows NT with 256MB of memory, a Pentium II™ processor running at 400 MHz, and an Intergraph Intense3D graphics card. Our geometric environment consists of a realistic model of a house containing some 45 megabytes of geometry and 19 megabytes of high-resolution texture data.

5.1   Overall Rendering Acceleration

We demonstrate the speedup achieved by our method by showing the polygon count and frame rate for a fixed path through the house model both with and without cell-based culling. Our method is able to maintain a frame rate between 10 and 20 frames/second in the house model. Naïve rendering is consistently slower than 5 fps for most views inside the house.

5.2   Breakdown of Time Per Frame

In Table 3, we show the amount of time our system spends on various tasks during each frame. These times are averaged over the duration of the same sample path through the model as in section 5.1.

5.3   Preprocessing

Table 2 shows a breakdown of time and resources spent on our preprocessing phase. Both the acquisition of far-field images and subsequent MPEG encoding to form video impostors can be easily parallelized. The encoding process can make use of as many graphics pipelines as are available. Runtime decoding is generally CPU-bound and benefits from a multiprocessor machine.

Table 2: Time and space requirements for each stage of preprocessing. These vary in direct proportion to the number of virtual cells in the model.

Preprocessing Stage	Time	Disk Space
Cell creation	<1 minute	30Kb
Impostor generation	21 min	2511MB
MPEG encoding	123 min	61 MB

Table 3: Breakdown of average frame time by task. Prefetching of textures happens in a separate thread and is not included.

Task	Avg. time per frame
Cell update	<1ms
Texture binding	32ms
Rendering	40ms
Total Frame Time	73ms

5.4 Analysis of Results

Our system is able to maintain an upper bound on the number of polygons rendered in any particular view of the model, as shown in Figure 7. This is a major step toward guaranteeing a minimum frame rate. However, we found that binding texture data in OpenGL is unexpectedly expensive on our PC graphics card. The regular downward spikes in Figure 8 are pauses between cells while the system binds the texture data for a new cell's video impostors. By comparison, the actual decoding of video impostors using MPL involves negligible computational overhead.

We also encountered problems at times matching colors between the model and the decoded video impostors, as can be seen in Figure 13. These appear to be due to the fact that different color-conversion formulae were used to convert from RGB to YUV space (during MPEG encoding) and from YUV back to RGB (during decoding).

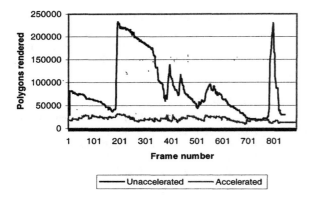

Figure 7: Polygon counts along a sample path, with and without acceleration. Our method imposes an upper bound of roughly 30000 polygons for any view of the model.

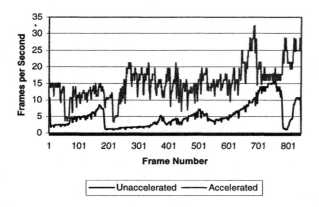

Figure 8: Frame rates along a sample path, both with and without video-based acceleration. Our system achieves an average frame rate of 16 frames per second.

6 Conclusions and Future Work

We have presented an algorithm for accelerating interactive walkthroughs of architectural environments by replacing portions of the model with video-based impostors. We have demonstrated this algorithm on a textured, radiositized model of a house. Our method achieves frame rates 8 times higher than is possible with naïve rendering on common hardware. Although this does not fully meet our goals for interactivity, it represents a considerable improvement over previous methods and suggests that future improvements can possibly yield an update rate of at least 30 frames per second. In terms of implementation and application, we dealt with several issues, including the following:

- compensating for color quantization artifacts in the video compression process
- managing limited texture memory and low host-to-graphics-pipe bandwidth
- choosing a sample density that gives acceptable results without excessive preprocessing overhead

We are exploring the following issues related to the sampling and storage of video impostors:

- Fully automatic generation of cells based upon free space within the model, including higher sample density in regions of interest. It may be possible to compute a Voronoi subdivision of free space and extract paths of maximum clearance to guide cell creation. Crowded areas of the model are natural targets for smaller cells and hence denser sampling of the far field.
- Better mappings from a 3D cell grid to a 1D stream of impostors. Video compression techniques will give better results if there are fewer discontinuities (as when the viewpoint passes through a wall) in the input stream. A mapping which stays within open regions of the model for as long as possible is more useful.
- Modifications to the encoding process to take advantage of the 3D source environment. Since we generate our video impostors from a synthetic environment using known camera parameters, it should be straightforward to estimate motion vectors during image generation rather than search for them during the encoding process. We are also investigating encoding schemes based on a 3D cell structure instead of a 1D stream of images. Such encodings could provide more efficient decoding and allow the use of impostors with fewer inherent artifacts.

7 Acknowledgements

We wish to thank some of the people whose assistance has been instrumental in this work. Matt Holliman of Intel's Media and Graphics Lab provided much-needed insight into problems with color quantization and compression. We are particularly grateful to the UNC Walkthrough team for allowing us access to the CAD model of the house and for providing infrastructure and model-translation assistance. We thank Bob Liang at Intel for inviting the first three authors to the MGL group during the summer of 1999. This research was also supported in part by

ARO contract DAAG55-98-1-0322, a DOE ASCI Grant, NSF grants NSG-9876914, DMI-9900157 and IIS-9821067, an ONR Young Investigator Award, and NIH Research Resource Award 2P41RR02170-13.

8   References

[Airey90] J. Airey, J. Rohlf, and F. Brooks, "Towards image realism with interactive update rates in complex virtual building environments", In *Proc. of ACM Symposium on Interactive 3D Graphics*, 1990, pp. 41--50.

[Aliaga96] D. G. Aliaga, "Visualization of Complex Models Using Dynamic Texture-based Simplification", *IEEE Visualization '96*, October 1996.

[Aliaga99] D. Aliaga et al., "MMR: An integrated massive model rendering system using geometric and image-based acceleration", *Proc. of ACM Symposium on Interactive 3D Graphics*, April 1999.

[Boyd98] J. Boyd, E. Hunter, P. Kelly, L. Tai, C. Phillips and R. Jain, "MPI-Video Infrastructure for Dynamic Environments", to appear in *IEEE International Conference on Multimedia Systems 98*.

[Brooks86] F. Brooks. Walkthrough: A dynamic graphics system for simulating virtual buildings. In *ACM Symposium on Interactive 3D Graphics*, Chapel Hill, NC, 1986.

[Carraro98] G. Carraro, J. Edmark and J. Ensor, " Techniques for Handling Video in Virtual Environments", *Proc. of ACM SIGGRAPH*, 1998, pp. 353-360.

[Chen93] S. Eric Chen and Lance Williams, "View Interpolation for Image Synthesis", In *Computer Graphics (SIGGRAPH '93 Proceedings)*, vol. 27, J. T. Kajiya, Ed., August 1993, pp. 279--288.

[Chen95] S. Chen, "Quicktime VR: An image based approach to virtual environment navigation", *Proc. of ACM SIGGRAPH*, 1995.

[Chim98] J. Chim, M. Green, R. Lau, H. Leong and A. Si, "On Caching and Prefetching of Virtual Objects in Distributed Virtual Environments", *Proc. of ACM Multimedia*, 1998, pp. 171-180.

[Cohen97] J. Cohen, D. Manocha, and M. Olano. "Simplifying Polygonal Models Using Successive Mappings". In *Proc. of IEEE Visualization*, Tampa, AZ, 1997.

[Erikson99] C. Erikson and D. Manocha, "GAPS: General and Arbitrary Polygon Simplification", *Proc. of ACM Symposium on Interactive 3D Graphics*, 1999.

[Funkhouser93] T. A. Funkhouser. "Database and Display Algorithms for Interactive Visualization of Architecture Model". Ph.D. thesis. CS Division, UC Berkeley, 1993.

[Garland97] M. Garland and P. Heckbert, "Surface simplification based on Quadric Error Metric", *Proc. of ACM SIGGRAPH*, 1997.

[Gortler96] S. J. Gortler, R. Grzeszczuk, R. Szeliski, and M. F. Cohen, "The Lumigraph" In *SIGGRAPH 96 Conference Proceedings*, August 1996, pp. 43--54.

[Greene93] N. Greene, M. Kass, G. Miller, "Hierarchical Z-buffer visibility", *Proc. of ACM SIGGRAPH* 1993.

[Hoppe96] H. Hoppe. Progressive Meshes. In *SIGGRAPH 96 Conference Proceedings*: ACM SIGGRAPH, 1996, pp. 99--108.

[Katkere97] A. Katkere, S. Moessi, D. Kuramura, P. Kelly and R. Jain, "Towards video-based immersive environments", Multimedia Systems, May 1997, pp. 69-87.

[Kender97] John Kender and B. Yeo, "Video Scene Segmentation via Continuous Video Coherence", IBM Research Report RC 21061, December 1997.

[Lastra99] A. Lastra, Private communication, University of North Carolina at Chapel Hill, 1999.

[Levoy96] M. Levoy and P. Hanrahan. "Light Field Rendering", in *SIGGRAPH 96 Conference Proceedings*, August 1996, pp. 31--42.

[Maciel95] W. C. Maciel and Peter Shirley. "Visual Navigation of Large Environments Using Textured Clusters." In *1995 Symposium on Interactive 3D Graphics*, April 1995, pp. 95-102.

[Mannoni97] B. Mannoni, "A Virtual Museum", Communications of the ACM, vol. 40, no. 9, pp. 61-62, 1997.

[McMillan95] L. McMillan and Gary Bishop, "Plenoptic Modeling: An Image-Based Rendering System", in *SIGGRAPH 95 Conference Proceedings*, August 1995, pp. 39-46.

[Millerson90] G. Millerson. *The Technique of Television Production*. Focal Press, Oxford, England, 1990.

[MPEG2] MPEG-2, ISO, ISO/IEC JTCI CD 13818, *Generic Coding of moving pictures and associated audio*, 1994.

[MPEG4] MPEG4 Home Page. In http://drogo.cselt.stet.it/mpeg.

[MSSG] MPEG Software Simulation Group home page, http://www.mpeg.org/MSSG.

[Patel98] Ketan Patel and Lawrence Rowe, "Exploiting Temporal Parallelism for Software-only Video Effects Processing", *Proc. of ACM Multimedia*, pp. 161-170, 1998.

[Rohlf94] J. Rohlf and J. Helman, "Iris Performer: A high performance multiprocessor toolkit for realtime 3D Graphics". In *Proc. of ACM Siggraph*, 1994, pp. 381--394.

[Shade96] J. Shade, D. Lischinski, D. Salesin, T. DeRose, and J. Snyder, "Hierarchical Image Caching for Accelerated Walkthroughs of Complex Environments", In *SIGGRAPH 96 Conference Proceedings*, August 1996, pp. 75--82.

[Shen95] K. Shen and E. J. Delp, "A fast algorithm for video parsing using MPEG compressed sequences", *International Conference on Image Processing*, vol. II, pp. 252-255, Oct. 1995.

[Teller91] S. Teller and C. H. Sequin. Visibility preprocessing for interactive walkthroughs. In *Proc. of ACM Siggraph*, 1991, pp. 61--69.

[Tu00] X. Tu and B. L. Yeo, "Interactive Video for E-Merchandising", Intel Internal Report, Jan. 2000.

[Wei97] Q. Wei, H. Zhang and Y. Zhong, "A robust approach to video segmentation using compressed data", *Proceedings SPIE Storage and Retrieval for Still Images and Video Databases V*, vol. SPIE 3022, pp. 448-456, Feb. 1997.

[Yeung97] M. Yeung and B. Yeo, "Video visualization for compact presentation and fast browsing of pictorial content", *IEEE Transactions on Circuits and Systems for Video Technology*, vol. 7, pp. 771-785, Oct. 1997.

[Yeo00] B.L. Yeo, M. M. Yeung, and V. Kuriakin. "MPEG Processing Library (MPL)", Intel Internal Report, Jan. 2000.

[Zhang93] H. Zhang, A. Kankanhalli and S. Smoliar, "Automatic partitioning of full-motion video", *Multimedia Systems*, vol. 1, pp. 10-28, July 1993.

[Zhang97] H. Zhang, D. Manocha, T. Hudson, and K. Hoff, "Visibility culling using hierarchical occlusion maps", In *Proc. of ACM Siggraph*, 1997.

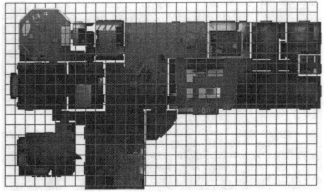

Figure 9: House model with cell grid overlaid in red. Each cell is 1 meter on a side and extends from the floor through the ceiling of the house.

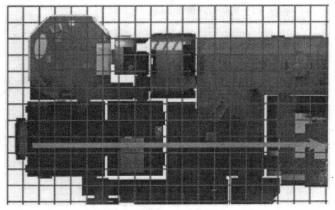

Figure 10: One row of cells through the model. These rows are used to map the cells into 1D streams for video encoding.

Figure 11: Video impostor showing correct perspective effects. The viewpoint is near the cell center in this image. Our system maintains a frame rate between 12 and 30 frames per second for such views.

Figure 12: A view of the house with impostors disabled, for comparison with the artifacts below. This view is rendered with a frame rate of roughly 2 frames/sec.

Figure 13: Example of perspective distortion caused by lack of depth parallax in impostors. The viewpoint is near the cell boundary in this image. Also note the color discontinuity between impostor and geometry.

Detecting topical events in digital video

Tanveer Syeda-Mahmood[*]
IBM Almaden Research Center
K57/B2, 650 Harry Road
San Jose, CA 95120
stf@almaden.ibm.com

S. Srinivasan
IBM Almaden Research Center
K57/B2, 650 Harry Road
San Jose, CA 95120
savitha@almaden.ibm.com

ABSTRACT

The detection of events is essential to high-level semantic querying of video databases. It is also a very challenging problem requiring the detection and integration of evidence for an event available in multiple information modalities, such as audio, video and language. This paper focuses on the detection of specific types of events, namely, topic of discussion events that occur in classroom/lecture environments. Specifically, we present a query-driven approach to the detection of topic of discussion events with foils used in a lecture as a way to convey a topic. In particular, we use the image content of foils to detect visual events in which the foil is displayed and captured in the video stream. The recognition of a foil in video frames exploits the color and spatial layout of regions on foils using a technique called region hashing. Next, we use the textual phrases listed on a foil as an indication of a topic, and detect topical audio events as places in the audio track where the best evidence for the topical phrases was heard. Finally, we use a probabilistic model of event likelihood to combine the results of visual and audio event detection that exploits their time co-occurrence. The resulting identification of topical events is evaluated in the domain of classroom lectures and talks.

Keywords

Topic of discussion events, multi-modal fusion, slide detection, topical audio events, query-driven topic detection.

1. INTRODUCTION

Despite the progress made in image and video content retrieval, making high-level semantic queries, such as looking for specific events, has still remained a far reaching goal. Yet, most practical applications embedding content-based retrieval require precisely a way to handle such queries. One such application is the domain of distributed or distance learning where querying the video content for events containing a topic of discussion is a desirable component of any

---

[*]Author for correspondence.

learning system. While a large number of studies have been done on event perception in various fields such as economics, perception, psychophysics, and artificial intelligence, the automatic detection of events has remained a challenging problem due to several reasons. First, the detection and understanding of events requires examining objects, actions, and their inter-relationships automatically. Secondly, events are often multi-modal requiring the gathering of evidence from information available in multiple media sources such as video and audio. Finally, identifying an event also requires identifying a duration over which it occurs (including the precise start and end times). Even with the best techniques for visual or audio scene analysis, event detection using the individual cues will continue to possess robustness problems due to detection errors. For example, the detection of objects and their relationships are well-known to be difficult problems in computer vision. Further, the localization inaccuracies with individual cue-based detection often lead to conflicting indications for an event at different points of time making their multi-modal fusion difficult. Previous work on the automatic detection of events has primarily focused on actions including event classification[12], and object recognition for capturing visual events. The automatic detection of auditory events, on the other hand, has been mainly limited to discriminating between music, silence and speech[15]. The notion of combining of audio-visual cues, though not for event detection, has also been explored by others. In general, the methods of combining cues have considered models such as linear combination[4] including Gaussian mixtures, winner-take-all variants[7], rule-based combinations[2], and simple statistical combinations[2].

In this paper, we address the problem of event detection in digital video by focusing on specific types of events, namely, topic of discussion or topical events. Topical events are defined here as points of time in a video where a specific topic as indicated in a given foil, was discussed. From a survey of the distance learning community, it has been found that the single most useful query found by students is the querying of topic of interest in a long recorded video of a course lecture. Such classroom lectures and talks are often accompanied by foils (also called slides) some of which convey the topic being discussed at that point in time. Figure 1c,f,i shows examples of such slides. When such lectures are video taped, at least one of the cameras used captures the displayed slide, so that the visual appearance of a slide in video can be a good indication of the beginning of a discussion relating to a topic. However, the visual presence alone may not be sufficient, since it is possible that a speaker flashes a slide without talking about it, or can continue to discuss the topic even after a slide is removed. In this paper, therefore, we focus on detecting topical events by combining visual and audio cues derived from the image and textual content of foils.

To our knowledge, no work has yet been done on the detection of topical events using a combination of visual and audio search of foils. The work reported here makes several novel contributions in that direction. First, we present a novel method of topical visual event detection by identifying points of time in video where a foil was displayed and captured in the video stream. The identification of specific foils exploits the color and spatial layout geometry of regions on foils using a technique called region hashing. Specifically, an illumination-invariant description of color is used for robust foil localization. Region hashing, being pose-invariant assures robust recognition of foils. Next, we present a novel method of topical audio event detection based on the phrasal content of foils. In particular, by relying on the phrases listed on a foil as a useful indication of the topic, we search the audio track for places where the phrases were spoken. The search uses a combination of word and phonetic recognition of speech and exploits the order of occurrence of words in a phrase to return points in video where one or more sub-phrases used in the foil were heard. The individual phrase matches are then combined into a topical match for the audio event using a probabilistic combination model that exploits the contiguity of occurrence to group phrasal matches into audio events. Finally, we present a novel method of multi-modal fusion for overall topical event detection that uses a probabilistic model to exploit the time co-occurrence of individual audio and video events. The automatic topical event detection method reported here has been extensively tested to demonstrate effective topic detection as part of a distributed learning system for the indexing and browsing of a large number of teaching and training videos.

2. TOPICAL VIDEO EVENT DETECTION

We begin by addressing the problem of topical video event detection through the detection of foils in a video. There has been some work done in the multimedia authoring community to address this problem from the point of synchronization of foils with video. The predominant approach has been to do on-line synchronization using a structured note-taking environment such as Zenpads[1] to record the times of change of slide electronically and synchronize with the video stream. Current presentation environments such as Lotus Freelance or Powerpoint have features that can also record the change time of slides when performed in rehearse modes. In distributed learning, however, there is often a need for off-line synchronization of slides since they are often provided by the teacher after a video recording of the lecture has been made. The detection of foils in a video stream under these settings can be challenging. There are a multitude of ways in which foils appear depending on the camera geometry used in taping lectures. The resulting appearance of slides in video can vary greatly in color, and the slides themselves could appear anywhere in the video frame. Figure 1a,d,g show examples of different slide appearances possible in videos. A solution to this problem for constrained camera geometries was presented in[9]. There, a solution was proposed for a two-camera geometry, in which

one of the cameras was fixed on the screen depicting the slide. Since this was a more-or-less calibrated setting, the boundary of the slide was visible so that the task of selecting a slide-containing region in a video frame was made easy. Further, corners of the visible quadrilateral structure could be used to solve for the 'pose' of the slide under the general projective transform. Our approach to foil detection is meant to consider more general imaging situations involving one or more cameras, and greater variations in scale, pose and occlusions. We break the foil detection problem into two phases, namely, 1) detecting foil-containing regions in video frames, and 2) recognizing which of a given set of foils appears in a slide-containing region of a video frame.

Detection of foil regions based on color

We detect slide containing regions within video frames using the background color of slides. Since there is considerable color variation in the appearance of the slide in a video frame from its original electronic or hardcopy form (see Figure 1), this can be a difficult problem even in cases where a uniform color background is used. To enable a robust detection of slide using the background color, we adopted an approach to describing color based on surface color classes as reported in an earlier work[18]. A surface color class is the set of surfaces with same spectral properties but different spatial distributions. It was shown in [16] that the eigenvector of the projected clusters from samples of such surface classes is an illumination-invariant description of the surface color class. We model the background color of slides (the largest region on a foil that encloses all other regions is taken to be the background region) in terms of this description. For cases in which multi-colored backgrounds are used, we describe it by multiple surface color class descriptions.

To detect foils in video, we first process the video to group into shots using conventional histogram-based scene clustering methods. Each such shot is represented by a keyframe. To handle videos with fixed camera settings that generate very few shots, we also allow a regular sampling of video (for eg., once per second) to ensure at least twice as many keyframes as the number of slides used in the talk. The method of detecting color regions using the specific color class description described in [16] was then applied to detect regions in the keyframes that contain one or more of the background colors of the specified foil set.

Figure 1b,e,h shows background color detection in sample video frames shown in Figure 1a,d,g using the query slides of Figure 1c,f,i respectively. As can be seen, the detection works well even under considerable changes in color appearance. A detailed analysis of the results of slide detection are reported in Table 1 and are discussed under the evaluation of topical event detection in Section 5.

Recognition of foils in video

Even though color-based selection points to candidate regions, it cannot be used to identify which of the foils is depicted in the region, as most foils of a set tend to have the same (slide master) background. Also, due to the scale at which these foils are imaged, it is not possible to decipher the individual words on a slide using an OCR algorithm. In addition, differences between successive slides can be small (eg. when a topic is continued) so that foil recognition requires a detailed modeling of spatial layout of the smaller regions constituting the foil. Such a modeling of spatial layout, however, must be pose-invariant, to account for effects of warping, rotation, and scaling that are often present due to the camera geometry used for taping the lectures. Finally, it should be robust to occlusion errors that are present often as speakers move in front of displayed screen, or when camera pans to the surrounding scene. A technique for recognizing objects by the spatial layout of regions called region hashing, was presented in an earlier paper[17]. In this paper, we apply region hashing to the problem of foil recognition. For this, we note that the foils or slides displayed on a screen can be modeled as planar regions in space, so that their transformation assuming orthographic projection, can be modeled as 2d affine distortion[1]. For constrained camera geometries, perspective effects can also be modeled as described in [9]. To model the spatial layout of foil regions using region hashing, we exploit the well-known observation that the shape of a 2d pattern can be described in a pose-invariant fashion by recording the affine coordinates of features within object, computed with respect to a triple of basis features chosen as an object-based reference frame[8]. The relative location of a pair of foil regions can be specified precisely and in a pose-invariant fashion through affine intervals, i.e. the interval in which affine coordinate values lie. Thus ideally, a region of a video frame can be recognized as containing a specific foil if the affine intervals of corresponding region pairs are identical. In practice, due to occlusions, the affine intervals overlap rather than register exactly. To account for missing data which cause affine intervals to be missing altogether, we compute affine intervals w.r.t multiple basis triples and region pairs on a given foil, and store them in a suitable index structure. This precomputation saves time during recognition of foils in video stream following the principle of geometric hashing[8].

The electronic foil images of a foil set are pre-processed to extract features. Specifically, curves are extracted from an edge map of a slide. Connected components of curves are used to form regions within the foil image. Consecutive features along curves are used to form basis points. The affine coordinates of all features of one region are then computed w.r.t. a basis triple of another region, and the range in which they lie are noted in the corresponding affine interval. The spatial layout of each foil is then represented as

$$\text{Object layout} = \{(R_i, C_{R_i})(R_j, C_{R_j}), \{Int_{ij}, B_{ik}\})\} 1 \leq i,j, \leq N \tag{1}$$

where N is the number of object regions, C_{R_i} is the color of the region R_i, and Int_{ij} is the affine interval information given by $< (\alpha_{jmin}, \beta_{jmin}), (\alpha_{jmax}, \beta_{jmax}) >$ of features F_j of region R_j computed with respect to kth basis B_{ik} of Region R_i. For slides containing single color text, the color of the region is not distinctive information. On the other hand, for slides containing diagrams and images, color can be useful for pruning false matches. The affine interval information is consolidated and represented in an index structure called the interval hash tree. The details of the interval hash tree

construction and search are reported in [17] and are skipped here for brevity.

Given a query foil-containing region in a video frame, an identical processing is done to generate the affine intervals with the exception that they are computed with respect to one basis triple per region. In our experiments we found the median basis triple of a curve to be a reliable choice. We then find evidence for overlap of query affine intervals of all query region pairs with a subset of database affine intervals, by indexing the interval hash tree used to store the affine intervals. Let the affine interval information retrieved for a query region pair $F_O = (R_{Oi}, C(R_{Oi}), R_{Oj}, C(R_{Oj}), < Int_{Oij}, B_{Oijm} >)$ after such indexing be denoted by $\{R_k, C(R_k), R_l Int_{kl}, B_{kln} >)\}$. We first discard region pairs if the corresponding region identities do not match i.e., $C(R_k) \neq C(R_{Oi})$ and $C(R_l) \neq C(R_{Oj})$, or their overlap is less than a certain threshold. The score of the basis retrieved B_{kln} is then incremented by the extent of interval overlap $\frac{2Int_{kl} \cap Int_{Oij}}{Int_{kl} \cup Int_{Oij}}$. We then select the top few basis, and declare their corresponding enclosing regions as matching region pairs, and the corresponding foils as candidate matching foils in the database. For each foil selected, we use the basis triple pair with the highest score in the region pair with the highest score as a candidate matching basis. Since these are three pairs of matching points, an affine transformation relating the object to its presence in the image is found and used to project the selected foil image at the foil-containing region in the video frame for verification. The sum of verification scores of all potential matches is used for normalization to render scores of matching positions as probabilities.

Examples

We now illustrate regions hashing for foil recognition through a few examples. Figure 1a,d,g shows examples of keyframes from sample videos. The recognized slide in each of video frames at the located slide region shown in Figure 1b,e,h are shown in Figure 1c,f,i respectively. More details on results of slide image matching for topical event detection are described in Section 5.

Topical video event detection

The above method of foil matching in video can now be applied to detect topical video events. Since the foil matching is performed on keyframes, the video event spanned by the foil topic based on image content is taken to be the duration between the scene changes of two consecutive foil matches. That is, let b_i, e_i be the shot duration corresponding to the keyframe F_i. Let ith match to the foil image Q_j be in frame F_k with probability of correctness p_k. Let F_l be the keyframe with the smallest $l > k$ where a match to foil $Q_m \neq Q_j$ was found (notice that the intermediate keyframes between F_l and F_k may be pure scene changes not depicting a slide). Then the topical video event duration of the ith match of foil image Q_j is (b_k, e_{l-1}). Notice here that we are regarding different match instances to a foil as separate events, even though they may be related.

---

[1]The region hashing formalism relying on the overlap of affine intervals also covers in most cases the usual effects of perspective projection.

Video	Number of foils	video frames	total keyframes	keyframes showing foils		Correct matches	false or no matches
				Detected	Actual		
1.	13	59457	20	11	10	9	1
2.	24	143900	196	61	46	42	7
3.	6	19318	25	10	6	6	0
4.	11	23398	25	12	12	12	0
5.	10	17054	161	14	9	8	4
6.	10	19176	127	16	10	10	1

Table 1: Precision in visual event detection.

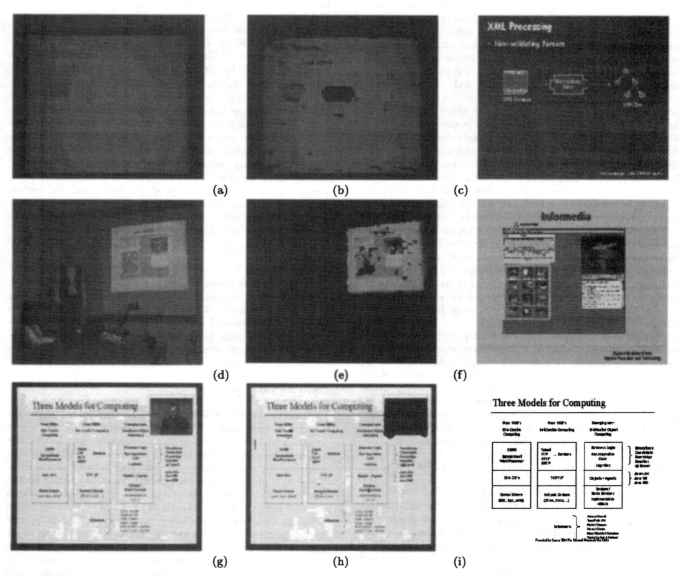

(a)   (b)   (c)

(d)   (e)   (f)

(g)   (h)   (i)

Figure 1: Illustration of foil detection and recognition. The first column shows the video frames, the second column shows the slide-containing regions detected based on background color, and the third column shows the corresponding recognized slide in the detected region.

88

3. TOPICAL AUDIO EVENT DETECTION

We now turn our attention to the detection of topical audio events in which topical phrases indicated on a foil were spoken. Detecting topical audio events is particularly useful in case of errors in foil recognition which can either cause portions of video discussing a topic to be entirely missed, or worse still, can point to the wrong point of time. It also becomes necessary in cases where the slide was not displayed, or displayed but not captured by the camera, so that only the audio can be relied upon to indicate topical information. The deduction of topics from transcribed audio or text documents is an area of intense exploration in the information and spoken document retrieval communities[6, 3, 5, 11]. Much of the research addresses topic discovery for large document collections, which can be referred to as intervideo topic discovery. These methods focus on the bottom-up detection of topics by exploiting the multiple occurrences of phrases (both local and global) to indicate their topical relevance. We take a different approach here by focusing on the problem of time-localized topical audio event detection (rather than topic detection) within a single video. Further, we take a query-driven approach in that we assume the desired topical event can be suitably abstracted in the topical phrases used on foils. For example, from the slide shown in Figure 2a we can guess that at the time the slide was displayed in the video, the speaker may have been discussing the details of an XML schema. Other slides such as those containing mostly graphics as shown in Figure 3a, need not give as clear an indication of the topic of discussion. In such cases, we can rely either on the visual cue, or other slides preceding or following the given foil to decipher the topic.

Thus a topical audio event in our case is defined as the set of contiguous points of time in an audio track where there is spoken evidence for the maximal number of textual phrases listed on a foil. It is detected by a 4-step algorithm that involves (i) word spotting of individual textual words on foils, (ii) consolidation of word matches into matches for text phrases on foils, (iii) grouping of matches to multiple text phrases on foils to identify candidate audio events, and finally, (iv) probabilistic ranking of the candidate events to identify most likely audio events. Each of these operations are desrcibed in detail below.

Word spotting for phrasal matching

The localization of points in time where topical phrases are spoken makes use of a word spotting algorithm that is based on a combined word and phonetic-based representation of audio. The details of word and phonetic-based retrieval algorithms are available in [13, 14], so that our discussion of them here will be brief.

We first analyze the audio track using a speech recognition engine (IBM ViaVoice^{TM} with a large (65,000) word vocabulary) to generate a word transcript. This is then filtered using a language model that imposes some sentence structure through tokenization and part-of-speech tagging. Thus for example, an original query word "growing" will be converted to "grow" during this stage. This is then followed by stop-word removal to prevent excess false positives during retrieval. To account for errors in word boundary detection, word recognition, and out-of-vocabulary words, we also ex-tract a phone-based representation of the audio to build a time-based phonetic index. The phonetic query representation is generated by converting the original query words to equivalent phone sequences. For example, the original query "growing" is converted to the phone sequence "G-R-OW". Finally, the word and phoneme indexes are represented as a tuple $(w, \{t_w, p_w\})$ and $(s, \{t_s, p_s\})$ respectively, where w, s are the word and phoneme strings, $\{t_w, t_s\}$ are points in time where they occur, and $\{p_w, p_s\}$ are their respective recognition probabilities.

These indexes are now used to peform word spotting as follows. We convert the original query comprising of a sequence of words into word and phonetic representations as described above. We then use the word-based query representation to retrieve an ordered list of matches in time using the word index. We refer to this as word-based retrieval. Next, we use the phonetic query representation to generate an ordered list of matches in time using the phone index. We refer to this as phonetic retrieval. We merge the two ordered lists in time, and compute a combined score for each of the matches. We empirically arrive at a threshold value for the score, and retrieve only those matches with a score above the threshold value.

Our word spotting algorithm has good performance bounds as described in Table 3 which lists the precision and recall numbers for word-based, phonetic and combined word-phoneme retrieval for the experimental data set outlined in Table 2.

Topical phrase detection

We now discuss the localization of points in time where topical phrases extracted from lines of text on foils are heard. The lines of text in electronic foils are extracted automatically using OLE code for Powerpoint or Freelance slides as described in [10]. Matches for each of the words in a phrase (line of text) are obtained using the word-spotting algorithm described above. Although the precision of our word spotting algorithm is good, an individual word may be spoken in multiple contexts so that the matches to individual words of a phrase tend to span wide sections of the audio track. The phrase-based retrieval, therefore, consolidates these matches such that the order of words in the query phrase is preserved in the matching spoken phrases found. That is, given a query phrase sequence $S_Q = (q_1, q_2, ...q_n)$, we retrieve matches to individual words q_i by recording the set $\{t_{qij}, p_{qij}\}$ where t_{qij} is the time at which there is a jth match to the ith query word q_i based on the word index or the phonetic index (or both), and p_{qij} is probability of relevance of a match. Here we use a simple linear combination of matching word and phone index term probabilities to arrive at p_{qij}. The resulting sets $\{t_{qi}, p_{qi}\}$ for all query phrase words are then arranged in time-sorted order to form a long match sequence

$$S_M = (s_1, s_2, ...s_m) \qquad (2)$$

where the ith match $s_i = (q_j, t_{qjk} = t_i, p_{qjk})$ in the combined sequence corresponds to a kth match for some query word q_j and m is the total number of matches to all the query words in the phrase. The best match to the overall query phrase that preserves the order of occurrence of words is then found by enumerating all common contiguous subsequences $W_q = (w_1, w_2, ...w_l)$ of S_M and S_Q. The sequence W_q is a contiguous subsequence of S_M if there exists a strictly increasing sequence $(i_1, i_2, ..i_l)$ of indices of S_M such that $w_j = s_{i_j}$ for $j = 1, 2, ..l$ and $i_j - i_{j-1} < \tau$. The threshold τ represents average time between two words in a spoken phrase. When the words are consecutive, this is typically of the order of 1 second for most speakers. The probabilities of relevance of each such subsequence is then computed simply as the average of the relevance score for each of its element matches, as the matches to the individual words can be assumed to be mutually exclusive. All those with probabilities of relevance above a chosen threshold are retained as matches to a query phrase. Thus the method of indexing for a phrase exploits the probabilities of relevance of individual matching words in the phrase, as well as their spoken order taking into account the average separation in time between spoken words in a phrase.

topical audio event detection

The above query phrase-based audio retrieval can be repeated for all query phrases on a foil to obtain places in the video where one or more of the query phrases were heard. Due to errors in speech recognition, and due to partial phrase matches, the match positions are again widely distributed potentially spanning the entire video. Figure 2b shows the phrasal match distribution in the audio to the phrases on slide depicted in Figure 2a. Similarly, Figure 3b shows the distribution for the phrases on the query slide shown in Figure 3a. While the individual matches to phrases can be widely distributed, we notice that there are points in time where a number of these matches either co-occur or occur within a short span of time. If such matches could be grouped based on inter-phrasal match distance, then it is likely that at least one such group corresponds to the place in the audio where the topic conveyed by the foil was discussed. *This is the central observation exploited in detecting the topical audio event.* To arrive at a suitable threshold for inter-phrasal match distance, we recorded the match distributions for phrases on over 350 slides and a collection of over 20 videos depicting one or more of the slides covering multiple speakers and course content. We then noted the inter-phrasal match distance difference during the duration over which the topic conveyed by the foil was actually discussed (as noted manually). The resulting distribution of the difference indicated a peak in the distribution between 1 and 20 seconds indicating that for most speakers and most topics, the predominant separation between utterances of phrases tended to be between 1 to 20 seconds apart. We, therefore, used a distance threshold of 20 seconds to group consecutive phrasal matches into time groups using a simple connected component algorithm. During grouping, we allowed multiple occurrences of a match to a phrase within a group to handle cases when a phrase emphasizing a point of discussion was uttered frequently. The resulting time intervals form the basic localization units of the topical event using the audio cue.

Not all such interval groups, however, are relevant to the topical audio event. That is, while it is common for multiple matches to occur for individual topical phrases that look equally good, a discussion containing all the topical phrases on a given foil are seldom repeated. To compute the probabilities of relevance of the derived interval groups to the topical audio event, we combine the probabilities of individual phrasal matches within the group. Let the topical audio event be denoted by E_a, and let the probability that a time interval group $G_j = (L_j(E_a), H_j(E_a))$ contains E_a be denoted by $P(G_j; E_a)$. Here $L_j(E_a), H_j(E_a)$ are the lower and upper end points of the time interval of the jth match for the topical audio event E_a. Let the time and probability of matches to query phrase qp_i be denoted as $\{(T_{qpij}, P_{qpij})\}$. Since the individual phrase matches within G_j occupy distinct time intervals, the mutual exclusiveness assumption holds, so that $P(G_j; E_a)$ can be assembled as

$$P(G_j; E_a) = \frac{\sum P_{qprs}}{\sum_{\text{all } i} \sum_{\text{all } j} P_{pqij}} \quad (3)$$

where the intervals $T_{pqrs} \in G_j$. The intervals ranked highest using the above probability of relevance then represents the best match to the topical event based on audio information.

Examples

We now illustrate indexing of topical audio events based on foil phrases. Figure 2a and 3a show two topical foils with text phrases representative of the topic of discussion. Figure 2b and 3b show the matches for the all the phrases on each of the slides (here phrase 1 match is indicated in red, (2-green) (3-blue) (4-cyan) (5-yellow) (6-magenta) (7-black), and so on). The result of grouping using the inter-phrase distance threshold of 20 seconds is shown in Figure 2c and 3c respectively, thereby identifying candidate durations for the topical audio event. The topical relevance scores are also listed in these figures. The results on the correctness of topic localization using the most probable match is discussed under Section 5.

4. TOPICAL EVENT DETECTION BY MULTI MODAL FUSION

We now discuss the detection of the overall topical event using the evidence for the event obtained by visual and audio clues. Since both foil indexing and phrase-based retrieval can have false negatives and positives, they can result in either a video segment being incorrectly weighted for relevancy to a topical event or indicating the same topic at a wrong location. The time co-occurrence of these matches, however, can be a strong clue to the correctness of the detected location for the topic. Simplistic combining methods for multi-modal fusion such as "AND" or "OR" of the intervals do not yield satisfactory solutions. That is, a simple AND of the durations can result in too small a duration to be detected for the overall topic, while an "OR" of the results can potentially span the entire video segment, particularly, when the audio and video matches are spread over the length of the video. Other combination methods such as winner-take-all[7] used in past approaches are also not appropriate here since the probabilities of relevance of durations for events given by neither the audio nor the video matches are particularly salient for clear selection. Finally, weighted linear combination methods are also not appropriate as they do not exploit time co-occurrence.

Number of Videos in Test Collection	6
Total Duration of Videos	4.5 hours
High fidelity Recording with Professional Speaker (35% WER)	1 hour
Low fidelity Recording with Amateur Speaker (65% WER)	3.5 hours
Average Number of In-Vocabulary Queries Per Video	8
Average Number of Matches Per Query	9 (ranges 2 – 43)
Average Query Length	1 word

Table 2: Test data statistics for word spotting experiments.

Retrieval System	Average Precision	Average Recall
Word-Based	0.98	0.59
Phonetic	0.87	0.73
Combined	0.89	0.75

Table 3: Word spotting performance data.

Video	Number of foils	Avg # of phrases	Avg. # of phrase matches	Number of times Correct	Actual Present
1.	13	5.9	4.3	9	13
2.	24	6.8	7.2	18	24
3.	6	7.2	3.8	5	6
4.	11	4.9	4.3	8	11
5.	10	8.3	6.8	7	10
6.	10	8.3	7.9	6	10

Table 4: Precision in audio event detection.

Video	Slide #	Topic duration detected							
		Foil image		foil text		Combined		Ground truth	
		start	end	start	end	start	end	start	end
1.	3	2:02	3:46	2:28	4:08	2:02	3:47	2:25	3:32
2.	6	6:33	7:36	6:29	8:09	6:33	7:36	6:33	7:29
3.	5	12:56	17:44	14:23	15:23	12:56	17:44	12:40	16: 02
4.	3	3:31	5:48	4:20	5:10	3:31	5:48	2:54	6:01
5.	4	16:04	16:49	12:22	14:24	16:04	16:49	15:29	17:01
6.	6	7:45	10:43	6:23	8:24	6:23	10:43	7:01	10:51

Table 5: Accuracy of topical event duration detection.

Video	# slides	Topic Ocurrences in top 10 matches			Topic Ocurrences in top 3		
		foil image	foil text	combined	foil image	foil text	combined
1.	10	9	10	10	8	6	9
2.	27	22	25	25	24	16	26
3.	32	28	30	31	26	20	28
4.	16	13	12	14	10	8	12
5.	23	16	19	20	14	14	19
6.	18	15	16	16	12	10	14

Table 6: Illustration of precision and recall of topical event indexing of videos using foils

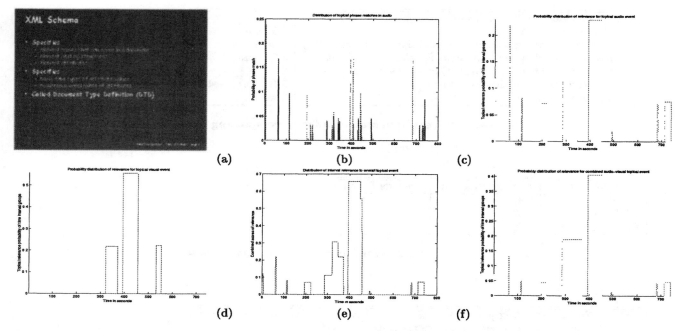

Figure 2: Illustration of topical event detection. (a) A query slide. (b) Phrasal match distribution in the audio track. The colors represent matches for the individual phrases. (c) Candidate audio events and their relevance probabilities obtained by grouping phrasal matches. (d) Topical visual event indicating appearance of foil in video track. (e) Cumulative distribution of combined topical audio and video events. (f) Segmentation of cumulative distribution to indicate combined topical event and their relevance probabilities.

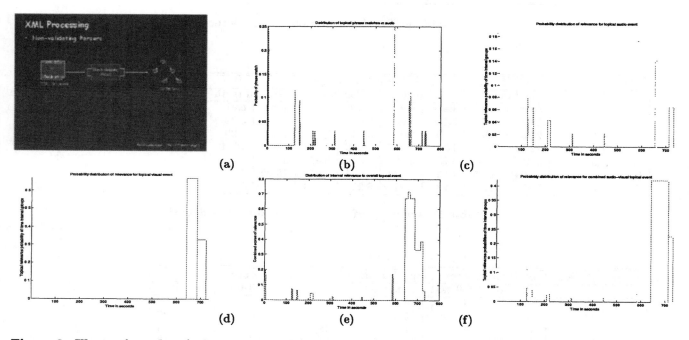

Figure 3: Illustration of topical event detection – Another example. (a) A query slide. (b) Phrasal match distribution in the audio track. The colors represent matches for the individual phrases. (c) Candidate audio events and their relevance probabilities obtained by grouping phrasal matches. (d) Topical visual event indicating appearance of foil in video track. (e) Cumulative distribution of combined topical audio and video events. (f) Segmentation of cumulative distribution to indicate combined topical event and their relevance probabilities.

Our approach to multi-modal fusion is based on the following guiding rationale. (a) The combination method should exploit the time co-occurrence of individual cue-based event detections. (b) The selected duration for the overall topical event must show graceful begin and end to match the natural perception of such events. (c) The combination should exploit the underlying probabilities of relevance of a duration to event given by individual modal matches.

The durations likely to contain the individual cue-based events can be denoted by $\{G_j(E_i), F_j(E_i)\}$, where $G_j(E_i) = (L_j(E_i), H_j(E_i))$ are the the lower and upper end points of the time interval of the jth match in time using the ith modal topical event E_i as defined earlier. In our case, E comprises of E_1 = topical video event where a visual match to a slide appeared in the video stream and E_2 = topical audio event where the text phrases on slide were heard in the audio track[2] Here $F_j(E_i)$ is the probability of relevance of interval G_j to the event $E_i = P(G_j(E_i)/E_i)$. In general, the probability that the time duration of the entire video contains the overall topical event E is given by

$$P(G; E) = P(G; E_1) + P(G; E_2) - P(G; E_1) * P(G; E_2). \quad (4)$$

To localize the duration most likely to contain the topical event E better, we can split the interval G based on the beginning and end times indicated by the individual modal events. That is, from the intervals $L_j(E_i), H_j(E_i)$, we get the end point sequence $e_1, e_2, ..e_{2M}$ where M is the total number of matches to all cues. The sequence of time intervals is then $\delta t_1, ... \delta t_{2M-1}$ where $\delta t_i = e_i - e_{i-1}$. The probability that each such interval is likely to contain the event E can now be given by

$$P(\delta t_i; E) = P(\delta t_i; E_1) + P(\delta t_i; E_2) - P(\delta t_i; E_1) * P(\delta t_i; E_2) \quad (5)$$

The individual values $P(\delta t_i; E_k)$ are then given as

$$P(\delta t_i; E_k) = \begin{cases} p(G_j; E_k) & e_i = H_j(E_k) \\ 0 & e_i = L_j(E_k) \end{cases} \quad (6)$$

The distribution of $P((\delta t; E)$ is often multimodal (unless all event matches co-occur), as shown in Figure 2e and 3e indicating that the overlap of time intervals of multi-modal matches grows and shrinks in cycles. By noting the local maxima of this distribution, and adjacent local minima around them, we form groups of time co-occurrence intervals (the local minima are those where there is a sign change in the derivative). The minima of the distribution correspond to situations where evidence from a cue disappears to be replaced next by evidence from another cue. These breakpoints are often the places where there is a graceful ending of the topic of discussion, a fact which has also been later verified through our experiments. Each such group δT_i is then taken as an indication of the localization of a match to the queried topical event. The probability of relevance $P(\delta T_i; E)$ is then taken to be simply $max\{P(\delta t_j; E), \delta t_j \in \delta T_i\}$. This is based on the rationale that once the individual time intervals t_j have been grouped as one time unit for the event, it is sufficient to consider the best evidence for it within the specified time interval.

---

[2] Although we do not show here, the method of multi-modal fusion described here can be easily generalized to more than two cues.

5. RESULTS

The indexing of topical events using foils was attempted as part of new distributed learning system that supports search and browse of multimedia documents based on text, image and audio content. The distributed learning system was delivered to a customer, and the following studies resulted during the evaluation phase prior to the delivery of the system.

The best way to view the results is by playing the corresponding indexed video segments for each query topical event indicated by sample foils, and noting the differences in the indicated time location using each of the cues. Since this is not possible in the paper version of the proceedings, we restrict to illustrating the results through the following studies.

Precision in visual event detection

We now report on our results of testing the precision of a match to a topical visual event. We have tested the slide matching technique on a total of 20 classroom videos collected from multiple university and training sources. The number of slides associated with each course varied, with the minimum being 10 and a maximum of 37, giving rise to a database of about 600 slide objects (generated from Powerpoint slides, Freelance graphics slides, and hardcopy slides or lecture notes respectively). For each of the videos, we evaluated the accuracy of foil detection using color, as well as accuracy of recognition in the frames detected to contain foils. The resulting performance is indicated in Table 1. Here we report the results for the duration most likely to contain the visual event as indicated by the verification scores of foil recognition. Note from the table that, for some videos, when a foil is projected for long time, multiple keyframes can indicate the same foil. Also, errors in keyframe extraction can miss the depiction of a foil. The color-based detection method is conservative as can be seen by Column 4 where the number of early detections are always more than the actual number of foils found. It can be concluded from Column 4,6,and 7 that both detection and recognition of foils in videos is reliable. In practice, though verification errors can leave more than one choice for a matching slide in a video frame, and can also cause some misses, particularly for badly occluded slides, or where zooming and panning effects leave only a small portion of a slide visible.

Precision in audio event detection

The test set to evaluate the precision in audio event detection remained the same as above. Here, however, we used the text phrases on each of the slides for querying the audio content. We then manually recorded the number of times the duration indicated to be most likely to contain the audio event, actually contained such an event. The result is indicated in Table 4. It can be seen from the table that while the most probable duration contained the audio event in most cases, the performance is not as good as for the slide image-based detection.

Precision in duration detection of topical events

Next, we evaluated the precision in the detection of the duration of the topical event using each of the cues. For this, we chose a set of 40 slide queries and 10 sample videos showing one or more of the slides. We indexed the video using slide image, slide text, and their combination, and in each case, noted the beginning and ending times. The result is shown in Table 5 for a sample of 10 slide queries in two sets of videos. Here rows 1- 5 are edited videos, in which the camera panned to the slide more or less around the time it was starting to be discussed. The second set of videos consisted of unedited videos, videos with single fixed camera and amateur videos taken with a handycam. Here we also record the ground truth beginning and ending times, as obtained by manual verification. From this table, we note that, the duration of the topic was spanned best by combining the two types of searches. The foil image-based indexing was accurate in identifying the beginning of a topic for edited videos, while the duration indicated showed a mismatch for unedited videos. This is understandable since the duration of the topic event indicated by foil image match is the time between two different consecutive slide appearances, which assumes that the camera pans to the slide as soon as it is displayed. Lastly, note that even with combined search, there is still a difference between the automatic and manually detected topic location and duration.

Precision and recall in topical event indexing

To test the precision and recall in topic indexing, we recorded the number of times a match to the topic was indicated in the top 10 results, and the number of times the correct match appeared in the top 3 results for a set of slides per video. The result is indicated in Table 6 for a topic search of a sample of slide queries in the corresponding videos in which they appear. The number of slides used for each video is shown in Column 2. As can be seen, the foil image-based search has fewer false positives, while foil text-based search has fewer false negatives in topic identification. The combined use of both cues, has fewer false positives and negatives.

6. CONCLUSIONS

In this paper we have tried to expose the challenges facing event detection in digital videos by focusing on topical events. In doing so, we have demonstrated a novel application of content-based retrieval of videos for the indexing of topics of discussion in classroom lecture/talk environments.

7. REFERENCES

[1] G. Abowd et al. Teaching and learning as multimedia authoring: The classroom 2000 project. In *Proc. ACM Multimedia*, pages 104–111, 1996.

[2] D.E. Appelt et al. Maestro: Conductor of multimedia analysis technologies. *cacm*, 43:57–63, February 2000.

[3] K. Bharat and M. Henzinger. Improved algorithms for topic distillation in a hyperlinked environment. In *Proc. 22nd Annual SIGIR Conference*, pages 326–327, 1999.

[4] J.C. Clark and N. Ferrier. Modal control of an attentive vision system. In *Proceedings of the International Conference on Computer Vision*, pages 514–523. 1988.

[5] G. Hauptmann, D. Lee, and P.E. Kennedy. Topic labeling of multilingual broadcast news in the informedia digital video library. In *Proc. ACM Digital Libraries/SIGIR MIDAS Workshop*, 1999.

[6] S. Jones and G. Paynter. Topic-based browsing within a digital library using keyphrases. In *Proc. 4th ACM Conference on Digital Libraries*, pages 114–121, 1999.

[7] C. Koch and S. Ullman. Selecting one among the many: A simple network implementing shifts in selective visual attention. Technical report, Artificial Intelligence Lab, M.I.T., AI-Memo-770, January 1984.

[8] Y. Lamdan and H.J. Wolfson. Geometric hashing: A general and efficient model-based recognition scheme. In *Proceedings of the International Conference on Computer Vision*, pages 218–249, 1988.

[9] S. Mukhopadhyay and B. Smith. Passive capturing and structuring of lectures. In *Proc. ACM Multimedia*, pages 477–488, 1999.

[10] W. Niblack. Slidefinder: A tool for browsing presentation graphics using content-based retrieval. In *Proc. IEEE Workshop on Content-based Access of Image and Video Libraries*, pages 114–118, 1999.

[11] R. Schwartz et al. A maximum likelihood model for topic classification in broadcast news. In *Proc. European Conf. on Speech Communication and Technology*, 1997.

[12] J.M. Siskind and Q. Morris. A maximum likelihood approach to visual event classification. In *European Conf. Computer Vision*, pages 347–362, 1996.

[13] S. Srinivasan et al. Query expansion for imperfect speech: Applications in distributed learning. In *Proc. IEEE Workshop on Content-based Access of Image and Video Libraries (CBAIVL-2000)*, 2000.

[14] S. Srinivasan and D. Petkovic. Phonetic confusion matrix-based spoken document retrieval. In *Proc. Special Interest Group on Information Retrieval (SIGIR) 2000*, 2000.

[15] S. Srinivasan, D. Petkovic, and D. Ponceleon. Towards robust features for classifying audio in the cuevideo system. In *Proc. ACM Multimedia*, pages 393–400, 1999.

[16] T. Syeda-Mahmood. Indexing of topics using foils. In *IEEE Conf. on Computer Vision and Pattern Recognition*, 2000.

[17] T. Syeda-Mahmood, P. Raghavan, and N. Megiddo. Interval hash trees: An efficient index structure for searching object queries in large image databases. In *IEEE Workshop on Content-based Access of Image and Video Libraries*, 2000.

[18] T.F. Syeda-Mahmood and Y-Q. Cheng. Indexing colored surfaces in images. In *Proceedings Int. Conf. on Pattern Recognition*, 1996.

Determining Computable Scenes in Films and their Structures using Audio-Visual Memory Models

Hari Sundaram   Shih-Fu Chang
Dept. of Electrical Engineering,
Columbia University,
New York New York 10027.

{sundaram, sfchang}@ctr.columbia.edu

ABSTRACT

In this paper we present novel algorithms for computing scenes and within-scene structures in films. We begin by mapping insights from film-making rules and experimental results from the psychology of audition into a computational scene model. We define a computable scene to be a chunk of audio-visual data that exhibits long-term consistency with regard to three properties: (a) chromaticity (b) lighting (c) ambient sound. Central to the computational model is the notion of a causal, finite-memory viewer model. We segment the audio and video data separately. In each case we determine the degree of correlation of the most recent data in the memory with the past. The respective scene boundaries are determined using local minima and aligned using a nearest neighbor algorithm. We introduce a periodic analysis transform to automatically determine the structure within a scene. We then use statistical tests on the transform to determine the presence of a dialogue. The algorithms were tested on a difficult data set: five commercial films. We take the first hour of data from each of the five films. The best results: scene detection: 88% recall and 72% precision, dialogue detection: 91% recall and 100% precision.

Keywords

Computable scenes, scene detection, shot-level structure, films, periodic analysis transform, memory models.

1. INTRODUCTION

This paper deals with the problem of computing scenes within films using audio and visual data. We also derive algorithms for shot-level structures that exist within each scene. The problem is important for several reasons: (a) automatic scene segmentation is the first step towards greater semantic understanding of the film (b) breaking up the film into scenes will help in creating film summaries, thus enabling a non-linear navigation of the film. (c) the determination of visual structure within each scene (e.g. dialogues), will help in the process of visualizing each scene in the film summary.

There has been prior work on video scene segmentation using image data alone [8], [19]. In [19], the authors derive scene transition graphs to determine scene boundaries. Their method assumes a presence of repetitive shot structure within a scene. While this structure is present in scenes such as interviews, it can be absent from many scenes in commercial films. This can happen, for example, when the director relies on fast succession of shots to heighten suspense or uses a series of shots to merely develop the plot of the film. In [8], the authors use a infinite, non-causal memory model to segment the video.

Prior work [14], [15], [20] concerning the problem of audio segmentation dealt with very short-term (100 ms) changes in a few features (e.g. energy, cepstra). This was done to classify the audio data into several predefined classes such as speech, music ambient sounds etc. They do not examine the possibility of using the long-term consistency found in the audio data for segmentation. Audio data has been used for identifying important regions [6] or detecting events such as explosions [9] in video skims. These skims do not segment the video data into scenes; the objective there is to obtain a compact representation.

There has been prior work on structure detection [19], [20]. There, the authors begin with time-constrained clusters of shots and assign labels to each shot. Then, by analyzing the label sequence, they determine the presence of dialogue. This method critically depends upon cluster threshold parameters that need to be manually tuned.

There are constraints on what we see and hear in films, due to rules governing camera placement, continuity in lighting as well as due to the psychology of audition. In this paper, we derive the notion of a computable scene by making use of these constraints. A computable scene exhibits long-term consistency with respect to three properties: (a) chromatic composition of the scene (b) lighting conditions and (c) ambient audio. We term such a scene as *computable*, since it can be reliably computed using low-level features alone. In this paper, we do not deal with the *semantics* of a scene. Instead, we focus on the idea of determining a computable scene, which we believe is the first step in deciphering the semantics of a scene.

We present algorithms for determining computable scenes and periodic structures that may exist within such scenes. We begin with a idea of a memory model [8]. Our memory model is causal and finite. The model has two parameters: (a) an analysis window that stores the most recent data (the attention span) (b) the total amount of data (memory).

In order to segment the data into audio scenes, we compute correlations amongst the envelopes of the audio features in the attention-span with feature envelopes in the rest of the memory. The video data comprises shot key-frames. The key-frames in the attention span are compared to the rest of the data in the memory to determine a coherence value. This value is derived from a color-histogram dissimilarity. The comparison takes also into account the relative shot length and the time separation between the two shots. In both cases, we use a local minima for detecting a scene change and the audio and video scene boundaries are aligned using a simple time-constrained nearest neighbor approach.

We introduce the idea of a periodic analysis transform to determine visual structure within each computable scene. The transform computes the degree of periodicity amongst a time-ordered sequence of images (key-frames of shots). We use the Student's t-test in conjunction with a simple rule on this transform, to detect the presence of a dialogue. In contrast to [19], [20] which require manually tweaked cluster diameter threshold parameters, this algorithm is almost parameter free. Our experiments show that the scene change detector and the intra-scene structure detection algorithm show good results.

The rest of this paper is organized as follows. In the next section, we formalize the definition of a computable scene. In section 3, we present an algorithm for the detection of such computational scenes. In section 4, we derive algorithms for automatically determining periodic structures within a scene. In section 5, we present our experimental results. In section 6 we discuss shortcomings of our model and finally in the section 7, we present our conclusions.

2. WHAT IS A COMPUTABLE SCENE?

In this section we shall define the notion of a computable scene. We begin with a few insights obtained from understanding the process of film-making and from the psychology of audition. We shall use these insights in creating our computational model of the scene.

2.1 Insights from Film Making Techniques

The line of interest is an imaginary line drawn by the director in the physical setting of a scene [4]. During the filming of the scene, all the cameras are placed on one side of this line (also referred to as the 180 degree rule). This is because we desire successive shots to maintain the spatial arrangements between the characters and other objects in the location. As a consequence there is no confusion in the mind of the viewer about the spatial arrangements of the objects in the scene. He (or she) can instead concentrate on the

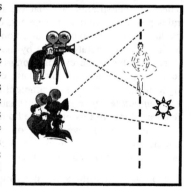

Figure 1: showing the line of interest (thick line) in a scene. We also see the fields-of-view of the two cameras intersecting.

dramatic aspect of the scene. It is interesting to note that directors willingly violate this rule only in very rare circumstances[1].

The 180 degree rule has interesting implications on the computational model of the scene. Since all the cameras in the scene remain on the same side of the line in all the shots, there is an overlap in the field of view of the cameras (see Figure 1). This implies that there will be a consistency to the chromatic composition and the lighting in all the shots.

Film-makers seek to maintain continuity in lighting amongst shots within the same physical location. This is done even when the shots are filmed over several days. This is because viewers perceive the change in lighting as indicative of the passage of time. For example, if two characters are shown talking in one shot, in daylight, the next shot cannot show them talking at the same location, at night.

2.2 The Psychology of Audition

The term *auditory scene analysis* was coined by Bregman in his seminal work on auditory organization [1]. In his psychological experiments on the process of audition, Bregman made many interesting observations, a few of which are reproduced below:

- Unrelated sounds seldom begin and end at the same time.

- A sequence of sounds from the same source seem to change its properties smoothly and gradually over a period of time. The auditory system will treat the sudden change in properties as the onset of a new sound.

- Changes that take place in an acoustic event will affect all components of the resulting sound in the same way and at the same time. For example, if we are walking away from the sound of a bell being struck repeatedly, the amplitude of all the harmonics will diminish gradually. At the same time, the harmonic relationships and common onset[2] are unchanged.

Bregman also noted that different auditory cues (i.e. harmonicity, common-onset etc.) compete for the user's attention and depending upon the context and the knowledge of the user, will result in different perceptions. However, the role played by higher forms of knowledge in grouping is yet to be ascertained.

Different computational models (e.g. [3]) have emerged in response to those experimental observations. While these models differ in their implementations and differ considerably in the physiological cues used, they focus on short-term grouping strategies of sound. Notably, Bregman's observations indicate that long-term grouping strategies are also used by human beings (e.g. it is easy for us to identify a series of footsteps as coming from one source) to group sound.

---

[1] This is so infrequent that directors who transgress the rule are noted in the film theory community. e.g. Alfred Hitchcock willingly violates this rule in a scene in his film *North by Northwest* thus adding suspense to the scene [4].

[2] Different sounds emerging from a single source begin at the same time.

2.3 The Computable Scene Model

The constraints imposed by production rules in film and the psychological process of hearing lead us to the following definition of a scene: It is a continuous segment of audio-visual data that shows *long-term*[3] consistency with respect to three properties:

- Chromaticity
- Lighting conditions
- Ambient sound

Table 1: Several scenarios are examined using our c-scene definition. These would normally be viewed as a single "normal" scene.

Scenario	Shot-sequence	C-Scenes	Explanation
Alice goes home to read a book.	(a) She is shown entering the room. (b) she picks up the book. (c) we see her reading silently (d) while she is reading, we hear the sound of rain.	2	One consistent visual but two consistent chunks of audio.
Alice goes to sleep.	(a) She is shown reading on her bed. (b) she switches off the light and room is dark.	2	Two consistent visuals but the audio is consistent over both video segments.
Bob goes for a walk	He switches on his handy-cam inside the house and walks out of the house. Note, this is one single camera take.	2	There are two consistent visuals (inside/outside) as well as two consistent chunks of audio.

We denote this to be a *computable* scene since these properties can be reliably and automatically determined using low-level features present in the audio-visual data. We need to examine the relationship between a computable scene (abbreviated as c-scene) and normal notions of a shot and a scene. A shot is a segment of audio-visual data filmed in a single camera take. A scene is normally defined to be sequence of shots that share a common semantic thread. Table 1 examines the impact of the c-scene definition for several scenarios.

The semantics of a normal scene within a film, are often difficult to ascertain. While a collection of shots may have objects that are meaningful without context (e.g. a house, a man, a woman the colors of the dress etc.), the collection of shots are infused with meaning only with regard to the context.

The context is established due to two factors: the film-maker and the viewer. The film-maker infuses meaning to a collection of

shots in three ways: (a) by *deciding* the action in the shots (b) the kind of shots that precede this scene and the shots that follow it (c) and finally by the manner in which he *visualizes*[4] the scene. All three methods affect the viewer, whose *interpretation* of the scene depends on his world-knowledge. Hence, if the meaning in a scene is based on factors that cannot be measured directly, it is imperative that we begin with a scene definition in terms of those attributes that are measurable and which lead to a consistent interpretation. We believe that such a strategy will greatly help in deciphering the semantics of the c-scene at a later stage.

2.4 The C-Scene Definition

We wished to validate the computable scene definition, which appeared out of intuitive considerations, with actual film data. The data was diverse with one hour segments from three English language films and two foreign films[5].

The definition for a scene works very well in many film segments. In most cases, the c-scenes are usually a collection of shots that are filmed in the same location and time and under similar lighting conditions. The definition does not work well for montage[6] sequences. However, in such sequences, we observed a long-term consistency of the ambient audio. We need to define a c-scene in order to accommodate different production styles. We now make two distinctions:

1. **N-type:** These scenes (or normal scenes) fit our original definition of a scene: they are characterized by a long-term consistency of chromatic composition, lighting conditions and sound.

2. **M-type:** These scenes (or montage/Mtv scenes) are characterized by widely different visuals (differences in location, time of creation as well as lighting conditions) which create a unity of theme by manner in which they have been juxtaposed. However, M-type scenes will be assumed to be characterized by a long-term consistency in the audio track. Transient scenes are M-type scenes that are characterized by shots of long duration[7].

In this paper, we narrow our focus to derive algorithms that detect two adjacent N-type scenes. We will not handle the two cases when we have either (a) two adjacent M-type scenes or (b) an N-type scene that borders an M-type scene. Analysis of the ground truth indicates that these two transitions constitute about 25% of all the transitions. Henceforth, for the sake of brevity, we shall use the term "scene" for our notion of a computable scene (c-scene).

---

[3] Analysis of experimental data (one hour each, from five different films) indicates that the scenes in the same location (e.g. in a room, in the marketplace etc.) are typically 40~50 seconds long.

[4] In order to show a tense scene, one film-maker may have fast succession of close-ups of the characters in a scene. Others may indicate tension by showing both characters but changing the music.

[5] The English films: *Sense and Sensibility, Pulp Fiction, Four Weddings and a Funeral.* The foreign films: *Farewell my Concubine (Chinese), Bombay (Hindi).*

[6] In classic Russian montage, the sequence of shots are constructed from placing shots together that have no immediate similarity in meaning. For example, a shot of a couple may be followed by shots of two parrots kissing each other etc. The meaning is derived from the way the sequence is arranged.

[7] Mtv videos are good examples of M-type scenes with shots of short duration. Transient scenes can occur when the director wants to show the passage of time e.g. a scene showing a journey.

3. DETECTING SCENES

We begin the process of scene detection by first detecting audio and video scene segments separately and then aligning the two by a simple nearest neighbor algorithm.

This section has four subsections. In section 3.1, we develop the idea of a memory model. In sections 3.2 and 3.3, we build upon some early techniques in [16], [17] for automatic audio and video scene detection. In section 3.4 we present a simple nearest-neighbor algorithm for aligning the two scene detector results.

3.1 A Memory Model

In order to segment data into scenes, we use a causal, first-in-first-out (FIFO) model of memory (figure 2). This model is derived in part from the idea of coherence [8].

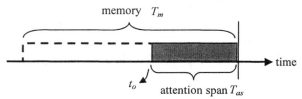

Figure 2: The attention span (T_{as}) is the most recent data in the buffer. The memory (T_m) is the size of the entire buffer. Clearly, $T_m \geq T_{as}$.

In our model of a listener, two parameters are of interest: (a) memory: this is the net amount of information (T_m) with the viewer and (b) attention span: it is the most recent data (T_{as}) in the memory of the listener. This data is used by the listener to compare against the contents of the memory in order to decide if a scene change has occurred.

The work in [8] dealt with a non-causal, infinite memory model based on psychophysical principles, for video scene change detection. We use the same psychophysical principles to come up with a causal and finite memory model. Intuitively, causality and a finite memory will more faithfully mimic the human memory-model than an infinite model. We shall use this model for *both* audio and video scene change detection.

3.2 Determining Audio Scenes

In this section we present our algorithm for audio-scene segmentation. We model the *audio-scene* as a collection of a few dominant sound sources. These sources are assumed to possess stationary properties that can be characterized using a few features. An audio-scene change is said to occur when the majority of the dominant sources in the scene change. A detailed description of audio scene segmentation can be found in [16].

3.2.1 Features and Envelope Models

We use ten different features [13], [14], [15], [16], [20] in our algorithm: (a) cepstral-flux (b) multi-channel cochlear decomposition (c) cepstral vectors (d) low energy fraction (e) zero crossing rate (f) spectral flux (g) energy (h) spectral roll off point. We also use the variance of the zero crossing rate and the variance of the energy as additional features. The cochlear decomposition was used because it was based on a psychophysical ear model. The cepstral features are known to be good discriminators [13]. All the other features were used for their ability to distinguish

between speech and music [14], [15], [20]. Features are extracted per *frame* (100ms. duration) for the duration of the analysis window.

Given a particular feature f and a finite time-sequence of values, we wish to determine the behavior of the envelope of the feature. The feature envelopes are force-fit into signals of the following types: constant, linear, quadratic, exponential, hyperbolic and sum of exponentials. All the envelope (save for the sum of exponentials case) fits are obtained using a robust curve fitting procedure [5]. We pick the fit that minimizes the least median error. The envelope model analysis is only used for the scalar variables. The vector variables (cepstra and the cochlear output) and the aggregate variables (variance of the zero-crossing rate and the spectral roll off point) are used in the raw form.

3.2.2 Detecting a Scene Change

Let us examine the case where a scene change occurs just to the left of the listeners attention span. First, for each feature, we do the following:

1. Place an analysis window of length T_{as} (the attention-span length) at t_o and generate a sequence by computing a feature value for each frame (100 ms duration) in the window.

2. Determine the optimal envelope fit for these feature values.

3. Shift the analysis window back by Δt and repeat steps 1. and 2. till we have covered all data in the memory.

We then define a local correlation function per feature, using the sequence of envelope fits. The correlation function C_f for each feature f is then defined as follows:

$$C_f(m\delta) = 1 - d(f(t_o, t_o + t_{as}), f(t_o + m\delta, t_o + m\delta + t_{as})) \quad (1)$$

where, $f(t_1, t_2)$ represents the envelope fit for feature f for the duration $[t_1, t_2]$. Now, $m \in [-N..0]$, where $N \equiv (T_m - T_{as})/\delta$. δ is the duration by which the analysis window is shifted back and d is the Euclidean metric[8] on the envelopes. For the vector and the aggregate data, we do not compute the distance between the windows using envelope fits but use a L^2 metric on the raw data. In our experiments we use $\delta = 1$ sec.

We model the correlation decay as a decaying exponential [16]: $C_i(t) = \exp(b_i t)$, $t < 0$ where C_i is the correlation function for feature i, and b_i is the exponential decay parameter. The audio-scene decision function $D(t_o)$ at any instant t_o is defined as follows: $D(t_o) = \sum_{i=1}^{N} b_i$. Where, N is the number of features and b_i are the estimates at t_o.

We chose the exponential decay model based on empirical observations on the correlation data. More sophisticated modeling techniques could be easily employed. The parameter δ, effectively determines the number of samples of the correlation data. This in turn affects our estimate of the parameter b_i. For example, in a

---

[8]This metric is intuitive: it is a point-by-point comparison of the two envelopes. More sophisticated predictor based schemes are being investigated at present.

typical case of memory (T_m) size of 31 sec and attention span (T_{as}) of 16 sec. and δ=1 sec., we have 16 data points.

The audio-scene change is detected using the local minima of the decision function. In order to do so, we use a sliding window of length $2w_a+1$ sec. to slide across the data. We then determine if the minima in the window coincides with the center of the window. If it does, the location is labeled as an audio scene change location. The result for a single film is shown figure 3. The figure shows that the results agree within an ambiguity window of w_a sec.

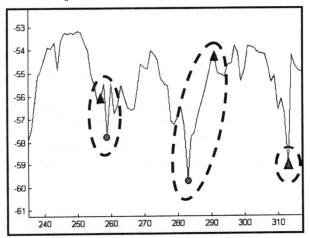

Figure 3: Audio detector results for a part of the audio track of the film *Sense and Sensibility*. The triangles show the ground truth label while the dots show the detector result. In the first two cases the result is very close while in the third case there is an exact match. The *x*-axis shows the time in sec. while *y*-axis shows the detector magnitude.

3.3 Determining Video Scenes

In this section, we shall describe the algorithm for video-scene segmentation. The algorithm is based on notions of *recall* and *coherence*. We model the video-scene as a contiguous segment of visual data that is chromatically coherent and also possesses similar lighting conditions. A video-scene is said to occur when there is a change in the long-term chromaticity and lighting properties in the video. This stems from the film-making constraints discussed in Section 2.1.

Ideally, we would like to work with raw frames and avoid having to detect shots. However, this would lead to an enormous increase in the computational complexity of the algorithm. Hence, the video stream is converted into a sequence of shots using a simple color and motion based shot boundary detection algorithm [10]. A frame at a fixed time after the shot boundary is extracted and denoted to be the key-frame.

3.3.1 Recall

In our visual memory model, the data is in the form of key-frames of shots (Figure 4) and each shot occupies a definite span of time. The model also allows for the most recent and the oldest shots to be partially present in the buffer. A point in time (t_o) is defined to be a scene transition boundary if the shots that come after that point in time, do not recall [8] the shots prior to that point. The idea of recall between two shots *a* and *b* is formalized as follows:

$$R(a,b) = (1 - d(a,b)) \bullet f_a \bullet f_b \bullet (1 - \Delta t / T_m), \qquad (2)$$

where, $R(a,b)$ is the recall between the two shots *a*, *b*. $d(a,b)$ is a L^1 color-histogram based distance between the key-frames corresponding to the two shots, f_i is the ratio of the length of shot *i* to the memory size (T_m). Δt is the time difference between the two shots.

The formula for recall indicates that recall is proportional to the length of each of the shots. This is intuitive since if a shot is in memory for a long period of time it will be recalled more easily. Again, the recall between the two shots should decrease if they are further apart in time.

We need to introduce the notion of a "shot-let." A shot-let is a fraction of a shot, obtained by breaking individual shots into δ sec. long chunks but could be smaller due to shot boundary conditions. Each shot-let is associated with a single shot and its representative frame is the key-frame corresponding to the shot. In our experiments, we find that $\delta = 1$ sec. works well. Figure 4 shows how shot-lets are constructed. The formula for recall for shot-lets is identical to that for shots.

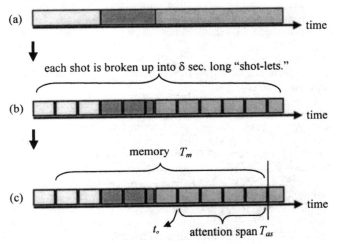

Figure 4: (a) Each solid colored block represents a single shot. (b) each shot is broken up into "shot-lets" each at most δ sec. long. (c) the bracketed shots are present in the memory and the attention span. Note that sometimes, only fractions of shots are present in the memory.

3.3.2 Computing Coherence

Coherence is easily defined using the definition of recall:

$$C(t_o) = \left(\sum_{a \in T_{as}} \sum_{b \in \{T_m \setminus T_{as}\}} R(a,b) \right) \Big/ C_{\max}(t_o) \qquad (3)$$

where, $C(t_o)$ is the coherence across the boundary at t_o and is just the sum of recall values between all pairs of shot-lets across the boundary at t_o. $C_{\max}(t_o)$ is obtained by setting $d(a,b)=0$ in the formula for recall (Equation (2)) and re-evaluating the numerator of Equation (3). This normalization compensates for the different number of shots in the buffer at different instants of time.

We compute coherence at the boundary between every adjacent pair of shot-lets. Then, similar to the procedure for audio scene detection, we determine the local minima. This we do by using a sliding window of length $2w_v+1$ sec. and determine if the minima in the window coincides with the center of the window. If it does, the location is labeled as a video scene change location.

3.3.3 The need for shot-lets

Shot-lets become necessary in films since they can contain c-scenes with shots that have a long duration. In [8], the authors evaluated their coherence function only at shot boundaries. Evaluating the coherence function ($C(t)$, Equation (3)) at shot boundaries has the effect of coarsely sampling the coherence function. This can cause problems in locating the scene change minima. For example, if in a segment of size 90 sec. if we have three shots, of 30 sec. each, where the first two belong to one scene and the third to another, then we cannot determine the minima as we will only have two values for coherence. A thought will indicate that interpolating the coherence values will not be of much use.

Shot-lets have two main advantages: (a) they preserve the location of existing shot boundaries and (b) they help us evaluate the coherence function at a fine time-scales. Simply uniformly segmenting the video stream into δ sec. chunks has two disadvantages: (a) shot boundaries are missed and (b) high computational complexity. Evaluating Equation (3) takes $O(k^2)$ operations where k is the number of shots in the buffer[9]. The idea of shot-lets can be shown to significantly improve the detection rate results in [17], [8].

3.4 Aligning the Detector Results

We generate correspondences between the audio and the video scene boundaries using a simple time-constrained nearest-neighbor algorithm. Let the list of video scene boundaries be V_i, where $i \in \{1..N_v\}$. Let the list of audio scene boundaries be A_i, where $i \in \{1..N_a\}$. The ambiguity window around each video scene is w_v sec. long. The ambiguity window width around each audio scene boundary is w_a sec long. Note that these sizes are the same size of the windows used for local minima location. For each video scene boundary, do the following:

- Determine a list of audio scene boundaries whose ambiguity windows intersect the ambiguity window of the current video scene boundary.

- If the intersection is non-null, pick the audio scene boundary closest to the current video scene boundary. Remove this audio scene boundary from the list containing audio scene boundaries.

- If the intersection is null, add the current video scene boundary to the list of singleton (i.e. non-alignable) video scene changes.

---

[9] The primary contributor to the computational complexity of Equation (3) is the distance computation in Equation (2). A little thought indicates that with some book-keeping, this is avoided with shot-lets.

At the end of this procedure, if there are audio scene boundaries left, collect them and add them to the list of singleton audio scene changes. Figure 5 illustrates this scenario.

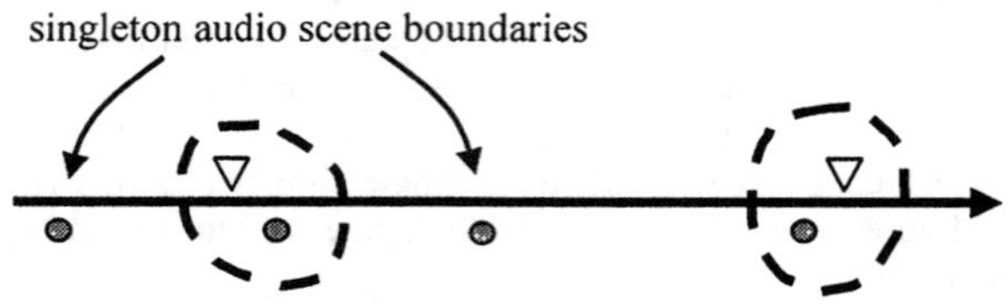

singleton audio scene boundaries

Figure 5: The figure shows video (triangles) and audio (solid circles) scene change locations. The dashed circles show audio/video scene boundaries which align.

Films exhibit interesting interactions between audio and video scene changes. Singleton audio and video scene boundaries can be caused due to the following reasons:

1. **Audio scene change but no video scene change:** this can happen for example : the director wants to indicate a change the mood of the scene, by using a sad / joyous sounding audio track. In *Sense and Sensibility,* one character was shown singing and once she was finished, we had conversation amongst the characters *in the same location.*

2. **Video scene changes within an audio scene:** This happens when a sequence of video scenes have the same underlying semantic . For example, we can have a series of video scenes showing a journey and these scenes will be accompanied by the same audio track.

Now that we have determined the scene boundaries, we will now present algorithms that determine structure within a scene.

4. THE SCENE LEVEL STRUCTURE

In this section we shall discuss possible structures that could exist within a scene and technique to detect and classify such structures. The detection of these structures will help in summarizing the scene. Here, we focus on detection of visual structures.

4.1 Postulating Scene-level Structures

We postulate the existence of two broad category of scenes: N-type (based on the initial definition) and the M-type scene. The N-type scenes are further subdivided into three types: (a) pure dialogue (b) progressive and (c) hybrid. We use an abstract graph representation for representing the shot structure within a scene. Each node in the graph represents one cluster of shots. Figure 6 shows a hybrid scene containing an embedded dialogue.

4.1.1 N-type Scenes

An N-type scene has unity of location, time and sound. We now look at three sub-categories:

Dialogue: A simple repetitive visual structure (amongst shots) can be present if the action in the scene is a dialogue. Note that sometimes, directors will *not* use an alternating sequence to represent a dialogue between two characters. He (or she) may use a single shot of long duration that shows both the characters talking. A repetitive structure is also present when the film-maker shuttles back and forth between two shots to indicate an idea (e.g. man watching television). We denote this as a thematic dialogue.

Progressive: There can be a linear progression of visuals without any repetitive structure (the first part of figure 6 is progressive). For example, consider the following scene: Alice enters the room looking for a book. We see the following shots (a) she enters the room (b) she examines her book-shelf (c) looks under the bed (d) locates the book and the camera follows her as she sits on the sofa to read.

Hybrid: This is the most common case, when we have a dialogue embedded in an otherwise progressive scene. For example, in the scene mentioned above, assume Bob enters the room while Alice is searching for the book. They are shown having a brief dialogue that is visualized using an alternating sequence. Then Bob leaves the room and Mary continues her search.

Figure 6: A hybrid scene with an embedded dialogue sequence.

4.1.2 M-type Scenes

In M-type scenes (in classic montage, commercials and MTV videos) we assume there to be no unity of visuals either in terms of location, time or lighting conditions[10]. However, we expect that the audio track will be consistent over the scene. This condition can be converted into a detection rule: A sequence of highly dissimilar shots with unity of sound will be labeled as a M-type scene. As noted earlier, transient scenes are M-type scenes with long shot durations.

4.2 Determining the Structure

In this section we shall describe techniques to identify structures within N-type scenes. We begin by first describing the periodic analysis transform. Then we show how to use this series in conjunction with statistical tests to determine the presence of a dialogue. Finally we show a simple algorithm that determines the exact location of the dialogue.

4.2.1 The Periodic Analysis Transform

The periodic analysis transform helps us estimate the periodicity in an time-ordered sequence of N key-frames. Let o_i where $i \in \{0, N-1\}$ be a time ordered sequence of key-frames. Then:

$$\Delta(n) \triangleq 1 - \frac{1}{N} \sum_{i=0}^{N-1} d(o_i, o_{\text{mod}(i+n, N)}), \qquad (4)$$

where, $\Delta(n)$ is the transform, d is the L^1 color-histogram based distance function, mod is the usual modulus function. The modulus function simply creates a periodic extension[11] of the

original input sequence. Note that the transform definition will work on *any* time ordered sequence of arbitrary objects, provided we define a suitable metric on the objects.

4.2.2 Statistical Tests

We shall use two statistical tests: the students t-test for the means and the F-test for the variances [12]. The F-test is used to determine the appropriate[12] Student's t-test. These tests are used to compare two series of numbers and determine if the two means and the variance differ significantly.

4.2.3 Detecting Dialogues

We can easily detect dialogues using the transform. In a dialogue, every 2nd frame will be very similar while adjacent frames will differ. This is also to observed in figure 7. Let us assume that we have a time-ordered sequence of N key-frames representing different shots in a scene. Then we do the following:

1. Compute the series $\Delta(n)$.

2. Check if $\Delta(2) > \Delta(1)$ and $\Delta(2) > \Delta(3)$.

3. A dialogue is postulated to exist if one of two conditions in step 2 is at least significant at $\alpha = 0.05$ and the other one is at least significant at $\alpha = 0.1$[13]. Note that $\Delta(n)$ for each n is the mean of N numbers. We use the Student's t-test to determine whether the two means are different in a statistically significant sense.

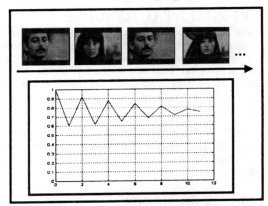

Figure 7: A dialogue scene and its corresponding periodic analysis transform. Note the distinct peaks at $n = 2, 4 \ldots$

We use a simple technique to make a distinction between thematic and actual spoken dialogue. From test data we observe that the average shot length for a thematic dialogue is much shorter than for a spoken dialogue. The reason is that there is a minimum time required to utter a meaningful phrase. In [7], the authors assume that phrases last between 5~15 sec. An analysis of hand-labeled data reveals that dialogues with average shot length of less than 4 sec. are thematic.

---

[10] There will be a unity of theme which shall be brought about by how the director assembles the component shots of the scene.

[11] Defining the transform using a symmetric extension should improve our detector results.

[12] There are two Student's t-tests depending upon whether the variances differ significantly.

[13] We are rejecting the null hypothesis that the two means are equal. We reject the hypothesis if we believe that the observed difference between the means occurred by chance with a probability less than α.

4.2.4 The Sliding Window Algorithm

We use a sliding window algorithm to detect the presence of a dialogue (thematic or spoken dialogue) within a hybrid N-type scene . Assuming that the total number of frames in the scene to be N, we set the size of the initial window to be k frames. Starting with the leftmost key-frame, the algorithm is as follows:

1. Run the dialogue detector on the current window.

2. If no dialogue is detected, keep shifting the window to the right by one key-frame to the immediate right until either a dialogue has been detected or we have reached the end of the scene.

3. If a dialogue has been detected, keep growing the window by adding the key-frame to the immediate right of the current window until either the end of the scene has been reached or the sequence of key-frames in the window is no longer a statistically significant dialogue. The dialogue is the longest statistically significant sequence.

4. Move the start of the new window to the immediate right of the detected dialogue. Go to step 1.

Setting the initial window size in terms of number of key-frames instead of time has the advantage of compensating for shot length variations across films.

5. EXPERIMENTAL RESULTS

In this section we shall discuss the experimental results of our algorithms. The data used to test our algorithms is complex: we have five one hour segments from five diverse films. There are three English films: (a) *Sense and Sensibility* (b) *Pulp Fiction* and (c) *Four Weddings and a Funeral*. We also have two foreign language films: (a) *Bombay* (Hindi) and (b) *Farewell my Concubine* (Chinese).

This section is organized as follows. We begin with a section that explains how the labeling of the ground truth data was done. The section following that section deal with the experimental results of the two detectors.

5.1 Labeling the Ground Truth

The audio and the video data were labeled separately (i.e. label audio without watching the video and label video without hearing the audio). This was because when we use *both* the audio and the video (i.e. normal viewing of the film) we tend to label scene boundaries based on the semantics of the scene. Only one person (the first author) labeled the data.

The video scene changes were labeled as follows. While watching the video if at any time there was a distinct change in lighting or color, this was labeled as a video scene change. This usually meant a change in location, but walking from a lit room to a dark one was also labeled as a scene change. Scene boundaries for M-type scenes (transient, montage) were difficult to locate. For example, if there was an M-type → N-type transition, we need to see a few shots from the N-type scene, to determine that the first N-type shot was not part of the previous M-type scene.

For audio, we adopted the following policy: label a scene change if it was felt that the ambient audio properties had changed. For example, if we heard the sounds of a marketplace immediately followed a conversation, this was labeled as a scene change. Correctly labeling the audio scene boundaries is challenging since we don't see the associated video. Often, with the beginning and the end of dialogues since there is silence, it becomes very hard to place the boundary accurately[14]. We need to wait to wait till the end of the silence and then work back to place the boundary.

Labeling the data became particularly challenging when labeling the Chinese film. Since the labeler (the first author) had no semantic understanding of the film, it became hard to determine if a conversation had ended if there was a pause after the last sentence or if the speakers had changed (if one dialogue sequence followed the other).

Table 2: The ground truth data derived from labeling the audio and video data of each film separately. Columns two and three show the number of audio and video scene changes. The last column shows the number of audio/video scene change locations that align. The table shows all changes including to and from M-type scenes.

Film	Audio	Video	Synchronized A/V Changes
Bombay	77	46	33
Farewell my Concubine	91	58	44
Four Weddings and a Funeral	76	57	37
Pulp Fiction	45	39	31
Sense and Sensibility	52	65	41

It is clear from the data in Table 2 that the audio and video scene changes in a film, are not random events i.e. there is a high degree of synergy between the two thus lending support to our joint audio-visual computable scene model.

5.2 Scene Change Detector Results

There are three parameters of interest in each scene change algorithm (i.e. audio and video). They are: (a) memory (T_m) (b) attention-span (T_{as}) and the (c) ambiguity-window size. For both audio and video scene change algorithms, the attention-span and the memory parameters follow intuition: results improve with a large attention-span and a large memory. For both scene change algorithms, large windows have the property of smoothing the audio decision function and the video coherence function. Larger windows decrease the number of false alarms but also increase the number of misses.

The audio and video ambiguity parameters[15] are used in the location of local minima in both scene change algorithms. Hits and misses are determined by looking at whether the time

---

[14] The accuracy in labeling that we refer to is with a comparison to the where the label would have been had we labeled the film with both audio and the video.

[15] This is half the size of the windows used for location of the audio and video minima (w_a and w_v sec. respectively).

difference between the scene change location and the ground truth location is less than the ambiguity window size (i.e. less than w_a and w_v sec.). The memory buffer parameters for the entire data set was fixed as follows: audio: T_m=31 sec. T_{as}=16 sec., video: T_m=16 sec., T_{as}=8 sec.

We now present results for the five films in Table 3. These results are for two adjacent N-type transitions only since our algorithms cannot handle N-type → M-type or M-type → M-type transitions. Note that: recall = hits/(hits + misses) while precision = hits/(hits + false alarms).

Table 3: The table shows c-scene change detector results for the five films. We only deal with adjacent N-type scenes, the other transitions were manually excluded. The columns are: Hits, Misses, False Alarms, Recall and Precision.

Film	H	M	FA	Recall	Precision
Bombay	24	3	9	0.88	0.72
Farewell my Concubine	28	9	10	0.75	0.73
Four Weddings and a Funeral	17	11	4	0.60	0.80
Pulp Fiction	19	9	11	0.67	0.63
Sense and Sensibility	27	7	7	0.79	0.79

The results show that our detector works well, achieving a best result of recall of 0.88 and precision of 0.72 for the film *Bombay*. There are two types of errors that decrease our algorithm performance: (a) uncertainty in the location of the audio labels due to human uncertainty and (b) misses in the video shot boundary detection algorithm. Shot misses cause the wrong key-frame to be present in the buffer, thus causing an error in the minima location.

Prior work done in video scene segmentation used visual features alone [19], [8]. There, the authors focus on detecting scene boundaries for sitcoms (and other TV shows) and do not consider films. However, since we expect the c-scenes in sitcoms to be mostly long, coherent, N-type scenes, we expect our combined audio visual detector to perform very well.

5.3 Structure Detection Results

The statistical tests that are central to the dialogue detection algorithm make it almost parameter free. These test are used at the standard levels of significance ($\alpha = 0.05$). We do need to set two parameters: The initial sliding window size T_w (8 frames) and the threshold for the thematic dialogue test (4 sec.).

The results of the dialog detector (Table 4) show that it performs very well. The best result is a precision of 1.00 and recall of 0.91 for the film *Sense and Sensibility*. The misses are primarily due to misses by the shot-detection algorithm. Missed key-frames will cause a periodic sequence to appear less structured. The thematic/true dialog detector's performance is mixed: with a best detection result (precision) of 0.84 for the Indian film *Bombay* and a worst result of 0.50 for *Pulp Fiction*. Thematic dialogues seem to vary significantly with the film genre and the directorial style; hence instead of global time threshold, an algorithm that

adapts to the film, perhaps based on the average shot length will work better.

Table 4: The table shows the dialogue detector results for the five films. The table includes both thematic and spoken dialogues. The columns are: Hits, Misses, False Alarms, Recall and Precision.

Film	H	M	FA	Recall	Precision
Bombay	10	2	0	0.83	1.00
Farewell my Concubine	10	2	1	0.83	0.90
Four Weddings and a Funeral	16	4	1	0.80	0.94
Pulp Fiction	11	2	2	0.84	0.84
Sense and Sensibility	28	3	0	0.91	1.00

6. DISCUSSING MODEL BREAKDOWNS

In this section we shall discuss three situations that arise in different film-making situations. In each instance, the 180 degree rule is adhered to and yet our assumption of chromatic consistency across shots is no longer valid.

1. **Change of scale:** Rapid changes of scale cannot be accounted for in simple model as they show up as change in the chrominance of the shot. For example, the director might show two characters talking in a medium-shot[16]. Then he cuts to a close up. This causes a change in the dominant color of the shots.

2. **Widely differing backgrounds:** This results from the two opposing cameras having no overlap in their field-of-view causing an apparent change in the background. This can happen for example, when the film shows one character inside the house, talking through a widow to another character who is standing outside.

3. **Background changes with time:** This can happen for example if the film shows several characters talking in a party (or in a crowd) . Then the stream of people in motion can cause the dominant chrominance/lighting of the scene to change.

If these situations occur over long time scales, they will cause errors (misses, incorrect boundary placement) in the segmentation algorithm. However, short time scale chromatic (or lighting) changes will be handled by our algorithm. Clearly, our computational model makes simplifying assumptions on the possible scenarios even when film-makers adhere to the 180 degree rule.

7. CONCLUSIONS

In this paper we have presented a novel paradigm for film segmentation using audio and video data and an algorithm for visual structure detection within scenes. We developed the notion of computational scenes. The computational model for the c-scenes was derived from camera placement rules in film-making and from experimental observations on the psychology of

---

[16] The size (long/medium/close-up/extreme close-up) refers to the size of the objects in the scene relative to the size of the image.

audition. A c-scene exhibits long-term consistency with regard to (a) lighting conditions (b) chromaticity of the scene (c) ambient audio. We believe that the c-scene formulation is the first step towards deciphering the semantics of a scene.

We showed how a causal, finite memory model formed the basis of our scene segmentation algorithm. In order to determine audio scene segments we first determine the correlations amongst the envelope fits for each feature extracted in the memory buffer. We then determine the decision function based on exponential fits to the envelope correlations. We use ideas of recall and coherence in our video segmentation algorithm. The algorithm works by determining the coherence amongst the shot-lets in the memory. A local minima criterion determines the scene change points and a nearest neighbor algorithm aligns the scenes.

We introduced the formulation of the periodic analysis transform to determine the periodic structure within a scene. We showed how one can use the Student's t-test to detect the presence of statistically significant dialogues.

The scene segmentation algorithms were tested on a difficult test data set: five hours from commercial films. They work well, giving a best scene detection result of 88% recall and 72% precision. The structure detection algorithm was tested on the same data set giving excellent results: 91% recall and 100% precision. We believe that the results are very good when we keep the following considerations in mind: (a) the data set is complex (b) the audio ground truth labeling was difficult and introduced errors (c) the shot cut detection algorithm had misses that introduced additional error.

There are some clear improvements possible to this work: (a) the computational model for the c-scene is limited, and needs to tightened in view of the model breakdowns pointed out in section 6. (b) we need to come up with a technique that handles N-type scenes that abut M-type scenes and also the case when M-type scenes are in succession. A possible solution is to introduce a short-term self-coherence function followed by audio-scene based grouping.

8. ACKNOWLEDGEMENTS

The authors would like to thank Di Zhong for help with the shot boundary detection algorithm.

9. REFERENCES

[1] A.S. Bregman *Auditory Scene Analysis: The Perceptual Organization of Sound*, MIT Press, 1990.

[2] M. Christel et. al. *Evolving Video Skims into Useful Multimedia Abstractions* Proc. of the Conference on Human Factors in Computing System, CHI'98, pp 171-178, Los Angeles, CA, Apr. 1998.

[3] D.P.W. Ellis *Prediction-Driven Computational Auditory Scene Analysis,* Ph.D. thesis, Dept. of EECS, MIT, 1996.

[4] Bob Foss *Filmmaking: Narrative and Structural techniques* Silman James Press LA, 1992.

[5] F. R. Hampel et. al. *Robust Statistics: The Approach Based on Influence Functions,* John Wiley and Sons, 1986.

[6] A. Hauptmann M. Witbrock *Story Segmentation and Detection of Commercials in Broadcast News Video* Advances in Digital Libraries Conference, ADL-98, Santa Barbara, CA., Apr. 22-24, 1998.

[7] Liwei He et. al. *Auto-Summarization of Audio-Video Presentations,* ACM MM '99, Orlando FL, Nov. 1999.

[8] J.R. Kender B.L. Yeo, *Video Scene Segmentation Via Continuous Video Coherence,* CVPR '98, Santa Barbara CA, Jun. 1998.

[9] R. Lienhart et. al. *Automatic Movie Abstracting,* Technical Report TR-97-003, Praktische Informatik IV, University of Mannheim, Jul. 1997.

[10] J. Meng S.F. Chang, *CVEPS: A Compressed Video Editing and Parsing System*, Proc. ACM Multimedia 1996, Boston, MA, Nov. 1996

[11] R. Patterson et. al. *Complex Sounds and Auditory Images, in Auditory Physiology and Perception* eds. Y Cazals et. al. pp. 429-46, Oxford, 1992.

[12] W.H. Press et. al *Numerical recipes in C, 2nd ed.* Cambridge University Press, 1992.

[13] L. R. Rabiner B.H. Huang *Fundamentals of Speech Recognition,* Prentice-Hall 1993.

[14] Eric Scheirer Malcom Slaney *Construction and Evaluation of a Robust Multifeature Speech/Music Discriminator* Proc. ICASSP '97, Munich, Germany Apr. 1997.

[15] S. Subramaniam et. al. *Towards Robust Features for Classifying Audio in the CueVideo System,* Proc. ACM Multimedia '99, pp. 393-400, Orlando FL, Nov. 1999.

[16] H. Sundaram S.F. Chang *Audio Scene Segmentation Using Multiple Features, Models And Time Scales,* ICASSP 2000, International Conference in Acoustics, Speech and Signal Processing, Istanbul Turkey, Jun. 2000.

[17] H. Sundaram S.F Chang *Video Scene Segmentation Using Audio and Video Features,* to appear in IEEE International Conference on Multimedia and Expo, New York, NY, Aug. 2000.

[18] S. Uchihashi et. al. *Video Manga: Generating Semantically Meaningful Video Summaries* Proc. ACM Multimedia '99, pp. 383-92, Orlando FL, Nov. 1999.

[19] M. Yeung B.L. Yeo *Time-Constrained Clustering for Segmentation of Video into Story Units,* Proc. Int. Conf. on Pattern Recognition, ICPR '96, Vol. C pp. 375-380, Vienna Austria, Aug. 1996.

[20] M. Yeung B.L. Yeo *Video Content Characterization and Compaction for Digital Library Applications,* Proc. SPIE '97, Storage and Retrieval of Image and Video Databases V, San Jose CA, Feb. 1997.

[21] T. Zhang C.C Jay Kuo *Heuristic Approach for Generic Audio Segmentation and Annotation,* Proc. ACM Multimedia '99, pp. 67-76, Orlando FL, Nov. 1999.

Automatically Extracting Highlights for TV Baseball Programs

Yong Rui, Anoop Gupta, and Alex Acero
Microsoft Research
One Microsoft Way, Redmond, WA 98052
{yongrui, anoop, alexac}@microsoft.com

ABSTRACT

In today's fast-paced world, while the number of channels of television programming available is increasing rapidly, the time available to watch them remains the same or is decreasing. Users desire the capability to watch the programs time-shifted (on-demand) and/or to watch just the highlights to save time. In this paper we explore how to provide for the latter capability, that is the ability to extract highlights automatically, so that viewing time can be reduced.

We focus on the sport of baseball as our initial target---it is a very popular sport, the whole game is quite long, and the exciting portions are few. We focus on detecting highlights using audio-track features alone without relying on expensive-to-compute video-track features. We use a combination of generic sports features and baseball-specific features to obtain our results, but believe that many other sports offer the same opportunity and that the techniques presented here will apply to those sports. We present details on relative performance of various learning algorithms, and a probabilistic framework for combining multiple sources of information. We present results comparing output of our algorithms against human-selected highlights for a diverse collection of baseball games with very encouraging results.

Keywords

Highlights, summarization, television, video, audio, baseball.

1. INTRODUCTION

Internet video streaming and set-top devices like WebTV [1], ReplayTV [2], and TiVo [3] are defining a new platform for *interactive* video playback. With videos being in digital form, either stored on local hard disks or streamed from the Internet, many sophisticated TV-viewing experiences can be supported. It has become possible to "pause" a live broadcast program while you answer the doorbell and continue from where you left off. The fact that video is stored on the hard disk (instead of tape) also allows for instant random access to the program content. This allows for rich browsing behavior by users based on additional meta-data associated with the video. For example, indices into TV news programs can permit users to focus only on subset of stories that are of interest to them, thus saving time. Similarly, meta-data indicating action-segments in a sports

program can permit viewers to skip the less interesting portions of the game.

The value of such meta-data was explored in a recent study by Li *et. al.*, where viewers were provided with metadata (manually generated) and instant random access for a wide variety of video content [4]. The ability to browse video was found to be highly valuable by users, especially for news, sports, and informational videos (e.g., technical presentations, travel documentaries). In addition to saving time watching content, the users appreciated the feeling of being in control of what they watched.

We also note a key difference between two models on how highlights may be made available to viewers. In the traditional TV broadcast model, e.g., CNN sports highlights, when they show a 1-minute highlight of a game, the user has no choice to watch anything more or less. In the new model, with set-top boxes and hard disks, we can make the assumption that the whole 2-hour game is recorded on the local hard disk, and the highlights act only as a guide. If the user does not like a particular selected highlight they can simply skip it with a push of a button on their remote control, and similarly at the push of a button they can watch more details. This new model allows for greater chance of adoption of automatic techniques for highlight extraction, as errors of automation can be compensated by the end-user.

In this paper we explore techniques to automatically generate highlights for sports programs. In particular, we focus on the game of baseball as our initial target---it is a very popular sport, the whole game is quite long, often there are several games being played on the same day so viewer can't watch all of them, and the exciting portions per game are few. We focus on detecting highlights using audio-track features alone without relying on expensive-to-compute video-track features. This way highlight detection can even be done on the local set-top box (our target delivery vehicle) using the limited compute power available.

Our focus on audio-only forces us to address the challenge of dealing with an extremely complex audio track. The track consists of announcer speech, mixed with crowd noise, mixed with remote traffic and music noises, and automatic gain control changing audio levels. To combat this, we develop robust speech endpoint detection techniques in noisy environment and we successfully apply support vector machines to excited speech classification. We use a combination of generic sports features and baseball-specific features to obtain our results, but believe that many other sports offer the same opportunity. For example, we use bat-and-ball impact detection to adjust likelihood of a highlight segment, and the same technology can also be used for other sports like golf. We present details on relative performance of various learning algorithms, and a probabilistic framework for combining multiple sources of information. The probabilistic framework allows us to avoid *ad hoc* heuristics and loss of information at intermediate stages of the algorithm due to premature thresholding.

We present results comparing output of our algorithms against human-selected highlights for a diverse collection of baseball games. The training for our system was done on a half-hour segment of one game, but we test against several totally distinct games covering over 7 hours of play. The results are very encouraging: when our algorithm is asked to generate the same number of highlight segments as marked by human subject, on average, 75% of these are the same as that marked by the human.

The rest of the paper is organized as follows. Section 2 discusses related work from both technology perspectives and video domains. In Section 3, we first examine the advantages and disadvantages of the information sources that we can utilize to perform baseball highlights extraction and then discuss the audio features that will be used in this paper. In Section 4, we present both the algorithm flowchart and the algorithm details that include noisy environment speech endpoint detection, excited speech classification, baseball hit detection and probabilistic fusion. Section 5 presents detailed descriptions of the test set, evaluation framework, experimental results, and observations. Conclusions and future work are presented in Section 6.

2. RELATED WORK

Video-content segmentation and highlight extraction has been an active research area in the past few years [5]. More recently, leading international standard organizations (e.g., MPEG of ISO/IEC [6] and ATVEF [7]) have also started working actively on frameworks for organizing and storing such metadata. Below we focus primarily on technologies used and the types of content addressed by such systems and organizations.

There are primarily three sources of information used by most video segmentation and highlight detection systems. These are analysis of video track, analysis of audio track, and use of close-caption information accompanying some of the programs. Within each of these, the features used to segment the video may be of a general nature (e.g., shot boundaries) or quite domain specific (e.g., knowledge of fact that a news channel segments stories by a triple hash mark "###" in the close caption channel).

When analyzing the video track, a first step is to segment raw video into "shots". Many shot boundary detection techniques have been developed during the past decade. These include pixel-based, histogram-based, feature-based and compressed-domain techniques [8]. However, video shots have low semantic content. To address real-world need, researchers have developed techniques to parse videos at a higher semantic level. In [5], Zhang et. al. present techniques to categorize news video into anchorperson shots and news shots and further construct a higher-level video structure based on news items. In [9], Wactlar et. al. use face detection to select the frame to present to the user as representative of each shot. In [10], McGee and Dimitrova developed a technique to automatically pick out TV commercials from the rest of the programs based on shot change rate, occurrence of black frames and occurrence of text regions. This allows users to quickly skip through commercials. In [11], Yeung et. al. developed scene-transition graphs to illustrate the scene flow of movies. As stated in the introduction, in this paper we do not focus on video-track features for computational reasons.

The audio-track contains immense amounts of useful information and it normally has closer link to semantic event than the video information. Some interesting early work was done by Arons [12] in trying to aggressively speed-up informational talks. He

noticed that relative-pitch increases for people when they are emphasizing points. In his Speech Skimmer system, he used that for prioritizing regions within a talk. He et al [13] further built upon Aron's work and constructed presentation summaries based on pitch analysis, knowledge of slide transitions in the presentation, and information about previous users' access patterns. The study showed that the automatically generated summaries were of considerable value to the talk viewers. As we will discuss later, we use pitch as one component for emphasis detection in this paper too.

Use of close-caption information (e.g., Informedia project [9]) is a special case of speech track analysis; ideally if speech-to-text conversion were perfect, one would not have to rely on close-caption information. However, we are far from ideal today, and close caption text is a powerful source to classify video segments for indexing and searching. For this paper, as is the case in practice, we assume close caption information is not available for baseball games.

As one moves away from relatively clean speech environments (e.g., news, talks), analysis of audio-track can become trickier. For example, in sports videos, there are several sources of audio—the announcer, the crowd, noises such as horns — are all mixed together. These sound sources need to be separated, if their features are to be used in analysis and segmentation of video. The CueVideo system from IBM [15] presents techniques to separate speech and music in mixed-audio environments. They use a combination of energy, zero-crossing rate, and analysis of harmonics. In [16], Zhang and Kuo developed a heuristic-based approach to classifying audio signals into silence, speech, music, song, and mixtures of the above. While both systems achieve good accuracy, the selection of many hard-coded thresholds prevents them from being used in a more complicated audio environment such as baseball games. As we discuss in later sections, the audio channel in TV baseball programs is very noisy, the sound sources more diverse, and we want to detect special features like baseball bat-and-ball impact that have not been addressed earlier.

Looking at related work in the sports domain, we see that relatively little work has been done on sports video as compared to news video. This is partly due to the fact that the analysis is more difficult for sports, for example, due to lack of regular structure in sports video (in contrast, news often has structured format: anchor person → clip from the field → back to anchor person) and more complex audio. In some early work, Gong et. al. [17] targeted at parsing TV soccer programs. By detecting and tracking soccer court, ball, players, and motion vectors, they were able to distinguish nine different positions of the play (e.g. midfield, top-right corner of the court, etc.). While Gong et al focused on video track analysis, Chang et. al.[18] primarily used audio analysis as an alternative tool for sports parsing. Their goal was to detect football touchdowns. A standard template matching of filter bank energies was used to spot the key words "touchdown" or "fumble". Silence ratio was then used to detect "cheers", with the assumption that little silence is in cheering while much more are in reporter chat. Vision-based line-mark and goal-posts detection were used to verify the results obtained from audio analysis. Our work reported here is similar in spirit though different in detail.

3. INFORMATION SOURCES

As discussed in previous section, the two primary sources of information are video-track and audio-track. Video/visual information captures the play from various camera distances and angles. One can possibly analyze the video track to extract *generic features* such as: high-motion scene or low-motion scene; camera pan, zoom, tilt actions; shot boundaries. Alternatively, as done by Gong *et. al.* and Chang *et. al* for soccer and football, we can detect *sport-specific features*. For baseball, one can imagine detecting situations such as: player at bat, the pitcher curling-up to pitch the ball, player sliding into a base, player racing to catch a ball. Given our goal of determining exciting segments, we believe sport-specific features are more likely to be helpful than the generic features. For example, interesting action usually happens right after the ball is pitched, so detecting the curled-up pitching motion sequences can be very helpful, especially when coupled with the audio-track analysis.

The technology to do such video-analysis while challenging seems within reach. However, we do not use video analysis in this paper. We had two reasons. First, visual information processing is compute intensive, and we wanted to target set-top box class of machines. For example, to compute the dense optical flow field of a 320x240 frame, it needs a few seconds on a high-end PC even using the hierarchical Gaussian pyramid [19]. Second, we wanted to see how well we can do with audio information only. As we discuss below, we thought we could substitute for some of the visual cues with cheaper-to-compute audio cues. For example, instead of detecting beginning of a play with a curled-up pitcher visual sequence, we decided to explore if we could locate it by detecting bat-and-ball impact points from the audio track.

There are four major sources mixed in: 1) announcers' speech, 2) audience ambient speech noise, 3) game-specific sounds (e.g. baseball hits), and 4) other background noise (e.g. vehicle horning, audience clapping, environmental sounds, etc.). A good announcer's speech has tremendous amount of information, both in terms of actual words spoken (if speech-to-text were done) and in terms of prosodic features (e.g., excitement transformed into energy, pitch, and word-rate changes). The audience ambient noise can also be very useful, as audience viscerally react to exciting situations. However, in practice this turns out to be an unreliable source, because automatic gain control (AGC) affects the amount of audience noise picked up by the microphones. It varies quite a bit depending on whether the announcer is speaking or not. Game specific sounds, such as bat-and-ball impact sound, can be a very useful indicator of the game development. However, AGC and the far distance from the microphones make detecting them challenging. Finally, vehicle horning and other environmental sounds happen arbitrarily in the game. They therefore provide almost no useful, if not negative, information to our task.

Based on the above analysis, in this paper, we will use announcers' speech and game specific sound (e.g., baseball hits) as the major information sources and fuse them intelligently to solve our problem at hand. We make the following assumptions in extracting highlights from TV broadcasting baseball programs:

1. Exciting segments are highly correlated with announcers' excited speech;

2. Most of the exciting segments in baseball games occur right after a baseball pitch and hit.

Under the above two assumptions, the *challenges* we face are: develop effective and robust techniques to detect excited announcers' speech and baseball hits from the mixed and very noisy audio signal, and intelligently fuse them to produce final exciting segments of baseball programs. Before we going into full details of the proposed approach in Section 4, we first examine various audio features that will be used in this paper.

3.1. Audio Features Used

3.1.1 Energy Related Features
The simplest feature in this category is the short-time energy, i.e., the average waveform amplitude defined over a specific time window.

When we want to model signal's energy characteristics more accurately, we can use sub-band short-time energies. Considering the perceptual property of human ears, we can divide the entire frequency spectrum into four sub-bands, each of which consists of the same number of critical bands that represent cochlear filters in the human auditory model [14]. These four sub-bands are 0-630hz, 630-1720hz, 1720-4400hz, and 4400hz and above. Let's refer them as $E_1, E_2, E_3,$ and E_4. Because human speech's energy resides mostly in the middle two sub-bands, let's further define $E_{23} = E_2 + E_3$.

3.1.2 Phoneme-level Features
The division of the sub-bands based on human auditory system is not unique. Another widely used sub-band division is the Mel-scale sub-bands [20]. For each tone with an actual frequency, f, measured in Hz, a subjective pitch is measure on a so called "Mel-scale". As a reference point, the pitch of a 1 kHz tone, 40 dB above the perceptual hearing threshold, is defined as 1000 Mels. In plain words, Mel-scale is a gradually warped linear spectrum, with coarser resolution at high frequencies. The Mel-frequency sub-band energy is defined accordingly. For automatic speech recognition, many phoneme-level features have been developed. Mel-frequency Cepstral coefficients (*MFCC*) is one of them [20]. It is the *cosine* transform of the Mel-scale filter bank energy defined above. *MFCC* and its first derivative capture fine details of speech phonemes and have been a very successful feature in speech recognition and speaker identification.

3.1.3 Information Complexity Features
There are quite a few features that are designed for characterizing the information complexity of audio signals, including bandwidth and entropy. Because of entropy's wide use and success in information theory applications, in this paper we will concentrate on entropy (*Etr*). For an N-point FFT of the audio signal $s(t)$, let $S(n)$ be the *nth* frequency's component. Entropy is defined as:

$$Etr = -\sum_{n=1}^{N} P_n \log P_n$$

$$P_n = |S(n)|^2 / \sum_{n=1}^{N} |S(n)|^2$$

3.1.4 Prosodic Features
The waveform of voiced human speech is a quasi-periodic signal. The period in the signal is called the pitch (*Pch*) of the speech. It has been widely used in human speech emotion analysis and synthesis [21]. Independent of the waveform shape, this period can be shortened or enlarged as a result of the speaker's emotion

and excitement level. There are many approaches to pitch estimation, including auto-regressive model and average magnitude difference function [16], etc. The pitch tracker we use in this paper is based on the maximum *a posteriori* (MAP) approach [22]. It creates a time-pitch energy distribution based on predictable energy that improves on the normalized cross-correlation and is one of best pitch estimation algorithms available.

3.1.5 Summary
We have discussed various audio features in this section. They are designed for solving different problems. Specifically, we will use E_{23}, Etr, and *MFCC* for human speech endpoint detection. E_{23} to E_4 are used to build a temporal template to detect baseball hits. Statistics based on E_{23} and *Pch* are used to model excited human speech.

4. PROPOSED APPROACH
In this section we will first give an algorithm overview and then discuss each sub-systems in full detail.

4.1 Algorithm Overview
As stated in Section 3, we base our algorithm for highlight detection on a model of baseball where we assume: (i) exciting segments are highly correlated with announcers' excited speech; and (ii) most exciting segments in baseball occur right after a baseball pitch and hit. As a result, we need to develop techniques to reliably detect excited human speech and baseball hits, and then fuse them intelligently to generate the final highlights segments. The following is the flowchart of the algorithm.

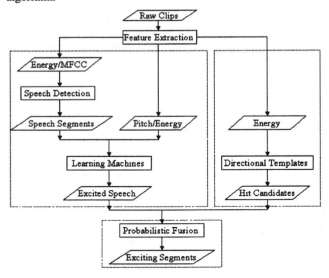

Figure 1. Algorithm Flowchart

The top-left block is the sub-system for excited speech classification, including the pre-processing stage of noisy environment speech endpoint detection. The top-right block is the sub-system for baseball hits detection. The bottom block is the sub-system for probabilistic fusion.

1. *Noisy Environment Speech Endpoint Detection:* In conventional speech endpoint detection, the background noise level is relatively low. An energy-based approach can

achieve reasonably good results. Unfortunately, in TV baseball programs, the noise presence can be as strong as the speech signal itself, and we need to explore more sophisticated audio features to distinguish speech from other audio signals.

2. *Classifying Excited Speech Using Learning Machines:* Once speech segments are detected, the energy and pitch statistics are computed for each speech segment. These statistics are then used to train various learning machines, including pure parametric machines (e.g., *Gaussian fitting*), pure non-parametric machines (e.g., *K nearest neighbors*), and semi-parametric machines (e.g., *support vector machines*). After the machines are trained they are capable of classifying excited human speech for other baseball games.

3. *Detecting Baseball Hits Using Directional Templates:* Excited announcers' speech does not correlated *100%* with the baseball game highlights. We should resort to additional cues to support the evidence that we obtained from excited speech detection. Sports-specific events, e.g., baseball hits, provide such additional support. Based on the characteristics of baseball hits' sub-band energy features, we develop a directional template matching approach for detecting baseball hits.

4. *Probabilistic Fusion*: The outputs from Steps 2 and 3 are the probabilities if an audio sequence contains excited human speech and contains a baseball hit, respectively. Each one of two probabilities alone does not provide enough confidence in extracting true exciting highlights. However, when integrated appropriately, they will produce stronger correlations to the true exciting highlights. We will develop and compare various approaches to fuse the outputs from Steps 2 and 3.

Based on the nature of each processing steps, different audio signal *resolutions* are used. All of the original audio features are extracted at the resolution of 10 msec (referred as *frames*). The frame-resolution E_{23} and E_4 are used in *directional template matching* to detect baseball hit candidates. In speech endpoint detection, human speech seldom is less than half a second. We therefore use 0.5 sec resolution (referred as *windows*). The statistics of *Pch* and E_{23} are extracted from each *window* to conduct excited speech recognition.

One thing worth emphasizing is that the whole proposed approach is established on a probabilistic framework. Unlike some of the existing work that uses heuristics to set hard thresholds, we try to avoid thresholding during the intermediate stages. In the thresholding approaches, early misclassifications cannot be remedied at later stages. The probabilistic framework approach will, on the other hand, produce probability values at each intermediate stage not a 0/1 decision. This probabilistic formulation of the problem allows us to avoid *ad hoc* procedures and solve the problem in a principled way.

5. Noisy Environment Speech Detection
Most of the traditional speech endpoint detection techniques make the assumption that the speech is recorded in a quiet room environment. In that case, E_{23} alone can produce reasonably good results. At a baseball stadium, however, human speech is almost always mixed with other background noise, including machinery noise, car horns, background conversations, etc [20].

In this case, E_{23}'s distinguishing power drops significantly, because microphone's AGC amplifies the background noise level when the announcers are not talking. The energy level of non-speech signal can therefore be as strong as that of speech.

In a recent work by Huang and Yang [23], they proposed to use a hybrid feature (product of energy E_{23} and entropy Etr) to perform noisy car environment speech endpoint detection. Based on our experiments, even though this approach is effective in car environment, its performance drops significantly in baseball stadium environment that has much more varieties of background interferences.

Inspired by the success of *MFCC* in automatic speech recognition, and the observation that speech exhibits high variations in *MFCC* values, we propose to use first derivatives of *MFCC* (delta *MFCC*) and E_{23} as the audio features. They are complimentary in filtering out non-speech signals: energy E_{23} helps to filter out low energy but high variance background interference (e.g., low volume car horns) and delta *MFCC* helps to filter out low variance but high energy noise (e.g., audience ambient noise when AGC produces large values). In Section 5, we compare the performance of the above three approaches: energy only, energy and entropy, and energy and delta *MFCC*.

5.1 Classifying Excited Human Speech

A good announcer's speech has tremendous amount of information, both in terms of actual words spoken (if speech-to-text were done) and in terms of prosodic features (e.g., excitement transformed into energy and pitch). As speech-to-text is not reliable in noisy environment, in this paper we concentrate on the prosodic features. Excited announcers' speech has good correlations with the exciting baseball game segments. Previous study has shown that excited speech has both raised pitch and increased amount of energy [21]. The features we use in this paper are therefore statistics of pitch Pch and energy E_{23} extracted from each 0.5 sec speech *windows*. Specifically, we use six features: maximum pitch, average pitch, pitch dynamic range, maximum energy, average energy, and energy dynamic range of a given speech *window*.

The problem of classification can be formulated as follows. Let C_1 and C_2 be the two classes to be classified (e.g., excited speech vs. non-excited speech). Let X be the observations of the features (e.g., the six audio features described above). Let $P(C_i | X)$, $i = 1, 2$, be the *posterior* probability of a data being in class C_i given the observation X. *Bayes* decision theory tells us that classifying data to the class whose *posterior* probability is the highest minimizes the *probability of error* [24]:

$$\arg \max_i P(C_i | X)$$

How to reliably estimate $P(C_i|X)$ is the job for learning machines. We next explore three different approaches.

5.1.1 Parametric Machines

Bayes rule tells us that $P(C_i | X)$ can be computed as a product of the *prior* probability and the conditional class density, and then normalized by the data density:

$$P(C_i | X) = \frac{P(C_i)p(X | C_i)}{p(X)}$$

As $p(X)$ is a constant for all the classes and does not contribute to the decision rule, we only need to estimate $P(C_i)$ and $p(X|C_i)$.

Priors $P(C_i)$ can easily be estimated from labeled training data (e.g., excited speech and non-excited speech). There are many ways to estimate the conditional class density $p(X|C_i)$. The simplest approach is the *parametric* approach. This approach represents the underlying probability density as a specific functional form with a number of adjustable parameters [24]. The parameters can be optimally adjusted to best fit the training data. The most widely used functional form is *Gaussian* (Normal) distribution $N(\mu, \sigma)$, because of its simple form and many nice analytical properties. The two parameters (mean μ and standard deviation σ) can be optimally adjusted by using the *maximum likelihood estimation* (MLE):

$$\mu = \frac{1}{n}\sum_{k=1}^{n} X_k \text{ , } \sigma^2 = \frac{1}{n}\sum_{k=1}^{n} (X_k - \mu)$$

where n is the number of training samples.

5.1.2 Non-Parametric Machines

Even though easy to implement, parametric machines are too restrictive in data modeling and sometimes result in poor classification results. For example, the pre-assumed function seldom matches the true underlying distribution function and it can only model unimodal distributions [24]. Non-parametric machines were proposed to overcome this difficulty. They do not pre-assume any functional forms, but instead depend on the data itself. There are non-parametric machines that can estimate the *posterior* probability $P(C_i | X)$ directly. *K nearest neighbor* is such a technique.

Let V be the volume around observation X and V covers K labeled samples. Let K_i be the number of samples in class C_i. Then the *posterior* probability can be estimated as [24]:

$$P(C_i | X) = \frac{K_i/nV}{\sum_i K_i/nV} = \frac{K_i}{K}$$

This estimation matches our intuition very well: the probability that a data sample belongs to class C_i is the fraction of samples in the volume labeled as class C_i.

5.1.3 Semi-Parametric Machines

Pure parametric machines are easy to train and fast to adapt to new training samples, but too restrictive. Non-parametric machines, on the other hand, are much more general but take more time to compute. To combine the advantages and avoid the disadvantages of the above two approaches, *semi-parametric* machines have been proposed [25]. These new set of machines include the *Gaussian mixture models*, *neural networks* and *support vector machines (SVM)*. Because of its recognized success in pattern classification [26], we will focus on SVM in this paper.

Let R be the actual risk (test error) and Re be the empirical risk (training error). For η, where $0 < \eta < 1$, with probability $1 - \eta$, the following bound holds [26]:

$$R \leq R_e + \sqrt{\frac{h(\log(2n/h)+1) - \log(\eta/4)}{n}}$$

where n is the number of training samples and η is a non-negative integer called the *Vapnik-Chervonenkis* (VC) dimension of a learning machine [26]. R (test error) represents a learning machine's ability to generalize to unseen data, after it is trained.

In any classification task, we want R to be minimized. It is not always true that R will be minimized when Re is minimized. The second term on the right-hand side determines the "mismatch" between training and testing situations, and it increases as the VC dimension increases. VC dimension characterizes the "capacity" of a learning machine. If the capacity is *too low*, the machine cannot learn and results in a high Re (thus high R). On the other hand, if the capacity is *too high*, even though Re can be arbitrarily small, the machine can be "over fit" and results in a high value of the second term (thus high R). The remarkable characteristic of SVM is that it can automatically find the required "capacity" to learn the training samples without being over trained. In another word, SVM learns in a principled way. SVM has found successes in many applications including face detection, hand writing recognition, and text categorization [26].

Standard SVM does not generate the *posterior* probability directly. In [27], Platt developed a new approach to first train a SVM and then to train an additional *sigmoid* function to map the SVM outputs into *posterior* probabilities. Because of its effectiveness, we adopted this method in our system:

$$P(C_i \mid X) = \frac{1}{1 + \exp(AX + B)}$$

where A and B are the parameters of the *sigmoid* function.

In Section 5, we give detailed comparisons between the above three learning machines' performance.

5.1.4 Post Processing

In real world, excited speeches never appear in just one *window* (0.5 sec). Instead, they appear in a much longer unit. Experimentally, we find a *segment* (5 sec) is the minimum length required by a coherent excited speech. Since each *window* contributes equally to a *segment*, we use the average *posterior* probability of the *windows* in the *segment* as the *posterior* probability for the *segment* $P(ES)$:

$$P(ES) = \frac{1}{M} \sum_{m=1}^{M} P(C_1 \mid X_m)$$

where C_1 represents the excited speech class, and M is the number of *windows* in a *segment*.

5.2 Baseball Hit Detection

Even though excited announcers' speech has good correlations with exciting baseball game segments, it is not sufficient or reliable to base the judgment solely on the excited speech. For example, the pitch tracker may perform poorly in noisy speech environment. More importantly, announcers' speech can become excited due to other reasons that are totally irrelevant with the development of the game (e.g., a joke from their partners or a balloon passing the stadium). If we were to use excited speech only, there would have been many false alarms.

In most of the sports, there exist sports-specific events. For example, *player gatherings* indicate the start of new attacks in football, and baseball hits manifest possible exciting segments a few seconds later in the game. These sports-specific events can help reduce the amount of false alarms. In this section, we will describe a *directional template matching* approach to detecting baseball hits.

In the audio signal spectrograms, when we examine a baseball hit in isolation, it is extremely difficult to distinguish it from a strong

speech fricative or a stop. However, when we look at it in the context of its surrounding signals, while the task is still difficult we have some hope: fricatives or stops normally are followed by vowels that exhibit high energy in E_{23} but low energy in E_4. To capture this temporal context, we build a baseball-hit template consisting of 25 *frames*, with the hit peak at the 8th *frame*. In this template, using only the absolute values of E_{23} and E_4 is not sufficient. To capture the shape of the energy curves over time, we further use the ratio of E_{23} and E_4 normalized by $E_{23}(8)$:

$$ER_{23}(i) = E_{23}(i) / E_{23}(8)$$
$$ER_4(i) = E_4(i) / E_{23}(8)$$

where $i = 1, ..., 25$.

The four 25-element templates are constructed based on labeled training data. Figure 3 shows the four templates (E_{23}, ER_{23}, E_4 and ER_4 in that order) built on 55 training samples.

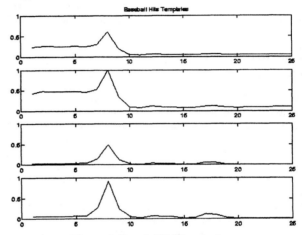

Figure 2. Baseball hit's template

We next discuss how we compute the probability that a data sequence (25 *frames*) contains a baseball hit. Let D be the Mahalanobis distance of a data sequence $\vec{X}$ from the template $\vec{T}$:

$$D^2 = (\vec{X} - \vec{T})^T \Sigma^{-1} (\vec{X} - \vec{T})$$

where both $\vec{X}$ and $\vec{T}$ are vectors of $4 \times 25 = 100$ elements, and Σ is the covariance matrix of $\vec{T}$. To simplify computation, we restrict Σ to be a diagonal matrix. The distance D can be converted to a probability value as follows [28]:

$$P(HT) = \exp(-\frac{1}{2} D^2) / (C + \exp(-\frac{1}{2} D^2))$$

where C is a suitable constant.

The above conventional (*un-directional*) template matching technique does not incorporate domain knowledge into the computation of D effectively. For example, domain knowledge (Figure 2) tells us that $E_{23}(8)$ should exhibit high value while other $E_{23}(i)$'s exhibit low values. But in the un-directional template matching, an over-mismatch data point of $E_{23}(8)$ is treated the same as an under-mismatch data point of $E_{23}(8)$. In reality, however, an over-mismatch should not only not to be punished, but also be encouraged. The *direction* from which the data point is approaching the template *is* important. We thus propose a *directional* template matching approach:

| (a) | (b) | (c) | (d) |

Figure 3. A typical presentation of an exciting segment: It starts with the pitcher throwing the ball (a). Then the hitter tries to hit the ball (b). If it is a good hit, then the hitter is running (c). The final part (d) is the audience cheering for the good play.

$$D^2 = (\vec{X} - \vec{T})^T I \times \Sigma^{-1} (\vec{X} - \vec{T})$$

where I is a diagonal indicator matrix. Its elements can be of various values to reflect the domain knowledge. For example, $I(8,8)$ takes a negative value when $E_{23}(8)$ is an over-mismatch to reduce the distance D but a positive value for an under-mismatch to increase the distance D. This new formulation makes template matching much more flexible to incorporate domain knowledge into the distance computation. Specifically, in this paper, when $E_{23}(i)$'s are over-matching, $I = diag[1, ..., 1, -1, 1, ..., 1]$, where the -1 is at location 8. When $E_{23}(i)$'s are under-matching the templates, $I = diag[-1, ..., -1, 1, -1, ..., -1]$, where the 1 is at location 8.

5.3 Probabilistic Fusion

In the previous two sections we have developed techniques to compute the probability that a *segment* is an excited speech segment ($P(ES)$) and the probability that a *frame* contains a baseball hit ($P(HT)$). The two assumptions we made in Section 3 tell us that if a segment has high $P(ES)$ and it occurs right after a high $P(HT)$ frame, it is very likely to be a true exciting segment. From the training data, we find that a hit can occur upto 5 sec ahead of the excited speech segment. In all the following discussions, we search a hit *frame* within the 5 sec interval of the excited speech segment. We next explore two techniques to fuse $P(ES)$ and $P(HT)$ into the final probability if a segment is an exciting segment ($P(E)$).

5.3.1 Weighted Fusion

In this approach, both $P(ES)$ and $P(HT)$ directly contribute to $P(E)$, with appropriate weights:

$$P(E) = W_{ES} P(ES) + W_{HT} P(HT)$$

where W_{ES} and W_{HT} are the weights that sum up to *1.0*. They can both be estimated from the training data, and we use values of *0.83* and *0.17*.

5.3.2 Conditional Fusion

In this approach, we try to capture the intuition that the key value of a detected hit P(HT) is not in directly adding to the probability that a segment is exciting P(E). Instead it contributes indirectly to P(E) by adjusting the by adjusting the confidence level of the $P(ES)$ estimation (e.g., that the excited speech probability is not high due to mislabeling a car horn as speech):

$$P(E) = P(CF)P(ES)$$

$$P(CF) = P(CF \mid HT)P(HT) + P(CF \mid \overline{HT})P(\overline{HT})$$

where $P(CF)$ is the probability that how much confidence we have in $P(ES)$ estimation, and $P(\overline{HT}) = 1 - P(HT)$ is the probability that there is no hit. $P(CF|HT)$ represents the probability that we are confident that $P(ES)$ is accurate *given* there is a baseball hit. Similarly, $P(CF \mid \overline{HT})$ represents the probability that we are confident that $P(ES)$ is accurate *given* there is no baseball hit. Both conditional probabilities $P(CF|HT)$ and $P(CF \mid \overline{HT})$ can be estimated from the training data and we obtain values *1.0* and *0.3*.

5.4 Final Presentation

Starting at the beginning of the algorithm, various probability values are computed and flow to the end of the algorithm. This probabilistic framework allows us to avoid information loss due to intermediate-step hard thresholding and can solve the problem in a principled way. At the end of the algorithm flow chart, there is only a single probability value ($P(E)$) associated with each segment.

When presenting an exciting segment to the end user, overlapping and close-by segments are merged into a single segment. In addition, because we already know the most likely baseball hit locations, each segment starts a few seconds before the hit. Figure 3 is a typical sequence of an exciting segment.

Depending on users' interest level and/or time available to view the game, the users can specify an interest threshold. This is the only threshold that a user needs to specify. Based on this threshold, the algorithm generates a summary of suitable duration.

Of course, the algorithm may generate false positives and negatives. Lowering the threshold will minimize false negatives (reduce missing exciting segments) though it may increase false positives (include non-exciting segments). Our belief is that if these are few, then the benefits of automation will far exceed the costs. In WebTV/TiVo/ReplayTV environments it is particularly easy for the end-user to skip incorrectly identified false positives due to the instant seek capability.

6. EXPERIMENTAL RESULTS

In this section, we will give detailed reports on our experiments to evaluate various proposed approaches. We will describe the data set used, evaluation framework, experimental results and observations.

6.1 Data Set

In most of the existing systems, only limited amount of tests have been conducted (e.g. less than 1 hr video in [15], 45 min in [18],

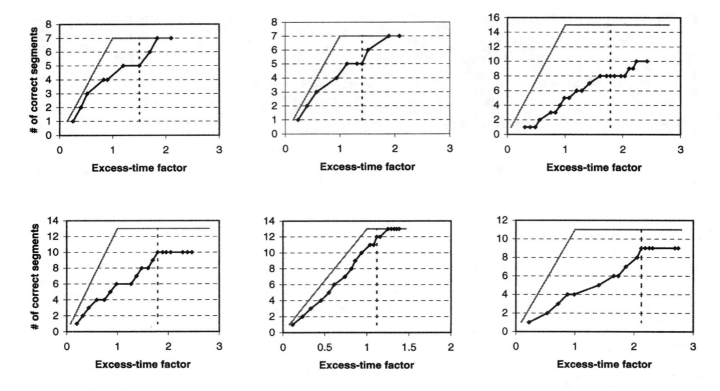

Figure 4. Overall performance curves for clips A through F, in raster scan order. Y-axis shows number of exciting segments identified correctly by the algorithm. X-axis indicates excess-time factor, i.e., duration of algorithmically selected segments divided by duration of human selected segments. For each graph, the left light-gray curves shows *ideal* performance, corresponding to choices made by human. Right dark curve shows our algorithm's performance assuming *E+MFCC* for speech selection, SVM for classifying exciting speech segments, and using conditional fusion for including baseball hit data. The vertical dash line indicates the time duration of algorithmically selected segments when threshold was set so that the number of segments selected was same as that generated by human. The overall graph was plotted with a slightly lower threshold, with number of generated segments being 1.5 times human segments. This allows us to see if we capture some more of the human selected segments if we lower the threshold.

Table 1. Data set. The clips cover about 7 hours of video, with 4 different announcers. The Energy Level is given as compared to maximum allowable level (in percentage).

Clip	Length	Announcer	Samp. Fr.	Energy Lev
A	1:10:05	A	16 KHz	50
B	1:05:34	A	16 KHz	55
C	1:01:54	B	16 KHz	80
D	0:41:14	C	16 KHz	80
E	1:58:26	A	11 KHz	30
F	1:06:19	D	16 KHz	120

and 30 min in [17]). To validate the effectiveness and robustness of the proposed approach, we have collected baseball game videos from various sources (see Table 1). In total we have seven hours of baseball games consisting of eight giga bytes of data. They come from different sources, digitized at different studios, sampled at different frequencies and amplitude, and reported by different announcers. The first half (35 min) of Clip A is used as the training data. The second half of Clip A is used as a *clip-dependent* test case. Clip B has many similar conditions as Clip A and is used as a *similar-clip* test case. Clips C and D differ significantly from Clip A, and are used as *clip-independent* test cases. To further stress test, we included Clips E and F. Clip E

is sampled at a lower frequency and may lose some higher frequency information, as needed in the algorithm. Clip F's audio level was over amplified (clipped), i.e., 20% over the limit of maximum allowable level. These two tapes represent the *stress* test cases. A summary of the six clips is given in Table 1.

6.2 Evaluation Framework

We wanted to compare our automatically generated highlight segments to the ones marked by humans. A human subject (not working on the project) was asked to watch the baseball games A-F and mark the exciting segments. Given the certain amount of subjectivity in what is exciting, we would have ideally liked multiple people to do such markings. The results are quite interesting nonetheless.

There are two methods we use to evaluate our results. The first called "segment-overlap method" is as follows. We vary the threshold until the number of segments selected by our algorithm is the same as that selected by the human. We then ask the question how many of these are the same as those selected by the human. The larger the overlap, clearly the algorithm is performing better. We can also do sensitivity analysis by letting our algorithm select fewer or more segments than that selected by the human.

The second method, called "excess-time method", is used to deal with a possible pitfall of the first method. For example, if the segments determined by an algorithm are very long (e.g., each is 2 minutes long) then obviously the probability of covering human-selected segments (each is typically about 10 seconds) would be higher, and first metric would indicate good results. However, that would not be as good as an algorithm that more tightly identifying the exciting segments. So in this method we plot the number of correctly generated segments as a function of T/T_0 (e.g., Figure 4). The numerator T corresponds to the duration of the algorithmically selected segments (ordered based on decreasing $P(E)$ values), and the denominator T_0 corresponds to the total duration of the human-selected segments. For example, a point on this graph could indicate that to get coverage of 5 of the 7 human-selected segments, we have to spend 1.4 times as long watching the video as duration of human-selected segments. These excess-time curves illustrate how the algorithm performs when more and more segments are added to the final presentation.

6.3 Overall Performance

We begin by comparing the performance of the best of our algorithms with the ground truth as marked by the human. The best overall algorithm combines energy plus delta *MFCC* for speech-endpoint detection, SVM for learning excited speech segments, and conditional fusion for including baseball hit information. Table 2 summarizes the performance when the threshold of our algorithm was set to pick the same number of segments as selected by human.

Table 2. Overall performance. Second row indicates # of segments selected by human. Third row indicates # of correct segments identified by algorithm, when asked to pick same number of segments as human.

Clip	A	B	C	D	E	F	Total
# human	7	7	15	13	13	11	66
# algorithm	5	5	8	10	12	9	49

Comparing the performance in Table 2, we see that algorithm identifies 49 out of 66 segments correctly (~75%). This is quite remarkable, if we consider that some of the exciting segments identified by the human start falling into the gray area, where there may have been others segments just as exciting to another human. The performance for clip C is poorest of all the clips (8 out of 15 correct), and this is due to pitch tracking reasons. We discuss this aspect in greater detail in Section 5.8 after discussing rest of results.

Figure 4 shows the overall performance using excess-time plots for all the clips (shown in raster-scan order). We also show the "ideal" curves corresponding to the ground truth, i.e., human selected segments. These represent the least amount of time to achieve the highest "correctness". The vertical dashed lines in each graph indicates the time duration of algorithmically selected segments when threshold was set so that the number of segments selected was same as that generated by human (the correctness at this threshold is 49 out of 66 as shown in Table 2). The location of these dashed lines indicate how much more time a viewer need to spend to view the same number of segments as the human marked ones. For example, if the vertical dashed line's location is 1.3, it says a viewer will spend 30% more time. The closer the line is to 1.0, the better the algorithm's performance. As can be

seen in the figure, except for Clip F, all the clips' vertical lines are within 2.0, with average of ~1.5.

This is a strong result indicating that the algorithm is not achieving its correctness by marking up excessively long duration segments. In fact, even this factor of 1.5 is partly due to the fact that the human in our case was particularly conservative in identifying the exciting segments. For example, he did not include the pitcher pitching the baseball and player hitting the baseball in his highlighted segments; he only included the action after that. Our instructions to the human were not so precise, and we did not want to change his markings after the fact.

The overall graphs in Figure 4 were plotted with a slightly lower threshold, with number of generated segments being 1.5 times human segments. Thus if human identifies 10 segments, we adjusted the algorithm to generate 15 segments. These portions of the curves cover the region on the right of the vertical line, and also provide useful information. If the curves continue upwards, it means it is still beneficial to include more segments into the presentation at the cost of increased viewing time. On the other hand, if the curves become flat after the vertical lines, it is almost of no advantage to include more segments. The curves in Figure 4 show that it is still beneficial to include more segments (other than for Clips D and F). By increasing our excess-time factor slightly, we can achieve correctness of 57 out of 66 segments (~86%).

After establishing the overall performance of the proposed approach, we next examine various algorithms in greater detail along three orthogonal dimensions: speech endpoint detection, excited speech classification, and probabilistic fusion.

6.4 Speech-Endpoint Detection

We had presented three speech-segment endpoint detection algorithms in Section 4.2: energy only (*E*), energy and entropy (*E+Etr*), and energy and delta *MFCC* (*E+MFCC*). We now explore the impact of the speech-endpoint detection algorithm on the overall end results. For this comparison, we fix the other control conditions: the learning algorithm is fixed to SVM (it was the best as we will show later), and the hit-detection and fusion algorithm to "conditional fusion".

The relative performance is summarized in Table 3. It is clear that overall *E+MFCC* does substantially better (49 out of 66 correct) than the other two approaches, while *E+Etr* does better than E alone (40 vs. 30 out of 66). *E+MFCC* does best for each of the six individual clips (A-F) too, while there are some performance reversals between *E* and *E+Etr* (clips C and F).

Table 3. Performance of various speech-endpoint detection algorithms. Second row indicates # of segments selected by human. Subsequent rows indicate correct segments identified by algorithm, when asked to pick the same number of segments as human.

Clip	A	B	C	D	E	F	Total
# human	7	7	15	13	13	11	66
E+MFCC	5	5	8	10	12	9	49
E+Etr	5	5	7	9	9	5	40
E	4	4	8	5	2	7	30

6.5 Excited Speech Classification

In Section 4.3, we discussed three approaches to excited speech classification: Gaussian fitting (*GAU*), K nearest neighbors

(*KNN*), and support vector machines (*SVM*). Table 3 summarizes the impact of the different learning machines on the overall end results. For this comparison, we fix the other control conditions: we use *E+MFCC* as the speech endpoint detection algorithm and use conditional fusion as the fusion algorithm.

While *SVM* performs the best in the three learning machines as we expected, the gain is not significant. After analyzing the data, we found one major reason accounting for this was the following. The input to all the learning machines was the pitch and energy statistics of each speech *window*(Section 4.3). Our proposed *E+MFCC* did a very good job in separating other audio signals from human speech. Once this is done, excited speech classification becomes less difficult and less sophisticated learning paradigms (e.g., *GAU* and *KNN*) can achieve reasonable good results. One thing worth pointing out is that, even though *KNN* achieves almost the same accuracy as *SVM*, it is the slowest of the three learning machines.

Table 4. Performance of the three learning machines. Second row indicates # of segments selected by human. Subsequent rows indicate correct segments identified by algorithm, when asked to pick the same number of segments as human.

Clip	A	B	C	D	E	F	Total
# human	7	7	15	13	13	11	66
SVM	5	5	8	10	12	9	49
GAU	5	5	8	9	12	7	46
KNN	5	5	8	9	12	9	48

6.6 Baseball Hits Detection

The output of the *directional* template matching (Section 4.4) is the probability if a *frame* contains a baseball hit. Even though there is no need to set any threshold at this intermediate stage, we can set a threshold (*TH*) for *evaluation* purpose. We vary *TH* from 0.05 to 0.5 and Table 5 summarizes the baseball hits detection performance for Clip D. (We did not do other Clips due to resource involved in marking the ground truth.) There are *58* true baseball hits in this clip. Considering many baseball hits are corrupted by background noise and even completely overlapping with announcers' speech, the proposed approach's performance is very encouraging. For example, at *TH = 0.20*, it detects 47 (81%) of all the true hits and only introduced 8 (less than 14%) of false positives. Among the undetected hits, for some the audio was too weak to be detected even by human, and in ground truth we simply assumed there was a hit based on video analysis.

Table 5. Baseball hits detection

TH	.05	.10	.15	.20	.30	.40	.50
Correct	53	50	47	47	41	32	23
False Alarms	23	13	9	8	2	2	1

6.7 Probabilistic Fusion

In Section 4.5, we proposed two methods to fuse *P(ES)* and *P(HT)*: weighted fusion and conditional fusion. Table 6 summarizes the performance between conditional fusion, weighted fusion, and no fusion – just use *P(ES)* and discard *P(HT)*. For this comparison, we fix the other control conditions: we use *E+MFCC* as the speech endpoint detection algorithm and use SVM as the learning machine for classifying excited speech.

We find no significant difference between the two fusion algorithms. When we looked at the details, we found that conditional fusion was giving more weight to hits than weighted fusion. As a result, when conditional fusion was used, if hits were correctly identified the algorithm did a better job. If, however, an actual hit was not detected, the algorithm often resulted in a mis-classification. On the balance, the results looked the same as weighted fusion, that gave an overall low level of importance to presence of hits.

Table 6 shows, however, that both conditional fusion and weighted fusion outperform no-fusion by about 8% (column Total in Table 6). This demonstrates that *sports-specific* features (e.g., baseball hits) provide useful cues to calibrate the accuracy of *generic* features (e.g. pitch estimation) and thus improve the overall system performance. We believe such features can also be valuable for sports like Golf, which have an impact involved and share the property with baseball of considerable slack time between exciting plays.

Table 6. Performance of the three learning machines. Second row indicates # of segments selected by human. Subsequent rows indicate correct segments identified by algorithm, when asked to pick the same number of segments as human.

Clip	A	B	C	D	E	F	Total
# human	7	7	15	13	13	11	66
Cond fusion	5	5	8	10	12	9	49
Wei. fusion	5	6	8	9	12	9	49
No fusion	5	5	8	7	12	8	45

6.8 Discussion

When we examine the highlights marked by the human subject, there are different exciting levels associated with the highlights. Some of highlights are clearly very exciting and most people will agree that they are exciting segments. Others, however, are subtle: they are exciting to some degree and from a certain perspective. After our experiments, we discussed with the human subject for some of the segments he marked but the algorithm missed, and some segments the algorithm detected but he did not select. He agreed that those segments belong to the "gray area", where even humans may have different answers. On the other hand, our algorithm almost never misses the really exciting segments. Considering the "gray area" effects, 49 out of 66 (75%) accuracy is a very encouraging result. In fact, if we ignore clip C for which the accuracy is the worst (we discuss clip C below), the overall accuracy increases to 41 out of 51 (~80%). We also have the possibility of increasing coverage by asking the algorithm to generate a larger # of segments than that generated by the human. While this would increase number of false positives, this might work well in practice, because given the instant-seek functionality provided by WebTV/TiVo/Replay boxes, it is very easy for end-user to skip incorrectly identified exciting segments.

The algorithm missed quite a few highlights in Clip C. When we carefully traced the reason, we found the pitch tracker was giving wrong estimations. The pitch tracker [22] we used in this paper is already one of the best in speech research community. However, like other pitch trackers, it is designed and tuned to clean speech pitch estimation. Even though it performs well in those situations, it failed when the background noise's level is almost comparable to that of human speech.

Baseball hits detection is still far from satisfactory. This *sports-specific* event is very useful in providing additional cues for highlights detection. If we had more accurate hit detection, the performance of conditional fusion and weighted fusion would have more significantly outperformed that of no-fusion. Even with current hit detection accuracy, conditional fusion and weighted fusion already exhibit clear performance advantage (around 8%) over no-fusion.

7. CONCLUDING REMARKS

In this paper, we have explored solutions to the challenging task of extracting baseball game highlights on set-top devices. Our task is highly constrained by the computing power and noisy audio data. We presented effective techniques to speech detection in noisy environment. We show that energy level plus delta MFCC performs best, and it improves the final performance considerably over alternatives. We discussed the relative strength of three types of learning machines and successfully applied SVM in excited speech classification. To incorporate domain knowledge more flexibly, we developed a *directional* template matching approach to baseball hits detection and achieved encouraging results. Finally, we developed probabilistic framework that intelligently integrates $P(ES)$ and $P(HT)$. The proposed probabilistic framework does not lose useful information at intermediate stages and allows us to solve the problem in a principled way.

We tested various methods over a diverse collection of six baseball games covering 7 hours of game time. The results are very encouraging. When our algorithm is asked to generate the same number of highlight segments as marked by human subject, on average, 75% of these are the same as that marked by the human. When asked to generate 1.5 times the number of segments, the overlap increases to 86%. At the same time, the total duration of the algorithmically generated segments is not significantly more than that of human segments.

Future work plans include real use of the proposed system, for example, to create highlights for the hundreds of games that are broadcast during a baseball season. An implementation on a PC acting as a TiVo/WebTV/Replay box will let us explore how end-users react to the availability of such highlight metadata. We also plan to explore use of visual features to improve the system performance. Given the computing power constraints, visual features will be used only after audio features have filtered clear-cut cases. Use of visual features is also possible when highlights are detected on a server and then communicated to the set-top box over the Internet.

8. ACKNOWLEDGMENTS

The authors want to thank John Platt and Liwei He for their valuable discussions, and thank JJ Cadiz for providing ground truth of the highlight segments in the baseball games.

9. REFERENCES

[1] WebTV, http://www.webtv.com.

[2] TVReplay, http://www.tvreplay.com

[3] Tivo Inc., http://www.tivo.com

[4] Li, F.C., *et al. Browsing Digital Video*. in *ACM CHI*. 2000. Hague, The Netherlands.

[5] Zhang, H., *et al. Automatic Parsing of News Video*. in *IEEE Conference on Multimedia Computing and Systems*. 1994.

[6] *MPEG-7: Context and Objectives (V.7)*. in *ISO/IEC JTC1/SC29/WG11 N2207, MPEG98*. March 1998.

[7] ATVEF, http://www.atvef.com

[8] Rui, Y., T.S. Huang, and S. Mehrotra, *Constructing Table-of-Content for Videos*. Journal of Multimedia Sys., Sept 1999. 7(5): p. 359-368.

[9] Wactlar, H.D., *et al., Lessons Learned from Building a Terabyte Digital Video Library*. IEEE Computer, 1999(Feb): p. 66-73.

[10] McGee, T. and N. Dimitrova. *Parsing TV Program Structures for Identification and Removal of Non-Story Segments*. in *SPIE Conf. on Storage and Retrieval for Image and Video Databases*. 1999. San Jose, CA.

[11] Yeung, M., B.-L. Yeo, and B. Liu, *Extracting Story Units from Long Programs for Video browsing and Navigation*, in *Proc. IEEE Conf. on Multimedia Comput. and Syss.* 1996.

[12] Arons, B. *Pitch-based Emphasis Detection for Segmenting Speech Recordings*. in *International Conference on Spoken Language Processing*. 1994.

[13] He, L., *et al. Auto-Summarization of audio-video presentations*. in *ACM Multimedia*. 1999.

[14] Liu, Z., Y. Wang, and T. Chen, *Audio Feature Extraction and Analysis for Scene Segmentation and Classification*. Journal of VLSI Signal Processing Systems for Signal, Image, and Video Technology, 1998. 20(1/2): p. 61-80.

[15] Srinivasan, S., D. Petkovic, and D. Ponceleon. *Towards Robust Features for Classifying Audio in the CueVideo System*. in *ACM Multimedia*. 1999. Orlando, FL.

[16] Zhang, T. and C.-C.J. Kuo. *Heuristic Approach for Generic Audio Data Segmentation and Annotation*. in *ACM Multimedia*. 1999. Orlando, FL.

[17] Gong, Y., *et al. Automatic Parsing of TV Soccer Programs*. in *IEEE Conf on Multimedia Computing and Systems*. 1995.

[18] Chang, Y.-L., *et al. Integrated Image and Speech Analysis for Content-Based Video Indexing*. in *IEEE Conf. on Multimedia Systems and Computing*. 1996.

[19] Rui, Y. and P. Anandan. *Segmenting Visual Action Units Based on Spatial-Temporal Motion Patterns*. in *IEEE Conf on Computer Vision and Pattern Recgonition*. 2000.

[20] Rabiner, L. and B.-H. Juang, *Fundamentals of Speech Recognition*. 1993.

[21] Dellaert, F., T. Polzin, and A. Waibel. *Recognizing Emotion in Speech*. in *IEEE ICASSP*. 1995.

[22] Droppo, J. and A. Acero. *Maximum A Posterior Pitch Tracking*. in *IEEE ICASSP*. 1999.

[23] Huang, L.-S. and C.-H. Yang. *A Novel Approach to Robust Speech Endpoint Detection in Car Environments (submitted)*. in *IEEE ICASSP*. 2000.

[24] Duda, R.O. and P.E. Hart, *Pattern Classification and Scene Analysis*. : p. 211-249.

[25] Bishop, C.M., *Neural Networks for Pattern Recognition*. 1994, Oxford, UK: Clarendon Press.

[26] Burges, C., *A Tutorial on Support Vector Machines for Pattern Recognition*, U. Fayyad, Editor. 1999, Kluwer Academic Publishers: Boston.

[27] Platt, J.C., *Probabilistic Outputs for Support Vector Machines and Comparisons to Regularized Likelihood Methods*, in *Advances in Large Margin Classifiers*, P.B. Alexander J. Smola, Bernhard Scholkopf and Dale Schuurmans, Editor. 1999.

[28] Ishikawa, Y., R. Subramanya, and C. Faloutsos, *MindReader: Query databases through multiple examples*, in *Proc. of the 24th VLDB Conference*. 1998: New York.

Stochastic Resource Prediction and Admission for Interactive Sessions on Multimedia Servers

Matthias Friedrich[*], Silvia Hollfelder, Karl Aberer
GMD–IPSI Integrated Publication and Information Systems Institute
Dolivostr. 15, 64293 Darmstadt, Germany
hollfelder@gmd.de

ABSTRACT

In highly interactive multimedia applications startup latency is significant, and may negatively impact performance and Quality of Service (QoS). To avoid this, our approach is to admit whole multimedia sessions instead of single media streams. For the prediction of the varying resource demands within a session, which are mainly correlated to user behavior, we model user behavior as Continuous Time Markov Chains (CTMCs). In this paper, we propose a mathematical analysis of the CTMC model. This allows to anticipate possible overload and in turn to plan an admission control policy. As a result, our approach provides better control on the tradeoff between server utilization and QoS. Simulation studies confirm this capability.

Keywords

Admission Control, Interactive Multimedia Applications, Continuous Time Markov Chains

1. INTRODUCTION

Interactive multimedia presentations are fundamental to many advanced application domains, like home entertainment (e.g., news on demand, interactive VoD, action games), e-commerce (e.g., electronic product catalogs), education and training (e.g., computer-based training - CBT), and multimedia production (e.g., video editing). In these applications, users interact frequently with the system for a variety of activities, including VCR-control and request for typically short media chunks, such as video scenes or text documents, and the selection of media combinations (e.g., synchronized audio and video). In the following, we understand a *multimedia session* as a user's successive requests of different media objects to fulfill his information needs for a specific content.

The presentation time of selected media objects is typically very short in these applications. High startup latency in between subsequent presentations are thus not tolerable [12],

---

[*]New address: Mummert und Partner Consulting AG, Kölner Strasse 44, 60327 Frankfurt, Germany

and intra- and intermedia synchronisation requirements must also be considered.

Admission control mechanisms are used to limit the number of clients to be served in order to meet each clients' Quality of Service (QoS) requirements and to achieve high resource utilization. Most classical admission control mechanisms, like those for video-on-demand applications, handle requests for a *single* media stream playout. In this case, the resource requirements are pre-specified in terms of constant rate or rate deviations [23] and calculated by stochastic ([18], [28]) or deterministic approaches ([27], [20]).

For highly interactive applications, the admission of single streams leads to intolerable startup delays *within* a multimedia session at high system load. We claim that admission control for such applications has to be granted at *session level* to reduce startup latency. But a session-oriented admission control schema needs to adequately take into account the *highly varying* resource requirements. These do not only vary due to bursty VBR-media presentations [21] and VCR-control, but also to users' selections of media objects (that can be encoded in different formats) and media object combinations to present.

To analyze the resource consumption of interactive multimedia sessions, we first develop a user behavior model which exploits domain specific knowledge. Second, we utilize the model to stochastically predict resource demands for admission control purpose. In our approach, we do not consider system component specific properties, such as disk bandwidth or buffer space, but we assume that system resources are available in terms of throughput of a multimedia system.

Our model restricts the subset of media that can be requested within a multimedia session. This is realistic, for example, when a user retrieves its media objects via a query. Another example is a preorchestrated SMIL document in which the temporal order and possible interaction points are predetermined [29]. In our approach, we represent an uncertain user behavior by means of a Continuous Time Markov Chain (CTMC) model [25], which enables to stochastically represent the presentation times of media objects and the interaction probabilities. In previous work, we demonstrated how the parameters of a CTMC can be deduced by employing application domain knowledge. For example, for video browsing the user behavior can be heuristically specified from a ranked query result list [2]. In [14], we specified how user behavior in electronic multimedia catalogs can be monitored and applied to data mining technologies. The main difficulty is that heuristic assumptions on how the users behave with regard to their interaction possibilities are required.

Future resource needs are stochastically predicted for a look-ahead time window based on the user behavior model.

The time window can be analyzed at various granularity levels. This prediction is then employed for admission control, when the server tests whether an overload situation occurs due to the admission of a pending client.

The level of granularity depends on various factors, like the ratio of total system resources and clients' resource requirements, the distribution of the resource requirements within a session, and the stability of the deviation patterns. For a large number of clients with uniform behavior, a simple method based on average resource consumption may suffice. Such a method is proposed in [2], where equilibrium analysis for the video browsing scenario is employed. However, equilibrium analysis can only be applied to specifically structured, so-called closed, CTMCs and is therefore more useful for long-lasting sessions.

For fewer clients with large deviations in consumptions, a more fine-grained analysis can be beneficial or even crucial. In this paper, we focus on a fine-grained admission control strategy. We perform a transient analysis on the CTMC that is much more precise than the equilibrium analysis, and is applicable to all types of CTMCs. As an additional advantage, the method is also flexibly adaptable to different application requirements by adjusting the time granularity in which the analysis is performed. Large timesteps smooth out the data rates and are adequate in scenarios with more uniform data rate demands, while decreasing the timesteps "zooms into" the temporal structure of the multimedia presentations, thus allowing more detailed predictions on resource consumption. In this paper, we focus on the mathematical analysis of the model.

The further content of the paper is structured as follows: In Section 2, we give a survey of the related work. We present our approach in detail, in Section 3, and show simulation results obtained by using our admission control strategy in Section 4. In Section 5, we conclude the paper with a result summary and some open issues.

2. RELATED WORK

Typically, admission control mechanism are classified by the service guarantees (i.e., predictive, stochastic, deterministic), and the system resources that are taken into account (e.g., buffer space, disk I/O, etc.). In the following, we take another focus and classify related work by the general idea behind. We evaluate approaches that support VCR-interactions or multimedia sessions with frequent changes in resource demands. However, there is no related work that covers both, interactivity and media object compositions, appropriately.

VCR-support for single streams can be given by a *priori reservation* of separate server bandwidth ([9], [3]), but leads to low system utilization or low QoS in case of highly varying resource demands. The *smoothing* of data rates for VCR-interactions aims to achieve a relatively constant workload ([24], [6], [5]). This proceeding is restricted to VCR-interactions, since it would lead to unacceptable quality degradations of media with originally high resource demands. A straightforward way for VCR-support is to *re-admit by priorities at interaction points* to reduce startup latency in case of high system load ([22], [8]). The problem here is that high variations in consumption rates due to media switches are neglected. *Server caching* for VCR-interactions ([30], [3]) needs applications with high probabilities for the access of same media data, such as news on demand.

Re-admission at media switches is proposed in [12] by

adressing interactive hypermedia sessions consisting of discrete and continuous data requests. This works well for low workload (e.g., 50 percent), but startup latency gets intolerable for higher workload.

From **pre-orchestrated presentations** knowledge on the exact resource demands can be employed when the users are not allowed to control the presentation process interactively. This information can be used for admission of whole multimedia sessions, as realized in the following. Prefetching and replication heuristics in multidisk environments are proposed in [10]. The goal is to achieve low latency for few additional memory requirements, assuming that disk bandwidth is the scarce system resource. This idea is not applicable for our purpose, since interactions are not allowed at all. The goal in [31] is to determine a starting point for a session so that no bottlenecks occur. The basic reservation model does not consider user interactions, but following extensions for *interactions* are suggested: (1) the specification of a minimum upper bound which is not efficient for our purpose and (2) re-admission at media switches as discussed previously. Another schema for the admission of composite multimedia presentations is proposed in [4]. The servers' buffer space is the critical, limited system resource. They briefly propose two extensions for interactive applications, namely re-admission at media switches and a priory reservation.

Observation-based admission. The general idea here is to assume that the past behavior is an indicator for the future. This approach can be employed for single media streams [26] as well as for whole multimedia sessions ([16], [13]). It is applicable for a large number of parallel sessions with even access patterns, but problems occur at low capacity with bursty or unpredictable client behavior.

A more detailed analysis of related work can be found in [11].

3. APPROACH

In the following we describe a stochastic admission control strategy for multimedia presentation scenarios. Our approach, called *Admission Control Based On Stochastic Prediction (ACSP)*, rests upon the prediction of the overload probability at the server resulting from the admission of an additional client. The precision of the prediction in terms of fine-granular time-intervals can be flexibly adapted by choosing the length of the *rounds* which will be statistically analyzed one by one. In this section, we describe the user behavior model representing an interactive session, the admission control system architecture, and the statistical approach to resource usage prediction.

3.1 Modelling of interactive client sessions

For modelling of user behaviors, we assign to each client an application class c ($c = 0, ..., C - 1$) which is further differentiated into a finite number of states i ($i = 0, ..., S_c - 1$) representing the different presentation modes. Each client is allowed to switch between the states of his class. At each point in time, a client is assigned to a unique current state. In our context a transition from one state to another is interpreted as an interaction of the client leading to another presentation mode.

Each class c models a set of clients with similar behaviors. This means that the *duration times in the states*, the *data rates requested on average* and the *transition behavior* of the clients belonging to class c are either identical or similar. The model can be flexibly used for different desired levels of accuracy, by combining subsets of clients according to different degrees of similarity in their behaviors.

For illustration purposes, we give the concrete example for a preorchestrated interactive multimedia application, where the temporal and spatial relationships of components within a session are modelled. In Figure 1 the nodes relate to presentation of media objects and the arrows represent the possible user interactions, i.e., a user selects another media object for presentation. Since our main problems to be solved in this paper are user interactions in general, we will neglect VCR-modelling, which is only one specific case. However, VCR-interactions can be simply added to each playback state by additional VCR-mode states and the corresponding transition probabilites to these states.

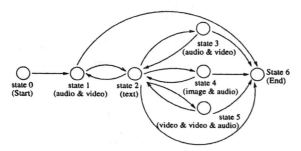

Figure 1: Example of a Preorch. MM Document

3.2 State Transitions and Data Rates

The transitions between the states of a client class are modelled as a stochastic process $X^c(t)$. $X^c(t)$ indicates the state of a client of class c at time t. For statistically modelling the state transition system, we use the Continuous Time Markov Chain model (CTMC). Such a process is stationary, time-continuous, and has the Markovian Property, i.e., it is memoryless. In scenarios with high user interaction probabilities, the CTMC assumption is realistic. For our model, the Markovian property means the following: If a client of class c leaves state i, the probability of his moving to state j is always p_{ij}^c, no matter how he attained state i. For the p_{ij}^c, which will subsequently be called *time-independent transition probabilities*, the following equations hold:

$$\sum_{j=0, j \neq i}^{S_c - 1} p_{ij}^c = 1. \qquad (1)$$

If a client moves to state j of class c, he stays there for a time interval being exponentially distributed with parameter v_j^c, independent of how he reached state j. We will subsequently call the v_j^c *leaving rates*.

The implementation of the ACSP requires the identification of the classes and their corresponding states, as well as the determination of the parameters p_{ij}^c and v_j^c. The latter could possibly be carried out by means of observation. In the subsequent part of this paper, we therefore assume that the time-independent transition probabilities as well as the leaving rates are known.

We distinguish two different types of states the client may reside in, namely *active states*, in which they request data at a specific data rate, and *idle states*, in which they are inactive. In active states, the requested average data amount per round for a client of class c is described by the random variable

N_{ci}. We assume N_{ci} to be rectangularly distributed, with minimum u_{ci} and maximum v_{ci}.

We consider the rectangular distribution for modelling the active states to be appropriate as it describes a corridor which the requested data amounts fall into. The width of this corridor $v_{ci} - u_{ci}$ captures the variability of the data rates requested by the clients. In the idle states, the clients request with probability 1 no data.

3.3 Implementation of the admission control module

Within the admission control module, we predict the probability of a situation in which the given server resources are smaller than the amount of resources requested by the clients. Such a situation is called *overload*. Our prediction is performed for a look-ahead time window W starting at time t_{start}. We further divide W into rounds which all have the same length l_r (see Figure 2). The statistical analysis in the prediction is performed for each round separately.

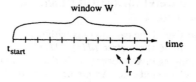

Figure 2: Time Window for Resource Prediction

In this analysis, the random variable T_s^t is the time the server needs in the round starting at time $t_{start} + t$ for serving the data requested by all clients to be served on average. Then an overload is the probability that T_s^t is greater than l_r. Thus, for each of the rounds in W, we calculate an upper bound $ub(t)$ for the probability that, within this round, an overload situation occurs. For $ub(t)$ the following holds:

$$ub(t) \geq P(T_s^t > l_r) \qquad (2)$$

The calculation of $ub(t)$ is the essential part in the ACSP. It is performed in two separate steps (see Figure 3). First, in a prognosis module 1, a matrix $M(t)$ is calculated which describes the predicted number of clients in each state of each class for the round beginning at time t including the client to be admitted. Second, in a prognosis module 2, $M(t)$ is used to calculate $ub(t)$. Note that this analysis can be precomputed and thereby computational overhead at admission time is reduced.

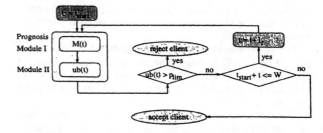

Figure 3: Flow Diagram of the ACSP Mechanism

Figure 3 shows how the admission control within the ACSP proceeds on the arrival of a new client. At the beginning of the ACSP process the time parameter t is set to the value t_{start}, i.e., to the beginning of the first round within W. Next, within the prognosis modules 1 and 2, the upper bound $ub(t)$ for that first round is calculated. This value is then compared with a value p_{lim} representing the maximal overload probability the system is willing to accept without rejecting the client. The value p_{lim} is a configuration parameter showing how optimistic or pessimistic the admission control proceeds. High values for p_{lim} lead to a larger number of admitted clients and therefore to more frequent overload situations. If $ub(t)$ is greater than p_{lim}, the client is rejected, otherwise the time parameter t is increased by l_r, the matrix $M(t + l_r)$ and the upper bound $ub(t + l_r)$ are calculated, and the algorithm proceeds as described before. If, for none of the rounds within W, the calculated upper bound of the overload probability is greater than p_{lim}, the new client is accepted to service. Otherwise, if $ub(t)$ exceeds p_{lim} for a single round, the client is rejected.

3.4 The determination of $M(t)$ in prognosis module 1

The objective of the calculations within prognosis module 1 is to determine the matrix $M(t)$. $M(t)$ is a $C \times S$ matrix with non-negative integers. S is the maximum number of states a class contains. An element m_{ci}^t of $M(t)$ represents the estimated number of clients being in state i of class c at the round beginning at time t. For the calculation of $M(t_{start})$, all admitted clients as well as the actual client requesting for admission are taken into account. We assume for the calculation that none of the clients will leave the system during the time window W, i.e., the following equations must hold:

$$\sum_{i=0}^{S_c-1} m_{ci}^t = \sum_{i=0}^{S_c-1} m_{ci}^{t_{start}} \qquad (3)$$

If, contrary to our assumption, one client stops requesting the server during the time window W, the predictions do not become invalid but only more conservative.

To calculate $M(t)$, we first determine the *time-dependent transition probabilities* $p_{ij}^c(t)$.

$$p_{ij}^c(t) = P(X^c(t) = j | X^c(0) = i) \qquad (4)$$

As the transition process $X^c(t)$ is stationary and has the Markovian Property, the $p_{ij}^c(t)$ can be interpreted as the probability that the client moves from state i to state j within t time units.

The $p_{ij}^c(t)$ must be clearly distinguished from the known p_{ij}^c. Whereas p_{ij}^c indicates the probability that a client of class c will eventually move from state i to state j, $p_{ij}^c(t)$ indicates the probability that a client of class c will move from state i to state j within time t.

The $p_{ij}^c(t)$ can be calculated via the *uniformization method* [25] using the given p_{ij}^c as well as the given leaving rates v_j^c as follows:

$$\overline{p}_{ij}^c = \begin{cases} \frac{v_i^c}{v^c} p_{ij}^c, & j \neq i \\ 1 - \frac{v_i^c}{v^c}, & j = i \end{cases} \qquad (5)$$

$$p_{ij}^c(t) = \sum_{k=0}^{\infty} e^{-vt} \frac{(vt)^k}{k!} \overline{p}_{ij}^{c(k)} \qquad (6)$$

$$\text{with } \overline{p}_{ij}^{c(k)} = \sum_{s=0}^{S_c-1} \overline{p}_{is}^{c(k-1)} \overline{p}_{sj}^c$$

$$\overline{p}_{ss}^{c(0)} = 1$$

$$\overline{p}_{sj}^{c(0)} = 0 \text{ for } j \neq s$$

$$v^c \geq v_i^c \, \forall \, i = 0, \cdots S_c - 1$$

Next, we use the $p_{ij}^c(t)$ to calculate the matrix $\overline{M}(t)$ giving the expected values for the numbers of clients in the individual states of the different classes.

$$\overline{M}(t) = \begin{pmatrix} \overline{m}_{0,0}^t & \cdots & \overline{m}_{0,S-1}^t \\ \cdots & \cdots & \cdots \\ \overline{m}_{C-1,0}^t & \cdots & \overline{m}_{C-1,S-1}^t \end{pmatrix} \qquad (7)$$

$$\text{with } \overline{m}_{ci}^t = \sum_{k=0}^{S_c-1} m_{ck}^{t_{start}} p_{ki}^c(t)$$

$$m_{ci}^{t_{start}} \in M(t_{start})$$

$$t \in \{0, l_r, 2l_r, \cdots, (W-1)l_r\}$$

Finally, we obtain $M(t)$ by rounding the values of the elements of $\overline{M}(t)$.

3.5 The determination of $ub(t)$ in prognosis module 2

Based on the matrix $M(t)$, we can calculate the upper bound $ub(t)$ according to equation (2). To achieve this, we first introduce a random variable N^t representing the amount of data the admitted clients and the new client request on average in the round starting at time $t_{start} + t$. We further assume that the following relationship between N^t and T_s^t holds:

$$T_s^t = \frac{N^t}{capacity} \qquad (8)$$

Equation (8) expresses a linear relationship between the amount of data the server has to transmit to the client and the time it takes the server to execute this transmission. The parameter *capacity* is a constant that gives the data amount the server is able to deliver in a single round[1]. To calculate $ub(t)$, we use the *Chernov Inequality* [15] which has the form

$$P(Y \geq x) \leq \inf_{\theta \geq 0} e^{(-\theta x)} G_Y(\theta) \qquad (9)$$

The Chernov inequality has been proven to be a good upper bound for many practical problems, such as in [19]. In this inequality, $G_Y(\theta)$ is the so-called *Moment Generating Function* of Y which is defined as [15]:

$$G_Y(\theta) = \int_{-\infty}^{\infty} e^{\theta y} f_Y(y) dy \qquad (10)$$

with $f_Y(y)$: density function of random variable Y

---

[1]We abstract from resource specific parameters, like buffer size, disk seek and transfer time, and rotational latency.

Between the Moment Generating Function G_Y and the so-called *Laplace Transformation* $F_Y^*(\theta)$ the following relationship exists [15]:

$$G_Y(\theta) = F_Y^*(-\theta) \qquad (11)$$

Inequality (9) applied to equation (2), leads to

$$ub(t) = \inf_{\theta \geq 0}(e^{-\theta l_r} G_{T_s^t}(\theta)) \qquad (12)$$

$$with \quad inf_{\theta \geq 0}(e^{-\theta l_r} G_{T_s^t}(\theta)) \leq P(T_s^t > l_r)$$

Thus, to find $ub(t)$, we first have to solve the problem of how to determine $G_{T_s^t}(\theta)$, i.e., the Moment Generating Function of T_s^t. To achieve this, we proceed as follows: First, we express T_s^t in terms of known random variables. Then, we use this expression to calculate the Laplace Transformation of T_s^t and derive from this Laplace Transformation the desired Moment Generating Function using equation (11).

For the first step, we observe that the random variable N^t for the total data consumption can be computed from the matrix $M(t)$ and the known random variables N_{ci} for the amount of data a client on average requests in one round if he is in state i of class c, as follows:

$$N^t = \sum_{c=0}^{C-1} \sum_{i=0}^{S_c-1} \sum_{k=1}^{m_{ci}^t} N_{ci} \qquad (13)$$

Thus, according to equation (8) T_s^t can be rewritten as follows:

$$T_s^t = \frac{1}{capacity} \sum_{c=0}^{C-1} \sum_{i=0}^{S_c-1} \sum_{k=1}^{m_{ci}^t} N_{ci} \qquad (14)$$

Next, we define a random variable M_{ci} as follows:

$$M_{ci} = \frac{1}{capacity} N_{ci} \qquad (15)$$

We have to distinguish between the idle and the active states of the clients. Within the latter, M_{ci} is rectangularly distributed, and the parameters u_{ci}' and v_{ci}' corresponding to the minimum and maximum of the rectangular distribution of M_{ci} as well as the distribution function can directly be deduced from those of N_{ci}:

$$P(M_{ci} \leq x) = \begin{cases} 0, & -\infty < x \leq u_{ci}' \\ \frac{x - u_{ci}'}{v_{ci}' - u_{ci}'} & u_{ci}' < x < v_{ci}' \\ 1, & v_{ci}' \leq x \end{cases} \qquad (16)$$

$$with \ u_{cs}' = \frac{u_{cs}}{capacity}, \ v_{cs}' = \frac{v_{cs}}{capacity}$$

For the idle states, the random variable M_{ci} has the value zero. Therefore, we can rewrite T_s^t in terms of known random variables as follows:

$$T_s^t = \sum_{c=0}^{C-1} \sum_{i=0}^{S_c-1} \sum_{k=1}^{m_{ci}^t} M_{ci} \qquad (17)$$

This is the form of T_s^t that we can use to calculate the Laplace Transformation of T_s^t. This calculation is based on the following observations [15]: The density function of a sum of random variables is equal to the convolution of the density functions of the individual terms of the sum. The Laplace Transformation of a convolution is equal to the product of the Laplace Transformations of the individual terms of the convolution, where the convolution is defined as [15]:

$$conv(y) = \int_{-\infty}^{\infty} f_{X_1}(y - x_2 - \cdots - x_n) * \cdots$$
$$\cdots * f_{X_2}(x_2) * \cdots * f_{X_n}(x_n) dx_n$$
$$\text{with } f_{X_i} : \text{density function of term } i$$
$$n : \text{number of terms}$$

Using equation (17), we can therefore calculate the Laplace Transformation $F_{T_s^t}^*(\theta)$ of T_s^t as follows:

$$F_{T_s^t}^*(\theta) =$$
$$F_{M_{0,0}}^*(\theta)^{m_{0,0}^t} \quad \times \cdots \times \quad F_{M_{0,S_c-1}}^*(\theta)^{m_{0,S_c-1}^t}$$
$$\times \cdots \times$$
$$F_{M_{C-1,0}}^*(\theta)^{m_{C-1,0}^t} \quad \times \cdots \times \quad F_{M_{C-1,S_c-1}}^*(\theta)^{m_{C-1,S_c-1}^t}$$
$$(18)$$

In this context $F_{M_{c,i}}^*(\theta)$ represents the Laplace Transformation of the random variable M_{ci}. As the exponents of the individual factors are the elements of the known matrix $M(t)$, the search for $F_{T_s^t}^*(\theta)$ can be reduced to determining $F_{M_{c,i}}^*(\theta)$, which has the following form:

$$F_{M_{c,i}}^*(\theta) = \frac{e^{-\theta u_{ci}'} - e^{-\theta v_{ci}'}}{\theta(v_{ci}' - u_{ci}')} \quad \text{(active states)}$$
$$F_{M_{c,i}}^*(\theta) = 1 \quad \text{(idle states)} \qquad (19)$$

Having determined $F_{T_s^t}^*(\theta)$ the Moment Generating Function $G_{T_s^t}(\theta)$ can be calculated using equation (11). Finally, we compute $ub(t)$ of equation (12) by a polynomial approximation.

4. SIMULATIONS

4.1 Simulation scenarios

For evaluation purposes, we model preorchestrated interactive multimedia presentations with highly varying resource requirements. As components of the presentations, we use three different media formats, namely the video formats MPEG-1 and MPEG-2 and the audio format MP3 [1]. We assume that an MPEG-1 video has a mean data rate of 1.5 Mbit/s. For an MPEG-2 encoded video, we assume a mean data rate of 4.5 Mbit/s. Both video formats are considered to be hardware encoded with a fixed IPB-pattern. Therefore, we assume the rates within a video stream to be rectangularly distributed with maximum or minimum values 20 per cent above or below the average data rate. We assume audio streams with CD-quality to be MPEG-1 encoded. For MP3 encoded audio streams, we use a data rate of 130 Kbit/s. Since text documents, images and VRML scenes require a relatively low amount of data in comparison with time-dependent media like audio and video, we ignore them within our simulations. The resource requirements of the different media formats are summarized in Table 1.

In our simulations, we consider three different application classes. The first one consists of 9 different states (see Figure 4). The values next to the arrows represent the time-

Media Format	Mean Data Rate	Distribution	Rate Deviation
MPEG-1	1.5 Mbit/s	rectangular	0.2
MPEG-2	4.5 Mbit/s	rectangular	0.2
MP3	130 Kbit/s	rectangular	0.2

Table 1: Resource Requirements

independent transition probabilities. Table 2 includes the media combinations, the mean data rates and the mean holding times of the users, within the single states of class 1.

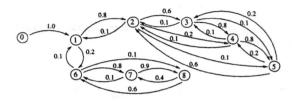

Figure 4: Class 1: States and Transitions

The second class represents a multimedia presentation consisting of 4 different states with extremely high variations in the requested data rates. The mean data rate in state 2, for example, is more than 80 times larger than that of states 0 and 3. The simulation parameters within the states of class 2 are summarized in Table 3. The time-independent transition probabilities are shown in Figure 5.

Finally the simulation parameters of the third class are summarized in Figure 5 and in Table 4, respectively. In this class which consists of 4 different states, the variations in the requested data rates are not as high as those in class 2. By default, an equal combination of these three classes is employed for simulation purpose.

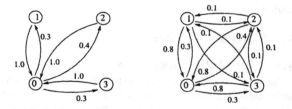

Figure 5: Class 2 (left side) and Class 3 (right side)

4.2 Experimental testbed

In our simulations, the time interval between the arrival of two successive clients in a given class is exponentially distributed. For each class, the parameter of the distribution is 0.05, i.e., every 20 seconds a new client asks for admission, on average. The presentation times of the clients are also exponentially distributed with a parameter of 0.003, i.e., the average presentation time is 300 seconds for each class. The server resources are set to 100000, that means, the server is able to deliver 100 Mbit/s. In all experiments, 3000 rounds are simulated. The single requests of the clients are scheduled according to the strategy Earliest Deadline First (EDF). Table 5 summarizes the default simulation parameters.

Parameter	Value
server resources	100000
number of rounds	3000
duration of a round	1 time unit
average arrival of new clients	20 time units
distribution of clients arrival	exponential
average duration of a presentation	300 time units
distribution of presentation duration	exponential

Table 5: Default Simulation Parameters

4.3 Experimental results

In this section, we present the simulation results we obtained by using the ACSP. We measure the server utilization and the ratio of requests served within their deadlines (*in-time-ratio*). Keeping the deadlines corresponds to *all* temporal QoS parameters, i.e., startup delays as well as intra- and intermedia constraints. This means that a startup request has the same priority as consecutive requests. For the simulations, we do not allow spatial QoS adaptations. Another goal of the simulations is to investigate if the ACSP leads to a stable system behavior, i.e., if the proposed model is able to recover from underload or overload periods. For the implementation of our simulations, we used the CSIM tool [17].

4.3.1 Experiment 1

First, we study the system behavior under variations of the time window W and the parameter p_{lim} (see Figures 6 and 7). For time windows of length 10, 20, 30 and 40 the system behavior becomes instable for small values of p_{lim}, i.e., the growing number of client requests cannot be handled by the server.

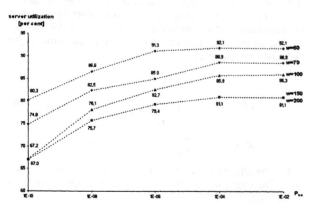

Figure 6: Server Util. for Variations of W and p_{lim}

For $W \geq 50$ the system becomes stable and it can be seen that, for a constant p_{lim}, a larger time window leads to a lower server utilization and to a better QoS level. This result can be explained as follows: For growing time windows W

State	Media Combinations	Mean Data Rates	Mean Holding Times
0	1 MP3 and 2 MPEG-1	3.13 Mbit/s	40
1	1 MP3	130 Kbit/s	30
2	1 MP3 and 1 MPEG-1	1.63 Mbit/s	20
3	1 MP3 and 2 MPEG-1	3.13 Mbit/s	100
4	2 MPEG-1	3 Mbit/s	80
5	1 MP3 and 1 MPEG-2	4.630 Mbit/s	100
6	1 MP3	130 Kbit/s	20
7	1 MP3	130 Kbit/s	100
8	1 MPEG-1	1.5 Mbit/s	100

Table 2: Class 1

State	Media Combinations	Mean Data Rates	Mean Holding Times
0	1 MP3	130 Kbit/s	30
1	1 MP3 and 1 MPEG-1	1.63 Mbit/s	200
2	1 MP3 and 2 MPEG-2 and 1 MPEG-1	10.63 Mbit/s	300
3	1 MP3	130 Kbit/s	100

Table 3: Class 2

the ACSP estimates the overload probability for a larger number of rounds as our algorithm looks further into the future. Thus, fewer clients are admitted to the service, the server utilization decreases and the rate of requests served within their deadlines increases.

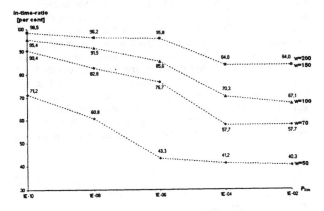

Figure 7: In-time-ratio for Variations of W and p_{lim}

Likewise we observe that, for a constant W, a higher value for p_{lim} leads to a lower server utilization and to a better QoS level. This correlation can be explained as follows: A low value for p_{lim} means that, for each round within the time window W, the estimated overload probability will be compared with this low value. In this case, it is more likely that the estimated overload probability exceeds p_{lim} and thus a newly arriving client is rejected than for a large p_{lim}. Therefore, a smaller value for p_{lim} means that less clients are admitted to the service, the server utilization decreases and the rate of requests served within their deadlines increases.

Furthermore, it can be seen that for $W = 200$ and $W = 150$ the simulations lead to the same values for the regarded variables, i.e., our application scenario converges into an equilibrium state for the given parameter values.

For $p_{lim} = 10^{-8}$ ($10^{-8} = 1E - 08$) and $W = 150$, more than 96 per cent of all requests are served within their deadlines and the average utilization has an acceptable value

about 75 per cent. Thus, this parameter combination is a good choice in the given scenario. If an even higher in-time-ratio is needed $p_{lim} = 10^{-10}$ can be employed leading to about 98.5 per cent of requests served within their deadlines. However, this would most probably lead to an 8 per cent reduction of the server utilization. Accordingly, if the in-time-ratio is of low importance, lower values for W and/or higher values for p_{lim} could also be preferred.

4.3.2 Experiment 2

Now, we evaluate how the system reacts if the data rate variations in the simulations and the data rate variation assumed in the ACSP model differ. We separately consider the situations in which the maximum respectively minimum values are between 20 and 100 per cent above respectively below the average data rate. That means that we study higher data rate variations in the states of all classes than assumed in the ACSP.

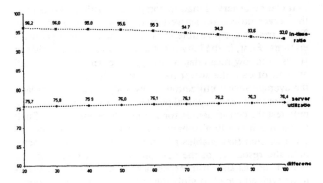

Figure 8: Behavior for differing Consumpt. Rates

The corresponding results for $p_{lim} = 10^{-8}$ and $W = 150$ in Figure 8 show that a higher variation leads to nearly the same result with respect to the server utilization and to a decreased value for the observed QoS level. These correlations can be explained as follows: A high variation in the requested data rate does not affect the average value in the long run. Therefore, the average server utilization does not vary, ei-

State	Media Combinations	Mean Data Rates	Mean Holding Times
0	1 MP3	130 Kbit/s	30
1	1 MP3 and 1 MPEG-1	1.63 Mbit/s	200
2	1 MP3 and 1 MPEG-1	1.63 Mbit/s	300
3	1 MP3 and 1 MPEG-1	1.63 Mbit/s	100

Table 4: Class 3

ther. On the other hand, a high variation in the requested data rate leads to a high amount of resource requests within single rounds. These, in turn, lead to violations of deadlines not only within the rounds they occur but also in subsequent rounds. Thus, the in-time-ratio decreases. Nevertheless, as the results show, the system behavior remains stable since the number of delayed requests are still strongly limited.

4.3.3 Experiment 3

Now, we assume that only clients of the second class are asking for admission, i.e., the server has to deal with excessively high variations in the requested data rates. The simulation results for $W = 100$, $W = 150$ and different values for p_{lim} are summarized in Figures 9 and 10.

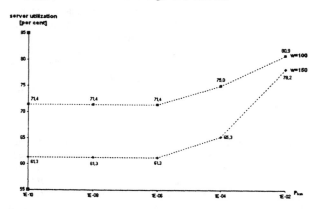

Figure 9: Server Utilization (only Class 2)

It can be observed that, in comparison with experiment 1, the server utilization as well as the in-time-ratio decrease. These results are plausible because of the following considerations: First, in the long run, the clients of class 2 reside in states with low mean data rates. In these periods the overall amount of data the server has to deliver is very low. Thus, the average server utilization is low, too, since our approach does not look for an optimal point in time to admit a client but only test the consequences for an immediate admission. Such an approach would also have drawbacks, such as to find another session that enables a better system utilization exactly until the resources of the new one will be needed. On the other hand, as shown in experiment 2, high data rate variations typically lead to violations of deadlines in subsequent rounds. As a result, the in-time-ratio decreases.

4.3.4 Experiment 4

Next, we evaluate how the system reacts with respect to changes of the parameter l_r (see Figure 11). In these simulations, p_{lim} was set to 10^{-8}, and we regarded a future time interval with a length of 150 time units. It can be seen that the average server utilization becomes better with growing values for l_r whereas the in-time-ratio decreases dramatically.

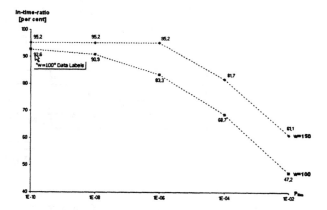

Figure 10: In-time-Ratio (only Class 2)

For $l_r = 10$, only about two third of all requests could be served in time. For $l_r \geq 11$, the system even became instable, i.e., the server could not deal with the growing resource claims. These results show that the granularity of the overload prediction is a critical parameter. Large values for l_r mean that the ACSP-predictions are based on the average client behavior and that peaks in the resource demands of the clients are not taken into account. Thus, large values for l_r correspond with a naive admission control mechanism regarding only the average behavior of the clients. This experiment clearly indicates that a less precise prediction in terms of the round length is not suitable for scenarios with high data rate variations.

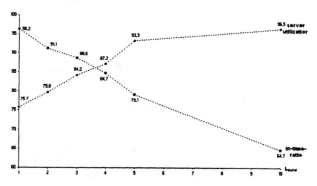

Figure 11: Behavior for Changes of l_r

4.3.5 Experiment 5

Finally, we study the system behavior under the assumption that the real data rate distributions are normal, exponential, erlang, and hyperexponential (Hyper). The system behaves well for normally distributed client requests. Thus, by employing the Central Limit theorem [7], even bursty client behavior is covered by our model. As described in Section 3, the ACSP assumes that the amounts of data the clients request are rectangularly distributed. The simulation results shown in Table 6 are very similar to those obtained in experiment 1 and show that our model is very robust against differences between the assumed and the real data rate distributions.

We summarize our simulation results as follows: For applications with highly varying resource requirements a precise prediction in terms of studying fine-grained rounds is required. Instable system behavior could only be observed for very small values for the parameter W and for large values of l_r. In the given environment, the time window should be set to a value of $W = 150$ and the parameter l_r should be set to a value of 1 to obtain a good system behavior. With p_{lim} set to a value of 10^{-8}, we achieved a very good QoS and a high server utilization, in most cases. We showed that the ACSP mechanism is even applicable if the real requested data rate differs from the assumed one in terms of mean variation and generating distribution function. In scenarios with unexpected behavior, the parameter p_{lim} should be set lower than in scenarios with more predictable behavior.

5. CONCLUSION AND FUTURE WORK

In this paper, we presented an admission control scheme that targets at the highly varying resource requirements of multimedia sessions. With our session-based approach, we are able to achieve continuous presentations and to reduce startup latency. This is of special importance for interactive applications with frequent media switches.

We model application classes using Continous Time Markov Chains (CTMCs) and stochastically predict the resource usage within a future time interval. Simulation results show that a high server utilization as well as a good Quality of Service are achieved.

Future work will be focused on the following aspects: First, we will consider specific user profiles. More precise information on user behavior, like their preferences for a specific content, enable a more precise parameter setting within the ACSP. Another aspect is the integration of discrete data requests (mixed workload). Especially VRML scenes seem to be interesting in our context since, on the one hand, no 'real' time-constraints are given, but, on the other hand, in case of high system load, the delivery of such discrete data may be very slow. This leads to high delays especially at the start of a VRML presentation because at this point in time a high amount of data is typically requested. A further topic is to use other mathematical theories as a basis for our model. In this context new stochastical bounds and distributions will be studied.

6. ACKNOWLEDGEMENTS

We would like to thank Aris Ouksel for his many helpful comments.

7. REFERENCES

[1] Audio compression MP3. http://www.iocon.com/das/.

[2] K. Aberer and S. Hollfelder. Resource prediction and admission control for interactive video browsing scenarios using application semantics. In *Proc. of Int. Conf. on Data Semantics - 8 (DS-8), Semantic Issues in Multimedia Systems, IFIP TC-2 Working Conference*, pages 27–46, January 1999.

[3] E. L. Abram-Profeta and K. G. Shin. Providing unrestricted VCR functions in multicast video-on-demand servers. In *Proc. of Int. Conf. on Multimedia Computing and Systems (ICMCS)*, pages 66–75, June/July 1998.

[4] N. H. Balkir and G. Ozsoyoglu. Delivering presentations from multimedia servers. *VLDB Journal. Special Issue on Multimedia Databases*, pages 297–307, December 1998.

[5] H.-J. Chen, A. Krishnamurthy, T. D. C. Little, and D. Venkatesch. A scalable video-on-demand service for the provision of VCR-like functions. In *Proc. of Int. Conference on Multimedia Computing and Systems*, pages 65–72, May 1995.

[6] M.-S. Chen, D. D. Kandlur, and P. S. Yu. Support for fully interactive playout in a disk-array-based video server. In *ACM Multimedia*, 1994.

[7] H. Cramer and M. Leadbetter. *Stationary and Related Stochastic Processes*. Wiley, 1967.

[8] J. K. Dey, S. Subhabrata, J. F. Kurose, and J. D. Salehi. Playback restart in interactive streaming video applications. In *IEEE Conference on Multimedia Computing and Systems*, pages 458–465, June 1997.

[9] J. K. Dey-Sircar, J. D. Salehi, J. F. Kurose, and D. Towsley. Providing VCR capabilities in large-scale video servers. In *ACM Multimedia*, pages 25–32, 1994.

[10] M. L. Escobar-Molano and S. Ghandeharizadeh. On coordinated diplay of structured video. *IEEE Multimedia Systems*, 4(3):62–75, July-September 1997.

[11] M. Friedrich, S. Hollfelder, and K. Aberer. Stochastic resource prediction and admission for interactive sessions on multimedia servers. GMD Technical Report 50, GMD, Sankt Augustin, Germany, March 1999.

[12] C. Gopal and J. F. Buford. Delivering hypermedia sessions from a continuous media server. In S. M. Chung, editor, *Multimedia Information Storage and Management*, pages pp. 209–235. Kluwer Academic Publishers, 1996.

[13] S. Hollfelder and K. Aberer. An admission control framework for applications with variable consumption rates in client-pull architectures. In A. D. Sushil Jajodia, M. Tamer Özsu, editor, *Proc. of Int. Workshop on Multimedia Information Systems MIS'98*, pages 82–97. Springer LNCS, September 1998.

[14] S. Hollfelder, V. Oria, and T. Özsu. Mining user behavior for resource prediction in interactive electronic malls. In *Int. Conference on Multimedia and Expo (ICME)*, July/August 2000. will appear.

[15] L. Kleinrock. *Queueing Systems, Volume I: Theory*. Wiley, 1975.

[16] C. Ludmila and P. Phaal. Session based admission control: A mechanism for improving the performance of an overloaded web server. HP Labs Technical Reports, External HPL-98-119, 980612, Hewlett Packard, June 1998.

[17] Mesquite Software, Inc. *CSIM17 Users' Guide*, 1994.

[18] G. Nerjes, P. Muth, and G. Weikum. Stochastic performance guarantees for mixed workloads in a multimedia information system. In *Proc. of the IEEE International Workshop on Research Issues in Data Engineering (RIDE'97)*, April 1997.

[19] G. Nerjes, P. Muth, and G. Weikum. Stochastic service guarantees for continuous data on multi-zone disks. In

Distr.	Rect.	Exp.	Normal	Hyper	Erlang
serv. utiliz.	75.7%	78.9%	78.0%	76.2%	76.4%
in-time-ratio	96.2%	91.4%	93.4%	94.9%	95.6%

Table 6: Results for diff. Data Rate Distributions

Proc. of the Symposium on Principles of Database Systems (PODS'97), pages 154–160, May 1997.

[20] B. Özden, R. Rastogi, A. Silberschatz, and P. S. Narayanan. The Fellini multimedia storage server. In S. M. Chung, editor, *Multimedia Information Storage and Management*. Kluwer Academic Publishers, 1996.

[21] T. Plagemann and V. Goebel. Analysis of quality-of-service in a wide-area interactive distance learning system. *Telecommunication Systems Journal*, 11(1-2):139–160, 1999.

[22] N. Reddy. Improving latency in interactive video server. In *Proc. of SPIE Multimedia Computing and Networking Conference*, pages 108–112, February 1997.

[23] S. S. Roa, H. M. Vin, and A. Tarafdar. Comparative evaluation of server-push and client-pull architectures for multimedia servers. In *Proc. of Nossdav 96*, pages 45–48, 1996.

[24] P. J. Shenoy and H. M. Vin. Efficient support for interactive operation in multi-resolution video servers. *Multimedia Systems*, 7(3):241–253, July 1999.

[25] H. C. Tijms. *Stochastic Models. An Algorithmic Approach*. Wiley series in probability and mathematical statistics. Wiley, 1994.

[26] H. M. Vin, A. Goyal, A. Goyal, and P. Goyal. An observation-based admission control algorithm for multimedia servers. In *Proc. of the First IEEE International Conference on Multimedia Computing and Systems (ICMCS)*, pages 234–243, May 1994.

[27] H. M. Vin, A. Goyal, and P. Goyal. Algorithms for designing large-scale multimedia servers. *Computer Communications*, March 1995.

[28] H. M. Vin, P. Goyal, A. Goyal, and A. Goyal. A statistical admission control algorithm for multimedia servers. In *Proc. of the ACM Multimedia*, pages 33–40, October 1994.

[29] W3C. Synchronized media integration language (SMIL), Boston Specification. http://www.w3.org/TR/smil-boston, February 2000.

[30] M. Y.Y.Leung, J. C. Lui, and L. Golubchik. Buffer and I/O resource pre-alocation for implementing batching and buffering techniques for video-on-demand systems. In *Proc. of Int. Conf. on Data Engineering (ICDE)*, pages 344–353, 1997.

[31] W. Zhao and S. K. Tripathi. A resource reservation scheme for synchronized distributed multimedia sessions. *Multimedia Tools and Applications*, 7(1/2):133–146, July 1998.

Application Performance in the QLinux Multimedia Operating System *

Vijay Sundaram **Abhishek Chandra** **Pawan Goyal†**

Prashant Shenoy **Jasleen Sahni‡** **Harrick Vin‡**

Department of Computer Science
University of Massachusetts
Amherst, MA 01003
{vijay,abhishek,shenoy}@cs.umass.edu

† Ensim Corporation
1215 Terra Bella Ave
Mountain View, CA 94043
goyal@ensim.com

‡ Department of Computer Sciences
University of Texas
Austin, TX 78712
{jks,vin}@cs.utexas.edu

ABSTRACT

In this paper, we argue that conventional operating systems need to be enhanced with predictable resource management mechanisms to meet the diverse performance requirements of emerging multimedia and web applications. We present QLinux—a multimedia operating system based on the Linux kernel that meets this requirement. QLinux employs hierarchical schedulers for fair, predictable allocation of processor, disk and network bandwidth, and accounting mechanisms for appropriate charging of resource usage. We experimentally evaluate the efficacy of these mechanisms using benchmarks and real-world applications. Our experimental results show that (i) emerging applications can indeed benefit from predictable allocation of resources, and (ii) the overheads imposed by the resource allocation mechanisms in QLinux are small. For instance, we show that the QLinux CPU scheduler can provide predictable performance guarantees to applications such as web servers and MPEG players, albeit at the expense of increasing the scheduling overhead. We conclude from our experiments that the benefits due to the resource management mechanisms in QLinux outweigh their increased overheads, making them a practical choice for conventional operating systems.

1. Introduction

Recent advances in computing and communication technologies have led to the emergence of a wide variety of applications with diverse performance requirements. Today's general purpose operating systems are required to support a mix of (i) conventional best-effort applications that desire low average response times but no absolute performance guarantees, (ii) throughput-intensive applications that desire high average throughput, and (iii) soft real-time applications that require performance guarantees from the operating system. To illustrate, PCs in office environments run a mix of word processors, spreadsheets, streaming media players and large compilation jobs, while large-scale servers run a mix of network file

*This research was supported in part by a NSF Career award CCR-9984030, NSF grants ANI 9977635, CDA-9502639, Intel, Sprint, and the University of Massachusetts.

services, web services, database applications and streaming media servers.

Whereas less demanding application mixes can be easily handled by a conventional best-effort operating system running on a fast processor, studies have shown that such operating systems are grossly inadequate for meeting the diverse requirements imposed by demanding application mixes [13, 15]. To illustrate, conventional operating systems running on even the fastest processors today are unable to provide jitter-free playback of full-motion MPEG-2 video in the presence of other applications such as long-running compile tasks. The primary reason for this inadequacy is the lack of service differentiation among applications—such operating systems provide a single class of best-effort service to all applications regardless of their actual performance requirements.[1] Moreover, special-purpose operating systems designed for a particular application class (e.g., real-time operating systems [12, 24]) are typically unable or inefficient at handling other classes of applications. This necessitates the design of an operating system that (i) multiplexes its resources among applications in a predictable manner, and (ii) uses service differentiation to meet the performance requirements of individual applications.

The QLinux operating system that we have developed meets these requirements by enhancing the standard Linux operating system with quality of service support. To do so, QLinux employs schedulers that can allocate resources to individual applications as well as application classes in a predictable manner. These schedulers are hierarchical—they support class-specific schedulers that schedule requests based on the performance requirements of that class (and thereby provide service differentiation across application classes). Specifically, QLinux employs four key components: (i) hierarchical start-time fair queueing (H-SFQ) CPU scheduler that allocates CPU bandwidth fairly among application classes [7], (ii) hierarchical start-time fair queueing (H-SFQ) packet scheduler that can fairly allocate network interface bandwidth to various applications [8], (iii) Cello disk scheduler that can support disk requests with diverse performance requirements [17], and (iv) lazy receiver processing for appropriate accounting of protocol processing overheads [6]. Figure 1 illustrates these components. We have implemented these components into QLinux and have made the source code freely available to the research community.[2]

---

[1] Rather than reduce the processor shares of all applications equally, an operating system that provides service differentiation might reduce the fraction of the CPU bandwidth allocated to best-effort compile jobs and thereby reduce the jitter in soft real-time video playback.

[2] Source code and documentation for QLinux is available from http://www.cs.umass.edu/~lass/software/qlinux.

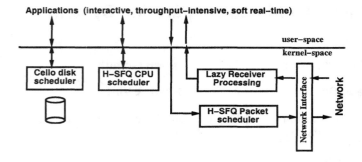

Applications (interactive, throughput-intensive, soft real-time)

Figure 1: Key components of QLinux.

In this paper, we make four key contributions. First, we show how to synthesize several recent innovations in OS resource management into a seamless multimedia operating system. Second, we consider several real-world applications and application scenarios and demonstrate that these resource management techniques enable QLinux to provide benefits such as predictable performance, application isolation and fair resource allocation. For instance, we show that QLinux enables a streaming media server to stream MPEG-1 files at their real-time rates regardless of the background load. Third, we show that existing/legacy applications can also benefit from these features without any modifications whatsoever to the application source code. Finally, we show that the implementation overheads of these sophisticated resource management techniques are small, making them a practical choice for general-purpose operating systems. For instance, we show that the context switch overhead due to the H-SFQ CPU scheduler increases from 1 μs to 4 μs, but the increased overhead is still substantially smaller than the quantum duration. Based on these results, we argue that conventional operating systems should be enhanced with such resource management mechanisms so as to meet the needs of emerging applications as well as existing and legacy applications.

The rest of this paper is structured as follows. Section 2 discusses the principles underlying the design of QLinux and briefly describes each component employed by QLinux. Section 3 presents the results of our experimental evaluation. Section 4 discusses related work, and finally, Section 5 presents some concluding remarks.

2. QLinux Philosophy and Overview

In this section, we first present the principles underlying the design and implementation of QLinux. We then briefly describe each resource management component employed by QLinux (these mechanisms are described in detail elsewhere [6, 7, 8, 17]).

2.1 QLinux Design Principles

The design and implementation of QLinux is based on the following principles:

- *Support for Multiple Service Classes:* Today's general purpose computing environments consist of a heterogeneous mix of applications with different performance requirements. As argued in Section 1, operating systems that provide a single class of service to all applications are inadequate for handling such diverse application mixes. To efficiently support such mixes, an operating system should *support multiple classes of service and align the service provided within each class with application needs.* For instance, an operating system

may support three classes of service—interactive, throughput-intensive and soft real-time—and treat applications within each class differently (interactive applications are provided low average response times, real-time applications are provided performance guarantees, and throughput-intensive applications are provided high aggregate throughput). Other operating systems such as Nemesis [16] have also espoused such a *multi-service* approach to operating system design.

- *Predictable resource allocation:* A multi-service operating system requires mechanisms that can multiplex its resources among applications in a predictable manner. Many operating systems (e.g., Solaris, UNIX SVR4) support multiple application classes using strict priority across classes. Studies have shown that such an approach can induce starvation in lower priority tasks even for common application mixes [13]. For instance, it has been shown that running a compute-intensive MPEG decoder in the highest priority real-time class on Solaris can cause even kernel tasks (which run at a lower priority) to starve, causing the entire system to "freeze" [13]. One approach to alleviate the starvation problem is to use dynamic priorities. Whereas the design of dynamic priority mechanisms for homogeneous workloads is easy, the design of such techniques for heterogenous workloads is challenging. Consequently, QLinux advocates rate-based mechanisms over priority-based mechanisms for predictable resource allocation. Rate-based techniques allow a weight to be assigned to individual applications and/or application classes and allocate resources in proportion to these weights. Thus, an application with weight w_i is allocated $\frac{w_i}{\sum_j w_j}$ fraction of the resource.[3] Observe that, rate-based allocation techniques are distinct from static partitioning of resources—they can dynamically reallocate resources unused by an application to other applications, and thereby yield better resource utilization than static partitioning.

- *Service differentiation:* Since different application classes have different performance requirements, an operating system that supports multiple service classes should provide service differentiation by treating applications within each class differently. To do so, QLinux employs hierarchical schedulers that support multiple class-specific schedulers via a flexible multi-level scheduling structure. A hierarchical scheduler in QLinux allocates a certain fraction of the resource to each class-specific scheduler using rate-based mechanisms; class-specific schedulers, in turn, use their allocations to service requests using an appropriate scheduling algorithm. The flexibility of using a different class-specific scheduler for each class allows QLinux to tailor its service to the needs of individual applications. Moreover, the approach is extensible since it allows existing class-specific schedulers to be modified, or new schedulers to be added.

- *Support for legacy applications:* We believe that only those mechanisms that preserve compatibility with existing and legacy applications are likely to be adapted by mainstream op-

---

[3]Such a resource allocation mechanism performs relative allocations—the fraction allocated to an application depends on the weights assigned to other applications. Rate-based mechanisms that allocate resource in absolute terms have also been developed. Such mechanisms allow applications to be allocated an absolute fraction f_i ($\sum f_i < 1$), or allocate x_i units every y_i units of time. We chose a relative allocation mechanism based on weights due to its simplicity.

erating systems in the near future. Hence, QLinux chooses an incremental approach to OS design. Each mechanism within QLinux is carefully designed to maintain full compatibility with existing applications at the binary level. We also decided that mere compatibility was not enough—we wanted existing applications to possibly benefit (but definitely not suffer) from the new resource allocation mechanisms in QLinux (although the degree to which they benefit would be less than new applications that are explicitly designed to take advantage of these features).

- *Proper accounting of resource usage:* An operating system that allocates resources in a predictable manner should employ mechanisms to accurately account and charge for resource usage. Whereas most operating systems employ mechanisms that can accurately track the amount of CPU bandwidth consumed by applications, resources consumed by kernel tasks are not accounted for in the same manner. For instance, many kernel tasks such as interrupt processing and network protocol processing occur asynchronously and get charged to the currently running process rather than the process that triggered these tasks. Other kernel tasks such as scheduling decisions or book-keeping operations are system-wide in scope in that they cannot be attributed to a particular process. Improper or inaccurate accounting of resource usage can cause the bandwidth allocated to an application to deviate significantly from its specified share. QLinux employs a two-pronged approach to deal with such accounting issues.

  - It employs lazy receiver processing [6], a technique to ensure that network protocol processing overheads are charged to the appropriate process (rather than arbitrarily charging it to the currently running process). This is achieved by deferring protocol processing from packet arrival time to the time a process attempts to receive the data from a network socket.

  - Since lazy receiver processing accounts only for protocol processing overheads, other mechanisms are required to account for kernel tasks such as interrupt processing and book-keeping operations. To address this limitation, QLinux employs a CPU scheduler that provides predictable performance even in the presence of fluctuating processor bandwidth. Specifically, the fairness guarantees provided by the CPU scheduler hold even when a varying amount of CPU bandwidth is used up by kernel tasks, thereby resulting in more predictable allocation [8].

Together, these two techniques ensure accurate accounting and predictable allocation of resources in QLinux.

Next, we describe the four key components of QLinux.

2.2 Hierarchical Start-time Fair Queueing (H-SFQ) CPU Scheduler

Hierarchical start-time fair queuing (H-SFQ) is a hierarchical CPU scheduler that fairly allocates processor bandwidth to different application classes and employs class-specific schedulers to manage requests within each class [7]. The scheduler uses a tree-like structure to describe its scheduling hierarchy (see Figure 2). Each process or thread in the system belongs to exactly one leaf node. A leaf node is an aggregation of threads and represents an *application class* in the system. Each non-leaf node is an aggregation of application classes. Each node in the tree has a weight

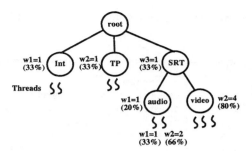

Figure 2: A sample hierarchy employed by the H-SFQ CPU scheduler. The figure shows three classes—interactive, throughput-intensive and soft real-time—with equal share of the processor bandwidth. The bandwidth within the soft real-time class is further partitioned among the audio and video classes in the proportion 1:4. Individual threads can also be assigned weights, assuming the leaf node scheduler supports rate-based allocation.

that determines the fraction of its parent's bandwidth that should be allocated to it. Thus, if $w_1, w_2, \ldots, w_n$ denote the weights on the n children of a node, and if B denotes the processor bandwidth allocated to the node, then the bandwidth received by each child node i is given by

$$B_i = \left(\frac{w_i}{\sum_j w_j} \right) * B$$

Each node is also associated with a scheduler. Whereas the scheduler of the leaf node schedules all threads belonging to the leaf, the scheduler of an intermediate node schedules all its children. Scheduling of threads occurs hierarchically in H-SFQ: the root node schedules one of its child nodes; the child node, in turn, schedules one of its children until a leaf node schedules a thread for execution. Any class-specific scheduler may be employed to schedule a leaf node. For instance, the standard time-sharing scheduler could be employed for scheduling threads in the interactive class, whereas the earliest deadline first (EDF) scheduler could be used to schedule soft real-time tasks. H-SFQ employs start-time fair queuing (SFQ) as the scheduling algorithm for a non-leaf node. SFQ is a rate-based scheduler that allocates weighted fair shares—bandwidth allocated to each child node is in proportion to its weight. Bandwidth unused by a node is redistributed to other nodes according to their weights. In addition to rate-based allocation, SFQ has the following properties: (i) it achieves fair allocation of CPU bandwidth regardless of variation in available capacity, (ii) it does not require the length of the quantum to be known a priori (and hence, can be used in general-purpose environments where threads may block for I/O before their quantum expires), and (iii) SFQ provides provable guarantees on fairness, delay, and throughput received by each thread in the system [7, 8].

H-SFQ replaces the standard time-sharing scheduler in QLinux. The default scheduling hierarchy in H-SFQ consists of a root node with a single child that uses the standard time-sharing scheduler to schedule threads. An application, by default, is assigned to the time-sharing scheduler, thereby allowing QLinux to mimic the behavior of standard Linux. The scheduling hierarchy can be modified dynamically at run-time by creating new nodes on the fly. Creating a new node involves specifying the parent node, a weight, and a scheduling algorithm, if the node is a leaf node (non-leaf nodes are scheduled using SFQ). QLinux allows processes and threads to

Table 1: System call interface supported by the H-SFQ CPU scheduler

System call	Purpose
hsfq_mknod	create a new node in the scheduling hierarchy
hsfq_rmnod	delete an existing node from the hierarchy
hsfq_join_nod	attach the current process to a leaf node
hsfq_move	move a process to a specified child node
hsfq_parse	parse a pathname in the scheduling hierarchy
hsfq_admin	administer a node (e.g., change weights)

Table 2: System call interface supported by the H-SFQ packet scheduler

System call	Purpose
hsfq_qdisc_install	Install HSFQ queuing discipline at a network interface
hsfq_link_mknod	create a node in the scheduling hierarchy
hsfq_link_createq	create a packet queue
hsfq_link_attachq	attach a queue to a leaf node
hsfq_link_moveq	move a queue between schedulers
hsfq_link_rmnod	delete the specified node
hsfq_link_rmq	delete the specified queue
hsfq_link_modify	change the weight of a node/queue
hsfq_link_parsenode	parse a pathname in the scheduling hierarchy
hsfq_link_getroot	get the ID of the root node at a particular network interface
hsfq_link_status	display the scheduling tree
setsockopt	attach a socket to a queue

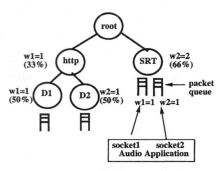

Figure 3: The H-SFQ network packet scheduler. The figure shows a sample scheduling hierarchy with two classes—http and soft real-time. The bandwidth within the http class is further partitioned among two web domains, $D1$ and $D2$, in the ratio 1:1. Note that individual sockets can either share a queue or have a queue of their own. Since each queue has its own weight, in the latter case, bandwidth allocation can be controlled on a per-socket basis.

Table 3: System call interface supported by Cello

System call	Purpose
cello_open	Open a file and associate it with the specified class
cello_read	read data using an optional deadline
cello_write	write data using an optional deadline
cello_set_class	associate a class with a process
cello_admin	administer a class (e.g., specify weights)

be assigned to a specific node at process/thread creation time; processes and threads can be moved from one leaf node to another at any time. Moreover, weights assigned to an application or a node in the scheduling hierarchy can be modified dynamically. QLinux employs a set of system calls to achieve these objectives (see Table 1). We have also implemented several utility programs to manipulate the scheduling hierarchy as well as individual applications within the hierarchy. These utilities allow existing/legacy applications to benefit from the features of H-SFQ since users can assign weights to applications without modifying the source code.

2.3 H-SFQ Packet Scheduler

An operating system employs a packet scheduler at each of its network interfaces to determine the order in which outgoing packets are transmitted. Traditionally, most operating systems have employed the FIFO scheduler to schedule outgoing packets. To better meet the needs of applications with different requirements, QLinux employs H-SFQ to schedule outgoing packets. As described in Section 2.2, H-SFQ can fairly allocate resource bandwidth among different application classes in a hierarchical manner. As in the case of CPU, the H-SFQ packet scheduler employs a multi-level tree-like scheduling structure to hierarchically allocate network interface bandwidth (see Figure 3). Each leaf node in the tree consists of one or more queues of outgoing network packets and any class-specific scheduler can be employed to schedule the transmission of packets from these queues; the default leaf scheduler is FIFO. A non-leaf node is scheduled using SFQ. Every node in the hierarchy

is assigned a weight; H-SFQ allocates bandwidth to nodes in proportion to their weights. Bandwidth unused by a node is reallocated fairly among the nodes with pending packets, thereby improving overall utilization.

The H-SFQ packet scheduler in QLinux replaces the FIFO scheduler employed by Linux. The default scheduling hierarchy in H-SFQ is a root node with a single child that employs FIFO scheduling. Packets sent by applications are, by default, queued up at this node, enabling QLinux to emulate the behavior of Linux. As in the case of the CPU scheduler, the scheduling hierarchy can be modified by adding new nodes to the tree or deleting existing nodes. QLinux allows applications to be associated to a specific queue at a leaf node (via the setsockopt system call); this association can be done on a per-socket basis. Packet classifiers [19] are then employed to map each transmitted packet to the corresponding queue at a leaf node. Table 2 lists the system call interface exported by the packet scheduler to achieve these objectives. We are currently implementing utility programs using these system calls that will enable existing applications to benefit from these features without having to modify their source code.

2.4 Cello Disk Scheduler

Unlike disk scheduling algorithms such as SCAN that provide a best-effort service to disk requests, QLinux employs the Cello disk scheduling algorithm to support multiple application classes. Cello services disk requests using a two level scheduling algorithm, consisting of a class-independent scheduler and a set of class-specific

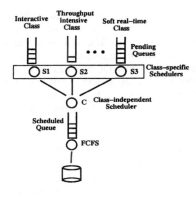

Figure 4: The Cello disk scheduling algorithm.

schedulers [17]. The class-independent scheduler is responsible for allocating disk bandwidth to classes based on their weights, whereas the class-specific schedulers use these allocations to schedule individual requests based on their requirements. Unlike pure rate-based schedulers that focus only on fair allocation of resources, Cello also takes disk seek and rotational latency overheads into account when making scheduling decisions (thereby improving disk throughput).

The implementation of Cello in QLinux supports three application classes—interactive, throughput-intensive and soft real-time. To do so, QLinux maintains three pending queues, one for each application class and a scheduled queue (see Figure 4). Newly arriving requests are queued up in the appropriate pending queue. They are eventually moved to the scheduled queue and dispatched to the disk in FIFO order. The class-independent scheduler determines *when* and *how many* requests to move from each class-specific pending queue to the scheduled queue, while the class-specific schedulers determine *where* to insert it into the scheduled queue. To maintain compatibility with Linux, Cello uses the interactive best-effort class as the default class to service disk requests. Applications can override this default by specifying a class for each file that is read or written. For the soft real-time class, an application must also specify a deadline with each read or write request. Table 3 lists the interface exported by Cello to achieve these objectives. Note that the current implementation of Cello supports bandwidth allocation only on a per-class basis; in the future, we plan to add support for bandwidth allocation on a per-application basis.

2.5 Lazy Receiver Processing

Consider the operation of a network subsystem within a typical operating system. When a packet arrives at a network interface card, it causes an interrupt. The OS then suspends the currently running process and invokes an interrupt service routine to process the packet. Typically this processing involves executing the protocols at the data link layer (e.g., ethernet), the network layer (IP), and the transport layer (TCP or UDP). Observe that, by using the CPU quantum of the suspended process to do protocol processing, these overheads get charged to this process rather than the process that will eventually receive the packet. Such accounting anomalies result in violation of performance guarantees provided to applications by a multimedia operating system, especially on servers running network applications (e.g., http servers). Lazy receiver processing (LRP) is a technique that overcomes this drawback [6]. LRP postpones protocol processing from packet arrival time to the time a

process actually receives data by reading it from a socket. Postponing protocol operations to socket read time enables the OS to charge these overheads to the process that actually receives the data. The key challenge in designing an LRP-based network subsystem is to ensure only those protocol operations are postponed that do not affect protocol performance or semantics. For instance, TCP performs asynchronous operations such as sending acknowledgements for received packets. Delaying acknowledgements can severely affect the throughput received by an application (since the window-based flow control mechanism in TCP won't permit the sender to send additional data without receiving acknowledgements). Since such asynchronous operations can not be postponed, LRP employs a special kernel thread for each application to perform these operations as and when required. The kernel thread executes independently of the application process and its CPU usage is charged to the parent process.

The implementation of LRP in QLinux employs a queue per socket in the data link layer and employs early demultiplexing of incoming packets—a technique that classifies packets into these queues immediately upon arrival. Thus, interrupt processing upon the arrival of a process only involves packet classification to the appropriate queue and does not involve any expensive protocol processing; these operations are deferred to socket read time. Special kernel threads are employed to handle asynchronous operations as well as to implement protocols such as ARP and ICMP that are not process-specific. Finally, observe that LRP is transparent to applications—no additional system calls are required to support it, nor do you need to modify applications.

3. Experimental Evaluation

In this section, we experimentally evaluate the performance of QLinux and compare it to vanilla Linux. In particular, we examine the efficacy of the resource allocation mechanisms within QLinux to (i) allocate resource bandwidth in a predictable manner, (ii) provide application isolation, (iii) support multiple traffic classes, and (iv) accurately account for resource usage. We use several real applications, benchmarks and micro-benchmarks for our experimental evaluation. In what follows, we first describe the test-bed for our experiments and then present the results of our experimental evaluation.

3.1 Experimental Setup

The test-bed for our experiments consists of a cluster of PC-based workstations. Each PC used in our experiments is a 350MHz Pentium II with 64MB RAM and runs RedHat Linux 6.1. Each PC is equipped with a 100 Mb/s 3-Com ethernet card (model 3c595); all machines are interconnected by a 100 Mb/s ethernet switch (model 3Com SuperStack II). The version of QLinux used in our experiments is based on the 2.2.0 Linux kernel; comparisons with vanilla Linux use the identical version of the kernel. All machines and the network are assumed to be lightly loaded during our experiments.

The workload for our experiments consists of a combination of real-world applications, benchmarks, and sample applications that we wrote to demonstrate specific features. These applications are as follows: (i) *Inf:* an application that executes an infinite loop and represents a simple compute-intensive best-effort application; (ii) *mpeg_play:* the Berkeley software MPEG-1 decoder; represents a compute-intensive soft real-time application; (iii) *Apache web server* and *webclient:* a widely-used web server and a configurable client application that generates http requests at a specified rate; represents an I/O-intensive best-effort application; (iv) *Streaming media server:* a server that transmits (*streams*) MPEG-1 files over

131

the network using UDP; represents an I/O-intensive soft real-time application; (v) *Net_inf:* an application that sends UDP data as fast as possible on a socket; represents an I/O-intensive best-effort application; (vi) *Dhrystone:* a compute-intensive benchmark for measuring integer CPU performance; (vii) *lmbench:* a comprehensive benchmark suite that measures various aspects of operating system performance such as context switching, memory, file I/O, networking, and cache performance.

In what follows, we present the results of our experimental evaluation using these applications and benchmarks. Since the code for the Cello disk scheduler was unstable at the time of writing, we have not included experimental results for Cello.

3.2 Supporting Multiple Application Classes using the H-SFQ CPU Scheduler

To demonstrate that the H-SFQ CPU scheduler can allocate CPU bandwidth to applications in proportion to their weights, we created two classes in the scheduling hierarchy and ran the *Inf* application in each class. We assigned different combination of weights to the two classes (e.g., 1:1, 1:2, 1:4) and measured the number of loops executed by *Inf* in each case. Figures 5(a) and (b) depict our results. Figure 5(a) shows the progress made by the two *Inf* applications for a specific weight assignment of 1:4. Figure 5(b) shows the number of iterations executed by the two processes at t=337 seconds for different weight assignments. Together, the two figures show that each application gets processor bandwidth in proportion to its weight.

Next, we conducted an experiment to demonstrate the fair work-conserving nature of H-SFQ. Again, we created two application classes and gave them equal weights (1:1). The *Inf* application was run in each class and as expected each received 50% of the CPU bandwidth. At t=250 seconds, we suspended one of the *Inf* processes. Since H-SFQ is work-conserving in nature, the scheduler reallocated bandwidth unused by the suspended processes to the running *Inf* process (causing it's rate of progress to double). The suspended process was restarted at t=350 seconds, causing the two processes to again receive bandwidth in the proportion 1:1. Figure 5(c) depicts this scenario by plotting the progress made by the continuously running *Inf* process. As shown, the process makes progress at twice the rate between $250 \leq t < 350$ and receives its normal share in other time intervals.

We then conducted experiments to show that real-world applications also benefit from H-SFQ. To show that the CPU scheduler can effectively isolate applications from one another, we created two classes—soft real-time and best-effort—and assigned them equal weights. The best-effort leaf class was scheduled using the standard time sharing scheduler, while the soft real-time leaf class was scheduled using SFQ. We ran the Berkeley software MPEG decoder (mpeg_play) in the soft real-time class and used it to decode a five minute long MPEG-1 clip with an average bit rate of 1.49 Mb/s. The Dhrystone benchmark constituted the load in the best-effort class. We increased the load in the best-effort class (by increasing the number of independent Dhrystone processes) and measured the CPU bandwidth received by the MPEG decoder in each case. We then repeated this experiment using vanilla Linux. Figure 6(a) plots our results. As shown in the figure, in case of QLinux, the CPU bandwidth received by the MPEG decoder was independent of the load in the best-effort classes. Since vanilla Linux employs a best-effort scheduler, all applications, including the MPEG decoder, are degraded equally as the load increases. This demonstrates that H-SFQ, in addition to proportionate allocation, can also isolate application classes from one another. To further demonstrate this behavior, we ran two Apache web servers in two different classes and gave them different weights. The *webclient* application

was used to send a large number of http requests to each web server and we measured the processor bandwidth received by each class. As shown in Figure 6(b), the H-SFQ scheduler allocates processor bandwidth to the two classes in proportion to their weights. These experiments demonstrate that QLinux can be employed for web hosting scenarios where multiple web domains are hosted from the same physical server. Each web domain can be allocated a certain fraction of the resources and can be effectively isolated from the load in other domains.

3.3 Supporting Multiple Traffic Classes Using the H-SFQ Packet Scheduler

To demonstrate that the H-SFQ packet scheduler can allocate network interface bandwidth to applications in proportion to their weights, we created two classes in the scheduling hierarchy and ran the *Net_inf* application in each class. The UDP packets sent by *Net_inf* were received as fast as possible by a receiver process running on a lightly loaded PC. We varied the weights assigned to the two classes and measured the number of packets sent by the two processes for different weight assignments. Figure 7(a) depicts the number of bytes received from each *Net_inf* for one particular weight assignment (1:4). As expected, both classes receive bandwidth in proportion to their weights. To demonstrate that bandwidth received by a class is independent of the packet size, we repeated the experiment using different packet sizes for the two classes. Figure 7(b) shows that, despite using different packet sizes, the two classes again receive bandwidth in proportion to their weights.

To demonstrate that real-world applications also benefit from these features, we conducted an experiment with two classes—soft real-time and best-effort. The streaming media server was run in the soft real-time class and was used to stream a five minute long variable bit-rate MPEG-1 clip (average bit rate of the clip was 1.49 Mb/s). We ran an increasing number of *Net_inf* applications in the best-effort class and measured their impact on the bandwidth received by the streaming media server. We then repeated this experiment on vanilla Linux. As shown in Figure 8, QLinux is able to effectively isolate the streaming media server from the best-effort class—the server is able to stream data at its real-time rate regardless of the best-effort load. Linux, on the other hand, is unable to provide this isolation—increasing the best-effort load reduces the bandwidth received by the streaming media server and also increases the amount of packet loss incurred by all applications.

3.4 Combined Impact of H-SFQ CPU and Packet Schedulers

To demonstrate the combined benefits of the CPU and packet schedulers, we considered a scenario consisting of a loaded web server and several I/O intensive applications. We created two classes in the CPU and packet scheduler hierarchies. We ran a simulated web server in one CPU/packet scheduler class and ran all the I/O-intensive *Net_inf* applications in the other CPU/packet scheduler class. Our simulated web server consisted of a sender application that reads an actual web server trace and sends data using TCP (each send corresponds to an http request in the trace file; the timing and size of each request was taken directly from the information specified in the traces). The publicly-available ClarkNet server traces were employed to simulate the web server workload [4]. We increased the number of *Net_inf* applications in the best-effort class and measured their impact on the throughput of the web server. The experiment was then repeated for vanilla Linux. Figure 9 depicts our results. Observe that, the web server simulates the http protocol which runs on TCP. TCP employs congestion control mecha-

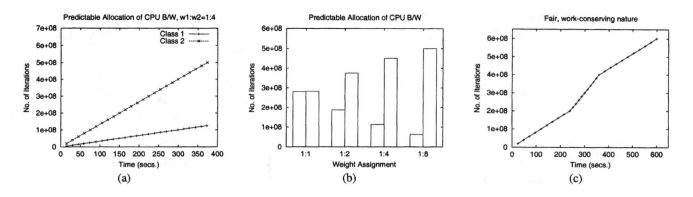

Figure 5: Predictable, fair allocation of processor bandwidth by the H-SFQ scheduler

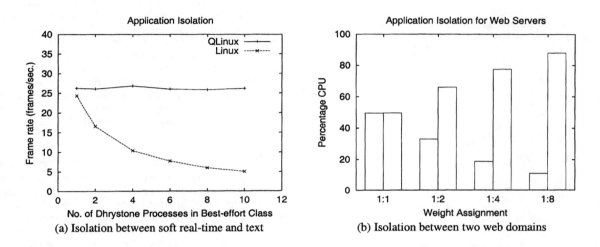

Figure 6: Application isolation and flexibility in the H-SFQ CPU scheduler.

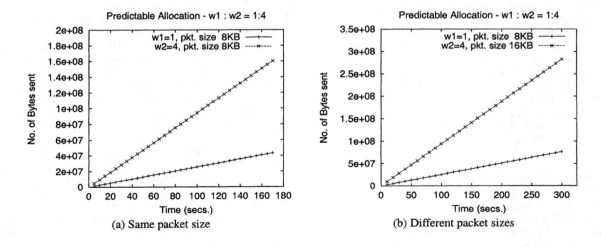

Figure 7: Predictable allocation in the H-SFQ Packet Scheduler.

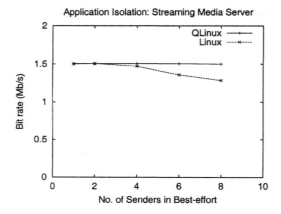

Figure 8: Application isolation in the H-SFQ Packet Scheduler.

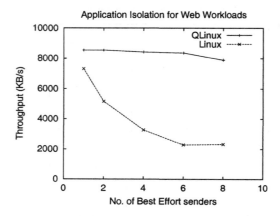

Figure 9: Impact of the H-SFQ CPU and packet schedulers on web workloads.

nisms that back off in the presence of congestion. Consequently, as the load due to *Net_inf* applications increases, congestion builds up in the ethernet switch interconnecting the senders and receivers (due to the presence of limited buffers at switches), causing TCP to reduce its sending rate. Both QLinux and Linux experience this phenomenon, resulting in a degradation in throughput for the web workload. However, since the QLinux CPU and packet schedulers reserve bandwidth for the web server, they can effectively isolate the web workload from the *Net_inf* applications. Hence, the degradation in throughput in QLinux is significantly smaller than that in Linux. This demonstrates that use of fair, predictable schedulers for each resource in an OS can yield significant performance benefits to applications.

3.5 Appropriate Accounting of Protocol Processing Overheads

To demonstrate the impact of lazy receiver processing, we ran two Apache web servers in QLinux. In the presence of a light load, the response time of a server to retrieve a 1.9KB file was measured to be 50.7ms. We then simulated a simple denial of service attack scenario, in which one server was bombarded with http requests at a high rate (300 reqs/s). In the presence of this load, the response time of the other server (which was lightly loaded) was found to

Table 4: Lmbench Results

Test	QLinux	Linux
syscall overhead	$1\ \mu s$	$1\ \mu s$
fork()	$400\ \mu s$	$400\ \mu s$
exec()	2 ms	2 ms
Context switch (2 proc/ 0KB)	$4\ \mu s$	$1\ \mu s$
Context switch (16 proc/ 64KB)	$286\ \mu s$	$283\ \mu s$
Local UDP latency	$47\ \mu s$	$53\ \mu s$
Local TCP latency	$83\ \mu s$	$82\ \mu s$
File create (0 KB file)	$21\ \mu s$	$21\ \mu s$
File delete (0 KB file)	$2\ \mu s$	$2\ \mu s$

be 70.1ms. We then repeated the experiment on vanilla Linux and found the response time of the lightly loaded web server to be 79.8ms. Since LRP ensures that protocol processing overheads for a packet are charged to the application receiving that packet, the lightly loaded server is not charged for the packets received by the overloaded server. Hence, it provides a better response time to its requests (note that, some degradation in response time is inevitable due to the congestion control mechanism in TCP and the increased load). Linux, on the other hand, does not account for protocol processing overheads in the same manner, resulting in a greater degradation in response time. This demonstrates that proper accounting of kernel overheads can improve application performance and help isolate unrelated applications during overloads or denial of service attacks.

3.6 Microbenchmarking QLinux: Scheduling Overheads

In the previous sections, we demonstrated that applications can benefit from the sophisticated resource management techniques employed by QLinux. In what follows, we measure the overheads imposed by these mechanisms using microbenchmarks.

To measure the overhead imposed by the CPU scheduler, we created a leaf node and ran a solitary *Inf* process in that class. We then progressively increased the depth of the scheduling hierarchy (by introducing intermediate nodes between this leaf and the root) and measured the bandwidth received by *Inf* in each case. Observe that, increasing the depth of the scheduling hierarchy may increase the scheduling overhead (since H-SFQ recursively calls the scheduler at each intermediate node until a thread in the leaf class is selected). A larger scheduling overhead will correspondingly reduce the bandwidth received by applications (since a larger fraction of the CPU time would be spent in making scheduling decisions). Figure 10(a) plots the number of iterations executed by *Inf* in 300 seconds as we increase the depth of the scheduling hierarchy. As shown in the figure, the bandwidth received by *Inf* is relatively unaffected by the increasing scheduling overhead, thereby demonstrating that the overheads imposed by H-SFQ are small in practice.

We then performed a similar experiment for the H-SFQ packet scheduler. The experiment consisted of running the *Net_inf* process in a scheduling hierarchy with increasing depth and measuring the bandwidth received by *Net_inf* in each case. As in the case of the CPU scheduler, the bandwidth received by *Net_inf* was relatively unaffected by the scheduling overhead (see 10(b)). Together, these experiments show that hierarchical schedulers such as H-SFQ are feasible in practice.

3.7 Benchmarking QLinux

In our final experiment, we employed the widely used *Lmbench*

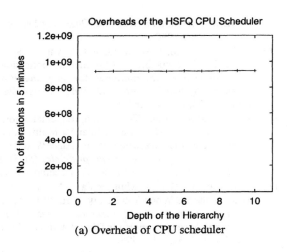

(a) Overhead of CPU scheduler

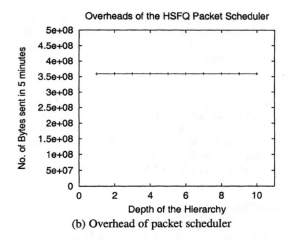

(b) Overhead of packet scheduler

Figure 10: Microbenchmarking QLinux: overheads imposed by the CPU and Packet Schedulers

benchmark to compare QLinux and Linux. Lmbench is a sophisticated benchmark that measures several aspects of system performance, such as system call overheads, context switch times, network I/O, file I/O and memory performance [10]. We employed Lmbench version 1.9 for our experiments. We first ran Lmbench in the default best-effort class on QLinux and then repeated the experiment on Linux. In each case, we averaged the statistics reported by Lmbench over several runs to eliminate experimental error. Table 4 summarizes our results (Lmbench produces a large number of statistics; we only list those statistics that are relevant to QLinux).

Note that the QLinux code is untuned, while Linux code is carefully tuned by the Linux kernel developers. Table 4 shows that the performance of QLinux is comparable to Linux; however, the increased complexity of the QLinux schedulers do result in a larger overhead. For instance, the context switch overhead increases from 1 μs to 4 μs for two active processes; however this overhead is still several orders of magnitude smaller than the quantum duration of 100 ms. The network latency for TCP and UDP, as well as file I/O overheads and system call overheads are comparable in both cases.

4. Related Work

The growing popularity of the multimedia applications has resulted in several research efforts that have focused on the design of predictable resource allocation mechanisms. Consequently, in the recent past, several techniques have been proposed for the predictable allocation of processor [7, 9, 14, 21, 22], network interface [3, 5, 8, 18] and disk [1, 11, 23] bandwidth. While each effort differs in the exact mechanism employed to provide predictable performance (e.g., admission control, rate-based allocation, fair queuing), the broad goals are similar—add quality of service support to an operating system. The key contribution of QLinux is to synthesize/integrate many of these mechanisms into a single system and demonstrate the benefits of this integration on application performance. Whereas the mechanisms instantiated in QLinux are based on our past work in this area, we believe that it would have been relatively easy to implement some other predictable resource allocation mechanisms and demonstrate similar benefits.

Some other recent operating system efforts have also focused on the design of predictable resource allocation mechanisms. The Nemesis operating system, for instance, employs mechanisms that provide quality of service guarantees when allocating processor,

network and disk bandwidth [1, 16]. Unlike QLinux, which employs weights to express resource requirements, Nemesis requires applications to specify their resource requirements in terms of tuples (s, p, x), where s units of the resource are requested every p units of time, and x is the additional bandwidth requested, if available. Nemesis is a multi-service multimedia operating system that was designed from the grounds up; QLinux, on the other hand, builds upon the Linux kernel and benefits from the continuing enhancement made to the kernel by the Linux developers. The Eclipse operating system, based on FreeBSD, is in many respects similar to QLinux [2]. Like QLinux, Eclipse employs hierarchical schedulers to allocate OS resources (the actual scheduling algorithms that are employed are, however, different). Eclipse employs a special file system called /reserv that is used by applications to specify their resource requirements [2]. QLinux and Eclipse are independent and parallel research efforts, both of which attempt to improve upon conventional best effort operating systems. Finally, many commercial operating systems are beginning to employ some of these features. High end versions of Solaris 2.7, for instance, include a resource manager that enables fine-grain allocation of various resources to processes and process groups [20].

5. Concluding Remarks

Emerging multimedia and web applications require conventional operating systems to be enhanced along several dimensions. In this paper, we presented the QLinux multimedia operating system that enhances the resource management mechanisms in vanilla Linux. QLinux employs four key components: the H-SFQ CPU scheduler, the H-SFQ packet scheduler, the Cello disk scheduler and the lazy receiver processing-based network subsystem. Together, these mechanisms ensure fair, predictable allocation of processor, network and disk bandwidth as well as accurate accounting of resource usage. We experimentally demonstrated the efficacy of these mechanisms using benchmarks as well as common multimedia and web applications. Our experimental results showed that multimedia and web applications can indeed benefit from predictable resource allocation and application isolation offered by QLinux. Furthermore, the overheads imposed by these mechanisms were shown to be small. Based on these results, we argue that all conventional operating systems should be enhanced with such mechanisms to meet the needs of emerging applications.

As part of future work, we plan to enhance QLinux along several dimensions. In particular, we are designing resource allocation mechanisms that will enable QLinux to scale to large symmetric multiprocessors and clusters of servers.

Acknowledgments

T R. Vishwanath helped us develop the initial version of QLinux. Raghav Srinivasan helped with implementation of the Cello disk scheduler in QLinux. Gisli Hjalmtysson provided useful inputs during the inception of QLinux in the summer of 1998. Finally, we thank the many users of QLinux and the research community for providing valuable feedback (and bug reports) for enhancing QLinux.

6. REFERENCES

[1] P. Barham. A Fresh Approach to File System Quality of Service. In *Proceedings of NOSSDAV'97, St. Louis, Missouri*, pages 119–128, May 1997.

[2] J. Blanquer, J. Bruno, M. McShea, B. Ozden, A. Silberschatz, and A. Singh. Resource Management for QoS in Eclipse/BSD. In *Proceedings of the FreeBSD'99 Conference, Berkeley, CA*, October 1999.

[3] S. Chen and K. Nahrstedt. Hierarchical Scheduling for Multiple Classes of Applications in Connection-Oriented Integrated-Services Networks. In *Proceedings of IEEE International Conference on Multimedia Computing and Systems, Florence, Italy*, June 1999.

[4] ClarkNet Web Server Traces. Available from the Internet Traffic Archive http://ita.ee.lbl.gov, 1995.

[5] A. Demers, S. Keshav, and S. Shenker. Analysis and Simulation of a Fair Queueing Algorithm. In *Proceedings of ACM SIGCOMM*, pages 1–12, September 1989.

[6] P. Druschel and G. Banga. Lazy Receiver Processing (LRP): A Network Subsystem Architecture for Server Systems. In *Proceedings of the 2nd Symposium on Operating System Design and Implementation (OSDI'96), Seattle, WA*, pages 261–275, October 1996.

[7] P. Goyal, X. Guo, and H.M. Vin. A Hierarchical CPU Scheduler for Multimedia Operating Systems. In *Proceedings of Operating System Design and Implementation (OSDI'96), Seattle*, pages 107–122, October 1996.

[8] P. Goyal, H. M. Vin, and H. Cheng. Start-time Fair Queuing: A Scheduling Algorithm for Integrated Services Packet Switching Networks. In *Proceedings of ACM SIGCOMM'96*, pages 157–168, August 1996.

[9] M B. Jones, D Rosu, and M Rosu. CPU Reservations and Time Constraints: Efficient, Predictable Scheduling of Independent Activities. In *Proceedings of the sixteenth ACM symposium on Operating Systems Principles (SOSP'97), Saint-Malo, France*, pages 198–211, December 1997.

[10] L. McVoy and C. Staelin. Lmbench: Portable Tools for Performance Analysis. In *Proceedings of USENIX'96 Technical Conference, Available from http://www.bitmover.com/lmbench*, January 1996.

[11] A. Molano, K. Juvva, and R. Rajkumar. Real-time File Systems: Guaranteeing Timing Constraints for Disk Accesses in RT-Mach. In *Proceedings of IEEE Real-time Systems Symposium*, December 1997.

[12] L. Molesky, K. Ramamritham, C. Shen, J. Stankovic, and G. Zlokapa. Implementing a Predictable Real-Time Multiprocessor Kernel–The Spring Kernel. In *Proceedings of the IEEE Workshop on Real-time Operating Systems and Software*, May 1990.

[13] J. Nieh, J. Hanko, J. Northcutt, and G. Wall. SVR4UNIX Scheduler Unacceptable for Multimedia Applications. In *Proceedings of 4th International Workshop on Network and Operating System Support for Digital Audio and Video*, pages 41–53, November 1993.

[14] J. Nieh and M S. Lam. The Design, Implementation and Evaluation of SMART: A Scheduler for Multimedia Applications. In *Proceedings of the sixteenth ACM symposium on Operating systems principles (SOSP'97), Saint-Malo, France*, pages 184–197, December 1997.

[15] J. Nieh and M. S. Lam. Multimedia on Multiprocessors: Where's the OS When You Really Need It? In *Proceedings of the Eighth International Workshop on Network and Operating System Support for Digital Audio and Video, Cambridge, U.K.*, July 1998.

[16] Timothy Roscoe. *The Structure of a Multi-Service Operating System*. PhD thesis, University of Cambridge Computer Laboratory, April 1995. Available as Technical Report No. 376.

[17] P Shenoy and H M. Vin. Cello: A Disk Scheduling Framework for Next Generation Operating Systems. In *Proceedings of ACM SIGMETRICS Conference, Madison, WI*, pages 44–55, June 1998.

[18] M. Shreedhar and G. Varghese. Efficient Fair Queuing Using Deficit Round Robin. In *Proceedings of ACM SIGCOMM'95*, pages 231–242, 1995.

[19] V. Srinivasan, G. Varghese, S. Suri, and M. Waldvogel. Fast Scalable Level Four Switching. In *Proceedings of the ACM SIGCOMM'98, Vancouver, BC*, pages 191–202, September 1998.

[20] Solaris Resource Manager 1.0: Controlling System Resources Effectively. Sun Microsystems, Inc., http://www.sun.com/software/white-papers/wp-srm/, 1998.

[21] B. Verghese, A. Gupta, and M. Rosenblum. Performance Isolation: Sharing and Isolation in Shared-Memory Multiprocessors. In *Proceedings of ASPLOS-VIII, San Jose, CA*, pages 181–192, October 1998.

[22] C. Waldspurger and W. Weihl. Stride Scheduling: Deterministic Proportional-share Resource Management. Technical Report TM-528, MIT, Laboratory for Computer Science, June 1995.

[23] R. Wijayaratne and A. L. N. Reddy. Providing QoS Guarantees for Disk I/O. Technical Report TAMU-ECE97-02, Department of Electrical Engineering, Texas A&M University, 1997.

[24] K. Zuberi, P. Pillai, and K G. Shin. EMERALDS: A Small-Memory Real-Time Microkernel. In *Proceedings of the 17th ACM Symposium on Operating Systems Principles (SOSP'99)*, pages 277–291, December 1999.

An Adaptive Protocol for Locating Programmable Media Gateways

Wei Tsang Ooi
Department of Computer Science
Cornell University
weitsang@cs.cornell.edu

Robbert van Renesse
Department of Computer Science
Cornell University
rvr@cs.cornell.edu

ABSTRACT

We describe a new control protocol called Adaptive Gateway Location Protocol (AGLP). In this protocol, a client requests a computation on a multimedia stream. AGLP discovers programmable Internet servers that process multimedia streams, and assigns the computation to one of these so-called *gateways*. AGLP continuously searches for alternate gateways, and, transparent to users, migrates computations between them to improve efficiency. The AGLP protocol uses soft-states for robustness and scale. Simulation results support that our protocol quickly locates gateways and migrates computations while keeping the load on the network low. We also outline planned enhancements to AGLP.

1. INTRODUCTION

There is a growing interest in adding multimedia processing capabilities into the network. For example, active services such as MeGa [1] allow an application-level gateway to transcode multimedia streams into lower-bandwidth streams suitable for slow links, while still allowing the senders to send high quality high bandwidth streams to other well-connected receivers. Here at Cornell University, the Degas project [10] extends the model of MeGa, by allowing receivers to upload a program into a gateway to customize the processing of RTP media streams. Examples include creating a picture in picture effect by merging two video streams, or switching between different streams automatically based on audio signals. With multiple gateways running in the network the question arises as to which gateway should be chosen to run such a program.

Running the program in a gateway that is strategically located in the network could use network bandwidth more efficiently. For example, if the output video stream has lower bandwidth than the input stream, then the program should be run on a gateway that is close to the sender. On the other hand, if the program outputs a higher bandwidth stream, the program should be run close to the receiver.

The problem of determining the best gateway is an optimization problem. However, the dynamic nature of the network prevents us from solving the problem using a centralized, combinatoric algorithm. Senders and receivers may join and leave video sessions, new gateways may be added and deleted, and the underlying network behavior changes continuously. Therefore, we opt for a distributed, adaptive algorithm in Degas.

In this paper, we present the Adaptive Gateway Location Protocol (AGLP) used in Degas for choosing a gateway that efficiently utilizes bandwidth. Although we design AGLP to work with Degas, we believe that it can be modified to suit other applications as well. AGLP is a soft-state protocol based on the announce-listen model widely used in MBone tools. The simplicity of the model allows us to build a scalable, robust protocol that is resilient to crashes and message loss. AGLP adapts to changing network conditions, as well as the birth and death of gateways, senders, and receivers, by migrating computations (also called *services*) between gateways. An additional requirement on our protocol is that it assigns a new service to a gateway rapidly.

We designed our protocol to be compatible with existing MBone tools. No changes are required at the senders. This means that traditional MBone tools such as vic [7] and ivs [13] can be used as the video sending application. This makes it possible to deploy our protocol without affecting the existing MBone community.

Our simulations support that AGLP achieves its goals of rapid assignment and adaptive placement, while keeping the load on the network low. The rate of migrations is small, and a good gateway for such a migration can be selected within a minute.

The rest of this paper is organized as follows. We describe the AGLP protocol in Section 2. We analyze the performance in Section 3. In Section 4, we discuss improvements to AGLP we plan to make. Related work is described in Section 5 and we conclude our paper in Section 6. Please note that an in-depth discussion about Degas is out of the scope of this paper. Therefore certain details about the gateways have been omitted to simplify the presentation. Interested readers should refer to [10] for a full description of the Degas system.

2. PROTOCOL DESCRIPTION

Before we describe our protocol, we present the symbols and terminology used in our description:

- g is a well-known multicast channel used for exchanging control messages among the gateways, and between the gateways and client. Every gateway and client listens to g.

- s is a multicast session.

- P is a program that specifies an input session s and the processing to be done on video streams from s.

- C is the client that requests some processing to be done on video streams.

- $G_0, G_1, .., G_m$ are gateways available for running a program requested by C. One of the gateway will be selected to service C. Without loss of generality, we let G_0 be the current gateway servicing C.

- $S_0, S_2, .., S_k$ are video senders participating in video session s. These senders can be normal MBone video sources. They need not be aware of the existence of the gateways or C.

For simplicity, we assume that each client can submit only one program at a time, and each program can read from only one session. We also assume that all participants run the network time protocol NTP [8], which we rely on to measure the propagation delay of a packet.

Our protocol consists of two phases (see Figure 1). The first phase, *Quick-Start Phase*, chooses a gateway G_0 that is close to C, without worrying about optimizing bandwidth utilization. The second phase, the *Adapting Phase*, optimizes the bandwidth utilization by migrating services to a better gateway. We describe these two phases in Section 2.1 and Section 2.2 respectively.

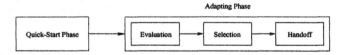

Figure 1: Different phases in the AGLP Protocol.

2.1 Quick-Start Phase

There are two reasons why the Quick-Start Phase is necessary. First, we want to reduce the start-up latency experienced by the user. Secondly, we do not have any knowledge about the behavior of the program requested by the client, nor do we know anything about the session (such as the identity of the senders, and bandwidth of incoming video streams). The gateway we select at the Quick-Start Phase serves as a temporary gateway. This gateway collects information so that further optimization can be done. The Quick-Start Phase works as follows (see Figure 2).

The client C who wants to request some processing to be done on the gateway first multicast a **request** message onto the common multicast channel g. A gateway G_i that receives the **request** message and is available to serve C replies

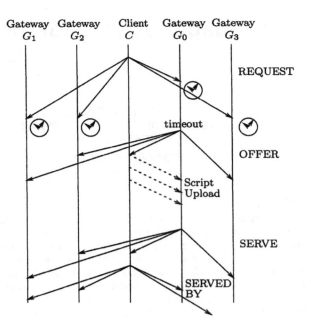

Figure 2: The Quick-Start phase of AGLP.

with a **offer**(C) message. However, instead of replying immediately, we employ a technique commonly known as Multicast Damping to reduce the number of **offer** messages received by C. Each G_i waits for time $T_{\text{offer},i}$ before multicasting the offer onto g. Moreover, a gateway will suppress its **offer**(C) message if it has received an **offer**(C) message from another gateway while waiting.

Client C listens to g and accepts the first offer that it receives. Without loss of generality, let the first offer that C receives be from gateway G_0. C subsequently creates a TCP connection with G_0 at port p, where p is a port number embedded in the **offer**(C) message. Subsequent offers from other gateways will be ignored by C.

C sends the necessary information needed for processing to G_0 using the TCP connection. This includes the multicast address of the input session, s, the multicast address of the output session, s', and a program that specifies how to process the incoming video streams.

After G_0 has received all the necessary information, G_0 joins the session s, processes incoming video streams, and multicasts the output onto channel s' (see Figure 3). C listens to channel s' to receive the post-processed video it requested. At this point, we enter a state where gateway G_0 is serving client C. G_0 and C periodically announce this relationship onto g. Every T_{serve} seconds, G_0 announces a **serve**(C) message onto g. Similarly, C sends a **served-by**(G_0) message to G_0 every $T_{\text{served-by}}$ seconds.

The receipt of **serve**(C) message by C indicates that the Quick-Start Phase has completed successfully. If C does not receive any **serve**(C) message in a period of length T_{request}, C will restart the whole process by sending another re-

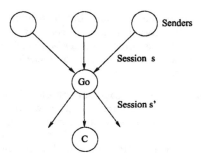

Senders

Session s

Go

Session s'

C

Figure 3: Gateway G_0 listens to session s and receives video streams from the senders. G_0 processes those streams and sends the result out onto session s', on which C is listening.

quest message. Otherwise, the Quick-Start is successful, and AGLP proceeds to the next phase.

2.2 Adapting Phase

During the adapting phase, a service for C may be migrated from the current gateway G_0, to another more suitable gateway, as more information about the session is discovered and changes in the environment are detected. The adapting phase consists of three stages: evaluation, selection and replacement (see Figure 4 for an example). In the evaluation stage, each gateway evaluates itself against G_0 to check if it is more suitable than G_0 for serving C. Once a gateway determine that it can serve G_0 better, it will notify G_0. G_0 periodically runs a selection process, to select the best alternate gateway. Once a replacement G_r is chosen, G_0 hands-off the service for C to G_r. We explain these three stages in greater detail in the following subsections.

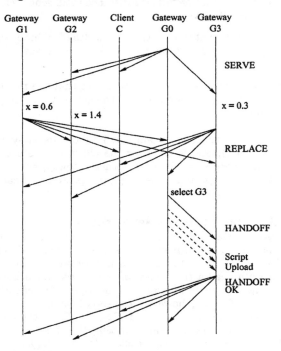

Figure 4: The Adapting phase of AGLP.

2.2.1 Stage 1: Evaluation

We first introduce a few variables that corresponds to the criteria used to perform evaluation:

- b_i: the bandwidth of video stream from sender S_i
- b_C: the bandwidth of the output video stream
- $d_{i,j}$: the distance between gateway G_i and sender S_j
- $d_{i,C}$: the distance between gateway G_i and client C

We now describe how this information is collected and how the evaluation is performed.

After joining session s, G_0 starts to collect information about the current session. This information includes the identity of the senders in the session, and bandwidth of the input streams and the output stream, and the distance (or latency) $d_{0,j}$ from each sender S_j. The identities and distances can be learned from RTCP [12] packets, while the bandwidth information can be gathered by simply counting the packets as they are being processed. This information is included in the **serve** messages and multicast onto group g.

Each gateway G_i, that is available to serve C, maintains a table of distances to itself from the sources, $D_{self} = d_{i,0}..d_{i,k}$. This table is maintained as soft-states, and is refreshed by periodically joining session s, and listening for RTCP packets. A distance can be calculated by subtracting the NTP timestamp of a sender's report from the arrival time.

Each gateway, upon receiving a **serve**(C, s) message from G_0, starts the evaluation test to compare the suitability of serving client C. The test produces a *score*, x_i. This score is calculated as follows. First, let U_i be

$$U_i = \sum_j (b_j \times d_{0,j}) + b_C \times d_{0,C}$$

Intuitively, U_i corresponds to the bandwidth utilization. We calculate x_i as

$$x_i = U_0 - U_i$$

A score $x_i > 0$ indicates that G_i is better than G_0 for serving C. Each gateway with a score larger than ϵ will try to replace the current gateway. We choose a threshold ϵ instead of 0 for two reasons. First, a score between 0 and ϵ indicates that the gateway is only slightly better than G_0. The small improvement that we gain is not worthy of the overhead caused by the replacement process. Second, by ignoring gateways that are only slightly better, we can avoid unnecessary oscillation caused by small changes in network conditions. In the next subsection, we discuss how a replacement is selected by G_0.

2.2.2 Gateway Replacement

After evaluation, each gateway with a score larger than ϵ will notify the current gateway, and wait for a reply. This process is similar to the Quick-Start Phase. Again, we use Multicast Damping for scalability reasons. The gateways start a timer and wait for $T_{replace,i}$ seconds. When the timer expires, gateway G_i multicasts a **replace**(C, x_i) message onto

139

g. If G_i receives another replace(C,x_j) message from another gateway G_j and $x_j > x_i$, then G_i suppresses its own replace message.

The current gateway keep tracks of the gateway with the lowest score so far, which we call the replacement gateway G_r. T_{adapt} seconds after G_0 receives the first replace message, gateway G_0 unicasts a message handoff(C,p), to G_r. G_0 then establishes a TCP connection to G_r at port p through which G_0 sends the program and input session address s to G_r. G_r subsequently starts the service, and multicasts a handoff-ok(C,G_0,s'') announcement, where s'' is a new multicast address where the processed media stream is going to be sent.

2.2.3 Service Handoff

G_r joins session s, starts processing the input video streams, and sends the output onto session s''. G_r also begins the periodical announcement of serve(C, s'') messages.

At this stage, both G_r and G_0 are providing service for C. Upon receiving both handoff-ok(C,G_0,s'') and serve(C,s''), C knows that another more suitable gateway has been found and this new gateway is ready to serve C. C can now switch from group s' to group s''. C stops announcing served-by(C,G_0) and starts announcing served-by(C,G_r). G_0 stops processing video streams from s eventually after no served-by(C,G_0) is received for T_{bye} seconds.

We provide a summary list of messages involved in this protocol in Table 1.

3. ANALYSIS AND SIMULATION

In this section we evaluate our protocol. In particular, we want to confirm that our protocol satisfies two desirable properties:

- robustness:
  - a gateway eventually runs the service requested by a client;
  - all services are eventually terminated when no client is listening;
  - the service is eventually moved to the optimal gateway.
- scalability:
  - as the number of gateways increases, the number of states maintained and the number of messages exchanged does not increase significantly.

3.1 Robustness

We achieve robustness by maintaining only soft-states which are periodically forgotten and need to be refreshed. Soft-state protocols are used in many light-weight protocols in MBone applications such as SDP [6] and RTCP [12]. Failure recovery is automatic in soft-state protocols, since the failure of a gateway or network link will cause refresh messages to be lost and states to be forgotten. Refresh messages in AGLP include serve and served-by—we illustrate how they support failure recovery by describing two scenarios below.

- Suppose that the gateway that is serving C crashes. The periodic serve message will cease and C will eventually forget that some gateway is servicing it. C will start requesting service again by entering the Quick-Start phase.

- Suppose that the message handoff-ok is lost on its way to C. C will not switch to the new gateway. Even though the new gateway has started serving C, it will not receive a served-by message from C. The new gateway will eventually timeout after T_{bye} seconds, and end its service.

We simulated AGLP in networks with up to 50% loss rate. Although this caused somewhat longer start-up/handoff latencies and redundant requests, the protocol still worked correctly.

3.2 Scalability — Memory Requirements

We envision that the number of gateways running in the network $|G|$ will be large (up to thousands), and the number of clients requesting service to be in the same range. The number of senders per client, $|S|$, however, is expected to be small (say, less than 10). Similarly, because the processing requested by client could be computation intensive, we expect the maximum number of clients that can be served by each gateway, $|C|$, to be small as well.

Each gateway maintains the following soft-states:

- A list of clients it is currently serving;
- The gateway with the best score so far;
- A table that records the distance to all senders for each client it serves;
- A table that records the bandwidth of all input streams and output streams for each client it serves.

On the client side, the only soft-states that are maintained are the sessions to listen to, and the gateway currently serving the client.

The size of the state maintained in the gateway is thus $O(|S| \times |C|)$, and is $O(1)$ for the client. Since a gateway does not keep state for every other gateway, and both $|S|$ and $|C|$ are expected to be small, our protocol is scalable in terms of memory size.

3.3 Scalability — Networking

Multicast Damping is a widely used technique to improve scalability in one-to-many protocols (*e.g.*, it is used in IGMP [4] and SRM [5]). As described in Section 2, we use Multicast Damping for the request-offer and serve-replace message exchanges to avoid implosion of messages. The effectiveness of this technique, however, depends heavily on the timeout values chosen, T_{offer} and T_{replace}. Even though there is extensive work done in analyzing the effect of timers in Multicast Damping (see, for example, [5] and [9]), there are some unique requirements for our timers. T_{offer} should be proportional to the distance from the client, so that the first request() A request for service by a client.

offer(C, p) A response to a request message from client C. Indicates that the sending gateway is available to serve C. C should contact this gateway at port p for details.

serve(C, S, D) The sending gateway is currently running a service for C. S is the list of session members, D is a vector containing distances from each member in S as well as the distance from C.

served-by(G) Response to the gateway serving C to notify that C is still listening to output from G.

replace(C, x) Notify others that the sending gateway is more suitable for serving C. x indicates how much better the sending gateway is.

handoff(C, p) Message from the current gateway to G' to indicate that G' has been chosen to replace the current gateway for serving C. G' should listen to port p for service specification.

handoff-ok(C, G, s') Announcement from a new gateway G' that it is ready to replace G to serve C. s' is the new multicast address where the output from the service will be sent.

Table 1: A summary of message types and their contents in AGLP

reply received by the client comes from the gateway that is closest to the client. For T_{replace}, the timer value should be inversely proportional to the score of a gateway. We discuss these two parameters in this section.

In order to evaluate the performance of AGLP under these parameters, we simulate our protocol using the ns2 network simulator and run it on a 500-node topology generated using the gt-itm toolkit [2]. We place gateways and the client at random locations in the generated network.

In AGLP, we set the value of T_{offer} to $k \times d$, where k is a constant and d is the propagation delay between gateway and client, measured using an NTP timestamp embedded in the request message. A small value of k results in a lower start-up latency, but a larger number of duplicates. The number of duplicates also depends on the distribution of gateways in the network. If gateways are sparsely distributed, then the number of duplicates increases.

We tried different values of k in our simulations. In Figure 5 we show the average number of duplicate offer messages received by the client for different values of k in cases where the number of gateways G is either 50, 100, or 200. A value of $k \geq 2$ causes the number of duplicates to stay below 3 even as the number of gateways increases up to 200. Figure 6 shows the latencies that the client experiences.

We conclude that $k = 2$ works well in reducing the number of duplicates while keeping the start-up latency within a reasonable time. In Figures 7 and 8 we show the behavior of Multicast Damping as a function of the number of gateways in more detail, along with a 95% confidence interval for each measurement. Our experiments indicate that AGLP scales well for $k = 2$. In the remaining experiments we are using this value for k.

We set the value of T_{replace} to k'/x, where x is the score. In Figure 9 we show the number of duplicate replace responses as a function of k'. We see that for $k' > 500$ the number of duplicates is under 10, which we consider acceptable. Figure

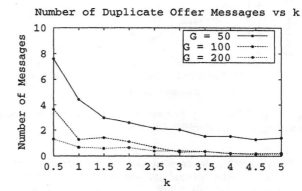

Figure 5: Duplicate offer messages for different values of k and G (the number of gateways).

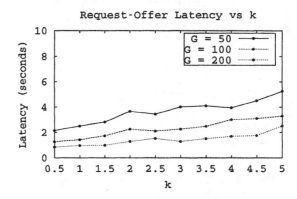

Figure 6: The delay between sending a request and receiving the first offer.

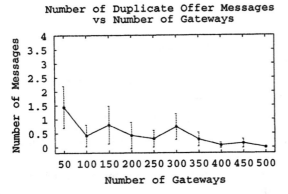

Figure 7: Duplicate offer messages for $k = 2$.

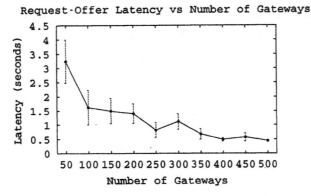

Figure 8: The delay between sending a request and receiving the first offer for $k = 2$.

10 shows that the average number of migrations before a service reaches the optimal gateway goes down with k'. We were surprised by this result. After all, as k' goes up, it becomes less likely that the client will receive a response from the optimal gateway within T_{adapt}. However, after further consideration we are able to explain this.

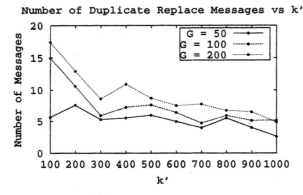

Figure 9: Duplicate replace messages.

After the current gateway gets the first replace response, it waits T_{adapt} seconds before selecting a gateway to hand-off to. That is, after sending the last serve message, it waits

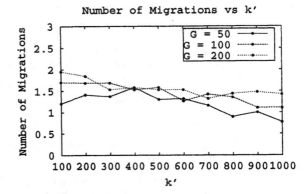

Figure 10: Number of migrations needed to migrate to an optimal gateway.

a total of $RTT_1 + k'/x_1 + T_{adapt}$ seconds, where RTT_1 is the round-trip time to the first responding gateway, and x_1 is the score at that gateway. In order for the optimal gateway's response to be received in time, we need to have the following condition (see Figure 11):

$$RTT_{optimal} + \frac{k'}{x_{optimal}} < RTT_1 + \frac{k'}{x_1} + T_{adapt}$$

We can rewrite this as:

$$\frac{RTT_{optimal} - RTT_1 - T_{adapt}}{(\frac{1}{x_1} - \frac{1}{x_{optimal}})} < k'$$

Thus, the larger k', the more likely that the optimal gateway responds in time, as reflected in Figure 10.

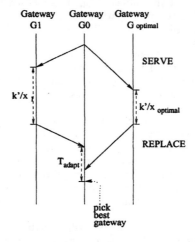

Figure 11: Exchanges of serve and replace messages.

In the following experiments, we use $k' = 1000$ as a conservative choice. For this value of k', we find that there are no more than 8 replace messages received (see Figure 12) even if we run a gateway on all 500 nodes in the network. There were at most two migrations in all runs of our simulations (see Figure 13 for averages and 95% confidence intervals). In Figure 14 we show how this translates into time. On average, all services were migrated to the optimal gateway within 60 seconds, which we find acceptable.

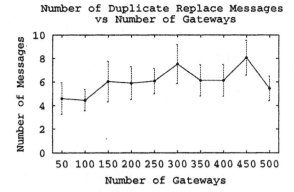

Figure 12: Duplicate replace messages received by a gateway for $k' = 1000$.

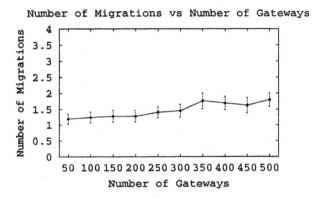

Figure 13: Number of migrations to migrate to an optimal gateway for $k' = 1000$.

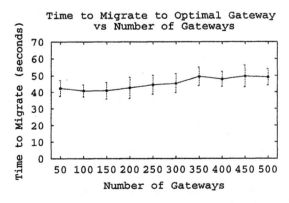

Figure 14: Time to migrate to an optimal gateway for $k' = 1000$.

4. ENHANCEMENTS TO AGLP

Our current implementation of AGLP, as described above, has many restrictions. For example, we assume that each service reads from only one multicast session, and outputs to another session. We also assume that each client can request one service at a time. As described below, we plan to relax these restrictions.

4.1 Multiple Receivers

Although so far we have assumed that the client is the only one who benefits from the service provided by the gateways, we can easily allow multiple clients to receive the post-processed streams from gateways. Since the post-processed video stream is multicast onto session s', any host that is interested in the post-processed stream can tune in to session s' to receive the stream. This can be done as follows.

We will augment the Session Description Protocol to include information about services currently provided by the gateways. A host can view the list of services available using a GUI front end, and join any session that it is interested in. The host will periodically announce **served-by** messages onto the common multicast channel g. The **served-by** messages from multiple receivers can be consolidated by using Multicast Damping: if a receiver R receives a **served-by** message, then R reschedules the announcement of its own **served-by** message. This reduces the total number of **served-by** message sent. If the original client C that initiated the service quits, the gateway will continue serving the other receivers as it is still receiving **served-by** messages.

Two problems arise. First, what if the gateway servicing the receivers fails after C quits? The other receivers do not have access to the original program submitted by C, and therefore cannot restart the service. One possible solution to the first problem is to have each receiver download the program from the gateway (if C permits it) as they join session s'. Another solution is to let the gateway periodically multicast the programs onto a separate channel.

The second problem concerns the calculation of scores during evaluation. Since the output from the gateway is now multicast to multiple receivers, how can we characterize the bandwidth utilization of the output stream? We can estimate the propagation delay from the gateway to all receivers by using receiver report RTCP packets, but since bandwidths are shared in the multicast tree, we cannot simply sum the products of the bandwidth and the distances. We plan to investigate both problems further.

4.2 Composable Services

So far we have tacitly assumed that each client requests service from only one gateway. We can extend AGLP to allow multiple services to be requested by a client. An interesting consequence of this is that the client can submit multiple programs that can be composed to perform a task.

For example, a client would like to create a "Quad Splitter" view of four video streams from some session s. One approach is to submit a program that says "take these four streams, scale each of them down by half, and arrange them to create a quad-splitter view." If the four video sources are located far from each other, this program is best run at a gateway somewhere in the middle of the four sources. However, if a client can request multiple services, then a better way to create a quad-splitter view is to write five programs: each of the first four programs reads from one video sender, scales it by half, and sends the scaled video out to a new session. The fifth program reads from the output sessions of the first four programs and creates the quad-splitter view. Our adaptive protocol will cause the scaling processes to be performed near the senders, resulting in more efficient use of bandwidth (see Figure 15)

Several modifications to AGLP are needed to support this. First, a gateway G needs to know whether it is receiving data from another gateway G'. This is needed so that when a service on G' is migrated to another gateway, G can detect the handoff and switch its input session to the output session of the new gateway. The client can indicate this information to G in the program uploaded to G. G can then pay attention to any handoff message from G', and switch accordingly.

Secondly, a gateway must be able to receive and process streams from multiple sessions. We have been assuming that a service reads multiple streams from a single session, and output to one session. This is inadequate if we want to allow composable services. For instance, say gateway G is receiving streams from two gateways G' and G''. Initially G' and G'' can send their outputs to a shared session, which G can listen to. As services on G' and G'' migrate to other gateways, G will have to listen to two different sessions to receive its inputs.

The third modification needed concerns failure recovery when a gateway G fails. One way to recover from the failure is to restart only the service that ran on that gateway. However, the client needs to maintain consistent information about where each of the gateways receives its input from and where they send their outputs to, so that the client can modify its program to indicate the new input or output session. Maintaining consistent information is hard because our protocol uses soft-states. We believe that a better solution is to let the client restart all services from scratch. Even though this is inefficient as it will cause all living gateways to stop running their service for C, this does provide a quick recovery from failures.

4.3 Load Balancing
We have implemented a simple method to balance the loads on gateways. Only a gateway with load lower than a certain threshold is eligible to offer services to a client. Ideally, we should take the available resources of a gateway into consideration. We should include metrics such as available CPU time, available memory, or the availability of special multimedia hardware into our evaluation function. However, it is not clear how to integrate these different metrics into one variable in order to decide which gateway is more suitable to service a particular client.

5. RELATED WORK
Many techniques that we use in AGLP are already widely used in the network community, especially in the MBone tools. For example, announce-listen based soft-state protocols are used in the Active Service Control Protocol (ASCP)

[1], the Internet Group Management Protocol (IGMP) [4], the Session Description Protocol (SDP) [6], and RTCP [12]. Among these protocols, ASCP is the closest to our work. ASCP is used to locate an active server in the network to perform a specified transcoding. However, ASCP does not adapt to network conditions, and the transcoding may not occur on a server that is strategically located. This may result in inefficient utilization of network bandwidth.

Other protocols for locating services existed. For example, DHCP [3] uses a centralized server at a known location to provide information about the location of the local DNS servers. DHCP is intended for local area networks only – DHCP does not scale, and its centralized design makes it vulnerable to crashes. SLP [14] uses another approach, where each server periodically announces the availability of services to a well-known multicast channel. A client who requires some service listens to the multicast channel to discover the services available. This approach is designed for local area networks, and suffers from a scalability problem when a large number of servers are available. [11] describes a wide-area version of SLP for locating Internet Telephony Gateway, but this work does not take network bandwidth into consideration.

MeGaDiP (Media Gateway Discovery Protocol) [15] uses centralized directory agents called *dealers* to find media gateways located along the end-to-end path between two end hosts. An end host contacts a local dealer to find a gateway. If no gateway is available, the dealer forwards the request to another dealer along the end-to-end path. List of dealers along the path are obtained using traceroute and modified DNS lookup. While both AGLP and MeGaDiP try to minimize network traffic, AGLP is distributed, does not require changes to DNS, and can support multiple end hosts.

The Conductor system [16] allows adaptors to be deployed at key locations in the network to adapt data flows to changing network conditions. Conductor uses a centralized algorithm to decide on deployments of adaptors into strategic locations in the network. The Conductor may produce a non-optimal plan because the complexity of calculating an optimal plan in a centralized location is prohibitive. We use a distributed, adaptive scheme that does not suffer from this problem. Conductor adapts TCP streams, but does not support the connection-less, RTP-based multicast packets that AGLP supports.

6. CONCLUSION
In this paper, we present an adaptive control protocol called AGLP for running services on media processing gateways in the Internet. Our protocol supports the following functionality:

- allowing the client to request a service, and submit media processing program to a gateway;

- deciding which gateway should be used to perform a service;

- migrating services to more suitable gateways (adaptability).

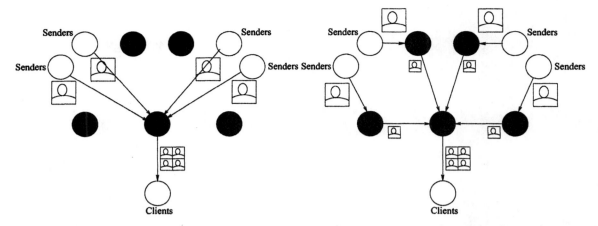

Figure 15: Composable Service is possible with AGLP. The left diagram shows a possible configuration when a client uses a single gateway to create a quad-splitter view. The right figure shows a possible configuration when multiple programs are used. Scaling the video near the sources may result in significant reduction in bandwidth usage.

AGLP builds on the announce-listen paradigm and uses soft-states to maintain information. As a result, our protocol is both scalable and robust. AGLP is compatible with existing MBone tools, so that no changes are required at the senders. Furthermore, the existence of gateways and clients is transparent to the senders.

Although AGLP was designed for the Degas system, the protocol can be modified for any application that needs to decide where to run certain services inside the network. With the increasing interest in the research community to move computation, traditionally performed at the edge of the network, into the network itself, we believe applications for AGLP will increase in the future.

7. REFERENCES

[1] E. Amir, S. McCanne, and Z. Hui. An application level video gateway. In *Proc. of 3rd ACM Intl. Multimedia Conf. and Exhibition*, pages 255–266, San Francisco, CA, November 1995.

[2] K. Calvert, M. Doar, and E. Zegura. Modeling internet topology. *IEEE Communications Magazine*, 36(6):160–163, June 1997.

[3] R. Droms. RFC 2131: Dynamic host configuration protocol, March 1997.

[4] W. Fenner. RFC 2236: Internet Group Management Protocol, version 2, November 1997.

[5] S. Floyd, V. Jacobson, C. G. Liu, S. McCanne, and L. Zhang. A reliable multicast framework for light-weight sessions and application level framing. *IEEE/ACM Transactions on Networking*, 5(6):784–803, December 1997.

[6] M. Handley and V. Jacobson. RFC 2327: SDP: Session description protocol, April 1998.

[7] S. McCanne and V. Jacobson. vic: A flexible framework for packet video. In *Proc. of 3rd ACM Intl. Multimedia Conf. and Exhibition*, pages 511–522, San Francisco, CA, November 1995.

[8] D. L. Mills. RFC 1305: Network time protocol (version 3) specification, implementation, March 1992.

[9] J. Nonnenmacher and E. W. Biersack. Scalable feedback for large croups. *IEEE/ACM Transactions on Networking 1999*, 7(3):375–386, June 1999.

[10] W. T. Ooi and B. Smith. The design and implementation of programmable media gateways. In *Proc. of 10th. Intl. Workshop on Network and Operating Systems Support for Digital Audio and Video (NOSSDAV'00)*, Chapel Hill, North Carolina, June 2000.

[11] J. Rosenberg and H. Schulzrinne. Internet telephony gateway location. In *Proc. of IEEE INFOCOM*, March 1998.

[12] H. Schulzrinne, S. Casner, R. Frederick, and V. Jacobson. RFC 1889: RTP: A transport protocol for real-time applications, January 1996.

[13] T. Turletti. The INRIA videoconferencing system. *ConneXions - The Interoperability Report Journal*, 8(10):20–24, October 1994.

[14] J. Veizades, E. Guttman, C. Perkins, and S. Kaplan. RFC 2165: Service location protocol, June 1997.

[15] D. Xu, K. Nahrstedt, and D. Wichadakul. MeGaDiP: a wide-area media gateway discovery protocol. In *Proc. of IEEE Intl. Performance, Computing and Communications Conf.*, Pheonix, Arizona, February 2000.

[16] M. Yarvis, A. A. Wang, A. Rudenko, P. Reiher, , and G. J. Popek. Conductor: Distributed adaptation for complex networks. Technical Report CSD-TR-990042, University of California, Los Angeles, Los Angeles, California, August 1999.

IRM: Integrated Region Matching for Image Retrieval*

Jia Li[†]
Palo Alto Research Center
Xerox Corporation
Palo Alto, CA 94304
jiali@db.stanford.edu

James Z. Wang[‡]
Dept. of Computer Science
Stanford University
Stanford, CA 94305
wangz@cs.stanford.edu

Gio Wiederhold
Dept. of Computer Science
Stanford University
Stanford, CA 94305
gio@cs.stanford.edu

ABSTRACT

Content-based image retrieval using region segmentation has been an active research area. We present IRM (Integrated Region Matching), a novel similarity measure for region-based image similarity comparison. The targeted image retrieval systems represent an image by a set of regions, roughly corresponding to objects, which are characterized by features reflecting color, texture, shape, and location properties. The IRM measure for evaluating overall similarity between images incorporates properties of all the regions in the images by a region-matching scheme. Compared with retrieval based on individual regions, the overall similarity approach reduces the influence of inaccurate segmentation, helps to clarify the semantics of a particular region, and enables a simple querying interface for region-based image retrieval systems. The IRM has been implemented as a part of our experimental SIMPLIcity image retrieval system. The application to a database of about 200,000 general-purpose images shows exceptional robustness to image alterations such as intensity variation, sharpness variation, color distortions, shape distortions, cropping, shifting, and rotation. Compared with several existing systems, our system in general achieves more accurate retrieval at higher speed.

1. INTRODUCTION

With the steady growth of computer power, rapidly declining cost of storage, and ever-increasing access to the Internet, digital acquisition of information has become increasingly popular in recent years. Digital information is preferable to analog formats because of convenient sharing and

*This work was supported in part by the National Science Foundation's Digital Libraries initiative. The authors would like to thank the help of Oscar Firschein and anonymous reviewers. An on-line demonstration is provided at URL: http://WWW-DB.Stanford.EDU/IMAGE/

[†]Research performed when the author was with Stanford University.

[‡]Also of Medical Informatics, Stanford University.

distribution properties. This trend has motivated research in image databases, which were nearly ignored by traditional computer systems due to the enormous amount of data necessary to represent images and the difficulty of automatically analyzing images. Currently, storage is less of an issue since huge storage capacity is available at low cost. However, effective indexing and searching of large-scale image databases remains as a challenge for computer systems. The automatic derivation of semantics from the content of an image is the focus of interest for most research on image databases. Image *semantics* has several levels: semantic types, object composition, abstract semantics, and detailed semantics.

1.1 Related Work

Content-based image retrieval is defined as the retrieval of relevant images from an image database based on automatically derived imagery features. The need for efficient content-based image retrieval has increased tremendously in many application areas such as biomedicine, crime prevention, military, commerce, culture, education, entertainment, and Web image classification and searching.

There are many general-purpose image search engines. In the commercial domain, IBM QBIC [3, 16] is one of the earliest developed systems. Recently, additional systems have been developed at IBM T.J. Watson [23], VIRAGE [5], NEC AMORA [14], Bell Laboratory [15], Interpix (Yahoo), Excalibur, and Scour.net. In the academic domain, MIT Photobook [17, 18] is one of the earliest. Berkeley Blobworld [1], Columbia VisualSEEK and WebSEEK [22], CMU Informedia [24], UIUC MARS [12], UCSB NeTra [10], UCSD, Stanford (EMD [19], WBIIS [26]) are some of the recent systems.

Existing general-purpose CBIR systems roughly fall into three categories depending on the signature extraction approach used: histogram, color layout, and region-based search. There are also systems that combine retrieval results from individual algorithms by a weighted sum matching metric [5], or other merging schemes [20].

Histogram search [16, 19] characterizes an image by its color distribution, or histogram. The drawback of a global histogram representation is that information about object location, shape, and texture is discarded. Color histogram search is sensitive to intensity variation, color distortions, and cropping.

The color layout approach attempts to mitigate the problems with histogram search. For traditional color layout indexing [16], images are partitioned into blocks and the average color of each block is stored. Thus, the color layout is essentially a low resolution representation of the original image. A later system, WBIIS [26], uses significant Daubechies' wavelet coefficients instead of averaging. By adjusting block sizes or the levels of wavelet transforms, the coarseness of a color layout representation can be tuned. The finest color layout using a single pixel block is merely the original image. We can hence view a color layout representation as an opposite extreme of a histogram. At proper resolutions, the color layout representation naturally retains shape, location, and texture information. However, as with pixel representation, although information such as shape is preserved in the color layout representation, the retrieval system cannot "see" it explicitly. Color layout search is sensitive to shifting, cropping, scaling, and rotation because images are characterized by a set of local properties.

Region-based retrieval systems attempt to overcome the deficiencies of color layout search by representing images at the object-level. A region-based retrieval system applies image segmentation to decompose an image into regions, which correspond to objects if the decomposition is ideal. The object-level representation is intended to be close to the perception of the human visual system (HVS).

Since the retrieval system has identified objects in the image, it is relatively easy for the system to recognize similar objects at different locations and with different orientations and sizes. Region-based retrieval systems include the NeTra system [10], the Blobworld system [1], and the query system with color region templates [23]. We have developed SIMPLIcity (Semantics-sensitive Integrated Matching for Picture LIbraries), a region-based image retrieval system, using high-level semantics classification [27].

The NeTra and the Blobworld systems compare images based on individual regions. Although querying based on a limited number of regions is allowed, the query is performed by merging single-region query results. Because of the great difficulty of achieving accurate segmentation, systems in [10, 1] tend to partition one object into several regions with none of them being representative for the object, especially for images without distinctive objects and scenes. Consequently, it is often difficult for users to determine which regions and features should be used for retrieval.

Not much attention has been paid to developing similarity measures that combine information from all of the regions. One effort in this direction is the querying system developed by Smith and Li [23]. Their system decomposes an image into regions with characterizations pre-defined in a finite pattern library. With every pattern labeled by a symbol, images are then represented by region strings. Region strings are converted to composite region template (CRT) descriptor matrices reflecting the relative ordering of symbols. Similarity between images is measured by the closeness between the CRT descriptor matrices. This measure is sensitive to object shifting since a CRT matrix is determined solely by the ordering of symbols. Robustness to scaling and rotation is not considered by the measure either. Because the definition of the CRT descriptor matrix relies on the

pattern library, the system performance depends critically on the library. Performance degrades if regions in an image are not represented in the library. The system in [23] uses a CRT library with patterns described only by color. In particular, the patterns are obtained by quantizing color space. If texture and shape features are added to distinguish patterns, the number of patterns in the library will increase dramatically, roughly exponentially in the number of features if patterns are obtained by uniformly quantizing features.

1.2 Overview of IRM

To reflect semantics more precisely by the region representation, we have developed IRM, a similarity measure of images based on region representations. IRM incorporates the properties of all the segmented regions so that information about an image can be fully used. Region-based matching is a difficult problem because of inaccurate segmentation. Semantically-precise image segmentation is extremely difficult [21, 11, 28, 7, 8] and is still an open problem in computer vision. For example, segmentation algorithm may segment an image of a dog into two regions: the dog and the background. The same algorithm may segment another image of a dog into six regions: the body of the dog, the front leg(s) of the dog, the rear leg(s) of the dog, the eye(s), the background grass, and the sky.

The IRM measure we have developed has the following major advantages:

1. Compared with retrieval based on individual regions, the overall similarity approach in IRM reduces the adverse effect of inaccurate segmentation, an important property that previous work has virtually overlooked.

2. In many cases, knowing that one object usually appears with another object helps to clarify the semantics of a particular region. For example, flowers typically appear with green leaves, and boats usually appear with water.

3. By defining an overall image-to-image similarity measure, the system provides users with a *simple* querying interface. To complete a query, a user only needs to specify the query image. If desired, the system can also be adjusted to allow users to query based on a specific region or a few regions.

To define the similarity measure, we first attempt to match regions in two images. Being aware that segmentation cannot be perfect, we "soften" the matching by allowing one region of an image to be matched to several regions of another image. Here, a region-to-region *match* is obtained when the regions are relatively similar to each other in terms of the features extracted.

The principle of matching is that the closest region pair is matched first. We call this matching scheme *Integrated Region Matching* (IRM) to stress the incorporation of regions in the retrieval process. After regions are matched, the similarity measure is computed as a weighted sum of the similarity between region pairs, with weights determined by the

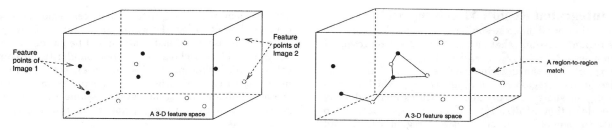

Figure 1: Region-to-region matching results are incorporated in the Integrated Region Matching (IRM) metric. A 3-D feature space is shown to illustrate the concept.

matching scheme. Figure 1 illustrates the concept of IRM in a 3-D feature space. The features we extract on the segmented regions are of high dimensions. The problem is much more sophisticated in a high-dimensional feature space.

1.3 Outline of the Paper

The remainder of the paper is organized as follows. In Section 2, the similarity measure based on segmented regions is defined. In Section 3, we describe the experiments we have performed and provide results. We conclude in Section 4.

2. THE SIMILARITY MEASURE
2.1 Image Segmentation

The similarity measure is defined based on segmented regions of images. Our system segments images based on color and frequency features using the k-means algorithm [6]. For general-purpose images such as the images in a photo library or the images on the World-Wide Web (WWW), precise object segmentation is nearly as difficult as computer semantics understanding. Semantically-precise segmentation, however, is not crucial to our system because we use a more robust integrated region-matching (IRM) scheme which is insensitive to inaccurate segmentation (Figure 2).

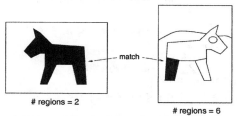

Traditional region-based matching

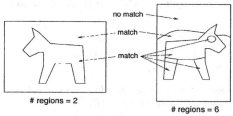

Integrated Region Matching (IRM)

Figure 2: Integrated Region Matching (IRM) is robust to poor image segmentation.

To segment an image, the system partitions the image into

blocks with 4×4 pixels and extracts a feature vector for each block. We choose this block size to optimize between texture effectiveness and segmentation coarseness. The k-means algorithm is used to cluster the feature vectors into several classes with every class corresponding to one region in the segmented image. An alternative to the block-wise segmentation is a pixel-wise segmentation by forming a window centered around every pixel.

The segmentation results are available on the demonstration web site. One main advantage of using the k-means clustering algorithm for segmentation is that blocks in each cluster does not have to be neighboring blocks. This way, we preserve the natural clustering of objects and allow classification of textured images [9]. The number of regions, k, is selected adaptively. Experimental results have shown that the system is insensitive to the number of regions segmented.

Six features are used for segmentation. Three of them are the average color components in a 4×4 block. The other three represent energy in high frequency bands of the wavelet transforms [2, 13], that is, the square root of the second order moment of wavelet coefficients in high frequency bands. We use the well-known LUV color space, where L encodes luminance, and U and V encode color information (chrominance).

To obtain the other three features, a Daubechies-4 wavelet transform is applied to the L component of the image. After a one-level wavelet transform, a 4×4 block is decomposed into four frequency bands: the LL, LH, HL, and HH bands [2]. Each band contains 2×2 coefficients. Without loss of generality, suppose the coefficients in the HL band are $\{c_{k,l}, c_{k,l+1}, c_{k+1,l}, c_{k+1,l+1}\}$. One feature is:

$$f = \left(\frac{1}{4} \sum_{i=0}^{1} \sum_{j=0}^{1} c_{k+i,l+j}^2 \right)^{\frac{1}{2}} .$$

The other two features are computed similarly from the LH and HH bands. The motivation for using the features extracted from high frequency bands is that they reflect texture properties. Moments of wavelet coefficients in various frequency bands have been shown to be effective for representing texture [25]. The intuition behind this is that coefficients in different frequency bands show variations in different directions. For example, the HL band shows activities in the horizontal direction. An image with vertical strips thus has high energy in the HL band and low energy in the LH band.

149

2.2 Integrated Region Matching (IRM)

In this section, we define the similarity measure between two sets of regions. Assume that Image 1 and 2 are represented by region sets $R_1 = \{r_1, r_2, ..., r_m\}$ and $R_2 = \{r'_1, r'_2, ..., r'_n\}$, where r_i or r'_i is the descriptor of region i. Denote the distance between region r_i and r'_j as $d(r_i, r'_j)$, which is written as $d_{i,j}$ in short. Details about features included in r_i and the definition of $d(r_i, r'_j)$ will be discussed later. To compute the similarity measure between region sets R_1 and R_2, $d(R_1, R_2)$, we first match all regions in the two images. When we judge the similarity of two animal photographs, we usually compare the animals in the images before comparing the background areas in the images. The overall similarity of the two images depends on the closeness in the two aspects. The correspondence between objects in the images is crucial to our judgment of similarity since it would be meaningless to compare the animal in one image with the background in another. Our IRM matching scheme aims at building correspondence between regions that is consistent with human perception. To increase robustness against segmentation errors, we allow a region to be matched to several regions in another image. A matching between r_i and r'_j is assigned with a significance credit $s_{i,j}$, $s_{i,j} \geq 0$. The significance credit indicates the importance of the matching for determining similarity between images. The matrix $S = \{s_{i,j}\}$, $1 \leq i \leq n$, $1 \leq j \leq m$, is referred to as the significance matrix.

Figure 3: Integrated region matching (IRM) allows one region to be matched to several regions.

A graphical explanation of the integrated matching scheme is provided in Figure 3. The figure shows that matching between images can be represented by an edge weighted graph in which every vertex in the graph corresponds to a region. If two vertices are connected, the two regions are matched with a significance credit being the weight on the edge. To distinguish from matching two sets of regions, we refer to the matching of two regions as they are *linked*. The length of an edge can be regarded as the distance between the two regions represented. If two vertices are not connected, the corresponding regions are either from the same image or the significance credit of matching them is zero. Every matching between images is characterized by links between regions and their significance credits. The matching used to compute the distance between two images is referred to as the *admissible matching*. The admissible matching is specified by conditions on the significance matrix. If a graph represents an admissible matching, the distance between the two region sets is the summation of all the weighted edge lengths, i.e.,

$$d(R_1, R_2) = \sum_{i,j} s_{i,j} d_{i,j} .$$

We call this distance the integrated region matching (IRM) distance.

The problem of defining distance between region sets is then converted to choosing the significance matrix S. A natural issue to raise is what constraints should be put on $s_{i,j}$ so that the admissible matching yields good similarity measure. In other words, what properties do we expect an admissible matching to possess? The first property we want to enforce is the fulfillment of significance. Assume that the significance of r_i in Image 1 is p_i, and r'_j in Image 2 is p'_j, we require that

$$\sum_{j=1}^{n} s_{i,j} = p_i, \ i = 1, ..., m$$
$$\sum_{i=1}^{m} s_{i,j} = p'_j, \ j = 1, ..., n .$$

For normalization, we have $\sum_{i=1}^{m} p_i = \sum_{j=1}^{n} p'_j = 1$. The fulfillment of significance ensures that all the regions play a role for measuring similarity. We also require an admissible matching to link the most similar regions at the highest priority. For example, if two images are the same, the admissible matching should link a region in Image 1 only to the same region in Image 2. With this matching, the distance between the two images equals zero, which coincides with our intuition. Following the "most similar highest priority (MSHP)" principle, the IRM algorithm attempts to fulfill the significance credits of regions by assigning as much significance as possible to the region link with minimum distance. Initially, assume that $d_{i',j'}$ is the minimum distance, we set $s_{i',j'} = \min(p_{i'}, p'_{j'})$. Without loss of generality, assume $p_{i'} \leq p'_{j'}$. Then $s_{i',j} = 0$, for $j \neq j'$ since the link between region i' and j' has filled the significance of region i'. The significance credit left for region j' is reduced to $p'_{j'} - p_{i'}$. The updated matching problem is then solving $s_{i,j}$, $i \neq i'$, by the MSHP rule under constraints:

$$\sum_{j=1}^{n} s_{i,j} = p_i \quad 1 \leq i \leq m, \ i \neq i'$$
$$\sum_{i:1 \leq i \leq m, i \neq i'} s_{i,j} = p'_j \quad 1 \leq j \leq n, \ j \neq j'$$
$$\sum_{i:1 \leq i \leq m, i \neq i'} s_{i,j'} = p'_{j'} - p_{i'}$$
$$s_{i,j} \geq 0 \quad 1 \leq i \leq m, \ i \neq i'; \ 1 \leq j \leq n .$$

We apply the previous procedure to the updated problem. The iteration stops when all the significance credits p_i and p'_j have been assigned. The algorithm is summarized as follows.

1. Set $\mathcal{L} = \{\}$, denote $\mathcal{M} = \{(i,j) : i = 1, ..., m; j = 1, ..., n\}$.

2. Choose the minimum $d_{i,j}$ for $(i,j) \in \mathcal{M} - \mathcal{L}$. Label the corresponding (i,j) as (i',j').

3. $\min(p_{i'}, p'_{j'}) \rightarrow s_{i',j'}$.

4. If $p_{i'} < p'_{j'}$, set $s_{i',j} = 0$, $j \neq j'$; otherwise, set $s_{i,j'} = 0$, $i \neq i'$.

5. $p_{i'} - \min(p_{i'}, p'_{j'}) \rightarrow p_{i'}$.

6. $p'_{j'} - \min(p_{i'}, p'_{j'}) \rightarrow p'_{j'}$.

7. $\mathcal{L} + \{(i', j')\} \rightarrow \mathcal{L}$.

8. If $\sum_{i=1}^{m} p_i > 0$ and $\sum_{j=1}^{n} p'_j > 0$, go to Step 2; otherwise, stop.

We now come to the issue of choosing p_i. The value of p_i is chosen to reflect the significance of region i in the image. If we assume that every region is equally important, then $p_i = 1/m$, where m is the number of regions. In the case that Image 1 and Image 2 have the same number of regions, a region in Image 1 is matched exclusively to one region in Image 2. Another choice of p_i is the percentage of the image covered by region i based on the view that important objects in an image tend to occupy larger areas. We refer to this assignment of p_i as the *area percentage scheme*. This scheme is less sensitive to inaccurate segmentation than the uniform scheme. If one object is partitioned into several regions, the uniform scheme raises its significance improperly, whereas the area percentage scheme retains its significance. On the other hand, if objects are merged into one region, the area percentage scheme assigns relatively high significance to the region. The current implementation of the system uses the area percentage scheme.

The scheme of assigning significance credits can also take region location into consideration. For example, higher significance may be assigned to regions in the center of an image than to those around boundaries. Another way to count location in the similarity measure is to generalize the definition of the IRM distance to $d(R_1, R_2) = \sum_{i,j} s_{i,j} w_{i,j} d_{i,j}$. The parameter $w_{i,j}$ is chosen to adjust the effect of region i and j on the similarity measure. In the current system, regions around boundaries are slightly down-weighted by using this generalized IRM distance.

2.3 Distance Between Regions

The distance between a region pair, $d(r, r')$, is determined by the color, texture, and shape characteristics of the regions. We have described in Section 2.1 the features used by the k-means algorithm for segmentation. The mean values of these features in one cluster are used to represent color and texture in the corresponding region. To describe shape, normalized inertia [4] of order 1 to 3 are used. For a region H in k dimensional Euclidean space $\mathfrak{R}^k$, its normalized inertia of order γ is

$$l(H, \gamma) = \frac{\int_H \|x - \hat{x}\|^{\gamma} dx}{[V(H)]^{1+\gamma/k}}$$

where $\hat{x}$ is the centroid of H and $V(H)$ is the volume of H. Since an image is specified by pixels on a grid, the discrete form of the normalized inertia is used, that is,

$$l(H, \gamma) = \frac{\sum_{x:x\in H} \|x - \hat{x}\|^{\gamma}}{[V(H)]^{1+\gamma/k}}$$

where $V(H)$ is the number of pixels in region H. The normalized inertia is invariant with scaling and rotation. The minimum normalized inertia is achieved by spheres. Denote the γth order normalized inertia of spheres as L_γ. We define shape features as $l(H, \gamma)$ normalized by L_γ:

$$f_7 = l(H, 1)/L_1 \ , \quad f_8 = l(H, 2)/L_2 \ , \quad f_9 = l(H, 3)/L_3 \ .$$

The computation of shape features is skipped for textured images because region shape is not perceptually important for such images. By a textured image, we refer to an image composed of repeated patterns that appears like a unique texture surface. Automatic classification of textured and non-textured images is implemented in our system (for details see [9]). For textured image, the region distance $d(r, r')$ is defined as

$$d(r, r') = \sum_{i=1}^{6} w_i(f_i - f'_i)^2 \ .$$

For non-textured images, $d(r, r')$ is defined as

$$d(r, r') = g(d_s(r, r')) \cdot d_t(r, r') \ ,$$

where $d_s(r, r')$ is the shape distance computed by

$$d_s(r, r') = \sum_{i=7}^{9} w_i(f_i - f'_i)^2 \ ,$$

and $d_t(r, r')$ is the color and texture distance defined the same as the distance between textured image regions, i.e.,

$$d_t(r, r') = \sum_{i=1}^{6} w_i(f_i - f'_i)^2 \ .$$

The function $g(d_s(r, r'))$ is a converting function to ensure a proper influence of the shape distance on the total distance. In our system, it is defined as

$$g(d) = \begin{cases} 1 & d \geq 0.5 \\ 0.85 & 0.2 < d \leq 0.5 \\ 0.5 & d < 0.2 \ . \end{cases}$$

It is observed that when $d_s(r, r') \geq 0.5$, the two regions bear little resemblance. It is then not meaningful to distinguish the extent of similarity by $d_s(r, r')$ because perceptually the two regions simply appear different. We thus set $g(d) = 1$ for d greater than a threshold. When $d_s(r, r')$ is very small, to retain the influence of color and texture, $g(d)$ is bounded away from zero. For simplicity, $g(d)$ is selected as a piecewise constant function instead of a smooth one. Because rather simple shape features are used in our system, color and texture are emphasized more than shape for determining similarity between regions. As can be seen from the definition of $d(r, r')$, the shape distance serves as a "bonus" in the sense that only when two regions are considerably similar in shape, their distance is affected by shape.

There has been much work on developing distance between regions. Since the integrated region matching scheme is not confined to any particular region distance and defining a region distance is not our main interest, we have chosen a distance with low computational cost so that the system can be tested on a large image database.

3. EXPERIMENTS

The IRM has been implemented as a part of our experimental SIMPLIcity image retrieval system. We tested the system on a general-purpose image database (from COREL) including about $200,000$ pictures, which are stored in JPEG format with size 384×256 or 256×384. These images were automatically classified into three semantic types: graph (clip art), textured photograph, and non-textured photograph [9]. For each image, the features, locations, and areas of all its regions are stored.

Compared with two color histogram systems [19] and the WBIIS (Wavelet-Based Image Indexing and Searching) system [26], our system in general achieves more accurate retrieval at higher speed. However, it is difficult to design a fair comparison with existing region-based searching algorithms such as the Blobworld system which depends on manually defined complicated queries. An on-line demonstration is provided[1]. Readers are encouraged to visit the web site since we cannot show many examples here due to limited space.

3.1 Accuracy

The SIMPLIcity system was compared with the WBIIS system using the same image database. As WBIIS forms image signatures using wavelet coefficients in the lower frequency bands, it performs well with relatively smooth images, such as most landscape images. For images with details crucial to semantics, such as pictures containing people, the performance of WBIIS degrades. In general, the SIMPLIcity system performs as well as WBIIS for smooth landscape images. Examples are omitted due to limited space.

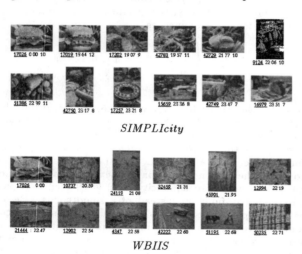

Figure 4: Comparison of SIMPLIcity and WBIIS. The query image (upper-left corner) is a photo of food. Best 11 matches are shown.

SIMPLIcity also performs well for images composed of fine details. Retrieval results with a photo of a hamburger as the query are shown in Figure 4. The query image is the image at the upper-left corner. The three numbers below the pictures from left to right are: the ID of the image in the database, the value of the similarity measure between the query image and the matched image, and the number of regions in the image. The SIMPLIcity system retrieves 10 images with food out of the first 11 matched images. The WBIIS system, however, does not retrieve any image with food in the first 11 matches. The top match made by SIMPLIcity is also a photo of hamburger, which is perceptually

[1] URL: http://WWW-DB.Stanford.EDU/IMAGE/

1. Sports and public events	2. Beach	3. Food
4. Landscape with buildings	5. Portrait	6. Horses
7. Tools and toys	8. Flowers	9. Vehicle

Table 1: Categories of images tested in our systematic evaluation.

very close to the query image. WBIIS misses this image because the query image contains important fine details, which are smoothed out by the multi-level wavelet transform in the system.

Figure 5: Retrieval by SIMPLIcity: the query image is a portrait image that probably depicts life in Africa.

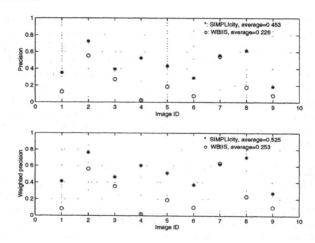

Figure 6: Comparison of SIMPLIcity and WBIIS: average precisions and weighted precisions of 9 image categories.

Another query example is shown in Figure 5. The query image in Figure 5 is difficult to match because objects in the image are not distinctive from the background. Moreover, the color contrast is small. Among the retrieved images, only the third matched image is not a picture of a person. A few images, the 1st, 4th, 7th, and 8th matches, depict a similar topic as well, probably about life in Africa.

3.2 Systematic evaluation

3.2.1 Performance on image queries

To provide numerical results, we tested 27 sample images chosen randomly from 9 categories, each containing 3 of the images. Image matching is performed on the COREL database of 200,000 images. A retrieved image is considered a match if it belongs to the same category of the query image. The categories of images tested are listed in Table 1.

Most categories simply include images containing the specified objects. Images in the "sports and public events" class contain humans in a game or public event, such as festival. Portraits are not included in this category. The "landscape with buildings" class refers to outdoor scenes featuring man-made constructions such as buildings and sculptures. The "beach" class refers to sceneries at coasts or river banks. For the "portrait" class, an image has to show people as the main feature. A scene with human beings as a minor part is not included.

Precision was computed for both SIMPLIcity and WBIIS. Recall was not calculated because the database is large and it is difficult to estimate the total number of images in one category, even approximately. To account for the ranks of matched images, the average of precisions within k retrieved images, $k = 1, ..., 100$, is computed, that is,

$$\bar{p} = \frac{1}{100} \sum_{k=1}^{100} \frac{n_k}{k},$$

$n_k = \#$ of matches in the first k retrieved images .

This average precision is referred to as the "weighted precision" because it is equivalent to a weighted percentage of matched images with a larger weight assigned to an image retrieved at a higher rank. For each of the 9 image categories, the average precision and weighted precision based on the 3 sample images are plotted in Figure 6. The image category identification number is assigned according to Table 1 scanned row wise. Except for the tools and toys category, in which case the two systems perform about equally well, SIMPLIcity has achieved better results than WBIIS measured in both ways. For the two categories of landscape with buildings and vehicle, the difference between the two system is quite significant. On average, the precision and the weighted precision of SIMPLIcity are higher than those of WBIIS by 0.227 and 0.273 respectively.

3.2.2 Performance on image categorization

The SIMPLIcity system was also evaluated based on a subset of the COREL database, formed by 10 image categories, each containing 100 pictures. Within this database, it is known whether any two images are of the same category. In particular, a retrieved image is considered a match if and only if it is in the same category as the query. This assumption is reasonable since the 10 categories were chosen so that each depicts a distinct semantic topic. Every image in the sub-database was tested as a query, and the retrieval ranks of all the rest images were recorded. Three statistics were computed for each query: the precision within the first 100 retrieved images, the mean rank of all the matched images, and the standard deviation of the ranks of matched images.

The recall within the first 100 retrieved images was not computed because it is proportional to the precision in this special case. The total number of semantically related images for each query is fixed to be 100. The average performance for each image category in terms of the three statistics is listed in Table 2, where p denotes precision, r denotes the mean rank of matched images, and σ denotes the standard deviation of the ranks of matched images. For a system that ranks images randomly, the average p is about 0.1, and the average r is about 500.

Category	Average p	Average r	Average σ
1. Africa	0.475	178.2	171.9
2. Beach	0.325	242.1	180.0
3. Buildings	0.330	261.8	231.4
4. Buses	0.363	260.7	223.4
5. Dinosaurs	0.981	49.7	29.2
6. Elephants	0.400	197.7	170.7
7. Flowers	0.402	298.4	254.9
8. Horses	0.719	92.5	81.5
9. Mountains	0.342	230.4	185.8
10. Food	0.340	271.7	205.8

Table 2: The average performance for each image category evaluated by precision p, the mean rank of matched images r, and the standard deviation of the ranks of matched images σ.

Similar evaluation tests were carried out for color histogram match. We used LUV color space and a matching metric similar to the EMD described in [19] to extract color histogram features and match in the categorized image database. Two different color bin sizes, with an average of 13.1 and 42.6 filled color bins per image, were evaluated. We call the one with less filled color bins the Color Histogram 1 system and the other the Color Histogram 2 system. Figure 7 shows the performance as compared with the SIMPLIcity system. Clearly, both of the two color histogram-based matching systems perform much worse than the SIMPLIcity region-based CBIR system in almost all image categories. The performance of the Color Histogram 2 system is better than that of the Color Histogram 1 system due to more detailed color separation obtained with more filled bins. However, the Color Histogram 2 system is so slow that it is impossible to obtain matches on larger databases. SIMPLIcity runs at about twice the speed of the faster Color Histogram 1 system and gives much better searching accuracy than the slower Color Histogram 2 system.

3.3 Robustness

We have performed extensive experiments to test the robustness of the system. Figure 8 summarizes the results. The graphs in the first row show the the changes in ranking of the target image as we increase the significance of image alterations. The graphs in the second row show the the changes in IRM distance between the altered image and the target image, as we increase the significance of image alterations.

The system is exceptionally robust to image alterations such as intensity variation, sharpness variation, intentional color distortions, intentional shape distortions, cropping, shifting, and rotation. Figure 9 shows some query examples, using the 200,000-image COREL database.

3.4 Speed

The algorithm has been implemented on a Pentium Pro 430MHz PC using the Linux operating system. To compute the feature vectors for the 200,000 color images of size 384×256 in our general-purpose image database requires approximately 60 hours. On average, one second is needed to segment an image and to compute the features of all regions. The speed is much faster than other region-based

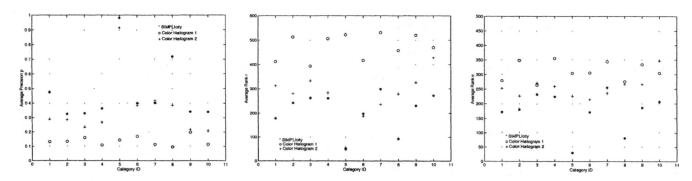

Figure 7: Comparing with color histogram methods on average precision p, average rank of matched images r, and the standard deviation of the ranks of matched images σ. *The lower numbers indicate better results for the last two plots (i.e., the r plot and the σ plot.* Color Histogram 1 gives an average of 13.1 filled color bins per image, while Color Histogram 2 gives an average of 42.6 filled color bins per image. SIMPLIcity partitions an image into an average of only 4.3 regions.

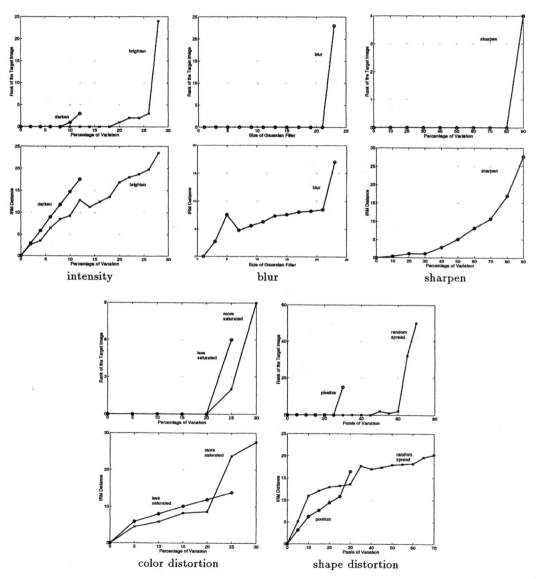

Figure 8: The robustness of the system to image alterations.

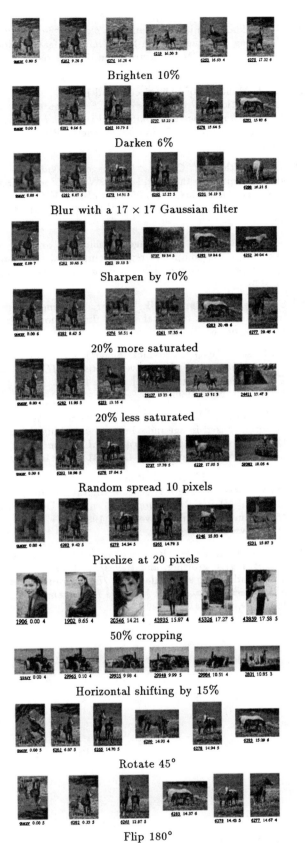

Brighten 10%

Darken 6%

Blur with a 17 × 17 Gaussian filter

Sharpen by 70%

20% more saturated

20% less saturated

Random spread 10 pixels

Pixelize at 20 pixels

50% cropping

Horizontal shifting by 15%

Rotate 45°

Flip 180°

Figure 9: The robustness of the system to image alterations. Best 5 matches are shown.

methods. For example, the Blobworld system developed by University of California at Berkeley segments each image in several minutes. Fast indexing has provided us with the capability of handling outside queries and sketch queries in real-time.

The matching speed is very fast. When the query image is in the database, it takes about 1.5 seconds of CPU time on average to sort all the images in the 200,000-image database using our similarity measure. If the query is not in the database, one extra second of CPU time is spent to process the query. Other systems we have tested are several times slower.

4. CONCLUSIONS AND FUTURE WORK

A measure for the overall similarity between images, defined by a region-matching scheme that incorporates properties of all the regions in the images. Compared with retrieval based on individual regions, the overall similarity approach in IRM reduces the influence of inaccurate segmentation, helps to clarify the semantics of a particular region, and enables a simple querying interface for region-based image retrieval systems. The application of the system to a database of about 200,000 general-purpose images shows more accurate and faster retrieval compared with existing algorithms. Additionally, the system is robust to various image alterations.

The IRM can be improved by introducing weights on different regions, refining the features, and allowing the user to turn off the scale-invariance and rotation-invariance characteristics. The interface can be improved by providing more intuitive similarity distances. We are also planning to extend the IRM to special image databases (e.g., biomedical), and very large image databases (e.g., WWW).

5. REFERENCES

[1] C. Carson, M. Thomas, S. Belongie, J. M. Hellerstein, J. Malik, "Blobworld: a system for region-based image indexing and retrieval," *Third Int. Conf. on Visual Information Systems*, D. P. Huijsmans, A. W.M. Smeulders (eds.), Springer, Amsterdam, The Netherlands, June 2-4, 1999.

[2] I. Daubechies, *Ten Lectures on Wavelets*, Capital City Press, 1992.

[3] C. Faloutsos, R. Barber, M. Flickner, J. Hafner, W. Niblack, D. Petkovic, W. Equitz, "Efficient and effective querying by image content," *Journal of Intelligent Information Systems: Integrating Artificial Intelligence and Database Technologies*, vol. 3, no. 3-4, pp. 231-62, July 1994.

[4] A. Gersho, "Asymptotically optimum block quantization," *IEEE Trans. Inform. Theory*, vol. IT-25, no. 4, pp. 373-380, July 1979.

[5] A. Gupta, R. Jain, "Visual information retrieval," *Comm. Assoc. Comp. Mach.*, vol. 40, no. 5, pp. 70-79, May 1997.

[6] J. A. Hartigan, M. A. Wong, "Algorithm AS136: a k-means clustering algorithm," *Applied Statistics*, vol. 28, pp. 100-108, 1979.

[7] J. Li, R. M. Gray, "Text and picture segmentation by the distribution analysis of wavelet coefficients," *Int. Conf. Image Processing*, Chicago, Oct. 1998.

[8] J. Li, J. Z. Wang, R. M. Gray, G. Wiederhold, "Multiresolution object-of-interest detection of images with low depth of field," *Proceedings of the 10th International Conference on Image Analysis and Processing*, Venice, Italy, 1999.

[9] J. Li, J. Z. Wang, G. Wiederhold, "Classification of textured and non-textured images using region segmentation," *Proceedings of the Seventh International Conference on Image Processing*, Vancouver, BC, Canada, September, 2000.

[10] W. Y. Ma, B. Manjunath, "NaTra: A toolbox for navigating large image databases," *Proc. IEEE Int. Conf. Image Processing*, pp. 568-71, 1997.

[11] W. Y. Ma, B. S. Manjunath, "Edge flow: a framework of boundary detection and image segmentation," *CVPR*, pp. 744-9, San Juan, Puerto Rico, June, 1997.

[12] S. Mehrotra, Y. Rui, M. Ortega-Binderberger, T.S. Huang, "Supporting content-based queries over images in MARS," *Proceedings of IEEE International Conference on Multimedia Computing and Systems*, pp. 632-3, Ottawa, Ont., Canada 3-6 June 1997.

[13] Y. Meyer, *Wavelets Algorithms and Applications*, SIAM, Philadelphia, 1993.

[14] S. Mukherjea, K. Hirata, Y. Hara, "AMORE: a World Wide Web image retrieval engine," World Wide Web, vol. 2, no. 3, pp. 115-32, Baltzer, 1999.

[15] A. Natsev, R. Rastogi, K. Shim, "WALRUS: A similarity retrieval algorithm for image databases," *SIGMOD*, Philadelphia, PA, 1999.

[16] ICASSPW. Niblack, R. Barber, W. Equitz, M. Flickner, E. Glasman, D. Petkovic, P. Yanker, C. Faloutsos, G. Taubin, "The QBIC project: querying images by content using color, texture, and shape," *Proc. SPIE - Int. Soc. Opt. Eng., in Storage and Retrieval for Image and Video Database*, vol. 1908, pp. 173-87, San Jose, February, 1993.

[17] A. Pentland, R. W. Picard, S. Sclaroff, "Photobook: tools for content-based manipulation of image databases," *SPIE Storage and Retrieval Image and Video Databases II*, vol. 2185, pp. 34-47, San Jose, February 7-8, 1994.

[18] R. W. Picard, T. Kabir, "Finding similar patterns in large image databases," *IEEE*, Minneapolis, vol. V, pp. 161-64, 1993.

[19] Y. Rubner, L. J. Guibas, C. Tomasi, "The earth mover's distance, Shimulti-dimensional scaling, and color-based image retrieval," *Proceedings of the ARPA Image Understanding Workshop*, pp. 661-668, New Orleans, LA, May 1997.

[20] G. Sheikholeslami, W. Chang, A. Zhang, "Semantic clustering and querying on heterogeneous features for visual data," *ACM Multimedia*, pp. 3-12, Bristol, UK, 1998.

[21] J. , J. Malik, "Normalized cuts and image segmentation," *Proceedings of IEEE Computer Society Conference on Computer Vision and Pattern Recognition*, pp. 731-7, San Juan, Puerto Rico, June, 1997.

[22] J. R. Smith, S.-F. Chang, "An image and video search engine for the World-Wide Web," *Storage and Retrieval for Image and Video Databases V (Sethi, I K and Jain, R C, eds), Proc SPIE 3022*, pp. 84-95, 1997.

[23] J. R. Smith, C. S. Li, "Image classification and querying using composite region templates," *Journal of Computer Vision and Image Understanding*, 2000, to appear.

[24] S. Stevens, M. Christel, H. Wactlar, "Informedia: improving access to digital video," Interactions, vol. 1, no. 4, pp. 67-71, 1994.

[25] M. Unser, "Texture classification and Chansegmentation using wavelet frames," *IEEE Trans. Image Processing*, vol. 4, no. 11, pp. 1549-1560, Nov. 1995.

[26] J. Z. Wang, G. Wiederhold, O. Firschein, X. W. Sha, "Content-based image indexing and searching using Daubechies' wavelets," *International Journal of Digital Libraries*, vol. 1, no. 4, pp. 311-328, 1998.

[27] J. Z. Wang, J. Li, D. , G. Wiederhold, "Semantics-sensitive retrieval for digital picture libraries," *D-LIB Magazine*, vol. 5, no. 11, DOI:10.10 45/november99-wang, November, 1999. http://www.dlib.org

[28] S. C. Zhu, A. Yuille, "Region competition: unifying snakes, region growing, and Bayes/MDL for multiband image segmentation," *IEEE Transactions on Pattern Analysis and Machine Intelligence*, vol. 18, no. 9, pp. 884-900, 1996.

Keyblock: An Approach for Content-based Image Retrieval

Lei Zhu and Aidong Zhang†
Department of Computer Science
SUNY at Buffalo
Buffalo, NY14260

{lzhu, azhang}@cse.buffalo.edu

Aibing Rao and Rohini Srihari
CEDAR
SUNY at Buffalo
Amherst, NY14228

{arao, rohini}@cedar.buffalo.edu

ABSTRACT

We propose a new framework termed *Keyblock* for content-based image retrieval, which is a generalization of the text-based information retrieval technology in the image domain. In this framework, methods for extracting comprehensive image features are provided, which are based on the frequency of representative blocks, termed keyblocks, of the image database. Keyblocks, which are analogous to index terms in text document retrieval, can be constructed by exploiting the vector quantization (VQ) method which has been used for image compression. By comparing the performance of our approach with the existing techniques using color feature and wavelet texture feature, the experimental results demonstrate the effectiveness of the framework in image retrieval.

1. INTRODUCTION

Tremendous work has been done on lower-level feature extraction for content-based image retrieval. Features from various points of view such as color [19], texture [10], and shape [20] have been extensively explored. Various systems such as QBIC [5], VisualSeek [17], PhotoBook [14] and Virage image management system[1] have been built for general or special image retrieval tasks. However, efficient and precise image retrieval still remains to be an open problem because of the extreme difficulty in image understanding. Hence, researchers working on content-based image retrieval are still seeking more comprehensive techniques for content-based image retrieval, with the goal of improving average precision and recall. Most of the work took the view of an image as a matrix of pixel intensity values and then applied mathematical analysis on the raw data to extract image features.

The view of image retrieval as a special case of information retrieval (IR) has motivated researchers to extend text-based techniques for image retrieval. Many keyword-based text information retrieval systems such as Yahoo, Lycos, and Google have achieved great success for indexing web sites. The success has also shed light on the area of content-based image retrieval because the relatively mature theories and techniques of text-based information retrieval can be applied to the image domain. One of the representatives is to annotate image with meta-data such as text keywords, captions and then to index the image database using text-based techniques on the meta-data. We observe that the text-based techniques may also be effectively used to represent image features and conduct image retrieval. Although an image is greatly different from text both syntactically and semantically, image and text have the same intrinsic property: both of them are information, but with different representation formats. Our goal is to generalize the techniques developed in text-based information retrieval to image retrieval.

Some initial work related to our approach was proposed by Indris and Panchanathan [7] and Lu and Teng [9]. In their method, an image is first compressed based on vector quantization (VQ), and then a code vector usage map or a code vector histogram is used as the image features. The work is a natural analogue of text-based techniques. A VQ-based compressed image is just an 1-dimensional vector of codes where each code corresponds to an entity of a pre-selected codebook, which is generated based on the clustering of all image blocks of some training images. Also, the concept of color histograms is another analogue of text-based techniques where the "words" are the colors after color quantization, the "text" is the 1-dimensional vector of the pixel colors of an image, and the histogram is the frequency of these "words" in the "text".

1.1 Text-based Information Retrieval

Baeza-Yates and Ribiero-Neto [2] presented a taxonomy of fifteen text-based information retrieval models. Among them two classic models, Boolean Model and Vector Model, are widely used and proved to be more suitable in text retrieval. These two models adopt keywords to index and retrieve documents based on the assumption that both documents in a database and queries can be described by a set of keywords, which are referred as index terms. For some full text search engines, a keyword is any word which appears in the documents.

For a given database of M text documents, after N keywords

---

*This research is supported by National Imaging and Mapping Agency (NIMA) and NCGIA at Buffalo.
†URL of demo: http://vangogh.cse.buffalo.edu:8080/

have been determined, a $M \times N$ matrix W, called *weight matrix*, is used. Each entry $w_{i,j}$ of W, associated with document d_i and keyword k_j, represents the importance of the keyword in describing the content of the document. For example, in Boolean Model, $w_{i,j}$ is 1 if k_j appears in d_i, 0 otherwise. Furthermore, a similarity metric is also needed. For different models, the weight matrices and the similarity metrics are defined differently and thus give rise to different retrieval performance. More detail of these models can be found in [2].

1.2 Text-based IR and Content-based Image Retrieval

The goal is to generalize the theories and the techniques of text-based IR to image retrieval domain. This goal is achievable due to the following consideration. In principle, text retrieval and image retrieval are the same because both of them are concerned with information retrieval, except that they deal with different data formats.

However, the generalization of IR from text domain to image domain is non-trivial. The greatest obstacle is due to the intrinsic difference between text and image as different media in representing and expressing information. First, in terms of representation, syntactically, a text document is 1-dimensional while an image is 2-dimensional. Second, in terms of expression, semantically, the units (words) of a text document, especially those keywords, carry direct semantics which are related to the semantics of text documents. In contrast, the units of an image, either in the pixel level or in the segment level after segmentation, provide generally no clue at all about the semantics of the image in the first case, or at most give unreliable object description in the second case. But content-based image retrieval doesn't assume a perfect object recognition. The analogue of text retrieval in image retrieval motivated us the following consideration. If there is a codebook of "keywords" for images, analogous as the dictionary for text documents, which has already been set up naturally in the evolution of human culture, an image can then be represented by a sequence of "keywords", just as a text document is summarized as a sequences of keywords. Consequently, the models of text IR can be easily generalized to image feature representation and retrieval. Thus, the central questions are:

- *What are "keywords" of an image?*

- *How to generate "keywords" from images?*

It is quite difficult to answer the first question according to the state of the art. What are the possible candidates as the "keywords" of an image? As we mentioned before, pixels are not good "keywords" because they don't reflect image semantics. Objects are good candidates since they represent a kind of "pictorial languages" and have been used by human beings even before languages existed. However, object recognition still remains to be an open problem! A compromising approach we adopted is: with a limited degree of sacrificing the accuracy, images are partitioned into smaller blocks, and then a set of representative blocks, which can somehow be used as standard blocks for reconstructing the image, are selected as "keywords". We term them as *"key-blocks"*.

To answer the second one, an analogue of lexical analysis in text retrieval should be proposed for image retrieval. This brings us to an interesting technique used for image compression: vector quantization.

1.3 Vector Quantization for Signal Compression

Vector quantization (VQ) is a technique proposed for signal compression and coding [6]. It is based on Shannon's theory[4] that coding systems can perform better if they operate on vectors or groups of symbols rather than on individual symbols. A vector quantizer Q is a mapping:

$$Q : R^k \longrightarrow C = \{c_1, ..., c_i, ..., c_N \mid c_i \in R^k\},$$

where R^k is Euclidean space of dimension k, C is usually called "codebook" of the quantizer, N is the codebook size, and c_i is the code vector.

Given a training sequence $T = \{t_1, ..., t_j, ..., t_M \mid t_j \in R^k\}$, the vector quantizer Q gives rise to a partition of T which consists of N cells $P = \{p_1, ..., p_i, ..., p_N\}$, where

$$p_i = \{t \mid t \in T, Q(t) = c_i\}.$$

For a given distortion function, $d(t_j, c_i)$, which is the distance between the input signal t_j and output code c_i (For example, the Euclidean distance, which is also called the square error), an optimal vector quantizer must satisfy the following optimality conditions:

- *Nearest Neighbor Condition:* For each p_i, if $t \in p_i$, then $d(t, c_i) \leq d(t, c_j)$, for all $j \neq i$.

- *Centroid Condition:* For a given partition P, the optimal code vectors satisfy

$$c_i = \frac{\sum_{t \in p_i} t}{k_i},$$

where k_i is the cardinality of p_i.

A VQ-based signal coding system consists of three steps: (1) Generate the codebook, (2) Encoding: each input vector is replaced by the index of the nearest entry in the codebook, and (3) Decoding: the decoder uses the index to reconstruct a vector by looking up the codebook.

Because Shannon's theory which provided theoretical basis for VQ didn't mention how to implement such a vector quantizer and how to design the codebook, these two problems have been active research issues and there have been a lot of general results and extensive applications in specific domains [6]. In particular, it has been used as a powerful source coding technique for the compression of image and video data [11, 3].

In VQ-based image compression, an image is decomposed into fixed-size blocks which are then used as the vectors. To generate the codebook, a clustering algorithm is applied to the set of all blocks obtained from a training set and then

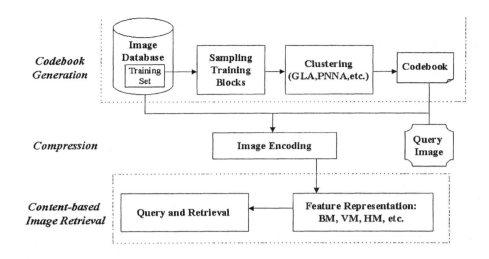

Figure 1: Flowchart of keyblock-based image retrieval.

the centroid of each cluster is used as a codebook entry. To encode an image, the image is partitioned into blocks of the same size and then each block is replaced by the index of the nearest entry on the codebook. Now each image is an matrix of indices. To reconstruct the image, each index is replaced by the code vector in the codebook which is actually a lookup table. Usually the reconstructed image is only an approximation of the original one, since VQ is a lossy compression.

Similarly to other compression strategies, VQ-based image compression tries to balance the compression rate and compression quality, while both of which are dependent on the size of the blocks and the size of the codebook. VQ is generally recognized as an effective data compression technique for low compression rate (≤ 1 bpp) applications.

With VQ-based image coding, code vectors (image blocks) in the codebook are now natural image "keywords", so-called keyblocks. They are representative units used to reconstruct image itself, hence they can be regarded as intrinsically semantic units of an image. Moreover, a compressed image, which is now a sequence of keyblocks, has the similar 1-dimensional linear structure as what a text document has. Therefore, the generalization of text-based IR is now natural.

1.4 Our Approach
In this paper, we present a keyblock-based approach for content-based image retrieval. This approach mainly consists of three main components: (1) Codebook generation: generates a codebook of the image database based on VQ which is performed on images in the training set, (2) Compression: encodes each image in the database as well as in the query using the keyblocks in the codebook, and (3) Content-based retrieval: creates image retrieval models and applies various text retrieval techniques such as term frequency and inverted files to generate the representations of image feature vectors on which image retrieval are con-

ducted. Figure 1 illustrates a flowchart of our approach.

This paper is organized as follows. Section 2 describes the VQ-based approach for generating keyblocks of images and for encoding images. Section 3 presents the keyblock-based image feature extraction and retrieval models. Section 4 presents the experiments of the proposed approach and the comparison to existing techniques. And finally, the conclusion is provided in Section 5.

2. KEYBLOCK GENERATION AND IMAGE CODING BASED ON VECTOR QUANTIZATION
Keyblock generation is critical to the proposed approach. In fact, VQ codebook design is an active area of research and a large number of design techniques have already been presented [6]. The goal is to find the codebook of a given size from a set of training image blocks. In theory, this goal can be achieved with any clustering algorithm. The most popularly used one is *Generalized Lloyd Algorithm* (GLA) and *Pairwise Nearest Neighbor Algorithm* (PNNA). We first introduce these two algorithms and then combine them to generate the codebook of keyblocks.

2.1 GLA
GLA is an iterative clustering algorithm with the goal of achieving the optimality conditions for the design of a vector quantizer. Explicitly, during each iteration, first, the training blocks are re-partitioned into cells according to the *nearest neighbor condition* based on the codebook generated at the previous iteration. Second, based on the *centroid condition*, the centroid of each cell is computed which will be the entry of the codebook generated at the current stage. Then the overall distortion is computed and the change of the distortion is tested. This process is repeated until the change of distortion is below a threshold. The algorithm can be summarized as follows:

Step 1: Given training sequence $T = \{t_1, ..., t_M\}$, initial codebook $C_1 = \{c_1, ..., c_i, ..., c_N\}$, and a suitable threshold δ, set the initial average distortion D_0 to a large value and iteration number $m = 1$.

Step 2: Use C_m to find the minimum distortion partition $P = \{p_1, ..., p_i, ..., p_N\}$ based on *nearest neighbor condition*, and compute the average distortion

$$D_m = \frac{\sum_{i=1}^{N} \sum_{t \in p_i} d(t, c_i)}{M}.$$

Step 3: If $\frac{D_{m-1} - D_m}{D_m} \leq \delta$, stop the iteration with C_m as the final codebook; otherwise continue.

Step 4: Form a new codebook C_{m+1} by finding the optimal code vector c_i for the partition p_i using the *centroid condition* $(i \in [1..N])$.

Step 5: Replace the old codebook C_m with the new codebook C_{m+1}, set $m = m + 1$, and go to step 2.

GLA cannot guarantee to find the optimal codebook. The iterations may converge to a local minimum if the initial codebook is poorly selected. Gersho and Gray [6] presented various ways to do initialization. Another problem is that GLA is somewhat computationally expensive. PNNA is more efficient.

2.2 PNNA

PNNA is a very simple clustering algorithm. It starts with the whole training sequence. At each iteration, two nearest code vectors are merged and replaced by their centroid. The codebook size is decreased by 1. This process is repeated until the desired final codebook size is reached. Note that each merge is optimal but the overall result might not be optimal, which is why PNNA is faster but slightly inferior to GLA.

2.3 Combining GLA and PNNA

In the VQ image compression, there is a tradeoff between the compression rate and the quality of the compressed image. Because retrieval is directly conducted on the compressed images, we are more concerned about the compressed image quality. There is a relationship between the average distortion and the retrieval performance which will be uncovered by the experiment results. Since an image database is usually very large, a good tradeoff between the efficiency and effectiveness of generating the codebook is expected. This is achieved by combining GLA and PNNA. We now describe the complete procedure for generating the codebook.

Let D be an image database. First, a sampling procedure is conducted to select a training set $I = \{i_1, ..., i_k, ..., i_t\}$. The larger the training set, the less the average distortion is. In the ideal case, the whole database D is used as the training set, but it will be too costly. The principle of the sampling is to select a set of images which represents D as much as possible.

Second, the training images are divided into blocks which are represented as vectors. The smaller the block size, the higher the resolution is. Consequently, we can achieve better quality for the compressed images. However, it is more computationally expensive. The block size is usually less than 16×16 to satisfy the minimal requirement of the quality.

Since the block size is small, the set of the training blocks B decomposed from the training image set I can still be very large. Even directly applying GLA on B is still too costly. For example, for an image of resolution 512×512, there are $65,536$ (2×2) blocks and $16,384$ (4×4) blocks. If the number of the training images is t, then there are $16,384 \times t$ vectors on which a clustering algorithm such as GLA will be applied in order to obtain the codebook of 4×4 blocks. To alleviate this problem, we need to reduce the size of the set of the training vectors. Of course, again, a sampling strategy can be applied to each training image to reduce the large factor, $16,384$ in the above example, to a relatively small size N. However, in order to keep the representative blocks in the training vector set, instead of applying the sampling strategy, we apply GLA to the blocks of each training image first and then use the resulting cluster centroids to form the training vector set. We can then apply PNNA to generate the codebook C. Also, we can optionally apply GLA again with C as an initial codebook to generate the final codebook. Below is the steps for generating keyblocks for image database D:

Step 1: Sample D to get the training set I. The sampling can be done either manually or automatically. For an automatic procedure, randomly sampling is one choice but the optimal representative set is not guaranteed. An expensive but effective choice is to apply existing feature extraction such as color histogram, texture or even shape to conduct a clustering of the whole database and then use the centroid of each cluster as a training image.

Step 2: For each training image i_k, decompose it into blocks of a fixed size to get a sequence of vectors, $T_k = \{t_1, ..., t_j, ..., t_M\}$ Then, apply GLA on T_k to extract an codebook C_k of size N, where the initialization is done randomly;

Step 3: Put all vectors in C_k into the training set T;

Step 4: Apply PNNA on T to get a codebook C';

Step 5(Optional): Apply GLA to T again with C' as an initial codebook to get the final codebook C_I.

If step 5 is not conducted, then C' is the final codebook.

2.4 Image Encoding

In this stage, for each image in the database, decompose it into blocks. Then, for each of the blocks, find the closest entry in the codebook and store the index correspondingly. Now each image is a matrix of indices, which can be regarded as 1-dimensional in scan order. This property is very similar to a text document which is considered as a linear list of keywords in text-based IR.

3. KEYBLOCK-BASED IMAGE FEATURE REPRESENTATION AND RETRIEVAL

We now present the generalization of text-based IR to image retrieval.

Definition. A general model of *keyblock-based image retrieval* is a quintuple $[D, K, W, Q, S]$ where

- $D = \{d_1, ...d_j, ..., d_n\}$ is the list of VQ compressed images.
- $K = \{k_1, ...k_i, ..., k_t\}$ is the list of keyblocks in the codebook.
- $W : K \times D \longrightarrow R^+$ is a mapping which maps a pair of a keyblock and an image to a non-negative number. Denote $w_{i,j} = W(k_i, d_j)$. So, W is represented as a matrix $(w_{i,j})_{t \times n}$, called the *weight matrix* with each element indicates the importance of a keyblock in an image. For each image d_j, there is a t-dimensional feature vector $\vec{d_j} = \{w_{1,j}, ..., w_{t,j}\}$. Let g_i, which has the form of $g_i(\vec{d_j}) = w_{i,j}$, be the projective function that returns the weight associated with keyblock k_i and image d_j.
- $Q = \{q_1, ...q_c, ..., q_l\}$ is the set of queries. A query-by-example approach is used. Each query has a feature vector, $\vec{q} = \{w_{1,q}, ..., w_{t,q}\}$, which is similar to the feature vector $\vec{d_j}$.
- $S : Q \times D \longrightarrow R^+$ is a similarity measure between a query and an image. This measure is used to generate the ranking in the retrieval stage.

In the following, two specific models: Boolean Model (BM) and Vector Model (VM) are described. A special case of VM, called Histogram Model (HM), is also listed for its own importance.

3.1 Boolean Model

BM generates the feature vectors of database images and queries by considering whether or not a keyblock appears. Thus, we have $w_{i,j}, w_{i,q} \in \{0, 1\}$, which are defined as

$$w_{i,j} = \begin{cases} 1 & if \quad f_{i,j} \geq T, \\ 0 & \text{otherwise,} \end{cases}$$

where $f_{i,j}$ is the frequency of keyblock k_i appearing in image d_j and T is a threshold.

Both $\vec{q}$ and $\vec{d_j}$ are binary strings of length t where the i-th bit indicates whether or not k_i appears. Comparison between $\vec{q}$ and $\vec{d_j}$ is bit by bit so that the similarity between image d_j and query q is defined as:

$$S_{BM}(q, d_j) = n_{11} * w_{11} + n_{00} * w_{00},$$

where

- n_{11} is the number of bits satisfying $g_i(\vec{d_j}) = g_i(\vec{q}) = 1$ if it is the i-th bit. In other words, n_{11} is the number of positions at which both $\vec{d_j}$ and $\vec{q}$ are 1;
- n_{00} is the number of bits satisfying $g_i(\vec{d_j}) = g_i(\vec{q}) = 0$ if it is the i-th bit. In other words, n_{00} is the number of positions at which both $\vec{d_j}$ and $\vec{q}$ are 0; and
- w_{11} and w_{00} are the weights assigned to n_{11} and n_{00}, respectively.

We believe that the appearance or disappearance of certain keyblocks in both d_j and q simultaneously has very important indication of the similarity between d_j and q. Moreover, "appearance" is more important than "disappearance" so that $w_{11} \geq w_{00}$. For example, in our implementation, we notice that $w_{11} = 1$, $w_{00} = 0.5$ give the best result. Suppose $\vec{q} = (1, 0, 0)$, $\vec{d_1} = (0, 1, 0)$, $\vec{d_2} = (1, 0, 1)$, then $S_{BM}(q, d_1) = 0 * 1 + 1 * 0.5 = 0.5$, $S_{BM}(q, d_2) = 1 * 1 + 1 * 0.5 = 1.5$, which indicates that d_2 is more similar to q than d_1.

3.2 Vector Model

VM is similar to its counterpart in text-based IR. Assume that there are n images in D and t keyblocks in K. Let $f_{i,j}$ be the frequency of $k_i \in K$ appearing in image $d_j \in D$ and n_i be the number of images in which k_i presents, as defined above. The normalized frequency $\hat{f}_{i,j}$ is given by

$$\hat{f}_{i,j} = \frac{f_{i,j}}{\max_{1 \leq l \leq t} f_{l,j}}.$$

Another important concept, analogous to *inverse document frequency* in text domain, is *inverse image frequency*, which is defined as

$$idf_i = log(\frac{n}{n_i}), \quad for \ k_i.$$

Keyblock frequency is a measure of how often a keyblock appears in the compressed image. But the keyblocks which appear in many images are not very useful for distinguishing relevance, just like the stop-words in the text case. VM compromises these two effects by defining the keyblock weights as

$$w_{i,j} = \hat{f}_{i,j} * idf_i.$$

The weights for query q, $w_{i,q}$, are computed similarly.

VM defines the similarity measure as the inner product of two unit feature vectors

$$S_{VM}(q, d_j) = \frac{\vec{d_j} \bullet \vec{q}}{\mid \vec{d_j} \mid \times \mid \vec{q} \mid} = \frac{\sum_{i=1}^{t} w_{i,j} * w_{i,q}}{\sqrt{\sum_{i=1}^{t} w_{i,j}^2} * \sqrt{\sum_{i=1}^{t} w_{i,q}^2}}.$$

3.3 Histogram Model

HM can be regarded as a special case of VM, which is important and simple. In this case, $w_{i,j} = f_{i,j}$, the frequency of k_i appearing in d_j. Similarly, $w_{i,q} = f_{i,q}$. The feature vectors $\vec{d_j}$ and $\vec{q}$ are the *keyblock histograms*. The similarity measure is defined as

$$S_{HM}(q, d_j) = \frac{1}{1 + dis(q, d_j)},$$

where the distance function is

$$dis(q, d_j) = \sum_{i=1}^{t} \frac{\mid w_{i,j} - w_{i,q} \mid}{1 + w_{i,j} + w_{i,q}}.$$

The weighted sum is to remove the excessive influence of the frequently appearing keyblocks on the similarity.

Because the above three models only focus on individual keyblock's appearance in images while the correlations between keyblocks are not counted in, we also proposed N-block models which are the generalization of the N-gram models [15] in language modeling to extract correlation features. The detail can be found in [8].

4. EXPERIMENTS

The experiments are conducted on two databases. One consists of web color images (denoted CDB), which is in favor of color feature, and the other consists of grey-scale Brodatz texture images (denoted TDB), which is in favor of texture feature. On CDB, the proposed models are compared with the traditional color histogram [19] and color coherent vector [13] techniques, and on TDB, it is compared with Haar and Daubechies wavelet texture techniques.

4.1 CDB and TDB Setup

The first database, CDB, consists of 500 images manually divided into 41 well-defined groups, where each of which has either 10 or 20 similar images. The criterion for manually similarity grouping is based on overall appearance. The image size varies from 364×369 to 807×1061. The images were down-loaded from various web sites so that no pre-restrictions such as different camera models and lighting conditions are assumed for the testing. CDB is just a small snapshot of the images on the Internet. There are 120 art images which are classified into 11 groups such as paintings, calligraphy, etc. In addition, there are 380 real life images which are categorized into 30 classes such as scenery, human activities, models, animals, arsenal, etc. This is the ground truth for evaluation. In order to select the training images for obtaining the codebooks, one image is randomly picked up from each group so that the training set has 41 images.

The other database, TDB, consists of 2240 grey-scale Brodatz texture images of size 96×96 which are divided into 112 categories. Each category consists of 20 images with similar texture. Again, for each category, one image is randomly selected so that the size of the training set is 112.

4.2 Codebook and Keyblock Generation

To generate keyblocks, three block sizes, 2×2, 4×4, and 8×8, are used for both CDB and TDB. In addition, CDB is also tested with the size of 16×16 because the images are in larger size than TDB. Intuitively, blocks with different sizes may capture information with different granularity. Usually smaller blocks exploit local information of the image content, such as edges and regions with high spatial frequency. Larger blocks may provide correlation among neighboring sub-blocks as well as an overview of the global variation.

For each block size, experiments have been performed to generate codebooks of four different sizes 256, 512, 1024 and 2048. In the implementation, the distortion, which is the objective function for optimization when generating a codebook, is the square error commonly used for image compression. The square error is the Euclidean distance between the vectors of the intensity values of an original block and that of the corresponding keyblock. In short, the testing is conducted with 16 (4 block sizes × 4 codebook sizes) codebooks for CDB, and with 12 (3 × 4) codebooks for TDB. After the codebooks are generated, all images in the databases are then encoded correspondingly.

As an example, Figure 2 shows an image (from CDB) and its

Table 1: Average distortion of the databases under different codebooks

	blocks	256	512	1024	2048
CDB	2×2	615.57	464.10	374.95	311.37
	4×4	1000.70	888.58	799.83	707.34
	8×8	1602.50	1444.33	1346.86	1258.06
	16×16	2373.23	2182.95	2084.16	1976.10
TDB	2×2	129.47	111.15	75.45	59.82
	4×4	485.96	423.99	354.98	314.33
	8×8	895.21	855.22	800.99	764.54

reconstructed images with different codebooks. Each codebook is obtained by applying the algorithm described in Section 2 on the selected training set.

Table 1 presents the average distortion of CDB and TDB with all of the codebooks. The average distortion for an image database D is calculated by

$$d_{avg} = \frac{\sum_{i \in D} d(i, \hat{i})}{|D|},$$

where i is an image and $\hat{i}$ is the reconstructed image after decoding. The table shows the relationship between the average distortion of a given database and the parameters for the VQ-based compression. For a given codebook size, the smaller the keyblock size, the lower the distortion. On the other hand, for a given block size, the larger the codebook, the smaller the distortion. Therefore, block size and codebook size would affect the retrieval performance because a large distortion leads to a large degradation of the quality of an image after the compression, thus might mislead the image retrieval.

4.3 Image Feature Representation, Retrieval and Comparison of Results

We have implemented three models as described in Section 3. Experiments are performed on CDB and TDB with different codebooks. For each given codebook, database images are encoded following the keyblock indexing procedure. The dimensions of the feature vectors are exactly the same as the codebook size, which is one of 256, 512, 1024 or 2048. In order to conduct the evaluation and the comparison, the database is also taken as the visual query set for testing. So, there are 500 query examples for CDB and 2240 query examples for TDB. For each query, the precision and recall pairs corresponding to the top 1, 2, ..., up to 40 retrieved images are calculated. Finally, the average precision and recall is calculated over all queries for a given database. Since CDB is designed in favor of color feature, two conventional color feature techniques, the traditional histogram proposed by Swain and Ballard [19] and the color coherent vector (CCV) proposed by Pass and Zabih[13] are used for the comparison on CDB. The feature vectors of CCV and color histogram are both of 2048 dimensions. On the other hand, since TDB is set up in favor of texture features, Haar and Daubechies wavelet texture techniques [16, 18] are used for the comparison on TDB.

Figure 3 presents the comparison results: (a) and (b) indicate that the performance of BM, HM, VM all outper-

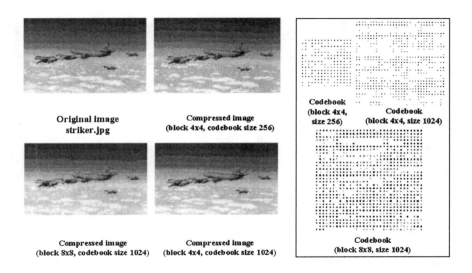

Figure 2: A raw image and the compressed images with different codebooks. Each codebook is obtained with the same training set.

form the traditional techniques. For example, in the case of CDB, almost 70% of all of the relevant images are among top 40 retrieved images with BM while only 40% are returned by CCV. In the case of TDB, at the recall level of 0.2, the precision is: 0.96 (HM), 0.91 (BM), 0.90 (VM), 0.88 (Haar wavelets) and 0.81 (Daubechies wavelets), hence HM performs best; (c), (d) are the comparison of the proposed models with fixed parameters, where the former shows that for codebooks (block 4 × 4, size 1024 or 512), BM performs best on CDB while HM performs best on TDB; (e), (f) demonstrate the effect of the codebook size on performance, taking BM with 4 × 4 keyblocks as an example. On CDB, the performance is not as sensitive as on TDB with respect to the codebook size. In addition, for a fixed keyblock size, the larger the codebook size, the better the performance. Together with Table 1, the assumption that a smaller distortion leads to better performance is verified. Of course, due to some hard-to-control factors such as VQ parameters, color space, and ground truth, there are exceptions.

Figure 4 presents the effect of the block size on three models. For each model, generally speaking, for a fixed codebook size, a smaller block size leads to better performance. Again, this verifies that good performance of a keyblock-based image retrieval model is based on a smaller distortion of the VQ based compression. This is especially true for TDB because it is a slightly simpler database. However, for both databases, in the extreme case of the least distortion when 1 × 1 blocks (pixels) is used, which reduces to the color quantization [12], the performance is not as good as the case with 2 × 2 and 4 × 4 blocks. For example, the best average precision with 1 × 1 blocks achieved at the top 5 retrieved images is only 0.65, which is less than 0.68 for the case of 2 × 2 blocks on CDB. The reason is that 1 × 1 blocks do not reflect local spatial information which is useful for retrieval. Moreover, it is too costly to compress an image with 1 × 1 blocks. Note that GLA has a complexity of $O(N * C * I)$, where N is the size of the training sequence, C is the codebook size

and I is the iteration times. Thus, the smaller the block size, the larger the training sequence. Also, the smaller the block size, the longer the image compression. Hence, it is more computationally expensive for smaller blocks. Therefore, there is a tradeoff. In our experiments, 4 × 4 is a good choice. Figure 4 also shows that HM is more sensitive to block size than the other two models and TDB brings more sensitivity to every model than CDB.

In real applications, the top ten retrieved images are normally paid more attention for a query. For this reason, Figure 5 compares the average precision and recall on top 5 and 10 retrieved images of each case. First, for each database, the highest precision/recall in each column is marked with "*", which corresponds to the best model for a given codebook size and a fixed block size. On CDB, in most of the cases, BM performs best; while on TDB, HM alway performs the best. Second, for a fixed codebook size and for each model, the highest precision/recall among different block sizes are underlined, which show that with blocks 2 × 2 and 4 × 4, performance is better than with 8 × 8 or 16 × 16. Third, for each model, the optimal performance is highlighted. For example, BM performs best on CDB with codebook (4 × 4, 1024) while HM performs best on TDB with codebook (2 × 2, 1024). Finally, the global optimal performance for each database is italicized, where BM with codebook (4 × 4, 1024) is the best on CDB while HM with codebook (2 × 2, 1024). This indicates that the optimal parameters and the model are database dependent. Notice that an oversized codebook may mislead the retrieval because the feature vectors become too sparse. On the other hand, a under-sized codebook may also be misleading because the feature vectors become too coarse.

5. CONCLUSION

A new approach for content-based image retrieval is proposed by exploiting analogous text-based IR techniques on compressed images based on the vector quantization. The

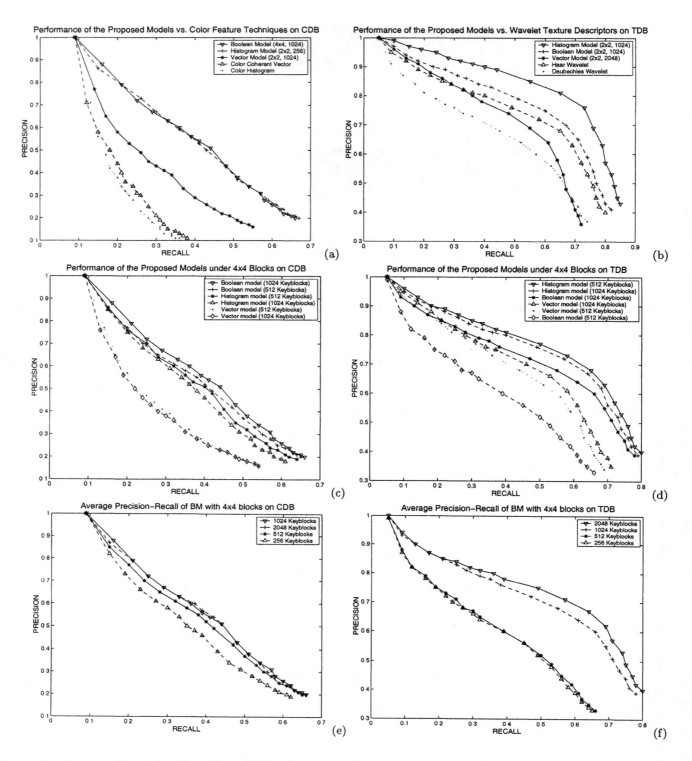

Figure 3: Average Precision-Recall on CDB and TDB: (a), (b) present the comparison of BM, HM, VM with CCV and Color Histogram on CDB, with Haar and Daubechies wavelets on TDB, respectively; (c), (d) present more comparison among BM, HM, VM for fixed parameters; (e), (f) reveal the effect of codebook size on the performance.

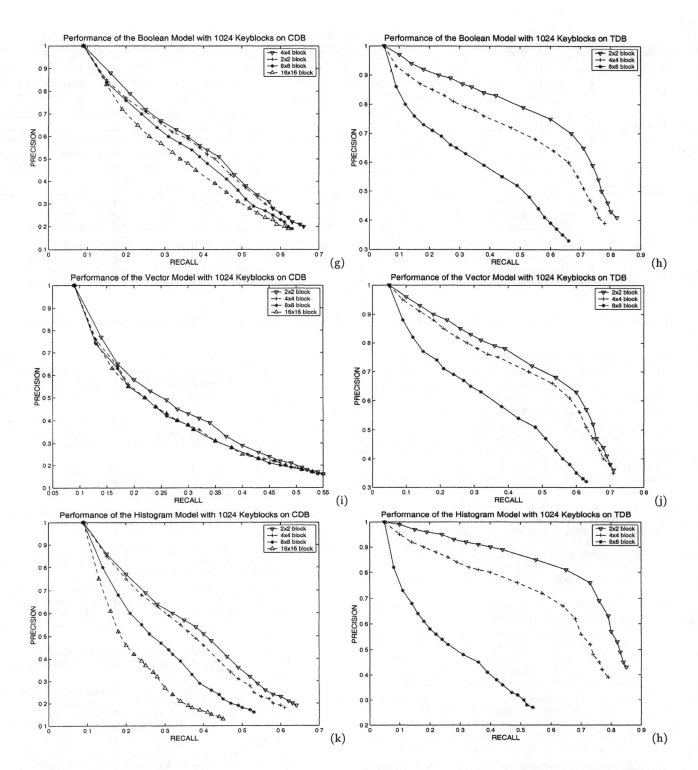

Figure 4: The effects of block size on the average precision-recall of each model on CDB and TDB: (g), (h) are for BM; (i), (j) are for VM; and (k), (h) are for HM. HM is more sensitive to block size than BM and VM. Moreover, it seems that TDB brings more sensitivity to every model.

Average Precision/ Recall for Top 5 and 10 Retrieved Images on Different Databases

Data Sets	Top Matches	Block Size / Model	Codebook Size 256				Codebook Size 512				Codebook Size 1024				Codebook Size 2048			
			2x2	4x4	8x8	16x16	2x2	4x4	8x8	16x16	2x2	4x4	8x8	16x16	2x2	4x4	8x8	16x16
Color Images (CDB)	5	BM	0.58/0.26	0.61/0.27	0.60/0.26	0.58/0.25*	0.61/0.27	0.65/0.28*	0.63/0.27	0.60/0.26*	0.86/0.29	0.68/0.30*	0.64/0.28	0.60/0.26*	0.67/0.29*	0.67/0.29*	0.65/0.28*	0.60/0.26*
		HM	0.67/0.30*	0.66/0.29	0.62/0.27	0.55/0.24	0.67/0.29*	0.64/0.28	0.60/0.26	0.51/0.22	0.64/0.28	0.63/0.28	0.55/0.24	0.46/0.20	0.62/0.28	0.59/0.26	0.51/0.22	0.40/0.17
		VM	0.53/0.23	0.50/0.22	0.48/0.21	0.48/0.21	0.53/0.23	0.51/0.22	0.49/0.21	0.49/0.21	0.54/0.23	0.50/0.22	0.50/0.22	0.50/0.22	0.54/0.23	0.51/0.22	0.50/0.22	0.50/0.22
		CCV	0.44/ 0.19								color histogram		0.41/ 0.18					
	10	BM	0.42/0.37	0.46/0.39	0.44/0.38	0.43/0.37	0.44/0.39	0.49/0.42*	0.47/0.40*	0.44/0.37*	0.50/0.43	0.51/0.45*	0.48/0.41	0.45/0.38*	0.51/0.44*	0.51/0.44*	0.49/0.42*	0.45/0.38*
		HM	0.50/0.43*	0.49/0.42*	0.45/0.39*	0.41/0.35	0.50/0.43*	0.48/0.42	0.43/0.38	0.36/0.31	0.48/0.42	0.46/0.40	0.39/0.34	0.32/0.28	0.45/0.40	0.42/0.37	0.35/0.30	0.28/0.24
		VM	0.38/0.33	0.35/0.31	0.36/0.31	0.35/0.30	0.38/0.33	0.37/0.32	0.36/0.31	0.36/0.31	0.39/0.34	0.36/0.32	0.36/0.31	0.36/0.31	0.39/0.34	0.38/0.33	0.36/0.31	0.37/0.32
		CCV	0.30/ 0.26								color histogram		0.28/ 0.24					
Brodatz Texture Images (TDB)	5	BM	0.87/0.22	0.75/0.19	0.67/0.17		0.89/0.22	0.75/0.19	0.72/0.18		0.90/0.23	0.85/0.21	0.73/0.18		0.90/0.22	0.85/0.21*	0.70/0.17	
		HM	0.94/0.24*	0.89/0.22*	0.72/0.18*		0.95/0.23*	0.89/0.22*	0.70/0.17		0.95/0.24*	0.88/0.22*	0.64/0.16		0.94/0.23*	0.81/0.20	0.51/0.13	
		VM	0.84/0.21	0.82/0.21	0.72/0.18*		0.85/0.21	0.84/0.21	0.74/0.19*		0.88/0.22	0.85/0.21	0.74/0.19*		0.88/0.22	0.85/0.21*	0.73/0.18*	
		HAAR	0.87/ 0.22								DAUB		0.81/ 0.20					
	10	BM	0.78/0.39	0.64/0.32	0.57/0.29		0.81/0.40	0.65/0.32	0.62/0.31		0.83/0.42	0.76/0.38	0.63/0.32*		0.83/0.41	0.78/0.39*	0.59/0.29	
		HM	0.87/0.44*	0.80/0.40*	0.62/0.31*		0.88/0.44*	0.81/0.40*	0.59/0.29		0.89/0.44*	0.80/0.40*	0.52/0.26		0.88/0.44*	0.72/0.36	0.39/0.19	
		VM	0.73/0.38	0.71/0.35	0.61/0.30		0.74/0.37	0.73/0.36	0.63/0.31*		0.78/0.39	0.75/0.37	0.63/0.32*		0.78/0.39	0.76/0.38	0.62/0.31*	
		HAAR	0.80/ 0.40								DAUB		0.73/ 0.36					

Figure 5: Performance of top 5 and 10 retrieved images in each model and different parameter combinations.

proposed approach provides methods for extracting image features which is not in favor of any particular low-level feature such as color or texture. Instead, the features extracted for an image is a comprehensive description of the content of the image which is more semantics-related than the existing lower-level features. Experimental results have demonstrated that the proposed models are superior not only to color histogram and color coherent vector approaches which are in favor of color features, but also to Haar and Daubechies wavelet texture approaches which are in favor of texture features.

6. REFERENCES

[1] J. Bach, C. Fuller, A. Gupta, A. Hampapur, B. Horowitz, R. Jain, and C. Shu. The virage image search engine: An open framework for image management. In *Proceedings of SPIE, Storage and Retrieval for Still Image and Video Databases IV*, pages 76–87, San Jose, CA, USA, February 1996.

[2] R. Baeza-Yates and B. Ribiero-Neto. *Modern Information Retrieval.* Addison Wesley, 1999.

[3] C. F. Barnes, S. A. Rizvi, and N. M. Nasrabadi. Advances in residual vector quantization of image: A review. *IEEE Transactions on Image Processing*, 5(2):226–262, Feb. 1996.

[4] T. M. Cover and J. A. Thomas. *Elements of Information Theory.* John Wiley & Sons, Inc., New York, 1991.

[5] M. Flickner, H. Sawhney, W. Niblack, J. Ashley, Q. Huang, and B. D. et al. Query by Image and Video Content: The QBIC System. *IEEE Computer*, 28(9):23–32, Sept. 1995.

[6] A. Gersho and R. M. Gray. *Vector Quantization and Signal Compression.* Kluwer Academic Publishers, 1992.

[7] F. Idris and S. Panchanathan. Algorithms for indexing of compressed images. In *Proceedings of International Conference on Visual Information Systems*, pages 303–308, Melbourne, Feb 1996.

[8] Lei Zhu, Aibing Rao and Aidong Zhang. Advanced feature extraction for keyblock-based image retrieval. In *Proceedings of International Workshop on Multimedia Information Retrieval (MIR2000)*, Los Angeles, California, USA. November 4 2000.

[9] G. Lu and S. Teng. A novel image retrieval technique based on vector quantization. In *Proceedings of International Conference on Computational Intelligence for Modelling, Control and Automation*, pages 36–41, Viana, Austria, Feb 1999.

[10] B. Manjunath and W. Ma. Texture Features for Browsing and Retrieval of Image Data. *IEEE Transactions on Pattern Analysis and Machine Intelligence*, 18(8):837–842, August 1996.

[11] N. M. Nasrabadi and R. A. King. Image coding using vector quantization: A review. *IEEE Trans. Commun.*, COM-36(8):957–971, August 1988.

[12] M. T. Orchard and C. A. Bouman. Color Quantization of Images. *IEEE Transactions on Signal Processing*, 39(12):2677–2690, December 1991.

[13] G. Pass, R. Zabih, and J. Miller. Comparing images using color coherence vectors. In *Proceedings of ACM Multimedia 96*, pages 65–73, Boston MA USA, 1996.

[14] A. Pentland, R. Picard, and S. Sclaroff. Photobook: Tools for Content-based Manipulation of Image Databases. In *Proceedings of the SPIE Conference on Storage and Retrieval of Image and Video Databases II*, pages 34–47, 1994.

[15] R. Rosenfeld. *Adaptive Statistical Language Modeling: A Maximum Entropy Approach.* PhD thesis, Carnegie Mellon University, 1994.

[16] J. R. Smith and S. Chang. Transform Features For Texture Classification and Discrimination in Large Image Databases. In *Proceedings of the IEEE International Conference on Image Processing*, pages 407–411, 1994.

[17] J. R. Smith and S.-F. Chang. VisualSeek: a fully automated content-based image query system. In *Proceedings of ACM Multimedia 96*, pages 87–98, Boston MA USA, 1996.

[18] G. Strang and T. Nguyen. *Wavelets and Filter Banks.* Wellesley-Cambridge Press, 1996.

[19] M. Swain and D. Ballard. Color Indexing. *Int Journal of Computer Vision*, 7(1):11–32, 1991.

[20] T. Syeda-Mahmood. Finding shape similarity using a constrained non-rigid transform. In *International Conference on Pattern Recognition*, 1996.

Semantic Based Image Retrieval: A Probabilistic Approach

Ben Bradshaw
Microsoft Research,
St. George House,
1 Guildhall St.,
Cambridge, England.
+44 1223 744808

bbradsha@microsoft.com

ABSTRACT

This paper describes an approach to image retrieval based on the underlying semantics of images. To extract these semantics a hierarchical, probabilistic approach is proposed. The labels that are extracted in this case are man-made, natural, inside and outside. The hierarchical framework combines class likelihood probability estimates across a number of levels to form a posterior estimate of the probability of class membership. Unlike previous work in this field, the proposed algorithm can determine probabilities at any point in the scene and only a small number of images are required to train the system. To illustrate the potential of such an approach a prototype image retrieval system has been developed, initial results from this system are given in this paper.

Keywords

Image retrieval, semantic image analysis, image statistics.

1. INTRODUCTION

Content-based Image Retrieval (CBIR) has become an active area of research in the last 5-10 years because of the increasingly large volumes of electronically stored information and the corresponding requirement for high performance systems to access and manipulate this information.

This paper describes an architecture that accurately generates localised semantic labels (in a probabilistic setting). Specifically, the problem of probabilistically labelling images, or parts of images, as being made up of man-made (e.g. buildings, roads, cars) or natural (e.g. clouds, forests, streams) objects is addressed, as is the problem of determining whether an image was taken inside or outside. The advantages of the presented approach are that it generates localised probabilities, only requires a few 100 images to train and is computationally efficient.

The first section of this paper reviews the current research into CBIR systems and the extraction of semantic content from images. Following this review, Sections 2-4 describe the proposed method for extracting semantic information. Section 5 quantitatively examines results from the method and Section 6 describes and evaluates a prototype image retrieval system based on the research in this paper.

1.1 Content-based Image Retrieval

The first CBIR systems (classed by the author as 'first generation'), indexed images based on low-level features such as colour and texture. Examples of such systems are the IBM Query By Image Content (QBIC) system (see Flickner et al., [2]) the Virage system (see Gupta et al., [4]) and the VisualSEEk system (see Smith et al., [14]). Each of these systems allows the user to specify a query in a number of ways based on the low-level features extracted by the system. The user is also often allowed to specify how much weight to attach to each of these features. It is now recognised that this explicit knowledge of the *low-level* feature space does not help the user formulate a query. The user (be they naive *or* experienced) finds it hard to determine which of the low-level features are appropriate for a given query.

In recent years there has been a proliferation in CBIR systems (which the author classifies as 'second generation') which deliberately hide the low level features from the user. Instead of specifying texture and colour combinations the user supplies an example image and asks for similar ones (termed Query By Example, QBE). Although this alleviates the problem of knowing which low level features are important for a given query it immediately introduces another one. Namely, the user must already have a good example of what they want prior to initiating the query. Examples of such systems are the 'Texture of textures' system devised by Debonet and Viola, [1] and the MARS system developed at the University of Illinois (see Rui et al. [13]). Note that the idea of introducing relevance feedback mechanisms into image retrieval systems, was first demonstrated in the latter system.

It is the author's belief that the next (third) generation of image retrieval systems will address the limitations of the second generation systems by replacing the low-level image feature space with a higher-level semantic space. Query formulation can then be performed using these higher level semantics, these being much more understandable to the user than the low level image features used previously.

Given the large amounts of research into image retrieval it is surprising to find out how little research has been undertaken into understanding how users organise photos or image collections. To the author's knowledge the only published works addressing this are Rodden [11] who concentrated on home users (and hence is most relevant to our research) and Jose *et al.* [5] who concentrated on design professionals' needs in a work environment. The former outlines the results of interviews with a number of people who have large collections of home photographs and their experiences in organising them, whilst the latter undertakes a comparative evaluation of two variants of an image retrieval system in a work environment. It is interesting to note that the user's interviewed by Rodden stated that one of the *least* useful searching mechanisms for photos would be by colour or texture.

1.2 Extracting semantic content

There are a number of papers that address the issue of extracting semantic content from images. One of the first was Gorkani and Picard, [3] who attempt to discriminate 'city' from 'landscape' scenes using a texture orientation approach that is based on a multi-scale steerable pyramid operating on 128 × 128 pixel blocks across an image. Yiu [20] uses an identical texture extraction approach but introduces colour information to try and classify indoor and outdoor scenes. The procedure used is based on a nearest neighbour approach combined with a support vector machine classifier.

Szummer and Picard [15] address the same problem but combine a number of feature extraction techniques the best of which is a combination of Ohta colour space histograms (see Ohta, [10]) and textural features based on a multi-resolution simultaneous autoregressive model (see Mao and Jain, [8]).

Two other papers are closer to the work presented here. The first by Torralba and Oliva [16] describes an algorithm that attempts to determine a set of real-valued 'semantic axes' in their chosen feature space. They recognise the importance of being able to assign real-values to each image in relation to each semantic label, rather than the more common binary classification approach, but do not extend these real-values to a probabilistic representation. The second paper, by Vailaya *et al.* [17] describes a system that performs a hierarchical categorisation of images using a Bayesian framework resulting in probabilistic labels for the images.

Note that all of the systems described above only output one binary or real value per image. The primary contributions of this paper are the localisation of the semantic labelling to a *small area* (if required) in an image (rather than the entire image), the low number of images required to train the system and the low computational complexity involved in performing classification. All these features are important when considering the problem of retrieval from a large set of images. The localisation ability of the labelling is illustrated in Figure 1 where the labels have been used to segment the image. Another important contribution is the representation of the localised labels by probabilities (a lo-

Figure 1: The proposed scheme can segment images based on the probabilistic labels. (a): Original image extracted from the Corel Gallery 1,000,000 collection. (b): Segmentation of the image highlighting those areas that are believed to be man-made. The threshold was set to only highlight those areas having probabilities greater than 0.5.

calised equivalent of the global probabilistic values obtained by the system described by Vailaya *et al.*). This gives a principled approach to combining results across a number of categories.

2. OVERVIEW

The technique outlined in this paper allows probabilistic, localised labelling of images. To achieve this the system aggregates data over a number of different block sizes and then combines the knowledge obtained from each of these levels. This gives rise to a significantly more robust algorithm than a single level approach. In this paper two sets of semantic labels are considered. The first set attempts to label small areas of the image as either natural or man-made (subsequently termed a 'local sampling procedure') whereas the second attempts to label the entire image as either having been taken from inside a building or outside (subsequently termed a 'global sampling procedure').

The local sampling procedure extracts data from different sized blocks from the image, each of which is centred at the current sampling point. Figure 2 illustrates this procedure. In using this approach, samples can be extracted at any position across the image, in the natural/man-made labelling the sample 'grid' was set to have a 16 × 16 pixel spac-

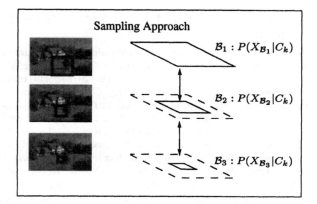

Sampling Approach

$\mathcal{B}_1 : P(X_{\mathcal{B}_1}|C_k)$

$\mathcal{B}_2 : P(X_{\mathcal{B}_2}|C_k)$

$\mathcal{B}_3 : P(X_{\mathcal{B}_3}|C_k)$

Figure 2: When classifying locally, blocks contributing to the same sample point are all centred at the same pixel position. At each level a feature vector from the corresponding block is extracted. After dimensionality reduction the likelihood of class membership can be estimated.

ing. Note that in so doing blocks from adjacent samples will overlap (thus applying an implicit smoothness constraint on the results of the labelling). Table 1 defines the levels used in both the local and global sampling procedures and their corresponding sizes. Note that all images used are either 256×384 pixels or 384×256 pixels in size, and have been extracted from the Corel Gallery 1,000,000 collection.

Table 1: Definition of levels and block sizes.

Level	Block Size
0	Whole image[1]
1	128×128
2	64×64
3	32×32
4	16×16

In order to obtain probabilistic labels probability densities representing the conditional class likelihoods must be estimated at each level. To achieve this a set of feature vectors is obtained for each class (in this case the natural/man-made categorisation is considered) at each level. This is done by selecting a set of natural and a set of man-made homogeneous images from which feature vectors can be extracted[2]. The feature vectors have 26 dimensions (these are described below); to make the task of estimating probability densities easier, dimensionality reduction is performed and then class likelihood densities estimated.

Once class conditional probability distributions have been

[1]Note that level 0 is only used when classifying on a global scale such as in the Inside/Outside case and is not used when classifying locally as in the Natural/Manmade case.

[2]In this paper, the term 'homogeneous' refers to scenes that only contain one class of image data (i.e. in the natural/man-made case the image consists of completely natural or completely man-made objects) whereas 'inhomogeneous' refers to scenes containing both classes.

determined labelling of an image can be performed. Feature vectors are extracted from all blocks at all levels. Class likelihoods are then estimated which, by the application of Bayes rule, allows posterior probabilities to be determined. In so doing, it is assumed that the class likelihoods at each level are statistically independent of each other. Note that in the two binary classification problems considered in this paper (natural/man-made and inside/outside) this results in probabilities (denoted as P(·)) such that:
P(Class 1) = 1 - P(Class 2).

One point that should also be mentioned is that the implicit smoothness constraint mentioned above implies that the proposed approach is unlikely to correctly label particularly small objects of either class (i.e. objects less than 16×16 pixels in size).

The following sections describe in detail how the feature vectors are extracted and the class likelihoods estimated.

3. EXTRACTING FEATURE VECTORS
3.1 Colour extraction
There are many different models to choose from when considering colour extraction. The primary aim when extracting colour is to obtain a set of values which are as decorrelated from each other as possible. Two common models used to achieve this are the Ohta colour model (see Ohta, [10]) and the HSV colour model (Hue, Saturation and Value). On comparing these methods, it was found that both the Ohta and HSV components had very similar correlation properties with both sets of components being significantly more decorrelated than those of the RGB model. Although they both give very similar results the Ohta transformation is more easily computed than the HSV transformation and so the former was used throughout the research described in this paper.

Subsequently, the three components of the Ohta colour transformation corresponding to image I are denoted as I_{o1}, I_{o2} and I_{o3}. The first of these corresponds to the luminance information, the latter two correspond to the chrominance information.

The chrominance information corresponding to block $\mathcal{B}_l$ (see Figure 2) is determined as follows:

$$C_1(\mathcal{B}_l) = \int_{\mathcal{B}_l} I_{o2}(\underline{r}) \, d\underline{r} \qquad (1)$$

$$C_2(\mathcal{B}_l) = \int_{\mathcal{B}_l} I_{o3}(\underline{r}) \, d\underline{r} \qquad (2)$$

where $\underline{r}$ denotes a particular pixel position in the image.

3.2 Texture extraction
The texture extraction approach is based on the complex wavelet transform (CWT). The CWT, developed by Kingsbury [6], is an efficient way of implementing a set of critically sampled Gabor-like wavelets. Gabor wavelets/filters have been used by a number of authors investigating both semantic content and classification problems, for example see Wood [19], Torralba [16], Rubner et al. [12] or Wiskott et al. [18]. They have also been shown to be similar in nature to the function of simple cells in the primary visual cortex of

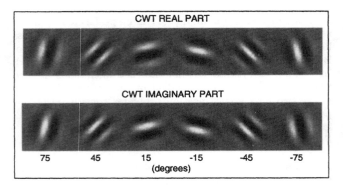

Figure 3: Illustration of the Gabor-like nature of the CWT which gives rise to directionally selective sets of filters.

primates (see Kruizinga [7] and Marčelja [9]). In this paper the CWT was used rather than Gabor wavelets because of the significantly reduced computational load[3].

Figure 3 illustrates the impulse responses obtained from the CWT at scale 4 in the decomposition. As described above these are Gabor-like in nature providing directional selectivity with 6 orientations at each scale. To succinctly represent the proposed procedure the following notation is introduced. The wavelet function at scale s, and orientation θ is denoted as ϕ_s^θ. The orientation can take one of six values $\Theta = \{15°, 45°, 75°, -75°, -45°, -15°\}$. The θ in the following text refers to an index into this vector i.e. $\theta \in \mathcal{I} : \{1 \ldots 6\}$. The response across the luminance image I_{o1}, extracted using the Ohta transformation, to each of the wavelet functions is determined as follows[4]:

$$I_s^\theta = I_{o1} * \phi_s^\theta \qquad (3)$$

The $o1$ has been dropped to aid clarity. The energy response to the wavelet function at scale s, and orientation θ is defined for block $\mathcal{B}_l$ as:

$$\mathcal{T}_s^\theta(\mathcal{B}_l) = \int_{\mathcal{B}_l} (I_s^\theta(\underline{r}))^2 \, d\underline{r} \qquad (4)$$

In this paper, wavelet functions corresponding to scales 1-4 are used with 6 orientations at each scale giving rise to 24 texture based features per feature vector.

The feature vectors have 26 dimensions, 24 texture features and 2 colour features. Using the terms defined above, the feature vector at a particular block $\mathcal{B}_l$ is found by concatenating the texture based features with the colour based features as follows:

$$\mathbf{X}_{\mathcal{B}_l} = [\mathcal{T}_1^1(\mathcal{B}_l), \mathcal{T}_1^2(\mathcal{B}_l), \ldots, \mathcal{T}_4^6(\mathcal{B}_l), \mathcal{C}_1(\mathcal{B}_l), \mathcal{C}_2(\mathcal{B}_l)] \qquad (5)$$

---

[3]Instead of requiring 2 dimensional convolutional operations the CWT combines results obtained from computationally efficient 1 dimensional convolutional operations.
[4]The * symbol denotes the convolution operator

4. PROBABILISTIC LABELLING PROCEDURE

Prior to describing how the class likelihoods are estimated the following nomenclature is defined. The two possible classes are denoted as C_k where $k \in 1, 2$ (in the natural/man-made case C_1 corresponds to natural, C_2 corresponds to man-made). Probabilities are denoted as $P(\cdot)$ and probability densities as $p(\cdot)$. Fisher's discriminant approach is used to reduce the dimensionality of the feature space. This technique gives a vector at each level l, denoted subsequently as $\mathbf{p}_l$, on to which feature vectors from that level are projected. This discriminative approach gives the 'best' vector onto which to project feature vectors in the sense that the projection maximises inter-class separation whilst minimising intra-class distance. This results in a 1 dimensional space, i.e. the projections onto the vector gives scalar values. The value obtained from projecting the feature vector extracted from block $\mathcal{B}_l$ onto $\mathbf{p}_l$ is denoted as $X_{\mathcal{B}_l} = \mathbf{p}_l^T \mathbf{X}_{\mathcal{B}_l}$.

Prior probabilities of class membership $P(C_k)$, likelihoods of class membership at a given block $P(X_{\mathcal{B}_l}|C_k)$ and a way of combining these likelihoods and priors is now required. Estimating the priors, $P(C_k)$, presents no problem; assuming that there is no knowledge about the images to be analysed they can be set at 0.5. However, to estimate the likelihoods at each position and level across the image, probability density estimation must be performed, this is discussed next.

4.1 Estimating the class likelihoods

The projection onto $\mathbf{p}_l$ at each level results in scalar values which makes probability density estimation very easy but throws away extra information that could possibly be used to discriminate between the two classes. This point is returned to in the summary.

Having determined the vector $\mathbf{p}_l$ for each level, probability densities for the class likelihoods can be estimated. The likelihoods are modelled using normal distributions this being based on the fact that when the dimensionality reduction step is undertaken it approximates to summing a set of independent, random variables and thus the central limit theorem can be invoked. The feature vectors for both classes are projected onto $\mathbf{p}_l$ and the mean and variance of the 1D normal distributions then found using the maximum likelihood approach. Figure 4 illustrates this class likelihood estimation process for the first three levels of the model in the natural/man-made case.

4.2 Combining class likelihoods

To estimate the probability of class membership, given data at a number of levels, it is assumed that the likelihoods at each level are statistically independent of each other; this assumption is addressed later in this section. In the following discussion the block index $\mathcal{B}$ is dropped to aid clarity. Given that data has been extracted from a number of block sizes, 1 to L, at a given sampling point the posterior conditioned on this data is:

$$P(C_k|X_1, \ldots, X_L) = \frac{P(X_1, \ldots, X_L|C_k)}{P(X_1, \ldots, X_L)} P(C_k) \qquad (6)$$

$$\approx \frac{\prod_{l=1}^L P(X_l|C_k)}{P(X_1, \ldots, X_L)} P(C_k) \qquad (7)$$

170

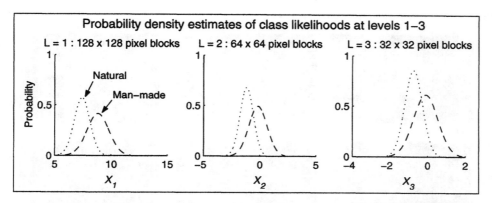

Figure 4: Estimates of the class likelihood probability densities. These correspond to the first three levels of the architecture obtained from the projected data X_1, X_2, X_3. Dotted: natural class likelihood $p(X_1|C_1)$. Dashed : Man-made class likelihood $p(X_1|C_2)$.

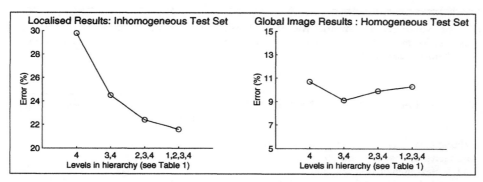

Figure 5: Natural/Man-made Results: Advantage gained from multi-level architectures. The left graph illustrates the classification error for all the samples (i.e. localised within each image). The right graph illustrates the error when the localised results for the homogeneous test set are averaged across each image to obtain a single classification result per image.

The denominator can be evaluated using the chain rule as follows:

$$P(X_1, \ldots, X_L) = P(X_L|X_{L-1}, \ldots, X_1) \ldots P(X_2|X_1)P(X_1) \quad (8)$$

Each factor in this expansion of the denominator can be evaluated by marginalising over the class variable and this then allows Equation 7 to be evaluated in a top down, recursive, manner.

As described above the likelihoods at each level are assumed to be statistically independent of each other. The reason that this assumption is made is to reduce the amount of data required to train the system. Thus, the system described in this paper can be trained using 100's of images rather than 1000's (as is required in other techniques).

5. RESULTS
5.1 Natural/Man-made
As described above, to estimate the class likelihoods a set of labelled data is required and so 120 'natural' and 120 'man-made' scenes were taken from the Corel Gallery 1000000 collection. Feature vectors for each of these sets of images were extracted for levels 1 to 4 (128×128 to 16×16 pixel

block size)[5]. Following this, the optimum vector to project onto at each of the levels was determined using Fisher's linear discriminant and estimation of the probability densities then performed. The resulting densities for the first three levels are shown in Figure 4.

Two test sets of images were used to assess the system. The first set consists of 240 homogeneous images. In this set there were 120 images containing only natural objects and 120 images containing only man-made objects. The second inhomogeneous test set consisted of 125 images containing both natural and man-made objects. These were hand-segmented to allow analysis of how well the system performed at a local scale. The images for both test sets were taken from the Corel Gallery 1000000 collection. Note that none of the images in either of the test sets were in the labelled set of images used to generate the class likelihoods.

Experiments were undertaken to evaluate the performance of a variety of architectures. Classification was based on thresholding the posterior probabilities such that samples

---

[5]To ensure that the system correctly identified sky as 'natural', those areas of the man-made scenes containing significant amounts of sky were ignored.

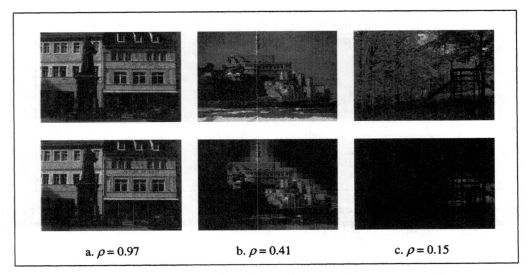

a. $\rho = 0.97$ b. $\rho = 0.41$ c. $\rho = 0.15$

Figure 6: Examples of Natural/Man-made Results: Top row: Original images. Bottom row: The brightness of each image block has been weighted with the posterior probability of being man-made. ρ : proportion of samples classified as being man-made.

with posteriors > 0.5 were 'in-class' otherwise they were 'out-of-class'.

Figure 5 shows the classification error for the samples obtained from the inhomogeneous test set and also shows the error obtained for the homogeneous test set when the localised results were averaged across each image to give a single classification result per image. These graphs illustrate two points.

- For images containing both natural and man-made objects, adding extra levels significantly increases the performance of the algorithm (as illustrated by the left graph). Using only level 4, for example, results in a classification error for the inhomogeneous test set of 29.8% whereas combining levels 1,2,3 and 4 reduces this to 21.6%.

- By averaging the localised results (as illustrated in the right graph), the system can accurately classify homogeneous images. The error in this classification is approximately 10%.

Figure 6 shows the results from a number of images having used an architecture consisting of levels 1,2,3 and 4. These examples illustrate that the proportion of samples, ρ, corresponds well with the proportion of the scene containing man-made objects.

5.2 Inside/Outside

The problem of classifying images as having been taken inside or outside is different to that of the natural/man-made problem in that there is no requirement to obtain localised results (i.e. the classification is a global property of the image). To take account of this an extra level was added to the hierarchy containing information aggregated across the

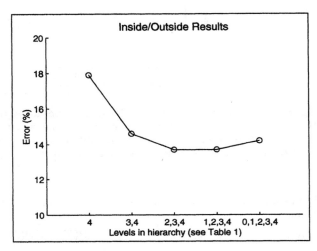

Figure 7: Inside/Outside Results: These results illustrate that the optimum performance is achieved when using at least 3 levels in the hierarchy.

entire image (see Table 1). 120 'inside' and 120 'outside' scenes were taken from the Corel Gallery 1000000 collection. Feature vectors for each of these sets of images were extracted for levels 0 to 4 (entire image through to 16 × 16 pixel block size). As with the natural/man-made case the optimum vector to project onto at each of the levels was determined using Fisher's linear discriminant and estimation of the probability densities then performed. Note that because inside/outside is a global property of the image samples were extracted using a 32 × 32 grid (rather than the 16 × 16 grid used in the natural/man-made case).

A test set of 240 images (none of which were in the training set) was used to determine the performance of the system.

172

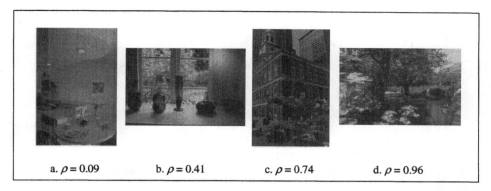

a. $\rho = 0.09$ b. $\rho = 0.41$ c. $\rho = 0.74$ d. $\rho = 0.96$

Figure 8: Examples of Inside/Outside Results. ρ : **proportion of samples classified as being outside.**

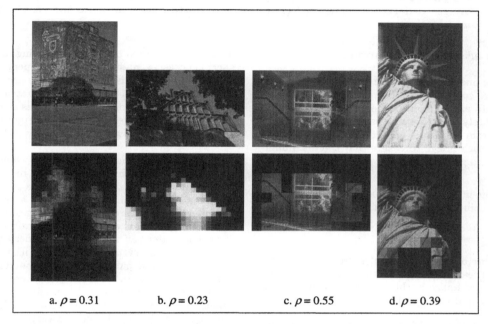

a. $\rho = 0.31$ b. $\rho = 0.23$ c. $\rho = 0.55$ d. $\rho = 0.39$

Figure 9: Four examples of errors in classification. Top row: Original images. Bottom row: Original images weighted by the relevant probabilities. (a),(b): Man-made classification; (c),(d): Outside classification. Note that in (b) the original image has been omitted to aid clarity.

Figure 7 shows the results illustrating that the optimum architecture consists of at least 3 levels giving rise to a classification accuracy of 86.3%. As with the natural/man-made case, using multiple levels gives better results although interestingly using the whole image (i.e. Level 0) degrades the performance slightly. This indicates that using features aggregated across the entire image can reduce the accuracy of an algorithm even in the cases where *global* attributes are trying to be extracted. Figure 8 shows a number of examples (having used an architecture consisting of levels 2,3, and 4).

5.3   Classification Errors

Figure 9 shows examples of where the classification process has gone wrong. In 9(a) the colours painted onto the building lead to about half of the building being incorrectly labelled as natural, thus biasing the overall result. In 9(b), the shadows cast onto the building from the surrounding trees are also incorrectly classified as natural (in this case the image has been omitted for clarity). In 9(c), the system

incorrectly labels the swimming pool and the window as corresponding to objects that occur in 'outside' scenes and thus the overall classification is biased towards an 'outside' result. 9(d) illustrates that the system labels dark, low texture areas as corresponding to images that have been taken inside which in this case results in an incorrect classification.

6.   IMAGE RETRIEVAL APPLICATION

To assess whether a system based on the algorithms outlined above can actually work in practice, a prototype image retrieval application was built using the author's digital photo archive as a database. A useful feature associated with digital cameras is that it is often possible to extract the date that each photo was taken, this extra information was used in the retrieval procedure as explained below. The archive consists of 800 images taken over the past 12 months. A daytime/night-time binary classification was added using a very similar procedure to that of the inside/outside to give extra information useful for retrieval. The resulting indexing

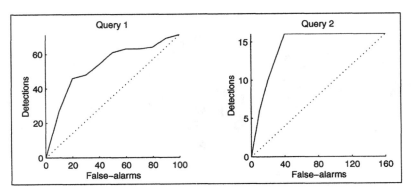

Figure 10: Receiver-Operator Characteristics: Query 1 : 'Find pictures of my holiday in Wales'. Images ordered in terms of P(Outside)×P(Natural). Query 2 : 'Find pictures of the evening spent with friends in a bar in Boston'. Images ordered in terms of P(Inside). The dotted lines indicate the results that would be obtained by random selection.

procedure for each image consists of two steps.

1. Rescaling the image. This is done firstly to reduce the computational complexity and secondly to ensure that the image data extracted from the photos corresponds to approximately the same area as that obtained from the images from the Corel collection. Thus, the system rescales each image to ensure that the maximum dimension is no greater than 400 pixels.

2. Processing the image and subsequently storing the extracted probabilities and also the date that the photo was taken.

Unlike the majority of image retrieval systems that have to store the actual feature vectors in the database, the resulting 'signature' per image in this case is extremely small consisting of a date and three probability values.

During retrieval the user is asked to specify the dates between which the image was likely to have been taken. This significantly reduces the number of photos that need to be searched. The user can then indicate whether the photo was taken inside or outside. If it was taken outside, the user can also indicate whether the image consists of mainly natural or man-made objects and/or whether the image was taken during the daytime or at night.

To give an indication of how well the system performs, the results of two queries presented to this prototype system are shown in Figures 11 and 12. In both cases the same sets of dates were chosen during which the author went on holiday to both Boston and Wales; this reduces the search from the entire database (800 images) to 171 images. The first query is based on trying to find pictures from the holiday in Wales and, knowing that the images contain a lot of scenery, the system is asked to return images in decreasing order of P(Outside'ness and 'Natural'ness. Out of the 171 images, 71 match this query (i.e. were taken whilst in Wales). The Receiver Operator Characteristic (a plot of the false-alarms vs detections) is shown in Figure 10 and the top 24 images, as returned by the system, are shown in Figure 11. Of the first 24 images, 17 are relevant to the query.

The second query is based on extracting images taken on a specific occasion, namely an evening spent with friends in a bar in Boston. In this case the images are ordered in terms P(Inside). Only 16 of the 171 images match this query, again the Receiver Operator Characteristic is shown in Figure 10 and the top 24 images are shown in Figure 12. Of the first 24 images, 9 are relevant to this query.

The prototype application presented above illustrates the potential of a semantic-based image retrieval application. The results show that combining date metadata with even this small number of categories gives a system that allows the user to find different types of images quickly and easily. The assumption on which this semantic retrieval is based is that the user can map from the query to the semantics extracted by the system (in query 1, illustrated above, the query was: 'Find pictures from the holiday in Wales' and the semantics used to retrieve images were 'outside-ness' and 'natural-ness'). Note that this mapping from query to semantic features is much more intuitive than the mapping from query to low-level image features.

7. SUMMARY

In this paper a probabilistic, multiple level approach to the semantic labelling of images has been proposed. The architecture is based on modelling class likelihoods at each of the levels separately and combining these to form an overall estimate of the posterior, conditioned on the data. The results that have been presented illustrate that using multiple levels significantly increases the accuracy of the posterior probabilities.

The binary semantic categories that have been investigated are natural/man-made and inside/outside. The results illustrate that the proposed technique can classify images with an accuracy of between 86-91% given a training set of only a couple of hundred images. The method outlined in this paper compares well with other, previously published, techniques such as that proposed by Vailaya *et al.*. Note that it is difficult to make quantitative comparisons between different retrieval systems because of the lack of consistent test sets of images. It is also acknowledged that the numbers of images used in the analyses presented in this paper are small. To this end, a much larger test set of images is currently being gathered and hand-labelled to allow more exhaustive testing of the algorithms described in this paper.

A prototype photo archive image retrieval system based on the probabilistic labelling procedure has been tested using the author's digital image archive. Using the date information combined with the semantic labels gave surprisingly good results and indicate that this is a very useful approach to image retrieval. It is clear that more needs to be learnt about how users would like to interact with such systems.

The primary limitations of the proposed system are a. it can only discriminate between classes that are linearly separable and b. the assumption of statistical independence between levels in the classification algorithm. Noting these limitations, there are a number of interesting areas of research to persue following from the work presented in this paper:

- Using more sophisticated techniques for the probability density estimation task such as kernel methods or Bayesian Belief Networks etc. These techniques are likely to improve upon the results presented here (and address the limitations of the current algorithm as described above).

- Finding other categories that are of use in this domain. An obvious category that is required in the photo archive domain is 'People'/'No people'. This leads onto more specific categories such as trying to locate particular types of object.

- Incorporating relevance feedback and Query By Example techniques into the system.

8. ACKNOWLEDGEMENTS

All the images used in this paper were extracted from the Corel Gallery 1,000,000 collection. Special thanks to Andrew Blake for helpful comments regarding this paper and to Nick Kingsbury for comments regarding the description of the CWT and for the 'donation' of Figure 3.

9. REFERENCES

[1] J. S. DeBonet. Novel statistical multiresolution techniques for image synthesis, discrimnation and recognition. Master's thesis, M.I.T. Learning and Vision Group, AI Lab,, 1997.

[2] M. Flickner, H. Sawnhey, W. Niblack, J. Ashley, Q. Huang, B. Dom, M. Gorkani, J. Hafner, D. Lee, D. Petkovic, D. Steele, and P. Yanker. *Intelligent Multimedia Information Retrieval*, chapter Query by image and video content: The QBIC system, pages 8–22. AAAI Press, 1997.

[3] M. M. Gorkani and R. W. Picard. Texture orientation for sorting photos 'at a glance'. In *Proc. of the IEEE Int. Conf. on Pattern Recognition*, October 1994.

[4] A. Gupta and R. Jain. Visual information retrieval. *Communications of the ACM*, 40(5):71–79, May 1997.

[5] J. M. Jose and J. Furner. Spatial querying for image retrieval: a user oriented evaluation. In *21st SIGIR Int. Conf. on Research and Development in Information Retrieval*. ACM, August 1998.

[6] N. G. Kingsbury. The dual-tree complex wavelet transform: A new efficient tool for image restoration and enhancement. In *EUSIPCO'98*, volume 1, pages 319–322. EURASIP, 1998.

[7] P. Kruizinga and N. Petkov. Nonlinear operator for oriented texture. *IEEE Trans. on Image Processing*, 8(10):1395–1407, October 1999.

[8] J. Mao and A. Jain. Texture classification and segmentation using multiresolution simultaneous autoregressive models. *Pat. Rec.*, 25(2):173–188, 1992.

[9] S. Marčelja. Mathematical description of the response of simple cortical cells. *Journal of the Optical Society of America*, 70:1297–1300, 1980.

[10] Y. Ohta, T. Kanade, and T. Sakai. Colour information for region segmentation. *Computer Graphics and Image Processing*, 13:222–241, 1980.

[11] K. Rodden. How do people organise their photographs? In *IRSG 99, 21st Colloquim on Information Retrieval*, pages 142–152. British Computer Society, April 1999.

[12] Y. Rubner and C. Tomasi. Texture-based image retrieval without segmentation. In *ICCV'99*, Corfu, Greece, September 1999.

[13] Y. Rui, T. Huang, S. Mehrotra, and M. Ortega. A relevance feedback architecture in content-based multimedia information retrieval systems. In *Proc of IEEE Workshop on Content-based Access of Image and Video Libraries*, 1997. in conjunction with CVPR'97.

[14] J. Smith and S. Chang. *Intelligent Multimedia Information Retrieval*, chapter Querying by colour regions using the VisualSEEk content-based visual query system, pages 23–41. AAAI Press, 1997.

[15] M. Szummer and R. W. Picard. Indoor-outdoor image classification. In *IEEE Int. Work. on Content-based Access of Image and Vid. Databases*, January 1998.

[16] A. B. Torralba and A. Oliva. Semantic organisation of scenes using discriminant structural templates. In *ICCV'99*, Corfu, Greece, September 1999.

[17] A. Vailaya, M. Figueiredo, A. K. Jain, and H.J. Zhang. Content-based hierarchical classification of vacation images. In *IEEE Conf. on Multimedia Computing and Systems*, volume 1, pages 518–523, 1999.

[18] L. Wiskott, J. Fellous, N. Krüger, and C. von der Malsburg. Face recognition by elastic bunch graph matching. In *IEEE Int. Conf. on Image Processing*, volume 1, 1997.

[19] M. E. J. Wood, N. W. Campbell, and B. T. Thomas. Iterative refinement by relevance feedback in content-based digital image retrieval. In *6th ACM Int. Multimedia Conference*, Bristol, September 1998. http://www.acm.org/sigmm/MM98/.

[20] E. C. Yiu. Image classification using colour cues and texture orientation. Master's thesis, Dept EECS, MIT, 1996.

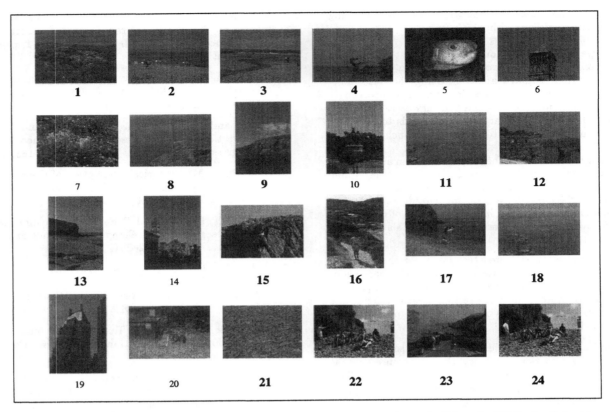

Figure 11: Image retrieval application: Query 1 : 'Find pictures of my holiday in Wales'. Selecting dates between May 1st and June 15th cuts down the search to 171 images which are then ordered in terms of P(Outside)×P(Natural). Out of the images shown here, 17 are relevant to the query. These are indicated by the larger, bold typeface numbers.

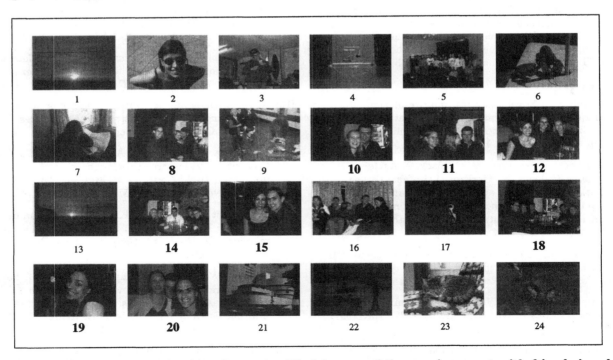

Figure 12: Image retrieval application: Query 2 : 'Find images of the evening spent with friends in a bar in Boston'. Selecting dates between May 1st and June 15th cuts down the search to 171 images which are then ordered in terms of P(Inside). 9 of the images shown here are relevant to the query. These are indicated by the larger, bold typeface numbers.

Virtual 3D Camera Composition from Frame Constraints

William Bares   Scott McDermott   Christina Boudreaux   Somying Thainimit
Center for Advanced Computer Studies
University of Lousiana at Lafayette
337-482-5697
whbares@cacs.louisiana.edu

ABSTRACT

We have designed a graphical interface that enables 3D visual artists or developers of interactive 3D virtual environments to efficiently define sophisticated camera compositions by creating storyboard frames, indicating how a desired shot should appear. These storyboard frames are then automatically encoded into an extensive set of virtual camera constraints that capture the key visual composition elements of the storyboard frame. Visual composition elements include the size and position of a subject in a camera shot. A recursive heuristic constraint solver then searches the space of a given 3D virtual environment to determine camera parameter values which produce a shot closely matching the one in the given storyboard frame. The search method uses given ranges of allowable parameter values expressed by each constraint to reduce the size of the 7 Degree of Freedom search space of possible camera positions, aim direction vectors, and field of view angles. In contrast, some existing methods of automatically positioning cameras in 3D virtual environments rely on pre-defined camera placements that cannot account for unanticipated configurations and movement of objects or use program-like scripts to define constraint-based camera shots. For example, it is more intuitive to directly manipulate an object's size in the frame rather than editing a constraint script to specify that the object should cover 10% of the frame's area.

Keywords
Virtual 3D Cameras, Constraints, User Interfaces.

1. INTRODUCTION

Automatically planning camera shots in virtual 3D environments requires solving problems similar to those faced by human cinematographers. In traditional cinematography parlance, a *shot* refers to a continuous stream of *frames* (individual images) recorded by a given camera. In the most essential terms, a shot typically communicates some specified visual message. Consequently, the camera must be carefully staged to clearly view the relevant subject(s), properly emphasize the important elements in the shot, and compose an engaging image that holds the viewer's attention [20, 23]. Expert cinematographers and film directors often design the initial concept of a camera shot using a *storyboard frame*, or rough sketch of how the shot should appear

[17]. It in effect defines the most essential visual composition elements of a shot. Visual composition elements include the size and position of a subject appearing in a camera shot. Given a storyboard frame, a camera operator then carefully surveys the given setting and chooses a camera position, orientation, and lens angle to create a shot closely matching that in the given storyboard frame. This division of labor allows the cinematographer to express the appearance of the shot at a high level leaving the details of camera placement to the camera operator. In addition the camera operator must be able to think on his or her feet by adjusting the camera to account for unanticipated obstacles or arrangements of objects [14].

Users interact with three-dimensional virtual environments by viewing the scene through the "eyes" of a virtual camera. A virtual 3D camera view is defined by parameters of camera position, aim direction vector, and field of view (lens angle). In many 3D applications, users directly control the camera view. Applications featuring complex interaction tasks or fast-moving action often delegate the task of camera control to automatic computer control allowing the user to focus on the task at hand.

Our approach to automatically computing camera shots in virtual 3D environments employs a constraint-based methodology. The desired appearance of a camera shot in a virtual 3D environment is encoded by constraints declaring how subjects should appear in the frame. For example, set the camera to obtain a close-up shot in which the subject fills the frame with the camera viewing its front right side. A constraint solver module then attempts to automatically find values for each camera parameter so that all constraints are satisfied in the context of a given 3D virtual environment. In contrast, some less sophisticated methods of automatically placing cameras in virtual 3D environments typically define shots by in effect pre-coding the camera parameters to properly view a set of anticipated situations. Constraint-based approaches have the flexibility to analyze the space of possible camera parameter values to successfully find satisfactory shots in spite of viewing obstructions or unanticipated object configurations typical in dynamic interactive 3D worlds.

A constraint-based virtual camera system should provide the following basic features if it is to be effective in a wide-range of applications and virtual 3D environments.

- *Visual Constraint Editor:* Provide a graphical WYSIWYG interface allowing users to directly "draw" how a desired camera shot is to appear. Constraints are then automatically extracted from the storyboard frame created by the user and exported to the constraint solver system.

- *Environmental Analysis:* The constraint solver should be able to analyze a virtual 3D environment to account for viewing obstructions or objects which may move into an infinity of possible configurations in dynamic or interactive 3D virtual environments.

- *Evaluation of Shot Quality:* The constraint solver should evaluate computed shots to determine how effectively they satisfy the desired visual constraints.

- *Interactive Performance:* The constraint solver should be able to compute solutions in real-time or near real-time to facilitate interactive 3D applications.

1.1 Current State of the Art

Automatic camera control assistants vary camera position to avoid occlusions of a goal object or satisfy screen-space constraints on how subjects appear on-screen [11, 24]. Automated camera navigation assistants adjust camera speed based on distance to the target or guide the camera along specified optimal vantages as a user navigates over a terrain [13, 19, 26, 27]. Both automated viewing and navigation assistants focus on controlling the camera at a low-level and frequently require considerable user inputs.

Other systems define camera shots by displacements relative from the subject(s) being viewed [1, 8, 16, 25]. For example, the "chase plane" view found in typical flight or driving simulators and popular third-person 3D adventure games automatically positions the camera a set distance behind and slightly above the player's vehicle or character. IBIS features multi-view illustrations and cutaways of occluding obstructions and CATHI has a facility for transparency [4, 9]. Idiom-based systems employ hierarchical encodings or planners to sequence prototypical shots of anticipated actions such as conversations between small groups of players [4, 5, 16, 18]. Most idiom-based systems use variants of the pre-specified relative camera method in lieu of more complex camera placement solvers. The Virtual Cinematographer employs Blinn's method to for example stage the camera so an object projects to a given point in the frame [3]. It can also reposition objects that are not in the anticipated locations to improve camera shots [18]. One recent effort employs a cognitive forumulation of the Virtual Cinematographer's Finite State Machines to film autonomous virtual creatures [10]. However, each of these systems can fail to find acceptable shots when multiple subjects occupy or move into unanticipated relative spatial configurations, structures in the world occlude the subject(s) of interest, or users wish to view unanticipated types of shots.

The CAMDROID constraint system supports a powerful set of camera constraints, but employs a numerical constraint solver that is subject to local minima failures [6, 7]. CAMPLAN utilizes genetic algorithms to generate-and-test candidate camera shots by "mating" those sets of camera parameters which best satisfy a given set of camera constraints specified from over eighteen types of constraints [12, 22]. A third constraint-based solver features real-time performance and a systematic solution for handling constraint failures by creating multiple shot solutions or relaxing less important constraints, but supports only four types of constraints [2]. Virtual Camera Man solves small sets of interval constraints to generate animations offline [15]. Our goal is to develop a constraint-based system that can provide real-time performance suitable for interactive applications, a large set of expressive constraints to create artful photographic compositions, and a graphical interface to facilitate rapid specification of constraints, especially by non-programmers.

1.2 Photographic Composition

Our camera constraints are based on established knowledge in photography and cinematography. Like photographs and shots in motion pictures, camera shots in virtual 3D environments should be composed to clearly depict the objects and actions of interest to the user. *Composition* is the artful arrangement of visual elements in an image [20, 21, 23]. These visual elements include:

- *Subject size:* The size of a subject in the frame can be expressed by the terms extreme close-up, close-up, medium, long, and extreme long shots in order of decreasing subject size. Camera positions nearer to the subject or narrower fields of view yield larger subject sizes.

- *Location:* Subjects may be carefully positioned in the frame to determine visual weight, balance, or emphasis. For example, subjects may be framed so that they form a triangle with the dominant subject at the apex of the triangle.

- *View angle:* The relative orientation from which the camera views the subject. For example, the camera may be positioned at a 45-degree angle from the front of the subject to create a *three-quarter shot.*

- *Occlusion:* Allowing subjects to partially overlap one another can provide an increased degree of interest or additional depth cues.

- *Exclusion:* Good compositions typically exclude unimportant or distracting objects from the frame.

- *Depth:* The camera can be positioned so that subjects lie at varying distances from the camera to better reveal the spatial distribution of objects in a scene.

2. STORYBOARD FRAME INTERFACE

A developer of an interactive 3D virtual environment would begin by creating constraint-based definitions of the types of shots needed. Our constraint solver module, integrated into a 3D application, would analyze the environment to compute camera shots. We have developed a graphical interface to facilitate the creation of constraint-based shot definitions. It is far more intuitive to manipulate an object's appearance so its size in the storyboard frame view defines a medium shot rather than using a constraint program script to specify that the object should cover 10% of the frame's area. The storyboard frame view (left half of Figure 1) is augmented by overhead or side views (right half of Figure 1) to allow the artist to more precisely indicate depth relationships between objects with respect to the camera.

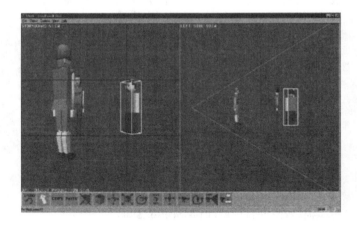

Figure 1: Storyboard Frame Editor Interface.

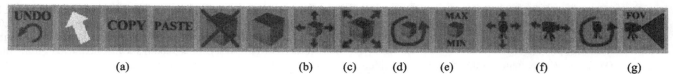

(a)   (b)   (c)   (d)   (e)   (f)   (g)

Figure 2. Storyboard Frame Editor Toolbar

The Storyboard Frame Editor provides the following functionalities via drop-down menus or a toolbar (Figure 2).

(a) Object Editing. Basic operations to select, copy, paste, delete, and create new storyboard objects.

(b) Location. Move the currently selected object in the storyboard frame view to vary its location in the frame. Or, move an object in the overhead or side views to vary its relative distance from the camera causing a corresponding increase or decrease in apparent subject size in the storyboard frame view.

(c) Size. The size of the currently selected object in the storyboard frame view may be varied by dragging the mouse also producing a corresponding decrease or increase in the object's relative distance from the camera in the overhead or side views.

(d) View Angle. Rotate the currently selected object to set the relative viewing angle between it and the camera.

(e) Minimum-Maximum Allowable Ranges. By default the previous object edit operations (location, size, and view angle) specify the optimal framing attributes for a given object in the shot. In complex, unpredictable, or dynamic interactive 3D environments it may not always be possible to obtain the optimal shot framing so our constraint-based method permits satisfactory solutions that are within a specified threshold away from the optimal shot depicted in the Storyboard Editor frame view. By enabling a toggle switch, the user can edit the allowable ranges of values for the selected attribute of the current object. An object's range of allowable minimum and maximum sizes in the frame are represented by two rectangular outlines. The outermost rectangle represents the maximum size that an object may assume in the frame, while the innermost rectangle represents its minimum size. The range of allowable locations in the storyboard is represented by one bounding rectangle (Figure 4). A transparent spherical patch surrounding the current object represents the range of allowable view angles of the camera relative to an object.

(f) Camera Pan, Dolly, and Rotate. The storyboard camera can be moved about to simultaneously change the framing properties of all objects in the shot. A pan moves the camera laterally, while a dolly moves the camera towards or away from the objects, and rotate swings the camera around the center of the object(s).

(g) Field of View. Change the field of view angle (zoom factor) of the camera lens to simultaneously vary the sizes of all objects.

(h) Field of View Inclusion and Occlusion. If an object is partially outside the frame, then this fact may be noted for export to the constraint system. If an object is partially occluded by another object, the user can specify that this overlap is required for a constraint solution (this is only available in the menu).

(i) Design Guides. Users may toggle the display of the "Rule of Thirds Lines" or a horizon plane. The Rule of Thirds suggests placing objects on or at the intersection of horizontal and vertical lines that split the frame into thirds in either dimension [21]. The horizon or ground plane can be used to assist in aligning objects.

3. CAMERA CONSTRAINTS

The camera constraint system supports fifteen types of constraints on either the camera's attributes or how objects appear in the camera shot. Constraint types are designed to support the visual composition elements from Section 1.2. Constraints specify optimal and allowable ranges of values for compositional attributes including subject size in the frame and relative view angles. Constraints may be applied to one (primary object) or two specified objects (primary and secondary objects) or to the camera itself. Some object constraints, may opt to apply the constraint to a designated point or region of space (bounded by a sphere) displaced from an object's midpoint. This optional construct is referred to as a *locus modifier*. For example, the object projection size constraint can apply a locus modifier to a figure's head requiring its projection to fill a given fraction of the frame.

3.1 Constraint Types

The following lists the constraint types featured in this paper.

1. OBJ_PROJECTION_SIZE: requires that the projection of the primary object's *projection source* cover a specified fraction of the frame. An object's projection source may be either its bounding box or its optional locus modifier sphere.

2. OBJ_PROJECTION_ABSOLUTE: Requires that the specified projection source of the primary object project to lie entirely inside a given rectangular region of the frame. The projection source may be a point, locus sphere, or bounding box.

3. OBJ_VIEW_ANGLE: requires the camera to lie at a specified orientation relative to the untransformed primary object. This relative orientation is expressed in spherical coordinates (horizontal angle theta -180° to 180° and phi -90° to 90°).

4. OBJ_IN_FIELD_OF_VIEW: requires the specified primary object to lie entirely or partially in the camera's field of view as specified by an optional inclusion fraction.

5. OBJ_OCCLUSION_MINIMIZE: requires that no more than the specified maximum allowable fraction of the given primary object is occluded by other object(s).

6. OBJ_OCCLUSION_PARTIAL: requires the fraction of the primary object occluded by other opaque object(s) to range between specified minimum and maximum allowable values. It is also possible to specify which object should contribute occlusion.

7. OBJ_EXCLUDE_OR_HIDE: requires that the primary object is either completely occluded by other object(s) or lies entirely outside the camera's field of view.

8. CAM_POS_IN_REGION: requires that the camera position lie within the specified region of space, which can be defined by one or more box, sphere, or space partitioning plane regions combined in a hierarchy using union and intersection operations.

Other implemented constraint types include relative projection locations of two objects in the frame (e.g. above, below, left of, or right of, etc.), relative depth of two objects from the camera, field of view angle, and aiming the camera at a specified point.

3.2 Storyboard Frame to Constraints

The Storyboard Frame Editor exports shot definition files, which are loaded into a separate 3D application program equipped with our constraint solver. Two forms of shot definition are exported when the user saves a shot in the Storyboard Frame Editor.

Relative Displacement Definition: The camera position and aim direction are expressed as vectors in a local coordinate system anchored at the first object in the storyboard frame. Our constraint solver includes an implementation of relative displacements to permit an instantaneous solution if the configuration of objects in a scene happens to match those of the Storyboard Frame Editor's internal 3D scene model.

Constraint Definition: The Storyboard Frame Editor automatically exports a set of constraints that define the key visual elements of the shot. These constraints are requirements on how various objects are to appear in the desired shot. Exported constraint definitions are scene independent allowing the same set of storyboard constraints to be used in a variety of different 3D virtual environments. A constraint-based shot definition may also be used to film differing configurations of objects in the same 3D virtual environment thus providing an allowance for object movement away from an anticipated configuration.

For example, the storyboard frame in Figure 3(a) depicts a medium three-quarter shot of a virtual actor. The user can manipulate the actor's appearance in the frame view to visually define the desired shot. Select the view angle tool and rotate the object so the camera views the front-left side of the figure. Next, use the size tool to move the object towards or away from the camera until the object appears at the desired size in the frame. With the size tool still selected, enable the minimum-maximum toggle switch to specify first the minimum allowed object projection size and then the maximum allowed object projection size. Do so by stretching the bounding rectangles marking the minimum and maximum allowed projection sizes (Figure 4). The Storyboard Frame Editor automatically extracts the essential visual composition constraints that define this shot. In this case, the image of the virtual actor covers 37% of the frame area and the camera is oriented 45 degrees to the left of the actor's front and is elevated by 15 degrees. Figure 3(b) is an abstractraction (for illustration only) of the constraint parameters for projection size and view angle. The parameter values for projection sizes (optimal, minimum, and maximum) are taken by dividing the area of the object or bounding rectangles by the total frame area. Values are encoded for the desired optimal values and allowable ranges for the virtual actor's OBJ_PROJECTION_SIZE,

OBJ_PROJECTION_ABSOLUTE and OBJ_VIEW_ANGLE constraints. Projection location parameters are encoded with (0,0) as the lower left corner of the frame and (1,1) as the top right corner. The constraints automatically extracted from the Storyboard Editor frame view in Figure 3 are given in the constraint script file listing on the following page (Listing 1). Note, a constraint to minimize occlusion of a subject is automatically exported unless otherwise specified by the user.

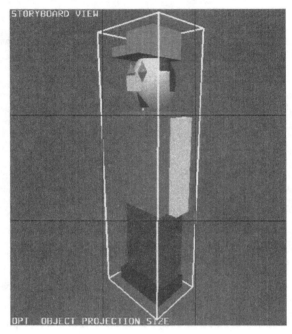

(a) Storyboard frame view of medium three-quarter shot.

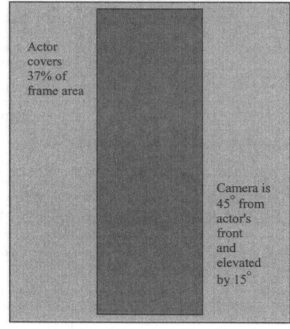

(b) Abstraction of constraints extracted from frame view.

Figure 3. Extraction of projection size and view angle constraints from Storyboard Editor frame view.

```
NumConstraints 5
  // Include BlueActor in camera field of view.
  Constraint OBJ_IN_FIELD_OF_VIEW
  { PrimaryObj BlueActor          Priority 1.0 }

  // Projection size of BlueActor
  Constraint OBJ_PROJECTION_SIZE
  { PrimaryObj BlueActor
    Parameters
    {
      Source BoundingBox
      MinSize 0.18   OptSize 0.37       MaxSize 0.63
    }
    Priority 1.0  }

  // BlueActor's 3D bounding box must project into the
  // specified rectangular region of the frame.
  Constraint OBJ_PROJECTION_ABSOLUTE
  { PrimaryObj BlueActor
    Parameters
    {
      Source BoundingBox
      BottomLeft 0.079801 0.006981
      TopRight 0.882977 1.044370
    }
    Priority 1.0  }

  // Relative view orientation to camera.
  Constraint OBJ_VIEW_ANGLE
  { PrimaryObj BlueActor
    Parameters
    {
      optHoriz 45.0  optElev 15.0
      AllowedHorizRange 0.0  90.0
      AllowedElevRange   0.0  35.0
    }
    Priority 1.0   }

  // Minimize occlusion by obstacles
  Constraint OBJ_OCCLUSION_MINIMIZE
  { PrimaryObj BlueActor
    Parameters
    {        MaxAllowable 0.10          }
    Priority 1.0   }
```

Listing 1. Exported constraint definition from figure 3.

As a second example, consider the shot of three virtual actors in conversation expressed in the Storyboard Editor frame view in Figure 4(a). Projection size, viewing angle, projection location, and occlusion constraints are exported for each character. Figure 4(b) illustrates the abstraction of the extracted optimal and maximum allowable projection size for the gray actor standing on the right side of the frame.

The user manipulates a bounding rectangle in the frame view to set the maximum allowable projection size of the subject in the frame. The Storyboard Frame Editor detects that the nearer blue actress partially obscures the green actress. The user can opt to export a constraint that specifies the optimal and allowed degree to which the green actress is occluded. This constraint is useful to add interest and depth cues to a shot.

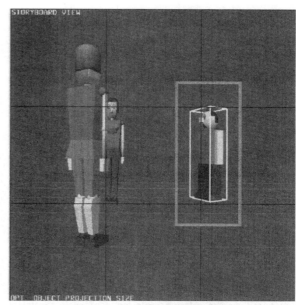

(a) Storyboard frame view of desired shot. User adjusts rectangle around rightmost actor to specify its maximum allowable projection size. Note the partial overlap of the other two figures.

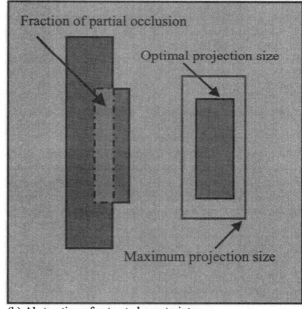

(b) Abstraction of extracted constraints.

Figure 4. Specification and extraction of maximum projection size and partial occlusion constraints.

3.3 Measuring Constraint Satisfaction

A computed *camera placement solution* is an assignment of values to the virtual camera's position, aim direction, and field of view angle. It's essential to determine how well a given camera placement satisfies the constraints. The satisfaction rating for a constraint is computed as a value in the range 0.0 to 1.0, which rates how near a camera placement solution is to the specified optimal value for that constraint. A cumulative constraint satisfaction rating is computed as shown in the below equation, where P_i is the relative priority of the ith constraint, which may be specified in a Storyboard Editor dialog box, S_i is the computed satisfaction rating of the ith constraint, and N is the number of constraints.

$$satisfaction = \sum_{1}^{N} (Pi \times Si)$$

This cumulative shot constraint satisfaction rating is used to determine the "best" shot found during the solution search process. Constraint priority values, which can be edited by the user in the Storyboard Frame Editor, normally range between 0.0 and 1.0. Constraints having priority values greater than 1.0 are mandatory and must have a non-zero individual constraint satisfaction rating; otherwise, the cumulative satisfaction rating for the shot is degraded to zero. The constraint priority weights distinguish between those that are mandatory for an acceptable shot and those that rank acceptable shots based on how near they are to the optimal shot given in the Storyboard Editor frame view. The constraint priority weights help select the returned solution shot from the set of candidate shots satisfying the given constraints. The selection of these priority weights is largely subjective based on the relative importance of each constraint assigned by an application or user.

Specialized evaluator functions are provided for each type of constraint. Object projection size, location, and inclusion or exclusion from the field of view are evaluated using the bounding box of the relevant object. For object projection size and location, the 8 vertices of an object bounding box are projected onto the camera's viewplane. Then a rectangle is computed to enclose the projected points in the frame of the shot. During solution searches, the evaluation of a shot terminates when it is certain that the shot's cumulative satisfaction rating is less than that of the best shot(s) found so far. Occlusion constraints are evaluated last since they tend to be more costly. The occlusion constraint evaluator can assume one of two variations:

Ray Casting: Cast rays from the camera position to each of the 8 vertices and midpoint of a potential obstruction's bounding box. The number rays resulting in a hit is used to estimate the fraction of the object in occlusion.

Frame Rendering: An object of interest is rendered into the OpenGL backbuffer with accompanying writes to a stencil buffer mask. Potential occluders are rendered using unique color codes. Non-zero pixels having values not equal to the id of the object of interest are added to the fraction of the object in occlusion.

3.4 Camera Constraint Solutions

Our heuristic search method uses the given constraint allowable minimum and maximum values to reduce the size of the 7 Degree of Freedom search space of possible camera positions (x,y,z), aim direction vectors (dx, dy, dz), and field of view angles. The Constraint Solver constructs *valid regions* of space, each of which represents the allowable range of virtual camera parameter values that will satisfy a particular constraint. The solver then examines candidate camera shots by stepping by discrete increments of the camera placement parameters (position, aim direction, and field of view angle) inside the respective valid regions. Each candidate camera placement is evaluated as described in Section 3.3 to determine how well it satisfies the set of constraints. If no camera

parameter values lie inside all of the respective valid regions, then the solver reports its failure to find a solution.

3.4.1 Valid Regions

First compute valid regions for those camera constraints that restrict the position of the camera. A view angle constraint requires the camera position to lie inside a spherical wedge, defined by (theta, phi) minima and maxima extending from the midpoint or locus modifier of an object (Figure 5). For example, the optimal 45 degree horizontal and 15 degree vertical elevation orientation between the camera and virtual actor shown previously in Figure 2 would require the camera to lie along a vector V. The allowable range of view angles would be defined by sweeping out by user-specified threshold angles along the horizontal and vertical dimensions.

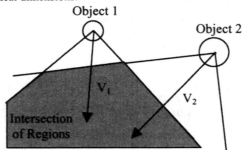

Figure 5: Viewing angle constraint valid regions.

Distance and object projection size constraints require the camera to lie inside two concentric spheres, representing the minimum and maximum distances from camera to object midpoint or locus modifier. For projection size constraints, frame area fractions are converted into corresponding camera to subject distances using the subject's bounding sphere and allowable range of camera field of view angles. If a projection size constraint requires a subject to fill most of the frame, then the camera must be positioned relatively near the subject and vice versa for small projection size.

The camera in region constraint directly expresses its valid region using a set of spatial region primitives including boxes, spheres, and space-partitioning planes combined using Boolean intersection and union operators. These regions keep the camera inside an irregular-shaped room interior of a 3D environment. The camera can be located only at those points, the so-called *valid camera positions*, lying inside the intersection of all of these valid regions which restrict the allowable camera positions.

Next, for a given valid camera position, determine the maximum allowable ranges for the field of view angle using each object's projection size constraint. Given a valid camera position, an object's minimum projection size constraint determines its maximum allowable field of view angle, while the maximum projection size determines its minimum allowable field of view angle. Its optimal field of view angle (FOV) may be likewise estimated from the given optimal projection size $f = \pi r^2 / A_F$ in Figure 6, where $A_R = \pi r^2$ is the area of the projection of the object's bounding sphere and A_F is the frame area. The equation giving the field of view angle is:

$$fov = \arctan \left(\frac{\sqrt{\pi r^2 / f}}{vpdist} \right)$$

where f is either the minimum, optimal, or maximum projection size fraction and *vpdist* is the distance to the projection plane. The per-object field of view ranges are intersected to estimate the valid field of view angle range for a given valid camera position.

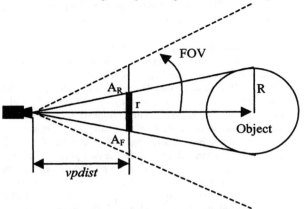

Figure 6: Projection size to field of view.

For a given candidate camera position and object geometry, the maximal allowable range of camera aim directions can be estimated using the OBJ_IN_FIELD_OF_VIEW, OBJ_NOT_IN_FIELD_OF_VIEW, LOOK_AT_POINT, and OBJ_PROJECTION_ABSOLUTE constraints. For example if point P must project into frame region T, then the valid range of aim directions S may be estimated using spherical coordinates (Figure 7). The valid aim directions for multiple constraints are intersected using (theta, phi) spherical coordinate intervals.

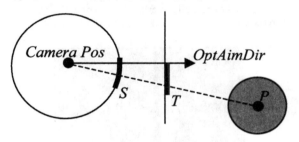

Figure 7: Valid regions for aim direction.

3.4.2 Heuristic Solver Algorithm

The constraint-solver algorithm utilizes a recursive heuristic search over the possible camera parameter values. The constraint valid regions limit the search to consider only those sets of parameter values that may be part of an allowable solution as defined by the given constraints. The search begins at a relatively coarse resolution generating-and-testing candidate shots. The best candidate shots are logged for further refinement of the search via recursion about these most promising candidates.

1. Initialize a log of the $\dot{N}$ best candidate shots found so far. In the examples, the log records the top 5 candidate shots.

2. Optimistically, compute and evaluate the relative-displacement shot. If its cumulative constraint satisfaction rating exceeds the given minimum constraint success threshold, then immediately return this shot as the solution to obtain instantaneous performance when objects are configured as anticipated.

3. Compute valid regions for constraints that limit the allowable camera positions. These constraints include projection size, object-to-camera distance, object view angle, and camera inside region. Form an axis-aligned bounding box *PosBBox* to enclose the intersection of these camera position valid regions.

4. Loop over candidate camera positions spaced along a regular grid of points spanning the space enclosed by *PosBBox*. The number of points generated is determined by the size of *PosBBox* and the desired degree of solution precision.

   4(a). For each valid camera position, use the projection size, projection location, aim direction, and camera field of view constraints to compute the allowable ranges and estimated optimal values for aim direction and field of view angle.
   4(b). Evaluate the shot using the estimated optimal aim direction and field of view angle and immediately return it as the solution if its cumulative constraint satisfaction rating exceeds the given minimum constraint success threshold.
   4(c). Update the log of the best N shot found so far.

5. If a candidate shot exceeding the given minimum constraint success threshold has not yet been found, then loop over each of the N best shots found so far to further refine the search.

   5(a) For each top candidate shot TS, initialize *PosBBox* to enclose space nearby the camera position of shot TS.
   5(c) Initialize a new log of best candidate shots for the next level of search to empty.
   5(c) Recursively execute the solver algorithm beginning from step number (4) if the maximum recursion depth has not been reached.
   5(d) If the best candidate shot returned by the recursive call in step 5(c) exceeds the minimum success threshold, then immediately return that shot as the solution.

6. Return the top-rated candidate shot from the log of best shots.

4. EXAMPLE CAMERA SOLUTIONS

For example, we might want a shot of player1's face as he speaks, in which player1 (gray) is viewed from a camera position behind and over-the-shoulder of player2. In order to compose the desired over-the-shoulder shot of player1 and player2, we could specify the following set of visual composition elements, or camera constraints, by editing the storyboard frame depicted in Figure 8.

- Player1 and player2 should appear entirely in the field of view, while the other three players are excluded or hidden.

- View the face of player1 who is speaking.

- Player1 (gray) should appear slightly to the right of player2 (blue) and centered in the frame (Absolute projection location constraint for each player).

- Player1 should be framed in a long shot and player2 should be in a medium shot (Projection size).

- Player1 should be partially occluded by player2 and player2 should not be occluded (Object partial and minimize occlusion constraints).

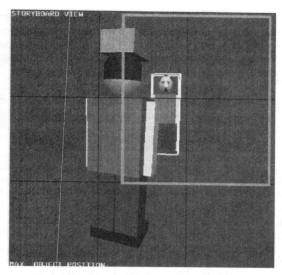

Figure 8: Given storyboard frame of a two shot.

Figure 9: Room interior scene featuring five players.

Figure 10: Computed two shot in given 3D scene.

The image depicted in this storyboard frame represents the optimal location, projection sizes, view angles, and occlusion of the two players. The range of allowable locations of player1 (the rightmost player in the frame) has been set by a bright red bounding rectangle. The optimal viewing angle for player1 is the front, and the optimal viewing angle for player2 is rear right.

We could then apply this storyboard frame to a 3D scene of five players, four standing around a table in a room ringed by stone columns with a fifth player standing on a balcony (Figure 9). The virtual camera will need to be carefully staged in order to capture the desired over-the-shoulder shot of player1 and player2, while excluding the three other players. The computed shot appears in Figure 10. A less sophisticated relative displacement method would place the camera behind and slightly to the right of player2. However, in this environment, such a shot leaves player2 partially occluded by a column. If the camera were moved in front of the column and directly behind player2 to avoid the occlusion, it would only partly include player2 in the shot and would also include the green player on the balcony. The heuristic search solver analyzed the environment to find a next-best shot within the allowable bounds specified in the given storyboard frame (Figure 10). This shot succeeds by taking a camera orientation farther to the side of the players than specified by the optimal storyboard frame definition in Figure 8. This example demonstrates the flexibility of a constraint-based approach, which enables developers of 3D virtual environments to compose desired camera shots (Figure 7) independent of the unanticipated configuration of objects in a given scene (Figure 9).

Figure 11 presents a triangle shot of three players where one of the players is required to partially overlap the balcony player. The storyboard frame used to create this shot appears in Figure 4.

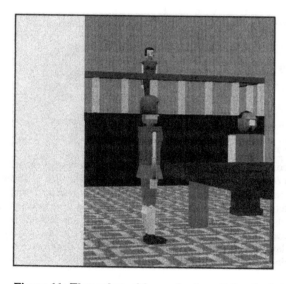

Figure 11: Three shot with required partial occlusion of balcony player by the blue player.

Next, suppose the blue player (standing on the left side) backs away from the table. We can still apply the same set of storyboard frame constraints to compute the acceptable solution depicted in Figure 12. Note how the partial occlusion is maintained by shifting the camera's vantage point.

Figure 12. Solution after player movement.

Figure 13: Cluttered long three-quarter shot.

Figure 14: Improved composition excludes distractions.

The next example, specifies a long three-quarter shot of a building. Figure 13 depicts the resulting heuristic search solution of the desired long three-quarter shot. However, the user feels that the cars surrounding the building clutter the shot distracting attention from the subject. The user then adds constraints to exclude each of the cars from the shot. The heuristic solver positions the camera to obtain the desired three-quarter angle and utilizes the flower arrangement to occlude the distracting cars, which also yields a dramatic low-angle composition (Figure 14).

5. PERFORMANCE EVALUATIONS

Table 1 provides benchmarks for several individual constraint evaluators. As described in Section 3.3, specialized evaluators are provided to determine how well a given shot satisfies a particular constraint. A typical constraint-based shot definition may include between 6 and 20 different constraints, each of which would be evaluated by its respective type of evaluator method.

Table 1. Constraint evaluator benchmark results.

Evaluator Function	Time in milliseconds
Projection size	0.009344
Projection location	0.009088
View angle	0.010140
Object in camera field of view	0.013505
Occlusion by ray casting	0.184320
Occlusion by frame rendering	10.78

Table 2 gives benchmarks of the heuristic search constraint solver using ray casting for evaluating occlusion. Times are given in milliseconds. The test system is a Pentium II 400 MHz Intergraph GL2 computer with 256 MB memory, and a VX113 AGP OpenGL accelerator. In all examples, the first level of search over candidate camera positions scanned a 9x9x9 grid, while the second recursive search over the top 5 shots scanned over a 4x4x4 grid. The third column records the total number of shots evaluated including shots tested to refine the camera field of view and aim direction per each candidate position tested. The fourth column lists the total number of candidate camera positions tested, while the fifth column records the number of candidate camera positions culled because they were not inside the constraint valid regions.

Table 2. Constraint solution benchmark results.

Figure	Time	Shots Tested	Positions	Culled Positions
10	4500 ms	5358	402	711
11	2872	4509	414	699
12	3461	5073	410	703
14	417	609	271	586

The solver can be configured to examine the search space at varying resolutions and can be directed to return the best shot found after having testing a specified maximum number of candidate shots. This allows an application to fine-tune the quality of the computed solutions and the amount of time allowed to find a solution. For comparison, our implementation of a simple relative displacement camera algorithm computes camera placements in 0.016 milliseconds. An exhaustive search was implemented for comparison purposes and its solution times range from about to 20 to 30 minutes in evaluating 2 million shots.

Table 3 gives the cumulative constraint success ratings of our heuristic search and our relative displacement solvers.

Table 3. Comparison of constraint satisfaction.

Figure	Heuristic Search	Relative Displacement
10	0.877109	0.0
11	0.850244	0.338701
12	0.774565	0.338701
14	0.810209	0.473219

6. CONCLUSIONS AND FUTURE WORK

Together the Storyboard Frame Editor interface and constraint solver provide tools for interactive 3D application developers to define how the virtual camera should film objects of interest leaving the low-level task of placing the camera to the automated constraint solver module. The constraint solver module is currently being integrated into several prototypical types of interactive 3D virtual environments. The search heuristics and constraint evaluators will be further optimized to obtain real-time performance necessary for many interactive applications. Additional constraint types can be implemented by coding new evaluators and script parsing functions. Techniques such as returning multiple shots or relaxing less important constraints will be added to handle failures to compute constraint solutions [2]. Studies of user interface effectiveness and aesthetics of the computed shots will also be performed.

7. ACKNOWLEDGEMENTS

We would like to thank James Lester and Lou Harrison for their assistance in reviewing the paper. Thanks to visual artists Robert Russett, Yeon Choi, and Patrick FitzGerald for their creative suggestions. Thanks also to Junwei Li for editing the 3D environments and Byungwoo Kim for assisting in testing the examples. This work is partly supported by the Louisiana Board of Regents through the Board of Regents Support Fund contract (1999-2002)-RD-A-48.

8. REFERENCES

[1] André, Elisabeth , W. Finkler, W. Graf, T. Rist, A. Schauder, and W. Walhster. WIP: The automatic synthesis of multimodal presentations. In M.T. Maybury, editor, *Intelligent Multimedia Interfaces*, chapter 3, AAAI Press, 1993.

[2] Bares, W. and J. Lester. Intelligent Multi-Shot Visualization Interfaces for Dynamic 3D Worlds. In *IUI-99: Proceedings of the 1999 International Conference on Intelligent User Interfaces*, Los Angeles, California, 1999, pages 119-126.

[3] Blinn, James. Where Am I? What Am I Looking At? In *IEEE Computer Graphics and Applications*, July 1988, pages 76-81.

[4] Butz, Andreas. Anymation with CATHI. In *IAAI-97: Proceedings of Innovative Applications of Artificial Intelligence*. Providence, Rhode Island, July 1997, pages 957-962.

[5] Christianson, David, Sean Anderson, Li-wei He, David Salesin, Daniel Weld, and Michel Cohen. Declarative camera control for automatic cinematography. In *Proceedings of the AAAI-96: Proceedings of the Thirteenth National Conference on Artificial Intelligence*, August 1996, pages 148-155.

[6] Drucker, Steven. *Intelligent Camera Control in Graphical Environments*. Ph.D. thesis, 1994, Massachusetts Institute of Technology, Cambridge, Massachusetts, 1994.

[7] Drucker, Steven and David Zeltzer. CamDroid: A System for Implementing Intelligent Camera Control. In *1995 Symposium on Interactive 3D Graphics*, 1995, pages 139-144.

[8] Feiner, Steven. APEX: An Experiment in the Automated Creation of Pictorial Explanations. In *IEEE Computer Graphics & Applications*, September, 1985, pages 29-37.

[9] Feiner, Steven and Dorée D. Seligmann. Cutaways and ghosting: satisfying visibility constraints in dynamic 3D illustrations. In *The Visual Computer*, August 1992, pages 292-302.

[10] Funge, John, Xiaoyuan Tu, Demetri Terzopouos. Cognitive Modeling: Knowledge, Reasoning and Planning for Intelligent Characters. In *Proceedings of ACM SIGGRAPH '99*, August 1999, pages 29-38.

[11] Gleicher, Michael and Andrew Witkin. Through-the-lens camera control. In Edwin E. Catmull, editor, *Computer Graphics (Proceedings of SIGGRAPH '92)*, 1992, pages 331-340.

[12] Halper, Nicolas and Patrick Olivier. CAMPLAN: A Camera Planning Agent. In *Smart Graphics 2000 AAAI Spring Symposium*, Stanford, California, March 2000, pages 92-100.

[13] Hanson, Andrew and Eric Wernert. Constrained 3D navigation with 2D controllers. In *Proceedings of IEEE Visualization '97*, 1997, pages 175-182.

[14] Hines, William. Operating Cinematography for Film and Video: A Professional and Practical Guide. Ed-Venture Publishers, Los Angeles, California, 1997.

[15] Jardillier, Frank and Eric Languénou. Screen-Space Constraints for Camera Movements: the Virtual Cameraman. In *Eurographics 1998 Computer Graphics Forum*, 17(3), 1998.

[16] Karp, Peter and Steven Feiner. Automated Presentation Planning of Animation Using Task Decomposition with Heuristic Reasoning. In *Graphics Interface '93*, 1993, pages 118-126.

[17] Katz, Steven. *Film Directing Shot by Shot*. Studio City, CA, Michael Wiese Press, 1991.

[18] Li-wei He, Michael F. Cohen, and David H. Salesin. The virtual cinematographer: A paradigm for automatic realtime camera control and directing. In *Computer Graphics (Proceedings of SIGGRAPH '96)*, 1996, pages 217-224.

[19] Mackinlay, Jock, S. Card and G. Robertson. Rapid controlled movement through a virtual 3D workspace. In *Proceedings of ACM SIGGRAPH '90*, 1990, pages 171-176.

[20] Mascelli, Joseph. *The Five C's of Cinematography*. Silman-James Press, Los Angeles, California, 1965.

[21] Millerson, Gerald. *Video Camera Techniques*. Focal Press, Oxford, England, 1994.

[22] Olivier, Patrick, Nicolas Halper, Jon Pickering, and Pamela Luna. Visual Composition as Optimisation. In *Artificial and Simulation of Intelligent Behavior (AISB) Workshop '99 Symposium on AI and Creativity in Entertainment and Visual Arts*. Edinburgh, UK, April 1998, pages 22-30.

[23] Peterson, Bryan. *Learning to See Creatively*. Watson-Guptill, New York, New York, 1988.

[24] Phillips, Cary B., Norman Badler, and John Granieri. Automatic viewing control for 3D direct manipulation. In David Zeltzer, editor, *Computer Graphics (1992 Symposium on Interactive 3D Graphics)*, volume 25, March 1992, pages 71-74.

[25] Seligmann, Dorée and Steven Feiner. Automated Generation of Intent-Based 3D Illustrations. In *Computer Graphics*, July 1991, pages 123-132.

[26] Ware, Colin and S. Osborn. Exploration and virtual camera control in virtual three-dimensional environments. In *1990 Symposium on Interactive 3D Graphics*, 1990, pages 175-184.

[27] Ware, Colin and Daniel Fleet. Context Sensitive Flying Interface. In *Proceedings of the Symposium on Interactive 3D Graphics*. Providence, Rhode Island, 1997, pages 127-130.

Using Java to implement a multimedia annotation environment for young children

Afrodite Sevasti
Computer Engineering and
Informatics Department,

University of Patras

and

Computer Technology Institute,
61 Riga Feraiou Str., GR-262 21
Patras, Greece

(+30)-61-960316

sevastia@cti.gr

Bouras Christos
Computer Engineering and
Informatics Department,

University of Patras

and

Computer Technology Institute,
61 Riga Feraiou Str., GR-262 21
Patras, Greece

+30-61-960375

bouras@cti.gr

ABSTRACT

The exceptional advent and dominance of interactive multimedia applications in our days has led to the need for their exploitation for educational, among many other, purposes. In this work, we present the design and implementation of a multimedia annotation environment for young children using the Java 2 Platform. This environment was developed to provide children of ages 4 to 8 with the opportunity to reflect upon and annotate episodes from their everyday life.

Our aim was to exploit the recent technological developments in the field of multimedia and the processing capabilities of contemporary personal computers, in order to build an annotation environment where children would be able to add multimedia annotations to videos. Apart, from the environment itself, design choices, interface realization, platform limitations and emerging solutions as well as media handling methods and performance issues are also presented.

Keywords

Interactive multimedia, video annotation, video browsing, Java, hypermedia interface, media integration and synchronization

1. INTRODUCTION

The fields of multimedia editing and annotating are currently among the rapidly evolving fields in the development of Instructional Computer Technology. Multimedia editing, to begin with, has been recognized as a widely promising tool in educational procedures. It can replace the two-dimensional written word with three-dimensional written, auditory or visual material, enriching all educational procedures and capturing the students' attention. In our days, there exist several commercial authoring applications in the field of multimedia editing and storyboarding for younger children. However, current educational software rarely offers either the child or the adult facilitator options for 'deeper interaction' and it hardly ever exploits powerful computer technologies.

In this paper we present the implementation work that took place within the framework of project "Today's Stories", part of the Long Term Research Task 4.4, (i3 –ESE, Project Nr. 29312). According to the "Today's Stories" project definition ([18]), one technological objective of the project is to develop a wearable device (actually a wearable video camera), that can capture short sequences of interest in the child's daytime. The crucial insight here is that apart from providing a fragmented history of the day of a child, recordings of an event from more than one child's perspective can be interrelated. This brings us to the second technological objective of the project, which is the development a multimedia editing tool that enables children to annotate a recorded episode with what they see, think, experience. Annotation uses expressive media, symbols (e.g., stylized faces to express various emotional states), or sound-effects (e.g., special effects to highlight for example surprise or fear). The resulting multi-medial document is to be kept as a memory and a document for future reference.

The work that took place within the scope of this second technological objective of the project, including design and implementation issues, is the subject of this paper. It must also be stated here that our work took seriously into consideration the pedagogical issues that are involved in the nature and use of such an application, as they have been approached by the "Today's Stories" consortium (see also the notion of personal autonomy as a central educational aim in [1]). After all, the project itself pays attention to social, cultural and ethical implications, as well as to the conditions for acceptance and success of deploying its technology.

For the implementation of this video exploring and annotating application, referred to from now on as the Diary

Composer (DC), the Java platform was elected. More specifically, the Java 2 SDK, Standard Edition, v 1.2.2, developed by Sun Microsystems, Inc. and the Java Media Framework (JMF) 2.0 API developed by Sun Microsystems, Inc. and IBM were used. This choice was made for several reasons, with the first one being to assure complete platform independence and that the final version of the application could also be accessible through the Internet, for future use from the children's home. The fact that Java programs are compiled for the Java Virtual Machine (JVM) enables Java programs to be executed on a variety of platforms, provided that the JVM is implemented for each one of these platforms [19].

Apart from that, the release of version 2.0 of the Java Media Framework (JMF) with a much richer set of features as well as the advanced features provided by the Swing 1.1.1 API (included in the Java Foundation Classes (JFC) API of Java 2 SDK, Standard Edition, v 1.2.2) made the Java 2 Platform appropriate for our implementation.

In this paper, we initially make a thorough presentation of the standardization, research and implementation attempts in the field of multimedia annotation. Consequently, we are presenting an overview of the DC design and architecture, describing briefly the functionality provided by the application. The remainder of the paper analyses the implementation techniques that were used for implementing that functionality as well as the limitations that were imposed by the platform used for the implementation, accompanied by performance issues. Finally, we are describing our future work on this application.

2. RELATED WORK

A worthwhile approach to the standardization of multimedia annotating is the work of the EBU/SMPTE Task Force for Harmonized Standards for the Exchange of Program Material as Bit streams. The Task Force has produced [7], which in section 4, 'Wrappers and Metadata' gives a thorough terminology and structure (close to that defined by the Digital Audio-Video Council (DAVIC)) for how physical media (video, audio, data of various kinds including captions, graphics, still images, text etc.) can be linked together, for streaming of program material and stored in file systems and on servers.

Another attempt towards the direction of standards for multimedia annotation was made by the Workshop on MMI (Metadata for Multimedia Information) conducted by the European Committee for Standardisation and Information Society Standardisation System (CEN/ISSS) from February 1998 until June 1999. The workshop resulted into deliverables on the requirements and model for metadata for multimedia information.

MPEG-7 is an ISO/IEC standard being developed by MPEG (Moving Picture Experts Group), formally named "Multimedia Content Description Interface". It aims to create a standard for describing the multimedia content data that will support some degree of interpretation of the information's meaning, which can be passed onto, or accessed by, a device or a computer code. In [11] it is stated that MPEG-7 *must* accommodate audio-visual material and take advantage of the ability to associate descriptive information within video streams at various stages of video production. As an example for this, information captured or annotated during shooting, and post-production edit lists are suggested. Based on these principles among others, MPEG-7 will

work on making a global standardisation for multimedia annotations.

Apart from standardisation efforts, a lot of research work is performed in the field of video editing and multimedia annotation. An interesting work that deals mainly with non-linear video navigation and organization is presented in [9]. The author introduces the notion of 'hypermovies': hyper-documents that only consist of movie nodes. These nodes are entities comprising not only of the video as content but also of additional cinematic information which is synchronized with the video and can be made visible on demand to support navigation. The MovieCatalog tool presented, uses the Apple Macintosh Finder look-and-feel in order to organize movie segments, by displaying on the screen one thumbnail for each one of them, while the Segmenter tool uses the multiple tracks that the Quicktime format supports, to add additional cinematic information to different tracks.

The multiple tracks provided by the Quicktime format, are also utilized for the development of a Movie Authoring and Design system called 'MAD' which is presented in [8]. MAD facilitates the process of creating dynamic visual presentations by simultaneously allowing easy structure creation or modification of motion pictures and visualization of the result of those modifications. The principles behind MAD include hierarchical multimedia document representation, the flexible inclusion and combination of words, images, sounds, and video sequences, and real-time playback of a rough version of the final film at any time in the process.

An effort to reinforce a document design methodology to a hypermedia document is presented in [15]. Here, the authors point out that hypermedia applications are real-time, dynamic and depend on user interactions and therefore authoring techniques usually postpone design validation to the run-time stage. Moreover, they emphasize the fact that hypermedia documents can contain inconsistencies, which are stemming from the temporal constraints that are applied to their components through various relationships among anchors. The document design methodology proposed, translates a high-level model of a hypermedia document into an RT-LOTOS formal specification, on which standard reachability analysis may be applied for verification purposes.

Another interesting work, the results of which were seriously taken into account while developing our DC application, is presented in [10]. Here, the authors investigate the users' assimilation and understanding of the informational content of multimedia clips, to conclude upon a significant result: The quality of video clips can be severely degraded without the user having to perceive any significant loss of informational content.

The authors of [14], developed 'CueVideo' in order to provide a solution to effective video cataloging and browsing. The first phase of the 'CueVideo' system involves the so-called integrated cataloging which includes segmenting the video files into shots and adding image, text, speech etc. as annotations. In this way, the user can incorporate the type of semantic information that automatic techniques would fail to obtain and which facilitates content characterization, browsing and retrieval. An interactive video authoring system that supports the video object annotation capability is presented in [6]. The so-called 'Zodiac' system allows users to associate annotations, such as text, image and audio, to moving objects in a video sequence. This work makes a step even further on the subject of video annotation, since it doesn't annotate video frames but objects in video frames.

The approach followed in the ACTS project no. AC082, called DIANE (Design, Implementation and Operation of a Distributed Annotation Environment) ([2],[3]), was to allow the recording if an arbitrary application output as the basic content of a multimedia document and to annotate it with all kind of media available to the user. This was achieved by the concept of a multimedia annotated document consisting of two distinct parts: recorded application output and annotations given by a user in various media including text, audio, video and pointer movements. By providing generic techniques to record output of arbitrary applications, DIANE implemented an annotations' recording tool independent of any application context.

A brief but thorough presentation of commercial authoring applications in the fields of multimedia editing for young children is given in [4]. These applications comprise worthwhile solutions to the direction of offering children the opportunity to experiment and create with the use of multimedia. However, none of them offers the functionality of adding annotations to videos and most of them include textual components for user interaction – something that we definitely wanted to avoid in our case.

A conclusion that can easily be drawn by this extensive research in the standardisation and implementation initiatives on annotation of multimedia is that the corresponding technologies have not matured yet. Standardisation efforts, with that of the MPEG-7 standard being the most significant, are still under development. The MPEG-7 standard for example is due to no sooner than 2001. Implementation efforts, on the other hand, tend to use their own method of annotating multimedia, making their solutions proprietary. In this work, we present our implementation solution for adding multimedia annotations to videos and we describe what our future work will focus on, in order to conform to the upcoming standards.

3. APPLICATION OVERVIEW

The DC application was designed so that it provides two distinct components and corresponding interfaces: one for making the video recordings accessible to the DC users, allowing navigation and selection of the video/videos to be annotated and one for providing the tools and infrastructure for annotation. We call the first component of the application the 'Video Explorer' and the second one the 'Annotation Panel'.

3.1 The Video Explorer

This component of the application was designed to provide the functionality of displaying a representative frame (actually the first frame) from each video recording stored into the DC system. These frames are called 'thumbnails' and it was a challenge of the design and implementation phase to organize and display them on screen in an efficient manner that would also be comprehensible to children of ages 4 to 8.

According to [20], all authoring interfaces use authoring metaphors for their implementation such as a slide-show metaphor, a book metaphor, a timeline metaphor, an icon metaphor etc. For the DC implementation, the set of videos recorded needed to be somehow structured and included in a multimedia database. The "Today's Stories" objectives indicated

that the storage and retrieval should avoid using textual categories.

For the implementation of the Video Explorer, the timeline metaphor was adopted. Generally speaking, a timeline metaphor is an authoring metaphor where objects and events are placed on the time scale in correct relationship. For the case of the Video Explorer, video thumbnails are organized in groups according to the identity of their owner, in other words, according to which child shot them. Each group of video thumbnails is then distributed along a timeline, which in interface terms is represented by a straight line extending from one point of real-world time to another. The distribution of video thumbnails along the timeline is proportional to the shooting time of each video recording.

Another significant component of the Video Explorer is the help feature, envisaged by the 'Genie' character. This 'Genie' has been implemented to have drag-and-drop features within the Video Explorer (it also appears in the Annotation Panel) environment. Dropping the 'Genie' on a certain visual component of the Video Explorer initiates an event that provides the DC user with an audio description and a brief listing of the visual component's functionality. This implementation of the help feature was based on the JFC/Swing Containment Model (see [12],[13]) which allows for placing interface components in different layers within the same container. More details on this will be provided in the 'Implementation Issues' further down.

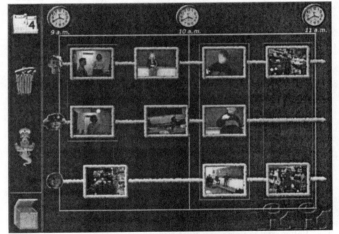

Figure 1. The Video Explorer layout

The Video Explorer supports simultaneous use of more than one users, by presenting more than one timelines in cases when more than one children share the same workspace (see Figure 1). During the videos' storing procedure, metadata that indicate which of the videos are shootings of the same incident by different children, are also stored in the system. During the implementation of the DC, several methods were developed that associate related video files and their visual representations on the Video Explorer interface. Thus, video files of the same incident shot from different perspectives, form a so-called 'hyper-video' in the DC. This hyper-video, containing one, two or three separate video files is the entity handled by the annotation methods of our DC application. It is actually treated as an autonomous unit (for annotation, auto-save etc. procedures) to which all annotations are added, from the moment it is realized.

The functionality supported by the Video Explorer component includes the 'delete' operation. This operation has been implemented in such a way that all annotations of an annotated video are erased when the video thumbnail is dragged and dropped upon the 'Dustbin' visual component of the interface. Future versions of the DC will also support navigating through videos from different dates, by the use of the 'Diary' visual metaphor (see Figure 1)

Each single video thumbnail or hyper-video comprises a 'hyperlink'. This 'hyperlink', when clicked or pressed upon (this depends on whether a mouse or a touch-screen is being used for interface I/O) initializes an annotation session, by opening the second component of the DC application, the so-called Annotation Panel.

3.2 The Annotation Panel

The second component of the DC has as its main functionality to provide the user with the tools to add image and sound annotations to the video/videos already selected via the Video Explorer.

The dominant still controversial features of the Annotation Panel implementation are its dynamic nature and simplicity. Bearing in mind that the tool aims at very young children and that the procedure of annotation actually can be broken into two phases (adding/removing annotations and playback of the video in its current state, containing all annotations previously added), appropriate methods had to be implemented. To be more specific an annotation procedure consists of the following steps:

- Start the video playback
- Pause playback
- Either drop one or more annotations to the video's visual component (add) or drag previously added annotations from the videos visual component (remove)
- Resume playback

The last three steps are iterated as many times as the user wishes to.

A playback procedure consists of the following steps:

- Rewind the video up to its first frame
- Start the video playback
- Pause and resume playback

Again, these steps can be iterated as many times as the user wishes to.

The design choice made was to merge the annotating and playback procedures so that the two distinct phases would become transparent to the users of the DC. The DC application allows for steps of the annotation procedure to be interrupted for initializing a playback procedure and vice versa. In other words, the user is provided with the ability to interrupt the annotation procedure, in order to go back and find out how he has done so far, but during playback he can still pause the video reproduction and add annotations. We have called this 'dynamic annotation' and more implementation details will be given in the 'Implementation Issues' section.

Apart from the 'Genie' character that implements the help feature in the Annotation Panel in an identical to that in the Video

Explorer way, the Annotation Panel provides the user with a totally different set of functionality. Three simple video control buttons are provided to the user for controlling playback of the hyper-video being annotated. According to the Video Explorer implementation, more than one videos might be chosen for simultaneous annotation, in cases more than one video recordings of the same incident, forming a hyper-video, exist. However, this hyper-video depicts the same incident from two or three different perspectives and there was no point in providing the users of the DC with the possibility to start/stop/resume each video component of the hyper-video separately. Therefore, the video control buttons are placed on one control panel, which is common to all the videos that are being annotated at the moment. From the implementation point of view, this approach required video synchronization techniques, which will be analyzed further in the 'Implementation Issues' section, to be adopted.

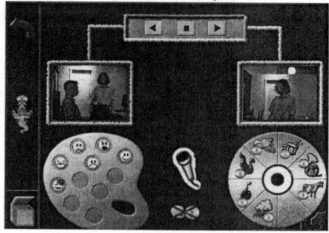

Figure 2. The Annotation Panel layout

For the current version of the DC, two types of annotation palettes were implemented: one for image annotations and one for sound annotations (represented by images as well for the purposes of the DC interface). The first palette (see bottom left of Figure 2), contains image annotations that are depicting emotions while the second one (see bottom right of Figure 2) contains image annotations that are depicting sounds but also represent sounds. The user is provided with the functionality of pausing the video at any moment and adding to it an unlimited number of image and sound annotations, in order to comment the incident that has been recorded.

Both image and sound annotations are implemented in such a way that present the users with a 'sticky' behavior: annotations can be dragged towards any direction within the DC interface but can be dropped only on one of the video frames. Dropping an annotation outside a video frame, results in the annotation moving back to its original position in the palette. The latter provides the users with the ability to remove annotations from a video, simply by dragging away any annotation that has been 'stuck' on the video and dropping it outside the video frame. Adding a sound annotation to a video frame does not only result into the correspondent icon being added to the video as an image annotation: it also 'adds' the sound associated with it to the sound track of the video, so that the sound annotation is reproduced during playback, at the time it was placed during annotation.

Apart from the predefined set of sound annotations, new sound annotations (e.g. spoken words) can also be inserted to the current hyper-video. The user has to pause video playback at the desired video frame and speak to his workstation's microphone while pressing the microphone icon between the two palettes (see Figure 2). In this way, all kind of sound annotations can be 'added' to the video's audio track.

Except for removing annotations one by one, the Annotation Panel provides the user with the opportunity to reset the hyper-video being currently annotated, thus removing all annotations at once (by pressing the small icon under the microphone in Figure 2). Finally, there is a 'Back' button that can be used from users to finish their annotating session and return to the Video Explorer either for further navigation through videos or for choosing another hyper-video to annotate.

4. IMPLEMENTATION ISSUES

4.1 Annotation

For the implementation of the annotation functionality in our DC application, we co-estimated the related work presented in section 2 of this paper and the requirements specified by the "Today's Stories" consortium as far the multimedia annotating application to be developed was concerned.

Due to the lack of mature standards and in order to achieve acceptable performance and platform independence in application execution and video supported formats, we designed a proprietary still open and configurable annotation system. The main idea was to create transparent to the end user data structures that would hold hyper-videos and all kinds of multimedia annotations attached to them in an efficient and consistent way. This way, we bypassed the limitations and performance issues rising from all our attempts to encode video and annotations together.

All of our annotation methods follow the principle of associating an annotation with the frame of the video to which the annotation was added. In this way, predefined images and sounds as well as recorded sounds are associated in dynamic data structures with the video frame being annotated by them. During the application runtime, this association is dynamic and configurable. This approach makes the feature of 'dynamic annotation' described in section 3.2 feasible.

The annotation procedure can be interrupted by the user at any time in order for him to be able to preview his annotations so far. The application then reads from those dynamic data structures in order to represent the annotated hyper-video playback to the user. This is achieved by displaying images and opening sound players at those positions during playback, where the data structures' contents appoint. At any moment, the user can remove any annotation he wishes. This functionality is internally implemented by removing the correspondent entries from these data structures and re-ordering the data structures' contents.

All these dynamic interactions are possible during an annotation session. As soon as the user wishes to interrupt the annotating procedure, annotation data together with the hyper-videos they refer to, are stored permanently to the system for future use. For the current version of the application, we have implemented a proprietary scheme for storing all this information.

The implementation approach described here has the following advantages:

- Supports a wide variety of video formats for the video files that are annotated within the application (in [16], a list of the supported by the JMF API media formats is provided)

- An unlimited set of different kinds and formats of multimedia data can be used as annotations (images, sounds etc.)

- Performance is preserved in satisfactory levels independently of the amount/type of annotations inserted, due to the fact that annotations are stored separately from the raw video data and not encoded within it.

The main disadvantage of our implementation approach is the fact that annotated hyper-videos are stored in a proprietary format, readable by our application alone. In section 5, we describe how our future work will proceed in order to eliminate this disadvantage.

4.2 User Interface

For the purposes of the annotation functionality, the implementation procedure exploited the potentials of the JFC/Swing Lightweight Component Framework and Containment Model ([12],[13]) so that the DC application was developed on a multi-containment, multi-layer infrastructure. The JFC/Swing Lightweight Component Framework and Containment Model were two of the major enhancements of Swing over the Abstract Window Toolkit (AWT) that the Java platform used to provide for User Interface (UI) development. Actually, the DC application would be impossible to implement without these two features of Swing.

The Lightweight Component Framework facilitated the implementation procedure in the sense that the application was organized in many different components, the most complicated of which contained the simpler ones, thus acting as containers. All methods implementing objects' behavior within the application itself and the application UI, were accessible by the appropriate levels of containment hierarchy in order to provide a consistent and reliable look and feel throughout the application. An indicative diagram that depicts a large proportion of the containment hierarchy of the DC implementation objects is shown in Figure 3.

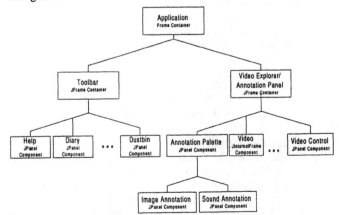

Figure 3. The multi-containment infrastructure

Root containers of the containment hierarchy have been implemented in such a way that act as mediators among their components. They listen for events from certain components (e.g.

a mouse 'click' event on a video control object) and generate other events according to the application's functionality protocol (e.g. starting, stopping or rewinding of the initiated video player/s depending on which video control object was triggered). In this way, leaf components of the containment hierarchy do not communicate directly with each other. Instead, each event climbs up in the hierarchy tree so that all listener objects are informed about it in order for the appropriate methods to be called.

The JFC/Swing Containment Model allows for organizing components in different layers within their container. Actually, this feature is provided by the group of the heavyweight container classes in Swing and is referred to as the nested-container hierarchy in [13]. According to this infrastructure, the Annotation Panel container was organized in layers: the background component controls and coordinates all other layers. Videos and video controls are placed two layers above on the so-called Modal layer while annotations are placed on the topmost Drag layer (see Figure 4).

This UI architecture was adopted for several reasons and resolved most of the implementation problems. One of these reasons was to make the heavyweight visual component of each video player cooperate with the rest of the application, being placed over the UI background and under the annotations' layer at the same time. Of course, this architecture facilitated the implementation of the drag and drop behavior of annotations and the 'Genie' object in the best possible way. Annotation and 'Genie' objects' behavior is defined by a set of methods that allow them to move on the UI drag layer, thus creating the impression that they 'float' over all other UI components. Their drag-and-drop behavior was implemented over the mouse listening interface that the Java 2 SDK provides.

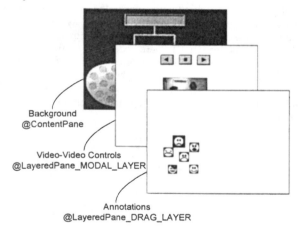

Background
@ContentPane

Video-Video Controls
@LayeredPane_MODAL_LAYER

Annotations
@LayeredPane_DRAG_LAYER

Figure 4. The multi-layer infrastructure

4.3 Media Handling

The release of version 2.0 of the Java Media Framework (JMF) API from Sun Microsystems, Inc. and IBM has undoubtedly provided Java platform programmers with a much wider set of features for inserting and handling multimedia in their applications. The major challenges that the DC implementation had to face was to ensure the best quality possible while loading more than one video/audio players, synchronize these players and monitor their behavior throughout the application runtime. In this section, we present how the JMF API was used for the DC

implementation and the design choices made in order to achieve the desired functionality.

According to [17], the JMF specification defines APIs for displaying time-based media. JMF players share a common model for timekeeping and synchronization and JMF clocks define the basic timing and synchronization operations. Also, according to [5], JMF does not build the functionality of constant media progression tracking into each media player. Based on the above, we had to implement several mechanisms for accessing video data by frame number instead of media time, for keeping track of the video data progression in frame numbers and for generating events according to the current video frame number.

One of the dominant components for video/audio management within the DC was the Frame Positioning Control (FPC) interface of the JMF API ([5],[16]). This interface was used for accessing the individual frames of each video file, a feature which is not built-in within JMF. This limitation produced the first obstacles in the Video Explorer implementation, where a player interface and consecutively an FPC interface for each video had to be initialized in order to access the first representative frame of each video and transform it to an image thumbnail. This procedure was very consuming in terms of resources in cases such as the one depicted in Figure 1, where ten different video thumbnails were to be created.

The design choice that was made here deviated this problem by removing from the DC implementation the processing burden of extracting a thumbnail from each video file. Instead, an asynchronous application that uses the FPC interface to produce a thumbnail, runs every time a new video file is stored in the DC infrastructure. This standalone application is transparent to the user and produces one image file for each video file, to be used as the video thumbnail in the Video Explorer.

In order for the annotation feature of the DC to be implemented, we had to keep track of the video progression in frame numbers or, in other words, be aware of the number of the current video frame being displayed on screen, during the annotation/playback procedure. Whenever video playback is paused and annotations are added to or removed from it, the current frame number is used to associate annotations with the video, as it has already been explained in section 4.1.

However, keeping track of the video progression in terms of frame number, required the combination of the FPC interface and its mapTimeToFrame method. Actually, calling this method on the FPC interface of a video player is the only way to monitor a video player's progression in frame numbers within JMF. This procedure is often performed during the DC runtime and more specifically every time the application needs to be informed about the exact video frame number to which one or more annotations have been added. This fact could not be ignored by our implementation and it is one of the major performance drawbacks of the DC application.

Things become even more complicated if we attempt to introduce the functionality of displaying annotations previously added to a video file, during playback. This functionality requires constant monitoring of the video player's current frame number, so that an annotation display event is initiated when the video playback approaches the video frame number where the annotation was added. For this functionality and since JMF players cannot produce such events themselves, we had to implement a thread running in parallel to the video player/s.

This thread has as its main duty to monitor the player status, and place annotations to their position inside a video's visual component, according to the data recorded during the annotation procedure. It receives as input the content of the data structures, where data, associating video frames with annotations, are stored. We will refer to these data as annotation data entries (ADE) from now on. Each ADE, consists of an annotation's insertion frame number (AIFN) and an annotation identifier (AI). In fact, the thread implemented complies with the following algorithm:

Thread activates itself only when video player is in "Started" state

Thread polls the video player for the current video frame number (CVFN)

Thread compares CVFN with the subset of ADEs for which AIFN<CVFN

WHILE (AIFN<CVFN+15 and AIFN>CVFN-15)

> *Add the annotation referred to by this ADE's AI to the video's visual component*

This algorithm ensures that although annotations are actually added to one frame of the videos (AIFN), they are displayed for a window of 30 video frames (starting from 15 frames before the AIFN and finishing at 15 frames after the AIFN) so that the user can perceive their existence. The main drawback of this approach has turned out to be the burden placed upon the application's performance by the thread introduced.

The implementation of the annotation functionality within the DC environment includes also synchronization techniques for the cases when two or three videos forming a hyper-video are being simultaneously annotated. Generally speaking, JMF provides the functionality of synchronization of multiple players in such a way that the programmer has to define a master player, the controls of which are responsible for all other players stated as 'slaves'. For the DC purposes we had to implement methods that designated as master player in a group of two or three videos the one with the maximum duration. We also made several experiments that resulted into the conclusion that equal frame rates among the members of a video group are ensuring best synchronization and performance behavior.

Finally, the JMF API does not provide a reliable mechanism for interfering with the video players' playback rate. In fact, not all players are guaranteed to allow their playback rate to be adjusted, that is reduced or increased. This fact prevented us from being able to provide videos' fast forward and rewind functionality within our application in its current version. This issue is part of our future work and might also be resolved in future versions of the JMF API.

4.4 Performance Issues-Memory management

A lot of performance issues occurred during the implementation procedure of the DC application, some of which have already been mentioned in previous sections of this paper.

A quantative amount of experimenting took place in order to determine the appropriate video format characteristics that would allow qualitative simultaneous playback of three different video files in the Annotation Panel component. Results designated as

the only solution recommended for good performance that of reducing the video files' frame rate to numbers less than or equal to 15 frames per second. According to the results of [10], we are allowed to do so for the sake of playback quality, without putting in stake significant loss of informational content.

Another significant issue related to performance, that had to be dealt with, was that of memory management. The nature of the DC application requires for tentative memory interactions and extensive care had to be taken for the introduction of efficient memory management into the application. Keeping in mind that Java does not provide sophisticated and automated mechanisms for memory management and garbage disposal, several methods were implemented for disposal of the extensive memory resources occupied by video players. These methods anticipate for master-slave relationships between video players and clean up most of the system's memory resources each time an annotation session is terminated.

5. FUTURE WORK-CONCLUSIONS

The DC application presented in this paper comprises the first fully functional version of a tool that will be further enhanced with functionality and improved. This will be done according to the feedback that will be provided from extended trials in school environments within the "Today's Stories" project time plan and the pedagogical analysis of the application's use and nature.

From the implementation point of view, functionality to be added includes:

- To make the DC environment accessible over the Internet

- An interface for the insertion of custom image annotations to the application

- A hierarchical structure that will support multiple annotation palettes, categorized according to different thematic categories

- A navigator-browser for the users' video recordings from previous dates

- More sophisticated video controls, such as fast forward and rewind

Apart from adding functionality to the existent tool, our future work will also investigate the possibilities to introduce multimedia annotations in widely accepted video content types such as QuickTime. QuickTime architecture and file format offer themselves for annotation insertion, since they organize media data in synchronized tracks. However, there are still limitations to the data types that can be used as annotations and of course to the platforms over which an annotated QuickTime movie can be presented. We are currently working with the QuickTime for Java API in order to make QuickTime and its annotation techniques accessible to all the Java compliant platforms.

Generally speaking, we can conclude that our work and all other efforts should move towards the direction of multimedia annotations' standardization. It is for sure that the upcoming MPEG-7 standard will contribute significantly towards this direction.

6. ACKNOWLEDGMENTS

We would like to thank all our partners in the "Today's Stories" consortium for their feedback and collaboration in the procedure of defining the functional specifications of the DC application.

We would also like to mention that the application's interface graphics and layout that appear in Figure 1 and Figure 2 were designed by the Assistive Technology & Human-Computer Laboratory, Institute of Computer Science, Foundation for Research & Technology-FORTH, Crete, Greece. The videos, the thumbnails of which appear in Figure 1 and Figure 2, were produced by Marilyn Panayi and David Roy and were shot in Denmark, at the KISS – NIS Laboratory and Nr. Brody Skole.

7. REFERENCES

[1] Aviram, A., *Personal Autonomy And The Flexible School*, International Review of Education 39(5), Kluwer Academic Publishers, printed in the Netherlands, 1993, 419-433

[2] Benz, H., Bessler, S., Fischer, S., Hager, M., and Mecklenburg, R. DIANE: "A Multimedia Annotation System" in *Proceedings of the Second European Conference on Multimedia Applications, Services and Techniques (ECMAST'97)* (Milan IT, May 1997), Fdida, S., and Morganti, M. (Eds.), Lecture Notes in Computer Science 1242, Springer Verlag, Berlin, 183-198.

[3] Benz, H., Fischer, S., Mecklenburg, R., and Dermler, G. DIANE - "Hypermedia Documents in a Distributed Annotation Environment" in *Proceedings of the Conference on Hypertext - Information Retrieval - Multimedia (HIM'97)* (Dortmund DE, September 1997), Norbert, F., Gisbert, D., and Tochtermann, K.(Eds.), Schriften zur Informatik, UVK Universitaetsverlag, Konstanz, 293-306.

[4] Bouras, C., Kapoulas, V., Konidaris, A., Ramahlo, M., Sevasti, A., and Van de Velde, W. "Diary Composer: Supporting Reflection on Past Events for Young Children" To appear at the *ED-MEDIA 2000-World Conference on Educational Multimedia, Hypermedia & Telecommunications*, Montréal (Canada), June 26-July 1, 2000.

[5] Carmo, L.de. *Core Java Media Framework*, Prentice Hall PTR, Upper Saddle River NJ, 1st edition (June 24, 1999).

[6] Chiueh, T., Mitra, T., Neogi, A., and Yang, C.K. Zodiac: A "History Interactive Video Authoring System" in *Proceedings of the 6th ACM International Multimedia Conference (Multimedia'98)* (Bristol UK, September 12-16, 1998), 435-443.

[7] EBU/SMPTE Task Force for Harmonized Standards for the Exchange of Programme Material as Bitstreams. Final Report: Analyses and Results, August 1998.

[8] Baecker, R., Rosenthal, A.J., Friedlander, N., Smith, E., and Cohen, A. "A Multimedia System for Authoring Motion Pictures" in *Proceedings of the 4th ACM International Multimedia Conference (Multimedia'96)* (Boston MA, November 18-22, 1996), 31-42

[9] Geissler, J. "Surfing the Movie Space: Advanced Navigation in Movie--Only Hypermedia" in *Proceedings of the 3rd ACM International Multimedia Conference (Multimedia'95)* (San Francisco CA, November 5-9, 1995), 391-400.

[10] Ghinea, G., and Thomas, J.P. "QoS Impact on User Perception and Understanding of Multimedia Video Clips" in *Proceedings of the 6th ACM International Multimedia Conference (Multimedia'98)* (Bristol UK, September 12-16, 1998), 49-54.

[11] International Organisation For Standardisation (ISO/IEC JTC1/SC29/WG11) - Requirements Group (Adam Lindsay, Editor), MPEG-7 Applications Document v.9 (ISO/IEC JTC1/SC29/WG11/N2861), (Vancouver CA, July 1999).

[12] Pantham, S. *Pure JFC Swing*, Sams Publishing, Indianapolis IN, 1999.

[13] Piroumian, V. *Java Gui Development: The Authoritative Solution*, Sams Publishing, Indianapolis IN, 1999.

[14] Ponceleon, D., Srinivasan, S., Amir, A., Petkovic, D., and Diklic, D. "Key to Effective Video Retrieval: Effective Cataloging and Browsing" in *Proceedings of the 6th ACM International Multimedia Conference (Multimedia'98)* (Bristol UK, September 12-16, 1998), 99-107.

[15] Santos, C.A.S., Soares, L.F.G., de Souza, G.L., and Courtiat, J.-P. "Design Methodology for Formal Validation of Hypermedia Documents" in *Proceedings of the 6th ACM International Multimedia Conference (Multimedia'98)* (Bristol UK, September 12-16, 1998), 39-48.

[16] Sun Microsystems Inc. *Java Media Framework API Guide*, September 3, 1999, v. 0.8.

[17] Sun Microsystems Inc., Silicon Graphics Inc., and Intel Corporation. *Java Media Players*, Version 1.0.5., May 11, 1998.

[18] Today's Stories: i[3] –ESE (Long Term Research Task 4.4) Project Nr. 29312, Project Web Site found at: http://stories.starlab.org/about.htm

[19] Weber, J.L. *Special Edition Using Java 2 Platform*, Que Publishing, 1999.

[20] Yoo, S. Multimedia Authoring/ Scripting. Course seminar. Oct. 14, 1995. Found at: http://mmlab.snu.ac.kr/course/mmseminar/temp/YsPres.html

Detection, Analysis and Rendering of Audience Reactions in Distributed Multimedia Performances

Nikitas M. Sgouros
Dept. of Informatics, Univ. of Piraeus
Karaoli & Dimitriou 80, Piraeus
185 34, Greece
+30 1 414 2270

sgouros@unipi.gr

ABSTRACT

Recent advances in distributed multimedia technologies encourage the development of interactive performance systems. These systems allow multiple users to take part in a performance either as players or spectators and influence its development in real time. However, in order for these applications to become effective they have to provide meaningful interaction capabilities and adequate means of expression to all the participants. This research provides an interaction framework that seeks to address these requirements. In particular, the system allows players and spectators to exchange messages during the performance. These messages describe player actions and audience reactions. Furthermore, the framework monitors the development of the event and analyzes the behavior of the participants in order to: (i) detect and render shared audience reactions (ii) achieve a high degree of audience engagement. Finally, the system synchronizes the presentation of audience reactions with performance developments at each site. This method has been applied in MISSION, a multi-player game on the Web.

Keywords

Multimedia tools, end-systems and applications, distributed multimedia applications, entertainment systems.

1. INTRODUCTION

Recent advances in distributed multimedia technologies encourage the development of interactive performance systems. These systems allow a large number of users to participate and influence the performance of an event in real time. Many of these applications offer to the user a single mode of interaction with the system, that of the performance player. Although interesting, this form of interaction can be quite restrictive since it covers only a subset of the possible performance types. In particular, there are many events in which 'performance' can be described as the execution of an activity by an individual or group (i.e., the *players* or *performers*) largely for the pleasure of another individual or group (i.e., the *spectators* or the *audience*). There

are numerous and quite popular examples including games with fixed rules, competitions, ritual and unstructured forms of 'play', drama or music performances. A common goal of all these events is to involve the audience in the performance and to allow it to express shared emotions, understandings or beliefs. Audience reactions, in this case, are largely festive and decorative, seeking to unify the participants and to mobilize sentiment and action during performance. In contrast, player actions are mainly purposeful since they serve the player's goals in the event.

This research provides a novel, interaction framework that enriches the types of interaction available in current distributed performance systems. In particular, this framework allows multiple users to participate in the performance either as *players* or *spectators*. A player influences directly the performance by taking part in it. For example, a player can control one of the characters in a multi-user game or play one of the instruments in a music performance on the Web. A spectator, on the other hand, is able to freely observe and comment on the event and to express his/her reactions by sending messages to the rest of the participants. The framework supports a centralized communication scheme in which a server module is responsible for relaying the messages generated by the participants. In addition, the framework analyzes the behavior of the users at each site and affects the presentation of the event locally in order to keep the spectators interested in the performance and provide efficient ways of expressing their shared reactions. Finally, the system seeks to synchronize the rendering of audience reactions with performance events at each site based on the number and rate of player actions.

This framework has been implemented in MISSION, a multi-player game on the Web that enables two players to participate in a 3-D space combat, while a group of spectators observes the game action and provides feedback during the performance.

Possible uses for this research include the development of novel, distributed multimedia applications similar to more traditional and highly popular forms involving public performance (e.g. sporting events, drama or music performances, festivals etc) and deployed over a number of different platforms (e.g. WWW, interactive TV, mobile phones etc). Furthermore this research can be used for the enhancement of existing applications, such as multi-user games or shared virtual environments, with capabilities for audience involvement. In addition, this research can be used for the creation of adaptive user interfaces for multimedia performances that control the way the information is presented based on audience feedback.

195

The rest of this paper is organized as follows. Section 2 describes in detail the framework architecture. Section 3 describes the analysis of audience behavior along with the strategies for audience engagement. Section 4 presents the synchronization heuristics for audience reactions. Section 5 describes the message aggregation techniques for rendering shared spectator reactions, while section 6 discusses the implementation of this framework in MISSION. Finally, section 7 presents related work, while section 8 provides conclusions and describes future work.

2. ARCHITECTURE

The framework assumes that each participant (player or spectator) is connected to a *Central Server Module* (*CSM*) that is responsible for distributing information related to the performance actions or to the audience reactions (see Figure 1). The system assigns a unique id to each participant site. CSM accepts two types of messages from each site; *action* and *reaction* messages.

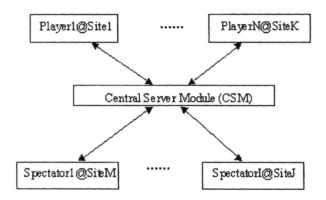

Figure 1: System architecture.

2.1 Action Messages

Action messages are produced by the players and describe their actions during the performance. The server automatically relays all these messages to the rest of the participants. For example, in the case of a multi-user game action messages may include information on the motion of a player in game space, while in the case of a music performance these can include MIDI messages generated by any of the players. The server assumes that all processing related to the rendering of action messages is handled locally at each participating site. Consequently, these messages can be short and only contain directions for updating the presentation locally at each site, thus conserving valuable network bandwidth. For example, in MISSION, the maximum length for an action message is 3 bytes. Table 1 describes the possible action messages in MISSION.

While player actions are relayed to the rest of the participants, the framework assumes that action outcomes are computed locally at each site. Therefore, no messages describing action outcomes need to be exchanged. For example, in MISSION each site determines locally whether a missile fired by a player will hit its target or not based on the missile trajectory and the current positions of the rest of the players. Table 2 describes the possible action outcomes in MISSION.

Table 1: Possible action messages for player X in MISSION.

#	Symbolic Form	Interpretation
1	Lturn(X)	Player X turns left
2	Rturn(X)	Player X turns right
3	Forward(X)	Player X moves forward
4	GainHeight(X)	Player X gains height
5	LoseHeight(X)	Player X looses height
6	Fire(X)	Player X fires a missile

Table 2: Possible action outcomes in MISSION.

#	Symbolic Form	Interpretation
1	MissedTarget(X)	Player X missed its target
2	HitTarget(X)	Player X hit its target
3	Damaged(X)	Player X was damaged by a missile
4	ShotDown(X)	Player X was shot down

2.2 Reaction Messages

Reaction messages are sent from audience members to the rest of the participants. They are generated as reactions to the content of the performance. Reaction messages allow each spectator to: (i) criticize current player actions, (ii) express his/her affective reactions towards the performance events. For example, Table 3 describes the possible reaction messages in MISSION.

Table 3: Possible reaction messages generated by a spectator (e.g. S) and their interpretation in MISSION.

Symbolic Form	Message Interpretation
Praise(S)	S praises an action outcome
Reject(S)	S rejects an action outcome
Support(S)	S supports the execution of an action
Oppose(S)	S opposes the execution of an action
Laugh(S)	S laughs with an action or outcome
Cry(S)	S cries with an action or outcome

In order to render reaction messages the system uses multimedia effects that are pre-stored at each site. Each one of these effects is executed automatically at each site with the arrival of a reaction message from CSM that specifies its use. Spectators are able to specify the particular effect that will be used for rendering every reaction message they send. For example, a message praising the outcome of an action in MISSION can be rendered either as an audio clip of an applause, as a text message reading "Go on!" or as an image of a trophy.

Only a subset of the reaction messages relayed by CSM is rendered at each site. In particular, when posting a reaction each spectator is free to decide on the subset of performers for which his/her message is relevant. In this case, the message is rendered only by those spectator sites in which the specified performers are currently visible/audible. Consequently, each spectator views only those reaction messages that are relevant to the part of the performance s/he is observing. In addition, a spectator can choose to send a message to all of the participants.

3. ANALYSIS OF AUDIENCE BEHAVIOR

One of the main criteria for judging the effectiveness of interactive media performances is their ability to keep the audience interested and to stimulate its participation during the event. To this end, the framework monitors audience behavior at each site and seeks to link the actions of the players and their outcomes with the spectator reactions they induce. The resulting links are then used to determine spectator preferences during the performance. Based on these preferences the system identifies and emphasizes critical points in the performance, i.e., points with a high dramatic potential for the spectator at each site. Whenever the system detects such a point, it executes a set of multimedia effects that affect the local rendering of the performance and try to convey its dramatic significance for the spectator. In the following, we refer to a site as S and to the spectator (user) at this site as U.

3.1 Linking Player Actions with Audience Reactions

In order to link player actions with audience reactions the system assumes that each spectator reaction is caused by a recent player action in the performance. In particular, if t is the time of occurrence of a reaction M by U in S, then the system assumes that the candidate player actions for inducing M are those that have been rendered by S during the time interval $[t - dt, t)$. We refer to this set of player actions as $Candidates_{M, t}$ and to the cardinal number of this set as $N_{M, t}$. The system assumes that dt is a reasonable maximum time lag between the rendering of a player action in S and the onset of a reaction by U to it. For example, dt has been empirically set at 3 seconds in MISSION. Furthermore, the system assumes that the actions in $Candidates_{M, t}$ are ordered in the chronological order in which they were rendered in S.

Based on $N_{M, t}$, S computes the probability p that each action in $Candidates_{M, t}$ has induced reaction M at time t as the inverse of $N_{M, t}$. Formally:

$$\forall A \in Candidates_{M, t} : p(A \mid M, t) = 1/ N_{M, t}.$$

For example, let us assume that in MISSION we have two players A and B and that 80 seconds after the start of the game U posts a Praise(U) signal to the rest of the participants. Then:

$$M = Praise(U), t = 80 \ sec.$$

Furthermore, let us assume that during the interval [80-3, 80) the following sequence of player actions have been rendered in S:

$$Lturn(A), Fire(A), Rturn(B).$$

Then:

- $Candidates_{Praise(U),80} = \{ Lturn(A), Fire(A), Rturn(B) \}$
- $N_{Praise(U),80} = 3$
- $p(Lturn(A) \mid Praise(U), 80) = 1/3 = 0.33$

- $p(Fire(A) \mid Praise(U), 80) = 0.33$
- $p(Rturn(B) \mid Praise(U), 80) = 0.33$

Whenever U posts a reaction message M, S appends the resulting $Candidates_{M, t}$ set to a superset containing all the groups of actions that have been associated with M during the performance. We refer to this superset as the *inducement history* for M (*InduceHistory_M*) and to its cardinal number as the *frequency* for M (*Freq_M*). Obviously, $Freq_M$ is equal to the number of times that U has posted reaction message M during the performance.

In the case of our previous example, if we assume that U had also posted a Praise(U) signal 45 seconds into the game with a candidate set equal to:

$$Candidates_{Praise(U),45} = \{ Lturn(A), Fire(A) \}$$

then:

- $p(Lturn(A) \mid Praise(U), 45) = 1/2 = 0.5$
- $p(Fire(A) \mid Praise(U), 45) = 0.5$

and:

- $InduceHistory_{Praise(U)} =$
  = \{ $Candidates_{Praise(U),45}$, $Candidates_{Praise(U),80}$\} =
  = \{ \{ Lturn(A), Fire(A), Rturn(B) \},\{ Lturn(A), Fire(A) \} \}
- $Freq_{Praise(U)} = 2$

Based on the inducement history and the frequency for a reaction message M, the system computes the probability for a player action (e.g. A) inducing M during the performance so far (i.e. $p(A \mid M)$). The computation of $p(A \mid M)$ consists of the following sequence of steps:

1. $p(A \mid M) = 0$;
2. For every $Candidates_{M, t}$ set in $InduceHistory_M$ do:

   if $A \in Candidates_{M, t}$ then

   $p(A \mid M) = p(A \mid M) + p(A \mid M, t)$;
3. $p(A \mid M) = p(A \mid M) / Freq_M$;

Based on our previous example the probability of all actions involved with the Praise(U) signal during the performance will be:

- $p(Fire(A) \mid Praise(U)) = (p(Fire(A) \mid Praise(U), 45) + p(Fire(A) \mid Praise(U), 80)) / Freq_{Praise(U)} = (0.5+0.33)/2 = 0.415$
- $p(Rturn(B) \mid Praise(U)) = 0.33/2 = 0.165$
- $p(Lturn(A) \mid Praise(U)) = 0.5/2 = 0.25$

Based on the probability of each player action inducing a reaction message M, the system forms the *strongest inducers* set for M (*S-Induce_M*). This set contains all the actions for which their probability of inducing M is greater than a pre-specified value *MaxAssoc*. Let us assume that in our example MaxAssoc has been set to 0.4. Then the strongest inducers set for the Praise(U) reaction will contain just one element:

$$S\text{-}Induce_{Praise(U)} = \{ Fire(A) \}.$$

3.2 Determining audience preferences

The system uses the strongest inducers sets for the Praise, Reject, Support and Oppose reactions posted by U to determine whether U is a fan or opponent of any of the players in the game.

Definition 2: U is a *fan (opponent)* of player P if:

1. more than half of the actions contained in the strongest inducers sets for the Praise and Support reactions involve (do not involve) player P

2. more than half of the actions in the strongest inducers sets for the Reject and Oppose reactions do not involve (involve) player P

In other words, U is a fan (opponent) of player P if s/he favors (opposes) more frequently actions that involve player P and oppose (favors) more frequently actions that do not involve P.

Furthermore, the system uses the strongest inducers sets for the Laugh and Cry reactions posted by U to identify performance actions or action outcomes with significant affective potential for U.

Definition 3: Event A is *comic* for U if:

$$A \in \text{S-Induce}_{\text{Laugh}(U)}.$$

In other words an event is comic if it has made the spectator post a Laugh reaction most of the time.

Definition 4: Event A is *tragic* for U if:

$$A \in \text{S-Induce}_{\text{Cry}(U)}.$$

i.e., an event is tragic if it has made the spectator post a Cry reaction most of the time.

Apart from classifying audience behavior, the system measures the overall frequency of the reaction messages generated by U. If this frequency is lower than a fraction of the average message frequency of all sites that send messages to S, then U is considered to be *idle*. Otherwise U is considered to be *active*.

3.3 Engaging the Audience

The system seeks to raise audience interest in sites classified as idle by emphasizing critical points in the performance. These are points in which:

Players have their physical or emotional state changed. Changes in the state of a performer can affect the emotional state of its fans or opponents as well. Consequently, if such changes occur and the user is a fan or opponent of the player involved, then the system triggers a series of multimedia effects associated with the emotional state induced on the user. For example, each time a player's spaceship is damaged in MISSION a sad audio clip is executed at every fan site for this player while a joyful audio clip is being heard at every opponent site.

Performance reaches a climactic point. For example, in a music performance a crescento can correspond to such a climactic point, while in many computer games the conflict between two players reaches a climax during their violent confrontation.

An action with a significant affective potential for a spectator occurs. In particular, the rendering of player actions that have been classified as comic or tragic for a spectator are accompanied by the execution of a multimedia effect that seeks to reinforce the mood of the event.

Structural changes occur in the performance. For example, in a drama performance a structural change occurs when the number of performers changes or when there is a change in the setting of the play. In a music performance structural changes occur when there is a change in tempo, while in a game a similar change occurs when new players appear. Structural changes herald fresh developments in the performance and their introduction is accompanied by appropriate multimedia effects that convey the suspense generated by these changes in the case of a drama performance or the mood induced by the changing tempo in a music performance.

4. SYNCHRONIZATION OF AUDIENCE REACTIONS

One of the main requirements from a distributed performance system is the synchronization of the appearance of audience reactions with the performance events. In particular, the system has to ensure that the audience will appear to react to a recent action, not to a past one. This is even more crucial in fast-paced, live events (e.g. games) where even a small loss of synchronization can lead to great confusion.

To this end, each site (e.g. S) attaches a *signature* (Sig_M) to each outgoing reaction message (e.g. M) that describes the state of the performance in S to which M corresponds. More specifically, Sig_M contains the total number of action messages processed (i.e., generated or received) by S from the start of the performance till the moment M was generated.

In addition, S measures constantly its *action rate* (AR_S). This rate counts the number of action messages processed per unit of time by S during the performance. Symbolically, if T_S is the amount of time elapsed from the start of the performance till the moment AR_S is computed, as measured by the system clock in S, and N_S is the total number of action messages processed by S during T_S, then $AR_S = N_S/T_S$.

For example, if S is 60 seconds into the performance and during this time it has processed 30 action messages then $AR_S = 30/60 = 0.5$ actions/sec.

Whenever S receives a reaction message (e.g. M) from the server, it tries to estimate the *lag* for M. This lag estimates how long ago M was generated, assuming that M was generated by S. If we assume that the signature for M is Sig_M, then S computes the lag (Lag_M) for M as:

$$Lag_M = (N_S - Sig_M) / AR_S$$

If $0 \leq Lag_M \leq MaxLag$, where MaxLag is a maximum time lag that can be tolerated by the performance, then S will render message M. Otherwise M will be discarded since it is not synchronized with the performance events.

Furthermore, if $Lag_M < 0$ then the sender of M has processed more performance actions than S. Therefore some action messages have not reached A at all. In this case, the system informs the user in S of this problem. The user then has the option to remain in the performance or leave.

In our previous example, if we assume that S receives a message M with $Sig_M = 26$, then the lag for M will be: $Lag_M = (30 - 26) /$

0.5 = 8 seconds. In this case the system estimates that M refers to a player action that occurred 8 seconds ago, therefore M should be discarded.

5. DETECTION OF SHARED AUDIENCE REACTIONS

A common goal of many types of performances is to allow the audience to express shared emotions, understandings or beliefs. Therefore, an interactive performance system should be capable of detecting and emphasizing shared reactions by the spectators. In our case, the framework assumes that shared reactions are those that occur at approximately the same point in the performance, have the same content and are caused by the same inducing actions. Consequently, in order to detect these reactions CSM examines the signatures, the content and the inducing actions of the reactions in its receiving queue.

Definition 5: Two reaction messages (e.g. A, B) are *common reactions* to the same performance event if they have:

1. the same content (e.g., both messages are Cry reactions)

2. different senders

3. approximately the same signatures ($Sig_A \approx Sig_B$)

4. at least one common inducing action ($Candidates_{A, tA} \cap Candidates_{B, tB} \neq \emptyset$)

Whenever CSM detects two common reactions A and B, it merges both messages into a single message (e.g. C) with the same content as A and B and with $Sig_c = max(Sig_A, Sig_B)$. C is then relayed to the participants. The server appends to C a *strength counter* that indicates the number of spectators behind it (i.e., the number of messages merged into C). Each site examines the strength counter of every message it receives in order to determine the emphasis with which each message will be presented. Emphasis is proportional to the value of this counter and it can be achieved locally through the manipulation of presentation parameters such as the screen space allocated for the display of each message, the intensity of the audio signal played, the number of messages displayed on the screen or the duration for which these messages are allowed to appear on screen.

6. AN EXAMPLE

The interaction framework has been implemented in MISSION, a simple, multi-player game on the Web. The game enables two players to confront each other in a 3-D space battle. A group of spectators can observe the game action on the Web and react during the performance. MISSION allows each player to see or hear the reaction messages sent to him/her by the spectators. On the other hand, each spectator can freely navigate in 3-D space so that s/he can view the game action from any view invisible from the players. Players and spectators navigate using the arrow keys in the keyboard.

A spectator can send reaction messages to either a certain player by placing the player inside a circular selector area in the screen, or to all of the players that are visible from his/her current position. Each possible reaction message has been associated with a key in the keyboard. A spectator views all the reaction messages concerning the players that are visible from his/her point of view.

Figure 2 shows a typical screenshot from the game. This shot depicts one of the player spaceships and two reaction messages. As the figure shows, text or image messages flash at random positions on the player's or spectator's screen. The small circle to the right side of the figure is used, in the case of players, as a targeting device during battle and in the case of spectators as a player selector area for sending messages to any player inside this area. In both cases, the outline of the area changes color whenever it contains a player.

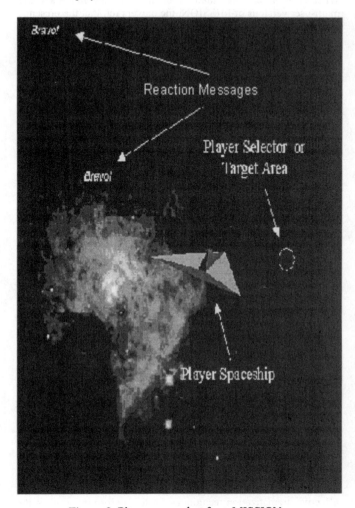

Figure 2. Player screenshot from MISSION.

Strategies for audience involvement use two kinds of multimedia effects: *suspense* and *atmospheric*. Suspense effects are triggered whenever there is a climactic point in the performance and they seek to capture audience interest. In the simple plot of MISSION, these points occur whenever there is a violent confrontation between the players. These confrontations are accompanied by the execution of a suspense audio clip at each spectator site viewing the incident.

Atmospheric effects seek to communicate the mood of the events and the nature of the relationships between the players in the performance. They are triggered whenever there is a change in the state of the players. For example, whenever a player misses its target, the system executes a sad audio clip at every fan site for this player and a joyful audio clip at every opponent site for this player. In addition, atmospheric effects are triggered whenever points with significant affective potential for a spectator occur in the performance.

Up to this date MISSION has been tested in two trial runs, each one involving two players and an audience of four spectators. Players and spectators were interviewed after the trials. Before each trial, the players used a single-user version of the game. When asked to compare their experience with the single and the multi-user versions of MISSION, the players felt that the presence of an audience increased their motivation to play. Furthermore, they thought that playing in the multi-user version was more demanding, since randomly flashing messages from the spectators sometimes distracted them from the game. Players felt that audio signals were the least unobtrusive.

Spectators found the system original and entertaining. In both trials, the participants reported that a lag of up to 3 seconds in the appearance of each message (i.e., MaxLag ≤ 3) was tolerable. The trials showed that a value of MaxAssoc greater than 0.7 was necessary in order for the classification of the behavior of audience members as fans or opposers of certain players to agree with the interpretation they gave for their behavior after the game.

7. RELATED WORK

Recently, there has been considerable research interest in the development and staging of interactive media performances. Work in this area has focused on supporting player actions during the performance by allowing the performers to interact physically or remotely with various forms of media (e.g. graphics, musical instruments, computer-controlled characters etc) [3, 5]. Other research work has focused on the creation of large-scale virtual reality systems for supporting crowds of participants. Work in this area has identified four major issues that have to be addressed in order for distributed virtual reality systems to scale up, namely; a reduction in the effects of network delays, scalable causal event delivery, update control and reliable communication [4]. In addition, relevant work has developed spatial models of interaction for crowds in virtual reality or interactive TV environments with different effects on mutual awareness and communication [2]. The results in this paper complement all this research focusing on the development of appropriate means of expression for shared reactions, on strategies for analyzing and encouraging audience participation and on methods for synchronization of spectator reactions.

Furthermore, there has been a significant amount of work on effective dramatization techniques for the performing arts, on the investigation of the relation between the performance and the audience and on the psychology of the crowd [1, 6, 7]. This research seeks to use the results of this work in the creation of a new generation of multimedia performance systems capable of creating engaging experiences for both the performers and the spectators of distributed performances.

8. CONCLUSIONS & FUTURE WORK

This paper describes a distributed interaction framework that supports and analyzes spectator reactions during multimedia performances. This research can be used for the development of a new generation of multimedia performance systems that allow meaningful audience participation and provide efficient means for the expression of shared reactions during the performance. In addition, it can be used for the enhancement of current multimedia applications, such as multi-user games or shared virtual environments, with capabilities for audience involvement. Finally, it can be used for the development of adaptive performances, i.e., performances that automatically analyze audience reactions in order to improve their staging.

Future work in this area will focus on running extensive user trials of the system in order to enrich and fine-tune the means of expression of the audience during the performance, the strategies for maintaining a high degree of audience involvement and the message synchronization methods. Furthermore, it will seek to extend the analysis of audience reactions in order to detect action sequences with significant affective potential for the spectators. Finally, future work will focus on coupling the analysis of audience reactions with dynamic plot generation methods for interactive stories similar to the ones in [8]. The goal of this coupling will be the creation of a new generation of interactive story performances that can dynamically modify their plot and presentation based not only on the actions of the protagonists but also on the audience reactions.

9. REFERENCES

[1] Aristotle, *Poetics*, (~340BC)

[2] Benford S.; Greenhalgh S.; and Lloyd D., Crowded Collaborative Virtual Environments, *Proceedings of CHI'97*, Atlanta GA, USA, (1997).

[3] Maldonado, H., Picard, A., Doyle, P., and Hayes-Roth, B., Tigrito: A Multi-Mode Interactive Improvisational Agent. *Proceedings of IUI'98*, San Francisco, CA, (1998).

[4] Roberts D.J.; Sharkey P.M., Maximizing Concurrency and Scalability in a Consistent, Causal, Distributed Virtual Reality System, whilst minimising the effect of network delays, *Proceedings of IEEE WETICE'97*, (1997).

[5] Sgouros, N. M. et al., Multimedia Presentation Techniques for Interactive Plots, *Proceedings of IEEE Conference on Multimedia Computing and Systems*, Ottawa, Canada, (1997).

[6] McQuail, D., *Mass Communication Theory*, Sage Publications (1994).

[7] Pfister, M., *The Theory and Analysis of Drama*, Cambridge University Press, (1988).

[8] Sgouros, N. M., Dynamic generation, management and resolution of interactive plots, *Artificial Intelligence*, 12(3), 29-62, Elsevier (1999).

Smart Rebinning for Compression of Concentric Mosaics

Yunnan Wu[a], Cha Zhang[b], Jin Li[c], Jizheng Xu[a]

[a]University of Science & Technology of China, Heifei 230026, China

[b]Electronic Engineering Department, Tsinghua University, Beijing 100084, China.

[c]Microsoft Research, China, 5F Research, Sigma Ctr, 49 Zhichun Road, Haidian, Beijing 100080, China.

Contact Email: jinl@microsoft.com

ABSTRACT

Concentric mosaics offer a quick solution to construct a virtual copy of a real environment, and navigate in the virtual environment. However, the huge amount of data associated with concentric mosaics is a heavy burden for its application. A 3D wavelet transform-based compressor has been proposed in previous work to compress the concentric mosaics. In this paper, we greatly improve the performance of the 3D wavelet coder with a data rearrangement mechanism called "smart rebinning". The proposed scheme first aligns the concentric mosaic image shots along the horizontal direction and then rebins the shots into multi-perspective panoramas. Smart rebinning greatly improves the cross shot correlation and enables the coder to better explore the redundancy among shots. Experimental results show that the performance of the 3D wavelet coder improves an average of 4.3dB with the use of smart rebinning. The proposed coder outperforms MPEG-2 coding of concentric mosaics by an average of 3.7dB.

Keywords

Image based rendering, concentric mosaics, compression, rebinning, multi-perspective panorama, 3D wavelet.

1. INTRODUCTION

Image-based rendering (IBR) techniques have received much attention in the computer graphic realm for realistic scene/object representation. Instead of referring to complicated geometric and photometric properties as the conventional model-based rendering does, IBR requires only sampled images to generate high quality novel virtual views. Furthermore, the rendering time for an IBR dataset is independent of the underlying spatial complexity of the scene, which makes IBR attractive for the modeling of highly complex real environments. Concentric mosaics[1] enable quick construction of a virtual copy of a real environment, and navigation in the virtual environment. By rotating a single camera

mounted at the end of a leveled beam, with the camera pointing outward and shooting images as the beam rotates, a concentric mosaic scene can quickly be constructed. At the time of the rendering, we just split the rendered view into vertical ray slits, and reconstruct each slit through similar slits captured during the rotation of the camera.

Though it is easy to create a 3D walkthrough, the amount of data associated with the concentric mosaics is tremendous. As an example, a concentric mosaic scene from [1] includes 1350 RGB images with resolution 320x240 and occupies a total of 297MB. Efficient compression is thus essential for the application of the concentric mosaics. In [1], a vector quantization approach was employed to compress the concentric mosaic scene with a compression ratio of 12:1. However, the size of the compressed bitstream is still 25MB, far too large for storage and transmission. Since the captured concentric mosaic shots are highly correlated, much higher compression ratio should be achievable.

Since the data structure of the concentric mosaics can be regarded as a video sequence with slowly panning camera motion, video compression techniques may be used to compress the concentric mosaics. We consider two major categories of video compression techniques. Existing standards, such as MPEGx and H.26x, adopt a prediction-based framework, where the temporal redundancy across frames is reduced through motion compensation and block residue coding. A reference block coder (RBC) has been proposed with a similar concept to compress the concentric mosaic scene [13].

Along a separate direction, three-dimensional (3D) wavelet video coders[2][3][4][5] present another category of video coding approaches that explore the temporal redundancy via wavelet filtering in the temporal direction. One attractive property of the 3D wavelet video coder is its spatial, temporal and quality scalability. Here the term scalability means that a 3D wavelet coder can compress a video into a single bitstream, where multiple subsets of the bitstream can be decoded to generate complete videos of different spatial resolution/temporal resolution/quality commensurate with the proportion of the bitstream decoded [6]. This is extremely useful in the Internet streaming environment where heterogeneous decoder/network settings prevail. Furthermore, since 3D wavelet based coders avoid the recursive loop in predictive coders, they perform better in an error prone environment, such as a wireless network. In previous work, we developed a 3D wavelet transform coding system to compress concentric mosaics[7]. However, the performance of that coder is inferior to that of RBC and MPEG-2. In this work, we investigate the performance bottleneck and further improve the compression performance of the 3D wavelet concentric mosaic coder.

In a 3D wavelet coder, wavelet transforms are applied separately along the horizontal, vertical and temporal directions to concentrate the signal energy into relatively few large coefficients. However, one common problem with the 3D wavelet compression schemes is that the temporal wavelet filtering does not achieve efficient energy compaction. In a prediction-based video / concentric mosaic coder, local motion can be specified on a per block basis, thus inter-frame correlation due to the moving object/camera can be explored which is very beneficial to the coding performance. However, local motion cannot be easily incorporated into the framework of 3D wavelet compression. Because of the nature of temporal filtering, each pixel can be engaged in one and only one transform.

Taubman and Zakhor [2] proposed a pan compensation module that aligned the image frames prior to the wavelet transform. In our former 3D wavelet concentric mosaic codec[7], a panorama alignment module was used to eliminate global translation. Wang *et al.* [3] proposed to register and warp all image frames into a common coordinate system and then apply a 3D wavelet transform with an arbitrary region of support to the warped volume. To make use of the local block motion, Ohm [4] incorporated block matching and carefully handled the covered/uncovered, connected/unconnected regions. By trading off the invertibility requirement, Tham *et al.* [5] employed a block-based motion registration for the low motion sequences without filling the holes caused by individual block motion. However, both Ohm and Tham's approaches are complex.

In this paper, a smart rebinning operation is proposed as a novel preprocessing technique for the 3D wavelet compression of the concentric mosaics. Rather than adapting the compression algorithm or the filter structure to the mosaic image array, we modify the data structure for easy compression by 3D wavelet. The proposed scheme begins with pair-wise alignment of the image shots. Then the original concentric mosaic scene is rebinned to form multi-perspective panoramas. The rearranged data have much stronger correlation across frames; and thus can be compressed more efficiently by the 3D wavelet coder.

This paper is organized as follows: The background for the acquisition and display of the concentric mosaics is provided in Section 2. The smart-rebinning operation and its rationale and potential benefits to the 3D wavelet codec are detailed in Section 3. Since the smart-rebinned concentric mosaics may no longer be of rectangular region of support, the associated 3D wavelet coding technique is discussed in Section 4. Experimental results are presented in Section 5. Finally, we conclude the paper in Section 6.

2. BACKGROUND: THE CONCENTRIC MOSAICS

A concentric mosaic scene is captured by mounting a camera at the end of a rotating beam, and shooting images at regular intervals as the beam rotates. We show the capturing device in Figure 1. Let the camera shots taken during the rotation of the beam be denoted as $F_n=\{f(n,w,h)|w,h\}$, where n indexes the camera shot, w indexes the horizontal position within a shot, and h indexes the vertical position. Let N be the total number of camera shots, W and H be the horizontal and vertical resolution of each camera shot, respectively. The entire concentric mosaic database can be

treated as a series of camera shots F_n, or alternatively be interpreted as a series of rebinned panoramas $P_w=\{f(n,w,h)|n,h\}$ where each individual panorama consists of vertical slits at position w of all camera shots. Three rebinned panoramas at different radii are shown in Figure 2. Panorama P_w can be considered as taken by a virtual slit camera rotating along a circle co-centered with the original beam with a radius $d=R\sin\theta$, where R is the radius of the rotation beam, d is the equivalent radius of the slit camera, and θ is the angle between ray w and the camera normal, which can be calculated as:

$$\theta=arctan\frac{2w\text{-}W}{W}.$$

Since the entire data volume P_w, $w=0,\cdots,W\text{-}1$ can be considered as a stack of co-centered mosaic panoramas with different radius, it is called the concentric mosaic[1].

Concentric mosaics are able to capture a realistic environment and render arbitrary views within an inner circle of radius $r=R\sin(FOV/2)$, where FOV is the horizontal field of view of the capturing camera. Rendering concentric mosaics involves reassembling slits from the captured dataset. Shown in Figure 3, let P be a novel viewpoint and AB be the field of view to be rendered. We split the view into multiple vertical slits, and render each slit independently. A basic hypothesis behind the concentric mosaic rendering is that the intensity of any ray does not change along a straight line unless blocked. Thus, when a slit PV is rendered, we simply search for the slit $P'V$ in the captured dataset, i.e., either in the captured image set F_n or the rebinned panorama set P_w, where P' is the intersection point between the direction of the ray and the camera track. Because of the discrete sampling, the exact slit $P'V$ might not be found in the captured dataset. The four sampled slits closest to $P'V$ may be P_1V_{11}, P_1V_{12}, P_2V_{21} and P_2V_{22}, where P_1 and P_2 are the two nearest captured shots, P_1V_{11} and P_1V_{12} are the slits closest to P_1V in direction in shot P_1, and P_2V_{21} and P_2V_{22} are closest to P_2V in shot P_2. We may choose only the slit that is closest to $P'V$ from the above four to approximate the intensity of PV. However, a better approach is to use bilinear interpolation, where all four slits are employed to interpolate the rendered slit PV. The environmental depth information may assist the finding of the best approximating slits and alleviate the vertical distortion. More detailed description of the concentric mosaic rendering may be found in [1].

3. SMART REBINNING: A CROSS SHOT DECORRELATION APPROACH

In the previous paper[7], we compress the 3D data volume of the concentric mosaics through the global alignment of the panorama and 3D wavelet coding. However, filtering in the temporal direction (mentioned as cross shot filtering, as there is no time domain in the concentric mosaic) has not been very efficient, and thus the compression performance of the 3D wavelet codec suffers. In recognition of the significant role of motion compensation in the 3D wavelet compression, we look for an efficient decorrelation scheme along the cross-shot direction. Since the concentric mosaics assume static scenery and the camera is slowly swinging within a planar circle, the motion between two successive images is predominantly horizontal translation, with little or non vertical motion. We can easily calculate the horizontal translation vector between each pair of consecutive shots. Let x_n denote the calculated horizontal displacement between shot F_n and F_{n+1}. Since the shots are circularly captured, shot x_0 is right next to shot x_{N-1}. We thus denote x_{N-1} as the displacement vector between frame F_0 and F_{N-1}. Note that the horizontal displacement vectors may not be equal for all frames. They are inverse proportional to the distance of the object, i.e., larger for shots with a close-by object, and smaller for shots with the far away background. We can maximize the correlation between neighboring shots by horizontally aligning them according to the calculated displacement vector, as shown in Figure 4. We term this approach horizontal shot alignment. We use 7 concentric mosaic image shots F_0, F_1, ···, F_6 as an example. Each shaded horizontal line in Figure 4 corresponds to one captured image. The vertical direction of the image is not shown since we are only concerned with horizontal translation. An additional virtual image F_0 is drawn right after the last image F_6 to show the circular capturing activity of the camera.

After the horizontal shot alignment, the concentric mosaics form a skewed data volume, which may be encoded by a 3D wavelet codec with horizontal, vertical and cross-shot filtering with a non-rectangular (arbitrary) region of support. The correlation across image shots is expected to improve, however, since the resultant data volume is highly sparse and is not rectangular, the compression efficiency may be compromised.

The proposed smart rebinning goes beyond horizontal shot alignment one step further. The idea is to cut and paste (i.e., to rebin) the skewed dataset into panoramas by pushing the skewed data volume downward in Figure 4, and form smartly rebinned panoramas. The details of the smart rebinning operation are shown in Figure 5. Let the horizontal displacement vectors between frames be x_0, x_1, ···, x_{N-1}. The original shots are divided into groups of vertical slits according to the horizontal displacement vectors, which are called stripes. As shown in Figure 5, frames are aligned according to the horizontal displacement vectors. The frame boundaries are shown as dashed lines, and stripes are the segments between the dashed lines. The stripe is the smallest integral unit in the smart rebinning. Let the stripe be denoted as $s_{n,j}$, where n indexes the image shot F_n that the stripe belongs to, and j indexes the stripe within F_n. The length of the first stripe $s_{n,0}$ is x_n, the horizontal displacement vector between frame F_n and F_{n+1}. The length of the jth stripe $s_{n,j}$ is $x_{(n+j) \bmod N}$, correspondingly. The number of stripes is not constant for all frames; it is inversely proportional to the horizontal displacement vector. Therefore, there are few stripes for the frame with a close-by object, and more stripes for that with the faraway background. We then downward stack the stripes and form the rebinned panorama set. We also warp the right part of the data volume to the left due to the circular nature of the camera shots. Let the maximum number of stripes for all frames be S. A total of S panoramas are obtained with equal horizontal length $x_0 + x_1 + \ldots + x_{N-1}$. The first rebinned panorama P_0 is constructed by concatenating the first stripes of all frames, i.e., the bottom of the downward-stacked data volume, which is shown in Figure 5 as the trace of the dotted circles. In general, a smartly rebinned panorama P_i consists of the ith stripes of all frames cut and paste sequentially, with the ith stripe of frame F_0 at the ith slot:

$$P_i = \{ s_{(-i) \bmod N, i}, \ s_{(-i+1) \bmod N, i}, \ \cdots, \ s_{(-i+N-1) \bmod N, i} \}, \ i = 0, 1, \cdots, S-1.$$

An illustration of the resultant rebinned panorama is shown in Figure 6. As shown in Figure 5, the sample concentric mosaic image array has a total of 7 frames with 12 slits each frame. The 7 horizontal displacement vectors for the frames are 2, 3, 3, 3, 2, 3 and 3 respectively. There are at most 5 stripes in any frame. As a result, the mosaic image array is rebinned into 5 panoramas with width $2+3+3+3+2+3+3=19$. The first panorama is consisted of the first stripes from all shots. The second panorama is consisted of the second stripes from all shots. To align the first and the second panoramas in the cross panorama direction, the second panorama is rotationally shifted so that the stripe from frame F_{N-1} is at the head. Some portions of the stripes in panorama P_4 contain no data, as the corresponding image shot do not have a full 5th stripe. The smart-rebinned panoramas are thus not of rectangular region of support. Special handling for coding those empty regions will be addressed in the next section.

With the smart rebinning approach, the unfilled regions of the skewed dataset are largely reduced, which makes the compression much more efficient and the implementation much more convenient. Filtering across the panorama is exactly equivalent to filtering across the image shots in the horizontal shot alignment approach shown in Figure 4. However, the horizontal filtering is changed from filtering within an image shot to filtering within the rebinned panorama. The newly generated panorama P_i is highly correlated internally, because each stripe consists of successive slits in one original shot image, and two neighbor stripes are smoothly connected because they are from the matching stripes in neighboring concentric mosaic image shots. Consequently, horizontal filtering is still pretty efficient.

A degenerated approach is to restrict all horizontal translation vectors to be exactly the same:

$$x_0 = x_1 = \cdots = x_{S-1} = x.$$

We call this approach simple rebinning. All image shots now have the same number of stripes. If there are unfilled slits at the last stripe, we simply fill them by repeating the last slit. Rebinning the stripes into panoramas, a set of panoramas with a rectangular region of support is formed. The approach is similar to the formation of the concentric mosaics $P_w = \{f(n,w,h) | n,h\}$ in [1]. The difference lies in that multiple slits are obtained from each shot to generate the rebinned panorama.

We show the volume of the original concentric mosaics in Figure 7. The rebinned concentric mosaics form a cube, with the front view showing a concentric mosaic panorama, the side view a camera shot, and the top view a cross-section slice at a certain height. We then show the smartly rebinned panorama volume in Figure 8 as a comparison. The smartly rebinned panorama forms volume of non-rectangular support, and the black region in Figure 8 identifies the unsupported region. We note that the area with a smaller region of support is closer to the capturing camera, because it has a larger horizontal displacement vector, and thus contains a smaller number of stripes. In comparison with the concentric mosaics, the smartly rebinned panorama appears to be more smooth and natural looking, as it adjusts its sampling density according to the distance of the shot to the object, and maintains a relative uniform object size as seen by the camera. The smartly rebinned panoramas have strong correlation across the panoramas. A set of rebinned panoramas at the same horizontal location is extracted and shown in Figure 9. We observe that most objects in the rebinned panoramas are well aligned. Only a few objects, such as the light bulb at the upper-left corner and the balloons behind the girl, show differences due to the gradual parallax transition among the rebinned panoramas. Such a well aligned data volume can be efficiently compressed by a 3D wavelet transform.

In fact, the smartly rebinned panorama belongs to a general category of *multi-perspective* panoramas that become popular recently in the computer graphic realm, such as manifold mosaics[8], multiple-center-of-projection image[9] and circular projection[10]. Multi-perspective panorama extends the conventional panorama by relaxing the requirement of having one common optical center and allows several camera viewpoints within a panorama. The idea of multi-perspective panorama construction via cutting and pasting stripes was first introduced in [8]. It has also been extended to enable stereo viewing in [10], where the stripes taken from the left side of each image shot generate the right eye panorama and those from the right generate the left eye view. However, in contrast to the work of [8][9] and [10], where only one or two panoramas are generated for their specific graphic application, we generate a whole set of rebinned panoramas to provide a dense representation of the environment, and to efficiently compress the concentric mosaic data set.

4. 3D WAVELET CODING OF REBINNED PANORAMAS

We further encode the rebinned panoramas with a 3D wavelet coder. Though other coders, such as the reference block coder (RBC) in [13] can also be applied, 3D wavelet coding is ideal because better alignment across image shots is more efficiently explored by the 3D wavelet coder. For the simple rebinning, straightforward 3D wavelet encoding may be adopted. In this work, we use a 3D wavelet codec with arithmetic block coding as proposed in our previous paper [7]. The data volume of the concentric mosaics is decomposed by multi-resolution 3D wavelet transform. The wavelet coefficients are then cut into fixed size blocks, embedded encoded, and assembled with a rate-distortion optimization criterion. For details of the 3D wavelet coding algorithm, we refer the reader to [7].

For smartly rebinned panoramas, a 3D wavelet coding algorithm that handles a data volume with an arbitrary region of support must be developed. Fortunately, there are wavelet algorithms designed to encode arbitrary shaped objects in the literature, most developed in the standardization process of MPEG-4[11]. A simple approach is to pad the unfilled arbitrary region of support to the tightest rectangular volume containing it and apply the rectangular 3D wavelet transform and coding algorithm to the padded data volume. In this work, we extend the low-pass extrapolation (LPE) adopted in MPEG4 for the padding work. The unsupported regions are first filled with the average pixel value of the boundary of the supported/unsupported region, and then a low-pass filter is applied in the unsupported region several times. Since in the unsupported region, all pixel values are initialized with the same average value, the effect of the low-pass filter is primarily at the boundary, where a gradual transition is built up. After the wavelet transform, coefficients in the unsupported regions will be mostly zeros, except at the boundary. The padded data volume is then compressed with the 3D wavelet codec described in [7]. Since the number of wavelet coefficients after padding is still

more than the number of pixels in the supported region, the padding increases the coding rate, and therefore the compression performance is affected. The advantage is that the padding involves the least change in the 3D wavelet codec, and is very easy to implement. Moreover, although the padding operation adds complexity in the encoder, it does not affect the decoder, which decodes the entire data volume and simply ignores the decoded pixels in the unsupported region.

Another feasible solution is to use an arbitrary shape wavelet transform [12] directly on the irregular region of support. For each directional wavelet transform, a set of straight lines parallel to the axis intersects the supported region and creates several segments. Each segment is then decomposed separately using a bi-orthogonal symmetric filter with symmetric boundary extension into the exact number of wavelet coefficients. We then store the coefficients in the wavelet domain, and record the region of support for the wavelet coefficients. The process can be recursively applied for multi-resolution decomposition, and can transform the arbitrarily supported concentric mosaic volume into an exact number of wavelet coefficients as that of the original data. For details of the scheme, we refer the reader to [12]. A block arithmetic coder with an arbitrary region of support in the wavelet domain is then used to compress the transformed coefficients. We call this codec the 3D arbitrary shape wavelet codec. It is observed that the arbitrary shape wavelet transform and coding is slightly superior in compression performance to padding the unsupported region. However, it is also more complex to implement, as we need to add support of the arbitrary shape region to both the transform and entropy coding module.

The smartly rebinned and 3D wavelet compressed concentric mosaic can be efficiently rendered as well. The rendering engine is very similar to the progressive inverse wavelet synthesis (PIWS) engine that we have proposed in [14]. According to the current viewing point and direction of the user, the rendering engine generates a set of slits which need to be accessed from the concentric mosaic data set. It then figures out the position of the accessed slits in the rebinned panorama set. After that, the PIWS engine is used to locate the wavelet coefficients in the rebinned panorama set and perform just enough computation to recover the accessed slits. Because smart rebinning can be considered as a preprocessing step of the 3D wavelet coder, the only extra step in rendering the smartly rebinned concentric mosaics is to locate the slits in the rebinned panorama, which can be easily performed with knowledge of the horizontal displacement vectors. The computational complexity of rendering the smartly rebinned concentric mosaics is thus similar to the rendering of 3D wavelet compressed concentric mosaics. With the PIWS engine, a rendering rate of 12 frames per second is achievable, which is fast enough for real time rendering applications.

5. EXPERIMENTAL RESULTS

The performance of the 3D wavelet concentric mosaic compression with smart rebinning is demonstrated with extensive experimental results. The test scenes are *Lobby* and *Kids*. The scene *Lobby* has 1350 frames at resolution 320x240, and the total data amount is 297MB. The scene *Kids* has 1462 frames at resolution 352x288, and the total data amount is 424MB. The *Kids* scene contains more details, and is thus more difficult to compress than the *Lobby* scene. The scenes are first converted from RGB to YUV color-space with 4:2:0 sub-sampling, and then compressed by different coders. We compress the *Lobby* scene at ratio 200:1(0.12bpp, 1.48MB) and 120:1(0.2bpp, 2.47MB), and the *Kids* scene at 100:1(0.24bpp, 4.24MB) and 60:1(0.4bpp, 7.07MB). The peak signal-to-noise-ratio (PSNR) between the original and decompressed scene is shown as the objective measure of the compression quality. We report the PSNRs of all three color components (Y, U and V) in Table 1, however, it is the PSNR result of the Y component that matters most. Therefore, we comment only on the Y component PSNR in the discussion.

We compare the proposed smart rebinning 3D wavelet coder with three benchmark algorithms. The first algorithm (A) compresses the entire concentric mosaics as a video sequence using a MPEG-2 video codec. The MPEG-2 software is downloaded from www.mpeg.org. In the MPEG-2 codec, the first frame is independently encoded as I frame, and the rest frames are predictively encoded as P frames. The second algorithm (B) is a direct 3D wavelet codec as reported in [7], where we rebin the concentric mosaic image shots into mosaic panoramas, align the panoramas and encode them with the 3D wavelet and arithmetic block coding. The third benchmark algorithm (C) is the reference block coder (RBC) reported in [13]. It is a prediction-based codec tuned for compression of concentric mosaics. We observe that direct 3D wavelet coding of the concentric mosaic scene (algorithm B) is not very efficient; it is 0.3 to 1.0 dB inferior to MPEG-2 with an average of 0.6 dB, and is inferior to the RBC codec with an average of 1.1dB.

We tested three different configurations of the 3D wavelet codec with smart rebinning. In the first configuration (algorithm D), we restrict the horizontal displacement vector between frames to be constant, i.e., the simple rebinning is used. The actual displacement vector is 2 and 3 pixels for the *Lobby* and *Kids* scenes, respectively. The resultant rebinned concentric mosaics form a rectangular panorama volume and are compressed by the exact same 3D wavelet and arithmetic block coder as algorithm B. It is observed that by simply rebinning multiple slits into the panorama, a large compression gain is achieved. In fact, compared with the direct 3D wavelet codec, the PSNR improves between 3.2 to 3.6dB, with an average of 3.5dB. The 3D wavelet coder with simple rebinning outperforms the MPEG-2 concentric mosaic codec by 2.9dB, and outperforms the RBC codec by 2.4dB.

We then apply the full-fledged smart rebinning algorithm. The horizontal displacement vectors are calculated by matching neighborhood concentric mosaic image shots. They are then stored in the compressed bitstream. After the rebinning operation, the bounding volume for the rebinned panoramas is 2832x162x240 for the *Lobby* scene and 5390x149x288 for the *Kids* scene. In the *Lobby* scene, object is of relatively constant depth to the camera, and the unsupported regions occupy only 6% of the bounding volume. However, in the *Kids* scene, 36% of the bounding volume is unsupported. We compress the rebinned panoramas through padding the data volume and applying the same 3D wavelet codec as the one used in the algorithm B and D (denoted as algorithm E); also, we use an arbitrary shape wavelet transform and coefficient coding algorithm (denoted as algorithm F). According to the results shown for algorithm F, the smart rebinning further improves the compression performance over simple rebinning by 0.7 to 1.0 dB, with an average of 0.8dB. The

average gain of the arbitrary shape wavelet transform (F) over the padding approach (E) is 0.3dB. Note that the system of algorithm E is very close in complexity to that of the simple rebinning (algorithm D), because both systems use rebinning, rectangular 3D wavelet transform, and arithmetic block coding. The only difference is that algorithm D rebins a fixed number of slits into the panorama, while algorithm E rebins a variable number of slits into the panorama, which is then padded before coding. In terms of PSNR performance, algorithm E outperforms algorithm D by 0.5dB on average. Therefore general smart rebinning with calculated horizontal translation vectors does have an advantage over simple rebinning, where a fixed translation vector is used for all image shots.

Overall, smart rebinning with arbitrary shape wavelet transform and coding is the best performer of the proposed approaches. It outperforms the MPEG-2 concentric mosaic codec by an average of 3.7dB, outperforms the direct 3D wavelet video encoder by 4.3dB, and outperforms the reference block coder by 3.2dB. The PSNR of the smart rebinning compressed *Lobby* at 0.12bpp is even superior to prior concentric mosaic codecs operated at 0.2 bpp. It is 2.1dB superior to the MPEG-2, 2.4dB superior to the direct 3D wavelet, and 1.5dB superior to the RBC compressed scene at 0.2bpp. Since the PSNR of the *Lobby* scene compressed at 0.2bpp is on average 2.1dB higher than the PSNR of the same scene compressed at 0.12bpp, the smart rebinning almost quadruples the compression ratio for the *Lobby* scene. We also observe that the smart rebinning nearly doubles the compression ratio for the *Kids* scene over prior approaches. Considering the huge amount of data of concentric mosaics, and considering the relatively large bitstream even after a high ratio compression has been applied (1.48-7.07MB), smart rebinning is a very effective tool to greatly reduce the amount of data of concentric mosaics.

Algorithm	Test Dataset	LOBBY (0.2 bpp)	LOBBY (0.12 bpp)	KIDS (0.4 bpp)	KIDS (0.24 bpp)
A	MPEG-2	Y: 32.2 U: 38.7 V: 38.1	Y: 30.4 U: 37.4 V: 36.9	Y: 30.1 U: 36.6 V: 36.7	Y: 28.3 U: 34.8 V: 34.9
B	3D Wavelet	Y: 31.9 U: 40.3 V: 39.9	Y: 30.0 U: 39.3 V: 38.9	Y: 29.4 U: 36.5 V: 37.2	Y: 27.3 U: 34.9 V: 35.7
C	RBC	Y: 32.8 U: 39.7 V: 40.5	Y: 29.8 U: 38.4 V: 39.0	Y: 31.5 U: 39.3 V: 38.9	Y: 28.7 U: 37.3 V: 36.6
D	Simple rebinning	Y: 35.5 U: 41.5 V: 40.9	Y: 33.6 U: 40.7 V: 40.2	Y: 32.8 U: 39.3 V: 40.1	Y: 30.5 U: 37.7 V: 38.5
E	Smart rebinning + padding	Y: 36.0 U: 41.6 V: 41.0	Y: 34.0 U: 40.9 V: 40.2	Y: 33.4 U: 39.9 V: 41.1	Y: 31.1 U: 38.4 V: 39.6
F	Smart rebinning +arbitrary shape wavelet codec	Y: 36.3 U: 43.9 V: 42.8	Y: 34.3 U: 42.9 V: 42.0	Y: 33.8 U: 41.1 V: 41.2	Y: 31.3 U: 39.5 V: 39.6

Table 1 Compression results for the concentric mosaic scenes

6. CONCLUSION AND EXTENSION

A technology termed smart rebinning is proposed in this paper to improve the 3D wavelet compression performance of the concentric mosaics. Through cutting and pasting stripes into a set of multi-perspective panoramas, smart rebinning greatly improves the performance of cross shot filtering, and thus improves the transform and coding efficiency of the 3D wavelet codec. The region of support after smart rebinning may cease to be rectangular, and a padding scheme and an arbitrary shape wavelet coding scheme have been used to encode the resultant data volume of smart rebinning. With the arbitrary shape wavelet codec, smart rebinning outperforms MPEG-2 by 3.7dB, outperforms a direct 3D wavelet coder by 4.3dB, and outperforms the reference block coder (RBC) by 3.2dB on the tested concentric mosaic image scenes. It nearly quadruples the compression ratio for the *Lobby* scene, and doubles the compression ratio for the *Kids* scene.

7. ACKNOWLEDGEMENT

The authors would like to acknowledge the following individuals: Harry Shum, Honghui Sun and Minsheng Wu for the raw concentric mosaic data; and Brandon Schwartz for proofreading the paper.

8. REFERENCES

[1] H.-Y. Shum and L.-W. He. "Rendering with concentric mosaics", *Computer Graphics Proceedings, Annual Conference series (SIGGRAPH'99)*, pp. 299-306, Los Angeles, Aug. 1999.

[2] D. Taubman and A. Zakhor, "Multirate 3-D subband coding of video", *IEEE Trans. on Image Processing*, vol. 3, no. 5, pp. 572-588, Sept. 1994.

[3] A. Wang, Z. Xiong, P. A. Chou, and S. Mehrotra, "3D wavelet coding of video with global motion compensation," *Proc. DCC'99*, Snowbird, UT, Mar. 1999.

[4] J. R. Ohm, "Three-dimensional subband coding with motion compensation", *IEEE Trans. on Image Processing*, vol. 3, no. 5, pp. 572-588, Sept. 1994.

[5] J. Y. Tham, S. Ranganath, and A. A. Kassim, "Highly scalable wavelet-based video codec for very low bit-rate environment", *IEEE Journal on Selected Areas in Communications*, vol. 16, no. 1, Jan. 1998.

[6] D. Taubman and A. Zakhor, "A common framework for rate and distortion based scaling of highly scalable compressed video", *IEEE Trans. On Circuits and Systems for Video Technology*, Vol. 6, No. 4, Aug. 1996, pp. 329-354.

[7] L. Luo, Y. Wu, J. Li, and Y.-Q. Zhang, "Compression of concentric mosaic scenery with alignment and 3D wavelet transform", *SPIE Image and Video Communications and Processing*, SPIE 3974-10, San Jose, CA, Jan. 2000.

[8] S. Peleg and J. Herman, "Panoramic mosaics by manifold projection", *IEEE Conference on Computer Vision and Pattern Recognition*, pp. 338-343, San Juan, Jun. 1997.

[9] P. Rademacher and G. Bishop, "Multiple-center-of-projection images", *Computer Graphics Proceedings, Annual Conference series (SIGGRAPH'98)*, pp. 199-206, Orlando, Jul. 1998.

[10] S. Peleg and M. Ben-Ezra, "Stereo panorama with a single camera", *IEEE Conference on Computer Vision and Pattern Recognition*, pp. 395-401, Fort Collins, Jun. 1999.

[11] MPEG-4 Video Verification Model 14.2. *ISO/IEC JTC1/SC29/WG11 5477*, Maui, Dec. 1999.

[12] J. Li and S. Lei, "Arbitrary shape wavelet transform with phase alignment", *Proc. Int'l. Conf. of Image Processing*, Chicago, IL, Oct. 1998.

[13] C. Zhang and J. Li, "Compression and rendering of concentric mosaic scenery with reference block codec (RBC)", *accepted by SPIE Visual Communication and Image Processing (VCIP 2000)*, Perth, Australia, Jun. 2000.

[14] Y. Wu, L. Luo, J. Li and Y. –Q Zhang, "Rendering of 3D wavelet compressed concentric mosaic scenery with progressive inverse wavelet synthesis (PIWS)", *SPIE Visual Communication and Image Processing (VCIP 2000)*, Perth, Australia, Jun. 2000.

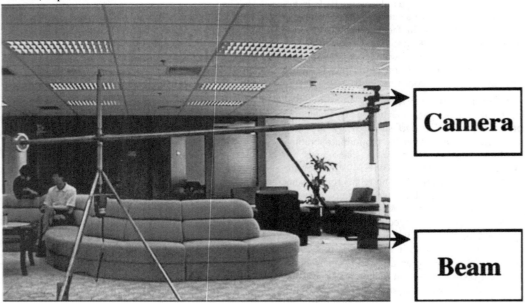

Figure 1: Capturing device of concentric mosaics.

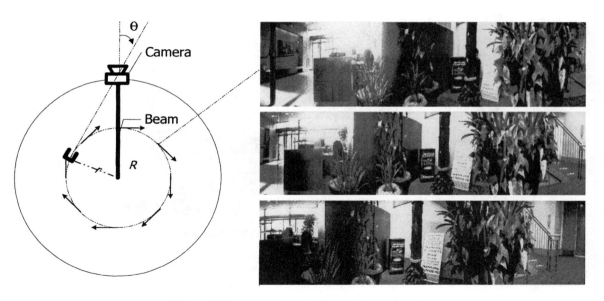

Figure 2 The concentric mosaic imaging geometry

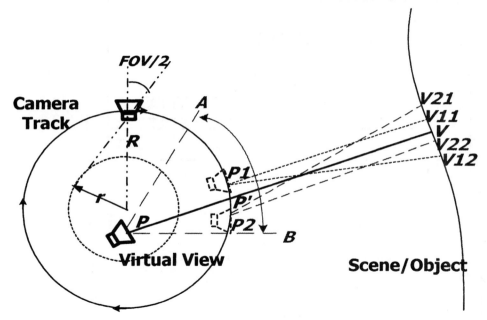

Figure 3 Rendering with concentric mosaics

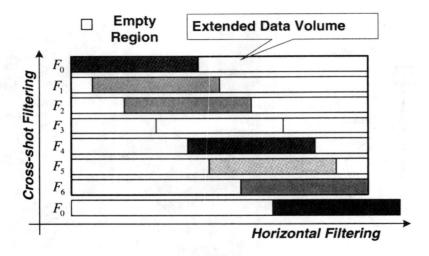

Figure 4 Horizontal shot alignment of concentric mosaic image shots.

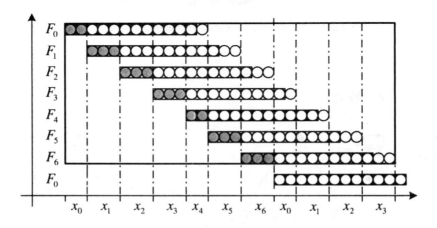

Figure 5 The smart-rebinning process

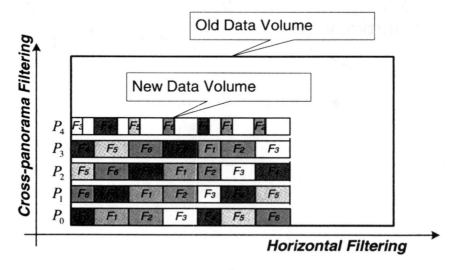

Figure 6 Smart-rebinned data volume

Figure 7 The volume of the concentric mosaics

Figure 8 Part of the volume of the rebinned multi-perspective panorama set

Figure 9 A set of smart-rebinned panoramas at the same horizontal location (note the parallex shown by the lightbulb and the balloon behind the girl).

Caption Processing for MPEG Video in MC-DCT Compressed Domain*

Jongho Nang, Ohyeong Kwon, Seungwook Hong

Dept. of Computer Science and Engineering, Sogang University

1 Shinsoo-Dong, Mapo-Ku, Seoul 121-742, Korea

+82-2-705-8494

jhnang@ccs.sogang.ac.kr

ABSTRACT

The (cinema) caption processing that adds descriptive texts on the sequence of frames is an important video manipulation function that video editor should support. This paper proposes an efficient MC-DCT compressed domain approach to insert the caption into the MPEG-compressed video stream. It basically adds the DCT blocks of the caption image to the corresponding DCT blocks of the input frames one by one in MC-DCT domain as in [5]. However, the strength of the caption image is adjusted in the DCT domain to prevent the resulting DCT coefficients from exceeding the maximum value that is allowed in MPEG. In order to adjust the strength of caption image adaptively, we should know the exact pixel values of input image that is a difficult task in DCT domain. We propose an approximation scheme for the pixel values in which the DC value of a block is used as the expected pixel value for all pixels in that block. Although this approximation may lead some errors in the caption area, it still provides a relatively high image quality in the non-caption area, while the processing time is about 4.9 times faster than the decode-captioning-reencode approach.

Keywords

Caption Processing, MC-DCT Domain, MPEG Video, MPEG Editing

1. INTRODUCTION

The (cinema) caption processing (or *subtitl*ing) which adds some descriptive information in a text form on the top of the sequence of the frames is an important video manipulation function that the video editor should support. The simplest approach to insert the caption for the MC-DCT (Motion Compensation – Discrete Cosine Transform) compressed video is to fully decode the video first, add the caption into the video data in a raw format, and then re-encode the resulting captioned video to the MC-DCT compressed form again. Since this decode-captioning-reencode approach requires a huge amount of computational and storage resources, there have been some researches [1, 2, 3, 4, 5, 6, 9] that directly manipulate the video in the MC-DCT domain. Among these researches, Meng's scheme [5] which inserts the visible watermark mask into the MC-DCT compressed video is a candidate that could be directly used for the caption processing, because basically the caption processing and embedding visible watermark require the same functionality that overlaps one image to another transparently or non-transparently. However, since usually the strength (or distinctness) of the caption is higher than that of visible watermark, the direct application of this scheme to caption processing may cause a problem in the referencing frame in MC-DCT compressed videos. This problem comes from the fact that they did not consider the case in which the strength of the visible watermark mask is too high so that the sum of original pixel value and watermark mask value may exceed a maximum value that is allowed in the MC-DCT compressed video. In this case, the resulting value is normalized to its maximum value and stored in the anchor frame. However, when this resulting (normalized) anchor frame is reconstructed to be referenced by the successive frames for their encodings, the watermark mask value should be subtracted from the stored value in order to build the original anchor frame. Since the watermarked value in the anchor frame is already normalized to its maximum value, the original image could not be reconstructed precisely so that there might be some data blocks with errors in the referencing frames.

* This work is supported by KOSEF (Project Title : *"Development of Non-Linear Editor for MPEG Video Stream,"* 1998.9 ~ 2000.8)

This paper proposes an efficient caption processing scheme that inserts the descriptive information into the MPEG compressed video frames in the MC-DCT compressed domain directly. Basically, it adopts the visible watermark embedding scheme proposed in [5] so that the DCT blocks of caption image are added to the DCT frames of the input video in the DCT or MC-DCT domain. In this scheme, for I frame or intracoded blocks of P- and B-frame, the DCT blocks of caption images are added directly to the DCT blocks of input frames. On the other hand, for the intercoded blocks in P- and B-frame, the DCT blocks of caption image added in the anchor frames are subtracted before adding the DCT block of current caption image to the DCT error residual blocks of current frame as in [5]. However, since just adding the DCT blocks of caption image to the DCT block of input anchor frame may cause a problem as mentioned before, the DCT coefficients of caption block are adjusted with respect to the DCT coefficients of corresponding target image block. This adjustment is designed to have a property that the sum of luminance values of pixel at (n,m) in the caption image and the input frame does not exceed the maximum allowed value. However, since we could not figure out the exact luminance value for each pixel in the input frame in DCT domain, the average of the luminance values of all pixels in the block of input video frame is used as an approximated luminance value for all pixels in that block. This average value is actually the DC coefficient of the block in the DCT domain, and could be obtained in the DCT domain easily. The proposed adjustment and approximation scheme contribute to minimize the errors in the caption processing for the both of intracoded and intercoded blocks in MC-DCT domain, while keeping the decoding and encoding overhead to be minimal. Upon our experiments on the caption processing for the MPEG video streams, although this adjustment may lead some errors in the caption areas because of the approximation of pixel luminance value, it still provides a relatively high image quality in the non-caption area, while the processing time is about 4.9 times faster than the decode-captioning-reencode approach. The caption processing scheme proposed in this paper could be used to insert the strong visible watermark or caption into the MPEG compressed video streams efficiently while keeping the video quality as high as possible with minimal decoding overheads.

2. Previous Works

The caption used in the TV programs and movies is either opaque or transparent and usually surrounded with black borders to maximize the visibility of the characters as shown in Figure 1. The process that inserts this caption to video frame in the spatial domain is formalized as follows [2, 9];

$$P_{new}(i,j) = \alpha(i,j) \times P_a(i,j) + (1 - \alpha(i,j)) \times P_b(i,j) \quad (1)$$

where P_{new}, P_a, P_b, and $\alpha(i,j)$ are the captioned video frame, the input video frame, the caption image, and the transparency factor ($0 \le \alpha(i,j) \le 1$), respectively. If $\alpha(i,j)$ is 1, it is an opaque caption. Otherwise, it is a transparent caption.

<Figure 1> An Example of Captioned Video Frame

The simplest way to insert the caption into an MPEG video is to fully decode the MPEG video stream to raw data, add the captions using Eq. (1) in the spatial domain, and reencode the resulting captioned video to MPEG video streams as shown in Figure 2. However, this approach requires not only a huge amout of computational resources for DCT/IDCT and motion estimation but also a large storages for storing the temporal raw video data. Furthermore, the image qualities of resulting captioned MPEG streams may be degraded because of the repeated quantization and dequantization processes. It has stimulated several researches [2, 3, 9, 10] on the manipulation of images and video streams in DCT or MC-DCT domain directly. Among these researches, there was an approach [8, 9] based on the convolution that directly mainipulated the compressed image and videos in DCT or MC-DCT domain. This approach could be formulated as follows;

$$DCT(P_{new}) = DCT(\alpha) \otimes DCT(P_a) + \\ DCT(1-\alpha) \otimes DCT(P_b) \quad (2)$$

where $DCT(A)$ represents the result of the DCT transformation of block A, and $\otimes$ represents the convolution in the DCT domain. It is actually a DCT domain representation of Eq. (1). Although there are some researches [9] to optimize the convolution process in DCT domain, it still requires too many computations to be used in the real environments.

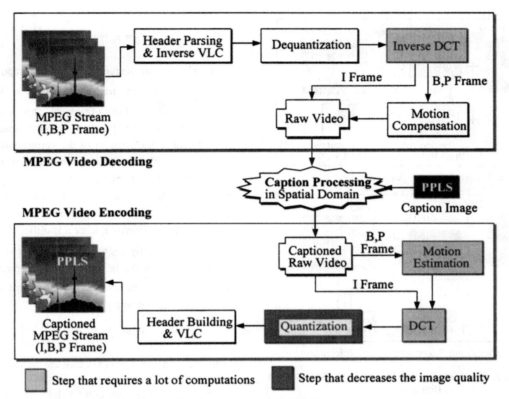

▨ Step that requires a lot of computations	■ Step that decreases the image quality

<Figure 2> Caption Processing in Spatial Domain

Recently, there was an approach [5] to embed the visible watermark to MPEG compressed video in the MC-DCT without the complex convolution operations. The key idea of this scheme is to adjust the strength of the watermark block by block (not pixel by pixel) adaptively with respect to the strength of the blocks in the input video frames so that the resulting watermark will have constant visibility. They show that this operation could be performed in MC-DCT domain directly using the motion compensation technique in DCT domain [2]. Since the embedding of the visible watermark and the caption processing requires the same functionality that overlaps one image to another transparently or non-transparently, we can use this scheme to insert the caption to MPEG video streams in MC-DCT domain. However, since usually the strength of the caption is stronger than that of watermark mask, a direct application of this scheme to caption processing may cause an artifact in the resulting captioned video streams. Let us explain this problem in more detail via an example in the MC-Spatial domain as shown in Figure 3. If the sum of luminance values of pixel at (n,m) of target video frame and the watermark image gets out of the luminance range allowed in MPEG which is [16, 235], the luminance value at (n,m) of resulting watermarked frame is normalized to its maximum value 235 (Figure 3-(a)). It causes a problem when this pixel is referenced by the successive frame in which the added watermark

luminance value is being subtracted again to reconstruct the original anchor frame without watermark. Since the resulting luminance value of the pixel in watermarked image is already normalized to its maximum value 235, the original reference frame could not be reconstructed properly with just subtracting the watermark value from the watermarked frame (Figure 3-(b)). If the strength of the watermark is weak enough (as in embedding visible watermark) so that the result of the addition does not exceed the maximum value, then there would be no problem. However, if the strength of the watermark is strong enough (as in the caption processing), the strength of the watermark should be adjusted adaptively so that the result of the addition would not exceed the maximum value. This problem is the same in the inverse motion compensation in the MC-DCT domain. This paper proposes a scheme to adaptively adjust the strength of the caption image in DCT domain so that the summation does not exceed the allowed range. Of course, Meng and Chang [5] proposed a scaling scheme that adaptively adjusts the strength of the watermark mask based on the local image content, but it was to provide a constant visibility of resulting watermark, not to prevent the errors in the anchor frame reconstruction process.

213

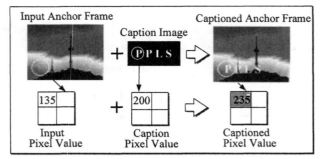

(a) Caption Processing for Anchor Frame

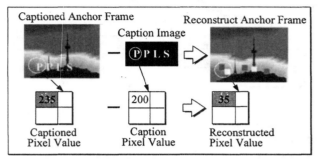

(b) Anchor Frame Reconstruction for Referencing

<Figure 3> An Example of Caption Processing in MC-Spatial Domain

3. A NEW CAPTION PROCESSING in MC-DCT DOMAIN with DC IMAGE

In this section, we propose a caption strength adjustment scheme according to the strength of the input frame in DCT or MC-DCT domain to minimize the errors in the motion compensation process.

3.1 Adaptive Caption Scaling with DC Image

For the errorless reconstruction of the anchor frames, the summation of the luminance values of the pixels in the captioned and input images should not exceed the maximum value allowed in MPEG that is 235 as explained in Figure 3. One way to adaptively adjust the strength of caption image is to decrease the strength of pixel in the caption image if the luminance of the corresponding pixel in the input image is high enough so that the summation would not exceed the maximum value. On the other hand, if the luminance of the corresponding pixel is low enough, the strength of the pixel in caption image is not changed. Since the luminance of pixel in the text area of the caption image usually takes the highest value (that is 235 in MPEG), this mechanism would produce the captioned image in which the luminance of the pixels in the caption area have their maximum values and others have their original values in the input image. One way to satisfy these requirements could be formulated as follows:

$$x'_i = x_i + w_i * \left(1 - \frac{x_i}{235}\right) \quad (3)$$

where x', x, w are the luminance block in captioned image, input image, and caption image, respectively, and x'_i, x_i, w_i are luminance values of their i-th pixels. This equation implies that the strength of the pixel in caption image is decreased proportional to the strength of the corresponding pixel in input image so that the summation would not exceed the maximum luminance value. As shown in Eq. (3), the strength of the each pixel in the caption image that are added adaptively to the input image could be calculated exactly if we know the luminance value of each pixel x_i. However, since it is difficult to know its value in DCT domain directly, the average luminance value of the pixels in the block x, $e(x)$, is used in the proposed scheme as an approximation for all pixels in x. Using this approximation, we obtain following equation from Eq. (3);

$$x'_i = x_i + w_i * \left(1 - \frac{e(x)}{235}\right) \quad (4)$$

In this equation, if $x_i < e(x)$, then the computed x'_i is as less as $w_i * \frac{x_i - e(x)}{235}$ than the exact value computed using Eq. (3). However, since the resulting value still does not exceed the maximum value, it would be no problem in the reconstruction phase. On the other hand, if $x_i > e(x)$, then the actual x'_i is as bigger as $w_i * \frac{x_i - e(x)}{235}$ than the exact value computed using Eq. (3). In this case, since the resulting value exceeds the maximum value, it may cause an error again in the reconstruction phase. The formulae in Eq. (4) could be transform to DCT domain as follows;

$$X' = X + W * \left(1 - \frac{DC(X)}{1880}\right) \quad (5)$$

where X', X, W are the DCT block of x', x, w, respectively, and $DC(X)$ is the DC coefficient of block x that can be easily obtained in the DCT domain.

3.2 Inserting Caption in DCT and MC-DCT Domain

The caption image is converted to a gray scale image because the caption is only added to luminance channel of the input video frame. All pixels in the transparent region are set to 0 so that the addition of their values to target image pixels has no effects on the captioned image. Let W' be the DCT coefficients of the block in caption image that are adjusted and added to the input image;

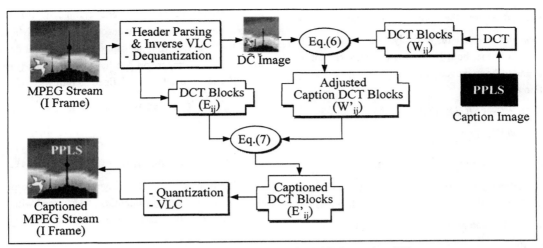

<Figure 4> Caption Processing in DCT Domain : I-Frame

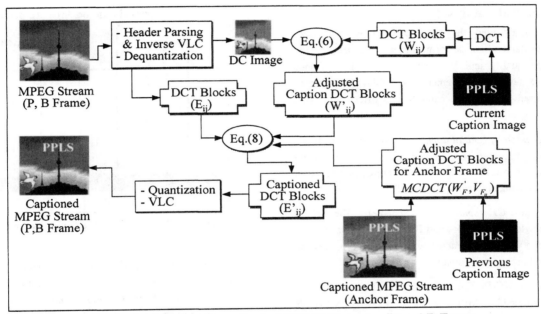

<Figure 5> Caption Processing in MC-DCT Domain : P- and B-Frame

$$W' = W * \left(1 - \frac{DC(X)}{1880}\right) \quad (6)$$

Once these DCT coefficients are computed for each block, they are inserted into the DCT frames of the input video differently for each of three macroblock types. This process is the same as the one for embedding the visible watermark in MC-DCT domain proposed in [5]. Let us explain this process roughly. For I-frame or intracoded blocks in B- or P-frames, the DCT of scaled watermark mask is added directly,

$$E'_{ij} = E_{ij} + W'_{ij} \quad (7)$$

where E'_{ij}, E_{ij}, and W'_{ij} are the ij-th DCT blocks of the

captioned frame, the input frame, and the adjusted caption image, respectively. This process is performed in DCT domain directly as shown in Figure 4.

For the blocks with forward motion vector in P frame (or backward motion vector in B frame), the caption image added in the anchor frame needs to be subtracted before adding the current caption image in the current frame. The resulting residual is,

$$E'_{ij} = E_{ij} - MCDCT(W'_F, V_{F_{ij}}) + W'_{ij} \quad (8)$$

where $MCDCT()$ is the motion compensation function performed in DCT domain as described in [2]. W'_F is the caption DCT used in the forward anchor frame, and $V_{F_{ij}}$ is the motion

215

vector. E_{ij} and E_{ij}' are the original and new motion compensation residual errors, respectively. For bidirectional predicted blocks in B frame, both forward and backward motion compensation needs to be averaged and subtracted while adding the current caption as follows;

$$E_{ij}' = E_{ij} - (MCDCT(W_F', V_{Fij}) + MCDCT(W_B', V_{Bij}))/2 + W_{ij}' \qquad (9)$$

where V_{Fij} and V_{Bij} is the forward and backward motion vector respectively. This process is performed in the MC-DCT domain as shown in Figure 5. Note that these processing mechanisms are basically the same as the one proposed in [5] except that W_{ij}' is computed differently.

4. Experimental Analyses

We have implemented the proposed caption processing scheme, and evaluated the performance with respect to the produced image quality and its speed. For the performance comparisons, we have also implemented the following schemes that could be used to insert the caption to MPEG compressed video;

- *Processing in totally Spatial domain* (Spatial Scheme): It is a decode-captioning-reencode method in which the MPEG compressed video is fully decoded, the caption is inserted in the spatial domain, and reencoded to MPEG video.

- *Processing in DCT domain* (DCT Scheme) : The MPEG compressed video with I-, P-, and B-frames is converted into MPEG video with only I-frames, and the caption processing is performed in the DCT domain.

- *Processing in MC-DCT domain* (MC-DCT Scheme): The caption is inserted into MPEG compressed video in MC-DCT domain using the method proposed in [5].

- *Processing in MC-DCT domain with DC Image* (Ours : MC-DCT(DC) scheme) : It is the same as the one proposed in [5], but the strength of the caption image is adjusted according to its DC image to prevent the errors in the motion compensation using Eq. (5).

All of above four implementations read the same MPEG stream, process the captions, and output the captioned MPEG stream. The GOP pattern of MPEG stream used in the experiments is IBBPBBPBBPBBPBB.

Let us first compare the image qualities of captioned MPEG streams produced by above four schemes. The resulting four captioned MPEG streams are decoded to PPM files with the public domain decoder [7], and compared with the captioned images that are generated by decoding the input MPEG streams to PPM files and inserting the caption in the spatial domain. For the image quality comparison, we have used PSNR (Peak Signal-to-Noise Ratio) values that are defined as follows;

$$PSNR(X,Y) = 20\log_{10} \frac{255}{\sqrt{\frac{1}{MN}\sum_{i=1}^{M}\sum_{j=1}^{N}(X_{ij} - Y_{ij})^2}} \ dB$$

where M and N are the sizes of the image, and X_{ij} and Y_{ij} are the (i,j)-th pixels in the image X and Y, respectively. The comparison of the image qualities is performed with respect to the areas that are influenced by the caption processing as shown in Figure 6.

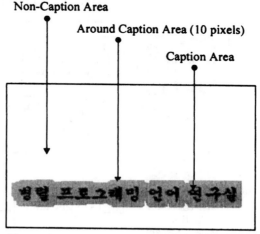

<Figure 6> Example of Image Divisions for Quality Comparisons

Figure 7 shows an experimental image quality comparison of the four caption processing schemes with respect to the three areas, while Figure 8 shows their examples visually. Let us analyze these experimental results in more details. Figure 7-(a) shows the experimental PSNR values of four caption processing schemes in the caption area. As shown in this figure, our approach (MC-DCT(DC)) produces a lower PSNR than the spatial and DCT domain approaches in caption area because it adaptively decreases the strength of the caption image according to the contents of the input image frame. On the other hand, it produces a higher PSNR value except I-frame than MC-DCT approach because it adjusts the strength of the caption image not to exceed the maximum value so that it could minimize the errors in the anchor frame reconstruction process. The image quality of the around caption area (10 pixels far from the caption) is also compared, and its experimental results is shown in Figure 7-(b). As shown in this figure, all processing schemes except Meng's scheme (MC-DCT) produce almost the same PSNR values. It is mainly because the

Meng's scheme did not adjust the caption strengths with respect to the strength of the input video frame image as explained in Figure 3. However, for the I-frames, both of the MC-DCT and MC-DCT(DC) schemes produce the same PSNR values because

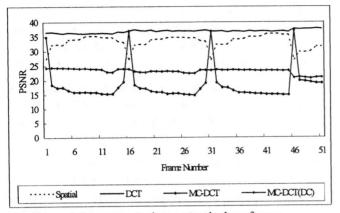

there is no motion compensation process in these frames.

(a) Image Quality in Caption Area

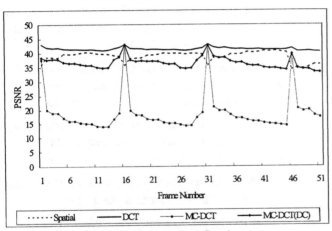

(b) Image Quality in Around Caption Area

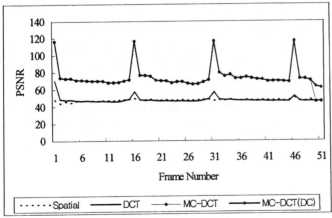

(c) Image Quality in Non Caption Area

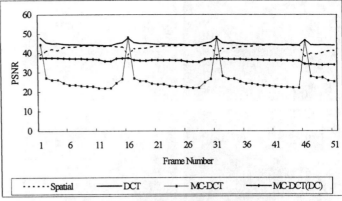

(d) Overall Image Quality

<Figure 7> An Experimental Image Quality Comparison

Since the non-caption area is not affected by the caption processing, theoretically there should be no image quality degradation in this area. However, since the spatial domain approach requires a full decoding of MPEG stream for the caption processing (VLC-Dequantization-MC-IDCT-CaptionProcessing-DCT-MC-Quantization-VLC), the image quality of the non-caption area is also degraded as shown in Figure 7-(c). Furthermore, the DCT domain approach also requires to convert the P- and B-frame to I-frame for caption processing and it requires to decode the video to the spatial domain, it also introduces a quality degradation. On the other hand, MC-DCT and MC-DCT(DC) approaches do not require the full decoding of MPEG stream for caption processing, the image quality could be kept in the non caption area as shown in Figure 7-(c). Actually, all steps except the quantization/dequantization are theoretically lossless compressions so that there would be no more errors in the other processes, but practically small errors in the DCT/IDCT could introduce a non-negligible error in quantization/dequantization process. It is the reason why MC-DCT and MC-DCT(DC) approach could produce a high image quality in the non-caption area. Figure 7-(d) shows the overall image qualities of the four caption processing schemes. As shown in this figure, the proposed scheme (MC-DCT(DC) approach) may produce a higher image quality than MC-DCT approach, and a lower image quality than spatial and DCT approaches. But since it processes the caption in MC-DCT domain so that could skip the DCT/IDCT and motion estimation process, the execution time is about 4.9 times faster than that of spatial domain approach as shown in Table 1. It shows the average caption processing time per frame of four schemes on Pentium PC.

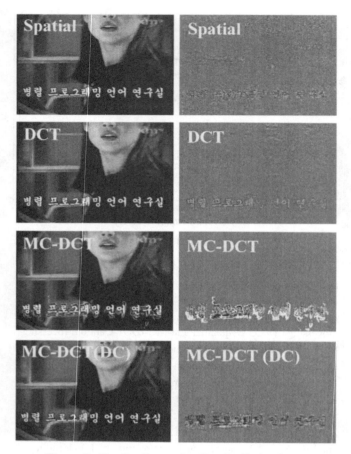

<Figure 8> Caption Processing Results (Left : Captioned Image, Right : Embedded Error Image)

<Table 1> Experimental Average Processing Time (Sec/Frame)

	Spatial	DCT	MC-DCT	MC-DCT(DC)
Time	0.53	0.41	0.11	0.11

5. CONCLUDING REMARKS

This paper proposes a caption processing scheme that could be directly applied in the MC-DCT domain while keeping the image quality as high as possible. This scheme basically follows the MC-DCT domain approach proposed in [5], however, it adjusts the strength of the caption image in order not to exceed the maximum value allowed in MPEG. To adjust the strength of the caption image, it uses the DC image of the input frame as an approximation of the source image. Since this DC value can be obtained in MC-DCT domain easily, the proposed scheme could adjust the caption strength easily while keeping the decoding overhead as small as possible. Upon on the experimental results, we could argue that although there are still some errors in the captioned image because of the approximation scheme, the proposed scheme could produce a higher quality captioned MPEG stream than the other MC-DCT domain scheme, while keeping the caption processing time to be about 4.9 times faster than the spatial domain approach.

6. References

[1] Soam Acharya and Brian Smith, "Compressed Domain Transcoding of MPEG," *Proc. of IEEE International Conference on Multimedia Computing and Systems*, Jul. 1998.

[2] Shih-Fu Chang and David G. Messerschmitt, "Manipulation and Compositing of MC-DCT Compressed Video," *IEEE Journal on Selected Areas in Communications*, Vol. 13, No. 1, Jan. 1995.

[3] Vrkrant Kobla and David Doerman, "Compressed Domain Video Indexing Techniques Using DCT and Motion Vector Information in MPEG Video," *Proc. of SPIE Conf. on Storage and Retrieval for Image and Video Databases V*, Vol. 3022, Feb.1997.

[4] Jianhao Meng and Shih-Fu Chang, "CVEPS: A Compressed Video Editing and Parsing System," *Proc. of ACM Multimedia 96 Conference*, Nov. 1996.

[5] Jianhao Meng and Shih-Fu Chang, "Embedding Visible Video Watermarks in the Compressed Domain," *Proc. of ICIP International Conference on Image Processing*, Oct. 1998.

[6] Neri Merhav and Vasudev Bhaskaran, *A Fast Algorithm for DCT-Domain Inverse Motion Compensation*, HPL Technical Report #HPL-95-17, Sep. 1995.

[7] MPEG Software Simulation Group, MPEG-2 Video Codec, Available from http://www.mpeg.org/MPEG/MSSG.

[8] Bo Shen and Ishwar K. Sethi, "Inner-Block Operations On Compressed Images," *Proc. of ACM Multimedia 95 Conference*, Nov. 1995.

[9] Bo Shen, Ishwar K. Sethi and Vasudev Bhaskaran, "DCT Convolution and Its Application in Compressed Video Editing," *Proc. of SPIE 3024 in Visual Communications and Image Processing*, Feb. 1997.

[10] Bo Shen, Ishwar K. Sethi, and V. Bhaskaran, "Closed-loop MPEG Video Rendering," *Proc. of IEEE Conference on Multimedia Computing Systems*, Jun. 1997.

New Enhancements to Cut, Fade, and Dissolve Detection Processes in Video Segmentation

Ba Tu Truong
Department of Computer Science
Curtin University of Technology
GPO Box U1987, Perth, 6845, W. Australia
truongbt@cs.curtin.edu.au

Chitra Dorai
IBM T. J. Watson Research Center
P.O. Box 704, Yorktown Heights
New York 10598, USA
dorai@watson.ibm.com

Svetha Venkatesh
Department of Computer Science
Curtin University of Technology
GPO Box U1987, Perth, 6845, W. Australia
svetha@cs.curtin.edu.au

ABSTRACT

We present improved algorithms for cut, fade, and dissolve detection which are fundamental steps in digital video analysis. In particular, we propose a new adaptive threshold determination method that is shown to reduce artifacts created by noise and motion in scene cut detection. We also describe new two-step algorithms for fade and dissolve detection, and introduce a method for eliminating false positives from a list of detected candidate transitions. In our detailed study of these gradual shot transitions, our objective has been to accurately classify the type of transitions (fade-in, fade-out, and dissolve) and to precisely locate the boundary of the transitions. This distinguishes our work from other early work in scene change detection which tends to focus primarily on identifying the existence of a transition rather than its precise temporal extent. We evaluate our improved algorithms against two other commonly used shot detection techniques on a comprehensive data set, and demonstrate the improved performance due to our enhancements.

Categories and Subject Descriptors

[Information Storage and Retrieval]: Information Search and Retrieval; [Database Management]: Systems—*Multimedia Databases*; [Multimedia]: Multimedia Processing and Coding

1. INTRODUCTION

Video segmentation, often performed by detecting transitions occurring between shots in a digital video stream, is a fundamental process in automatic video analysis since it results in disjoint contiguous video segments that can serve as basic units to be indexed, annotated, and browsed. A shot in a video is defined as an unbroken sequence of images of a real or animated world captured between a camera's "record"

and "stop" operations [7]. Shots are joined together in the editing stage of video (post) production with either sharp cuts between them or using gradual visual effects such as fades and dissolves to form a complete story sequence and to provide a certain narrative structure to events portrayed in the video. Detecting shots and the type of transitions used to link them is extremely useful in analyzing the inter shot relationships for high level video interpretation and program genre categorization. It is also useful in improving video compression [1].

The purpose of this paper is to revisit the problem of shot transition detection (STD) and study techniques for automatic STD in the light of requirements relating to robustness, accuracy of detection, and precise temporal characterization, all stemming from our ongoing work on building video annotation systems that are expected to function reliably in real-world scenarios. Due to the fundamental importance of the problem of shot detection and the existence of many different types of transitions such as cut, fade, dissolve, and wipe, automatic STD has received wide attention in the research community and many excellent techniques have been proposed [1, 2, 5, 7, 10, 19]. However, we found in our study of several of these that many enhancements could be designed to render them more accurate and robust especially when dealing with a wide range of ways in which transitions are produced in videos of many different genres. In detecting gradual transitions, we also realized that the existing techniques do not focus as much on accurately classifying and measuring the temporal extent of transitions as needed in automatic video processing systems for deployment in digital studios. Further, we aimed to test the algorithms on a comprehensive data set. Presently, we limit our attention to cuts, fades, and dissolves in our work, since we observed with our experimental video collection that wipe transitions are quite uncommon, accounting for less than 0.5 percent of all transitions and found that we could safely ignore wipe detection without any consequences on our system goals.

This paper proposes the following enhancements to algorithms that detect scene changes. First, building on the current work on shot transition detection [19], we propose a new adaptive thresholding mechanism that would reduce the effects of noise, motion, and other artifacts on the frame histogram difference curves, and at the same time accentuate peaks caused by real shot cuts. This leads to notable improvements in the performance of the hard cut detector.

We next augment existing approaches based on production models for detecting fades and dissolves [1, 2] with our new two-step algorithms. In our approach, instead of selecting thresholds based on traditional *trial-and-error* mechanisms, robust adaptive thresholds are derived analytically from the mathematical models of these transitions. Third, we propose a simple, yet effective technique for eliminating false positives from a list of detected transitions. This process is performed after cut, fade, and dissolve detectors have been executed on video streams. Finally, our algorithms have been tested on variety of data and their performance shown to be more accurate and reliable when compared with two commonly used STD methods including a commercial software.

2. PREVIOUS WORK

Among many aspects of video editing, our paper focuses on (i) the moment chosen to change from one shot to another (*cutting point*) and (ii) how the change is made (cut, fade, dissolve, and other effects) and the speed of this transition in produced videos of different genres.

Among the types of shot transitions considered, {cut, fade, dissolve}, the cut is an instantaneous change from one shot to another and can be seen as the shortest distance between two shots. There are two types of fades: fade-in and fade-out. A fade-out occurs when the picture information gradually disappears, leaving a blank screen. A fade-in occurs when the picture gradually appears from a blank screen. A fade-in from or fade-out to black is the most common; however, it is possible to fade-in or fade-out from any other colour. A dissolve occurs when one whole picture fades away while another whole picture is appearing.

2.1 Review of STD Techniques

For a comprehensive review of STD techniques, we refer the reader to [17]. The earliest and simplest technique for hard cut detection uses pixel-wise comparision of successive frames [15]. Some well known hard scene cut detection techniques employ color histograms which are compared using different metrics [19, 16] or with *twin-comparison* [21]. The algorithms primarily differ in the selection of an appropriate color space to compute the histograms and in the functions used to determine the similarity between two histograms.

Much research in gradual transition detection has been carried out by analyzing the production models of these effects [7, 6]. Instead of exploiting intensity changes in individual pixels in video frames, [1], [14], [2], and [12] investigate the effect of the production models on frame luminance mean and variance. During an ideal dissolve or fade, the mean changes in a linear manner, while the variance has a parabolic or half parabolic shape. [1] detects dissolves by first recording all negative spikes in the second order derivative of frame variances and ensuring that the luminance means within a dissolve region do not change sign. [14] records all successive peaks and the valleys between them on the variance curve as indications of parabolic

regions caused by dissolves. Conditions are further imposed to verify that the dissolves are wide enough and the valleys are deep enough. [2] detects fades by recording all negative spikes in the second derivative of the variance curve and ensuring that the first derivative of the mean curve is relatively constant next to a negative spike. [12] detects fades by fitting a regression line on the frame standard deviation curve. Other algorithms, some based on edges [20, 12] and some using temporal analysis of slices obtained from video sequences [9] also exist. Some techniques [4, 19, 14, 11] utilize information available in MPEG compressed video streams such as DCT coefficients, bit rate, motion vectors, and macro block types to detect scene discontinuities.

2.2 Threshold Selection Mechanisms

While finding appropriate features and metrics to compare two consecutive frames is well researched, the problem of interpreting the frame difference values such that certain values can be selected to indicate shot changes, continues to be a major challenge. Proper selection of difference values is usually done by setting thresholds. [21] proposes a statistical approach for determining the threshold, based on the mean value μ and the standard deviation δ of frame-to-frame differences. A window based approach in which shot detection takes place at the center value of a temporal window [19, 3, 8], also investigated in our work, can improve thresholding since it is more appropriate to treat a shot change as a local activity. One requirement with the window-approach is that the window size should be set so that it is unlikely that two shots occur within the window. Therefore, the center value in the window must be the largest frame-to-frame difference in the window. [19] selects the threshold based on the second largest value within the window. [3] divides all points within the window into two clusters depending on the distance from each point to the largest and the lowest points. The threshold is then set based on the distance between the two clusters. If the distance is below a threshold, the threshold will be set just above the upper cluster; otherwise, it will be set as half of the distance between the clusters. [8] combines the sliding-window approach and general statistical models for the frame-to-frame difference curve to detect hard cuts.

3. IMPROVED HARD CUT DETECTION

Color histogram difference has proved to be the most simple, yet effective method for detecting hard cuts. The color histogram of a frame, f_i whose width and height are given by $\mathbb{N}_1^X$ and $\mathbb{N}_1^Y$ respectively is computed from its pixel luminance as:

$$f_i^{\mathcal{H}}[k] = |\mathcal{B}_k|, \quad \mathcal{B}_k = \{(x, y) \in \mathbb{N}_1^X \times \mathbb{N}_1^Y \mid f_i(x, y) = k\}. \tag{1}$$

The color histogram difference, $t_i^{\mathcal{H}}$ between two consecutive frames f_i and f_{i+1} is then computed as the sum of absolute bin-wise differences:

$$t_i^{\mathcal{H}} = \sum_{k=1}^{K} (|f_i^{\mathcal{H}}[k] - f_{i+1}^{\mathcal{H}}[k]|), \quad K \text{ is the number of bins.} \tag{2}$$

Unlike approaches using global thresholds on the difference of color histograms, we propose a simple adaptive thresholding technique to detect peaks in the histogram difference curve.

For each frame transition t_i that stands for a feature vector containing all features computed jointly from frame f_i and f_{i+1}, which in this case is the histogram difference, we consider a sliding window of size $2w+1$ along the temporal axis, $\mathcal{T}$ that covers frame transitions $t_{i-w}, \ldots, t_{i+w}$. A hard cut between frame f_i and f_{i+1} is declared if all the following conditions are satisfied.

1. $t_i^{\mathcal{H}}$ has the maximum value within the window. This means $t_i^{\mathcal{H}} \geq t_j^{\mathcal{H}}, i-w \leq j \leq i+w$. This step is similar to one used in [19].

2. We additionally employ the fact that in a true cut, $t_i^{\mathcal{H}}$ is some α times greater than the mean of all $t_j^{\mathcal{H}}$ within the window excluding $t_i^{\mathcal{H}}$ itself. In order to guard against the case when f_i and f_{i+1} are surrounded by "freeze" frames that result in the value of this mean being approximately zero, in which case it is difficult to select an appropriate threshold, we add a constant c to both mean and the value of $t_i^{\mathcal{H}}$. The value used for c is 0.8. Thus, the adaptive threshold for this scene cut is determined to be the one that satisfies

$$t_i^{\mathcal{H}} + c \geq \alpha \frac{\sum_{j=i-w, j\neq i}^{i+w}(t_j^{\mathcal{H}} + c)}{2w}. \qquad (3)$$

There are some ways to further enhance the algorithm and reduce the computation time. First, we can use a global threshold to determine all potential cut transitions t_i, and sliding windows are applied only to these frames, and all the rest can be ignored. This global threshold should be small allowing all cuts to be detected. In addition, if t_i is declared as a cut transition, then it is possible to proceed directly to t_{i+w+1} without checking $t_{i+1}, \ldots, t_{i+w}$, since the color histogram difference of these frames will be less than t_i and the first criterion [19] will not be satisfied.

In fact, if we map the color histogram difference curve into the local mean-ratio space (the value at each frame is now equal to its original value divided by the mean of the window by which it is enveloped; we also add the constant c to it), then the adaptive threshold presented above becomes a fixed threshold i.e., α. The value of the new curve at frame i is computed as:

$$t_i^{\mathcal{H}^*} = \frac{t_i^{\mathcal{H}} + c}{\frac{\sum_{j=i-w, j\neq i}^{i+w}(t_j^{\mathcal{H}} + c)}{2w}}. \qquad (4)$$

Figure 1(a) shows the color histogram difference curve with a global threshold and with the curve connecting our adaptive thresholds. Figure 1(b) shows the transformed color histogram difference for a window of size $w = 5$ and threshold $\alpha = 1.2$. All cut points, whose histogram difference is beyond the computed threshold, are marked by little circles. Under close examination, the global threshold causes a false positive at near frame 200, while the adaptive threshold does not. More importantly, Figure 1(a) shows other potentials for false positives due to object and camera motion near frame 200, 300, 500 600, and 800 if a global threshold is used, while these artifacts are significantly reduced in Figure 1(b). Two important aspects of this improved algorithm can thus be summarized to be (i) the use of local mean-ratio to reduce the effect of noise and motion, and (ii) the addition of a constant to accentuate peaks caused by real shot cuts and to ease the process of selecting an appropriate threshold.

4. ENHANCED FADE DETECTION

We start with the production model of a fade as presented in [2]. Fade-in and fade-out often occur together as a *fade group*. More specifically, a fade group starts with a shot fading out to a color $\mathcal{C}$ which is then followed by a sequence of monochrome frames of color $\mathcal{C}$, and it ends with a shot fading in from color $\mathcal{C}$. Fade groups formed this way are often referred to as a single fade. Alattar [2] detects fades by recording all negative spikes in the second derivative of the frame luminance variance curve and ensuring that the first derivative of the mean curve is relatively constant next to a negative spike. [12] proposes detecting fades by fitting a regression line on the frame standard deviation curve. We present further extensions to these techniques.

During fade transitions, as detailed in [17], frame luminance mean values move linearly towards $\mathcal{C}$, the fading color (see Figure 2(a)), while variance curves of fade-out and fade-in frame sequences have a half-parabolic shape independent of $\mathcal{C}$ (see Figure 2(b) showing the variance curve for a video segment with 2 pairs of fade-in/fade-out).

The salient features of our enhanced two-step fade detection algorithm are the following:

1. Existence of monochrome frames is a very good clue for detecting all potential fades, and they are used in our algorithm as the first step in recognizing the existence of a fade. In a quick fade, the monochrome sequence may last only one frame while in a slower fade it would last up to 100 frames. However, we can apply a smaller constraint (e.g., 2 sec.) on the length of fade-in and fade-out components. Therefore, locating monochrome frames forms our algorithm's first step.

2. Earlier work [2] shows that large negative spikes appear near the start of a fade-out and near the end of a fade-in on the second derivative curve of luminance variance. While [2] uses only these negative spikes for detecting dissolves, we observe that motion also would cause such spikes. It can be seen from our simulations shown in Figure 3(a) that two relatively large negative spikes are actually present at the end of the fade-in (near frame 420), and only the second spike corresponds to a real boundary. Therefore, for robustness we should search for all spikes near a monochrome sequence until conditions discussed in the next step (3) are not satisfied. This forms the second step of our algorithm.

3. The first derivative of mean remains relatively constant and does not change its sign during a fade-out or a fade-in (see Figure 3(b)). Since in real videos, the mean feature would be distorted by motion, some

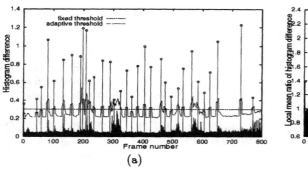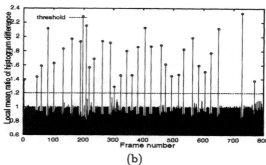

Figure 1: Hard cut: (a) Color histogram differences $t_i^{\mathcal{H}}$; (b) the local mean-ratio transform $t_i^{\mathcal{H}^*}$.

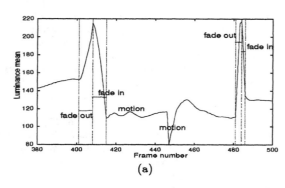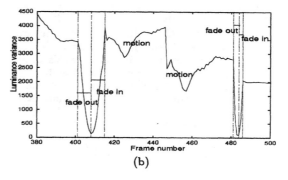

Figure 2: (a) Mean and (b) variance curves during a fade.

smoothing operation needs be applied to the mean difference curve before examining *the constancy of its sign* within a potential fade region. Similarly, as shown in Figure 2(b), depending on whether it is a fade-in or a fade-out, the variance of fading frames will increase or decrease rapidly. This establishes another constraint for testing the existence of fades in our algorithm.

4. We also limit the variance of the starting frame of a fade-out and the ending frame of a fade-in to be above a threshold to eliminate false positives caused by dark scenes, thus preventing them from being considered as monochrome frames.

5. IMPROVED DISSOLVE DETECTION

Our approach to dissolve detection is based again on the production model of an ideal dissolve. A fade can be considered as a special dissolve where one shot is composed of monochrome frames. Therefore, similar to a fade, during a dissolve transition, the luminance mean curve changes in a linear fashion, while the luminance variance curve has a parabolic shape. This means the first order difference of the mean curve should be constant during a dissolve (see Figure 4(a)), while that of the variance curve should change in a linear fashion (Figure 4(b)). If we take the second order difference of the luminance variance curve, two large negative spikes should appear at the start and end of the dissolve similar to the case of fade transitions. In fact, this feature is the basis for dissolve detection approach proposed by [1]. However, our study of real dissolves suggests that these neg-

ative spikes are not easily obvious during a dissolve when compared to fades due to noise and motion. Therefore, we ignore these negative spikes in our dissolve algorithm. Instead, we look for other clues that can signal the existence of a dissolve, and for various constraints to eliminate false positives. Let the two shots producing the dissolves be with luminance variances v_1 and v_2, respectively. We assume that shots making up a dissolve have variance of at least T_v and that the duration of a dissolve never exceeds T_l frames (T_l depends on the video frame rate). The first assumption can at times lead to misses, since dissolves near monochrome frames do exist, albeit relatively uncommon. The second assumption is very reasonable, since it is unlikely to have a dissolve lasting longer than 2 seconds. Based on these assumptions, the following steps form the basis of our dissolve detection algorithm.

1. Developing further the mathematical model of a dissolve starting at frame s and ending at frame e presented in [1], we algebraically establish that the first order difference t_i^v of the variance curve changes linearly from a negative value of $-\frac{2(e-s)-1}{(e-s)^2}v_1$ $(< -\frac{2T_v-1}{T_l})$ at frame s to a positive value of $\frac{2(e-s)-1}{(e-s)^2}$ $(> \frac{2T_v-1}{T_l})$ at frame $e-1$ (See appendix for the derivation of these formulae). Therefore, the existence of all dissolves can be triggered by all zero crossing sequences in the t_i^v curve whose start value is below a negative threshold, which then continuously increases, and then the end value is above a positive threshold. Figure 4(b)

222

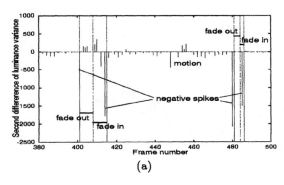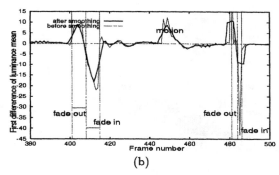

(a)   (b)

Figure 3: Fade: (a) The second derivative of luminance variance values during a fade; (b) the first derivative of luminance mean values.

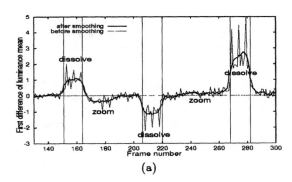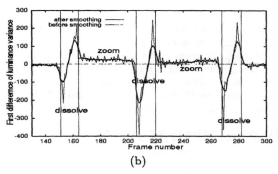

(a)   (b)

Figure 4: Dissolve: The first order difference of (a) mean and (b) variance curves during a dissolve.

illustrates clearly this property. In the actual implementation, to reduce the effect of noise and motion we smooth out the curve before searching for these zero crossing sequences.

2. Due to the smoothing operation, the position of the negative and positive peaks of the t_i^v curve caused by a dissolve is no longer coincident with its actual position in the ideal case. We can adjust these positions by moving the position of the negative peak backward until the value of t_i^v increases beyond a negative threshold. Similarly, the position of the positive peak is moved forward until the value of t_i^v drops below a positive threshold.

3. The variance curve f_i^v has a parabolic shape during a dissolve. Solving the quadratic equation 8 with respect to i shows that this parabolic curve attains the minimum value of $\frac{v_1 v_2}{v_1 + v_2}$ at frame number $\eta = \frac{ev_1 + sv_2}{v_1 + v_2}$ (we ignore the fact that frame number must be an integer). From this, we have:

$$f_s^v - f_\eta^v = \frac{v_1^2}{v_1 + v_2} \text{ and } f_e^v - f_\eta^v = \frac{v_2^2}{v_1 + v_2}. \quad (5)$$

Figure 5(a) simulates the the plotting of $\frac{v_1^2}{v_1 + v_2}$ against v_1. This and the plot of the second part of this equation in Figure 5(b) together show that all points lie below a line, say $y = x/4 - 200$; therefore, the difference between the start frame and the middle frame of a dissolve should be greater than $\frac{v_1}{4} - 200$. The

same condition applies to the difference between the end frame and middle frame of a dissolve. In addition, we have:

$$f_s^v + f_e^v - 2f_\eta^v = \frac{v_1^2 + v_2^2}{v_1 + v_2} > \frac{v_1 + v_2}{2}. \quad (6)$$

By now we already have a set of constraints on the shape of the parabolic curve to eliminate false positives caused by motion. However, these conditions only guide us to set appropriate thresholds. In order to cope with the effects of noise and motion, in the algorithm implementation we use lower thresholds.

6. FALSE POSITIVE TRANSITION ELIMINATION

Excluding complex graphics transition effects, changes in lighting, noise, object and camera motion all lead to false detection by STD algorithms. While those caused by long and fast camera operation can be eliminated by performing the "motion transition removal" test [10, 21], we propose a simple method based on color histogram differences for eliminating other kinds of false positives. Frames belonging to the same shot should be similar if there is no transition in the scene space, say due to camera movements. After detecting cuts, fades and dissolves, for each declared transition, we examine the shot preceding the transition and the shot succeeding it. This transition is deemed a false positive if the difference between an arbitrary frame from the

223

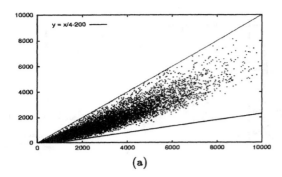 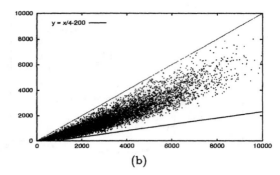

Figure 5: **Hints for threshold selection in dissolve detection: (a) Plot of** $\frac{v_1^2}{v_1+v_2}$ **against** v_1; **(b) Plot of** $\frac{v_2^2}{v_1+v_2}$ **against** v_2.

first shot and some arbitrary frame from the second shot is less than an empirically determined threshold. This technique can effectively prevent common effects such as flash lights, close-up objects moving in front of the camera, key-in, and other momentary noise. For computational efficiency, quantized color histograms can be stored in disks, thereby avoiding the second decoding of videos.

7. EXPERIMENTAL RESULTS

In order to test our enhanced transition detection algorithms on a diverse data set, we collected around 8 hours of video data from TV programs of news, commercials, sports, music, and cartoons telecast on different channels on different days and at different times, and encoded them in the MPEG-1 format. Some clips were recorded more than 5 years ago. A portion of this set (about 1 and 1/2 to 2 hours of data) was used to test the proposed algorithms and it contained a total of 1373 cuts, 297 dissolve transitions, and 111 fades. Table 1 summarizes the data used for testing shot transition detection algorithms in terms of number of cuts, dissolves, fades and their total duration for each video genre. We compared the performance of our algorithms with WebFlix, a commercial tool available for editing MPEG videos and also with an implementation of a simple version of the twin-comparison technique [21]. Instead of fine tuning the latter [21], we employed 5 pairs of thresholds, and for each test video and for each type of transition, we chose its best result and used it for comparison.

7.1 Performance Parameters

Recall and precision concepts from the IR field [18] have been often used to evaluate the performance of cut detectors. Unlike cuts, gradual transitions cover a range of frames; therefore, we need to adapt the concepts of recall and precision to include the characteristics of gradual transitions. Let $\bar{\Psi}^x = \{\bar{S}_1^x, \bar{S}_2^x, \ldots, \bar{S}_{k_x}^x\}$ denote the set of all transitions of type x as declared by an automatic detector, while $\Psi^x = \{S_1^x, S_2^x, \ldots, S_{k_x}^x\}$ denote the set of all real (existing) transitions of type x with $x \in \{cut, fade, dissolve\}$. Let Φ denote the set of frames covered by high motion graphic scenes and other special effects such as wipes, and morphing. Note that we do not consider a declared transition false positive if it is caused by special frames of set Φ, since none of algorithms to date are designed to deal with special effects. We consider a declared transition of type x to be correctly detected if it

overlaps with at least one real transition of type x. Recall and precision then are defined as follows.

DEFINITION 1. *Given the set* Ψ^x *of real transitions of type* x, *the set* Φ *of special effects frames, the set* $\bar{\Psi}^x$ *of transitions of type* x *as declared by its automatic detector, the recall level of the detector with respect to a video sequence* $\mathcal{V}$ *is defined as:*

$$\mathcal{R}^x = \frac{N_{correct}^x}{N_{correct}^x + N_{miss}^x} 100\%,$$

where

$$N_{correct}^x = |\Upsilon|$$

with

$$\Upsilon = \{S_i^x \quad i \in \mathbb{N}_1^{k_x} \mid \exists j \in \mathbb{N}_1^{k_x} \ and \ S_i^x \cap \bar{S}_j^x \neq \emptyset\},$$

and

$$N_{miss}^x = |\Upsilon|$$

with

$$\Upsilon = \{S_i^x \quad i \in \mathbb{N}_1^{k_x} \mid \forall j \in \mathbb{N}_1^{k_x} \ and \ S_i^x \cap \bar{S}_j^x = \emptyset\}.$$

DEFINITION 2. *Given the set* Ψ^x *of real transitions of type* x, *the set* Φ *of special effects frames, the set* $\bar{\Psi}^x$ *of transitions of type* x *as declared by its automatic detector, the precision level of the detector with respect to video sequence* $\mathcal{V}$ *is defined as:*

$$\mathcal{P}^x = \frac{N_{correct}^x}{N_{correct}^x + N_{false}^x} 100\%,$$

where

$$N_{false}^x = |\Upsilon| \quad with \quad \Upsilon = \{\bar{S}_i^x \quad i \in \mathbb{N}_1^k \mid \bar{S}_i^x \cap \Phi = \emptyset$$
$$and \ \forall j \in \mathbb{N}_1^{k_{cut}} \bar{S}_i^x \cap S_j^{cut} = \emptyset$$
$$and \ \forall j \in \mathbb{N}_1^{k_{fade}} \bar{S}_i^x \cap S_j^{fade} = \emptyset$$
$$and \ \forall j \in \mathbb{N}_1^{k_{dissolve}} \bar{S}_i^x \cap S_j^{dissolve} = \emptyset\}.$$

Table 1: Test data for shot transition detection experiments.

Categories	Cuts	Dissolves		Fades	
		number	duration (frm)	number	duration (frm)
Cartoons	334	9	152	17	463
Commercials	336	70	1017	28	761
Music	202	34	147	51	1545
News	239	77	973	5	50
Sports	262	107	852	10	260
Total	1373	297	3141	111	3079

Recall and precision parameters as defined here, do not take the detector accuracy into consideration in determining gradual transition boundaries which are important in video segmentation and classification. The boundaries of detected gradual transitions do not always coincide with the real boundaries. We reuse cover-recall and cover-precision parameters proposed by [13] to evaluate the detector ability to accurately locate the start and end of a fade or dissolve. While [13] includes both miss and false detections in the coverage evaluation, we believe that it is more appropriate to evaluate these parameters only on correctly detected transitions. For each correctly detected transition S_i^x, let $\bar{S}_{\alpha_i}$ denote the corresponding segment in the set of declared transitions Ψ^x. Since a video sequence may contain more than one dissolve or fade, we take the average of cover-recall and cover-precision of all correctly detected transitions to measure the cover-recall and cover-precision rates of the detector with respect to the whole video sequence. We define cover-recall and cover-precision precisely as follows:

DEFINITION 3. *The cover-recall of a transition detector with respect to a video sequence $\mathcal{V}$ is defined as:*

$$\mathcal{R}_{cov}^x = \frac{\sum_{i=1}^{k_x} \theta_i}{|\Upsilon|},$$

with

$$\Upsilon = \{S_i^x \quad i \in \mathbb{N}_1^{k_x} \mid \exists j \in \mathbb{N}_1^{k_x} \text{ and } S_i^x \cap \bar{S}_j^x \neq \emptyset\},$$

$$\theta_i = \begin{cases} 0, & \text{if } S_i^x \notin \Upsilon \\ \frac{|S_i^x \cap \bar{S}_{\alpha_i}|}{|S_i^x|} 100\% & \text{otherwise.} \end{cases}$$

DEFINITION 4. *The cover-precision of a transition detector with respect to video sequence $\mathcal{V}$ is defined as:*

$$\mathcal{P}_{cov}^x = \frac{\sum_{i=1}^{k_x} \theta_i}{|\Upsilon|},$$

with

$$\theta_i = \begin{cases} 0, & \text{if } S_i^x \notin \Upsilon \\ \frac{|S_i^x \cap \bar{S}_{\alpha_i}|}{|\bar{S}_{\alpha_i}|} 100\% & \text{otherwise.} \end{cases}$$

These four parameters allow a better evaluation of shot transition detection algorithms than those employed in other previous efforts which only assess the performance of shot transition detectors with respect to the presence of *editing*

effects in general, but not their ability to accurately classify and locate the temporal extent of transitions.

7.2 Results and Discussion

The shot transition detection results measured with respect to performance parameters described in the previous section are presented in Table 2. It can be seen from Table 2 that our algorithms outperform the twin-comparison method and WebFlix in almost all aspects.

As for hard cut detection, our adaptive thresholding technique decreases the number of false positives and obtains a precision of 98%, while still maintaining a very good level of recall of 98% on the experimental data. Most flashlight effects in music videos are detected by the histogram verification step and removed; therefore, the performance of our algorithm on music sequences is still very high. While the twin-comparison method obtains a reasonable good level of recall, its precision is much lower than our algorithm, since it fails to deal adequately with artifacts caused by object and camera motion. In contrast, while the precision of the WebFlix algorithm is good, too many cuts are missed by this algorithm. Most noticeably, it detects less than 50% of all cuts in music sequences. Under close examination, we discover that WebFlix has problems with detecting changes in very dark scenes.

Our algorithm for detecting dissolves performs better than WebFlix and the twin-comparison approach. It obtains a reasonably good level of recall of around 82%, while with the twin-comparison method, it is 76%. This suggests that our algorithm would be able to detect those dissolves whose color histogram differences between two consecutive frames is small, and which are not detected by the twin-comparison method. The accuracy of our algorithm is also much better, since most of the false positives are eliminated by different thresholds set on mean and variance curves. The performance of WebFlix in detecting dissolves is quite poor, as it misses nearly 50% of dissolves while only around 25% of its dissolves is correct. The twin-comparison approach obtains a good level of cover-precision, since it is uncommon for fast motions to occur at the boundary of a dissolve so that a correctly detected dissolve by twin-comparison would include false frames. However, the cover-recall by the twin-comparison method is rather low (65%), since interframe differences at the start and end of a dissolve are very small and cannot be detected by its threshold. Apart from a slight improvement in cover-precision, our algorithm offers a much better level of cover-recall of 82%. The performance of our dissolve detection algorithm on cartoon and music sequences

Table 2: Shot transition detection results on the test set.

Categories	Cuts		Dissolves				Fades			
	$\mathcal{P}$	$\mathcal{R}$	$\mathcal{P}$	$\mathcal{R}$	$\mathcal{P}_{cov}$	$\mathcal{R}_{cov}$	$\mathcal{P}$	$\mathcal{R}$	$\mathcal{P}_{cov}$	$\mathcal{R}_{cov}$
Proposed Alg.	96.0	99.4	53.8	77.8	97.8	88.2	93.3	82.4	96.0	94.2
WebFlix	90.7	66.8	24.2	88.9	-	-	-	-	-	-
Twin-Comp.	91.2	96.4	12.7	77.8	91.7	87.5	-	-	-	-
(a) Results for cartoon sequences										
Proposed Alg.	97.0	97.0	79.2	87.1	97.2	80.8	89.7	92.9	94.9	99.6
WebFlix	90.6	80.1	54.3	62.9	-	-	-	-	-	-
Twin-Comp.	84.4	83.6	41.2	70.0	96.7	66.6	-	-	-	-
(b) Results for commercial sequences										
Proposed Alg.	98.7	96.7	82.4	79.2	96.0	84.0	62.5	100.0	100.0	100.0
WebFlix	97.4	78.2	20.1	39.0	-	-	-	-	-	-
Twin-Comp.	90.0	93.7	67.0	87.0	88.4	65.2	-	-	-	-
(c) Results for music sequences										
Proposed Alg.	98.5	98.5	64.7	64.7	93.9	52.4	92.5	96.1	98.5	99.2
WebFlix	86.2	46.5	26.7	70.6	-	-	-	-	-	-
Twin-Comp.	90.9	94.1	36.5	67.6	70.8	11.6	-	-	-	-
(d) Results for news sequences										
Proposed Alg.	98.1	97.7	73.2	86.9	94.7	84.6	90.0	90.0	91.5	98.8
WebFlix	93.4	86.3	16.0	48.6	-	-	-	-	-	-
Twin-Comp.	87.6	94.3	44.4	73.8	86.2	68.3	-	-	-	-
(e) Results for sports sequences										
Proposed Alg.	97.5	97.9	75.1	82.2	96.0	81.9	89.6	92.8	96.6	98.5
WebFlix	92.0	72.8	23.3	53.2	-	-	-	-	-	-
Twin-Comp.	88.6	92.1	43.7	75.8	90.4	65.0	-	-	-	-
(f) Overall results										

is not as good as on other categories. The reason for this is dissolves in cartoons are relatively uncommon, and therefore, false positives tend to dominate, while dissolves in dark music videos are missed by our algorithm.

The performance of our fade detection algorithm is very good. Overall, it can detect 93% of fades, and 90% of declared fades are correct. In addition, the algorithm obtains a very high score of 97% and 99% in cover-precision and cover-recall, respectively. The lowest performance of our fade detection algorithm is with news sequences, and it obtains a precision level of only 63%. However, this only slightly affects the overall results, since fades are uncommon in newscasts. The precision of fade detection would be further improved, if frames are divided into equal regions, e.g. 4 × 4, and fade characteristics described in Section 4 are examined for each sub-region, since this approach will take into account the local and global natures of a fade operation.

8. CONCLUSION

In this paper we have presented our algorithms for detecting different types of shot transition effects such as cuts, fades, and dissolves. We improve conventional cut detection methods using color histogram differences by utilizing an adaptive threshold computed from a local window on the luminance histogram difference curve. Based on the mathematical models for producing ideal fades and dissolves, different clues (e.g., monochrome frames) for discovering the existence of these effects are proposed, and constraints on the characteristics of frame luminance mean and variance curves are derived analytically in our approach to eliminate false

positives caused by camera and object motion during gradual transitions. We also present an effective technique for eliminating false positives from a list of detected transitions. We evaluate our algorithms against two other methods for shot transition detection, WebFlix and twin-comparison, on a variety of videos and demonstrate the better performance of our techniques in terms of recall, precision, cover-recall, and cover-precision.

9. REFERENCES

[1] A. M. Alattar. Detecting and compressing dissolve regions in video sequences with a DVI multimedia image compression algorithm. In *Proceedings of 1993 IEEE International Symposium on Circuit and Systems*, pages 13–16, 1993.

[2] A. M. Alattar. Detecting fade regions in uncompressed video sequences. In *Proceedings of 1997 IEEE International Conference on Acoustics Speech and Signal Processing*, pages 3025–3028, 1997.

[3] M. Ardebilian, X. Tu, and L. Chen. Improvement of shot detection methods based on dynamic threshold selection. In *Proceedings of SPIE Conference on Multimedia Storage and Archiving Systems*, volume 3229, Dallas, USA, Nov. 1997.

[4] F. Arman, A. Hsu, and M.-Y. Chiu. Image processing on compressed data for large video databases. In *ACM Multimedia'93*, pages 267–272, California, July 1993.

[5] B. Furht, S. W. Smolliar, and H. Zhang. *Video and*

Image Processing in Multimedia Systems. Kluwer Academic Publishers, 1995.

[6] L. Gu, K. Tsui, and D. Keightley. Dissolve detection in MPEG compressed video. In *Proceedings of IEEE International Conference on Intelligent Processing Systems*, volume 2, pages 1692–1696, 1997.

[7] A. Hampapur, R. Jain, and T. Weymouth. Digital video segmentation. In *Proceedings of the Second ACM International Conference on Multimedia (MULTIMEDIA '94)*, pages 357–364, New York, Oct. 1994. ACM Press.

[8] A. Hanjalic, R. L. Lagendijk, and J. Biemond. A novel video parsing method with improved thresholding. In *Third Annual Conference of the Advanced School for Computing and Imaging, ASCI'97*, , Neitherland, 1996.

[9] H. Kim, S.-F. Park, J. Lee, W. M. Kimg, and S. M.-H. Song. Processing of partial video data for detection of wipes. In *Proceedings of SPIE*, 1999.

[10] V. Kobla, D. DeMenthon, and D. Doermann. Special effect edit detection using Video Trails: a comparison with existing techniques. In *Proceedings of SPIE conference on Storage and Retrieval for Image and Video Databases VII*, Jan. 1999.

[11] T. C. Kuo, Y. Lin, A. L.P.Chen, S.-C. Chen, and C. Ni. Efficient shot change detection on compressed video. In *Proceedings of International Workshop on Multimedia Database Management Systems*, pages 101–108, 1996.

[12] R. Lienhart. Comparison of automatic shot boundary detection algorithms. In *Proceedings of SPIE, Image and Video Processing VII*, volume SPIE 3656-29, 1999.

[13] G. Lupatini, C. Saraceno, and R. Leonardi. Scene break detection: a comparison. In *Proceedings of 8th Workshop on Continuous-Media Databases and Applications*, pages 34–41, 1998.

[14] J. Meng, Y. Juan, and S.-F. Chang. Scene change detection in a MPEG compressed video sequence. In *IS&AT/SPIE Symposium Proceedings Vol 2419*, Feb. 1995.

[15] A. Nagasaka and Y. Tanaka. Automatic video indexing and full-motion search for object appea rance. In *Proceedings of Second Working Conference on Visual Databases Sys tems*, pages 113–127. Elsevier Science Publishers B.V., 1992.

[16] N. V. Patel and I. K. Sethi. Compressed video processing for cut detection. In *IEE Proceedings: Vision, Image and Signal Processing*, volume 134, pages 315–322, Oct. 1996.

[17] B. T. Truong. Video genre classification based on shot segmentation. Honours Thesis, Curtin University of Technology, Western Australia, November 1999.

[18] I. H. Witten, A. Moffat, and T. C. Bell. *Managing Gigabytes; Compressing and Indexing Documents and Images.* Van Nostrand Reinhold, New York, 1994.

[19] B.-L. Yeo and B. Liu. Rapid scene analysis on compressed video. *IEEE Transaction on Circuits and Systems for Video Technology*, 2:533–544, 1995.

[20] R. Zabih, J. Miller, and K. Mai. A feature-based algorithm for detecting and classifying production effects. *Multimedia Systems*, 7(2):119–128, 1999.

[21] H. Zhang, A. Kankanhalli, and S. Smoliar. Automatic partitioning of full-motion video. *Multimedia System*, 1:10–28, 1993.

APPENDIX

Consider a dissolve starting at frame s and ending at frame e. Let g and h denote the shot preceding and succeeding this dissolve, respectively. We assume g and h are two static shots with luminance variances v_1 and v_2. The content of frames around this dissolve can then be modeled as:

$$f_i(x,y) = \begin{cases} g(x,y), & \text{if } i < s; \\ \left(1 - \dfrac{i-s}{e-s}\right)g(x,y) + \dfrac{i-s}{e-s}h(x,y), & \text{if } s \leq i \leq e \\ h(x,y), & \text{if } i > s. \end{cases} \tag{7}$$

where x, y and i are variables that represent the horizontal, vertical and temporal dimensions of a video sequence, respectively. The variance of frames around the dissolve region then can be derived as:

$$f_i^v = \begin{cases} v_1, & \text{if } s < i; \\ \left(1 - \dfrac{i-s}{e-s}\right)^2 v_1 + \left(\dfrac{i-s}{e-s}\right)^2 v_2, & \text{if } s \leq i \leq e; \\ v_2, & \text{if } i < s. \end{cases} \tag{8}$$

The first order difference $t_i^v = f_{i+1}^v - f_i^v$ of the variance curve around this dissolve region segment can be computed as:

$$t_i^v = \begin{cases} 0, & \text{if } i < s; \\ \dfrac{-(2(e-i)-1)v_1 + (2(i-s)+1)v_2}{(e-s)^2}, & \text{if } s \leq i < e; \\ 0, & \text{if } i \leq e. \end{cases} \tag{9}$$

Therefore, we have:

$$t_s^v = -\frac{2(e-s)-1}{(e-s)^2}v_1, \tag{10}$$

and

$$t_{e-1}^v = \frac{2(e-s)-1}{(e-s)^2}v_2. \tag{11}$$

Efficient and Robust Multiple Access Control for Wireless Multimedia Services *

Yu-Kwong Kwok
Department of Electrical and Electronic
Engineering
The University of Hong Kong, Pokfulam Road,
Hong Kong

ykwok@eee.hku.hk

Vincent K. N. Lau
Department of Electrical and Electronic
Engineering
The University of Hong Kong, Pokfulam Road,
Hong Kong

knlau@eee.hku.hk

ABSTRACT

In this paper, we propose a new multiple access control (MAC) protocol for wireless distributed multimedia systems based on ATM, in which user demands are highly heterogeneous and can be classified as CBR, VBR, and ABR. Our protocol is motivated by two of the most significant drawbacks of existing protocols: (1) channel condition is ignored or not exploited, and (2) inflexible or biased time slots allocation algorithms are used. Indeed, existing protocols mostly ignore the burst errors due to fading and shadowing, which are inevitable in a mobile and wireless communication environment. A few protocols take into account the burst errors but just "handle" the errors in a passive manner. On the other hand, most of the existing protocols employ an inflexible or biased allocation algorithm such that over-provisioning may occur for a certain class of users at the expense of the poor service quality received by other users. Our proposed protocol, called SCAMA (synergistic channel adaptive multiple access), does not have these two drawbacks. The proposed protocol works closely with the underlying physical layer in that through observing the channel state information (CSI) of each mobile user, the MAC protocol first segregates a set of users with good CSI from requests gathered in the request contention phase of an uplink frame. The MAC protocol then judiciously allocates information time slots to the users according to their traffic types, CSI, urgency, and throughput, which are collectively represented by a novel and flexible priority function.

Keywords: Wireless multimedia, ireless ATM, multiple access control, FDD, adaptive protocol, TDMA.

*This research was jointly supported by research initiation grants from the HKU CRCG under contract numbers 10202523 and 10202518, a seed funding grant from the HKU URC under contract number 10203010, and a grant from the Hong Kong Research Grants Council under contract number HKU7124/99E.

1. INTRODUCTION

Wireless ATM [12], a natural extension of the wired broadband communication infrastructure (e.g., B-ISDN), is aimed at providing seamless accommodation of tetherless mobile users with QoS-based networked multimedia data services such as voice telephony, video-conferencing, or web access. However, realization of a fully functional wireless ATM system involves tackling a number intricate tasks not encountered in the fixed-wire environment. Notorious examples include multiple access control (MAC), location management, routing, etc [12]. Among these chores, MAC is one of the most important problems because the service quality and capacity of the system critically depend on the effectiveness of a MAC protocol. A MAC protocol for wireless ATM distinguishes itself from other MAC protocols in that various mechanisms are required to handle the diverse traffic demands of different services such as constant bit rate (CBR), variable bit rate (VBR), and available bit rate (ABR). CBR traffic such as voice telephony, VBR traffic such as video-conferencing, and ABR traffic such as file data have very different service requirements in terms of delay and loss tolerance, and throughput. Multiplexing these diverse services harmoniously such that reasonable QoS is maintained while at the same time maximizing the utilization of the precious channel bandwidth is a daunting and challenging task. Thus, while traditional ALOHA-type MAC protocols can handle homogeneous traffic efficiently, different techniques are needed for a wireless ATM system. As such, there are many efficient MAC protocols reported in the literature that are specially designed for wireless ATM.

Despite that these recent MAC protocols are shown to be able to handle the diverse service requirements, they still have a number of common drawbacks. Firstly, while sophisticated slot assignment strategies with articulated frame structures are proposed in these methods, none of them considers the effect of burst channel errors on protocol performance, let alone the investigation of exploiting the error characteristics to enhance performance. Essentially, these previous protocols are designed and analyzed based on the assumption that data transmission through the wireless channel is error-free. However, because the geographically scattered mobile users inevitably suffer from different degrees of *fading* and *shadowing* effects, indeed a common drawback of previous MAC protocols is that they assume the underlying physical layer always delivers a constant throughput, and as such, they may not be able to effectively utilize the precious bandwidth when the channel condition is swiftly varying among different users. Secondly, the slot allocation methods are quite inflexible in that they are designed to optimize the performance of VBR and/or CBR users only. This lack of fairness control may lead to starvation of ABR users. Furthermore, over-provisioning becomes inevitable in these protocols. Thirdly, an important QoS metric, namely the delay jitter, is usually ignored and the protocol performance in this aspect is unknown. In view of these drawbacks, in this paper we propose a new FDD-based MAC protocol for wireless ATM with the following distinctive features:

- The proposed MAC protocol works closely with the underlying physical layer in that through observing the channel state information (CSI) of each mobile user, the MAC protocol first segregates a set of users with good CSI from requests gathered in the request contention phase of an uplink frame. The MAC protocol then judiciously allocates information time slots to the users according to their traffic types, CSI, urgency, and throughput, which are collectively represented by a novel priority function.

- The priority function used in our MAC protocol is designed to be very flexible to dynamically adjust the relative priorities of different users, both within and between traffic classes.

- Furthermore, our protocol can also minimize the delay jitter of user transmissions.

Our proposed protocol, called SCAMA (synergistic channel adaptive multiple access), also has a *request queue* which stores the previous requests that survive the contention but are not allocated information slots. This is to reduce the unnecessary contention loading during the contention phase. The SCAMA protocol has been implemented and compared with previous protocols. The simulation results indicate that SCAMA can support a much larger user population with diverse traffic requirements. This paper is organized as follows. In Section 2, we describe in detail the physical layer of our SCAMA protocol. In Section 3, we describe the multiple access operations and characteristics of the proposed SCAMA protocol. Experimental results and their interpretations are included in Section 5. The last section concludes the paper.

2. THE CHANNEL-ADAPTIVE PHYSICAL LAYER

2.1 Wireless Channel Model

The wireless communication environment considered in this paper is the reverse-link situation of a wireless system where a number of mobile terminals contend to transmit ATM cells to an ATM server. The wireless link between a mobile ATM terminal and the ATM server is characterized by two components, namely the *microscopic fading* component and the *macroscopic shadowing* component. Microscopic fading is caused by the superposition of multipath components and is therefore fluctuating in a fast manner (on the order of a few msec). Macroscopic shadowing is caused by terrain configuration or obstacles and is fluctuating in a relatively slow manner (on the order of one to two seconds).

Let $c(t)$ be the combined channel fading which is given by:

$$c(t) = c_l(t)c_s(t)$$

where $c_l(t)$ and $c_s(t)$ are the long-term macroscopic and short-term microscopic fading components, respectively. Both $c_s(t)$ and $c_l(t)$ are random processes with coherent time on the order of a few milli-seconds and seconds, respectively.

Short-Term Microscopic Fading:

Without loss of generality, we assume $\mathcal{E}[c_s^2(t)] = 1$ where $\mathcal{E}[]$ denotes the expected value of a random variable. The probability distribution of $c_s(t)$ follows the Rayleigh distribution which is given by:

$$f_{c_s}(c_s) = c_s \exp\left(-\frac{c_s^2}{2}\right)$$

In this paper, we assume the maximum mobile speed is 40 km/hr and hence, the Doppler spread [16], $f_d \approx 50$Hz. It follows that, the *coherent time*, T_c, is approximately given by:

$$T_c \approx \frac{1}{f_d} \tag{1}$$

which is about 20 msec.

Long-Term Macroscopic Shadowing:

The long-term fading component, $c_l(t)$, is also referred to as the *local mean* [16], which, as shown by field test measurement, obeys the *log-normal* distribution, $f_{c_l}(c_l)$. That is,

$$f_{c_l}(c_l) = \frac{4.34}{\sqrt{2\pi}\sigma_l c_l} \exp\left(-\frac{(c_l(dB) - m_l)^2}{2\sigma_l^2}\right)$$

where m_l, σ_l are the mean (in dB) and the variance of the log-normal distribution, i.e., $c_l(dB) = 20\log(c_l)$. Since $c_l(t)$ is caused by terrain configuration and obstacles, the random process fluctuates over a much longer time scale. Again, from field test results, the order of time span for $c_l(t)$ is about one second. Since mobile terminals are scattered geographically across the cell and are moving independently of each other, we assume the channel fading experienced by each mobile terminal is independent of each other.

2.2 Variable Throughput Channel Coding

Redundancy is incorporated to the information packet for error protection. To exploit the time-varying nature of the wireless channel, a variable rate channel-adaptive physical layer is employed as illustrated in Figure 1(a). Channel state information (CSI), $c(t)$, which is estimated[1] at the receiver, is fed back to the transmitter via a low-capacity *feedback channel*. Based on the CSI, the level of redundancy and the modulation constellation applied to the information cells are adjusted accordingly by choosing a suitable transmission mode[2]. Thus, the instantaneous throughput is varied

---

[1]In this paper, we assumed CSI is estimated by the pilot-symbol approach [10].

[2]Transmission mode refers to the combination of channel encoding rate and modulation constellation level.

according to the instantaneous channel state. In our study, a 6-mode variable rate adaptive bit-interleaved trellis coded modulation scheme (ABICM) is employed [10]. Transmission modes with *normalized throughput*[3] varying from 1/2 to 5 are available depending on the channel condition. For real-time sources such as CBR or VBR, the physical layer employs a variable throughput forward error correction (FEC) code. For a non-real-time source such as ABR, the physical layer employs a variable throughput error correction code embedded with error detection and retransmission.

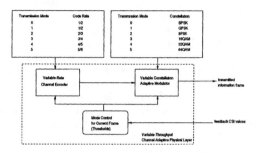

Figure 1: A conceptual block diagram of the variable throughput channel adaptive physical layer.

Information cells per user are transmitted in the assigned traffic slots of a TDMA frame. Since the coherence time of short-term fading is around 20 msec, the CSI remains approximately constant within a traffic slot duration. Hence, all the transmitted symbols of the traffic slot (per user) share the same transmission mode, which is determined by the current CSI level. Specifically, transmission mode q is chosen if the feedback CSI, $\hat{c}$, falls within the *adaptation thresholds*, (ζ_{q-1}, ζ_q). Here, the operation and the performance of the ABICM scheme is determined by the set of adaptation thresholds $\{\zeta_0, \zeta_1, \ldots\}$. Furthermore, we operate the ABICM scheme in the *constant BER* mode [10]. That is, the adaptation thresholds are set optimally to maintain a target transmission error level over a range of CSI values. When the channel condition is good, a higher mode could be used and the system enjoys a higher throughput. On the other hand, when the channel condition is bad, a lower mode is used to maintain the target error level at the expense of a lower transmission throughput. Note that when the channel state is very bad, the adaptation range of the ABICM scheme can be exceeded, making it impossible to maintain the targeted BER level. Given the above considerations about the channel state, the instantaneous throughput offered to the MAC layer, ρ, is also variable and is therefore a function of the CSI, $c(t)$, and the target BER, P_b, denoted by $\rho = f_\rho(c(t), P_b)$.

3. THE SCAMA PROTOCOL
In the following, we describe our proposed fully channel-adaptive MAC protocol based on D-TDMA framing. The proposed protocol also provides a convenient structure to accommodate different service requirements of CBR, VBR, and ABR effectively. We briefly review existing MAC protocols for wireless ATM before discussing the detailed operation of our MAC protocol.

---

[3]Normalized throughput refers to the number of information bits carried per modulation symbol.

3.1 Background
D-TDMA (dynamic TDMA) was first introduced for satellite communications [4] and has been proposed recently as a candidate MAC protocol for wireless ATM. There are many variations of D-TDMA based MAC protocols. The DQRUMA and DTDMA/PR are well known examples of D-TDMA based MAC protocols. Despite that these protocols are different in many detailed aspects, they can nevertheless be described by a common framework. Time on the channel is divided into a contiguous sequence of TDMA frames, which are subdivided into request slots and information slots. The information slots are sometimes further classified into CBR/VBR and ABR/UBR slots. There are two types of packets being transmitted in the channel, namely the *request packet* and the *information packet*. A request packet is used for the request of information slot (either voice or data slots). It often includes only very small of amount of information, namely the origin and the destination addresses, and is therefore usually much shorter than an information packet. The request subframe is usually operated using the slotted-ALOHA protocol.

A terminal generating a new stream of data cells transmits an appropriate request packet in one of the request slots of the next frame. If there are more than one packet transmitted in the same request slot, collision occurs and depending upon whether the capture effect [2] is considered, one or none of the requests will be correctly received (both with and without capture are considered in our study). At the end of each request slot, the successful or unsuccessful request will be identified and broadcast by the base station. Due to the short propagation delay in a FDD-based wireless ATM network, the mobile terminals can immediately know the request result. An unsuccessful user can retry in the next request slot. On the other hand, a successful user then transmits his/her information packet in the corresponding information slot in the current frame.

In most of the previous schemes [13], bandwidth allocation in the MAC layer for a certain traffic type is essentially based only on a first-come-first-serve strategy. Some of the previous MAC schemes even do not consider CBR and VBR separately. For those MAC schemes that treat CBR, VBR, and ABR seperately, no mechanism is incorporated to adjust the priority between classes in a flexible way. Most importantly, these protocols do not take into account of the CSI in the bandwidth allocation process. However, in a wireless communication system where burst errors due to fading are inevitable, CSI is a critical factor in achieving a higher overall utilization of the precious bandwidth in the system. This motivates our proposed new MAC protocol, called SCAMA (synergistic channel adaptive multiple access), which works closely and synergistically with the underlying channel adaptive physical layer. Specifically, the protocol adaptively assigns information slots to users based on their CSI ranking. Furthermore, this proposed protocol could accommodate CBR, VBR, and ABR traffic effectively with a very flexible priority adjustment between different classes.

3.2 Frame Structure
Figure 2 shows the uplink and the downlink frame structure of the proposed MAC protocol. To incorporate the channel-

adaptive feature of the proposed MAC protocol, the TDMA frames for the uplink and downlink are divided into subframes as follows.

In the uplink, a frame is divided into three subframes as illustrated in Figure 2(a). They are the *request subframe*, the *traffic subframe*, and the *reporting subframe*. Specifically, there are N_r mini-slots in the request subframe for CBR, VBR, and ABR requests requests contention. Note that an ABR user is not allowed to make reservation in the sense that even if an ABR user is granted traffic slot(s) in the current frame, it has to contend again in the next frame for the remaining data cells. On the other hand, CBR and VBR users can reserve slots in succeeding frames. Specifically, when a CBR or VBR user successfully makes a transmission request in one of the N_r mini-slots, the user does not need to contend again in the next period and the request will be automatically generated in the MAC layer until the current burst ends. There are N_i information slots in the traffic subframe for the transmission of CBR, VBR, or ABR packets. Finally, there are N_b mini-slots in the reporting subframe. The functions of the three subframes will be elaborated in detail later in Section 3.3. The frame duration is 2.5 msec. Such a short frame duration has the advantage of shorter delay and is practicable in wideband systems [15].

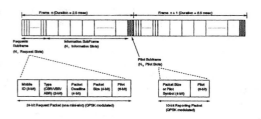

(a) uplink frame structure

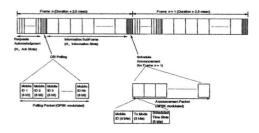

(b) downlink frame structure

Figure 2: Frame structures of the proposed SCAMA protocol for CBR, VBR, and ABR users.

A downlink FDD frame is similarly partitioned into four subframes, namely the *acknowledgment subframe*, the *polling subframe*, the *traffic subframe*, and the *announcement subframe*. The frame duration is also 2.5 msec and the number of slots in the subframes are given by N_r, N_b, N_i, and N_b, respectively. The functionality and operation of each subframe are described in Section 3.3. Note that in both uplink and downlink, variable throughput adaptive channel coding

and modulation is applied to traffic slots only. For the mini-slots of the other subframes, traditional QPSK modulation is applied.

3.3 Protocol Operations

The operation of the SCAMA protocol is divided into two phases, namely the *request phase* and *transmission phase*. In the request phase, mobile terminals which have packets to transmit will send a request packet in one of the N_r request mini-slots, governed by the respective permission probability. The request packet is very short (24 bits), occupying only a mini-slot, as illustrated in Figure 2(a). It contains the mobile terminal ID, request type (CBR, VBR, or ABR), data deadline, number of information data cells desired to transmit as well as pilot symbols for CSI estimation. If more than one mobile terminals send request packets in the same request mini-slot, collision occurs and all the request packets are lost if capture effect is not considered (if capture is considered, the request with the highest signal energy may be successfully received). After each request mini-slot, an acknowledgment packet will be broadcast from the base-station through the acknowledgment mini-slot in the downlink frame. The acknowledgment packet contains only the successful request packet ID. Mobile terminals that fail to receive an acknowledgment will retransmit the request packet in the next request mini-slot, again governed by the permission probability. On the other hand, successfully acknowledged users will wait for announcement on the allocation schedule of the traffic slots from the base-station.

Unlike traditional MAC protocols, the base-station will collect all requests in the current request phase as well as the *backlog requests* from the previous frames before allocation of traffic slots. All the requests will be assigned priorities according to the deadline, CSI, service type (CBR, VBR, or ABR), as well as the waiting time of the request (i.e., the number of elapsed frames since the request is acknowledged). Since the physical layer offers a variable throughput which is dependent on the CSI, the rationale behind the SCAMA MAC protocol is to give higher priority to the mobile terminals that are in better channel condition in the bandwidth allocation process. The motivation of this strategy is that a user with better channel condition, with the support of the variable rate channel encoder, can enjoy a larger throughput and therefore, can use the system bandwidth more effectively. Nevertheless, for fairness's sake, information slots should also be allocated to mobile terminals that are approaching their deadlines, despite their possibly worse channel states; otherwise, the queued information packets will be dropped.

3.4 Priority Function for Slots Allocation

In the SCAMA protocol, we employ a general priority function which could provide a flexible balance of the above conflicting goals. Furthermore, the slots allocation mechanism is also very flexible for incorporating other types of allocation algorithms such as deficit round robin [14], weighted fair queueing [3], and class based queueing [5].

Specifically, the *priority metric* of the i-th request (which may be a new request or a backlog request), μ_i, is given by the following equation:

$$\mu_i = \begin{cases} g_{CBR}(CSI^{(i)}, T_d^{(i)}) = f_\rho(CSI^{(i)}) + \\ \lambda_{CBR}(T_d^{(i)})^{-\beta_{CBR}} + \Delta_{CBR} & \text{for CBR request} \\ g_{VBR}(CSI^{(i)}, T_d^{(i)}) = f_\rho(CSI^{(i)}) + \\ \lambda_{VBR}(T_d^{(i)})^{-\beta_{VBR}} + \Delta_{VBR} & \text{for CBR request} \\ g_{ABR}(CSI^{(i)}, T_w^{(i)}) = f_\rho(CSI^{(i)}) + \\ \lambda_{ABR}(T_w^{(i)})^{\beta_{ABR}} & \text{for ABR request} \end{cases}$$
(2)

where $T_d^{(i)}$, $T_w^{(i)}$, λ_{CBR}, λ_{VBR}, λ_{ABR}, β_{CBR}, β_{VBR}, β_{ABR}, Δ_{CBR}, and Δ_{VBR} are the deadline, the waiting time, the *forgetting factors* of the CBR, VBR and ABR requests, as well as the *priority offsets* assigned to the CBR, VBR, or ABR users, respectively. From Equation (2), the first term is aimed to enforce that a higher priority for requests with a higher throughput. The second term is to maintain fairness[4] within each of the service classes. Finally, the last term is responsible for maintaining priority between different classes. As will be demonstrated in Section 5, the balance between the three goals could be easily adjusted by tuning λ and Δ.

Thus, in the allocation phase, traffic slots are allocated to service requests according to the sorted priority metrics. If there are not sufficient traffic slots to service all requests, remaining requests are queued and re-considered in the next frame[5]. After the request phase, the results of traffic slot allocation will be broadcast in the *announcement subframe* of the downlink frame. The announcement packet contains the traffic slot allocation schedule as well as the transmission mode as illustrated in Figure 2(b). Mobile terminals will then start to transmit information packets on the allocated traffic slot(s).

3.5 Handling Heterogeneous Users Requirements

The SCAMA protocol is reservation based for CBR and VBR users only. As mentioned earlier, for a ABR user, even if traffic slots have been assigned for its successfully acknowledged request, the allocation is meant only for the current frame and the ABR user has to initiate another request for any remaining data cells. By contrast, for a CBR or VBR user, when traffic slots have been assigned for its successfully acknowledged request, additional requests will be *automatically generated* by the base-station (hence, reservation) periodically at 20 msec (i.e., taking voice as an example CBR source) and 40 msec (i.e., taking video as an example VBR source) time intervals for CBR and VBR respectively. Thus, the CBR or VBR user does not need to contend for request mini-slots anymore in the current talk-spurt. By avoiding unnecessary requests, the advantage of this reservation strategy is the reduction of the contention collisions in the request phase. For a CBR user, the number of cells generated per CBR period is constant and hence, this basic reservation scheme works fine. However, for a VBR user, the number of cells generated per VBR period is a random variable and hence, this information needs to be updated per VBR period in order to make proper reservation

---

[4]The second term will be large for requests with a urgent deadline or long waiting time.

[5]If the deadline for a remaining request has expired, this request will not be queued anymore. The information packet at the mobile terminal will be dropped.

for VBR. The mechanism for VBR updating is illustrated in the following section.

3.6 CSI Determination

On the other hand, a critical component in the proposed SCAMA MAC protocol is the determination of the current CSI for each user. As mentioned earlier, we assume that the coherence time for short-term fading is around 20 msec as illustrated in Section 2 while the frame duration is only 2.5 msec. Thus, the CSI remains approximately constant for at least two frames. For a new request, known pilot symbols are embedded in the request packets so that the current CSI can be estimated at the base station and this estimated CSI is valid for the next few frame duration. However, for a backlog request, the estimated CSI value obtained previously during a past request phase may be obsolete and thus, a mechanism is needed to obtain update the CSI.

Both the VBR reservation and the CSI update relies on a special updating procedure, which is illustrated in Figure 3.

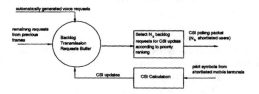

Figure 3: Information (CSI or VBR demands) updating mechanism for backlog requests

At the beginning of each frame, the base-station short-lists N_b backlog requests (those with the CSI values expired or those requiring VBR reservation update) according to their priorities. A *polling packet* is then broadcast to the mobile terminals in the *polling subframe*. The CSI polling packet contains the mobile terminal IDs that are short-listed by the base-station. The structure of the polling packet is shown in Figure 2(b). Mobile terminals listed in the polling packet respond at the appropriate reporting mini-slot according to the order specified in the polling packet. If the short-listed request is of CBR type with CSI value expired, the mobile station will transmit pilot symbols in the reporting mini-slot. Otherwise, the mobile station will transmit a VBR demand update packet as shown in Figure 2(a). The VBR demand update packet contains the number of VBR cells generated in the current frame as well as pilot symbols for CSI updating.

Thus, the base station could update the VBR reservation requests as well as backlog requests' CSI values (which are valid for at least two consecutive frames). The estimated CSI value is used to determine the transmission mode in the physical layer as well as to determine the priority of the request in the MAC layer. With the above considerations, the SCAMA protocol is outlined below in pseudo-code format.

```
1: loop
2:    contention phase {requests are acknowledged but no
      slot is assigned}
3:    {CSI of each request is recorded}
4:    merge the new requests to the request queue
```

5: sort the request queue according to the request priority
6: assign information slots according to the request queue order
7: remaining unassigned requests are queued
8: **end loop**

4. SOURCE MODELS

The wireless ATM system considered in this paper is aimed to support integrated CBR, VBR, and ABR services. As such, we assume that there are only three types of mobile terminals, namely the CBR terminal, the VBR terminal and the ABR terminal in the system. Both CBR and VBR cells are assumed to be delay sensitive while ABR cells are assumed to be delay insensitive. Thus, CBR and VBR cells are labeled with *deadlines*. The cells will be dropped by a mobile terminal if the deadline expires before being transmitted. Such cells dropping has to be controlled to within a certain limit (e.g., below 1% for voice as indicated in [6]) in order to have acceptable quality of service for CBR and VBR users. The source and contention models are summarized below.

- **CBR Source Model:** We use voice as an example CBR source. The voice source is assumed to be continuously toggling between the talkspurt and silence states. The duration of a talkspurt and a silence period are assumed to be exponentially distributed with means t_t and t_s seconds, respectively (as indicated by the empirical study in [11], $t_t = 1$, and $t_s = 1.35$). We assume a talkspurt and a silence period start only at a frame boundary. Finally, as mentioned above, a voice source cannot tolerate a cell loss rate higher than 1% in order to achieve a reasonable service quality [6].

- **VBR Source Model:** We use video teleconference as an example VBR source. In the model we use [9], the number of cells per VBR period (i.e., 40 msec for a 25 fps frame rate) is govern by the DAR(1) model, which is a Markov chain characterized by three parameters: the mean, the variance, and ρ. The transition matrix is computed as:

$$P = \rho I + (1 - \rho)Q \qquad (3)$$

where ρ is the autocorrelation coefficient and I is the identity matrix. Furthermore, each row of Q is identical and consists of the negative binomial probabilities $(f_0, \ldots, f_K, F_K)$, where $F_K = \sum_{k<K} f_k$, and K is the peak rate. Similar to a voice source, a video source can only tolerate a 1% cell loss rate [9].

- **ABR Source Model:** The arrival time of data generated by a ABR data terminal is assumed to be exponentially distributed with mean equal to one second. The data size, in terms of number of cells, is also assumed to be exponentially distributed with mean equal to 100 cells. An ABR user will not drop cells because there is no deadline constraint. Again we assume that the cells arrive at a frame boundary.

- **Terminal Contention Model:** As in most previous studies, to avoid excessive collisions, even if a user has some cells awaiting to be sent, the user will attempt to send a request at a request mini-slot only with a certain *permission probability*. The permission probability for CBR, VBR and ABR users are denoted by p_c, p_v and p_a, respectively. The protocol also has a *request queue* which stores the previous requests that survive the contention but are not allocated information slots.

It is also interesting to investigate the performance of the proposed SCAMA protocol under situations with and without capture. Thus, the capture process is also implemented. Specifically, suppose there are k requests, with signal power denoted by $P_1, P_2, \ldots, P_k$, contending for a request mini-slot. A request j can be captured if [2]:

$$\frac{P_j}{\sum_{i \neq j} P_i} > \gamma$$

where γ is the SNR threshold.

5. RESULTS AND INTERPRETATIONS

In this section, we present the performance results of our proposed protocol. In our simulation study, we assume a transmission bandwidth of 1.36 MHz for the TDMA frames. CBR bit rate is 8 kbps while the average VBR bit rate is 128 kbps. Table 1 summarizes the parameters we used.

Table 1: Simulation parameters.

Parameter	Value
N_r	10
N_i	40
N_b	20
t_t	1000 msec
t_s	1350 msec
p_c	0.3
p_v	0.3
p_a	0.2
channel bandwidth	1.36MHz
CBR (voice) data rate	8 kbps
VBR (video) data rate	128 kpbs
ABR data rate	16 kbps
number of simulated frames	2×10^6

5.1 Adjusting Priority between Traffic Classes

As described in Section 3.4, the priority function employed proposed protocol is very flexible in adjusting priority between different traffic classes. This is illustrated in Figure 4(a) where the variation of the cell loss rates of CBR and VBR users (with a particular combination of Δ_{CBR} and Δ_{VBR}) against Δ_{CBR} (Δ_{VBR} is fixed at 40) are shown. As can be seen, the cell loss rate of CBR improves while that of VBR increases as Δ_{CBR} is increased. This indicates that priority could be shifted to the CBR users by increasing Δ_{CBR}. This robustness of the priority function can be employed to dynamically adjust the relative service quality of different user classes depending on the traffic condition. For example, if we find that the current number of admitted VBR users is small, say less than 25, then we can increase the value of Δ_{CBR} to further improve the service quality of the CBR users without significantly degrading the service quality of the VBR users. This can be done similarly for VBR users if needed.

5.2 Adjusting Priority within a Traffic Class

The proposed priority function is also very flexible in adjusting the priority and hence the fairness, within each class. As mentioned in Section 3.4, although it is efficient to give a higher priority to a request with a high CSI value, it would also be unfair to those requests with inferior CSI values because such requests may have to wait for a long time in the request queue to get service. Thus, there is a design trade-off between system efficiency and fairness. Depending upon the desired service conditions, fairness could be promoted by adjusting the priority within a traffic class, which could be easily done by changing λ in Equation (2). As an example, we observe the delay jitter of the ABR users with background CBR and VBR traffic against λ, which is shown in Figure 4(b). Clearly, by choosing an appropriate value of λ, the delay jitter of ABR users can be easily controlled to fall within the desired range.

5.3 Comparison with Previous MAC Protocols

We compare the MAC performance of the proposed SCAMA protocol with well-known ATM MAC protocols such as DQRUMA and DTDMA/PR. However, one may argue that the performance gain of the proposed scheme is entirely due to the variable-throughput physical layer, which has been shown to offer a larger average throughput compared with traditional fixed-throughput physical layers [1]. To better illustrate the superiority of our scheme, we compare with an additional MAC protocol, namely the DTDMA/VR, which employs the same variable-throughput physical layer as ours. For completeness, the characteristics of these three protocols are briefly summarized below. The reader is referred to the respective references for further details.

- **DQRUMA:** The DQRUMA (distributed queueing request update multiple access) protocol proposed by Karol, Liu, and Eng [7] is a well known MAC protocol for wireless ATM. In simple terms, being a FDD (frequency division duplex) protocol, DQRUMA works by dividing the uplink frame into two sections with the first section for requests contention, whereas the second section for information data transmissions. A nice and novel feature of the DQRUMA protocol is the use of a piggyback reservation field, with which a VBR user can update the traffic slot demand without the need of an extra contention. Another novel feature of the DQRUMA protocol is that if needed, the base-station can convert one information slot into a number of request slots so as to alleviate the contention.

- **DTDMA/PR:** Similar to DQRUMA, the DTDMA/PR (dynamic TDMA with piggyback reservation) proposed by Qiu, Li, and Ju [11] also allows VBR users to update time slots requirements using a piggyback field in an uplink information slot. A distinctive feature of DTDMA/PR is that the information slots are classified as long-term and short-term reservable. Specifically, long-term slots are for CBR and VBR users, while short-term ones are for ABR users.

- **DTDMA/VR:** In the DTDMA/VR [8] protocol, the MAC layer assigns information slots to the users on a

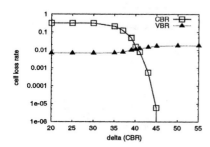

(a) effect of Δ with 80 CBR users and 25 VBR users (Δ_{VBR} is fixed at 40)

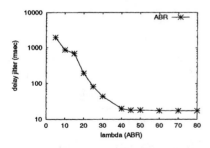

(b) effect of λ with 30 CBR users, 30 VBR users, and 30 ABR users

Figure 4: Effects of Δ and λ.

First-Come-First-Serve basis. The DTDMA/VR protocol also considers the effect of burst errors by employing a channel adaptive physical layer. However, the DTDMA/VR does not consider the synergistic interaction between the MAC and physical layers as ours and therefore, it is not a fully adaptive protocol.

All the three protocols incorporate a piggybacking mechanism for VBR users to update their traffic demands. All of the schemes are compared based on the same bandwidth, BER level and the average transmitted power.

5.3.1 CBR Performance

The service quality for CBR users, being voice sources, is governed by the average cell loss rate, P_{loss}, which is contributed by two factors: cell dropping at the mobile and cell loss during transmission. On one hand, voice cell is delay sensitive and hence, voice cells are labeled with deadlines. A voice cell has to be discarded if its delay exceeds the deadline[6]. Such discarding constitutes the cell dropping at the voice terminal. On the other hand, transmitted cells could be corrupted due to channel error and thus, cell transmission error results. The cell loss rate P_{loss} is then given by:

$$P_{loss} = \frac{N_{tx} - N_{rv}}{N_{tx}} \qquad (4)$$

where N_{tx} and N_{rv} are the number of transmitted voice cells and the number of voice cells received without error, respectively. Figure 5(a) shows the cell loss rate performance of our proposed SCAMA protocol as well as the other three previous protocols. In this set of experiments, we fixed the number of ABR users to be 25 and that of VBR users to be 25 also. As can be seen, the DQRUMA and DTDMA/VR protocols perform much worse compared with the DTDMA/PR and SCAMA protocols. Indeed, the former two protocols achieve a cell loss rate which is higher than the 1% tolerance threshold for a voice source [6], while the latter two offer a two order of magnitude lower cell loss rate. This can be explicated by the fact that the DQRUMA and DTDMA/VR protocols do not incorporate any prioritization mechanism in the time slots allocation process. That is, the time slots are essentially allocated in a first-come-first-serve manner. Thus, as VBR and ABR users usually have a much larger chunk of cells for transmission, the CBR users suffer from the "convoy" effect (i.e., a large request blocks a number of subsequent small requests), and thus, cell droppings occur quite frequently. The latter two protocols, however, allocate slots according to the requests' priorities. In particular, isochronous users such as CBR and VBR users are given a higher priority than the ABR users. The cell loss due to dropping can be avoided almost completely.

5.3.2 VBR Performance

Similar to CBR users, the service quality of VBR users is also sensitive to loss (e.g., the image quality degrades if some cells are lost in a vidoe-conferencing application). Also, being a isochronous source, cells have deadlines such that missing the transmission deadlines render the cells useless. Thus, we also evaluate the performance of the protocols using the

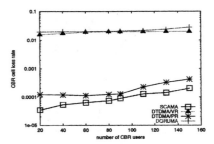

(a) CBR performance (25 ABR users and 25 VBR users)

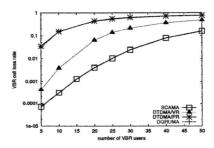

(b) VBR performance (25 ABR users and 50 CBR users)

Figure 5: Performance of the protocols for CBR and VBR users.

---

[6]In this paper, the deadline of voice cell is assumed to be 20 msec after it is generated by the source.

cell loss rate for VBR users. Figure 5(b) depicts the VBR cell loss rate performance of the four protocols. We can see that in contrast to CBR performance, the DTDMA/PR protocol performs quite poorly for VBR users in that the cell loss rate is much higher than the 1% threshold even for 5 VBR users. This phenomenon is a result of assigning priority to CBR users in the DTDMA/PR, which concurs with the results presented in [11]. The DQRUMA protocol also gives similar performance as the DTDMA/PR protocol. The DTDMA/VR protocol, however, outperforms the previous two protocols by a large margin for VBR users. This is because the variable-throughput physical layer offers almost two times the average throuhgput compared with traditional fixed-throughput physical layers and is reflected in the performance of DTDMA/VR. Finally, we can see that the proposed SCAMA protocol considerably outperforms the DTDMA/VR protocol. This illustrates the synergy that could be achieved by the judicious requests prioritization (based on CSI, urgency, and throughput) process in the former.

5.3.3 ABR Performance

ABR cells are delay insensitive and as such, they will not be discarded at the mobiles. However, ABR cells may experience transmission errors when the channel condition is poor. Thus, lost cells are retransmitted (through the data-link layer). This inevitably introduces additional delay due to retransmissions. Here, different from CBR and VBR users, ABR users' performance is quantified by two measures: delay and throughput. The average ABR data throughput, $\bar{\rho}$, is defined as the average number of cells successfully received at the base-station per frame. The average delay, $\bar{D}_d$, is defined as the average time that a cell spends waiting in the transmitter buffer until the beginning of the successful transmission. Figure 6 illustrates the performance of data terminal in terms of $\bar{\rho}$ and $\bar{D}_d$ respectively. When the traffic load is high, the system is in a highly congested state so that the average per-user throughput drops and the average per-user delay also increases dramatically. These adverse phenomena are detrimental to the data users' quality of service (QoS), which depends critically on the parameters pair `(delay, throughput)` as describe above. Before the system gets into the congested state, the proposed SCAMA protocol consistently offers a much lower delay and a much higher throughput compared to the other three protocols. In other words, given a certain QoS level, the SCAMA protocol can support a much larger ABR user population. For example, at a QoS level of `(1 sec, 0.25)`, the SCAMA protocol can support more than 200 ABR users while the second best protocol, the DTDMA/VR protocol, can only support 100 ABR users.

5.4 Interpretations

From the simulation results shown above, the proposed SCAMA protocol is robust and outperforms two recently proposed efficient protocols by a considerable margin. In this section, we further provide some interpretations of the performance results.

First, a CBR terminal may experience a deep fading for a long time when it is affected by shadowing. In the other three protocols (including DTDMA/VR), bandwidth allocation in the MAC layer is carried out regardless of the current channel condition as detected in the physical layer. Thus,

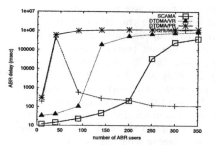

(a) ABR delay (10 VBR users and 20 CBR users)

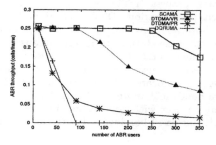

(b) ABR throughput (10 VBR users and 20 CBR users)

Figure 6: Performance of the protocols for ABR users.

information slots could also be allocated to such a user and the transmitted packets will be very likely lost due to the poor channel condition. In other words, assigned slots are simply wasted. This kind of wasteful allocation is avoided in the SCAMA protocol.

Secondly, selection diversity is implicitly incorporated in the SCAMA protocol. Through the priority-based assignment process, every frame is packed with a selected group of information cells with good channel states. Thus, the effective delivered throughput per frame achieved in SCAMA can be much higher than that in DTDMA/VR and other protocols. In SCAMA, a large number of transmission requests are collected first before allocation of information slots. From the collection of requests, there is a high likelihood that a sufficient number of requests with good channel states can be selected to fully utilize the information slots in an effective manner (i.e., high throughput). For those requests with poor instantaneous channel states, their transmissions are deferred until when the CSI improves or the deadlines are approaching. By contrast, in the DTDMA/VR and DQRUMA protocols, requests are served in a first-come-first-serve manner due to the traditional strategy of immediately assigning slots upon successful receipt of requests. Thus, the channel states of such requests are highly diverse and, most importantly, some requests with bad channel states (hence very low throughput) are also served, whereby causing inefficient the bandwidth utilization. For example, a CBR terminal may experience a very good CSI for a long time (out of shadowing). In protocols without considering CSI in the prioritization process (DTDMA/PR) or those even without explicit prioritization (DTDMA/VR and DQRUMA), this user, however, may fail to successfully transmitted a request to the base-station, probably because of excessive collisions in the request phase. In comparison, our proposed scheme gathers a large number of requests through successive frames, and allocate time slots to the users that can use the system bandwidth more effectively. Thus, the likelihood of "missing" a user with good channel state is much lower and the utilization of bandwidth is therefore higher.

6. CONCLUSIONS

We have presented a new channel-adaptive MAC protocol for wireless distributed multimedia systems based on ATM. The proposed protocol, called SCAMA, employs a judicious prioritization and scheduling mechanism, which takes into account all the critical performance parameters such as channel condition, urgency, and throughput. In particular, the prioritization is robust and flexible in that it can be easily adapted to suit the needs of a certain class of users (e.g., the CBR users). Our simulation results indicate that the performance of the SCAMA protocol is superior to three state-of-the-art wireless ATM MAC protocols.

7. REFERENCES

[1] S. M. Alamouti and S. Kallel, "Adaptive Trellis-Coded Multiple-Phase-Shift Keying for Rayleigh Fading Channels," *IEEE Transactions on Communications*, vol. 42, no. 6, pp. 2305-2314, June 1994.

[2] J. C. Ambak and W. van Blitterswijk, "Capacity of Slotted ALOHA in Raleigh Fading Channels," *IEEE Journal on Selected Areas in Communications*, vol. SAC-5, no. 2, pp. 261-268, Feb. 1987.

[3] A. Demers, S. Keshav, and S. Shenker, "Analysis and Simulation of a Fair Queueing Algorithm," *Proceedings of the ACM SIGCOMM'89*, pp. 1-12, Sept. 1989.

[4] G. Falk, J. S. Groff, W. C. Milliken, M. Nodine, S. Blumenthal, and W. Edmond, "Integration of Voice and Data in the Wideband Packet Satellite Network," *IEEE Journal on Selected Areas in Communications*, vol. SAC-1, no. 6, pp. 1076-1083, Dec. 1983.

[5] S. Floyd and V. Jacobson, "Link-sharing and Resource Management Models for Packet Networks," *IEEE/ACM Transactions on Networking*, vol. 3, no. 4, pp. 365-386, Aug. 1995.

[6] J. Gruber and L. Strawczynski, "Subjective Effects of Variable Delay and Speech Clipping in Dynamically Managed Voice Systems," *IEEE Transactions on Communications*, vol. COM-33, no. 8, pp. 801-808, Aug. 1985.

[7] M. J. Karol, Z. Liu, and K. Y. Eng, "Distributed-Queueing Requests Update Multiple Access (DQRUMA) for Wireless Packet (ATM) Networks," *Proceedings of INFOCOM'95*, pp. 1224-1231, 1995.

[8] M. Kawagishi, S. Sampei, and N. Morinaga, "A Novel Reservation TDMA Based Multiple Access Scheme Using Adaptive Modulation for Multimedia Wireless Communication Systems," *Proceedings of VTC'98*, pp. 112-116, 1998.

[9] T. V. Lakshman, A. Ortega, and A. R. Reibman, "VBR Video: Tradeoffs and Potentials," *Proceedings of the IEEE*, vol. 86, no. 5, pp. 952-973, May 1998.

[10] V. K. N. Lau, "Performance of Variable Rate Bit-Interleaved Coding for High Bandwidth Efficiency," *Proceedings of VTC'2000*, Tokyo, May 2000, accepted for publication and to appear.

[11] X. Qiu, V. O. K. Li, and J.-H. Ju, "A Multiple Access Scheme for Multimedia Traffic in Wireless ATM," *ACM/Baltzer Mobile Networks and Applications*, vol. 1, pp. 259-272, 1996.

[12] D. Raychaudhuri, "Wireless ATM Networks: Technology Status and Future Directions," *Proceedings of the IEEE*, vol. 87, no. 10, pp. 1790-1806, October 1999.

[13] J. Sanchez, R. Martinez, and M. W. Marcellin, "A Survey of MAC Protocols Proposed for Wireless ATM," *IEEE Network*, vol. 11, no. 6, pp. 52-62, Nov./Dec. 1997.

[14] M. Shreedhar and G. Varghese, "Efficient Fair Queuing Using Deficit Round Robin," *Proceedings of the ACM SIGNCOMM'95*, Sept. 1995.

[15] A. Urie, M. Streeton, and C. Mourot, "An Advanced TDMA Mobile Access System for UMTS," *Proceedings of the IEEE PIMRC'94*, 1994.

[16] M. D. Yocoub, *Foundations of Mobile Radio Engineering*, McGraw Hill, 2nd edition, 1986.

Dynamic-CBT and ChIPS – Router Support for Improved Multimedia Performance on the Internet

Jae Chung and Mark Claypool
Computer Science Department
Worcester Polytechnic Institute
Worcester, MA 01609
1-508-831-5357

{goos|claypool}@cs.wpi.edu

ABSTRACT

The explosive increase in the volume and variety of Internet traffic has placed a growing emphasis on congestion control and fairness in Internet routers. Approaches to the problem of congestion, such as active queue management schemes like Random Early Detection (RED) use congestion avoidance techniques and are successful with TCP flows. Approaches to the problem of fairness, such as Fair Random Early Drop (FRED), keep per-flow state and punish misbehaved, non-TCP flows. Unfortunately, these punishment mechanisms also result in a significant performance drop for multimedia flows that use flow control. We extend Class-Based Threshold (CBT) [12], and propose a new active queue management mechanism as an extension to RED called Dynamic Class-Based Threshold (D-CBT) to improve multimedia performance on the Internet. Also, as an effort to reduce multimedia jitter, we propose a lightweight packet scheduling called Cut-In Packet Scheduling (ChIPS) as an alternative to FIFO packet scheduling. The performance of our proposed mechanisms is measured, analyzed and compared with other mechanisms (RED and CBT) in terms of throughput, fairness and multimedia jitter through simulation using NS. The study shows that D-CBT improves fairness among different classes of flows and ChIPS improves multimedia jitter without degrading fairness.

Keywords

Multimedia, Router, Queue management, Congestion, Fairness, Jitter

1. INTRODUCTION

The Internet has moved from a data communication network for a few privileged professions to an essential part of public life similar to the public telephone networks, while assuming the role of the underlying communication network for multimedia applications such as Internet phone, video conferencing and video on demand (VOD). As a consequence, the volume of traffic and the number of simultaneous active flows that an Internet router

handles has increased dramatically, placing new emphasis on congestion control and traffic fairness. Complicating traditional congestion control is the presence of multimedia traffic that has strict timing constraints, specifically *delay* constraints and variance in delay, or *jitter* constraints [3,11]. This paper presents a router queue management mechanism that addresses the problem of congestion and fairness, and improves multimedia performance on the Internet. Figure 1 shows some of the current and the proposed router queue mechanisms.

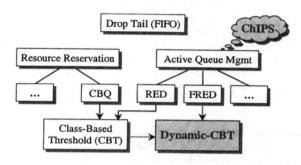

Figure 1. Router Queue Mechanisms (shaded are proposed)

There have been two major approaches suggested to handle congestion by means other than traditional drop-tail FIFO queuing. The first approach uses packet or link scheduling on multiple logical or physical queues to explicitly reserve and allocate output bandwidth to each class of traffic, where a class can be a single flow or a group of similar flows. This is the basic idea of various Fair Queuing (FQ) disciplines such as DRR [13] and the Class-Based Queuing (CBQ) algorithm [7]. When coupled with admission control, the mechanism not only suggests a solution to the problem of congestion but also offers potential performance guarantees for the multimedia traffic class. However, this explicit resource reservation approach would change the "best effort" nature of the current Internet, and the fairness definition of the traditional Internet may no longer be preserved. Adopting this mechanism would require a change in the network management and billing practices. Also, the algorithmic complexity and state requirements of scheduling make its deployment difficult [12].

The second approach, called Active Queue Management, uses advanced packet queuing disciplines other than traditional FIFO drop-tail queuing on an outbound queue of a router to actively handle (or avoid) congestion with the help of cooperative traffic sources. In the Internet, TCP recognizes packet loss as an indicator of network congestion, and its back-off algorithm reduces transmission load when network congestion is detected [4]. One of the earliest and well-known active queue management mechanism is Random Early Detection (RED), which prevents congestion through monitoring outbound buffers to detect impending congestion, and randomly chooses and notifies senders of network congestion so that they can reduce their transmission rate [6]. While fairly handling congestion for TCP flows, RED reveals the critical problem that non-TCP flows that are unresponsive or have greedier flow-control mechanisms than TCP can take more share of the output bandwidth than TCP flows [10,12]. In the worst case, it is possible for non-TCP flows, especially for unresponsive ones, to monopolize the output bandwidth while TCP connections are forced to transmit at their minimum rates. This unfairness occurs because non-TCP flows reduce transmission load relatively less than TCP flows or do not reduce at all, and the same drop rate is applied to every flow.

This unfairness could be a serious problem in a near future as the number of Internet multimedia flows increases. Delay sensitive multimedia applications typically use UDP rather than TCP because they require in-time packet delivery and can tolerate some loss, rather than the guaranteed packet delivery with potentially large end-to-end delay that TCP produces. Also, they prefer the periodic packet transmission characteristics of UDP rather than the bursty packet transmission characteristics of TCP that can introduce higher receiver side jitter. Multimedia UDP applications either do not use any flow-control mechanism or use their own application-level flow control mechanisms that are rate-based rather than window based and hence tend to be greedier than that of TCP taking the multimedia Quality of Service (QoS) requirements into account.

In addressing the problem of fairness, there have been strong arguments that unresponsive or misbehaving flows should be penalized to protect well-behaved TCP flows[1] [5]. Fair Random Early Drop (FRED) is an active queue management approach that incorporates this argument [10]. FRED adds per-active-flow accounting to RED, isolating each flow from the effects of others. It enforces fairness in terms of output buffer space by strictly penalizing unresponsive or misbehaving flows to have an equal fair share while assuring packets from flows that do not consume their fair share are transmitted without loss. FRED achieves its purpose not only in protecting TCP flows from unresponsive and misbehaving flows but also in protecting fragile TCP connections from robust TCP connections. However, FRED has a potential problem that its TCP favored per-flow punishment could unnecessarily discourage flow-controlled interactive multimedia flows. Under FRED, incoming packets for a well-behaved TCP flow consuming more than their fair share are randomly dropped applying RED's drop rate. However, once a flow, although flow-controlled, is marked as a non-TCP friendly flow, it is regarded as an unresponsive flow and all incoming packets of the flow are dropped when it is using more than its fair share. As a result, a flow-controlled multimedia UDP flow, which may have a higher chance to be marked, will experience more packet loss than a TCP flow and be forced to have less than its fair share of bandwidth.

Another major concern with FRED is that the per-active-flow accounting is expensive and might not scale well.

Core-Stateless Fair Queueing (CSFQ) [14] addresses the scalability problem by deploying hierarchical distribution of the per-flow accounting workload. In CSFQ, edge routers are distinguished from core routers, where edge routers calculate per-flow state information in terms of rate estimates and label outgoing packets, and core routers use the rate estimates to achieve fair allocation of the output bandwidth without maintaining per-flow states. The accuracy of CSFQ relies heavily on the assumption that all packets from a flow travel along the same path.

Jeffay et al., [12] propose a new active queue management scheme called Class-Based Threshold (CBT), which releases UDP flows from strict per-flow punishment while protecting TCP flows by adding a simple class-based static bandwidth reservation mechanism to RED. In fact, CBT implements an explicit resource reservation feature of CBQ on a single queue that is fully or partially managed by RED without using packet scheduling. Instead, it uses class thresholds that determine ratios between the number of queue elements that each class may use during congestion. CBT defines three classes: tagged (multimedia) UDP[2], untagged (other) UDP and TCP. For each of the two UDP classes, CBT assigns a pre-determined static threshold and maintains a weighted-average number of enqueued packets that belong to the class, and drops the incoming class' packets when the class average exceeds the class threshold. By applying a threshold test to each UDP class, CBT protects TCP flows from unresponsive or misbehaving UDP flows, and also protects multimedia UDP flows from the effect of other UDP flows. CBT avoids congestion as well as RED, has less overhead and improves multimedia throughput and packet drop rates compared to FRED. However, as in the case of CBQ, the static resource reservation mechanism of CBT could result in poor performance for rapidly changing traffic mixes and is arguably unfair since it changes the best effort nature of the Internet.

To eliminate the limitations due to the explicit resource reservation of CBT while preserving its good features from class-based isolation, we propose *Dynamic-CBT (D-CBT)*. D-CBT fairly allocates the bandwidth of a congested link to the traffic classes by dynamically assigning the UDP thresholds such that the sum of the fair share of flows in each class is assigned to the class at any given time. In addition, as a means to improve multimedia jitter, we propose a lightweight multimedia-favored packet scheduling mechanism, *Cut-In Packet Scheduling* (ChIPS), as an alternative to FIFO packet scheduling under D-CBT and possibly under other RED like active queue management mechanisms. ChIPS monitors average enqueue rates of tagged and the other flows, and is invoked when the tagged flows are using a relatively smaller fraction of bandwidth than the TCP flows. On transient congestion in which the queue length is greater than the average queue length, ChIPS awards well-behaved (flow-controlled) multimedia flows by allowing their packets to "cut" in the queue to the average queue length.

---

[1] A *well-behaved flow* (or TCP friendly) is defined as a flow that behaves like a TCP flow with a correct congestion avoidance implementation. A flow-controlled flow that acts different (or greedier) than well-behaved flow is a *misbehaving flow*.

---

[2] Tagged (multimedia) UDP flows can be distinguished from other (untagged) UDP flows by setting an unused bit of the Type of Service field in the IP header (Version 4).

To evaluate the proposed mechanisms, we use an event driven network simulator called NS (version 2) that simulates a variety of IP networks [15]. NS implements most of the common IP network components including RED. We implement CBT in NS, extend it to D-CBT, add ChIPS into D-CBT, and compare the performance of D-CBT and D-CBT with ChIPS with that of RED and CBT. In the evaluation, our primary focus is on the effect of heterogeneously flow-controlled traffic on the behavior of the queue management mechanisms especially on fairness, and the effect of queue management on the performance of well-behaved (flow-controlled) multimedia flows.

2. PROPOSED MECHANISMS

This section presents the design and implementation of Dynamic-CBT (D-CBT) and Cut-In Packet Scheduling (ChIPS) in detail. Before describing D-CBT and ChIPS, we present the design of Class-Based Threshold (CBT) [12] which D-CBT extends. As discussed briefly in Section 1, the main idea behind the design of CBT is to apply class-based isolation on a single queue that is fully or partially managed by RED without using packet scheduling. Instead of using packet scheduling on multiple logical queues, CBT regulates congestion-time output bandwidth for n classes of flows using a RED queue management mechanism and a threshold for each of the $n-1$ classes of flows, which is the average number of queue units that a class may use. The conceptual view of the first CBT design is shown in Figure 2.

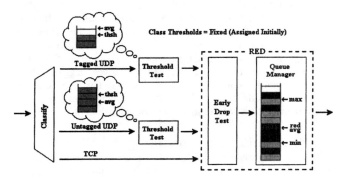

Figure 2. CBT (with RED for all) Conceptual View

CBT categorizes flows into three classes, which are TCP, tagged (multimedia) UDP and untagged (other) UDP, and assigns a pre-determined static threshold for each of the two UDP classes, assuming that UDP flows are mostly unresponsive or misbehaving and need to be regulated. When a UDP packet arrives, the weighted-average for the appropriate class is updated and compared against the threshold for the class to decide whether to drop the packet before passing it to the RED algorithm. For the TCP class, CBT does not apply a threshold test but directly passes incoming packets to the RED test unit. This is the first design of CBT, called "CBT with RED for all". In the second design, called "CBT with RED for TCP", only TCP packets are subjected to RED's early drop test, and UDP packets that survive a threshold test are directly enqueued to the outbound queue that is managed by RED. Another difference from the first design is that RED's average queue size is calculated only using the number of enqueued TCP packets. CBT with RED for TCP is based on the assumption that tagged (multimedia) UDP flows as well as untagged (other) UDP flows are mostly unresponsive, and it is of

no use to notify these traffic sources of congestion earlier. D-CBT is extended from CBT with RED for all. In the rest of this paper, CBT refers to CBT with RED for all.

2.1 Dynamic-CBT (D-CBT)

D-CBT enforces fairness among classes of flows, and gives UDP classes better queuing resource utilization. Figure 3 shows the design of D-CBT. The key difference from CBT is (1) the dynamically moving fair thresholds and (2) the UDP class threshold test that actively monitors and responds to RED indicated congestion. To be more specific, by dynamically assigning the UDP thresholds such that the sum of the fair average queue resource share of flows in each class[3] is assigned to the class at any given time, D-CBT fairly allocates the bandwidth of a congested link to the traffic classes. Also, the threshold test units, which are activated when RED declares impending congestion (i.e. $red\_avg > red\_min$), coupled with the fair class thresholds, allow the UDP classes to use the available queue resources more effectively than in CBT, in which each UDP class uses the queue elements an average of no more than its fixed threshold at any time. Looking at it from a different view, D-CBT can be thought of a Class-Based FRED-like mechanism that does *per-class-accounting* on the three classes of flows.

As in CBT, D-CBT categorizes flows into TCP, tagged UDP and untagged UDP classes. However, unlike the class categorization of CBT in which flow-controlled multimedia flows are not distinguished from unresponsive multimedia flows (all tagged), D-CBT classifies UDP flows into flow-controlled multimedia (tagged) UDP and other (untagged) UDP. The objective behind this classification is to protect flow-controlled multimedia flows from unresponsive multimedia flows, and encourage multimedia applications to use congestion avoidance mechanisms, which may be different than those of TCP. We believe that there are advantages in categorizing UDP traffic in this way for the following reasons: first, multimedia applications are the primary flows that use high bandwidth UDP; second, by categorizing flows by their congestion responsiveness characteristic (i.e. TCP friendly, flow-controlled but misbehaving multimedia and unresponsive flows), different management can be applied to the classes of differently flow-controlled flows.

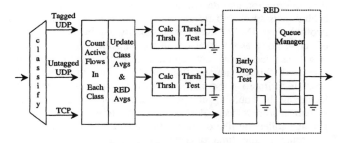

* Threshold Test is activated when $red\_avg > red\_min$

Figure 3. Design of Dynamic-CBT (D-CBT)

---

[3] Fair class shares are calculated based on the ratio between the number of active flows in each class.

In fact, in determining the fair UDP thresholds, D-CBT calculates the fair average output buffer share of the tagged UDP class from the average queue length that is maintained by RED, and that of untagged UDP class from the RED's minimum threshold (plus a small allowance). This is based on the assumption that tagged flows (or flow-controlled multimedia) can respond to network congestion and will actively try to lower the average length of a congested queue on notification of congestion. Therefore, they are allowed to use the impending congestion state queue buffers (i.e. *red_avg – red_min* when *red_avg > red_min*) up to their fair share of the average. However, unresponsive (untagged) flows, which have no ability to respond to network congestion, are not allowed to use the impending state queue buffers at impending congestion. Actually, we allow the unresponsive UDP class to use a small fraction of the impending state queue buffers, which is 10% of (*red_max – red_min*) * *untagged_UDP_share* when the maximum early drop rate is 0.1, to compensate for the effect of needless additional early drops for the class.

In the design of D-CBT, the existence of the active flow counting unit is a big structural difference from CBT. In order to calculate a fair threshold (or average queue resource share) for each class, D-CBT needs class state information, and therefore keeps track of the number of active flows in each class. Generally, as in FRED, active flows are defined as ones whose packets are in the outbound queue [10]. However, we took slightly different approach in detecting active flows, in that an active flow is one whose packet has entered the outbound queue unit during a certain predefined interval since the last time checked. In D-CBT, an active flow counting unit that comes right after the classifier maintains a sorted linked list, which contains a flow descriptor and its last packet reception time, and a flow counter for each class. Currently, the flow descriptor consists of a destination IP address and the flow ID (IPv6). However, assuming IPv4, this could be replaced by source and destination address, although this would redefine a flow as per source-destination pair.

For an incoming packet after the classification, the counting unit updates an appropriate data structure by inserting or updating the flow information and the current local time. When inserting new flow information, the flow counter of the class is also increased by one. The counting unit, at a given interval (set to 300ms in our implementation), traverses each class' linked list, deletes the old flow information and decreases the flow counter. The objective behind this probabilistic active flow counting approach is twofold: First, D-CBT does not necessarily require an exact count of active flows as do other queue mechanisms that are based on flow-based-accounting, although a more exact count is better for exercising fairness among flow classes. Second, it might be possible to improve the mechanism's packet processing delay by localizing the counting unit with the help of router's operating system and/or device. For example, the traversing delete is a garbage collection-like operation that could be performed during the router's idle time or possibly processed by a dedicated processor in a multiprocessor environment. In our simulator implementation, we used a sorted linked list data structure that has inserting and updating complexity of $O(n)$, and traversing complexity of $O(n)$, where n is the number of flows of a class. Assuming that a simple hash table is used instead, the complexity of inserting and updating operation drops to $O(1)$, while the complexity of the traverse delete will remain $O(n)$. Future work suggests more thorough measurement of added overhead.

When an incoming packet is updated or inserted according to its flow identification to its class data structure at the counting unit, D-CBT updates the RED queue average, the tagged UDP average and the untagged UDP average, and passes the packet to an appropriate test unit as shown in Figure 3. Note that for every incoming packet all of the averages are updated using the same weight. This is to apply the same updating ratio to the weighted-averages, so that a snapshot in time at any state gives the correct average usage ratio among the classes. Using the three averages and the active flow count for each class, the UDP threshold test units calculate the fair thresholds for the tagged and untagged UDP classes, and apply the threshold test to incoming packets of the class when the RED queue indicates impending congestion. UDP packets that survive an appropriate threshold test are passed to the RED unit along with the TCP flows as in CBT.

Thus, D-CBT is designed to provide traditional fairness between flows of different characteristics by classifying and applying different enqueue policies to them, and restrict each UDP class to use the queue buffer space up to their share in average. We hypothesize that the advantages of D-CBT are the following: First, D-CBT avoids congestion as well as RED with the help of responsive traffic sources. Second, assuming that the flows in a class (especially the tagged UDP flows) use flow control mechanisms of which the congestion responsiveness characteristics are almost the same, D-CBT will fairly assign bandwidth to each flow with much less overhead than FRED, which requires per-flow state information. Even if the tagged flows do not use their fair share, D-CBT will still successfully assign bandwidth fairly to each class of flows, protecting TCP from the effect of misbehaving and unresponsive flows and also protecting the misbehaving (flow-controlled multimedia) flows from the effect of unresponsive flows. Lastly, D-CBT gives tagged (flow-controlled multimedia) flows a better chance to fairly consume the output bandwidth than under FRED by performing per-class punishments instead of the strict per-flow punishment.

2.2 Cut-In Packet Scheduling (ChIPS)

ChIPS is a light-weight multimedia favored packet scheduling mechanism that can replace the FCFS enqueue style packet scheduling of a RED-managed queue for CBT, D-CBT and possibly other RED-like mechanisms, which is specifically targeted to improve multimedia jitter. ChIPS monitors the average enqueue rates of tagged and the other flows, and is activated when the tagged flows are using a relatively smaller fraction of bandwidth than the TCP flows. On transient congestion in which the queue length is greater than the average queue length, ChIPS awards tagged (flow-controlled multimedia) flows by allowing their packets to "cut" in the line of queue to the average queue length. Figure 4 shows the design of ChIPS.

By inserting tagged UDP packets at the average queue length on transient congestion, ChIPS improves flow-controlled multimedia jitter. However, this could harm the TCP flows and even make them time out by introducing a large extra delay when the multimedia traffic is taking a considerable portion of the output bandwidth. Under the normal RED queue mechanism that has no means to regulate the queue buffer usage among the classes of flows, it is essential for ChIPS to monitor the average enqueue ratio between the tagged and other flows and turn on its function only when the ratio is small. However, under CBT, in which the tagged threshold can be explicitly set to use a small fraction of the available queue buffer, this automatic turn on/off function is not really necessary. When used with D-CBT, the ratio that turns off ChIPS could be set relatively large (tested for up to 50% in our simulations with a RED minimum threshold of 5 and the maximum of 15) without degrading the fairness because of the "self-adjusting" ability of D-CBT. When a relatively large number of tagged flows compete for bandwidth with TCP flows, ChIPS could instantly lower the throughput of the TCP flows. However, this will also lower the average queue length of the queue, and therefore the fair threshold for the tagged class will be reduced and the tagged class throughput will be reduced as well. Thus, ChIPS may cause the average queue length to fluctuate a bit more but should not reduce fairness significantly. Section 5 has detailed results.

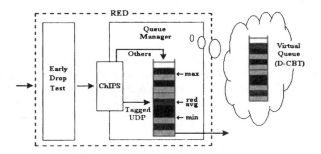

Figure 4. Design of ChIPS (Tagged Packet Insertion on Transient Congestion)

Another issue in implementing ChIPS is that the increment of the tagged packet dequeue rate caused by the insertion could degrade the fairness when the packet enqueue decision makes use of each class' buffer usage as in CBT and D-CBT. This faster tagged packet drain rate is not an issue for RED since its enqueue decision has nothing to do with the drain rate. However, in CBT and D-CBT, the faster drain rate lowers the average number of enqueued packets for the tagged class, which could result in the tagged class getting more bandwidth than its fair share. To prevent this effect, we used a virtual FIFO queue for counting the number of enqueued packets for the UDP classes, in which the class information of an enqueuing packet is always enqueued at the end, even though ChIPS cuts a tagged packet in the line of the real queue. In this way, the virtual queue can help more fairly count the class averages by telling if the tagged packets that have been transmitted already are still in the queue. Thus, the actual tagged packet drain rate does not affect the calculation of the average number of enqueued packets for the tagged class.

Looking at the complexity of the design, ChIPS has $O(1)$ behavior, since the insertion complexity is $O(1)$ and the virtual queue maintenance complexity is also $O(1)$. We believe that ChIPS, which noticeably improves tagged flow (flow-controlled multimedia) jitter, along with D-CBT would further encourage multimedia applications to use a flow control mechanism. An important issue that is not addressed in this paper is how to monitor and tag the flow-controlled multimedia flows. This issue of packet marking is beyond the scope of this paper, but can be extended from research into Diffserv scenarios [1]. We believe that this job should be done at the Internet Service Provider (ISP)

or at the local network management level at the gateways to the public networks, and leave the routers free from this issue. The next section presents the methods we used to evaluate D-CBT and ChIPS.

3. PERFORMANCE METRICS

This section presents the fairness and jitter measurement metrics used to evaluate our proposed mechanism. To measure the fairness among the three different classes of flows and also to visualize the system's fairness on individual flows, we use the following two metrics. The first metric is an indicator of how fairly the output bandwidth is assigned to each class considering the number of flows in the class, called the *direct comparison of the average per-flow throughput in each class*. This is an average aggregated class throughput divided by the number of flows in the class. As the second fairness measurement metric, *Jain's fairness index* is used to visualize the fairness among individual flows [8]. Figure 5 shows the formula that calculates Jain's fairness, which gets the average throughputs of the flows (x_i) of which the fairness is measured as an input, and produces a normalized number between 0 and 1, where 0 indicates the greatest unfairness and 1 indicates the greatest fairness.

$$f(x_0, x_1, x_2, \cdots, x_n) = \frac{\left(\sum_{i=0}^{n} x_i\right)^2}{n \sum_{i=0}^{n} x_i^2}$$

Figure 5. Jain's Fairness Index Equation

Another network performance factor we measure is multimedia stream jitter (Figure 6). Jitter can is primarily measured in one of two ways: *variance in inter-frame arrival time* at the receiver, and *variance in end-to-end delay*. While the former is a receiver-oriented observation on the variance, the latter is a more network-oriented observation of the variance. Measuring jitter as variance in inter-frame arrival time (ex, r2 – r1) is useful when a traffic source's frame transmission interval is fixed. However, it may not be a good measure of jitter when the transmission interval varies as in the case of flow-controlled multimedia applications which may not transmit a frame in response to congestion. Measuring jitter in terms of end-to-end delay (ex, r2 – s2) is more direct indicator of a system's performance on multimedia streams, since it eliminates the inter-frame transmission periods of the source.

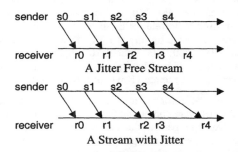

Figure 6. Multimedia Jitter – *si* **is the time at which the sender transmits frame** *i*. **r***i* **is the time at which the receiver receives frame** *i*.

In real environments, it is hard to measure jitter in terms of variance in end-to-end delay because of asynchronized clocks at the source and destination. However, in our simulation environment where only one logical clock is used for the whole system, it is easy to measure the variance in the end-to-end delay. Moreover, this method can even visualize the effect of queuing delays of a single router on jitter well. Therefore, we measured jitter in terms of variance in end-to-end delay.

4. SIMULATION

We ran a simulation for each of RED, CBT, D-CBT and D-CBT with ChIPS. Every simulation had exactly the same settings except for the network routers, each of which was set to use one of the above four outbound queue management mechanisms. The network topology and the traffic source schedules are shown in Figure 7.

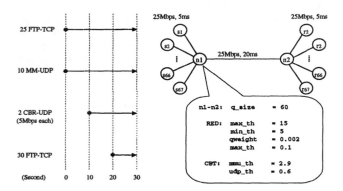

Figure 7. Simulation Scenario and Network Setup

In each simulation, we had 67 source nodes connected to one router and 67 destination nodes connected to the other router, which are interconnected by a link with 25Mbps bandwidth and 20ms of delay. Each link that connects a source (or destination) node and a router was set to have 25Mbps of bandwidth and 5ms of delay. For traffic sources, 55 FTP, 10 flow-controlled multimedia traffic generators called MM_APP [2] (tagged) and 2 CBR (untagged) traffic generators were used, where FTP used TCP Reno and the others used UDP as the underlying transport agent. All the TCP agents were set to have a maximum congestion window size of 20 packets and maximum packet size of 1Kbyte. The UDP agents were also set to have maximum packet size of 1Kbyte, so that all the packets in the network were the same size. The MM_APP traffic generators, which react to congestion using 5 discrete media scales with a "cut scale by half at frame loss, up scale by one at RTT" flow control mechanism, used 300, 500, 700, 900 and 1,100Kbps for scale 0 to 4 transmission rates, with a fixed packet size of 1Kbyte. The CBR sources were set to generate 1Kbyte packets at a rate of 5Mbps.

We scheduled the traffic sources such that 25 TCP flows and 10 MM_APP flows were competing for the bandwidth during 0 to 10 seconds. At this period the fair bandwidth share for each connection was about 714Kbps (25Mbps / 35 flows). In the next period (10 to 20 seconds), the two high bandwidth CBR blasts joined trying to aggressively use the output bandwidth of which the average fair share was about 675Kbps (25Mbps / 37 flows). Later at 20 seconds, 30 more TCP flows came into the network

lowering the average fair share during the last 10 seconds to about 373Kbps (25Mbps / 67 flows).

Network routers were assigned a 60-packet long physical outbound queue. The RED parameters, which are shown in Figure 7, were chosen from one of the sets that are recommended by Floyd and Jacobson [6]. For CBT, besides the RED parameters, the tagged and untagged class thresholds (denoted as *mmu_th* and *udp_th* in the figure) were set to 2.9 packets and 0.6 packets respectively to force each UDP flows to get about their fair bandwidth shares during 0 to 20 seconds. Assuming the average queue size is 10 packets, by reserving an average of a 2.9-packet space, the tagged class could get an average bandwidth of 7,250Kbps (25Mbps * 2.9 / 10) at congestion, which is about 10 times (10 tagged flows) the fair flow share during 0 to 10 seconds. Likewise, by reserving 0.6-packet space in the queue, the untagged class could get an average of 1,500Kbps, that is little bit more than 2 times (2 untagged flows) the fair flow share during 10 to 20 seconds.

D-CBT also shares the RED settings, but since each threshold is assigned dynamically to the fair share of each class, no threshold setup was necessary. Finally, ChIPS was set to turn off its cut-in scheduling feature when the ratio between the number of tagged flows and the other flows are greater than 50%. However, under our simulation, ChIPS was always on since the ratio was always under 50%.

Thus, the simulations were designed to give an environment under which all three queue management mechanism manage output bandwidth fairness during the first 10 seconds, RED fails during the second 10 seconds, and CBT fails during the last 10 seconds. Then, we examine if D-CBT dynamically offers fair bandwidth allocation in every situation. Also, by comparing the results (fairness and jitter) of D-CBT with ChIPS with basic D-CBT, we examine the effect of ChIPS on fairness and multimedia jitter.

5. RESULTS AND ANALYSIS

We measured the performance of RED, CBT, D-CBT, and D-CBT with ChIPS in terms of fairness and multimedia jitter. We also compared TCP throughput under ChIPS and basic D-CBT as well as packet drop percentages.

5.1 Class' Average Per-Flow Throughput

Figure 8 (a) through (d) compares the periodic (i.e., 0-10, 10-20 and 20-30 seconds) average per-flow throughput for each class under the four queue mechanisms.

As shown in Figure 8 (a), RED absolutely failed to assign bandwidth fairly to each class of flows from 10 seconds when the two high bandwidth untagged UDP flows (unresponsive CBR) join transmitting at a total of 10Mbps, about 40% of the link bandwidth. During 0-10 seconds, when 25 TCP and 10 tagged (flow-controlled MM_APP) flows were competing for the bandwidth, it was somewhat unfair as a tagged flow got an average of 37% more bandwidth than a TCP flow, but RED was able to manage the bandwidth. However, when the untagged UDP blast came into the system, RED was totally unable to manage bandwidth. The 2 untagged UDP flows got most of the bandwidth they needed (average of 4.68Mbps out of 5Mbps), and the remaining flows used the leftover bandwidth. Especially, the 25 TCP flows got severely punished and transmitted at an average of 293Kbps per flow as they often went back to slow start and even timed out. Fairness got worse as 30 more TCP flows joined at 20 seconds and experienced starvation.

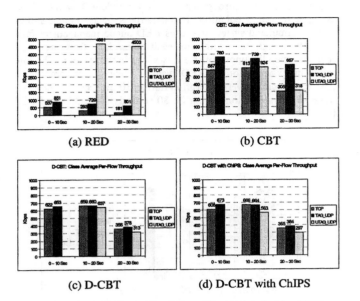

(a) RED   (b) CBT

(c) D-CBT   (d) D-CBT with ChIPS

Figure 8. Average Per-Flow Throughput for TCP, Tagged UDP and Untagged UDP Classes under RED, CBT, D-CBT and D-CBT with ChIPS

Figure 8 (b) shows that CBT can avoid the great unfairness of RED using fixed thresholds for the UDP classes. However, CBT was not assigning the output bandwidth to each class as expected. When designing the simulation, we set the UDP thresholds such that during 0-10 seconds each tagged UDP flow should get about 725Kbps on average. During 10-20 seconds, we expected that each tagged flow's average bandwidth would remain the same and each untagged UDP flow would get an average of 750Kbps. Also, we expected that during 20-30 seconds, the tagged and untagged flows would get a large portion of the bandwidth the same as during 10-20 seconds and the TCP flows would get much less than the fair share during this period. However, the simulation result shows that the tagged UDP class got more bandwidth than the expected values especially during the last period, while the untagged UDP class got much less bandwidth than expected.

We found that this is mainly due to how and when CBT updates each UDP class threshold and RED queue average. CBT updates each UDP class average only for incoming packets that belong to the class, and the RED unit updates its queue average for all incoming TCP packets and for UDP packets that passed an appropriate threshold test. Therefore, the class averages and the RED queue average are almost independently updated at different speeds that are closely related the number of incoming packets that belong to the class. In addition, the RED average has a higher chance of being updated faster than the UDP class averages. In this situation, which we call *unsynchronized weighted-average updates*, whoever (i.e. a class) updates its weighted-average more often will get less bandwidth by having a larger weighted-average than the average of others for the same

amount of class output bandwidth, and the output bandwidth is controlled using the averages at the UDP threshold test units.

Figure 9 shows this effect by comparing two situations where a UDP class that has an initial class weighted-average of 1, a weight of 0.1 and a class threshold of 1.02, is experiencing two different incoming packet rates. Figure 9 (a) is the case when the incoming packet rate is 0.5 packets per packet transmission delay, and Figure 9 (b) is the case when the class is receiving packets at the rate of 1.0 packets per packet transmission delay. In this example, it is assumed that the traffic sources are unresponsive CBR applications. One thing to note in the figure is that the class average shown at the left bottom of each queue in each state is its value before making the enqueue admission decision for an incoming packet at that state. As you can see in the figure, as the number of incoming packets for a class increases, packets are enqueued in a bursty manner, and more importantly, its class average gets larger. As the average is updated more frequently, not only is a newly enqueued packet added to the average (with the weight of 0.1), but also the existence of the other already enqueued packet are added to the average. For example, the existence of the first packet is added to the average 2 times more for the second situation than for the first situation. Note that Figure 9 (a) enqueues more packets but has a lower class average.

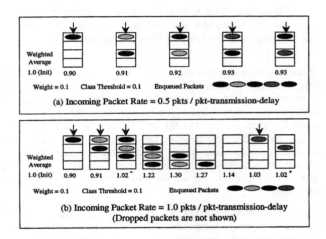

(a) Incoming Packet Rate = 0.5 pkts / pkt-transmission-delay

(b) Incoming Packet Rate = 1.0 pkts / pkt-transmission-delay
(Dropped packets are not shown)

Figure 9. A CBT Class's *Weighted Average* under Two Different Incoming Packet Rates

The weighted-average calculation method works fine when the purpose of measuring an average queue size is to detect impending congestion as in RED. However, when the method is used to assign bandwidth to different classes of flows by comparing each class' weighted-average number of enqueued packets, we have determined that all the weighted-averages should be updated at the same time and at an equal frequency to give a correct output bandwidth utilization ratio among the classes. In the case of CBT, by measuring each UDP class average and the RED average independently, the classes' bandwidth utilization could not measured correctly by comparing the class averages. By comparing the fairness measurement in Figure 8 (b) and CBT's outbound queue averages in Figure 10, especially for 20-30 seconds, one can easily see that CBT's attempt of using unsynchronously updated weighted-averages to regulate class bandwidth was misleading. Figure 10 indicates that during 20-30 seconds, 10 tagged flows used an average of about 2.5 packet-spaces in the queue that is 0.25 packet-spaces per each flow, and the 2 untagged flow used an average of about 0.6 packet-spaces that is 0.3 packet-spaces per each flow. However, as shown in Figure 8 (b), each tagged flow used about 657 Kbps of bandwidth and each untagged flow used about 318 Kbps, about one half of the per-flow bandwidth of a tagged flow.

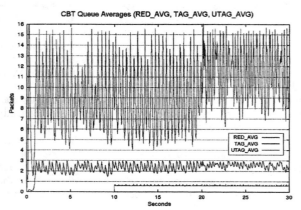

Figure 10. CBT Queue Averages – The top line is the RED average, the middle is the tagged UDP average and the lower is the untagged average.

From the above observation, we conclude that the current CBT design can only prevent a great unfairness caused by unresponsive or misbehaving flows, and it needs some adjustment on weighted-average calculation. Indeed, we tried the average calculation method that is used in D-CBT in CBT and got a much better result, that is the ratio between the three averages indicates the ratio between the actual classes' bandwidth utilization. However, we did not include the result in this paper, since the method is used in only D-CBT and we are presenting D-CBT in the next paragraph.

Figure 8 (c) shows the D-CBT results, which indicates that D-CBT fairly managed bandwidth during all periods by dynamically allocating the right amount of output queue space to each flow class. It also shows that by updating each class and RED average at the same time in a synchronized manner, the ratio between the averages is a good indicator of the ratios between each class' bandwidth utilization. One thing to note in the figure is that although we strictly regulate the untagged class by assigning a fair threshold calculated from RED's minimum threshold, the untagged class did get most of its share. This is because the high bandwidth untagged (unresponsive) packets were allowed to enter the queue without a threshold test, when RED indicated no congestion.

Figure 8 (d) shows the result of D-CBT with ChIPS. The result confirms that ChIPS, when used with D-CBT, does not affect fairness between each class of flows, due to the virtual queue and D-CBT's self adjusting capability described in Section 2.2. In the simulation, the ratio between tagged flows and all flows was about 28% during 0-20 seconds, and was about 15% during the last 10 seconds.

5.2 Jain's Fairness Measurement

Figure 11 visualizes the simulated systems' fairness on individual flows using Jain's Fairness Index, where the periodic (0-10, 10-20 and 20-30) average throughput of each individual flow was given as input to Jain's equation. Jain's fairness measurement shows that the simulated system that uses RED queue management fails to fairly assign bandwidth to each individual flow from 10 seconds when the unresponsive flows join in the system. The low Jain's index value for the RED system indicates that some flows are experiencing severe starvation during 10-20 seconds and even more severe starvation during 20-30 seconds when 30 extra TCP flows join.

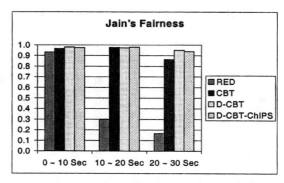

Figure 11. Jain's Fairness Comparison

The system that uses the CBT queue management mechanism was fair overall in distributing bandwidth to each flow. However, during 20-30 seconds, the system's fairness was degraded because the 10 tagged (multimedia) flows got about twice as much bandwidth as the other flows. One thing to note is that CBT's fairness was pre-engineered. In a circumstance where traffic mixes change a lot, CBT might show more degraded fairness.

On the other hand, the systems that use D-CBT or D-CBT with ChIPS were dynamically adjusting to changing flow mixes, and were very fair not only to the classes of flows but also to individual flows as Jain's index numbers indicate. Jain's fairness measurement results on D-CBT and D-CBT with ChIPS also reconfirmed that ChIPS did not degrade the system's fairness.

5.3 Analysis of ChIPS

Now that we have shown that D-CBT outperforms RED and CBT in managing bandwidth, and that the use of ChIPS does not degrade the performance of D-CBT, this section presents the performance of ChIPS on multimedia jitter and TCP throughput. Figure 12 shows tagged UDP (or multimedia) jitter by comparing a MM_APP application's end-to-end frame delay under D-CBT and D-CBT with ChIPS.

The result indicates that ChIPS does improve tagged stream jitter by inserting tagged packets into the line of the queue to which the RED average points on transient congestion. Under ChIPS, the maximum tagged-UDP jitter was about 5ms (36ms – 31ms) while it was about 12ms (43ms – 31ms) under normal D-CBT. Noting that the maximum threshold of RED was set to 15 packets, which gives about 3ms (15pkts * 8Kbits / 25Mbps) of queuing delay, ChIPS was able to regulate the maximum tagged stream jitter around the queuing delay of the RED's maximum threshold.

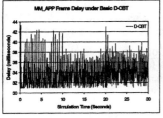
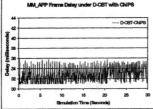

(a) Basic D-CBT   (b) D-CBT w/ ChIPS

Figure 12. ChIPS Effect on Multimedia Jitter

We believe that ChIPS effect on improved multimedia jitter could be very significant because of the following two reasons. First, what we show in Figure 12 is the jitter gain due to a single router. When multiple routers are involved, the jitter gain due to ChIPS could be larger. Second, in the simulation, we used multimedia frames that are the same size as that of a network packet, meaning that no frame fragmentation occurs in the IP layer. Assuming that a multimedia application uses frames that are larger than a network packet and are chopped into multiple packets in the network, the jitter improvement due to ChIPS could be even more significant, since the multimedia packets have a better chance to be transmitted close to each other at routers. Thus, we believe that the potential for ChIPS to improve multimedia jitter is larger than shown in our experiments.

Table 1. TCP Packet Accounting (0 ~ 30 Seconds)

	TCP Packets Delivered	TCP Packet Drop Rate	TCP Throughput
D-CBT	66,648 pkts	4.46 %	17,773 Kbps
D-CBT w/ ChIPS	66,386 pkts	4.44 %	17,703 Kbps

Table 2. Tagged (MM) Packet Accounting (0 ~ 30 Seconds)

	Tagged Packets Delivered	Tagged Packet Drop Rate
D-CBT	21,126 pkts	11.85 %
D-CBT w/ ChIPS	21,519 pkts	12.95 %

Lastly, we present TCP packet accounting and tagged packet accounting for the simulation in Table 1 and Table 2. Table 1 shows the TCP packet drop rate and throughput under ChIPS is very compatible with those of basic D-CBT. The TCP throughput under ChIPS was about 99.6% of the throughput under basic D-CBT. This indicates that ChIPS, when used along with D-CBT, may not significantly affect the TCP throughput. Comparing the TCP throughput loss with the multimedia jitter gain, ChIPS compensates 14.3% ((42*ms* - 36*ms*) / 42*ms* * 100) of multimedia jitter gain for 0.4% of TCP throughput loss for the simulation.

Table 2 shows the multimedia packet drop rate of the system that used ChIPS is very compatible with that of the system that used basic D-CBT. This result shows that ChIPS has a high potential to improve end-user multimedia performance (perceptual quality) on the Internet by improving jitter without increasing the multimedia packet drop rate, which is another important factor in multimedia perceptual quality and for congestion control and system utilization.

6. CONCLUSION

In this paper, we have presented the design and evaluation of our proposed router queue mechanisms, Dynamic Class-Based Threshold (D-CBT) and Cut-In Packet Scheduling (ChIPS), by comparing their performance with that of RED and CBT. D-CBT is a new active queue management mechanism that addresses the problem of fairness by grouping flows into TCP, tagged (flow-controlled multimedia) UDP and untagged (other) UDP classes and regulating the average queue usage of the UDP classes to their fair shares. ChIPS is a multimedia-favored lightweight packet scheduling mechanism that can substitute the FCFS enqueue style packet scheduling part of a RED-managed queue for D-CBT and possibly for other RED-like queue mechanisms.

As expected, RED, previously shown to be fair among TCP flows, showed an extreme unfairness with mixed traffic. CBT that uses a fixed threshold on UDP classes was able to avoid extreme unfairness. However, during the analysis, we found that CBT suffers from "unsynchronized weighted-average updates". That is, the ratio between independently updated UDP class averages and RED average does not correctly indicate the actual class bandwidth utilization ratio, since whichever class updates the average more frequently will have higher weighted-average than the others will, although they all use the same amount of bandwidth.

D-CBT fixes CBT's problem by synchronizing all the average updates, and better manages bandwidth by dynamically determining the UDP thresholds to cooperate with RED by fairly assigning the output bandwidth to each class for all traffic mixes. That is, through class-based accounting, D-CBT fairly protects TCP from the effect of UDP flows and also fairly protects tagged UDP flows from untagged flows. We have also shown that ChIPS, when used with D-CBT, can improve multimedia jitter without degrading fairness.

There exist many possible areas for future work and still remain many performance aspects to be evaluated. Recently, we implemented CBT and D-CBT into the Linux kernel [9], which currently works both for IPv4 and IPv6. Our current ongoing work is in measuring and analyzing the overheads of D-CBT using the Linux implementation and in optimizing it. Another area for future work is to measure the effect of the threshold test of D-CBT on multimedia QoS with currently available responsive multimedia applications, since bursty multimedia packet drops when the class average reaches the class threshold may degrade the multimedia quality noticeably.

Another possible future project would be to extend this study to evaluate the limitation of ChIPS on the fairness and the link utilization offered by D-CBT. As noted in Section 2.2, ChIPS introduces an additional delay to other traffic which may affect TCP throughput. Therefore, in order for the use of ChIPS to be more practical, future work suggests an extended study to determine the maximum average ChIPS enqueue ratio between tagged and the other classes of flows without degrading fairness or link utilization. An additional project would be to evaluate D-CBT and ChIPS under the environment where fragile and robust

TCP connections as well as multimedia connections with different end-to-end delays coexist in the system. Another study that we could not do due to the lack of time but suggest as a future work is to compare the performance of the D-CBT with that of FRED. We expect that D-CBT could give better throughput performance for tagged UDP flows than FRED, since it frees flow-controlled multimedia flows from the strict per-flow punishment.

7. ACKNOWLEDGMENT
The authors are grateful for the detailed suggestions by several anonymous reviewers.

8. REFERENCES

[1] Bernet, Y. et. Al. "A Framework for Differentiated Services", February 1999, Internet Draft, draft-ietf-diffserv-framework-02.txt

[2] Chung, J. and Claypool, M., "Better-Behaved, Better-Performing Multimedia Networking", *SCS Euromedia Conference*, Antwerp, Belgium, May 8-10, 2000

[3] Claypool, M. and Tanner, J., "The Effects of Jitter on the Perceptual Quality of Video", *ACM Multimedia Conference*, Volume 2, Orlando, FL, October 30 - November 5, 1999

[4] Floyd, S., "TCP and Explicit Congestion Notification", *Computer Communication Review*, October 1994

[5] Floyd, S. and Fall, K., "Promoting the Use of End-to-End Congestion Control in the Internet", *IEEE/ACM Transactions on Networking*, February 1998

[6] Floyd, S. and Jacobson, V., "Random Early Detection Gateways for Congestion Avoidance", *IEEE/ACM Transactions on Networking*, August 1993

[7] Floyd, S. and Jacobson, V., "Link-sharing and Resource management Models for Packet Networks", *IEEE/ACM Transactions on Networking*, Vol. 3 No. 4, August 1995

[8] Jain, R., "The Art of Computer Systems Performance Analysis: Techniques for Experimental Design, Measurement, Simulation, and Modeling", John Wiley & Sons, Inc., New York, NY, 1991

[9] Leazard, N., Maldonado M., Mercado, E., Chung, J. and Claypool, M., "Class-Based Router Queue Management for Linux", *Technical Report WPI-CS-TR-00-15*, Computer Science, Worcester Polytechnic Institute, April 2000

[10] Lin, D. and Morris R., "Dynamics of Random Early Detection", In *Proceedings of SIGCOMM '97*, Cannes, France, September 1997

[11] Multimedia Communications Forum, Inc. "Multimedia Communications Quality of Service", *MMCF/95-010, Approved Rev 1.0*, 1995, URL: http://www.luxcom.com/library/2000/mm_qos/qos.htm

[12] Parris, M., Jeffay, K. and Smith, F. D., "Lightweight Active Router-Queue Management for Multimedia Networking", *Multimedia Computing and Networking*, SPIE Proceedings Series, Vol. 3020, San Jose, CA, January 1999

[13] Shreedhar, M. and Varghese, G., "Efficient Fair Queueing using Deficit Round Robin", In *Proceedings of SIGCOMM '95*, Boston, MA, September 1995

[14] Stoica, I., Shenker, S. and Zhang, H., "Core-Stateless Fair Queueing: Achieving Approximately Fair Bandwidth Allocation in High Speed Networks", In *Proceedings of SIGCOMM '98*, Vancouver, Canada, September 1998

[15] VINT, "Virtual InterNetwork Testbed, A Collaboration among USC/ISI, Xerox PARC, LBNL, and UCB", URL: http://netweb.usc.edu/vint

A Window-based Congestion Control for Reliable Multicast based on TCP Dynamics

Koichi Yano[*]
University of California, Berkeley

Steven McCanne
FastForward Networks

Abstract

The limitation of the current multicast model led to the development of embedded network assist and new service models for reliable transport. We show a viable solution for one of the hardest problems in reliable multicast – congestion control – through the deployment of a new forwarding service model, *"Breadcrumb forwarding service"* (BCFS). Our proposed reliable multicast transport, *"Rainbow"*, is built on top of this model. In our approach, each receiver maintains its own congestion window and individually runs window control modeled after TCP. To enhance Rainbow's scalability and support asynchronous receiver subscriptions, Rainbow utilizes Digital Fountain at the source. This allows receivers to exercise asynchronous and autonomous behavior while simultaneously enjoying the performance benefit of synchronous multicast communication with fast group establishment of BCFS. In this paper, we detail the congestion control of Rainbow and demonstrate its efficiency and scalability through simulation and analysis. According to simulation results, Rainbow shows more TCP-fair behavior than RLC, which is a TCP friendly congestion control scheme based on layered multicast.

1. Introduction

As content distribution of large data such as video over the Internet becomes commonplace, an efficient and reliable transport protocol for data dissemination to a large number of receivers becomes increasingly important. In addition, such a protocol must coexist friendly with TCP, the dominant transport protocol in the Internet. However, congestion control for reliable multicast remains one of the hardest problems. As the session size grows, a sender cannot keep track of each receiver's condition for controlling a sending rate. In addition, packet loss reports that only notify lost packets to sender result in overestimation of loss rate, known as the loss path multiplicity problem [1]. Further, using a single sending rate that conforms to the slowest receiver causes underutilization of a high bandwidth path. Finally, congestion control scheme must be designed in a TCP friendly way to co-exist with current Internet traffic.

MTCP [14] solves the loss path multiplicity problem and

[*]On leave from Canon Inc..

realize TCP-like congestion control by placing agents within the network. However, a source has to slow down the transmission rate according to the slowest path, because a MTCP source sends out a single data stream to all receivers. Thus this solution is inherently unsatisfying for deployment under a heterogeneous environment [15].

Alternatively, the source can send to multiple multicast groups allowing receivers to individually adjust their reception rate by joining and leaving multicast groups [12, 18, 19]. RLC [18] is a TCP friendly congestion control scheme based on layered multicast, which imitates TCP's behavior of additive increase and multiplicative decrease by layer organization and control timing. Unfortunately, the granularity of the layers limits the degree of adaptation, and the design of a control law that can manage receiver memberships in a scalable and robust fashion is a hard problem that has not been satisfactorily solved.

Much research advocates the strategic placement of intelligence within the network infrastructure, given the limitation of the end-to-end scheme [5] based on the current multicast service model. For example, RMTP [11], LRMP [8], and RMX [4] deploy service nodes within and across the network to carry out localized retransmission and to accommodate network heterogeneity. Other works address the problem of how one might jointly optimize the design of a new multicast service with complementary end-to-end transport protocols, thereby retaining many of the merits of the end-to-end approach. In LMS [13], multicast routers conspire to arrange the receivers into a tree-based hierarchy that is congruent with the underlying network topology. A similar, though less modular, approach has been undertaken in PGM [16], where routers are enhanced with transport-level knowledge and an end-to-end protocol is built on top of this transport-aware network infrastructure yielding a monolithic solution for reliable multicast loss recovery. PGM-aware routers coalesce NACKs by maintaining per-packet sequencing state in the routers. This state, in effect, forms a "trail of breadcrumbs" from the receivers missing a piece of data to the source of the data. A retransmission from the source follows the breadcrumbs and simultaneously tears down the breadcrumb state. This loss recovery scheme is optimal in the sense that retransmissions are sent to only those receivers that are in need of that data.

Some research and standardization efforts have tried to generalize the PGM-like network service, intending to be deployed for general multicast end-to-end transport protocols beyond efficient loss recovery. *Breadcrumb Forwarding Service* (BCFS) [20] defines a PGM-like reusable network service, abstracting data identifiers as labels and combining with EXPRESS-like multicast service model [7], as an explicit-source multicast service that is optimized for fast

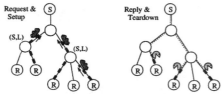

Figure 1: Basic Service Model by BCFS.

group establishment and teardown. GRA [3] is an IETF's effort to generalize PGM to a general network service, defining an architecture which specifies a router's function as filters. These novel network services have potential to be deployed for different types of multicast transport, although a transport protocol other than loss recovery has not been examined yet.

In this paper, we propose a novel multicast congestion control scheme for reliable bulk data transfer, named *Rainbow*, which is designed on top of a new multicast forwarding service, BCFS. By utilizing dynamic group establishment of BCFS, we try to realize the characteristics which are difficult to achieve at once based on the current IP multicast service model: 1) window based congestion control, 2) scalability to large scale session, 3) high utilization of network links under heterogeneous environment, 4) TCP friendly behavior. Unlike most other reliable multicasts, our protocol is built exclusively upon the BCFS service model. Also, unlike previous works, Rainbow includes a window-based congestion control algorithm that is modeled after TCP and thus provides a viable solution for congestion-controlled reliable multicast. In this approach, each receiver maintains its own congestion window and runs slow-start and congestion avoidance [9] individually by driving the equivalent of the TCP "ack clock" with breadcrumb requests. To enhance Rainbow's scalability and support asynchronous receiver subscriptions, Rainbow utilizes Digital Fountain [2] at the source to temporally decorrelate what data to send from when it must be sent. This approach allows receivers to exercise asynchronous and autonomous behavior while simultaneously enjoying the performance benefit of synchronous multicast communication.

In the remainder of the paper, we illustrate the BCFS in section 2. In section 3, we detail congestion control algorithm of Rainbow. In section 4, efficiency, scalability and TCP fairness of Rainbow is examined through a variety of simulation settings and analysis. We discuss open issues and future work in section 5 and conclude in section 6.

2. Breadcrumb Forwarding Service

The Breadcrumb Forwarding Service (BCFS) [20] unifies the EXPRESS service model and the network component of PGM into a single, flexible multicast service model. To this end, BCFS provides a single-source, request-based multicast service, where groups can be efficiently set up and torn down in tandem with data exchange. BCFS is thus optimized for ephemeral groups that come and go rapidly and is consequently well-suited as a building block for multi-group reliable multicast schemes.

To avoid unnecessary transport-level dependence, BCFS uses an abstract "label" to identify a particular request with respect to some source. The source/label pair (S,L) thus induces an group-oriented address architecture that is precisely analogous to the source/channel (S,E) framework proposed in EXPRESS. BCFS differs from EXPRESS, how-

ever, in that messages are sent from the receivers toward the source along the multicast tree and are suppressed if a message with the same label has already been sent up the tree. The group membership protocol is exposed to and run at the application layer, and arbitrary messages can be piggybacked onto these control messages. Figure 1 illustrates this breadcrumb forwarding model. Request messages for some piece of data drop breadcrumbs along the path to a source: the breadcrumbs, in turn, guide the reply message from the source back to all requesting receivers. Each breadcrumb is identified by an (S,L) pair to differentiate the forwarding paths for all labels in use. The breadcrumbs in networks are deleted during the reply message is forwarded.

To enhance the range of transport services that can be built on top of BCFS, the forwarding model includes a level-numbering scheme for selectively tearing down the breadcrumb state. Each breadcrumb carries with it a level number and each request and response includes a level number in the header of the packet. A request packet is propagated up the tree toward the sender only if its level number exceeds the level number in the breadcrumb stored at the router (or if no such breadcrumb exists). Similarly, breadcrumb state is torn down by a response packet only if the level number is equal to or exceeds the breadcrumb level stored in the router. More detailed explanation of BCFS appears in [20].

Based on this multicast forwarding service, called BCFS, we propose a congestion control scheme, Rainbow, which is detailed in the following section.

3. Rainbow on Digital Fountain

We propose a reliable multicast transport scheme, called Rainbow, (ReliAble multicast by INdividual Bandwidth adaptation using windOW), built on BCFS. Even though BCFS is modeled after PGM's network element, Rainbow differs quite substantially from PGM. In particular, our protocol exhibits a viable solution to one of the hardest problems in reliable multicast, namely congestion control.

Heterogeneity amongst receivers makes congestion control a hard problem. Because end-to-end available bandwidth varies for each receiver, a single multicast group and a single sending rate cannot satisfy all the receivers' available bandwidth. In order to tame this heterogeneity, layered scheme using multiple multicast groups has been proposed [12, 18]. Receivers can adjust their reception rates individually by subscription of multicast groups. However, the granularity of layers limits the flexibility of adaptation and the prune delay of the current multicast could cause poor performance of adaptation.

To address these problems, our proposed scheme, Rainbow, deploys BCFS as a multicast service model to take advantage of its fast group establishment feature. In addition, it places Digital Fountain [2] at the source to realize asynchronous access and scalability. A key property of the Digital Fountain is that based on forward error correction, (almost) any subset of packets may be used to decode, thereby alleviating any need for feedback from the receivers to the source. Thus, Digital Fountain provides a robust mechanism for "implicit" multicast loss recovery.

Rainbow is designed to accomplish the following

- A receiver receives data at its available rate as if there were a unicast TCP connection between a source and a receiver (i.e., the protocol dynamics are "TCP friendly")

- A bottleneck link in a multicast distribution tree is efficiently shared by data aggregation among many receivers

- The source need not manage state on a per-receiver basis, which would otherwise limit the protocol's scalability.

3.1 Congestion Control and Data Aggregation by using BCFS

In order to provide data at a different rate for each receiver without deteriorating network condition, congestion control is structured on BCFS as follows

- **Individual TCP-like window control:** Each receiver independently executes TCP-like window control [9]. Data transmissions are triggered by the arrival of breadcrumbs at the sender. Packet arrivals at the receiver cause that host to increase its congestion window (either by one for each packet received in slow start or one per round-trip in congestion avoidance mode). The invariant we maintain is that the number of breadcrumbs outstanding is less than or equal to the congestion window. Thus, the number of packets in transit from the source to the receiver is bounded by the congestion window. In addition, the congestion window is controlled in response to lost packets according to measured congestion conditions on the path from the source to that receiver. Since the window control behaves as if there were a TCP session between a source and a receiver, each receiver utilizes bandwidth in a TCP-friendly way.

- **Transmission request and data aggregation by BCFS:** A receiver sends a TRQ (transmission request) as a BCFS request using as many labels as its window size. This means that receivers which have the same window size use the identical labels for TRQs, and a receiver that has a smaller window uses a subset of the labels that are used by a receiver with a larger window size. Suppose a receivers sends a TRQ with a label, and followed by the same label TRQs from other receivers, some TRQs arrive at a BCFS router before the reply message of the first TRQ arrives. Then, the TRQs are aggregated and the copies of the identical data packet are sent to all receivers which send the TRQs with the label. TRQ corresponds to ACK in TCP in the sense that it is sent at packet reception. However it does not need to include sequence numbers of received packets.

- **Simple reply by a Digital Fountain source:** By using a Digital Fountain, the source can merely respond to each TRQ by sending one packet after another as a BCFS reply, which includes the same label as the TRQ.

Figure 2 (a) illustrates Rainbow/BCFS data aggregation, where two receivers have a shared bottleneck link. In the ideal case, the two receivers have the same window size according to the bottleneck bandwidth, and it is expected that most TRQs are aggregated at the link. As a result, most of the data packets from a source are directed to both receivers. In Figure 2 (b), two receivers have bottlenecks at down-links and one link has half the bandwidth of the other link. The slower receiver receives a subset of the data directed to the faster receiver, copied at the diverging point. Using Digital Fountain as source, a receiver receives different packets and reliability is guaranteed by continuously sending TRQs until enough packets have arrived to reconstruct the original data. Packet loss can be detected based on whether a TRQ

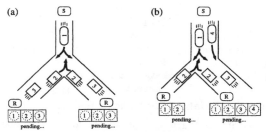

Figure 2: Congestion Control using BCFS.

is replied. If loss is detected, higher level BCFS request message is used for TRQ to prevent request suppression by intervening nodes in networks.

There is no guarantee that all packets are delivered efficiently as in the example above, because sending TRQ of each receiver is not synchronized in any explicit coordinated way, and a receiver accesses data asynchronously. However when receivers have a shared bottleneck link, it is likely that the same packet loss pattern causes same window control timing, and thereby, behave in a nearly synchronous way. Thus, networks can enjoy efficient multicast transmission, and receivers can receive data at the end-to-end available bandwidth. Simulation results in section 4 demonstrate this aggregation efficiency.

3.2 Window Adaptation Algorithm

In Rainbow, each receiver maintains its congestion window independently. The window control algorithm of Rainbow imitates TCP-Reno in the sense that it increases window size by one when the entire window's packets are received, and decreases it by half when a packet loss is detected. It also has a slow start phase in which the window size is increased by one at every packet reception.

Figure 3 shows parameters that each receiver maintains. cw is the size of the current window size. In the following sections, we detail how cw is controlled. For the purpose of checking the data packets of a whole window are received and detecting reordered packet arrival, the receiver keeps track of the round number of data exchange in terms of window, cur_count. cur_count should be increased by one when all the current window's data are delivered.

As described in section 3.1, each receiver sends TRQ's using as many kinds of labels as the window size and maintains some variables tied with each label. count tied with a label is the round number for each TRQ and it is increased by one when a TRQ is sent. cur_count must be the minimum count among the numbers for all TRQs maintained by the receiver. Thus, the data packets whose count is equal to cur_count are expected to arrive prior to others.

pending shows that a data packet for the TRQ arrives but another TRQ is not sent yet because the TRQ is replied one round earlier than others. lost means that the request or reply data packet for TRQ is considered to be lost in networks. level is the level number for the former TRQ packet. After a packet is lost, the state tied with the label must be left in network and cause suppression of the request with the same level. In order to avoid this suppression, when lost is true, the receiver sends a TRQ with a level one higher than the former TRQ.

3.2.1 Increase of window size

A receiver waits for arrival of data packets which have

```
cw:                   Window size
trq[i]:               i:label, i <= cw
trq[i].count :        the round number of TRQ.
trq[i].pending :      status if the TRQ is pending.
trq[i].lost :         status if packet loss is detected.
trq[i].level :        level number of TRQ.
cur_count:            current count
```

Figure 3: Variables that each receiver maintains.

a label within the current window size and whose count is current count. Immediately after the arrival of such an expected data packet, another TRQ with the same label should be sent toward the source again. In addition, its window size should be increased according to the receiver's condition.

A receiver starts its window size from one (cw=1) when it sends the first TRQ. Because the receiver is in slow start phase, the receiver increase the congestion window size by one at every packet reception. It means that when a data packet arrives, the receiver sends two TRQs, one with the label in the data packet and one with the new label.

Once loss is detected and TRQ resumes, the receiver is in congestion avoidance mode, in which window size is increased by one when all the data packets of current window size are received. When a data packet is received in congestion avoidance mode, the receiver sends a TRQ which includes the label in the data packet and checks whether all the packets in the window are received. If count of all labels are more than the current count, which means an entire window TRQs must be replied, the receiver increases window size by one and sends a TRQ with the new label.

3.2.2 Loss detection and halving the window

When a data packet arrives at the receiver with the label which has one round ahead of current count, packet loss might have happened in the networks. The TRQ for the label should be pending until all the data packets of the current count arrive. When the number of pending TRQs is more than a threshold ($cw/4$), the receiver considers that packets as lost from congestion.

Rainbow has another mechanism to detect packet loss based on timer expiration. Each receiver measures the time span between request and reply data arrival and regards the time as a round-trip time measurement, and estimates the round-trip time from the measurement like TCP. When a TRQ is sent, the timer is set based on the round trip time estimation. If the timer expires before the reply data packet arrives, the packet is considered lost.

When a loss is detected, the window size is decreased by half. After the loss detection the receiver should not send TRQs immediately because there must exist extra outstanding packets in the networks for the prior window size. Thus the receiver should be placed in congestion phase after loss detection and does not allow to send a TRQ in that phase.

When the number of outstanding packets become less than the new halved window or the timer which is set when loss is detected expires, the receiver gets out of the congestion phase and resumes sending TRQ based on the new window size. The number of outstanding packets is estimated by the difference between the prior window size and pending TRQ number. The estimation of the number of outstanding packets is decreased when a data packet arrives during the congestion phase. When loss state of a label is true, the TRQ is sent with higher level than level, maintained tied with the label, to avoid TRQ being suppressed.

In Rainbow, reordering of packets is expected to happen frequently, because some TRQs go up all the way to the source but other TRQs are suppressed at an intervening node and reply for another receiver's TRQ is directed to the receiver. It could cause the receiver to take such reordering for packet loss. If the receiver receives all the supposed lost packets during congestion phase, halving of window should be undone. Then the window size is restored to the prior window size and sending TRQ resumes.

4. Evaluation

We have implemented BCFS and Rainbow in the network simulator ns-2 [17]. In this section, we present simulation results that study how Rainbow adapts to heterogeneous receivers and network conditions. In section 4.1, we explore the basic behavior of Rainbow based on small scale sessions with simple topologies. In section 4.2, we evaluate the performance of Rainbow more comprehensively through larger scale simulations and comparison with RLC [18]. TCP fairness of Rainbow and RLC is examined in section 4.3.

4.1 Exploring the behavior of Rainbow

We explore the dynamics of Rainbow with relatively small scale sessions, as shown in Figure 4. To satisfy each receiver, the receiving rate should become close to end-to-end available bandwidth for each sender-receiver pair. However, 100 % utilization of available bandwidth is not expected because of TCP-like oscillating window control.

In the perfect scenario, receivers sharing the same link would observe complete aggregation. However, this cannot be always realized because of lack of explicit synchronization mechanism. It is still expected that a "bottleneck" link should be shared efficiently by BCFS data aggregation mechanism. Another point to explore is whether clusters of receivers under the same link can share the link fairly.

4.1.1 Topologies and Settings

We simulated two scenarios shown in Figure 4. The topology of Scenario A-(i) consists of one shared up-link and five different down-links. One down-link is narrower than the shared up-link, but others have broader link capacity than the shared bottleneck. Through this topology, adaptation to heterogeneous receivers and sharing bandwidth at a bottleneck link is investigated. While four faster receivers should receive the same service at up-link capacity, the slowest receiver should receive a portion of the data directed to faster ones at its down-link capacity.

Scenario A-(ii) has two clusters of five receivers with the shared backbone link (L1) by all receivers and the same capacity down-link for each cluster. For the shared backbone link, we use three different bandwidth. Receivers in both clusters should receive data at the same rate in all situations in terms of intra-session fairness, and the degree of data aggregation should change depending on the backbone capacity. We expect that as the backbone capacity becomes narrower, more packets are aggregated at the link and all the receivers come to receive the same data packets if the backbone becomes an end-to-end bottleneck.

In all simulations, the data packet size is 512 bytes, and the simulation run comprises 2000 packets, which means a receiver stops sending TRQs after receiving 2000 packets. All routers are RED gateways with a queue size of 10 packets. To "randomize" each run, each receiver initiates its

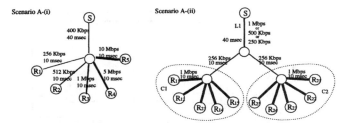

Figure 4: Simulation Settings: Exploring behavior.

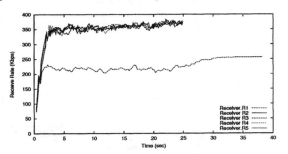

Figure 5: Scenario A-(i): Rate for five receivers.

session at a uniformly random start time in [0...5] seconds. In each scenario, 100 simulations are executed with randomized different start time of receivers and average results are shown in the following sections.

4.1.2 Scenario A-(i)

The results for scenario A-(i) are illustrated in Figure 5. The slowest receiver receives data at over 200 Kbps against its 256 Kbps bottleneck capacity and the average receiving rate throughout the duration of the simulation is 224.1 Kbps. This average is calculated from all 100 simulation runs, and we use the average rate for later explanation of simulation results. The receiving rate of all four faster receivers reaches around 350 Kbps against 400 Kbps up-link bottleneck bandwidth after slow start phase and the average rate of four receivers is 346.2 Kbps.

In this scenario, four faster receivers should be dealt with as if on a single multicast channel because they share the identical bottleneck link. The overhead of sent packets through the shared link is 8.3 %, which is calculated by four times of the packet number sent from the source over the total packet number received by the four faster receivers during the stable condition, between 10 and 20 second in the simulation. Furthermore, 1237.4 packets out of 1265.6 packets for the slowest receiver (R1) are shared with at least one of other faster receivers while at least one other receiver is receiving data.

From this simulation, we have seen all receivers can receive at their appropriate rates according to each available bandwidth through data aggregation at bottleneck link. Some overhead exists even for receivers sharing a bottleneck link, but this overhead is not expected to grow as the number of receivers increases, because the more receivers exist under the same bottleneck link, the higher the probability TRQs are aggregated. As a result, the same data packet is sent to more receivers at the same time.

4.1.3 Scenario A-(ii)

In Table 1, the average receiving rate for each cluster of five receivers and the average total packet number sent from

the source are shown for different bandwidth backbone (L1) cases of scenario A-(ii). According to the average receiving rate in Table 1, receivers on both subtrees (C1,C2) attain approximately equal throughputs, around 225 Kbps, for all bandwidth cases.

When the shared backbone link has enough bandwidth (1 Mbps) to accommodate the two down-links, all receivers would receive data at the down-link capacity rate. In this case, packet aggregation at link L1 is not expected because there is no mechanism for synchronization. The packets for receivers under the bottleneck link (i.e. within C1) is totally aggregated as if they were on the same multicast channel as receiving rate around 225 Kbps in Table 1 shows. As a result entire behavior becomes similar to the situation where two multicast groups are formed for each subtree. The average total number of sent packets is 3326.9, which is less than the double of the necessary packet number for a single receiver because some packets are eventually aggregated across the clusters.

When the bandwidth of the shared backbone link is 500 Kbps, its capacity is a little less than aggregation of down-links bandwidth. Even in this case, the same receiving rate is realized as in 1 Mbps case, as shown in Table 1. The reason is that more packets are aggregated at the the backbone link (L1) and directed to more receivers at the same time, which is also evident by less total sent packets than 1 Mbps case in Table 1.

When the shared backbone link is 250 Kbps, the link becomes the bottleneck and all receivers should be dealt with as if on one multicast channel. In Table 1, a decrease in overall packets shows that more data are aggregated at the node of the backbone link. Further, average receiving rates for both clusters are consistent independent of backbone capacity.

As the results show, depending on the placements of bottleneck link, Rainbow aggregates data packets in different ways, and as a result, traffic behaves as if a subtrees of bottleneck link is formed as the same multicast channel without explicit coordinated mechanism for synchronization.

Table 1: Scenario A-(ii): Rate for two clusters and total packet number.

L1 Bandwidth	Average rate (Kbps)		Packet number
1 Mbps	C1	226.2	3326.9
	C2	224.8	
500 Kbps	C1	224.2	3241.7
	C2	223.5	
250 Kbps	C1	226.3	2411.2
	C2	226.0	

4.2 Scalability Evaluation

In this section, we present more comprehensive simulation results to investigate scalability to large scale session and adaptation to heterogeneous environments. We also compare results of Rainbow with those of RLC [18], which is a TCP-friendly congestion control scheme based on layered multicast. The detail of deployment of RLC for Digital Fountain is described in [2].

4.2.1 Topologies and Metrics

Figure 6 shows the topologies used in the simulations for

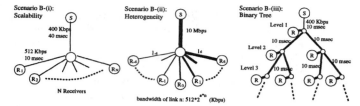

Figure 6: Simulation Settings: Scalability.

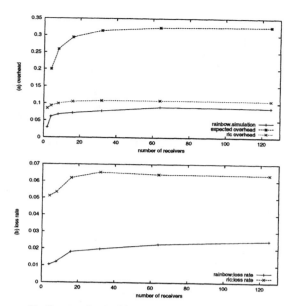

Figure 7: Scenario B-(i): Scalability to large session.

investigating scalability of Rainbow. The topology in scenario B-(i) consists of one sender and N receivers. The N receivers are homogeneous: they have the same bandwidth and delay, and the shared up-link is narrower than a downlink for each receiver. The number of receivers N varies from 2 to 125. We examine how overhead changes as the number of receivers N increases. The total number of packets sent to a cluster of receivers through the shared bottleneck link characterizes efficient network resource utilization. In ideal case, if there are N homogeneous receivers under the bottleneck link and all the data are shared by all the N receivers, the total number of packets received by all the N receivers is N times of the number of packets transmitted through the shared bottleneck link.

$$overhead = \frac{N * s}{\sum_{i=1}^{N} r_i} - 1 \qquad (1)$$

is used as a metric of overhead, where s is the number of packets transmitted through the shared link and r_i is the number of packets received by the ith receiver. If all data packets are aggregated at the shared link and provided to all receivers, it results in 0% overhead. However, unsynchronized behavior of each receiver's congestion control and packet loss at the shared link cause overhead.

Scenario B-(ii) has one sender and 13 heterogeneous receivers with different bandwidths. The nth receiver R_n's link bandwidth is $r_n = 2^{\alpha n} r_0$ ($n : -6...6$). Thus, α indicates the degree of heterogeneity, which increases as α increases. We investigate how Rainbow and RLC adapt to such a heterogeneous environment and whether they can realize high utilization for each link. In this scenario, we set r_0 to 512 Kbps, and α varies from 0.0 to 0.5. When α is 0.0, receivers are homogeneous with 512 Kbps links. In the most heterogeneous case, or $\alpha = 0.5$, the bandwidth of the narrowest link is $r_{-6} = 64$ (Kbps) and the bandwidth of the broadest link $r_6 = 4$ (Mbps). We investigate the link utilization of each link:

$$utilization = \frac{average\,transmisson\,rate}{link\,bandwidth} \qquad (2)$$

Scenario B-(iii) deploys binary tree topologies. Under the single shared bottleneck link, receivers are placed for each node of the binary trees, depth of which change from 2 to 5. The average receiving rate on different levels of a tree is investigated.

For RLC, the base layer's sending rate is 32 Kbps, synchronization points for base layer come every second, and leave delay from a multicast group is one second. For all scenarios, 100 simulation runs are executed and each session starts at uniformly randomized time in [0...5] seconds.

4.2.2 Scenario B-(i): Large-scale homogeneous session

Figure 7 (a) illustrates the results of overhead and Figure

7 (b) shows loss rate for Rainbow and RLC as the number of receivers increases.

Overhead of RLC does not depend on the number of receivers, because receivers conduct synchronized congestion control of joining or leaving a layer. However, the overhead of RLC is larger than Rainbow, which comes from lost packets as shown in Figure 7 (b). On the other hand, Rainbow's overhead increases with the number of receivers because of unsynchronized window control at each receiver. However, this overhead does not diverge to infinity and converges at around 10 %.

Intuitive reason of the convergence of overhead is shown in Figure 8, which illustrates expected overhead in the case of two asynchronous window controls. If there are two receivers, running unsynchronized window control, each receiver increases window size up to maximum value W additively and reduce window in half to $W/2$ in reaction to packet loss. In the region where two congestion window sizes overlap in Figure 8, TRQs are aggregated because one receiver's "breadcrumbs" are a subset of the other receiver's. In this case, overhead against a single receiver's session is regarded as the meshed areas. Extending this idea to N receivers and supposing that the window control start timings are uniformly distributed, the expected value of overhead is calculated as $(N - 1)/3(N + 1)$ through order statistics (the proof is omitted because of lack of space.). As N approaches infinity, the expected overhead converges to 33%. This is also intuitively obvious from Figure 8 because the meshed areas extend to triangle regions as N grows. This expected overhead is also plotted in Figure 7 (a).

Actual overhead by simulations is less than this expectation. The reason of this better convergence is considered as window synchronization effect like concurrent TCP flows. Furthermore, some lost packets are probable to be shared by many receivers because of data aggregation. This shared packet loss could result in more synchronized behavior of window control among receivers and thereby reduce overhead. In other words, the expected value is considered as the worst case bounds of overhead without synchronization.

254

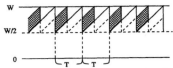

Figure 8: Overhead by two individual window controls.

4.2.3 Scenario B-(ii): Bandwidth Heterogeneity

Figure 9 (a) shows the results of link utilization for Rainbow and RLC as the heterogeneity index α increases. Average utilization of all receivers are calculated and displayed. The best and the worst utilization among all 13 links are also plotted for each α. For both of Rainbow and RLC, the utilization of the worst link degrades as heterogeneity increases. In the case of Rainbow, the worst utilization goes down to 33%, and in the case of RLC to 13%, and mostly these worst results come from the broadest bandwidth link (l_6). As for RLC, the best utilization increases as the heterogeneity increases although loss rate also increases as shown in Figure 9 (b). Both of this best utilization and high loss rate of RLC are results from the narrowest link (l_{-6}).

As for Rainbow, the reason of this poor utilization for high bandwidth link is that heterogeneous link bandwidth causes many reordered packets. Reordering occurs because some TRQs are aggregated at an intervening node and reply data packets for other receivers are copied and sent to the link, but other TRQs have to go up all through the tree to the source and then reply packets are sent. In the heterogeneous case, receivers have different window sizes and send TRQs at different rates. Thus, the more heterogeneous the receivers' link bandwidth is, the more probable the reordering happens. This reordering makes receivers misunderstand that packet loss occurs and fail to extend window size large enough for high bandwidth links.

In the case of RLC, it does not have slow start phase (exponential increase) and synchronized points when join experiments are executed become more infrequent for higher layer. This causes slow adaptation for higher bandwidth links. Based on parameters that are used for this simulation, appropriate layer for 4 Mbps link is 7th or 8th layer and join experiments for 7th layer are executed every 32 seconds. We can adjust parameters for high bandwidth case. However, the current parameters have the high loss rate problem for low bandwidth link, although high utilization is realized by the aggressive behavior. Parameters tuned for high bandwidth will make the loss problem of the low bandwidth case worse, although the high loss rate in Figure 9 (b) is unacceptable considering coexistence with other traffic.

In conclusion, RLC has a specific range of bandwidth which can be applied well, depending on parameters. Thus, it is difficult for RLC to cover heterogeneous receivers. On the other hand, Rainbow can apply to wider range of bandwidth as the fact that Rainbow can adjust rate in the single receiver case shows (the results are omitted because of lack of space.). However, Rainbow also has problems when applied to heterogeneous environment because of difficulty of dealing with complicated behavior of reordered packets.

4.2.4 Scenario B-(iii): Binary tree

In this scenario, we examine the case that a bottleneck link is shared by receivers which are connected under a binary tree. Figure 10 shows the average receiving rate of each level

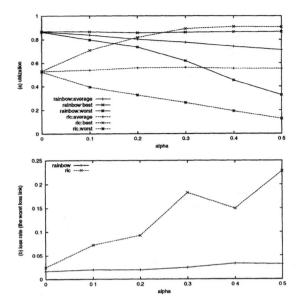

Figure 9: Scenario B-(ii): Heterogeneity.

of the tree, and four lines show the results from the different sizes of binary trees. Receiving rate degrades as receivers are placed farther from the source and depth of a whole tree becomes deeper, even though all receivers share the same bottleneck link.

This unfair behavior comes from the different appropriate window sizes among receivers. A receiver with longer transmission delay must have a larger window size to realize the same receiving rate. Thus, a farther receiver have to use more kinds of "breadcrumbs" than a closer receiver. One possibility under this condition is that the node of the bottleneck link has forwarding state tied with as many kinds of labels as necessary for the longer delay receiver. In this case, some portion of data packets through the link are directed only to the farther receiver because the closer receiver maintains less kinds of labels for TRQ. It results in lower receiving rate for the closer receiver compared with bottleneck link bandwidth. As another possibility, if just as many kinds of labels as necessary for the closer receiver are used for TRQ, the farther receiver cannot get enough bandwidth share because the window size (kinds of labels) is not large enough. In either way, it is impossible to realize full utilization of bottleneck link for both receivers. From the simulation results, the latter is considered to happen. Before farther receivers increase window size to large enough, closer receivers fill up the queue of the bottleneck link node, and farther receivers fail to get enough bandwidth share.

Rainbow has a problem on intra-session fairness. A receiver with longer transmission delay get less share of bandwidth. In other words, Rainbow inherits TCP's property of unfairness on transmission delay.

4.3 TCP Fairness Evaluation

4.3.1 Topologies and Metrics

Figure 11 shows topologies for investigating TCP fairness of Rainbow. In scenario C-(i), two receivers of TCP and Rainbow (or RLC) share a bottleneck link. The ratio of Rainbow (or RLC) and TCP's receiving rate is examined for

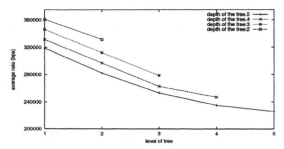

Figure 10: Scenario B-(iii): Binary tree.

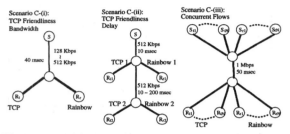

Figure 11: Simulation Settings: TCP fairness.

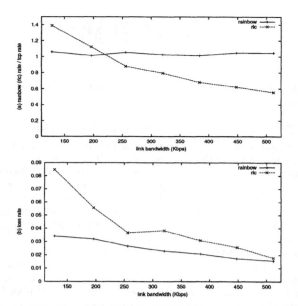

Figure 12: Scenario C-(i): TCP fairness (bandwidth dependence).

different bottleneck bandwidth cases, from 128 to 512 Kbps. According to the results of section *4.2.3*, RLC's behavior is not TCP-friendly especially for a low capacity link.

In Scenario C-(ii) of Figure 11, four receivers, two of which are for TCP and the other two are for Rainbow (or RLC), share the same bottleneck link. Two receivers, one for Rainbow (or RLC) and one for TCP, have longer delay than the other two receivers. The difference in the transmission delay changes from 10 to 200 msec. The bandwidth share of Rainbow and TCP with the same delay (*TCP fairness*) and the bandwidth share within Rainbow (or RLC) receivers with different delay (*intra-session fairness*) are examined.

In scenario C-(iii), n Rainbow sender-receiver pairs and n TCP sessions share a bottleneck link. As the number of sessions $2n$ changes from 4 to 16, TCP fairness of Rainbow and RLC is examined. When the bottleneck is shared evenly by all $2n$ sessions, the bandwidth share should be similar to the case of scenario C-(i). The fairness metric [10],

$$fairness = \frac{(\sum x_i)^2}{n \sum x_i{}^2} \quad (3)$$

is used, where x_i is normalized throughput of measured throughput T_i over fair throughput O_i,

$$x_i = T_i/O_i \quad (4)$$

Fair throughput O_i is a fraction of a shared link bandwidth over a total number of Rainbow (or RLC) and TCP flows. The maximum value of the metric is one, which means bandwidth is shared evenly among all receivers.

TCP NewReno implementation in ns-2 [17] is used. Other settings are the same as those of the former sections.

4.3.2 Scenario C-(i): Bandwidth dependence

We study how a link is shared between TCP and Rainbow (or RLC) flows for different bandwidths. Figure 12 (a) shows the ratio of average receiving rate of Rainbow (or RLC) and TCP. A value of more than 1.0 means Rainbow's (or RLC's) average rate is over TCP's average rate. Packet loss rate at the shared link is shown in Figure 12 (b). Ac-

cording to Figure 12 (a), Rainbow's bandwidth ratio to TCP is around 1.05 and stable for all bandwidth cases. In contrast, RLC gets 40 % more bandwidth share than TCP in the low bandwidth case, but about half of TCP bandwidth in the high bandwidth case. As Figure 12 (b) shows, packet loss rate of RLC is high and more than 8 % in the case of low bandwidth bottleneck.

RLC behaves too aggressively for low bit rate link and causes packet drops because parameters of RLC are tuned for higher capacity link as explained in section *4.2.3*. As a result, such high loss rate prevents TCP from increasing its congestion window and causes TCP's less share of bandwidth. In the case of high bandwidth, RLC's slow adaptation causes failure of getting enough bandwidth. In contrast, Rainbow shows fair behavior against TCP independent of the bottleneck bandwidth because of similarity of the adaptation algorithm.

4.3.3 Scenario C-(ii): Delay dependence

Scenario C-(ii) examines TCP fairness and intra-session fairness in the presence of transmission delay differences. Figure 13 (a) shows the ratio of average rate of Rainbow (or RLC) to TCP with the same delay (i.e. in Figure 11, Rainbow1/TCP1, Rainbow2/TCP2, ...). Two solid lines, which are results of Rainbow, show that Rainbow and TCP get almost the same bandwidth share independent of transmission delay, if they have the same transmission delay. On the other hand from the results of dashed lines, RLC receivers get more share of bandwidth than TCP, as transmission delay grows.

From the same simulation, Figure 13 (b) shows the ratio of average rates between the same kind of traffic, Rainbow, RLC, or TCP, with the different transmission delay to investigate intra-session fairness (i.e. Rainbow2/Rainbow1, TCP2/TCP1, ...). Two solid lines show the results of Rainbow and TCP co-existence and almost overlap with each other. For both of Rainbow and TCP, receivers get less share of bandwidth as the transmission delay becomes longer. In

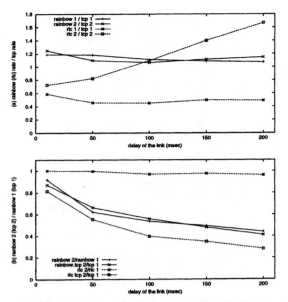

Figure 13: Scenario C-(ii): TCP fairness (delay dependence).

contrast, as the upper dashed lines shows, RLC shows fair behavior between themselves independent of transmission delay. However, co-existent TCP flows have delay dependence on bandwidth share as the lower dashed line shows.

In terms of intra-session fairness, RLC shows stable results because of synchronization mechanism among receivers. However, this causes unfair behavior against TCP depending on transmission delay. As a result, RLC affects TCP traffic and causes the worse result on TCP's delay dependence of bandwidth share, as the lowest dashed line in Figure 13 shows. On the other hand, Rainbow's delay dependence on bandwidth share is very similar to that of TCP. In other words, Rainbow realizes TCP fairness at the cost of intra-session fairness.

4.3.4 Scenario C-(iii): Concurrent flows

Scenario C-(iii) examines TCP fairness in the case of multiple sessions of Rainbow (RLC) and TCP. Figure 14 (a) shows the fairness metric. RLC shows unfair behavior (around 0.95 by the metric) both for a few sessions and many sessions case, although it shows very fair (around 0.99) for a specific number of sessions. On the other hand, Rainbow shows more stable results on the fairness metric (around 0.97 - 0.98) than RLC for all session size.

Figure 14 (b) shows the ratio of average rate of Rainbow (or RLC) to TCP. The ratio of Rainbow is stable for all session numbers around 1.3, which means get more bandwidth share than TCP. In contrast, RLC's ratio rises as the number of sessions grows. When session number is 4, RLC get less than 70 % of TCP bandwidth. However, when session number grows to 16, RLC's bandwidth share is 40 % more than TCP.

These results are similar to scenario C-(i) by reversing the x-axis as expected from the similar appropriate share of bandwidth. As the session number increases and the appropriate share of bandwidth becomes narrower, RLC behaves more aggressive than TCP and loses TCP fairness as it is also illustrated high loss rate in Figure 14 (c).

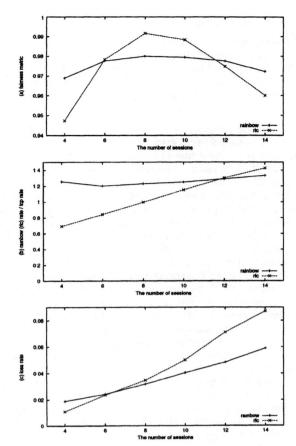

Figure 14: Scenario C-(iii): TCP fairness (concurrent flows).

Rainbow shows more stable TCP fair behavior than RLC independent of session number, but get somewhat more share of bandwidth than TCP. This is from the difference on loss detection and restoration of window size between TCP and Rainbow. In TCP-Reno, packet loss is detected by a sender through reception of three duplicate ACKs. On the other hand, in Rainbow, loss is conceded by a receiver and the receiver has to wait for more reordered packets reception before loss detection because ordered delivery cannot be expected. In addition, Rainbow does not apply exponential backoff which TCP has.

5. Discussions and Open Issues

In this section, we discuss some issues on Rainbow derived from simulation results.

- **Intra-session Fairness or TCP Fairness:** As shown in section 4.3, Rainbow shows TCP friendly but not intra-session fair behavior. On the other hand, RLC shows intra-session fairness but is not TCP friendly. According to [6], TCP fairness cannot be realized by rate based control like RLC. In contrast, RTT-based window control like Rainbow has delay dependence on fairness that TCP also has. It seems impossible to realize the both properties at the same time. More studies are needed to determine whether solution for both of intra-session fairness and TCP fairness is possible and which yields better whole system fairness.

- **Heterogeneity:** We believe that Rainbow has potential to tame heterogeneity. However, Rainbow suffers from degradation of link utilization in face of heterogeneous receivers, as shown in section *4.2.3*, because of its complicated packet reordering behavior. More studies on packet aggregation dynamics are necessary.

- **RTT measurement:** In Rainbow, RTT is measured as a time span between sending TRQ and arrival of its reply packet. Some measurements are much shorter than actual RTT between the source and the receiver, because some TRQs are aggregated at an intervening router. One reason that Rainbow works well in spite of this false RTT measurement is that we calculate RTT estimation by adding the mean measurement to its standard deviation. Consequently Rainbow can absorb the problem of false RTT measurements because deviation is large when that aggregation occurs. Further, Rainbow is robust against variability of RTT measurements, unless inaccurate measurements cause frequent timeouts in loss detection. In fact, we implemented infrastructure assist in BCFS to measure accurate RTT. Based on this assist in BCFS, we conducted simulations of the binary tree (Scenario B-(iii)), which is affected by false RTT measurements the most. This change in the BCFS infrastructure does not impact the performance of Rainbow much. In addition, this infrastructure assist increases a router's load badly because it has to rewrite the header of each reply packet differently for each link. In any event, more investigation is needed for whether this kind of infrastructure assist is worth being implemented.

- **Cost of Router State:** Detailed implementation issues of BCFS is left for future work [20]. However, the maximum state which a router has to maintain for a single Rainbow session is bounded by the maximum window size among receivers.

6. Conclusion

We propose a novel congestion control scheme, Rainbow, based on new multicast forwarding service model, BCFS. The congestion control is designed to achieve TCP fairness through window based congestion control, high utilization for each link through a receiver's individual window maintenance, and scalability to large and heterogeneous sessions.

We demonstrate the scalability of Rainbow through simulations for wide range of topologies and analysis. In general, Rainbow shows better performance than RLC, especially in terms of TCP fairness. Rainbow still has problems on heterogeneity and intra-session fairness, and needs more work in algorithmic refinement and analysis. Implementation issues such as memory requirement in a router and processing load for forwarding state renewal also need to be addressed.

A novel transport design like Rainbow should be tackled along with efforts of designing new multicast network service. We believe Rainbow is a truly TCP-friendly reliable multicast protocol and gives a new direction for deployment of a new multicast service model.

7. Acknowledgments

We thank Gene Cheung, Hisayuki Hara and Tina Wong for their thoughtful discussion and comments on this paper.

8. REFERENCES

[1] S. Bhattacharyya, D. Towsley, and J. Kurose. The Loss Path Multiplicity Problem for Multicast Congestion Control. In *Proceedings of IEEE Infocom '99*, New York, NY, March 1999.

[2] J. Byers, M. Luby, M. Mitzenmacher, and A. Rege. A Digital Fountain Approach to Reliable Distribution of Bulk Data. In *Proceedings of Sigcomm '98*, Vancouver, Canada, September 1998.

[3] B. Cain, T. Speakman, and D. Towsley. Generic Router Assist (GRA) Building Block, Oct. 1999. Internet Draft (Work in Progress).

[4] Y. Chawathe, S. Fink, S. McCanne, and E. Brewer. A Proxy Architecture for Reliable Multicast in Heterogeneous Environments. In *Proceedings of ACM Multimedia*, Bristol, England, September 1998.

[5] S. Floyd, V. Jacobson, C. Liu, S. McCanne, and L. Zhang. A Reliable Multicast Framework for Light-weight Sessions and Application Level Framing. *IEEE/ACM Transactions on Networking*, 1995.

[6] J. Golestani and K. Sabnani. Fundamental Observations on Multicast Congestion Control in the Internet. In *Proceedings of IEEE Infocom '99*, New York, NY, March 1999.

[7] H. Holbrook and D. Cheriton. IP Multicast Channels: EXPRESS Support for Large-scale Single-source Applications. In *Proceedings of Sigcomm '99*, Cambridge, MA, September 1999.

[8] H. Holbrook, S. Singhal, and D. Cheriton. Log-Based Receiver-Reliable Multicast for Distributed Interactive Simulation. In *Proceedings of Sigcomm '95*, Boston, MA, Sept. 1995. ACM.

[9] V. Jacobson. Congestion avoidance and control. In *Proceedings of Sigcomm '88*, Stanford, CA, Aug. 1988.

[10] R. Jain, A. Durresi, and G. Babic. Throughput Fairness Index: An Explanation, Feb. 1999. ATM Forum/99-0045.

[11] J. Lin and S. Paul. RMTP: A Reliable Multicast Transport Protocol. In *Proceedings IEEE Infocom '96*, pages 1414–1424, San Francisco, CA, Mar. 1996.

[12] S. McCanne, V. Jacobson, and M. Vetterli. Receiver-driven layered multicast. In *Proceedings of Sigcomm '96*, Stanford, CA, Aug. 1996. ACM.

[13] C. Papadopoulos, G. Parulkar, and G. Varghese. An Error Control Scheme for Large-Scale Multicast Applications. In *Proceedings IEEE Infocom '98*, San Francisco, CA, March 1998.

[14] I. Rhee, N. Ballaguru, and G. Rouskas. MTCP: Scalable TCP-like Congestion Control for Reliable Multicast. In *Proceedings of IEEE Infocom '99*, New York, NY, March 1999.

[15] D. Rubenstein, J. Kurose, and D. Towsley. The Impact of Multicast Layering on Network Fairness. In *Proceedings of Sigcomm '99*, Cambridge, MA, September 1999.

[16] T. Speakman, D. Farinacci, S. Lin, and A. Tweedly. PGM Reliable Transport Protocol Specification, Aug. 1998. Internet Draft (Work in Progress).

[17] UCB/LBNL/VINT. Network Simulator - ns (version 2). http://www-mash.cs.berkeley.edu/ns/.

[18] L. Vicisano, L. Rizzo, and J. Crowcroft. TCP-like congestion control for layered multicast data transfer. In *Proceedings of Infocom '98*, San Francisco, CA, March 1998.

[19] L. Wu, R. Sharma, and B. Smith. Thin Streams: An Architecture for Multicasting Layered Video. In *Proceedings of NOSSDAV*, St. Louis, Missouri, May 1997.

[20] K. Yano and S. McCanne. The Breadcrumb Forwarding Service: A Synthesis of PGM and EXPRESS to Improve and Simplify Global IP Multicast. *ACM Computer Communication Review*, 30(2), Apr. 2000.

A Generic Late-Join Service for Distributed Interactive Media

Jürgen Vogel, Martin Mauve, Werner Geyer, Volker Hilt, Christoph Kuhmünch
Praktische Informatik IV
University of Mannheim
L15, 16
68131 Mannheim
{vogel,mauve,geyer,hilt,cjk}@informatik.uni-mannheim.de

ABSTRACT

In this paper we present a generic late-join service for distributed interactive media, i.e., networked media which involve user interactions. Examples for distributed interactive media are shared whiteboards, networked computer games and distributed virtual environments. The generic late-join service allows a latecomer to join an ongoing session. This requires that the shared state of the medium is transmitted from the old participants of the session to the latecomer in an efficient and scalable way. In order to be generic and useful for a broad range of distributed interactive media, we have implemented the late-join service based on the Real Time Application Level Protocol for Distributed Interactive Media (RTP/I). All applications which employ this protocol can also use the generic late-join service. Furthermore the late-join service can be adapted to the specific needs of a given application by specifying policies for the late-join process. Applications which do use a different application level protocol than RTP/I may still use the concepts presented in this work. However, they will not be able to profit from our RTP/I based implementation.

Keywords
Distributed Interactive Media, Late-Join, Generic Service, RTP/I

1. INTRODUCTION

The term *distributed interactive medium* is used to denote a networked medium which involves user interactions with the medium itself [9]. Typical examples of distributed interactive media are shared whiteboards [3][14], networked computer games [2], and distributed virtual environments [5]. One fundamental problem that applications for these media need to address is the support for participants who arrive late and wish to join an ongoing session. This is known as the *late-join problem*.

The late-join problem is challenging since distributed interactive media typically employ a *replicated distribution architecture*. That is, the application of each participant maintains a local copy of the medium's shared state. For example, in a shared whiteboard application this state may comprise the text shown on each whiteboard page as well as annotations and modifications that have been made by participants over the course of the session. Without

information about the current shared state of the medium it is not possible to participate in a session. The application of a latecomer therefore needs to take special actions to retrieve the relevant parts of the shared state information.

In general a solution to the late-join problem has to perform two tasks:

1. It must identify those pieces of the shared state that are needed by the latecomer to participate in the ongoing session.

2. It needs to provide the late coming application with this information at the appropriate point in time in an appropriate way.

The first task is important since a large part of the medium's shared state may not be immediately relevant for a latecomer. In a shared whiteboard session, for example, only the state of the current page may be required to enable a latecomer to participate in the session. The state of other pages may be needed only when they become visible later on. A solution to the late-join problem therefore needs a way to explore which pieces of shared state are available in a session, and under which conditions a certain piece of the shared state is required.

Once it has been decided when the pieces of shared state are needed the second task is to retrieve those pieces at the appropriate time. This is a complex task since pieces of the shared state may be required at different times, e.g. immediately (the current page of a shared whiteboard), or later on triggered by some user action (an old shared whiteboard page that becomes visible). Furthermore the state information needs to be retrieved in a way that does not overload the network or the participating applications. This is especially difficult since distributed interactive media often involve large groups of users.

A solution to the late-join problem is called a *late-join algorithm* or *late-join service*. The application program of the latecomer is a *late-join client*, while those applications that transmit state information to the late-join client are called *late-join servers*. The role of late-join clients and late-join servers is dynamic, i.e., a late-join client may become a late-join server for another late-join client later on.

In this paper we present a generic late-join service. It can be used for arbitrary distributed interactive media. We implemented the service using the information provided by the Real Time Application Level Protocol for Distributed Interactive Media (RTP/I) [10]. RTP/I captures the common aspects of distributed interactive media and thereby enables the development of reusable functionality without any medium-specific information. The concepts presented in this paper are independent of RTP/I and may also be used for applications that use other application level protocols. However, these application will not be able to profit from our implementation of the late join service.

The generic late-join service is highly customizable to the needs of diverse applications. Furthermore it minimizes the burden that is placed on the network and the participants of a session. The generic late-join service has been implemented in Java and is currently used by a 3D telecooperation application. Other applications are being converted to use RTP/I and the late-join service.

The remainder of this paper is structured as follows. In Section Two existing approaches to solve the late-join problem are examined. In Section Three we present our media model for distributed interactive media. This model allows us to discuss the late-join problem in a media-independent way. A short presentation of the Real Time Application Level Protocol for Distributed Interactive Media is given in Section Four. The generic late-join service is discussed in detail in Section Five. The sixth section contains a summary of our experiences with integrating the generic late-join service into an existing 3D telecooperation application. This paper is concluded by a summary and an outlook to future work.

2. EXISTING APPROACHES

Existing late-join algorithms can be separated into approaches that are handled by the transport protocol and those that are completely realized at the application level. Application level late-join algorithms can be subdivided further into centralized algorithms and distributed approaches.

Representatives of the first category are reliable multicast transport services that offer late-join functionality. An example of such a protocol is the Scalable Reliable Multicast protocol (SRM) [1]. A reliable multicast protocol can offer the late-join service by using its loss recovery mechanism to supply the late-joining application with all data packets missed since the beginning of the session. The application then reconstructs the current state from these packets.

The usage of transport protocol functionality to solve the late-join problem has four major drawbacks:

1. It is inefficient since a large part of the transmitted information may no longer be relevant. For example an image on a shared whiteboard page which has already been deleted in the meantime.

2. It is generally more efficient to transfer state information than to transmit all transport packets that have lead to that state. When editing a text, for example, it makes sense to transmit the state of the text rather than all the packets that contain the description of a character that has been typed or deleted. This becomes even more important when the overhead for packet headers is taken into account.

3. The application either has to be able to reconstruct every packet that has ever been transmitted, or the transport service needs to buffer the transmitted packets indefinitely. This is clearly not acceptable for a large number of applications.

4. The state of certain media may not be easily reconstructible from a simple replay of packets. The problem here is that for certain media (such as an networked action game) an event is only valid at a certain point in time. In order to reconstruct the state of such a medium from outdated packets, the application would have to perform a timewarp to the beginning of the session and then a rapid replay of states and events. It is by no means guaranteed that all, or even a significant number of, application will be able to perform this task.

Because of these problems we generally view the replay of packets as inappropriate for late-join support. Instead the current shared state should be explicitly queried by the latecomer. This leads us to existing late-join approaches at the application level.

The distinct advantage of application level approaches is the usage of application knowledge to optimize the late-join process. *Centralized* late-join approaches require that a single application exists that is able to act as the late-join server for the shared state. When a late coming application joins the session it may contact the state server which will in turn deliver the relevant state information. An example where a centralized state server is used for late-join purposes is the Notification Service Transport Protocol [12].

A centralized state server results in the typical disadvantages of all centralized solutions. Main problems are the existence of a single-point-of-failure (lack of robustness), and the high application load for the server, which might become a bottleneck. Because of these drawbacks we have decided not to use a centralized late-join server for our generic late-join service.

Distributed late-join approaches seek to avoid the problems of a centralized approach by involving multiple applications in the late-join process. In particular, many applications may be able to assume the role of a late-join server for any given piece of shared state. The failure of any single application can generally be tolerated without preventing a latecomer from joining the session. Applications that use a distributed late-join approach are the network text editor (NTE) [6] and the digital lecture board (dlb) [3].

The innovative idea of the method used for the dlb is to employ a separate (multicast) group for the data that is transmitted to latecomers. Requests for the state of a page are transmitted to the regular session by the late-join clients. Replies are sent to the late-join group by the applications that act as late-join servers. An application may leave the late-join group once it has received all required information about the shared state. A reply implosion of the potential late-join servers is prevented by using an anycast mechanism that is based on random timers.

The approach used for the dlb has several positive characteristics. First, it limits the burden of the late-join activity that is placed on session participants who are not latecomers. These participants just need to check whether they have been selected as late-join servers. The transmitted state information is only received by those applications that have not yet finished their late-join activity. Second, for the same reason, the approach also minimizes the network load: state information is only transmitted over those parts of the network that lead to an application still lacking late-join information. Third, the dlb late-join effectively prevents a reply implosion when more than one participant is able to act as a late-join server.

However, there are also some areas in which the dlb solution can be further improved:

1. In addition to preventing a reply implosion, a request implosion should also be avoided. This is particularly important if a user action (such as changing the page in a shared whiteboard) may trigger the need for additional state information. In this case multiple late-join clients might require the same state information simultaneously.

2. Some applications that represent potential late-join servers should join the late-join group. Requests for state information could then be transmitted to the late-join group, so that uninvolved applications do not have to handle requests for state information. Only as a fall-back solution should the request be sent to the original group. This requires to give criteria that decide which potential late-join servers should enter or leave the late-join session.

3. The dlb approach is application-dependent. It is not based upon a generic application level protocol, and it is not easily customizable to the diverse needs of different distributed interactive media.

Because of its positive characteristics we have chosen the dlb approach as the basis for our generic late-join service. Upon this basis we have developed an improved and generic late-join service for distributed interactive media.

3. MEDIA MODEL

In order to provide a generic service that is reusable for a whole class of media it is important to investigate the media model of this media class. In the following we give a brief overview of the characteristics of the distributed interactive media class. A more detailed discussion can be found in [9].

3.1 States and Events

A *distributed interactive medium* has a *state*. For example, at any given point in time the state of a shared whiteboard is defined by the content of all pages present in the shared whiteboard. In order to perceive the state of a distributed interactive medium a user needs an *application*, e.g. a shared whiteboard application is required to see the pages of a shared whiteboard presentation. This application generally maintains a local copy of (parts of) the medium's state. Applications for distributed interactive media are therefore said to have a *replicated distribution architecture*. For all applications participating in a session the local state of the medium should be at least reasonably similar. It is therefore necessary to synchronize the local copies of the distributed interactive medium's state among all participants, so that the overall state of the medium is *consistent*.

The state of a distributed interactive medium can change for two reasons, either by *passage of time* or by *events*. The state of the medium between two successive events is fully deterministic and depends only on the passage of time. Generally, a state change caused by the passage of time does not require the exchange of information between applications, since each user's application can independently calculate the required state changes. An example of a state change caused by the passage of time is the animation of an object moving across the screen.

Any state change that is not a fully deterministic function of time is caused by an *event*. Generally events are (user) interactions with the medium, e.g. the user makes an annotation on a shared whiteboard page. Whenever events occur, the state of the medium is in danger of becoming inconsistent. Therefore, an event usually requires that the applications exchange information - either about the event itself or about the updated state once the event has taken place.

3.2 Partitioning the Medium - Sub-Components

In order to provide for a flexible and scalable handling of state information it is desirable to partition an interactive medium into several *sub-components*. In addition to breaking down the complete state of an interactive medium into more manageable parts, such partitioning allows the participants of a session to track only the states of those sub-components in which they are actually interested. Examples of sub-components are 3D objects (an avatar, a car, a room) in a distributed virtual environment, or the pages of a shared whiteboard. Events affect only a *target* sub-component. Sub-components other than the target are not affected by an event.

4. RTP/I

While the media model provides an important insight into the distributed interactive media class, the design and implementation of a generic late-join service requires a more formal foundation. The Real Time Application Level Protocol for Distributed Interactive Media (RTP/I) [10] provides such a foundation. While our implementation of the generic late join service makes use of RTP/I, the concepts presented here may also be used by applications which do use other application level protocols.

RTP/I consists of two parts: a data transfer protocol for the transport of event and state information, and a control protocol for meta-information about the medium and the participants of a session:

- The *data transfer protocol* (RTP/I) frames the transmitted states and events of the medium with information that is common to the distributed interactive media class. With this information a generic service, like the late-join service presented here, can interpret the semantics of the information without knowing anything about the medium-specific encoding. Typical examples for the information contained in the RTP/I data framing are a timestamp which indicates at what time an event happened or a state was calculated, an identifier for the affected sub-component and the type of the data (event vs. state information). In addition to state and event transmission RTP/I is also used to request the state of a sub-component in a standardized way.

- The *RTP/I control protocol* (RTCP/I) conveys information about the participants of a session. This includes the participants' names and email addresses. This information can be used to establish a light-weight session control. Moreover RTCP/I provides information about the sub-components that are present in a session. Information about each sub-component is regularly announced. The announcement contains three types of information: (1) the ID of the sub-component, as it is also used in the framing of the data transfer protocol. (2) An application level name for the sub-component. This name allows an application to identify the sub-component. A typical example for an application level name could be the title of a shared whiteboard page. (3) An announcement whether this sub-component is actively used by any participating application in order to present the medium to the user. The visible pages of a shared whiteboard presentation would belong to the class of active sub-components, while the invisible pages would belong to the class of passive sub-components. All three types of information can be used by the late-join service and the application using the late-join service to determine the relevance of sub-components.

RTP/I is closely related to the Real Time Transport Protocol (RTP) [7] which is mainly used for the transmission of audio and video. However, while RTP/I reuses many aspects of RTP it has been thoroughly adapted to meet the needs of distributed interactive media.

5. GENERIC LATE-JOIN SERVICE

The architecture of the generic late-join service is depicted in Figure 1. The late-join service intercepts the data (events, states, and requests for states) that arrives from the base session. Since this data is transmitted using RTP/I the generic late-join service can understand the semantics of this data to a degree sufficient to provide the late-join functionality. Knowledge about the medium-specific encoding is not required. After examining the data the late-join service forwards it to the application.

The application transmits all regular data directly to the base RTP/I session without informing the late-join service. late-join information is handed from the application to the late-join service. An example for this type of information is the state of a sub-component that is required by the late-join service to support a remote latecomer. The reason for passing this data to the late-join service instead of transmitting it over the base RTP/I session is as follows: the generic late-join service maintains an additional late-join RTP/I session. This session is used to transmit all late-join oriented data. The late-join service joins and leaves this additional RTP/I session at appropriate times. This ensures that only a small subset of all participants need to handle late-join data.

Finally there exists a generic services channel. This channel is shared by all generic services (there may be multiple generic services present in a single application). It is used to convey signalling data for the generic services. In order to limit routing effort at the network level the generic services channel has the same network address as the base RTP/I session. Transport layer multiplexing is used to separate the generic services channel from the base RTP/I session. An application remains a member of the generic services channel for the lifetime of a session.

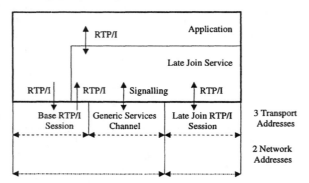

Figure 1: Architecture of the late-join service

When joining an ongoing session the late-join service will learn about the sub-components that are present in a session through the RTCP/I reports on sub-components. Whenever a new sub-component is detected the late-join service informs the application and requests information on how the late-join should be performed. The application may choose between a set of policies, ranging from no action to immediate retrieval of the sub-component's state. In addition to the sub-component ID the application may use the information which is delivered via RTCP/I (application level name, and whether the sub-component is active for at least one user) to determine which policy is appropriate for a given sub-component.

When the condition occurs that was specified by the policy the state of the sub-component is requested by the late-join service. This is done by transmitting RTP/I state queries to the late-join group using a message implosion avoidance mechanism. This mechanism makes sure that no message implosion occurs if multiple latecomers want to request the state of the same sub-component at the same time. A similar mechanism was first used by SRM [1] to achieve a scalable reliable multicast. In order to avoid a message implosion the late-join service waits a random time before transmitting an RTP/I state query. The value of the random timer is evenly distributed in an interval that depends on the distance (in terms of network delay) to the participant who transmitted the report of the sub-component. The smaller the distance, the smaller is the upper bound on the timer. Therefore it is likely that applications which are close to the origin of a report will reply first. Any other late-join service that wants to send a state query for the same sub-component suppresses this message when it sees that the message has already been transmitted by someone else. In this way a message implosion can be prevented effectively.

The request is repeated if there is no answer after a certain amount of time. If multiple requests for the sub-component's state remain unanswered, it is concluded that there is no late-join server for that sub-component present in the late-join group. In this case the late-join service uses the generic services channel to request that a participant which holds the state of the sub-component joins the late-join session and transmits the state. If this fails, too, then the application is informed.

When the late-join service receives the desired state information it passes it on to the application and marks this sub-component as complete. When there are no new sub-components detected for a period of time and all sub-components are marked as complete, then the late-join is finished. At that time the late-join service may

leave the late-join group. If, at any later point in time, a new sub-component is detected, then the application may ask the late-join service to resume its duty and join the late-join group again. When new sub-components are introduced in an ongoing session this can be used to conveniently request the state of the new sub-components in a way that is policy-driven.

5.1 Late-Join Policies

An application that uses the generic late-join service may specify a late-join policy for each sub-component that has been discovered by the late-join service. Setting different policies for sub-components makes it possible to retrieve different sub-components with different priorities; some may be retrieved immediately, others when network capacity is available or when they become important for the presentation to the user. The use of policies ensures high flexibility and an easy adaptation to the needs of individual applications. Existing solutions to the late-join problem, such as the one used for the digital lecture board, lack this ability.

The generic late-join service offers five late-join policies:

- event-triggered late-join,
- no late-join,
- immediate late-join,
- network-capacity-oriented late-join, and
- application-initiated late-join.

An application may change the late-join policy for a given sub-component at any time. We will examine the event-triggered late-join policy in more detail while the other policies are only outlined briefly.

5.1.1 Late-Join Policy: Event Triggered Late-Join

An application may decide that a sub-component is required only when it is the target of an event. For example, if a page in a shared whiteboard becomes the active page by means of an "activate page" event. This is supported through the event-triggered late-join policy. Besides deferring the request of state information until it is actually needed, this policy also increases the likelihood that multiple latecomers may profit from a single state transmission if multicast is used. The reason for this is that the late-join service may refrain for a long time (until the first event for the sub-component occurs) from requesting the state of a sub-component with an event-triggered late-join policy. All latecomers who join during that period will profit from a single transmission of the sub-component's state.

The finite state machine for the event-triggered late-join policy is shown in Figure 2. The name of the initial late-join state is "sub-component discovered" (SD). At the time the application chooses the late-join policy the late-join state changes to "wait-for-event" (WFE). In the WFE state the late-join service listens to incoming RTP/I packets and checks whether they contain an event or a state for the sub-component. If a state is received then the state is handed to the application, and the late-join state becomes "complete" (COMP) for the sub-component. This may happen when a state is transmitted for some reason (e.g., as a means of resynchronization) in the base RTP/I session.

When an event for the sub-component is received, then the late-join state for the sub-component becomes "sub-component needed" (SN), and a random timer is set. The random timer prevents a request implosion in the case that the sub-component is required by multiple latecomers at the same time. If the state of the sub-component is received while the request timer is running a transition from SN to complete (COMP) is performed.

262

When the random timer expires before the state of the sub-component has been received, then an RTP/I *state query* packet is transmitted to the late-join group, another random timer is set, and the late-join state changes to "sub-component requested I" (SR I). When a reply to this request is received then the late-join is complete for that sub-component. If no reply is received before the timer expires, then a new request is transmitted. In the case that a remote request for the sub-component is received, the timer is reset (not shown in Figure 2).

If multiple requests fail, then there is not appropriate late-join server for this sub-component in the late-join group. In this case the late-join state for this sub-component changes to "sub-component requested II" (SR II), and a join request is transmitted on the generic services channel. Upon receiving this request potential servers check whether they should join, using a join implosion avoidance mechanism similar to the one used for request implosion avoidance. When an application decides to join, it also transmits the required information to the late-join group.

When repeated requests for state information fail, the application is informed, and the state is set to WFE. A new event for the sub-component triggers another request round. This makes sense since an event indicates that the problem has been repaired and that a late-join server for this sub-component should be available.

5.1.2 Late-Join Policy: No Late-Join
This policy is chosen by the application to indicate that it is not interested in the sub-component. In a distributed virtual environment this policy could be used for sub-components that the user will never be able to see. By choosing the "no late-join" policy the overall amount of state information that is required for the initialization of the late-join client is reduced. This has a positive effect on the initialization delay as well as on the network and the application load. When the late-join service is notified that the application has chosen this policy for a sub-component, then the sub-component is marked as complete.

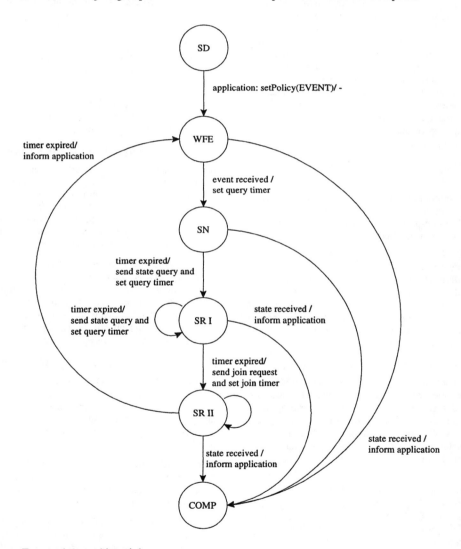

Figure 2: Event-triggered late-join

263

5.1.3 Late-Join Policy: Immediate Late-Join

An application may choose the immediate late-join policy when the sub-component is required at once to present the medium to the user (e.g., the currently visible pages of a shared whiteboard). An application can derive the information whether a sub-component is required immediately from the sub-component ID, from the application level name, or from the fact that it is needed to display the medium to at least one user.

The finite state machine for the immediate late-join policy is similar to the one of the event triggered late-join policy. The main difference is that there exists no wait for event (WFE) state. Instead the late-join state becomes "sub-component needed" as soon as the application sets the immediate late-join policy for a sub-component.

5.1.4 Late-Join Policy: Network-Capacity-Oriented Late-Join

For sub-components where the state is not immediately required an application may choose the network-capacity-oriented late-join policy. With this policy the late-join service monitors the incoming and outgoing network traffic of the application. This replaces the WFC state from the event-based late-join policy. If the traffic falls below a threshold set by the application then a transition to the "sub-component needed" state is performed. Whenever a state query is about to be transmitted, the network traffic is checked. Only when it is still below the threshold, is the query actually transmitted. Otherwise the query is delayed further. In all other aspects the network-capacity-oriented late-join policy is identical to the event-triggered late-join policy.

5.1.5 Late-Join Policy: Application-Initiated Late-Join

At any point in time the application may choose to change the late-join policy of a sub-component. In this way it is possible to upgrade policies like "no late-join" or "network capacity oriented late-join" to any other policy if this becomes necessary.

The application can define new late-join policies by initially setting the late-join policy for a sub-component to "no late-join". When the application-defined policy indicates that the state of the sub-component should be retrieved then the application can change the policy to "immediate late-join". This should be used only for experimental purposes. If another late-join policy becomes important for certain applications, then the late-join service should be expanded to include it.

5.2 Joining and Leaving the Late-Join Session

Unlike existing approaches, the generic late-join service allows a small number of applications which have completed their late-join process to stay in the dedicated late-join group. If these applications are chosen well they can assume the role of late-join servers for future latecomers, while the vast majority of applications (those that have completed their late-join process and that are not member of the late-join group) are completely uninvolved in the late-join process.

This approach raises the question of who should be member of the late-join group? Obviously all applications that have not yet finished the late-join process for all sub-components should stay in the late-join group. A late-join service could theoretically leave the late-join group as soon as the late-join for all sub-components has been completed. However, it should not do so without further consideration since this could leave the late-join group without a late-join server for certain sub-components. This would increase the time that a late-join client has to wait before it gets the state of a sub-component. It is therefore important to define an algorithm that decides which applications should stay members of the late-join group, even if they have completed their own late-join operations for all sub-components.

There are a number of criteria that need to be considered for an algorithm that decides whether an application should stay in the late-join group or not:

- **Group size.** The late-join group should be as small as possible. The smaller the group, the less network traffic is generated, and the fewer the applications that are involved in late-join management. A small group also decreases the likelihood that more than one late-join server will reply to the state query of a late-join client.

- **Sub-component presence.** Ideally each sub-component for which the state is likely to be requested should have a late-join server in the late-join group. This reduces the delay for late-join clients.

- **Group invariance.** The number of join and leave operations should be small for the late-join group since each of these operations is associated with overhead at the network layer (e.g., multicast routing).

- **Simplicity.** The applications should be able to perform the algorithm with a minimal effort in computation and communication.

Let us consider three different approaches to decide which applications should remain in the late-join group to act as late-join servers: distributed, isolated, and application controlled.

5.2.1 Distributed Membership Management

In distributed membership management the applications exchange information about their capabilities to act as late-join servers. This can be done via the generic services channel. With this information an optimal set of potential late-join servers can be determined. For example, the participants who are able to provide late-join server functionality for many sub-components should be preferred as members of the late-join group.

The main drawback of the distributed membership management is its complexity. Applications need to exchange additional information to allow for this kind of membership management. This information needs to be transmitted and processed, which may lead to significant overhead, especially for large sessions. For these reasons we have chosen not to use distributed membership management for our generic late-join service.

5.2.2 Isolated Membership Management

Isolated membership management seeks to avoid additional messages and processing overhead by using local information. Each application decides on its own whether it should join or leave the late-join group. Isolated membership management therefore seeks to increase simplicity at the cost of a slight reduction in the other quality criteria.

Our generic late-join service uses isolated membership management. Applications will leave the late-join group by means of a 'smart timeout', and they enter the late-join group upon the request of a late-join client.

An application leaves the late-join group if it has not answered any state queries for a certain amount of time. This amount of time is not fixed, but is calculated based on three values:

1. An average late-join group membership time provided by the application. In this way the application can give a hint to the late-join service on how fast applications should leave the late-join session.

2. The number of sub-components that the application can provide as a late-join server compared to the total number of sub-components present in the session. In this way applications that can serve a large percentage of the sub-components will stay longer in the late-join group.

3. The number of late-join state queries that could have been answered by the late-join server compared to the number of late-join state queries that actually have been answered by this application and not by some other late-join server. The lower this percentage is, the less important is the presence of the application in the late-join group.

When the timer expires the application leaves the late-join group. It may happen that the late-join group contains no late-join server for a given sub-component. If there is no late-join activity for a prolonged time the late-join group may even become empty. Generally this is a good thing, since it saves resources in the event that late-joins are infrequent. However, there must also be a way to allow applications to re-join the late-join group if a new late-join client appears.

As described above, a late-join client transmits a message on the generic services channel if the state queries for a sub-component remain unanswered in the late-join group. All applications that are able to become a late-join server for this sub-component use an SRM style implosion-avoidance mechanism to decide who will actually join the late-join group. The generic service of the selected application transmits an acknowledgment to the generic services channel, joins the late-join group, and transmits the requested state of the sub-component.

5.2.3 Application-Controlled Membership Management

In some cases the application may want to decide explicitly who should join the late-join group rather than leaving this decision to the late-join service. For example, in a medium that uses a floor control mechanism only the floor holder may be able to transmit the state of a sub-component. Since there is only one candidate for joining the late-join session, it would be wasteful to use an implosion avoidance mechanism. Therefore our late-join service allows the application to specify that it should immediately enter the late-join group if the state of a certain sub-component is requested.

In order to determine when an application should leave the late-join session, the smart timeout mechanism described above is also used for application-controlled membership management. This is reasonable since an application will generally not be able to determine with a higher accuracy than the late-join service when it is no longer needed as a late-join server.

5.3 Generic Late-Join Service API

The interface to the late-join service is depicted in Figure 3. The first two functions are called when RTP/I and RTCP/I data is received for the original RTP/I session. Based on this information the late-join service discovers new sub-components and triggers requests for the state of sub-components.

When a new sub-component is discovered, then the late-join service asks the application about the late-join policy that should be associated with the sub-component. If all sub-components should be treated with the same policy then it is possible to set a default policy by means of setDefaultPolicy. The late-join service will then refrain from asking the application about late-join policies for individual sub-components.

An application can at any time call setPolicy to assign a new late-join policy to a sub-component. This may also be called on a sub-component for which a late-join has already been completed.

The late-join may be used in this way to recover the state of sub-components in a late-join policy driven fashion.

The application may specify the policy for joining the late-join group and the base time for leaving it. When the late-join service needs to transmit the state of a sub-component as a late-join server, then it requests the sub-component's state from the application by means of the getSubComponentState method. Finally the application may be informed of an unsuccessful late-join attempt through a ljFailed call.

In order to allow others to experiment with this service, we provide an open source implementation of RTP/I and the late join service. The Java source code of this implementation can be downloaded from our web site [13]. It includes a more detailed specification of the late-join API and a full Javadoc documentation.

```
Implemented by the generic late-join service:
void rtpiDataReceived(RTPIData rtpiData)
void rtcpiPacketReceived(RTCPIPacket
                              rtcpiPacket)
void setPolicy(LJPolicy policy, long subID)
void setDefaultPolicy(LJPolicy policy)
void setJoinGroupPolicy(JGPolicy policy)
void setLeaveGroupBaseTime(long baseTime)


Implemented by the application:
LJPolicy askForPolicy(long subID)
RTPIData getSubComponentState(long subID)
void ljFailed(long subID)
```

Figure 3: Generic late-join service API

5.4 Consistency and the Generic Late-Join Service

A distributed interactive medium generally needs to take specific actions to maintain a consistent shared state for all participants of a session. This includes ensuring that events are applied to the state of the medium in the correct order at the appropriate point in time. It may also be necessary to realize state repair functionality to recover from network partitioning or lost events. The piece of software that is responsible for these actions is called a *consistency service*.

The generic late-join service provides the application and the consistency service with an initial state of the sub-components in a policy driven and efficient way. It is not the task of the late-join service to realize the functionality that should be provided by a separate consistency service. This would limit the applicability of the generic late-join service, since different distributed interactive media may have different requirements regarding consistency while having the same requirements for a late-join service. In addition to the generic late-join service presented here we have designed and implemented a consistency service for distributed interactive media which are continuous (i.e. these media require that events are applied to the state of the medium at a given point in time). A detailed description of the algorithm for this consistency service can be found in [11].

6. EXPERIENCES

We have used the generic late-join service for a 3D telecooperation application called TeCo3D - a shared workspace for dynamic and interactive 3D models [8]. TeCo3D was developed to allow users to share collaboration-unaware VRML (Virtual Reality Modeling Language) models, i.e. models which have not been specifically developed to be used by more than one user at a time. With this functionality it is possible to include arbitrary VRML content, as generated by standard CAD or animation software, into teleconferencing sessions.

TeCo3D was developed by reusing a Java3D VRML loader as 3D presentation and execution engine and employs a completely replicated distribution architecture with reliable multicast as means of communication. When a user imports a local VRML object, the VRML code is parsed and the parts which are responsible for user interactions are replaced with custom components turning the collaboration-unaware object into a collaboration-aware model. User initiated operations are captured by the custom components and are transmitted to all peer instance in the session, where they are injected into the local model. In order to provide access to the shared state of items on the shared workspace we have enhanced the VRML loader by a method to get and set the state of arbitrary VRML objects.

The media model for distributed interactive media provides a good fit for TeCo3D. The sub-components are the VRML objects. The state of these objects represent the state of the sub-components while the events are user interactions with the objects. TeCo3D uses RTP/I as application level protocol.

TeCo3D uses a floor control based consistency service. Like the late-join service presented in this work, the consistency service is RTP/I based and generic. The floor of a sub-component identifies the participant with a valid state of a VRML object. Only this participant is able to transmit states and events for the VRML object.

The generic late-join service has been developed completely separate from TeCo3D using a simple demo application. The integration of the generic late-join service into TeCo3D was straight forward. It took less than 5 hours to complete the integration. The following choices were made for adapting the generic late-join service to the needs of TeCo3D:

- The late-join policy for those sub-components that are currently visible for at least one participant is set to immediate late-join.

- The late-join policy for those sub-component that are not visible for any user is set to event triggered.

- The late-join group join policy is set to application defined. This is reasonable since the consistency service of TeCo3D allows only a single participant to reply to state queries for a given sub-component.

The simple and straight forward integration, as well as the easy way of adaptation shows that the generic late-join service is indeed generic and useful for distributed interactive media. First experiences with the performance of the late join service show that the time required for the selection of the late-join server remains in an acceptable range (below 2 seconds) even when no late-join server is present in the late-join session and when packet loss is not negligible.

7. CONCLUSION AND OUTLOOK

In this paper we have presented a generic, RTP/I based, late-join service for distributed interactive media. This service enables latecomers to join and participate in an ongoing session. Since the late-join service does not use any media specific information it can be employed by arbitrary applications that use RTP/I as application level protocol.

The two main innovations of the generic late-join service are its efficiency and its flexibility. The efficiency of the generic late-join service is realized by the usage of a dedicated late-join session. Unlike than in existing approaches, only members of this session will be regularly involved in the late-join process. Members of the base session are not burdened with the late-join activity. The membership of potential late-join servers in the late-join group is controlled by means of a smart time-out and join signals from latecomers.

The flexibility of the late-join service is realized by means of diverse late-join policies for the sub-components of the distributed interactive medium. The late-join policies allow the simple tailoring to the individual needs of application. Furthermore the application can decide on the policy for joining the dedicated late-join session.

We have integrated the generic late-join service into an existing, RTP/I based, 3D telecooperation application called TeCo3D. This integration was simple and needed less than 5 hours. The source code of the generic late-join service is available for download.

Currently we are working on a C++ port of the late-join service. Furthermore we will integrate the late-join service into two additional applications: a shared whiteboard and distributed Java animations for teleteaching purposes. We expect to get important information about how to improve the late-join service from these items of future work.

8. REFERENCES

1. S. Floyd, V. Jacobson, C. Liu, S. McCanne and L. Zhang. A reliable multicast framework for leight-weight sessions and application level framing. In: *IEEE/ACM Transactions on Networking*, Vol. 5, No. 6, 1997, pp. 784 - 803.

2. L. Gautier, C. Diot. Design and Evaluation of MiMaze, a Multi-player Game on the Internet. In: *Proc. of IEEE International Conference on Multimedia Computing and Systems*, Austin, Texas, USA, 1998, pp. 233-236.

3. W. Geyer and W. Effelsberg. The Digital Lecture Board - A Teaching and Learning Tool for Remote Instruction in Higher Education. In: *Proc. of 10th World Conference on Educational Multimedia (ED-MEDIA) '98*, Freiburg, Germany, 1998. Available on CD-ROM.

4. W. Geyer, J. Vogel, and M Mauve. An Efficient and Flexible Late Join Algorithm for Shared Whiteboards. To appear in: *Proc. of the Fifth IEEE International Symposium on Computers and Communications, ISCC'2000*, Antibes, France, July, 2000.

5. O. Hagesand. Interactive multiuser VEs in the DIVE system. In: *IEEE Multimedia*, Vol. 3, No. 1, 1996, pp. 30 - 39.

6. M. Handley, and J. Crowcroft. Network text editor (NTE): A scalable shared text editor for the MBone. In. Proc. of the ACM SIGCOMM'97, Cannes, France, 1997, pp. 197 - 208.

7. V. Jacobson, S. Casner, R. Frederick and H. Schulzrinne. *RTP: A Transport Protocol for Real-Time Applications*, Internet Draft, Audio/Video Transport Working Group, IETF, draft-ietf-avt-rtp-new-04.txt, 1999. Work in progress.

8. M. Mauve. TeCo3D: a 3D telecooperation application based on VRML and Java. In: *Proc. of SPIE Multimedia Computing and Networking (MMCN) '99*, San Jose, CA, USA, published by SPIE, Bellingham, Washington, USA, January 1999, pp. 240 - 251.

9. M. Mauve, V. Hilt, C. Kuhmünch and W. Effelsberg. A General Framework and Communication Protocol for the Transmission of Interactive Media with Real-Time Characteristics. In: *Proc. of IEEE Multimedia Systems (ICMS) '99*, Florence, Italy, published by IEEE Computer Society, Los Alamitos, California, USA, June 1999, Vol. 2, pp. 641 - 646.

10. M. Mauve, V. Hilt, C. Kuhmünch, J. Vogel, W. Geyer and W. Effelsberg. *RTP/I: An Application Level Real-Time Protocol for Distributed Interactive Media*. Internet Draft: draft-mauve-rtpi-00.txt, 2000. Work in progress.

11. M. Mauve. *Consistency in Continuous Distributed Interactive Media*. Technical Report TR-9-99, Reihe Informatik, Department for Mathematics and Computer Science, University of Mannheim, November 1999.

12. J. F. Patterson, M. Day and J. Kucan, Notification servers for synchronous groupware. In: *Proc. of the ACM conference on Computer supported cooperative work (CSCW) ' 96*, Boston, USA, 1996, p. 122.

13. RTP/I. The RTP/I homepage. http://www.informatik.uni-mannheim.de/ informatik/pi4/projects/RTPI/index.html

14. T. L. Tung. MediaBoard: *A Shared Whiteboard Application for the MBone*. Master's Thesis, University of Calafornia, Berkeley, California, USA, 1998.

The Good, the Bad, and the Muffled:
the Impact of Different Degradations on Internet Speech

Anna Watson
Department of Computer Science
University College London
Gower Street
London, WC1E 6BT
+44 (0)20 7679 3643

A.Watson@cs.ucl.ac.uk

M. Angela Sasse
Department of Computer Science
University College London
Gower Street
London, WC1E 6BT
+44 (0)20 7679 7212

A.Sasse@cs.ucl.ac.uk

ABSTRACT

This paper presents an experiment comparing the relative impact of different types of degradation on subjective quality ratings of interactive speech transmitted over packet-switched networks. The experiment was inspired by observations made during a large-scale, long-term field trial of multicast conferencing. We observed that user reports of unsatisfactory speech quality were rarely due to network effects such as packet loss and jitter. A subsequent analysis of conference recordings found that in most cases, the impairment was caused by end-system hardware, equipment setup or user behavior. The results from the experiment confirm that the effects of volume differences, echo and bad microphones are rated worse than the level of packet loss most users are likely to experience on the Internet today, provided that a simple repair mechanism is used. Consequently, anyone designing or deploying network speech applications and services ought to consider the addition of diagnostics and tutorials to ensure acceptable speech quality.

Keywords

Internet audio, speech, media quality assessment, subjective assessment, multicast conferencing.

1. INTRODUCTION

Over the past 5 years, there has been increasing interest and growth in the use of multicast technology over the Internet in areas such as distance education and remote project meetings. It is well established that good-quality audio is a necessary condition for usable multimedia conferencing [e.g. 8, 16], and a great deal of research effort in the telecommunications arena has been directed at combating the effects of packet loss, jitter and delay [e.g. 2, 3, 9]. To date, there has been an implicit assumption in the networking community that many of these issues will be resolved through increased bandwidth [6, 24]. If

this is true, given the level of provision in the US and western Europe today, the quality of speech users experience in Internet conferences should be good. Yet, in a recent large-scale field trial, users reported speech quality problems in one out of three multimedia conferencing activities, where sufficient bandwidth was available.

The PIPVIC-2 (Piloting IP-based VideoConferencing) project [12] involved 13 UK academic institutions and 150 participants in a range of educational activities running from December 1998 to October 1999. The project gathered both subjective (user opinion) and objective (network behavior) performance data, and developed methods of matching these two types of data more closely.

Subjective data was gathered through paper-based questionnaires at the end of each particular course; group workshops with the tutors and students; and through web-based opinion scales completed at set points during a conference. This latter method was used since it is notoriously difficult to gather reliable subjective opinions of the quality delivered in lengthy multimedia conferences. Waiting until the end of a conference leaves the user open to primacy and recency memory effects, whilst taking continuous readings throughout a conference leads to task interference [18]. Collecting subjective quality data at certain set points during the conference seemed a reasonable compromise. In an hour-long conference, these data were collected approximately every 20 minutes – after the sound and volume check at the start of the conference, midway through the conference, and at the end of the conference.

Objective data was collected through modification of the audio and video conferencing tools such that they logged the reception reports received from the other participants in the conference. These statistics could then be matched in time with the web-based opinion ratings.

The remainder of this paper describes an experiment informed by the main finding from the PIPVIC-2 project: that many reported speech quality problems are due not to network conditions, but rather to end-user behavior and equipment problems. We investigated both the subjective ratings and the physiological responses (blood volume pulse and heart rate) of listeners to samples of Internet speech degradations. Results confirm that the impact of volume discrepancies and voice feedback affect perceived quality more adversely than the levels of packet loss typically experienced in the project. Initial physiological results indicate that poor-quality microphones and too high volume levels are particularly stressful to users.

2. BACKGROUND TO EXPERIMENT

2.1 Rationale for conditions chosen

The user assessment of the conferencing sessions in the PIPVIC-2 trials showed that three factors were most often reported as problematic: missing words or incomplete sentences; variation in volume between participants; and variation in quality between participants. These problems, and their likely causes, are summarized in Table 1.

Table 1 Key audio problems reported by users in the PIPVIC-2 field trials

Problem	Likely causes
Missing words or incomplete sentences	Packet loss; silence suppression clipping beginnings and endings of words; machine 'glitching'
Variation in volume between participants	Insufficient volume settings; poor headset quality
Variation in quality between participants	High background noise; open microphone; poor headset quality

Although 'missing words' were frequently cited as a problem, the outcome from the project's network monitoring activities showed that, in general, the level of packet loss on both the SuperJANET[1] multicast service, and participants' local area networks, was low during the trial. The project collected RTP (Real-time Transport Protocol) reception report statistics from the participants in various conferences. Reception reports are generated once every 2-5 seconds, and can be used to produce an overall picture of the level of loss experienced at different end sites in a conference. One such picture is shown in Figure 1, where reception reports reflecting the level of loss received by a participant in Glasgow from a participant in London are shown.

The overall results indicated that packet loss on the audio stream was relatively rare, and in general occurred at a level of 5% loss or below. Higher levels of packet loss tended to appear in very short-lived bursts, but could reach levels of 20% or greater.

In view of these findings, we designed a controlled experiment investigating the impact of different factors on subjective opinion.

2.1.1 Codec, packet size and packet loss repair method

In the PIPVIC-2 project the Robust Audio Tool, RAT [13], was used. RAT is one of the two most commonly used software audio tools in the multicast community (the other being LBL's Visual-Audio Tool, VAT [5]). RAT offers greater functionality than VAT, in particular packet loss repair mechanisms.

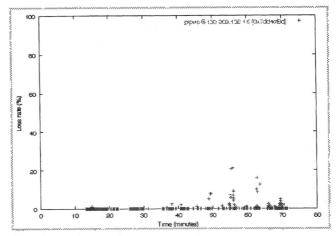

Figure 1 Loss reported from UCL by a Glasgow conference participant over a one-hour project meeting

In selecting the codec and packet size to investigate in the experiment, we decided to use the RAT version 3 default settings that had been available to users in the field observations, even though in recent months these defaults have been changed and are now likely to produce better perception[2]. Therefore the experimental speech material that was generated was coded in DVI [14], using 40 ms packets, and repaired with the receiver-based packet loss repair method packet repetition.

Packet repetition (also known as waveform substitution) fills in the space from a missing packet by repeating the last received packet. This technique works best when the packet size is small (20 ms): when the packet is large (80 ms), the speech signal is likely to have changed significantly within the missing packet, meaning that the repaired speech can sound faintly synthetic or metallic where the repaired waveform does not connect smoothly.

2.1.2 Packet loss rates

As a result of the PIPVIC-2 findings reported above, for the experiment we selected 5% as a lower level of packet loss, which is representative of the level of packet loss users are likely to experience on the SuperJANET multicast service today. The figure of 20% was chosen as a higher level for the experiment presented here because it is known from previous research that this is the level at which perceived quality of repaired speech starts to drop significantly, but where speech intelligibility is maintained [18, 19][3].. Since this level of packet loss is known to

---

[1] SuperJANET is the UK's national broadband network for the education and research community.

[2] At the time of writing, the defaults in RAT version 4 are 20 ms packets, with pattern matching as the preferred method of receiver-based packet loss repair.

[3] It was an explicit aim of the study that the intelligibility of the speech should not be affected. Intelligibility and perceived

cause severe degradation, it would act as a reference point in the planned study.

2.1.3 'Bad' microphone

A poor-quality microphone was chosen as a condition because during the field trials users had reported and complained about 'tinny' or 'hummy' microphones. The selection of a 'bad' microphone is, of course, somewhat subjective. In addition, a microphone that produces 'bad' audio when used with one soundcard will not necessarily be a 'bad' microphone for another, making the matter more complicated. However, the effect of microphone distortion was still felt to be worthwhile investigating, since so many subjective comments refer to how the voice sounds, and whether it is pleasant to listen to [11]. The microphone chosen for the experiment was an Altai A087F.

2.1.4 Volume differences

Many users in the field trials complained of extreme volume differences between participants in multi-way conferences. Although it is possible to alter the incoming volume from a particular participant by adjusting the incoming volume slider in RAT, users tend not to adjust the slider when the next speaker is louder or softer, since it becomes tedious and interferes with the ongoing purpose of the conference. We decided to investigate the subjective effects of one speaker at 'normal' volume, and the other at 'too loud', and also the impact of 'normal' and 'too quiet'. Again, it is recognized that determining what is 'too loud' or 'too quiet' is a subjective decision to be taken by the experimenter, but by piloting the experiment with both network audio experts and novices we were able to determine levels that were commonly agreed to be 'too loud' or 'too quiet'.

2.1.5 Echo

Echo, or feedback, commonly occurs in multicast conferences when people are working in individual offices and using a speaker and open microphone, and forget to mute their microphone when not speaking, or when 'leaky' headsets are used (i.e. the headphones leak sound into the microphone). Although the echo effect is primarily annoying to the speaker, it is also distracting to other listeners.

2.2 Measurement methods

The most common listening quality rating scale in use is the ITU-recommended 5-point listening quality scale (resulting in a Mean Opinion Score, or MOS) [4]. This scale has come under criticism from an increasing number of researchers in recent years [7, 10, 18] for a number of reasons, not least of which is the fact that the labels on the scale (*Excellent, Good, Fair, Poor, Bad*) are not appropriate for the level and type of degradation experienced in speech over the Internet, since the quality encountered will rarely be described as *excellent*. The other key reasons are:

1. Although treated as such, the scale is not an interval scale as represented by its 5 qualitative labels (*Excellent, Good, Fair, Poor, Bad*) [7, 17, 23]. *Fair*,

quality are not the same thing - it is possible to get high intelligibility with speech that receives very poor quality ratings e.g. with synthetic speech, but not vice versa.

for example, is not indicative of a midpoint to most people.

2. Use of the 5-point scale leaves the experimenter ignorant of the subject's perspective and rationale for positioning on the scale [10].

3. Quality is a *multi*dimensional phenomenon [11, 23], and means are required by which the dimensions that have the largest effects can be identified.

On-going research at UCL has been investigating a number of novel methods [18, 19, 1, 21] for measuring received quality in conferences over the Internet, and in particular has developed what we believe to be a more suitable rating scale for the subjective assessment of Internet media. This method will be discussed in the following section.

2.2.1 Subjective measurement

The unlabelled scale that was described in [18, 19] has evolved into a scale where the end-points are bounded by 1 and 100 (see Figure 2). (This development was necessary when gathering data in the PIPVIC-2 project via web-based evaluation forms.)

We fully subscribe to the point made by [11], that speech quality should not be treated as a unidimensional phenomenon, since one or many different dimensions may affect the listener's opinion. This is why there are no descriptive labels other than at the end points on the 100-point scale. Instead we ask subjects to describe how the sample sounded, and why a certain rating was awarded. This allows us to gain a deeper insight into factors that affect perceived quality, with a long-term view to producing a series of diagnostic scales along different quality dimensions. The background to this research lies in the observation that the vocabulary that is used by Internet audio experts is rarely matched by novice users when describing how Internet communication sounds to them [18].

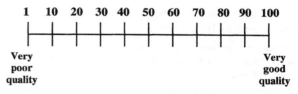

Figure 2 The 100-point quality rating scale

2.2.2 Objective (physiological) measurement

A traditional Human-Computer Interaction (HCI) approach should take into account *user cost* as well as user satisfaction [21]. User cost addresses the level of fatigue, discomfort, physical strain etc. that people experience in performing a certain task. We have recently begun to investigate the effect of different media quality on user stress, as measured by Blood Volume Pulse (BVP) and Heart Rate (HR). Using a ProComp[4] unit, we place sensors on the fingers of subjects, making it possible to monitor their physiological responses to different

---

[4]Manufactured by Thought Technology,

http://www.thoughttechnology.com/

types of impairment. This enables us to assess the relationship between expressed opinion and user cost.

BVP is an indicator of blood flow which decreases when a person is under stress. Under stress, HR increases in order to increase blood flow to the muscles (the 'fight or flight' reflex). Therefore the physiological indicators of increased user cost would be a decrease in BVP and an increase in HR, compared to the levels recorded in a resting state.

3. THE EXPERIMENT

3.1 Experimental material

A two-person conversation was scripted from recordings of multicast project meetings, with names and locations changed from the original recordings. This script was acted out by two male actors without regional accents. The actors sat at Sun Ultra workstations at different locations on the same local network for the duration of the recording. (Only audio was recorded: video did not play a part in this study.) The recording was made at 16 bit linear quality and recorded via the record facility in RAT. Silence suppression was left on and both microphones were kept open during the recording. The actors wore identical Canford DMH12OU headsets. Different parts of the conversation were subject to manipulation by the experimenter such as the volume and feedback of one of the speakers, and the headset in use. The resulting recordings were then split into 2-minute files and coded into DVI, at 8kHz sampling rate, and 40 ms packets. Packet loss and repair (packet repetition) were generated on the files where required, using the software program **test_repair**[5].

The conditions that were generated were:

- **reference**: a no-degradation reference condition;

- **5% loss**: 5% packet loss generated on both voices, and repaired with packet repetition;

- **20% loss**: 20% packet loss generated on both voices, and repaired with packet repetition;

- **echo**: one person using an open microphone and speaker rather than headset, such that the other person generates echo/feedback ;

- **quiet**: one voice recorded at a low volume, the other at a normal volume;

- **loud**: one voice recorded at a high volume, the other at a normal volume;

- **bad mic**: one person using a poor quality microphone.

Three Internet audio experts agreed that the conditions were identifiable as containing the degradations we aimed to test, and also that the intelligibility of the recorded speech was not affected by the impairments A pilot study of the recorded samples with 6 subjects (all first-time users of Internet audio) confirmed the expert assessment.

---

[5] **test_repair** is a component verification program included in the RAT version 4 application.

3.2 Subjects

Twenty-four subjects (12 men and 12 women) participated in the study. They all had good hearing and were aged between 18 and 28. None of them had previous experience in Internet audio or videoconferencing.

3.3 Procedure

The subjects each listened to the seven 2-minute test files twice (to determine the consistency of subjects' scores on the 100-point scale). The files were played out through the program Audio Tool[6] on a Sun Ultra workstation. Each subject listened to the files wearing a Canford DMH12OU headset. There was no accompanying video image. The test files were preceded by a 1-minute file which had no degradations. The function of this file was for the subjects to assess whether the volume playout level was acceptable to them, but they were also instructed that the volume test file should be taken as indicative of the best quality they would encounter in the following test files. This ensured that the subjects knew what the upper limit of quality would be. The order of the test files was randomized, with one exception: the **reference** (no degradation) condition was always heard first and eighth. The 7 conditions were therefore all heard once before they were repeated in a different order.

Baseline physiological readings were taken for each subject for 15 minutes before the listening part of the study, using the Procomp measurement device[7]. Sensors were placed on the left hand of each subject, taking measurements of blood volume pulse (BVP) and heart rate (HR).

After each test file the subject was asked to provide a quality rating, for the file as a whole, from the 1-100 scale where 1 represents *Very Poor Quality* and 100 represents *Very Good Quality* (see Figure 2). The subject was then asked to explain why that rating was awarded i.e. how the speakers had sounded to him/her. These answers were tape-recorded.

4. RESULTS

4.1.1 Quantitative results

The mean results and standard error for the perceived quality ratings are shown in Figure 3. The graph suggests that a 'normal' level of packet loss (5%) when repaired with packet repetition has little impact on perceived quality when compared to the **reference** (no degradation) condition. As expected, **20% loss** repaired with packet repetition has a profound effect on perceived quality, but it appears a loud-normal volume discrepancy, and an echo effect also affect perceived quality adversely. Are these apparent differences statistically significant?

Analyses of variance were carried out on the data. A two-factor with replication ANOVA at the 1% level of probability revealed that there is a highly significant effect of condition ($F_{6, 322}$ =

---

[6] Audio Tool is an OpenWindows DeskSet application for recording, playing and simple editing of audio data.

[7] The Procomp, manufactured by Thought Technology, encompasses physiological measurement sensors and software.

62.25, p < 0.01), and that there is no significant difference between the quality ratings awarded on 1st presentation and those awarded the 2nd time of hearing (F 1, 322 = 0.799).

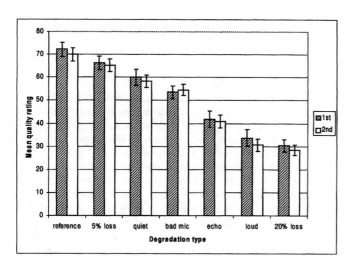

Figure 3 Mean quality rating awarded for different degradation types, on 1st and 2nd occasion of hearing

Table 2 Combined subjective rating means for 1st and 2nd presentation of the conditions

	Ref	5%	quiet	bad	echo	loud	20%
1	77.5	67.5	62.5	50	37.5	27.5	30
2	77.5	78.5	49.5	67.5	35	51	29.5
3	81.5	81	81.5	71	30	18.5	17
4	83.5	73.5	51	52.5	60	31.5	32.5
5	72.5	60	27.5	40	20	10	25
6	60	50	65	52.5	17.5	25	9
7	58.5	45	59	44	30	10.5	19
8	60	60	47.5	50	42.5	24	27.5
9	77.5	50	60	62.5	40	17.5	34
10	90	90	50	57.5	42.5	27.5	32.5
11	35	50	40	35	25	20	15
12	87	81.5	76	66.5	60	66	47.5
13	72	73.5	80	57	51	34	27.5
14	65	59	67.5	52.5	37.5	27.5	37.5
15	67.5	62.5	56	51.5	52.5	50	40
16	82.5	65	60	65	75	30	35
17	90	80	79	66.5	50	27.5	21.5
18	80	72.5	67.5	70	57.5	52.5	45
19	72.5	62.5	52.5	37.5	30	35	40
20	60	60	57.5	40	32.5	42.5	20
21	77.5	72.5	62.5	55	45	30	30
22	75.5	77	79	72.5	57.5	61	42.5
23	60.5	68.5	54	47.5	41.5	31	33
24	42.5	38	37.5	32.5	22.5	21	14
Mean	71.08	65.75	59.27	54.02	41.35	32.12	29.35

Since we know that there is no significant difference between the 1st and 2nd presentation ratings, we can take the mean response for each person. These results are presented in Table 2. An analysis of variance on these combined means again confirms that there is a highly significant main effect of condition at the 1% level of probability (F 6, 161 = 36.598, p < 0.01). Post hoc analyses (Tukey HSD) allow further statements to be made as to where these significant differences lie. There is no significant difference between the **reference** condition and the **5% loss** condition (Qcrit = 4.88, Qobt = 1.97) or the **quiet** condition (Qobt = 4.36). The differences between the **reference** condition and all other conditions are significant. The **5% loss** condition is not significantly different from the **quiet** condition (Qobt = 2.39), but it is rated significantly higher than the **echo** (Qobt = 9), **loud** (Qobt = 12.41) and **20% loss** (Qobt = 13.43) conditions at the 1% probability level, and higher than the **bad mic** condition at the 5% level (Qcrit = 4.17, Qobt = 4.33). Although **20% loss** gives the worst performance according to the graph, the difference between this condition and the **echo** and **loud** conditions is not significant at the 1% level (Qobt = 4.43 and 1.02 respectively).

4.1.2 Physiological results

The mean HR and BVP readings for each condition were calculated, and are shown in Figures 4 and 5 respectively. The graphs show a different order of severity for the different conditions compared to that seen in the subjective results (Figure 3). Are these differences significant?

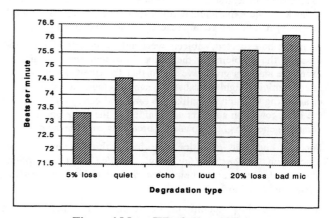

Figure 4 Mean HR of all participants

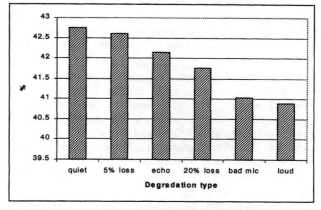

Figure 5 Mean BVP of all participants

273

A multivariate analysis of variance (MANOVA) revealed significant effects of condition for both HR (F 5,115 = 4.106, p < 5) and BVP (F 5,115 = 3.316, p < 0.05) signals. Pairwise comparisons revealed that, for both HR and BVP, **bad mic**, **loud** and **20% loss** were all significantly more stressful than **quiet** and **5% loss** at the 5% level of probability. **Echo** was found to be significantly more stressful than quiet in the HR signal only, at the 5% level of probability.

In contrast to the subjective ratings, therefore, the **20% loss** condition did *not* produce the worst physiological ratings: the **loud** and **bad mic** conditions produced significant increases in HR and significant decreases in BVP, indicating that these two conditions were the most stressful for the subjects to listen to. The least stressful conditions appear to be the **quiet** and **5% loss** conditions.

The significance of these findings will be discussed in section 5. (For a detailed presentation and discussion of the physiological results, the reader is referred to [22].)

4.1.3 Qualitative results
In addition to providing a rating on the 100 point scale, subjects were asked to describe why they had awarded each rating. The primary aim of this part of the study was to search for common descriptive terms used by non-expert users to describe different types of degradations to aid in the building of diagnostic scales, as discussed in section 2.2.1. The descriptions also functioned as a check on the experimental conditions by enabling us to check that users had perceived and reacted to the effect intended.

As might be expected, subjects were able to clearly identify and describe the problems in the **quiet**, **loud** and **echo** conditions. From the answers given, we found that the **quiet** condition was rated relatively highly because the subjects found it not *too* quiet or annoying to listen to, unlike the **loud** and **echo** conditions. In the **loud** condition subjects complained of the increased level of noise in general e.g. the speaker's breathing could be heard.

For the **bad mic** condition, we found three main types of description: *'distant'* or *'far away'*, *'muffled'*, and descriptions likening the speaker to being *'on the telephone'*, or *'walkie-talkie'*, or *'in a box'*.

In the **5% loss** condition, the terms that appeared most frequently were *'fuzzy'* and *'buzzy'*, (mentioned by 13 of the subjects) with *'metallic'*, *'robotic'* and *'electronic'* appearing slightly less often (7 times) than might have been anticipated. This fuzziness/buzziness is due to the speech waveform changing in the missing packet, and not being catered for well enough in the repeated packet.

In the **20% loss** condition, the descriptive terms used most often were words that suggested the mechanical nature of the sound: *'robotic'*, *'metallic'*, *'digital'*, *'electronic'* (mentioned by 15 of the subjects), in addition to terms such as *'broken up'* and *'cutting out'* (10 times). Compared to the **5% loss** condition, *'fuzzy'* and *'buzzy'* were generated infrequently - just twice each. Interestingly, 5 subjects described the impairment as *'echo'*, and 10 of the subjects described major volume variations in the file.

The frequency with which the subjects ascribed volume differences (in the **20% loss** condition especially, but also in the

5% loss and **bad mic** conditions) as a problem was surprising. Since the original recordings did not have volume differences, and because subjects were not consistent in attributing the problem to the first or second speaker, we have to conclude that users do not always reliably identify the cause of a degradation. This has implications for the type of support that users require, as will be argued in the following sections.

5. DISCUSSION
The results of the experiment have shown that the typical PIPVIC-2 level of packet loss (which was generally below 5%), when repaired with a method such as packet repetition, does not affect users' subjective ratings adversely when compared to a no-loss condition, whereas non-network factors such as volume discrepancies between speakers, poor quality microphones, and echo or feedback do. It is not the case that the users do not *notice* the degradation in the **5% loss** condition (since their descriptions of the files are different from those of the **reference** condition), but rather that it has less impact on perceived quality than other types of degradation. We have demonstrated that users will rate the different conditions consistently on a 100 point rating scale. However, we have observed that, although their ratings and descriptions may be consistent, users often attribute impairments inaccurately, suggesting there is a need for a diagnostic tool to aid users in correctly identifying the source of different impairments, and then enable them to take appropriate steps to correct them.

The physiological results are intriguing in that they indicate that users are more adversely affected by the **bad mic** condition and less affected by the **20% loss** condition than the subjective rating results suggest. In a previous study looking at the impact of video frame rate on both subjective ratings and user cost, it was found that viewers did not notice (subjectively) the change in frame rate from 5 to 25 frames per second (fps), but their physiological measurements changed significantly in the direction of stress [21]. These types of findings emphasize the importance of carrying out research of this nature, combining subjective ratings with measurements of user cost - we believe that subjective results alone do not provide a wholly accurate picture.

We believe that the method outlined in this paper, using field trials to inform the design of controlled experiments, is a meaningful and practical way forward in terms of understanding the complexity of factors affecting perceived quality in multimedia conferencing across the Internet. As discussed in section 1, gathering subjective opinions of the quality delivered in multimedia conferences is not straightforward, since memory effects or task interference can occur, depending on the method used. The approach described here allows us first to identify the main effects affecting real users performing real tasks, then to perform controlled experiments to confirm and assess the relative impact of these effects. The experimental step is of great importance since users are often unable to correctly identify what is responsible for the problem in a conferencing environment, due to the complexity of many interacting factors and media. For example, it is known that audio quality can affect the rating of video quality [15]. The experiment reported here has shown that speech quality problems can be attributed to the wrong source, highlighting the importance of ascertaining as much subjective explanatory data as possible.

However, the work reported here is merely the first step in a logical research progression – there is a danger in making assumptions about quality required without careful consideration of the task being undertaken. It is very likely, for example, that both speech and video quality variables would be rated differently in an interactive experiment, and depending on the task being performed in that experiment, different factors will be important.

6. CONCLUSIONS AND RECOMMENDATIONS

The experiment has clearly demonstrated that the perceived quality of network audio is *not* primarily affected by the level packet loss we observed in the large-scale field trial (provided that a packet loss repair method such as packet repetition is in use). Volume discrepancies, poor quality microphones and echo have a greater impact on the user, meaning that it is possible to have perfect transmission from a network viewpoint, but still have poor quality audio from a user's viewpoint. The solutions envisioned mainly involve raising and improving user awareness, both of what the problem is, and how to solve it. These can be low-cost solutions – a huge amount of people-support should not be required once audio tools are better set up to support non-expert users.

By further analyzing how people describe different types of degradation, it should be possible to provide improved fault diagnosis to novice users. For example, a help menu on an audio tool should provide a list of problems described in terms that users most commonly generate, such as *'fuzzy'* and *'buzzy'* which, as we have seen, are related to a specific type of packet loss repair (packet repetition). The user could search down this list for the terms that describe his or her problem, then follow the solution suggested (e.g. change the receiver-based packet loss repair method to another, such as pattern matching).

There is perhaps less that a user can do about someone else's bad microphone, other than tell them that they sound *'muffled'*, *'distant'*, or like they're *'on the phone'*. One solution would be a pre-session diagnostic that would reflect the user's audio as heard by other participants, since at present the user cannot hear what he/she sounds like. We propose developers design a tool to perform an expert-system style diagnostic of a user's speech stream and point to likely causes of problems. After a system is initially set up, users could be required to record sample sentences – as in a voice recognition package for word processing, for example – and only be allowed onto the network once the quality of the sample files is matched or recognized as providing satisfactory quality.

The key problems highlighted in the study also provide a strong case for the inclusion of aspects such as automatic gain control and reliable echo suppression in Internet audio tools. These are already present in RAT version 4, but they are optional settings – users need guidance on when to apply them.

7. FUTURE WORK

There is a clear need to quantify the exact levels of degradation that were imposed in this study, in order to identify the levels that represent enough, too much, or too little of a certain quality variable. By establishing these levels, suitable input to designers of future tool diagnostics can be provided.

As discussed in section 1, the research community has focused on investigating the effects of objective degradations such as delay and jitter. Future work should therefore consider the relative weights of these factors against user and hardware variables, as has been done with packet loss in the present study.

An obvious further step will be to recreate the experimental conditions presented in this paper in an interactive task environment, and have people engage in active conversations as opposed to passive listening. It can be hypothesized that the effects of the factors investigated here will be altered in this setting. We can predict that the effect of echo, for example, will have an even more negative effect when a subject is trying to engage in a conversation with another person, but keeps hearing their own voice fed back to them. It will also be important to introduce a video channel into the set-up, and observe the impact of audio-visual interactions.

Another important aspect to investigate will be the effects of the interaction *between* different impairment types, for example one person with a bad microphone conversing with someone speaking too loudly. Again, presenting this scenario as an interactive experiment is likely to lead to different results.

Future work will continue to gather physiological data, to gain a better understanding of the user cost of different types of degradations, and the relationship between user cost, subjective opinion, and task performance.

8. ACKNOWLEDGMENTS

Our thanks go to Gillian Wilson at UCL, who carried out the physiological measurements. We gratefully acknowledge the technical advice and assistance of Orion Hodson and Colin Perkins, also at UCL. Partners on the UKERNA funded PIPVIC-2 project also merit recognition and thanks. The research reported here was funded under the EPSRC project ETNA (GR/M25599).

9. REFERENCES

[1] Bouch, A., Watson, A. and Sasse, M.A. QUASS: A tool for measuring the subjective quality of real-time multimedia audio and video. Poster presented at HCI '98 (Sheffield, England, September 1998).

[2] Gruber, J.G. and Strawczynski, L. Subjective effects of variable delay and speech clipping in dynamically managed voice systems. IEEE Transactions on Cummunications, 1985, 33(8), 801-808.

[3] Hardman, V., Sasse, M.A., Handley, M.J. and Watson, A. Reliable audio for use over the Internet. Proceedings of INET '95 (Honolulu, Hawaii, June 1995), 171-178.

[4] ITU-T P.800 Methods for subjective determination of transmission quality. Available from http://www.itu.int/publications/itu-t/iturec.htm

[5] Jacobson, V. vat manual pages, Lawrence Berkeley Laboratory, USA. Software available from http://www-nrg.ee.lbl.gov/vat/

[6] Jayant, N.S. High-quality coding of telephone speech and wideband audio. IEEE Communications Magazine, Jan. 1990, 10-20.

[7] Jones, B.L. and McManus, P.R. Graphic scaling of qualitative terms. SMPTE Journal, November 1986, 1166-1171.

[8] Kawalek, J. A user perspective for QoS management. Proceedings of 3rd International Conference on Intelligence in Broadband Services and Network (IS & N '95, Crete, Greece).

[9] Kitawaki, N. and Itoh, K. Pure delay effects on speech quality in telecommunications. IEEE Journal on Selected Areas in Telecommunication, 1991, 9(4), 586-593.

[10] Knoche, H., De Meer, H.G. and Kirsh, D. Utility curves: Mean opinion scores considered biased. Proceedings of IWQoS '99 (London, England, May 1999), 12-14.

[11] Preminger, J.E. and Van Tasell, D.J. Quantifying the relationship between speech quality and speech intelligibility. Journal of Speech and Hearing Research, 1995, 38, 714-725.

[12] PIPVIC-2 Project web site at http:// www-mice.cs.ucl.ac.uk/multimedia/projects/pipvic2/

[13] RAT (Robust Audio Tool). Available for download from http://www-mice.cs.ucl.ac.uk/multimedia/software

[14] Recommended practices for enhancing digital audio compatibility in multimedia systems (version 3.00). Technical Report, Interactive Multimedia Association, Annapolis, MD, 1992.

[15] Reeves, B. and Nass, C. The Media Equation. Cambridge University Press/CSLI Publications, 1996.

[16] Sasse, M.A., Bilting, U., Schulz, C-D. and Turletti, T. Remote seminars through multimedia conferencings: Experiences from the MICE project. Proceedings of INET'94/JENC5.

[17] Teunissen, K. The validity of CCIR quality indicators along a graphical scale. SMPTE Journal, March 1996, 144-149.

[18] Watson, A. and Sasse, M.A. Measuring perceived quality of speech and video in multimedia conferencing applications. Proceedings of ACM Multimedia '98 (Bristol, England, September 1998), ACM Press, 55-60.

[19] Watson, A. and Sasse, M.A. Multimedia conferencing via multicast: Determining the quality of service required by the end user. Proceedings of AVSPN '97 (Aberdeen, Scotland, September 1997), 189-194.

[20] Watson, A. and Sasse, M.A. Distance education via IP videoconferencing: Results from a national pilot project. Poster to be presented at CHI 2000 (The Hague, The Netherlands, April 2000).

[21] Wilson, G. & Sasse, M.A. Do users always know what's good for them? Utilising physiological responses to assess media quality. To be presented at HCI 2000, September 5th - 8th, Sunderland, UK.

[22] Wilson, G. & Sasse, M.A. Investigating the impact of audio degradations on users: Subjective vs. objective measurement methods. Submitted to OZCHI 2000. Available as UCL Computer Science research note RN/00/36.

[23] Virtanen, M.T, Gleiss, N. and Goldstein, M. One the use of evaluative category scales in telecommunications. Proceedings of Human Factors in Telecommunications, 1995, 253-260.

[24] Zhang, L., Deering, S., Estrin, D., Shenker, S. and Zappala, D. RSVP: A new resource ReSerVation Protocol, IEEE Network Magazine, 1995, 7(5), 8-18.

Multi-Modal Haptic Device
For Large-Scale Virtual Environment

Laroussi Buoguila
P&I, Tokyo Institute of Technology
4259 Nagatsuta, Midori ku,
226-8503 Yokohama - Japan
Phone: +81 45 924 5050

laroussi@pi.titech.ac.jp

Masahiro Ishii
P&I, Tokyo Institute of Technology
4259 Nagatsuta, Midori ku,
226-8503 Yokohama - Japan
Phone: +81 45 924 5050

mishii@pi.titech.ac.jp

Makoto Sato
P&I, Tokyo Institute of Technology
4259 Nagatsuta, Midori ku,
226-8503 Yokohama - Japan
Phone: +81 45 924 5050

msato@pi.titech.ac.jp

ABSTRACT
The paper aims to present a new human-scale haptic device for virtual environment named Scaleable-SPIDAR (Space Interface Device for Artificial Reality), which provide to both hands different aspects of force feedback sensations, associated mainly with weight, contact and inertia within a cave-like space. Tensioned string techniques are used to generate such haptic sensations, while keeping the space transparent and unbulky. The device is scaleable so as to enclose different cave-like working space. Scaleable-SPIDAR is coupled with a large screen where a computer generated virtual world is displayed. The used approach is shown to be simple, safe and multi-modal interface for human-scale virtual environment (VE).

Keywords
Human-Scale, Virtual Environment, Force Feedback.

1. INTRODUCTION
The uses of high quality computer-generated imagery, auditory and interactive scenes have recently been applied to many cave-like virtual environments. Accurate simulations and graphical display of these virtual environments are being used to impart users with realistic experiences. As well as, to provide a more comprehensive understanding of specific problems. However, visual and auditory cues alone do not allow the user to clearly perceive and understand physical interactions such as contact, pressure and weight. The importance of such sensory modality in virtual workspace had already been showed in many researches. To create an immersible human-scale virtual environment, the ability to interact physically with virtual environment, as well as the full and direct use of both hands are indispensable to control over objects and to develop a physical skill. However, to provide such capability of perception and action in a human-scale virtual

environment, usually some mechanical equipment attached to a stationary ground as well as to the operator's body are required [7]. This direct contact between hard equipment and operator limits the range of movement and may occlude the graphical display. As well, the weight and the bulk of the mechanical attachments are clearly perceived by the operator, figure 1.

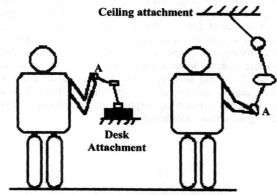

Figure 1: Typical mechanical attachment

Although GROPE-project [1] may be the most famous human-scale virtual environment system with force display. Yet, most of the current haptic devices are designed for desktop usage and display force feedback to only one hand. Unlike video and audio, force information is very difficult to send through air. To form a 3D force at a certain point, say point A, lead a "hard" mechanical device from a "force source" to point A may be the only "simple" and precise way. If A is moveable, then the force display device will become much more complicated in structure compared with video and audio display. Particularly, when the virtual environment workspace becomes larger, that is the point A may go far away from the force source, the haptic device structural strength needs to be enhanced to keep the precision. This enhancement usually makes the whole system bulky, heavy and expensive, as well limits the user's moving freedom. On the other hand, the machinery based forces displays are usually low dynamic performance. In a mechanical system, the dynamic performance is mainly decided by system's weight and moment of inertia. As the haptic devices in human-scale virtual environment are heavy, they would have lower dynamic performance than the ones in a relatively small system, desktop devices. Unfortunately, the task in large working space tends to need higher moving speed and bigger acceleration. How to balance precision and dynamic performance? While improving both of them are the key points to realize usable and accurate force display in human-scale virtual environment.

We propose a new approach, based on tensioned string techniques, to display force feedback sensation on both operator's hands in a large space. While allowing smooth movement and keeping the space transparent.

In the next sections, we explain the features of Scaleable-SPIDAR. A trial system was developed and tested through experiments. Additionally, an application was developed to evaluate the profitability of our device. In the last section, the remaining problems are discussed.

2. CONCEPT OF SCALEABLE-SPIDAR

The device is derived from the original desktop SPIDAR device, which was introduced late in 1990 by Makoto Sato *et al* [3]. As shown in figure 2, Scaleable-SPIDAR is delimited by a cubic frame that enclose a cave-like space, where the operator can move around to perform large scale movements. The experimental prototype is $27m^3$ size (3m x 3m x 3m). Within this space, different aspect of force feedback sensations associated mainly with weight, contact and inertia can be displayed to the operator's hands by means of tensioned strings. The front side of the device holds a large screen, where a computer-generated virtual world is projected. Providing such a combination of haptic and visual feedback cues is indispensable to lets the operator's eyes and hands work in concert to explore and manipulate objects populating the virtual environment.

fingering; next subsection gives more detail about forces and position computation. In order to control the tension and length of each string, one extremity is connected to the fingering and the other end is wounded around a pulley, which is driven by a DC motor. By controlling the power applied to the motor, the system can create appropriate tension all the time. A rotary encoder is attached to the DC motor to detect the string's length variation, Figure 3-a. The set of DC motor, pulley and encoder controlling each string is fixed on the frame.

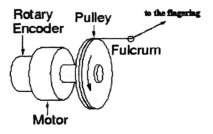

Figure 3-a: Motor and rotary encoder

2.1 Force Control

Scaleable-SPIDAR uses the resultant force of tension from strings to provide force display. As the fingering is suspended by four strings, giving certain tensions to each of them by the means of motors, the resultant force occurs at the position of the fingering, where transmitted to and felt by the operator's hand.

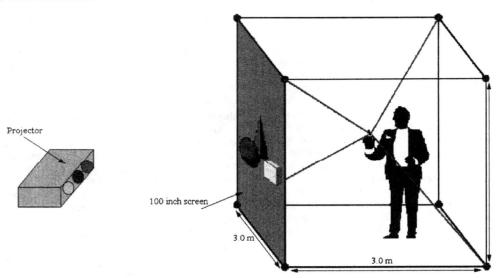

Figure 2: Overview of Scaleable-SPIDAR

The device uses tensioned string techniques to track hands position as well as to provide haptic feedback sensations. The approach consists mainly on applying appropriate tensions to the four strings supporting each fingering worn by the operator. The force feedback felt on the operator's hand is the same as the resultant force of tension from strings at the center of the

Let the resultant force be $\vec{f}$ and unit vector of the tension be $\vec{u}_i$ ($i=0,1,2,3$), figure 3-b, the resultant force is:

$$\vec{f} = \sum_{i=0}^{3} a_i \vec{u}_i \qquad (a_i > 0)$$

Where a_i represents the tension value of each string. By controlling all of the a_i the resultant force of any magnitude in any direction can be composed [5].

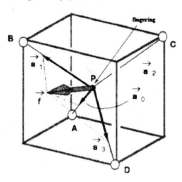

Figure 3-b: Motor and rotary encoder

2.2 Position Measurement

Let the coordinates of the fingering position be $P(x,y,z)$, which represent in the same time the hand position, and the length of the ith string be l_i $(i=0, ..., 3)$. To simplify the problem, let the four actuators (motor, pulley, encoder) A_i be on four vertexes of the frame, which are not adjacent to each other, as shown by figure 4 [2]. Then $P(x,y,z)$ must satisfy the following equations (Eqs).

$$(x + a)^2 + (y + a)^2 + (z + a)^2 = l_0^2 \qquad (1)$$

$$(x - a)^2 + (y - a)^2 + (z + a)^2 = l_1^2 \qquad (2)$$

$$(x - a)^2 + (y + a)^2 + (z - a)^2 = l_2^2 \qquad (3)$$

$$(x + a)^2 + (y - a)^2 + (z - a)^2 = l_3^2 \qquad (4)$$

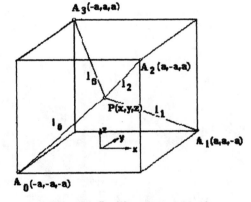

Figure 4: Position measurement

After differences between the respective adjacent two equations among equation (1)-(4) and solve the simultaneous equations, we can obtain the position of a fingering (hand) as the following equation (5):

$$\begin{cases} x = \dfrac{(l_0^2 - l_1^2 - l_2^2 + l_3^2)}{8a} \\[2mm] y = \dfrac{(l_0^2 - l_1^2 + l_2^2 - l_3^2)}{8a} \\[2mm] z = \dfrac{(l_0^2 + l_1^2 - l_2^2 - l_3^2)}{8a} \end{cases} \qquad (5)$$

3. IMPROVEMENT IN POSITION MEASUREMENT

In this section, we describe the reason why it is possible to revise the error of position measurement, and propose a general revise method and give two concrete revision models for improvement on the error.

3.1 Dynamic Position Measurement Error

As we introduced above, the strings we used to measure finger position are linked to motors. When we offer a motor a certain electric current, the maximal angular acceleration of the motor is fixed. If the user's hand acceleration is larger than this, the string is no longer straight, but form a suspend curve because of its weight, figure 5. Hence, the length of a string does not reflect the exact distance between user's hand and the fulcrum. Thus, the position measurement is no longer precise.

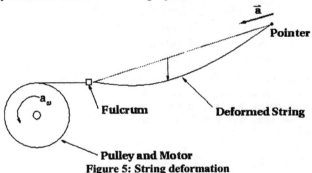

Figure 5: String deformation

3.2 Error Revision

From equations (1) to (4) we can find that it is redundant to use four known quantities (length of strings) to obtain three unknown quantities x, y and z. So it is possible to find an error revision method using this redundancy.

General Revise Method: As in figure 4, let the position of P be (x, y, z), and the string lengths obtained from encoders be l_0, l_1, l_2 and l_3. We can obtain x, y, and z as equation (5).

Let the distance between P and fulcrums A_i $(i = 0, 1, 2, 3)$ be l_i^*. By substituting equation (5) into equations (1) to (4), equation (6) is derived.

$$l_i^{*2} = l_i^2 + \frac{1}{64a^2}\left\{4(l_0^2 + l_1^2 + l_2^2 + l_3^2 + 64a^4) \right.$$
$$\left. - (l_0^2 + l_1^2 + l_2^2 + l_3^2 + 8a^2)^2\right\} \qquad (6)$$

If all strings' length are correctly measured, then $l_i^* = l_i$. We define J as equation (7) to show the degree of error.

$$J = \sum_{i=0}^{3} (l_i^{*2} - l_i^2)^2$$

$$= \frac{4}{(64a^2)^2} \left\{ 4(l_0^2 + l_1^2 + l_2^2 + l_3^2 + 64a^4) \right. \tag{7}$$

$$\left. - (l_0^2 + l_1^2 + l_2^2 + l_3^2 + 8a^2)^2 \right\}^2$$

When there is no error for all l_i of equation (7), J = 0 should be held. For string length with error, let

$$l_i^* = l_i + \gamma \delta_i \quad (i = 0,1,\ldots,3) \tag{8}$$

Where $\gamma \delta_i$ is the error term. δ_i is a function depends on revision model which can be obtained directly. γ is the only variable. By substituting equation (8) into equation (7) and let equation (7) equal to 0, equation (9) is derived, assuming that $|\gamma \delta_i|$ is small enough.

$$16 \sum l_i^3 \delta_i \gamma + 24 \sum l_i^2 \delta_i^2 \gamma^2 - 4(\sum l_i \delta_i)^2 \gamma^2$$
$$- 2(\sum l_i^2 + 8a^2) \sum \delta_i^2 \gamma^2 = 0 \tag{9}$$

From equation (9) we can obtain

$$\gamma = \frac{16 \sum l_i^3 \delta_i}{2(\sum l_i^2 + 8a^2) \sum \delta_i^2 - 24 \sum l_i^2 \delta_i^2 + 4(\sum l_i \delta_i)^2} \tag{10}$$

Which can give us the variable γ. Thus, we can use equation (8) to revise the strings length and calculate the position of P by using the equation (5).

Revision Models: As δ_i is a function depending on the revision model. And since the deformation is caused by the hands acceleration, it is better to use a model based on the acceleration of the hand represented by the pointer P, figure 4. One such revised model is:

$$\delta_i = \phi\left(\vec{a}_p \cdot \frac{\vec{l}_i}{\|\vec{l}_i\|} \right) \tag{11}$$

Where,

$$\phi(x) = \begin{cases} x & x > 0 \\ 0 & x \le 0 \end{cases} \tag{12}$$

In equation (11), $\vec{a}_p$ is the acceleration of pointer P, $\vec{l}_i$ is the string vector pointing from P to the corresponding fulcrum and $\vec{a}_p \cdot \frac{\vec{l}_i}{\|\vec{l}_i\|}$ is the projection of $\vec{a}_p$ in the direction of $\vec{l}_i$. Using equation (11) as the revision model is based on the understanding that the larger the acceleration on $\vec{l}_i$ direction, the larger deformation will be of $\vec{l}_i$. Equation (12) is used to make sure that the revision will only proceed when the acceleration is toward the fulcrum.

We can calculate $\vec{a}_p$ and $\vec{l}_i$ as follow:

$$\vec{a}_p(t) = \frac{\vec{v}_p(t) - \vec{v}_p(t-1)}{T}$$

$$= \frac{P(t) - 2P(t-1) + P(t-2)}{T^2}$$

$$\vec{l}_i(t) = F_i - P(t)$$

Where $\vec{v}_p(t)$ is the velocity of the pointer P. $P(t)$ and F_i are respectively the coordinate of P at time t and the coordinate of fulcrums. T is the time of sampling cycle.

Figure 6 shows the average position measurement error J before and after the revision. After revision, we can reduce the error (J) to nearly 1/3 when the deformation is large.

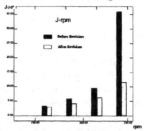

Figure 6: Position measurement error (J)

4. EXPERIMENTAL PROTOTYPE

The experimental prototype provides two fingerings to be worn by the operator on both hands, Figure 7-b. The fingerings are made of light plastic material and the size can fit to any operator. As well, this small device leaves the hand free and easy to put on and off. Although the operator can wear the fingering on any finger, middle finger is most recommended. The bottom of this finger is close to the center of hand, and the force feedback applied on this position is felt as being applied to the whole palm.

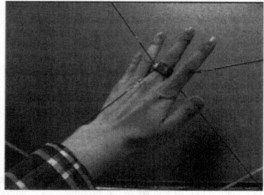

Figure 7-b: The fingering

To provide the appropriate tensions and lengths of the strings, a personal computer (PC) is used to control an 8-bits D/A , A/D converter and a VME bus, which control respectively the currents entering the motors and detect the changes occurred on each rotary encoder. The PC is connected to a graphics workstation that provides a real-time video image of the virtual world. The apparatus of the prototype is shown by Figure 7-a.

Figure 7-a: Apparatus of the Scaleable-SPIDAR

4.1 Performance of Scaleable-SPIDAR

Position Measurement Range: the coordinates origin are set to the center of the framework. The position measurement ranges of all x, y and z in[-1.50m, +1.50m].

Static Position Measurement Error: the absolute static position measurement errors are less than 1.5cm inside the position measurement range.

Force Feedback Range: within the force displayable sphere[7], force sensation range is from $0.005N$ (minimum) to $30N$ (maximum) for all directions.

System Bandwidths:

- ❖ Video: 10 ~ 15 Hz

- ❖ Audio: 22 kHz (stereo)

- ❖ Position measurement and force display: > 1200 Hz (depends also on hardware installation)

Comparison With Other Haptic Devices: the next tabular shows the performance of Scaleable-SPIDAR compared with two other well-known force display devices, PHANToM [4] and Haptic-Master[6].

Haptic device	work space	position resolution (mm)	peak force (kgf)	inertia
Haptic Master	40x40x40	0.4	2.1	220
PHANToM	20x27x38	0.03	0.87	75
Scaleable-SPIDAR	300x300x300	15	3.0	50

5. EXPERIMENTS AND APPLICATION

In this section, the implementation of a haptic feedback experience with Scaleable-SPIDAR and an evaluation application are described.

5.1 Experiments

An investigation is carried to state the feasibility and the effect of the Scaleable-SPIDAR's force feedback on an interactive task. As

"Space-Pointing" movements are considered as basic operations in any virtual reality applications and they are expected to be performed accurately within the minimum of time, a pushing button task was simulated to study how perfectly the operator can perform this task with and without force feedback. The operator is provided with a virtual flat wall, where five hemisphere shaped buttons are fixed on it; one of them is lighted red and the others are green. A graphical representation of the hand is displayed to give visual feedback cues. The apparatus of the setting is presented in figure 8. The operator is asked to move his hand on the top of the red button and push it to a certain deep. If he succeed, an audible bell is displayed and the red button changes to green while the next green button is lighted up to red. The order is the same as writing the letter "Z". The times spent from a button was lighted up to red until it is successfully pushed are recorded as "Task Times" (TTs) under the following conditions:

- *Condition 1: Visual Cues Only:* in this condition, the operator is only able to get visual feedback cues, force feedback information is not available; hence, operator's hand can pass through the buttons and the wall.

- *Condition 2: Visual and Force Feedback Cues:* in this case the operator can feel force feedback when his hand comes into contact with the wall or any of the button. The spherical shape of the buttons and the flatness of the wall are haptically perceived.

- *Condition 3: Force Feedback Cues Only:* after the operator has remembered the buttons' positions in his mind, the hand's visual feedback cues are disabled; thus the operator can not "see" the position of his hand in the simulated scene. That is he do not know whether his hand is moving close to the button or not, but only "feel" force feedback reactions when the hand runs over the virtual wall or the buttons.

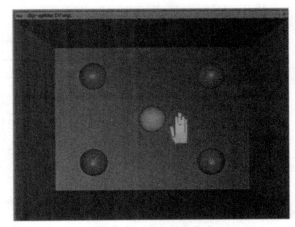

Figure 8:Space-pointing task

Four right-handed subjects participated in the experiment, including two of the authors. None of them reported any haptic deficiencies. Although it was not necessary for the experiment, all subjects were familiar with haptic devices and virtual environment. Each subject was told about the three different conditions and the task to be performed. There was three different sessions of trials for all subject. In each session the red button should be pushed successfully 40 times. Before any session a short time of practice was given.

5.2 Results

TTs' means and variances are presented in figure 9 under the different conditions. When force feedback is available together with visual information. The "push button" task can be performed faster and only cost about 65% of the time needed for the "visual feedback only" condition. At the mean while, after plenty of practice even with the "force feedback only" condition, the user can still finish the "push button" task faster than the "visual feedback only" condition. This is because after practices, and by trials the operator has remembered the space positions of the buttons and can quickly move his hand toward the red button since the order is fixed and previously known.

It was found also, that in condition 1 80% of the TTs is devoted exclusively to push the button, whereas only 20% of the TTs is needed for positioning the hand in front of the red button. Nearly the opposite situation is present for trials done under condition 3, where 30% of the TTs is devoted exclusively for the pushing task and the other 70% of times are used to localize the targeted button. Also, as it can be seen from figure 9 that, the TTs variance are smaller when force feedback is available.

The difference of time spending in both condition 1 and 3 is significant. In the former one subjects have mainly a lack of depth perception, but good navigational performance. The later condition shows better capability of manipulation and interaction with objects, although the navigation is slow. The combined influence of visual and haptic modalities has a clear effect on the subject's performance in the second condition.

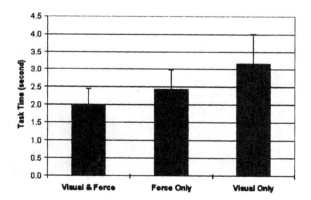

Figure 9:Mean task-time of different conditions

As conclusion, Scaleable-SPIDAR's force feedback system is shown to be able to improve the interaction with objects. Such haptic capability and enhancement is not only desirable but could be indispensable for dexterous manipulation.

5.3 Experimental Application

Scaleable-SPIDAR is used to simulate the experience of the basketball's free throw shot, which is considered a skillful action that requires large space to play and where the haptic sensation of

the ball is crucial to shoot a hoop. Being inside the playing space, the operator face a large screen where a 3D basketball's playground, backboard and a ball are displayed. As well, a graphic representation of the player's hands to give a visual feedback cues, figure 10.

In order to control the ball and perceive haptically its weight and shape, the player has to wear the two fingering on both hands. As the player start moving inside the frame the system tracks the hands' position, and when they come into contact with the virtual ball appropriate forces are displayed, such as its weight. If the player doesn't hold tight enough or open her/his hands, the ball will fall down and bounds on the floor. After making a shot, the ball begins a free falling movement determined by the hand's velocity and orientation while freeing the ball. If the ball doesn't go through the hoop, it may rebound from the backboard, basket's ring or objects surrounding the playground. The virtual ball is designed 40cm in diameter and weights 300g.

Figure 10: Virtual basketball

To show the force feedback effectiveness in such skillful operation, we asked two users to play this game, while recording the distance between their hands. Two session was organized, one with force feedback, that is the user can fell haptically the spherical shape of the ball as well as its weight. And a second session, where only visual feedback cue is provided. The results of this experiment is shown by figure 11a,b. The horizontal axes show the time and the vertical show the distances between the two hands. Time spent for each trial is devised into three parts. Part A where the user is trying to catch the ball. Part B is when the ball is hold by the user. During this part the user start first by ensuring the fact of holding a ball (B1), this part is still characterized by some vibrations due to user's behavior as well as software optimization. Then the user brings his attention to the backboard and aims the hoop (B2) and finishes this part by throwing the ball toward the basket (B3). At last in part C the hands become free again.

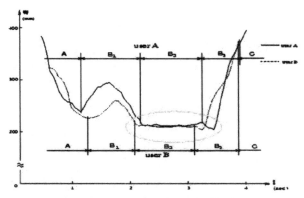

Figure 11-a: With force feedback

The part to which we are interested is B2, where there is a direct and full contact between the virtual ball and user's hands. As the figures 9a-b show, the distance between the two hands is more stable when force feedback is displayed. In this case the user unintentionally does not think about the ball, instead he is concerned about the game and his skills to shoot a hoop. Without force feedback, the user cannot easily keep his hands in right distance to hold the ball. The only thing he can do while holding a ball, is to keep looking whether or not his hands are deep inside the ball.

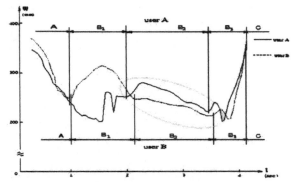

Figure 11-b: Without force feedback

Other results of this interactive experience showed that, with force feedback sensation the player improve considerably his performance of scoring up to 60% better than throwing the ball without force feedback. Haptic sensation is revealed to be indispensable to show the real skills while manipulating virtual object.

6. DISCUSSION AND CONCLUSION

Tensioned strings techniques are used to realize force feedback sensation on both hands in a large space. The approach makes the human scale device very light and easy to use as well as safe. The tracking accuracy and force feedback display of the system are shown to be effective and sufficient for skillful object manipulation and interaction within VE. The only remaining problem rises from crossing deeply both hands. Actually, this backdrop is inevitable for any system using direct contact attachment with the operator to generate force feedback. Another

problem, that was partially improved by [2] but still remain, occurs when the operator moves her/his hands with a very high speed. This kind of movement makes the string no longer strait and causes a length miscalculation, which affects the precision of hands' position.

The concept of the Scaleable-SPIDAR is new and unique and it offers possible application in a wide variety of fields. Its main features, are the ability to display different aspects of force feedback within different size cave-like space without visual disturbance; As well, the device is not bulky, and easy to use; Another distinguishing characteristic of Scaleable-SPIDAR, is that the operator does not think in terms of manipulating an input device, instead he has a full and direct use of his hands.

Recently we are investigating the use of scaleable-SPIDAR in a visual-less virtual environment that is to explore what can be accomplished within an "invisible" but audible and tangible virtual environment. Such system has a great deal of interest in building new computer interfaces for blind persons.

7. REFERENCES

[1] F.P. Brooks, M.O.Young, J.J.Batter and P.J.Kilpatrick (1990)" Project GROPE- Haptic Display for Scientific Visualization" Computer Graphics, Proc. ACM SIGGRAPH'90, Vol.24, No4, pp. 177-185.

[2] Y. Cai, M. Ishii, and M. Sato, "Position Measurement Improvement on a force Display Device Using Tensioned Strings". IEICE TRANS. INF. &SYST. Vol. E77-D, N°6 June 1996.

[3] Y. Hirata, M.Sato and H.Kawarada, ``A Measuring Method of Finger Position in Virtual Work Space'' Forma, Vol.6, No.2, pp.171-179(1991)

[4] http://www.sensable.com/product.htm

[5] Ishii and M.Sato, 1994a, "A 3D Spacial Interface Device Using Tensioned Strings," Presence-Teleoperators and Virtual environments, Vol. 3. No 1, MIT Press, Cambridge, Ma, pp 81-86

[6] H. Iwata: ``Artificial Reality with Force-Feedback: Development of Desktop Virtual Space with Compact Master Manipulator,'' (Computer Graphics), 24(4), 165-170(1990)

[7] Salisbury, J. and M. Srinivasan, 1992, "Virtual Environment Technology for Training (VETT)" BBN Report No 7661, VETREC, MIT, Cambridge, MA.

[8] Fukuda T. (1984) "The stepping test: two phases of the labyrinthine reflex". In: Statokinitic reflexes in equilibrium and movement. University of Tokyo press; Chap. 8, 110-123

[9] Laroussi B. Masahiro I. Makoto S. "Integrating Walking-in-Place with Turntable to Move Around Large-Scale Virtual Environment: a New Locomotion Metaphor" Human Interface symposium 2000. Tsukuba –Japan. Sept.20-22 2000. To appear

On Face Detection in the Compressed Domain

Huitao Luo and Alexandros Eleftheriadis
Advent Group, Columbia University
{luoht, eleft}@ctr.columbia.edu

Abstract

We propose a fast face detection algorithm that works directly on the compressed DCT domain. Unlike the previous DCT domain processing designs that are mainly based on skin-color detection, our algorithm analyzes both color and texture information contained in the DCT parameters, therefore could generate more reliable detection results. Our texture analysis is mainly based on statistical model training and detection. A number of fundamental problems, e.g., block quantization, preprocessing in the DCT domain, and feature vector selection and classification in the DCT domain, are discussed.
Key words: face detection, DCT, JPEG, MPEG.

1 Introduction

Human face detection is an interesting research topic. In the literature, many works have been reported with different application backgrounds. They could be classified into two groups, *i.e.*, color based approaches and texture based approaches.

Color based approaches have been popular in multimedia community because of their relative simple design and fast performance. In general, this type of algorithms tries to model human skin color in different chromatic spaces (RGB, YCbCr, HSV, *etc.*) with various statistical models. Typical skin color modeling works include: *mixture of Gaussian* [13], *linear region approximation* [7], *Bayesian minimal cost decision rule* [18], *etc.* In addition to color modeling, a number of recent works seek to include additional heuristics such as texture, symmetry, region ratio, region segmentation and merging, *etc.* [2, 19, 1]. In order to further improve the processing speed, Wang and Chang [18] proposed to detect human faces directly on the compressed MPEG macroblocks. In their work, JPEG pictures and MPEG I frames are partially decoded (entropy decoded and de-quantized) to restore DCT parameters in their block structure. Their algorithm then works directly on the decoded DCT parameters. Color information is used as the major detection clues in their algorithm. A skin color model is created at the macroblock level in the YCbCr color space. In addition, they also use some texture information by grouping the DCT parameters into bins and evaluating the energy distribution patterns based on bin statistics. This algorithm has interesting fast performance, but it shares the same problem with those typical color-based algorithms designed in the pixel domain, *i.e.*, it has good detection rate, but suffer from high false alarm rates when the backgrounds have skin like colors.

In contrast, texture based works detect face directly from the picture grayscale information. Most texture based methods are developed from face recognition algorithms, because in the recognition sense, color information does not help much in distinguishing different individual's faces. Instead, it is the face texture that we use to recognize different persons. Typical examples [1] based on this observation includes Sung and Poggio [16]' system developed at MIT AI lab and Rowley and Kanade [15]'s system developed at CMU Robotic Institute. Both systems use similar preprocessing algorithms and multi-scale searching mechanism, except that Sung and Poggio's system uses multimodal Gaussian clustering method as classifier while Rowley and Kanade's system uses neural network as classifier. Similar systems available in the literature also include: Lew [9]'s work that uses information theory, Collobert *et al.* [5]'s and McKenna [10]'s works that use neural networks, Yang and Ahuja [20]'s work that uses factor analyzer and Osuna *et al.* [14]'s work that uses support vector machine (SVM) as classifiers. They all reported close detection performance on some common testing pictures, for example the CMU testing database. In general, texture-based algorithms are more reliable than color based algorithms, but they are also more complex and slower.

In this paper, we propose a face detection algorithm that combines both color and texture information in order to find a good balance between speed and detection reliability. We design the algorithm to work on the com-

---

[1] We do not intend to give a comprehensive survey of face detection algorithms. Instead only a group of similar algorithms that our work bases on is covered.

pressed DCT domain in a similar way as Wang [18]'s work. However, our work extends theirs by building up an independent texture-based detection module in the compressed DCT domain, i.e., we study how to map the successful texture-based face pattern detection algorithms such as [16, 15, 20, 14] from the traditional pixel domain to the DCT transform domain. With the new texture-based detection model included, face detection problems can be solved more reliably in the compressed domain, as compared with Wang and Chang [18]'s work. We believe this algorithm is especially valuable for fast content analysis of large amount of visual media data stored in the compressed formats such as JPEG and MPEG. In the following of this paper, when mentioning compressed DCT domain, we refer to JPEG pictures and MPEG I frames that are partially decoded (entropy decoded and de-quantized) and have their DCT parameters restored in 8 pixel by 8 pixel block structures, if not expressed clearly otherwise.

The structure of this paper is as follows. First in Section 2, we give a simple survey of the texture-based face detection design in the pixel domain. In Section 3 we discuss in detail the texture-based face detection algorithm design in the compressed DCT domain. In Section 4, the texture-based face model is extended to include color information and a new combined texture-based and color-based face detection algorithm is developed with experimental results. Finally in Section 5 we conclude the paper.

2 Texture Based Face Detection in the Pixel Domain

In this work, we seek to map the successful texture-based face detection algorithms from the original pixel domain to the transformed DCT domain. Therefore, before going directly to the DCT domain, we first take a close look at the available works in the pixel domain.

In the available face detection works designed on the pixel domain, successful algorithms such as [16, 15, 20, 14] generally share similar processing procedures and structures. In these works, the face pattern is represented as a rectangle or square window of pixel plane. In order to detect face patterns, the systems scan the input image plane at every location. That is, the image is divided into multiple (possibly overlapping) subimages of the model window size. Each window is compared with a previously trained "face" model to tell whether it is a face pattern or not. In order to detect faces in multiple scales, the input image is downscaled to a series of scales (for example, by scales of $1.2^n, n = 1, 2, \ldots$) and the detection process is repetitively applied to each scale. Or in other words, to tell a windowed image a face or not, the window is always first scaled to the size of the model, and then compared with it.

The details of this processing flow chart are illustrated in Fig. 1. As we can see from Fig. 1, to detect faces, the input image is scaled and cropped to generate a windowed image pattern. The pattern is processed with a preprocessing module to remove illumination noise and normalize the grayscale ranges. The normalized image pattern is then fed to a classifier to see if it is a face pattern. To create a face model, a database of frontal faces is generally used. Each face is scaled and moved to align its common facial feature points such as

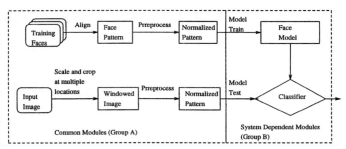

Figure 1: Illustration of common face detection procedures in the pixel domain

corner of eyes, tip of nose, etc. to specified positions in the model window. The windowed image pattern is then processed by a preprocessor, and finally applied to train a classifier.

In all the four detection systems [16, 15, 20, 14], their basic structures are generally the same (as indicated in modules covered by the dashed rectangle in the left (Group A) of Fig. 1). The only different part is the classifier, i.e., classifier's internal structure, its training and detection operation (as indicated in modules covered by the dashed rectangles in the right (Group B) of Fig. 1.

Based on the summery as depicted in Fig. 1, the detection complexity is M times of the processing in Group A plus the processing in Group B. M depends on the image size, the model size, and the range of the face sizes that are to be detected by the system.

However, the essence of the complexity issue is the size of the face model, which determines directly the complexity of the classifier, i.e., how complex the classifier should be, in order to separate the *face patterns* from the *nonface patterns*. Though there is no clear measure available to judge the complexity of face pattern classification, most reported papers use similar face model sizes. For example, Sung [16] uses a (masked) 19-pixel by 19-pixel square window, Rowley [15] uses a (masked) 20-pixel by 20-pixel square window, and Collobert et al. [5] uses a 15-pixel by 25-pixel rectangle window. Therefore, the face detection problem is (at most)[2] a 2-dimensional pattern classification problem at the size of about 20 pixels by 20 pixels. If we stack up the pixels row by row as in [16], the problem is then converted to a 1-dimensional pattern classification problem at the size of about 200-400 dimension.

3 Texture Based Face Detection in the DCT domain

3.1 Feature Representation in the Block DCT Domain

3.1.1 The DCT Transform

In principle, pattern detection models should not be influenced by converting the problem to the DCT domain

---

[2]Sung [16]'s work indicates that the classification problem can be projected to subspaces in much lower dimensions. But there is no clear quantitative boundary on how low this dimension could be.

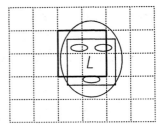

Figure 2: Illustration of the block quantization problem in face detection.

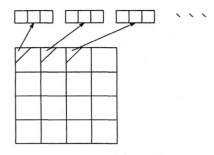

Figure 3: Illustration of the feature vector creation from DCT parameters

if we do not consider the blocks and quantization errors incurred. Because DCT is an orthonormal transform, both the *Euclid distance* and the *Mahalanobis distance* are unchanged after the transform. If we follow the Gaussian clustering approach as discussed in [16], it is easy to proof that the Gaussian model remains a Gaussian model in the DCT domain. In addition to the invariant features, the DCT domain is better than the pixel domain for pattern classification problems in that DCT transform reduces the dependence among individual components and compresses the feature energy to the low frequency parameters. Therefore, it is much easier to choose feature components from DCT parameters than from direct pixel values.

3.1.2 Block Quantization Problem

However, to apply model-based algorithms directly to the compressed domain of JPEG and MPEG, a major problem to overcome is that the image frames are divided into 8 by 8 blocks before DCT transform. Therefore, any detection work based on DCT parameters has to be done at the locations of blocks rather than pixels. That is, the blocks reduce the spatial resolution of the system by 8, which makes it hard to detect small faces without fully decoding the image from the block based DCT parameters to pixels. We refer to this problem as *block quantization* in this work.

More specifically, the block quantization problem influences face detection in the following three aspects.

First, because the DCT parameters are organized in a block structure, in order to detect a face, a face model cannot be used to search the picture pixel by pixel. Instead, this search can only done block by block in the DCT domain. This problem is better illustrated in Fig 2, in which the rectangle in light solid lines represents the actual location of a face, while the rectangle in dark solid lines is the closest searching window that the system can arrive at based on 8 by 8 block quantization. Therefore, in order to detect faces that are not aligned with block positions, we need to introduce certain translation invariant feature in face model training. Or in order words, when training the face model, more images patterns should be included as positive training examples than the corresponding procedure that designed in the pixel domain.

Second, in addition to the feature aligning problem, block quantization also introduces some background noise when the searching window is not well aligned with the actual face region, which influences the accuracy of both

model training and detection.

Third, in the block-based DCT domain, it is hard to obtain resolution transformation. Though several papers [8, 11, 4] have discussed the issue of fast resolution transform in the compressed DCT domain, it is still too expensive to carry out resolution transforms in arbitrary ratios, *e.g.*, to down-sample the image by 1.2. Therefore, in order to detection faces in multiple scales, we have to design models individually for each scale. We call this solution as a *multi-model* approach in this work, as compared to the multi-scale approach commonly used in the original pixel domain.

To sum up, the block quantization reduces the distribution density of the face patterns in the feature space, as well as introduces background noises and the scaling problem. Therefore, to detect human face patterns within the block based DCT domain is more difficult than to do it in the pixel domain.

3.1.3 Feature Vector Design

In this work, we design face detection as a 1-dimensional vector classification problem similar to Sung [16]'s system. In the DCT domain, feature vectors are created directly from (block based) DCT parameters as follows. Suppose the size of the face model is M block by M block and the desired length of the feature vector is N, then in each DCT block, the lowest d DCT parameters are used for feature vector creation, where

$$d = N/(M * M).$$

This is better illustrated in Fig. 3, in which the lowest d DCT parameters from each block is stacked up to form a N dimension feature vector.

In order to choose the first few low frequencies from a 2-D DCT block, we number the 64 DCT parameters according to the typical DCT quantization table design as reported in [17], *i.e.*, the larger the quantizer is, the less important its corresponding DCT parameter is for low frequency representation of the picture. In Eq.1, we show the positions of the first 16 parameters.

$$\begin{pmatrix} 1 & 2 & 3 & 10 \\ 4 & 5 & 7 & 13 \\ 8 & 6 & 11 & 15 \\ 9 & 12 & 14 & 16 \end{pmatrix}. \tag{1}$$

Based on the complexity analysis in Section 2, the complexity of face detection problem should be pro-

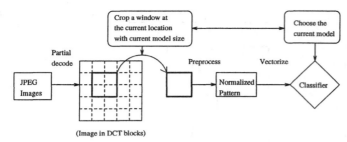

Figure 4: Illustration of the face detection procedures in the DCT domain.

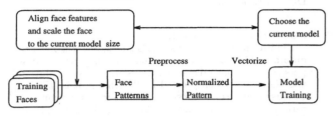

Figure 5: Illustration of the face model training procedures in the DCT domain.

cessed adequately over a rectangle window of 19 pixel by 19 pixel, therefore, the feature vector length in this work should be in the range of 200-400 dimension. For example, if a 5 block by 5 block face model is to be created, and we choose the feature vector length to be 300, then for each DCT block, its lowest 12 DCT parameters are used to create the feature vector for training and classification.

In principle, this approach of choosing the lowest few DCT parameters in each block is actually to downscale the windowed image to a *unit* model size, saying 19 pixel by 19 pixel, as used in the pixel domain. In other words, to tell a windowed image pattern a face or not, in the pixel domain, the face is downscaled to the unit model size, *e.g.*, 19 by 19 pixel, and compared with the face model. In the DCT domain, the correspondence is that the low frequent DCT parameters in each block of the windowed image pattern are used to form a feature vector, which is then compared with the face model. In this mapping, as long as the lowest few DCT parameters have maintained the image features at the resolution of 19 by 19 pixels (approximately)[3], we have reason to believe that those parameters have maintain the necessary information for face detection, based on our complexity analysis in Section 2. The benefit in this domain mapping is that unlike the bilinear downsampling in the pixel domain, choosing the lowest few DCT parameters is an easier and better way to do downsampling in the DCT domain. This is also noticed and discussed by Dugad and Ahuja [4] in their paper on fast DCT domain downsampling design.

---

[3]That is, if the image is decoded with only these low frequent parameters and then downscaled to 19 by 19 pixels, the image quality is still comparable with direct downloading the original image in the pixel domain.

3.2 Face Detection System Design

Based on the analysis in Section 2, a multi-model DCT domain face detection system is designed that combines algorithm capabilities and performance efficiencies.

3.2.1 Multi-Model Detection System

Due to the block quantization problem as discussed in Section 3.1.2, model-based face detection in the block-based DCT domain faces two problems, *i.e.*, aligning problem and scaling problem.

For the aligning problem, because the block size is 8 pixels, there are totally 64 possible spatial setups at the every searching position in the DCT domain. To solve the aligning problem, one might train 64 models for one model size, with each one representing a face pattern at a different aligning position. However, this approach is obviously not efficient because 64 models are hard to store as well as to apply. In addition, there are redundancies in the 64 models as the spatially neighboring models are similar to each other. Therefore, the trade-off has to be made between model efficiency and model accuracy. In addition, to overcome the scaling problem in the DCT domain, multiple models have to be created in order to detect faces in different scales, which further improves the burden of choosing too many models in one scale.

In this system, we create face models in six scales, and the model windows are designed to be squares in side length of 5, 6, 7, 8, 9, and 10 DCT blocks. That is, faces in the range of 40 by 40 pixels to 80 by 80 pixels are covered by the system. For each scale, one face model is trained for faces in all the possible aligning positions, *i.e.* the model represents variations in different face features as well as in different aligning positions (all the 64 possible positions).

The processing procedures for each model size is generally the same as those in the pixel domain (refer to Fig. 1), except that the works are moved to the DCT domain. We illustrate the DCT domain detection procedures and model training procedures separately in Fig. 4 and Fig. 5. The details of the processing modules are discussed in the following sections.

3.2.2 Preprocessing and Masking in the DCT Domain

To remove the signal variance introduced by different illuminations and different grayscale dynamic range, a number of preprocessing steps are used in the works designed in the pixel domain. In the DCT domain, we find it also possible to implement their correspondences. More specifically, our system includes the following pre-processing steps:

1. **Masking.** Similar to Sung [16]'s work, we introduce binary face masks on top of DCT blocks. For face patterns, these masked blocks often represent background regions. Removing them from the feature vectors ensures that the subsequent modeling work does not wrongly encode any unwanted background structures. Based on different sizes of the face model, different masks are designed to represent different spatial resolutions. In Fig. 7, we show the six masks we used in our system for face

models in six different scales. Note that the face models are actually in different sizes. They are scaled to the same size in Fig. 7 for ease of illustration. Each block in the model windows is of size 8 pixel by 8 pixel.

2. **Illumination Linear Factor Correction.** In order to remove shadowing effect, a 2-dimensional linear function is fitted to the DC plane of the face region in the DCT domain. The fitted function is then removed from the DC plane.

3. **Histogram Equalization.** This nonlinear process is applied directly to the DC components of the face region DCT blocks. In addition, the AC components in each block are changed linearly to reduce the block effects. That is, for each DCT block, if its DC component d is mapped to d' according to the histogram equalization, then its AC components a_i are also mapped linearly to a_i' with $a_i' = a_i * d'/d$.

Fig. 6 shows an example of preprocessing (the picture is taken from Olivetti face database[4]). Fig. 6(a) is a cropped face region, (b) is the face region with a grayscale linear factor removed, and (c) is the final result of face region preprocessing. We can see that the shading in the original face is effectively removed (in subfigure (b)). In addition, the histogram equalization based on DC components introduces certain blocking effect, but the general quality is acceptable (in subfigure (c)).

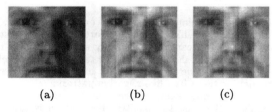

(a)   (b)   (c)

Figure 6: An example of preprocessing results on block based DCT domain

3.2.3 Distribution Based Classifier Design

For face detection purpose, a number of classifiers have been used. These include: unimodel Gaussian [12], multimodel Gaussian [16], neural networks [15, 10] and support vector machine [14]. Among them, neural networks and support vector machine have been shown to have theoretical merits for high dimensional vector classification problems. Especially SVM is proved capable of finding optimal classification boundary in that it can minimize structural risk [3]. However, both neural networks and SVM are hard to train, i.e., to organize the positive and negative training samples in order to make the classifier converge to the optimal status.

In this work, we have to train multiple face models for faces in multiple scales, therefore, we choose to use

[4]http://www.cam-orl.co.uk/facedatabase.html

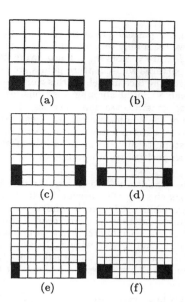

(a)   (b)

(c)   (d)

(e)   (f)

Figure 7: Illustration of binary face masks design for models in different sizes.

multimodal Gaussian model as the classifier, which is a trade-off between model training complexity and classification performance.

The essence of multimodal Gaussian model is to approximate the feature vector distribution with a number of Gaussian clusters. Though Gaussian distribution is a general purpose statistical model that has been extensively used, unimodel Gaussian distribution is shown by Sung [16] inadequate to model face patterns' distribution in the high dimensional feature space. Multimodal Gaussian model is a natural extension of unimodal Gaussian models that has worked well in complex and high dimensional distribution problems. It also has moderate training complexity as compared with neural networks and SVMs. In this work, in order to improve classification performance, we use two groups of multimodal Gaussian models to approximate separately the distribution of face patterns and nonface patterns.

Positive Training Samples The basic idea of this approach is to approximate the distribution of face feature vectors with high dimensional Gaussian clusters. To study the distribution of face patterns in the DCT domain, 300 frontal faces are collected from various sources such as MIT face database, Yale face database, Olivetti face database, University of Sterling face database[5] and some anchorperson images from the NBC news video database stored at AT&T research lab. Four feature points of each face, i.e., the inner and outer corners of both eyes, are marked manually. Each face is moved and scaled to align these feature points with specific positions in a model window. The face image is then cropped with the model window, and converted to the DCT domain. After that, the feature vector is obtained

[5]Most of them are downloadable from http://www.cs.rug.nl/~peterkr/FACE/face.html

from the DCT parameters as described in Section 3.1.3. Because we train only one model for one modeling window size, feature vectors should also be created to represent face patterns whose feature points are not perfectly aligned with the face model. In this work, we use 16 out of 64 possible spatial aligning positions for each training face to generate training samples. In addition, to make use of the symmetric property, each training face is flipped and used as a new training sample. Therefore, in this system, totally $16 * 2 * 300 = 9600$ feature vectors are used as positive training samples.

Clustering Algorithm We cluster the face feature vectors into six clusters of Gaussian distribution. The clustering algorithm used here is similar to the K-means algorithm, except that the *Euclidean distance measure* is replaced by a *logarithmic Gaussian distance measure*. If we denote each cluster with a Gaussian distribution $N(\mathbf{v}_i, \mathbf{C}_i)$. A new feature vector's distance to each cluster is defined to be a *logarithmic Gaussian distance* as:

$$d = \frac{1}{2}(N \ln 2\pi + \ln |\mathbf{C}_i| + (\mathbf{v} - \mathbf{v}_i)^T \mathbf{C}_i^{-1} (\mathbf{v} - \mathbf{v}_i)),$$

where N is the dimension of the feature vectors. Because N is a rather high dimension in this problem ($200 \sim 400$), we actually use Karhunen-Loeve transform to reduce the above equation into a lower dimension problem as:

$$d = \frac{1}{2}\left[M \ln 2\pi + \sum_{k=0}^{M-1} \ln |\lambda_k| + \sum_{k=0}^{M-1} \frac{y_k^2}{\lambda_k}\right],$$

where y_k^2 are the principle components and λ_k are the eigenvalues. M is the number of eigenvectors used to approximate the system. Generally $M \ll N$.

The detailed clustering steps are as follows.

1. Initialize the clustering process by grouping the feature vectors into six groups in *Euclidean* distance space, *i.e.*, a vector is put into the group whose center is the closest to it among the six groups. And the covariance matrix for each cluster is initialized to be unit matrix.

2. Re-compute the data centers of each cluster to be the center of the current cluster partition.

3. Based on the current cluster centers and covariance matrixes, re-assign the data partition by assigning the feature vectors to the cluster that is closest to it in the *logarithmic Gaussian distance* space. If the difference between the new data partition and the old one is bigger than a threshold and the inner loop time (Step 2 and Step 3) is less than the maximal time, goto Step 2, otherwise goto Step 4.

4. Re-compute the covariance matrixes of the 6 clusters based on the current data partition.

5. Based on the current cluster centers and covariance matrixes, re-assign the data partition by assigning the feature vectors to the cluster that is closest to it in the *logarithmic Gaussian distance*

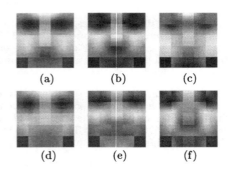

(a)	(b)	(c)
(d)	(e)	(f)

Figure 8: *Average faces* of the six face clusters when the face model size is 5 blocks by 5 blocks.

space. If the difference between the new data partition and the old one is bigger than a threshold and the outer loop time (Step 2 to Step 5) is less than the maximal time, goto Step 2. Otherwise, return the created mean vector and covariance matrix of each cluster.

In Fig. 8, we give the clustering results on the 9600 face feature vectors. The model size used is 5 blocks by 5 blocks. Fig. 8(a) to (f) are the average faces of the six clusters at the time of convergence. Because only the 4 lowest frequent DCT parameters (the choice of 4 will be discussed later in this section) in each block are used for feature vector creation, the block effect is noticeable. But in general the six mean faces represent mainly the variances in face textures rather than those in different spatial aligning positions.

Negative Training Samples In our experiments, we find many face like "nonface" patterns in our testing examples that can not be simply separated from face patterns by thresholding. In order to reduce the misclassification rate, we further create a multimodal Gaussian model for these face like negative patterns.

The training samples are collected in a *boot-strap* fashion. That is, the positive face model is first created by the clustering algorithm as previously discussed. Based on this model, a face detector is designed, which is then applied to the training pictures. The nonface patterns misclassified as faces by the face detector are used as negative samples.

In this way, we collect about 9000 negative nonface samples and cluster them into eight clusters. The clustering algorithm used is the same as positive face sample clustering. The clustering result of model size 5 blocks by 5 blocks is shown in Fig. 9, in which each subfigure represents an average nonface pattern for the eight clusters.

Classification The classification problem is based on the distance measures from the input feature vector to the positive and the negative clusters. Let's denote the input vector as $\mathbf{v}$, the six positive clusters as $N(\mathbf{C}_k^{(p)}, \mathbf{v}_k^{(p)})$, $k = 1, 2, \cdots, 6$, and the eight negative clusters as $N(\mathbf{C}_k^{(n)}, \mathbf{v}_k^{(n)})$, $k = 1, 2, \cdots, 8$. Then a 6-dimension positive distance vector could be defined as

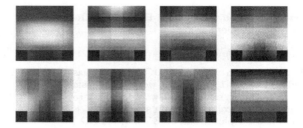

Figure 9: *Average nonfaces* of the eight nonface clusters when the face model size is 5 blocks by 5 blocks

$\mathbf{d}^{(p)} = (d_1^{(p)}, d_2^{(p)}, \cdots, d_6^{(p)})$, where

$$d_k^{(p)} = \frac{1}{2}(N\ln 2\pi + \ln|\mathbf{C}| + (\mathbf{v} - \mathbf{v}_k^{(p)})^T \mathbf{C}^{-1}(\mathbf{v} - \mathbf{v}_k^{(p)})), \tag{2}$$

where N is the dimension of the feature vector $\mathbf{v}$. In practice, because the input feature vectors are in high dimension, the covariance matrix $\mathbf{C}$ is always decomposed with KL transform:

$$\mathbf{C} = \mathbf{T}\mathbf{\Lambda}\mathbf{T}^{-1},$$

where $\mathbf{T}$ is the eigen-matrix and $\mathbf{\Lambda}$ is the diagonal matrix of eigenvalues. With only the first M eigenvectors of the eigen-matrix $\mathbf{T}$ used to span the feature space, the distance Eq. 2 is decomposed into two parts: the distance in the feature space (DIFS) and the distance from the feature space (DFFS),

$$\text{DIFS} = \frac{1}{2}\left[M\ln 2\pi + \sum_{k=0}^{M-1}\ln|\lambda_k| + \sum_{k=0}^{M-1}\frac{y_k^2}{\lambda_k}\right],$$

$$\text{DFFS} = \frac{1}{2}\left[(N-M)\ln 2\pi + (\ln|C| - \sum_{k=0}^{M-1}\ln|\lambda_k|) + \frac{\Delta^2}{\rho}\right],$$

where y_k is the principle components and $\Delta^2 = \|\mathbf{v}\| - \sum_{k=0}^{M-1}y_k^2$ is the residue. ρ is a weighting factor based on the estimation of eigenvalues $\lambda_k, (k = M, M+1, \cdots, N)$. In this work, the distance measure is therefore defined as:

$$d_k^{(p)} = \frac{1}{2}\left[N\ln 2\pi + \ln|\mathbf{C}| + \sum_{k=0}^{M-1}\ln|\lambda_k| + \eta\frac{\Delta^2}{\lambda_M}\right], \tag{3}$$

where η is an adjustable weighting factor.

Similarly, an 8-dimension negative distance vector is defined as $\mathbf{d}^{(n)} = (d_1^{(n)}, d_2^{(n)}, \cdots, d_8^{(n)})$, with respect to the eight negative clusters.

Therefore, the classification problem is reduced from a high dimension problem ($N = 200 \sim 400$) to a lower dimension problem with $N = 14$, which is then solved with a simple minimal distance classification algorithm in our work, *i.e.*, if

$$\min_{k=(1,\cdots,6)} d_k^{(p)} \leq \min_{k=(1,\cdots,8)} d_k^{(n)},$$

the pattern is detected as a face, otherwise it is a nonface.

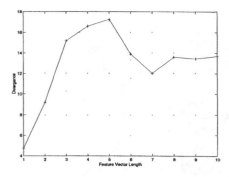

Figure 10: Illustration of the relation between the feature vector length and the divergence of the face and nonface patterns.

In implementing the classifier on practical face images, we tried to select feature vectors of a variety of lengths. Based on the complexity analysis in Section 2, the complexity of the face detection problem requires feature vectors of length in the range of 200-400 dimensions. However, we notice that when feature vectors coming from various spatial aligning positions are included as positive training samples (due to the block quantization problem), the high frequency DCT parameters become unstable in both face model training and face detection functions. In order to illustrate this problem, an experiment is carried out to measure the *separability* feature between the 9600 positive samples and the 9000 negative samples under the condition of different feature vector lengths.

The measure we used here is the *divergence* measure as defined in [6]. The divergence measure of two Gaussian distributions $N(\mathbf{v}_1, \mathbf{C}_1)$ and $N(\mathbf{v}_2, \mathbf{C}_2)$ is given as

$$\text{Div} = \frac{1}{2}(\mathbf{v}_1 - \mathbf{v}_2)^T(\mathbf{C}_1^{-1} + \mathbf{C}_2^{-1})(\mathbf{v}_1 - \mathbf{v}_2) + \frac{1}{2}\text{tr}[(\mathbf{C}_1 - \mathbf{C}_2)(\mathbf{C}_2^{-1} - \mathbf{C}_1^{-1})] \tag{4}$$

To study the influence of the feature vector length on the separability of the problem, both the 9600 positive samples and the 9000 negative samples are projected to the six positive clusters, which generates two groups of feature vectors in Gaussian distribution (in $\mathcal{R}^6$). Their divergence is then computed according to Eq. 4. In this experiment, we used a model size of 5 blocks by 5 blocks (40 by 40 pixels). The feature vector length is changed from 23 to 230, or 1 parameter per DCT block to 10 parameters per DCT block. The corresponding divergence is computed and their relation is illustrated in Fig. 10.

From Fig. 10, we notice that the divergence increases with the feature vector length from 1 to 5 (parameters per block), and then drops when the feature vector length further increases. That is, the more DCT parameters are included into the feature vector, the less likely that the face patterns are able to be separated from the nonface ones. This problem comes mainly from the high frequency components in each DCT blocks. When we try to build up one model to represent face patterns in all the 64 different spatial aligning positions (with respect to the current model window), the high frequent

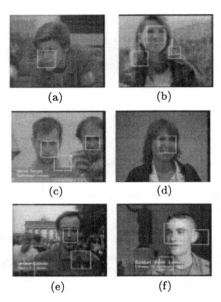

(a)	(b)
(c)	(d)
(e)	(f)

Figure 11: Several detection results of our texture-based face detection algorithm (in the compressed domain)

parameters in the feature vectors experience large variation from sample to sample, which makes them contribute negatively to the separation problem. As indicated by Fig 10, for the specific case of model size 5 block by 5 block, the ideal feature vector length should be 4 to 5 DCT parameters per block, or of about 100 parameters for the entire feature vector.

Based on this observation, we determine the feature vector lengths for all the 6 models in our system, which is listed in Table. 1. Note that the feature vector lengths are all shorter than those used for pixel domain detection. This difference is mainly, as have already been pointed out, due to the block quantization problem in the DCT domain.

3.3 Experiments

The texture based face detection algorithm is tested on a variety of pictures, which include: CMU database[6], CMU online face database[7], key frames of news video clips from CNN and NBC as well as pictures downloaded from Internet and scanned from magazines and books. Though coming from different sources and formats, the pictures are all compressed into JPEG format with Adobe Photoshop 5.0 (quality option *medium*, quantizer index 3) before processed. Some detection results are shown in Fig 11.

Compared with the pixel-domain detection algorithms, our algorithm is less accurate because of block quantization, especially the false detection rate is relatively high. This can be seen from Fig 11. To overcome this problem, we seek to combine the texture-based algorithm with a color-based algorithm.

---

[6]http://www.ius.cs.cmu.edu/IUS/eyes_usr17/har/har1/usr0/har/faces/test/

[7]http://www.ius.cs.cmu.edu/IUS/usrp0/har/FaceDemo/gallery-inline.html

4   Combined Color-Based and Texture-Based Face Detection in the DCT Domain

4.1   Generating Color Similarity Map

Color-based face detection work in the DCT domain was first discussed by Wang [18]. In this work, our basic design is similar to theirs, except that we do not try to setup a threshold at the color detection stage.

We assume the color pictures in JPEG and MPEG I frames are compressed in $4:2:0$ format. The pictures are partially decoded to restore their DCT parameters in the block structures. The skin color is modeled and detected at the macroblock level. That is, in each macroblock, the DC components of the Cb and Cr blocks are used as the average chromatic feature vector. A Gaussian model $N(\mathbf{v}_s, \mathbf{C}_s)$ for the skin color is created by training over a manually labeled picture database. Based on this skin color model, a color similarity map is generated for each picture at the macroblock level. For macroblock (i,j), if we denote its color feature vector as $\mathbf{v}_{(i,j)}$, then its skin color similarity map entry is

$$\text{color}(i,j) = -\frac{1}{2}\left[\ln 2\pi + \ln|\mathbf{C}_s| + (\mathbf{v}_{(i,j)} - \mathbf{v}_s)^T \mathbf{C}_s^{-1}(\mathbf{v}_{(i,j)} - \mathbf{v}_s)\right]$$
(5)

4.2   Color Constrained Face Pattern Detection

With the color map available, the face detection problem is further extended from the previous texture domain to the color domain. That is, given an input color picture in its YCbCr format, we can apply the texture-based pattern detection on the Y component and the skin-color map based pattern detection on the CbCr components[8]. Because both detection designs have a statistical expression, it is easy to combine them with a statistical framework, either in a parallel or sequential structure. Though theoretically the parallel structure has the merit of delayed judgment and thus better detection performance, sequential structure is simpler and faster. In addition, the color based detection module is not a balanced module as compared with the texture based detection module in the detection accuracy and reliability sense[9]. Therefore we choose the sequential structure in our system design. A skin color map is at first created by the color analysis module to generate a skin color map as follows. Given a windowed image pattern $\mathcal{W}$, its average skin-color similarity

$$\frac{\sum_{(i,j)\in\mathcal{W}}\text{color}(i,j)}{\sum_{(i,j)\in\mathcal{W}}1},$$

(where $\text{color}(i,j)$ is defined in Eq. 5), is compared with a threshold T. Only the windows with an average similarity higher than the threshold are further processed by the texture analysis module as discussed in Section 3.

---

[8]Because the skin-color similarity map is a map of scalar values, it is straight-forward to design a face pattern detection algorithm based on this similarity map, which should be, in principle, the same as the one we have designed on the texture map.

[9]In this work, we do not spend time to create an example based face pattern on top of the skin-color similarity map as we do in Section 3 on top of the texture map (though it is possible).

	model size (in block)	model size (in pixel)	masked block numbers	parameters per block	feature vector length
1	5	40	23	4	92
2	6	48	32	3	102
3	7	56	45	2	90
4	8	64	60	2	120
5	9	72	77	2	154
6	10	80	92	1	92

Table 1: Feature vector length at different model sizes

This combination, though simple, is better than both texture-only and color-only algorithms. Compared with texture-only algorithms, the color similarity map offers an additional constraint, which eliminates false alarms in the background without a skin-color appearance as well as improves the processing speed. Compared with color-only algorithms, the texture analysis module helps reduce false alarms introduced by skin-like backgrounds. In addition, the texture analysis module is also useful in locating faces when skin-like backgrounds are close to actual faces, in which case the simple shape analysis modules commonly used in the color-based algorithms always fail.

4.3 Experiments

We tested our face detection algorithm based on combined texture and color information over many pictures. The testing picture set we used in Section 3.3 is also used here, except the CMU database and CMU online database are not used because they are grayscale pictures. In Fig. 12, we show some detection results on pictures from various sources.

To evaluate the performance of our algorithm quantitatively, we use the key frames of one day's NBC Nightly News (Feb. 18, 1999, totally 586 frames) as our testing data set. Within this data set, there are 42 faces and 36 of them are frontal and upright ones that are within the coverage of our texture-based face model. The detection performance is listed in Table 2. In Table 2, the new combined texture and color based face detection algorithm (column a) is compared with a color-based detection algorithm (column b). Because the color-based algorithm works in the pixel domain, while the combined texture and color based detection algorithm works in the compressed DCT domain, the comparison is focused on the detection performance, but not the spatial location accuracy of the detected faces.

As we can see from Table 2, the combined texture and color based algorithm has less false alarms than the color-based algorithm because the texture processing module has removed some false alarms introduced by the skin-color backgrounds. In addition, fewer faces are missed by the combined color and texture based algorithm than by the color-based algorithm. This difference is mainly due to the different ability of the two algorithms to detect faces surrounded by skin-like backgrounds. That is, in color-based algorithms, skin-color regions are first detected with a skin-color model based detector and then processed with a shape analysis module. Only the regions have specific aspect ratios are accepted as face regions. When some skin-like back-

	(a)	(b)
total faces	42	36
face detected	34	30
face missed	7	5
false alarm	9	4
detection rate	81%	83%
detection accuracy	79%	88%

Table 2: Performance of the combined color and texture based face detection algorithm

grounds are close to the actual faces, the detected skin-color regions always get connected, which makes the shape of the detected regions no longer have a face-like shape. In contrast, the texture based approach is not influenced by the backgrounds, as long as they do not *look like* face patterns in the grayscale sense.

As a result, the combined texture and color based algorithm exhibits better *detection rate* (*i.e.*, the ratio of correctly detected faces v.s. total faces that should be detected) as well as better *detection accuracy* (*i.e.*, the ratio of correctly detected faces v.s. the total detected faces) in this experiment.

In speed performance, the texture analysis module is the most time consuming part in our algorithm. However, its complexity depends on the actually size of the detected skin-color map. On the mentioned CIF size 586 key frames, the average speed of our algorithm is about 1 second per frame on a 366 Celeron PC. We expect to achieve better performance on a better PC with some software optimizations.

5 Concluding Remarks

In this paper we mainly developed a texture-based face detection algorithm that works in the compressed DCT domain. This is a new work on compressed domain processing. Our work is based on the previous face detection works designed in the pixel domain, but we discussed major problems we met in the compressed DCT domain, such as block quantization problem, feature vector selection, preprocessing design in the DCT domain, and multi-model based system structure. Due to the block quantization problem, we have to use shorter feature vector than the face detection designs in the pixel domain. Therefore, the proposed texture-based detection algorithm is not as good as its counterparts in the pixel domain. To solve this problem, we proposed to combine the texture-based algorithm with a face color detection algorithm. Experiments indicate

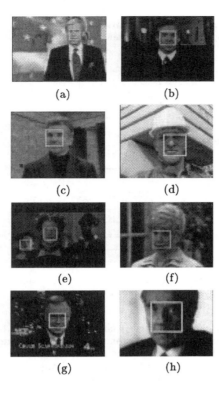

Figure 12: Face detection examples

that the combined texture and color based detection algorithm works better than both texture-only and color-only algorithms.

To sum up, this work is interesting because it first proposed to do traditional pattern detection work on the compressed DCT domain, which is a promising research direction for multimedia content analysis. In addition, in this work we also proposed, for the first time, to combine texture and color information for face detection. This is especially useful for multimedia processing, in which most visual data are in color formats.

References

[1] M. Abdel-Mottaleb and A. Elgammal. Face detection in complex environments from color images. In *IEEE ICIP*, Kobe, Japan, 1999.

[2] A. Albiol, C.A. bouman, and E.J. Delp. Face detection for pseudo-semantic labeling in video databases. In *IEEE ICIP*, Kobe, Japan, 1999.

[3] C.J.C. Burges. A tutorial on support vector machines for pattern recognition. *Data Mining and Knowledge Discovery*, 2(2), 1998.

[4] R. Dugad and N. Ahuja. *A Fast scheme for image size change in the compressed domain*, April 1999. Manual under review.

[5] M. Colobet *et al.* LISTEN: a system for locating and tracking individual speakers. In *Proc. of the 2nd Intl. Conf. on automatic face and gesture recog.*, pages 283–288, Killington, VT, 1996.

[6] K. Fukunaga and W.L.G. Koontz. Application of the karhunen-loeve expansion to feature selection and ordering. *IEEE Trans. on Computers*, 19(4), 1970.

[7] C. Garcia and G. Tziritas. Face detection using quantized skin color regions and wavelet packet analysis. *IEEE Trans. on Multimedia*, 1(3), 1999.

[8] J.B. Lee and B.G. Lee. Transform domain filtering based on piplining structure. *IEEE Trans. on Signal Processing*, 40:2061–2064, 1992.

[9] M. Lew. Information theoretic view-based and modular face detection. In *Proc. of the 2nd Intl. Conf. on automatic face and gesture recog.*, pages 198–203, Killington, VT, 1996.

[10] S. McKenna and S. Gong. Tracking faces. In *Proc. of the 2nd Intl. Conf. on automatic face and gesture recog.*, pages 271–275, Killington, VT, 1996.

[11] N. Merhav and V. Bhaskaran. Fast algorithms for DCT-domain image downsampling and for inverse motion compensation. *IEEE Trans. on CSVT*, 7(3), 1997.

[12] B. Moghadda and A. Pentland. Probalilistic visual learning for object detection. In *Proc. Intl. CVPR*, pages 786–793, Cambridge, MA, 1995.

[13] N. Oliver, A. Pentland, and F. Berard. LAFTER: A real-time lips and face tracker with facial expression recognition. In *Proc. Intl. CVPR*, S.Juan, Puerto Rico, June 1997.

[14] E.E. Osuna, R. Freund, and F. Girosi. Support vector machines: training and applications. Technical report, MIT AI Lab, March 1997. A.I.Memo 1602.

[15] H.A. Rowley, S. Baluja, and T. Kanade. Neural network-based face detection. *IEEE Trans. PAMI*, 20(1), 1998.

[16] K.K. Sung. *Learning and Example Selection for Object and Pattern Detection*. PhD thesis, MIT AI lab, 1996. also available as MIT tech. Report AITR 1572.

[17] A.M. Tekalp. *Digital Video Processing*. Prentice Hall, 1996.

[18] H. Wang and S.-F. Chang. A highly efficient system for automatic face region detection in mpeg video. *IEEE Trans. CSVT*, 7(4), 1997.

[19] M.-H. Yang and N. Ahuja. Detecting human faces in color images. In *IEEE ICIP*, Chicago, IL, 1998.

[20] M.-H. Yang and N. Ahuja. Face detection using a mixture of factor analyzers. In *IEEE ICIP*, Kobe, Japan, 1999.

Model-Based Varying Pose Face Detection and Facial Feature Registration in Video Images

Lixin Fan and Kah Kay Sung
School of Computing
National University of Singapore
Singapore, 117543
{fanlixin, sungkk}@comp.nus.edu.sg

ABSTRACT

This paper presents an automatic method for simultaneous human face detection and facial feature registration from colour video images. At the first stage, we use a skin colour Gaussian model to identify possible face locations under varying pose. Secondly, we compare image patterns with a varying pose face model in terms of shape and texture differences, using a combined feature-texture similarity measure (FTSM). False detections from the first stage are eliminated by setting an appropriate FTSM threshold. Moreover, one can also register the facial features (eyes, nose and mouth) by aligning a prototype face with the unknown pose faces. Experimental results show that the proposed method can achieve reliable face detection and feature registration under various conditions, including different poses, face appearances, and lighting conditions.

1. INTRODUCTION

Detecting human face in video frames is an important task in many computer vision applications, such as human-computer interface [7][19], video conferencing [3], and multimedia retrieval [9]. Moreover, the ability to extract detailed facial features (e.g. eyes, nose and mouth) and estimate pose orientation allows these vision systems to interact more intelligently with environments [1][12][24]. While the last decade has witnessed significant advances in face detection [20][25] [21][30], these methods are developed mainly for fixed pose (frontal) face detection, and need retraining in order to detect face images under different poses (e.g., side view faces [21]). A reliable face detection method which can handle *varying pose* faces is still open to research.

To reliably detect human faces, one must take into account image variations caused by different factors such as face appearance, lighting condition and pose. Pentland *et al.* represent the *texture* variations of frontal face patterns with an eigenface parametric model [15][26]. In order to represent

varying pose faces variations, Beymer, Jones, Vetter and Poggio [4][14][27], Craw [6], and Cootes and Taylor [5] independently proposed a *non-linear* model which combines two parametric models (one for texture differences, the other for structural/pose differences) by using *image warping* techniques. Once the model is learnt from training faces, one can then formulate face detection as a *model-based image matching* problem, in which face images synthesized by the model are compared against different locations in the input image. Furthermore, when good matches are found, one can use the known position of facial features in the warped model to locate facial features in the image. Recently, Fan and Sung [8] extended the model to deal with larger amount of pose variations by using a combined feature-texture similarity measure during the matching process.

Meanwhile, there are other cues, such as colour, motion and depth information that can be used for face detection. For example, one can use a statistical colour model capturing variations of different skin-colours for face detection, and the method was proven to be fast and robust for varying pose faces [18][28]. Nevertheless, false detection of nonface skin-coloured objects is inevitable for a purely colour-based face detector (see Section 2). In addition, it is also hard to extract detailed facial features and infer pose orientation, based on colour information only. It has been shown that integrating different cues can significantly improve the reliability, robustness and speed of face detection, and seems a promising solution in unconstrained environments [7][19][24].

In this paper, we present a fast automatic method for simultaneous human face detection and facial feature registration from colour video images by using *colour, shape*[1], and *texture* information about faces. Given an image, we first use a Gaussian skin colour model introduced in [18][28] to coarsely detect varying pose face candidates. At the second stage, we use the varying pose face model to (1) eliminate false detections from the first stage by setting appropriate thresholds on a feature-texture similarity measures; (2) extract facial features (eyes, nose and mouth) by aligning a prototype face with unknown pose faces. The explicit use of both shape and texture information in our second stage is unique, which makes varying pose face detection more robust. Note that using colour information makes our method rely on the acquisition of colour images, and we believe that this requirement can be satisfied in an indoor environment,

Figure 1: Left to Right: Original image, skin colour converted image, and face detection result.

Figure 2: False Detection: A skin-coloured book and a hand are false detected.

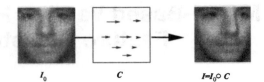

Figure 3: Feature based image warping. Original image I_0, feature points correspondence map C, and corresponding warped image I are shown from left to right.

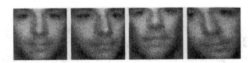

Figure 4: Left to right: Reference image I_0, and warped images with first three eigenvectors, given pose parameter=1000 ($I_0 \circ 1000E_i$, $i = 1, 2, 3$).

given the widespread use of digital cameras nowadays. Our main objective is to develop a face detection system which can handle pose changes existing in many applications including human-computer interface, video conferencing and multimedia retrieval etc..

For the rest of this paper, we first briefly review in Section 2 the skin colour based face detection. In Section 3, we describe how to use the varying pose face model to refine face detection and register facial features. Experimental results and discussions are presented in Sections 4 and 5 respectively. Section 6 concludes the paper.

2. SKIN COLOUR DETECTION

Colour information can be used to quickly segment interesting image regions for further processing [23]. To make colour based face detection robust to different fleshy tones and illumination conditions, we adopt *brightness normalized colour space* and *Gaussian color distribution model* introduced in [18][28] to locate skin-coloured regions in an image. With this technique, we implemented a real-time skin colour detector, which can reliably respond to human faces of different races under various pose, and lighting conditions at a frame rate of greater than 10 f/s on a Pentium 200MHz Linux PC without using any special hardware. An example of colour-based face detection is depicted in Figure 1.

This skin colour detector responds to all skin-coloured objects, even though they may look very different from faces in terms of structure (see Figure 2). In addition, it is difficult to derive detailed facial features and infer pose from colour information only. To solve these problems, one can also rely on texture and shape information of faces.

3. VARYING POSE FACE DETECTION BY TEXTURE AND SHAPE

In this section, we first review a varying pose face model, which takes into account both texture and structural(pose)

[1]We use *shape, structure* and *pose* interchangeably throughout this paper.

differences of faces. We then introduce a combined feature-texture similarity measure to quantify the difference between a given image and model image, and finally, we show how to eliminate false colour-based detections and extract facial features by using the varying pose face model.

3.1 A Varying Pose Face Model

We adopt a varying pose face model described below, which combines two separate parametric models representing frontal face textures and pose changes *independently*.

3.1.1 Texture Variation Modeling
Pentland *et al.*[15][26] and others approximate the distribution of frontal face texture patterns with a linear combination of eigenfaces:[2]

$$I \approx \widehat{I} = \Phi_T \cdot \alpha \qquad (1)$$

where Φ_T is a eigenface matrix obtained by applying PCA on training face images, and discarding small eigenvectors. The transformation coefficient $\alpha = \Phi'_T \cdot I$ determines texture variations caused by face appearance as well as lighting change in reconstructed faces. We refer to α as *texture* parameters below.

In our method, we use PCA to model both *facial appearance* and *lighting* variations. The justification of using PCA to model lighting variations lies in the fact that, for a convex Lambertian surface, its image under arbitrary lighting conditions can be represented as a linear combination of three images taken under any fixed lighting directions, provided no self-shadowing exist [16][22]. For face images, the assumption of convex Lambertian surface may not hold for all parts of faces, nevertheless, one still can use the linear combination model with more than three eigenvectors to represent a novel face [11][10].

[2]We use notations that (1) all m-by-n images are lexicographically ordered to form image vectors $I \in \Re^{N=mn}$; (2) images are subtracted by the average of training images; (3) "′" represents transpose of matrix.

296

3.1.2 Pose Variation Modeling

When faces change in pose, normally there are only minor changes in intensity at most pixels, but very obvious *spatial* movement of some distinctive feature points (e.g. eyes, nose, mouth). Accordingly, we can use a sparse *feature points correspondence map*(FPCM) between distinctive feature points of two images, to represent structural(pose) differences in two images. A FPCM consists of a set of *displacement vectors*, which map corresponding distinctive feature points (e.g eyes, nose, mouth) between two images (see Figure 3 for an example). On the other hand, given an initial image I_0 and a feature point correspondence map C, one can also synthesize a new image I by using a *feature based image warping* technique (see Figure 3):

$$I = I_0 \circ C \qquad (2)$$

where $\circ$ denotes a warping process, which involves (1) finding a dense pixelwise correspondence map by **interpolating** the sparse FPCM C, and (2) shifting image pixels accordingly. We refer readers to [2] for detailed warping procedures. Note that the dense pixelwise correspondence maps and the sparse FPCMs are in fact identical concepts, except that they contain different numbers of point matches. Unless otherwise stated, we will use them interchangeably below.

To learn varying pose model from example varying pose face images, one can first construct sparse FPCMs of these images with respect to a frontal prototype face by manual registration[3], then apply PCA on the constructed FPCMs. Figure 4 shows examples of warped images transformed using the first three eigenvectors of the learned pose change model. Note that these warped images roughly correspond to three types of pose changes (i.e. in depth left-right rotation, in depth up-down rotation, and in plane rotation). With this model, arbitrary pose variations from the frontal pose can be approximated as a linear combination of these basic warping operations. According to [4][5][14], the associated FPCM (C) represented by a $\Re^{2N}$ vector can be approximated by:

$$C \approx \widehat{C} = \Phi_P \cdot \gamma \qquad (3)$$

where N is the number of feature points, Φ_P is an eigenvector matrix obtained by applying PCA on training FPCMs and discarding the small eigenvectors. The transformation coefficient $\gamma = \Phi'_P \cdot C$ is referred as *pose* parameters below.

3.1.3 Combining Texture and Pose Variations

Combining linear subspaces of face texture and pose change, one can model an unknown pose face image as:

$$I \approx I^M(\alpha, \gamma) = (\Phi^T \alpha) \circ (\Phi^P \gamma) \qquad (4)$$

where Φ^T, Φ^P and α, γ are defined above.

The image warping process actually introduces a *non-linear* transformation on the distribution of frontal face images, and results in a complex manifold in image space. Figure 5

---

[3]When we learn the varying pose model, FPCMs are found by manual registration for all example images with respect to a prototype frontal face. When we match the model against a given image pattern, FPCMs are found by a binary edge map matching method, see Section 3.2.

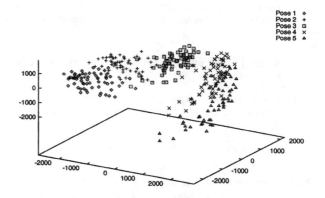

Figure 5: Distribution of the first 3 principle components of varying pose faces (Pose 1: right rotation; Pose 2: minor right rotation; Pose 3: frontal; Pose 4: minor left rotation; and Pose 5: left rotation).

shows the distribution of the first 3 principal components of a set of frontal face images and its warped counterparts under 4 non-frontal poses, synthesized by the proposed model. One can find out that the overall distribution of varying pose faces forms a *non-convex* and connected region across the view sphere.

3.2 A Combined Feature-Texture Similarity Measure

With the above proposed model, varying pose face detection involves comparing examined image patterns I at candidate locations (e.g. segmented regions from the skin colour detection) against model approximations I^M using an appropriate similarity measure, and reporting a "face" where a closely matching model approximation can be found. In order to accurately quantify the difference between the given image pattern (I) and model approximation I^M, we need a similarity measure that accounts for both texture and pose differences, since methods using only brightness differences [4][5][6][14][27] do not reflect image differences due to large pose-changes well. In [8], we introduce a combined feature-texture similarity measure(FTSM), which includes both a Pose Aligned Intensity Difference component reflecting texture differences, and a Feature Based Similarity Measure(FBSM) component capturing structural(pose) differences between distinctive feature points in the two images I and I^M. We briefly review the proposed similarity measure below.

3.2.1 Feature Point Correspondence Map

First, we present a method for computing the feature point correspondence map(FPCM) between two given images. To find the FPCM between two overlapping images I_1 and I_2, we employ a simple *binary edge map matching* method, which consists of following steps:

1. Compute the binary edge maps E_1 and E_2 fo the two given images;

297

2. For each edge point e_i in E_1, find the spatially closest edge point e_i' in the other edge map E_2, and obtain the *displacement vector* $\vec{d_i}$ from two matched edge points:

$$\vec{d_i} = (x_i' - x_i, y_i' - y_i) \tag{5}$$

where (x_i, y_i) and (x_i', y_i') are coordinates of e_i and e_i' respectively;

3. Construct the feature point correspondence map (FPCM) from displacement vectors of all edge points in image E_1:

$$C_{E_1 \to E_2} = \{\vec{d_i}(e_i \to e_i')|e_i \in E_1, e_i' \in E_2\} \tag{6}$$

Note that the FPCM is *directed*, which means $C_{E_1 \to E_2}$ and $C_{E_2 \to E_1}$ are not necessarily, and very unlikely, to be identically reversed for a given pair of edge maps E_1 and E_2. This implies that the proposed correspondence map based similarity measure should also be directed.

3.2.2 *Feature Based Similarity Measure*
Using computed FPCMs, one can quantify how close two sets of image features resemble each other by defining a *feature based similarity measure*(FBSM) as follows:

$$S_{feat}(I_1, I_2) = \max(s(E_1, E_2), s(E_2, E_1)) \tag{7}$$

where $s(E_a, E_b)$ is the root mean squared length of displacement vectors in the *directed* FPCM $C_{E_a \to E_b}$:

$$s(E_a, E_b) = \frac{1}{N} \sum_{i \in E_a} \left\| \vec{d}_i \right\|^2 \tag{8}$$

in which N is the number of feature points in E_a. This similarity measure is in fact a modification of the classical Hausdorff measure, which takes maximum of displacement vectors' lengths [13]. Note that since this similarity measure is proportional to the *spatial* distances between two sets of feature points, a pose alignment algorithm including this measure in its error function, will attempt to merge two sets of points and eventually align facial feature points in the two images.

3.2.3 *Pose Aligned Intensity Difference*
Given a FPCM C associating image I_1 with image I_2, one can quantify "texture differences" between the two images as :

$$S_{text}(I_1, I_2) = SSD(I_1, (I_2 \circ C)) \tag{9}$$

where $SSD()$ is the sum of square distance.

3.2.4 *Combined Feature-Texture Similarity Measure*
Combining both feature(pose) and texture similarities (Equations 7 and 9), we can define a combined feature-texture similarity measure (FTSM):

$$S(I_1, I_2) = K_f \cdot S_{feat} + K_t \cdot S_{text} \tag{10}$$

where K_f and K_t are two user-specified weighting parameters. The selecting of these two terms is heuristic based on user's priori knowledge of object textural and structural components. If no priori knowledge is accessible, one can simply set them with equal values(e.g. 1.0) without emphasizing either aspect.

Note that the FTSM not only measures the pose aligned texture similarity, which capture intensity differences between correctly corresponding pixels, but also takes into account the structural differences between feature points. We note that this property is crucial to align facial features between various pose faces, especially when initial poses are faraway (see [8] for detailed discussion).

3.3 Face Detection and Feature Registration

3.3.1 *Model-based Image Matching*
With the proposed parametric varying pose face model, one can first formulate the model-based image matching as an optimal parameter estimation problem, with objective to minimize the FTSM between the original image (I) and the model image (I^M). The optimal texture and pose parameters are estimated by using the *maximum likelihood* principle:

$$(\alpha^*, \gamma^*) = \arg \min_{\alpha, \gamma} S(I, I^M(\alpha, \gamma)) \tag{11}$$

We outline a face alignment algorithm below which, for a given input face image, alternates between estimating texture and pose parameters in an iterative manner:

1. Set α_0^* and γ_0^* such that I^M corresponds to a prototype frontal face image (see Figure 6);

2. With fixed α_{i-1}^*, estimate $\gamma_i^* (i = 1, 2, 3, ...)$ with objective to minimize $S(I, I^M(\alpha_{i-1}^*, \gamma_i^*))$ using FPCM based hill-climb method [8];

3. With fixed γ_i^*, estimate α_i^* with objective to minimize $S(I, I^M(\alpha_i^*, \gamma_i^*))$ using Levenberg-Marquardt method [17];

4. **if** ($S >$threshold) $\{i = i + 1$; and go to step 2; $\}$ **else** stop looping;

5. Output (α_i^*, γ_i^*), $S(I, I^*(\alpha_i^*, \gamma_i^*))$ and $I^M(\alpha_i^*, \gamma_i^*)$;

The algorithm starts from an initial frontal view face prototype (Figure 6), and warps the model image to match the given images. Once the final match is found, one can compute the optimal FPCM based on estimated pose parameter γ^* using Equation 3, and apply it to prototype feature points to obtain the warped feature points which are aligned with given face poses.

3.3.2 *Face Detection*
Next, we can compare the minimized FTSM with a preset threshold to decide whether the examined image patch does contain a face pattern. Ideally, a non-face image results in large FTSM, while a face image gives small FTSM. Figure 9 depicts the measured FTSMs for two non-face objects (book and hand), and three sequences of varying pose face. It is shown that by setting appropriate thresholds on FTSM (e.g. $t = 31$), one can easily eliminate false detections from the skin-colour face detector.

298

Figure 6: A face prototype and feature points.

iterations	$\gamma_{[0]}$	$\gamma_{[1]}$	$\gamma_{[2]}$	Error
0	0.00	0.00	0.00	39.38
1	-1007.21	-23.65	65.31	34.10
5	-1325.43	-100.66	150.17	29.36
9	-1599.95	-155.83	198.18	27.05

Table 1: Pose parameters (first three components) and error measures ($K_f = 1.0$, $K_t = 1.0$).

3.3.3 Facial Feature Registration

Finally, one can compute the optimal FPCM based on estimated pose parameter γ^* using Equation 3, then apply it to prototype feature points to locate the feature points of unknown pose faces. The recovered γ^* provides information on how known points on a prototype face pose map to locations in the examined image. With this information, one can infer where interesting facial features (e.g eyes, nose and mouth) are located in the unknown pose faces. An intermediate face registration result is illustrated in Figure 7 and Table 1 (see [8] for more results).

We note that the estimated pose parameters also provide useful information for pose estimation. For instance, comparing the final pose parameter in Table 1 with eigenvectors in Figure 4, one can find out that the first component($\gamma_{[0]} = -1599.95$) and the second component($\gamma_{[1]} = -155.83$) correspond to a left and slightly downward in-depth rotation respectively, which is a fairly accurate semantic description of face pose in Figure 7. Learning a mapping between pose parameters and face pan-tilt angels is one direction of our current research.

4. EXPERIMENTAL RESULTS

To detect faces and register facial features using texture and shape information, we first construct a frontal face subspace model and a varying pose model, using a subset of the MIT Beymer face database as training data. The training set includes 60 different people' face images (100x100 pixels), under 5 fixed poses (300 face images in total). All frontal training faces are shape-normalized to align feature points. Training FPCMs are obtained by manual registration of non-frontal face images with respect to a prototype frontal face. As the feature point correspondences can only be found when they are not self-occluded, the pose change

Figure 7: Unknown pose face alignment with feature points located (Left to Right: Iteration 0,1,5 and 9).

Figure 8: The experiment setup

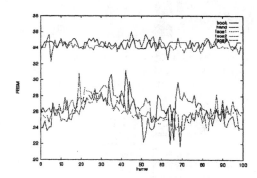

Figure 9: Comparison of FTSMs for non-faces and faces.

in our training images are limited in the range of $[-60^0, 60^0]$ right-left rotations, and $[-10^0, 10^0]$ up-down rotations. Correspondingly, the pose change in testing images are also roughly limited in this range.

The proposed face detection and feature registration algorithm was tested over a number of test sequences of human subjects turning their faces in the range of allowed pose changes. The test sequences belong to four (3 male and 1 female) different people, in which none are present in the training data. Test sequences are taken in an indoor environment under various lighting condition. The camera image size used is 240x180 pixels, and the face size change from approximately 50x50 to 100x100 pixels. Figure 8 shows the setup of our experiment system, where the camera is on top of the monitor.

Experiment 1: Face Detection

In this experiment, we test our method under different conditions, such as varying pose faces, false skin-colour detection and partial occlusion. Some experimental results are depicted in Figure 10. We note that in our indoor experimental environment, the detection is generally reliable for varying pose faces, as long as facial features are not entirely occluded. Partial occlusions are tolerable subject to the feature-texture similarity measures still below given threshold. For false detections at skin-coloured objects (e.g. hands), as they are rather different from faces in terms of structure, and thus can be eliminated by comparing FTSMs

Figure 10: Face Detection Results. Row 1: Varying pose face detection. Row 2: Partial Occlusion. Row 3: False Detection eliminated (compared with Figure 2).

	#Frames	Face size	Good	Fair	Mis.
Seq. 1	100	100x100	54	42	4
Seq. 2	100	100x100	48	47	5
Seq. 3	100	80x80	65	35	0
Seq. 4	100	50x50	54	45	1
Seq. 5	100	80x80	49	46	5
Seq. 6	100	80x80	60	37	3
Overall	600	-	330	252	18

Table 2: Feature Registration Results - we define a good registration as having feature points at most 5% of face size away from correct positions, and a fair registration at most 10% of face size away, otherwise, a mis-registration (see Figure 11).

with a preset threshold (say $t = 31$).

Experiment 2: Facial Feature Registration

The facial feature registration results is summarized in Table 2, and Figure 11 illustrates some feature registration results. It is shown that the proposed feature registration algorithm is generally robust and effective, with more than 55% faces well registered, 42% fairly registered and 3% faces mis-registered, under various conditions including different individuals, lighting conditions, face appearances and sizes.

Finally, it is worth mentioning that the feature registration results are obtained at a frame rate greater than 1f/s on a Pentium 200MHz Linux PC without using any special hardware. We believe that running the algorithm on a faster machine will improve the speed to meet requirements of real world applications.

5. DISCUSSIONS

5.1 Comparison with Previous Face Detection and Registration Methods

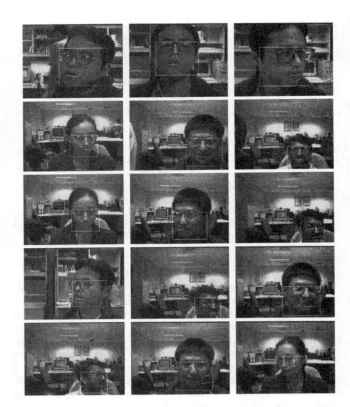

Figure 11: Feature Registration Results (rows 1 to 3: good registration; row 4: fair registration; row 5: mis-registration).

We briefly compare this method with three different types of face detection and registration approaches in the literature: (1) the statistical face detection methods [15][25][20][21][30]; (2) the colour-based face detection methods [28][18][29]; (3) the morphable model-based registration [4] [5].

1. The statistical methods are normally trained with *fixed pose* (frontal) face images. While small (realistic or synthetic) variations in pose changes are included in the training images, these methods are fundamentally pose sensitive, and detecting faces under varying poses requires retraining with face images under different poses. In fact, Schneiderman and Kanade [21] proposed to train two face detectors with frontal view and side view face images separately. Unlike these methods, we adopt a different approach to handle pose variations by learning a pose change model, obtained from the example correspondence maps between varying pose face images. The advantage of separating pose variations from the facial appearance and lighting variations is that one can synthesis new pose faces from a fixed (frontal) pose (see Figure 4), and thus does not need to retrain the face detector for a particular new pose.

2. As mentioned earlier, coloured-based face detection methods are pose-insensitive, but naive skin-colour detectors respond to all skin-coloured objects, which may not be faces. To eliminate false detections, Yang and Ahuja [29] proposed to inspect the shape of detected

regions, and assume that faces must be elliptic regions. In our method, we compare the candidate regions with a varying pose face model in terms of textural and structural variations, and eliminate false detection by thresholding FTSM.

3. The idea of using a linear subspace to model pose variations was also used in the morphable mode-based registration methods [4] [5]. While these methods use *texture* based similarity measures to quantify differences between model image and images to be matched, we use a combined *feature-texture* similarity measure, which better reflect the structural variations across larger pose changes, and can align faces even when initial poses are far off. We refer to [8] for detailed comparison and discussions.

5.2 Feature Based Correspondence

We note that our method work well only when feature-based correspondences can be reasonably established. While this has been largely true for the face edge maps detected in our experimental environment, and Huttenlocher et. al. [13] have even reported reliable feature-based alignment results under more challenging conditions, we believe that more discriminative feature matching methods will be needed to deal with significant image clutter. This is one direction of our current research.

6. CONCLUSIONS

This paper presents a fast method for detecting face and extracting facial features in video images. The skin-colour detection first quickly locates possible face candidates. A more selective model-based method then discards false detections from the first stage, and extracts facial features by comparing image patterns with a varying pose face model learned from training images. Taking into account both texture and structural information leads to more robust face detection. Experimental results show that the proposed method can achieve reliable face detection and feature registration under various conditions, including different poses, face appearances, and lighting conditions. To extend this work in future, we can easily derive pose information from the optimal pose parameter, by learning a mapping between pose parameters and face pan-tilt angles. These information can be used to infer user intentions in human-computer interface.

7. ACKNOWLEDGEMENTS

We thank Dr. David Beymer and the MIT Artificial Intelligence Laboratory for making available the Beymer face database. Ms. Zeng Ying helped us manually label the training data. Lixin Fan is supported by NUS research scholarship. This research is supported by a NUS ARF Research Grant: RP3960623.

8. REFERENCES

[1] P. Ballard and G. C. Stockman. Computer Operaton via Face Orientation. In *Proceedings of 11th IAPR International Conference on Pattern Recognition*, volume 1, pages 407 – 410, 1992.

[2] T. Beier and S. Neely. Feature-based image metamorphosis. In *SIGGRAPH'92 Proceedings*, pages 35 – 42, 1992. Chicago, IL.

[3] O. Bernier and et. al. MULTRAK: A System for Automatic Multiperson Localization and Traking in Real-time. In *Proceedings of 1998 IEEE ICIP*, volume 1, pages 136 – 140, 1998.

[4] D. Beymer. Vectorizing Face Images by Interleaving Shape and Texture Computations. AI Lab, Memo 1537, MIT, Sept. 1995.

[5] T. Cootes and C. Taylor. Active Appearance Models. In *Proc. of ECCV*, volume 2, pages 484 – 498, 1998.

[6] I. Craw, N. Costen, T. Kato, and S. Akamatsu. How should we represent faces for automatic recognition? *IEEE Trans. on PAMI*, 21:725 – 736, Aug. 1999.

[7] T. Darrell, G. Gordon, J. Woodfill, and M. Harville. A Virtual Mirror Interface using Real-time Robust Face Tracking. In *Proceedings of Third IEEE International Conference on automatic Face and Gesture Recognition*, pages 616 – 621, 1998.

[8] L. Fan and K. K. Sung. A Combined Feature-Texture Similarity Measure for Face Alginment Under Varying Pose. In *Proc. of IEEE Conference on Computer Vision and Patter Recognition*, pages 308 – 313, 2000.

[9] C. Garcia and G. Tziritas. Face Detection Using Quantized Skin Colour Regions Merging and Wavelet Packet Analysis. *IEEE Trans. on Multimeida*, 3:264 – 276, Sept. 1999.

[10] A. Georghiades, P. N. Belhumeur, and D. J. Kriegman. Illumination-Based Image Synthesis: Creating Novel Image of Human Faces Under Differing Pose and Lighting. In *Proc. of IEEE Workshop on Multi-View Modeling and Analysis of Visual Scenes*, 1999.

[11] P. Hallinan. A Low-dimensional Representation of Human Faces for Arbitrary Lighting Conditions. In *Proc. of IEEE Conference on Computer Vision and Patter Recognition*, pages 995 – 999, 1994.

[12] H. Hongo, A. Murata, and K. Yamamoto. Consumer Products User Interface Using Face and Eye Orientation. In *Proceedings of 1997 IEEE International Symposium on Consumer Electronics*, pages 87 – 90, 1997.

[13] D. P. Huttenlocher, G.A.Klanderman, and W.J.Rucklidge. Comparing Images Using the Hausdorff Distance. *IEEE Transactions on PAMI*, 15:850 – 863, Sept. 1993.

[14] M. J. Jones and T. Poggio. Model-Based Matching by Linear Combinations of Prototypes. AI Lab, Memo 1583, MIT, Nov. 1996.

[15] B. Moghaddam and A. P. Pentland. Prbabilistic visual Learning for Object Detection. Technical Report 326, Media Lab, MIT, June 1995.

[16] S. Nayar and H. Murase. Dimensionality of Illumination Manifolds in Appearance Matching. In *In Int. Workshop on Object Representations for Computer Vision*, 1996.

[17] W. H. Press, S. A. Teukolsky, W. T. Vetterling, and B. P. Flannery. *Numerical Recipes in C*. Cambridge University Press, second edition, 1992.

[18] R. Raja, S. McKenna, and S. Gong. Tracking and Segmenting People in Varying Lighting Conditions Using Colour. In *Proc. of FG'98*, 1998.

[19] J. Rehg, M. Loughlin, and K. Waters. Vision for a Smart Kiosk. In *Proceedings, IEEE CVPR*, pages 690 – 696, 1997.

[20] H. Rowley, S. Baluja, and T. Kanade. Neural Network-based Face Detection. *IEEE Transactions on PAMI*, 20(1):23 – 38, Jan. 1998.

[21] H. Schneiderman and T. Kanade. Probabilistic Modeling of Local Appearance and Spatial Relationships for Object Recognition. In *Proc. of IEEE Conference on Computer Vision and Patter Recognition*, 1998.

[22] A. Shashua. On Photometric Issues to Feature-based Object Recognition. *International Journal on Computer Vision*, 21:99 – 122, 1997.

[23] W. Skarbek and A. Koschan. Colour Image Segmentation - A Survey. Technical report, Univ. of Berlin, 1994.

[24] R. Stieflhagen, J. Yang, and A. Waibel. A Model-Based Gaze Tracking System. In *Proc. of IEEE International Symposium on Intelligigence and Systems*, pages 304 – 310, 1996.

[25] K.-K. Sung and T. Poggio. Example-based learning for view-based human face detection. *IEEE Transactions on PAMI*, 20(1):39 – 51, Jan. 1998.

[26] M. A. Turk and A. P. Pentland. Eigenfaces for Recognition. *Journal of Cognitive Neuroscience*, 3(1):71 – 86, 1991.

[27] T. Vetter, M. J. Jones, and T. Poggio. A Bootstrapping Algorithm for Learning Linear Models of Object Classes. AI Lab, Memo 1600, MIT, Feb. 1997.

[28] J. Yang and A. Waibel. A real-time face tracker. In *Proceedings of the Third IEEE Workshop on Applications of Computer Vision*, pages 142 – 147, 1996.

[29] M.-H. Yang, N. Ahuja, and D. Kriegman. Detecting Human Faces in Color Images. In *Proceedings of the IEEE International Conference on Image Processing*, pages 127 – 130, 1998.

[30] M.-H. Yang, N. Ahuja, and D. Kriegman. Face Detection Using Mixtures of Linear Subspaces. In *Proceedings of the IEEE International Conference on Image Processing*, 1999.

302

An Integrated Scheme for Object-based Video Abstraction

Changick Kim and Jenq-Neng Hwang
Information processing Laboratory
Dept. of Electrical Engineering, Box#352500
University of Washington, Seattle, WA 98195
{cikim, hwang}@ee.washington.edu

ABSTRACT

In this paper, we present a novel scheme for object-based key-frame extraction facilitated by an efficient video object segmentation system. Key-frames are the subset of still images which best represent the content of a video sequence in an abstracted manner. Thus, key-frame based video abstraction transforms an entire video clip to a small number of representative images. The challenge is that the extraction of key-frames needs to be automated and context dependent so that they maintain the important contents of the video while remove all redundancy. Among various semantic primitives of video, objects of interest along with their actions and generated events can play an important role in some applications such as object-based video surveillance system. Furthermore, on-line processing combined with fast and robust video object segmentation is crucial for real-time applications to report unwanted action or event as soon as it happens. Experimental results on the proposed scheme for object-based video abstraction are presented.

Keywords

Video abstraction, object-based key frame extraction, video object segmentation, MPEG-4/MPEG-7.

1. INTRODUCTION

The traditional video coding standards, such as MPEG-1/MPEG-2 and H.261/H.263, lack high-level interpretation of video contents. The MPEG-4 [1] video standard introduces the concept of Video Object Layer (VOL) to support content-based functionality. Its primary objective is to support the coding of video sequences which are segmented based on video contents and to allow separate and flexible reconstruction and manipulation of contents at the decoder. Thus, video object segmentation, which emphasizes to partition the video frames to semantically meaningful video objects and background, becomes an important issue for successful use of MPEG-4/MPEG-7. As an example in the MPEG-7, segmented results based on the frame-to-frame motion information or abrupt shape change can be utilized for a

high-level (object-level) description .

Most of the traditional key frame extraction algorithms are rectangle frame based. Popularly used visual criteria to extract key frames are shot-based criteria, color-feature-based criteria, and motion-based criteria [4]. However, they are limited to rely on low-level image features and other readily available information instead of using semantic primitives of video, such as interesting objects, actions and events. The attempt to object-based key frame extraction has been reported in [7], where the ratio of the number of I-macroblocks (MBs) to the total number of (encoded) MBs in a Video Object Plane (VOP) in intra mode was used as the key frame selection criteria. When the ratio exceeds a certain threshold the frame is labeled as a key frame. However, the scheme requires an MPEG-4 encoder as well as pre-segmented VOPs and the accuracy of using the ratio of I-MBs is too low to be effective. In this paper, we extended previous work on VOP extraction [17] and propose a new object-based framework for video abstraction, where changes in contents are detected through observations made on the objects in the video sequence. Naturally, the efficient video object segmentation scheme is necessary for successful object-based key frame extraction.

This paper is organized as follows. In Section 2, an efficient video object segmentation algorithm is described as the first step of the object-based video abstraction system. The object-based key frame extraction algorithm using distance measure is introduced in Section 3, promising simulation results are also reported in this section. Conclusion is followed in Section 4.

2. VIDEO OBJECT SEGMENTATION

Many of video segmentation algorithms that specifically address VOP generation have been recently proposed due to the development of the new video coding standard, MPEG-4 [1]. The change detection for inter-frame difference is one of the most popular video segmentation schemes [5][6][9] because it is straightforward and enables automatic detection of new appearance. While the algorithms, which are based on inter-frame change detection, enable automatic detection of objects and allow larger non-rigid motion comparing to object tracking methods [10], the drawback is the noise (small false regions) created by decision error. Thus small holes removal using morphological operation and removal of false detection parts like uncovered background by motion information are usually incorporated [6][9][16]. Another drawback of change detection is that object boundaries are irregular in some critical image areas due to the lack of spatial edge information. This drawback can be overcome by using spatial edge information to smooth and adapt the object boundaries in the post-processing stage. Nevertheless, we believe that the spatial edge information should be incorporated in the motion detection stage to simplify algorithm and generate better results. A desirable video object segmentation for real-time object-based applications should meet the following criteria.

- Segmented objects should conform to human perception, i.e., semantically meaningful objects should be segmented.

- Segmentation algorithm should be efficient and achieve fast speed.

- Initialization should be simple and easy for user to operate (human intervention should be minimized).

2.1. Extraction of Moving Edge (*ME*) Map

Our segmentation algorithm [17] starts with edge detection which is the first and most important stage of human visual processing as discovered by Marr and *et al.* [2]. While edge information plays a key role in extracting the physical change of the corresponding surface in a real scene, exploiting simple difference of edges for extracting shape information of moving objects in video sequence suffers from great deal of noise even in stationary background (see Fig. 1-(a)). This is due to the fact that the random noise created in one frame is different from the one created in the successive frame. The difference of edges is defined as

$$\left|\Phi(f_{n-1}) - \Phi(f_n)\right| = \left|\theta(\nabla G * f_{n-1}) - \theta(\nabla G * f_n)\right|, \quad (1)$$

where the edge maps $\Phi(f)$ are obtained by the Canny edge detector [8], which is accomplished by performing a gradient operation ∇ on the Gaussian convoluted image $G*f$, followed by applying the non-maximum suppression to the gradient magnitude to thin the edge and the thresholding operation with hysteresis to detect and link edges. On the other hand, edge extraction from difference image in successive frames (see Eq. (2)) results in a noise-robust difference edge map DE_n because Gaussian convolution included in the Canny operator suppresses the noise in the luminance difference.

$$DE_n = \Phi(\left|f_{n-1} - f_n\right|) = \theta(\nabla G * \left|f_{n-1} - f_n\right|). \quad (2)$$

Fig. 2 shows the block diagram of our segmentation algorithm. After calculating edge map of difference of images using Canny edge detector (see Fig.1-(b)), we extract the moving edge ME_n of the current frame f_n based on the edge map DE_n of difference $\left|f_{n-1} - f_n\right|$, the current frame's edge map $E_n = \Phi(f_n)$, and the background edge map E_b. Note that, E_b contains absolute

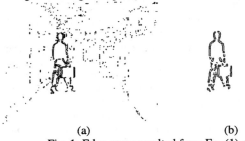

(a)   (b)

Fig. 1: Edge maps resulted from Eq. (1) and (2)

background edges in case of a still camera and is set at the first stage to increase the extraction performance. For video surveillance sequences, such as 'Hall Monitor', which contain no moving objects in the beginning of video clip, edge map of the first frame is used as a background edge map. For sequences which have temporarily still objects from the beginning, such as 'Miss America' or 'Akiyo', the background edge map E_b can be created by manually deleting moving edges of target objects (see Fig. 3). We define the edge model $E_n = \{e_1, \cdots, e_k\}$ as a set of all edge points detected by the Canny operator in the current frame n. Similarly, we denote $ME_n = \{m_1, \cdots, m_l\}$ the set of l moving edge points, where $l \leq k$. The edge points in ME_n are not restricted to object boundary, but can also be in the interior of the object boundary. If DE_n denotes the set of all pixels belonging to the edge map from the difference image, then the moving edge model generated by edge change is given by selecting all edge pixels within a small distance T_{change} of DE_n, i.e.,

$$ME_n^{change} = \left\{e \in E_n \mid \min_{x \in DE_n} \|e - x\| \leq T_{change}\right\}. \quad (3)$$

Some ME_n might have scattered noise, which need to be removed before proceeding to the next steps. In addition, previous frame's moving edges can be referenced to detect temporarily still moving edges, i.e.,

$$ME_n^{still} = \left\{e \in E_n, e \notin E_b \mid \min_{x \in ME_{n-1}} \|e - x\| \leq T_{still}\right\}. \quad (4)$$

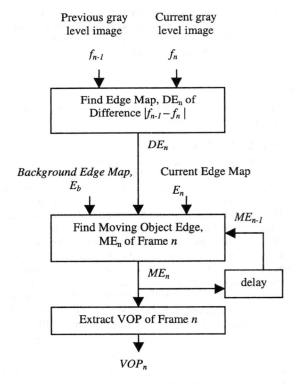

Figure 2: Block diagram of the segmentation

304

(a)   (b)

(c)   (d)

Fig.3: Finding initial edge maps: (a) The first frame, I_0 , (b) edge map of 1st frame, E_0, (c) Background edge map, E_b , (d) Moving edge map of first frame, $ME_0 = E_0 - E_b$

Finally, the moving edge model for current frame, f_n, is given by combining the two components.

$$ME_n = ME_n^{change} \cup ME_n^{still} . \qquad (5)$$

For initial moving edge map ME_0, just a blank image is required in case of surveillance video such as 'Hall Monitor'. For head-and-shoulder type of video, such as 'Miss America' or 'Akiyo', we need to manually delineate the moving object (e.g., by outlining the outer contour of the objects of interest) in the first frame. Note that in case of little movement in the beginning frames, there is no way to detect moving edges, i.e., correct moving edges are not generated until we encounter the frame in which objects begin to move. Thus, to facilitate correct moving edge extraction, ME_0 is calculated by the equation, $ME_0 = E_0 - E_b$ (see Fig. 3-(d)). Note that such a manual initialization is not needed for the surveillance type of sequences, because moving objects will not appear in the very beginning of the sequences.

2.2 Extraction of VOP

With moving edge map ME_n, as shown in Figure 5-(a), detected from DE_n , we are ready to extract the VOPs (see Figure 4). The horizontal candidates are declared to be the region inside the first and last edge points in each row (see Fig.5-(b)) and the vertical candidates for each column. After finding both horizontal and vertical VOP candidates, the intersection regions (see Fig. 5-(c)) through logical AND operation are further processed by alternative use of morphological operations. For video sequences, such as 'Miss America', which contain only a partial moving object instead of the whole object, a rule is added to declare image boundary points as moving edge points if either of horizontal or vertical candidates touch image boundary points. This process for finding candidates is repeated to extract VOP.

ME_n

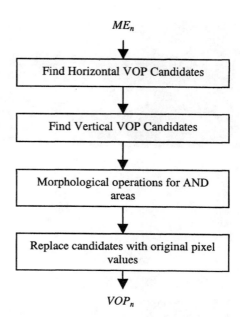

Figure 4: Block diagram of VOP extraction

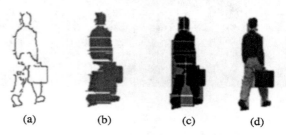

(a)   (b)   (c)   (d)

Figure 5: The VOP extraction process. (a) moving edge map, ME_{45}, (b) horizontal candidates, (c) logical AND (black areas) of horizontal and vertical candidates, (d) extracted VOP after morphological operations.

2.3 Simulation Results

In this section, the algorithmic performance of the proposed VOP extraction is illustrated through the subjective and objective evaluation .

2.3.1 Subjective Evaluation

The proposed algorithm was applied to 'Hall Monitor', which contains small moving objects and complex background in CIF format. It was also applied to 'Miss America' and 'Akiyo' sequences, which are typical head-and-shoulder type video in QCIF and CIF format respectively. Fig. 6 and Fig. 7 show several results, which show that the proposed algorithm is quite efficient on both surveillance and head-and-shoulder type sequences. Both of T_{change} and T_{still} values are 1. In order to eliminate small false regions, morphological opening can be applied. In our simulations, the morphological operations were only applied to 'Hall Monitor', which has floating noise in the background through the sequence. The entire resulting VOPs for 'Akiyo' sequence is accessible at our web site [12].

| (a) | (b) |

| (c) | (d) |

Fig.6: Extracted VOPs from 'Hall Monitor'
(a) fr.46 (b) fr.55 (c) fr.105 (d) fr.294

2.3.2 Objective Evaluation of Performance

For objective evaluation of the proposed segmentation scheme, Wollborn and Mech [14] proposed a simple pixel-based quality measure. The spatial distortion of an estimated binary video object mask at frame t is defined as

$$d(O_t^{est}, O_t^{ref}) = \frac{\sum_{(x,y)} O_t^{est}(x,y) \oplus O_t^{ref}(x,y)}{\sum_{(x,y)} O_t^{ref}(x,y)}, \qquad (6)$$

where O_t^{ref} and O_t^{est} are the reference and the estimated binary object masks at frame t, respectively, and $\oplus$ is the binary "XOR" operation. The temporal coherency $\eta(t)$ is defined by

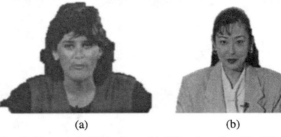

| (a) | (b) |

Fig. 7: Extracted VOPs from (a) Miss America (fr. 16) and (b) Akiyo (fr.148)

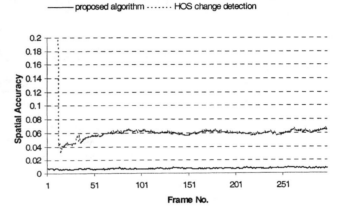

(a)

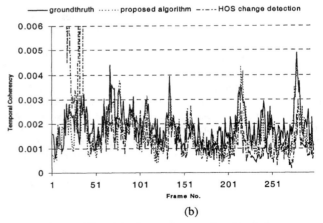

(b)

Figure 8 : The objective evaluation for objects from 'Akiyo' CIF sequence. (a) spatial accuracy and (b) temporal coherency

$$\eta(t) = d(O_t, O_{t-1}), \qquad (7)$$

where O_t and O_{t-1} are binary object masks at frame t and t-1, respectively. Temporal coherency $\eta^{est}(t)$ of the estimated binary mask O^{est} should be compared to temporal coherency $\eta^{ref}(t)$ of the reference mask O^{ref}. Any significant deviation from the reference indicates a bad temporal coherency.

The segmentation performance of the proposed algorithm is evaluated by using both subjective and objective criteria described above. The corresponding results of the "Akiyo" sequence in CIF format are shown in Fig. 8. For the reference binary VO mask, the manually segmented mask from the original sequence is used. More specifically, edge map is taken from each frame and the background edges are manually deleted. Next, for the broken edges along the object boundary, manual linking is also performed. Finally, the inner area of an object is filled using 'paint bucket tool' in Adobe Photoshop software. In Fig. 8-(a), the dot line is obtained by using higher order statistics change detection described in [9] while the solid line is from our proposed algorithm. We see that the spatial accuracy of the proposed edge-based algorithm is much better than the inter-frame change detection scheme. The error is less than 1% in every frame. In Fig. 8-(b), the solid line denotes the reference mask while the dot line the proposed scheme. The temporal coherency curve from the proposed algorithm closely follows the curve from the reference mask. We see from these results that our moving-edge-based segmentation gives good spatial accuracy as well as temporal coherency since it provides accurate object boundary information.

3. OBJECT-BASED KEY-FRAME EXTRACTION

Object-based key-frames are extracted in a sequential manner through the sequence. Figure 9 illustrates the proposed integrated scheme for object-based key-frame extraction (KFE). It relies on two criteria to extract key-frames from a video shot.

3.1 Key Frames by Event

The first criterion is based on the change of the number of regions between the last declared key frame and the current frame. There are two cases for change in numbers of regions. If the number reduces, this implies either disappearance of one or more objects, or overlap of two or more objects. If the number increases, it also implies either new appearance of one or more objects, or separation of two or more overlapped objects. In either cases, we declare the current frame as a new key-frame assuming an important event occurs. For this decision, connected components labeling [11] is first conducted to label separate regions. Specifically, we adopt a row-by-row labeling algorithm, which makes two passes over the image: the first pass to record equivalence and assign temporary labels; and the second pass to replace each temporary label by the label of its equivalence class. In between the two passes, the recorded set of equivalence, stored as a binary relation, is processed to determine the equivalence classes of the relation. These labeled regions are also used in the key-frame extraction by action change which will be explained in the next subsection.

3.2 Key-Frames by Action (or Shape) Change

In case the number of labeled regions in the last selected key-frame and current frame are same, the KFE problem is modeled as choosing a compact set of samples (key-frames) given feature vectors from sequential frames. We assume that we have a data set Δ of L frames in an n-dimensional feature space belonging to two different classes +1 (=key-frames) or −1 (=non-key-frames)

$$\Delta = \left\{ (\mathbf{x}_k, y_k) \mid k \in \{1, \cdots, L\}, \mathbf{x}_k \in \Re^n, y_k \in \{+1, -1\} \right\} \qquad (8)$$

where L denotes the number of sequential frames in which the number of labeled regions is consistent.

A binary classifier that maps the points from their feature space to their label space can be used.

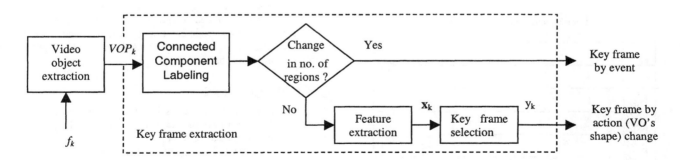

Fig.9: Block diagram for Integrated system for object-based key frame extraction

$$f : \Re^n \rightarrow \{+1, -1\}. \qquad (9)$$

$$\mathbf{x}_k \mapsto y_k$$

Our classification is based on the distance measure between two frames. If two frames are denoted as F_i and F_j, and they contain the same number of labeled regions as $R_i = \{r_{i,m}, m = 1, \cdots M\}$ and $R_j = \{r_{j,m}, m = 1, \cdots M\}$, then the distance between these two frames can be defined as

$$D(F_i, F_j) = \max[d(r_{i,1}, r_{j,match_{ij}(1)}), d(r_{i,2}, r_{j,match_{ij}(2)}), \cdots,$$

$$d(r_{i,M}, r_{j,match_{ij}(M)})], \qquad (10)$$

where $match_{ij}(m)$ denotes the closest spatially labeled region in F_j for the m-th labeled region in F_i. We take city block distance [3] between center points of two regions to measure spatial closeness. We define the distance (weighted Euclidean distance) between two regions as

$$d(r_{i,m}, r_{j,n}) = \sum_p w_p \left[x_{i,m}(p) - x_{j,n}(p) \right]^2, \qquad (11)$$

where w_p is the weighting constant and $\mathbf{x}_{i,m}$ is a shape feature vector. The 7-dimensional feature vector $\mathbf{x}_{i,m}$ of the m-th labeled region in frame F_i is generated using seven Hu moments [15][3], which are known as reasonable shape descriptors in a translation- and scale-invariant manner. In order to reduce the range of values, the *log* of 7 moments are used.

If a distance $D(F_{last}, F_k)$ between the last selected key-frame and the current frame is greater than predefined threshold value, we regard the existence of quite different action or shape change from the last key frame. Details of our object-based key frame selection method is given as followed.

The first frame in a shot is always chosen as a key frame. Then, the numbers of objects are computed for the current frame F_k and the last extracted key-frame F_{last}. If the numbers are different each other, the frame F_k is declared as a key-frame, otherwise the distance $D(F_{last}, F_k)$ is computed between the current frame F_k and the last extracted key-frame F_{last}. If this difference exceeds a given threshold T_d, the current frame is selected as a new key-frame, that is

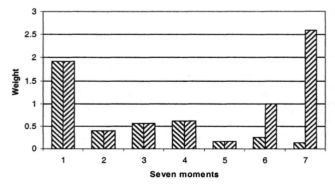

Fig. 10. Weights used for Eq. (11) in this experiments

*Step*1: $\forall k \in [1, N], \ y_k = -1$

*Step*2: $y_1 = +1, last = 1, k = 1$

*Step*3: $k = k + 1,$

if $n_k \neq n_{k-1}$ and $k - last > T_f \Rightarrow y_k = +1, last = k$

otherwise

if $D(F_{last}, F_k) > T_d$ and $k - last > T_f$

$\Rightarrow y_k = +1, last = k$

*Step*4: Iterate step3 until $k = N$.

Here, N is the number of frames within a shot and n_k is the number of labeled regions in F_k.

4. Experimental Results

In this section, we present experimental results on the MPEG-4 test sequence 'hall monitor'. For VOP extraction, we used morphological closing with structuring element (S.E.) 9×19 followed by 5×11 size of opening. The latter opening with structuring element of 5×11 suppresses small false regions. In feature extraction stage, 7 Hu moments are calculated from the ground-truth object masks manually generated for the first VO in 'hall monitor'. Weight vector $\mathbf{w}$ (see the first columns in Fig.10) is first selected by taking inverse of variances for each moment. We found the 6th and 7th moments are more influential to discriminate shapes from others. Thus we set weight vector with more weight on 6th and 7th moments (see the second column in Fig.10). Two threshold values used are 3.0 and 10 for T_d and T_f, respectively. In our labeling stage, the regions smaller than the size of 100 pixels are regarded as noise and ignored.

In order to evaluate the performance of the proposed key-frame extraction scheme, the ground-truth object masks are used, which are generated by the method explained in Subsection 2.3.2. The experimental results are shown in Figure 11, which reports important events in the sequence, such as birth (appearance) and death (disappearance) of two objects (see (a), (d), (l) and (q) in Fig. 11), and distinguishable action changes, such as different walking or turning scenes (see (b), (c), (e), (h), (i), (j), (k), (m), (n), (o) and (p) in Fig. 11), and bending scenes to put/take something (see (f) and (g) in Fig.11). Fig. 12 shows the experimental results applied to our integrated system. Note that the proposed automatic segmentation system has been used for this experiment. It shows little difference from Fig. 11, capturing important events and shape changes.

5. CONCLUSION

We have shown an integrated scheme for object-based video abstraction. The contributions and characteristics of the proposed scheme are summarized as followings:

- Efficiency: Easy to implement and fast to compute.

- Effectiveness: Able to capture the salient contents based on observations made on objects.

- On-line processing: Easy to be implemented on-line since it only depends on the last selected key frame and the current frame. The novel selection scheme for weight vector in

Equation 11 is needed. Firstly, the effect of each moment should be studied carefully.

- Open framework: In this paper, we used Hu moments for similarity measure. A combination with any useful features is possible. The feasible low level features to describe an object are color, texture, shape, spatial relationship, motion, etc. Performance study for each feature will be conducted to find some crucial features.

In this paper, the terminology of 'event' and 'action' has been used in a broad sense. Eventually, our scheme should be able to discriminate semantic aspects of different roles, actions, and events for better abstractions of visual signs.

6. REFERENCES

[1] T. Sikora, "The MPEG-4 video standard verification model," *IEEE Trans. Circuits Syst. Video Technology*, vol. 7, pp.19-31, Feb. 1997.

[2] William E. Grimson, *From Images to Surfaces*, The MIT press, pp3-5, 1981.

[3] Rafael C. Gonzalez, Paul Wintz, *Digital Image Processing*, Addison Wesley, 2nd edition, pp173-174, 1987.

[4] H.J.Zhang et al. "An Integrated system for Content-based Video Retrieval and Browing", Pattern recognition, vol. 30, No.4, pp.643-658, 1997.

[5] Til Aach, Andre Kaup, Rudolf Mester, "Statistical model-based change detection in moving video", *Signal Processing*, Vol. 31, No. 2, pp. 165-180, March, 1993.

[6] R. Mech and M. Wollborn, "A noise robust method for segmentation of moving objects in video sequences", *ICASSP97*, Vol.4, pp.2657-2660, April 1997.

[7] A.M.Ferman *et al.*, "Object-Based Indexing of MPEG-4 Compressed Video", SPIE-3024, pp. 953-963, Feb. 1997, San Jose, CA.

[8] J.F. Canny, "A Computational Approach to Edge Detection," *IEEE Transactions on Pattern Analysis and Machine Intelligence*, 6(6) pp.679-698, November 1986.

[9] A. Neri et al., "Automatic Moving Object and background Separation," *Signal Processing*, vol.66, pp219-232, 1998.

[10] C. Gu and M-C Lee, "Semantic Segmentation and Tracking of Semantic Video objects," *IEEE Trans. Circuits Syst. Video Technology*, vol. 8, pp.572-584, Sep. 1998.

[11] L. Shapiro, *"Computer Vision,"* Prentice Hall, to be published.

[12] http://students.washington.edu/cikim/cidil/mos/mos3.html

[14] M.Wollborn and R. Mech, "Refined procedure for objective evaluation of video generation algorithms," Doc. ISO/IEC JTC1/SC29/WG11 M3448, March, 1998.

[15] M. Hu, "Visual pattern recognition by moment invariants", IRE Trans. Information Theory, IT-8(2), pp. 179-182, Feb. 1962.

[16] Ju Guo *et al.*, "Fast and accurate moving object extraction technique for MPEG-4 object-based video coding," SPIE, vol.3653, pp.1210-1221, January, 1999.

[17] Changick Kim and Jenq-Neng Hwang, "Fast and Robust Moving Object Segmentation in Video Sequences," *IEEE international conference on Image Processing* (ICIP'99), Kobe, Japan, Oct. 1999.

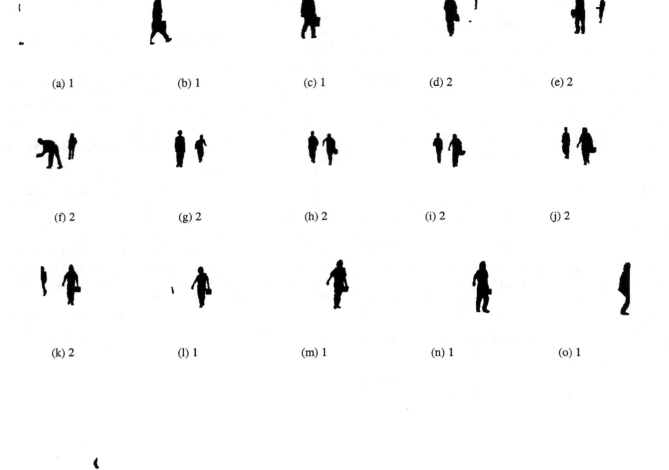

(a) 1   (b) 1   (c) 1   (d) 2   (e) 2

(f) 2   (g) 2   (h) 2   (i) 2   (j) 2

(k) 2   (l) 1   (m) 1   (n) 1   (o) 1

(p) 1   (q) 0

Fig.11: Extracted key frames from ground truths. Frame no. (a)15, (b)26, (c)48, (d)77, (e)88, (f)111, (g)151, (h)197, (i)210, (j)221, (k)239, (l)250, (m)274, (n)292, (o)307, (p)318, (q)329. Numbers denote the number of labeled regions in the frame. Note that some regions smaller than a predefined size are ignored in the KFE stage.

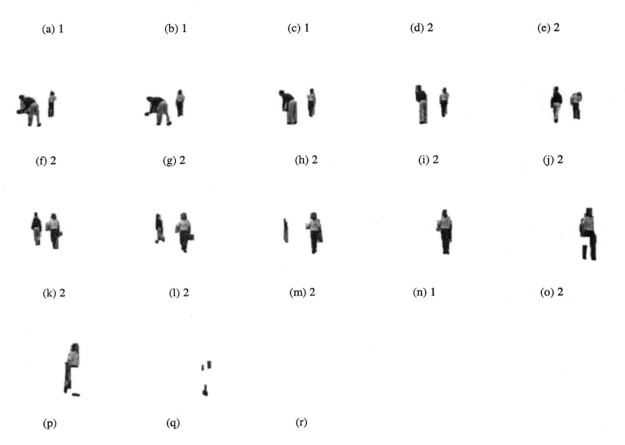

(a) 1   (b) 1   (c) 1   (d) 2   (e) 2

(f) 2   (g) 2   (h) 2   (i) 2   (j) 2

(k) 2   (l) 2   (m) 2   (n) 1   (o) 2

(p)   (q)   (r)

Fig.12: Extracted key frames generated by the integrated system. Frame no. (a)15, (b)26, (c)51, (d)76, (e)87, (f)106, (g)117, (h)132, (i)143, (j)164, (k)203, (l)235, (m)246, (n)257, (o)293, (p)304, (q)315, (r)326. Numbers denote the number of labeled regions in the frame. Note that some regions smaller than a predefined size are ignored in the KFE stage.

Evaluating Strategies and Systems for Content Based Indexing of Person Images on the Web*

Yuksel Alp Aslandogan
Navigation Technologies Corporation
10400 W. Higgins Rd.
Rosemont, IL 60018 USA
yaslando@chi.navtech.com
yaslando@eecs.uic.edu

Clement T. Yu
Department of EECS
University of Illinois at Chicago
Chicago IL 60607
yu@eecs.uic.edu

ABSTRACT

Content based indexing of multimedia has always been a challenging task. The enormity and the diversity of the multimedia content on the web adds another dimension to this challenge. In this paper, we examine ways of combining visual and textual information for content based indexing of multimedia on the web. In particular, we examine different methods of combining evidences due to face detection, Text/HTML analysis and face recognition for identifying person images. We provide experimental evaluation of the following strategies: i) Face detection on the image followed by Text/HTML analysis of the containing page; ii) face detection followed by face recognition; iii) face detection followed by a linear combination of evidences due to text/HTML analysis and face recognition; and iv) face detection followed by a Dempster-Shafer combination of evidences due to text/HTML analysis and face recognition. These strategies were implemented in an automatic web search agent named **Diogenes**[1] and compared against some well known web image search engines. The latter includes commercial systems such as AltaVista, Lycos and Ditto, and a research prototype, WebSEEk. We report the results of our experimental retrievals where Diogenes outperformed these search engines for celebrity image queries in terms of average precision.

Keywords

Content based image retrieval, Dempster-Shafer theory, evidence combination, web image retrieval, face detection and recognition.

---

*Research supported in part by NSF grants ISR-95 08953 and NSF-IIS-9902792

[1] After philosopher Diogenes of Sinope, d.c. 320 B.C. who is said to have gone about Athens with a lantern in day time looking for an honest man.

1. INTRODUCTION

Past are the days when database and information management systems had to deal with simple data types such as numbers, character strings and dates. Today, support for multimedia data types along with the traditional ones is widespread[5]. The capability to handle multimedia is typically offered in the form of special plug-in modules. Informix "data blades", Oracle's "cartridges" and IBM DB2's "multimedia extensions" are examples of such specialized modules. Content based indexing of multimedia is an important part of this integration which may require different mechanisms for extracting and possibly integrating multiple features. Loosely structured, vast collections such as the web bring another dimension to this already challenging task. While some companies could have a "copy" of the whole web during the early years of web's development, today even powerful search engines such as AltaVista and Excite only index a fraction of the web. A common thread between these very different environments is the need to index and effectively retrieve multimedia content.

In this work we evaluate mechanisms for finding and classifying facial images on the World Wide Web (the *web* in the sequel) by combining evidences due to different types of information. A web-based image search agent called **Diogenes**[3] retrieves web pages and associates a person name with each facial image on those pages. To accomplish its goal, Diogenes relies on two types of evidence: Visual and textual. A face detection module examines the images on the web page for human faces. A face recognition module identifies the face by using a database of known person images. A text/HTML analysis module analyzes the body of the text with the aim of finding clues about who appears in each image. The outputs of the face detection, text/HTML analysis and face recognition modules are merged using different evidence combination mechanisms to classify each image.

A key contribution of this paper is the quantitative evaluation of various search engines for person image retrieval from the web. We have evaluated three commercial systems and a research prototype in terms of their average precision in answering person image queries and compared them with Diogenes. Results of both individual searches and average precision-recall characteristics are reported. In these experiments, Diogenes had better average precision than the other four search engines.

Another contribution is the evaluation of different evidence combination methods for combining visual and textual clues in classifying person images as implemented by Diogenes. These methods include the following:

- *Using face detection as screening for text/HTML analysis:* Images on a retrieved web page are first screened by a face detector module. If there is any image that contains a human face, then this page is further analyzed by the text/HTML analysis module.

- *Face detection combined with face recognition:* Images that contain a human face are submitted to the face recognition module which assigns a degree of similarity between the retrieved image and the images selected from our database. the selection is based on whether a person's name is mentioned in the tag text or full text of the web page.

- A linear combination of the evidence due to text/HTML analysis and that due to face recognition.

- A Dempster-Shafer combination of the evidence due to text/HTML analysis and that due to face recognition.

In the rest of the paper we first look at the related work in the area of content based image retrieval from the web. We then give an overview of the system architecture of Diogenes in section 3. This section also introduces the visual and textual features used by the image classifier. In sections 4.1, 4.2 and 4.3 we describe the simple, Linear and Dempster-Shafer methods for evidence combination respectively and how each is applied to the image retrieval domain. The results of our quantitative evaluation of web image search engines and evidence combination strategies are given in section 5. Finally, section 6 summarizes key points of the paper and proposes areas for further research.

2. RELATED WORK

A number of web image search engines have been been built in recent years including both research prototypes and commercial ones. Among the former category are WebSeer [23], WebSEEk[2] [22], ImageScape[3], Amore[4] [14], WebHunter [15], ImageRover [24, 12], and PicToSeek [9]. Commercial web text search engines such as Lycos, AltaVista and Yahoo also offer image search facilities. Commercial image search engine Ditto emphasizes timely celebrity image searches. Among these systems, WebSEEk, WebSeer, WebHunter, AltaVista, Lycos and Ditto are the most similar to our system in terms of their functionality and scope. We will overview some of these systems in terms of the features they use to index images and how they resemble or differ from Diogenes.

On a web (HTML) page, there are two kinds of text: The *tag* texts are the pieces of text enclosed in special HTML tags. They contain information such as the name or the URL (the web address) of the image, and an alternative

---

[2]http://www.ctr.columbia.edu/webseek
[3]http://www.wi.leidenuniv.nl/home/lim/image.scape.html
[4]http://www.ccrl.com/amore/

text which appears in place of the image on a text-only web browser. The *full text* or the body text are the pieces of text that are not part of any HTML tag in the body of the page. Both WebSEEk and to a large extent WebSeer rely on the words found in the image *tag* text to index images. **Diogenes** on the other hand uses both the tag text and the *full text* of the web page.

Both WebSEEk and WebSeer analyze their images visually, but for different purposes. WebSEEk emphasizes the color information in images to facilitate visual query by example. The user can either select an existing image and retrieve similar images, or construct an image by using graphic elements [22]. WebSEEk indexes video clips by content in addition to images. WebSeer on the other hand uses several visual criteria to classify images as graphs, cartoons, photographs, clip art, etc. Both systems organize their images into conceptual categories. A user interested in people images is directed to the "people" category. WebSEEk apparently uses only textual information for this conceptual categorization. WebSeer goes one step further in image analysis by integrating a face detector. Consequently its accuracy is much better than WebSEEk in people queries. Diogenes uses both a face detector and a face recognition module in analyzing images visually. The image search engine Ditto also has conceptual categories such as animals, architecture, science, sports and people. However, it was not possible to limit a search to a specific category at the time of this writing.

WebHunter is a portrait image search engine for the web [15]. This system relies on web text search engines for an initial set of pages. The user describes the pictures he is interested in with a query. This query is submitted to a web text search engine such as AltaVista. The resulting pages returned from AltaVista are further analyzed. Words from the title of the document, image links and the matching words between the query and the full text of the page are assigned weights. A visual analysis module examines the images with a model of a portrait. If the image fits the model, it is indexed according to the result of the textual analysis.

To the authors' knowledge, the retrieval performances of WebSeer or WebHunter are not reported in the literature and no web interfaces were available as of this writing.

The commercial image search engines, Lycos[5] and AltaVista[6] apparently do not perform visual analysis and rely heavily on the *tag* text.

In addition to using tag and full texts and a face detector, Diogenes incorporates a face recognition module and uses Dempster-Shafer evidence combination method with object recognition and automatic, local uncertainty assessment. When a text/HTML analysis module or a visual analysis module assigns a degree of similarity between an image and a person name, there are degrees of uncertainty associated with both these values. In Diogenes' case, both of these modules produce numeric values indicating their degrees of uncertainty. These values are obtained *automati-*

---

[5]http://multimedia.lycos.com
[6]http://jump.altavista.com/st_im

cally (without user interaction) and *locally* (separately for each retrieval/classification).

3. OVERVIEW

Diogenes is a web-based, automated image search agent designed specifically for person facial images. It travels the web off-line and builds an index. In response to a query for "Bill Gates" it searches its index and prepares a page containing Bill Gates images. Figure 1 shows a snapshot of Diogenes search results for "Bill Gates" query.[7] Diogenes works with

Figure 1: A snapshot of Diogenes search results for Bill Gates.

the web pages that contain a facial image accompanied by a body of text. The approach is to take advantage of the *full text* and HTML structure of web pages in addition to the visual analysis of the images themselves and to combine the two pieces of information.

The first step in this process is to retrieve pages from the World Wide Web. This is done by the "Crawler" which is a web client program that uses HTTP protocol to request

---

[7]Although a web interface could not be provided for Diogenes as of this writing, sample result pages are available at http://www.eecs.uic.edu/~yaslando/diogenes. Please note that some images appear much smaller than their original size on this page because they were scaled down making the person's face indistinguishable in certain cases. To view the full images when the thumbnail is too small, use your browser's "view image" function. Also, images which are essentially the same but found on different web sites are not eliminated following the convention of other research and commercial image search engines. Please contact the first author for further information about the web interface.

pages from web servers. The crawler initially submits a text query to full text search engines such as Google, AltaVista, and Snap. It merges the returned lists of URLs and visits each URL for analysis. A face detector analyzes each page to detect facial images. The output of this module is input to two other modules: A text/HTML module and a face recognition module. The text and HTML structure of the page is analyzed to locate person names and determine their degree of association with each image. The face in each image is input to the face recognition module. Based on the outputs of these modules and depending on the combination mechanism, Diogenes associates each image containing a face with a person name. We describe the visual and text/HTML features used by the classifier further below.

3.1 Visual Features

The visual features used by the classifier of Diogenes consists of the outputs of face detection and face recognition modules. The neural network-based face detection module [16] examines an image to find a human face. If a face is found, the location is indicated to an intermediate module which crops (cuts out) the facial portion and submits it to both text/HTML analysis and face recognition modules. Diogenes uses a face recognition module which implements the eigen-face method [25, 18]. This module uses a set of known facial images for training. Each of these training images has an associated person name with it. At recognition time, a set of distance values between the input image and those of the training set are reported. These distances indicate how dissimilar the input image is to the training images. In addition, a global distance value called "Distance From Face Space" or DFFS is also reported. This is the global distance of the input image from the facial image space spanned by the training images. Diogenes uses this latter value to determine the uncertainty of the recognition.

3.2 Text/HTML Features

The text/HTML analysis module of Diogenes determines a degree of association between each person name on a web page and each facial image on that page. This degree of association is based on two factors: Page-level statistics and local (or structural) statistics. Page-level statistics such as frequency of occurrence and location-within-the-page (title, keyword, body text etc.) are independent of any particular image. Local/structural statistics are those factors that relate a name to an image. In an earlier work [1, 2], we have shown that structured queries and image descriptions provide a better framework for matching different descriptions of the same phenomenon as opposed to free text descriptions. Diogenes takes advantage of the HTML structure of a web page in determining the degree of association between a person name and an image. The factors of interest include whether the name occurs in proximity of the image, whether they are enclosed in the same HTML tag, whether the name is part of the image URL/path. We describe these further below:

- *Frequency:* The significance of a name is proportional to its number of occurrences within the page and inversely proportional to its number of occurrences on the whole web. This is known as the $tf * idf$ (term frequency times inverse document frequency) formula

[17, 26]. It captures the premise that if a rare word appears frequently on a page then it is very significant for that page. If a common word, on the other hand appears frequently on a page, it may not be as significant. In either case, the higher the local frequency, the higher the significance. Here we assume that the significance of a person name on a web page is proportional to the likelihood that he/she will be depicted in an image on that page.

- *Name or URL Match:* A name that is a substring of the image name or the image URL is assigned a higher significance.

- *Shared HTML Tags:* Names that are enclosed in the same HTML tags with an image are more likely to be associated with that image. For instance, a caption for an image is usually put in the same HTML table on the same column of adjacent rows.

- *Alternate Text:* The alternate text identified by the "ALT" HTML tag generally serves as a suitable textual replacement for an image or a description of it.

4. EVIDENCE COMBINATION
Once the visual and text/HTML features are computed for a particular web page, they can be combined in a number of ways. In the following we examine three approaches for evidence combination: Simple, Linear and Dempster-Shafer. These approaches have been implemented and evaluated experimentally.

4.1 Simple Evidence Combination
Since web queries tend to be very short, the user's intent may be ambiguous. When the user issues a query like "Abraham Lincoln" there is no way of knowing if the user is interested in images of former US president Abraham Lincoln or USS aircraft carrier Abraham Lincoln without further feedback from the user. Hence some of the images returned may be very irrelevant to the user. For people image queries, Diogenes overcomes this problem by incorporating a face detector into its search mechanism.

When a page is retrieved together with any images on it, each image is analyzed by a face detector. If a face is found in one of the images on the page then the text of the page is submitted to the text/HTML analysis (TA) module.

In the next two sections, we will look into ways of combining the output of text/HTML analysis module with that of the face recognition module.

4.2 Linear Evidence Combination
A simple linear combination is a weighted sum of normalized individual features. Diogenes implements a feature-value combination scheme:

$$Score_{combined} = \omega_1 * Score_{FR} + \omega_2 * Score_{TA}$$

Where $Score_{FR}$ and $Score_{TA}$ are the numeric "degree of association" scores assigned to each pair of person name and facial image on a web page by the face recognition and text/HTML analysis modules respectively.

The simplest approach is to assigning weights to classifier inputs is to use constant weights. A more sophisticated approach might improve these weights by various learning algorithms. In the experiments reported in this paper we used a simple arithmetic average, i.e. $\omega_1 = \omega_2 = 0.5$.

4.3 Dempster-Shafer Evidence Combination
Dempster-Shafer Theory of Evidence (a.k.a. Mathematical Theory Of Evidence) is intended to be a generalization of Bayesian theory of subjective probability [19]. It provides a method for combining independent bodies of evidence using Dempster's rule.

4.3.1 Dempster's Rule for Evidence Combination
Suppose we are interested in finding the combined evidence for a hypothesis C. Given two **independent** sources of evidence m_1 and m_2, Dempster's rule for their combination is as follows:

$$m_{1,2}(C) = \frac{\sum_{A,B \subseteq \Theta, A \cap B = C} m_1(A)m_2(B)}{\sum_{A,B \subseteq \Theta, A \cap B \neq \emptyset} m_1(A)m_2(B)}$$

Here $m_{1,2}(C)$ is the combined Dempster-Shafer probability for C. m_1 and m_2 are the basic probabilities assigned to sets A and B respectively by two independent sources of evidence. A and B are sets that include C. A and B are not necessarily proper supersets and they may as well be equal to C.

The numerator accumulates the evidence which supports a particular hypothesis and the denominator conditions it on the total evidence for those hypotheses supported by both sources.

4.3.2 Using Dempster-Shafer Theory in Image Retrieval
In this study, we are interested in classifying person images obtained from the web. We have two sources of evidence: The output of a face recognition module (FR) which classifies the image and the output of a text/HTML analysis module (TA) which analyzes the text that accompanies the image. Both modules attempt to identify the person in the image based on different media. We assume that if more than one person appears in an image, identifying one of them is sufficient. We designate the two pieces of evidence as m_{FR} and m_{TA} respectively. By default, these two modules operate independently: The results of face recognition module does not affect the text/HTML score and vice versa. Hence the independence assumption of the theory holds. The text/HTML analysis module determines a degree of association between every person name-facial image pair on the web page. It assigns numerical values to different person names for each image indicating this degree of association. The face recognition module assigns a distance value to each person in our database of known person images. We convert these values to similarity scores. We assume that for any person for which we have no stored image, the face recognition similarity score is zero. If we use Dempster's Rule for combination of evidence we get the following:

$$m_{FR,TA}(C) = \frac{\sum_{A,B \subseteq \Theta, A \cap B = C} m_{FR}(A)m_{TA}(B)}{\sum_{A,B \subseteq \Theta, A \cap B \neq \emptyset} m_{FR}(A)m_{TA}(B)}$$

316

In the case of classification of person images, it is possible to simplify this formulation. Our face recognition and text/HTML analysis modules give us information about individual images and the uncertainty of the recognition/analysis. This means we have only beliefs for singleton classes (persons) and the body of evidence itself ($m(\Theta)$). The latter is the belief that we can not associate with any hypothesis: It accounts for our "ignorance" about those subsets of Θ for which we have no specific belief. Thus, the basic probability assignment to Θ represents the *uncertainty* of the evidence:

$$m(\Theta) = 1 - \sum_{A \subset \Theta} m(A)$$

If in a body of evidence the basic probabilities assigned to proper subsets of Θ add up to 1, then this would make $m(\Theta) = 0$ meaning we have very high confidence in this body of evidence and no uncertainty.

For our image ranking problem, the Dempster combination formula can be simplified as follows:

$$rank(P_C) \propto m_{FR}(P_C)m_{TA}(P_C) + m_{FR}(\Theta)m_{TA}(P_C) \\ + m_{FR}(P_C)m_{TA}(\Theta) \quad (1)$$

Here $\propto$ represents 'is proportional to' relationship. Later on, we shall replace "$\propto$" with "$=$". $m_{FR}(P_C)$ and $m_{TA}(P_C)$ are the beliefs assigned to person P_C by the face recognition and text/HTML analysis modules respectively. $m_{FR}(\Theta)$ and $m_{TA}(\Theta)$ represent the uncertainty in the bodies of evidence m_{FR} and m_{TA} respectively. The beliefs and uncertainties have the following relationships.
For face recognition:

$$m_{FR}(\Theta) = 1 - \sum_{A \subset \Theta} m_{FR}(A)$$

For text/HTML analysis:

$$m_{TA}(\Theta) = 1 - \sum_{A \subset \Theta} m_{TA}(A)$$

The derivation with examples can be found in [4].

The simplified Dempster-Shafer evidence combination formula for image retrieval was originally described by Jose et al. in [11]. In this work, a (non-facial) photograph retrieval system, called **Epic**, that uses Dempster-Shafer evidence combination is reported. The primary difference between Epic and Diogenes is how they obtain and use the uncertainty values: Epic works with non-facial images and does not employ an automatic object recognition module. It lets its users input their confidence in the bodies of evidence prior to retrieval. Diogenes on the other hand uses a face recognition module and automatically determines uncertainty values for both text/HTML and face recognition based on system performance parameters.

The values of the uncertainties $m_{FR}(\Theta)$ and $m_{TA}(\Theta)$ are obtained as follows: For face recognition, we have a "distance from face space" (DFFS) value for each recognition. This value is the distance of the query image to the space of eigenfaces formed from the training images [25]. Diogenes uses the DFFS value to estimate the uncertainty associated with face recognition. If the DFFS value is small, the recognition

is good (uncertainty is low) and vice versa. The following is Diogenes' formula for the uncertainty in face recognition:

$$m_{FR}(\Theta) = 1 - \left(\frac{1}{ln(e + DFFS)} \right)$$

For text analysis, uncertainty is inversely proportional to the maximum value among the set of degree of association values assigned to name-image combinations.

$$m_{TA}(\Theta) = \frac{1}{ln(e + MDA)}$$

Where MDA is the maximum numeric "degree of association" value assigned to a person name with respect to a facial image among other names. As described in section 3.2, each degree of association for an image name pair is a function of the frequency of occurrence of that name, location relative to the image, HTML tags shared with the image, etc.

Both face recognition and text analysis uncertainties are obtained locally, i.e. for each retrieval and automatically without user interaction. This feature distinguishes Diogenes from other applications where the users provide the uncertainties [11].

The following example illustrates the application of the Dempster's combination formula to a simple image classification task:

EXAMPLE 4.1. Let's consider a simple image database containing images of Bill Clinton, Newt Gingrich and Bob Dole. For an input image, we are interested in determining the owner of the image using the Dempster combination formula. For each of these persons we assume the following values for our parameters:

$$
\begin{aligned}
m_{FR}(Clinton) &= 0.25 \\
m_{FR}(Gingrich) &= 0.10, \\
m_{FR}(Dole) &= 0.05 \\
m_{TA}(Clinton) &= 0.10 \\
m_{TA}(Gingrich) &= 0.25 \\
m_{TA}(Dole) &= 0.25 \\
m_{FR}(\Theta) &= 0.6 \\
m_{TA}(\Theta) &= 0.4
\end{aligned}
$$

By (1),

$$
\begin{aligned}
m_{FR,TA}(Clinton) &= 0.25 * 0.10 + 0.25 * 0.40 + 0.10 * 0.60 \\
&= 0.185
\end{aligned}
$$

$$
\begin{aligned}
m_{FR,TA}(Gingrich) &= 0.10 * 0.25 + 0.10 * 0.40 + 0.25 * 0.60 \\
&= 0.215
\end{aligned}
$$

$$
\begin{aligned}
m_{FR,TA}(Dole) &= 0.05 * 0.25 + 0.05 * 0.40 + 0.25 * 0.60 \\
&= 0.1825
\end{aligned}
$$

Hence, according to our Dempster-Shafer-based classifier, Gingrich is the most likely owner of this image among the three candidates because the combined evidence for Gingrich is the largest of the three. The ranking is 1. Gingrich 2. Clinton and 3. Dole. Note that $m_{TA}(Gingrich) =$

$m_{FR}(Clinton)$ and $m_{FR}(Gingrich) = m_{TA}(Clinton)$ but TA has a lower degree of uncertainty than FR. This makes Gingrich rank higher than Clinton.

5. EXPERIMENTAL RESULTS

A set of experimental retrievals were performed where search engines were compared in terms of average precision in answering people image queries. Ten popular person names were chosen randomly from among the people who appeared in the news headlines during the course of development of Diogenes. Four search engines were available for this evaluation: WebSeek, Lycos (multimedia/picture search), AltaVista, and Ditto. Among the other systems mentioned in the introduction, WebSeer project was discontinued and hence the web interface was not available for this evaluation. Also, no web interface was available for WebHunter. The people images database of Yahoo Image Surfer[8] was too limited to be included in this study[9]. For AltaVista, the image search feature was used with the following options: Photos only, web only (no image collections), and no banners.

An image retrieved by a search engine was regarded as relevant if the person named in the query was clearly recognizable in the image. Banners were excluded and cartoons were counted as failures. Since WebSEEk did not allow for multiple word queries, a convention was adopted: Only the last name of the celebrities were used and if there were multiple celebrities with the same last name, anyone was accepted as relevant.

In reviewing the following results it should be noted that not all image search engines are tuned to find person images. Although they index mostly person images they may also index other images of interest such as document images and inanimate object images. An evaluation accepting any image of interest as relevant in response to a person query may reveal different results than what is reported here. Another important point is that the retrieval performance of search engines change over time as they index more material. They may change their search algorithms as well. The numbers reported in this paper represent only a snapshot of their performances as of this writing.

Table 1 and Figure 2 show the search results of this experiment. In Table 1 we report the average precision of different search engines over top 20 images for 10 queries. In Figure 2 we report the global average precision for the same set of engines for different number of images retrieved.

In Table 1 there are two rows for each search engine. The first row shows the average precision: the number of relevant images among the top 20 retrieved images. The number 20 was chosen based on the observation that users of web search engines typically do not browse beyond the top two pages of results and a typical results page contains 10 images. Although usage statistics exclusively for web image search engines are not readily available, there are indications that this number may be higher for image search engines[10].

For this reason, we also report the average precision over top 30 and 40 images in Figure 2. The second row in Table 1 shows the total number of images returned for the query. If the total recall number is less than 20, then the precision is computed over this total.

The average precision of Diogenes in Table 1 (0.94) is higher than the average precision of each of the other three search engines. Its total recall is much better than that of WebSEEk. Due to the limited amount of time available to Diogenes to retrieve its images, its average recall is not as high as AltaVista or Lycos[11], but comparable to Ditto.

In Figure 2 we report the average precision of the same set of search engines, namely AltaVista, Lycos, Ditto and Diogenes, over varying number of images. This figure illustrates that Diogenes' lead over the other search engines continues over a larger range of images. An interesting point to observe in this figure is that the average precision of Diogenes and Ditto decreased uniformly as the interval for the average was increased. This may indicate that these two systems rank their resulting images more effectively than the others.

Table 2 shows how the different combinations implemented by Diogenes fare against each other. As before, the number in each cell shows the average precision over the top 20 retrieved images for a particular query. The first row shows the retrieval results based on text/HTML evidence preceded by face detection. In other words, the page is analyzed by the text/html module only if it contained a facial image. The second row shows the results when the search agent relied on face detection and recognition alone. The third row is for linear evidence combination as described in section 4.2 and the fourth row is for Dempster-Shafer evidence combination approach.

The comparison of retrieval results in Table 2 for text/html analysis with face detection, linear combination and dempster shafer combination reveals that neither of the combination strategies was able to provide any further improvement in precision beyond text/HTML analysis following face detection. Elsewhere [3], we have shown that when the average precision of individual methods are far from the optimum, Dempster-Shafer evidence combination mechanism provides significant improvement. In Table 2 ,however, since the average precision obtained by the screening combination (face detection followed by text/HTML analysis) was near the optimum, neither of the evidence combination mechanisms improved the performance any further. The circumstances under which the evidence combination strategies provide the most benefit is currently being investigated.

6. CONCLUSION AND FUTURE WORK

We have presented the results of our experimental evaluation of different strategies and systems for content based person image retrieval from the web. The web offers a rare opportunity for indexing multimedia: A significant amount of multimedia content is accompanied by textual context.

---

[8] http://ipix.yahoo.com
[9] For instance, the "Bill Clinton" query returned only seven images three of which were irrelevant.
[10] See, for instance, the web search engine usage statistics at http://www.alexa.com and http://www.searchenginewatch.com.
[11] In a sequel to this experiment where Diogenes retrieved more URLs, it has matched and sometimes surpassed the total retrieval numbers of Lycos and Ditto.

Srch. Eng.		Q1	Q2	Q3	Q4	Q5	Q6	Q7	Q8	Q9	Q10	Avg.
WebSEEk	prec.	.70	.55	.67	N/A	1.0	.05	1.0	.55	0	N/A	.57
	total	43	9	3	0	5	107	2	13	1	N/A	
AltaVista	prec.	.60	.40	.40	.70	.80	.65	.70	.70	.70	.55	.62
	total	16112	3786	2304	2146	568	13864	1321	650	1039	1307	
Lycos	prec.	.60	.90	.75	.80	.85	.90	.80	.65	.65	.35	.73
	total	1234	355	98	283	123	839	72	129	89	27	
Ditto	prec.	1.0	.65	.95	.95	.82	.90	.50	.90	.95	.50	.81
	total	622	426	79	385	17	307	4	44	127	48	
Diogenes	prec.	.90	.90	.1.0	1.0	.95	.85	1.0	.85	.1.0	.95	.94
	total	445	266	124	285	89	61	56	43	95	113	

Table 1: Performance comparison of different search engines over 10 queries. Legend: Avg.: Average precision over 10 queries; prec.: Average precision for a single query over top 20 images; Q1:Bill Clinton Q2:Hillary Clinton Q3:Kenneth Starr Q4:Monica Lewinsky Q5: Madeleine Albright Q6: Bill Gates Q7:Benjamin Netanyahu Q8:Boris Yeltsin Q9:Rush Limbaugh Q10:OJ Simpson

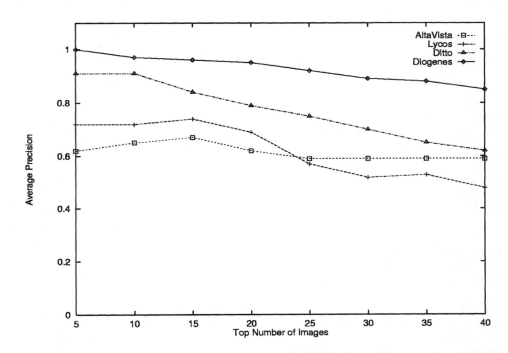

Figure 2: Average precision plots of different search engines as a function of number of images at the top.

Retrieval Method		Q1	Q2	Q3	Q4	Q5	Q6	Q7	Q8	Q9	Q10	Avg.
FD,Text/HTML	precision	.90	.90	1.0	1.0	.95	.95	1.0	.85	1.0	.85	.94
	total	480	335	326	346	166	65	79	58	120	124	
Face Recognition	precision	.30	.65	.25	.75	.55	.50	.40	.30	.50	.85	.56
	total	447	247	221	219	105	46	57	113	101	107	
Linear	precision	.85	.90	1.0	1.0	.95	.85	1.0	.85	1.0	1.0	.94
	total	445	266	124	285	89	61	56	43	95	113	
Dempster-Shafer	precision	.90	.90	1.0	1.0	.95	.85	1.0	.85	1.0	.95	.94
	total	445	266	124	285	89	61	56	43	95	113	

Table 2: Performance comparison of different retrieval strategies implemented by Diogenes. Legend: Avg.: Average precision over 10 queries; Q1:Bill Clinton Q2:Hillary Clinton Q3:Kenneth Starr Q4:Monica Lewinsky Q5: Madeleine Albright Q6: Bill Gates Q7:Benjamin Netanyahu Q8:Boris Yeltsin Q9:Rush Limbaugh Q10:OJ Simpson

This enables search agents such as Diogenes to take advantage of both textual and visual clues in indexing this content. Unfortunately, the textual descriptions are far from being structured and the quality of multimedia may be low. To address these challenges different evidence combination mechanisms were implemented by Diogenes, a person-image search agent. The strategies include using face detection as screening and combining text, face detection and face recognition via different mechanisms.

The performance of Diogenes was compared with those of other image search engines such as WebSEEk, AltaVista, Lycos and Ditto. The results obtained suggest the potential of evidence combination mechanisms in indexing multimedia on the web and in other collections.

Other evidence combination mechanisms which we haven't experimented with in this work include Bayesian combination, neural networks and fuzzy sets[27]. These mechanisms and others have been proven to be effective in various contexts including image retrieval[10, 12]. In text retrieval, combining different query expressions and results of different retrieval algorithms have also been shown to be effective [13, 6].

Our research is currently focused on incorporating user feedback mechanisms into Diogenes. Giving the user the ability to designate images as relevant or irrelevant have been demonstrated to improve retrieval performance in both text and image retrieval systems [8, 24, 21]. Another promising area of research is the use of spatial relationships [20]. Since a number of objects can now be identified with the help of computer vision modules, the relationships among these objects can be used to express concept queries [7].

Acknowledgments

We would like to thank Matthew Turk (work done at MIT), Alex Pentland (MIT), Takeo Kanade (CMU) and Henry A. Rowley(CMU) for making software available for this project.

7. REFERENCES

[1] Y. Alp Aslandogan, Charles Thier, and Clement T. Yu. A System for Effective Content Based Image Retrieval (Prototype Demonstration). In *Proceedings of ACM Multimedia Conference*, pages 429–430, Boston, MA, November 1996.

[2] Y. Alp Aslandogan, Charles Thier, Clement T. Yu, Jun Zou, and Naphtali Rishe. Using Semantic Contents and WordNet(TM) in Image Retrieval. In *Proceedings of ACM SIGIR Conference*, Philadelphia, PA, 1997.

[3] Y. Alp Aslandogan and Clement Yu. Multiple Evidence Combination in Image retrieval: Diogenes Searches for People on the Web. In *Proceedings of ACM SIGIR 2000, Athens, Greece*, July 2000.

[4] Y. Alp Aslandogan and Clement Yu. Multiple Evidence Combination in Image retrieval: Diogenes Searches for People on the Web. Technical Report UIC-EECS-00-1, Department of EECS, University of Illinois at Chicago, January 2000.

[5] Y. Alp Aslandogan and Clement T. Yu. Techniques and Systems for Content Based Image and Video Retrieval. *IEEE TKDE Special Issue on Multimedia Retrieval*, 11(1):56–63, January 1999.

[6] Nicholas J. Belkin, Paul B. Kantor, Edward A. Fox, and J. A. Shaw. Combining the Evidence of Multiple Query Representations for Information Retrieval. *Information Processing and Management*, 31(3):431–448, 1995.

[7] Chua, T., Pung, H., Lu, G., and Jong, H. A Concept Based Image Retrieval System. In *IEEE Int'nl Conf. on system Sciences*, pages 590–598, January 1994.

[8] Faloutsos C., Barber R., Flickner M., Hafner J., Niblack W., Petkovic D., and Equitz W. Efficient and Effective Querying by Image Content. *Journal of Intelligent Information Systems*, 3(1):231–262, 1994.

[9] Theo Gevers and Arnold W. M. Smeulders. PicToSeek: A Content-Based Image Search System for the World Wide Web. In *Proceedings of SPIE Visual 97*, 1997.

[10] David L. Hall. *Mathematical Techniques in Multisensor Data Fusion*. Artech House, 1992.

[11] Joemon M. Jose, Jonathan Furner, and David J. Harper. Spatial Querying for Image Retrieval: A User Oriented Evaluation. In *ACM SIGIR*, pages 232–240, 1998.

[12] Marco LaCascia, Saratendu Sethi, and Stan Sclaroff. Combining Textual and Visual Cues for Content-based Image Retrieval on the World Wide Web. In *Proceedings of IEEE Workshop on Content-Based Access of Image and Video Libraries*, June 1998.

[13] Joon Ho Lee. Analyses of Multiple Evidence Combination. In *Proceedings of ACM SIGIR*, pages 267–275, 1997.

[14] Sougata Mukherjea, Kyoji Hirata, and Yoshinori Hara. AMORE: A World Wide Web Image Retrieval Engine. *World Wide Web*, 2(3):115–132, 1999.

[15] Olaf Munkelt, Oliver Kaufmann, and Wolfgang Eckstein. Content-based Image Retrieval in the World Wide Web: A Web Agent for Fetching Portraits. In *Proceedings of SPIE Vol. 3022*, pages 408–416, 1997.

[16] Henry A. Rowley, Shumeet Baluja, and Takeo Kanade. Neural Network-Based Face Detection. *IEEE Transactions on Pattern Analysis and Machine Intelligence*, 20(1):23–38, Jan 1998.

[17] Salton, G. *Automatic Text Processing*. Addison Wesley, Mass., 1989.

[18] A. Samal and P. A. Iyengar. Automatic Recognition and Analysis of Human Faces and Facial Expressions. *Pattern Recognition*, 25(1):65–77, February 1992.

[19] Glenn Shafer. *A Mathematical Theory of Evidence*. Princeton University Press, 1976.

[20] P. A. Sistla, C. T. Yu, and A. Haddad. Reasoning about Spatial Relationships in Picture Retrieval Systems. In *Proceedings of the 20th VLDB Conference*, pages 570–581, Santiago, Chile, 1994.

[21] Alan F. Smeaton and Ian Qigley. Experiments on Using Semantic Distances Between Words in Image Caption Retrieval. In *Proceedings of ACM SIGIR Conference*, 1996.

[22] J. R. Smith and S. F. Chang. Visually Searching the Web for Content. *IEEE Multimedia*, 4(3):12–20, July-September 1997.

[23] Michael J. Swain, Charles Frankel, and Vassilis Athitsos. WebSeer: An Image Search Engine for the World Wide Web. Technical Report TR-96-14, University of Chicago, Department of Computer Science, July 1996.

[24] Leonid Taycher, Marco LaCascia, and Stan Sclaroff. Image Digestion and Relevance Feedback in the ImageRover WWW Search Engine. In *Proceedings of SPIE Visual 97*, 1997.

[25] M. Turk and A. Pentland. Eigenfaces for Recognition. *Cognitive Neuroscience*, 3(1):71–86, 1991.

[26] Clement T. Yu and Weiyi Meng. *Principles of Database Query Processing for Advanced Applications*. Data Management Systems. Morgan Kaufmann, 1998.

[27] Lotfi Zadeh. A Simple View of the Dempster-Shafer Theory of Evidence and Its Implications for the Rule of Combination. Technical Report 33, The Institute of Cognitive Studies, University of California at Berkeley, November 1985.

A Situated Computing Framework for Mobile and Ubiquitous Multimedia Access using Small Screen and Composite Devices

Thai-Lai Pham
Multimedia/Video Department
Siemens Corporate Research, Inc.
755 College Road East
Princeton, NJ 08540
001 609 734 3344

pham@scr.siemens.com

Georg Schneider
Multimedia/Video Department
Siemens Corporate Research, Inc.
755 College Road East
Princeton, NJ 08540
001 609 734 3651

gschneider@scr.siemens.com

Stuart Goose
Multimedia/Video Department
Siemens Corporate Research, Inc.
755 College Road East
Princeton, NJ 08540
001 609 734 3391

sgoose@scr.siemens.com

ABSTRACT

In recent years, small screen devices, such as cellular phones or Personal Digital Assistants (PDAs), enjoy phenomenal popularity. PDAs can be used to complement traditional computing systems to access personal multimedia information beyond the usage as digital organizers. However, due to the physical limitations accessing rich multimedia contents and diverse services using a single PDA is more difficult. Hence, the Situated Computing Framework (SCF) research project at Siemens Corporate Research (SCR) aims to develop a ubiquitous computing infrastructure that facilitates nomadic users to access rich multimedia contents using small screen devices. This paper describes a new distributed computing concept, the *Small Screen/Composite Device (SS/CD)* framework, which offers mobile users new classes of ubiquitous and mobile multimedia services without to limit the diversity and the richness of the provided services.

Keywords

Situated computing, mobile and ubiquitous computing, composite devices, WWW

1. INTRODUCTION

The World Wide Web (WWW) has significantly changed and is still continuing to change the information society. It has never been easier to access such a giant resource of information by using just simple mouse clicks. Concurrent, Internet technologies as well as standards facilitate the representation of information in Multimedia format. Much effort was invested to build systems and infrastructures for one to appreciate multimedia WWW contents/services and to ensure reliable Internet traffic.

However, the majority of these activities are focusing on desktop computing systems. Nowadays, small screen computing devices, such as Personal Digital Assistants (PDAs), Handheld PC (H/PC) or cellular phones, enjoy enormous popularity. The phenomenal growth and rising demand as well as reliance of nomadic users to access Internet content anywhere at any time have further driven the future of computers towards to mobile and ubiquitous computing. That is to break away from a desktop-centric world and to move into the world that surrounds the users. The discipline *situated computing* [14] investigates techniques to provide a more ubiquitous and user-centric computing environment. While the last two decades was marked by the *immobile* Internet, we are now witnessing the strong move towards to the *mobile* Internet, which rather complements and extends traditional systems than replacing it.

At Siemens Corporate Research (SCR), one research focus has been identified to investigate techniques and methodologies to provide mobile users access to rich multimedia information and diverse services by using small screen devices. This research effort is aimed to provide a framework that offers small screen device users the possibility to retrieve the same variety of multimedia information and access the same diversity of services as is given by traditional desktop systems while being on the move. This paper describes an innovative distributed architecture, the *Small Screen/Composite Device (SS/CD)* architecture, that implements a more *user-centric* and small screen device focused communication system. We define a composite device as compositions of available hardware resources that surround user's current location, such as PCs, workstations, high-resolution monitors, TV set etc. Depending upon the user's current position and situation, the *SS/CD* framework provides a computing infrastructure to incorporate and to outsource computing tasks redirected to computing resources in the close vicinity.

The remainder of this paper is structured as follow: Section 2 provides a brief overview about situated computing. The related work is summarized in section 3. The research motivation is discussed in section 4. Section 5 describes a SCF application scenario. The SCF design goals are described in section 6. Section 7 illustrates and describes the high-level SCF system architecture. Sections 8 and 9 describe the core component of SCF. The status about the current stage is given in section 10. Finally, a discussion about future research directions and conclusion is given in section 11.

Also in the remainder of this paper, the term PDA is used to represent the class of small screen devices.

2. SHORT OVERVIEW OF UBIQUITOUS AND SITUATED COMPUTING

The origin of ubiquitous computing derived from the idea to make any kind of computing devices invisible. That is to create an environment, in which computers are fulfilling tasks for us in the background without being the object of interest [31]. The ubiquitous computing environment is an environment, in which different kind of computers and devices are surrounding us and provide computing services customized and tailored to our needs and demands.

Situated computing is one research direction within the ubiquitous computing research. By considering environmental factors, such as user location, identity, profile etc. [14], situated computing is aimed to provide techniques for developing situation, context-aware and more intelligent mobile computing systems. Hence, these systems are first capable to sense and to detect resources and social events in the surrounding environment of the mobile user. Second, these systems are able to process and to interpret this information as well as to react to it. Third, such systems are further characterized by a more user-centric approach. Consequently, situated computing pursues concrete application scenarios to provide new classes of mobile application and services with a more personal and appropriate behavior. Concurrent, it embodies new methodologies to exploit and to use hardware resources and physical location in a different context.

3. RELATED WORK

This section provides a brief overview about related research activities. Also, it aims to provide an historical view about the conducted research activities in the ubiquitous and mobile computing society since the first discussions.

Many research activities have been conducted since the first discussions and the pioneer work of mobile and ubiquitous computing were published in the early 90s [31,32,33,29]. While the contributions by Weiser [31,32,33] expressed the vision of using computing devices as natural as using pen and paper, the Active Badge System [29] is a system that tracks the current position of people wearing badges in an office environment. Due to the lack of available handy- and pocket-sized computing hardware, many succeeding works are focused on wearable computing systems, such as the Touring Machine by Feiner et al [7] or the Metronaut system by Smailagic et al [26]. A typical wearable computing system consists of a backpack computer, a handheld computer and a head mounted display (HMD). Feiner et al incorporate position tracking and augmented reality technologies to provide virtual urban information on HMD that is overlaid on the actual view of the environment to guide people through university campus [7]. Similar, Smailagic's Metronaut system offers users guidance service and scheduling negotiating possibility [26], but without using augmented reality technology and HMDs. The combination of wearable computer and augmented reality is further explored by the research activities of Rekimoto [21,22,23] and Billinghurst [3]. Both researchers investigate methodologies for mobile virtual collaborative working space that allows users to interact with the real world [21,22,23] and to communicate and collaborate with each other in virtual conference spaces via wearable computers [3]. Therefore,

Rekimoto develops a technique that enables the attachment of digital information to physical devices [22]. In Billinghurst's virtual conference space [3] people equipped with wearable computers and HMDs can walk around and discuss about HTML contents displayed on their HMDs.

Several researchers have focused on methodologies to build service and maintenance systems with more multimedia capabilities. Siewiorek et al [25] develop the mobile service and maintenance system Adtranz that allows mobile service technicians to communicate using media, such as digital data, image and audio, with help desk personnel for remote aid on repairing tasks. Accordingly, technicians have access to HTML structured manual data via a standard web browser on the mobile PC tablet that even offers document annotation and collaboration capability, e.g. application sharing [25]. Audio communication is enabled over a wireless LAN network and IP based telephony software. Although more multimedia is provided, the Adtranz system as well as the above guiding systems are heavy and bulky and therefore are not very pleasant to carry.

Context-awareness issue is a further focus of ubiquitous systems. The Cyberguide system by Abowd et al [1] provides mobile tour guides to university campus. Knowledge of physical user location at present time and in the past, which is identified as context information, is used to provide a guiding system that aims to simulate real guide tours. Although focusing on positioning infrastructure and exploiting context information, Apple's Newton MessagePad [1] is used as the Cyberguide mobile hardware that is in comparison to above described wearable systems much smaller and more convenient to carry.

A most other recent research direction of mobile and ubiquitous computing is the intelligent home [16] and classroom practices [2,15] or in general smart spaces [20]. This group of researches aims to incorporate computing technologies and pervasive devices to enhance human daily life environment and to facilitate it. The Cyberfridge as presented in [15] always informs users about the actual content of the fridge and allows placing of virtual notes for other users on a display mounted on the fridge's door. Smart spaces can provide further services, e.g. to adjust a specific room temperature or to control the room light depending upon the situation and users preference.

Meyers et al [17] describe the application Pebbles that allows multiple PDAs to connect to a PC for collaborative works. Pebbles provides a simple method for a group of people to in turn control applications running on a PC. Although, in Pebbles PDAs are simply used as an additional input device for a group of people to conduct meetings, it demonstrates a new perspective of using this class of devices other than the typical organizer functionalities, such as address book, calculator or memo pad.

With the rising popularity of small screen devices primarily dominated by the PalmPilot, a product line by Palm Inc. [18], one research direction has been focused on developing middleware approaches to deliver multimedia information and services to thin clients. Fox et al [8] develop an adaptive middleware proxy and a graphical web browser for PalmPilot [8] that enables the access of multimedia content on the PalmPilot. That is achieved by adapting the contents into the format that the PalmPilot is able to perform. Smith et al [27] describe in Infopyramid a content adaptation framework to deliver multimedia content, such as video, image, text and audio, to pervasive devices. Infopyramid provides two methodologies, translation and summarization [27], to create different varieties of media data to fit on thin clients.

As described in the literature review many researchers have been active to develop ubiquitous and situation aware systems. However, not many activities have been conducted to build user-centric and PDA-centric systems that are pocket-sized and concurrent enabling the access of rich multimedia content/services. The situated computing framework with the underlined *Small Screen/Composite Device* (SS/CD) architecture approach that is presented in the remainder of this paper, is the first attempt to build such a system.

4. MOTIVATION

Having acknowledged the activities of the mobile and ubiquitous research society and observing future mobile technology trends, we conclude that:

- Small screen device capabilities will change towards more processing power and high-resolution displays.

- Wireless networks and protocols will improve towards more bandwidth. The third generations of wireless network protocols such as GPRS (General Packet Radio Service) [9] and UMTS (Universal Mobile Telecommunications System) [28] offer a much higher bandwidth in comparison to today's available technologies such as CDMA (Code Division Multiple Access) [5]. (CDMA: 9.6 kbps; GPRS: 171.2 kbps; UMTS: 2 Mbit/s) [12].

- The multimedia content and services will change, e.g. trend from *e*-Commerce towards to *m*-Commerce (mobile commerce).

- Due to the requirement of the PDA to be pocket-sized, the maximum physical size of the small screen display will remain the same. While it is likely that the PDA screen resolution and quality will improve, the display size is anticipated to remain constant for a longer period

Being aware of the display limitations and thus the limited graphical user interface of small screen devices, at SCR one research focus has been identified to build a mobile computing and communication system called the Situated Computing Framework (SCF), that differs from previous and current activities in many ways. The SCF aims to provide a system that is:

- *User-centric*: The SCF intends to provide a system that is customized to the need of nomadic users. That is to enable high flexibilities to access multimedia information and services while being mobile.

- *Pervasive:* The SCF is designed to use a pervasive device such as a PDA. This is significant since we aim to build a system that not abuses users by having to carry bulky and heavy devices such as wearable computing systems with HMD. Instead, we use light and pocket-sized devices as access devices.

- *Full multimedia capable:* Although, SCF is a user-centric and PDA-centric concept, it should enable users to access to rich multimedia contents and services without having to compromise much in quality and diversity.

- *To exploit composite devices:* To overcome the conflict of *full multimedia capability* and the *screen display limitations*, the SCF provides an infrastructure to incorporate

surrounding resources in order to offer rich multimedia content and services as the proposed *SS/CD* framework by Pham *et al* [19].

The innovative *SS/CD* approach allows mobile PDA users to access rich multimedia content and services without having to shrink or to tailor the content to match the capabilities of the PDA as e.g. proposed by Fox *et al* [8]. Further, the PDA-centric approach of the *SS/CD* framework avoids users having to carry heavy and bulky equipments, e.g. wearable computing system as used by some related research activities. Hence, the SCF provides the means to dynamic exploit and seek for surrounding available composite devices and to outsource the requested information/services via the PDA redirected to the most appropriate composite elements to fulfill.

5. SCF APPLICATION SCENARIO

The SCF was designed to be adaptable to different working environments depending upon the required services and composite device infrastructure. This section outlines in brief a practice area, which demonstrates the value of the SCF.

Situated Computing in Healthcare Environment

The scenario briefly describes the concept of using a small screen device and the incorporation of composite devices to enhance rich multimedia access on a small screen device. It demonstrates the use of the PDA as a unique communication and access interface. Also, tasks that are not suitable for the PDA to perform are outsourced to more appropriate devices.

Multimedia and ubiquitous computing techniques can be exploited to support the transition of paper-based structure of healthcare environment, such as hospital, towards a more digital-based or hypertext-based infrastructure as proposed by Hsu *et al* [13]. That is the use of hypermedia as innovative means to archive patient data record in a hypertext data structure. Concurrent multimedia can be used to create multimedia reports including annotations. Such kind of dynamic multimedia annotation system is proposed by Sastry *et al* [24].

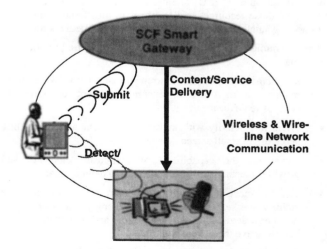

Figure 1. SCF for healthcare scenario

Complementary ubiquitous computing infrastructure provides doctors and nurses with the ability to access these data at any time while being mobile within the hospital vicinity. This kind of communication infrastructure facilitates and provides a better point of care service at patient's bed.

Thus, the SCF can be deployed within a hospital as depicted in figure 1. Each doctor is equipped with a PDA affording wireless access to the hospital patient information system. Visiting a patient, the doctor wishes to query the patient's medical history, including symptoms, diagnoses, prescriptions and x-rays. The PDA first detects the presence of a TV and a telephone in the room using the infrared interface. The PDA then communicates the doctor's request together with details about the detected devices to the SCF gateway server. After authorizing the doctor access and verifying a secure connection, the SCF gateway routes symptoms, diagnoses, and prescriptions directly to the doctor's PDA. As SCF server is aware of the PDA physical limitations, the x-ray image is transmitted via RF to the TV for viewing. The doctor then uses the infrared capability of his PDA to annotate a region of the x-ray. SCF then establishes a telephone call to the patient's original doctor for consultation. This arrangement provides a convenient infrastructure for the doctor to access, view, interact and collaborate upon the multimedia information.

6. AIMS AND DESIGN GOALS
The conflict of physical device limitations and full multimedia capability is overcome by using the PDA and composite device approach. That is to use the PDA as mobile and unique access interface to request structured multimedia information and services. The request performance is outsourced and redirected to the most appropriate element(s) of the composite device available in the close user's vicinity to fulfill. The focus is to avoid having to use a single PDA to perform all tasks. Instead of tying users to the traditional computing environment, we actively seek to exploit it. That is possible, since our daily living environment, both working and home, is evermore equipped with electronic and computing hardware resources (composite elements), such as PCs, workstations, high-resolution monitors, TV, telephones, beamer, etc. Hence, the SS/CD architecture provides techniques to "borrow" these resources and to use it in a different context by supporting small screen devices to process multimedia content.

Hence, a number of design goals have been identified to build the SCF that:

- has the ability to organize, arrange, manage and synchronize multimedia in order to ensure sufficient deliveries to composite devices.

- offers interactivity with multimedia content and controlling services via small screen device.

- recognizes the capabilities of composite elements and provides mechanisms to adapt media to device capabilities.

- able to detect a pool of computing resources in the close vicinity and reacts to its dynamic changing number that is when new devices are available to join and registered devices have to leave the device pool.

- does not require special software to be installed on the PDA and composite devices, except the prerequisites of a WWW browser and the remote invocation ability. Thus, the PDA

user interface is a Web browser, which communicates with the server via standard HTTP protocol.

Overall, the research focus of the SCF can be summarized in to two major steps: First is the development of a new distributed computing infrastructure consisting of composite device(s) and small screen devices that enables rich multimedia access using small screen devices and allows to redirect server responses to composite device(s). Second to provide smart mechanisms for media processing and delivery to composite device(s). The next few sections describe the architecture of SCF that fulfills the design goals.

7. HIGH LEVEL SCF ARCHTECTURE
As described in the earlier section, the SCF is designed to be adaptable to different working environments. A precise system architecture relies upon the concrete application scenario that the SCF is deployed for. Figure 2 illustrates the SCF high-level architecture. As can be appreciated from this picture, the SCF is comprised of a set of components on the server side and client side. The description of each component is given in the next sections.

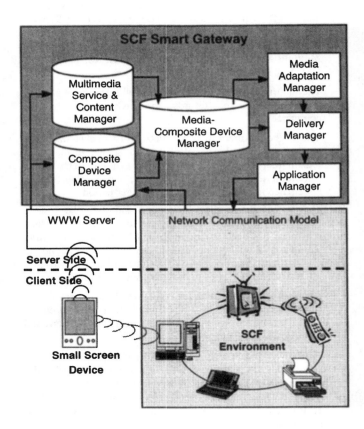

Figure 2. SCF System Architecture

7.1 Server Side Components
The SCF server side is primarily comprised of the WWW server and the SCF Smart Gateway (SG). The following describes in brief the task of each element within the system.

7.1.1 The WWW Server

The WWW server is the entry point for the PDA to access services and contents provided by the SCF network. The use of HTML and HTTP protocol facilitate the access interface significantly. Thus, the WWW server offers the selection of available SCF service and information that users can choose from. Concurrent, the WWW server is able to interpret server side scripting commands that allows the PDA to dynamically update the smart gateway with changes about available composite devices via a markup language structured interface, such as HTML. That strengthens our goal to limit the tasks running on the PDA and to outsource as much as possible to the server side.

7.1.2 SCF Smart Gateway (SG)

The Smart Gateway (SG) is the significant part of the SCF system and is the main research focus of our SCF research. In principal, it fulfills the task of outsourcing user requests to the most appropriate composite elements to ensure reliable performances. It is responsible for the success of the composite device communication infrastructure, which is an alternative paradigm for ubiquitous situated computing to exploit rich multimedia contents and services. The essential components of the SG are (see figure 2):

- *Composite Device Manager*: Primarily the composite device manager maintains the database of available composite elements that can be used to perform certain tasks. Important is the knowledge of the capability(ies) of each composite element. E.g. if a PC is equipped with soundcard and speakers or the monitor resolution of a workstation. This is essential to support the Media-Composite Device Manager (see description below) to assign the selected services and information request to the most appropriate device for the performance. The number of composite elements and its availability is either updated by the PDA or directly by the pool of composite elements on the client side.

- *Multimedia Service & Content Manager*: This component provides and manages the pool of available multimedia services and information. Depending upon the selection and requested content it handles the communication with the corresponded content storage server, such as streaming media server. E.g., in the described scenario it enables specific applications based on the doctor's location, identity and privileges.

- *Media-Composite Device Manager*: The media-composite device manager is another important component of the smart gateway. It is responsible for the assignment of requested services and information to the most appropriate composite element to perform the tasks. As shown in the scenario, the x-ray image is redirect to the TV for display instead sending it to the PDA. The mechanisms for decision making is described in more details in a later section.

- *Media Adaptation Manager:* In cases, when the available composite devices are not capable to handle requested contents and services, this component will provide a set of different techniques to adapt the media to the capabilities of the composite devices. For example, a user queries a multimedia video message via his PDA, but only a PC without speakers and a telephone are available. The media

adaptation manager will split the video into a visual part for the PC and an audio part for the telephone.

- *Delivery Manager:* The order and sequence of service delivery are essential when multiple services are selected. This is important to avoid the performance of all service requests at the same time. Therefore, the device manager maintains a number of criteria that can be used to calculate an optimal service delivery.

- *Application Manager:* The abilities of the SG to offer services to users, identifying appropriate devices for the performance of selected media, the conversion of media if necessary and the determination of an appropriate delivery order are crucial. But important is also the ability of the SG to invoke processes running remotely on available output devices and to control and interact with the invoked application (see section 9), which are tasks of the application manager. The remote process invocation on composite devices requires the SG to be authorized to access the composite elements and special security settings. Furthermore, the application manager hosts a pool of controls or helper applications that can be downloaded by the composite device to perform requested services.

Section 8 describes some aiding components that assist the SG fulfilling its tasks.

7.1.3 SCF Network Communication Model

As depicted in figure 2, the communication model is an overlapping component between server and client side. In principal, its task is to manage the convergence of wireless and wire line networks, as well as the corresponding communication protocols. This is necessary to ensure a seamless device communication and data transmission. The network communication model includes short-range wireless communication used by the PDA to detect available output devices in user's vicinity and cellular or wireless network to support the interaction between the PDA and the SG. In addition, it provides the network infrastructure to enable SG and composite device communication for the redirection of requested information as well as remotely invoking processes on composite elements to deliver requested services.

7.2 Client Side Components

The client side of the SCF system consists mainly of the PDA, SCF Environment and a network communication infrastructure that is part of the network communication model.

Three main and important functions are primarily designated to the PDA. First, the PDA is used as a unique interface to access information and services provided by the SCF system. Second, the PDA detects and reserves available composite elements in the close vicinity and informs the SG. Third the PDA's task is to control the invoked services or to provide users possibilities to interact with requested information and services.

The SCF Environment primarily describes the current physical location of the SCF service user and a pool of available output devices. Due to the diverse number of hardware devices as well a variety of standard communication and network protocols, we recognize the need to predefine virtual and collaborative environments (the SCF Environment) in order to facilitate the development of SCF systems. Therefore, SCF environment represents typical output devices available at certain location, whereby the number and type of devices are varying significantly from physical location to location. E.g. the office environment typically consists of high performance computing devices and high-resolution monitors. Whereas, the home area is more likely equipped with entertainment devices, such as TV or VCR

At the client side, the network communication model covers the wireless short-range sensing and communication. That is required to allow two-ways *PDA-Device-Communication* in order to detect output devices. A wireless bi-directional *PDA-Gateway-Communication* is further prerequisite for the PDA to update the SG with location information (available output devices) and to submit user's requests.

8. DECISION SUPPORTING COMPONENTS

A key focus of the SCF research project is to develop sophisticated methods for intelligent information distribution to such a distributed system that comprises of the PDA and composite device. The characteristic of the distributed PDA–Composite-Device-Architecture is the fact that the PDA initiates the server requests and server responses are redirected to the composite device. Thus, a typical client server communication is not taking place. The high-level SCF system architecture presented above highlights the importance of the SG that is responsible for the smart media preparation and distribution to composite devices. Therefore, this section describes the components that assist the SCF-SG fulfills its tasks. Figure 3 illustrates the essential steps of the SG workflow.

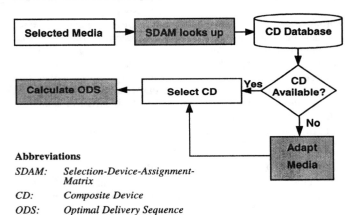

Abbreviations

SDAM: *Selection-Device-Assignment-Matrix*

CD: *Composite Device*

ODS: *Optimal Delivery Sequence*

Figure 3. High-Level Flow Diagram of SCF Smart Gateway

The components support the SG to make decisions are Selection-Device-Assignment-Matrix, the Media Adaptation and the Optimal Delivery Sequence. The descriptions of these aiding components are given in the following.

8.1 Selection-Device-Assignment-Matrix

A crucial part of the SCF system is the determination of the most appropriate output device to perform selected media. To support the SG calculating the best assignment schema, we introduce the Selection-Device-Assignment-Matrix $\mathcal{M}_{sd} = \mathcal{S} \times \mathcal{D}$, which consists of users selections $\mathcal{S}$ and available composite devices $\mathcal{D}$. The

selections $\mathcal{S}$ represents the media and services that are requested by the users, whereas $\mathcal{D}$ summarizes the available composite devices are submitted via the PDA by users:

$$\mathcal{M}_{sd} = \begin{bmatrix} m_{11} & \cdots & m_{1d} \\ \vdots & \ddots & \vdots \\ m_{s1} & \cdots & m_{sd} \end{bmatrix}$$

Through the selection $\mathcal{S}$ the type of media is determined. Concurrent, the media-composite device manager searches the database of the composite device manager for the most appropriate device to perform the selected media type and calculate the assignment. That is possible since the composite device manager maintains the exact information about the capabilities of each output device. The media-composite device manager dynamically generates the matrix $\mathcal{M}_{sd}$ any time a selection is made. In cases when the user selects another service or the number of available output devices has changed, it recalculates the matrix again to ensure a precise assignment schema. This can happen when e.g. the device is occupied by its owner or new devices are detected and are available as output devices. The result of the calculation process is then presented to the users via a HTML based interface on their PDA. Users can either accept system suggestion or can manually make their own assignment.

8.2 Media Adaptation

We recognize the ability of the system to have the flexibility and intelligence to offer alternatives of calculating appropriate media device schema. As described above in 7.1.2, in some cases no appropriate device is available to perform the selected media types. That is the case when the device owner meanwhile occupies the output device or running other processes and thus drops out the pool of available output devices. Before generating the matrix $\mathcal{M}_{sd}$ the SG will adapt the selected media type to the capabilities of available output devices. Although, the specific adaptation methods rely upon the concrete application scenario, we are experimenting with three different techniques to adapt the media type to multiple output devices with varying capabilities as well as the changing number of devices (see figure 4):

- *Splitting*: Intelligent content separation. E.g. a user wants to view a video message in an environment where only a PC without sound card and a telephone exist. In this case the media adaptation manager would prepare the content and split video into audio and video part that then can be individually redirected it to the available telephone and the PC.

- *Conversion*: Media conversion techniques, such as text to speech [10], can be offered when no appropriate devices are available.

- *Filtering*: Content extraction and delivery of the sub-content, which can be rendered by the output device. E.g. delivery of only the audio part of the video message to a telephone.

To make the decision, which of the techniques has to be deployed, the media adaptation manager can refer to the device capability and media type database as depicted in figure 4. Depends upon the capabilities of available composite devices, it can select the most appropriate technique to prepare and adapt the media for further processing. The results will then use by the matrix $\mathcal{M}_{sd}$ to assign the adapted media type to a particular output device for the performance.

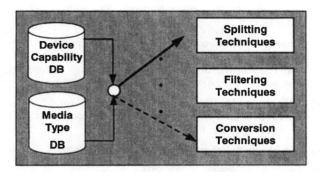

Figure 4. Media Adaptation Techniques

8.3 Media Delivery Sequence

We acknowledged the need of having a smart service delivery order. That is important for SCF system users and facilitates the process of editing the requested services on output devices. As mentioned above, the SCF system differs from typical distributed systems in the client-server communication schema. The initiator of server requests is not the recipient of server responses. Instead, the server needs to distribute the responses to multiple clients. That complicates the situation for users to appreciate the services, when all the responses are distributed simultaneously. Thus, we consider different standard values to calculate an Optimal Delivery Sequence to assist the SG delivery manager:

- *Frequency of service request*: The frequency a service is requested can be used as a standard value for the order of service delivery.
- *Urgency:* Urgent messages shall be displayed first.
- *Type of media:* Time critical media (e.g. live streaming media) shall be displayed before static media (e.g. Email).
- *Type of output device:* Converted media shall be displayed before unconverted media. This is useful to gain computing time for computing intensive media conversion.

9. SYSTEM INTERACTIVITY

The PDA-Composite Device-Architecture of the SCF system requires the development of a newly user interface to control and interact with requested services. In many cases users cannot rely upon the input possibilities of the output devices to control and interact with the invoked applications. We recognize in addition the need of providing a kind of *mobile user interface* on the PDA that enables users to interact, control and collaborate with the invoked processes. Therefore, we anticipate three situation dependent interaction and application control modes:

- *Abdicative*: In this case the PDA hands over the control to the output device. E.g. once an application is invoked on the PC mouse and keyboard can be used as input devices.
- *Cooperative*: PDA and input capabilities of the output device can jointly be used to control the application. E.g. a slideshow can be annotated either using the mouse and

keyboard of the output device or through a specialized and simplified user interface for the PDA

- *Exclusive*: The only input device is the PDA. This is especially important for output devices where no input facilities are available (e.g. a TV).

The cooperative and the exclusive modes require a special *mobile user interface* on the PDA. As such, we intend to introduce two possibilities, which strongly rely upon the specific application scenario:

- *Wireless Mouse Cursor Control via PDA*

  In this case, it is anticipated that the application control interface and the application are operating on the output device. The mouse cursor of the output device is controlled wireless via the PDA. Thus, all mouse commands are entered on the PDA display using the PDA stylus. Such a solution as proposed by Meyers *et al* [17] can be deployed, but need to be improved to support wireless communication ability.

- *Representation of the Application Control Interface on PDA*

  This user interface is a more advance interface and more challenging approach. Unlike the first approach, the application control part of the application is represented on the PDA screen. Users can directly operate the application from the PDA and all the commands are transferred wirelessly to the output client running the application, whereby these commands need to be synchronized with the running application. A challenging task is further the awareness of the SG to provide multiple application control interfaces for multiple applications at different time depend upon the delivery order of the services.

These interfaces are ideal to serve the *cooperative* and *exclusive* mode as well in general to allow a group of users to collaborate with each other and interact with the application.

10. IMPLEMENTATION

The realization status of SCF is still at early stage. The design of SCF as presented in this paper involves a various number of research disciplines that need to be individually and carefully investigated. Yet, with the current implementation status, we have successfully built a network communication infrastructure that will serve as a fundament for our future research activities as well as testbed for future experimental evaluations. Hence, at current stage we have not considered issues such as security and privacy aspects or QoS delivery concepts that we will incorporate in future versions of the prototype. Also, the deployment of SCF for a concrete application scenario will also facilitate to identify the necessary requirements.

Further, the relatively short existence of the PDA and the continuous introduction of new devices and functionality prevent the definition of standards upon which to rely. Instead, we recognize the initial realization of the SCF concept requires making decisions about specific computing platform, such as a wireless IR or RF interface and HTTP/HTML or WAP/WML (Wireless Application Protocol/Wireless Markup Language) [30]. Thus, we attempt to choose as much standard or de facto standard elements as possible to design the SCF concept, which is flexible enough to adapt upcoming technologies.

The SCF has been deployed for an office environment. We have successfully developed a demonstration system to verify the SCF concept. At the client side a PDA running Windows CE is used to represent the class of small screen devices. The pool of composite devices comprises of a PC running Windows 98, a Windows NT and a Windows 2000 workstation, and a TV, attached with a camera, connected via RF link to a Windows 98 running desktop. All composite elements are equipped with IR serial interfaces. At the server side a Windows NT server workstation hosts the system SG and the WWW server. The SG offers Microsoft Exchange webmail services, streaming media distribution and Microsoft Netmeeting videoconferencing services. The network communication model is a combination of a LAN network, a Cellular Digital Packet Data (CDPD) network as wireless network and IR as short-range communication network.

The IR interface of the PDA enables the detection available composite devices via the IR short-range communication. The PDA and SG communication is realized using HTTP over the CDPD network. That allows the PDA to submit the detected composite devices and access SCF system services, which is represented in HTML interfaces. Depending upon the selection of the user, the SG calculates the most appropriate service-device schema, which the user can either confirm or manually modify. The demonstrator allows the user to request the streaming of media files to one workstation, to redirect the webmail service to another and to conduct a videoconferencing session on the TV. The remote invocation of the application processes running on composite devices via the SG is realized using the Distributed Component Object Model (DCOM) [11], without the requirement of using any "special" software on composite clients. The combination of HTML/HTTP as user interface and communication protocol requires only a WWW browser and additional functionality supported through the browser extension mechanisms as prerequisite on the PDA as well as on composite devices.

11. CONCLUSION AND FUTURE WORK

This paper has presented a new conceptual framework that allows the class of small screen devices to access rich multimedia information and services. In comparison to related activities the SCF concept consequently avoid the performance of heavy computing tasks on a single small screen device or to shrink and tailor services and information to match the limitations of these devices. The *SS/CD* approach solves several problems of using small screen devices for ubiquitous rich multimedia information access. First, the outsourcing of requests to appropriate devices for the performance enables the possibility to offer a diverse range of services and information. Second, the user interface limitation of such devices is overcome by a better exploitation of available hardware resources.

Currently, we are working on the integration of different composite devices and using a WAP [30] cellular phone as a different small screen device to access of multimedia information. Concurrent, new technologies, such as Bluetooth [4], are investigated to improve the short-range network communication infrastructures and new standard protocols, e.g. the working draft protocol Composite Capability/Preference Profiles (CC/PP) [6], are considered to add more intelligence to the system. Further, our future activities research includes the development of methods and techniques to realize the *mobile user interfaces* as proposed in

section 9 and on concepts to integrate the SCF into different application scenarios.

12. REFERENCES

[1] Abowd, G. D., et al. *Cyberguide: A mobile context-aware tour guide.* ACM Wireless Networks Vol 3 (5), 1997, pp. 421-433

[2] Abowd, G. D. *Classroom 2000: An Experiment with the Instrumentation of a Living Educational Environment.* IBM Systems Journal, Special issue on Pervasive Computing, Volume 38, Number 4, pp. 508-530, October 1999.

[3] Billinghurst, M., Bowskill, J., Jessop, M., Morphett, J. *A Wearable Spatial Conferencing Space*, Proceeding of IEEE Second IWSC, Oct 1998, pp. 76-84

[4] The Bluetooth Forum, http://www.bluetooth.com

[5] Code Division Multiple Access (CDMA), http://www.cdg.org/

[6] Composite Capability/Preference Profiles (CC/PP): http://www.w3.org/TR/NOTE-CCPP/

[7] Feiner, S., MacIntyre, B., Hoellerer, T., Webster, A. *A Touring Machine: Prototyping 3D Mobile Augmented Reality Systems for Exploring Urban Environment.* Proceedings of IEEE First ISWC 1997, pp. 74-84

[8] Fox, A., Goldberg, I., Gribble, S., Lee, D., Polito, A., Brewer, E. *Experience With Top Gun Wingman: A Proxy-based Graphical Web Browser for the 3Com PalmPilot*, Proceeding of IFIP International Conference on Distributed Systems Platforms and Open Distributed Processing, 1998

[9] General Packet Radio Service (GPRS), http://www.gsmworld.com/technology/gprs.html

[10] Goose, S., Wynblatt, M. and Mollenhauer, H., *1-800-Hypertext: Browsing Hypertext With A Telephone* Proceedings of the ACM International Conference on Hypertext, June, 1998, pp. 287-288.

[11] Grimes, R. Professional DCOM Programming. *Wrox Press,* 1997.

[12] Helal, A., et al *Any time, Anywhere Computing; mobile computing concepts and technology.* Kluwer Academics Publisher, Boston, 1999

[13] Hsu, L.-H.; Johnson-Laird, B; Vjaygiri, S. *Authoring, Managing and Browsing of Large-Scale Hyperlinks in Multimedia Product Documentation*, Markup Technologies Conference, November 1998.

[14] Hull, R., Neaves, P., Bedford-Roberts, J. *Towards Situated Computing.* Proceeding of IEEE First ISWC, Oct 1997, pp. 146-153

[15] Khai, N. T., Abowd, G. D. *StuPad: Integrating Student Notes with Class Lectures.* Proceedings of ACM CHI Conference '99, May 1999. pp. 208-209.

[16] Mankoff, J., Somers, J., Abowd, G.D. *Bringing People and Places Together with Dual Augmentation.* Proceedings of Collaborative Virtual Environments (CVE), June 1998. pp. 81-86.

[17] Myers, B. A., Stiel, H., Garggiulo, R., *Collaboration Using Multiple PDAs Connected to a PC*, Proceedings of the ACM Conference CSCW, Nov 1998, pp. 285-294

[18] The PalmPilot product series, http://www.palm.com/

[19] Pham, T-L., Schneider, G., Goose, S., Pizano, A. *Composite Device Computing Environment: A Framework for Augmenting the PDA using surrounding Resources*, ACM CHI 2000 Conference Workshop "Situated Interaction in Ubiquitous Computing", April 2000.

[20] Raskar, R., Welch, G., Cutts, M., Lake, A., Stesin, L., Fuchs, H. *The office of the future: a unified approach to image-based modeling and spatially immersive displays*, Proceedings of the 25th annual ACM Conference on Computer Graphics SIGGRAPH. pp. 179 - 188

[21] Rekimoto, J. *"TransVision: A hand-held augmented reality system for collaborative design"*, International Conference on Virtual Systems and Multimedia (VSMM), 1996, pp. 85-90

[22] Rekimoto, J., Ayatsuka, Y., Hayashi, K. *Augment-able Reality: Situated Communication through Digital and Physical Space*, Proceedings of IEEE Second IWSC, Oct 1998, pp.68-75

[23] Rekimoto, J., Nagao, K. *The World through the Computer: Computer Augmented Interaction with Real World Environments*, Proceedings of UIST, 1995, pp.29-36

[24] Sastry, C., Lewis, D., Pizano, A. *Webtour: A System to Record and Playback Dynamic Multimedia Annotations on Web Document Content*, Proceedings ACM Multimedia, 1999, pp 175-179.

[25] Siewiorek, D., Smailagic, A., Bass, L., Siegel, J., Martin, R., Bennington, B. *Adtranz: A Mobile Computing System for Maintenance and Collaboration*, Proceeding of IEEE Second IWSC, Oct 1998, pp. 25-32

[26] Smailagic, A., Martin, R., *Metronaut: A Wearable Computer with Sensing and Global Communication Capabilities*. Proceeding of IEEE First ISWC, Oct 1997, pp. 116-122

[27] Smith, J., Mohan, R., Li, C-S. *Scalable Multimedia Delivery for Pervasive Computing*, Proceeding of ACM Multimedia Conference, 1999, pp. 131-140

[28] Universal Mobile Telecommunications System (UMTS), http://www.umts-forum.org/

[29] Want, R. Hopper, A., Falcao, V., Gibbons, J. *The Active Badge Location System*, ACM Transactions on Information Systems, Vol. 10, 1992

[30] Wireless Application Protocol Specification and Wireless Markup Language specification, http://www.wapforum.com/what/technical.htm

[31] Weiser, M. *The Computer for the 21st Century*, Scientific American, 1991

[32] Weiser, M. *Some computer science issues in ubiquitous computing*. CACM, *36(7)*: 74-83, July 1993. In Special Issue, Computer-Augmented Environments

[33] Weiser, M. *Hot topic: Ubiquitous computing*. IEEE Computer, Oct 1993, pp. 71-72

A Practical Query-By-Humming System for a Large Music Database

Naoko Kosugi, Yuichi Nishihara, Tetsuo Sakata, Masashi Yamamuro, and Kazuhiko Kushima
nao@isl.ntt.co.jp

NTT Laboratories, 1-1, Hikarinooka, Yokosuka-shi, Kanagawa, 239-0847, Japan

Abstract

A music retrieval system that accepts hummed tunes as queries is described in this paper. This system uses similarity retrieval because a hummed tune may contain errors. The retrieval result is a list of song names ranked according to the closeness of the match. Our ultimate goal is that the correct song should be first on the list. This means that eventually our system's similarity retrieval should allow for only one correct answer.

The most significant improvement our system has over general query-by-humming systems is that all processing of musical information is done based on beats instead of notes. This type of query processing is robust against queries generated from erroneous input. In addition, acoustic information is transcribed and converted into relative intervals and is used for making feature vectors. This increases the resolution of the retrieval system compared with other general systems, which use only pitch direction information.

The database currently holds over 10,000 songs, and the retrieval time is at most one second. This level of performance is mainly achieved through the use of indices for retrieval. In this paper, we also report on the results of music analyses of the songs in the database. Based on these results, new technologies for improving retrieval accuracy, such as partial feature vectors and or'ed retrieval among multiple search keys, are proposed. The effectiveness of these technologies is evaluated quantitatively, and it is found that the retrieval accuracy increases by more than 20% compared with the previous system [9]. Practical user interfaces for the system are also described.

1 Introduction

The use of multimedia data has spread throughout the world with the availability of high-performance, low-cost personal computers, and this has led to a need for accurate, efficient retrieval methods for large multimedia databases. General retrieval systems accept only key words as queries. However, many users experience difficulty in formulating a query in words when they want to retrieve something from a multimedia database. Content-based retrieval is seen as a solution to this problem [4, 7, 10, 15, 21].

Content-based retrieval accepts data-type queries, e.g., drawings for an image database and sung tunes for a music database. As content-based retrieval enables users to represent what they want directly, it makes the retrieval system easier to use.

The authors have developed a data-type retrieval system called *ExSight* [17, 20] for an image database. We are currently studying a content-based music retrieval system for a music database, which we call *SoundCompass* [8].

In a content-based retrieval system, it is possible for the users to make a query key from erroneous input. This makes it difficult to obtain an accurate result through a matching with the key. Thus, similarity retrieval is useful because retrieval results contain multiple alternatives ranked according to the closeness of the match. Users can select what they want from the list even though they cannot make an accurate query.

The authors have developed the *HyperMatch* engine [2], a high-speed similarity retrieval engine based on distance measurement employing multiple high-dimensional feature vectors. Each vector retains feature information, and similarity is represented as a weighted combination of the search results from individual feature vector spaces.

This paper describes our music retrieval system that accepts a hummed tune as a query. Our ultimate goal for this system is to have it retrieve the correct song for the hummed tune as the first item in the retrieved results list. This means that our system's similarity retrieval eventually should allow for only one correct answer.

When matching is done between songs in the database and the hummed tunes, we have to consider the following problems:

- We do not know which segment of the song will be hummed a priori.
- The song may be sung out of tune.
- The tempo may be wrong.
- Users may hum the wrong note, because their memory of the song is incorrect.
- The transcription may contain a mistake.

We have already described techniques for handling these problems in a query-by-humming system [9, 13]. The previous system was demonstrated at ACM Multimedia '99. Since then, the database has been enlarged, for eventual practical use of the retrieval system. As a result, the problems became more complex, and the technologies for improving performance and accuracy of the retrieval system became more challenging. This paper describes in detail the technologies for improving the performance and accuracy of the query-by-humming system for a large music database. We first report on the results of music analyses on all the songs in the database. Then, these results are incorporated in new technologies for database construction and hummed tune processing. The effectiveness of these technologies is evaluated quantitatively. Practical user interfaces for the system are also described.

2 Related Work

We'll begin by reviewing some of the research on content-based retrieval for audio databases [4]. With respect to "for what it searches", we can find research on identifying a specific rhythm or sound of an instrument [6, 12], and research on identifying a song from a melody segment given as a query [7, 9, 11]. With respect to "by what means it searches", we can find research on search by sound file in ".au" format [6], search by segment of a MIDI file [18], search by a string representing pitch direction [1], and search by hummed tune [7, 9, 11, 14]. Content-based retrieval using similarity requires that one clarify "for what" and "by what means" it searches.

String matching is the most often used method of melody and song retrieval from a music database [1, 7, 11, 14, 18]. This is because music can be represented by a sequence of notes, and this sequence can be converted into a string of letters. Pitch direction is often used [1, 7, 11, 14] instead of the pitch itself to construct the string. There are two reasons for this choice: one is that it ignores the key difference between a music in a database and an inputted tune, and the other is that for a hummed tune as input, it realizes robust retrieval even though the hummed tune may have variations in tone and tempo. However, for a large database, retrievals using only this information can not provide a high enough resolution. Thus, optional retrievals using rhythm information and accurate intervals have been provided as an advanced search feature in [11], and a more detailed specification describing pitch direction according to pitch differences has been proposed in [1].

Errors in input data also have to be considered in a searching method [7]. Errors in a hummed tune may include not only variations in tone and tempo, but also fragmentations, insertions and deletions of notes [11]. Dynamic Programming (DP) can be applied to string matching, which allows errors in inputs. Similarity is calculated by *edit distance* in DP matching. In edit distance, costs for insertions, deletions, and the substitutions of specific pairs of characters are defined. The smaller the cost, the more the two strings are regarded as being similar to each other. DP matching usually has a high retrieval accuracy [11]. However, its retrieval time depends on the size of the database because the search is done by brute force [7]. Thus, a state matching algorithm [19] has been used in [11] to improve the speed of retrieval. However, the authors of [11] also reported that the similarity cannot be sufficiently specified, after inclusion of the state matching. The authors in [18] investigate how to best represent the music data and how to calculate the similarity between two pieces of music by examining different combinations of measures (edit distance, n-gram measures, and so on) and representations (contour, exact interval, and so on).

Besides string matching, retrievals that use high-dimensional feature vectors in which similarity is represented by the distance between vectors have been proposed [6, 9]. Euclidean distance or cosine distance is used as the measure. In this case, since indices are used for retrieval, the larger the size of the database, the higher the retrieval performance.

To transcribe the inputted tune as accurately as possible, the user is asked to utter a specific syllable rather than actually hum. Thus, "humming" here does not mean the ordinary humming but instead "singing with only the syllable *ta* or *da*" [9, 11].

Many music databases for melody/song retrieval hold music data in MIDI format. The number of songs in the database usually ranges from a few hundred [7] to over 10,000 [18]. Notice that we cannot know the exact size of the database only from the number of songs it contains because its size actually depends on the length of each song and the number of the notes in each song.

3 Music Analysis

In this section, the results of an analysis of the over 10,000 songs in our database are presented. These results gave us many important clues on MIDI data processing to make a database and process hummed tunes.

3.1 MIDI Data Information

We currently have 10,069 songs stored in MIDI format. The division of all the songs is 480. Thus, the length of a quarter-note is 480 tick times. An interval is represented by a whole number between 0 and 127. An interval of 1 tone in MIDI is the same as a half step in the normal musical scale.

3.2 Note Distribution

The 10,069 songs include many musical genres. Some are short, simple songs such as nursery songs and folk songs, and some are long, complex pop and rock songs. The total number of notes is 3,676,773, and the mean number of notes per song is 365.16, which is about seven times greater than that of the average folk song that can be downloaded via the Internet. Figure 1 shows the distribution of the total number of notes in each song.

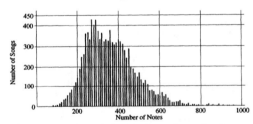

Figure 1: Distribution of the total number of notes per song.

We also investigated the distribution of the length of notes in the songs. All songs specify the length of a quarter-note as 480 in tick time, so Figure 2 shows that eighth-notes are overwhelmingly dominant. Note that the slower the

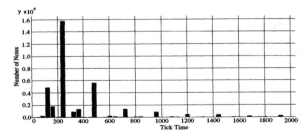

Figure 2: Distribution of the note length of all songs.

tempo is, the greater the number of notes there are whose length is 120, and the faster the tempo, the greater the number of notes whose length is 480. This result implies that there is not a wide variation in the length of the notes that human beings can sing.

3.3 Repetition Structure of Music

Music is generally self-similar [5], and many songs have a repetitive structure consisting of two or three similar verses. Figure 3 shows the ratio of songs that contain identical parts within themselves, with the song chopped up into overlapping parts every four beats with a length of 16 beats. The figure shows that about 50% or 60% of the parts of the songs are exactly the same. This implies that many songs may

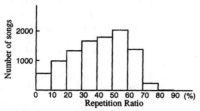

Figure 3: Ratio of songs that have a x% identical portion.

have a second verse. Most of the songs that have a high ratio of repetition (i.e., more than 80%) are highly rhythmical songs, such as dance music, and very easily learned songs, such as cheering songs for sports events.

3.4 Tempo Analysis

When people sing, they themselves decide what tempo to maintain, and it may well happen that the tempo they choose is not the same as that of the song in the database.

Figure 4 shows the distribution of the tempo of all the songs. We found that the faster a song is, the more people will use a tempo that is only half the correct one. This point is also relevant to the discussion in Section 3.2.

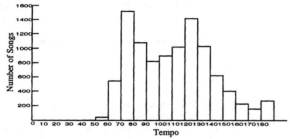

Figure 4: Distribution of tempo of all songs.

Why is that people sing a faster song at a tempo that is half the correct one? Let us consider two songs, A and B (Figure 5 – 6). The tempo of song A is 180 and that

Figure 5: Segment of song A. The tempo is 180.

Figure 6: Segment of song B. The tempo is 90.

of song B is 90. These songs may seem to be very different from each other, but they are performed in the same way with respect to the note length. This is because an eighth-note in tempo 90 is performed with the same length as that of a quarter-note in tempo 180.

3.5 Interval Distribution

Generally, there is not a wide range of difference in the pitch between successive notes in many songs. Figure 7 shows the distribution of the pitch difference between successive notes. In MIDI data, a difference of a half step is represented with

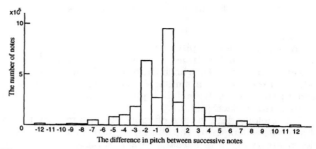

Figure 7: Distribution of the pitch difference between successive notes.

the numeral 1, so +12 represents a tone an octave higher, and -12 represents a tone an octave lower.

As shown in Figure 7, the difference in successive notes is concentrated in 0, -2, and +2. This means that most of the notes are either the same or within one step of each other. Another interesting point is that the difference for six half steps is much less than that for 5 or 7. This interval is called "tritone" and is the most dissonant interval.

4 Music Retrieval System

This section describes how we generated a query-by-humming system based on the analysis in Section 3.

4.1 Database Construction

We chose MIDI music data for the database elements. A lot of MIDI music data, including the latest pop hits, can be easily obtained in Japan because of the popularity of karaoke. MIDI music data can be regarded as musical indicators for each channel. Most karaoke recordings store the melody data on one channel. This allows the melody to be easily recognized.

To construct a music database, the melody data have to be extracted first. Currently, only melodies are used for matching because most people remember a song by its melody.

Then, the song is analyzed according to its tempo. As described in Section 3.4, for faster songs users tend to choose a tempo that is half the correct one. Thus, for fast tempos, two copies of the song data are made: one at the correct tempo and another at half that tempo. As a result, users can retrieve the same song by humming at either tempo.

Next, all the chords are deleted. A chord here means "notes that partially overlap each other in time". Chords that are found in accompaniments are not included because the melody data are extracted by the process described above. Most of the chords are made from a succession of notes that partially overlap (overlaps are included as MIDI performance effects by the manufacturer). However, most people cannot sing two tones at the same time when they hum. Thus, chord deletion is done to enable the melody data information to be coordinated with that from the hummed tunes. The note in a chord that occurred earliest is deleted. For example, if note B begins to sound while note A is sounding, the note A part of the chord is deleted (see Figure 8). If two notes start to sound simultaneously, the higher note

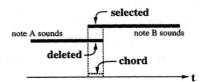
Figure 8: Chord deletion.

is kept.

In addition, double-pitch errors are corrected. This type of error exists in the transcriptions of the hummed tunes. However, we require that both the hummed tunes and melody data be processed in a similar fashion. So this correction step is performed on both data types. This correction method is described in Section 4.2.2.

The melody data is then chopped up into melody pieces of a constant length by the sliding window method[9]. The pieces are defined as *subdata*. Each subdata is given redundancy with respect to its predecessor and successor by letting the length of the slide be shorter than the length of the window. Chopping up the melody data into subdata of exactly the same length is necessary for correct similarity calculation, while chopping up the melody data into overlapping subdata allows a user to select whichever part of a song he or she wishes to hum.

Next, feature information is extracted from each subdatum. Multiple features are extracted and converted into high-dimensional feature vectors. The features are described in detail in Section 5.

Then, subdata which make the same feature vectors are deleted (duplication deletion). To put it concretely, subdata which make the same vectors for all features are detected for each song, and only one subdatum among them is kept for the database.

Finally, the feature vectors are loaded to the system's memory. The vectors are individually indexed according to feature and entered in the database's server. Indices are made based on an improved version of VAMSplit R-tree [2], which provides faster retrieval.

4.2 Hummed Tune Processing

This section describes the method of generating the query key from the hummed tune. The process is similar to the database construction process. However, before making a query, some corrections have to be made to the information obtained from the hummed tune because these tunes may contain various errors.

4.2.1 How to Hum?

The hummed tune is recorded through a microphone and is converted into MIDI format by commercial composition software [16]. The user is required to clearly hum the song notes using only the syllable "ta" . This is done so that the hummed tune can be transcribed as accurately as possible. Note that tunes hummed with the syllables "da" and "la" produce transcription errors.

Moreover, users are required to hum following the beats of a metronome. This is done to enable people to hum in constant tempo; casual singers usually have difficulty in keeping a constant tempo without any guidance. Moreover, we have to know the tempo information that the singer followed because we use beat-based processing [13]. Of course, the user may adjust the metronome to the desired tempo.

4.2.2 Modifications and Making the Search Key

Noise is deleted from the hummed tune after the tune has been converted into MIDI format. The noise deletion method is described in detail in Section 8.1.

Double-pitch errors are then corrected. In a double-pitch error, a note is transcribed at an octave lower in pitch than the correct one. Errors of this type arise in the pitch detection part of the transcription software [16]. The fact that sound waves of a relatively long wave length are weighted in processing to establish priority when the pitch is extracted by the auto-correlation function may cause these errors [3]. The method of correcting double-pitch errors is as follows: if the difference in pitch between a note and its successor falls within a certain range, raise that note one octave.

Next, the hummed tune is chopped up into hummed pieces of the same window size and sliding length as that of the subdata. During the chopping, a waver correction is also performed. The waver correction compensates for the subtle variation in tempo of a hummed tune. This correction adjusts the chop point to be at the start of the note that is nearest the chop point.

Finally, the same kinds of features as those extracted from subdata are extracted from each hummed piece. These are also converted to feature vectors and used for queries.

4.3 Similarity Measurement, Similarity Retrieval

The similarity retrieval finds vectors in each feature's vector space that are close to the vectors generated by the hummed tune. Dissimilarity is calculated for each subdatum by using the weighted linear summation of the distance between the vectors. Euclidean distance is used for the measurement. The shorter the distance to the subdata is, the higher the ranking of the retrieval results. The final retrieval result is a weighted combination of the search results from individual feature vector spaces and is presented as a ranked list of songs.

Figure 9 presents an image of the content of this section.

5 Feature Vectors

This section explains how feature vectors are generated from each subdatum and each hummed piece. The parameters used for the generation of the vectors are based on the results in Section 3. Section 7 describes these parameters in detail. The feature vectors are chosen so that a correct answer could be obtained from as little feature information as possible.

5.1 Tone Transition Feature Vector

People can usually identify a song they know by hearing a only part of it, even if the hummed tune is somewhat out of tempo or tune. They also tend to think that timewise transitions in the pitch and duration of tones are the most important feature of music. Thus, it is useful to define a feature vector that can represent a timewise transition, hereafter called a *tone transition feature vector* [9].

A tone transition feature vector is a sequence of tones in which each tone sounds within successive constant beats (resolution beat "r"). This is why we describe our query-by-humming system as being beat-based and not note-based. The value of each dimension of a feature vector is a typical tone in a succession of resolution beats. So, problems such as note fragmentation and note insertion [11] have no affect on matching. A tone is considered to be representative, if it is the longest tone in the resolution beat. Thus, a short note that is incorrectly transcribed (due to variation in tone) does not affect the generation of the feature vector.

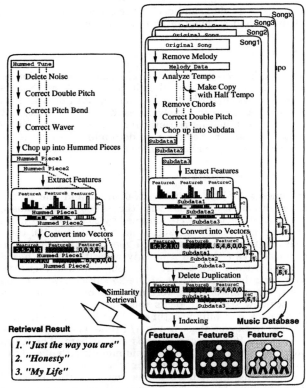

Figure 9: Steps in construction of the music database and processing the hummed tune.

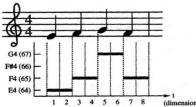

Figure 10: Image of making a tone transition feature vector.

Figure 10 shows how to make a tone transition feature vector from a tune with the resolution of an eighth-note. E4, F4, and G4 are MIDI codes, and the numbers to their right are the MIDI note number. Thus, an eight-dimensional feature vector, (64, 64, 65, 65, 67, 67, 65, 65), can be made from this four-beat tune. In addition, a vector that does not depend on the key difference between a hummed tune and a melody data in the database can be made if each value in the vector represents pitch relative to a certain tone (called *base tone*). For example, if the most common tone in the tune in Figure 10 is selected as a base tone (65) and let it be "0", the final feature vector of eight dimensions is (-1, -1, 0, 0, 2, 2, 0, 0).

5.2 Partial Tone Transition Feature Vector

As described in Section 4.1 and Section 4.2.2, both melody data in the database and hummed tunes are chopped up into subdata and hummed pieces respectively of the same length in every slide length by the sliding window method. Since we cannot know which portion of a song a user will

sing a priori, this redundant chopping generally makes it possible for a user to hum any part of a song (usually users tend to hum the beginnings of a song or its phrases) in order to retrieve the song. However, this of itself is not enough, because people do not always remember a song by its beginning or its phrases. Thus, the beginning of the hummed tune is not always the beginning of the song or the beginning of a phrase. Furthermore, the beginnings of subdata are not always the beginnings of phrases or bridges. In particular, in many current pop songs, the start beat of songs is inconsistent with the start beats of the phrases and the bridges.

Let us consider the tune shown in Figure 11. The

Figure 11: A tune in which the start beat of the beginning part (A) is different from the start beat of the bridge part (B).

bridge begins at the fourth beat (B) of the third bar, and the start of the song is at the first beat (A) of the first bar. This means that this tune is an example of an anacrusis with respect to the bridge. All of the starts of the subdata made from this tune are at the first beat of each bar if the slide length of the sliding window method for chopping is four beats. Thus, when the user hums the bridge, there is no subdata in the database whose start is consistent with the start of the hummed tune. That is to say, between the starts of the subdata and the starts of the hummed pieces, there can actually be a gap that is as much as half the slide length when melodies and hummed tunes are chopped up automatically in the sliding window method.

We therefore propose another tone transition feature vector to solve this problem. Of course, the length of the slide can be reduced; however, this increases the size of the database. Thus, we invented a partial tone transition feature vector to solve this problem without increasing the database. In a partial tone transition feature vector, the starts of the vectors are inconsistent with the starts of the subdata and hummed pieces.

The vector is made by picking out the values of $(w - s) \times r + 1$ dimensions from the values of $w \times r$ dimensions, where r is the resolution of the feature vector, w is the window size, and s is the slide length. The start of the vector is selected according to a certain rule from the values within s beats. For example, suppose that the tune in Figure 10 is the four beats of the beginning of a certain subdata. The value of s is four here. If we let the place where the highest tone initially appears be the beginning of the vector, the fifth place of G4 is the start of the vector and a $(w - 4) \times 2 + 1$-dimensional vector is generated.

Using the same parameters, let us make another vector from the tune in Figure 11. Vectors whose starts are consistent with the starts of the subdata are generated up to the fourth vector; however, the start of the fifth vector is different from the start of the subdata because the start of the fifth vector is the place marked C in the figure. Thus, if a user hums the bridge part including the fifth bar, the retrieval system can find a vector whose start is consistent with the start of a vector made from the hummed tune in the database.

5.3 Tone Distribution Feature Vector

The partial tone transition vector proposed in Section 5.2 can solve the inconsistency of the starts of the vectors generated by both the subdata and the hummed pieces. However, some of the starts of the vectors in the database will still be inconsistent with the starts of the vectors generated from the hummed tune. Furthermore, feature vectors that enable us to roughly grasp the characteristics of the hummed tune are needed because there may be variations in tempo and tone in the hummed tune. Thus, we have introduced another type of feature vector that represents the distribution of tones of each subdatum [9]. This type of vector can represent the total number of occurrences of each tone and represent the total number of beats that each tone sounds. Figure 12 depicts a histogram which shows the total number of beats that each tone sounds. A four-dimensional tone distribution feature vector (2,4,0,2) can be made, if we define 64 as the lowest tone and 67 as the highest.

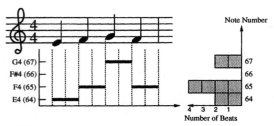

Figure 12: Image of making a tone distribution feature vector.

6 Or'ed Retrieval among Search Keys

As described in Section 4.2.2, hummed tunes are also chopped up into hummed pieces of the same length with the sliding window method. Thus, multiple search keys can be generated from a hummed tune, if the user hums for a time period longer than that specified by the window size. Since most tunes are not hummed well at the very beginning or at the very end, we made a search key for the middle part of a hummed tune by requiring users to hum for a period of time a little longer than the window size [8]. However, some people hum in tune only at the beginning, while others become more in tune the longer they hum. Moreover, some parts of songs are easy to hum, while others are more difficult.

We propose generating multiple search keys from the entire hummed tune, if a user hums for a period of time that is longer than the window size, and retrieving songs using all keys.

We also propose making the final results by or'ing each result of search keys.

Let us illustrate this with the following example. Suppose that a user hums a little longer than the time period specified by the window size, and as a result, three search keys, h_1, h_2, and h_3, are generated. There are four songs, A,B,C, and D, in the database. Suppose that these three keys retrieve the results shown in Table 1. The values in parenthesis are dissimilarities calculated from each subdata. The retrieval result can be made as follows. First, the re-

Table 1: Retrieval Results of Each Hummed Key of a Hummed Tune.

key	result(dissimilarity)			
h_1	D(0.9)	B(1.5)	C(1.8)	A(5.8)
h_2	A(0.3)	B(1.2)	C(2.0)	D(5.9)
h_3	B(1.0)	C(1.2)	D(1.5)	A(6.0)

sults are gathered for each song, then we let the minimum dissimilarity within the results of each song be the dissimilarity of the song. The result is presented as a ranked list of songs in ascending order of dissimilarity. This method makes use of the fact that a vector made from a subdatum that correctly matches a vector made from a hummed piece must have minimum dissimilarity. As a result, we can obtain

the final result, A(0.3) D(0.9) B(1.0) C(1.2), by processing the results in Table 1, and decide the correct answer is song A. This method is called *or'ed retrieval among search keys*.

7 Evaluation

In this section, we present retrieval accuracy evaluation results for the database (described in Section 4.1) and for the feature vectors (described in Section 5), both of which are generated based on the analysis results given in Section 3. We also present another retrieval accuracy evaluation for the method proposed in Section 6 to determine the final result and a performance evaluation of the use of indices.

7.1 System Parameters

Experiments for the accuracy evaluation and the performance evaluation were done with the 10,069-song database.

A total of 258 tunes were hummed by 25 people (21 males and four females). Of the 258 tunes, we selected 186 tunes which are transcribed into MIDI representation and were recognizable as a part of a melody when they were heard. All the 186 tunes are a part of a song which is registered in our song database. Most of the 25 subjects were casual singers, but some of them were members of a choral group.

A window size of 16 beats was chosen for chopping up melody data and hummed tunes. This is because most of the songs in the database are in 4/4 time, and in that case, the length of 16 beats corresponds to four bars. The length of four bars was found to be the minimum length of a phrase or a unit of a part of a melody for many songs.

A slide length of four beats was chosen. With this length a few hummed pieces can be made from a tune that is hummed for a period of time that is a little longer than the window size.

For successive notes, a difference in the MIDI note number ranging between -10 and -14 was chosen to be the range for double-pitch error correction. This point is also relevant to the discussion in Section 8.1. Figure 7 shows that about 97.5% of the entire tone differences in successive notes were in the range between -12 and +12. Though more radical changes in tones can be seen when the next phrase starts, it appears that users seldom hum a tune that has overlapped phrases. As the figure also shows, the difference in successive notes is concentrated around 0, -2, and +2. Thus, a double-pitch error may be found in the range between -12-2 and -12+2 in tones of successive notes. As a result, the range between -14 and -10 of MIDI notes determines the thresholds of double-pitch error correction.

A DELL PowerEdge 2300 with twin 500MHz Pentium 3's and 1GB main memory was used as the database server for the performance evaluation.

Figure 13 shows the structure of the experimental system. A database server and a client PC were connected

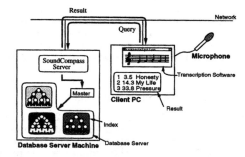

Figure 13: Experimental system structure.

338

through a network. The query-by-humming system server (*SoundCompass Server*), a master program that handles queries, and a database server worked together in the server machine. The database server housed the indices of feature vectors. A microphone was connected to the client PC, which included a GUI and the transcription software for the query-by-humming system. Hummed tunes input through the microphone were transcribed and converted into MIDI format and sent to the SoundCompass Server. The server processed the hummed tunes in MIDI according to the method described in Section 4.2 and then sent a query to the master program. The master then sent the query to the database server and the server returned the retrieval result to the SoundCompass Server. The SoundCompass Server sent the result to the client PC, and the results were displayed by the GUI.

7.2 Evaluation for Size of Database

As shown in Figure 3, about 60% of the subdata of a song have a duplicate structure. By chopping up the 10,069 melody data with a 16-beat window size and a four-beat slide length, 938,028 subdata can be generated. After the duplication deletion, the number of subdata was reduced to 548,195. As a result, we were able to reduce the size of the database by 38.6%. The accuracy of the retrieval results obtained from the smaller database was the same as the results obtained from the large database.

Fast-tempo songs were copied to make half-tempo songs. According to Figure 4, the number of songs with tempo 150 or more is 1,063, which is 10% of the total number of songs in the database. Thus, our database held 11,132 song versions (10,069 songs). As a result, songs that had not been retrieved because of tempo errors could be retrieved.

The maximum number of songs that can be copied depends on the size of the database to be managed. We thought that copying only songs with tempo 150 or more might not completely ensure retrieval. However, users did not seem to make any tempo mistakes for songs with tempo 140 or less. By copying these songs, an additional 70,017 subdata units were generated but that number was reduced to 52,146 by deleting the duplication of identical subdata.

The number of subdata before duplication deletion was 938,028. However, after the deletion, it became 600,342 (a 36% reduction in size) even when subdata generated from half-tempo songs were added. As a result, we were able to obtain a smaller database and more accurate retrieval results.

7.3 Evaluation for Feature Vectors

In this section, the effects of feature vectors on retrieval accuracy are examined.

7.3.1 Evaluation of Resolution

As shown in Figure 2, the eighth-note is the most frequently occurring note. To determine the effective resolution for tone transition feature vectors, accuracy of the retrieval results is compared with the results generated through the use of tone transition feature vectors whose resolution is an eighth-note, and the results generated through the use of vectors whose resolution is a quarter-note. Figure 14 shows the results obtained. The figure shows the percentage of times in which a correct song name appears within the rank. In the figure, the x axis represents rank, and the y axis represents percentage of correct retrieval. For example, in 65% of the 186 hummed tunes the correct answer was retrieved within the 10th rank when the eighth-note was used as the resolution for tone transition feature vectors.

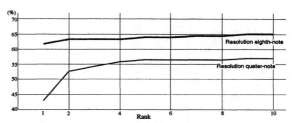

Figure 14: Evaluation of resolution for tone transition feature vectors.

Figure 14 reveals that the eighth-note is better than a quarter-note as the resolution for tone transition feature vectors.

7.3.2 Evaluation of Partial Feature Vector

A partial tone transition feature vector was proposed in Section 5.2 to solve the problem that the starts of tone transition feature vectors generated from melody subdata are not always consistent with the starts of the vectors generated from hummed pieces.

Figure 15 shows the retrieval results for examining the effect of the partial tone transition feature vectors on retrieval accuracy. The figure shows the percentage of times

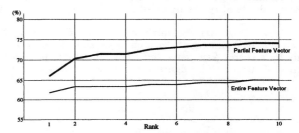

Figure 15: Evaluation of the partial tone transition feature vector.

in which a correct song name appears within the rank. In the figure, the x axis represents rank, and the y axis represents percentage. For example, in 70% of the 186 hummed tunes the correct song name was retrieved within the second rank when the partial feature vector was used.

Figure 15 reveals that the partial feature vector is an extremely good measure for retrieval. The main reason for this improvement in accuracy is that hummed tunes that could not be retrieved correctly because of the gaps between the starts of vectors became retrievable.

7.3.3 Evaluation of Combination of Tone Transition Feature Vector and Tone Distribution Feature Vector

The functions of tone transition feature vectors and/or tone distribution feature vectors were investigated based on the discussion in Section 5.

The partial tone transition vector alone seems to be good enough for retrieval, however, it may retrieve multiple possible answers with an identical similarity. On the other hand, the tone distribution feature vector alone can not retrieve as many correct answers as the tone transition feature vector does. However, through the combined use of the two, more accurate retrieval results can be obtained because the addition of the extra information helps the system narrow down the number of possible correct answers. The figure shows the percentage of times in which a correct song name

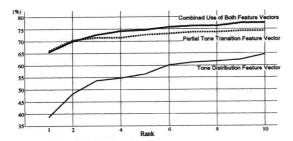

Figure 16: Evaluation of combination.

appears within the rank. In the figure, the x axis represents rank, and the y axis represents percentage of correct retrieval. For example, in 75% of the 186 hummed tunes the correct answer was retrieved within the fifth rank when both tone transition feature vector and tone distribution feature vector were used.

Thus, this figure reveals that the combined use of both feature vectors can increase the retrieval accuracy.

7.4 Evaluation for Or'ed Retrieval

In Section 6, retrieval was done by making multiple search keys from a hummed tune when a user hummed for a period of time longer than the window size for chopping, and getting the final result by or'ed retrieval among the search keys.

Figure 17 shows the retrieval results obtained by the or'ed retrieval among the search keys and those obtained only by a search key generated from the middle part of the hummed tunes. The figure shows the percentage of times

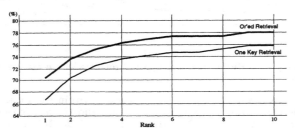

Figure 17: Evaluation for or'ed retrieval.

in which a correct song name appears within the rank. In the figure, the x axis represents rank, and the y axis represents percentage. For example, in 74% of the 186 hummed tunes the correct answer was retrieved within the second rank when or'ed retrieval among the search keys was used.

Thus, this figure reveals that or'ed retrieval among the search keys provides more accurate results than can be obtained with a single search key.

7.5 Evaluation of Performance

Figure 18 shows the execution times in the database server. One line represents the retrieval time when indices are used, and the other was obtained through the use of brute force searching. Songs to make subsets of the database for this experiment were chosen randomly.

This figure reveals that the greater the size of the database is, the higher the efficiency the indices provide. It also reveals that the database server with indices can provide a result within one second for the database with all 11,132 song versions.

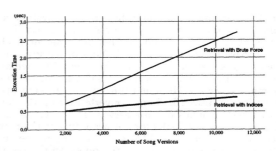

Figure 18: Performance evaluation.

7.6 Summary of Evaluations

In our music retrieval system, a database that holds copied half-tempo songs and has no duplicated subdata was generated. Partial tone transition feature vectors are used instead of the entire tone transition feature vectors. Their resolution is an eighth-note. Both a partial tone transition feature vector and a tone distribution feature vector are used. Multiple search keys are generated from a hummed tune and the result obtained by or'ed retrieval among the search keys becomes the final result. Indices are used for retrieval.

As a result, this music retrieval system is able to provide correct answers within the fifth rank for about 75% of hummed tunes that are recognizable as a part of a song. The answer, which is the combination of each result generated from multiple feature vector spaces, can be obtained in at most one second.

8 Towards Practical Use

This section describes a practical query-by-humming system that we hope to offer commercially in the near future. We visualize a system that will be used, for example, in the following situation:

> **Situation example:**
> Some people are singing happily in a karaoke room about three meters square. Person A is singing, and it's Person B's turn next. Person B knows the song he wants to sing but not its title. So while A is singing, B retrieves the song title by humming it, so now he can enter the title into the karaoke system so he can sing it.

In this section, problems related to noise and note fragmentation are discussed in addition to the problems presented in Section 4.2.

The tunes in Figure 19 and 20 are from the same song and were hummed by the same person. The one in Figure 19 was hummed in a quiet place, and the other in Figure 20 was hummed in a noisy place. These scores are used as aids in the following discussion.

Figure 19: Hummed tune of a song C in a quiet place.

Figure 20: Hummed tune of a song C in a noisy place.

8.1 Noise Deletion

Noise is a note that was recorded when the hummed tune was recorded, but has nothing to do with the melody. Noise is caused by the singing of others, e.g. A in the situation example, and by mistakes made by the hummer. For example, in Figure 20, there are 21 notes, and three notes, 1, 4, and 14, are definitely noise notes. Noise notes must be deleted from hummed tunes to extract correct features from the tunes and then to make effective feature vectors.

As shown in Figure 7, successive notes seldom have big differences in pitch. Thus, we propose these rules for deleting noise note.

1. If there is a duration of silence of more than m beats within n beats from the beginning of the recording, the part before the silence is deleted.
2. A note which has a wide range of difference exceeding a threshold p in pitch for a mean tone is regarded as a noise note and hence is deleted. The checking of noise notes is done twice in a tune, once in timewise normal order, and then in timewise opposite order.

The mean tone is recalculated whenever the tones of the notes are checked. In this recalculation, notes whose tone exceeds the threshold p are not used for the calculation. As a result, the more the recalculation is done, the more accurate the mean tone becomes.

8.2 Note Fragmentation

The number of relatively short notes in a tune hummed in a noisy place is greater than those of one hummed in a quiet place, even if the same person hummed both in the same way. This may be caused by confusion of the transcription software, which cannot decide whether or not a tone to be recorded has been sounded in a noisy environment. Thus, note processing of the hummed tune is not appropriate when the tune is recorded in a noisy place. Fortunately, our system uses beat processing rather than note processing, as described in Section 4.2.1. Thus, note fragmentation has no effect on our system performance.

8.3 Evaluation of Noise Deletion

A query-by-humming experiment in a noisy place was conducted to evaluate the noise deletion method described in Section 8.1. In this experiment, 8, 4, and 15 were selected as parameters for m, n, and p respectively. From our experience, we had found that there are few songs with relatively long rests (four beats) at the beginning of a phrase. Thus, we selected eight beats as the threshold to detect a long rest and delete the midi data before the rest as noise notes.

A threshold of 15 in tone difference for noise deletion was chosen. This is also relevant to the discussion in Section 7.1, which showed that there may be double-pitch errors in tone difference in the range between -12-2 and -12+2. The value of ± 15, which exceeds the threshold for double-pitch error correction, was selected as the threshold for the noise note deletion.

For example, the tune in Figure 21 was obtained from the hummed tune in Figure 20 after deleting noise notes with the method described in Section 8.1 and correcting double-pitch errors with the method described in Section 4.2.2. In other words, two noise notes (1 and 4) can be deleted, but one (14) can not be. The third note (3) was a double-pitch note, and it was corrected by the method described in Section 4.2.2.

In this experiment, 31 hummed tunes were recorded in a noisy place. Two people, one male and one female, recorded their hummed tunes in a room where four kinds of background music with vocals were played very loudly. The total

Figure 21: Hummed tune of a song C after noise removal.

number of hummed notes was 1,492. There were 87 noisy notes which were definitely judged as noise, and 61 noise notes were deleted, while 20 notes that were not noise were deleted.

Figure 22 shows the results of the accuracy evaluation of the retrieval for these 31 hummed tunes. A noise deletion routine was added to the retrieval system described in Section 7.6.

The figure shows the percentage of times in which a correct answer appears within the rank. In the figure, the x axis represents rank, and the y axis represents percentage.

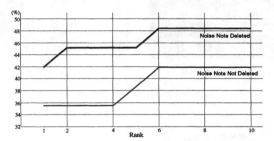

Figure 22: Evaluation for noise note deletion.

This figure reveals that the method for noise deletion proposed in Section 8.1 is efficient because accuracy was increased.

8.4 GUI and User Interface Hardware

We created the graphics and prepared equipment shown in Figure 23 for practical use, where (a) to (c) show the graphics and (d) shows the equipment for the user interface.

Figure 23(a) shows a graphic for the opening. In the graphic, the title "Query by Singing" appears in large Japanese letters. The doll on the right is a character named "Onpu-chan". Its head is an eighth-note and it is named after the term "note" in Japanese. It tells users to sing clearly with the syllable "ta" and also tells them to keep tempo by moving its body right and left.

Figure 23(b) is a graphic for recording hummings. Here, Onpu-chan moves its body right and left again as a metronome. The speed can be adjusted using the direction bar under Onpu-chan. Onpu-chan requires the user to find the tempo at which it is easy for them to sing and then push the record button.

Figure 23(c) is a graphic showing the retrieval results. When the user pushes the retrieval button after recording a hummed tune in Figure 23(b), this graphic appears within a few seconds. In this graphic, the scores registered for each song are shown in addition to the song title. The score is calculated from the dissimilarity of the match using a certain function. For example, "Love Train" was retrieved as the second match in the database, and the system says the hummed tune was similar to "Love Train" with a score of 80 out of 100.

Figure 23(d) shows the equipment for the user interface: a microphone with a headphone and a game pad for user input. Tempo can be recognized by listening to the ticks of a metronome through the headphone, as well as by following the movements of Onpu-chan. The game pad is used for input because it is familiar to young people in Japan.

(a) Opening

(b) Recording a Hummed Tune

(c) Retrieval Result

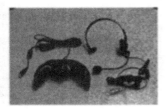

(d) Microphone and Game Pad

Figure 23: Practical query-by-humming system.

9 Conclusion

This paper describes a music retrieval system that accepts hummed tunes as queries. The database currently holds 11,132 song versions (10,069 songs), and the database server is able to retrieve songs from the database in at most one second. The hummed tunes can be any part of a song. In about 75% of the retrievals, the correct song name of recognizable hummed tunes is listed within the fifth rank. In addition to this result, medleys that included a part of a song that had a part similar to the hummed tune were also retrieved. The previous system [9] provided correct song names within the fifth rank for about 50% of the hummed tunes. Thus, the accuracy of retrieval increased by more than 20% over that of the previous system.

To achieve these results, we introduced partial tone transition feature vectors, implemented or'ed retrieval among the search keys, made copies of fast songs at half-tempo, decreased the size of the database, and corrected double-pitch errors based on the results of music analyses. Furthermore, in aiming towards the development of a practical service, we prepared graphics and equipment for users and proposed a noise note deletion method.

10 Future Directions

We are still researching this music retrieval system in the hope of improving its performance and accuracy. We also hope to decrease the size of the database without removing any songs, and make the retrieval system easier to use. This research represents our first step in the development of a query-by-humming system for practical use with a large music database. Further investigations and evaluations will be needed.

A very wide range of issues, e.g., from the technical side, such as the implementation of more efficient feature vectors, to fundamentals, such as what the similarities in music are, remain as future work.

It is well known that people can often identify a song by hearing only a part of it hummed, even if the humming is out of tempo or tune. Our system has significant tolerance to input errors but does not approach the ability of most people when it comes to identifying hummed tunes of music they are familiar with. Our future research will focus on making the system more human-like in this regard.

Acknowledgment

We would like to thank Daiichi Kosho Co., Ltd., in particular Mr. Yuji Namekata, for providing the 10,069 MIDI song data.

References

[1] S. Blackburn and D. DeRoure. A Tool for Content Based Navigation of Music. In *Proc. ACM Multimedia 98*, 1998.

[2] K. Curtis, N. Taniguchi, J. Nakagawa, and M. Yamamuro. A comprehensive image similarity retrieval system that utilizes multiple feature vectors in high dimensional space. In *Proceedings of International Conference on Information, Communication and Signal Processing*, pages 180–184, September 1997.

[3] J. J. Dubnowski, R. W. Schafer, and L. R. Rabiner. Real-Time Digital Hardware Pitch Detector. *IEEE Trans. on Acoustics, Speech, and Signal Processing*, ASSP-24(1):2–8, February 1976.

[4] J. Foote. An overview of audio information retrieval. In *Multimedia Systems 7*, pages 2–10. ACM, January 1999.

[5] J. Foote. Visualizing Music and Audio using Self-Similarity. In *Proc. ACM Multimedia 99*, pages 77–80, November 1999.

[6] J. T. Foote. Content-Based Retrieval of Music and Audio. In *Proc. SPIE, vol3229*, pages 138–147, 1997.

[7] A. Ghias, J. Logan, and D. Chamberlin. Query By Humming. In *Proc. ACM Multimedia 95*, pages 231–236, November 1995.

[8] N. Kosugi, Y. Nishihara, S. Kon'ya, M. Yamamuro, and K. Kushima. Let's Search for Songs by Humming! In *Proc. ACM Multimedia 99 (Part 2)*, page 194, November 1999.

[9] N. Kosugi, Y. Nishihara, S. Kon'ya, M. Yamamuro, and K. Kushima. Music Retrieval by Humming. In *Proceedings of PACRIM'99*, pages 404–407. IEEE, August 1999.

[10] W. Y. Ma, B. S. Manjunath, Y. Luo, Y. Deng, and X. Sun. NETRA: A Content-Based Image Retrieval System. http://maya.ece.ucsb.edu/Netra/.

[11] R. J. McNab, L. A. Smith, D. Bainbridge, and I. H. Witten. The New Zealand Digital Library MELody inDEX. http://www.dlib.org/dlib/may97/meldex/05written.html, May 1997.

[12] Muscle Fish LLC. http://www.musclefish.com/.

[13] Y. Nishihara, N. Kosugi, S. Kon'ya, and M. Yamamuro. Humming Query System Using Normalized Time Scale. In *Proceedings of CODAS'99*, March 1999.

[14] P. Y. Rolland, G. Raskinis, and J. G. Ganascia. Musical Content-Based Retrieval: an Overview of the Melodiscov Approach and System. In *Proc. ACM Multimedia 99*, pages 81–84, November 1999.

[15] J. R. Smith and C. S. Li. Image classification and querying using composite region templates. In *Journal of Computer Vision and Image Understanding*, 1999.

[16] WILDCAT CANYON SOFTWARE. AUTOSCORE. http://www.wildcat.com/Pages/AutoscoreMain.htm.

[17] N. Taniguchi and M. Yamamuro. Multiple Inverted Array Structure for Similar Image Retrieval. In *IEEE Multimedia '98*, pages 160–169, 1998.

[18] A. Uitdenbogerd and J. Zobel. Melodic Matching Techniques for Large Music Database. In *Proc. ACM Multimedia 99*, pages 57–66, November 1999.

[19] S. Wu and U. Manber. Fast Text Searching Allowing Errors. *Communications of the ACM*, 35(10):83–91, October 1996.

[20] M. Yamamuro, K. Kushima, H. Kimoto, H. Akama, S. Kon'ya, J. Nakagawa, K. Mii, N. Taniguchi, and K. Curtis. ExSight – Multimedia Information Retrieval System. In *20th Annual Pacific Telecommunications Conference, PTC'98 Proceedings*, pages 734–739, 1998.

[21] A. Yoshitaka and T. Ichikawa. A Survey on Content-Based Retrieval for Multimedia Databases. *IEEE Trans. Knowledge and Data Engineering*, 11(1):81–93, Feb. 1999.

Curricula and Resources for Courses about Multimedia

Edward A. Fox
Virginia Tech
Dept. of Computer Science, M/C 0106
Blacksburg, VA 24061 USA
+1-540-231-5113

fox@vt.edu

Wolfgang Effelsberg
University of Mannheim, L 15,16
Praktische Informatik IV
68131 Mannheim, Germany
+49 621 292 3300

effelsberg@pi4.informatik.uni-
mannheim.de

Nicolas Georganas
University of Ottawa (SITE)
161 Louis Pasteur Priv., Room A-613
Ottawa, Ont. Canada K1N-6N5
+1 -613-562-5800 Ext 6225

georganas@mcrlab.uottawa.ca

Rachelle S. Heller
George Washington University
School of Engineering and Applied Science
801 22nd Street NW; Washington DC
+1-202-994-5906

sheller@seas.gwu.edu

Ralf Steinmetz
Institutsleiter GMD IPSI
GMD Forschungszentrum Informationstechnik GmbH
Dolivostr. 15 • 64293 Darmstadt, Germany
+49 615 186 9869

ralf.steinmetz@darmstadt.gmd.de

ABSTRACT

This panel will discuss a recommendation for curricula guidelines for courses about multimedia. Based on conference input, the guidelines will be modified for review prior to future publication by ACM (with other groups). The recommendation will be one of the main results of a June 2000 Dagstuhl workshop led by 4 of the panelists. Dr. Heller, the 5th panelist, also attended that workshop, and is co-PI with the panel moderator on a directly related NSF project, Curriculum Resources in Interactive Multimedia, CRIM, see http://ei.cs.vt.edu/~crim. Each of the panelists has taught courses about multimedia. Each is interested in developing tools/demonstrations/resources to help in those courses. Each has a particular area of interest in the multimedia field. Together they constitute a representative group among those who will contribute to and benefit from curricula resources in multimedia.

Keywords

Dagstuhl, education, guidelines, knowledge modules, laboratory, learning, syllabi, teaching, tools, training

1. INTRODUCTION

The panelists will report on the CRIM project and the June 2000 Dagstuhl workshop, engaging the audience through a series of straw polls. Conference attendees will be asked to comment on how recommended syllabi fit in with their own experiences as teachers, trainers, employers, and students.

The proposed syllabi are based on analysis of existing courses surveyed around the globe. They address not only focused courses, like an undergraduate or a graduate overview course on multimedia, but also specialized/smaller "knowledge modules" that could fit into related courses such as: computer graphics, database management, human-computer interaction, image processing, information retrieval, networking/communications, operating systems, programming languages, software engineering.

As of July 2000, the IEEE/ACM Computing Curriculum 2001 (see http://computer.org/educate/cc2001, an update and revision of Curriculum 91) report of the Information Management Focus Group includes a number of knowledge units related to multimedia. These are:

- Hypertext and Hypermedia
- Multimedia Information and Systems
- Advanced Multimedia/Hypermedia Information and Systems

The panel discussion will explain these as well as other modules.

In addition, there will be discussion of requirements for, availability of, and review criteria for, educational resources to support such courses and knowledge modules. These will be related to the Computer Science Teaching Center (www.cstc.org) and the new ACM Journal of Educational Resources in Computing (JERIC). In particular, there will be a brief preview of the inaugural issue of JERIC, guest edited by Dr. Heller, that will be based on the Dagstuhl meeting.

Comments will be solicited from all those in the audience who have: developed demonstrations, built tool-kits, devised interesting applets, assembled labs for multimedia research/education, or otherwise engaged in related efforts.

2. DAGSTUHL WORKSHOP

The Dagstuhl Workshop on Multimedia for Multimedia: Learning and Teaching in the Next Decade was attended by all of the panelists, and coordinated by Steinmetz with the assistance of Effelsberg, Fox, and Georganas.

Viewed abstractly, it dealt with three layers:
- Archives (e.g., digital objects + metadata),
- Mappings (including hypertext paths and "sibyls"), and
- Services (e.g., for learning),

while addressing a number of approaches and issues, such as appliances, brokers/recommenders, cases, collaboration, conceptual structures, course builders, digital lecture halls, distance education, evaluation, learning environments, learning objects, learning processes, log analysis, modules, ontologies, tele-teaching, and virtual laboratories.

Following is a slightly edited version of Section 1 of the proposal for the Dagstuhl Workshop on Multimedia for Multimedia: Learning and Teaching in the Next Decade, attended by all of the panelists, and coordinated by Steinmetz with the assistance of Effelsberg, Fox, and Georganas:

We understand multimedia as being characterized by the integrated computer-controlled generation, manipulation, presentation, storage, and communication of independent discrete and continuous media.

Since the beginning of the nineties, learning and teaching at universities has tried to take advantage of multimedia technology and applications. Here we must distinguish between "teleteaching/ telelearning" and "multimedia courseware", which are very often combined or mixed:
- Teleteaching/telelearning means to learn and to teach at different locations (making use of networking facilities to communicate audio, video and other data) in a similar way as regular classes at universities take place. In such a typical set-up at the location of the instructor, many students take part in the lesson; simultaneously this event is conveyed to one or more remote locations (where other students take part in this class).
- Multimedia courseware means to focus on the learning and teaching material: How shall the contents be structured, accessed, presented? Which media shall be used? How can this be adapted to the teaching/learning situation? How can we support the learning in a team (or, possibly, distributed teams with cooperative environments)?

A wide range of experience from conferences and workshops in this area shows us that these issues are topics of interest in many research communities. However, very often the contributions are (sorry to say) somehow superficial. Hence, we want to work in Dagstuhl on a very narrow focus but from many different perspectives. We want to focus our workshop on multimedia courseware; we even want to restrict our view to courses on multimedia on multimedia.

The seminar should bring together researchers from the different areas interested and working on "multimedia in multimedia": Experts in multimedia technology and applications, pedagogical and cognitive aspects, curricula on multimedia, lectures of multimedia—and related publishers. New/up-coming leading & visionary researchers shall be explicitly involved and encouraged to demonstrate both the state-of-the-art and work in progress.

The participants will investigate what new requirements are emerging, to exchange experiences in teaching and learning in this area (also with many demonstrations to be shown), to identify commonalities all over the world, to discuss what is possible with the advent of new multimedia technology, and how this can be achieved (even with the severe problem of material rapidly going "out of date"). Hence, the goal of the seminar is not only to present each others' contributions but also to elaborate on common experiences in order to build up a worldwide network of experience to be used in the future by the whole research community interested in "multimedia on multimedia". Hence we will discuss:
- What should be in a multimedia classroom or laboratory so that students can best learn about multimedia?
- What to teach, how to teach, about multimedia?
- How students best learn about multimedia?
- What should be in a learning environment to help students learn about multimedia?

Topics to be treated at the seminar include:
- Existing curricula on multimedia (teaching on multimedia in multimedia)
- Potential and problems with sharing of high quality and expensive media elements
- Demonstration of tools
- Exploration of existing media contents (i.e., to explore how we can develop, collect, review, archive, distribute these resources/contents)
- Potential of up-coming media formats (e.g., virtual environments)
- Related multimedia document formats
- Usability testing of multimedia courseware
- Quality of service considerations
- Asynchronous vs. synchronous learning
- Next generation Internet and its impact
- Educating the multimedia educators
- Social economic issues of multimedia learning
- Identification of challenging issues

3. PANELISTS

Edward Fox holds a Ph.D. and M.S. in Computer Science from Cornell University, and a B.S. from M.I.T. Since 1983 he has taught at Virginia Tech (VPI&SU) where he serves as Professor of Computer Science. He directs the Digital Library Research Laboratory, Internet Technology Innovation Center at Virginia Tech, Networked Digital Library of Theses and Dissertations, and Curriculum Resources in Interactive Multimedia. For ACM he served 1988-91 as a member of the Publications Board and as editor-in-chief of ACM Press Database Products. He also served from 1987-95 as vice chair and then chair of the Special Interest Group on Information Retrieval, from 1992-94 as founder and chairman of the Steering Committee for the ACM Multimedia series of conferences, and from 1995-1998 as founding chairman of the Steering Committee for the ACM Digital Libraries series of conferences. He is General Chair for the 2001 Joint Conference on Digital Libraries, and was Program Chair for ACM DL'99, ACM DL'96 and ACM SIGIR'95. He has served as lead guest editor for Communications of the ACM special issues of July 1989, April 1991, April 1995, April 1998, and April 2001. He is a founder and co-editor-in-chief for the new ACM Journal of Education Resources In Computing (JERIC) and is editor for the Morgan Kaufmann Publishers series on Multimedia Information and Systems. He also serves on the editorial boards of Electronic Publishing (Origination, Dissemination and Design), Information Processing and Management, Journal of Educational Multimedia and Hypermedia, Journal on Multimedia Systems, Journal of Universal Computer Science, IEEE Multimedia, and Multimedia Tools and Applications.

Professor Effelsberg received his Diploma in Electrical Engineering in 1976 and the Dr.-Ing. degree in Computer Science in 1981 from the Technical University of Darmstadt, Germany. From 1981-1984 he worked in the United States. He was an Assistant Professor at the University of Arizona in Tucson, then a Post-Doctoral Fellow at IBM Research in San Jose, California. In 1984 he returned to Germany where he joined IBM's newly founded European Networking Center in Heidelberg. From 1984-1989 he led a research group working on the design and implementation of communication protocols and applications for the emerging OSI networks. In 1989 he joined the University of Mannheim as a full professor of computer science where he now teaches computer networks and multimedia technology. In 1997 he spent a four-month sabbatical at the International Computer Science Institute in Berkeley, California. Dr. Effelsberg's current research interests include communication protocols for multimedia systems, protocols for high-speed networks, distributed multimedia systems, and multimedia content processing. He is co-author of a book on multimedia communications, editor/co-editor of five other books, a book series on multimedia engineering for Vieweg-Verlag, and has published a number of papers in national and international journals and conferences. He is a member of the editorial board of IEEE Multimedia, and serves on the program committee for the ACM and IEEE multimedia conferences and many other national and international conferences. He is a member of ACM, IEEE and Gesellschaft für Informatik. Professor Effelsberg's research interests include multimedia systems, media content analysis, and application layer protocols for high-speed networks.

Nicolas D. Georganas is Professor and Director of the Multimedia Communications Research Laboratory (MCRLab) at the School of Information Technology and Engineering, University of Ottawa, Canada. He has been leading multimedia application development projects since 1984. He was General Chair of the IEEE Multimedia Systems'97 Conference (ICMCS97, June 1997, Ottawa) and is General Co-Chair of ACM Multimedia'2001. He is on the editorial boards of the journals Multimedia Tools and Applications, ACM/Springer Multimedia Systems, ACM Computing Surveys, Performance Evaluation, Computer Networks, Computer Communications, and was an editor of the IEEE Multimedia Magazine. He is Fellow of IEEE, Fellow of the Canadian Academy of Engineering, Fellow of the Engineering Institute of Canada, and Fellow of the Royal Society of Canada. In 1998, he was honored as the University of Ottawa Researcher of the Year and also received the University 150th Anniversary Gold Medal for Research. In 1999, he received the T.W. Eadie Medal of the Royal Society of Canada, for contributions to Canadian and International Telecommunications. In 2000, he received the A.G.L. McNaughton Medal and Award, the highest distinction of IEEE Canada, the Julian C. Smith Medal of the Engineering Institute of Canada and the President's Award of the Ottawa Centre for Research and Innovation.

Dr. Rachelle Heller holds a Ph.D. in Computer Science with a focus on education from the University of Maryland. Dr. Heller is the co-editor of the peer-reviewed journal "Computers & Education: An International Journal" by Pergamon Press. She is a lecturer for the Association of Computing Machinery and the IEEE. Dr. Heller is the co-principal investigator of four National Science Foundation grants. The first, "Bringing Young Minority Women to the Threshold of Science," is designed to raise the interest of young women to studies in science and engineering. The second, "TEAMSS, Teacher Enhanced Application for Middle School Science with Hypermedia," is designed to enable teachers to use and re-use videodisc technology in their classrooms. FORWARD in SEM is a focus on reaching women for academics, research and development in Science, Engineering and Mathematics. It is an implementation project for the recruitment and retention of women in advanced science, engineering and mathematics careers in conjunction with Gallaudet University. Curriculum Resources in Interactive Multimedia (CRIM) is a project in conjunction with Professor Fox at Virginia Tech. She is also the Co-PI for the VISIT System, a multimedia kiosk project designed to provide information about the park and to collect visitor preference data in US National Parks.

Ralf Steinmetz is Professor at the Departments of Electrical Engineering and Information Technology and Computer Science at the Darmstadt University of Technology. His research group in multimedia communication was newly founded in 1996. Since then 18 researchers have joined the KOM staff. Since January 1997 he has been the Director of the GMD (German – National Research Center for Information Technology) Institute IPSI (Integrated Publications and Information Systems Institute) in Darmstadt. About 100 full time employees work at his GMD institute. In 1999 he founded the httc (Hessian Telemedia Technology Competence Center) with focus on applied networked multimedia services being applied to education projects. He was among the core multimedia group that initiated the ACM/Springer Multimedia Journal and the IEEE Multimedia Magazine. He has served as editor and member of the editorial advisory board of several journals and as chair, vice chair, and member of numerous program and steering committees for workshops and conferences (recently as general co-chair of the ACM Multimedia '98 and chair of the itg/GI KIVS'99 - communications in distributed Systems '99 in Darmstadt. He wrote the first in-depth technical book on multimedia systems, with the most recent version published in German in 2000; a co-authored and restructured version of the edition in English published in 1995 is planned for the end of 2000.

Multimedia Copyright Enforcement on the Internet

James M. Burger
Dow, Lohnes & Albertson

Christopher J. Cookson
Warner Bros

Darko Kirovski
Microsoft.

David P. Maher
InterTrust

Miodrag Potkonjak
Computer Science Dept.
UCLA

Jeremy Welt
Maverick Records

Keywords:

copyright, intellectual property protection,
digital rights management, digital media, MP3

Panel Statement.

Technology has made it simple and economical to reproduce, distribute, and publish digital information. While enabling increased legitimate uses of digital media, the potential for misuse is multiplied many fold. Increasing Internet piracy is already producing a billion dollar loss in revenues per year to the music industry. As Internet bandwidth increases, the movie industry is expected to follow the same path. The dynamics of the process is disturbing; for example, Napster's music download web site has experienced a nearly six-fold traffic increase in the second quarter of 2000.

It appears that the content publishers have only few options to fight this agonizing problem: (i) seek for legal ways to enforce their copyright, (ii) change their business model e.g., by collecting revenues, through advertisement rather than music sales, and/or (iii) research new technologies that will raise effective barriers for illegitimate use of digital content.

While technology is progressing fast, the judiciary system is slowly adjusting to new situations. In the case of content "hard-copying", the legal recipe is to seek for damages from the recording (e.g., CD) plant. However, this model does not translate well to content "soft-copying". Although, Napster and Scour, as main enablers of free multimedia content distribution on the Internet, are facing a number of lawsuits, it is not clear how the current laws apply to these cases.
* Which party is liable in the process of up/downloading pirated content to/from a server?
* What are the legal issues with transferring pirated content using different Internet technologies such as email and push?
* Where are the boundaries between legal and illegal copying?
* How to address the copyright enforcement problem worldwide?

Many content publishers are already investigating ways to change their business models and adjust better to the Internet era. The most commonly mentioned business model is free content distribution and collection of revenues through advertisement. The total spending on advertisement in the US economy in 1999 totaled $218B. Advertising on the Internet accounted for a small part of that sum, however, it is the most rapidly growing sector: currently $1.8B per quarter with approximately 50% quarter-to-quarter increase.
* Is this a viable source of revenues for content publishers? The music industry collected $15B in 1999 in the US alone. The IFPI and RIAA claim revenues in excess of $38B annually for the music industry worldwide.
* What is the right business execution of this model?
* How is this going to affect the relations of artists with the content publishers? Will artists be able to publish their work into the Internet space without the Hollywood management?

Some believe that digital rights management (DRM) technologies are the only road for multimedia content publishers. The industry has already created an initiative, the SDMI (Secure Digital Music Initiative), to address the problem for screening digital content from illegal use. However, this problem is complex from a technical point of view. Multimedia watermarking has a crucial role in such systems as the only known protection technique that can survive D/A and A/D conversion of the signal. For example, by encrypting or scrambling a signal, a DRM system can only enforce copyright protection while the signal is in the protected form; once it is decrypted or unscrambled, it can be recorded or copied (in its digital or analog form) and freely distributed.

A number of techniques have been proposed for watermarking text, audio, images, and video to enable the enforcement of copyrights. Although each of the corresponding media industries desperately calls for a consensus on standards, the associated technical standards initiatives, such as the SDMI, have had little success due to a variety of reasons: legal and business model issues, DRM system design, inability to provide adequate testing, and lack of reliable watermarking technologies.
* Is it possible to guarantee prevention of illegitimate copying using an information technology?
* What are the bounds of watermarking? Why watermarking is hard? What are realistic scenarios for watermark use?
* How (or is it possible) to build an effective DRM system?

Multimedia copyright enforcement on the Internet is a complex issue involving aspects of technology, the law, economics, sociology and public policy. The breadth of this panel reflects the multidisciplinary nature of the problem. Each panel member is an expert with a different perspective and a strong point of view.

PANEL MEMEBERS
James M. Burger represents a wide variety of computer hardware, software and online companies on intellectual property, communications and government policy matters arising from the confluence of digital technology, content protection and government regulation. Jim has participated in resolving such complex issues as DVD copy protection and download and sale of music on the Internet - representing the Computer Industry Group in negotiations developing the DVD Content Scrambling System copy protection rules as well as the Secure Digital Music Initiative. Jim also represents clients in negotiating hardware acquisition, software licensing and online agreements. Prior to joining Dow, Lohnes, Jim occupied senior positions in Apple Computer's Law Department. For five years, he chaired the industry's intellectual policy committee at ITIC. Education: B.A., with honors, New York University; M.A., New York University Graduate School; J.D., cum laude, New York University School of Law.

Christopher J. Cookson is EVP & CTO for Warner Bros. He oversees the operation of the Technical Operations Division, which is responsible for all video mastering, duplication, physical and broadcast distribution, reservation/archiving/restoration of film and tape for WB's motion picture and television divisions. As CTO, Mr Cookson is further engaged in defining standards for secure digital distribution of Warner Bros.' intellectual property. He has been instrumental in the development and launch of DVD and The WeB, a new technology architecture for delivery of The WB Television Network. Mr. Cookson joined Warner Bros. in 1992 from CBS in New York where he was VP/GM, Operations and Engineering for the CBS Television Network. He is a fellow of SMPTE, a member of ATAS and a founding member of the Museum of Television and Radio Technical Council. He holds more than 17 U.S. patents and has been awarded two Emmys. Mr. Cookson holds a BSE degree and an MBA from Arizona State University.

Darko Kirovski received the Ph.D. degree from the Computer Science Department at the University of California, Los Angeles in 2000. He has been with Microsoft Research since April 2000. His research interests include: intellectual property protection, multimedia digital rights management, embedded systems security and design. He has co-authored more than 30 technical papers in journals and conferences and holds four US patents. Dr. Kirovski has received the Microsoft Graduate Fellowship in 1998 and the Design Automation Conference Fellowship in 1999.

David P. Maher has served as chief technology officer of InterTrust since July 1999. Before joining InterTrust, he was an AT&T Fellow, Division Manager, and Head of the Secure Systems Research Department at AT&T Labs where he was working on secure IP networks and secure electronic commerce protocols. He joined Bell Labs in 1981, where he developed secure wideband transmission systems, cryptographic key management systems, and secure communications devices. He was chief architect for AT&T's STU-III secure voice, data, and video products used by the President and US Intelligence and Military personnel for Top Secret communications. In 1992 Maher was made a Bell Labs Fellow in recognition of his work on Communications Security. He was also Chief Scientist for AT&T Secure Communications Systems overseeing Secure Systems R&D at Bell Labs, Gretag Data systems in Zurich and Datotek Systems in Dallas. Maher has published papers in the fields of Combinatorics, Cryptography, Number Theory, Signal Processing, and Electronic Commerce. He has been a consultant for the National Science Foundation, National Security Agency, National Institute of Standards and Technology, and the Congressional Office of Technology Assessment. He has a Ph.D. in Mathematics from Lehigh University, and he has taught Electrical Engineering, Mathematics, and Computer Science at several institutions.

Miodrag Potkonjak is an Associate Porfessor at the UCLA Computer Science Department. He received his Ph.D. degree in Electrical Engineering and Computer Science from University of California, Berkeley in 1991. In 1991, he joined C&C Research Laboratories, NEC USA, Princeton, NJ.
Since 1995, he has been with Computer Science Department at UCLA. He received the NSF CAREER award, OKAWA foundation award, UCLA TRW SEAS Excellence in Teaching

Award and a number of best paper awards. His recent watermarking-based intellectual property protection research formed a basis for the Virtual Socket Initiative Alliance developing standard. His research interests include embedded systems, communication and multimedia system design, computational security, and intellectual property protection.

Jeremy Welt (bio not available at press time)

Posters

Study of Shot Length and Motion as Contributing Factors to Movie Tempo

Brett Adams
Department of Computer Science
Curtin University of Technology
GPO Box U1987, Perth, 6845, W. Australia
adamsb@cs.curtin.edu.au

Chitra Dorai
IBM T. J. Watson Research Center
P.O. Box 704, Yorktown Heights
New York 10598, USA
dorai@watson.ibm.com

Svetha Venkatesh
Department of Computer Science
Curtin University of Technology
GPO Box U1987, Perth, 6845, W. Australia
svetha@cs.curtin.edu.au

ABSTRACT

This work seeks to lay the framework of film grammar over the video to be analyzed. We use the shot attributes of motion and shot length to produce a novel continuous measure of one of the aesthetic elements of films, namely the movie tempo. We refer to our previous work detailing the study of this construct and its automatic derivation, and also demonstrating its usefulness as an expressive element and as a sound basis for higher semantic descriptions such as dramatic events and story elements. Initial assessment of tempo was performed in our study on the basis that the relative importance of both shot length and motion in formulating the tempo function was the same. In this paper, we analyze their relative contributions to tempo, and demonstrate how these two factors can be manipulated to influence audience perception of movie time.

1. INTRODUCTION

Film "grammar" [3, 5] outlines the cinematic conventions that are employed by directors to manipulate film elements such as the shot, the movement, and the types of editing to convey a narrative structure of a story. Inspired by the existing film grammar, we propose a unique approach to computationally determine the expressive elements of motion pictures conveyed by the manipulation of editing, motion, colour etc. for high level video understanding and annotation. We seek to find computational elements that can map to the "expressiveness" of the medium, and determine thematic movie sections underscored by the expressions.

In our previous work [2, 1], we concentrated on a computational understanding of movie tempo or pace, that manifests in the sense of a story's *experienced* time. Sobchack says that "[tempo] is usually created chiefly by the rhythm of editing and by the pace of motion within the frame" ([5,

p. 103]). Encyclopedia Britannica [4] defines tempo as being influenced "in three ways: by the actual speed and rhythm of movement and cuts within the film, by the accompanying music, and by the content of the story". We proceeded from this artistic definition to formulate a computable measure, briefly recapitulated below, of tempo/pace for a given film.

As a new contribution in this paper, we analyze the relative impact of shot length and motion on our tempo function, and demonstrate how the two factors can be manipulated to influence audience's perception of time. Film grammar tells us that different directors and different genres will make use of these complementary techniques with differing measures. We conduct experiments on films of different genres and find that tilting the sensitivity of the tempo function toward one or the other of its constituents causes different "flavours" of movie tempo to be emphasized accordingly.

2. EXTRACTION OF MOVIE TEMPO

We first proposed tempo/pace function of a video sequence in [2] and improved it in [1] as:

$$P(n) = \alpha(W(s(n))) + \frac{\beta(m(n) - \mu_m)}{\sigma_m}, \quad (1)$$

where s refers to shot length, m to motion magnitude, and n to shot number. The shot length, s, is computed in frames (from source 25 frames/sec) for each shot detected in the video, and m is the absolute value of the sum of pan and tilt values computed for every frame pair in a shot, and averaged for each shot. In addition to the per shot data, the mean, μ and the standard deviation, σ of these features are calculated for the entire film for normalization. $W(s(n))$ is a novel two-part normalization scheme proposed for shot length in [1] where it is defined to be more sensitive near the overall shot length median. For the motivation and derivation of this normalization scheme, see [1]. The weights α and β affect the contributions of shot length and motion to the perception of pace, and are given values of 1. $P(n)$ is smoothed with a bank of Gaussian filters as a response to the neighbourhood nature of pace, and as a means to multi-resolution video analysis.

3. SHOT LENGTH VS. MOTION

While it has been recognized that both motion and shot length contribute to the perception of pace, it is not as simple to make statements about their relative impact.

Our research on $P(n)$ has thus far used unit weights for α and β, assuming that motion and shot length contribute equally to the perception of time. It is possible, however, that under certain circumstances one or the other of these two impact more heavily on the audience perception of time. Such circumstances might include sparing use of a technique. For example, a director who makes minimal use of quick cutting techniques might do so only at particularly important junctures in a film's development. Conversely, a director might rely heavily upon one technique to clarify the story. An example of this might be films crafted by montage directors, who make use of shot characteristics (e.g., length) for the purpose of carrying artistic expression to the exclusion of other cinematic factors like motion. This results in one technique being used to influence semantic interpretation, thus relegating other techniques such as motion to a position of secondary importance.

In order to explore this further, we carried out two experiments on the movies, Colour Purple (CP) and Lethal Weapon 2 (LW2). For each movie, edges were automatically detected in its $P(n)$ using Deriche's multi-scale edge detection algorithm and the resulting story sections manually labeled, since significant pace changes as indicated by the edges often accompany dramatic events, or are precipitated by story/scene boundaries. The results of our equal weights-based pace scheme for LW2 can be seen in [1] as an example of this process. These two movies have been chosen as good representatives of a slow thoughtful movie and an action movie respectively. Having computed their reference pace functions with the equal weights-based pace scheme, experiments reported in this paper consist of tilting the weights α and β, in effect adjusting the sensitivity of $P(n)$ to motion or shot length respectively.

3.1 Increase Sensitivity to Less Used Technique

For the first experiment the weight corresponding to the "least" used technique is increased. For CP, this is motion (α), with an overall average of only 0.58 indicating that it is not a very visually dynamic movie. Conversely, for LW2 it is shot length (β), due to its large motion average of 0.83 (as expected for an action movie). In each case, the amplified mode receives a weighting of 1.5, while the other weighting is dropped to 0.5. Figures 1(a) and 1(b) show pace plots for the two movies, using the normal and amplified weighting schemes. See Table 1 for edges of $P(n)$ from new weightings.

For LW2 the most obvious effect is a small swing towards less "action" oriented edges. That is, edges more to do with character/plot development and background than with the dynamic action sequences that are the hallmark and raison d'etre of this genre of film. This is to be expected as the technique of crafting shot length is generally much more dominant in such scene types as dialogue, character development etc. (to well made scenes of these types at least). As such, these events often serve as breathers to the main action of the film, or provide vital pieces of information to the dramatic development of the plot that serve to clarify and justify its existence.

As an example of this, consider edge "B" from Table 1, labelled "Murtaugh's daughter on commercial". The scene takes place at Murtaugh's home. Family, friends and Riggs have gathered to watch Murtaugh's daughter on her small screen debut. The result is a mixed reaction of disbelief, anger, and humour as it turns out to be quite an embarrass-

ing situation for her poor father. The event is an occasion to see the family bonds that exist, the friendship between Riggs and Murtaugh, and also serves as a breather from the hectic pace of the surrounding scenes. Detection of this event would be desirable as it provides a useful index to the overarching story, but in this case we see that it would be lost in the mass of action oriented edges that arise when no special consideration is given to edges of this type.

The results from CP are not as amenable to clear conclusions. The reason for this becomes clear after a consideration of the movie. Unlike LW2, the story told by CP is by nature "amotion", i.e., motion not used to such a degree, with the centrepiece of the story being the relationships that exist between the characters. This is the essence of the story. Rather than forcing motion on the story to alter time perception, the more readily avaliable and natural method open to the director is shot rate change. Thus highlighting motion is missing the point somewhat. In other words, of the methods available to the director to manipulate the perception of time for CP, shot length is much more appropriate and fits seamlessly with the story. Therefore amplifying the effect of any incidental motion is unjustified and results in meaningless edges. No resulting clear trend exists and fits with the fact that we are amplifying *semantic noise*.

3.2 Increase Weight of Primary Technique

For the second experiment the weight corresponding to the most used mode is increased. This results in an emphasis on the opposite modes as compared to the previous experiment. For LW2 motion is emphasized, for CP it is shot length. Once again, the amplified mode is given a weighting of 1.5, with the remaining mode receiving a weighting of 0.5. This second experiment in effect says "we recognize that this mode is predominant, and therefore we're going to pay special attention to it as the director seems to be placing much upon it". Refer to Figures 2(a) and 2(b) for comparative pace plots, and Table 2 for edge descriptions.

Table 1: Experiment 1 - Resulting significant edge changes in $P(n)$ (cf. Figures 1(a), 1(b)).

Gained and Lost Edges			
Lethal Weapon 2 Edges			
A	-	End of car chase	action
B	+	Murtaugh's daughter on commercial	tense/humour
C	+	Riggs talks about his wife's death	tense/sad
D	+	Riggs meets the baddies in room	tense
Colour Purple Edges			
A	+	Mr asks to marry Nettie	tense
B	-	Mr slaps Celie	tense
C	+	Harpo's wedding	lively

For LW2 we observe an effect opposite to that found in the first experiment. There is a shift towards action based events, those noted above as being the trademarks of this kind of film. We also find better resolution of different events within larger action sequences. Edge "D" is an example of this; a scene entailing the destruction of the crooks house.

A second observation has to do with the fact that, especially with this kind of intense film, both motion and shot length techniques are often used to compound their effects to cause a greater impact on the viewer. Both techniques are often used together to overwhelm the audience visually. Given this, where one set of data is subject to error (par-

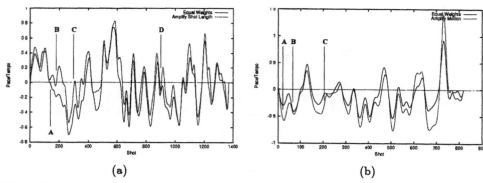

Figure 1: (a) LW2 - Unit Weights vs. Amplified Shot Length; (b) CP - Unit Weights vs. Amplified Motion.

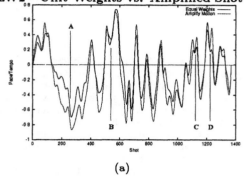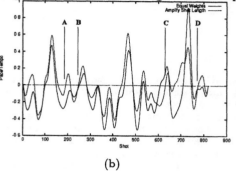

Figure 2: (a) LW2 - Unit Weights vs. Amplified Motion; (b) CP - Unit Weights vs. Amplified Shot Length.

Table 2: Experiment 2 - Resulting significant edge changes in $P(n)$ (cf. Figures 2(a), 2(b)).

Gained and Lost Edges			
Lethal Weapon 2 Edges			
A	-	End of Rian's TV debut	tense/humour
B	-	After gun fight at crooks house	action breather
C	+	Riggs fights back (caravan scene)	action
D	+	Crooks house begin to shake	action
Colour Purple Edges			
A	+	Sophia talks to Mr about Harpo	tense/dialogue
B	+	Shug Avery arrives	rising tension
C	→	Celie about to kill Mr	rising tension
D	+	Shug and others join Church	climax

ticularly the shot index), the other technique may be used to locate edges that would otherwise be missed. This may be viewed as taking advantage of a form of inherent redundancy. Edge "C" offers an example of this observation. The scene involves the gunship attack on the caravan in which Riggs lives. Originally only the edge marking the start of the attack was detected. There is however a dip in shot rate just before Riggs retaliates, that is not captured in the shot index due to the fact that it is a darkly lit scene. There is also a motion pause in concert with this shot rate drop which is now detected with amplified motion.

The converse is true for CP. There is a swing towards dramatic events. Given the discussion above of the relatively minor role of motion in the fashioning of this story, it is to be expected that the result of desensitizing the pace function to motion is to more faithfully bring out the ebb and flow of the story. Edge "C" is "shifted" to the point where Spielberg brings his increasing metric montage to a climax. In addition to this improved accuracy, edges "A", "B", and "D"

refer to dramatic events that have been detected in this new configuration, with the lessening of the motion *noise* (i.e., not indicative of events) in the pace measure.

4. CONCLUSIONS

We have shown how the film grammar relating to the production of motion pictures can be exploited for the purpose of creating tools that can extract semantic information from motion pictures. A function for the calculation of the expressive element, pace or tempo has been briefly outlined and demonstrated. Further, we have experimented with the relative contribution of each of the two fundamental components of pace, namely shot length and motion. The results indicate that it is possible to sensitize the pace function to different flavours of dramatic event. They also serve as further impetus to sift the body of film grammar for aid in the task of extracting useful information from the film medium.

5. REFERENCES

[1] B. Adams, C. Dorai, and S. Venkatesh. Role of shot length in characterizing tempo and dramatic story sections in motion pictures. In *IEEE Pacific-Rim Conference on Multimedia*, Sydney, Australia, December 2000.

[2] B. Adams, C. Dorai, and S. Venkatesh. Towards automatic extraction of expressive elements from motion pictures: Tempo. In *IEEE International Conference on Multimedia and Expo*, New York City, USA, July 2000.

[3] D. Arijon. *Grammar of the film language.* Silman-James Press, 1976.

[4] E. Britannica. Encyclopedia Britannica Online, 1999.

[5] T. Sobchack and V. Sobchack. *An introduction to film.* Scot, Foresman and Company, 1987.

User-defined Music Sequence Retrieval

Masoud Alghoniemy and Ahmed H. Tewfik
Department of Electrical Engineering, University of Minnesota
Minneapolis, MN 55455
masoud, tewfik@ece.umn.edu

Abstract

A system for retrieving a sequence of music excerpts or songs based on users and producers requirements is proposed in this paper. Our system provides a flexible way to retrieve music pieces based on its contents as well as user-defined constraints. The proposed system allows online users to extract a sequence of songs whose first and last tracks are known and at the same time the in-between songs have minimum inter-track differences and satisfy predefined requirements. We model the problem as a constrained minimum cost flow problem which leads to a binary integer linear program (BILP) that can be solved in a reasonable amount of time.

1 Introduction

Online music distribution centers have proved its effectiveness in distributing high quality music and at the same time avoiding the disadvantages of buying physical CD's [1, 2]. This is due to the high quality of digital audio compression standards, the affordability and the high capacity of portable players, the easiness of accessing online music and finally the feasibility of building your own style of songs. On the other hand, buying physical CD's has its own limitations. Most of the time people buy a certain CD to listen only to two or three songs and rarely enjoy the whole collection. Secondly, with high probability the successive tracks inside the CD have no correlation between them which may not be preferable if you enjoy listening to a style of songs rather than to individual songs. In this paper, terms like songs, music excerpts, titles and tracks are used interchangeably. It should be noted that current online music retrieval systems do not provide users with the full flexibility in designing their listening style. The problem stems from the traditional textual query which asks for the singer name, the song title or the year of release. These information may not be available to the user at the time of request. There are other factors add to the limitations of the current systems. First, lack of users awareness to music/songs which they may like in the database due to the huge number of titles and the

diverse styles. Second, the difficulty in searching for listening styles rather than for individual songs in such a huge collection which requires an enormous amount of time. We should mention that producers have certain requirements, as well, in exploiting previous catalogs to reach a balance among themselves, which seems to be a hard constraint to impose in the current systems. Finally, it is also infeasible in the current systems how can they provide the personal distribution service based on customers requirements [3, 4]. For example, how can you extract a sequence of songs which starts with a hard rock and ends with a classic one and at the same time satisfy your listening style and producers needs?. This seems to be infeasible in the current systems.

2 Problem Formulation

In our formulation to the problem we follow the same notations described by the authors in [4] which are repeated here to avoid confusion. We assume that we have a database consists of M songs/music excerpts, each of them consists of N attributes. The attributes can be musical characteristics, singer gender, type of tempo, kind of instruments, etc. In this paper we assume that the attributes have already been extracted, manually or automatically [5, 6]. Each song is represented as a binary vector, V_k, of dimension N. For example, assume that the kth song is represented as $V_k = [1\ 0\ 0\ 1\ 0\ 1\ 1]^T$, here $N = 7$, then this song satisfies attributes number 1, 4, 6, and 7 while the attributes 2, 3, and 5 are not satisfied. Assume that the required sequence consists of L titles starts with a song, S, and ends up with a song, T. Let us name S as a source and T as a sink to be suited with our model as explained later. Define two types of requirements which should be satisfied in the sequence as constraints, absolute and coherence constraints. Absolute constraints deal with the percentage of each attribute, the at most and the at least constraints, which has to be satisfied in the constructed sequence. On the other hand coherence constraints deal with the correlation between successive songs in the sequence [4]. Absolute constraints can be imposed by defining C_{min} and C_{max} as the $N \times 1$ vectors whose i^{th} element contains the *minimum* and the *maximum* number of attribute i to be satisfied in the retrieved sequence. For example, consider $C_{min} = [4\ 0\ 2\ 3\ 0\ 0\ 1]^T$ and $C_{max} = [L\ 6\ 7\ L\ 5\ L\ L]^T$ then the retrieved sequence should have at most 6 out of its L songs satisfy the second attribute and at the same time at least two and at most 7 of them satisfy the third attribute. It should be noted that placing L in the ith position in C_{max} denotes that the maximum number is unbounded. Similarly placing 0 in the ith position in C_{min} indicates that the minimum number of attribute i is unbounded. Coherence constraints are imposed by minimizing the discontinuity between the successive songs to be at most D.

2.1 Network Flow Model

Consider a network which has M nodes and there is a flow going out from the source node, S, and ending in the sink node, T. Each node k is represented by a binary vector V_k in the N dimensional space. Fig. 1 shows a simplified network of 5 nodes.

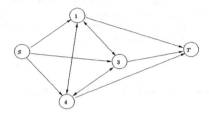

Figure 1: Network with 5 nodes

In order to relate our problem to the network flow problem both coherence and absolute constraints are imposed by associating each arc with two quantities, costs and weights.

2.1.1 Coherence Constraints

Coherence constraints are imposed in order to minimize the discontinuity between successive songs. We model it by associating a cost for each arc in the network. The cost of going from node i to node j, c_{ij}, is

$$c_{ij} = \begin{cases} 1 & if \quad \|V_i - V_j\|_1 \leq D \\ \alpha & otherwise \end{cases} \qquad (1)$$

where α is a large number and D is an integer represents the maximum allowable difference between successive songs. It is clear that finding the path with the minimum cost between the source and the sink would satisfy the coherence constraints but not the absolute constraints.

2.1.2 Absolute Constraints

Absolute constraints guarantee that the retrieved sequence of songs will satisfy users requirements by bounding the percentage of each attribute in the sequence. To impose absolute constraints in the network model, define the vector weight of the arc connecting node i to node j as W_{ij}. As it is clear from Fig. 1 the network has a directed graph, which means that $W_{ij} \neq W_{ji}$. The weights are defined as follows

$$W_{ij} = \begin{cases} 2V_i - V_j & if \quad i \neq S, \ j \neq T \\ V_i - V_j & if \quad i = S, \ j \neq T \\ 2V_i + V_j & if \quad i \neq S, \ j = T \end{cases} \qquad (2)$$

Assigning the weights as in (2) guarantees that the total weight of any path from S to T will be equal to $\sum_{k=S}^{k=T} V_k$.

The objective now is to find a continuous path connecting the source and the sink which has a minimum cost and at the same time has a constrained weights. This can be formulated by the following minimization problem

$$\min_{i,j} \sum_{i=S}^{j=T} c_{ij} \qquad (3)$$

$$subject \ to \quad C_{min} \leq \sum_{i=S}^{j=T} W_{ij} \leq C_{max}$$

3 Solution Strategy

In this section, we put (3) in an integer linear program context which can be solved using the branch and bound algorithm [7].

3.1 Adjacency Matrix

To correctly define the variables in the linear program, an Adjacency Matrix (AM) need to be defined. The adjacency matrix is another form of representing a network which makes it easier to relate variables together. In general, a network of M nodes has an AM of size $M \times M$ and each cell in the matrix represents an arc in the original network and its value is the cost of this arc as in (1). For illustration purposes we will consider the adjacency matrix of the network in Fig. 1. The network in Fig. 1 has only 5 nodes from which $S = 2$ and $T = 5$ and its AM is shown in Fig. 2. As pointed ear-

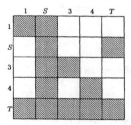

Figure 2: Adjacency Matrix for the Network in Fig. 1

lier, each cell in the AM represents an arc in the original network. For example, the cell whose coordinate is (4,3) represents an arc going from node 4 to node 3 and its value is c_{34}. Note that the filled cells in Fig. 2 represent invalid cells in the sense that their coordinates do not represent a valid cell in the network. It is clear that the second column of the AM is invalid, this is true since it is not allowed to go to the source, $S = 2$, from any other node. The same is true for the fifth row and the diagonal cells. It should be noted that the cell $AM(S,T)$ is also invalid to avoid a direct transition from the source to the sink. Invalid cells are assigned high costs, α, in the AM to avoid considering them in the solution of (3). For a general network, the previous rules apply as well. Let $y_{ij} \in \{0,1\}$ be the variable associated with the cell $AM(i,j)$ and Γ be the set of valid cells, then we can rewrite the network constraints as follows.

$$\sum_{i \in \Gamma} y_{Si} = 1 \qquad (4)$$

$$\sum_{i \in \Gamma} y_{iT} = 1 \qquad (5)$$

$$\sum_{k \in \Gamma} y_{ki} = \sum_{j \in \Gamma} y_{ij}, \quad i \notin \{S, T\} \qquad (6)$$

$$\sum_{i \in \Gamma} x_{ij} \in \{0, 1\}. \qquad (7)$$

$$x_{ij} + x_{ji} \in \{0, 1\}. \qquad (8)$$

Constraints (4) and (5) ensure that the sequence starts from the source and ends in the sink respectively. On the other hand (6) and (7) guarantee the continuity of the path, with only one arc, at each node. Finally constraint (8) is imposed to avoid oscillation between any two nodes.

3.2 Linear Programming

Transforming the problem into a linear program form is performed by lexicographically ordering the AM into the vector $\mathbf{f}$ of dimensionality $M^2 \times 1$, which consists of the costs of each arc, and transforming y_{ij} into $x_k \in \{0, 1\}$ according to the mapping

$$k = (i - 1)M + j \qquad (9)$$

The network constraints described in the previous subsection can now be imposed into the constraint matrix $\mathbf{A}$ and the corresponding constraint vector $\mathbf{a}$. Similarly absolute constraints can be represented by the $N \times M^2$ constraint matrix $\mathbf{C}$ and the corresponding constraint vectors C_{max} and C_{min}. Columns of $\mathbf{C}$ consist of vector weights described in (2) and arranged according to (9). Then it is required to solve the following binary optimization problem

$$\min_{\mathbf{x}} \mathbf{f}^T \mathbf{x} \qquad (10)$$

$$subject \ to \begin{cases} \mathbf{Ax} = \mathbf{a} \\ \mathbf{Cx} \geq C_{min} \\ \mathbf{Cx} \leq C_{max} \\ \mathbf{1}^T \mathbf{x} = L - 1 \\ x_k \in \{0, 1\} \end{cases}$$

where $\mathbf{1}$ is a $M^2 \times 1$ vector of all ones. It should be noted that the $M^2 \times 1$ solution vector $\mathbf{x}$ should only have $L - 1$ ones as indicated by the constraints. This ensures that we have exactly a sequence of L tracks. It is clear that (10) follows the standard form of the BILP which can be solved using the branch and bound algorithm [7].

$$\hat{R} = \begin{bmatrix} 0 & 0 & 0 & 0 & 0 & 1 & 1 & 1 & 1 & 1 & 1 & 1 \\ 1 & 1 & 1 & 0 & 0 & 0 & 0 & 0 & 0 & 0 & 0 & 0 \\ 0 & 0 & 1 & 1 & 1 & 1 & 1 & 1 & 1 & 1 & 1 & 1 \\ 1 & 1 & 1 & 1 & 1 & 1 & 0 & 0 & 0 & 0 & 1 & 1 \\ 0 & 1 & 1 & 1 & 1 & 1 & 1 & 1 & 1 & 0 & 0 & 0 \\ 0 & 0 & 0 & 0 & 0 & 0 & 0 & 0 & 0 & 0 & 0 & 0 \\ 1 & 1 & 1 & 1 & 1 & 1 & 1 & 1 & 1 & 1 & 1 & 0 \\ 0 & 0 & 0 & 0 & 0 & 0 & 0 & 1 & 1 & 1 & 1 \\ 1 & 1 & 1 & 1 & 0 & 0 & 0 & 0 & 0 & 0 & 0 & 0 \\ 1 & 1 & 1 & 1 & 1 & 1 & 1 & 0 & 0 & 0 & 0 & 0 \end{bmatrix}$$

4 Simulation Results

We simulated a collection of $M = 100$ songs each has $N = 10$ attributes by a randomly distributed binary matrix of dimension 10×100. The required sequence of songs should contain $L = 12$ songs with a maximum inter-track diferences $D = 1$. The first track $S = [0 \ 1 \ 0 \ 1 \ 0 \ 0 \ 1 \ 0 \ 1 \ 1]^T$ while $T = [1 \ 0 \ 1 \ 1 \ 0 \ 0 \ 0 \ 1 \ 0 \ 0]^T$. The minimum number of allowable attributes $C_{min} = [4 \ 2 \ 6 \ 6 \ 6 \ 0 \ 8 \ 0 \ 2 \ 5]^T$

while the maximum allowable number of attributes $C_{max} = [8 \ 5 \ 10 \ 10 \ 8 \ 9 \ 11 \ 6 \ 5 \ 7]^T$. The retrieved sequence of tracks is listed in the columns of the matrix $\hat{R}$. Examining the columns of $\hat{R}$ justifies the imposed constraints. First, the first track is the same as the source, S, while the last track is exactly T. Second, the maximum difference between any two successive tracks is at most 1. Third, the maximum and the minimum attributes in the retrieved sequence is bounded by C_{min} and C_{max} as expected.

5 conclusion

In this paper we proposed a system for retrieving music pieces from a database based on users preferences. The proposed system allows users to specify the first and the last required track, their attribute preferences and the maximum allowable inter-track discontinuity.

6 Acknowledgment

This work was suported by the AFRL under grant AF/F3060298 C-0176.

References

[1] http://www.mp3.com

[2] http://www.emusic.com

[3] F. Pachet, P. Roy, and D. Cazaly, "A Combinatorial Approach to Content-based Music Selection," *Proc. International Conference on Multimedia Computing and Systems,* Vol. 1, pp. 457-462, Italy, June, 1999.

[4] Masoud Alghoneimy and Ahmed H. Tewfik, "Personalized Music Distribution," *Proc. International Conference on Acoustics Speech and Signal Processing,* (ICASSP) Turkey, June 2000.

[5] Masoud Alghoniemy and Ahmed H. Tewfik, "Rhythm and Periodicity Detection in Polyphonic Music," *Proc. IEEE third Workshop on Multimedia Signal Processing,* pp. 185-190, Denmark, September. 1999.

[6] Scheirer, E. D., "Tempo and Beat Analysis of Acoustic Musical Signals," *Journal of the Acoustical Society of America,* 103(1), pp.588-601, 1998.

[7] F. Hillier and G. Lieberman, "Introduction to Mathematical Programming," McGraw-Hill, 1995.

Pricing Considerations in Video-on-Demand Systems[*]

Prithwish Basu
Dept. of Electrical and Computer Engg.
Boston University
8 Saint Mary's St., Boston, MA, USA
pbasu@bu.edu

Thomas D.C. Little
Dept. of Electrical and Computer Engg.
Boston University
8 Saint Mary's St., Boston, MA, USA
tdcl@bu.edu

ABSTRACT

Video-on-demand (VoD) has been an active area of research for the past few years in the multimedia research community. However, there have not been many significant commercial deployments of VoD owing to the inadequacy of *per user* bandwidth and the lack of a good business model.[1] Significant research efforts have been directed towards reduction of network bandwidth requirements, improvement of server utilization, and minimization of start-up latency. In this paper, we investigate another aspect of VoD systems which has been largely neglected by the research community, namely, pricing models for VoD systems. We believe that the price charged to a user for an on-demand video stream should influence the rate of user arrivals into the VoD system and in turn should depend upon quality-of-service (QoS) factors such as initial start-up latency. We briefly describe some simple pricing models and analyze the tradeoffs involved in such scenarios from a profit maximization point of view. We further explore secondary content insertion (ad-insertion) which was proposed elsewhere [1] not only as a technique for reducing the resource requirements at the server and the network, but also as a means of subsidizing VoD content to the end user. We treat the rate of ad insertion as another QoS factor and demonstrate how it can influence the price of movie delivery.

Keywords

Video-on-demand, pricing models, service aggregation

1. INTRODUCTION

With the explosive growth of the Internet and broadband cable networks in the mid- and late nineties, inter-

---

[*]This work is supported by the NSF under grant No. NCR-9523958.

[1]Several VoD field trials have been conducted in the US and elsewhere [5], but most of them have been reported to be unsuccessful from a business point of view, so far.

active video-on-demand (VoD) had been touted to be one of the most promising future applications for such networks. Unfortunately, inadequacy of bandwidth for serving a significant user population has stymied the growth in deployment of VoD on a large scale. Hence, lot of research efforts have been directed towards finding a scalable solution to the bandwidth problem using different techniques for serving *aggregates* of users [2, 3, 4]. These techniques use CATV broadcast or IP multicast as dissemination mechanisms. One aspect of VoD systems that has been largely neglected by the research community is pricing of VoD services. In this paper we briefly investigate several factors that can affect the price of a video stream delivered to the user, and also analyze some economic tradeoffs that exist in that context. Such an analysis can help in establishing a sound economic basis for a large scale deployment of VoD.

We develop models for pricing three different types of VoD service. First, in Sec. 2, we start with a simple interactive VoD system which provides each user with a dedicated channel and show how an optimal price can be calculated for maximization of profit. In Sec. 3, we describe how a QoS factor like start-up latency can affect the price of an on-demand movie in a staggered broadcast delivery system, and then we again show how profits can be maximized in such a setup. In Sec. 4, we describe how ads can be used to subsidize VoD to users, and speculate how varying degrees of ad insertion can affect the price and the interest of the users. We also demonstrate how profits can be maximized in such a scenario. Sec. 5 concludes the paper and gives some directions of future work.

2. OPTIMAL PRICE SELECTION

A VoD system consists of a video server which can serve users on N channels at any point of time. Users arrive into the system with an average rate of λ per unit time. For simplicity, suppose that the VoD system is not aggregation based, i.e., each channel supports only one user, because the service is fully interactive. Suppose that the movie is L time units long, and that the users remain in the system for some more video time $T_{int} > 0$, on average, due to pauses and rewinds.[2] We can treat the system as an $M/G/N$ queue, where M stands for Poisson arrivals, G stands for a general service time which has a deterministic part L and a stochastic part T_{int} ($T_s = L + T_{int}$), and N stands for the number of servers. For stability of the queue, i.e., for bounded waiting

---

[2]A large number of fast forward interactions may result in T_{int} being negative, but that is unlikely in a paid service.

359

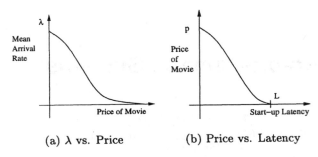

(a) λ vs. Price   (b) Price vs. Latency

Figure 1: Interdependence of Parameters

times, the condition $\lambda T_s < N$ must hold, hence N should be chosen properly.

Now suppose each user is charged a price p for viewing a movie. Intuitively, the mean arrival rate λ will depend on the price of the movie as depicted by Fig. 1(a). However, the exact function $\lambda(p)$ can only be known from marketing experiments such as user polls and surveys. Suppose the VoD service provider (VoDSP) incurs a cost b per channel per unit time. Therefore in time T, the cost incurred will be NbT. In that time the VoDSP will receive λT user requests. If no user is rejected (by bounding of waiting time due to appropriate selection of N), the revenue earned will be $p\lambda(p)T$. The profit per unit time is given by $P = p\lambda(p) - Nb$. Now, we have an optimization problem at hand given by:

Maximize: $P(p, N) = p\lambda(p) - Nb$
Subject to: (1) $p > 0$ and (2) $N > \lambda(p)T_s$

Optimality is achieved when the second constraint has an equality, and the optimal price p^* is given by the solution to the the equation: $(bT_s - p^*)\lambda'(p^*) = \lambda(p^*)$. We should point out here that there is an issue with the above analysis: when the second constraint is relaxed to an equality, the variability in arrivals may result in larger waiting times, and hence the assumption that the waiting times are low and do not affect user arrival, may fail. However, by over-engineering the system (i.e., by allocating a larger N than predicted by the optimal solution), we can approach a near-optimal solution. Also, if the function $P(p, N)$ is not *convex*, then first derivative techniques may be inadequate to solve the optimization problem. However, since the function is bounded, it will have a maxima, and that can be found using other more sophisticated (perhaps numerical) techniques.

3. BROADCAST DELIVERY SYSTEMS

Recently, staggered broadcast delivery systems have become popular with researchers in this area since they can be used to provide VoD service over CATV networks to a large user population with a *constant* number of "staggered" broadcast channels per movie. The basic idea is to divide the whole movie into a constant number of smaller segments and then broadcast each smaller segment repeatedly on a different channel. The client listens on one or more of these channels for downloading the video data before consumption. The simplest scheme which does not need any buffering on the clients is to distribute a movie of length L into an equal number of parts. In this case, the worst case start-up latency, t_{sl} is inversely proportional to the total number of broadcast channels, n ($n = \frac{L}{t_{sl}}$). The worst case start-up latency is a QoS parameter which can affect the price that is charged to a user by the VoDSP. We show by simple analysis

how this parameter can be adjusted by the VoDSP for maximizing their profits. More sophisticated broadcast schemes like Skyscraper Broadcast [4] can reduce the startup latency by dividing the movie into segments of increasing size and by intelligent use of client buffering. However, the basic pricing model is similar in that case as n can be expressed as a function of t_{sl}.

As in the previous section, let us assume that the VoDSP incurs a cost b per video stream per unit time. Since they allocate $n = \frac{L}{t_{sl}}$ streams for a movie, the total cost incurred by the VoDSP in time T is $\frac{L}{t_{sl}}bT$. Suppose the mean arrival rate into the system is λ per unit time. Hence the total number of users that have arrived in the system in time T is λT. Suppose the price p charged to a user varies with t_{sl}. We depict the price by some function $p(t_{sl})$ which intuitively should be a decreasing function of t_{sl} (a possible function is depicted graphically in Fig. 1(b)). As in Sec. 2, the exact shape of this curve too can be characterized by marketing techniques such as polls and surveys. The revenue earned by the VoDSP in time T is $\lambda T p(t_{sl})$, and the profit per unit time, P is given by $P = \lambda p(t_{sl}) - \frac{L}{t_{sl}}b$. P is maximized at $t_{sl} = t_{opt}$ when $P'(t_{sl}) = 0$, i.e., $\lambda p'(t_{opt}) + \frac{L}{t_{opt}^2}b = 0$. If the equation has multiple roots, then the VoDSP can choose either of those operating points depending upon other factors like viewer utility, which we do not consider in this paper.

4. AD-INSERTION BASED SYSTEMS

Secondary content insertion (or ad insertion) has been proposed for reduction in server and network bandwidth requirements, and for subsidizing the cost of VoD to the end user [1]. First, we consider ads only as a means of subsidizing the cost to the user. We consider a scenario where all users are uniformly shown ads at a rate α ($0 \le \alpha \le 1$).[3] Intuitively, the price of a movie, p to a user should be a decreasing function of α. If $\alpha \ge \alpha_0$, the movie is streamed to the users for free. Price p should be *maximum* when no ads are shown, i.e., $\alpha = 0$. An interesting topic to study is how the price varies with α in the interval $[0, \alpha_0]$. Two possible curves have been shown as I and II in Fig. 2(a).

Initially, let us suppose that the mean arrival rate λ is constant, and hence the number of movie channels needed to support that rate (N) is also constant. In this case, the VoDSP has two sources of revenue, namely, a broadcast advertisement channel, and the price of movies that it charges its users. If a video server can stream out N streams concurrently,[4] and if b is the cost per stream per unit time, the cost incurred in time T is NbT. If the VoDSP charges a per unit time to the advertisers, the revenue earned from the ad channel in time T is aT. Since the advertisers are willing to pay more money if they know that more people are watching ads at any point of time, a can be represented as an increasing function of α. With respect to the above model, the profit per unit time is given by $P = \lambda p(\alpha) + a(\alpha) - Nb$, and it is maximized at $\alpha = \alpha^*$ which satisfies the equation $\lambda p'(\alpha^*) + a'(\alpha^*) = 0$.

Now we consider the case when the mean arrival rate may be influenced by the price p and the quality of service factor α. Fig. 2(b) shows a tentative schematic of the effect of α on

---

[3] $\alpha = \frac{A_{max}}{A_{max} + V_{min}}$, where A_{max} is the maximum continuous ad time and V_{min} is the minimum video time between ads.
[4] For bounded waiting time: $\lambda L < N$.

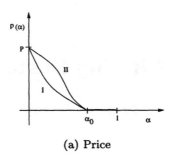

(a) Price

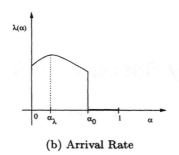

(b) Arrival Rate

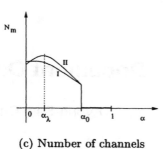

(c) Number of channels

Figure 2: Effect of Ad-Ratio

the arrival rate of users into the system in the steady state.[5] As mentioned previously, these functions can be characterized more exactly by conducting marketing experiments. As α increases, the price drops and hence more people are attracted to the system. But for $\alpha > \alpha_\lambda$, the high rate of ad insertion acts more as a deterrent, and λ decreases. Also, in this case, the number of channels that are needed to support a particular arrival rate is lower bounded by $N(\alpha) > \lambda(\alpha)L$. Therefore we have an optimization problem akin to the one discussed in Sec. 2:

Maximize: $P(\alpha) = \lambda(\alpha)p(\alpha) + a(\alpha) - N(\alpha)b$

Subject to: (1) $0 \le \alpha < \alpha_0$ and (2) $N(\alpha) > \lambda(\alpha)L$

P is maximized for a particular value of $\alpha = \alpha^*$, where α^* is a root of the following equation:

$$p'(\alpha)\lambda(\alpha) + a'(\alpha) + (p(\alpha) - L)\lambda'(\alpha) = 0$$

Stream Merging Based Systems. Constrained ad insertion has been proposed for reducing the server and network bandwidth requirements by reducing the temporal skews between adjacent streams receiving the same content [1]. Essentially, a leading stream is put onto a multicast ad channel for A_{max} time units and then is shown video for V_{min} time units, in a cyclic manner, while a trailing stream continuously receives video until it merges with the leading stream. The merging algorithm ensures that no stream receives ads at a rate greater than α.

In order to support users arriving into the system at a rate $\lambda(\alpha)$, in steady state, the number of channels needed is given by $N_m(\alpha)$ which is an decreasing function of α for a constant arrival rate λ. However, since the arrival rate is influenced by the ad ratio, $N_m(\alpha)$ may not be a strict decreasing function. For $\alpha > \alpha_\lambda$, $N_m(\alpha)$ drops due to the drop in the arrival rate, and due to greater ad insertion. But for $0 \le \alpha \le \alpha_\lambda$, $N_m(\alpha)$ is dictated by two opposing behaviors: increase in arrival rate (which tends to increase N_m) and greater ad insertion (tends to decrease N_m). Hence the cumulative effect of these two forces may result in either an increasing or a decreasing function of α. It is very hard to characterize $N_m(\alpha)$ analytically, but it can be characterized by simulations. Two curves that could possibly characterize $N_m(\alpha)$ are shown in Fig. 2(c). Again, we are faced with a profit maximization problem as before:

Maximize: $P(\alpha) = \lambda(\alpha)p(\alpha) + a(\alpha) - N_m(\alpha)b$

Subject to: (1) $0 \le \alpha < \alpha_0$

P is maximized for $\alpha = \alpha^*$ where α^* is a root of the following equation:

$$p'(\alpha)\lambda(\alpha) + p(\alpha)\lambda'(\alpha) + a'(\alpha) - bN'_m(\alpha) = 0$$

---

[5]$a(.)$ may not be an increasing function in this case.

5. CONCLUSION AND FUTURE WORK

We investigated pricing related tradeoffs involved in different types of VoD system deployments. Three different settings were analyzed: (1) a simple interactive VoD system with a dedicated channel per user, (2) a staggered broadcast delivery system, and (3) an aggregation system based on ad-insertion. We demonstrated in this paper how a multitude of factors such as price, QoS level (start-up latency and ad ratio), and user arrival rates can influence each other, and how the optimal price of a VoD service can be obtained (from a profit maximization perspective) in each of the above settings. We believe that such an analysis of pricing models can help in establishing a sound economic basis for wide deployment of VoD in future.

There are some open issues that need investigation. Waiting times in VoD systems due to queueing (we have addressed waiting times due to batching) can be another QoS factor for pricing.[6] Also, a good model of user behavior with respect to factors such as price is needed (by extensive survey) for proper characterization of the functions mentioned in this paper.

6. REFERENCES

[1] P. Basu, A. Narayanan, W. Ke, T. D. C. Little, and A. Bestavros. Optimal scheduling of secondary content for aggregation in video-on-demand systems. In *Proceedings ICCCN '99, Boston-Natick, MA*, pages 104–109, October 1999.

[2] A. Dan, P. Shahabuddin, D. Sitaram, and D. Towsley. Channel allocation under batching and VCR control in video-on-demand systems. *Journal of Parallel and Distributed Computing*, 30(2):168–179, November 1995.

[3] L. Golubchik, J. Lui, and R. Muntz. Adaptive piggybacking: A novel technique for data sharing in video-on-demand storage servers. *ACM/Springer Multimedia Systems*, 4:140–155, 1996.

[4] K. A. Hua and S. Sheu. Skyscraper broadcasting: A new broadcasting scheme for metropolitan video-on-demand systems. In *Proceedings ACM SIGCOMM '97, Cannes, France*, pages 89–100, September 1997.

[5] Interactive TV trials. URL – http://www.teleport.com/~samc/cable4.html.

---

[6]Large waiting times can result in loss of revenue due to *reneging*.

Document Ontology Based Personalized Filtering System

Kyung-Sam Choi

Chi-Hoon Lee

Phill-Kyu Rhee

IM Laboratory
In Ha Univ. Incheon , Korea
82-32-875-0742

g1981342@inhavision.inha.ac.kr

g1991259@inhavision.inha.ac.kr

pkrhee@inha.ac.kr

ABSTRACT

We propose the use of the personalized ontology model to improve the effectiveness of web documents filtering process. One important feature of this model is that by constructing the user specific ontology, web documents can be classified by using the user oriented meta data that reflects the user's view about the documents concept. Another is that by applying the user model to searching the classified documents, we achieved the effective document search performance. To find the user's preference, Bayesian Learner accepts user's interests flow as an input and writes output to users profile. Based on those user profiles, user specific ontologies are constructed to provide efficient search environment.

Keywords

Ontology, Personalized System, User Modeling, Document Filtering System.

1. INTRODUCTION

As the information on the Internet increases rapidly, it is difficult to find information appropriate to each user's interests. Many researches have been done among IR or search engine societies to provide user specific information. Most popular methods are collecting or filtering Web documents based on users' Web access patterns. However, most of them fail to produce good results reliably, because they consider not users' search tendency and their interests, but query history.

In response to the problems posed by the current state of information retrieval system, researchers such as A. Tan and Pazzani have attempted to process the web documents by using user model which is based on users' interests and favor. In PIN, to search the personalized news information, A. Tan proposed the method of constructing and updating user profile that specifies

user's interest. Also, Pazzani proposed SysKill&Webert that finds web document appropriate to user's needs and interest[1]. In above two retrieval system, user profiles act as a filter of user favorite web documents or news group information. However, those systems cannot automatically keep track of changing user's needs, because user profiles must be indicated explicitly by the user. Another system, Mlandenic's WebWatcher monitors user's behavior and adapts itself to the user's needs. This system uses unsupervised learning method and collects web documents based on monitored user behavior. Those collected documents are used to make user profile and this profile helps the system to find proper documents to the user[2,3,4].

Although mentioned systems provide documents relevant to each users' interests, they classify documents based on specific algorithms that do not consider each users' view(concept)[5,6]. To resolve the above problem, we propose the use of personalized ontology model to improve the effectiveness of web documents filtering process. By constructing the user specific document ontology, web documents can be classified by the user oriented meta data that reflect the user's view about the document concept. And, we apply the user model to searching the classified documents.

2. THE PERSONALIZED DOCUMENT ONTOLOGY MODEL
2.1 Ontology

In the context of the AI, a specification of a representational vocabulary for a shared domain of discourse - definitions of classes, relations, functions, and other objects -- is called an ontology[7]. Similarly, in the knowledge sharing field, the term "ontology" is to mean a specification of a conceptualization[8,9]. That is, an ontology is a description(like a formal specification of a program) of the concepts and relationships that can exist for an agent or a community of agents[11]. In brief, ontology is to help computer systems communicate with system users or another systems. Currently, ontology is popularly used to explain the information structure. For example, it is adopted to construct domain knowledge in CBR(Content Based Retrieval) system or to show the relationships among image data in the graphic image database.

2.2 The role of ontology

The systems that adopt this traditional notion of ontology can just provide predefined or structured information of the certain domain, because only one ontology is constructed for all users. Since users want to find information that corresponds to their view, the system should adapt itself to user's concept(viewpoint). In our proposed model, the personalized document ontology represents the user's concept towards some domains. As term "personalized" indicates, each user has his/her own ontology, so that documents that are relevant to the users are obtained based on those user-specific ontology.

When constructing ontology, since it is not an ideal approach to give the users responsibility for assigning category information, every ontology is constructed by analyzing user interactions with the system. Our ontology model chose hierarchical structure to express user specific web document. The initial step to build an ontology is defining categories in which documents are located. Each document is indexed according to the keywords, and words frequencies are recorded in the inversed file. By using those information, each document is classified and located in proper category.

2.3 MetaData extraction for document classification

We employ two kinds of metadata in this paper. They are user specified metadata and document metadata. The user specified metadata is the keywords that user enters when he/she registers document and document metadata is the results of TF·IDF method. These two kinds of metadata are not necessary same, but result shows that they are almost same. These two metadata are combined to generate new MetaData of the documents that contains user's view towards document.

After extracting MetaData, we use a K-means algorithm based on document's MetaData to place every document in a proper category. Figure 1 illustrates the block diagram of document classification process.

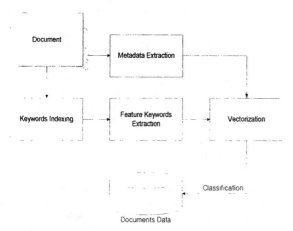

Figure 1. Document Classification Process

3. USER MODEL CONSTRUCTION
3.1 Bayesian learning for user adaptation

User modeling is the process of knowing about the user in terms of computer system. User model is constructed by analyzing user's interaction with the computer systems and the constructed user model helps computer systems provide user specific services to each user. There are many learning methods for doing this work. In our system, we employed Bayesian Learning algorithm among many learning methods.

What we want to obtain by executing learning algorithm is to know whether the user likes the documents or the set of document that the computer systems provide. Bayesian Learner calculates the probability that user will satisfy the proposed documents after learning user's document preference.

Figure 2 shows the block diagram of schematic leaning process.

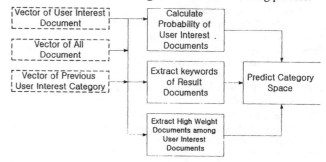

Figure 2. Conceptual Model of Bayesian Learning

3.2 User profile

User profile consists of ID and category edge weights information among documents for learning process. While user interacts with the system, user might rate the degree of satisfaction about the documents or download the certain documents. Learning module extracts high weighted keywords of those documents and calculates the similarity between extracted keywords and document's vector value of search results. We used cosine measure to calculate two vectors' similarity, where the input of cosine measure is the result of the Bayesian Learning algorithm.

Obtained results(keywords list) of learning algorithm are updated to the user profile as weight information. Since keywords list in user profile obtained by above process can be category information that the user is interested in, those keywords play an important role in building a personalized ontology.

Document Link Information Matrix of the user profile contains the edge weights information between 192 document's category and their high level nodes. By adjusting edge weights which are obtained from learning process, each user's interested and non interested categories are recognized by the system. Therefore, this process yields user specific ontology for documents.

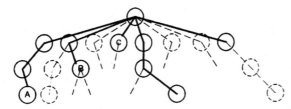

Figure 3. Personalized Category Tree

Figure 3 is one of the personalized category trees whose interest domains or knowledge depth can be expressed according to the depth of the user specific category. Based on those interest domains and knowledge depth, it is possible to classify users for better user specific document filtering services.

4. EXPERIMENTS

Experiments were conducted on abstracts of computer related papers. The Collaboration, Recall and Precision were measured to find how well the proposed system works for each user. We performed experiment in two way to compare non-adaptive system and user adaptive system that employs our proposed ontology model. Total 75 users are asked to query 100 times to each system. Figure 4 and 5 show that performance of the user-adaptive system is substantially higher than non-adaptive system. The average Recall and Precision values of non-adaptive system are 0.53 and 0.41, respectively. However, user-adaptive system's average Recall and Precision values are 0.74 and 0.66.

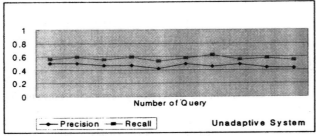

Figure 4. Non Adaptive System

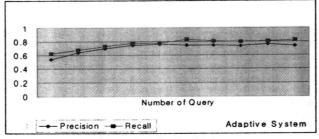

Figure 5. Adaptive System

5. CONCLUSION

Traditional user adaptive system requires user's explicit indication of his/her preference. This approach cannot keep track of changing user's interests. Therefore, we propose a document ontology based personalized filtering system that satisfies the user's needs and provides user specific search environment. Document ontology of each user is dynamically constructed according to the user's opinion toward the proposed documents from the system. We have seen that dynamic construction of the ontology can help the system work well. Thought just text document is the domain of consideration in our system, we are continuing to apply this approach to the multimedia domains such as sound or image, etc.

6. REFERENCES

[1] M. Pazzani, J. Muramatsu and D. Billsus, Syskill and Webert : "Identifying interesting web sites," proceedings of the Thirteenth national Conference on Artficial Intelligence and the Eighth Innovate Applications of Artficial Intelligence Conference, pp54-61, 1996

[2] Tom Kalt, "A New Probabilistic Model of Text Classification and Retrieval", University of Massachusetts, January 25, 1996

[3] Dnuja Mlandenic, Personal WebWatcher: Design and inplementation, Technical Report IJS-DP-7472, October 1996

[4] A. Tan and C. Teo, "Learning User Profiles for Personalized Information Dissemination," Proceedings of 1998 IEEE International Joint conference on Neural Networks, pp. 183-188, May 1998

[5] Atsuo Yoshitaka, Setsuko Kishida, Masahito Hirakawa, and Tadao Ichikawa, "Knowledge-Assisted Content-Based Retrieval for Multimedia Databases," Hiroshima University, Japan

[6] Patrick J.M. Keane, "Applied Research in Concept Clustering," 51th annual Eastern Colleges Scientific Conference, Hartford, CT., An Argument for Conceptual Clustering

[7] M. Blazquez, M. Fernandez, "Building Ontologies at the Knowledge Level using the Ontology Design Environment," Journal of IEEE Intelligent Systems, pp. 37-45, Feb, 1999.

[8] Guarino N., Welty, C. *Ontological Analysis of Taxonomic Relationships.* LADSEB/CNR Internal Report 05/2000 (DRAFT). April, 2000.

[9] N. Friedman, L. Getoor, D. Koller and A. Pfeffer, "Learning Probabilistic Relational Models," *Proceedings of the 16th International Joint Conference on Artificial Intelligence* (IJCAI), Stockholm, Sweden, August 1999.

[10] A. Farquhar, R. Fikes, & J. Rice, "A Tool for Collaborative Ontology Construction," Knowledge Systems Laboratory, KSL-96-26, September 1996

[11] Sean Luke, Lee Spector, David Rager and James Henler, "Ontology-based Web Agents," School of Cognitive Science and Cultural Studies Hampshire College amherst

Video Keyframe Production by Efficient Clustering of Compressed Chromaticity Signatures

Mark S. Drew and James Au
School of Computing Science, Simon Fraser University,
Vancouver, B.C. Canada V5A 1S6
{mark,ksau}@cs.sfu.ca

ABSTRACT

We develop a new low-dimensional video frame feature that is more insensitive to lighting change, motivated by color constancy work in physics-based vision, and apply the feature to keyframe production using hierarchical clustering. The new feature has the further advantage of more expressively capturing image information and as a result produces a very succinct set of keyframes for any video. Because we effectively reduce any video to the same lighting conditions, we can produce a *universal basis* on which to project video frame features. We carry out clustering efficiently by adapting a hierarchical clustering data structure to temporally-ordered clusters. Using a new multi-stage hierarchical clustering method, we merge clusters based on the ratio of cluster variance to variance of the parent node, merging only adjacent clusters, and then follow with a second round of clustering. The second stage merges clusters incorrectly split in the first round by the greedy hierarchical algorithm, and as well merges non-adjacent clusters to fuse near-repeat shots. The new summarization method produces a very succinct set of keyframes for videos, and results are excellent.

1. INTRODUCTION

Amongst expressions of video summarization, keyframes remain the most natural and immediate means of reducing video information to a concise form. As well, if we adopt keyframes as our goal then "inverse Hollywood" techniques, such as graph-based pruning [1] or other hierarchical representations of video sequences [2, 3, 4] can be brought to bear.

Ferman and Tekalp [5] applied a clustering approach to intra-shot keyframe selection, based on average color histogram [3] and intersection histogram [6]. Other algorithms advanced have used comparison to the first frame in a shot using color and motion [7], accumulating frame differences [8], algorithms based on geometric metaphors, e.g. [9], and other means but here we mean to set out a more effective algorithm that is also simpler.

Ferman and Tekalp [5] extract keyframes by clustering, and then go on to prune as well as augment the number of frames identified as keyframes, using a number of criteria. Firstly, since lighting changes can bias the average histogram adversely, outliers with respect to luminance are added to the list of keyframes. Secondly, clusters that contain only a few frames are eliminated. Thirdly, clusters with centers closer in color distance than a threshold T_C are merged. Finally, within each cluster, if the cluster radius exceeds T_C two representative frames are chosen that are (1) closest to the center, and (2) farthest from the center. The authors use the

Y-Cb-Cr color space.

We have found that applying some of the techniques above yield poor results for keyframe extraction in quite common situations. E.g., we considered the sequence shown in Fig. 1 [1] and found that lighting changes seen there as the child steps out of the shadows confound the algorithm in [5] because of the change in pixel values under different lighting. The method in [5] applied to such real outdoor lighting change from shadowing produces many keyframes, when in fact we wish to see only one.

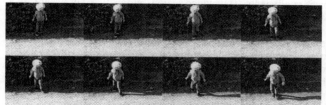

Figure 1: Video with lighting change.

In this paper we set out a method that performs correctly under this common lighting difficulty and moreover *performs better* overall on any video. Here, we utilize knowledge about color formation for lighting and surfaces, from physics-based vision, to cast the clustering problem into the form of projection of frames onto a basis derived offline. This basis is precomputed from a large training set and then applies equally to all subsequent videos.

Lighting is first discounted by normalization of color-channel bands [10]. This step approximately but effectively removes dependence on both luminance and lighting *color*. Then image frames are moved into a chromaticity color space. As well as reducing the dimensionality of color to 2 this also has the effect of removing shading. In order to make the method fairly robust to camera and object motion, and displacements, rotations, and scaling, we go over to a 2D histogram derived from DC components of frames. In this paper we use 128×128 histograms. Chromaticity histograms are then *compressed* — i.e., we treat the histograms as *images* (see [11, 10]). Here, we use a wavelet-based compression because this tends to strike a balance between simple low-pass filtering and retaining important details. Using a 3-level wavelet compression we arrive at 16×16 histograms.

However, we found that compression of histograms could be improved if the histograms are first *binarized*, i.e., entries are replaced with 1 or 0. The rationale for this step is that chromaticity histograms are a kind of color signature for an image, similar to a palette. In work involving recovering the plausible illuminant from pixel values in an image [12] it was found beneficial to utilize this kind of color signature. Here, the step of binarizing the histogram not only reduces the computational burden, since true chromaticity

---

[1] See http://www.cs.sfu.ca/~mark/ftp/AcmMM00/ for videos and full text of longer version of paper.

histograms need not be computed, but also has the effect of producing far fewer negatives in the compressed histogram. Finally, we found that one further step could substantially improve the energy compaction of the representation: we carry out a 16×16 Discrete Cosine Transform (DCT) on the compressed 16×16 histogram. After zigzag ordering, we keep 21 DCT coefficients.

The main utility of color-channel normalization and then chromaticity space is that every image approximately *goes over into the same lighting conditions*. That is, we perform a kind of universal normalization of images. Since every image now lives in approximately the same lighting, we can in fact precompute a *basis* for the DCT 21-vectors, offline, that can then be reused for any new image or video. Here we find a basis set by the Singular Value Decomposition (SVD) of the DCT 21-vectors (cf. [13] which used SVD on motion vectors and was considerably more complex than the method presented here). We found that 12 components in the new basis represent the entire DCT vector very well and that energy compaction worked better using a spherical chromaticity, rather than the usual linear one.

Thus the method we set out here is to precompute a set of 12 basis vectors, once and for all, and then form the 12-vector coefficients for any video frame with respect to this basis. Then keyframe extraction by clustering can be carried out very efficiently, using only 12-component vectors, and need not be performed only intra-shot, as in [5].

Each keyframe is associated with a length-12 feature vector of basis coefficients. Thus video search, retrieval, and browsing are a fast and simple matter once keyframe production has occurred.

The clustering method we adopt is a variant of hierarchical clustering, adapted to video. Firstly, only adjacent frames are merged, as we wish to maintain the temporal order of keyframes (as opposed to discarding temporal order, as in [14]). This permits an efficient data structure for the clustering tree and distance matrix. Also, an initial clustering is followed by an additional step on clusters found, marking some keyframes as representing near-repeated shots.

The threshold we use to control the number of clusters is the *variance ratio*; we can efficiently calculate variance for all subclusters (maintained in the hierarchical tree structure) and threshold on the ratio of intra-cluster variance to variance of the parent node. We find that a universal threshold of $T_{VR} = 0.25$ variance ratio performs quite well.

Testing performance for keyframe extraction involves a comparison of keyframes generated to those that *should* be generated, and for ground truth we must here rely on human opinion. With that proviso, we find that the method presented here does agree well with human notions of what frames most expressively summarize a video sequence.

2. ILLUMINATION CHANGE AND NORMALIZATION

The motivation for color-channel normalization lies in making images approximately independent of illumination. To understand how color normalization effects illuminant independence, firstly we note that several justifications can be made [15] for a *diagonal model* for illumination change. For consider pixel values ρ^x at camera retinal position x. Under lighting $E(\lambda)$, if the light impinges on a Lambertian surface with reflectance function $S(\lambda)$ from direction a, the RGB camera value produced is

$$\rho^x = a \cdot n^x \int E(\lambda) S^x(\lambda) q(\lambda) d\lambda \qquad (1)$$

where $q(\lambda)$ are three camera sensitivity functions, and n^x is the surface normal at position x. Now, the usual *factor model* approxi-

mation used in computer graphics can be employed:

$$\rho_k^x \simeq a \cdot n^x s_k^x e_k / \sigma_k , \quad k = 1..3 \quad \text{with} \qquad (2)$$

$$s_k^x = \int S^x(\lambda) q_k(\lambda) d\lambda , \; e_k = \int E(\lambda) q_k(\lambda) d\lambda , \; \sigma_k = \int q_k(\lambda) d\lambda$$

providing the light is fairly white [16]. Therefore under a lighting change $E \to E'$, $a \to a'$, pixel values transform according to

$$\rho_k^x \to \rho_k^{x'} = (e_k'/e_k)\rho_k^x \qquad (3)$$

Hence normalizing each color channel effectively removes the lighting. In fact, division of an N-pixel image by the mean amounts to seeing the image as it would appear in lighting $e_k = N \sigma_k / \sum_x a \cdot n^x s_k^x$. Thus under the common "gray-world" assumption, every image goes into the same lighting.

Going over to a 2D chromaticity $(r, g) = (R, G)/(R + G + B)$ removes the shading term $a \cdot n^x$. Here, for reasons discussed in §3, we actually use a spherical chromaticity $(r, g) = (R, G)/\sqrt{R^2 + G^2 + B^2}$.

Because we reduce all images to approximately the same color domain, we can calculate offline a basis on which to project each video frame. In [10] we used a wavelet-based compression method, applied to histograms as if they were images.

A further low-pass filter was applied by forming the DCT image of the resulting histogram, and truncating. However, that method can be improved in several substantive ways. Firstly, if an image essentially consists of only a few uniformly-colored patches it produces a histogram comprising a few sharp spikes. As a consequence, the wavelet-based compression gives rise to some negatives. A more well-behaved compression results if, instead, we replace the histogram with a *binarized* one, i.e., with entries either 0 or 1. In a sense, this shows a kind of color *signature* for the image, like a color palette. Now the percentage of negative counts in the compressed histogram goes down substantially.

As well, the DCT produces better energy compaction if we go over to a nonlinear definition of chromaticity, based on squared (or higher) powers of pixel values: $(r, g) = (R, G)/(R^p + G^p + B^p)^{1/p}$. The reason is that, since linear chromaticity obeys $r + g \leq 1$, there can exist a straight diagonal edge in a chromaticity histogram resulting in a DCT image that shows a ringing effect. In terms of a spherical definition of chromaticity (with $p = 2$), the straight edge is replaced by a circle and the ringing disappears. The resulting DCT image for the compressed histogram is quite concentrated.

As a final step, we form the SVD basis for the first 21 DCT coefficients, in zigzag order, for a large training set of images.

3. CLUSTERING INTRA-/INTER-SHOTS
3.1 Clustering strategy

Fig.2 shows the clustering scheme we use. We cluster using the 12-vector features outlined above. Although these vectors are longer than those used in [5], they carry much more information about the video than do the 2-vectors used there since they are grounded in a physics-based vision approach that arises from the underlying physics of color formation.

To begin with, we compute the 12-vector features for each frame, projecting onto a pre-determined basis. Because the feature space is relatively low-dimensional, and especially because we merge only adjacent frames, frame clustering is very fast. With buffering, this means that we could effectively carry out clustering on data from a temporal window of streaming video, presenting only keyframes to the user.

Only adjacent clusters are merged. The threshold used is the Variance Ratio = (intra-cluster variance)/(variance of parent node). As well, we apply a minimum variance threshold. The reason for this is that we found that if the entire video consists of only one scene, the ratio becomes meaningless. To fix this, we introduce a minimum variance threshold that would identify such uniform videos. Fortunately, these kinds of videos contain total variance that is usually much smaller than those of complex videos (by about a factor of 20). Thus we are able to select a global threshold that can work on most types of videos.

Finally, we carried out a second clustering step, on the clusters found. This has the effect of dropping whole shots that are near-repeats, as in the sequence ABCADEF.

3.2 Clustering algorithm

In detail, the steps used in the clustering algorithm are as follows:

1. Perform bottom-up hierarchical clustering using minimum L_2 distance between cluster means. Only adjacent clusters are merged. Spherical clusters containing contiguous frames are produced.

2. Extract top-level clusters that satisfy both the variance ratio threshold (intra-cluster variance) < (parent node variance) * T_{VR} and the minimum variance threshold. This gives us an initial set of clusters.

3. Merge adjacent initial clusters that satisfy thresholds. This step is needed to correct errors in the greedy hierarchical clustering algorithm in step 1: we merge similar adjacent clusters that were split in the early rounds.

4. Detect transitions and mark them: all contiguous clusters of size ≤ 3 are merged and marked as a transition.

5. Hierarchically merge non-adjacent non-transition clusters that result in lower variance: if cluster AB's variance is lower than either cluster A or B, then the two are merged.

6. Finally, one keyframe closest to its cluster centroid is extracted from each resulting cluster.

4. RESULTS

Table 1 shows results for the algorithm compared to the algorithm in [5], as specified there. Not only are the summarizations much more succinct, they are correctly unresponsive to changes in illumination, and also agree very well with human summarizations. In general, even given perfect transition detection, the method [5] generates too many keyframes whereas the present method does not; without perfect transition detection, [5] misses many more keyframes than the present method. Results may be viewed at http://www.cs.sfu.ca/~mark/ftp/AcmMM00/ .

5. CONCLUSIONS

Results produced are excellent, yielding a very succinct summarization that agrees well with human expectations, with almost no redundancy and very few misses. The success of the method depends on both the new approach to color histograms and the multistage hierarchical clustering algorithm.

However, we did find that wipe transitions becomes clusters on their own and thus create keyframes which are redundant or "half-wipe" frames. We intend to pursue this problem, applying the wipe detection in [17]. Misses mostly occur when the new scene's colors do not vary enough from the previous scene.

6. REFERENCES

[1] B.-L. Yeo and M.M. Yeung. Classification, simplification and dynamic visualization of scene transition graphs for video browsing. In *SPIE Storage and Retrieval for Image and Video Databases VI*, 1998.

[2] M.M. Yeung and B. Liu. Efficient matching and clustering of video shots. In *ICIP '95*, pages 338–341, 1995.

[3] D. Zhong, H. Zhang, and S.-F. Chang. Clustering methods for video browsing and annotation. In *SPIE Storage and Retrieval for Image and Video Databases IV*, pages 239–246, 1996.

[4] J. R. Kender and B. L. Yeo. Video scene segmentation via continuous video coherence. In *CVPR '98*, pages 367–373, 1998.

[5] A.M. Ferman and A.M. Tekalp. Efficient filtering and clustering methods for temporal video segmentation and visual summarization. *J. Vis. Commun. & Image Rep.*, 9:336–351, 1998.

[6] A.M. Ferman and A.M. Tekalp. Multiscale content extraction and representation for video indexing. In *SPIE Multimedia Storage and Archiving Systems II*, 1997.

[7] H.J. Zhang, S.Y. Tan, S.W. Smoliar, and Y. Gong. Video parsing, retrieval and browsing: An integrated and content-based solution. In *ACM Multimedia '95*, pages 15–24, 1995.

[8] A. Hanjalic, M. Ceccarelli, R.L. Lagendijk, and J. Biemond. Automation of systems enabling search on stored video data. In *SPIE Storage and Retrieval for Image and Video Databases V*, pages 427–438, 1997.

[9] D. DeMenthon, V. Kobla, and D. Doermann. Video summarization by curve simplification. In *ACM MM98*, 1998.

[10] M.S. Drew, J. Wei, and Z.N. Li. Illumination–invariant color object recognition via compressed chromaticity histograms of color–channel–normalized images. In *ICCV98*, pages 533–540. IEEE, 1998.

[11] J. Wei, M.S. Drew, and Z.N. Li. Illumination invariant video segmentation by hierarchical robust thresholding. In *Electronic Imaging '98: Storage and Retrieval for Image and Video Databases VI*, pages 188–201. SPIE Vol. 3312, 1998.

[12] G.D. Finlayson, P.M. Hubel, and S. Hordley. Colour by correlation. In *Fifth Color Imaging Conf.*, pages 6–11, 1997.

[13] E. Sahouria and A. Zakhor. Content analysis of video using principal components. *IEEE Trans. Circ. Sys. Vid. Tech.*, 9:1290–1298, 1999.

[14] A. Girgensohn and J. Boreczky. Time-constrained keyframe selection technique. In *IEEE MM Sys.*, pages 756–761, 1999.

[15] M. S. Drew, J. Wei, and Z.N. Li. Illumination–invariant image retrieval and video segmentation. *Pattern Recognition*, 32:1369–1388, 1999.

[16] C.F. Borges. Trichromatic approximation method for surface illumination. *J. Opt. Soc. Am. A*, 8:1319–1323, 1991.

[17] Mark S. Drew, Ze-Nian Li, , and Xiang Zhong. Video dissolve and wipe detection via spatio-temporal images of chromatic histogram differences. In *ICIP'00*, 2000. To appear.

14 Videos (~10,000 frames)				
Method	Correct	Generated	Redundant	Missed
Signatures	61	60	9	10
HistInt	61	347	288	2

Table 1: Keyframes generated, compared to algorithm in [5]. "Signatures" indicates present algorithm. "HistInt" indicates method in [5], with $k = 3$ and $T_c = 3000$ as specified there.

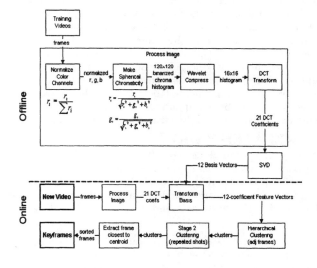

Figure 2: Clustering algorithm.

Techniques for Interactive Video Cubism

Sidney Fels
Dept. of Electrical and
Computer Engineering
University of British Columbia
Vancouver, BC, Canada
ssfels@ece.ubc.ca

Eric Lee
Dept. of Electrical and
Computer Engineering
University of British Columbia
Vancouver, BC, Canada
elee@ece.ubc.ca

Kenji Mase
ATR M.I & C. Research
Laboratories
Seika-cho, Soraku-gun
Kyoto, Japan
mase@mic.atr.co.jp

ABSTRACT

This paper presents an interactive video visualization technique called video cubism. With this technique, video data is considered to be a block of three dimensional data where frames of video data comprise the third dimension. The user can observe and manipulate a cut plane or cut sphere through the video data. An external real-time video source may also be attached to the video cube. The visualization leads to images that are aesthetically interesting as well as being useful for image analysis.

1. INTRODUCTION

We introduce a new technique for visualizing video data. In this novel scheme, video data is considered to be a volume of data. The dimensions of width and height are the usual X and Y axes of a frame of video data. The third dimension is derived from layering frames of video data sequentially in time as shown in the diagram (figure 1). Normal video viewing can be considered a cut plane that is parallel to the X-Y plane and advancing from the first frame to the last frame along the T axis as shown in figure 2 .

Now, imagine rotating the cut plane to a different location and moving it. For example, consider moving the cut plane so that it is parallel to the X-T axis and advancing it along the Y dimension. At each cut you are seeing all of the X dimension values for all the frames at a given position in the Y dimension as shown in the diagram in figure 3. Figure 4 shows an arbitrary rotation and positioning of the cut plane. Next, imagine a cut sphere instead of a plane as shown in figure 5. Here, we get a non-linear cut through the video data. We have implemented both a cut plane and a cut sphere which can be manipulated in real-time. Additionally, real-time video data can be streamed into the video cube.

2. RELATED WORK

Viewing video data along the X-T axis and Y-T axis has appeared in several forms in the literature. Most recently, [4] has developed a technique, called the *tx-transform*, for use with film. In their work, the different cut planes are always aligned with the basis axis and are used for creating aes-

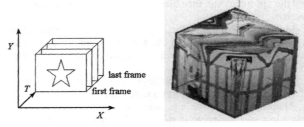

Figure 1: Video frames are stacked together to form a volume. The right figure shows a video cube with 7 seconds of data (210 frames; 212X160 pixels). The scene is a room with camera panning and zooming.

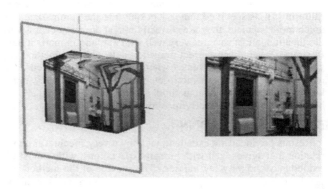

Figure 2: Cutting the video cube parallel to the X-Y plane shows a single video frame at some point in time. Animating along the T axis in this manner displays normal video. The image on the right is the cut plane viewed head-on.

thetically interesting dynamic viewpoints of film data. The work, *The Invisible Shape of Things Past* [5] also represents video as a three dimensional object where the topology is determined by the characteristics of the video camera. In [1], they describe epipolar-plane analysis for tracking objects in motion. In this work, the cut plane images through the video cube are are analysed for straight lines or hyberbolic curves to track objects during camera motion on a mobile robot. In their work, they consider the effect of moving a camera in straight lines relative to a fixed scene. In video cubism, the camera and the objects are free to move. The complex patterns that form are due to the plane or sphere cutting

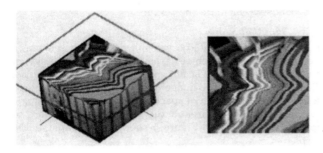

Figure 3: Cutting the video cube parallel to the X-Z plane. Stationary objects leave a smooth "trail" due to camera movement.

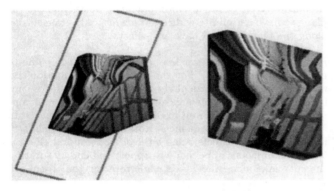

Figure 4: An arbitrary cut through the video cube. Camera movement translates to an interesting "bending" effect on the door.

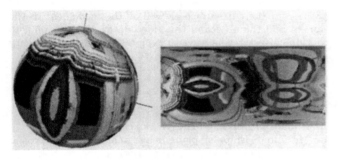

Figure 5: A spherical cut applied to the cube. The image on the right is the texture map applied to the surface of the sphere. Two "doors" appear in the image; one from front of the original cube and the other from the back.

through the epipolar lines allowing multiple representations of the spatiotemporal data.

The main distinctions this work has are that the cut plane or sphere used to view the video data can be manipulated in real-time and that real-time video data can be streamed into the video cube. This provides an opportunity to interactively explore the video cube from many different angles to get both aesthetically interesting static images as well as motion effects.

3. VIDEO CUBISM

Video cubism has three main parts, the video data buffer, the virtual cube and the cut surfaces. The video data buffer is formed from frames of video data. The virtual cube is the representation of the video data in virtual coordinates. Finally, the cut surface cuts through the virtual video cube which in turn displays the corresponding video data.

3.1 The Video Data Buffer

The first component of the system is the video data buffer. The complete video data is stored in memory as a 3D array consisting of a sequence of frames of video data. Currently, we are using RGB values for video frames that are 212x160pixels. Using the full 3D array representation made addressing individual video data (vixels) that are on the cut plane simple. In contrast to [3], the video buffer may also dynamically receive data either from a video capture card instead of a file.

The video data is used to form textures which are mapped onto appropriate faces of the video cube and cut surface.

3.2 The Video Cube

The video cube is an abstract representation of the video buffer discussed in section 3.1. The appropriate vixel data from the video buffer is texture mapped onto the six faces, with the most recent frame mapped to the front of the cube and the oldest frame at the back. Note that the dimensions of the cube can be selected arbitrarily; the texture map will stretch the vixel data to fit accordingly. This is similar to the technique used by [2]. In this implementation, we use a video cube centred at the origin, with dimensions 1.0x0.75x1.0. The dimensions were chosen to preserve the 4:3 aspect ratio of the video frames.

The video cube is represented as an unordered set of twelve line segments, one for each edge of the cube. The faces of the cube are divided into triangles, with each triangle texture mapped separately. Tessellating the faces simplifies the implementation and makes it consistent with the texture mapping process for the cut plane's intersection polygon, discussed in section 3.3.1. The cube can also be arbitrarily rotated around the origin in the world coordinate system. We use a single composite matrix, composed from rotation, scaling, and translation matrices to convert from video cube (x,y,z) coordinates to video buffer (X,Y,T) coordinates.

3.3 The Cut Surfaces

Two cut surfaces have been implemented: the cut plane and the cut sphere. The techniques used for these cuts can be extended to other cut surfaces.

3.3.1 The Cut Plane

The cut plane allows the user to move a planar window inside the video cube and examine the corresponding imagery (see figure 6). Every time the cube or the plane is moved, an intersection polygon must be calculated and a texture map computed.

The vertices of the intersection polygon can be computed by finding the points of intersection between each line segment representing the edges of the cube with the cut plane.

The intersection points are sorted into an ordered list of vertices for a convex polygon. Coordinates of the intersecting

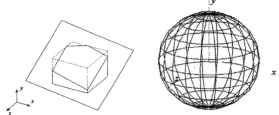

Figure 6: The cut plane and sphere. The intersection of the cut plane and cube is a polygon. This polygon can have three to six sides, depending on the orientation of the cut plane and cube. Shown is a wire frame cut sphere divided into 10 stacks and 20 slices.

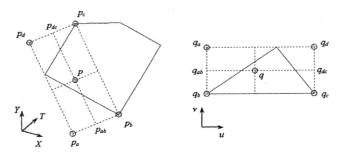

Figure 7: Computing the video buffer coordinates, p, of a point in the texture map, q, using a weighting function based on the four corners of a bounding box.

polygon are used to determine the texture map vixels.

In contrast to [3], we tessellate the intersection polygon into triangles and texture map each triangle separately. Using this procedure, we iterate over the pixels inside each triangle directly, eliminating any per-pixel bounds check. Furthermore, instead of rotating each pixel from texture map coordinates to video buffer coordinates, we rotate only the four corners of the bounding box of the triangle we are mapping. Then, we interpolate the interior texels based on the coordinates of the four corners of the bounding box to determine their video buffer coordinates. Figure 7 illustrates this process.

Given the texture map coordinates q_{ab} and q_{dc} for a particular row of the texture map, the corresponding values p_{ab} and p_{dc} in video buffer coordinates can be calculated. Then p is calculated using the following equation:

$$p = \frac{(p_{dc}-p_{ab})(q-q_{ab})}{q_{dc}-q_{ab}} + p_{ab} = C(q - q_{ab}) + p_{ab}$$

Note that the values C, q_{ab} and p_{ab} are constant for each row; thus, the number of operations has been reduced to only three multiplications and six additions/subtractions for each texel.

Profiling on a 650MHz PentiumIII processor, we found that the computation time for a triangle takes from 7 to 11 milliseconds, depending on the size of the triangle. From this, we estimate that the largest intersection polygon requires 36

milliseconds to calculate the texture.

3.3.2 The Cut Sphere

We have also implemented a cut sphere. In this scheme, a sphere is placed in the centre of the cube, and data outside of the sphere is removed. The cut sphere is interesting because, unlike the cut plane, the image on the surface of the sphere is a non-linear distortion of space and time. We use a single texture map wrapped around the surface of the sphere to display the video data. Figure 5 shows an example of the cut sphere.

4. INTERACTION CONTROLS

Using the mouse as a virtual trackball, the user is able to rotate or translate the entire scene, the video cube, or the cut plane. Alternatively, the rotations and translations may be specified absolutely using the keyboard, or by manipulating sliders on a control panel. Note that since we assume the cut plane to have an infinite width and height, only translations along the plane normal have any effect.

For the cut plane, the user may animation the cut plane to move along its normal. For the cut sphere, animation dynamically change the size of the sphere which has a "zooming" effect. If the cut plane is aligned along the normal, animating the plane will result in each frame being displayed in its normal or reverse sequence. Rotating the plane slightly induces temporal effects. One interesting temporal effect is that solid objects can be made to appear to bend by rotating the cut plane along the z axis while rotating the object.

5. CONCLUSIONS

With video cubism it is possible to interactively explore video data in all three dimensions simultaneously. The main purpose is to explore some of the aesthetics of looking at video data from a variety of perspectives. The images can be abstract or concrete depending upon the orientation and position of the cut surface as well as the movement of the camera and the object in the video data. We also plan to continue investigating ways to explore the dynamic imagery possible with the video cube.

Acknowledgments
The authors thank Ivan Poupyrev for helpful discussions.

6. REFERENCES

[1] Robert C. Bolles, H. Harlyn Baker, and David H. Marimont. Epipolar-plane image analysis: An approach to determining structure from motion. *International Journal of Computer Vision*, 1(1):7–55, 1987.

[2] S. S. Fels and K. Mase. Iamascope: A graphical musical instrument. *Computers and Graphics*, 2:277–286, 1999.

[3] S. S. Fels and K. Mase. Interactive video cubism. In *Proceedings of the Workshop on New Paradigms for Interactive Visualization and Manipulation (NPIVM)*, pages 78–82, Nov 1999.

[4] Martin Reinhart. tx-transform. http://www.tx-transform.com/frame_e.htm , 1998.

[5] Joachim Sauter and Dirk Lusebrink. The invisible shape of things past. Available from: http://www.artcom.de/projects/invisible_shape/welcome.en, 1997.

A Modular Middleware Flow Scheduling Framework*

Alexandre R.J. François and Gérard G. Medioni

Integrated Media Systems Center
University of Southern California, Los Angeles, CA
{afrancoi,medioni}@iris.usc.edu

ABSTRACT

Immersive, interactive applications require on-line processing and mixing of multimedia data. In order to realize the *Immersipresence* vision, we propose a *generic, extensible, modular* multimedia system software architecture. We describe here the Flow Scheduling Framework (FSF), that constitutes the core of its middleware layer. The FSF is an *extensible* set of classes that provide basic *synchronization* functionality and composition mechanisms to develop data-stream processing components. In this dataflow approach, applications are implemented by specifying data streams and their path through processing nodes, where they can undergo various manipulations. We describe the details of the FSF data and processing model that supports stream synchronization in a concurrent processing framework. We illustrate the FSF concepts with a *realtime* video stream processing application.

Keywords

Multimedia middleware; dataflow programming; synchronization.

1. INTRODUCTION

We present a Flow Scheduling Framework (FSF) to support generic processing and synchronization of data streams in a modular multimedia system.

Immersive, interactive applications require on-line processing and mixing of multimedia data such as pre-recorded audio and video, synthetic data generated at run-time, live input data from interaction sensors, media broadcast over a non synchronous channel (e.g. the internet), etc. Such applications present numerous challenges researched in many separate fields such as signal processing, computer vision, computer graphics, etc. Besides, several solutions can be developed for a given problem. Independent, partial solutions must therefore be gathered and integrated into working applications. Collecting, understanding and adapting independently developed components is always a challenging exercise. A common platform, providing a unifying data model, would facilitate the development and exploitation of multimedia software components and applications.

Recent multimedia architectures addressing on-line processing include MIT's VuSystem [2] and BMRC's Continuous Media Toolkit [3]. Both systems implement modular dataflow architecture concepts. They are designed primarily for audio and video processing with a strong emphasis on capture and replay aspects, and do not seem to easily scale up to applications involving immersion, interaction and synthetic content mixing. Earlier, De Mey and Gibbs proposed an object-oriented Multimedia Component Kit [4], that implements a framework for rapid prototyping of distributed

multimedia applications. Our approach is based on the same concepts: object-oriented, component-based extensible middleware and dataflow-based visual composition of multimedia application. The difference is in our definition of multimedia application: in order to realize the *Immersipresence* vision, we propose the *generic, extensible, modular* multimedia system software architecture presented in figure 1. A *middleware layer* provides an abstraction level between the low-level services and the applications, in the form of software components. An *application layer* allows to compose and execute multimedia applications using the software components in a dataflow-based, immersive programming environment.

The object of this paper is the description of the Flow Scheduling Framework (FSF) that is the core of the middleware layer. It is an extensible set of classes that provide basic synchronization functionality and composition mechanisms to develop data-stream processing components in the context of the proposed multimedia system architecture. In this dataflow approach, an application is the specification of data streams flowing through processing nodes, where they can undergo various manipulations. The FSF specifies and implements a *common generic data and processing model* designed to support stream synchronization in a concurrent processing framework. This extensible model allows to encapsulate existing data formats and standards as well as low-level service protocols and libraries, and make them available in a system where they can inter-operate.

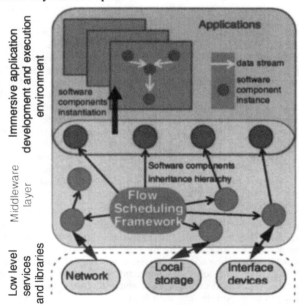

Figure 1. A modular multimedia system software architecture

*This research has been funded by the Integrated Media Systems Center, a National Science Foundation Engineering Research Center, Cooperative Agreement No. EEC-9529152, with additional support from the Annenberg Center for Communication at the University of Southern California and the California Trade and Commerce Agency.

371

2. OVERVIEW OF THE FSF CONCEPTS

Information is modeled as data *streams*. A stream represents one or several synchronized multimedia objects, i.e. expressed in the same time referential. An application is specified by a number of streams of various origins and the manipulations they undergo as they pass through processing nodes called *cells*. *Intra-stream processes* include formatting, alteration and presentation. A stream can originate from local sources such as local storage or input devices, or can be received from a network. It can also be created internally as the result of the manipulation of one or several other streams. As a stream goes through different cells, it can be altered. After processing, a stream can be stored locally, sent to output devices or sent on a network. *Inter-stream operations* are necessary for synchronization, as time referential transformations require the exchange or re-organization of data across streams. Streams occur in an application as time samples, which can represent instantaneous data, such as samples describing the state of a sensor at a given time, or integrated data describing, at a given time, the state of one or several objects over a certain period of time. Furthermore, the nature of the object(s) represented by a stream dictates the parameters of sample traffic in the stream. While some streams represent a steady flow of uniform time rate samples (e.g. captured frames from a video camera), others represent occasional arrival of samples at random time intervals (e.g. user input). Finally, we make a distinction between *active streams*, that carry volatile information, and *passive streams*, that hold persistent data in the application. For example, the frames captured by a video camera do not necessarily need to remain in the application space after they have been processed. Process parameters however must be persistent during the execution of the application.

3. DATA MODEL

We define a structure that we call *pulse*, as a carrier for all the data corresponding to a given time stamp in a stream. In an application, streams can be considered as pipes in which pulses can flow (in one direction only). The time stamp characterizes the pulse in the stream's time referential, and it cannot be altered inside the stream. Time referential transforms require inter-stream operations.

As a stream can represent multiple synchronized objects, a pulse can carry data describing time samples of multiple individual objects as well as their relationships. In order to facilitate access to the pulse's data, it is organized as a mono-rooted composition hierarchy, referred to as the pulse structure (see figure 3). Each node in the structure is an instance of a *node type* and has a *name*. The node name is a character string that can be used to identify instances of a given node type. The framework only defines the base node type that supports all operations on nodes needed in the processing model, and a few derived types for internal use. Specific node types can be derived from the base type to suit specific needs, such as encapsulating standard data models. Node attributes can be *local*, in which case they have a regular data type, or *shared*, in which case they are subnodes, with a specific node type. Node types form an inheritance hierarchy to allow extensibility while preserving reusability of existing processes.

4. PROCESSING MODEL

We designed a processing model to manage generic computations on data streams. We define a generic cell type, called *Xcell*, that supports basic stream control for generic processing. Custom cell types implementing specific processes are derived from the Xcell type to extend the software component base in the system. In particular, specialized cell types can encapsulate existing standards and protocols to interface with lower-level services provided by the operating system, devices and network to handle for example distributed processing, low-level parallelism, stream presentation

to a device, etc.

In an Xcell, the information carried by an active stream (*active pulses*) and a passive stream (*passive pulses*) is used in a process that may result in the augmentation of the active stream and/or update of the passive stream (see figure 2). Each Xcell thus has two independent directional stream channels with each exactly one input and one output. Part of the definition of the Xcell type and its derived types is the process that defines how the streams are affected in the cell. The base Xcell only defines a place-holder process that does not affect the streams.

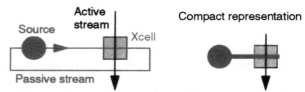

Figure 2. Generic processing unit

4.1 Flow Control

In an Xcell, each incoming active pulse triggers the instantiation of the cell process, to which it is the input data. The process can only read the active pulse data and add new data to the active pulse (i.e. augment its structure). *Existing data cannot be modified.*

Process parameters are carried by the passive stream. A passive stream must form a loop anchored by exactly one source that produces a continuous flow of pulses reproducing its incoming (passive) pulses. The passive pulse arriving at the cell at the same time as the active pulse is used as parameters for the corresponding process instance. The process can access and may update both the structure and the values of the passive pulse.

When the process is completed, the active pulse is sent to the active output. The passive pulse is transmitted on the passive output, down the passive loop, to ultimately reach the source where it becomes the template for generated pulses. Note that the continuous pulsing on passive loops is only a conceptual representation used to provide a unified model. In order to make application graphs more readable, passive loops are represented in compact form as self terminating bidirectional links (see figure 2).

In this model, the processing of different active pulses of the same active stream can occur in parallel, as pulses are received by the cell. However a given active pulse being processed in a cell is not output until the process is complete. Furthermore, a cell cannot alter the time stamp of an active pulse. Time referential transformations, such as buffering or pulse integration, require to make the active pulse data persistent *via* a passive loop, as described later.

4.2 Filtering

In an Xcell derived cell, the process is defined as a function that takes as input data an active pulse and a passive pulse, and may augment the active pulse and/or modify the passive pulse. The process description includes the specification of the associated input and parameter types, i.e. substructures to look for in the active and passive pulses structures respectively. When designing custom cells, corresponding local data types and node types must be defined if not already available. A partial structure type is specified as a *filter* or a composition hierarchy of filters (see figure 3). A filter is an object that specifies a node type, a node name and eventual subfilters corresponding to subnodes. The filter composition hierarchy is isomorphic to its target node structure. When an active pulse is received, the cell process input structure must be identified in the active pulse, and similarly the parameter structure must be identified in the passive pulse before the process can be started (see figure 4). Finding substructures in pulses is called filtering,

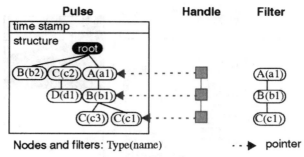

Pulse   **Handle**   **Filter**

Nodes and filters: Type(name)   ⋅⋅▸ pointer

Figure 3. Pulse filtering

and is a subtree matching operation. In order to provide efficient access to relevant data in the pulses, filtering operations return *handles*, that are used in the process for direct access to the relevant structure nodes. A handle is a pointer to a pulse node. Handles can be organized in composition hierarchies isomorphic to filter and node structures. A handle or composition hierarchy of handles is formed as the result of the filtering of a pulse's structure.

The Node names specified in filters to identify instances can be exact strings or string patterns to allow multiple matches. The filtering process thus returns a list of handles, one for each match. The interpretation of multiple matches in the active pulse is part of a specific process implementation. For example, the process can be applied to each match, thus allowing to define operations on objects whose count is unknown at design time.

Filtering efficiency is a major issue especially on active streams, since it must be performed independently on each new active pulse. In traditional dataflow models, data resulting from processes is not accumulated in a structure, but simply output from a processing node. Type checking can therefore occur at application design time, and there is no need to look for the relevant data in the incoming stream. After experimenting with this approach, we found that in multimedia applications, where synchronization is a major constraint, keeping data synchronized in our pulse structure is more efficient than separating data elements for processing and later having to put synchrone samples, distributed in independent storage nodes, back together. Our hierarchical structuration of the pulse data is suitable for efficient implementation of filtering. Furthermore, the filtering approach allows to apply a same process to an undetermined number of objects in an active pulse while preserving the temporal relationship of the object samples. It also makes it possible for several cells on a passive loop to share part or totality of their parameters.

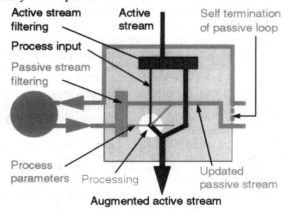

Figure 4. Inside an Xcell

5. APPLICATION COMPOSITION
5.1 Stream Routing

An application is specified by a graph of cells with two independent sets of links: active and passive. Active and passive connections are different in nature, and cannot be interchanged.

There is no limitation on the number of cells on a same passive loop. Feed-back can thus be implemented either with cells that directly update their parameters in their process, or with separate cells for processing and update, if the update depends on some subsequent processes, as shown in figure 5. Updated parameters are used in processes as they become available on the corresponding passive loop, thus feed-back loops cannot create any interlock.

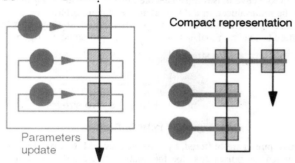

Figure 5. Parameter feed-back on a passive loop

The set of active connections between the cells is a *dependency graph*. A cell using as input the result of another cell must be traversed after the cell on which it depends in order for its process to be executed (otherwise the filtering fails and pulses are transmitted without any process). Independent cells can be traversed in arbitrary order, and their processes can occur in parallel. To take advantage of this parallelism, we define the *Scell* type, which is a stream splitter (see figure 6). An Scell has one active input and two active outputs. Scells transmit incoming input active pulses on both active outputs simultaneously.

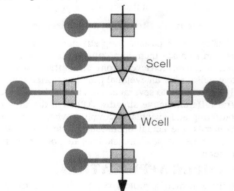

Figure 6. Stream routing for parallel execution

The only local synchronization enforced in the cells is that an active pulse does not reach a given cell before it has been completely processed by the previous cell on the active path. In order to enforce this constraint when a stream follows several parallel paths, we introduce the *Wcell* (see figure 6), which has two active inputs and one active output. A Wcell is needed when a cell depends on several independent cells traversed in parallel: the Wcell waits until it receives the same pulse on both its active inputs before sending it to its active output.

There is no *a priori* assumption on the time taken by cell processes. If the processing time in the upstream cells varies from pulse to pulse, active pulses might reach a given cell out of order. If simple time consistency can be enforced in cell processes, more elaborate synchronization mechanisms are usually required.

5.2 Synchronization

In our framework, synchronization reduces to time referential transformations. As already pointed out, each active stream has its own time referential, to which the pulses' time stamps relate. All passive streams share the same system time referential. The time referential in a stream cannot be altered. Time referential transformations thus require the transfer of pulses across different streams. To do so, active pulses must be stored in a passive loop before they can be reintroduced in a different active stream. Intuitively, if any time reorganization of the active pulses is to occur, they must be buffered. The minimal setup required is presented in figure 7.

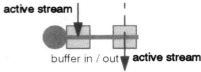

Figure 7. Pulse buffering

Active pulses are buffered, by a specialized cell, to a passive loop in which the pulses describe the content of the buffer at a given time. Buffered pulses may undergo a time transform. Another specialized cell on the same passive loop can retrieve the pulses from the buffer and restitute them in an active stream at the desired rate, determined either by a dedicated timer or by incoming active pulses. This operation may involve resampling.

More generally, if two active streams are to be combined in one single active stream (see figure 8), the pulses from both streams

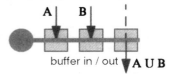

Figure 8. Streams synchronization

must be buffered in a passive loop structure after undergoing a time transform to place them in a common time referential. Synchrone pulses can be retrieved from the buffer and placed in a same active pulse, after an eventual time transformation. This pattern easily generalizes to several active streams being recombined into several different active streams. Although the time transformation, buffering and eventual resampling when de-buffering are generic concepts, the actual operations to carry are data (node) type and cell process dependent, and thus are not part of the framework definition.

6. EXAMPLE APPLICATION

We have implemented a prototype FSF, in the form of a C++ library for the Windows 2000 operating system (the library can easily be ported to other multitasking operating systems). Using this prototype FSF library, we have developed the components needed to build an adaptive color background model-based video-stream segmentation application, nicknamed "blue-screen without a blue screen" (based on [1]). The corresponding application graph is presented in figure 9. The application runs at *thirty* 240x180 frames per second on a dual Pentium III 550 MHz, a frame rate far superior to the one achieved in our previous stand alone implementations. The multithread processing model makes real-time processing possible.

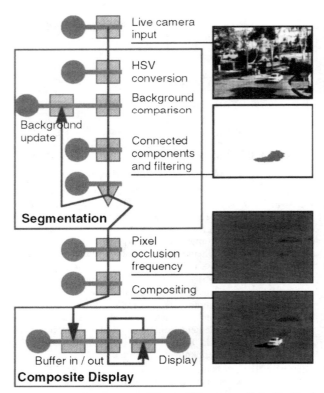

Figure 9. The "blue-screen without a blue screen" application

7. CONCLUSION

We have presented the Flow Scheduling Framework, foundation of the middleware layer of our generic, extensible, modular multimedia system software architecture to support immersive, interactive applications.

The FSF is an *extensible* set of classes that provide basic synchronization functionality and composition mechanisms to develop data-stream processing components in the context of the proposed multimedia system architecture.

We have described the FSF data and processing model to support stream synchronization in a concurrent processing framework, and shown how to build component-based applications in this model. We have demonstrated a prototype FSF implementation with a *real-time* video processing and compositing application.

8. REFERENCES

[1] François A.R.J. and Medioni G.G. Adaptive Color Background Modeling for Real-Time Segmentation of Video Streams. In Proc. Int. Conf. on Imaging Science, Systems, and Technology, pp. 227-232, Las Vegas, NA, June 1999.

[2] Lindblad C.J. and Tennenhouse D.L. The VuSystem: A Programming System for Compute-Intensive Multimedia. IEEE Jour. Selected Areas in Communications, 14(7), pp. 1298-1313, September 1996.

[3] Mayer-Patel K. and Rowe L.A. Design and Performance of the Berkeley Continuous Media Toolkit. In Multimedia Computing and Networking 1997, pp 194-206, Martin Freeman, Paul Jardetzky, Harrick M. Vin, Editors, Proc. SPIE 3020, 1997

[4] de Mey V. and Gibbs S. A Multimedia Component Kit. In Proc. ACM Int. Multimedia Conf. (MM'93), 1993.

Towards Virtual Videography

Michael Gleicher
Department of Computer Sciences
University of Wisconsin-Madison
Madison, WI 53706
gleicher@cs.wisc.edu

James Masanz
Department of Computer Sciences
University of Wisconsin-Madison
Madison, WI 53706
aranduil@cs.wisc.edu

ABSTRACT

Videographers have developed an art of conveying events in video. Through choices made in cinematography, editing, and post-processing, effective video presentations can be created from events recorded with little or no intrusion. In this paper, we explore systems that bring videography to situations where cost or time issues preclude application of the art. Our goal is to develop *virtual videography,* that is, systems that can help automate the process of creating an effective video presentation from given footage. In this paper, we discuss how virtual videography systems can be constructed by combining image-based rendering to synthetically generate shots with image understanding to help choose what should be shown to the viewer. To this, visual effects can be added to enhance the presentation, lessening the degradation caused by the medium.

Categories and Subject Descriptors

I.3.3 [**Computer Graphics**]: Picture/Image Generation; I.4.6 [**Image Processing**]: Segmentation; I.4.9 [**Image Processing**]: Applications

Keywords

Educational technology, videography, automatic presentation

1. INTRODUCTION

Portraying an event, such as a performance, lecture, or sporting event, in video is an art form practiced at many levels. While the experience of watching an event on screen is different from being there, well produced video can provide a differently effective experience for the viewer. Skillfully produced video can compensate for the limitations of the medium by exploiting the power of cinematic media to manipulate time and space and artificially enhance images, as well as to avoid some of the problems with attending a real event, such as being restricted to a given seat.

Videographers have a number of tools at their disposal for capturing and portraying an event. Multiple cameras, with various lenses, provide multiple viewpoints. The raw "footage" provided by the cameras is edited together to point the viewer's attention to where it is most needed and to control the timing of the presentation: compressing time by skipping over unimportant segments, or dilating it by replay or slow-motion.

The hardware demands of videography are a barrier to its use. Equally barring is the skill required at each phase of the process. Skilled camera operators are needed to capture the significant events with movements that will not induce motion sickness. Skilled editors and directors are needed to choose which shots should be used and when. These two phases are tightly coupled: the director often guides the cameras to insure needed footage is available, but ultimately must choose among what is provided, sometimes augmented with archived footage or synthetic images.

The challenge of videography is related to, but different than, traditional cinematography. The videographer has limited control over the events that are being filmed: there is no mise-en-scène [5]. Ideally, the videographer would unobtrusively observe and record what happens, although this ideal is sometimes compromised (for example by an intrusive wedding photographer).

Unfortunately, many applications do not afford the use of videography. Often, cost and intrusiveness considerations limit the number of cameras and their mobility. Cost and availability concerns often preclude the use of skilled practitioners, both during filming and production.

2. VIRTUAL VIDEOGRAPHY

Our goal is to construct a system and methodology for recording events with minimal intrusion, and to produce effective video from this footage in as automated a manner as possible.

Consider the task of creating video presentations from class lectures. In such a setting, cost and intrusion considerations preclude the use of more than a small number of non-mobile cameras. We would not expect to either recreate the experience of being in the class, or the video that might have been created were the whole event designed as a video. We do not want to affect either the instructor's presentation, nor the experience of the students in the class.

We are beginning by focusing on off-line systems. Some applications, such as live broadcast, require real-time, on-line systems. No application would be hurt by a system having an on-line capability, and such an on-line system has been explored by Bianchi [4]; however, in an off-line system we have certain advantages:

- Looking ahead in time can help us anticipate the action. In an on-line application, more knowledge of the event is required to help predict what will happen if unpleasant surprises are to be avoided.

- By looking at durations of the presentation simultaneously, we can better enforce temporal constraints, for example avoiding jittering and adhering to the 180 degree rule [5].

- Information from previous or future frames can be used to create special effects.

- The system need not operate in real-time.

Our target medium is to create "standard" video; a linear presentation. While interactivity offers potential for a novel presentation medium, we prefer to limit ourselves to a more traditional medium where presentation techniques are better understood. Much of the art in cinematography is in guiding the viewer's attention. Determining how to employ the existing art is challenging enough.

2.1 An Example Problem

We have chosen a specific, limited domain in which to explore virtual videography: medium sized classes given by a single lecturer in "chalkboard" style. This domain shows the need for virtual videography: while there is clearly value in making such material available to those unable to attend the lecture, cost considerations preclude the use of a professional video staff. Placing one or two static cameras in the back of the lecture hall is practical. Not surprisingly, these static camera videos are considerably less interesting to watch than the original lecture itself.

Our goal is to be minimally intrusive, not requiring the lecturer to change the presentation at all. Our view is that we are recording an event, not creating a different one. The presentation is really meant for the students in the class, and the instructor should be free to teach using whatever method they have honed for best communicating in this setting. We will use this simple domain as a running example through the paper.

LectureBrowser [15] also aims to non-intrusively record university lectures and create video presentations. They synchronize the observed lectures with display of other digital media, and rely on a known lecture format, tracking hardware, and apply cut-only editing between two fixed views.

The Classroom 2000 Project [1] makes a record not only of the lecturer, but also of the lecturer's notes and notes taken by students. The project does not aim to be completely non-intrusive; it aims to capture the entire event, including a record of the students notes.

3. SUBPROBLEMS

Producing "real" videography requires a team, or at least a multi-talented practitioner. Similarly, a virtual videography system requires a range of components. In this section, we survey these components and the issues that must be addressed.

Each component of a virtual videography system is an open-ended research topic in its own right. However, all afford a number of simpler solutions that can be constructed today without major extensions to the state of the art. In each of the following subsections, we note not only the potential for future systems and research directions, but also our initial experiments in the example domain.

3.1 Data Sufficiency

Given the fixed limited set of source images, we must first ask whether or not there is enough information to create the desired result. This problem is inherent in off-line production, not a consequence of virtual videography. A human editor faces this same problem when presented with the same raw footage.

The sufficiency questions arise at all levels. For instance, if there is insufficient information to see some detail, then there is simply no way to show that to the viewer. These sufficiency questions can be difficult to determine: what may be unreadable at first might be curable using image enhancement, or by combining elements from several sources. At a higher level, if a topic is not discussed in a presentation, it is unlikely that it can be explained in the resulting video.

Sufficiency issues lead to two general questions: How does the recorder of the event determine if there will be enough information in the "sampling" being recorded to create a good result? And how do we best use these bits to communicate a desired message? For example, when we record an event, can we know if two cameras are sufficient? If so where should we place them? And, given the output from these cameras for a given performance, how do we best use their images to convey the presentation? In our example domain, we have little control over the amount of data that we can obtain, and focus on the last question.

3.2 Image Understanding

More understanding about what is occurring in the source video footage enables more informed choices in how to utilize it. A virtual videographer must use computer vision to interpret its footage, or rely on manual intervention. A virtual videographer's needs are standard vision issues, such as person tracking and gesture recognition.

The vision task is simplified for the virtual videography application because precise results are not necessary. Initially we may further simplify the problem by limiting the scope of our application to a constrained and structured environment, allowing user intervention, and demanding only coarse grained information from the vision system. In our example domain, the static camera and knowledge that the only moving object is the presenter allows simple techniques, such as change detection and skin-color classifiers[9] to be effective.

To relax these restrictions, more sophisticated image comprehension allows for the automatic identification and interpretation of the action. For example, we might not only identify that there is a person gesturing, but that they are pointing at a particular object. Understanding where the action is taking place or where the attention of the people in the scene is focused suggests where the videographer should direct the viewer's attention.

3.3 Computational Cinematography

Much of the power of cinematography comes from the

Figure 1: Simulated medium shot.

Figure 2: A Compositing Effect.

ability to control the viewpoint. Through this control, the limited portal of the screen can be expanded through motion, as well as focusing the viewer's attention [12]. A virtual videography system chooses what viewpoints to show. Care must be taken to not only properly guide the viewer's attention, but also to not confuse them (unless it is intentional). When done correctly, such continuity-editing can seamlessly guide the viewer through time and space. Cinematography and editing is an art form unto itself.

In computer graphics, there have been various attempts to codify the art of cinematography. Karp and Feiner [11] use planning techniques to make cinematographic decisions based on knowledge of communicative goals, while He et. al. [8] explore automating cinematography in the context of animated conversations.

For creating video presentations, the choices are more limited. Bianchi [4] shows how a simple set of heuristics can be effective for videography, while LectureBrowser [15] gives an even smaller and simpler set to make cuts between a wide and close-up. In our example domain, we plan to mimic these heuristics, and extend them using our ability to look forward and backward in time to insure sufficient continuity and variety. Creating a presentation using heuristics is in contrast to the use of authoring tools such as MAD [3] that leave editing decisions to the author, and systems that give the viewer choices during playback, such as STREAMS [6].

3.4 Image-Based Rendering

We define the virtual videography problem as beginning with a set of source images. However, this set might be smaller than would be desirable, especially since no director was available to guide the shooting. This would mean that there would be a very limited selection of viewpoints. However, graphics and vision researchers have been exploring methods for generating novel viewpoints based on an initial set. While general solutions to the view interpolation are on the horizon, interesting methods have emerged for various special cases, for example those of Manning and Dyer [14], Seitz [16], and Avidan and Sashua [2].

A very simple form of novel view generation can be created by assuming that the camera only zooms and rotates around its optical center. The mapping between any two images taken from a camera with a fixed center is a projective deformation [17]. Therefore, panning and zooming can be implemented using a projective warp, as shown in Figure 1, where a dynamic close view has been created by re-sampling a longer, static one.

3.5 Shot Generation (Camera Operation)

Image-based rendering addresses the problem of creating a view, however, we still must control it. In analog to real videography, image-based rendering creates the camera,

however we still need to implement the cameraman. Camera operation must consider both the spatial aspects, how the "individual pictures" look, as well as the temporal aspects, to create motions that do not confuse or sicken the viewer.

Ultimately, a virtual videography system may encode heuristics that define the art of photography and cinematography. This has been explored in a constraint-based framework by Drucker [7] in the context of 3D virtual environments. Initially, our virtual videography experiments use simple algorithms to frame important elements, and we use filtering to avoid the generation of jittery motions. Implementing the filtering by fitting known good movement patterns, such as ease-in/out, will further improve the results.

3.6 Special Effects

Applying special effects is another form of shot creation. There are a wide range of effects that can be put to use: super-imposition, transparency, transitions, titling, picture-in-picture, etc. In our example domain, we imagine highlighting what a presenter points to. Traditional methods of emphasis, such as pointing, often obscure the very thing to be emphasized. With special effects we have the opportunity to emphasize something without obscuring it further.

Figure 2 is an example of another effect useful in our examples. In the original frame (left), the instructor obscures the partially drawn diagram. By combining this image with a later one, the obscured text is revealed, as is a sense of where the instructor is going. The right frame was constructed by overlaying a partially dissolved copy of the original frame over a frame taken from later in the video when the writing on the board is complete.

The inclusion of special effects make other aspects of the videography problem more difficult. The system must determine when and where to use them and what source footage is necessary to best generate them. There is also the question of whether such visual devices are effective, or are they confusing and distracting. Avoiding these latter problems will require developing ways to cue the viewer to what is happening.

4. INITIAL EXPERIMENTS

As stated earlier, a virtual videography system has a number of components, each with an open research agenda. Our approach to virtual videography is to aim for building a complete end-to-end system, with engineering "place-holders" for each component. Once such a system is demonstrated, we can further address each component in the context of a complete application. In this section, we describe our initial experiments and prototype.

For our initial explorations, we recorded an entire semester of lectures in an undergraduate course using DV camcorders.

Generally, a single static camera placed in the rear of the room was used, although a limited number of lectures were filmed with two cameras.

4.1 Proof of Concept

Our first efforts aim to show that there is in fact sufficient information in our source materials to create our targets. Given the extremely limited source material, is it possible to produce video of the sort we aim for? If not, how much more should we sample the lecture, or what concessions to invasiveness should be made? To experiment with this, we have chosen a "Wizard of Oz" prototyping approach [13] [10] where a user manually does the process envisioned by the final system. We have done this by attempting to produce video using commercial video production tools.

Some findings:

- Standard production software is not especially suited to our task.

- Manipulation of audio is not required, despite the moving viewpoint.

- Care must be taken with placement of the camera to make sure the chalkboard is readable on tape.

4.2 Initial Prototype

Our initial virtual videography system is designed so we can construct a working system as quickly as possible to explore the ideas, yet we can easily expand and improve it.

Ideally, the system will do a good enough job that human collaboration will be unnecessary when the expectations for the presentation are not too high. Initially, we rely on user interaction to compensate for simplified pieces of the system.

Our prototype is implemented on Windows NT workstations using our PyVideo Toolkit which relies on Video for Windows, Python, and the FlTk interface toolkit. Our initial experience shows that some very simple methods can produce interesting results, however many aspects of the problem require further exploration.

Acknowledgments

Rob Iverson implemented the majority of the PyVideo toolkit. This research was supported by NSF Career award CCR-9984506, a grant from Microsoft Research, and a hardware donation from Intel.

5. REFERENCES

[1] G. Abowd, C. Atkeson, A. Feinstein, C. Hmelo, R. Kooper, S. Long, N. Sawhney, and M. Tani. Teaching and learning as multimedia authoring: The classroom 2000 project. In *ACM Multimedia '96*, 1996.

[2] S. Avidan and A. Shashua. Novel view synthesis in tensor space. In *CVPR97*, pages 1034–1040, 1997.

[3] R. Beacker, A. Rosenthal, N. Friedlander, E. Smith, and a Cohen. A multimedia system for authoring motion pictures. In *ACM Multimedia '96*, 1996.

[4] M. Bianchi. Autoauditorium: a fully automatic, multi-camera system to televise auditorium presentations, 1998.

[5] David Bordwell and Kristin Thompson. *Film Art: An Introduction*. The McGraw-Hill Companies, Inc., 1997.

[6] G. Cruz and R. Hill. Capturing and playing multimedia events with streams. In *ACM Multimedia '94*, 1994.

[7] S. Drucker and D. Zeltzer. Camdroid: A system for implementing intelligent camera control. *1995 Symposium on Interactive 3D Graphics*, pages 139–144, April 1995.

[8] L. He, M. Cohen, and D. Salesin. The virtual cinematographer: A paradigm for automatic real-time camera control and directing. *Proceedings of SIGGRAPH 96*, pages 217–224, August 1996.

[9] M. Hunke and A. Waibel. Face locating and tracking for human-computer interaction, 1994.

[10] Todd Hovanyecz John D. Gould, John Conti. Composing letters with a simulated listening typewriter non-traditional interactive modes. *Proceedings of Human Factors in Computer Systems*, pages 367–370, 1982.

[11] P. Karp and S. Feiner. Automated presentation planning of animation using task decomposition with heuristic reasoning. *Graphics Interface '93*, pages 118–127, May 1993.

[12] S. Katz. *Film Directing Shot by Shot: Visualizing from Concept to Screen*. Michael Wiese Productions, 1991.

[13] J. F. Kelley. An iterative design methodology for user-friendly natural language office information applications. *ACM Transactions on Office Information Systems*, 2(1):26–41, 1984.

[14] R. Manning and C. Dyer. *Confluence of Computer Vision and Computer Graphics*, chapter Dynamic View Interpolation without Affine Reconstruction. Kluwer, 2000.

[15] Sugata Mukhopadhyay and Brian Smith. Passive capture and structuring of lectures. In *ACM Conference on Multimedia*, 1999.

[16] S. M. Seitz. *Image-Based Transformation of Viewpoint and Scene Appearance*. PhD thesis, University of Wisconsin - Madison, October 1997.

[17] R. Szeliski. Image mosaicing for tele-reality applications. In *WACV94*, pages 44–53, 1994.

Computer-Aided System Integration for Data-Intensive Multimedia Applications*

Sami J. Habib AND Alice C. Parker
University of Southern California
Electrical Engineering-Systems
3740 McClintock Avenue, Room 300B
Los Angeles, CA 90089-2562 USA

{shabib,parker}@eve.usc.edu

ABSTRACT

In this paper we describe a computer-aided design (CAD) tool for automatically designing and integrating network and data management hardware for data-intensive multimedia applications, such as the animation film studio. The tool determines the network strategy, interconnection hardware required, number and location of proxies and servers, and file allocation.

1. INTRODUCTION

Effective and efficient networking and data management are a requirement for data-intensive applications like digital post-production. Designing a cost-effective network and data management hardware configuration that supports the execution of all tasks is a complex design problem because multimedia applications rely not only on raw network bandwidth, but also on how well the network and database components are integrated together to achieve acceptable performance.

Such application environments are not only characterized by massive data storage and bandwidth requirements, but by requirements that are heterogeneous, that vary depending on each particular required task, and the geographical locations of the workstations. According to Weinberg [5], digital media production has rapidly become a highly distributed collaborative activity involving teams of people and digital resources in different locations. Budget limitations usually disallow the choice of the fastest possible networking hardware for the entire installation, forcing heterogeneous solutions with components that vary in cost and performance across the network. Literally millions of possible

*This work was supported in part by a USC Zumberge funding and in part by the Defense Advanced Research Projects Agency (DARPA) under contract 53-4503-9319 and monitored by the Federal Bureau of Investigation (FBI) under contract J-FBI-94-161.

network architectures could be used for a given project, and this number is magnified by possible variations in the number, location and capability of the file servers. It would be impossible for a human designer to examine all possibilities for typical large installations.

Finding solutions to system integration for post-production is an ideal application for CAD software. CAD techniques have been used widely to optimize the circuits used in digital systems, and for many aspects of system design. Applying CAD techniques to design distributed systems, to determine their networking and data management strategies, is the next logical step.

A research project is underway to demonstrate the feasibility of automated network and data management design for multimedia applications like an animation studio intranet. This intranet synthesis problem includes determining

1. file server/proxy placement,

2. file allocation (still images, audio and video in the case of animation), and

3. network architecture.

The file server/proxy placement problem is to determine the number, type, capacity and capability of servers/proxies that can be used by the clients to store/retrieve shared files, while minimizing the servers'/proxies' placement costs. The file allocation problem is to find a number of locations to store copies of the most frequently accessed files by clients in their local servers/proxies, while minimizing the storage and retrieval costs. The network architecture problem entails the allocation of network hardware resources, such as ATM, Ethernet, router, bridge, leased-line, and/or SONET, that will enable all clients to communicate and access file servers, while minimizing the network hardware cost.

Because the above three problems are interrelated, we have formulated them as one combined optimization problem. Each problem is known to be NP-complete; therefore, searching for optimal solutions would require a prohibitive amount of time, so the CAD software attempts instead to achieve good solutions.

The automatic synthesis of an application-specific intranet configuration problem has not been reported in the research literature. Some related problems have been reported in the literature (for example [2, 3]).

2. PROBLEM MODEL AND EXAMPLE

An online digital post-production system involves processing, storing and retrieving a huge amount of multimedia data in order to produce an animated film. A typical studio is divided into a number of collaborative tasks, such as live-action, audio, background, special-effect, management and drawing, where each task is composed of many distinct subtasks and each subtask is located in a distinct, possibly geographically distributed location. Digital post-production is redefining film production from a manual process into an online process. This can be seen especially in animation, and animation integrated with live action. An animated film comprises many shots, that each describe part of the story. Each shot comprises a number of frames. The film *Toy Story 2* has 122,699 frames of up to 4 gigabytes per frame [4]. This data reflects the finished film, which means that an enormous quantity of data is created within all tasks to develop the finished film.

We have modeled the problem as hierarchy of tasks. Each *site* in an enterprise represents a major task for the application, and is referred to as a site task. Each site task comprises a number of distinct *group* tasks. For example, the live-action site task consists of two group tasks: creating live-action and retrieving live-action. Also, each group task is composed of a number of distinct *client* tasks. These clients need to communicate among themselves and with other clients from other site tasks; moreover, these clients also need to access file servers to store/retrieve files efficiently, so they can carry out all tasks in a certain order and within a time bound.

The animation film studio intranet and other intranet applications is described by one matrix and two tables:

1. a traffic flow matrix represents the average traffic requirements among all clients in term of bits per second,

2. a client location table represents the physical location of each client within the studio and its allocation to a group task and a site task. In other words, clustering the clients into groups and clustering groups into sites are assumed to represent the behavior of the application ideally, and

3. a data request table represents the access rate of each file by all clients.

To clarify the presentation of the tasks, we model the group tasks and their communications graphically as a task flow graph (TFG), where a node represents a group task and an edge represents the communication between two group tasks. Figure 1 depicts a partial task flow graph for animation film studio's group tasks. This graph is a hierarchical hypergraph. Each node (group task) contains a set of client tasks; a collection of related group tasks forms a site task. Thus, we are dealing with a three-level hierarchical network design problem: group, site and backbone. It is a hypergraph, since each edge represents the communication among an arbitrary subset of clients of the two group tasks. Later, we intend to use the flow of tasks as additional information to be used during network design.

The goal is to synthesize an intranet hardware configuration to support execution of all tasks according to the traffic flow matrix, client location table and data request table. The intranet hardware configuration is specified in

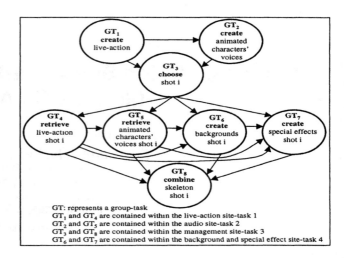

Figure 1: Partial task flow graph for animation film studio.

term of the number, locations, capacities and capabilities of the file servers, the allocation of storage space for all files and the number, type and capacity of the network hardware resources. A possible intranet hardware configuration for the given partial task flow graph in Figure 1 is shown in Figure 2.

3. PROBLEM FORMULATION

The design problem is to configure simultaneously data management and three-level network structures for the given application, in order to perform all tasks in a certain order and within a time bound, while minimizing the intranet hardware configuration cost. We have used an informal mixed integer non-linear programming notation to represent the combined optimization problem, which consists of set of design and performance constraints and an objective function. The entire problem model is a quite large. Here we highlight some of the core network and data management constraints.

3.1 Network Design Problem

The network design constraints are used to insure a correct and complete design of the three-level network hierarchies: group, site and backbone. The group network constraints insure that one group network-connector (GNC), which can be either a switch or a multi-access device, is allocated and bound for each group task; moreover, all clients (workstations) within a group task are connected to its GNC. Equations 1-2 represent some of the core constraints for a group task and similar equations are used to represent the core constraints for site and backbone tasks, but with more network technology choices, such as routers, leased-lines and SONET for example.

$$\sum_{\forall GNC_o} \mathcal{A}_o \times \phi_{o,e} = 1 \qquad (1)$$

GNC_o is a design parameter that indicates the group network connector to be selected and the index o indicates the GNC's identification. GT_e is a group task, which is an input parameter, and the index e indicates the GT's identification. $\mathcal{A}_o$ is an allocation variable (binary); $\mathcal{A}_o = 1$ indicates that

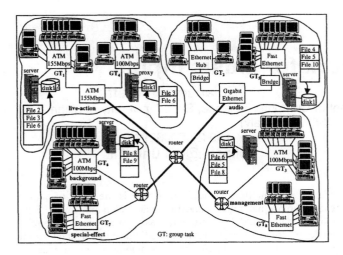

Figure 2: Synthesized animation film studio intranet.

a GNC_o is being included in the synthesized intranet. $\phi_{o,e}$ is a binding variable (binary); $\phi_{o,e} = 1$ indicates that an allocated GNC_o is bound to GT_e. Constraint (1) insures that only one GNC_o is allocated ($\mathcal{A}_o$) and bound ($\phi_{o,e}$) to a group task GT_e.

$$\sum_{CT_d \in GT_e} \omega_{d,e} \leq (NP_{GNC_o} - \mathcal{G}) \qquad (2)$$

CT_d is a client task, which is an input parameter, and the index d indicates the CT's identification. $\omega_{d,e}$ is a binding variable (binary); $\omega_{d,e} = 1$ indicates that a client task d is contained within a group task e. NP_{GNC_o} is an integer value that refers to the maximum number of ports within GNC_o and this value is given by the GNC design library. $\mathcal{G}$ is a variable set by another constraint to insure that one or more ports are dedicated to connect a site network and/or a file server/proxy. Constraint (2) insures that the allocated GNC_o has a sufficient number of ports, NP_{GNC_o}, to connect all clients CT_d (workstations) within a GT_e.

3.2 Data Management Problem

The data management design constraints consist of two sets: data management hardware placement and file allocation. Equations 3-4 represent some of the core constraints for server placement and file allocation respectively:

$$1 \leq \sum_{\forall GS_n} \beta_n \leq E \qquad (3)$$

GS_n is the selected group server, which is a design parameter to be determined, and the index n indicates GS's identification. β_n is an allocation variable (binary); $\beta_n = 1$ indicates that GS_n is being included in the synthesized intranet. Constraint (3) insures that there is a least one allocated (β_n) group server GS_n in the synthesized intranet and the total number of GS_n must not exceed the total number of group tasks E in the intranet.

$$\sum_{\forall i} k_{j,n,i} \leq 1 \qquad (4)$$

$k_{j,n,i}$ is a binding variable (binary); $k_{j,n,i} = 1$ indicates that an instance i of the jth file is stored in GS_n. Constraint (4) insures that only one instance of a file is stored in a GS_n.

3.3 Performance Problem

We use two performance methods to evaluate the synthesized intranet configuration. The first method, a quick performance method based on an analytical model, views the intranet configuration as a network of M/M/1 queues. This is widely used due to its fast approximation and simplicity [1] and it is embedded within the CAD system integration tool. The second method, a detailed performance method, is based on a simulation model. Its goal is to give the intranet planners a complete evaluation of the synthesized configuration. This method will be used after the CAD system integration tool is terminated.

4. CAD SYSTEM INTEGRATION TOOL

We are in the process of constructing a CAD tool to synthesize networks based on genetic algorithms. The tool reflects the integer non-linear constraints in the problem model. The tool creates an initial population of intranet configurations by selecting all network and database hardware resources randomly. The software analyzes and evaluates each configuration in the current population, selects the most fit configurations, modifies some and discards the rest. After several generations, if any of the configurations meet all the design and performance constraints and their costs are satisfied by the designer, then the tool terminates.

5. REFERENCES

[1] M. Gela and L. Kleinrock. On the Topological Design of Distributed Computer Networks. *IEEE Trans. on Communications*, COM-25:48–60, January 1977.

[2] K. Irani and N. Khabbaz. A Methodology for the Design of Communication Networks and the Distribution of Data in Distributed Supercomputer Systems. *IEEE Trans. on Computers*, C-31(5):419–434, May 1982.

[3] D. Mitra, J. Morrison, and K. Ramakrishnan. VPN DESIGNER: A Tool for Design of Multiservice Virtual Private Networks. *Bell Labs Technical Journal*, 3(4):15–31, October-December 1998.

[4] J. Slaton. Toys Will Be Toys. http://www.wired.com/news/culture/0,1248,32591,00.html

[5] R. Weinberg. Producing Content Producers. *IEEE Communications Magazine*, 33(8):70–73, August 1995.

A Multimodal Framework for Music Inputs

Goffredo Haus

Emanuele Pollastri

L.I.M.-Laboratorio di Informatica Musicale, Department of Computer Science, State University of Milan
via Comelico, 39; I-20135 Milan (Italy)

+39-2-55006222

haus@dsi.unimi.it

+39-2-55006297

pollastri@dsi.unimi.it

ABSTRACT

The growth of digital music databases imposes new content-based methods of interfacing with stored data; although indexing and retrieval techniques are deeply investigated, an integrated view of querying mechanism has never been established before. Moreover, the multimodal nature of music should be exploited to match the users' expectations as well as their skills. In this paper, we propose a hierarchy of music-interfaces that is suitable for existent prototypes of music information retrieval systems; according to this framework, human/computer interaction should be improved by singing, playing or notating music. Dealing with multiple inputs poses many challenging problems for both their combination and the low-level translation needed to transform an acoustic signal into a symbolic representation. This paper addresses the latter problem in some details, aiming to develop music-interfaces available not only to trained-musician.

Keywords

Multimodality, Music Interfaces, Music Information Retrieval, Pitch-Tracking, Singing Voice Analysis.

1. A MULTIMODAL FRAMEWORK

Recent advances in computer technologies and the general availability of audio/MIDI files over the Internet have spread out the diffusion of digital music databases. Research related to this field has been receiving growing interest, especially for its possible commercial exploitation. Since the pioneer work of Ghias et al. [3], query-by-humming and in general query-by-music-content are deeply investigated from the point of view of retrieval and indexing techniques, but the support of various input modes is quite omitted. Relying upon our previous experience in the *Music Archive Project* for *Teatro alla Scala in Milan* [4], this paper would be a first step to fill this gap.

In every multimedia system, human/computer interaction plays a fundamental role; human communication typically relies on multiple senses employed simultaneously and the same interaction should be desirable for human/computer communication, too. Referring to this use of multiple modalities to encode information, we use the term *multimodality* [1]. With the addiction of music-

sources into multimedia databases, there is the need of another channel more naturally bound to musical communication. Since musical data could be represented as notated music (graphical mode or visual domain) and performed music (acoustic/electronic mode or gestual domain), its presentation is multimodal by definition. Previous prototypes on music retrieval concentrate themselves on only a mode of input; for example, Ghias et al.[3], McNab et al.[8] and Rolland et al. [11] used vocal input while Uitdenbogerd and Zobel [12] preferred the MIDI input. The key point is finding a way of interaction that is more suitable for users and effective to filter useful data. It is indubitable that for a musician her/his instrument represents the most appropriate tool in communicating music but the same doesn't hold for the layman who would prefer her/his voice. Since the usefulness of every multimedia system is largely due to the way it matches the users' expectations as well as their skills, particular care must be taken in designing the overall structure of input modes.

2. HIERARCHY OF MUSIC-INTERFACES

Previous observations lead us to a hierarchy of music-interfaces that reflects the level of expertise of a particular type of user (figure 1); the textual input is placed at the top of the hierarchy as the easiest mode of interaction while the score representation lays at the last position as the most difficult one. In other words, the musician who is able to write a musical query on a score could typically play it with a musical instrument or sing it, but the layman could only sing or query by textual data.

Interfacing with a digital music library, we suggest to use, at least, a *bi-modality* where textual input is combined with a specific music-interface; the human/computer interaction is improved by using the possibilities of singing, playing or notating a melody. Supplying multiple modalities of input will gain system capabilities in filtering useful information. Textual input should delimit the scope of the musical query (for example, "find all Mozart works in which you find *this* melody") or it should be

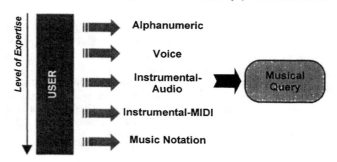

Figure 1. A hierarchy of input modalities for musical query.

restricted by (for example, "find all authors that used *this* melody") [2].

The use of multimodality for music applications is limited by technological issues. As a matter of fact, the richness of a musical performance can't be translated into all its dimensions (e.g. melody, harmony and rhythm) as input to a digital music library. There isn't a device that can reliably transcribe a polyphonic piece like a *piano sonata* and nevertheless there isn't an automatic tool that can understand the interpretation of a performance, for query like: "I want all the pieces where this melody is played *rubato*". Currently available technologies supply reliable translation of a monophonic input (voice or musical instruments played 'one note a time') into a sequence of notes; that is to say, the musical input can be only a melody.

Some of these difficulties could be overcome adopting interfaces less subject to human interpretation and/or system errors; it is the case of MIDI performance and musical notation. With this kind of input, graphical interface holds a special meaning: easiness of the input tools and feedback from entered data must be assured. User interfaces that enable *Common Musical Notation* input are essential; where they cannot be supply, widespread support of music score file formats like MIDI, ENIGMA, NIFF or SMDL can be a good compromise.

3. TRANSLATING AUDIO INPUTS

In the framework of the reference hierarchy introduced above, audio sources are the most difficult to deal with: low level translation is needed to pass from the acoustic domain to the symbolic domain. Thus, we will concentrate ourselves on transcribing an audio-query into a symbolic representation where the source could be either an acoustic signal captured by a microphone or an electronic signal driven through a 'line in' input. Singing voice and acoustical instruments lay in the first category and electronic instruments like synthesizers are in the second one; due to the peculiar aspects of human voice, this case will be treated separately from the one of musical instruments

3.1 Musical Instrument

We developed a system for pitch extraction that extends the sinusoidal model of McAulay and Quatieri [7]. In our model, we explicitly take into account the nearly-harmonic properties of sounds; in the case of real acoustic instruments, the frequency partials are not in the integral ratio but show a slight deviation from the ideal harmonic sound. The distance from the ideal harmonic case is weighted with an error function introduced by Maher and Beauchamp [6]. To validate our method, a software tool based on an interactive GUI was implemented. A general setting of parameters effective for monophonic translation has been configured and embedded into the La Scala's Music Archive, where a melodic query could be entered in the system by means of a graphical form with audio recording extensions. The error rate of such a configuration is negligible in comparison to an older algorithm developed for the same project where an error rate of less than 10% was reported [9].

A more challenging goal is the polyphonic transcription, for which we are currently testing our algorithm; it could serve the purpose of extending a melodic query over an harmonic one; in fact, a valuable mode of interfacing with a digital music database for a musician could be entering a series of chords for a query like "Find out all the pieces containing this harmonic structure"- playing it on a piano keyboard. To investigate this possibility, tests have been performed on the transcription of polyphonic pieces of music with synthesized sounds and transcription of chords generated by one or more real acoustic instruments. In the first case, a straightforward validation procedure could be settled, since we know exactly pitches and durations; an example is given in figure 2, where a piece in three voices (violin, oboe, double bass) is transcribed with only one higher octave error. In the second case, the aim is to test our system against nearly all the possible harmonic mixtures; random and exhaustive tests for bi-chords generated by 5 instruments were conducted. Results indicate that note recognition is very successful but the introduction of spurious notes or segmentation errors can reduce system accuracy. On average, in 89% of trials played notes were recognized, in 14% with spurious notes and in 10% with repeated notes.

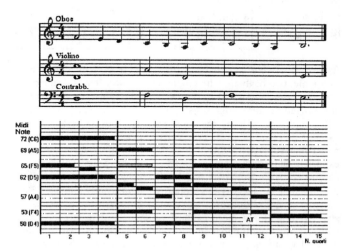

Figure 2. Transcription of a piece of music in three parts; gray note indicates an error.

3.2 Singing Voice

The human singing voice is one of the most difficult audio sources to automatically understand, due to its acoustical properties and to the inevitable connection with human language articulation. People sing approximately a melody, introducing deviation from the ideal case both in rhythm and in pitches; nevertheless, errors are constant-sized in respect to the overall melodic line [5]. Pitch information is conveyed by the vocal tract only, while the non-vocal tract has a state similar to impulsive noise [10]; thus, it is better estimating pitch only on the basis of the vocal part. Furthermore, allowing users to sing with lyrics enormously complicates the task of segmenting the signal into notes; for this reason, we force users to sing humming, like "hmm, hmm" or "haa-haa", or starting with a consonant, like "lalalla" or "na-na-na"; in the latter case rhythmic information are better preserved than in the former. Starting from these observations, we developed a pitch tracking algorithm dedicated to the singing voice. The system continuously adapts the input level to the optimum value monitoring background noise during user's pauses and clipping threshold during user's sing; unvoiced regions are detected and filtered; weak and strong consonant are distinguished and their relative positions are stored. In each stage, pitches are measured in fraction of semitones to improve the importance of relative distance between tones. Rounded intervals and durations that minimize the average deviation of the estimated melody are the ultimate sequence of notes.

Tables 1-2. Results of Singing Voice translation algorithm; on the left , table 1 shows the estimated intervals and base notes for the shortest piece of our test-set (8 notes–7 intervals long) interpreted by 6 subjects: gray cells indicate errors. On the right, table 2 summarizes the results for five pieces, indicating the percentage of right/wrong notes; among the wrong notes, error rate only due to subject 6 is made clear in column "Error Subject 6".

INTERVALS piece 1	N0 (midi note)	N1	N2	N3	N4	N5	N6	N7
Right Sequence	-	0	-3	3	4	-4	-3	5
Subj.1/Female	63.923	0	-3	3	4	-4	-3	5
Subj.2/Male	63.888	0	-3	3	4	-4	-3	5
Subj.3/Male	64.180	0	-3	3	3	-4	-3	5
Subj.4/Male	62.013	0	-3	4	4	-4	-3	5
Subj.5/Female	63.990	0	-3	3	4	-4	-4	6
Subj.6/Male	48.568	0	-4	5	3	-4	-4	6

	Right %	Wrong %	Error Subject 6 %	Total Number of Notes
piece 1	79	21	11	42
piece 2	89	11	6	72
piece 3	81	19	5	168
piece 4	87	13	6	78
piece 5	82	18	7	120

Experiments were carried out with six subjects, two female and four male, two of them with singing experience. It was decided to use five short songs well known to all subjects, who were encouraged to sing in the tonality they preferred; songs are 8-28 notes long. In table 1, intervals estimated during tests on the shortest piece are shown; gray cells indicate an error. It can be noted that subject number 6 introduced the most errors; it was expected, since his singing ability was very poor. This fact is confirmed by the summary in table 2: excluding tests carried out on this subject, success rates improve significantly (86%÷95%). Although very promising, we should consider these results a starting point for a more exhaustive session of tests conducted with an important collection of music pieces. A test session devoted to investigate performance on note lengths is currently under going.

4. CONCLUSION AND FURTHER WORK

The proposed hierarchy of music-interfaces is intended to offer an actual and flexible interaction between users and digital music databases; moreover, it could be a framework for a future development of finer interaction from the musicological point of view and for audio databases; in the former case, it could be generalized to other musical dimensions like harmony; in the latter case, we can imagine that querying by example or by timbral attributes (i.e. with a short clip or with a sound) could be its first natural extension. Much work needs to be done in different directions: besides current and already cited on-going experiments, we are measuring the effectiveness of combining different musical inputs in a complete environment for music information retrieval.

5. ACKNOWLEDGMENTS

This project has been partially supported by the Italian National Research Council in the frame of the Finalized Project "Cultural Heritage" (Subproject 3, Topic 3.2, Subtopic 3.2.2, Target 3.2.1). Authors are mainly indebted to Elena Ferrari, Giuseppe Frazzini, Maurizio Longari, Alessandro Meroni and Fabrizio Trotta.

6. REFERENCES

[1] Blattner, M.M., Dannenberg, R.B. Multimedia Interface Design. Addison-Wesley/ACM Press, 1992.

[2] Ferrari, E. and Haus, G. The Musical Archive Information System at Teatro alla Scala. In Proc. IEEE Int. Conf. on Multimedia Computing and Systems Florence, Italy, Jun. 1999.

[3] Ghias, A., Logan, D., Chamberlin, D., Smith, S.C. Query by humming – musical information retrieval in an audio database. In Proc. ACM Multimedia'95, San Francisco, Ca., Nov. 1995.

[4] Haus, G. Rescuing La Scala's music archive. IEEE Computer, Vol. 31, No. 3, pp. 88-89, March 1998.

[5] Lindsay, A. Using contour as a mid-level representation of melody. M.I.T. Media Lab, M.S. Thesis, 1997.

[6] Maher, R.C. and Beauchamp, J.W. Fundamental frequency estimation of musical signals using a two-way mismatch procedure. J. Acoust. Soc. of America, Vol. 95, No. 4, pp. 2254-2263, Apr. 1994.

[7] McAulay, R.J., Quatieri, T.F. Speech analysis/synthesis based on a sinusoidal representation. IEEE Trans. on Acoustic, Speech and Sig. Proc., Vol. 34, No. 4, pp.744-754, Aug. 1986.

[8] McNab, R.J., Smith, L.A., Witten, C.L., Henderson, C.L., Cunningham, S.J. Towards the digital music libraries: tune retrieval from acoustic input. In Proc. Digital Libraries Conference, 1996.

[9] Pollastri, E. Melody retrieval based on approximate string-matching and pitch-tracking methods. In Proc. XIIth Colloquium on Musical Informatics, AIMI-University of Udine, Gorizia, Oct. 1998.

[10] Rabiner, L.R. and Schafer, R.W. Digital signal processing of speech signals. Prentice-Hall, 1978.

[11] Rolland, P., Raskinis, G., Ganascia, J. Musical content-based retrieval: an overview of the Melodiscov approach and system. In Proc. ACM Multimedia'99, Orlando, Fl., Nov. 1999.

[12] Uitdenbogerd, A. and Zobel, J. Melodic matching techniques for large music databases. In Proc. ACM Multimedia'99, Orlando, Fl., Nov. 1999.

Detecting Video Shot Boundaries up to 16 Times Faster

Kien A. Hua
Computer Science Program, School of EECS
University of Central Florida
Orlando, FL 32816-2362, U. S. A.
kienhua@cs.ucf.edu

JungHwan Oh
Computer Science Program, School of EECS
University of Central Florida
Orlando, FL 32816-2362, U. S. A.
oh@cs.ucf.edu

ABSTRACT

Shot boundary detection (SBD) is the first fundamental step to managing video databases. Existing automatic SBD techniques, however, are based on sequential search, and therefore too expensive for practical use. To address this problem, we investigate a non-linear approach in which most video frames do not need to be compared. It can improve their performance substantially. Our experiments show that this idea speeds up a conventional method based on color histograms up to 16 times (five times on average) while preserving the same accuracy.

Keywords

Shot boundary detection, non-linear shot boundary detection, video data segmentation.

1. INTRODUCTION

In general, it is more beneficial to store a video as a sequence of *shots*, defined as a collection of frames recorded from a single camera operation. This requirement calls for technique to segment videos into shots, a process that is referred to as *shot boundary detection* (SBD).

Many techniques have been developed to automatically detect transitions from one shot to the next. These schemes differ mainly in the method for computing the inter-frame difference. The difference can be determined by comparing the corresponding pixels of the two images [1]. Color or grayscale histograms can also be used [5, 6]. Alternatively, a technique based on changes in the edges has also been developed [7]. Other schemes use domain knowledge [8, 3] such as predefined models, objects, regions, etc. Hybrids of the above techniques have also been investigated [2, 4]. In this paper, we refer to all these techniques as the *linear approach* due to the fact that they sequentially measure inter-frame differences and study their variance values. Since they need to compare every two consecutive frames in a given video stream, this approach is very expensive and unsuitable for large video databases.

To address the aforementioned problem, we investigate the *non-linear approach* in this paper. Our idea is motivated by the following two facts. First, there is little difference between consecutive frames within a shot. Thus, most comparisons under linear techniques are wasteful. Second, frames do not have to be examined in the order they appear in the video clip. Based on the above observations, we propose to process the video frames non-linearly. That is, we can develop search techniques to skip over unnecessary comparisons much in the same way that binary search skips over data items which have no chance of being matched. Since we need to examine only a fraction of a given video, non-linear solutions can potentially outperform existing linear techniques by order of magnitude.

The remainder of this paper is organized as follows. The proposed non-linear approach is presented in Section 2. In Section 3, we discuss our experimental results. Finally, we give our concluding remarks in Section 4.

2. NON-LINEAR APPROACH TO SBD

The existing SBD techniques usually scan the entire video stream and process the frames in the linear order as illustrated in Figure 1(b). But, we can skip over unnecessary comparisons. To illustrate this idea, we introduce two such techniques in this section.

2.1 Two Non-linear SBD Techniques

We assume that a shot has at least two frames. This assumption is generally true in practice. To gain insight on the benefits of the non-linear idea, let us consider the following strategies:

- **Regular Skip:** We compare every other d^{th} frames. As an example, "$d = 2$" is illustrated in Figure 1 (c). We compare the first frame with the third, the third with the fifth, and so forth. When two frames, say i and $i + 2$, are identified to be in two different shots, we compare frame i with frame $i + 1$ to determine the shot boundary. If frame i and frame $i+1$ are identified to be in two different shots, the shot boundary lies between frame i and frame $i + 1$. Otherwise, it lies between frame $i+1$ and frame $i+2$. We do not have to compare frame $i+1$ with frame $i+2$ since a shot must have at least two frames. Once a shot boundary has been identified, the same procedure is then repeated for the next shot starting from its first frame. This scheme is very simple; but we can already reduce the number of comparisons almost in half. We note that shot boundary detection is a cpu-bound process. The

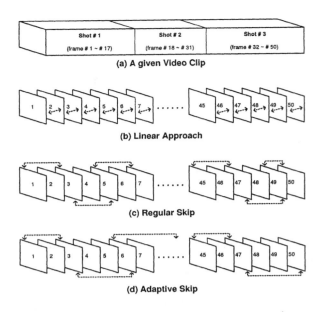

Figure 1: Various Non-linear SBD strategies

(a) A given Video Clip

(b) Linear Approach

(c) Regular Skip

(d) Adaptive Skip

number of comparisons dictates the performance of the algorithm.

- **Adaptive Skip**: The optimal value of d in Regular Skip varies from video to video. In the Adaptive Skip strategy, we determine d dynamically. In each iteration, the algorithm determines how many frames to skip by comparing the current frame with the one last examined (Figure 1 (d)). If this comparison is more similar than the last comparison, we increase d for the next comparison. If it becomes less similar, we decrease d. On the other hand, if the current comparison indicates that the two frames are in two different shots, we scan backward to look for the boundary using, say Regular Skip in the reverse direction. Once the boundary has been determined, we can scan forward again using the same procedure. Obviously, this adaptive strategy can also provide very significant savings compared to linear techniques.

We note that how to compare the video frames are intentionally left out in the description of Regular Skip and Adaptive Skip techniques. Any of the inter-frame comparison techniques, discussed in Section 1, can be used in a non-linear scheme to determine if two frames are in the same shot. Thus, we can achieve the same accuracy of the linear technique, but at a remarkably lower cost.

2.2 Rough Assessment of Performance

To illustrate the benefits of the non-linear approach, let us consider the video stream, shown in Figure 1(a), which consists of three shots. We compare the linear and non-linear schemes in term of the number of inter-frame comparisons (N_c) performed by each technique.

Let us compute N_c^{linear} for the linear approach as shown in Figure 1 (b). Since every two consecutive frames are compared, N_c^{linear} can be calculated as $F - 1$, where F is the total number of frames in the video. Since F is 50 this our example (Figure 1 (a)), $N_c^{linear} = 49$.

In Regular Skip (Figure 1 (c)), the odd numbered frames are compared; and when two frames are identified to be in two different shots, one additional comparison is necessary to determine the shot boundary. Thus, the number of comparisons required by Regular Skip can be computed as $N_c^{regular} = \lfloor \frac{F}{2} \rfloor + s$, where s is the number of shot boundaries in a given video. Since the video stream, shown in Figure 1(a), has 50 frames and two shot boundaries, $N_c^{regular} = 27$. This represents an impressive 45% saving over the linear approach.

If we apply Adaptive Skip to the sample video in Figure 1(a), $N_c^{adaptive} = 20$ which is a 59% improvement over the linear approach. Let us look at how the first boundary is detected to gain insight on the advantages of Adaptive Skip. First, we compare frame # 1 and frame # 3 ($d = 2$). Since they are in the same shot (shot # 1), frame # 3 and frame # 6 ($d = 3$) are compared next, and similarly, frame # 6 and frame # 10 ($d = 4$) are compared. This comparison continues until frame # 15 and frame # 21 ($d = 6$) are compared. Since frame # 15 and frame # 21 are in two different shots, we scan backward to find the shot boundary between frame # 17 and frame # 18. For simplicity, we use Regular Skip, with $d = 2$, to do the backward scan. In total, we need to perform only eight frame comparisons although the shot has 17 frames. In practice, a shot is typically much longer than 17 frames; and we can expect Adaptive Skip to provide substantially better saving.

3. EXPERIMENTAL RESULTS

To assess the performance of our non-linear schemes, we compare them with a linear technique in our experimental studies. To be fair, all three methods use the color histogram method (CHD) to compute the inter-frame differences. For convenience, we will refer to the three strategies, Linear, Regular Skip, and Adaptive Skip as 'Linear', 'Regular', and 'Adaptive', respectively, in this section. They are evaluated in terms of the *total time for execution* (T_c) and the *total number of frame comparisons* (N_c).

Our test video set consists of 18 video clips which represent six different categories as shown in Table 1. In total, this test set lasts more than 4 hours. Our video clips were digitized in AVI format at 30 frames/second. The resolution of our video clips is 160×120 pixels. Each pixel is encoded in 24 bits (8 bits for each red, green and blue).

The execution efficiency of Linear, Regular, and Adaptive techniques, according to our experiments, is shown in Table 1. We included Regular Skip with a minimum skipping distance of 2 in our study to investigate the minimum saving guaranteed by the non-linear approach. The results are shown in Table 1. We observe that Regular Skip reduces the costs of the linear technique in half, 53.4% in terms of total execution time and 51.0% in terms of total number of frame comparisons. This is consistent with our analysis in the last section. In general, this saving is achievable regardless of the videos. One can expect to at least "double" the performance when using a non-linear strategy. In practice, we would typically use bigger skipping distances to achieve much better performance.

One would expect Adaptive Skip to perform significantly better than Regular Skip with a minimum skipping distance. The results for Adaptive Skip are also included in Table 1. It shows that on average Adaptive Skip save more than 80% of the computation when compared with the linear approach.

Type	Name	Duration (min:sec)	Total Frames	Shots	Total Compl. Time (T_c, sec.)			Total Frame Comparisons (N_c)			Average Shot Length	
					Linear	Regular	Adaptive	Linear	Regular	Adaptive	frames	sec.
TV Programs	Silk Stalkings (Drama)	10 : 24	18718	95	787.49	409.52	118.91	18717	9476	2695	160	5.4
	Scooby Doo Show (Cartoon)	11 : 38	20941	106	869.95	429.60	136.58	20940	10614	3581	145	4.8
	Friends (Sitcom)	10 : 22	18655	116	846.76	449.75	149.03	18654	9467	3358	133	4.4
	Star Trek Deep Space Nine	12 : 27	22413	111	1019.40	541.66	156.99	22412	11324	3003	190	6.4
	General Hospital (Soap Opera)	11 : 20	20415	110	945.09	470.18	136.09	20414	10327	3021	170	5.7
	Sally (Talk Show)	11 : 19	20374	90	967.25	468.28	131.55	20373	10287	2669	204	6.8
	TV Commercials	31 : 25	56550	967	2910.80	1589.37	1129.01	56549	29869	22247	35	1.2
News	National (NBC)	14 : 45	26550	202	1217.95	668.05	294.74	26549	13606	6505	80	2.7
	Local (ABC)	30 : 27	54811	176	2749.51	1506.30	324.44	54810	27663	6193	212	7.1
	News Conference	9 : 19	16761	10	835.72	431.86	50.05	16760	8395	1056	1117	37.2
Movies	ATF	11 : 52	21356	224	985.11	541.79	288.64	21355	11074	6406	54	1.8
	Simon Birch	11 : 08	20040	164	949.65	510.22	219.37	20039	10220	4729	100	3.3
Sports Events	Mountain Bike Race	15 : 12	27360	143	1157.76	632.67	178.30	27359	13859	4569	153	5.1
	Football	21 : 26	38581	163	1801.27	968.32	239.57	38580	19472	4861	211	7.0
Docu- mentaries	Today's Vietnam	10 : 29	18868	93	850.54	459.28	142.04	18867	9572	3245	136	4.5
	For All Mankind	16 : 50	30305	127	1434.48	771.37	212.30	30304	15313	4455	188	6.3
Music Videos	Kobe Bryant	3 : 53	6987	53	307.35	168.48	63.62	6986	3547	1509	129	4.3
	Alabama Song	4 : 24	7915	65	346.68	190.51	74.19	7914	4035	1757	101	3.4
	Total	248 : 40	447600	3015	20982.76	11207.21	4045.42	447582	228120	85859	148	4.9

Table 1: Test Video Clips and Comparisons of Computation Costs

The exact savings depend on the lengths of the shots in the video. The average shot lengths of the test videos in the number of frames and seconds are given in Table 1. We observe that the savings are more for videos with longer shots. For instance, the average shot length of "News Conference" is 1,117 frames (or 37.2 seconds). In this case, Adaptive Skip can detect the shot boundaries using only 6% of the computation needed for the linear approach. That is, Adaptive Skip is more than 16 times better.

We note that the improvements due to Adaptive Skip are still respectable under videos with very short shots. As an example, let us consider 'TV Commercials' which is a sequence of TV commercials. The shot lengths of this video clip range from 16 to 33 frames, approximately one second. This is typical for TV commercials. Although the shots are short, Adaptive Skip can still skip over many frames to provide a significant saving of about 60% over the linear technique. At first sight, one might expect a higher saving since there are about 30 frames in each shot. The smaller saving obtained is due to the fact that we have to scan the video backward to find the shot boundary every time we detect two dissimilar frames. This step could be optimized by recursively applying Adaptive Skip to the video segment between the two dissimilar frames.

4. CONCLUDING REMARKS

The high costs of today's shot boundary detection techniques have hindered their use in practice. We have addressed this problem with a non-linear approach, in which not every video frame needs to be examined. We started with a very simple strategy that scans every other frame (Regular Skip). Even this plain scheme can reduce the cost almost in half. To really exploit the benefits of the non-linear idea, we also investigated the Adaptive Skip method. This technique determines the skipping distances dynami-

cally to achieve much better performance. Our experiments show that this idea speeds up a conventional method based on color histograms up to 16 times (five times on average) while preserving the same accuracy.

5. REFERENCES

[1] E. Ardizzone and M. Cascia. Automatic video database indexing and retrieval. *Multimedia Tools and Applications*, 4:29–56, 1997.

[2] H. Jiang, A. Helal, A. K. Elmagarmid, and A. Joshi. Scene change detection techniques for video database system. *Multimedia Systems*, pages 186–195, 1998.

[3] C. Y. Low, Q. Tian, and H. Zhang. An automatic news video parsing, indexing and browsing system. In *Proc. of ACM Int'l Conf. on Multimedia*, pages 425–426, Boston, MA, November 1996.

[4] J. Oh and K. A. Hua. An efficient and cost-effective technique for browsing and indexing large video databases. In *Proc. of 2000 ACM SIGMOD Intl. Conf. on Management of Data*, pages 415–426, 2000.

[5] M. A. Smith and M. G. Christel. Automating the creation of a digital video library. In *Proc. of ACM Multimedia '95*, pages 357–358, 1995.

[6] H. Yu and W. Wolf. A visual search system for video and image databases. In *Proc. IEEE Int'l Conf. on Multimedia Computing and Systems*, 1997.

[7] R. Zabih, J. Miller, and K. Mai. A feature-based algorithm for detecting and classifying scene breaks. In *Proc. of ACM Multimedia '95*, pages 189–200.

[8] H. Zhang, S. Y. Tan, S. W. Smoliar, and G. Yihong. Automatic parsing and indexing of news video. *Multimedia Systems*, 2:156–266, 1995.

Touring Into the Picture using Hand Shape Recognition

Eu-Mi Ji
C.S. Department HyeChen College
San 15-3 BogSuDong SeoGu
Taejeon, KOREA
+82-42-580-6208

emji@hcc.ac.kr

Ho-Sub Yoon
I.P. Div. CSTL in ETRI
161, KaJungDong, YuSung
Taejeon, KOREA
+82-42-860-5233

yoonhs@etri.re.kr

Younglae J.Bae
I.P. Div. CSTL in ETRI
161, KaJungDong, YuSung
Taejeon, KOREA
+82-42-860-5720

yljb@etri.re.kr

ABSTRACT

The purpose of this study is to prove that using gesture recognition through implementing the method of touring into the picture makes navigation very convenient and easy compared to navigation using mouse and keyboard. The method of touring into the picture is a simple technique that converts an 2D image into 3D animation. This study shows how to convert 2D image into 3D navigation, implementing the method previously proposed by Horry and Phy on the personal computer. Hand shape gesture recognition which functions as a user interface has been developed into three types: Type-1 means pause; Type-2 means showing directions on 2D; Type-3 is designed to assign upper and lower depth in space. These three types play the role as virtual mouse and keyboard in 3D-rendering image. Above all, using hand-shaped gestures contributes to the ease of user's navigation of 3D space..

Keywords

Hand Shape Recognition, 3D interface, Image Touring

1. INTRODUCTION

A gesture is the physical expression of a mental concept and must be an important tool for enhancing the communication level of HCI. Among the variety of gestures such as hand gesture, body gesture and facial expression, hand gesture is the more expressive and the frequently used one. In this dissertation, a gesture is defined as the motion or the posture of the hand in order to communicate with a computer.

From this assumption, this paper describes the hand shape recognition system for touring into the picture in 3D domain and the purpose of this study is to prove that using gesture recognition through implementing the method of touring into the picture makes navigation very convenient and easy compared to navigation using mouse and keyboard.

Most conventional approaches to hand gesture recognition have employed external devices such as datagloves and makers. But, for

more natural interface, hand gesture must be recognized from visual images without the aid of external devices.

This paper is composed of five sections. In Section II, we explain the touring algorithm proposed by Horry and Phy. Section III explains the method of hand shape recognition. In Section IV, experimental results between hand shape recognition and 3D touring are described. Finally, we give conclusions in Section V.

2. TOURING INTO THE PICTURE

Horry[1] and Phy[2] develop the 3D touring system TIP(Tour Into the Picture) that use the perspective information from 2D image and make the virtual 3D space. The user can input the vanish point and inner rectangle location that limit the distance range of camera such as figure 1 (a) user input. And then, system recofigurate to the 3D background model from 2D image using information from user that can be able to navigate the inner picture. Figure 1 (b) shows the 3D polygon model for background generation. The next step, environment model generation algorithm, processes the modeling and calculates the coordinate to the polygon from foreground object that segmented by user. Finally, the user decides the camera position and renders the environment model.

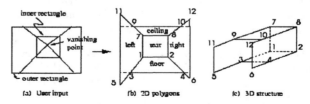

(a) User input   (b) 2D polygons   (c) 3D structure

Figure 1. Background model of Horry.

3. HAND SHAPE RECOGNITION

There are many potential constrains that if we used mouse or keyboard for interaction of man-machine communication in the touring of 3D space. Because mouse and keyboard actions are not suitable to defined the 3D actions such as up and down direction. To solve this problem, hand gesture interface is more reasonable method than the other methods. The general interface device in the 3D virtual reality area is a dataglove that simulates the actions from hand gesture through the electronic sensor. However, the dataglove is not general device in the common PC environments and is not easy to use.

Hand gesture recognition using visual devices has a number of potential applications in HCI (human computer interaction), VR(virtual reality), and machine control in the industrial field. Most previous approaches to hand gesture recognition have employed special color makers. For a more natural interface, however, hand gesture must be distinguishable from visual images without any constrains.

This paper describes the 3D mouse system using hand shape recognition that analyze input image from captured by CCD camera using image processing method. The results of hand shape recognition are converted to the commands in the 3D space. The type of hand shape commands are waiting, selecting 2D direction and selecting 3D direction. Figure 2 shows the three types of hand shape command.

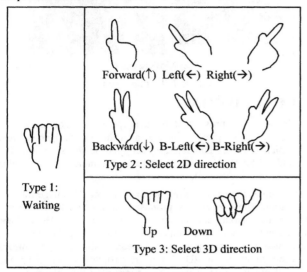

Type 1: Waiting

Forward(↑) Left(←) Right(→)

Backward(↓) B-Left(←) B-Right(→)

Type 2 : Select 2D direction

Up   Down

Type 3: Select 3D direction

Figure 2. The three types of hand shape command.

Following flowchart of figure 3 explains the detail image processing method for hand shape recognition. The first step, Detect Skin Color, has comparing processing with previous hand color information and detecting the skin color using threshold value. The second step has distinction between noise and skin region using a prior knowledge about skin regions. The third step is final selection of hand region from all candidate skin regions using hand region information about size, orientation, location and so on.

For more detail matching between hand shape and 3D commands, the finger counting method and finger direction search method are used. The run-length scanning is used for finger counting method such as figure 4. We scan the image from left to right from each horizontal line. If several horizontal lines have only one white run, then this hand image has one straight finger.

Finger direction search method calculates the momentum values that are very useful and accurate method for object direction detection. Final step for hand shape recognition is a dividing method of type 3 commands such as figure 5. Basically, type 3 commands have long horizontal length then vertical length. We can divide between type 2 and type 3 commands using this condition: Type 2 = horizontal length < vertical length, Type 3 = horizontal length > vertical length. The area1 of figure 5 means left half area including only white hand pixel and the area2 means the right half area in opposite direction. If area1 is bigger then area2, we decide that this hand image means the Up command, otherwise Down command.

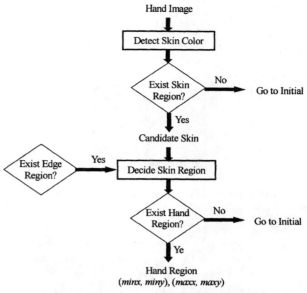

Figure 3. The flowchart of Hand region detection.

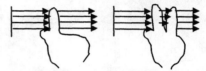

Figure 4. Run-length method for finger counting.

Area 1 < Area 2 ➔ Up   Area 1 > Area 2 ➔ Down

Figure 5. Decide of Type 3 commands.

4. EXPERIMENTAL RESULTS

The proposed system was implemented on a personal computer with an image capture board (Matrox Meteor II). Also, an input image sequences were captured by CCD camera with the resolution 640x480. The computing power is 10 ~ 15 frames per second using dual Pentium II 400 Mhz. Since our computer can process over 5 frames per second, it is possible to view the proposed system for real-time interface system. The recognition software is implemented in Visual C++ 6.0 and OpenGL library on Windows 98.

Figure 6 shows the description of image processing window and figure 7 shows the testing results of hand shape recognition system.

Input Image From Camera	Candidate Hand Region
Hand Region	Text Output of Results

Figure 6. The description of image processing window.

(a) Preparation of navigation (horizontal line setting)

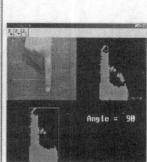

(b) Moving forward

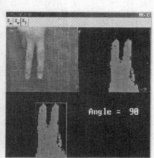

(c) Moving Backward

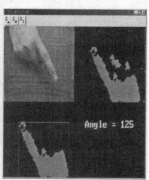

(d) Moving left

(e) Moving right

Figure 7. Testing results.

5. CONCLUSION

The paper is to prove that hand shape recognition under the touring into the picture in 3D area makes navigation very convenient and easy compared to using mouse and keyboard. The method of touring into the picture is a simple technique that converts an 2D image into 3D animation image.

This study shows converting algorithm from 2D image into 3D navigation using previously proposed the method by Horry and Pho on the personal computer with OpenGL Library. Hand shape gesture recognition which functions as a user interface has been developed into three types: Type-1 means waiting; Type-2 means showing directions on 2D; Type-3 is designed to assign up and down depth in space. These three types play the role as virtual mouse and keyboard in 3D-rendering image. From the proposed system, the hand-shaped gesture contributes to the ease of user's navigation of 3D space.

6. REFERENCES

[1]Youich Horry, Chen, S. E. and Williams, L. "View Interpolation for Image Synthesis", Proc. SIGGRAPH '93, pp. 279-288.

[2] Soon-Hyoung Pyo. Tour Into The Picture (TIP) Using A Vanishing Line. Master'sthesis, CS Dept., KAIST, 1999.

[3] Foley, J. D., van Dam, A. Feiner, S. K., and Hughes, J. F. *Computer Graphics: Principle and Practice*, Addison-Wesley, Reading, Mass., 1990.

[4] Chen, S. E. "QuickTime VR -An Image-based Approach to Virtual Environment Navigation", PROC. SIGGRAPH '95, pp.29-38.

[5] Ken-ichi Anjyo, Kiyoshi Arai, "Tour into the Picture: Using a Spidery Mesh Interface to Make Animation from a Single Image", SIGGRAPH-97, pp.225-232.

[6] P. A. Harling, "Gesture Input using Neural Networks", B.S. Thesis, Dept. of C. S., University of York, 1993.

[7] R. C. Gonzalez, R. E. Woods, Digital Image Processing, Addison-Wesley, 1992.

[8] Dvid Saxe, Richard Foulds, "Toward Robust Skin Identification in Video Images", International Workshop on Automatic Face and Gesture Recognition, Vermont, pp. 379-384. 1996.

Dissolve Transition Detection Algorithm Using Spatio-Temporal Distribution of MPEG Macro-Block Types

Sung-Bae Jun   Kyoungro Yoon   Hee-Youn Lee

LG Electronics Institute of Technology
16 Woomyeon-Dong, Seocho-Gu, Seoul, Korea 137-724
+82-2-526-4131

sbjun@ lge.com, {yoonk, hylee}@LG-Elite.com

ABSTRACT
Almost every shot change detection algorithm detects abrupt transition (hard cut) without difficulty, but gradual transitions such as fades, dissolves, wipes are left as hard-to-detect problems. Dissolve effect, among the various gradual transition effects, is one of the most frequently used shot transition methods with special semantic meaning such as scene transition. Information of the shot change type can also be the basis for the shot clustering algorithms. In this paper, we present a fast and effective dissolve-transition detection algorithm based on the spatio-temporal distribution of the macro block types in MPEG-compressed video. In the proposed algorithm, the ratio of forward macro blocks in the B-type frames and the spatial distribution of forward/backward macro blocks are utilized for detecting dissolve transition. After finding such sequence of frames, we apply 2 heuristic rules: (1) The global color distributions of the frames at which dissolve starts and terminates are very different, and (2) The duration of dissolve transition is typically more than 0.3 second.

Keywords
Video Segmentation, MPEG, Shot change detection, Dissolve, Fades, Macro block type distribution.

1. INTRODUCTION
Shot segmentation [4,5,6,7,9,10] and clustering [2,8] technologies have been developed for non-linear video browsing and searching during the last decade. Shot segmentation represents a process of extracting temporal information, such as frame numbers, of each shot of a video based on the transition detection, and shot clustering represents a process of extracting structural information of multiple shots to compose story units such as scenes. A shot can be defined as a single sequence of frames in a motion picture obtained by one camera without interruption, and is regarded as a basic unit of constructing/analyzing a video content. Many

researches have been concentrated on shot change detection that finds shot boundaries for segmentation. Among them, algorithms based on the global color distributions are known to be the most effective for detecting abrupt (discontinuous) shot changes. However, it is very hard to detect gradual (continuous) shot changes such as fade, dissolve and wipe transition.

In this paper, we propose an efficient and robust dissolve-transition detection algorithm for the MPEG-compressed video streams. The proposed algorithm is based on the observation of the spatio-temporal distribution of the forward/backward macro blocks, which requires only partially decoded domain processing. In dissolve transitions, it is observed that the ratio of forward macro blocks to forward and backward macro blocks in the sequence of B-frames are fluctuating, and the amplitude is very high compared to non-dissolve regions. It is also found that the spatial distribution of forward/backward macro blocks of a B-frame can be used to distinguish the dissolve transition effect among various gradual transitions. The forward and backward macro blocks tend to be scattered over the entire spatial region of the image in the B-frames.

Relevant researches are described in section 2, and our dissolve detection algorithm is described in section 3. Based on the algorithm, we are currently working on building digital library and non-linear video browser of MPEG video streams, and initial test results performed using MPEG-7 Content set and Korean news broadcast streams are shown in section 4. In section 5, conclusion and remarks are given.

2. RELATED WORKS
A number of shot segmentation algorithms detect gradual transitions. Twin comparison method [10] is the first attempt to detect and classify abrupt transitions and gradual transitions. In [10], dual threshold values are applied to the difference of intensity histogram in order to detect gradual transitions. With the twin comparison method, gradual transitions are partially detected. However, it cannot easily detect the dissolves between two shots involving camera or object motion, requires many times of comparison of intensity histograms, and doesn't classify the types of gradual shot transitions.

The most popular dissolve detection method which utilizes the intensity variance of successive frames are developed by Meng et. al. in [4]. It works on a partially decoded domain and utilizes 2 criteria: (1) The depth of the intensity variance valley must be large enough and (2) The duration of the fades or dissolve region must be long enough. The algorithm proposed in [4] produces good result and the processing speed of algorithm is very fast. But there still exist false alarms and false dismissals. False alarms are due to fast camera motion or object motion, and false dismissals are caused by the fact that there are some dissolve regions which do not satisfy 2 criteria of this algorithm.

An algorithm for editing effect detection and classification based on calculating edge change fraction in temporal domain was proposed by Zabih et. al. in [9]. It not only detects shot transitions but also classifies the types of shot transition using the change of fraction of entering/exiting edges. The experimental result shows the performance of the algorithm is very good, but this algorithm requires too much processing time (e.g.: calculation of pixel-wise image difference to extract the fraction of entering/exiting edges) for real-time application.

3. DISSOLVE-TRANSITION DETECTION

A dissolve-transition is a transition from one scene to other scene by linearly decreasing the intensity of the first scene and linearly increasing the intensity of the second scene in the mixed region [4]. Based on the spatio-temporal distribution of macro block types, a fast and robust dissolve-transition detection algorithm for partially decoded MPEG video stream is developed. In this algorithm, sequences of frames which have specific spatio-temporal macro block distribution are selected first as candidate sequences. Then, time constraints and color distribution characteristics are applied to the candidate sequences to make final decision.

3.1 Detection with Macro Block Type

In order to select candidates for dissolve transition in the compressed domain, we examine the spatio-temporal macro block type distribution of each B-type frame which is located right before or after anchor frame in display sequence. An anchor frame is a reference frame used for motion prediction and compensation. Figure 1 shows a typical GOP structure of an MPEG video stream. I and P frames are anchor frames, and shaded frames denote B frames adjacent to an anchor frame.

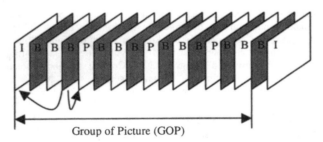

Group of Picture (GOP)

Figure 1. A typical MPEG video sequence

Use of the spatio-temporal macro block type distribution for dissolve detection is based on the characteristics of the MPEG encoded dissolve sequence as shown in Figure 2. In Figure 2, each selected frame is B-type frame adjacent to an anchor frame. The temporal macro block type distribution characteristic of dissolve sequence can be expressed using FMBR (Forward Macro Block Ratio) defined as follows:

$$FMBR = \begin{cases} M_{fwd}/(M_{fwd} + M_{bwd}) & \text{if } M_{fwd} + M_{bwd} \neq 0 \\ N/A & \text{otherwize} \end{cases}$$

where M_{fwd} denotes the number of forward type macro blocks in a frame and M_{bwd} denotes the number of backward type macro blocks in a frame.

The ratio of forward macro block (FMBR) in the collected sequence of B-type frames adjacent to anchor frames changes alternately from very high to very low and from very low to very high in a dissolve sequence. Figure 3 shows the temporal characteristic of FMBR in typical dissolve region and non-dissolve region.

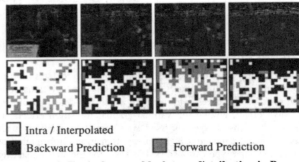

☐ Intra / Interpolated

■ Backward Prediction　■ Forward Prediction

Figure 2. Typical macro block type distribution in B frames when a dissolve transition occurs

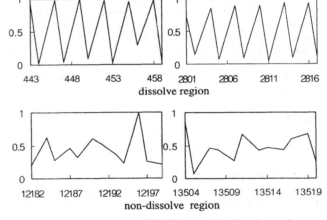

Figure 3. Typical FMBR graph in dissolve and non-dissolve region

The temporal distribution of macro block types can be simplified using the following 3 prediction states of B-type frames adjacent to anchor frame.

F_{none} : $M_{fwd} + M_{bwd} = 0$ or $1-\tau_r \leq FMBR \leq \tau_r$

F_{fwd} : $FMBR > \tau_r$

F_{bwd} : $FMBR < 1-\tau_r$

Where $\tau_r > 0.5$

In a dissolve transition, the alternating prediction state sequence such as [F_{fwd}, F_{bwd}, F_{fwd}, F_{bwd}, ..., F_{fwd}] appears in the collected sequence of B frames adjacent to anchor frames.

Another condition used to detect dissolve transitions is spatial macro block type distribution. In dissolve transitions, the forward and backward predicted macro blocks are scattered over the entire spatial region of the B-frame adjacent to anchor frames. The temporal characteristics of the macro block type distribution can also appear in some wipe transitions and in frames with fast object movement or camera motion. However, the spatial distribution of forward/backward macro blocks in a B-type picture of a wipe sequence or a fast object motion sequence is quite different from that of a dissolve sequence. Figure 4 shows a typical spatio-temporal macro block type distribution of wipe shot transition which is much different from that of dissolve transition.

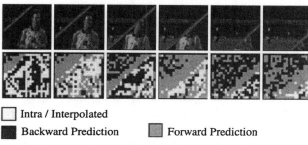

▢ Intra / Interpolated

◼ Backward Prediction   ▧ Forward Prediction

Figure 4. Typical macro block type distribution in B frames when a wipe transition occurs

Based on the above two conditions on macro block type distribution, candidates for dissolve transition are selected. Note that only B-type frames which is adjacent to anchor frames are considered in this stage. This stage of the proposed dissolve detection algorithm is summarized as [R1].

[R1] Find the sequence [b,e] which satisfies R[1.1] and R[1.2]

   [R1.1] if ($S_{cur} = F_{none}$) then return false

      else   if ($S_{prev} = S_{cur}$) then return false

              else return true.

   [R1.2] if ($S_{cur} = F_{none}$) then return false

      else   if ($SpatDist$(MinType) > τ_s) then return true

              else return false

In [R1.1], S_{cur} denotes the prediction state of current B-type frame and S_{prev} denotes the prediction state of previously checked B-type frame. In [R1.2], MinType is Fwd when $M_{fwd} > M_{bwd}$, else MinType is Bwd. $SpatDist$(A) is a spatial distribution measure of the macro blocks of type A. If A is Fwd, we calculate spatial distribution measure for forward predicted macro blocks and if the A is Bwd, calculate spatial distribution measure for backward predicted macro blocks. The spatial distribution function of macro blocks of type A, $SpatDist$(A), can be calculated by various methods. Among them, we choose the following method for its simplicity.

$$SpatDist(A) = C_A / T_A$$

   where T_A is the total number of macro blocks of type A

C_A is the number of connected component of type A.

The more macro blocks of the type A are scattered over the entire image, the higher the $SpatDist$(A) is. A more sophisticated algorithm can replace the measure for the spatial distribution of forward or backward macro blocks.

After applying [R1], we obtain the start and the last frame numbers of dissolve transition candidate sequence [b,e] (b is the first frame number and e is the last frame number of the dissolve candidate sequence). These candidates frequently have false alarms, and are used as input of [R2] and [R3].

3.2 Refinement with Duration of Dissolve

Since, the duration of a dissolve transition is typically longer than 0.3 sec, many algorithm uses time constraints for dissolve detection [4]. We also apply time constraint to the output of [R1], [b,e]. If [b,e] satisfies [R2], [b,e] is used as an input for [R3] and if [b,e] does not satisfy [R2], the [b,e] is regarded as non-dissolve region.

   [R2] if $Duration$(e-b) > τ_t return true else return false.

In [R2], the $Duration$(n) means the normal play time for n frames under the consideration of frame rate of the given video stream.

3.3 Refinement with Color Distribution

Since the dissolve transition is a type of shot transition method, the color distributions of the first frame and the last frame of a dissolve transition are very different as any other shot changing frames. Many hard cut detection algorithms [5,10] use color histogram difference measure to detect abrupt shot transitions. In order to improve the speed of our algorithm, we change the starting and the ending frame of a dissolve shot transition as [b',e'], where b' is the largest I-type frame number which is smaller than b and e' is the smallest I-type frame number which is larger than e. The I-type frame is selected since we can decode the picture without decoding other pictures. To further reduce the processing time, only the DC-image introduced in [4] is decoded. After the DC-images of frame b' and e' are decoded, the difference of color histogram is measured. In our sytem, if [b',e'] satisfies following rule [R3], our algorithm declares the dissolve candidate [b,e] as a dissolve region.

   [R3] if($HistDiff$($f_{b'}$,$f_{e'}$) > τ_{color}) return true. Else return false.

In [R3], the $HistDiff$($f_{b'}$,$f_{e'}$) is the color histogram difference between frame $f_{b'}$ and frame $f_{e'}$: f_i denotes frame whose frame number is i: and τ_{color} is a threshold value for color histogram difference.

4. EXPRIMENTAL RESULT

We have tested the algorithm on a soccer game video in MPEG-7 content set(CD #18) and 2 kinds of Korean news programs. The total running time of test material is about 115min 54sec long. Table.1 summarizes the performance of the presented dissolve detection algorithm.

The overall performance of the algorithm is very promising for video segmentation and it can be used as a basic input for shot clustering algorithms such as [2,8]. Since most of dissolve transitions satisfies proposed algorithm ([R1] to [R3]), the recall ratio is very high and the miss ratio is very low. Some of miss detection occurs when two similarly dim shots are connected with dissolve effect. These false positives can be minimized by applying adaptive threshold values to [R3]. If the global brightness of the start and the last dissolve transition candidates are relatively low, we can apply smaller τ_{color} to [R3]. The precision, on the other hand, is relatively low since it detects some of fast camera motions and wipes as fade or dissolve transition. Wipe detection algorithms like [7] can improve the precision of dissolve detection algorithm since there are few cases that dissolve and wipe occurs concurrently. Similarly, camera/object motion detection algorithms are able to improve the precision of the proposed dissolve detection algorithm since there are few cases that each of two shots connected with dissolve effect has camera/object motion.

Table 1. Experimental Result

Video (# of frames)	# of Fade/ Dissolve Transition	Experimental Result		
		# of Detected	Recall	Precision
Soccer (23502)	16	15	93%	68%
News1 (91208)	65	60	92%	72%
News2 (90256)	22	19	86%	70%
Total (204966)	103	94	91%	71%

In these experiments, we applied the same threshold values regardless the type of the video with an assumption that the video genre information is not available. However, with genre information or genre extraction algorithm, further optimization of parameters would give better performance. We also believe that the algorithm proposed in [4] can be incorporated with our algorithm for the performance improvements, since two algorithms share many low-level processing modules while exploiting different properties. One way of merging two algorithms is setting weight to each algorithm, and the other way is selecting one algorithm as pre-filter and the other as post-filter. Since the recall ratio of our algorithm is very high and it is fast, we believe that our algorithm is suitable for pre-filter.

5. CONCLUSION AND REMARKS

In this paper we presented a fast and effective algorithm for dissolve detection. Basically, our algorithm utilizes spatio-temporal distributions of macro block types to detect dissolve candidate sequences. The candidates are examined with the consideration of time constraints and global color distribution difference between the starting and the ending pictures. Based on the first stage experimental results, the proposed algorithm is expected to give very promising results with parameter optimization and further research. This algorithm can also be used

to detect fade-in/fade-out transition, since fade-in/fade-out are special cases of dissolve transitions where one of the first or the last frame of the dissolve sequence is either black or white frame.

Like other dissolve detection algorithms, certain kinds of fast camera/object motions and wipe transitions are detected as dissolves. In order to improve the precision of the proposed algorithm, camera/object motion detection algorithm will be added in the near future and wipe transition detection result will be taken into account. Further research will be focused on the parameter optimization or setting adaptive threshold and incorporation with other algorithm such as presented in [4] or [9]. The executable file for online video segmentation is downloadable at http://my.dreamwiz.com/jsb91 and MPEG codec used for developing our algorithm is MDC [1] which is downloadable at http://zeus.cs.wayne.edu/~dil/research/mdc/.

6. REFERENCES

[1] Dongge Li, and Ishwar K. Sethi, "MDC: A Software Tool for Developing MPEG Applicatoins," *Proc. IEEE International Conference on Multimedia computing and Systems (ICMCS'99),* vol. I, 445-450 (June 1999)

[2] Hanjalic, A., R. Lagendijk, and J. Biemond, "Automated Segmentation of Movies into Logical Story units," *IEEE Transactions on Circuits and Systems for Video Technology* (1999)

[3] Lagendijk, R. L., A. Janjalic, M. Ceccarelli, M. Soletic, and E. Persoon, "Visual Search In a SMASH System," *ICIP '96,* Lausanne, CH (1996)

[4] Meng, J., Y. Juan, and S. F. Chang, "Scene Change Detection in a MPEG Compressed Video Sequence," *SPIE2419,* 14-25 (1995)

[5] Nagasaka, A., and Y. Tanaka, "Automatic Video Indexing and Full-Video Search for Object Appearances," *Visual Database Systems II,* 113-127, Elsevier Science Piblishers (1992)

[6] Ishwar K. Sethi, and N. Patel, "A Statistical Approach to Scene Change Detection," *Proc. Storage and Retrieval for Image and Video Databases III,* SPIE2420, 329-339, San Jose, CA (Feb. 1995)

[7] Wu, M., W. Wolf, and B. Liu, "An Algorithm for Wipe Detection," *ICIP '98,* Chicago (1998)

[8] Yong, R., T. S. Huang, and S. Mehrotra, "Constructing Table-of-Content for Videos," *Multimedia Systems,* 7(5), 359-368 (1999)

[9] Zabih, R., J. Miller, and K. Mai, "A feature-based algorithm for detecting and classifying production effects," *Multimedia systems,* 7, 119-128 (1999)

[10] Zhang, H. J., A. Kankanhalli, and S.W. Smoliar, "Automatic partitioning of full –motion video," *Multimedia Systems,* 1(1) 10-28 (1993)

Analyzing Blood Cell Image to Distinguish Its Abnormalities

K.S. Kim, P.K. Kim
School of Computer Engineering
Chosun University
Kwangju, Korea, 501-759
Tel: +82-62-230-7636

{kskim, pkkim}@media.eas.asu.edu

J.J. Song, Y.C. Park
Media Laboratory
Arizona State University
Tempe, AZ, 85287-5406, USA
Tel: +1-480-965-1207

{jjsong, ycpark}@media.eas.asu.edu

ABSTRACT

In this paper, we show the blood-cell image classification system to be able to analyze and distinguish blood cells in the peripheral blood image. To distinguish their abnormalities, we segment red- and white-blood cell in an image acquired from microscope with CCD camera and then, apply the various feature extraction algorithms to classify them. In addition to, we use neural network model to reduce multi-variate feature number based on PCA(Principal Component Analysis) to make classifier more efficient. Finally we show that our system has a good experimental result and can be applied to build an aiding system for pathologist.

Keywords

blood cell image analysis, abnormal cell classification.

1. INTRODUCTION

In the medical field, there have been many proliferations of image data to be analyzed, to be stored, and to be retrieved. Also, there have been many researches to automate analysis and recognition of medical images together with advanced artificial intelligence techniques, image processing techniques, and computer graphics techniques[2][5][7][8][18]. Due to these, it is possible to construct diagnosis systems to aid medical doctor. In this paper, we have designed and implemented the system to be able to analyze and distinguish the human being's peripheral blood cell.

We can see human being's peripheral blood dyed by Wright method through microscope. It consists of red blood cell, white blood cell, platelet and plasma. Specially, according to the shape of neucleus and cytoplasm, white blood cell is divided into Neutrophil, Eosinophil, Basophil, Lymphocyte and Monocyte such as figure2.

In this paper, we classified 15 kinds of abnormality of red blood cells including normal one, referencing hemotology literatures[15][17] and just 5 kinds of normal white blood cell because there are many kinds of abnormality in case of white blood cell.

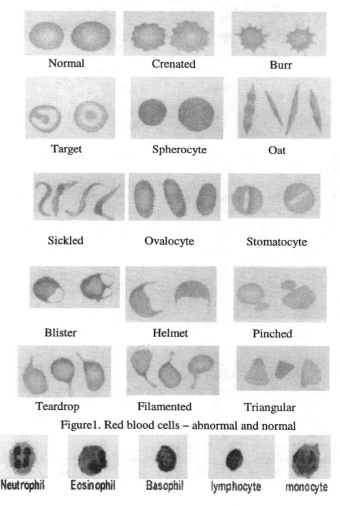

Figure1. Red blood cells – abnormal and normal

Figure2. White blood Cells

2. CLASSIFICATION OF BLOOD CELLS

2.1 Preprocessing

The input images are captured to magnify four hundred times from the color CCD camera attached to microscope with resolution 640x480. In general, the clinical pathologist examines ideal zone which has few folded cells. So, we select it for experiment. Firstly, we binarize the input image by using fuzzy measure[6] and label each cells. Figure4 shows labeled cells enclosed by minimum rectangle.

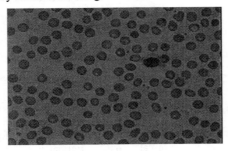

Figure3. Input image

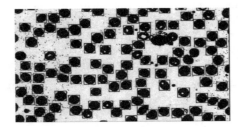

Figure4. Labled image

In the preprocessing step, the labeled cells are classified into red blood cell, white blood cell, plasma and platelet using their features, size and color. White blood cell has nucleus in it, so, it is very important to correctly separate neuclus and cytoplasm from the cell to classify them. The process is the follows. We enhance the edge and remove noise through nonlinear anisotropic diffusion in the first step[12]. And then, we apply watershed algorithm to the image and fusion nearest regions by C-means algorithm using color information[10][11].

Figure5. Segmentation of white blood cell

2.2 Feature Extraction

After the preprocessing, the features to classify are extracted from segmented cells. For red blood cells, the feature extraction is divided into two steps. We used UNL Fourier transform[14]. Outmost contour is used in the first step. Normal, spherocyte, target and stomatocyte belong to same class. In the second step, all edge information of the four class cell is used. The number of extracted features is 76. For white blood cell, we chose the best

features 60, among many kinds of features which are circularity, eccentricity, elongatedness, convexity of nucleus, ratio, intensity, perimeter and features related to the textures of neuclus and cytoplasm[1][3][4][16].

Figure6. Feature extraction process of red blood cell

2.3 Classification based on neural network model

We construct the two hierarchical neural network model with 3 layers to classify red and white blood cells using back propagation learning model[9][13]. The classifying of red blood cell consists of two steps. We assume that normal, target, spherocyte and stomatocyte are included in the same class, so called class having circular contour. So, the input cell is classified into one of 11 classes in first step. If the cell has circular contour, it will be classified into one of 4 classes in second step. The system to classify white blood cell is same with it to classify red blood cell but use different parameters.

FEATURES RECOGNITION STEP	ORIGINAL FEATURES	REDUCED FEATURES
FIRST STEP (12 CLASSES)	87	87
SECOND STEP (4 CLASSES)	94	94
AVERAGE RECOGNITION RATE	91	91

Table1. Average recognition rate of red blood cells(%)

RESULT	MONO CYTE	BASOP HIL	NEUTR OPHIL	ESINOP HIL	LYMPH OCYTE
MONOCYTE	55	0	2	0	13
BASOPHIL	0	38	2	10	0
NEUTROPHIL	11	0	97	8	4
ESINOPHIL	0	2	6	42	0
LYMPHOCYTE	18	0	4	0	98

Table2. Confusion matrix of the classification result of white blood cells

3. EXPERIMENTAL RESULTS

We use Wright dyed blood images of two hundred patient. To train classifier, the number of learning data for 15 classes of red blood cell is 680 and 410 for 5 class of white blood cell. We select the leave-one-out method[9] for the test and apply to PCA(Principal Component Analysis) to reduce the dimension of features. The original feature dimension is reduced from 76 to 38 in the first recognition step and 67 in the second recognition step for the red blood cell. Table1, the result of red blood cell recognition, shows that the recognition result after applying PCA is same. Table2 shows the recognition result of white blood cell using confusion matrix.

4. CONCLUSION

We have designed and implemented the system to recognize the abnormality of red blood cells and normal white blood cells in human being's peripheral to help pathologist. In special, we classified the abnormality of red blood cells in two steps, using the inner and outer edge information and classify normal white blood cell using various kinds of features about neucleus and cytoplasm. The experiment of results show that the complexity of neural networks can be reduced and can construct more efficient system, providing that principal component analysis is applied to the extracted features from cells.

In future, it needs to detect and classify immature red and blood cell in bone marrow image. Specially, we can see many kinds of abnormal cell in patient's bone marrow image having leukemia. We will try to classify many kinds of leukemia.

5. REFERENCES

[1] Babu M. Mehtre, M.S. Kankanhalli and Wing F. Lee, "Shape Measures For Content Based Image Retrieval : A Comparison", Technical Report95-195-0, Institute of Systems Science, National University of Singapore, 1995.

[2] Brent K. Stewart and Steve G. Langer, "Medical Image Databases and Infomatics", IEEE International Conf. on image processing, Oct, 4-7, Chicago, Ilinois, pp.29-33, 1998.

[3] B.S. Manjunath, W.Y. Ma, "Texture features for Browsing and Retrieval of Image Data", IEEE Trans. On Pattern Analysis and Machine Intelligence, Vol.18, No.8, pp.837-842, 1996.

[4] G. John, R. Kohavi, K. pfleger, "Irrelevant features and the subset selection problem", In proceedings of 11th Int'l Conf. on Machine Learning, pp.121-129, 1994.

[5] H. Nagata, H. Mizushima, "World Wide Microscope : New Concept of Internet Telepathology Microscope and Implementation of the Prototype", MEDIINFO 98, pp.286-289, 1998.

[6] Huang L.K, and M. J. Wang, "Image thresholding by minimizing the measures of fuzziness", Pattern Recognition, Vol.28, 1:41-51, 1995.

[7] http://sun16.cecs.missouri.edu/jpark/introduction.html

[8] http://vizlab.rutgers.edu/~comanici/demo.html

[9] James A. Freeman and David M. Skapura, Neural Networks: Algorithms, Applications and Programming, Techniques, Addision-Wesley Publishing, 1991.

[10] L. Majman, M. Schmitt, "Geodesic Saliency of Watershed Contours and Hierarchical Segmentation", IEEE Trans. on Pattern Analysis and Machine Intelligence, Vol.18, No.12, pp.1163-1173, Dec. 1996.

[11] N. A. Moga, M.. Gabbouj, " Parallel image component labeling with watershed transformation", IEEE Trans. on Pattern Analysis and Machine Intelligence, Vol.19, No.5, pp.441-450, 1997.

[12] P. Perona, M. Malik, "Scale-space and edge detection using anisotropic diffusion", IEEE Trans. on Pattern analysis and machine intelligence, Vol.12, No.7, pp.629-639, 1990.

[13] S. Seker, M. Bagriyanik, F. G. Gabgriyanik, "An application of shannon's entropy for Neural Architecture", Proc. of the 15th IASTED, pp.33-36, Innsbruck, 1997.

[14] T.W. Rauber, "Two-Dimensional Shape description", Technical Report Gruninova-RT-10-94, Universidade Nova de Lisboa, Lisboa, Portugal, 1994.

[15] Korea Medical Publisher, Illustrated Hemotology Book, Korea Publishing, 1995.

[16] K.S. Kim, Y. K. Kim, Y. S. Lee, Y. B. Lee, P. K. Kim, "Shape feature extraction method using discrete cosine transform", KIPS Journal, Vol.5, No.5, 1998.

[17] H. I. Cho, Practical Hemotology, Korea Publishing, 1995.

[18] Y. H. Jang, "Optimal Neural Network Classifier for Chromosome Karyotype Classification", KIEE Journal, Vol.46, No.7, Jul, pp.1129-1134, 1997.Anderson, G. E.. and B. R. Smith.

An Application-level Multicast Architecture for Multimedia Communications

Kang-Won Lee, Sungwon Ha, Jia-Ru Li, Vaduvur Bharghavan
Coordinated Science Laboratory, University of Illinois at Urbana-Champaign
Email: {kwlee, s-ha, juru, bharghav}@timely.crhc.uiuc.edu

1. INTRODUCTION

In recent years, interactive and real-time multimedia applications such as video teleconferencing and multimedia streaming have become increasingly popular in the Internet. The emergence of such applications has created two new phenomena: (a) *multicast* support is becoming critical, since they typically have multiple participants, and (b) the data streams are becoming *heterogeneous* in nature (e.g. a typical video conference session consists of text data, audio and video streams with different importance). Our target set of applications thus requires sophisticated multimedia support for small to medium multicast groups.

Supporting multicast communications of multimedia applications introduces unique challenges hitherto unaddressed in traditional network architectures: (a) Multicast groups consist of *heterogeneous* receivers, i.e. receivers in the same multicast group may have different processing capability and may perceive different connection qualities; and (b) Multimedia data streams are often *multi-resolution*, consisting of interleaved sub-streams with different importance.

Taking the environment and application requirements into consideration, we identify the two *desired behaviors* that we want our multicast architecture to satisfy: (i) *Each receiver must receive the highest priority portion of the heterogeneous data stream that its connection quality can sustain;* and (ii) *The receivers in the same group must be loosely synchronized, i.e. they must perceive approximately the same progress of the multimedia session even at the expense of losing low priority packets.*

In related work, a *layered multicast* approach has been proposed for multicasting prioritized data streams [1], [2], [3], [4]. Essentially, the approach is to decompose the *multiresolution* data stream into component *single resolution* streams, establish a distinct multicast group for each component stream using standard IP multicast, and let each receiver decide which multicast groups it wants to join based on the perceived connection quality or on the coordinated control mechanism. This approach has the charm of being intuitively simple, and of not requiring special mechanisms from the network. However, it also has several inherent limitations imposed by layering such as the coarse granularity of adaptation, slow reaction to network dynamics, destructive interference by concurrent adaptation by multiple receivers, and overhead of decomposition and resynchronization of the

multimedia stream at the end hosts.

In this paper, we present an overlay network architecture called MHPF (Multicast Heterogeneous Packet Flows) that supports multicast communications of heterogeneous data for small to medium multicast groups without decomposing them into component homogeneous data streams. MHPF exhibits the 'desired behaviors' of the multimedia multicast communications mentioned above without incurring the drawbacks of the layered approach, but at the expense of introducing specialized 'MHPF servers' inside the multicast tree. MHPF is composed of two key components: (a) an adaptive transport protocol called HPF (Heterogeneous Packet Flows) [5], which provides end-to-end transport of heterogeneous packet flows, and (b) a network of collaborating MHPF servers, which provides an application level overlay structure to support multicasting heterogeneous packet flows. The focus of this paper is the latter component.

2. MHPF DESIGN

HPF provides end-to-end unicast transport for heterogeneous packet flows [5]. Using HPF, the sender *interleaves packets with different priorities in a single transport layer stream* and enables the receiver to receive as much high priority packets as the connection quality can sustain. HPF allows an application to specify per-frame policies for priority, deadline, and dependency information, and implements the end-to-end framing, flow control, congestion control, and goodput control mechanisms for the heterogeneous data stream.

MHPF extends the idea of HPF to the multicast domain. Briefly, MHPF works as follows. For each session, MHPF abstracts a multicast tree T composed only of MHPF servers and multicast tunnels between them, which constitutes the overlay network on top of the IP multicast infrastructure. The HPF protocol at the sender interleaves packets with different priorities and transmits them in a single heterogeneous data stream. The MHPF servers implement a specialized packet forwarding behavior (rate adaptation and priority-based filtering on each multicast tunnel)[1] so that only the highest priority packets that can be accommodated on a path downstream are transmitted along the path.

Each receiver periodically generates feedback that contains the information on the bandwidth on the path leading to itself. The feedback from the receivers travels upstream along the multicast tree T and gets aggregated at the MHPF servers.

The feedback aggregation is done in such a way that when the feedback reaches the sender, it contains the information on the available bandwidth on the fastest paths in the multicast tree, so that the sender can service the receiver con-

---

[1] We have judiciously identified these minimum functionalities at each MHPF server that achieves the desired service model of MHPF in [7].

nected via the fastest path. For the other slower receivers, the network of MHPF servers performs rate adaptation and packet filtering so that only the highest priority packets are forwarded downstream (Figure 1).

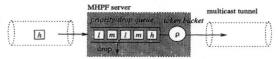

Figure 1: MHPF server and tunnel abstraction

We now first present the core mechanisms of MHPF, i.e. rate adaptation and priority-based packet filtering, with respect to a single multicast session, then present a session aggregation mechanism that alleviates per-session control and processing at each MHPF server.

2.1 Rate Adaptation Mechanism

When the sender transmits a packet, it inserts the *epoch id* in the packet header. Each receiver counts the number of packets it received in each epoch. Periodically each receiver generates a rate feedback containing *recv, epoch*, where *recv* indicates the number of received packets during *epoch*. The rate feedback is propagated back to the sender along the reverse direction of the multicast tree T.

```
1    Variables at the tunnel source i
2    ρi        // sending rate of i in the current epoch
3    ρg        // sending rate of parent tunnel source g in the current epoch
4    ρN        // new downstream (estimated) bottleneck rate for next epoch
5    sent      // number of packets sent on i in the current epoch
6    recv      // number of packets received by the receiver connected via
7              // the fastest path in the subtree in the current epoch
8    At the start of each epoch
9    The tunnel source of parent MHPF server g informs its sending rate
10   The tunnel source i updates ρg
11   After this update, the tunnel source i performs
12       if (ρg < ρi − α)
13           increase_constant ← 0
14       else
15           increase_constant ← 1
16   At the end of each epoch
17   The tunnel source i receives recv, and ρN from the child
18       if (recv = sent)          // additive increase
19           ρi ← min(ρN, ρi + increase_constant)
20       else                       // multiplicative decrease
21           ρi ← min(ρN, ρi × 0.5)
```

Figure 2: Rate adaptation at the MHPF server

When an MHPF server receives rate feedback on one of its downstream tunnel, it performs the rate control on the tunnel, according to the rate adaptation algorithm shown in Figure 2. Essentially the rate adaptation algorithm is the popular additive increase multiplicative decrease (AIMD) congestion control: if there was no packet loss in the last epoch (on the fastest path in the subtree rooted at the tunnel source i), i.e. $recv = sent$, then increase the sending rate to probe for more available bandwidth; otherwise, detect congestion and decrease the sending rate.

The algorithm presented in Figure 2 has additional conditions so that the rate control algorithm enables the tunnel source to quickly synchronize its sending rate with the downstream bottleneck sending rate[2] by taking the minimum of the calculated sending rate and the estimated downstream bottleneck rate (Figure 2, lines 19, 21).

In addition, we introduce 'increase_flag' in order to ensure that the sending rate of a tunnel source i does not increase

---

[2]The bottleneck sending rate on a path p is the sending rate of a tunnel source k whose immediate downstream multicast tunnel is the bottleneck on the path p. The downstream bottleneck sending rate at a tunnel source i is the bottleneck sending rate on the fastest path in the subtree of the tunnel source i.

without bound when the bottleneck tunnel is located upstream[3] (Figure 2, lines 12 − 15, line 19). The constant $\alpha \geq 0$ controls the amount of bandwidth that the tunnel source i can increase over the estimated sending rate of the upstream bottleneck. For the rate feedback aggregation, the MHPF server calculates the maximum of all the *recv* values from its children and forwards upstream, along with the maximum of the sending rates on the downstream tunnels. After the aggregation, the *recv* contains the number of received packets by the receivers connected via the fastest path in the subtree rooted at the MHPF server i. This provides the information for rate adaptation performed by the HPF sender and the upstream MHPF servers.

2.2 Priority-based Packet Dropping

In [7], we have identified that priority-based packet filtering is one of the major components to achieve the 'desired behaviors.' Essentially the filtering ensures that when the incoming data rate to the packet queue is greater than the outgoing data rate, only the highest priority data packets that are sustainable by the outgoing rate get forwarded by preferentially dropping low priority packets.

```
1    Variables for session i
2    bi        // the number of packets in the buffer for session i
3    Bi        // the buffer bound for the session i
4    For incoming packet p
5    pri ← p.priority
6    if (bi = Bi)              // if queue is full, then priority-drop
7        p' ← find_lowest_priority_packet (i)
8        if (p' < pri) drop (p'), then enqueue (p)
9        else drop (p)
10   else enqueue(p)
```

Figure 3: Pseudo code of the priority drop algorithm

The algorithm for priority dropping is quite straightforward (Figure 3). When the queue receives a new packet p, if the queue is full, then it searches for the lowest priority packet already in the queue. Then it compares the priority of the selected packet, say p', with the incoming packet p, and drop the lower priority packet of the two. Priority dropping involves fairly simple operations, and we typically anticipate only a few priority levels in practice.

2.3 Session Aggregation

We have thus far described all the mechanisms with respect to a single multicast session. Although we need to maintain state information and perform feedback aggregation on per-session basis, it will become impractical for MHPF servers to provide rate adaptation and priority dropping for individual multicast session as the number of on-going multicast sessions increases. We now briefly outline a computationally simple approximation that allows the tunnel sources of MHPF servers to perform rate control and priority-drop for each *tunnel* rather than for each *session*.

The basic idea of session aggregation is the following: when there are multiple on-going sessions, the tunnel source multiplexes them in a single output packet queue. The transmission rate of the tunnel is set to the sum of the data rates of all the sessions (i.e. $\rho_{tunnel} = \sum_i \rho_i$, $\forall i \in active\ session$), and the buffer bound of the queue is set to the sum of the buffer bounds (i.e. $B_{tunnel} = \sum_i B_i$, $\forall i \in active\ sessions$) of all the sessions on the tunnel. We then adopt the *dynamic queue management* mechanism [6], which provides

---

[3]In other words, the bottleneck sending rate on the path from the sender to the tunnel source i is smaller than the downstream bottleneck sending rate of i.

loose bandwidth assurances to each flow without requiring per-flow mechanisms.

We now briefly outline the dynamic queue management mechanism. Each flow has a buffer bound in a shared FIFO queue. A flow cannot enqueue a packet into the shared queue if *both* of the following conditions fail: (a) the aggregate queue size has exceeded the aggregated bound, i.e. $\sum_i b_i = B_{tunnel}$, and (b) the flow's queue size has exceeded its own buffer bound, i.e. $b_i = B_i$. Condition (a) allows for multiplexing the shared queue while condition (b) provides a minimum buffer allocation in the shared queue to each flow. It has been shown that this simple mechanism enables a reasonable level of long-term bandwidth assurances for individual flows as well as an efficient multiplexing on aggregate flows [6]. In our context, we approximate the rate adaptation mechanism simply by changing the buffer bound for the flow in the shared FIFO priority-dropping queue, and updating the aggregate sending rate on the tunnel.

3. PERFORMANCE RESULTS

We have tested the performance of MHPF using *ns* simulator. In this section, we summarize the major findings from the performance comparison of MHPF with RLM (receiver-driven layered multicast) [1]. Performance comparison with the later enhancements to RLM [2, 3, 4] is an on-going work.

Let us consider a network topology shown in Figure 4. The one-way link latency was set to 10 msec for all the links, and the operation parameters of RLM were adopted from [1]. We used 2.2 Mbps synthetic data flow with three priority levels with the ratio of high:medium:low at 1:2:3.

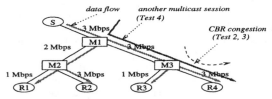

Figure 4: A simple two-level topology

- *Test 1. Steady State Performance* With a small amount of network buffers, the AIMD-based rate adaptation of MHPF achieves about 75 % of the bandwidth. With sufficient buffering at MHPF servers, the utilization is close to 100 %. In case of RLM, we observe variable performance: over 80 % for R_1 and R_3, but only about 50 % for R_2.

- *Test 2. Long-term Congestion* We instantiated 1 Mbps CBR flow on the link $M_3 \rightarrow R_4$ during $30 - 50$ second period. In ideal case, we expect that only R_4 sees a temporary performance degradation, which is true for both protocols. However, the performance degradation of RLM is greater than that of MHPF.

- *Test 3. Series of Short-term Congestions* On $M_3 \rightarrow R_4$, we instantiated 2 Mbps CBR flows during $30 - 31$, $40 - 41$, $50 - 51$, and $60 - 61$ second time windows. Overall, the performance degradation of R_4 in MHPF case is marginal (around 5 %) compared with Test 1. However, with RLM, R_4 sees around 40 % decrease even with short-term congestions.

- *Test 4. Effect of Aggregation* We have instantiated another multicast session sharing the same multicast tunnel as shown in Figure 4. We assigned the same buffer bound to both sessions, thus expect to observe approximately the same throughput for both sessions. The effective throughput of the original multicast session is 1.39 Mbps, and the new session is 1.29 Mbps, which are fairly close to each other in this simple case.

We performed tests using a larger multicast group of 8 and 16 receivers organized in a 2-level and 4-level binary tree, respectively. Two important lessons from the tests are: (a) when network condition is dynamically changing, RLM degrades to the case of long term congestion, whereas MHPF effectively adapts to the condition, and (b) as the number of receivers increases the performance of RLM degrades dramatically whereas the performance of MHPF degrades gracefully.

There can be several reasons for the progressively poor performance of RLM with the increase of the number of receivers and the network dynamics: (a) coarse grain adaptation, (b) interference of join/leave operations of independent receivers, and (c) incorrect congestion information propagated and maintained by the shared learning mechanism.

To sum up, the issue of MHPF versus layering is really an issue of *filtering* versus *layering*. MHPF promotes the idea of sending a single heterogeneous data stream, and filtering through the highest priority component of the data stream along each path of the multicast tree so that each receiver receives the most important data at the rate that its path can sustain, whereas layering promotes the idea of purely end-to-end mechanisms with the aim of minimizing the complexity inside the network or the multicast tree. With the advent of application-level overlay networks or end-system multicast architectures [8], we believe that exploring the filtering approach as a viable technical alternative to layering and understanding the trade-offs between the two is important, and preliminary evaluations seem to indicate that MHPF can provide improved service at the expense of sophisticated support from the network of MHPF servers.

4. REFERENCES

[1] S. McCanne and V. Jacobson. Receiver-driven Layered Multicast. *ACM SIGCOMM*, August 1996.

[2] L. Vicisano, J. Crowcroft, and L. Rizzo. TCP-like Congestion Control for Layered Multicast Data Transfer. *IEEE INFOCOM*, March 1998.

[3] L. Wu, R. Sharma, and B. Smith. ThinStreams: An Architecture for Multicasting Layered Video. *NOSSDAV*, May 1997.

[4] X. Li, S. Paul, and M. H. Ammar. Layered Video Multicast with Retransmissions (LVMR): Evaluation of Hierarchical Rate Control. *IEEE INFOCOM*, March 1998.

[5] J. Li, S. Ha, and V. Bharghavan. Transport Layer Adaptation for Supporting Multimedia Flows in the Internet. *IEEE INFOCOM*, March 1999.

[6] S. Ha, K.-W. Lee, and V. Bharghavan. Performance Evaluation of Scheduling and Resource Reservation Algorithms in an Integrated Services Packet Network Environment. *IEEE Symposium on Computers and Communications*, July 1998.

[7] K.-W. Lee and V. Bharghavan. An Application-level Multicast Architecture for Multimedia Communications in the Internet. *TIMELY Group Technical Report* available at http://timely.crhc.uiuc.edu/~kwlee/psfiles/mhpf.ps, Decempber 1999.

[8] Y. Chu, S. Rao, and H. Zhang. A Case for End System Multicast. *ACM SIGMETRICS*, June 2000.

Texture compression with adaptive block partitions

Leonid Levkovich-Maslyuk
The Keldysh Inst. of Appl. Math.,
4, Miusskaya Sq.,
Moscow, Russia,125047
(7-095)-250-78-56

levkovl@spp.keldysh.ru

Pavel Kalyuzhny
Lomonosov Moscow State University
Russia, Moscow, GSP119899, MSU,
Computer Science Faculty
(7-095)-939-01-90

kaluzhny@graphics.cs.msu.su

Alexander Zhirkov
Lomonosov Moscow State University
Russia, Moscow, GSP119899, MSU,
Computer Science Faculty
(7-095)-939-01-90

zh@graphics.cs.msu.su

ABSTRACT

We present image compression method based on block palletizing. Image block is partitioned into four subsets, and each subset is palletized by 2 or 4 colors from the quasioptimal local palette, constructed for the whole block. Index map for the whole block, being the union of index maps for subsets, is thus only 1 or 2 bits deep, while the local palette may consist of 8 or even 16 colors. The local palette has a specific geometrical configuration in RGB color space, determined by only 2 colors. These two colors are stored explicitly, and the rest are reconstructed at the decompression stage. Compressed block consists, essentially, of the index map, palette description and partition description. This format allows fast access to randomly chosen pixels, and high reconstruction quality for compression ratios from 8 to 12, which is useful for texture storage in 3D graphics applications where real-time *decompression* is crucial.

Keywords

Texture compression, image compression, fast rendering, local palletizing

1. OUTLINE OF THE METHOD

To avoid complex geometrical computations, it is common to use textures in 3D real-time graphics. In this context, textures are appropriate images (e.g., photos of a building façade) that are 'glued' upon a 3D 'wire frames'. Texture compression methods oriented at this class of applications must allow fast access to arbitrary chosen texels (pixels of the texture image). Mostly for this reason, virtually all texture compression techniques are block-based. For example, the well known S3TC algorithm [1] uses 4-by-4 image blocks, and the compressed block consists of a local palette (four colors) and the index map. The index map is a 4-by-4 array of 2-bit words, each word being index of the palette color replacing the original color of the corresponding pixel. Substantial idea behind S3TC is to represent the local palette as a line segment in RGB color space, optimally approximating total of 16

colors in the block. Only the endpoints of this segment are stored, while the other 2 colors are reconstructed at decompression stage. This allows to achieve compression ratio 6 for true color images with 24 bit color depth.

We suggest a different compression method, based on two main ideas. The first idea is to use more complex palette geometries than line segment, in order to represent more colors, closer adapting the palette to the original color distribution in the block. However, as the number of colors increase, the index map is becoming too large because indices must contain more bits. This makes compression ratio impractically low.

The second idea allows to cope with this problem. It is independent palletizing of block subsets by small (2 or 4 colors) "subpalettes" of the palette for the whole block. For example, 8-color palette would normally require 3 bit indices. But if a subpalette of 2 colors is used for each subset, index map is only 1 bit deep, i.e. becomes 3 times smaller.

However, in this case one has to store additional information: subpalettes description and partition description. Subpalettes can be specified by fixing an order of the palette entries, so that the first two entries are the first subpalette, e.t.c. For example, in case of the 8-color palette and four 2-color subpalettes we need a string of eight 3-bit words. Another way is to specify a small number of fixed subsets of the palette as possible subpalettes. Both approaches were implemented in our algorithms.

Since it is impossible to compactly represent an *arbitrary* block partition, we used a fixed collection (dictionary) of partitions. In this case, partition is specified by its index in the dictionary. We worked with 8-by-8 blocks, and partitioned them into 4 subsets. It turned out that even this very restricted collection of 256 'typical' partitions allowed to obtain good reconstruction quality. In this case partition is specified by 8-bit word.

Compression of each block is performed in 2 steps. At the first step, a quasioptimal palette for the whole block is constructed. At the second step, an optimal partition together with an appropriate collection of subpalettes is determined so that the total block distortion is minimal. Thus, the compressed block consists of: index of the selected partition; palette description; subpalettes description; index map.

Decompression of a texel is performed by: determination of the containing block (trivial calculation), reconstruction of the palette (essentially, a sequence of linear interpolations and equally simple operations), finding the partition subset containing the texel (simple masking operation), and output of the palette entry according to the index map.

Now let us consider some important details of the algorithms based on this approach.

2. DETAILS OF THE ALGORITHMS

2.1 Palettes geometry

We implemented two algorithms, (denote them A12 and A8), with compression ratios 12 and 8, respectively. A12 uses 8-color palette for the block, and 2-color subpalette for each of the four block subsets. A8 uses 16-color palette for the block, and 4-color subpalette for each of its four subsets. Both algorithms use the same dictionary of 256 block partitions.

Figure 1 shows the palette geometries for A8 and A12.

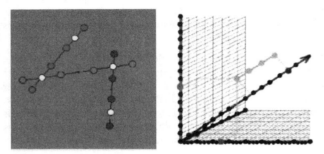

Figure 1. A8 (left) and A12 (right) palette

For A8 palette, white circles are the base colors that are stored. They are vertices of a tetrahedron in RGB color space. Sets of points shown by green, red, blue and white circles, each form a 4-color subpalette. Each subset of the chosen partition is palletized by one of these subpalettes. The A12 palette consists of two segments (four points on each) in the color space RGB. One of the two segments is shown in light-brown in Fig.1. Starting point of each segment is stored in RGB(4,5,3) format. The endpoint has the same (U,V) components (in the standard YUV color space), but its Y-component is different, and is defined by a 4-bit number (Y axis is shown, conventionally, in black in Fig.1). Hence, the palette is determined by $2 \cdot (4+5+3+4)=32$ bits. Subpalettes can be arbitrary 2-color subsets of the palette.

2.2 Examples of partitions

Block partitions are obtained by discretization of 'typical' quadratic functions level sets. Figure 2 shows how an original 8-by-8 pixel block (a) is compressed by A8 (b) and by A12 (c). These pictures are examples of the partitions from the dictionary.

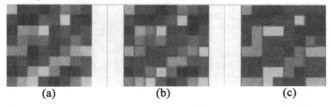

(a)   (b)   (c)

Figure 2. (a) Original image block. (b) A8-compressed block. (c) A12-compressed block.

Subsets boundaries are shown in green. Fidelity of reconstruction

decreases with the increase of compression ratio, but the informative features of the block remain visible.

2.3 Compression and decompression processes

A12 compression and decompression flowcharts for a single block

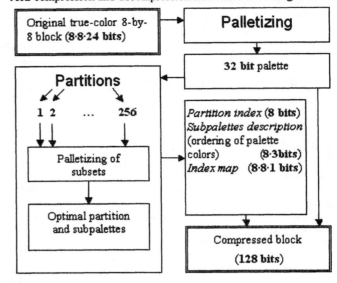

Figure 3. A12 Compression flowchart.

are shown in Figures 3 and 4, respectively.

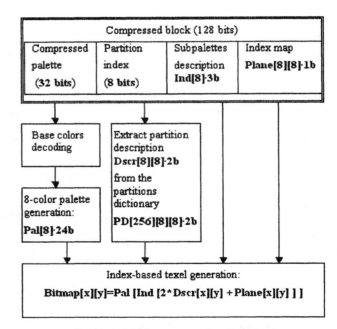

Figure 4. A12 Decompression flowchart.

3. TEST RESULTS

We have performed extensive testing of the algorithms A12 and A8 on a collection of images of various nature, with the aid of various distortion measures. In all cases, A8 algorithm (8 times compression) outperformed S3TC (6 times compression). A12 (12 times compression) has shown somewhat lower reconstruction quality than S3TC. Visual quality can be subjectively estimated as 'good' for A12 and 'excellent' for A8. PSNR values presented in the Table 1 give a quality estimate for two test images in terms of PSNR. "Portrait" image (Figure 5), turned out to be the most difficult among the 'natural' images for all the three algorithms A8, A12 and S3TC. "Lena" image was included here because of its popularity.

It should be noted that for *any* compression method based on reduced palette for small blocks, it is easy to construct artificial images for which visual distortion will be very noticeable. Indeed, any pattern composed of blocks with colors uniformly distributed in RGB color space will suffer drastic distortion after palletizing. Fortunately, this is practically never the case for images one meets in applications.

PSNR computations for RGB color images were performed for the distortion of standard intensity $Y=0.3R+0.59G+0.11B$.

Table 1. PSNR values for the three algorithms

	A12	S3TC	A8
"Portrait"	28.4	32	33.6
"Lena"	35	38.95	40.9

4. CONCLUSION

A method for image compression based on palletizing of small block subsets by subpalettes of compactly stored local palette was developed. Two algorithms using this method have compression ratios 12 and 8 for true color images, and allow fast random access to distinct pixels. High quality of reconstructed images suggests that the algorithms can be useful for texture storage in 3D graphics applications where fast decompression is important. Ideas of the work can be further developed by optimizing the dictionary of block partitions (with the aid of, for example, coding theory techniques), and by improving palette geometry in color space.

Figure 5. Test image "Portrait"

5. AKNOWLEDGMENTS

We are grateful to Yuri Bayakovski (Lomonosov Moscow State University) for helpful discussions, and to Jim Hurley and Alexander Reshetov (Intel Corporation) for their attention to the work. The work was supported by the Intel Corporation Research Contract.

6. REFERENCES

[1] S3TC DirectX 6.0 Standard Texture Compression, Savage 3D white papers (1998).

A Presentation Semantic Model for Asynchronous Distance Learning Paradigm

Sheng-Tun Li
National Kaohsiung First University of Science and Technology
Department of Information Management
1 University Road, Yenchao, Kaohsiung
Taiwan 824, R.O.C.
stli@ccms.nkfust.edu.tw

Shu-Ching Chen
Florida International University
School of Computer Science
Miami, FL 33199, USA
chens@cs.fiu.edu

Mei-Ling Shyu
University of Miami
Department of Electrical and Computer Engineering
Coral Gables, FL 33124, USA
shyu@miami.edu

ABSTRACT

This paper presents a presentation semantic model that is based on the augmented transition network (ATN) for asynchronous distance learning system called Java-based Integrated Asynchronous Distance Learning (JIADL) system. The JIADL system can support diverse asynchronous distance learning services. Unlike most related work in the literature, we integrate RealPlayer and Java technology so that the superiority of both models can be complemented. A course sample is illustrated to validate the effectiveness of the paradigm proposed. How to use the proposed multimedia ATN model to model the diverse requirements of a distance learning multimedia presentation is also discussed. The multimedia ATN model is powerful in modeling the asynchronization for distance learning multimedia presentations. Furthermore, in addition to supporting asynchronous distance learning, our system can be applied to a wide range of potential value-added applications.

1. INTRODUCTION

Recently, with the innovation of new network infrastructures, the development of multimedia technology and the diverse requirements asked by end-users, distance learning has become the mainstream of computer-based training (CBT). The seamless integration of the overwhelming WWW and the emerging Java technology [1] further endorses the universal accessibility to diverse distance learning services. In this paper, we present a project supported by Ministry of Education, R.O.C. and implemented at National Kaohsiung First University of Science and Technology (NKFUST). This project is aimed at digitizing and distributing video tapes recorded in a synchronous distance learning classroom to improve curriculums, to provide another channel for learning, and to complement synchronous/asynchronous learning. In order to broaden the functions and the effectiveness of such service, a number of interactive and cooperative services are integrated by mainly applying Java technology, which results in the paradigm of Java-based integrated asynchronous distance learning system (JIADL).

In this paper, a multimedia semantic model based on the augmented transition network (ATN) is proposed to model the distance learning multimedia presentations for the JIADL system. The proposed multimedia ATN model differs from the original ATN model by allowing the modeling of the multimedia presentations in addition to the sentence grammar checking. Multimedia input strings are used as the inputs for the multimedia ATN model. The multimedia input strings have the capabilities to capture the temporal relationships of the media streams, and to model the concurrent and optional displaying of the media streams in a distance learning multimedia presentation.

The proposed JIADL system integrates both the RealPlayer and Java technology. An example course is used to illustrate how a distance learning course can be modeled by the multimedia ATN model. The multimedia ATN model is powerful in modeling the asynchronization for distance learning multimedia presentations. Furthermore, in addition to supporting asynchronous distance learning, this JIADL system which is based on the multimedia ATN semantic model can be used in many potential value-added applications such as cultural heritage multimedia applications, marketing for electronic commerce, multimedia digital libraries, and lifelong learning.

The remaining of the paper is as follows. Section 2 outlines the components in the JIADL system with an example course. Section 3 introduces the multimedia ATN model and how to use the multimedia ATN model to model the example course. Section 4 concludes this paper.

2. THE JIADL PARADIGM

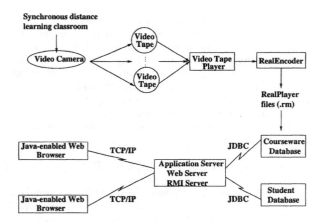

Figure 1: The JIADL paradigm.

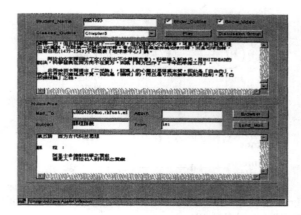

Figure 2: The CyberLearn subsystem.

The high-level architecture of the JIADL paradigm is outlined in Figure 1. The archived lecture contents are converted into RealVideo files by RealEncoder in advance and are stored in the Courseware database. Mobile learners may download the system applets from Web Server and retrieve the courseware of interest via the JDBC mechanism. The student database keeps records of students' learning progresses and personal registration information. RMI Server supports the collaborative learning in chat rooms. Currently, the platform for Application Server, Web Server, and RMI Server is on NT4.0. An example course offered by the Center of General Education at NKFUST had been experimented on the JIADL Paradigm. The lecture was broadcast in live video from NKFUST to four neighboring universities via three ISDN dedicated lines at 384K.

There are three subsystems in the JIADL system.

- **StudDBMS.** Any students including ones in the classes can log into the JIADL system by registering it in advance. The StudDBMS subsystem allows learners to query and modify personal information besides registration.

- **CourseDBMS.** The CourseDBMS subsystem endows the lecturers or administrators to manage the digitized courseware.

- **CyberLearn.** The CyberLearn subsystem is the kernel part of the JIADL paradigm as shown in Figure 2. It allows the student to browse the static lecture notes and/or the corresponding video lecture.

Empowered by Real Player G2 [2], the student is granted to the capability in controlling voice and lecture progress. Other further functionality like lecture clips can also be easily implemented. One important supplementary function for mobile learners is the Notes Area (the bottom area in Figure 2), in which the learners may write down the notes and send them via the SMTP protocol. One notes that the capability of attaching MIME objects from the local learning environment is incorporated. From the learning theory, learners of distance learning are not expected to sit still and stare at the lectures consistently. To improve the learning

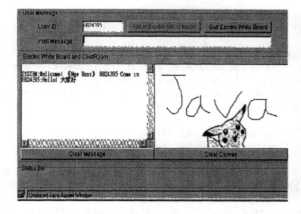

Figure 3: The whiteboard subsystem.

interaction, an interactive multi-user chat room and a collaborative real-time whiteboard are offered, which are based on Java RMI distributed computing model. Figure 3 depicts the layout of such services, where a number of vivid images can be added into the whiteboard.

3. USING MULTIMEDIA ATNS TO MODEL PRESENTATIONS IN JIADL

The augmented transition network (ATN), developed by Woods [5], has been used in natural language understanding systems and question answering systems for both text and speech. The proposed multimedia ATN that is based on the ATN with modifications can model multimedia presentations, multimedia database searching, the temporal, spatial, or spatio-temporal relations of various media streams and semantic objects, and multimedia browsing [3].

A multimedia ATN consists of nodes (states) and arcs. Each state has a state name and each arc has an arc label. Each arc label represents the media streams to be displayed in a time duration. Therefore, time intervals can be represented by a multimedia ATN. In the multimedia ATN, a new state is created whenever there is any change of media streams in the presentation. The two situations for the change of media streams are shown as follows.

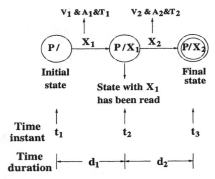

Figure 4: A multimedia ATN for an example multimedia presentation.

(1) Any media stream finishes to display;
(2) Any new media stream joins to display.

Figure 4 is a multimedia ATN for an example multimedia presentation in the JIADL system. There are three time instants (t_1 to t_3) and two time durations (d_1 and d_2). There are two occurrences of media stream combinations at each time duration and they are:

(1) Duration d_1: V_1, A_1, and T_1.
(2) Duration d_2: V_2, A_2, and T_2.

As shown in Figure 4, there are three states and two arcs which represent three time instants and two time durations, respectively. State names are in the circles to indicate the presentation status. State name $P/$ means the beginning of the multimedia ATN (presentation) and state P/X_i represents that presentation P just finishes to display X_i and the presentation can proceed without knowing the complete history of the past. For example, state name P/X_1 denotes the state after X_1 has been read. The reason to use X_i is for convenience purposes. In fact X_1 can be replaced by $V_1^*\&A_1^*\&T_1^*$. State name P/X_2 is the final state of the multimedia ATN to indicate the end of the presentation. Each arc label X_i in Figure 4 is created to represent the media stream combination for each duration. For example, arc label X_1 represents media streams V_1, A_1, and T_1 display together at duration d_1. A new arc is created when new media streams V_2, A_2, and T_2 start to display.

When an ATN is used for language understanding, the input for the ATN is a sentence which consists of a sequence of words with linear order. In a multimedia presentation, when user interactions such as user selections and loops are allowed, then we cannot use sentences as the inputs for a multimedia ATN. In our design, each arc in a multimedia ATN is a string containing one or more media streams displayed at the same time. A media stream is represented by a letter subscripted by some digits. This single letter represents the media stream type and digits are used to denote various media streams of the same media stream type. For example, T_1 means a text media stream with identification number one. A multimedia input string consists of one or more media streams and is used as an input for a multimedia ATN. Multimedia input strings adopt the notations from regular expressions. Regular expressions [4] are

useful descriptors of patterns such as tokens used in a programming language. Regular expressions provide convenient ways of specifying a certain set of strings. A multimedia input string may consist of several input symbols and each of them represents the media streams to be displayed at a time interval. In our framework, multimedia input strings are used to represent the presentation sequences of the temporal media streams. A multimedia input string goes from the left to right, which can represent the time sequence of a multimedia presentation as shown in string (1).

Multimedia input string: $(V_1^*\&A_1^*\&T_1^*)(V_2^*\&A_2^*\&T_2^*)$ (1)

In string (1), the "&" between two media streams indicates these two media streams are displayed concurrently. The "*" symbol is used to indicate the media stream which can be dropped in the on-line presentation. For example, $V_1^*\&A_1^*\&T_1^*$ represents media streams V_1, A_1, and T_1 being displayed concurrently but each of them can be dropped if Show_Outline and/or Show_Video buttons are not highlighted.

4. CONCLUSION

In this paper, we presented the JIADL system which is based on the proposed multimedia ATN model for supporting asynchronous distance learning. The inputs for a multimedia ATN are modeled by the multimedia input strings. The multimedia input strings have the capabilities to capture the temporal relationships of the media streams, and to model the concurrent and optional displaying of the media streams in a distance learning multimedia presentation.

As far as the references surveyed, our work presented is the pioneering study in the literature towards integrating RealPlay G2 and Java JMF in the distance learning application. In addition to supporting asynchronous distance learning, the paradigm has a variety of potential value-added applications. For example, The National Palace Museum of R.O.C. had published a series of video tapes, a preview function can be simply provided in the JIADL paradigm.

5. REFERENCES

[1] *Java JMF API*, http://www.javasoft.com/products/java-media/jmf/index.html.

[2] *RealPlayer for Java*, http://www.real.com/.

[3] S.-C. Chen and R. L. Kashyap. A spatio-temporal semantic model for multimedia presentations and multimedia database systems. *IEEE Transactions on Knowledge and Data Engineering*, accepted for publication 2000.

[4] S. Kleene. *Representation of Events in Nerve Nets and Finite Automata, Automata Studies*. Princeton University Press, Princeton, N.J., 1956.

[5] W. Woods. Transition network grammars for natural language analysis. *Comm. of the ACM*, 13:591–602, October 1970.

Explicit Query Formulation with Visual Keywords

Joo-Hwee Lim

RWCP * Information-Base Functions KRDL Lab †

21 Heng Mui Kent Terrace, S(119613), Singapore

joohwee@krdl.org.sg

ABSTRACT

This paper presents a novel framework called visual keywords for indexing and retrieving digital images. Visual keywords are flexible and intuitive visual prototypes with semantics. A new query method based on visual constraints allows direct and explicit content specification. Last but not least, we have developed a digital album prototype to demonstrate query and retrieval based on visual keywords.

1. INTRODUCTION

In this paper, we present a new content-based retrieval framework known as visual keywords (patent pending) and a query method based on visual constraints with experimental focus on home photos. In essence, *visual keywords* are intuitive and flexible visual prototypes specified perceptually from sample domain images. A visual content is described and indexed by spatial aggregation of soft presence of visual keywords, upon results of multi-scale view-based detection.

Visual keywords are linked to both specific and more general concepts by textual labels in a vocabulary and thesaurus to provide relevant semantics to the domain. Common labels of visual keywords form an equivalence class of visual synonyms. This concept-oriented visual thesaurus differs from the visual relations of R.W.Picard [3], which are founded on similarities between low-level visual features.

In a nutshell, each image is indexed as a spatial tessellation of visual keyword distributions, which is the core signature of its visual content for retrieval and classification tasks. The steps to derive such a visual description (i.e. index) for an image are summarized in Fig. 1. First a visual vocabulary and thesaurus is constructed from samples of a visual content domain. Then an image to be indexed is compared against the visual vocabulary to detect visual keywords automatically. The fuzzy detection results are registered in a *Type Evaluation Map* (TEM) and further aggregated spatially into a *Spatial Aggregation Map* (SAM). With visual

---
*Real World Computing Partnership
†Kent Ridge Digital Labs

thesaurus, it can be further abstracted and reduced to a simpler representation, *Concept Aggregation Map* (CAM).

2. VISUAL KEYWORDS

2.1 Vocabulary Construction

Visual keywords are visual prototypes specified with an appropriate visual tool. Domain-relevant regions are cropped from sample images and assigns sub-labels and labels to form vocabulary and thesaurus respectively. Suitable visual features (e.g. color, texture) are computed for each cropped region into a feature vector. i.e.

$$c_i : (s_{i1}, v_{i1}), (s_{i2}, v_{i2}), \cdots, (s_{ij}, v_{ij}) \cdots \quad (1)$$

where c_i are concept labels, s_{ij} are sub-labels for specific instances of concept i, and v_{ij} are feature vectors for regions ij. Fig. 2 to 4 show some of the visual keywords used in our prototype system. For instance, the sub-labels for the visual keywords shown in Fig. 4 are far-gray, far-brown, yellow-mosque, indian-temple, and balcony respectively. In our experiments, we use color (YIQ model) and texture (Gabor features) to characterize visual keywords.

Figure 2: Some visual keywords for face

Figure 3: Some visual keywords for crowd

Figure 4: Some visual keywords for building

2.2 Indexing

An image to be indexed is scanned with windows of different scales. Each scanned window is a visual token reduced to a feature vector τ compatible (i.e. same feature types and

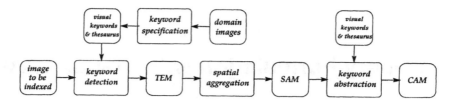

Figure 1: Indexing by spatial aggregation of visual keywords

dimension) to those of the visual keywords v_{ij} in Equation (1). More precisely, given an image I with resolution $M \times N$, a TEM $\mathcal{T}$ has a lower resolution of $P \times Q, P \leq M, Q \leq N$. Each pixel (p, q) covers to a two-dimensional region in I. The feature vector τ_{pq} computed for a region (p, q) is compared against the feature vectors v_{ij} of all visual keywords to derive a fuzzy membership vector $\mu(\tau_{pq}, v_{ij})$.

Likewise, SAM $\mathcal{S}$ tessellates over TEM with $A \times B, A \leq P, B \leq Q$ pixels. Each SAM pixel (a, b) aggregates the fuzzy memberships for visual keyword ij over those TEM pixels (p, q) covered by (a, b),

$$\mathcal{S}(a, b, i, j) = \sum_{(p,q) \in (a,b)} \mathcal{T}(p, q, i, j). \quad (2)$$

As a sub-label s_{ij} for visual keyword v_{ij} describes a specific appearance of the concept labelled by c_i, they are visual synonyms that allow abstraction by further aggregation over visual keywords sharing identical concept labels,

$$\mathcal{C}(a, b, i) = \sum_j \mathcal{S}(a, b, i, j), \quad (3)$$

3. QUERY BY VISUAL CONSTRAINTS

A query ξ is an intention or a means to define a *relevance* set R, with respect to some information need, over a given (visual) document space X. In principle, for each document x, one can compute a posterior probability $P(R|\xi, x)$ of relevance and rank the documents in decreasing degree of relevance. Here we adopted a fuzzy-theoretic equivalent. We propose a query formulation method, *Query by Visual Constraints* (QVC), that allows a user to specify a query in terms of *what* and *where*. We regard a *Visual Query Term* (VQT) $\xi(v_{ij}, \pi(a, b))$ as a fuzzy constraint to specify R with a visual keyword v_{ij} and a spatial extent $\pi(a, b)$. For any image x in the database, we can compute the fuzzy membership of x to the relevant set constrained by ξ. Mathematically,

$$\mu_\xi(x, R) = \mathcal{S}(a, b, i, j), \quad (4)$$

or if the visual keyword specified is a visual concept,

$$\mu_\xi(x, R) = \mathcal{C}(a, b, i). \quad (5)$$

Then a complex query Q can be specified as a disjunctive normal form of visual query literals (visual query term with or without negation),

$$Q = (q_{11} \wedge q_{12} \wedge \cdots) \vee \cdots \vee (q_{c1} \wedge q_{c2} \wedge \cdots) \quad (6)$$

where the logical operators are defined as,

$$\bar{\xi}(x, R) = 1 - \xi(x, R), \quad (7)$$
$$\xi_i(x, R) \wedge \xi_j(x, R) = \min(\xi_i(x, R), \xi_j(x, R)), \quad (8)$$
$$\xi_i(x, R) \vee \xi_j(x, R) = \max(\xi_i(x, R), \xi_j(x, R)). \quad (9)$$

4. TEST RESULTS

We have built a digital photo album prototype (C core engine and Java GUI) with 500 genuine family photos. While the highly diversified content of these photos presents a very challenging task for content-based retrieval, its reasonable size makes the verification of precision more tractable. For this album, we have created 85 visual keywords with a GUI. They are grouped into 8 equivalent classes of visual synonyms to allow abstraction. Some of them are shown in Fig. 2 to 4. In our performance test, we only show the top 15 images retrieved, ranked and displayed in descending order of relevance to the query in top-down and left to right sequence.

With QVC, a user issues a query as a disjunct of conjuncts of visual constraints (equation (6)) as described above. First an intuitive visual interface is provided for a user to specify a visual keyword by selecting its corresponding icon from a palette. To specify a spatial extent, the user can use the mouse to draw a box within a canvas, which could be presented as a landscape or portrait layout. After completed the specification of any visual query term (i.e. what visual keyword in which part of image), the user can apply a negation operator if necessary. Next the user can continue to specify more visual query terms in a conjunct or start a new conjunct in the disjunctive normal form until a complete query formulus has been specified.

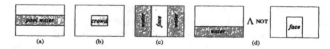

Figure 5: Queries by visual constraints

Fig. 5(a) and (b) denote two queries to look for images with swimming pool and crowd at specific spatial regions respectively. Their query results are shown in Fig. 6 and 7 respectively. For the query on swimming pool (Fig. 5(a) and Fig. 6), 9 out of the 10 photos with sizable swimming pool (images $1 - 8, 12$) were retrieved among the top 15 images. The query on crowd at the center of image (i.e. group photos) (Fig. 5(b)) pulls out 10 relevant photos (images $1 - 4, 6 - 9, 11, 15$) in the top 15 images of Fig. 7.

Fig. 5(c) and (d) present two queries that involve conjuncts of visual query terms. The intention is to search for images that simultaneously satisfy multiple visual constraints. In Fig. 5(c), the query is to find photos with faces (or people) appearing between water. 11 out of 12 relevant photos in the whole album are returned by the system (all images except $3, 6, 9, 15$ in Fig. 8). Another conjunctive query (Fig. 5(d)) involves a negated visual query term. The intention is to look for images with water at the bottom of an image and without people at the lower center of an image. The top 15 images retrieved by the system are presented in

Figure 6: Search for *swiming pool*

Figure 7: Search for *crowd*

Fig. 9. All images except $2, 5-7, 11, 12, 14$ satisfy the visual constraints. In fact, the small faces in most of these images cannot be detected reliably even with the state-of-the-art face detector.

Figure 8: Search for *people between water*

5. DISCUSSION

In the past, global measures of primitive features such as color, texture, and shape are exploited to index and retrieve images (e.g. [2]). However, this approach often produce results incongruent with human expectations as it does not consider spatial localities and higher-level perceptive cues. Images sharing similar overall color distribution can differ greatly in semantic content. This paradigm roughly corresponds to pre-attentive similarity matching which is a low-level function in human visual perception. In contrast, recent region-based methods (e.g. [1]) pre-segment an image by color (or both color and texture) into regions and compute the similarity between two images in terms of the features of these regions. But image segmentation is generally unreliable. A poor segmentation can result in incongruent regions for further similarity matching.

The visual keywords approach proposed here strives to go beyond primitive features and segmented regions. Based on view-based object detection with spatial aggregation, the proposed description scheme captures intuitive visual semantics specified for a given visual content domain. An

Figure 9: Search for **water at bottom without people in center**

alternative view of visual keywords is to regard them as coordinates that span a new pseudo-object feature vector space. The scale on each of these dimensions is the fuzziness ($\in [0, 1]$) of that visual keyword being detected at a specific spatial locality in the visual content. In this sense, visual keywords span an object-driven feature space beyond conventional feature space [2].

Query by visual example is an intuitive metaphor though it has bootstrapping problem. It does not allow explicit composition of visual semantics in a query. Query by Canvas (or Composition) (e.g. [2]) allows a query to be specified in terms of shapes with colors and textures using a graphical editor. However it tends to specify things/stuff of interest in an indirect way using primitive features. For example, one would draw an orange circle and expect the system to know that it represents the sun, though it can also represent an orange, an orange balloon etc. In effect, the system has to guess the semantics from what a user draws.

Query by Visual Constraints let user specifies the semantics directly. For example, a user can specify "pool water" and "crowd" if they are part of the visual vocabulary. In the case of query by canvas, to specify "pool water" and "crowd" is unnatural, if not impossible.

6. CONCLUSIONS

In this paper, we have presented a novel content-based framework based on visual vocabulary. It is independent of the feature measures and object detectors employed to characterize and realize the visual keywords. If shape descriptor is important for the domain or/and robust face detectors are available, they can be deployed as well. The approach can also be seen as a new pseudo-object level feature measure for visual content representation and matching, which does not rely on image segmentation. We also proposed and demonstrated an explicit query formulation method based on spatial specification of visual keywords.

7. REFERENCES

[1] Carson, C. et al. (1999). Color- and texture-based image segmentation using EM and its application to image query and classification. Submitted to *IEEE Tran. PAMI*.

[2] Niblack, W. et al. (1993). The QBIC project: querying images by content using color, textures and shapes. In *Storage and Retrieval for Image and Video Databases, Proc. SPIE 1908*, pp. 13-25.

[3] Picard, R.W. (1995). Toward a Visual Thesaurus. In *Proc. of Springer-Verlag Workshops in Computing, MIRO'95, Glasgow, Sep. 1995*.

MDS: A Multimodal-based Dialog System

Jiyong Ma[1], Wen Gao[1,2], Xilin Chen[2], Shiguan Shan[1],Wei Zeng[2] , Jie Yan[3], Hongming Zhang[2],
Jiangqin Wu[2],Feng Wu[3],Chunli Wang[4]

[1] Institute of Computing Technology, Chinese Academy of Sciences, Beijing 100080,China

[2] Department of Computer Science, Harbin Institute of Technology, Harbin, China

[3] Microsoft Research China

[4] Department of Computer Science, Dalian University of Technology, Dalian, China

{wgao,jyma,sgshan, wzheng,hmzhang,jyan,jqwu,clwang}@ict.ac.cn

1. ABSTRACT

This paper describes MDS: a Multimodal-based Dialog System that supports communication between the hearing impaired and hearing-abled. The system converts sign language to speech, and combines speech with gesture and lip motion using a human face. The features of the human face are derived by doing a 3D feature extraction of the speaker's face, so that the "virtual face" similar to the actual speaker. The main technologies associated with the system include sign language recognition, sign language synthesis and the synchrony of the lip movement and speech. Integration of the sign language recognition, sign language synthesis, speech recognition, speech synthesis and 3D virtual human technologies provides a new way to interact with computers for the hearing impaired.

Keywords

Sign language recognition, Virtual human synthesis, Human facial feature extraction, Communication between deaf people and hearing society.

2. INTRODUCTION

Multimedia interfaces are rapidly evolving to facilitate human-computer communication. Nevertheless, the audio media is inaccessible to the hearing impaired. The need to use tools for the hearing-impaired leads us to develop a system for non-verbal communication for the hearing-impaired based on sign language recognition and sign language synthesis. One challenge in developing this system is to transcribe sign language to text. The other is 3D virtual human synthesis. It includes automatic extraction feature points used for automatic generation of 3D-face mesh, 3D virtual human modeling and gesture synthesis. This paper will discuss the solutions of these challenges.

The reason we used sign language and speech as input modalities

is as following

1) Inputting Chinese characters into computer is difficult for most Chinese.

2) Sign language is a natural means of communication for the hearing impaired, and speech is a natural means of communication for the hearing-abled.

3) To explore new input modalities for easy use of computers.

The emphasis of this paper is focused on an overview of the integrated system, rather than on detail of each component.

The organization of this paper is as follows: we begin with the system setup, then proceed to a discussion sign language recognition, and human facial feature extraction for 3D virtual face synthesis for a given person. Thirdly, we present the system assessment. Finally, we provide a summary and conclusion.

3. SYSTEM SETUP

The architecture of MDS: a Multimodal-based Dialog System is demonstrated in Fig.1.

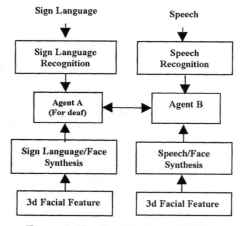

Figure 1. The Architecture of MDS

Except the speech recognition module we developed others. It was implemented on two personal computers. One computer is for a person with hearing ability and the other for the hearing impaired. These two computers are connected via a LAN with two different user interfaces. The agent A is responsible for the interaction of the hearing impaired person facing the virtual human with respect to the person with hearing ability at the other side. The agent B is responsible for the interaction of the person with hearing ability facing a 3-D synthetic face of the hearing impaired person at the other side. The person with hearing ability can speak to the computer and the agent B transfers the text recognized by speech recognition module to the language performed by the 3-D virtual human. The hearing impaired can understand the meaning of the text via the synthetic hand gestures. If the hearing-impaired person wants to "talk with" the person with hearing ability, he/she can perform gestures to the computer. The gesture recognition module recognizes the gestures and transfers the text to the agent B. When the agent B has received the text, it drives the 3-D synthetic face to speak the text accompanying speech and lip motion.

In fact, both sides should have a camera respectively. For simplicity of system design, only one camera at the side of Agent B was used to collect face images of users at the both sides. And both sides should have a 3D human face generator respectively. For simplicity of system design, only a 3D human face generator the side of Agent B was designed in the system. The sign language recognition and sign language synthesis are two main parts for agent A. The facial expression synthesis, lip motion, speech synthesis and speech recognition are four main parts for agent B.

4. SIGN LANGUAGE RECOGNITION

Researches on machine sign language recognition began at the end of 80's. For large vocabulary recognition, Ho-Sub Yoon recently [1] reported that a sign vocabulary consisting of 1,300 alphabetical gestures were recognized using HMMs. And C.Vogler and D.Metaxas[2] pointed that the major challenge for sign language recognition is to develop approaches that will scale well with increasing vocabulary size.

In baseline system for sign language recognition, the data collected by the gesture-input devices are fed to the feature extraction module; then, the feature vectors are input to the fast match models. The fast match finds a list of candidates from a word dictionary. The Bigram model uses word transition probabilities to assign, *a priori*, a probability to each word based on its context. The system combines the fast match score to obtain a list candidates, each of which is then subject to a detailed match, the decoder controls the search for the most likely word sequence using Viterbi search algorithm. When the word sequence is output from the decoder, each word drives the speech synthesis module and 3D-virtual human gesture animation module to produce the speech and gesture synchronously.

Sign position independent feature extraction is very important to practical applications because it is not necessary to restrict a singer to a certain position when the signer is gesturing. The more detailed approach to extraction of sign position independent feature can be found in our previous work [3].

Considering the scalability problems in sign language recognition, we propose the following approach. For each sign, a continuous HMM [4] is trained using training data. For each stream such as left hand shape, right hand shape, left hand position, right hand position, left hand orientation and right hand orientation, the HMM parameters of all signs are clustered. This greatly reduces

the amount parameters of signs, therefore reduces the computation load greatly without loss noticeable performance.

5. SIGN LANGUAGE SYNTHESIS

Our early synthesis system of sign language, speech and the corresponding facial expression driven by text was reported in [5]. A Chinese sentence is input to the text parser module that divides the sentence into basic words. The parser algorithm is the Bi-directional maximum matching with backtracking. After the words are matched, each word in the sentence is then input to the sign language synthesis module and speech synthesis module. For the time being, the word library consists of 5500 words.

6. SYNCHRONOUSLY DRIVING: SPEECH, GESTURE AND LIP MOVEMENT

Prerecorded speech was used to synthesize speech. To synchronously drive speech, gesture and lip motion, we align the display time of gesture and lip motion to the time of playing speech so that human perceives it comfortably. The underlying assumption of this approach is that the display speed of gesture and lip motion is faster than that of playing speech. Fortunately, high performance computers can satisfy this requirement. The quality of speech is better than that of speech generated by most Chinese TTS systems. Because the basic unit used in our system is Chinese phrase not a single Chinese word.

7. FACIAL FEATURE EXTRACTION

For extraction frontal features, we use our previous approach [6] to localize the face in an input image, which can give the location of the face and its approximate size. The second step is feature extraction of the frontal face. Deformable template [7] is an effective method to extract the locations and shapes of facial salient organs such as eyes, mouth and chin. For extraction of profile feature points, thirteen feature points are defined in the profile model. These points belong to feature points proposed in MPEG4. And they reflect main geometrical features of a profile.

8. AUTOMATIC GENERATION OF 3D-FACE MODEL FOR A GIVEN PERSON

Feature points are automatically extracted as mentioned in the preceding section. But some errors may occur. In order to rectify these errors, an interactive mechanism to modify feature points is introduced. According to these features points, the general 3D-face model is adjusted to fit a given person's face characteristics. Then multi-direction texture mapping is utilized to enhance the reality of the synthetic face. Finally, expression synthesis and lip motion syntheses are realized.

Global transform and local transform are designed in order to modify the general 3D neutral face model to the given person's 3D neutral face model. Global transform is used to adjust the global contour of the face and the position of the organs on the face. It is accomplished by scaling the coordinate values of each vertex of the model. The scaling factor can be calculated using the coordinates of the feature points before and after transform. While local transform aims at adjusting the shape of the organs such as the eyes, eyebrows, mouth, nose and the chin to fit the given person. Fig.2 illustrates the adjusting procedure of model.

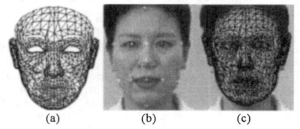

(a)   (b)   (c)

Figure 2. Modification from the General Face Model to the Given Person's Face Model (a) General Face Model (b) Feature Points Extracted (c) Given Person's Face Model

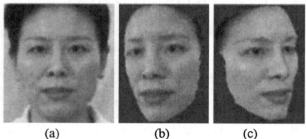

(a)   (b)   (c)

Figure 3. (a) Original Front Image (b) and (c) Synthetic face

Texture mapping provides a valuable technique to further enhance the reality of the synthetic human face. A texture mapping is constructed from two images, one frontal face image and one profile. For each Bézier surface patch of face surfaces, the corresponding texture image is determined by mapping the boundary curve of the Bézier patch to the face image. Which image to be chosen depends on the whole direction of the Bézier patch. When the angle of directional vector is less than 30 degree, frontal face image is used. Otherwise profile image is used. Fig.3 illustrates the result of one given person's synthetic face.

9. EXPERIMENTS AND EVALUATION

The integrated system was implemented on PIII-450. The first experiment was on a dialog between a sign language teacher and a hearing-abled. The database of gestures consists of 220 words and 80 sentences. Each sentence consists of 2 to 15 words. No intentional pauses were placed between signs within a sentence. Within 80 sentences, the deletion (D), insertion (I), and substitution (S) errors are D=3, S=2,I=2 respectively. The word recognition rate is 98.2%. The second experiment was carried on large vocabulary signs. The recognition rate of 5177 isolated signs is 94.8% in real time. For continuous sign recognition, the word correct rate is 91.4% for 200 sentences. A sign language teacher performed the signs. The average system response time is about 2 seconds delay after a sentence was performed. The performance of the sign language recognition system is almost the same with that of ViaVoice98. During the dialog, a few errors may occur for both the speech recognition and sign language recognition. These errors can be recovered by repeating the wrongly recognized sentence. A few errors may also occur for 3D-feature extraction module due to poor illuminant conditions, but the user can rectify these errors with the interactive mechanism.

The main difficult tasks for the integrated system are in recognition and the synchrony of the lip movement with speech.

10. SUMMARY AND CONCLUSION

We have described *MDS*: a Multimodal-based Dialog System using speech, sign language and 3D virtual human technologies for free communication between deaf people and hearing society. Although, we have designed and implemented the system, there are still some works to be improved.

1) Signer independent sign language recognition;

2) Understandable sign language synthesis;

3) 3D lip synthesis and its synchrony with speech.

ACKNOWLEDGMENTS

This work is a key project supported by Chinese NSF.

REFERENCES

[1] Ho-Sub Yoon. Jung Soh. Byung-Woo Min. Hyun Seung Yang. Recognition of alphabetical hand gestures using hidden Markov model. IEICE Transactions on Fundamentals of Electronics Communications & Computer Sciences, vol.E82-A, no.7, July 1999, pp.1358-66.

[2] Vogler C. Metaxas D. Parallel hidden Markov models for American Sign Language recognition. Proceedings of the Seventh IEEE International Conference on Computer Vision. IEEE Comput. Soc. Part vol.1, 1999, pp.116-22 vol.1. Los Alamitos, CA, USA

[3] Jiyong Ma,Wen Gao,Jiangqin Wu and Chunli Wang, A Continuous Chinese Sign Language recognition system, pp428-433, 28-31 March, FG'2000, Grenoble, France.

[4] L. Rabiner and B. Juang. An introduction to hidden Markov models. *IEEE ASSP Magazine*, Jan. 1996,pages 4-16.

[5] Wen Gao,Yibo Song,Baocai Yin, Jie Yan and Ying Liu. Synthesis of sign language ,sound and corresponding facial expression driven by text in multimodal interface. In *Proceedings of the First International Conference on Multimodal Interface*, 1996, 244-248.

[6] Wen Gao,Mingbao Liu. A hierarchical approach to human face detection in a complex background. In *Proceedings of the First International Conference on Multimodal Interface*,1996,289-292.

[7] Yuille, A.L., Hallinan, P.W. & Cohen, D.S.Feature extraction from faces using deformable templates. *International Journal of Computer Vision*, 1992,8, 99-111

ARTE – An Adaptive Rendering and Transmission Environment for 3D Graphics

Ioana M. Martin
IBM T. J. Watson Research Center
P. O. Box 704
Yorktown Heights, NY 10598
ioana@us.ibm.com

ABSTRACT

Thus far, a significant body of work has been devoted to the challenges of universal access related to the delivery of traditional multimedia content such as text, images, audio, and video. Less attention has been focused on three-dimensional (3D) digital content, as true market opportunities for 3D graphics over networks have just begun to emerge. In this paper, we present ARTE, an Adaptive Rendering and Transmission Environment that facilitates the delivery of 3D models in heterogeneous environments by monitoring the resources available and by selecting appropriate transmission modalities.

Keywords

3D graphics over networks, transcoding, universal access.

1. INTRODUCTION

Existing methods for transmission of complex 3D models over networks do not differentiate based upon the resources available. Therefore, technologies that can adapt the transmission of 3D graphics to various types of clients are critical. In this paper, we present an Adaptive Rendering and Transmission Environment (ARTE) that facilitates the delivery of 3D models over networks to match the resources and capabilities of diverse clients. ARTE consists of four key components: (a) an environment monitor that keeps track of the dynamically changing characteristics of the environment in which model transmission and rendering take place; (b) a hierarchical organization scheme for 3D models that allows multiple representation modalities to be associated with each model component; (c) an adaptive selection mechanism that takes into account environment characteristics, model structure, and user preferences to determine the most suitable modality for each model component that fits within a given resource budget; and (d) a transcoding engine that incorporates a number of transcoding modules that

perform the actual conversions of the 3D data to modalities selected by the adaptive selection mechanism.

Geometric models are viewed as collections of components. The geometry of each component is converted, i.e., transcoded into modalities with different quality and transmission characteristics. Associated with each component is a *perceptual importance* value that quantifies the contribution of that component to the perception of a final rendering of the model.

2. BACKGROUND

Adaptive delivery of 3D data over networks is a natural extension of similar efforts for multimedia types such as text, images, audio and video (e.g., [5]). A number of optimization technologies regarding both transmission and rendering of 3D models have been developed. Such methods include 3D model compression (e.g., [7]), model simplification (see [1] for a survey) and level-of-detail management (e.g., [2], [4]), streaming techniques (e.g., [3]), as well as various image-based methods (e.g., [4]). Each of these methods works well for certain types of models and system configurations, and are either not applicable or less efficient for others. In the present work, we expand and implement the idea of adaptive 3D transfer we introduced in [6] in a number of ways. We view models as collections of one or more components and we use a transcoding engine to generate different modalities for each component. Combining modalities for representing model components can achieve better transmission and rendering performance than the use of a "one-size-fits-all" strategy. Our modality selection mechanism accounts for the importance of each component to the final rendering of the model. It also estimates the resources available to predict the performance of a modality in a given context.

3. SYSTEM DESIGN

A schematic representation of the design of ARTE and the relationships between its components is illustrated in Figure 1. The model database contains the 3D models available to clients, as well as all the precomputed modalities cached with each model. When a client makes a request for a 3D model to a server, it first receives meta-data information about the requested model. This information allows the framework to estimate the performance characteristics for each of the modalities available. The perceptual importance of each model component is also estimated. An adaptive mechanism selects the best modality available for each component that fits into the budget and delivers it to the client. The components are processed in decreasing order of their importance. An application-level protocol supports the efficient transfer of modalities between servers and clients.

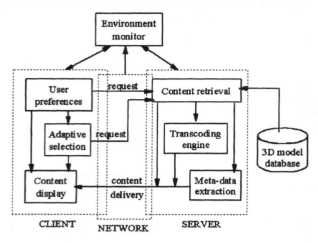

Figure 1: Logical flow of control in an adaptive client-server setup: a monitoring tool records the characteristics of the environment, such as server load, network delay, client and server rendering capabilities. This data is used in conjunction with information about the model to select suitable modalities for transmission and rendering of the model components.

3.1 Environment Monitoring

The characteristics of the environment in which model transfer and rendering takes place determine how suitable a particular modality is for use in that environment. Since the state of the environment may change over time, a monitoring tool is necessary to record the actions taking place in a client-server setting and to provide quantitative information to the selection process on that basis.

In ARTE the *state* of a given client-server configuration is characterized in terms of four parameters: the rendering capability of the client, the rendering capability of the server, the load on the server, and the performance of the communication link between the two. Instead of using absolute values of low-level performance counters such as CPU speed, memory available, and nominal bandwidth, we measure values of high-level quantifiers that are easier to interpret from an application's perspective. Hence, we describe the rendering capabilities of a machine (client or server) in terms of the average frame rate as a function of the model size; we measure server load as the average time between the receipt and the processing of a request; and we evaluate network performance in terms of latency and bandwidth. For each of the state parameters we maintain *history* information. The history is updated dynamically with actual measurements recorded as the data is transferred.

3.2 The Transcoding Engine

The transcoding engine converts original 3D content into various 3D and 2D modalities that can be used individu-

ally or in combination to deliver 3D models to clients under various conditions. It consists of a collection of transcoding modules that perform content conversion either on-line, upon selection of a desired modality, or off-line, at model creation time. The types of modalities available for each model component are described in the meta-data information associated with the model. Examples of modalities include polygonal mesh representations using indexed face sets, progressive meshes, depth images (i.e., 2D images enhanced with depth information at each pixel), bounding boxes with or without textures, and basic shapes (sphere, cylinder, cone, box). Each of these modalities can be generated and delivered at various levels of resolution.

4. ADAPTIVE SELECTION

Each component of a model requested by a client can be delivered to that client by using one of the several modalities associated with it. We define a set of performance parameters that allow various modalities to be compared in terms of the resources they require and the values they offer. If m denotes a modality associated with a model component, the performance parameters considered are: $T(m)$, the total estimated time to deliver m to a client, $Q(m)$, the estimated quality associated with rendering m, and $I(m)$, the degree of interaction supported by m.

The *estimated delivery time* T is defined as the sum of estimates of the time T_g it takes the transcoding engine to generate a modality, the time T_t to transfer it over the network, and the time T_r to render it for the first time on the client: $T(m) = T_g(m) + T_t(m) + T_r(m)$.

The *estimated quality* Q reflects how closely the rendering of a model component using a particular modality resembles the rendering of the full-detail data. We define quality as a dimensionless number between 0.0 and 1.0 that is modality specific.

The *degree of interaction* I represents the number of degrees of freedom when interacting with a particular modality. It can assume values between 0 and 7 for the three principal axes of rotation, translation, and the field-of-view.

The meta-data is used initially to display an outline of the requested model and to allow a user on the client side to define viewing preferences. Based on the meta-data and user preferences, the client computes visibility and perceptual importance for each component. The perceptual importance reflects the contribution of a model component to the final rendering. Starting with the component with the highest perceptual importance value, the selection algorithm identifies the most suitable modality for a component C, as follows. The performance parameters T, I, and Q are evaluated for all modalities available for C, based upon the characteristics defined in the meta-data. Among the modalities with T less than a given time budget T_B, the one with the highest quality Q is selected.

5. IMPLEMENTATION AND RESULTS

The design ideas previously described have been incorporated into an implementation of ARTE that supports adaptive downloading of 3D models between a server and multiple clients. For transmission and storage purposes, 3D data is encoded in MPEG-4 compressed format using the Topological Surgery compression scheme for 3D meshes described in [7]. The modalities currently available for representing

Client	Model	OS	CPU (MHz)	Display adapter
1	ThinkPad 770 ED	Win 95	266	Trident Cyber
2	Thinkpad 600 E	Win 98	300	NeoMagic Magic Media
3	Intellistation M Pro	Win NT	400	Intense 3D Pro
4	Intellistation Z Pro	Win NT	400	Intense 3D WildCat
5	This client runs on the same machine as the server			

Table 1: Platform configurations used in the adaptive experiment reported in this paper.

each model component are the indexed face set polygonal representation and the depth image, which can be delivered at various resolutions. These modalities determine an implicit partitioning of model components for hybrid rendering on the clients.

Data pertaining to content adaptation is shown in Figure 2 for a configuration consisting of a server and five clients. The clients make requests for two models of different complexities: an engine with 218 components (70275 vertices) and an automobile with 48 components (12733 vertices). The server is installed on an Intellistation Z Pro, running Windows NT 4.0, with a dual Pentium II 450 MHz processor and an Intergraph Intense 3D Pro 3400-GT graphics adapter. The clients are connected to this server over combinations of 16Mbps Token Ring, 10Mbps Ethernet, and 100Mbps Ethernet connections. Table 1 summarizes the configurations of the five clients.

Figure 2 shows the percentage of the geometry downloaded to the five clients given a rendering budget of 15 frames-per-second (fps) for each client. The geometry is downloaded progressively, in order of visibility and taking into account the approximate projected screen size of each component. Clients 1 and 2 have only software support for 3D rendering. Hence, they can handle only a small fraction of the total geometry at 15fps. Of the three clients with hardware support for 3D rendering, client 3 has the graphics adapter with the lowest performance, whereas the Intense 3D WildCat adapter of client 4 delivers the most performance. This behavior is captured by our adaptive system, which supplies a larger portion of the model geometry to clients 4 and 5, and less geometry to client 3.

The difference in the final quality received by the clients is affected by the restriction imposed on the rendering time. In the case of the automobile model, the high-end workstations (clients 4 and 5) receive the full model in the end. The other clients, receive only a fraction of the model geometry, according to their rendering abilities. A similar behavior may be observed with the engine. Note that in the case of this larger model, a partial geometric representation is downloaded to all the clients, as none is capable of rendering the engine at 15 fps.

The components for which geometry is not downloaded may be displayed on the client using the coarse geometry stored in the meta-data or may be rendered into a depth image on the server and delivered to the requesting client as context information. In the latter case, the resolution of the context image is adaptively chosen taking into account the transfer budget and the server load and rendering capability.

6. CONCLUSIONS

In this paper, we have described the architecture of ARTE, a system for adaptive delivery of 3D models in heterogeneous networked environments. This system enables efficient access to these models by clients with diverse graphics capabilities and network connections. An environment monitor keeps track of the resources available and provides the data necessary to estimate performance parameters for a given model and transmission context. These estimates are used by an adaptive selection mechanism to determine the combination of modalities best suited for transmission and rendering in that context. A transcoding engine drives the actual conversions between the original 3D data and the modalities selected.

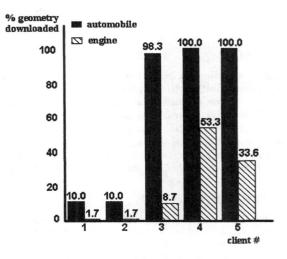

Figure 2: The percentage of the total geometry downloaded from a server to five clients (see Table 1) for a target frame rate of 15 fps and two models of different complexity.

7. REFERENCES

[1] P. Cignoni, C. Montani, and R. Scopigno. A comparison of mesh simplification algorithms. *Computers and Graphics*, 22:37–54, 1998.

[2] T. A. Funkhouser and C. H. Sequin. Adaptive display algorithm for interactive frame rates during visualization of complex virtual environments. In *Proceedings of SIGGRAPH 93*, pages 247–254, 1993.

[3] H. Hoppe. Progressive meshes. In *Proceedings of SIGGRAPH 96*, pages 99–108, 1996.

[4] P. Maciel and P. Shirley. Visual navigation of large environmnts using textured clusters. In *Proceedings of 1995 Symposium on 3D Graphics*, pages 95–102, 1995.

[5] R. Mohan, J. R. Smith, and C.-S. Li. Adapting multimedia internet content for universal access. *IEEE Transactions on Multimedia*, 1(1):10–19, 1999.

[6] B.-O. Schneider and I. M. Martin. An adaptive framework for 3d graphics over networks. *Computers and Graphics*, 23:867–874, 1999.

[7] G. Taubin and J. Rossignac. Geometric compression through topological surgery. *ACM Transactions on Graphics*, 17(2):84–115, 1998.

Experimental Evaluation of Forward Error Correction on Multicast Audio Streams in Wireless LANs

Philip K. McKinley and Suraj Gaurav
Department of Computer Science and Engineering
Michigan State University
East Lansing, Michigan 48824

{mckinley,gauravsu}@cse.msu.edu

ABSTRACT

This paper describes an experimental study of a proxy service to enhance interactive multicast audio streams when transmitted across wireless local area networks. The architecture of the proxy is presented, followed by results of a performance study conducted on a mobile computing testbed. The main contribution of the paper is to evaluate the effectiveness of forward error correcting codes on improving the quality of audio channels for collaborating mobile users.

1. INTRODUCTION

New wireless data communication services and advances in portable computing devices are rapidly changing the nature of distributed computing. One class of applications that can benefit from this expanding and heterogeneous infrastructure is collaborative computing. Examples include computer-supported cooperative work, computer-based instruction, telemedicine, and crisis management systems. A diverse infrastructure enables individuals to collaborate via widely disparate technologies. One approach to accommodating heterogeneity is to introduce a layer of *middleware* between applications and underlying transport services.

Towards this end, we are developing Pavilion [1], an object-oriented middleware framework for collaborative web-based applications. Pavilion enables a developer to construct new applications by inheriting and extending its default functionality. In addition, Pavilion provides services designed to mitigate differences in the performance and functionality of the network connections and devices used by participants. One focus area of the Pavilion project is on supporting collaborative applications in which some of the participants are connected via wireless LANs (WLANs); typical settings include schools, offices, factories, and hospitals.

Extending collaborative applications to wireless domains requires the redesign of communication services to accommodate relatively high packet loss rates and generally lower bit rates. Many approaches to solving this problem involve the use of proxy servers [2], which represent wireless receivers to the rest of the wired network. In earlier papers, we have described the use of Pavilion proxies to support distributed caching of web resources, collaborative web browsing via handheld computers, and forward error correction (FEC) on reliable multicast transmissions.

In this paper, we continue our study of FEC by exploring its application to multicast audio streams. While a number of analytical and theoretical studies have addressed real-time data streams on wireless LANs, the process of actually building and testing systems, even small-scale prototypes, can reveal component interactions and performance bottlenecks not otherwise apparent. The main contribution of this paper is to present our initial experimental results on the efficacy FEC applied to multicast audio streams. Additional details can be found in a companion technical report [3].

2. BACKGROUND

The Pavilion framework itself is written primarily in Java, but includes components written in other languages. Like other frameworks that support the development of collaborative applications, Pavilion can also be used in a "default" mode, in which it operates as a collaborative web browser. A participant can gain control of the session by simply selecting a URL in his/her browser. A set of threads monitor the state of each browser and reliably multicast URLs and web resources to the other browsers; see [1] for details.

A goal of the Pavilion project is to develop a uniform model for collaborative middleware that can adapt to heterogeneous client systems and dynamic network conditions. Figure 1 depicts an example in which adaptive components operate as plug-ins on participating hosts and their proxies. Some plug-ins (observers) monitor the system for conditions that may affect the operation or performance of the application, such as changes in the quality of a network connection and disparities among participating devices. Other plug-ins (responders) are programmed to handle to such events by instantiating new components or modifying the behavior of a communication protocol. For example, the audio proxy discussed herein is instantiated automatically when the first mobile host on a WLAN joins an ongoing Pavilion session.

The performance of group communication services, such as audio multicasting, is affected by three characteristics of WLANs: dynamic channel loss rates and the behavior of the 802.11 CSMA/CA MAC layer (no link-level acknowledgements for multicast frames), and the impact of a shared channel on effective bandwidth. Since CRC-based detection of an error at the data link layer typically results in the re-

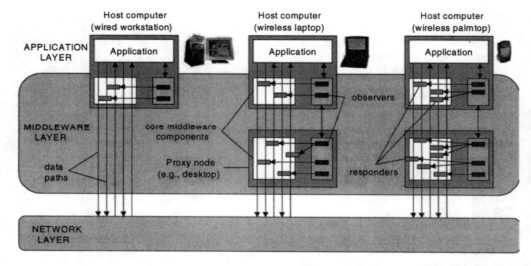

Figure 1: Configuration of Pavilion adaptive middleware components.

moval of the corrupt packet(s) from the stream, much of the FEC-related work in the networking community deals with recovering from *erasures* [4]. An (n, k) *block erasure code* converts k data packets into a group of n encoded packets, such that any k of the n encoded packets can be used to reconstruct the k data packets. In this paper, we use only *systematic* (n, k) codes, in which the first k encoded packets are identical to the k data packets. The remaining $n - k$ packets as referred to as *parity* packets. The advantage of using block erasure codes for multicasting is that a single parity packet can be used to correct independent single-packet losses among different receivers. For the FEC encoding in the Pavilion audio proxy, we used Rizzo's public domain FEC encoder/decoder library [4].

3. PROXY ARCHITECTURE

Figure 2 shows the components that constitute the FEC audio proxy. Each component comprises one or more threads in the implementation. Let us first consider delivery of an audio stream to mobile users. The `WiredReceiver` object receives multicast data packets over the wired network and delivers them to a `PacketBuffer`. The `FEC_Encoder` collects the data packets into FEC data blocks of size k. When a group of k packets is full, encoding routines are invoked to produce $n - k$ parity packets. Both the data and parity packets are forwarded to the `WirelessSender`, which uses IP multicast to transmit them on the WLAN. To enable mobile users to speak to other group members, the proxy also contains a `WirelessReceiver`, which receives data and parity packets on the wireless network interface. An `FEC_Decoder` extracts the audio data and forwards the resulting packets to a `WiredSender`, which forwards them to participants accessible via the wired network.

4. PERFORMANCE EVALUATION

Our testbed currently includes conventional workstations connected by a 100 Mbps Fast Ethernet switch, two WLANs (Lucent WaveLAN and Proxim RangeLAN2), and several handheld and laptop computer systems. All tests reported here were conducted on the WaveLAN network, which has

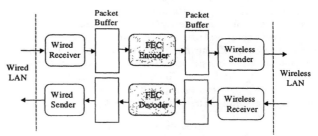

Figure 2: Operation of Pavilion audio proxy.

a raw bit rate of 2 Mbps (soon to be upgraded to 11 Mbps). The WaveLAN access point and the wired participating stations were located in our laboratory. The audio proxy was executed on a dual-processor 450 MHz desktop, and the mobile nodes were three 300 MHz laptops equipped with WaveLAN network interface cards.

The walls in our building are constructed of concrete, dramatically affecting packet loss rates for wireless stations. In our experiments, we varied the location of the mobile system farthest from the access point. Location 1 is just outside our laboratory; loss rates are near zero. Location 2 is approximately 25 meters down a corridor; without FEC, audio is intelligible at this location, but exhibits some jitter. Location 3 is approximately 50 meters down a corridor; without FEC, audio is unintelligible at this location.

We recorded audio in Windows PCM-based waveform audio file format (.WAV) at a rate of 8000 samples per second for two 8-bit/sample stereo channels. Experience with the recording API showed that using buffer sizes of either 400 or 800 bytes (hence, 25 or 50 milliseconds of audio) worked well in avoiding jitter in low-loss environments. However, we also tested several different *packet* sizes, by segmenting buffers prior to transmission, to determine which size resulted in the lowest loss rate. Figure 3 gives the raw receipt rate of data sent using four different packet sizes (50, 100, 200, 400 bytes) to each of the three target locations. All four sizes produced high receipt rates at the first two locations, but only the 100-byte packet produced a receipt rate over 80 percent at location 3. We conclude that 50-byte

417

packets overburden the receivers, while that 200- and 400-byte packets result in lost data that could be delivered with smaller packets (bit errors are localized within the packet). In the remaining test results described here, we used 800-byte recording buffers and 100-byte packets.

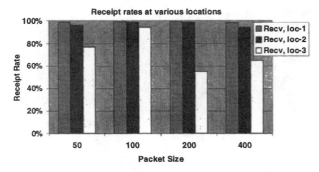

Figure 3: Effect of packet size on raw receipt rate.

Next, we measured the packet loss distributions. In wireless domain, however, losses are more commonly due to external factors such as interference, alignment of antennae, and ambient temperature, rather than congestion. Figure 4 shows a sample of the results, gathered from location 3. While some large bursts occur, the vast majority are under 3 packets long, and most "burst" errors comprise a single packet loss. Such results support the use of block erasure codes with a small value of n (and $n - k$).

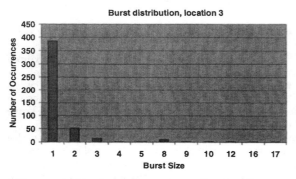

Figure 4: Packet burst error distribution, loc-3.

We experimented with several different sets of FEC parameters. In each test, we measured the raw and net packet receipt rate. Net receipt rate includes both packets received intact as well as those that can be reconstructed using FEC. Each test corresponds to 35 seconds of audio reception. At each location, we conducted three runs with various FEC configurations: (12,8), (8,4), (6,4). Figure 5 shows a plot of raw and reconstructed receipt rate at location 2, using a (6,4) FEC configuration. The average raw receipt rate is already quite high, but even these small losses result in noticeable degradation in the quality of the audio. Using FEC, the reconstructed packet rate increases to nearly 100%, producing very clear audio quality. At location 3, near the periphery of the wireless cell, the average raw receipt rate (86.74%) produced an is unintelligible channel without using FEC. The use of FEC(12,8) smoothed the losses to a great extent, and improved the net receipt rate to 96.44%, producing intelligible audio reception.

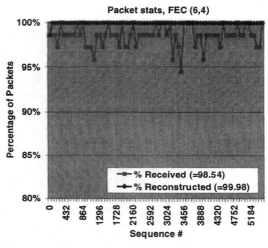

Figure 5: Trace data for location 2 with FEC(6,4).

5. CONCLUSIONS

In this paper, we have described our initial studies in the use of proxy services to support multicast audio streams across WLANs. Our results show that the use of FEC can extend audio services to the periphery of the WLAN cell, where the audio would otherwise be unintelligible. Our continuing work in this area involves dynamically adapting the rate of redundancy to in response to changes in packet loss rate and testing FEC techniques proposed for Internet audio traffic [5] on WLANs. Given the increasing presence of WLANs in homes and businesses, we envision immediate application of the proposed techniques to improve performance of collaborative applications involving users who roam within a WLAN environment.

Further Information. Related papers of our Communications Research Group are available via the World-Wide Web at: http://www.cse.msu.edu/~mckinley/crgweb.

Acknowledgements. The authors would like to thank Aaron Malenfant and Arun Mani for their contributions to this work. This project was supported in part by the NSF grants CDA-9617310, ANI-9706285, and CCR-9912407.

6. REFERENCES

[1] P. K. McKinley, A. M. Malenfant, and J. M. Arango, "Pavilion: A distributed middleware framework for collaborative web-based applications," in *Proceedings of the ACM SIG-GROUP Conference on Supporting Group Work*, pp. 179–188, November 1999.

[2] B. R. Badrinath, A. Bakre, R. Marantz, and T. Imielinski, "Handling mobile hosts: A case for indirect interaction," in *Proc. Fourth Workshop on Workstation Operating Systems*, (Rosario, Washington), IEEE, October 1993.

[3] P. K. McKinley and S. Gaurav, "A study of FEC-enhanced audio services for wireless LANs," Tech. Rep. MSU-CPS-00-12, Department of Computer Science, Michigan State University, East Lansing, Michigan, June 2000.

[4] L. Rizzo, "Effective erasure codes for reliable computer communication protocols," *ACM Computer Communication Review*, April 1997.

[5] J. Bolot, S. Fosse-Parisis, and D. Towsley, "Adaptive FEC-based error control for interactive audio in the Internet," in *Proceedings of IEEE Infocom'99*, (New York), March 1999.

mediacaptain – an interface for browsing streaming media

Florian Mueller

FX Palo Alto Laboratory
3400 Hillview Avenue, Bldg. 4
Palo Alto, CA 94304, USA

floyd@mediacaptain.com

ABSTRACT

The increase of bandwidth and streaming technology has made video on the Web the current "killer-app" of the dot-com world. However, users still face many problems. Users have to find the right video and the right segment within the video. Locally stored files provide easy (but still not very sophisticated) access to individual points in the video by utilizing a seek slider. If the video is streamed over the Internet, this slider loses much of its attraction. Every accessed point in the video requires the video player to buffer, which causes a time lag.

The mediacaptain is a system that addresses this issue by using supplementary material like text and graphics to provide indices. This time-aligned material is used to help the user make an informed decision on whether they want to watch a video and if so, what portions. This web-enabled prototype called mediacaptain emerged from user surveys and is demonstrated on several content types and represents an advanced experience with video on the Web.

Keywords

Streaming media, streaming video, buffering, supplementary text, supplementary graphics, video on the Web, video and text, user interface.

1. INTRODUCTION

Streaming media is "the" reason for a broadband Internet. Advancements in video technology and digital postproduction allow home users as well as traditional content providers in the television/movie market to produce quality video content easily, which they can distribute over the Web. Both parties use streaming technology to free the user from long waits. Once the streaming media player finishes downloading a predetermined amount of data, the video starts playing although the entire video data is not received so far. This so called "buffering" is necessary to intercept possible dropouts during the playback.

This greatly reduces the time for the user to wait due to bandwidth limitations.

Streaming technology facilities the user's experience, but is still far from easy -meaning instant- access to video on the Web. What if the user does not want to start watching from the beginning? Or quickly wants to jump to the next chapter? For each jump, buffering takes place making the user wait. These arbitrary jumps can be avoided by providing entry points in order to allow the user to make an informed assessment on where to jump within the video. Several solutions exist that create such index points, either authored in terms of annotations [1] or automatically generated [2]. The first utilizes textual content to retrieve index points, the later visual features within the video.

The mediacaptain is a system that tries to combine the advantages of both into a complete video-text or video-graphics solution that helps the user to determine, with contextual and visual support, the right point within a video to jump to. If this is achieved, it saves the user a lot of time waiting for the player to buffer and then realizing that this is not the point where the user wanted to start watching.

2. QUESTIONNAIRE

Due to the adolescent stage of video on the Web, it is important to see what the users' experience has been so far, what their needs are and where they see ways for improvement with streaming media.

A questionnaire was made available over the Internet to a selected audience, all of them very computer-literate. Of the 98 survey participants, only 66 had ever watched a video on the Web, and only 34 of them had actually searched for video at least once. None of the participants who watched video on the Web were satisfied with it: most of them criticized the poor quality and generally described their video on the Web experience as "too slow."

The users were asked further what they think would be the best representation for a video. They were introduced to the results in [3], which suggests a salient image with corresponding text as a good summary. If this could not be provided, the participants had to choose between three alternatives: just the image (23%), just the sentence (16%) or a combination of both, but the sentence would not really relate to the image (because it was done by a computer) (22%). Most of the participants were not able to make a decision (39%). Different users showed different needs, and this led to the design decision to incorporate text with a high level of user authoring possibilities.

The subjects also had to evaluate what they would see as a good representation of a sample video. Three possible solutions were presented:

1. An animated gif containing six keyframes extracted from a video in isochronous timeframes

2. A larger frame extracted from exactly the middle of the video, with the spot's title next to it

3. A sequence of three keyframes

The animated gif was favored by 66 participants out of the 92 who answered this question. Answer choices 2 and 3 were equally chosen by the remaining participants. These numbers changed little after the users were told what the video was about. This led to the design decision to emphasize the "moving images" character in the representation of a video, without utilizing a video skim, as also advised against in [4].

The study gave insights on the user's experience with streaming media, and it especially showed the current flaws of the technology. Two of the biggest complaints were the insufficient quality and the delays users had to face. Study participants complained that they sometimes do not want to start watching the video from the beginning, and this is where the annoyance of the buffering shows up repeatedly: Every time the seek slider is moved to an arbitrary point, the video has to buffer, most of the time just to show the user, that this is not the point the user wanted to jump to. So with the reduction of unnecessary jumps, which causes buffering, the delay time for the user can be dramatically reduced.

3. MEDIACAPTAIN
These findings led to the mediacaptain, which provides access points into the video. They are not only of textual or graphical content, but also provide visual aid from the video for the decision-making process of deciding whether this is the right point to start the video from, all without requiring the video to buffer.

A screenshot of the current implementation can be seen here:

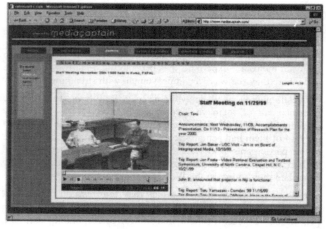

Every screen consists of two main parts. On the left, the video window is embedded, on the right is the supplementary material, mostly text, positioned in an extra frame. The text is in HTML format and therefore allows easy formatting and supports all layout capabilities of the web browser.

In addition to that, the text exhibits additional functionality: If the mouse is moved over any parts of the text, the keyframe (a JPEG) for that exact point in the video is displayed overlaying the video. So instead of having multiple keyframes all displayed at once as mentioned earlier, they are displayed "on demand". If the user wants the visual information of what happened in the video at this

point in the text, the user moves the mouse over and gets it right there.

The images, which are compressed JPEGs can be either preloaded or downloaded on demand. They are small in file size, so they can be quickly downloaded, and have the same dimensions as the video. The JPEGs are displayed overlaying the video, so it is clear for the user that they are part of the video, and before the user starts the movie, there is already a visual aid of what is going to be displayed upon a press on the start button.

For the user, it looks like the video would advance to the specific point and show the keyframe. In reality, it is not the video showing it (because this would require buffering), but pictures overlaying the video window.

If the mouse is moved along while reading the text, it can become like a slideshow of changing images. The user can basically play the video, with a very small frame rate and no audio, at any speed. This is coherent with the results of the user survey, where the users favored the animated gif instead of static images.

By clicking on the text, the video starts playing at that particular point. While the video is playing, the active text segment is highlighted and scrolls into view. It is a bi-directional connection, which means interaction on one side triggers action on the other side.

In case of text as supplementary material, the user can also easily retrieve the desired index point by simply utilizing the search functionality of the web browser.

3.1 Interaction vs Buffering
The restrictions of streaming media require an interface design, which guides the user's interaction with the video. The following graphic shows a major concept of the mediacaptain:

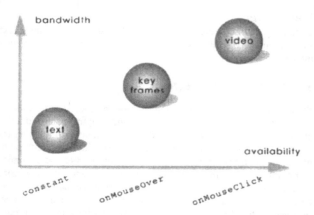

The more bandwidth a medium requires, the more intervention from the user is necessary to access it. This way, the loading and buffering times are kept to an absolute minimum.

Text is almost instantly loaded, therefore, it is available immediately and displayed constantly on the web page. The user can start exploring the text and decide whether the video is of any interest. If the text does not give enough information to assess relevance, the user can use the visual information of the keyframes to support this process. Keyframes require more bandwidth, so they are only available if the user requests them by moving the mouse over the point of interest. If the combination of text and keyframes provided sufficient information and the user decides to watch the movie at this point, a mouse click starts the video.

The more bandwidth that is needed, the more action is required from the user. The system leads the user to use text, keyframes and video in this order to assure that bandwidth is used optimally.

Users should not need to wait for a video to start. If they have to, the system functions as a guide to make sure that the user has chosen the right video and it starts playing at the right point.

3.2 Video and Graphics

"This sounds nice, but what if I don't have text? What if I have a graphic along with the video?"

The following shows a possible application with video content shot by a real estate agent. Important supplementary material to the video is not so much of a textual character, but more graphical, here a floor plan. With it, the potential buyer will get an idea of what the house will look like before even going there. The video is a taped tour the real estate agent made, which can be followed on the floor plan.

Below the video the floor plan is displayed. If the user moves the mouse over a room or any important marked area on the plan, the keyframe from the video will be displayed overlaying the video area. The keyframe is extracted at the point when the real estate agent in the video is entering the chosen room. If the mouse is clicked, the video starts playing at that point. While the video plays, the room that is being shown is highlighted in a different color. This way, the user knows which room on the floor plan the real estate agent is showing at the moment.

3.3 Only one file to author

The file format chosen to synchronize the video with the supplementary material is a text format that includes time-stamps, which is normally used for closed captioning for web content. It is called SAMI (Synchronized Accessible Media Interchange) and is a "…simple format optimized for authoring captions…in a single document." [5] It follows the XML specification and is therefore easily readable by human beings.

Sophisticated nesting of the tags needed for the mediacaptain and the SAMI specific XML tags allows creating one file: it is read in by the video, which controls the highlighting of the text, and is

also read in by the text frame, and controls there the mouseOver and the display of the appropriate keyframes. This means, if anything in the text needs to be changed, there is only one file to alter.

4. CONCLUSION

The mediacaptain gives the user a better interface to browse streaming video. Through the implementation of text, graphics, keyframes and video, the user can make an informed choice on which medium to use for which purpose. Each medium has advantages in its area of representation and can be used interchangeably.

The user is guided along an interaction path that is required by bandwidth constraints. Text, keyframes and video are available to the user, but require different kind of interaction levels. These levels correspond to the bandwidth requirements of the text, keyframes and video.

A two-way connection between the text and the video allows the video to control the text, and vice versa, and also gives the user permanent feedback on the question, "Where am I?"

Users can use the textual index points to access specific parts in the video faster. They have a variable rather than a sequential way to browse the video, without losing the temporal aspect of the medium.

5. DEMO

A demo can be seen at http://www.mediacaptain.com, which is also mentioned in the demo section of the ACM Multimedia 2000 proceedings.

[1] Bargeron, D., Gupta, A., Grudin, J., and Sanocki, E. "Annotations for Streaming Video on the Web: System Design and Usage Studies," (1998), ftp://ftp.research.microsoft.com/pub/tr/tr-98-60.doc

[2] Foote, J., Boreczky, J., Girgensohn, A., and Wilcox, L. "An Intelligent Media Browser using Automatic Multimodal Analysis." In *Proceedings of Multimedia '98*, ACM Press, pp. 377 (1998), http://www.fxpal.xerox.com/PapersAndAbstracts/papers/foo98.pdf

[3] Ding, W., Marchionini, G., and Soergel, D. "Multimodal Surrogates for Video Browsing," http://www.clis.umd.edu/faculty/soergel/soergeldl99wdgmds.pdf

[4] Uchihashi, S., Foote, J., Girgensohn, A., and Boreczky, J. "Video Manga: Generating Semantically Meaningful Video Summaries." In *Proceedings ACM Multimedia*, ACM Press, pp. 384 (1999), http://www.fxpal.xerox.com/PapersAndAbstracts/papers/uch99b.pdf

[5] Closed Captions for Web Multimedia, http://www.microsoft.com/enable/sami/details.htm

Design and Implementation of the Parallel Multimedia File System Based on Message Distribution

Seung-Ho Park, *Si-Yong Park, Gwang Moon Kim, Ki Dong Chung

Department of Computer Science Pusan National University
*Department of Multimedia Co-operation Course Pusan National University

Kumjeong-Ku, Pusan, Korea

Tel.No. +82-51-518-7502

{shpark, sypark, gmkim, kdchung}@melon.cs.pusan.ac.kr

ABSTRACT

The two-layered distributed clustered server architecture consisting of a control server and a group of storage servers has been widely used to support multimedia file systems. With this kind of the server architecture, it is easy to sustain disk load balancing and scalable disk bandwidth. However, it brings about the communication overhead between the control server and storage servers. Therefore, to reduce such overhead, media data should be transmitted from the storage servers to the users directly without the intervention of the control server. In addition, the file system must support the effective data placement and disk scheduling policies and should be designed to sustain portability and flexibility in any hardware or software environment to cope with rapidly developed hardware and software technologies.

So, to fulfill such requirements described in the above statements, we designed and implemented a parallel file system named PMFS(Parallel Multimedia File System) and analyzed its performance by comparing it with PVFS(Parallel Virtual File System). As a result of our experimental simulation, we came to conclusion that the PMFS shows better performance than the PVFS does in real time data processing.

Keywords

Parallel file system, multimedia, Message Distribution

1. INTRODUCTION

With the recent development of computing and communicating technology, multimedia services such as web-based multimedia applications including NOD(News On Demand) and digital libraries have been evolved rapidly into promising new multimedia services. As is widely known, those applications deals with multiple data types such as text, image, audio and video. Therefore, file systems for these multimedia applications must support not only non real-time data but also real-time data efficiently.

In particular, multimedia file systems must have high I/O bandwidth to support the number of concurrent clients isochronously[1]. Generally, to support these file systems, the two-layered distributed clustered server architecture consisting of a control server and a group of storage servers has been widely used[3]. With the two-layered distributed clustered server architecture, it is easy to exploit disk load balancing and scalable disk bandwidth. However, it brings about the communication overhead between the control server and storage servers[2]. Therefore, to reduce such overhead and improve the performance of the file systems in the two-tiered distributed architecture, media data should be transmitted from the storage servers to the users directly without the intervention of the control server. In Figure 1, we briefly introduce the data transmission process in the two-layered architecture. In this environment, the control server deals only with metadata in terms of data delivery, which indicate the attributes of the real data whereas the storage servers are responsible for the real data delivery. In this system, media objects are striped and then stored over a group of storage servers. Therefore, for data delivery, the data request message is sent to the group of distributed servers(we call this *message distribution*). Then data blocks that are stored in the group of servers are sent to the users and then rearranged in the client's side. Moreover, it is desirable that the file system should be designed to sustain portability and flexibility in any hardware or software environment to cope with the rapidly changing hardware and software technologies[4]. The file system should provide the users with the effective data placement and disk scheduling policies as well.

In this paper, to fulfill such requirements described in the above statements, we design and implement a parallel file system named PMFS(Parallel Multimedia File System) and analyze its performance by comparing it with PVFS(Parallel Virtual File System).

The rest of the paper is organized as follows. Section 2 reviews the related works in the areas of parallel file systems and cluster server architectures and introduces data placement techniques and real time scheduling policies. Section 3 presents the architecture and features of our proposed file system(PMFS). Section 4, we show that the results of the performance analysis for the PMFS. Finally we draw a conclusion with summary of our research results and refer to the future research in Section 5.

2. Related work

In this section, we refer to the related works in the area of parallel file systems and architectures of cluster server and introduce data placement techniques and real time scheduling policies.

O Parallel File System

Some parallel file systems have been implemented for non real-time applications in the scientific and statistic area : Galley, PVFS(Parallel Virtual File System), Vesta, GFS(Global File System)[7]. Other parallel file systems are implemented to operate on top of special hardwares ; PFS(Parallel File System for Intel Paragon), PIOFS(IBM SP2), SciFS(SCI Cluster)[7]. In the areas of multimedia applications, parallel file systems should be designed to support real-time data delivery : Symphony, Tiger shark, Fellini, Mitra, Video Server Array[7]. Among these, the Symphony file system is the only one to support both the real-time data and non real-time data.

O Cluster Server Architectures

The architectures of the clustered multimedia storage server is classified into 'Flat architecture' and '2-Tier architecture' based on the physical location of the control server and storage servers[5]. Or, these are classified into 'independent architecture' and 'distributed architecture' according to data placement policies.

O Data placement techniques

To maximize I/O bandwidth and keep disk load balance, it is important to find out how to place data on disks in the clustered storage server. The studies on data placement policies in the multi-disks have been done on different disk configurations : homogeneous disks or heterogeneous disks. These policies include Round Robin, staggered striping, Random permutation[6], RIO[8].

O Real time scheduling policies

EDF(Earliest Deadline First), LLF(Least Laxity First), RMS(Rate Monotonic Scheduling), QEDF(QoS-driven EDF), QLLF(QoS-driven LLF)[9] have been widely known as real time scheduling algorithm(We use EDF policy in the propose file system).

3. Design and Implementation of PMFS

PMFS is designed and implemented for multimedia data service based on the two-layered distribution architecture with extendibility and portability.

3.1 PMFS's Architecture

A storage group consists of a number of disks in multi storage nodes and a file is striped over a storage group in the PMFS. There are two kinds of daemon processes to manage metadata and process disk IO: MGR(Manager Daemon) and IOD(IO Daemon). MGR, which exists in the control server, manages metadata of all media objects in the PMFS whereas an IOD, which exists per storage server, deals with file reads and writes. The schematic architecture of PMFS is depicted in Figure 1.

3.1.1 PMFS's internal structure

PMFS runs as a high-level file system like EXT2 and consists of a group of user library function interfaces to support disk IOs. Its

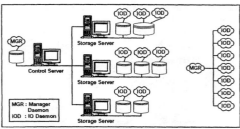

[Figure 1] Structure of PMFS

function library is composed of nine basic functions, which are similar to Unix file interfaces and two extended functions added to support multimedia data delivery : pmfs_setdeadline() to set I/O deadline and pmfs_settarget() to set transmission target respectively. pmfs_create() , which is similar to create() call in Unix file systems, is used to create a file. However, unlike Unix's create() function, it enables users to set file processing attributes such as data placement policy, media type, block size and replication policy at his or her will.

3.1.2 Data structure and file I/O of PMFS

< Data structure of I-node >

Like Unix file systems, in PMFS, an I-node is used to store metadata of a file. Those are not only general file system information as is stored in an Unix file's I-node but also additional information to support to continuous media data delivery and fault tolerance.

1) File read

pmfs_read() is the PMFS's version of read() function to read a file. For file reads, pmfs_read() sends read requests to each IOD and each IOD reads data blocks and then transmits them to the target address. At this point in time, the target address is set using pmfs_settarget() but if the target address is not set, the data blocks are transmitted to pmfs_read()(See in Figure 2).

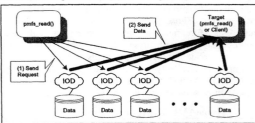

[Figure 2] Structure of pmfs_read()

An IOD consists of a Request reader, a Job scheduler and a Transmission scheduler. The Request reader is responsible for reading I/O requests and then inserting them to the job list. The Job scheduler schedules and then executes jobs in the job list using EDF algorithm. If data delivery deadline is not set, the Job scheduler schedules the jobs in the job list based on FIFO algorithm. The Transmission scheduler will transmit data using FIFO algorithm if data exists in the data list. We use non-blocking I/Os to read data in real time such that if pmfs_read() can't read data within the deadline, then the IOD marks the disk where the requested data resides as failure and then reads the data blocks in the disks where the replica of the requested data blocks reside. (See Figure 3).

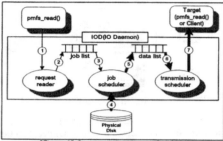

[Figure 3] Structure of pmfs_read() in IOD

2) File write

Pmfs_write() is similar to write() in the Unix file system in that it is used to write data to a file. However, unlike pmfs_read() with which all read requests are queued in the job list and then serviced , write requests are not scheduled in the job list. Instead, their requests are executed directly by the Request reader. This is because, if pmfs_write() sends a request for file writes in the job list, the Job scheduler has to read the requested block on behalf of pmfs_read(). Therefore, it is highly likely that the Request reader and the Job scheduler would compete for system resources such as socket if more than two requests are issued concurrently. It would be one solution if one socket per request is given but it will cause the system overhead for extra socket calls. To avoid this, the Request reader deals with file writes directly. pmfs_write() sends file write requests with additional information such as data placement policy, block size, I-node information and replication policy through the file pointer to each IOD(See Figure 8).

4. Performance evaluation and analysis

4.1 Experiment environment

For performance evaluation, we implemented the two-layered distributed cluster server that consists of a control server and three storage servers. Those servers are connected with each other through Fast Ethernet and internal switching hub and user requests are generated from the remote server. We did experiments about file writes and reads using 600 data objects consisting of randomly selected text, image, audio(MP3), video(MPEG1, MPEG2) which are stored in eight disks. Table 1 ,2 and 3 show some system parameters used in this experiment.

[Table 1] H/W environment using experiment

CPU	Intel Pentium II 300 MHZ Dual(1), Pentium 100 MHZ(2)
Main Memory	256 Mbyte(1), 32 Mbyte(2)
SCSI Card	Adaptec AIC-7860 Ultra SCSI
Network Interface Card	Intel EtherExpress Pro 100
Switching Hub	OmniSTACK Hub
HDD	Segate ST34520W(5), ST34371W(2), ST39140W(1)

[Table 2] S/W environment using experiment

Operating system	Linux Kernel 2.2.9
Placed media	Text, Image, Audio(MP3), Video(MPEG1)
User input pattern	User request arrival interval is Exponential distribution

4.2 Performance evaluation

We select the deadline miss ratio as a performance metric. To evaluate PMFS's performance, we compare PMFS with PVFS in terms of the dead line miss ratio as a function of users arrival rates.

[Table 3] System specification of PVFS and PMFS

File system	PVFS	PMFS
Server Architecture	2-layered distributed cluster	2-layered distributed cluster
Operating system	Linux 2.x	Linux 2.x , Solaris, FreeBSD
Protocol	TCP/IP	TCP/IP, UDP/IP
Data transmission type	Centralized Shared Data	Centralized Shared Data Distributed Message Based
Data placement policies	Static starting block – Round Robin	Random starting block – Round Robin, Staggered striping
Scheduling policy	FIFO	EDF

As shown in Figure 4, D-R-Staggered policy shows better result than other policy and PVFS. The performance of PVFS is similar to that of PMFS with C-S-RR placement policy but the higher the load, the better the performance of PMFS. Particularly, even when the system load is low, PMFS with D-R-Staggered shows good performance and as the system load gets higher, the performance of PMFS gets better. This is because, PMFS has a scheduling policy based on IO tasks' deadline and is implemented using message distribution technique that it could reduce the scheduling load of the control server. Moreover, D-R-Staggered striping could reduce the disk scheduling overhead by avoiding disk request collision. The experimental results are shown in Figure 4.

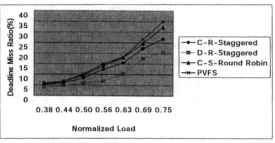

[Figure 4] Deadline miss ratio with different numbers of users

4.3 File read

4.3.1 Performance evaluation with different data placement policies

We measured the performance of R-Staggered, S-Staggered, R-Round Robin and S-round robin placement policies to check which placement policy fits well with multimedia data in PMFS.

1) Static starting block VS. random starting block placement policy

Experimental results show that random starting block placement policy shows the low deadline miss ratio about 7-14% compared to the static starting block placement policy. In case of static starting block placement policy, the disk(s) holding the initial portions of the requested data happened to be accessed heavily , which causes the disk load unbalance.

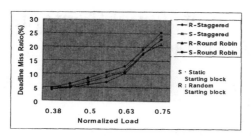

[Figure 5] Deadline miss ratio according to Data placement policies by Message Distribution

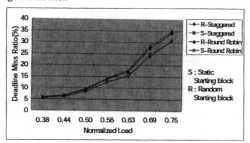

[Figure 6] Deadline miss ratio according to Data placement policies Centralized Shared Data structure

However, in case of random starting block placement policy, we show that performance show the moderate results because the starting blocks are dispersed over all disks fairly.

2) Round Robin VS. Staggered striping

Experimental results show that staggered striping placement policy shows the low deadline miss ratio about 3-16% compared to the round robin block placement policy. This is because, with staggered striping, IO requests for disks could be reduced more than with round robin striping policy

4.4 File write

As shown in Figure 7, we compared PMFS with PVFS in terms of data block size. PMFS is 5% better than PVFS on the average and the larger block size, the better the PMFS. When block size is 128K, PMFS shows the best performance.

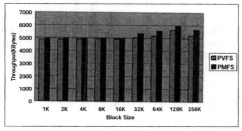

[Figure 7] Comparison of throughput with different block size

5. Conclusion and future works

In this paper, we designed and implemented a parallel multimedia file system called PMFS, which is optimized for multimedia applications and designed to run at the application level. PMFS is designed for the two-layered distributed cluster server consisting of a control node and multiple storage nodes. It uses a message distribution techniques for I/O among user library functions, the control node and storage nodes. Storage nodes directly transmit data to the clients in order to reduce the overhead of the control node and internal network traffic. Moreover, to support both real-time and non-real time multimedia data, PMFS provides multiple types of data placement policies including Round Robin, staggered striping and DIS. PMFS is designed to be installed and transplanted to any operating system. Moreover, it provides users with the flexibility to adjust block size, select data placement policy and replication policy and set IO deadline at users' will.

Through the perform evaluation, we showed that PMFS shows the best performance when data is placed using by DIS policy combined with random starting block placement policy and data is transferred using message distributed technique. Moreover, PMFS showed better performance than PVFS did in case of heavy system load. As a further research, we will do study about the effect of various real-time scheduling policies in terms of response time in case of IODs failure.

6. REFERENCES

[1] Asit Dan, Dinkar Sitaram, "An Online Video Placement Policy based on Bandwidth to Space Ratio(BSR)", Proceedings of ACM SIGMOD International Conference on Management of Data, 1995.

[2] R. L. Haskin, "The Shark Continuous Media File Server," Proc. of IEEE 1993 Spring COMPCON, pp. 12-17, 1993

[3] Asit Dan, M.Kienzle, D.Sitaram, "A dynamic policy of segment replication for load balancing in video-on-demand servers", Proc. of Multimedia Systems 3:93~105, 1995.

[4] Roger Zimmermann, "Continuous Display Using Heterogeneous Disk Subsystems", Ph.D Dissertation, University of Southern California, Computer Science Department, 1998.

[5] R. Tewari et.al., "Design and performance tradeoffs in clustered video servers," Proc. Of International Conference on Multimedia Computing and Systems pp 144-150, 1996

[6] Robert Flynn, William Tetzlaff, "Disk Striping and Block Replication Algorithms For Video File Servers," IEEE Conference on Multimedia Computing and Systems, 1996.

[7] Heinz Stockinger, "Dictionary on Parallel Input/Output", Master's Thesis, University of Vienna, Austria, 1998.

[8] Frank Fabbrocino, Jose Renato Santos, Richard Muntz, "An Implicitly Scalable, Fully Interactive Multimedia Storage Server", 2nd International Workshop on Distributed Interactive Simulation and Real Time Applications, 1998.

[9] D. J. Gemmel, "Disk Scheduling for Continuous Media," Multimedia Information Storage and Management, chapter 1, Kluwer Academic Publishers, 1996.

Efficient Tools for Power Annotation of Visual Contents: A Lexicographical Approach

Youngchoon Park
Roz Software Systems, Inc.
4417 N Saddlebag Trail, #3
Scottsdale, AZ 85251
Telephone number: +1(480) 941-2226
ypark@rozsoftware.com

ABSTRACT

Techniques for content-based image or video retrieval are not mature enough to recognize visual semantic completely. Whereas retrieval based on color, size, texture and shape are within the state of the art, our investigations on human factor analysis indicate that it is necessary to use captions or text annotations that are associated with photos and videos in content access of visual data. In this paper, a framework for integration of textual and visual content searching mechanism is presented. The framework includes ontology-based semantic query expansion, database navigation in a conceptual hierarchy, and a computational model for degree of term similarity calculation. The proposed method is embedded and evaluated in our novel content-based image database system called PicDB™.

Keywords

Concept indexing, image database, multimedia

1. INTRODUCTION

Advances in Internet, still and motion picture capturing and compression and the proliferation of multimedia information systems have lead to the generation of large on-line collections of images and videos, creating a demand for new methodologies to retrieve specific images and videos. To satisfy the demand, recent research has generated significant improvements in visual information retrieval (VIR). Content-based visual information retrieval has emerged as a promising yet challenging research area in the last decade. As a consequence of the research activities, several prototype systems and commercial retrieval engines have been developed [1],[3],[5],[6]. Such systems support various query modes such as query by example, query by sketch, query by color, query by spatial color distribution, as well as a mixture of several different query modes incorporated within a single or multi-feature based searching techniques.

Inspite of those extensive research activities, still content-based image or video retrieval is not capable of complete understanding of visual information, in particular, semantics of visual

information. Matching based on color, size, texture and shape are within the state of the art. However. moving beyond visual characteristics into the actual content (or semantic) of visual data is considerably more difficult [5]. Conceptual classification of visual data, for example, identification of person in an out-door scene, has received preliminary attentions, however is not yet mature. Even when the technology matures, there are elements of meaning that visual data may not convey. Such data are contextual, consisting of temporal, spatial, or instance information. In other words, semantic interpretation of visual data is incomplete without some mechanism for understanding semantic content that is not directly visible. For this reason, human assisted content-annotation through natural language is the one of most common methods, particularly in multimedia retrieval applications, and provides a means for exploiting syntactic, semantic as well as lexical information. A simple form of human-assisted semantic annotation is an attachment of textual description (i.e, a keyword, or a simple sentence) to visual data. Textual annotations may convey name of a visual object, property of a visual object, event happening in visual context, and action performed by an individual visual object or a group of visual objects. With proper structuring of those text descriptions, natural language based query may be used in content access of visual information. In retrieval of visual data with associated textual information, morphology (interpretation of word elements such as suffixes) is simple to implement and more accurate than wild cards. Inflectional morphology is far more important than derivational morphology. Thesaurus can be used in synonym matching. Hence, users do not need to guess which words to use -- auto racing should retrieve car racing. In fact, a semantic net is superior to a synonym list or thesaurus, since it includes a knowledge hierarchy. Term expansion can be performed on the query.

2. HUMAN FACTORS IN VISUAL CONTENT ACCESS

Ordinary users tend to use a noun or noun phrase to give a name of an image rather than use a complete sentences. The average number of the words used in picture naming is 4.7 (including articles and adjectives, 2.3 for noun and verbs). However, in semantic description, most participants (92.8%) try to use complete sentences followed. The most common grammatical elements in annotation are noun, verb and complement. The number of sentences that are used to describe the content of an image are correlated to the number of objects in an image. In our experiments, we observed that 93% of people use nouns as main querying terms. Even in action or activity retrieval, participants used nouns. Based on these results, we may conclude that one of the most demanding capabilities of visual information retrieval is *visual object retrieval in semantic recognition level* such as: "Find an image containing "President Clinton addressing out of space aliens". Simple and complex information retrievals benefit from representations that handle concepts expressible in natural language by more than one word.

From the experiments, we have noticed that retrieving a visual object based on mental experiences (later, we will call this as "Conceptual entity") tend to show lesser existence of subjectivities. Even though, denumerable symbolic descriptions of a visual object may exist in computational world.

3. ROZ's POWER ANNOTATION

Content-based image or video access systems provide only appearance based retrieval modes with keyword match (exact matching). However, most users want to find visual information based on the semantics of visual contents such as actions happening in a scene, etc. However, state-of-the art technologies for visual semantic analysis are not mature yet. However, simple keyword based retrieval requires users to memorize all the annotated keywords. In order to resolve this problem we use concept-based retrieval of annotated visual semantics.

One way of representing the semantic contents for a certain conceptual domain is an ontological organization that may be represented by means of a digraph. In a digraph, a point represents a distinct concept (which may be verbalized in more than one way and may have more than one label, and to which is appended a set of syntactic, semantic and usage features) and a line represents an instance of some set of operators which act on the verbalizations or labels of a point according to the features of that point to yield the parametric values of another point. It should go without saying that the complete portrayal of a dictionary according to this model requires a considerable amount of further work; nonetheless, we believe that the model provides the appropriate framework for conceptual retrieval of visual content access.

Terms in an ontology must be selected with great care, ensuring that the most fundamental (abstract, or foundational) concepts and distinctions are defined and specified. The terms chosen form a complete set, whose relationships to one another are defined using formal techniques. It defines the relationships that provide the semantic basis for the terminology chosen. Although taxonomy contributes to the semantics of a term in a vocabulary, ontologies include richer semantic (or conceptual) relationships between terms. These rich relationships enable the representation of domain-specific knowledge, without the need to include domain-specific terms. The adoption of a shared ontology allows us to interoperate without misunderstanding, retain a high degree of autonomy, flexibility and agility. In addition, an information retrieval system can have benefits with formalized and structured ontology. Benefits are (1) Reduction of the number of trial-and-errors to find correct keywords, (2) Improvement of precision rates by eliminating the polysemy in description, and (3) Improvement of recall rates through conceptual hierarchy navigation.

When we want to use a conceptual annotation in visual information retrieval, similarity based retrieval should be involved rather than a filtering approaches. Typically, textual annotations are used in filter processing in visual information retrieval. For instance, in QBIC and Excalibur, when a keyword and a visual content (i.e., shape) is provided as a query, the systems then retrieve images that contains the given keyword annotation and perform similarity search on the visual content. However, stepping down or expending the concept is required in search, as well as search weight assignment on each retrieval options. For instance, a weight combination may look like "50% on conceptual match, 40% on color match and 10% of texture match". We assume that users proper to use keywords such as visual object names, actions and events in retrieval with conjunction with various visual query options.

3.1 Computation of conceptual distance

The basic motivation in the development of similarity measurement of textual concept is that a conceptual structure (in general, it is a lattice) can be converted into a graph. The graph is organized based on the **conceptual hierarchy** (See Figure 1). In the hierarchy, conceptual entities are abstracted from bottom to top. In the top (root concept) is an empty concept denoted by ∅.

As discussed previously, most users use nouns in information retrieval because they capture most conceptual entities. Therefore, it is reasonable to consider a noun as a conceptual entity. With this mind, we use WordNet™[2] which provides one of the most complete collections of English nouns with acceptable conceptual hierarchy. However, it dose not have proper level of word classification at higher level to map human conceptual entity to corresponding words. The reason is that relationships between concepts established based on the linguistic criteria do not often correspond obviously to relationships between classes of conceptual entities in mental world. The restriction is applied in annotation. Annotation must have a concept type appeared in WordNet™.

To develop a distance measurement metric between two distinct conceptual entities, we assumed that a conceptual organization structure is a graph. And the graph represents a conceptual hierarchy, we can say that if conceptual entities are in the same level and have the same relations on the concept located at the immediate upper level, then those conceptual elements are conceptually very close.

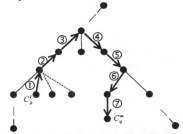

Figure 1. Conceptual distance calculated is based on the travel cost

Definition 1. From the given paths $\mathbf{P} = \{P_1, P_2, ..., P_n\}$, a semantic distance between two adjacent conceptual entities C_i^l and C_j^{l-1} connected through link P_i is as follows. Where C_i^l and C_j^{l-1} are i^{th} and j^{th} conceptual entities located at level l and $(l\text{-}1)$, respectively, and have a conceptual relation on path i.

$$S_{P_i}^s(C_i^l, C_j^{l-1}) = \delta \varphi w_{l \Rightarrow (l-1)}^{P_i}$$

Where δ is an inter-level discrimination constant, φ is an intra-level discrimination constant, and $w_{l \Rightarrow (l-1)}^{P_i}$ is a travel cost from C_i^l to C_j^{l-1} defined by the conceptual relation between

C_i^l and C_j^{l-1}. In WordNet™, possible relations among nouns are ISA, HAS_PART, MEMBER_OF, and HAS_SUBSTANCE. δ is responsible for maintaining conceptual distance within a single level. If δ is large, then conceptual distance among concepts within a certain level in hierarchy is getting increased. Similarly, φ is responsible for management of distance between levels. When φ is getting larger then conceptual distance among levels in hierarchy is getting larger. φ is decreased from top to bottom. A typical φ is appeared as $\varphi = C \times (\text{Max\_Level} - \text{Current\_level})$. C is a scaling factor for intra-level discrimination. A formula for φ has to be designed carefully.

Definition 2. From the given paths $\mathbf{P} = \{P_1, P_2, ..., P_n\}$. A similarity distance, S^s of two conceptual entities C_p^l and C_q^m is defined as follows:

$$S^s(C_p^l, C_q^m) = \sum_{i=1}^{NoOfLinks} S_{P_i}^s$$

Definition 3. A similarity distance, S^s of two conceptual entities C_p^l and C_q^m is a symmetric.

$$S^s(C_p^l, C_q^m) = S^s(C_q^m, C_p^l)$$

Definition 4. A content similarity between two visual object i and j; $S_c(VO_i, VO_j)$ is defined as follows:

$$S^c(VO_i, VO_j) = \alpha S^s(VO_i, VO_j) + \beta S^v(VO_i, VO_j)$$

Where, α and β are weight factors for conceptual similarity and visual similarity, respectively. S^v is a visual similarity measurement between two visual objects. For instance, Histogram similarity or shape similarity are belonging to S^v.

Based on the formulation, similarity matching is a straight forward.

δ	1	1	1	1		1	1
φ	9*9	9*8	9*7	9*6		9*5	9*4
level	1	2	3	4		5	6

"∅→entity→object→artifact⟨ covering→footwear→boot
instrumentation→transport→vehicle→motor vehicle→automobile↓boot

level	1	2	3	4	5	6	7	8	9
φ	9*9	9*8	9*7	9*6	9*5	9*4	9*3	9*2	9*1
δ	1	1	1	1	1	1	1	1	1.5

In similarity comparison, the distance calculation is done by counting the cost to travel from C_p^l = "automobile#boot" and C_q^m = "footware#boot". By the definition of similarity measurement, $S^s(automobile\#boot, footware\#boot)$ is $(9\times1.5+9\times2+9\times3+9\times4+9\times5+9\times6)+(9\times6+9\times5+9\times4) = 328.5$. Let us consider three conceptual entities, "covering", "transport", and "automobile". Conceptually, a concept "automobile" is closer to the concept "transport" than covering. The number of links from covering to transport, and from automobile to transport is the same (they are 3). With our calculation, $9\times6+9\times6+9\times5 = 153$ is the distance from covering to transport. However, $9\times2+9\times3+9\times4 = 81$ is the distance from automobile to transport.

So far we have demonstrated how semantic distance of conceptual entities appeared as noun in a conceptual hierarchy.

4. IMPIRICAL ANALYSIS

To evaluate the retrieval performance of the proposed methods, we use the two traditional metrics, namely, precision and recall. Recall measures the ability of the systems to retrieve all images that are relevant, whereas precision measures the ability of the system in retrieving only images that are relevant. In this experiments, 11,822 images were considered as a test set. We ran 10 different test queries against this image set. To verify the correctness of retrieval, we manually investigated the retrieval-answers. The host system for the tests was a Pentium III machine with a 600 MHz processor and 512 MB of memory.

The result tells us there are significant improvements in both precision and recall rate.

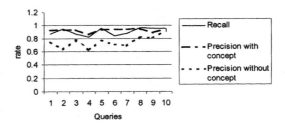

Figure 2. Comparison of query result with/without concept

5. CONCLUSION

A framework for integration of textual and visual content searching mechanism is presented. The framework leads us to develop ontology-based semantic query expansion, database navigation in a conceptual hierarchy, and a computational model for degree of term similarity calculation. The proposed similarity measuring technique can be easily expanded to handling for indexing and retrieval of multiple concepts.

6. REFERENCES

[1] Y.-H. Ang, et al, "Image information retrieval systems", in C.H. Chen, et al, (Eds.) Handbook of Pattern Recognition and Computer Vision, pp 719-739. World Scientific, 1993.

[2] Christiane Fellbaum (ed.), WordNet: An Electronic Lexical Database MIT Press, 1998

[3] M. Flickner et al. "Query by image and video content: The QBIC system", IEEE Computer, 28(9), pp23-32, 1995.

[4] Peter Gardenfors, "Frameworks for properties: Possible worlds vs. conceptual spaces", Language Knowledge and Intentionality (Acta Philosophia Fennica vol.49) pp 383-407, 1991

[5] F. Golshani, Y.C. Park, "Content-based Image Indexing and Retrieval in ImageRoadMap", Proc. SPIE Conf. on Multimedia Storage and Archiving Systems II, Dallas, TX, 1997.

[6] J. Z. Wang, et al, "Semantics-sensitive Retrieval for Digital Picture Libraries" D-Lib. Magazine,

A Digital Television Navigator

Chengyuan Peng
Telecommunications Software and
Multimedia Laboratory,
Helsinki University of Technology,
P.O. Box 5400, FI-02015 HUT, Finland.
Tel. +358 9 4515720

pcy@tcm.hut.fi

Prof. Petri Vuorimaa
Telecommunications Software and
Multimedia Laboratory,
Helsinki University of Technology,
P.O. Box 5400, FI-02015 HUT, Finland.
Tel. +358 9 4514794

Petri.Vuorimaa@hut.fi

ABSTRACT

Digital television is a new, interesting, and rich platform for developing next generation multimedia services. One of the key digital television standards is Multimedia Home Platform (MHP) which includes hardware devices and software architecture. Navigator is the most important multimedia service of digital television. It acts the main index of all the services available in set-top box. In this paper we presented a Java Navigator developed in Future TV project.

Keywords

Navigator, digital television, MHP, set-top box, multimedia service, SI, transport stream, Java, network.

1. INTRODUCTION

The Multimedia Home Platform (MHP) is specified by the Digital Video Broadcasting (DVB). It is a common platform for user to transparently access a range of multimedia services. Its hardware devices consist of the home terminal (set-top box, TV, PC), its peripherals, and the in-home digital network.

Digital television platform fulfils the DVB-MHP requirements for implementation of multimedia services.

Navigator is a resident application in set-top box for enhanced broadcasting (without a return channel). It is a part of the system software. The Navigator is typically provided by the set-top box manufacturer. Its functionality and look & feel are also determined by the manufacturer.

The viewers of tomorrow will receive a multitude of channels with their set-top box. These services range from interactive television, to near video-on-demand, and to specialized programs. The viewer needs help. The Navigator is the guide of the viewer to select services and applications, initiate interoperable applications, boot loading, and store user profiles.

The DVB-SI broadcast specifications provides the information structures necessary for the development of a basic Navigator. The Navigator uses the DVB-SI data supplied by the network operator or the broadcaster.

The DVB-SI data is multiplexed together with MPEG-2 compressed video and audio data streams to form a transport stream. The multiplexed transport stream must be demultiplexed in the set-top box before the Navigator can use it. The DVB-SI adds information that enables set-top box to tune automatically to particular services and allows services to be grouped into categories with relevant schedule information.

The viewer can activate the Navigator at any time with a remote control. Usually there is a button labeled *"Navigator"* in the remote control. When the viewer presses the *"Navigator"* button, the main graphical user interface will be displayed, through which the viewer then can navigate the services provided by set-top box manufacture, broadcaster, and service provider.

2. TRANSPORT STREAM AND DVB-SI

Transport stream packets are derived from elementary streams, service information, private data, and conditional access control. All the packetized elementary streams, including video and audio, that are multiplexed together are converted into transport packets. Similarly, the DVB-SI data, private data, and conditional access control data are converted into transport packets.

The resulting transport packets are then output sequentially to form an MPEG-2 transport packet stream. Null transport packets are used to soak-up any spare multiplex capacity, which can also appear in the transport stream.

MPEG-2 allows a separate Service Information system to be used to complement its Program Specific Information (PSI). The DVB-SI with accompanied DVB signals can be used by set-top box. Therefore the viewer may navigate through the array of offered services.

The DVB-SI is based on four service information tables (PSI), plus a series of optional tables. Each table contains ordinary fields and descriptors fields outlining the characteristics of the services/events being described.

The PSI data is structured in four tables, i.e. *Program Association Table (PAT), Conditional Access Table (CAT), Program Map Table (PMT),* and *Network Information Table (NIT).*

In addition to the PSI, the additional data is needed to provide identification of services and events carried by different multiplexes, and even on other networks. This data is structured in the following tables: *Bouquet Association Table (BAT)*, *Service Description Table (SDT)*, and *Event Information Table (EIT)* (including present/following and schedule tables), etc.

The DVB-SI tables are transmitted in sections. Each table must be segmented into one or more sections with the same *table_id* as the table before being inserted into transport stream packets. A section is in fact a syntactic structure. Sections may be variable in length. Each section is uniquely identified by the combination of the five fields in a section, such as *table_id, section_number*, etc.

3. NAVIGATOR FUNCTIONALITY

There are five main functions in the Navigator (cf. Fig. 1): *Channel Info Bar*, *Channel Guide*, *Program Guide* (i.e., EPG), *Services*, and *Configuration*. All these views can be accessed via the main user interface. Pushing the *"Navigator"* button on the remote control displays the main menu of the Navigator. Next, the viewer presses the *"up"* or *"down"* arrow and *"OK"* button to select a particular function of the Navigator (cf. Fig. 1).

Fig. 1. The Main Menu of the Navigator.

3.1 Channel Info Bar

The purpose of the *Channel Info Bar* is to show the information of the current program/event immediately. Thus the viewer does not need to browse the newspaper or textTV.

When the viewer presses a *"TV"* button, the *Channel Info Bar* is displayed on the screen (cf. Fig. 2). The *Channel Info Bar* displays current channel and program/event information (i.e., service/channel name, channel logo, event name, detailed information about the current event, and the date and time of the set-top box).

The information comes from the EIT present/following table and SDT table. Two descriptors are used in the *Channel Info Bar* (i.e., *Short Event descriptor* and *Extended Event Descriptor*). The *Short Event Descriptor* transmits the name and a short text description for the event. The language code indicates in which language the text was written. The *Extended Event Descriptor* provides a detailed text description of the event.

Fig. 2. The Channel Info Bar.

3.2 Channel Guide

The *Channel Guide* (cf. Fig. 3) is used to help the viewer to browse the present and following program/event of all the channels/services available in the broadcasting network. The right panel shows the present (upper part) and following (lower part) program information about current selected channel. It has the same data information carried in the EIT present/following table as the *Channel Info Bar*.

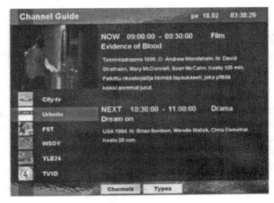

Fig. 3. The Channel Guide User Interface.

The left upper part is a MPEG-1 video stream which was used to show the selected channel video. The left lower panel shows channel information (i.e., channel logos and channel names).

The channel information is read from the SDT table. Its *Service Descriptor* field contains service name and service provider name.

3.3 Program Guide

The *Program Guide* is a simple EPG. It has seven days program schedule information for the channels. Fig. 4 shows the *Program Guide* user interface. It has the same date and real time clock display as the *Channel Guide* user interface.

The right upper part displays one day's program schedule of the selected channel. The *"up"* or *"down"* arrows can be used to browse the program schedule information. At the same time, the detailed text information of the program is displayed on the lower part of the Fig. 4. The video will not change, thus the viewer can still watch the current program when browsing the schedule information of the programs. When the viewer presses the "TV" button, the Navigator returns to full screen video from the *Program Guide*.

The Navigator can also store EPG data in set-top box in order to save searching time.

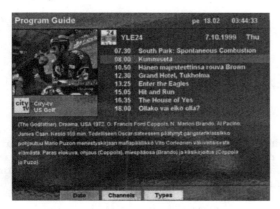

Fig. 4. The Program Guide User Interface

3.4 Services
The *Services* provides a list of multimedia services, e.g., www, Email, Home-shopping, and Screen Information service.

3.5 Configuration
The *Configuration* function is used to initialize and set up the set-top box. Initialization includes caching network information in the NIT table from transmission and downloading drivers, operating system, and applications from transmission or modem. Setting contains setting up network connections, look & feel of the user interface, and user preferences, such as aspect ratio, subtitle language, etc.

The Navigator stores NIT information in a binary file instead of non-volatile memory as suggested in ETS. The stored information includes the name of a physical network, the information about transport streams of the delivery system, a list of all services carried in all the transport streams, and the physical parameters for each transport stream in the network. These physical parameters come from delivery system descriptors These parameters are frequency, orbital-position, polarization, modulation, symbol rate, etc.

4. IMPLEMENTATION
The Navigator initialization is done when the set-top box is initialized, or a new version of the Navigator is downloaded. There is no need for the viewer to initiate it often, because searching the network takes quite a lot of time.

The following initialization includes scanning all accessible networks, storing all the services and types transmitted in multiplexed transport streams. Finally, the Navigator initializes the components of Java user interface (i.e., the look & feel).

Fig. 5 illustrates the first level data flow diagram of the Navigator. It was used to model information flow of the navigation process.

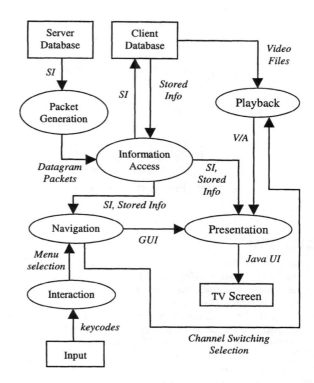

Fig. 5. Data Flow Diagram of the Navigator.

5. CONCLUSIONS
In this paper, we have described the process of implementing a basic set-top box Navigator in Java. This work demonstrated that parsing transport streams and decoding the DVB_SI data in the set-top box are the key functions of the Navigator for retrieving and updating its data information. Furthermore, Java is a good platform for coding the Navigator and accessing data from files and network. It is especially suitable for coding remote control events, the graphical user interface, etc.

Our work constitutes a basis for developing other multimedia services in the set-top box (e.g., Near Video-on-Demand, mosaic services, enhanced Teletext service, etc), designing the user interface of these services, decoding, displaying and controlling subtitles in the set-top box, etc.

We plan to embed the Navigator bytecodes in our system and make it work with other system functions and services in real broadcasting environment. Another goal is to develop other multimedia services as mentioned above in conjunction with DSM_CC (Digital Storage Media Command and Control) data carousels and object carousels. We also plan to improve the data access functions, e.g., reading EPG data from Teletext info, getting channel logos by decoding subtitles information, etc.

6. ACKNOWLEDGMENTS
The Future TV project is funded by the National Technology Agency of Finland together with major Finnish television, telecommunications, and digital media companies.

The author would also like to thank Nokia Oyj Foundation for the support.

From *Coarse to Fine* Skin and Face Detection

Hichem Sahbi
Imedia Research Group
INRIA, BP 105, F-78153
Le Chesnay, France
Email: Hichem.Sahbi@inria.fr

Nozha Boujemaa
Imedia Research Group
INRIA, BP 105, F-78153
Le Chesnay, France
Email: Nozha.Boujemaa@inria.fr

ABSTRACT

A method for fine skin and face detection is described that starts from a coarse color segmentation. Some regions represent parts of human skin and are selected by minimizing an error between the color distribution of each region and the output of a compression decompression neural network, which learns skin color distribution for several populations of different ethnicity. This ANN is used to find a collection of skin regions, which is used in a second learning step to provide parameters for a Gaussian mixture model. A finer classification is performed using a Bayesian framework and makes the skin and face detection invariant to scale and lighting conditions. Finally, a face shape based model is used to decide whether a skin region is a face or not.

Keywords

Color segmentation, Image Indexing, Bayesian classifier, Face detection, Neural Networks.

1. INTRODUCTION

The indexing of very large databases is a key challenge and an important issue in data mining. Several systems retrieve information using multiple descriptors, which include the color histogram, Fourier transform and edge orientation. Some descriptors suitable for face databases have been introduced and include ISS, flexible images [6] and eigenfaces. However the application of such descriptors on databases containing human faces is significant only if these descriptors are applied to the regions of interest (faces in our case), which means that a face localization process is required.

Several methods are discussed in the literature, including that developed by Rowley et al [4] who tests for the existence of faces of different sizes at each image position using a neural network. Leung et al [8] use a graph-matching method to find probable faces from detected facial features. These graphs are generated from the detected features and the true faces are detected among the candidates by random graph

matching. Goshtasby et al [5] use the chrominance invariant color space (ab) to learn skin color, using a Gaussian mixture model for color learning and face detection is performed using a template matching process.

Fleuret and Geman [3] have developed an algorithm, which is entirely based on the edge configurations, and does not take into account color information. This algorithm visits a hierarchical partition of the face pose space (the face pose is defined by the translation, orientation and scale parameters), and for each cell of this partition they compute the response of a dedicated detector. Each of these dedicated detectors estimates how many edge arrangements of a given set are present in the picture, and rejects the "face" hypothesis if a certain threshold is not obtained. Both the arrangement sets and the thresholds are estimated during a training stage with the ORL database.

In this paper we present an approach to precise skin and face detection based on the use of color space properties. This approach aims to track the variation in skin color distribution from one person to another. A coarse skin color learning stage from a very large population ethnicity is performed offline. This color model is used to seek skin regions and a finer color learning step is performed using a maximum confidence scheme in order to adapt parameters of the skin model to persons present in the scene. In the final stage, a skin/no-skin classification is performed using a mixture model and a Bayesian framework in order to have greater precision and a face shape based model is used to validate the face hypothesis.

2. *OFFLINE* TRAINING MODEL AND SKIN REGIONS DETECTION

To perform a better skin color learning process based on the conditions of the input image, we search for a distribution of pixel colors which is the most likely to be from human skin. An ad-hoc method, which attempts to search for every subset of the image pixels and to measure a distance for every combination from a given skin color model, is very time consuming. So we start by a coarse initial segmentation such as the DFDM method [9]. This segmentation provides connected regions which have a homogeneous local color distribution in the image space. Among these regions R_i, we have skin parts (noted S_{Ri}) which are detected using a distance E given by :

$$E(R_i) = \frac{1}{\|R_i\|} \sum_{(x,y)\in R_i} (\Phi(c_{(x,y)}) - c_{(x,y)})^2 \quad (1)$$

Here $c_{(x,y)}$ is the color of a pixel (x,y) represented in the normalized RGB color space. Φ is the output of a neural network trained over a large population of skin colors collected from the World Wide Web and Voila database[7]. A quadratic or more generally a nonlinear function such as one hidden layer neural network is a good choice for a satisfactory approximation of skin color distribution. The learning is performed using traditional back-propagation [1], and our network performs no linear PCA since for every color $c_{(x,y)}$ in the training set, the difference between the input and output is minimized.

For each candidate region to be a skin part, we use a decision rule based on computing an error between this region R_i and the learned model using (1). Our approach does not aim to classify each pixel directly into skin or no skin according to the ANN only. Indeed, a decision based on a direct computation of the error function E to each pixel color can cause an increase in the number of false positives and false negatives, related to noisy data and lighting variations (see Fig.(3).B). In order to reduce these effects, we learn the skin color under the lighting conditions of the input image, so the goal is to have a set of color pixels (which may even be small), in order to perform a second color training process for a better classification. Thus we summarize the "coarse-to-fine" algorithm as follows:

1. Learn the Neural Network weights from a skin color population which is different from the input image (Off-line Step).

2. For every request image I (On line step):

   - Do a coarse segmentation to have a collection of candidate regions R_i $i = 0...L$.

   - Classify each candidate region R_i as a skin or no skin region, which is undertaken by considering the regions where the error $E(R_i)$ is below a given threshold.

3.   *ACCURATE* FACE DETECTION

By considering K and $L - K$ clusters for both skin and noisy regions respectively, we make a decision rule for whether a pixel $X = (x,y)$ is a skin point given its color observation $c_{(x,y)}$, this decision rule is based on the following condition:

$$P(Y = 1|c_{(x,y)}) > P(Y = 0|c_{(x,y)}) \qquad (2)$$

Here $Y = 1$ (resp $Y = 0$) denotes the event which expresses that a pixel (x,y) is a skin (resp no-skin) point and $X = s_i$ (resp $X = n_i$) the event expressing that a pixel (x,y) is in the color distribution of S_{Ri} (resp N_i: The noisy region). The two members of equation (2) are given by:

$$P(Y = 1|c_{(x,y)}) = \sum_{i=1}^{K} \frac{P(c_{(x,y)}|X = s_i).P(X = s_i)}{P(c_{(x,y)})}$$

$$P(Y = 0|c_{(x,y)}) = \sum_{i=1}^{L-K} \frac{P(c_{(x,y)}|X = n_i).P(X = n_i)}{P(c_{(x,y)})}$$

We can fix the priors $P(Y = 1)$, $P(Y = 0)$ (the mixture parameters) to be equal, but a better characterization of

these coefficients is given by:

$$P(Y = 1) = \frac{1}{N.M} \sum_{i=1}^{K} \sum_{xy}^{N.M} P(X = s_i|c_{(x,y)})$$

$$P(Y = 0) = \frac{1}{N.M} \sum_{i=1}^{L-K} \sum_{xy}^{N.M} P(X = n_i|c_{(x,y)})$$

Here N and M are dimensions of the input image and the density function $P(X = s_i|c_{(x,y)})$ is modeled as a Gaussian having parameters which are estimated as explained in the following section.

3.1   Accurate online training Model

Let $x_1, ..., x_k, ..., x_{n_i}$ to be a quantification of colors in a skin region S_{Ri}, and $h_1, ..., h_k, ..., h_{n_i}$ the related histogram which denotes the color frequencies. The average μ_i and the variance-covariance Σ_i matrices, respectively are given by:

$$\mu_i = \frac{\sum_{k=1}^{n_i} h_k x_k}{\sum_{k=1}^{n_i} h_k}, \ \Sigma_i = \frac{\sum_{k=1}^{n_i} h_k (x_k - \mu_i)(x_k - \mu_i)^T}{\sum_{k=1}^{n_i} h_k}$$

During the generation of the parameters of the Gaussian model, the noisy points in a skin region S_{Ri} affect μ_i and Σ_i estimation quality. In order to reduce the effect of outliers, we model each skin region as two clusters which contain relevant and noisy skin points respectively. After we compute for each color in S_{Ri} the confidence coefficient [2] given by:

$$U_{pk} = \frac{1}{\sum_{q=1}^{2} [(d_{pk})^2/(d_{qk})^2]^{\frac{1}{(m-1)}}} \qquad (3)$$

$$J(U, v) = \sum_{p=1}^{2} \sum_{k=1}^{n_i} (U_{pk})^m (d_{pk})^2 \qquad (4)$$

Here U_{pk} expresses the color membership of a pixel color x_k to the cluster p (p is either skin or a noisy cluster) and d_{pk} is a simple Mahalanobis distance of the color x_k to the cluster p. Relating to [2], we perform a 2-mean fuzzy clustering of points present in each skin region into noisy and relevant skin points. This is carried out by minimizing the functional (4) which reaches its global minimum when each pixel color is assigned to its relevant (noisy or skin) cluster. This preprocessing step gives much greater accuracy to the learned parameters of the Gaussian model, which are now modified as follows:

$$\mu_i = \frac{\sum_{k=1}^{n_i} h_k U_{skin,k} x_k}{\sum_{k=1}^{n_i} h_k U_{skin,k}}, \ \Sigma_i = \frac{\sum_{k=1}^{n_i} h_k U_{skin,k}(x_k - \mu_i)(x_k - \mu_i)^T}{\sum_{k=1}^{n_i} h_k U_{skin,k}}$$

The coefficients $U_{skin,k}$ are introduced as weighting values to reduce the noise effects when computing the Gaussian model's parameters.

3.2   Shape model for frontal face detection

Given a skin region, a shape model is used to make a decision as to whether this region is a face or not. We compute two histograms corresponding to the horizontal and vertical sum of gray level information in the X and Y coordinates as shown in figure,1. These two histograms are smoothed using a Gaussian filtering function to eliminate high frequency components. A skin region is taken to be a frontal face if these two conditions are satisfied:

- The number of local extrema are three both in the horizontal and the vertical histograms and noted $x1,x2,x3$ and $y1,y2,y3$ respectively (see fig.1).

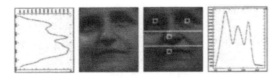

Figure 1: X and Y gray level histrogram projections used for frontal face feature detection.

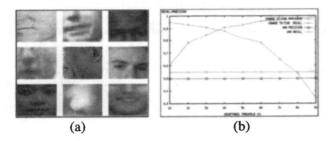

<table>
<tr><td>(a)</td><td>(b)</td></tr>
</table>

Figure 2: (a). A sample of skin maps from the WWW and Voila database used during the Off line learning process. (b)Recall and precision of skin classification for both (1) ANN direct classification (2) coarse to fine approach.

- We estimate the likelihood for $(x1, y1), (x3, y1), (x2, y2)$ and $(x2, y3)$ to be respectively eyes, nose and mouth coordinates using a learning model. A Gaussian mixture model is used where each cluster attempts to capture the statistical distribution of the (X,Y) coordinates of the related feature. A decision rule is made using a Bayesian classifier.

4. EXPERIMENTAL RESULTS

To evaluate the performance of our approach we collected a set of face maps from the World Wide Web, Voila and TF1 TV Channel databases. These images were chosen to span a wide range of environmental conditions (blur, noise,etc), with people of different ethnicity and various skin colors. The detection performances are estimated using the precision recall curves (see equations.(5),(6)) with respect to the acceptance rate σ which represents the fraction of accepted and used skin colors (considered as relevant) during the on-line learning step.

$$Precision = \frac{relevant\ detected\ skin\ pixels}{detected\ skin\ pixels} \quad (5)$$

$$Recall = \frac{relevant\ detected\ skin\ pixels}{all\ correct\ skin\ pixels} \quad (6)$$

According to the results (see fig3), even though the segmentation algorithm does not provide a good result, each detected skin region contains a significant part of skin color distribution, which is sufficient to perform a successful learning process. Figure 2.(b) presents the precision-recall curves in both direct color filtering (using the ANN directly) and the coarse-to-fine approach. From this diagram, a considerable improvement is observed in both precision and recall for our method with respect to the direct filtering approach.

5. CONCLUSION

A "coarse to fine" method is presented for a finer skin detection based on the combination of two coarse approaches.

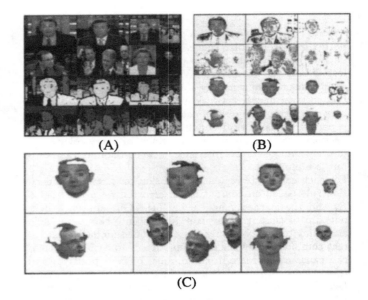

<table>
<tr><td>(A)</td><td>(B)</td></tr>
<tr><td colspan="2">(C)</td></tr>
</table>

Figure 3: (A) Segmentation using the DFDM.(B) Skin detection using repectively ANN and coarse to fine approaches (C) Frontal face detection using the shape model.

We start from a coarse segmentation method, which performs a subdivision of an image into regions of homogeneous color properties and a neural network skin detector provides a vote to select regions of interest among candidates. We can use our skin classifier as an input to Rowely et al face detector [4] to obtain a finer and fast face detection. This can be performed by applying their ANN detector only in the skin regions detected by our algorithm.
In future work we propose a shape model able to handle large variations in face pose to decide whether a skin region is a face or not. Minimizing an error based on the unification of face shape and skin color seems to be a promising approach and allows greater accuracy of face detection.

Acknowledgment: We would like to thank TF1, the French TV Channel for providing us images for tests.

6. REFERENCES

[1] C. Bishop. *Neural Networks for Pattern Recognition.* CLARENDON PRESS OXFORD, 1995.

[2] R. N. Dave. Characterization and detection of noise in clustering. *Pattern recognition*, 12(11):657–664, 1991.

[3] F. Fleuret and D. Geman. Graded learning for object detection. *Statistical and Computational Theories of Vision workshop at CVPR*, 1999.

[4] S. B. H. Rowley and T. Kanade. Neural network-based face detection. *IEEE Transactions on Pattern Analysis and Machine Intelligence*, 20(1):23–38, 1998.

[5] A. G. J. Cai. Detecting humans faces in color images. *Image and Vision Computing*, 18(1):63–75, 2000.

[6] C. Nastar and A. Pentland. Matching and recognition using deformable intensity surfaces. *In Proc. IEEE Sym. on Comp. Vision*, 1995.

[7] J. E. V. R. Féraud, O. Bernier and M. Collobert. A fast and accurate face detector for indexation of face images. *fourth IEEE Int. Conf on Automatic Face and Gesture Recognition, Grenoble*, 2000.

[8] M. B. T. Leung and P. Perona. Finding faces in cluttered scenes using random labelled graph matching. *Fifth Int. Conf on Computer Vision ICCV*, 1995.

[9] A. Winter and C. Nastar. Differential feature distribution maps for image segmentation and region queries in image databases. *CBAIVL workshop at CVPR*, 1999.

A Formal Approach for the Presentation of Interactive Multimedia Documents

P.N.M. Sampaio, J.P. Courtiat

LAAS – CNRS

7 Av. du Colonel Roche

31400   Toulouse – France

Tel: (33) 5.61.33.62.44

{psampaio, courtiat}@laas.fr

ABSTRACT

This paper presents the on-going work using a formal approach for the design of Interactive Multimedia Documents (IMDs) based on the RT-LOTOS formal description technique. The present work extends this approach proposing the scheduling of IMDs based on a simple and operational model obtained as a result from the reachability analysis. One important breakthrough of this model is that it is a scheduling graph that provides the control of the occurrence of non-deterministic events, such as user interactions, within valid temporal intervals so that the global synchronization constraints of the document can be fulfilled during its presentation. Further on, some scheduling policies are also presented based on this model. Finally, we introduce some characteristics of the player actually available for the presentation of IMDs based on this new model.

Keywords

Formal Methods, LOTOS, RT-LOTOS, Multimedia and Hypermedia Documents

1.   INTRODUCTION

The design of Interactive Multimedia Documents (IMDs) has been largely addressed by the proposal of several models, languages and authoring tools. For instance, SMIL [1], NCM [2], Firefly [3], IMAP [4], MADEUS [5], etc. Most of these works concern the specification of synchronization constraints and authoring requirements, but few of them address the identification and analysis of consistency properties of an IMD [3, 5, 6].

The methodology presented in this paper aims to provide a framework for the design (specification, verification and presentation) of complex *Interactive Multimedia Documents (IMDs)* which relies on the Formal Description Technique RT-LOTOS [7], and its associated verification/simulation tool RTL, developed at LAAS-CNRS. Using this formal approach for the design of IMD's has three main advantages. First, it provides a formal semantics to the high-level authoring model, describing without any ambiguity the behavior of the document during its

presentation. Second, it enables to check consistency properties on the formal specification derived from the authoring model, using standard verification techniques. Finally, it provides a consistent and operational representation for the scheduling of the document.

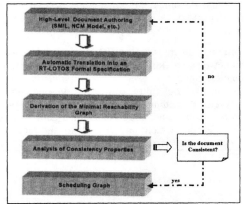

Figure 1   Formal design methodology of IMDs

The methodology applied for the formal design of IMD's is illustrated in Figure 1. This methodology provides a high flexibility for the author during the edition of the IMD since he is able to describe his document using the authoring model of his preference, such as SMIL [1], NCM [2], etc. Then, the logical and temporal structure of the document can be automatically translated into an RT-LOTOS specification which describes completely the semantics of the document. It is important to emphasize that the RT-LOTOS specification is, then, kept totally hidden to the author during the specification and verification phases.

Once the RT-LOTOS specification for the respective IMD is available, a minimal reachability graph can be obtained as a result to some verification techniques developed and implemented for RT-LOTOS within the RTL software tool [7]. Later on, based on the reachability graph, we are able to verify the temporal consistency of the document. Thus, some reachability properties can be determined in order to ensure that all the temporal constraints associated with the components of the document are fulfilled during its presentation. Furthermore, aggregation techniques can also be applied in order to avoid the state space explosion problem that may come up with the utilization of labeled transition systems.

If all the temporal constraints of the document can be fulfilled (if the document is consistent), then we are able to perform the scheduling of its presentation. The scheduling is, then, accomplished based on an appropriate representation (scheduling graph) which is obtained from the reachability graph. The scheduling graph is simple and operational enough and still provides the controllability of the document during its presentation. In opposite, if the document is still inconsistent after the reachability analysis, its high-level description must be revisited. For this purpose, the reachability analysis provides a feedback for the author proposing valid solutions for the presentation of the document. In particular, with respect to the occurrence of non-controllable events, such as user interactions.

The next section details the verification of consistency for IMD's with an illustrative example, and furthermore, presents how IMD's can be scheduled.

2. CONSISTENCY ANALYSIS AND SCHEDULING OF INTERACTIVE MULTIMEDIA DOCUMENTS

The formal verification of consistency of IMD's using RT-LOTOS has been previously addressed in [6, 8, 9]. In [6], a document was considered as *consistent* if the action characterizing the *start* of the document presentation is necessarily followed (some time later) by an action characterizing the *end* of the presentation.

This definition was revisited in [9] in order to make a clear distinction between two kinds of events that may lead to temporal inconsistencies, namely: *Internal non-deterministic* events which are related to the flexibility of media presentation duration (themselves related to admissible QoS adjustments for the media), as well as to incomplete timing constraints, and; *External non-deterministic* events which are related to the occurrence of external events, such as user interactions on anchors, network

delays and processing results from data-base queries, scientific simulations, and so on. Thus, temporal inconsistencies may be the consequence of either *internal* or *external* non-determinism, or even both. Basically, the temporal consistency of a document can be determined by the identification of the inconsistency sources of a temporal scenario and, then, checking whether they can be handled by a temporal formatter.

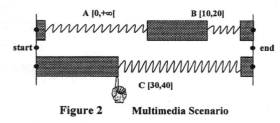

Figure 2   Multimedia Scenario

To illustrate the utilization of this methodology, let us consider Figure 2 which depicts a multimedia scenario that describes the simultaneous presentation of a sequence of two media objects (*A* and *B*) with the interactive media object *C*. Media object *A* has an unknown presentation duration, that is, it is comprised within [0,+∞[seconds. In opposite, the presentation duration of media object *B* is comprised within [10,20]. *C* is an interactive media object and its maximal presentation duration is 40 seconds; it can be interrupted by the user at anytime within [30,40] seconds. If there is no user interaction, the presentation of *C* finishes therefore at 40 seconds. As synchronization constraints, the presentation of media objects *A* and *C* must start together, and presentation of media objects *B* and *C* must terminate together. In this example, observe that a valid temporal interval must be determined for the presentation of object *A* so that the synchronization constraints of the scenario can be satisfied.

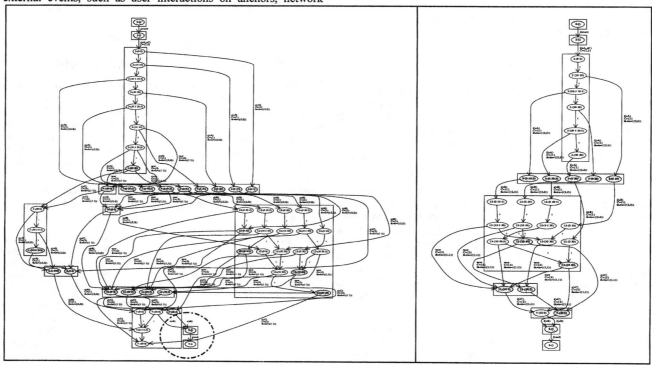

(a) Inconsistent Graph   (b) Consistent Graph

Figure 3   Reachability graph for the previous scenario

Once the temporal and logical behavior of this scenario is translated into RT-LOTOS, we are able to accomplish the reachability analysis and, then, to verify the temporal consistency of the document. The reachability graph for the previous scenario is illustrated in Figure 3(a). Note that, on this reachability graph all the branches that lead to the configuration 9-(), also lead to occurrence of the action *end* of the document's presentation. Although, potential inconsistent branches (those branches that do not lead to the action *end*) still occur in this reachability graph. These branches are associated either with the occurrence of *internal* (e.g., time progression), and/or external (e.g., user interaction) *non-deterministic events*, since they occur outside the valid temporal limit that satisfies the synchronization constraints of the scenario.

If a potential inconsistent branch is generated by the occurrence of an *internal non-deterministic event*, this inconsistency can be handled by the presentation system. However, if this branch is generated by the occurrence of an *external non-deterministic event*, it can not be ignored by the system to avoid an inconsistency situation (since the occurrence of this event is not controllable) [9]. The latter concept makes the previous scenario inconsistent since there are some inconsistent branches on its reachability graph that are generated by the occurrence of an external *non-deterministic event* (e.g., user interaction). In other words, this event can be produced outside the valid temporal interval for the presentation of the scenario.

The reachability graph is representative enough for the verification of consistency properties. Although, for scheduling purposes, an operational and simple scheduling graph can be obtained from a consistent reachability graph (all the branches lead to the occurrence of the action *end*). For this reason, when a potential inconsistent branch is generated by the occurrence of an *internal non-deterministic event*, this branch is cut out of this graph (since this event is controllable). However, when a potential inconsistent branch is generated by the occurrence of an *external non-deterministic event*, this branch can also be cut out of this graph in order to provide the controllability (determine a valid temporal interval for the presentation) of the scenario. The resultant consistent reachability graph is illustrated in Figure 3(b). In this sense, a scheduling graph is obtained from the consistent reachability graph. It is called *a Time Labeled Automaton* (TLA in short) and has been formalized in [10].

A TLA has as many clocks (called timers) as there are states in the automaton, and each timer (t_i) measures the time during which the automaton remains in a state (i). The timer associated with a state is reset when the automaton enters the state, and it is frozen to its current value when the automaton leaves the state. Each transition on the TLA is associated with two timed conditions: (1) a mandatory *firing window* (denoted as W) and; (2) an optional *enabling condition* (denoted as K). These conditions are expressed as inequalities and define temporal constraints to be satisfied for firing the associated transition.

The transitions of a TLA describe all the events (*start* and *end* of presentation of media objects) to be executed during the presentation of a multimedia scenario. For instance, consider the TLA for the previous scenario, as illustrated in Figure 4. Initially, event *sA_sC* (between states 1 and 2) takes place at t=0 seconds (absolute time). This event denotes the *start* of the simultaneous presentation of *A* and *C*. Then, event *eA* (end of *A*) occurs within [10,30] seconds. *Note that the TLA provides the controllability for the occurrence of this event within a valid temporal interval*. This event is immediately followed by event

eB (between states 3 and 12). In state 12, either a user interaction (*user*) or the end of presentation of media object *C* (*eC*) can take place. These events are controlled by the TLA so that *eC* occurs at 40 seconds and *user* takes place within [30,40] seconds. It is important to note that only one transition will be triggered among all the transitions associated with the event *user*, according to their different *enabling condition (K)* which expresses the time elapsed on previous states. Finally, both events *user* and *eC* lead to the occurrence of event *eB* (which denotes the end of presentation of media object *B*) and, then, to the *end* of the presentation. As we can note, the TLA provides the control of the presentation of media object *A* (which initially had non-defined duration according to the author's requirements) within a valid temporal interval (10<=t2<=30) so that it can respect the synchronization constraints of the scenario.

The scheduling of an IMD using the TLA can be accomplished based on the definition of some important issues, such as handling *active* and *passive* events. An event is *active* if its occurrence does not depend on the environment of the system (e.g., end of presentation of an image), and it is represented by the symbol "!". In opposite, an event is *passive* if its does depend on the environment of the system to occur (e.g., a user interaction, or the end of presentation of a continuous media), and it is represented by the symbol "?".

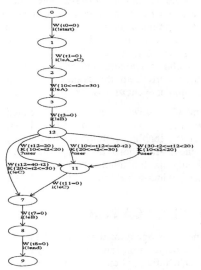

Figure 4   TLA for the previous scenario

The notion of *active* and *passive* events enables us to determine scheduling policies for the execution of *start* and *end* actions of media objects:

(1)   *Active events* may be related to start and end events of all media objects (e.g., video, audio, text, image, etc.). These events can be generated as soon as the scheduler decides when to trigger them based on their associated temporal firing window described on the TLA. It is important to note that the firing window associated with an *active* event may be defined by (a) an equality (e.g., t12=40-t2), or (b) an inequality (e.g., 10<=t2<=30). An equality implies at which time the event should occur. In the case of an inequality, different scheduling policies are applied in the following order to decide when the event must be triggered, such as: (1) the definition of a preferred duration (provided by the author of the document), (2) the availability of the intrinsic duration of the media object,

437

and finally, (3) the minimal duration satisfying the temporal constraint expressed by the associated firing window.

For instance, in the above example, the events *!sA_sC* (composition of two *active* start events *sA* and *sC*), *!eA*, *!sB*, *!eB* and *!eC* are *active* events. The firing window associated with *!sA_sC*, *!sB* and *!eB* are expressed by an equality which defines when the events should occur. Note also that *the* firing window associated with *!eC* (transition between states 12 and 7) is also an equality *(t12=40-t2)* which expresses how to compensate the time elapsed previously for the occurrence of event *!eA*. Finally, the firing window for the occurrence of event *!eA* (transition between states 2 and 3) is expressed by an inequality. Supposing that no explicit duration (not preferable, nor intrinsic duration) is associated with media *A*, the scheduler assumes presently the minimal valid duration for *A (e.g., t2=10s)*.

(2) In opposite, *passive* events can be related either to the end of streaming media objects (which can also be *active*, as seen previously) and to user interactions (which are always *passive*). It is important to note that the occurrence of passive events can not be predicted, but can be controlled within the valid temporal firing window of their associated action on the TLA. Thus, the scheduler waits until these events are generated and ensures that they are generated inside the temporal firing window of their associated action. In this case, it is still important to emphasize that the firing window associated with a *passive* event is defined within a temporal interval (an inequality) inside which the occurrence of this event can be controlled. In the above example, event *user* is the only passive event.

In the general case, several transitions, associated either with *active* or *passive* events, may be enabled within a state (depending on the enabling conditions of the TLA). During the scheduling, these transitions are considered as independent threads, and only one transition can be triggered as soon as its associated firing window becomes enabled.

3. THE TLA PLAYER

At this moment, an operational version of the TLA player is available. This player was implemented using Java (JDK1.2) based on the scheduling policies described previously. Figure 5 depicts a snapshot of a TLA player presentation. The TLA player presents multimedia documents based on their respective TLA and Resource files. The first one describes the logical and temporal synchronization of the document, and the latter describes all the presentation characteristics of the document (content and spatial synchronization). During the presentation of the document the user still is able to follow the execution based on the values of the clocks for the states in the TLA.

Figure 5   **Snapshot of the TLA Player**

4. CONCLUSION

This paper has presented an approach for the scheduling of Interactive Multimedia Documents based on a new temporal model called Time Labeled Automaton (TLA in short). The TLA is automatically derived from the RT-LOTOS reachability analysis and it provides a complete controllability for the presentation of a document, since it enables the controlling of the occurrence of non-deterministic events, such as user interactions, within valid temporal intervals. Further on, scheduling policies can also be defined using the concepts of *active* and *passive* events, what makes the scheduling based on the TLA an straightforward approach. Finally, the effective presentation of IMDs is accomplished by means of the TLA player which expresses the correct temporal semantics of the document respecting their real-time constraints .

5. ACKNOWLEDGMENTS

The first author is supported by a grant of the Brazilian Government (CAPES).

6. REFERENCES

[1] W3C Recommendation. Synchronized Multimedia Integration Language (SMIL) Boston Specification. URL: http://www.w3.org/TR/2000/smil-boston, february, 2000.

[2] Soares, L.F.G.; Rodriguez, N.L.R.; Casanova, M.A. Nested Composite Nodes and Version Control in an Open Hypermedia System.   Information Systems Journal, Sep.1995. pp.501-519.

[3] Buchanan, M.C.; Zellweger, P.T. Automatically Generating Consistent Schedules for Multimedia Documents. Multimedia Systems Journal, v.1, n..2,1993. pp.55-67

[4] Vazirgiannis, M; Boll, S. Events in Interactive Multimedia Applications: Modeling and Implementation Design. In: Proc of IEEE International Conference on Multimedia Computing and Systems (ICMCS'97), Ottawa - Canada, June, 1997.

[5] Layaida, N.; Sabry-Ismail, L. Maintaining Temporal Consistency of Multimedia Documents Using Constraint Networks. In Proc. of the 1996 Multimedia Computing and Networking, San-José, USA, Feb.1996, pp.124-135

[6] Courtiat, J.-P.; Oliveira, R.C. Proving Temporal Consistency in a New Multimedia Synchronization Model. In Proc. of ACM Multimedia'96, Boston, USA, Nov. 1996. pp.141-152.

[7] Courtiat, J.P.; Santos, C.A.S.; Lohr, C.; Outtaj, B. Experience with RT-LOTOS, a temporal extension of the LOTOS formal description technique. *In Computer Communications* Vol..23, No. 12, pp. 1104-1123, July 2000.

[8] Santos, C.A.S.; Soares, L.F.G.; Souza, G.L.; Courtiat, J.-P. Design methodology and formal validation of hypermedia documents. In: Proc. of ACM Multimedia'98, Bristol, UK, Sep. 1998. pp.39-48.

[9] Santos, C.A.S.; Sampaio, P.N.M.; Courtiat, J.-P. Revisiting the Concept of Hypermedia Document Consistency. ACM Multimedia'99, Orlando, USA, November, 1999.

[10] Lohr, C.; Santos, C.A.S.; Sampaio, P.N.M.; Courtiat, J.-P. Time Labeled Automata. (Technical Report LAAS N. 2000134)

Implementation of Aural Attributes for Simulation of Room Effects in Virtual Environments

Kenji Suzuki
University of Aizu
Spatial Media Group
Aizu-Wakamatsu, Fukushima
Japan 965-8580
www.u-aizu.ac.jp/~m5041116

m5041116@u-aizu.ac.jp

Yuji Nishoji
Lam Research Japan
Sagami-hara, Kanagawa
Japan 229-1105

yuji.nishoji@lamrc.com

Jens Herder
University of Aizu
Spatial Media Group
Aizu-Wakamatsu, Fukushima
Japan 965-8580
www.u-aizu.ac.jp/~herder

herder@acm.org

ABSTRACT

The audio design for virtual environments includes simulation of acoustical room properties besides specifying sound sources and sinks and their behavior. Virtual environments supporting room reverberation not only gain realism but also provide additional information to the user about surrounding space. Catching the different sound properties by the different spaces requires partitioning the space by the properties of aural spaces. We define soundscape and aural attributes as an application and multimedia content interface. Calculated data on an abstract level is sent to spatialization backends. Part of this research was the implementation of a device driver for the Roland Sound Space Processor. This device not only directionalizes sound sources, but also controls room effects like reverberation.

1. INTRODUCTION

Sound environment modeling can be through two major approaches [7]. A physical approach describes room geometry and surface properties. A perceptual approach describes an audio scene based upon parameters known from reverberator effect units (e.g., reverberator Yamaha REV 500). Both approaches have their applications. In the approach for our implementation the interface is strongly influenced by reverberators. This article contributes to the discussion on the Physical-Modeling Extensions to AudioBIFS in MPEG-4 Version 2 (which will become international standard as ISO 14496) in which nodes like AcousticScene and AcousticMaterial are proposed [8].
The Sound Spatialization Framework (SSF) [5], a toolkit and development environment for creating virtual spaces, was extended to support sound environment modeling using aural attributes. The scenegraph-based framework follows the VRML97 ISO/IEC 14772-1 specification [2] regarding

sound processing, but has an additional node for representing a sound sink, enabling independent listening and viewing point as well multiple listening locations. Extensions to VRML for better modeling of acoustic scenes have been proposed before [3]. The aural attribute parameters, inspired by the Java3D AuralAttributes class [9], are used to create virtual acoustical spaces for this development. These parameters are used for controlling devices, such as the Acoustetron II, the Pioneer Sound Field Controller (PSFC) [1], and the Roland Sound Space Processor (RSS-10). The later two sound spatialization backends (devices) are able to render aural attributes. The device interfaces are different as well their models. As a result of this parameterization, soundscape[1] and aural attributes are rendered in a scenegraph, and a combination of parameters for backend devices creates a sound with resemblance to that heard in an ordinary world. For this approach, two different kinds of rooms, a small bathroom and a large living room, are modeled using the API of the Sound Spatialization Framework. These rooms are modeled for rendering soundscapes with different aural attributes; thus when a sound sink[2] moves through two rooms, the context of the sink switches and different sound is obtained. Aural attribute parameters are obtained from the scenegraph, room size, and wall and floor materials.

This approach of setting the parameters of aural attributes is one style of calculation; but there are also other more computationally intensive approaches such as beam tracing and room acoustic prediction based on geometrical acoustics using octave-band echograms [6]. The beam tracing method [4], a geometric-based room acoustic model, is a relatively recent technique for calculating reflections efficiently. An implementation based on geometrical acoustics is CATT-Acoustic, a PC-based software tool for room acoustics and auralization prediction. This system processes digital signals with context information, and the calculation of binaural room impulse response is sent to a convolution engine, a dedicated signal processor and transaural converter representing a realistic sound in an anechoic room. Finally, the calculated data must be sent to spatialization backends.

The RSS-10 has room effect parameters like reverberation

---

[1]The MPEG-4 corresponding node is called AcousticScene.
[2]The MPEG-4 corresponding node is called ListeningPoint but differs in the fields.

which contribute to the acoustic environments' simulation. For the purpose of adding a new sound node which can control room effects parameters, a device driver for the RSS-10 was implemented on SGI workstations for the SSF. This device driver allows a listener to perceive room presence like reverberation and define the aural attributes easily.

This paper is guided by the abstraction levels going from the API to a device-independent interface to a device-specific interface.

2. TOOLS DESCRIPTION

The node SfSoundScape describes the effective area of sound and aural attributes. This area is expressed as a bounding box, and multiple boxes can exist in a single scenegraph. The SfSoundScapes has fields of two vector parameters to define a box and describes the attributes for each soundscape. The SfAuralAttributes, a node regarding aural parameters, has fields like AuralAttributes in Java3D [9]. This effect is held until the sink enters another bounding box. The fields and the mapping of these fields to the device specific level are shown in Table 1. Most of these fields are defined in and compatible with AuralAttributes class by the same name. A parameter of frequency changes after reflection is not defined in that class, so two fields wallColor and floorColor are added to define the property of the wall/floor reflection pattern of frequency respectively.

2.1 Visualization and Manipulation

The Sound Spatialization Framework has a module for visualizing and editing sound objects at runtime. A soundscape is visualized as a translucent box, representing the region in which aural attributes are valid (see Figure 1). Sound sink is in the right bounding box; right box is active and highlighted. By using a preference dialog, the visualization of soundscapes can be switched on and off. The sound sink is represented as bright sphere. The shown active sound source has a darker color. All visualizations are updated at

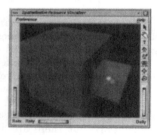

Figure 1: Soundscape visualization at runtime of a scene graph; translucent boxes presents the scope of aural attributes; the current active soundscape is highlighted

runtime. Dialogs to edit the different sound objects (i.e., nodes) can be invoked by clicking on their visual representation.

3. THE ROLAND RSS-10 SOUND SPACE PROCESSOR

In the RSS-10 system, direction is controlled with Azimuth and Elevation, distance is controlled with Distance parameter, presence is simulated with reverberation which is localized in 3D space, and movement is simulated with Doppler

effect to render 3D sounds. The RSS-10 system assumes that the listener hears the sound at a certain height above an imaginary floor. Reproducing 3D sounds depends on how the RSS-10 is used. The RSS-10 supports three output modes: speaker, headphones, and binaural. The 3D sound field can be controlled with MIDI system exclusive messages. All control of the RSS-10 is performed through the class library for the RSS-10. Figure 2 shows the connection between the SGI workstation and the RSS-10. The RSS-10 has room effect parameters described below.

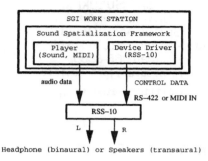

Figure 2: Connection from the workstation to the RSS-10 sound processor

Reverberation parameters. Room size and reverberation time parameters contribute to the perceived auditory spaciousness of the simulated environment. Wall color contributes to the simulation of the reverberant space characteristics. Reverb level controls the attenuation of reverberation. Roll off contributes to the atmospheric condition (wet/dry) that the simulated sound travels through and controls the absorption of high frequency by the air.

Floor parameters. Floor color contributes to the floor characteristics simulation. Floor reflection controls the attenuation of sound reflected off the floor. Floor distance is for setting the height of the listeners' ear from the floor. By controlling these parameters, the RSS-10 can represent many kinds of acoustic environments: hall, church, dead room, reflective room, free field, and more.

3.1 Abstract Backend Interface Specification

All information including listener movements, sound source location, direction, and intensity are passed by our abstract interface for spatialization backends (updateSink and update Source). Room control parameters; room size, reverberation time, and the like are passed by updateAuralAttributes. Table 1 shows the mapping of parameters to the device driver. The challenge for defining such interface is covering all features of known spatialization backends. From the Java 3D API documentation [9], reflectionCoefficient is the decay of gain at the initial-early-reflections on surfaces, reverbDelay is the time between start of sound and reverberation, and distance and frequencyCutOff are pairs of array for a low-pass-filtered function. Note that rolloff is used to model atmospheric changes from the normal speed of sound in Java 3D, but our RollOff parameter is defined as the distance-dependent high frequency attenuation level. Therefore, rolloff is not mapped to RollOff. wallColor and floorColor use 0 and 1.0 for applying low/high-pass-filter function respectively, and 0.5 for no change.

API level				examples		Device Specific level
	parameters	default	range	bathroom	living room	RSS-10
float	attribute_gain	1.0	≥ 0.0	0	0	no
float	rolloff	1.0	≥ 0.0	0	0	no
float	reflection_coeff	0.0	$0.0 - 1.0$	.9375	.86	ReverbLevel
float	reverb_delay	0.0	$\geq 0.0\ ms$	16	36	RoomSize, ReverbTime
int	reverb_order	0	≥ 0	15	2	ReverbTime
float[]	distance	null	≥ 0.0	0	0	RollOff
float[]	frequencyCutOff	null	≥ 0.0	0	0	RollOff
float	frequencyScaleFactor	1.0	≥ 0.0	0	0	no
float	velocityScaleFactor	0.0	≥ 0.0	0	0	no
float	wallColor	0.5	$0.0 - 1.0$	.7	.25	WallColor
float	floorColor	0.5	$0.0 - 1.0$	.5	.5	FloorColor

Table 1: Fields of the SfAuralAttribute node

4. COMPARISON WITH OTHER SOUND SPATIALIZATION BACKENDS

Two device drivers for sound spatialization backends previously developed, the PSFC and Acoustetron II, were selected for comparison. Table 2 shows the different features of three spatialization backends.

feature	PSFC	Acoustetron II	RSS-10
Doppler effect	no	yes	yes
distance cue	yes	yes	yes
azimuth	all angle	all angles	all angles
elevation	$0° \leq \theta \leq 90°$	all angles	all angles
reflection pattern (floor/wall color)	fixed	no	yes
reverberation	yes	no	yes
room size	yes	yes	yes
mixels (sound sources)	2	8 or 12	1 or 2

Table 2: Comparison between different spatialization backends

The PSFC features realtime configuration of an entire sound field, including sound direction, virtual distance, and simulated environment for each of two sources. Since the base of the PSFC speaker hemisphere is above head level (≥ 3 m), it has limitations regarding sound distance and elevation.

In the Acoustetron II, sound sources are spatialized using head-related transfer functions (HRTFs) for headphones. Since the Acoustetron II system does not provide reverberation for distance cues or room impression, a reverberator is needed to express room presence.

5. CONCLUSIONS AND FUTURE WORK

This development of a soundscape extends the Sound Spatialization Framework and establishes one way of changing sound by the environment surrounding the source and sink. Rendering aural attributes in virtual space provides users with more realistic sound. This development has some areas which can be improved. For example, the soundscape class can create only rectangular regions, and there is difficulty calculating reflection parameters. In the future, aural parameters should not only be settable by users, but also calculated automatically using properties of surrounded objects.

The implementation decision for using fields wallColor and floorColor was backend-specific, and normalized values were used. Other backends allow different control over early reflections (e.g., PSFC), which could be better supported using an AudioMaterial node as suggested for MPEG-4 [8, p. 247]. An implementation of such a node, mapping its data to a backend, is more complicated than the approach described in this article. It is also arguable if the designes of an acoustic virtual space can intuitively choose natural-sounding material properties.

6. REFERENCES

[1] K. Amano, F. Matsushita, H. Yanagawa, M. Cohen, J. Herder, W. Martens, Y. Koba, and M. Tohyama. A Virtual Reality Sound System Using Room-Related Transfer Functions Delivered Through a Multispeaker Array: the PSFC at the University of Aizu Multimedia Center. *TVRSJ: Trans. of the Virtual Reality Society of Japan*, 3(1):1–12, Mar. 1998. ISSN 1342-4386.

[2] G. Bell, R. Carey, and C. Marrin. ISO/IEC 14772-1:1997: The Virtual Reality Modeling Language (VRML97), 1997. http://www.vrml.org/Specifications/VRML97/.

[3] S. Ellis. Towards More Realistic Sound in VRML. In VRML 98, pages 95–100, Monterey CA, USA, 1998.

[4] T. Funkhouser, I. Carlbom, G. Elko, G. Pingali, M. Sondhi, and J. West. A beam tracing approach to acoustic modeling for interactive virtual environments. In *SIGGRAPH'98 conference*, held in Orlando, Florida, July 1998.

[5] J. Herder. Sound Spatialization Framework: An Audio Toolkit for Virtual Environments. *Journal of the 3D-Forum Society, Japan*, 12(3):17–22, Sept. 1998.

[6] M. Kleiner. Auralization a DSP approach. *Sound and Video Contractor*, Sept. 1992.

[7] R. Koenen. ISO/IEC jtc1/sc29/wg11 n3156: Mpeg-4 Overview - (maui version), Dec. 1999. http://drogo.cselt.stet.it/mpeg/standards/mpeg-4/mpeg-4.htm.

[8] E. D. Scheirer, R. Väänänen, and J. Huopaniemi. Audiobifs: Describing Audio Scenes with the MPEG-4 Multimedia Standard. *IEEE Transactions on Multimedia*, 1(3):237–250, Sept. 1999.

[9] H. Sowizral, K. Rushforth, and M. Deering. Java 3D 1.2 API Documentation. Web site, Sun Micro Systems inc., 1999. http://java.sun.com/products/java-media/3D/.

Topic Segmentation of News Speech Using Word Similarity

Seiichi Takao
Dept. of Electronics and Informatics
Ryukoku University
Seta, Otsu-shi, 520-2194, Japan
tail@arikilab.elec.ryukoku.ac.jp

Jun Ogata
Dept. of Electronics and Informatics
Ryukoku University
Seta, Otsu-shi, 520-2194, Japan
ogata@arikilab.elec.ryukoku.ac.jp

Yasuo Ariki
Dept. of Electronics and Informatics
Ryukoku University
Seta, Otsu-shi, 520-2194, Japan
ariki@rins.ryukoku.ac.jp

ABSTRACT

Conventional topic segmentation utilizes *cosine* measure as the similarity between consecutive passages. However, the *cosine* measure has a problem that it can not reflect the similarity unless exactly the same words are included in the passages. To solve this problem, in this paper, we propose a method to acquire the word similarity between different words from the input data directly and automatically by managing to collect the same topic sections. Further more, we propose a method to compute the passage similarity based on the word similarity. Finally we propose a method of topic segmentation based on the passage similarity in an unsupervised mode.

1. INTRODUCTION

Recently, many news programs are broadcast owing to its digitization. In this situation, viewers require to quickly select and watch his interesting news stories. From this viewpoint, news on demand systems have been developed[1][2]. In the systems, it is required to segment news programs into individual news story automatically using mainly news speech data, because manual segmentation is almost impossible due to a large amount of news programs.

In automatic topic segmentation [3]-[4], a small passage is compared with the successive passage and if the similarity between them is smaller than some threshold, the topic boundary is found between them. As the similarity measure, *cosine* is usually utilized between two vectors which are produced from the consecutive passages by counting the frequencies of the important words as the vector elements. However, the *cosine* measure has a problem that it can not reflect the similarity unless exactly the same words are included in the passages. To solve this problem, word similarity between different words is required before computing the *cosine* similarity.

In order to acquire the word similarity automatically, a large amount of training data is usually required. However,

newly input data (evaluation data or test data) is different from the training data so that the word similarity acquired from the training data is sometimes useless. To solve this problem, it is effective to acquire the word similarity directly from input data, not from the training data. For that purpose, time sections, where the same topic continues, have to be collected from the input data. We define this time sections as *topic sections*.

In the context of news program, the topic sections correspond with the time sections where the same video caption continues. From this viewpoint, in this paper, we propose a method to acquire the word similarity from the input data directly by collecting the topic sections. Further more, we propose a method to compute the passage similarity based on the word similarity. Finally a method of topic segmentation is proposed based on the passage similarity in an unsupervised mode.

In this paper, we describe the conventional unsupervised topic segmentation in section 2. A proposed method of topic segmentation on the basis of passage similarity and word similarity is described in 3. Speech transcription and video caption detection are described in section 4 and 5. Finally the experimental results will be described in 6.

2. CONVENTIONAL SEGMENTATION

2.1 Outline

In conventional methods for topic segmentation, a small passage is compared with the successive passage and if their similarity is less than some threshold, the topic is segmented at the passage. This method is called an unsupervised topic segmentation. In the context of news program, the process is summarized as follows;

1. Speech transcription is carried out for Japanese broadcast continuous news speech.
2. Topic vectors in each passage (analytical window) is constructed by using term weighting method and the analytical window is shifted.
3. The similarity between consecutive topic vectors, constructed from the analytical windows, is computed.
4. Topic boundary is detected where similarity is lower than some threshold.

2.2 Topic Vectors for Passages

Word frequencies in each analytical window are counted. Then weighting degree is computed for each word by using

Permission to make digital or hard copies of all or part of this work for personal or classroom use is granted without fee provided that copies are not made or distributed for profit or commercial advantage and that copies bear this notice and the full citation on the first page. To copy otherwise, to republish, to post on servers or to redistribute to lists, requires prior specific permission and/or a fee.
ACM Multimedia 2000 Los Angeles CA USA
Copyright ACM 2000 1-58113-198-4/00/10...$5.00

442

a term weighting method. We describe this method later. Finally, a vector for each analytical window is constructed by extracting words showing higher weighting degree than a threshold. We call this vector as *topic vector*.

The term weighting method we employed is mutual information incorporating TF-IDF due to the following reason. The conventional mutual information shows high value even when occurrences of word w_i are low, because mutual information is computed based on probability, not on word frequency. This is a weak point of the conventional mutual information.

On the other hand, TF counts the occurrences of word w_i and compensates for a weak point of the conventional mutual information. IDF shows the degree how word w_i depends on topic t_k by counting the number of topics which include word w_i. Therefore it can be said that IDF shows the co-occurrence of word w_i and topic t_k in different viewpoint from mutual information. This is the reason we employed here the combination of the mutual information and TF-IDF as shown in Eq.(1) to extract important words. We call this method as mutual information incorporating TF-IDF.

$$
\begin{aligned}
i(t_k; w_i) &\times (TF - IDF) \\
&= (i(t_k) - i(t_k|w_i)) \cdot TF(w_i, t_k) \cdot IDF(w_i) \\
&= (\log \frac{P(t_k, w_i)}{P(t_k)P(w_i)}) \cdot TF(w_i, t_k) \cdot IDF(w_i) \quad (1)
\end{aligned}
$$

2.3 Similarity Between Topic Vectors

A topic vector can be created from each analytical window. The elements of the topic vector are important words selected using the term weighting method (mutual information incorporating TF-IDF) already mentioned. Therefore an inner-product of the topic vectors can now be used to find the vocabulary overlap between any two topic vectors. Eq.(2) shows the similarity between two topic vectors X_k and X_l.

$$
\begin{aligned}
\cos\theta &= (X_k, X_l) \\
&= (x_{1k}, x_{2k}, \cdots, x_{nk})(x_{1l}, x_{2l}, \cdots, x_{nl})^T \\
&= (x_{1kc}, x_{2kc}, \cdots, x_{nkc})(x_{1lc}, x_{2lc}, \cdots, x_{nlc})^T \\
&= \sum_i x_{ikc} \cdot x_{ilc} \quad (2)
\end{aligned}
$$

where x_{ikc} and x_{ilc} are the normalized frequency of words appearing in both X_k and X_l. If $\cos\theta$ nearly equals 1, the similarity between two passages (analytical windows) is regarded as high.

After the similarity between consecutive passages is computed by using Eq.(2), topic boundary is detected as the point where the similarity is lower than some threshold.

3. PROPOSED SEGMENTATION

3.1 Problem of Conventional Methods

The *cosine* measure used in the conventional topic segmentation has a problem that it can not reflect the similarity unless exactly the same words are included in the passages. To solve this problem, similarity between different words has to be computed before the *cosine* similarity computation.

In order to obtain this type of word similarity automatically, a large amount of training data is usually required.

However, newly input data (evaluation data or test data) is usually different from the training data so that the word similarity obtained from the training data is sometimes useless. To solve this problem, it is effective to compute the word similarity directly from input data, not from the training data. For that purpose, time sections, where the same topic continues, have to be collected from the input data. We define this time sections as *topic sections*.

In the context of news program, the topic sections correspond with the time sections where the same video caption continues. From this viewpoint, in this paper, we propose a method to compute the word similarity from the input data by collecting the *topic sections*.

3.2 Word Distance and Word Similarity

We propose, in this paper, word distance in a word space to compute the word similarity. The word space is three dimensional, constructed by values of mutual information, TF and IDF. The word distance between word w_i and w_j is computed as follows;

$$
\begin{aligned}
WD(w_i, w_j) &= \frac{1}{m}\sum_m ((TF(w_i, t_m) - TF(w_j, t_m))^2 \\
&\quad + (IDF(w_i) - IDF(w_j))^2 \\
&\quad + (i(t_m; w_i) - i(t_m; w_j))^2)^{\frac{1}{2}} \quad (3)
\end{aligned}
$$

In Eq.(3), $TF(w_i, t_m)$ shows the term frequency that word w_i occurs in *topic section* t_m, $IDF(w_i)$ shows inverse document frequency of the word w_i, $i(t_m; w_i)$ shows mutual information of word w_i in *topic section* t_m. The m also shows the number of *topic sections*. Then the word distance shows the distance between word w_i and w_j in all *topic sections* in the word space (Mutual-TF-IDF). The word similarity is computed as the inverse of the word distance.

3.3 Passage Similarity

Eq.(2) counts only the number of overlapping words, but it doesn't take into consideration of the word similarity. This causes the decreasing of topic segmentation performance in the case where the analytical window is short, because similarity between consecutive analytical windows can not be correctly computed by using only word overlapping shown in Eq.(2). If the analytical window is long, this problem may be solved. But it becomes difficult to detect the topic boundaries precisely.

To solve this problem, similarity between consecutive analytical windows (passage similarities) has to be computed by using not only word overlapping but also word similarity. The passage similarity based on the word similarity can be computed using Eq.(4).

$$
(X_k, X_l) = \sum_i \sum_j x_{ik} \times x_{jl} \times \frac{1}{WD(w_i, w_j)} \quad (4)
$$

where x_{ik} and x_{jl} are the normalized frequency of word w_i and w_j in passage t_k and t_l respectively as shown in Eq.(2).

4. SPEECH TRANSCRIPTION

4.1 Experimental Condition

We carried out automatic speech transcription[5] for the NHK Japanese broadcast continuous news speech, using a language model and an acoustic model. The language model is the word bigram constructed from RWC text database which was produced by morphologically analyzing the MAINICHI Japanese newspaper of 45 months from 1991 to 1994. The number of the words in the dictionary is 20,000. The word bigram was back-off smoothed after cutting off at 1 word.

Speaker independent cross-word triphone HMMs were constructed. They were trained using 21,782 sentences spoken by 137 Japanese males. These speech data is taken from the database of acoustic society of Japan. The acoustic parameters are 39 MFCCs with 12 Mel cepstrum, log energy and their first and second order derivatives. Cepstrum mean normalization was applied to each sentence to remove the difference of input circumstances. Table1 shows the experimental conditions for acoustic analysis (AA) and HMM.

In the transcription experiment, we used HTK (HMM Toolkit) as the decoder which can perform Viterbi decoding with beam search using above mentioned language model and acoustic model.

Table 1: Acoustic Analysis(AA) and HMM

A A	Sampling frequency	12kHz
	High-pass filter	$1 - 0.97z^{-1}$
	Feature parameter	MFCC,Pow,Δ, $\Delta\Delta$ (39th)
	Frame length	20ms
	Frame shift	5ms
	Window type	Hamming window
H M M	Learning method	Concatenated training
	Type	Left to right continuous HMM
	Number of states	5 states with 3 loops
	Number of mixtures	8

4.2 Transcription Result

The automatic transcription was carried out for the NHK Japanese continuous news speech for 20 minutes in 1998. We show the transcription result in Table 2. In the table, the "Corr" indicates the correctness and the "Acc" indicates the accuracy of the speech transcription.

The reason why the transcription result is a little lower is explained as follows. The language model was constructed from the MAINICHI Japanese newspaper published from 1991 to 1994. On the other hand, the test data was NHK spoken news broadcast in 1998. This time difference caused the lower transcription result. This transcription result is used for topic segmentation.

Table 2: Transcription result(%)

	Corr	Acc
19980820-12:00NHK	77.83	75.57

5. DETECTION OF TOPIC SECTION

In this section, we describe a method [6] to correctly detect the *topic sections* where the same video caption continues. When the characters of video captions appear, edge correspondence between present frame and next frame shows high value. Therefore edge ratio defined by Eq.(5) changes along time at the following three sections; the character appearing section, character stable section and character disappearing section.

Edge ratio equals almost 1 in character stable section. Consequently, the *topic section* is determined by extracting the character stable section. Experimental results of topic section detection is shown in Table.3.

$$Edge\ ratio = \frac{Edge\ correspondence(present, next)}{Edge\ correspondence(present, previous)} \quad (5)$$

Table 3: Detection of topic sections

	Correct	Accuracy
19980820-12:00NHK	70.1% (47/67)	75.8% (47/62)

6. EXPERIMENTAL RESULTS

We compared two topic segmentation techniques for the transcription results shown in Table2, conventional unsupervised method and proposed topic segmentation method using the word similarity. Experimental results are shown in Table.4. The measure to evaluate the topic segmentation is recall, precision and F-measure. F-measure is the combination of recall and precision as defined in Eq.(6). If evaluated by F-measure, the proposed topic segmentation on the basis of word similarity showed about 10% superiority to conventional topic segmentation. From Table4, it can be said that the computation of word similarity and passage similarity using the *topic sections* in the test data is effective in topic segmentation.

Table 4: Topic Segmentation Results

	recall	precision	F-measure
Conventional	80.00%	41.37%	54.54%
Proposed	73.33%	57.89%	64.70%

$$F - measure = \frac{2 \times Recall \times Precision}{Recall + Precision} \quad (6)$$

7. CONCLUSION

In this paper, we proposed a new topic segmentation method based on passage similarity and word similarity in a word space which is constructed from the *topic sections* in the test data itself. The proposal method showed about 10% superiority to the conventional topic segmentation method.

8. REFERENCES

[1] F.Kubala, A.Colbath, D.Lie, A.Srivastava and J.Makhoul: "Integrated technologies for indexing spoken language", Communications of the ACM, Vol.43, No.2, pp.48-56, 2000.

[2] SRI MAESTRO Team: "MAESTRO:conductor of multimedia analysis technologies", Communications of the ACM, Vol.43, No.2, pp.57-63, 2000.

[3] J.P.Yamron, I.Carp, L.Gillick, S.Lowe, and P.van Mulbregt: "A Hidden Markov Model Approach to Text Segmentation and Event Tracking", ICASSP98, Volume I, pp.333-336, 1998.

[4] P.van Mulbregt, I.Carp, L.Gillick, S.Lowe and J.Yamron: "Text Segmentation and Topic Tracking on Broadcast News Via A Hidden Markov Model Approach", ICSLP98, Volume VI, pp.2519-2522, 1998.

[5] Y.Ariki and J.Ogata, "Indexing and Classification of TV News Articles Based on Speech Dictation Using Word Bigram", ICSLP98, Volume 7, pp.3265-3268.

[6] Y.Ariki and S.Takao, "Extraction and Recognition of Open Captions Superimposed on TV News Articles", to appear in ACCV00, 2000.

Automating the Linking of Content and Concept

Robert Tansley†, Colin Bird*, Wendy Hall†, Paul Lewis† and Mark Weal†

†IAM Research Group, University of Southampton, UK
*IBM UK Laboratories, Hursley Park, UK
rht96r@ecs.soton.ac.uk

ABSTRACT

In previous work we have described a multimedia system, MAVIS 2, supporting content and concept based retrieval and navigation. A central component of the system is a multimedia thesaurus in which media content is associated with appropriate concepts in a semantic layer. A major challenge is identifying and constructing these associations in a particular application without requiring a huge amount of manual effort. In this paper we propose a two phase approach to the problem. In the first phase, latent semantic analysis is used to associate metadata available for some media objects with concept class descriptions. This facilitates automatic associations to be made with the concept layer for those media objects. In the second phase, media content matching is used to classify media objects without metadata through their similarity to media objects classified in phase 1.

1. INTRODUCTION

Many multimedia information systems (MMISs) allow searching and navigating of multimedia objects based on associated textual *metadata*. The approach typically relies on the availability of suitably controlled metadata and the availability of people's time to enter it. Increasingly, we see MMISs which support retrieval of multimedia objects based on their content[2]. A small number also support hypermedia navigation based on content[6, 4]. However, it has become clear that, in many cases, the available low-level features of media objects are insufficient to determine whether or not two media objects pertain to the same real-world *concept*.

We have recently reported the development of an MMIS called MAVIS 2, Multimedia Architecture for Video, Image and Sound[1], which encapsulates both the information retrieval and hypermedia information discovery paradigms. It features a semantic layer component as part of a *multimedia thesaurus(MMT)* which is central to the MMIS architecture.

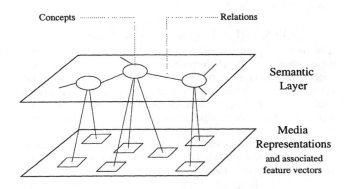

Figure 1: Multimedia Thesaurus Architecture

The semantic layer of the MMT consists of *concepts* connected by *relationships*. Each concept is an abstract entity corresponding to a real-world "object". Each concept is associated with one or more *media representations*, i.e. multimedia objects that represent the concept. These representations may be a text term or phrase, a portion of an image, a segment of video or any other medium. Thus, one concept may have many representations in many different media. This is illustrated in figure 1. Media representations are associated with feature vectors (signatures) extracted from the representation using media processing algorithms. Modules providing the media processing can be integrated in an incremental way as new techniques are developed and IBM's QBIC technology[3] has been incorporated to provide additional signatures and illustrate the extensible nature of the architecture.

The semantic layer architecture can support any number of arbitrary semantic relationships between concepts, but initially we implemented only the two common types used in existing thesauri: a hierarchical specialisation/generalisation relation, and a *related* relation. The *equivalence* relation for media representations is implicit in the architecture. Different media representations of the same concept are considered equivalent and are called *synonyms*, even if they are of different media types. They are linked to the same concept in the semantic layer.

Media representations may also constitute or contain source and destination anchors of hypermedia links. These links may be *generic links*; that is, the link may be followed not only from the source anchor itself, but also from any other portion of media that matches the source anchor. Matching is achieved using the signatures mentioned above and the distances generated are combined using a normalised ranking system.

The MAVIS 2 system uses the multimedia thesaurus architecture in a variety of ways. Content-based navigation can be enhanced by supplementing the available links with links from *synonyms* or by widening or narrowing the scope through the concept generalisation and specialisation relations. The results of 'find similar object' queries may also be enriched using synonyms of retrieved media or query expansion through generalisation. Additionally, the concept layer provides a useful means of navigation in itself and a concept browser is provided as an additional entry point for navigation or retrieval.

2. CONSTRUCTION PROBLEMS

The usefulness of a semantic layer has been reasonably well established, but a major problem with the development of such systems is how to construct the semantic layer and create the appropriate associations between media representations and the concepts in the semantic layer which they represent, without a substantial amount of manual effort.

The basis of the semantic layer developed for this application is a subset of the Dewey Decimal Classification (DDC) system, a widely used classification system with a broad scope. The DDC is a large set of classes, designed for libraries with potentially millions of volumes to index. We used a suitable subset of the classification relating to the subject domain of the images in our test in order to establish the semantic layer. One of the advantages of using the DDC is that one subset can be 'attached' to another with a wider scope. In this way two subsets (and hence multimedia thesaurus assisted collections) can be merged however much or little the subject areas overlap.

The core of the multimedia collection used in this trial application were a set of 1023 images of artefacts from the Victoria and Albert Museum, London. This image collection was compiled during the first phase of a previous project concerning electronic access to distributed image collections called the Electronic Library Image Service for Europe, or ELISE [7]. A wide range of artefacts are depicted; they include paintings, sculptures, clothing, furniture and textiles. Some text metadata is associated with some of the images but not all. Only a fraction of the images had an appropriate amount of associated metadata, and not all images with metadata have the same fields.

Fortunately, related work in the previously mentioned ELISE project is also of use here. As part of the ELISE project, a selection of DDC classes was chosen for representing the contents of image collections, particularly for museums. Each class was given a number of associated keywords. Largely, these keywords (and indeed the class names) do not appear in the image metadata, so simple text matching cannot be used to tie image metadata to DDC classes.

The subset the ELISE project used was designed with several museum collections in mind, and is thus still rather

700	The Arts; Fine and Decorative
730	Plastic Arts; Sculpture
736	Carving & Carvings
738	Ceramic Arts
738.2	Porcelain
738.4	Earthenware & Stoneware
739	Art Metalwork
740	Drawing and Decorative Arts
741	Drawing & Drawings
746	Textile Arts
748	Glass
749	Furniture & Accessories

Table 1: Dewey Decimal Classification

widely-scoped for the Victoria and Albert collection used in this application. A subset has been chosen with the scope of this collection in mind, and not so deep that it will be sparsely represented. Part of the chosen subset is shown in table 1. The indentation shows the hierarchy.

Each concept is made an abstract entity in the concept layer; the text label (for example, "Glass"), is held as a media representation in the media representation layer. In this way a suitable set of concepts is obtained for the semantic layer and for each concept a set of descriptive keywords was also available. We also have a set of images, of which only some have associated metadata. We now face the challenge of connecting the images to the concepts they represent without creating each association manually.

Our approach involves a two-phase process for associating the images with the appropriate concepts. Firstly, the images for which we have sufficient associated metadata are connected to the appropriate concepts by using Latent Semantic Analysis (LSA) to give a measure of correspondence. Secondly, low-level features are used to classify the remaining images, by using the image-concept associations created in the first stage as a ground truth.

3. PHASE 1: USING LATENT SEMANTIC ANALYSIS

Given two sets of text, the latent semantic analysis (LSA) technique developed at the University of Colorado[5] will return a value indicating how closely related the two pieces of text are, even if the terminology in each piece of text differs. The value is the cosine of the angle between vectors derived to represent the two pieces of text in a particular semantic space. Thus, to establish which concept is most appropriate for a particular image, the metadata associated with the image can be compared with the DDC class keywords to give a measure of correlation.

Initially, it might be assumed that since the Dewey class keywords and image metadata comprise a relatively small corpus of text, the effectiveness of the technique would be poor. However, several "ready-trained" semantic spaces are publicly available, in a variety of subject areas. Reviewing the subject areas revealed that the *encyclopedia* set holds the most relevant information on museum objects and artefacts and is likely to produce the best results.

The LSA Web site also offers on-line access to LSA software. We developed a simple Java based tool to send batches of pairs of text pieces and receive the resulting similarity values. Using the image metadata, concept keywords and the LSA tool, cosines were calculated indicating the degree of similarity between the images and the DDC classes (and hence, the appropriate concepts in the semantic layer). The next problem was how these values would be used to assign images to classes?

Two associators were built. One implements a *knn*-style classifier, which assigns images to concepts based on the highest cosine generated by the LSA process. The second implements a simple decision tree, propagated down to the descendent (narrower concept) with the highest cosine. Some preliminary testing established that the *knn*-style associator produces the best results.

The LSA based classification was performed with 106 images that had associated ELISE metadata. The relevant images were associated with the appropriate concepts in MAVIS 2 using a batch process that sent relevant messages to import the images to the MAVIS system and create the associations with the appropriate concept in the semantic layer. Once the main categorisation has been done, the resulting network was browsed using the concept browser to find and move any images that were obviously out of place. Ninety five of the 106 images were correctly associated with concepts using the automatic LSA technique. A script that quickly allowed the reassigning of an image to another class was used and the process of correctly associating the 11 misclassified images took about 15 minutes.

4. PHASE 2: USING IMAGE FEATURE MATCHING

The remainder of the Victoria and Albert Museum images were classified using only image features. No text metadata associated with either the images or the concepts was used. To facilitate this, another "batch classifier" facility was developed. The process is given a number of media objects to classify and these are used to form CBR queries to the MAVIS 2 system. The corresponding results are used to determine a best-matching concept. Associations are then made between the media representations and their appropriate concepts. The process is fully automatic.

The batch classification had a high rate of success in identifying *Glassware* and *Furniture & Accessories*. Images depicting paintings were more prone to misclassification. On the whole the content matching stage resulted in less reliable results than the LSA stage and an explanation for this is the great visual variability, particularly of the painting images, and the relatively small number of LSA classified images we used to act as prototypes. The signatures used were essentially, colour, spatial colour and texture measures and the classification would clearly benefit from the use of more pertinent features if they were available. Finally, the classification used a basic 'nearest neighbour' approach and more sophisticated techniques should produce more robust results.

5. CONCLUSIONS AND FUTURE WORK

We have presented a brief overview of an approach to the automatic building of a multimedia thesaurus in a small trial application of our MAVIS 2 multimedia information system. While this procedure was not entirely robust for the reasons cited above, it demonstrates that such an approach is feasible with the semantic layer architecture adopted and accelerates the creation of a the MMT to support both content and concept based retrieval and navigation. In future trials, we plan to use larger numbers of media objects in the LSA stage in order to provide a larger set of prototypes for phase 2 of the classification process. We are also investigating more robust classification techniques and improving the range and pertinence of signatures available for content matching.

Acknowledgements
The authors are grateful to the Victoria and Albert Museum for the use of their image collection, the ELISE project for their metadata and to the EPSRC for support through research grant GR/L03446. The authors also wish to thank David Dupplaw, Dan Joyce and Mark Dobie for useful discussions.

6. REFERENCES
[1] M. Dobie, R. Tansley, D. Joyce, M. Weal, P. Lewis, and W. Hall. A flexible architecture for content and concept based multimedia information exploration. In *Proceedings of the Challenge of Image Retrieval (CIR'99)*, pages 1–12, Newcastle, UK, Feb. 1999.

[2] J. Eakins and M. Graham. Content based image retrieval. Technical Report 39, U.K. JISC Technology Application Programme, Oct. 1999. Available at http://www.jtap.ac.uk/.

[3] M. Flickner, H. Sawhney, W. Niblack, J. Ashley, Q. Huang, B. Dom, M. Gorkani, J. Hafner, D. Lee, D. Petkovic, D. Steele, and P. Yanker. Query by image and video content: The QBIC system. *IEEE Computer*, 28(9):23–32, Sept. 1995.

[4] K. Hirata, S. Mukherjea, Y. Okamura, W.-S. Li, and Y. Hara. Object-based navigation: An intuitive navigation style for content-oriented integration environment. In *Proceedings of ACM Hypertext '97*, pages 75–86, Southampton, UK, Apr. 1997. ACM, ACM Press.

[5] T. K. Landauer, P. W. Foltz, and D. Laham. An introduction to latent semantic analysis. *Discourse Processes*, 25:259–284, 1998.

[6] P. H. Lewis, H. C. Davis, S. R. Griffiths, W. Hall, and R. J. Wilkins. Media-based navigation with generic links. In *ACM Hypertext 96 Proceedings*, pages 215–223, 1996.

[7] A. Seal. The creation of an electronic image bank: Photo-CD at the V&A. *Managing Information*, 1(1):42–44, 1995.

VIDEX: An Integrated Generic Video Indexing Approach

Roland Tusch, Harald Kosch, and Laszlo Böszörmenyi
Department of Information Technology
University Klagenfurt
9020 Klagenfurt, Austria

{rtusch, harald, laszlo}@itec.uni-klu.ac.at

ABSTRACT

This paper presents an integrated generic technique for low- and high-level video indexing. The proposed approach tries to integrate the advantages of existing low- and high-level video indexing approaches by reducing their shortcomings. Furthermore, the model introduces concepts for a detailed structuring of video streams, and for correlations of low- and high-level video objects. The proposed model is called generic, as it only defines a framework of classes for an integrated video indexing system. It has been verified by implementing a prototype of a distributed multimedia information system supporting content-based video retrieval.

Categories and Subject Descriptors

H.3.1 [**Information Storage and Retrieval**]: Content Analysis and Indexing—*abstracting methods, indexing methods*

1. INTRODUCTION

In recent years a number of video indexing models have been proposed, mostly covering either low-level (physical) ([14],[4]) or high-level (semantic) visual features ([6]) of video streams. Dealing only with physical or semantic indexes has certain disadvantages. On the one hand, low-level visual features can only provide very preliminary video classification and do not allow high-level content-based video queries. On the other hand, high-level semantic-based indexes, not being based on corresponding low-level video features, may lead to semantic inconsistencies and to exhaustive manual indexing work. Inconsistencies may appear through biased subjective content interpretations of different people during the video indexing process. Some approaches even tried to index videos by both physical and semantic features ([7],[8]). They provide integrated video indexing schemes which do not lack the shortcomings of the separate ones. But there are still some weaknesses concerning the segmentation of video streams and the high-level annotation process.

The main contribution of this paper is the definition of an integrated generic video indexing model based on low-level visual features and typed, high-level semantic objects. The proposed model allows the integration of a number of existing tools during the video indexing process. First, automatic and manual methods for segmenting video streams can be used to give videos a hierarchical structure. Second, mechanisms for extracting and tracking low-level visual objects need to be used to physical index videos. The extracted objects may be spatially, temporarily or spatio-temporarily related to each other. And third, tools for grouping low-level objects together to typed high-level, semantic objects are supported. These semantic objects can further be related to physical or logical video segments.

2. THE VIDEX MODEL

Our integrated generic video indexing model, presented in figure 1, integrates low- and high-level content information by picking up the advantages of existing models and reducing their shortcomings. Concerning content descriptions it is similar to the MPEG-7 standard. The differences are first, that our indexing model denotes a generic object-oriented model for low- and high-level video indexing, defining an indexing framework. The data model can be easily extended for a specific application domain, as we will demonstrate it on the example of the soccer domain in section 3. Second, we explicitly specify different granularities of video segments for video structuring. Here we take advantage of concepts of the *VideoSTAR* model [6]. Furthermore, we also provide a video hyper-link concept similar to the one presented in [7]. And finally, we integrate concepts of the MPEG-4 [9] standard in our model to be able to specify content-annotations to elementary video streams. The proposed model is a successor of the generic video indexing model presented in [12], which primarily focuses on high-level, semantic-based indexes.

2.1 The Video Segmentation Part

One main drawback of related approaches is that in most of them scenes are the only possibility to structure video streams. However, scenes do not form the basic structure of videos as they denote video units, which already incorporate the underlying semantics of physical video streams. As proposed in [6], [8] and [11], a multi-level video structuring approach should rather be followed. The higher the level, the more semantic information is covered.

Our model defines a video stream to be physically structured by so-called *PhysicalVideoUnits*. A physical video unit specifically can be a *Shot*, a *Scene* or a *Sequence*. Shots,

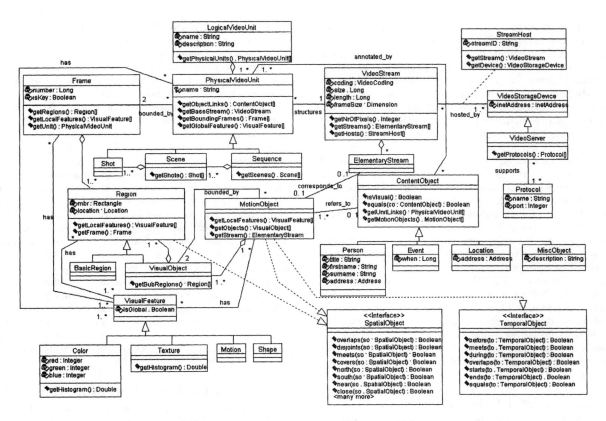

Figure 1: The generic VideX data model in UML notation

which are the smallest physical video units, consist of one or more consecutively generated and recorded frames, representing continuous actions in time and space [3]. A continuous usually is marked by physical boundaries like camera breaks and editing points. These boundaries are the most important shot transition indicators used by automatic shot boundary detection algorithms. Shot boundaries are usually represented by their first and last frames, denoting two of their key frames.

A key frame, represented as class *Frame* with key-property in the *VideX* model, is a video frame representing a still image including spatial features of its contained video objects. These features can be used for satisfying spatial conditions in video queries. In our model, frames are not considered as the smallest physical video unit, as they do not have a temporal extent. Frames only allow the definition of spatial relations between sub-objects not regarding temporal or spatio-temporal relations between them.

Shots are not sufficient for a meaningful video browsing and retrieval for mainly two reasons [11]. First, there are too many shots in a long video to be presented to the user. And second, shots do not capture the underlying semantic structure of a video since users might want to browse or retrieve videos at a semantic level, and not by physical shots or key frames. Therefore, all shots, which are related semantically in time and space, are grouped together to form the *scene* level.

Scenes represent the first abstraction level which take into account the underlying semantics of video streams. They are marked by semantic boundaries, which makes the scene

boundary detection a much more difficult task in comparison with shot boundary detection. However, in [11] an algorithm for automatic construction of scene structures is proposed. Scenes deliver very usable video units for retrieval in content-based video queries, due to their ability in structuring large video streams by semantic content.

In some cases it might be necessary to relate several scenes to *sequences*. As a scene only represents semantically related shots, the granularity might even be too small for browsing very long video streams effectively. Consider e.g. a video capturing a whole soccer match with a duration of at least 90 minutes and a lot of events occurring in it. Within this domain one shot could be e.g. the happening of a foul from player A on player B, another shot could be the execution of the following free-kick which results in scoring a goal. Both shots can be semantically grouped together to form a goal scene. Now, if someone would also be interested in some previous actions and events in the match, which lead to this foul, all the previous actions forming several scenes should be returned together with the goal scene. The whole returned unit denotes a sequence consisting of scenes, which together give a meaning [6]. The definition of sequences needs human assistance due to the very difficult task of keeping sequences semantically consistent.

For video authoring, our model provides the concept of logical video units (class *LogicalVideoUnit*). They allow the assembling of different physical video units to form user-created video documents. Thereby, the physical video units may belong to more than one physical video stream.

To be able to construct a reliable and consistent video

structure, it is necessary that the low-level video abstractions are made accurately. For this reason as well as for performing the video segmentation process in a more efficient way, the shots and maybe the scenes should be automatically extracted from the physical video streams. Therefore appropriate shot and scene boundary detection algorithms have to be used. The effectiveness of the algorithms concerning accuracy and robustness depends on the kind of video being segmented [2]. In the case of videos with abrupt camera transitions as e.g. in medical videos, where the noise level caused by camera and object motion is low, any of the known shot detection algorithms can be used. However, in videos with many gradual transitions and object motions the histogram-based approach using twin-comparison is preferable [13]. Histogram-based shot detection techniques give a good tradeoff between robustness and speed.

As extension to the video segments described above, our model provides means to integrate elementary video streams of the MPEG-4 standard described in [9]. An elementary stream in terms of the MPEG-4 standard is a coded data stream that can belong to a media object within an audio-visual MPEG-4 scene. Thus, one media object may consist of one or more coded elementary streams, which contain the coded physical object or some parts of it. In our model, elementary streams can be related to tracked objects over time, which further can correspond to high-level, semantic-based objects.

2.2 The Low-level Video Indexing Part

A number of existing video indexing techniques stop at the frame-level rather than exploring its sub-frame granularities. This shortcoming disables content-based video queries including spatial and spatio-temporal constraints on low-level visual objects.

In our model, the class *Frame* denotes the entry point for low-level video access. Within a physical video unit, a frame is uniquely identified by its number and may represent a key-frame. It consists of one or more regions (abstract class *Region*), which specifically can be *BasicRegions* or *VisualObjects*. A region is a spatial object, as it implements the interface *SpatialObject*. This interface defines a set of methods for implementing qualitative spatial relations including topological, directional and distance relations. Topological relationships between spatial objects are defined by neighbor or incidence relations between them. Two spatial object may i.e. intersect (*overlap*), touch externally (*meet*) or internally (*covers*), or be disjoint. A complete set of topological relationships between two spatial objects, called the *4-intersection-model*, is presented in [5]. Directional relations describe the relative positions between two given spatial objects. In [10], a complete set of 169 directional relationships is presented. It includes e.g. *north*, *south*, *above-left* and *above-right*. And finally, the distance relations describe the space range between spatial objects, including i.e. *far*, *near*, *close*. In the *VideX* model, regions are currently geometrically represented by *minimum bounding rectangles* (MBRs), as this kind of object approximation needs only a few points for their representation. Furthermore, MBR approximations are used to efficiently retrieve candidates that could satisfy a spatial query.

A *BasicRegion* in our model is a region which can be considered as being atomar, i.e. it does not consist of any other sub-regions. If a region represents an aggregation of sub-

regions, then it is called a *VisualObject*. Such a visual object could e.g. be a person, where the visual object *person* consists of two visual sub-objects *head* and *body*. The body further could consist of the regions *hands*, *trunk*, and *feet*. As a visual object is a special type of a region, it also implements the interface *SpatialObject*.

The concept of visual objects is required for tracking compound objects over time, which results in *MotionObjects*. A motion object denotes a sequence of visual objects and is bounded by a starting and ending visual object. As a visual object may consist of visual sub-objects, a motion object implicitly may consist of sub-motion objects. Using the previous example, a person-object could be tracked over time. As the person consists of the sub-objects *head* and *body*, implicitly two sub-motion objects would be tracked. As motion objects are tracked objects over time, they also have a temporal extent. Therefore, the class *MotionObject* implements the interface *TemporalObject*. This interface declares a set of methods for implementing temporal interval relations between temporal objects. The interface implicitly includes the 13 temporal interval relations proposed in [1], although it only defines seven. The basic temporal interval relations are: *before*, *meets*, *during*, *overlaps*, *starts*, *ends* and *equals*. All temporal relations except *equals* have inverse ones, which are implicitly covered by the return values of the methods.

2.3 The High-Level Video Indexing Part

The high-level indexing part of the model denotes that set of classes, which specifies typed, semantic-based content annotations to physical video units. These annotations are necessary since users usually do not want to search for videos by specifying constraints on their low-level visual features. Furthermore, content annotations allow a semantic-based browsing of video streams, not having to deal with unrelated sequences of key frames or shots.

In our *VideX* model, the basic class for content annotations is the *ContentObject* class. It represents an abstract class providing elementary functionalities for an arbitrary typed content object. It may refer to a low-level motion object for dealing with spatial, temporal or spatio-temporal characteristics of its physical pendant. As in most video streams, in which humans usually are interested in, objects like persons, locations and events are contained, the model even keeps track of these objects in its generic form. Furthermore, we are providing a class *MiscObject*, which can be any miscellaneous object that cannot be categorized as person, location or event. These four elementary concrete classes define the entry points for further specialization in specific application domains. In our prototype implementation, which is discussed in section 3, we illustrate the specialization in the case of soccer videos.

The model also includes the concept of video hyper-links, as described in [7], by relating content objects to physical or logical video units. There are mainly two different types of hyper-links. First, all content objects related to the same physical unit are hyper-linked together. These hyper-links are called *object-links* and delivered by method *getObjectLinks()* of class *PhysicalVideoUnit*. And second, all physical video units referenced by the same content object are hyper-linked together. These links are called *unit-links* and returned by method *getUnitLinks()* of class *ContentObject*. There are implicitly two further types of hyper-links, namely object-links of logical video units and logical unit-links of content objects. Video hyper-links allow a non-linear browsing of video story units. A non-linear browsing is much more effective and flexible than sequential approaches based on key-frames are.

3. THE SOCCER-BASED PROTOTYPE IMPLEMENTATION

We implemented a prototype of a distributed multimedia information system based on soccer videos. The system consists mainly of three interacting parts. First, a parallel video server providing selective access to physical video streams and their segments. Second, an index database capturing actually the segment and high-level indexing-part of the *VideX* model contains structural and semantic meta-information about the stored soccer streams. The video indexing model for the soccer domain extends the high-level indexing part of the generic *VideX* model with a rich set of soccer-specific classes. There are special events like e.g. *goals*, *free kicks* and *fouls* and special persons like *players* and *referees*. And third, a Java-based client provides users with graphical user-interfaces for video annotation, query specification and parallel browsing the video segments of the query results. Users may run queries against the system like:

"Find all video sequences, where a given player A scored a goal by head after a cross from the right over at least 30 meters, executed by player B."

The Java-based client requests the retrieved video segments from the video server and presents the received segment streams to the user in a parallel fashion. This is achieved by using Sun's *Java Media Framework*.

4. CONCLUSION

The main contribution of this paper to the research area of multimedia systems was the presentation of an integrated generic approach for indexing video streams. The proposed indexing model, called *VideX*, integrates both low- and high-level visual objects. Thereby, it tries to pick up the advantages of existing models and to reduce the number of their possible shortcomings. Additionally, it introduces extensions for structuring video streams and correlations of low- and high-level video objects. Video units are annotated by typed semantic video objects, as they facilitate an exact query formulation by using standard query languages. The *VideX* model is called generic, as it defines only the basic classes for an integrated video indexing system. It can be easily extended for specific application domains.

Future work concerns the integration of low-level features in the indexing part, as they are actually not contained by the database. To reduce semantic ambiguity during the annotation process, we will provide access to all low-level visual and motion objects known by the database. Then users will be able to associate directly high-level objects with low-level ones.

5. REFERENCES

[1] J.F. Allen, *Maintaining knowledge about temporal intervals*, Communications of the ACM **26** (1983), no. 11, 832–843.

[2] J.S. Boreczsky and L.A. Rowe, *A comparison of video shot boundary detection techniques*, Journal of Electronic Imaging **5** (1996), no. 2, 122–128.

[3] G. Davenport, T.G.A. Smith, and N. Pincever, *Cinematic primitives for multimedia*, IEEE Computer Graphics and Animation, Special Issue on Multimedia, 1991, pp. 67–74.

[4] Y. Deng and B.S. Manjunath, *NeTra-V: Toward an object based video representation*, IEEE Transactions on Circuits and Systems for Video Technology **8** (1998), no. 5, 616–627.

[5] M. Egenhofer and R. Franzosa, *Point-set topological spatial relations*, International Journal of Geographic Information Systems **5** (1991), no. 2, 161–174.

[6] R. Hjelsvold and R. Midtstraum, *Modeling and querying video data*, Proceedings of the 20th VLDB Conference, 1994, pp. 686–694.

[7] H. Jiang and A.K. Elmagarmid, *Spatial and temporal content-based access to hypervideo databases*, The VLDB Journal **7** (1998), no. 4, 226–238.

[8] International Standardization Organization, *MPEG-7 context and objectives*, ISO/IEC JTC1/SC29/WG11 N2460, October 1998.

[9] ———, *MPEG-4 overview (melbourne version)*, ISO/IEC JTC1/SC29/WG11 N2995, October 1999.

[10] D. Papadias and Y. Theodoridis, *Spatial relations, minimum bounding rectangles, and spatial data structures*, International Journal of Geographic Information Systems **11** (1997), no. 2, 111–138.

[11] Y. Rui, T.S. Huang, and S. Mehrotra, *Exploring video structure beyond the shots*, IEEE International Conference on Multimedia Computing and Systems, 1998, pp. 237–240.

[12] Roland Tusch, *Content-based indexing, exact search and smooth presentation of abstracted video streams*, Master's thesis, Klagenfurt University, Department of Information Technology, 1999.

[13] H.J. Zhang, A. Kankanhalli, and S.W. Smoliar, *Automatic partitioning of full-motion video*, ACM Multimedia Systems **1** (1993), no. 1, 10–28.

[14] D. Zhong and S.-F. Chang, *Video object model and segmentation for content-based video indexing*, IEEE International Symposium on Circuits and Systems (ISCAS'97), 1997, pp. 1492–1495.

SURFing the Home with Your TV

Dimitrios Voutsas
University of California, Los Angeles
Department of Computer Science
Los Angeles, CA 90095

dimitris@hotmail.com

Christine Halverson
IBM Research
650 Harry Rd E3/456
San Jose, CA 95120
1-408-723-1925
krys@us.ibm.com

ABSTRACT

SURF (Simple UI to Retrieve Favorites) is a system with which a user can interact, through a TV, both with electronic devices inside the house and with the World Wide Web (WWW). The user communicates with the TV by voice in two modes: reactive and proactive. We illustrate how, by speaking naturally, the user can check on locations in the home, or get information from appliances and specific information from the Internet, in a manner that does not interrupt the TV viewing experience.

Keywords

Internet TV, Interactive Television, Home Devices, Speech Recognition, Natural Language, Information Extraction, Information Representation.

1. INTRODUCTION

SURF (Simple UI to Retrieve Favorites) is a system that aims to transform a TV into an information portal [1] through which a user can interact with electronic devices inside the house, and also retrieve information from the World Wide Web (WWW) while continuing to watch TV [2]. Although a TV set can be used as a very efficient output device because of the screen's large area, it is limited in how it can receive input since the remote control is not adequate for tasks such as typing. Even though a keyboard could be connected to the TV, most people would not like having one on a table next to a sofa. Moreover, the primary task of the user in this case is watching TV, and this task should not be interrupted for more than a few seconds. Otherwise, the user gets distracted and the system does not satisfy the user's needs [3, 4].

These are some of the problems that every system, designed to bring interactivity to the TV, must tackle. SURF addresses these problems and attempts to overcome them by providing more "natural" means of interaction between the user and the system. SURF aims to enhance the TV viewing experience, not replace it.

The system uses speech recognition to receive input from the user and natural language techniques to understand the user's request. The information that is to be displayed, after an event has occurred or when the results of a query have returned, is usually short and therefore takes up only a small top portion of the TV screen. Larger amounts of information are either displayed in scrolling marquees or on the entire screen in the form of HTML pages. In the latter case, the TV program that the user was viewing is always preserved and keeps running in a smaller window on the screen.

2. BACKGROUND
2.1 Related Work

The idea of having the user interact with the TV is not new. There are many platforms available in the market that claim to offer various interactive features and access to the Internet through the TV. One of these platforms is WebTV. However, the WebTV platform [5] makes it difficult to view TV and browse the Internet at the same time (unless the Web page is written especially for the WebTV platform) since the user is forced to choose one of two modes, 'web' or 'tv'. Liberate [6] also is based on the concept of access to the Internet through TV. This platform allows the user to browse the Internet and watch TV at the same time by dedicating the top portion of the screen for the TV program and the rest for viewing Web pages. The system receives input from the user by a remote control and a keyboard.

None of these systems addresses interaction with other devices inside the house. If ubiquitous computing [7] is to become a reality, then interaction between them should exist. In contrast, our approach is to allow such interaction and let the users accomplish all their tasks, without interfering with their primary activity – watching TV. As an example, we describe a scenario of how SURF can be used [8].

2.2 Scenario

While the user is relaxing in the living room and watching his favorite show on TV, he hears a noise in the kitchen. Curious to find out what happened, but not willing to sacrifice his favorite show, he clicks the push-to-talk button on the remote and asks "Show me the kitchen". Instantly, a small window appears on the top left corner of the screen showing the kitchen from the view of a panoramic camera that is placed there. It was a false alarm, and everything looks fine.

Feeling hungry, and not wanting to interrupt his show, he asks "What's in the fridge". An HTML page is displayed on the screen, listing all the items that have been scanned before being placed in the refrigerator. On the top of the page, in a window of a size that the user can watch comfortably, his favorite show continues to play (see Figure 1). After viewing the contents he clicks on the window and the TV show uses the full screen again.

Figure 1: TV program in small window at top and the list of refrigerator contents below.

On a commercial break, he rushes to the kitchen to make his sandwich. He places a cup of tea in the microwave oven, sets the oven for tea, and returns to the living room. At the right temperature for tea, a sensor inside the oven detects that the desired temperature has been reached and sends a message to the TV. Our user, back watching TV, sees the message that pops up on the top of the screen, saying "Your tea is ready" (see Figure 2).

Figure 2: Message from the microwave oven, displayed over program, saying "Your tea is ready".

Later, he thinks about his trip to Miami in a few hours. He wonders about the weather there, so that he will know what clothes to take. So, he asks "What's the weather in Miami now?". The text, with the results, is displayed in a scrolling marquee, since it will be longer than the screen's width, on the top of the TV screen (see Figure 3).

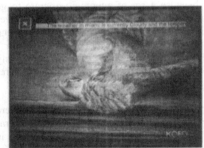

Figure 3: Information about the weather in Miami is extracted from Yahoo's weather website and displayed.

2.3 Open Agent Architecture (OAA)

Connection to other devices is possible because of the distributed agent architecture provided by SRI's Open Agent Architecture (OAA) [9]. OAA is a framework in which a community of software agents running on distributed machines can work together. An agent is defined as being software that conforms to the communication and functional standards imposed by the platform. So that multiple agents can cooperate, OAA agents delegate and receive work requests through a Facilitator agent. Thus, there is no need for each agent to interface with others, but simply to interface with the Facilitator. Requests are expressed in an Interagent Communication Language common to all agents. In addition, agents possess a common set of functionalities, such as the ability to install local or remote triggers.

3. SYSTEM IMPLEMENTATION
3.1 Logical Infrastructure

SURF uses the WebTV platform (1) to add interactive features to the TV viewing experience by displaying HTML content and a TV program at the same time and (2) to use Internet connectivity to interface with other devices and to retrieve information from the Internet. Information is presented in the form of HTML pages designed especially for the WebTV platform so that HTML content and a TV program can co-exist simultaneously.

The system uses the Nuance speech recognizer [10] to interpret the user's voice input. The recognizer is robust and, most important, it is speaker independent and thus requires no training for a specific user. The latter advantage is significant because the system is not intended for a single user, but would be used by all the members of a family.

Embedded inside the remote control is a microphone. The user clicks a push-to-talk button on the remote to activate the microphone. On the top left corner of the TV screen is a virtual button that provides visual feedback. When the push-to-talk button is clicked, the color around the displayed button changes from yellow to green, so the user knows that the speech recognizer has been activated and is listening for a request. SURF has two modes from which the user can select. In *confirmation* mode, after the speech recognition process is completed, the system asks for the user's confirmation by displaying the recognized text and two options: continue or cancel. This mode has been designed for surrounding environments with loud noise, where the speech recognizer might produce false recognition results. In the other mode, the recognized speech is automatically transferred for execution without a request for confirmation, thus decreasing the overall reply time and not forcing the user to issue multiple inputs (input + confirmation) for a single request.

The recognized speech is transferred to a natural language parser [11] that decides what the task is that the user requested. This information is passed to an interface process entity, which either routes the request to the appropriate agent for execution (when the request concerns a device inside the house) or goes to the Internet to retrieve the requested information. Results of the request are represented to the user on an HTML page, which is displayed on the screen without interruption of the TV program. The link between our system and the WebTV set-top-box is a JAVA servlet that accepts requests by using the GET method and replies by sending the generated HTML page to the set-top-box. The logical information flow is depicted in Figure 4.

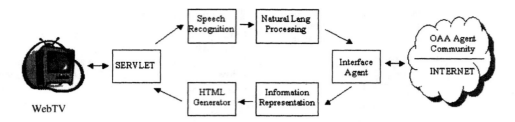

Figure 4: Logical information flow of SURF.

3.2 Interfacing with Other Devices

Using the OAA architecture, the agents can communicate with each other by exchanging messages through their Facilitator. SURF interfaces to multiple devices inside the house by having a special agent that sends messages and queries to the various devices according to the user's request. One of these devices is the refrigerator, Collaborative Home e-Fridge (CheF) [12]. CheF "knows" what items are in it because they have RFID tags that are scanned as each item passes through the door. Other home devices are panoramic cameras that can be placed anywhere inside the house, a microwave oven, a clock, and a caller-id device on the telephone. All these devices are separate agents that receive queries when SURF requests information or send messages when an event occurs.

When the user asks "What's in the fridge", after the request is recognized and understood, the Interface Agent sends a query to the fridge, asking it to list all the items that are inside. The fridge returns the results in the form of a list, which is passed to another agent that produces an HTML page. This page is projected on the screen, with the TV program that the user was watching in a window on top, and the items listed below.

This case illustrates the *reactive* mode of SURF, where the user requests something. In another case, the message from the microwave oven pops up on the screen. The user has not asked for this information explicitly, but implicitly, by placing the cup of tea with the temperature sensor in the microwave oven. Similarly, the caller-id device sends a message to the system when an incoming call arrives, informing the user of the number that is calling. These two last cases show the *proactive* mode of SURF where an event occurs and the user is informed without explicitly asking for information.

3.3 Information Retrieval from the WWW

Using the connection to the Internet provided by WebTV, SURF retrieves various kinds of information. One example is the weather forecast for any city. The system receives this request and executes a WebL [13] script, which goes live to the Yahoo Weather Web site and retrieves the weather forecast for that city. The HTML page returned by the Web server is parsed and the forecast is extracted. The text with the result is constructed and displayed to the user in a scrolling marquee on the top of the TV screen.

The OAA agent designated for this task was developed for another project. With the OAA architecture, this agent was easily adapted to the SURF agent community. Similarly, the user can ask for stock quotes. The process is exactly the same as the weather request.

4. DISCUSSION

SURF was designed and implemented with the motivation that the user is not in front of a computer, and interaction with the system must be adapted to the special conditions of a TV set. Speech recognition with natural language capability is used so that the burden of issuing and processing the input is on the system's side. This allows the user to focus without interruption on the primary activity, which is watching TV. Furthermore, even in the voice navigational systems that exist, the user is allowed to use voice only for handling menus and selecting items in them in a step-by-step fashion.

In SURF, on the other hand, the user uses voice to state the end goal without worrying about intermediate stages or the route that must be followed for this goal to be achieved. In this way, speech recognition provides a shortcut to the user for defining the goal, and the application designer provides the mechanism for its success. Finally, by embedding the microphone inside the remote control, the user does not need any additional device except the one that has been always used for viewing TV.

The same conditions and restrictions also apply to displaying output. When SURF needs to display information to the user, it blends this information with the TV program being viewed so that it will not be interrupted. When the user asks for the weather forecast, the system could simply redirect him to the appropriate Web page where the information is located. Although this solution provides the answer to the user's request, it is not the most efficient one because the user is asked to stop his current activity and start a new one. In SURF, the initial activity does not have to stop because a set of agents co-operate to get the Web page that answers the user's request, locate the answer inside the page by parsing it, extract it, and reconstruct a new message with the answer that will be displayed to the user in a scrolling marquee. This allows the user to simultaneously continue watching the TV program and view the results of his request.

5. CONCLUSION

We have demonstrated an approach that makes interacting with other devices and the Web possible without detracting from viewing TV. Our focus on interaction with TV and in the home extends earlier work based on distributed agent architectures and multimodal interfaces. As computers become invisible, methods of interaction become more important and the underlying architecture must support multiple interaction methods. We have shown a first step in how to do this with SURF.

6. ACKNOWLEDGMENTS

This work was done while both authors were part of the Computer Human Interaction Center (CHIC!) at SRI International.Many thanks to the entire CHIC! Group at SRI International for supporting this project and especially to the following people: Luc Julia and Adam Cheyer for providing both conceptual and technical ideas, Didier Guzzoni for support in the OAA-related parts of the system, and Ruth Lang for help in organizing the ideas for this paper. We also thank Bob Bolles for his help capturing some very nice screenshots.

7. REFERENCES

[1] T. Regan. *Taking Living Worlds into People's Living Rooms.* Third Symposium on Virtual Reality Modeling Language, Monterey, California, 1998.

[2] S. J. Mountford, P. Mitchell, P. O'Hara, J. Sparks, M. Whitby. *When Computers Are Computers Are TVs* (panel). Conference Proceedings on Human Factors in Computing Systems, Monterey, California, 1992.

[3] D. Herigstad, A. Wichansky. *Designing User Interfaces for Television.* Proceedings of CHI 98: Human Factors in Computing Systems, Los Angeles, California, 1998.

[4] J. O'Brien, T. Rodden, M. Rouncefield, J. Hughes. *At Home with the Technology: An ethnographic study of a set-top-box trial.* ACM Transactions on Computer-Human Interaction, Volume 6, Issue 3, 1999.

[5] E. Darnell. *Design brief: WebTV Networks.* Interactions, Volume 7, Issue 2, 2000.

[6] J. Palmer, J. Fulker, A. Liston, D. Misconish, P. Arnold. *Design brief: Liberate.* Interactions, Volume 7, Issue 2, 2000.

[7] M. Weiser. *The Computer for the 21st Century.* Scientific American, 265 (3), 66-75, 1991.

[8] General information about the SURF demo is at http://chic.sri.com/projects/OpenHouse/welcome.html and video is part of the CHIC-on-TV video at http://chic.sri.com/projects/videos.html.

[9] D. L. Martin, A. J. Cheyer, and D. B. Moran. *The Open Agent Architecture: A framework for building distributed software systems.* Applied Artificial Intelligence, Volume 13, pp. 91-128, January-March 1999.

[10] www.nuance.com. Nuance is a spin-off of SRI's Speech Technology and Research (STAR) Laboratory.

[11] J. Dowding, J.M. Gawron, D. Appelt, J. Bear, L. Cherny, R. Moore, D. Moran. *Gemini: A natural language system for spoken language understanding.* 31st Annual meeting of the Association for Computational Linguistics, Columbus, Ohio, 1993.

[12] L. Julia. *Augmenting Humans' Experiences.* OzCHI 99, Wagga Wagga, Australia, November, 1999.

[13] Thomas Kistler and Hannes Marais. *WebL: A Programming Language for the Web.* 7th International World Wide Web Conference Full Programme, Brisbane, Australia, April, 1998.

Data Allocation Algorithms for Distributed Video Servers*

James Z. Wang
School of Electrical Engineering & Computer Sci.
University of Central Florida
Orlando, FL 32816-2362, USA
zwang@cs.ucf.edu

Ratan K. Guha
School of Electrical Engineering & Computer Sci.
University of Central Florida
Orlando, FL 32816-2362, USA
guha@cs.ucf.edu

ABSTRACT

In this paper, We discuss the server level data allocation problems in the distributed Video-on-Demand systems. We proposed two data allocation algorithms, Bandwidth Weighted Partition (BWP) algorithm and Popularity Based (PB) algorithm, based on the bandwidth and storage capacity limits of the distributed multimedia servers. We compare those two algorithms with the traditional Round Robin (RR) algorithm. The analysis and simulation studies show that PB algorithm is a simple and practical video data allocation algorithm for the distributed video servers. It provides near optimal system performance in any system condition.

1. INTRODUCTION

There are many studies reported on data management for multimedia servers [1, 2, 3, 4, 5, 6]. However, only a few of them deal with the distributed multimedia environment [5, 6]. In this paper, we study the problems associated with the data allocation among the distributed multiple video servers located in different geographical locations across a WAN environment. Recent works discussing the data allocation issues in the distributed multimedia environment have focused on how to manage the multimedia data among the different storage devices [5, 6]. The objective of those data management schemes is to efficiently allocate and migrate the multimedia data between different storage devices in order to provide smaller user request latency and larger system throughput. We categorize those data management schemes as device level data management. In this study, we discuss the server level data management. At the server level, we only see the online multimedia data, i.e., data ready to be delivered to the clients when requests arrive. How to make the data online is the problem of the device level data management. We discuss three video data allocation algorithms and compare their performance using simulation studies.

*partial support by Army Research Contract No. DAAH04-95-1-0250.

The rest of the paper is organized as follows. In section 2, We propose the distributed multimedia data allocation algorithms. In section 3, we use simulation to model the distributed VOD servers and compare the proposed algorithms based on the system performance in terms of the average user request latency time. We have our concluding remarks in section 4.

2. DATA ALLOCATION ALGORITHMS FOR DISTRIBUTED VIDEO SERVERS

We discuss the video allocation algorithms based on two most important performance factors, server bandwidth and storage capacity, in the following paragraphs.

2.1 Round Robin Allocation Algorithm

Conventionally we assume each server has similar process power, i.e., they can handle equal number of concurrent streams at the same streaming rate. So the task of the video data allocation is to evenly distribute the hot video objects to the distributed servers so that no one server will have to handle most of the user requests. Let us assume the video object set is $V = \{v_1, v_2, \cdots v_m\}$ with the corresponding user access frequencies to the video objects is $F = \{f_1, f_2, \cdots f_m\}$ where $\sum_{i=1}^{m} f_i = 1$. Without losing generality, we also assume $f_1 \geq f_2 \geq \cdots \geq f_m$. We assume the server set is $\{S_1, S_2, \cdots S_n\}$ with the storage capacities $\{C_1, C_2, \cdots, C_n\}$, respectively.

Table 1: Round Robin video data allocation

S_1	S_2	......	S_{n-1}	S_n
v_1	v_2	......	v_{n-1}	v_n
v_{2n}	v_{2n-1}	......	v_{n+2}	v_{n+1}
...	...	......	...	...

The idea of the *Round Robin* (RR) algorithm is presented by Table 1. The actual algorithm varies slightly from the above basic idea because we need to consider the storage capacity of the servers.

2.2 Bandwidth Weighted Partition Algorithm

Instead of letting a single server handle the user requests for a specified object, we allow video servers to coordinate the delivery of the data for a single video object to the client's workstations. We partition each video object into the video servers in the way that the servers with higher server bandwidth will be allocated with a larger portion of the video data. Table 2 presents the BWP algorithm. We assume the server set is $\{S_1, S_2, \cdots S_n\}$ with the respective server bandwidths $\{B_1, B_2, \cdots, B_n\}$. For the object v_i, we

456

partition its data into n continuous chunks $v_{i_1}, v_{i_2}, \cdots, v_{i_n}$ where $size(v_{i_j}) = size(v_i) \cdot \frac{B_j}{\sum_{k=1}^{n} B_k}$.

Table 2: Bandwidth Weighted Partition Algorithm

S_1	S_2	......	S_{n-1}	S_n
v_{11}	v_{12}	......	$v_{1,n-1}$	v_{1n}
v_{21}	v_{22}	......	$v_{2,n-1}$	v_{2n}
...	...	......	...	...

This algorithm partition the video data based on the server bandwidth. It balances the server bandwidth utilization very well and hence derives excellent system performance.

2.3 Popularity Based Data Allocation Algorithm

The idea of the PB algorithm is to let the server with higher bandwidth handle larger portion of the user requests. Besides the same assumption as in the RR algorithm, We assume the respective server bandwidths are $\{B_1, B_2, \cdots, B_n\}$ for the servers $\{S_1, S_2, \cdots S_n\}$. Without losing generality, we further assume the access to each object requires equal server bandwidth. To allocate the video objects, we first calculate what percentage of the total user requests a certain video server may handle based on its server bandwidth. We transform the server bandwidths $\{B_1, B_2, \cdots, B_n\}$ into their normalized server bandwidths $\{\bar{B}_1, \bar{B}_2, \cdots, \bar{B}_n\}$ where $\bar{B}_i = \frac{B_i}{\sum_{j=1}^{n} B_j}$. Obviously we have $\sum_{i=1}^{n} \bar{B}_i = 1$. Since we have $n \ll m$, it is reasonable to assume $f_i < \bar{B}_j$ for any $i \in [1, m]$ and $j \in [1, n]$. It is also reasonable to assume the total storage capacity of the servers is not less than the entire video database size, i.e., $\sum_{i=1}^{n} C_i \geq \sum_{j=1}^{m} Size(v_j)$. Thus the ideal video data allocation algorithm divides the video set V into n subsets $\{V_1, V_2, \cdots, V_n\}$ and allocates subset V_i to server S_i where $i \in [1, n]$, so that we have $C_i \geq \sum_{j=1}^{k} Size(v_{i_j})$ and $\bar{B}_i = \sum_{j=1}^{k} f_{i_j}$ for video subset $V_i = \{v_{i_1}, v_{i_2}, \ldots, v_{i_k}\}$. However, implementing such an ideal algorithm requires $C_m^n = \frac{n \cdot (n-1) \cdots (n-m+1)}{m \cdot (m-1) \cdots 2 \cdot 1}$ computation complexity. Furthermore, there is no guarantee the optimal solution exists. So we design the approximate video allocation algorithm as depicted in Figure 1.

```
Algorithm: Popularity_Based_Allocation
for(i=1; i≤n; i++) { RB(i) = B̄i; RC(i) = Ci; }
ServerNum = n;
for(i=1; i≤m; i++) {
    Find the server j with largest RB.
    if(RC(j) ≥ Size(i)) {
        RC(j) -= si;  RB(j) -= fi;
        Allocate Object i to Server j.
        Consider all servers for the next object.
        ServerNum = n;
    }
    else { /* This server is full */
        Delete server j from consideration.
        ServerNum = ServerNum - 1; i = i - 1;
        if(ServerNum = 0)
            Fail due to lack of storage capacity.
    }
}
```

Figure 1: Popularity Based Data Allocation Algorithm

3. PERFORMANCE STUDY

We have developed a simulator to compare the performance of the proposed data allocation algorithms. Our simulator consists of *Request Generator*, *Dispatcher*, and *Servers*. The request generator is responsible for creating requests. The dispatcher routes the requests to the server where the requested object is located. There are four servers in our simulator. User requests are modeled using a Poisson process. The access frequencies of objects in the database follow a Zipf-like distribution. The access frequency for each video object, v_i, is determined as $f_i = \frac{1}{i^z \cdot \sum_{j=1}^{m} 1/j^z}$, where m is the number of objects in the system, and $0 \leq z \leq 1$ is the z-factor [1]. We summarize the simulation parameters in Table 3. We use those parameters to perform our simulation unless otherwise stated. Because users are most concerned about the latencies of their requests, we use average request latency as our performance metric.

Table 3: Simulation parameters

Server Storage Capacity	700,000 MB ($\approx$ 685 GB)
Playback rate B_p	6 Mbits/sec
Zipf factor	0.7
Requests inter-arrival time	5 seconds
Number of objects	1000
Object size	2,800 MB
Number of requests	20,000

In addition to the parameters listed in Table 3, we also need to determine a reasonable server bandwidth for us to compare the difference of the algorithms. Through simulation study, We choose the average server bandwidth to be 580 MB/sec in the rest of performance study.

3.1 Performance under various data skew condition

In this simulation, We varied the skew factor between 0.0 and 1.0. The results are plotted in Figure 2. It shows the BWP algorithm does not affect by data skew condition and its performance is the best in this situation. When the data skew condition was mild (less than 0.5), the RR algorithm performed well with the average latency less than 40 seconds. However, when the data skew condition became severe, the average latency for this algorithm increased drastically. The PB algorithm performed very well in any access skew condition. All of its latencies were less than 40 seconds which is practical for a 1-hour video.

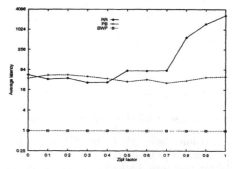

Figure 2: Performance under different access skew

3.2 Servers have different bandwidths

In the real distributed Video-On-Demand systems, the server bandwidths are different in different video servers. We studied system performance under this condition. We let the servers have an average bandwidth of 580 MB/sec. Their individual server bandwidth were different as $B_1 = 505$ MB/sec, $B_2 = 555$ MB/sec, $B_3 = 605$ MB/sec and B_4

= 655 MB/sec. We also assume each server has enough storage capacity to complete all three algorithms. We varied the skew factor between 0.0 and 1.0 as in the previous simulation. The results are plotted in Figure 3. It shows the RR algorithm is practically useless in this situation. On the other hand, BWP algorithm and PB algorithm performed very well.

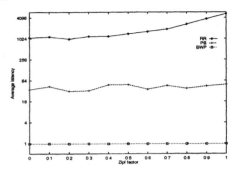

Figure 3: Servers have different bandwidths

3.3 The impact of the server storage capacity

In the previous simulations, we assumed all the servers have enough storage capacity to distribute the objects by the algorithms. However, in a real VOD system, it is not always the case. In this situation, BWP algorithm and PB algorithm will have to comply with storage limitation on the servers. We studied the similar situation using our simulator. We let all servers have same storage capacity of 685 GB. The server bandwidth in the servers were $B_1 = 505$ MB/sec, $B_2 = 555$ MB/sec, $B_3 = 605$ MB/sec and $B_4 = 655$ MB/sec. Because the servers have equal storage capacity, the data partition in the BWP algorithm should not be based on the server bandwidth. Each server has to store equal portion of an object. We also varied the zipf factor in the simulation, the results are presented by Figure 4.

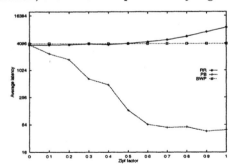

Figure 4: Impact of the server storage capacity

The simulation shows that the RR algorithm and the BWP algorithm are practically useless in this situation. When the zipf factor was zero, i.e., all objects had equal opportunity being accessed, the average latency for the PB algorithm was almost the same as that for the other two algorithms. This result is not surprising at all because there is no way for the PB algorithm to distribute the user requests to the servers based on their server bandwidth because of the server storage constraints. However, when the data skew factor is increased, PB algorithm takes advantage of the data access skew condition and put the hotter objects in the higher bandwidth servers. Hence, the average latency

dropped. When the zipf factor was greater than 0.5, the average latency time dropped below 1 minute. It is reasonable for 1-hour video objects. Based on the results of simulation we expect the PB algorithm will perform very well in the real distributed VOD systems.

4. CONCLUDING REMARKS

In this paper, we thoroughly discussed the data allocation problems in the distributed Video-On-Demand environment. We proposed two different algorithms, *Bandwidth Weighted Partition* (BWP) algorithm and *Popularity Based* (PB) algorithm, to address the problems that affect the system performance. Through our analysis and simulation, we found the BWP algorithm balanced the server bandwidth utilization very well if the server storage capacity is not limited. Its performance is not affected by the user request patterns. In the ideal situation, the BWP algorithm provides the optimal system performance. This algorithm requires larger storage capacities for the higher bandwidth servers. The ideal situation is the server storage capacity proportional to the server bandwidth. But those conditions are not guaranteed in the real VOD systems. On the other hand, partitioning the data across the servers causes problems in video presentation. We need extra processing effort and extra bandwidth to ensure there is no jitter or delay when switching from one data server to another data server. The PB algorithm does not partition the video objects. It allocates the video objects based on their access frequencies. This algorithm not only factors in all resource constraints in video servers but also takes advantage of the access skew to the video objects. The simulation results show it provides near optimal results in any condition. Thus in the VOD systems where the data access skew condition is usually severe, the PB algorithm is an excellent video data allocation algorithm.

5. REFERENCES

[1] James Z. Wang and Kien A. Hua. A bandwidth management technique for hierarchical storage in large-scale multimedia servers. In *Proc. of IEEE Int'l Conf. on Multimedia Computing and Systems*, pages 261–268, Ottawa, Ontario, Canada, June 1997.

[2] Y. Wang and D. Du. Weighted striping in multimedia servers. In *Proc. of IEEE Int'l Conf. on Multimedia Computing and Systems*, pages 102–109, Ottawa, Ontario, Canada, June 1997.

[3] T.-S. Chau, J. Li, B. Ooi, and K-L. Tan. Disk striping strategies for large video-on-demand servers. In *Proc. of ACM Multimedia*, pages 297–306, Boston, MA, November 1996.

[4] S. Berson, S. Ghandeharizadeh, R. Muntz, and X. Ju. Staggered striping in multimedia information systems. In *Proc. of ACM SIGMOD Conf.*, pages 79–90, May 1994.

[5] D. W. Brubeck and L. A. Bowe. Hierarchical storage management in a distributed VOD system. *IEEE Multimedia*, pages 37–47, Fall 1996.

[6] Jamel Gafsi and Ernst W. Biersack. Performance and reliability study for distributed video servers: Mirroring or parity? In *Proc. of IEEE Int'l Conf. on Multimedia Computing and Systems*, volume 2, pages 628–634, Florence, Italy, June 1999.

Identify Regions of Interest(ROI) for video watermark embedment with Principle Component Analysis

Roy Wang[1]   Qiang Cheng[1]   Thomas Huang[1]

University of Illinois at Urbana Champaign
[1]Beckman Institute, 405 N. Matthew Av. Urbana, IL 61801
{rwang,qcheng,huang}@ifp.uiuc.edu

ABSTRACT

The temporal redundancy of video provides a greater space than images for information hiding at the expense of invitation towards many forms of spatial and temporal attacks, such as frame dropping, frame averaging that are not common in images. With video, the active change of watermark placement location serves as an effective counterattack measure. In this paper, we utilize principal components of joint feature observation of video frames to robustly determine the location of watermark embedment. The approach eliminates the need of storing original sequence and is robust against common attacks.

Keywords

Principal Component Analysis, PCA, Video Watermarking, Region of Interest, Clustering.

1. INTRODUCTION

Principal Component Analysis (PCA) has been used extensively in pattern recognition and classification community for various aims. It has been employed to find basis supports such as eigenfaces [1], feature space reduction in image databases, and classifying video streams [2]. Our view of PCA in the watermark case is a feature-space generation tool, which may give one a more robust representation of data distribution against possible noise contaminant. With PCA, we are able to put a virtual ownership stamp on a video frame using all its helpful cues. The byproduct of this ownership stamp is the freedom of having a self-contained watermark verification that does not need original video.

Some recent video watermark work are listed here. Hsu and Wu [12] describe a video watermarking method for compressed video, which requires the original video frames for the detection stage.

Hartung and Girod [8] propose spread-spectrum based watermarks for uncompressed frame sequences and a compressed-domain embedment scheme on top of MPEG. Langelaar et al. [9] proposed a video watermarking method by selectively discarding the high frequency energy of the DCT coefficients. Statistical method to choose the parameters in their scheme was given. Swanson et al. [6] proposed a multi-scale watermarking method making use of the temporal wavelet transforms. They also suggest embedding watermarks into objects to resist the statistical attack, since the watermark in the low temporal frequency components is susceptible to the statistical analysis. How to define and segment objects is an open research issue in itself. Hartang and Kutter [7] provide an excellent review on video watermarking scheme.

We use PCA along with clustering to identify two regions of interests in a given video. Of the two regions of interests, one has a higher mean absolute motion activity than the other. The basic motivation behind having two motion-separated classes is to counterattack statistical analysis by attackers. Swanson [6] illustrates how to use temporal wavelet transform to mark object and static regions to put watermarks in. However, in general, one has no notion of what object is and segmentation is hard to come by. When the camera-induced background motion is involved, the object and background are often switched in their places in motion domination. Since our goal is to have one class drifting faster in time and the other drifting slower. The dichotomist separation into high motion class and low motion class are adequate low-level representation that serves this purpose.

The paper is organized as the following. In section 2, we discuss how to perform PCA to identify regions of interests on data features extracted based on the MPEG1/2 platform. We also illustrate how to insert video watermarks based on the regions of interests. In section 3, we study various clustering options and watermark attacks commonly seen in videos. We then draw our conclusion in section 4.

2. Representation, Embedment, and Retrieval

2.1 PCA representation

Experimentally, one observes that small amount of image degradation can make otherwise visually similar frames have quite different motion distributions with block matching motion estimation or other types of motion estimation. Thus, the motion field itself alone is hardly a sole reliable ownership indicator. PCA leads an elegant way to combine a set of different features (motion, spatial coordinates, and intensity values etc.) to give a robust and compact representation that serves as a strong ownership indicator of a given video frame. We have this representation only locally in time (considering just 1 video frame's features) to prevent any localized attack such as frame dropping.

To illustrate our approach, we denote the number of rows of macroblocks in the frame as M, the number of columns of macroblocks as N. So there are total M*N macroblocks, or observations in our data matrix **U**. Each row of data matrix U_i is a 6-d vector. We column-scan the macroblocks into the data matrix **U**, which has the dimension of M*N by 6.

$$U = \begin{bmatrix} U_{11} & U_{12} & .. & U_{16} \\ .. & .. & .. & .. \\ U_{M*N1} & U_{M*N2} & .. & U_{M*N6} \end{bmatrix} \qquad (1)$$

All the U_{ij} values are either directly retrieved from the compressed stream or indirectly computed based on decoded frame sequences. Before we perform PCA, we first Gaussian normalize each dimension.

$$\forall U_j \ni U, U'_{ij} = \exp(-\frac{(U_{ij} - E(U_j))^2}{Var(U_j)}) \qquad (2)$$

$$\{i \ni [1, M*N], j \ni [1,6]\}$$

where U_j is the jth column or jth dimension of the data set **U**, and **U'** is the newly formed dataset. By normalizing each dimension, we ensure that sparse outliers would not severally influence PCA results by their large distance to data center [5].

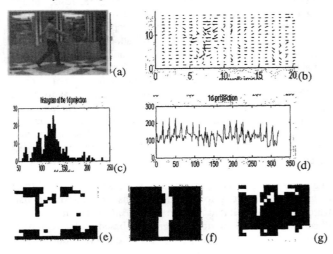

Figure 1. (a)Frame 38 'roywalk', (b)motion field, (c) histogram of 1-d projection data, and (d)1-d projection data created by PCA on column-scanned macroblocks.(e)the 2-class Fuzzy c-mean clustering results on the 1-d projection data (f) 40 macroblocks from high motion class picked out based on spatial constraints (g)100 macroblocks from low motion class picked out based on spatial constraints. Note: the spatial locations of blocks in

generally may not correspond to semantics-level object segmentation.

2.2 Watermark Insertion and Retrieval

<u>Watermark Embedding Stage:</u> After determining the principal direction of projection, we perform a two-class fuzzy c-mean clustering to determine the two binary support maps M1 and M2 for two regions of interest. Inserting watermarks W1 and W2 with equation (3) forms a new watermarked image.

$$I' = I + W_1*M_1 + W_2*M_2. \qquad (3)$$

<u>Watermark Retrieval Stage:</u> Similarly, We extract ROI's by applying PCA and clustering. Then, we use a correlation based watermark tester to examine the presence of watermark. Our video embedment scheme enables any correlation-based watermark to be used without the storage of original video.

3. Experiments

Some notations we use in this section are '*HMC*', *which* stands for High Motion Class and '*LMC*', *which* stands for Low Motion Class. They are the two class classification outcomes of PCA followed by c-mean. The one with higher mean absolute motion magnitude is found to be high motion class. '*Overlap Block Count*' refers to how two spatial block masks differ by checking how many blocks they have in common. '*Region of Interest*' is referred to a set of macroblock indices where watermarks are either to be inserted or though to contain watermarks. '*Block*' refer to the MPEG macroblocks.

3.1.1 On moving correlation of Region of Interest

We start with a frame and get its two-class region of interest masks and we check every nine frames (one GOP in our test MPEG stream), and see how much overlapping the subsequent frame has against the current frame. Figure 2 gives an intuitive feel of how moving correlation differs between HMC and LMC. It shows how HMC drifts faster than the LMC.

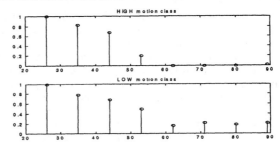

Figure 2. Plot of % of overlap against start frame v.s. frame # of the 'roywalk' sequence. The top one is for HMC, and bottom one is for LMC.

3.1.2 PCA to aid the consistency of Region of Interest.

In this study, we compare PCA followed with classification against classification only to see how consistent the ROIs are against compression attack. The study is performed with 'coast_guard' sequence undergoing various compression attacks.

Table 1

Compression Level	Visual quality	PCA with fuzzy c-mean	Fuzzy c-mean only
the pair of parenthesis has the # of overlapped blocks against uncompressed case. 1st value for High motion class, and 2nd for low motion class.			
Uncompress	Original	(40,100)	(40,100)
Jpeg 60%	Good	(40, 99)	(36, 96)
Jpeg 20%	Blurry	(39,100)	(36, 95)
Jpeg 5%	Extremely Blocky	(38, 97)	(27, 82)

3.1.3 On common video watermark attacks

The following experiments show the effectiveness of our ROI combined with correlation-based, DCT-domain watermark

Table 2

Columns are compression level, visual quality and watermark score respectively. The pairs of parenthesis have two scores, one for high motion class and low motion class.

Uncompressed	Original	(0.9426,1.0000)
Jpeg Quality 60%	Good	(0.9347,1.0000)
Jpeg Quality 20%	Burry	(0.9558,1.0000)
Jpeg Quality 5%	Extremely Blocky	(0.6455,0.5989)

Table 3

Columns are # of frames dropped, visual quality, overlap block count for HMC and LMC, watermark correlation score for HMC and LMC.

0	Unchanged	40	100	0.89	1
1	Unnoticeable	40	100	0.89	1
2	Slight jump	40	100	0.89	1
6	Obvious jump	0	0	0.07(0.36)	0.02(1)

Numbers in parenthesis are the correlation score of current class image against the other class' watermark (e.g. correlation of HMC features against LMC stored watermark). Extreme cases have the two classes switched in place due to motion distortion.

Table 4

Columns are # of frames averaged, visual quality, overlap block counts for HMC and LMC, watermark correlation scores for HMC and LMS.

0	Unchanged	40	100	0.8907	1
5	Edge Blurry	40	100	0.8907	1
10	Blurry Edge& Interior	40	100	0.8907	1
15	Blurry Edge& Interior	40	100	0.8907	1

4. The Conclusion

In this paper, we have presented a PCA-based framework that uses multiple cues to identify the ownership of a video frame. The ownership is expressed as two region of interests derived from a two-class classification result of the projected 1 dimensional subspace. One class drifts with a larger speed in the sequence than the other one. The dual watermark and their location provide a strong ownership stamp to a video frame without referring to the original sequence. In section 3, we have demonstrated the robustness of our scheme against various attacks. Some issues that we have not addressed are possible computational reduction techniques and feature selections.

5. Acknowledgement

The work is partly supported under NSF grant CDA 96-24396.

6. REFERENCES

[1] M.A Turk, A.P. Pentland "Face recognition using eigenfaces", *Computer Vision and Pattern Recognition* 1991

[2] Emile Sahouria and Avideh Zakhor, "Content Analysis of Video Using Principal Components" *IEEE Transaction on Circuits and Systems for Video Technology* Vol. 9, No.8 December, 1999

[3] L.T. Jolliffe, *Principal Component Analysis* New York: Springer-Verlag, 1986

[4] Pierre F. Baldi and Kurt Hornik, "Learning in Linear Neural Networks: A survey", *IEEE transactions on neural networks* , vol. 6, no. 4, July 1995

[5] David M.J. Tax, Rober P.W. Duin "Support vector domain description", *Pattern Recognition Letters* 20(1999) 1191-1199

[6] M. D. Swanson, B. Zhu and A. H. Tewfik, "Multiresolution and Object-Based Video Watermarking Using Perceptual Models", Wavelet, Subband and Block Transforms in Communications and Multimedia 1999.

[7] F. Hartung and M. Kutter, "Multimedia Watermarking Techniques", *Proceedings of IEEE* vol. 87, July 1999.

[8] F. Hartung and B. Girod, "Digital Watermarking of Uncompressed and Compressed Video" *Signal Processing*, vol. 66, March 1998.

[9] G. Langelaar, R. Lagendijk, and J. Biemond, "Watermarking by DCT coefficient removal: Statistical approach to optimal parameter settings," *Proceedings of SPIE*, vol. 3657, Jan. 1999.

[10] I. Cox, J. Kilian, T. Leighton, and T. Shammoon, "Secure Spread Spectrum Watermarking for Multimedia," *IEEE Trans. Image Processing*, vol. 6, NO. 12, 1997.

[11] C. Podilchuck and W. Zeng, "Image-Adaptive Watermarking Using Visual Models", *IEEE Journal of Selected Areas Communication* vol. 16, NO. 4, May 1998.

[12] C. T. Hsu and J. L. Wu, "Digital watermarking for video" *Proceedings of Digital Signal Processing* 97.

Handling Sporadic Tasks in Multimedia File System*

Youjip Won
Div. of Elec. and Comp. Engineering
Hanyang University, Seoul, Korea
yjwon@ece.hanyang.ac.kr

Y.S. Ryu
Div. of Info. and Comm. Engineering
Hallym University, Chunchon, Korea

ABSTRACT

Handling mixed workload in streaming server becomes important issue as integrated file system gets momentum as the choice for next generation file system. In this article, we present novel approach of handling sporadically arriving non-playback related disk request while minimizing its interference with the timely retrieval of data blocks for ongoing playbacks. The main idea of our approach is to extend the length of *period* in period based disk scheduling in multimedia streaming and subsequently a certain fraction of each period can be set aside for handling unexpected I/O request. We develop the analytical model to establish the relationship between the length of period, request arrival rate, request service time, and P(jitter). This model is used to precisely compute the length of period and the respective buffer size. We present the result of simulation based experiment.

Key Word: multimedia, streaming, mixed workload, disk scheduling

1. INTRODUCTION

Characteristic intensive demand on I/O subsystem, e.g, disk bandwidth, disk space, I/O bus bandwidth, to support multimedia playback requires sophisticated modeling of various system resources, to maintain the continuity of the playback. As on-line interactive multimedia services over the Internet, e.g. distance learning, Movie-On-Demand, etc get popular, supporting the multimedia stream with less amount of system resources become one of the prime issues in designing multimedia server software and also in planning the capacity of such server. In this work, we consider the situation where single server provides the streaming service as well as handles the requests for non-playback related data, e.g. text based web documents, gif images, etc. For this type of server, it is mandatory that the server handles multimedia

---

*This work was supported by grant No. 1999-1-303-001-3 from the Interdisciplinary Research Program of the KOSEF

data retrieval along with occasional text or image based file retrieval/storage simultaneously and seamlessly.

Recent study showed that it is more economical to have single integerated file system for various media types rather than to have dedicated file system for each media type[5, 4]. For multimedia playback, a certain amount of memory buffer needs to be dedicated to each stream to synchronize the synchronous playback operation and asynchronous disk retrieval operation. To minimize the system resource consumption for multimedia playback, the server software needs to be stringent upon allocating the memory buffer to individual stream. However, since stringent allocation of the memory buffer does not leave much slack for I/O operations other than playback related disk I/O, unexpected I/O task can easily interfere with the on-going playback and subsequently can either cause jitter on on-going multimedia playbacks or suffer from non trivial amount of I/O latency . In this article, we present novel approach in handling this aperiodic I/O request while prohibiting this I/O request to interfere with the on-going multimedia playbacks. A number of research efforts proposed the model for quantifying the system resource requirement for continous media server[1, 6].

2. APERIODICITY IN STREAMING

To maintain *jitter free* playback, a certain amount of disk bandwidth needs to be guranteed for timely supply of data block to the application. To compromise the discrepency between synchronous playback and asynchronous disk retrieval operations, a certain amount of memory buffer is dedicated to individual streams. Most of the disk scheduling technique for continous media streaming adopts period based disk retrieval approach. In period based disk retrieval, time is divided into fixed time interval called *period* such that the data blocks read from the disk during the period are suffient for the stream to playback during the same amount of time. Various period based disk scheduling approach are discussed in [8].

Fig. 1 illustrates the playback of multiple continuous media streams from storage subsystem. In the period based scheduling the continuity requirement can be represented with two condition. The first condition is that the number of data blocks retrieved during T should be greater than the amount of data blocks needed for playback for same period of time: $T \cdot r_i \leq n_i b$. This condition should hold for each stream, $i = 1, \cdots, m$. The second condition is that it should take less than T to retrieve the data blocks for all streams: $T \geq \left\{ \sum_{i=1}^{m} \frac{n_i b}{B_{max}} \right\} + \mathcal{O}(m)$. n_i, m, b and r_i are the number of data blocks read during the period T, the number of streams, size of I/O unit, and playback rate of stream i, respectively. B_{max} stands for maximum transfer rate of the disk. $\mathcal{O}(m)$ is the disk movement overhead such as seek and latency in reading the data blocks for m streams. It is important to note that $\mathcal{O}(m)$ is determined by the disk scheduling policy, e.g. *SCAN, FIFO*, and etc. Solving these two equations, the total buffer size increases asymtotically following $\mathcal{O}(\frac{1}{1-\rho})$, where ρ is disk utilization, $\frac{\sum_{i=1}^{m} r_i}{B_{max}}$ [2, 8].

In Fig. 1, disk subsystem supports three playbacks. Each playback is fed chunk of data blocks required for T period's playback and disk subsystem can retrieve the data blocks for these playbacks within less than T interval. It also services sporadic I/O requests which are irrelevant to multimedia playback. In Fig. 1, there is sufficient amount of idle time in each period and non playback related I/O request can be serviced without affecting the timely retrieval of multimedia data. When the sporadic tasks arrive in burstier manner, storage subsystem may not afford to service them within idle slack of the period and may interfere with retrieval of the multimedia data. Prospective way of resolving this situation is to make the period length T long enough such that there is sufficient idle slack for each period and that *most* of the sporadic tasks can be handled without affecting the retrieval for on-going playbacks. Extending the period entails the increase in the synchronization buffer as well as the increase in the start-up latency of on-demand request. Hence, it is important to carefully determine the length of period to meet the specific requirement of the system.

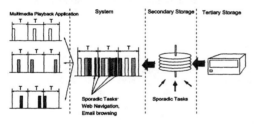

Figure 1: Supporting Multimedia Sessions along with sporadic tasks

3. HANDLING APERIODICITY

In Fig. 2, data blocks for each period needs to be retrieved from the disk at the beginning of each period. At the beginning of the period P_2, three non-playback related tasks were serviced. In the course of servicing these non-plyaback related tasks, retrieving the data blocks for P_2 is delayed by $(T_2 - T_1)$ time and subsequently it entails jitter. While Fig. 2 illustrates data retrieval based on FIFO disk scheduling strategy[3], sporadic tasks can cause jitter independent of disk scheduling strategy. To cope with this problem, we propose to extend the length of period such that occasional non-playback related I/O request does not affect the timely retrieval of the multimedia data blocks. The objective is to determine the length of period such that there is sufficient slack in each period to handle the sporadically arriving

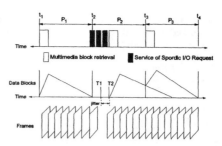

Figure 2: Impact of Handling Sporadic Tasks on Ongoing Playbacks

tasks. In Fig. 1, timeliness of the multimedia block retrieval is not affected by the sporadic tasks since the slack is large enough to handle the sporadic I/O requests.

Our approach provides the statistical guarantee on a maximum probability of jitter, $P(jitter)$ by extending the length of period. $P(jitter)$ is the probability that the sporadic tasks cannot be serviced within the slack of a period, i.e. $N_{sp} \cdot t_{sp} > P_{slack}$ where T_{slack}, N_{sp} and t_{sp} are the length of slack of a period, the number of sporadic tasks in a period and its service time, respectively. We develop a formulation for finding the new buffer size when period T is extend by some fraction to incorporate the sporadic tasks. $\alpha(> 1.0)$ is a coefficient to extend the period. $\alpha = 1.1$ means that $\frac{\alpha-1}{\alpha}$ fraction of a period is set aside to handle randomly arriving disk jobs. Let T be the period which does not contain the slack for handling sporadic tasks. Extending the period by α requires that the data blocks read in a period should be sufficient for αT's playback and time to retrieve that data blocks should be less than T to leave the room for handling sporadic tasks. Thus, finding the new buffer size with extension factor α is equivalent to solving Eq. 1 and Eq. 2.

$$\alpha T r_i \leq n_i b \qquad (1)$$

$$T \geq \left\{ \sum_{i=1}^{m} \frac{n_i b}{B_{max}} \right\} + \mathcal{O}(m) \qquad (2)$$

Solving these equations, we can obtain the new period length αT and the new buffer size as in Eq. 3. Detailed derivation steps can be found in [7].

$$\mathbf{n} \geq \frac{O(\mathbf{m})\mathbf{r}}{\frac{b}{\alpha B_{max}} \left(B_{max} - \alpha \sum_{i=1}^{n} r_i \right)} \qquad (3)$$

Once the length of slack is determined, we can find $P(jitter)$ given the arrival rate, λ and service time, t_{sp} of sporadic task. Our objective is to determine *how much additional buffer is allocated to handle sporadic tasks?*. Thus, actual steps towards solving our problem can be described as follows: *given λ, t_{sp}, and maximum allowable jitter, find α, length of period T and the respective buffer size.*

$$P(jitter) \leq P \left(N_{sp} \geq \left\lfloor \frac{T(\alpha - 1.0)}{t_{sp}} \right\rfloor \right) \qquad (4)$$

With Eq. 2, Eq. 3 and Eq. 4, we can obtain the buffer size and the extention factor α. Service time of sporadic tasks t_{sp} can be as large as *full seek* + data transfer time and actually is governed by the disk scheduling strategy adopted in underlying system. [4] proposed an disk scheduling algorithm for mixed workload. Statistical characteristics of L governed by various scheduling policy can be embedded in our framework.

4. SIMULATION

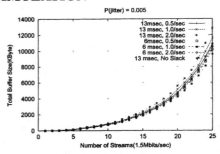

Figure 3: Arrival Rate vs. Buffer Size

There are a number of factors which govern the overhead of handling sporadic tasks: *arrival rate of the sporadic tasks*, *request service time*, and *P(jitter)*. Varying these three parameters, we conduct simulation based experiment and observe the buffer overhead of handling non-playback related sporadic tasks. Disk used in our simulation has 6720 cylinders and the rotational speed is 7200 RPM with 0.6 msec 4KByte block access time. We consider MPEG-1 stram of 1.5Mbits/sec(187KByte/sec) playback rate. In obtaining the buffer size, n, we need to find the extension factor α supporting $P(jitter)$. Finding closed form formulae for the buffer size n in terms of α, $P(jitter)$ from Eq. 2, Eq. 3 and Eq. 4 is non-trivial task. Instead, we take the numerical approach in finding the buffer size, n. Fig. 3 and Fig. 4 illustrate the simulation results. Fig. 3 illustrates the effect of

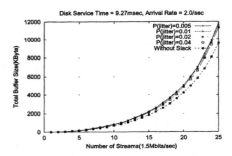

Figure 4: P(jitter) vs. Buffer Size

the request arrival rate of the sporadic tasks and the effect of the request service time on the total buffer size. Maximum allowable jitter probability, $P(jitter)$ is set to 0.005. Request service time is 6 msec and 13 msec. We assume that sporadic tasks arrives in Poisson manner. Simulation is conducted based on three different arrival rate 0.5/sec, 1.0/sec, 2.0/sec. As we can observe, the overhead of handling sporadic tasks increases as there are frequent sporadic request arrivals.

In Fig. 4, we observe the relationship between the buffer size and $P(jitter)$. We vary the $P(jitter)$ as 0.005, 0.01, 0.02, and 0.04. As can be observed, to guarantee smaller jitter probability, larger amount of buffer is required. It is observed that even though we degrade the jitter probability by eight fold(from 0.005 to 0.04), the respective reduction in buffer size is not significant.

5. CONCLUSION

In this article, we present novel approach of handling sporadically arriving non-playback related disk request while guaranteeing a certain level of service quality to ongoing playbacks. Handling mixed workload in the streaming server becomes important issue as integrated file system gets momentum as the choice for next generation file system. This is particulary important when small to medium size streaming server also needs to handle non-trivial amount of http request which is usually for text based web documents, or gif images. The main idea of our approach is to extend the length of *period* in period based I/O scheduling in multimedia streaming and subsequently a certain fraction of each period can be set aside *idle* for the case unexpected I/O request arrival. We develop the framework to obtain the length of period and the respective buffer size to gurantee a certain level of jitter probability given request arrival rate and request service time.

6. REFERENCES

[1] D. Gemmell, H. Vin, D. Kandlur, P. Rangan, and L. Rowe. Multimedia Storage Servers: A Tutorial. *COMPUTER*, 28(5):40–49, May 1995.

[2] D. Kenchammana-Hosekote and J. Srivastava. Scheduling Continuous Media on a Video-On-Demand Server. In *Proc. of International Conference on Multi-media Computing and Systems*, Boston, MA, May 1994. IEEE.

[3] P. Rangan, H. Vin, and S. Ramanathan. Designing an on-demand multimedia service. *IEEE Communication Magazine*, 30(7):56–65, July 1992.

[4] Y. Rompogiannakis, G. Nerjes, P. Muth, M. Paterakis, P. Triantafillou, and G. Weikum. Disk scheduling for mixed-media workloads in a multimedia server. In *Proceedings of ACM Multimedia '98*, pages 297–302, Bristol, UK, 1998.

[5] P. Shenoy, P. Goyal, and H. Vin. Architectural considerations for next generation file systems. In *Proceedings of ACM Multimedia Conference*, pages pp. 457–467, Orlando, FL, USA, Nov. 1999.

[6] R. Wijayaratne and A. Reddy. Providing qos guarantees for disk i/o. *Multimedia Systems*, 8(1):pp. 57–68, 2000.

[7] Y. Won. Handling mixed workloads in multimedia file system. Technical report, Divison of Electrical and Computer Engineering, Hanyang University, Seoul, Korea, In Preparation.

[8] Y. Won and J. Srivastava. "smdp: Minimizing buffer requirements for continuous media servers". *ACM/Springer Multimedia Systems Journal*, 8(2):pp. 105–117, 2000.

Content-based Video Similarity Model

Yi Wu   **Yueting Zhuang**   **Yunhe Pan**

Institute of Artificial Intelligence, Zhejiang University

Microsoft Visual Perception Laboratory of Zhejiang University

Hangzhou, 310027, P.R.China

Tel:86-571-7951853

wu_yi_77@yahoo.com   yzhuang@cs.zju.edu.cn   panyh@sun.zju.edu.cn

Abstract

The most commonly used method for content-based video retrieval is query by example. But the definition of video similarity brings great obstacle to further research. This paper puts forward a new approach to solve the difficulty. Firstly, it advances centroid feature vector of shot in order to reduce the storage of video database. Secondly, considering all the factors existing in human vision perception, it introduces a new comparison algorithm based on multi-granularity of video structure, which has great flexibility. Thirdly, after getting the similar video set, we take a brand-new method of feedback to adjust weight based on video similarity model. In this way, retrieval result can be optimized greatly.

Keywords

Content-based video retrieval, centroid feature, feedback

1.Introduction

Content-based video retrieval system is one of the important issues of multimedia design, mainly depending on its visual and spatio-temporal characteristic. But till now, there still exists some concept and technique unsolved:

(1) Video is not a simple frame sequence but a hierarchy of video-shot-keyframe[1], so the video similarity measurement is based on multi-level structure.

(2) The visual feature of whole video is based on that of keyframe. For a large video, the storage and comparison of high-dimensional visual features cost considerably.

(3) Whether two videos are similar depends on human realization. Different preponderance should be taken into account. We need to design not only a video similarity model, but also a reasonable feedback algorithm.

Dimitiova Abdel-mottaleb[2] regards the average distance of all the corresponding frames as two videos' similarity and defines that video frame sequence must obey temporal order. Lienhart et. al[3] considers video similarity from different levels and defines it with congregation degrees on presentation set. But the measurement factors they consider are too limited.This paper proposes a unified video retrieval model to solve the above problems. Given an arbitrary video, we can find similar ones from large video repository within time limitation, and integrating with feedback, the results can be adjusted according to user's preference. Section 2 introduces the centroid feature

vector of shot to reduce keyframes' visual feature storage. Section 3 proposes a new approach to compare shot. Section 4 presents video similarity model on the whole. Section 5 introduces feedback of video retrieval. At last we show the experimental result and evaluation.

2.Centroid feature vector of shot

Video can be seen as a hierarchy, composing of video- shot-keyframe, in which keyframe's visual feature summation presents the visual feature of the video.

Now the system extracts two visual features: color and texture. Color feature is defined by histogram in *HSV* space, presented as a 32-floating point in the range of [0,1]. Texture feature is composed of 3- floating point: *Coarseness, Contrast* and *Direction*[4]. On the whole, visual feature of keyframe is expressed as a vector of 35-dimension.

Considering that high dimensional vector is of low efficiency in comparison or storage. Furthermore, keyframes within the same shot still have great redundancy to be utilized, we can use centroid feature vector $\overline{K} = \{\overline{K}_{hv}, \overline{K}_t\}$ to describe the visual features of all keyframes within one shot *S*. where $\overline{K}_{hv}$ represents color feature, $\overline{K}_t$ texture feature.

Because there is little difference among the visual feature of keyframes within the same shot, so using $\overline{K}$ to replace keyframe feature will not arouse great error, but the storage of video database can be reduced considerably.

3. Shot similarity algorithm

The similarity of video is based on that of shot. Shot similarity algorithm searches similar shots in the range of video database for every S_{qi} *(i=1~n)* in V_q. Assume V_q is the video for query; S_{qi} is the shot in V_q; V_d is the video in the database. In the below, we analyze how to measure similarity between two arbitrary shots *S1* and *S2*. The similarity measurement of *S1* and *S2* equals to that of 35-dimensional centroid feature vector $\overline{K}^1$ and $\overline{K}^2$.

The 32-value color feature $\overline{K}_{hv}$ has been normalized to [0,1], so the similarity of color feature can be computed as:

$$Simlarity_c = \sum_{h=8}\sum_{v=4} w_{hv} \cdot D_{hv}\left(\overline{K}_{hv}^1 \cdot \overline{K}_{hv}^2\right) \quad (1)$$

Where *D* means Euclidean distance between two vectors.

On the other hand, the 3-value texture feature $\overline{K}_t(i)$ (i=1...3, each corresponding to *Coarse, Contrast, Direction*) is in the different range. So we firstly use Gauss normalization to convert them into the same range of [-1,1].

For totally *k* shots, we firstly calculate the mean μ and covariance σ of the *k* shots' texture, then normalize them to the range of [−1, 1] as follows:

$$D\left(\overline{K_1^1}, \overline{K_1^2}\right) = \left[\frac{D_1\left(\overline{K_1^1(1)}, \overline{K_1^2(1)}\right) - \mu_1}{\omega\sigma_1} \cdots \frac{D_3\left(\overline{K_1^1(3)}, \overline{K_1^2(3)}\right) - \mu_3}{\omega\sigma_3}\right]^T \quad (2)$$

When $\omega = 3$, 99% of value lies in $[-1,1]$. Other value larger than 1 is set to 1 and that smaller than -1 is set to -1. Then we calculate the similarity of texture and convert it to $[0,1]$.

$$Similarity_T = \sum_{i=1}^{3} w_n \frac{D_i\left(\overline{K_1^1(i)}, \overline{K_1^2(i)}\right) + 1}{2} \quad (3)$$

At last, we calculate the similarity of $S1$ and $S2$ in terms of color and texture weight of W_c and W_t.

$$Similarity(\overline{K^1}, \overline{K^2}) = W_c \cdot Similarity_C + W_t \cdot Similarity_T \quad (4)$$

All mentioned above only considers the shot difference in visual feature, but ignores that of shot duration. The factor of shot duration "Dur" must be taken into account, for it can measure the difference between the longer and shorter edition of the same shot.

$$Dur = 1 - \frac{|Dur_{qi} - Dur_{di}|}{Dur_{qi}} \quad (5)$$

Overall similarity between shots is measured by (6), whose result is in the range of $[0,1]$. '1' indicates the most similar, '0' indicates totally different.

$$S\_Similarity(S_1, S_2) = Dur * Similarity(\overline{K^1}, \overline{K^2}) \quad (6)$$

4. Video similarity algorithm

Video is comprised of several shots. After the calculation of section 3, for each S_{qi}, we get $S\_Similarity_s^i$ $(s=1 \sim K)$ representing the similarity degree between S_{qi} and all the shots in the video library(Assume there are K shots in the whole). Among the K values, which should the similar shots have? In fact, this question equals to finding $Threshold^i$ dynamically in $S\_Similarity_s^i$ $(s=1 \sim K)$.

We use clustering algorithm(7) to find $Threshold^i$ for $S\_Similarity_s^i$ $(i=1 \sim n)$:

$$Threshold^i = \{S\_Similarity_s^i \mid Max(\frac{\sum_{j=s+1}^{K} S\_Similarity_j^i}{K-s} - \frac{\sum_{j=1}^{s} S\_Similarity_j^i}{s}), s=1,2,...K\} \quad (7)$$

Compared with the normal approach of predefined threshold, clustering algorithm is more flexible in that it can find similar shots dynamically in the whole database. The corresponding relation of S_{qi} $(i=1 \sim n)$ with video set V_d_set of $\{V_{di}\}$ is shown in Figure.1, in which the line connects a pair of similar shots. Below introduces how to get the similarity degree between V_q and V_d based on similar shots corresponding graph.

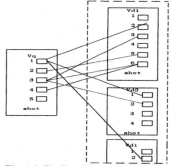

Figure1. Similar shot corresponding graph

4.1 Similarity between S_{qi} and V_d

Firstly, we compute the similarity between S_{qi} and V_d. In Figure.1, there exist many corresponding relation possibilities between S_{qi} and the shot in V_d:

1)S_{qi} has only one similar shot S_{dj} in V_d. This is the simplest situation. In addition to the difference of $S\_Similarity$, the order

of similar shot in V_d must be taken into account. For example, in Figure.1, S_{q1} is similar to S_{d2} of V_{d1} and S_{q2} is similar to S_{d5} of V_{d1}. For S_{q2}, $lastmaxid=2$(the id of S_{q1}'s similar shot S_{d2})We define $dis(j,lastmaxid)=|j-lastmaxid|+1$(in avoidance of zero division), so S_{d5}'s distance from $lastmaxid$ is 4. The nearer their distance, the more similar they are.

$$Sim(S_{qi}, V_d) = \frac{duration_{qi}}{Totalduration_q} * \frac{S\_Similarity_j^i}{dis(j, last\max id)} \quad (8)$$

Where $S\_Similarity_j^i$ represents the $S\_Similarity$ between S_{qi} and S_{dj}; $duration_{qi}$ represents the duration of S_{qi}; $Totalduration_q$ represents the duration of V_q; the fraction of $\dfrac{duration_{qi}}{Totalduration_q}$ means that the longer the S_{qi}, the more important it contributes to the whole V_q for query.

2) S_{qi} have several similar shots in the same V_{dk}, for example, S_{d3} and S_{d6} of V_{d1} are both similar to the S_{q3}. Assume they form the set of $\{S\_Set\}$. Also taken the same schema as above, we consider the "$S\_Similarity$" and "dis" for every similar shot in $\{S\_Set\}$, then find the most similar one.

With (9), we find S_{dk} in $\{S\_Set\}$, which maximizes the function of $\dfrac{S\_Similarity_j^i}{dis(j, last\max id)}$. S_{dk} is deemed as most similar to S_{qi}. With (10), the similarity between S_{qi} and V_d can be calculated. $lastmaxid$ is set as k in the next iteration for $S_{q(i+1)}$.

$$S_{dk} = \underset{S_{dj} \in \{S\_Set\}}{Max} (\frac{S\_Similarity_j^i}{dis(j, last\max id)}) \quad (9)$$

$$Sim(S_{qi}, V_d) = \frac{duration_{qi}}{Totalduration_q} * \frac{S\_Similarity_k^i}{dis(k, last\max id)} \quad (10)$$

4.2 Similarity between V_q and V_d

In this section, we compute the similarity between V_q and V_d.

The similar corresponding may not appear in the same temporal order, for example, in Figure.1, the 2nd and 3rd shot of V_q are similar to the 5th and 3rd one of V_{d1} respectively, whose order is reverse. "forward" records the sequential similar shot corresponding number between V_q and V_d; "backward" records the reverse one. In (11), We use "Seq" whose range is $[0,1]$ to measure the factor of the sequential and reverse corresponding between V_q and V_d.

$$Seq = \frac{forward}{forward + backward} \quad (11)$$

Assume V_q and V_{di} have n, m shots and n', m' similar shots each. Under the situation of $n>n', m>m'$, V_q and V_{di} each has some scattered shots which can not find similar counterpart in the other. In Figure1, the 1st, 3rd shot in V_{d1} and the 5th shot in V_q have no corresponding similar relation. The more these scattered shots are, the less similar the pair of videos is.

$$continuity = \frac{n'}{n} \times \frac{m'}{m} \quad (12)$$

At last, the overall video similarity between V_q and V_d is calculated as below:

$$V\_Similarity = Seq * Continuity * \sum_{i=1}^{queryshot} (w_i * Sim(S_{qi}, V_d)) \quad (13)$$

Where w_i shows the weight of every shot in the video during the procedure of human vision perception.

466

5. Relevance feedback of video retrieval
5.1Relevance feedback in video level

System gives the initial weight $1/n$ for every shot, and after the calculation of section 4, we get a list of similar videos.

$$L_v=\{V_d \mid S(V_d, \ [Q]) > Threshold, <S_{qi}, W_i> \} \qquad (14)$$

where L_v=the similar video list; S_{qi}=shot of V_q; W_i=weight of S_{qi}; Q=Query; S=function of similarity;

For every V_k in L_v, user gives relevant evaluation. "High relevant" means '$Feedback_k$ =1'; "no opinion" means '$Feedback_k$ =0'; "No relevant" means '$Feedback_k$ =-1'.

We compute the similar video list $L_v^i=[V_1^i,...,V_k^i,...,V_M^i]$ solely based on the weight of S_{qi}. The more L_v and L_v^i overlap, the more S_{qi} contributes to the whole video similarity. Assume that V_i is one overlapped video in L_v and L_v^i set. The corresponding feedback is $Feedback_i$

if $Feedback_i < LastFeedback_i$ (the feedback $Feedback$ of last overlapped video),

then W_i +=$Feedback_i$ +1/N;

else W_i +=$Feedback_i$; $\qquad (15)$

After such calculation dependent only on S_{qi}, the weight of S_{qi} is updated as: $W_i'=\dfrac{W_i'}{\sum W_i'} \qquad (16)$

Here we take into account not only the overlapping degree, but also the element order in the set of L_v^i and that of $Feedback_i$. If the $Feedback_i$ of overlapped video is decreasingly arrayed, the video rank obtained exclusively according to S_{qi} is the same with user's realization. So the weight of S_{qi} should be larger.

5.2Relevance feedback in shot level

The similarity in shot level (section 3) is measured by feature of $f_{sk}=(Similarity_C, Similarity_T), k=2$.

Assume that in L_v there are m videos whose $Feedback_i$ is larger than 0. The shots of V_q have relation with those of m videos, thus forming m sets, $Set_1=\{S_1^1,...,S_j^1...S_{N1}^1\},...$ $Set_i=\{S_1^i,...,S_j^i...S_{Ni}^i\},...$ $Set_m=\{S_1^m,...,S_j^m...S_{Nm}^m\}$, where Set_i represents the similar relation between V_q and V_{di}; S_j^i means a pair of similar shots and the corresponding property used in shot similarity computation, described by a two-value set $\{Similarity_C, Similarity_T\}$.

Add up $Similarity_C, Similarity_T$ of every S_j^i in Set_i, and compute their average value, thus getting a two-value set of $(average\_Similarity_C^i, average\_Similarity_T^i)$ for Set_i.

$average\_Similarity_C^i=\sum Similarity_C /N_i$;

$average\_Similarity_T^i=\sum Similarity_T /N_i$; $\qquad (17)$

m Set_i form a matrix of $m \times k, k=2$. We calculate the covariance σ_k of every column whose value represents the similarity of this column. The smaller the covariance is, the more similar this column value is, and the more weight f_{sk} contributes to the overall similarity:

$$W_{sk}=1/\sigma_k \qquad (18)$$

Finally W_{sk} is computed as:

$$W_{sk} = \frac{W_{sk}}{\sum W_{sk}} \qquad W_{sk}'= (W_c, W_t) \qquad (19)$$

In this way, the weight of shot level and that of video level can both be updated according to user's various preponderance.

6.Results

Feedback in Section 5 updates weight from shot and video level, and the new weight is recalculated in video similarity model(in Section 4). With the feedback times increasing, the result will be more close to user's need. In the below, we will show some examples to reflect the system performance.

We submit the first line of video "sunrise" in Figure.2 as example for querying. From top to bottom listing the similar video's shots ranked by similarity degree. Every line represents all the shots in this video.

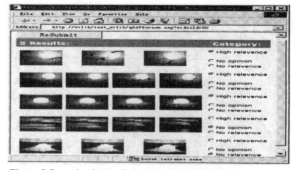

Figure.2 Querying by the first video "sunrise" as example

Next, user marks the 1st, 2nd and 3rd video as "High relevant"; marks the 4th video as "No opinion" and the 5th video as "No relevant". The initial weight is adjusted by feedback opinion and system recalculates similar videos. The returned results are listed in Figure.3 by similar order.

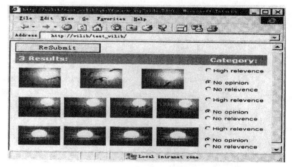

Figure3. Feedback of Figure.2

Generally speaking, in the first time, most of the results returned by video similarity model are up to user's requirement. But for video's complex content, distinct users may pay attention to different aspects, they have various understanding to the same video. Then with feedback system gets new similar rank. From the example shown, we can conclude that after feedback, some imprecise results are thrown off. In this way, the performance of results can be optimized greatly.

7. Acknowledgement
Our work was sponsored by the National Natural Science Foundation of China, Foundation of Education Ministry for Excellent Young Teacher, and College Key Teacher Supporting Plan.

8.Reference
[1] Madirakshi Das and Shih-Ping Liou. "A new Hybrid Approach to Video Organization for Content-Based Indexing".IEEE Multimedia System'98.

[2] Nevenka Dimitrova and Mohamed Abdel-Mottaled, "content-based Video retrieval by example video clip." In:SPIE 3022,1998

[3]Rainer Lienhart, Wolfgang Effelsberg, Ramesh Jain, "VisualGREP: A systematic methord to compare and retrieval video sequences". In: SPIE Vol.3312, pp.271-282,1997.

[4] H.Tamura, S.Mori,and T.Yamawaki, "Texture features corresponding to visual perception," IEEE Trans. on Sys, Man, and Cyb,vol.SMC-8,no.6,1978.

Demos

ACM

Image watermarking for owner and content authentication

Jean-Luc Dugelay
Institut Eurécom
Dept. Multimedia Communications
2229, route des Crêtes, B.P. 193
06904 Sophia Antipolis - France

jld@eurecom.fr

Christian Rey
Institut Eurécom
Dept. Multimedia Communications
Tel. +33 (0)4 93 00 26 26
Fax. +33 (0)4 93 00 26 27

christian.rey@eurecom.fr

ABSTRACT
The aim of this technical demonstration is to present the ongoing performance of our R&D watermarking scheme software for copyright and image content authentication. The proposed demonstration cover a large panel of original images (in gray levels and colors), signatures and attacks. Evaluation is performed according to ratio, visibility and robustness.

Keywords
Image, Security, Watermarking.

1. INTRODUCTION
Image watermarking [1] is an emerging technique which allows to hide, in an invisible and robust manner, a message inside a picture. According to the desired service, the message can contain some information about the owner (copyright), the picture itself (content authentication or indexing) or the buyer (non repudiation). It is then possible to recover the message at any time, even if the picture has been modified following one or several non destructive attacks (malicious or not). We propose to present preliminary results obtained in the field of still image watermarking for owner, users or content authentication using an original approach [2], derived from a basic data hiding algorithm [3] which exploits the properties of the fractal transform.

2. PROPOSED TECHNICAL DEMONSTRATION
More precisely our demonstration prototype for PC works under Windows 95/98/NT, as follows:

- **Owner authentication:**

Signer: The inputs of the marking tool are an image in '.ppm' format, a message to hide of 8 ASCII's (say, 64 bits), and a secret key of 8 digits. The signer inserts the message within a few seconds (PC Pentium II 400 Mhz, 128Mo RAM).

Retriever: To retrieve a mark, you have to specify an image, your secret key of 8 digits, and a level of extraction (express mode of extraction or advanced one).

- **Content authentication:**

For image authentication, the basic idea is to hide some features of the image within itself, then to check the invariance of theses characteristics from the transmitted and possibly tampered image. Contrary to the owner authentication application, this service requires a high capacity of insertion for embedding enough relevant attributes of the image.

3. PRELIMINARY RESULTS

Each of the services we investigate, is based on a robust invisible watermark.

3.1 Typical example of owner authentication
A satisfactory trade-off has been achieved between technical constraints (see figure 1):
- **Capacity:** the message can include up to 64 bits, which is the expected capacity for the emerging standards such as JPEG-2000 and MPEG-4;
- **Visibility:** the quality of the protected image is about the same as the one obtained after a JPEG compression, with a factor of quality equal to 80%;
- **Robustness:** the proposed algorithm defeats many (non-destructive) attacks including random geometric distortions (e.g. Stirmark 3.1 [4]);
- **Blind extraction:** the message can be identified from the protected image (possibly modified) alone. No information about the original image, nor about the expected watermark is necessary in the extraction step.

3.2 Typical example of copyright authentication
In this example, the original image has been protected using the block mean luminance (figure 2.a). Using *Paint Shop Pro* we have replaced the kiwi fruit, in the bottom-left hand corner of the image, by a lemon (figure 2.b). Figure 2.c. shows the regions that have been identified by our system as altered regions. Thanks to

such a system, the viewer is able to know that the image has been tampered with. In order to provide an authentication service for still images, it is important to distinguish between malicious manipulations, which consist of changing the content of the original image (captions, faces, etc.) and manipulations related to the usage of an image such as format conversion, lossy compression, filtering, etc.

4. CONCLUDING REMARKS

Similar demonstration prototypes for video and audio are under investigation. *More information can be found at the following address: http://www.eurecom.fr/~dugelay/WM/wm.html.*

5. ACKNOWLEDGMENTS

This work is partly supported by the National French Telecom project RNRT Aquamars [5] and the European project IST Certimark [6].

6. REFERENCES

[1] Handbook on Information Hiding Techniques for Steganography and Sigital Watermarking, Artech House Book, 1999, ISBN 1-58053-035-4.

[2] Dugelay J.-L. And S. Roxhe, "Process for Marking a Multimedia Document, such an Image, by generating a Mark", pending patent EP 99480075.3.

[3] Dugelay J.-L., "Method for Hiding Binary Data in a Digital Image", pending patent PCT/FR99/00485.

[4] Stirmark:

http://www.cl.cam.ac.uk/~fapp2/watermarking/stirmark/

[5] RNRT Aquamars:

http://www.telecom.gouv.fr/rnrt/projets/paquamars.htm

[6] IST Certimark: http://www.certimark.org

| Original image | Hidden message: "EURECOM" + Secret key | Watermarked image (distortion 38.08 dB) | Attack: Stirmark (cracker) + horizontal flip + rotation 3° | Attacked image (message recovered: "EURECOM") |

Figure 1. Example of copyright authentication.

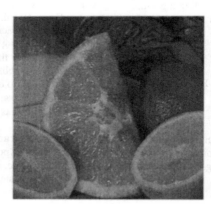

(a) *(b)* *(c)*

Figure 2. (a) original image (protected), (b) tampered image, (c) detection of tampered regions.

Demonstration of Dynamic Class-Based Router Queue Management

Jae Chung and Mark Claypool
{chung|claypool}@cs.wpi.edu

Computer Science Department
Worcester Polytechnic Institute
100 Institute Road
Worcester, MA, 0609, USA

Introduction

The explosive increase in the volume and variety of Internet traffic has placed a growing emphasis on congestion control and fairness in Internet routers. Two approaches for dealing with Internet congestion at the router are *resource reservation* and *active queue management.*

Resource reservation uses packet or link scheduling on multiple logical or physical queues to explicitly reserve and allocate output bandwidth to each class of traffic, where a class can be a single flow or a group of similar flows [8]. However, explicit resource reservation changes the current, effective "best effort" nature of the Internet, and the algorithmic complexity and state requirements of scheduling make its deployment difficult [11].

Active queue management uses packet queuing disciplines on an outbound router queue to actively handle (or avoid) congestion with the help of cooperative traffic sources, such as TCP. One of the earliest and best-known active queue management mechanism is Random Early Detection (RED) [7]. RED which prevents congestion through monitoring outbound buffers to detect impending congestion, and randomly chooses and notifies senders of network congestion so that they can reduce their transmission rate. While fairly handling congestion for TCP flows, RED has been shown to be extremely unfair in the presence of unresponsive UDP flows [9].

Complicating the above traditional congestion control approaches is the presence of multimedia traffic that has strict delay and jitter constraints [1], forcing multimedia flows to use network protocols other than TCP, some of which may be unresponsive to congestion [11, 9]. In addition, traditional router queue management techniques may cause jitter [3] which can severely degrade the quality of a multimedia flow [6].

In order to better manage congestion in the face of varied traffic and in order to better support multimedia flows, we propose *Dynamic-CBT (D-CBT)*. D-CBT extends the work of [11] and recognizes responsive multimedia flows while protecting them and TCP flows by adding a simple class-based static bandwidth reservation mechanism to RED. D-CBT fairly allocates bandwidth by dynamically assigning thresholds to each traffic class such that the sum of the fair share of flows in each class is assigned to the class at any given time. In addition, as a means to improve multimedia jitter, we propose a lightweight packet scheduling mechanism called *Cut-In Packet Scheduling (ChIPS)* which monitors average enqueue rates of tagged and the other flows, and, on transient congestion awards well-behaved (flow-controlled) multimedia flows by allowing their packets to 'cut' in the queue to the average queue length.

To evaluate our proposed mechanisms, we implemented D-CBT and ChIPS in a simulator called NS [10] and compared the performance to that of CBT and RED. Our studies showed that D-CBT improves fairness among different classes of flows and ChIPS improves multimedia jitter without degrading fairness. Details can be found in [4, 2].

Demonstration

Figure 1 depicts a screen shot after an NS run using a modified version of the Network Animator (nam). The interface is showing 3 flows traveling through a bottleneck router (node 6). Each flow is a different color, representing a TCP flow, an unresponsive UDP flow and a tagged, responsive UDP flow (a multimedia flow). The interface displays statistics on the number of drops for each class of traffic and the throughput at the bottom of the window. The effects of ChIPS can observed by monitoring scheduling of the different colored packets in the outbound queue. The speed of progression of the simulation is varied using the slider in the upper left-hand corner.

Further details on the technology and performance analysis can be found at: http://perform.wpi.edu/. All source code used in the demonstration is available at the same URL.

References

[1] Multimedia Communications Quality of Service. Technical Report MMCF/95-010, Multimedia Communications Forum, Inc., 1995.

[2] Jae Chung. Dynamic CBT - Router Queue Management for Improved Multimedia Performance on the Internet. Master's thesis, Worcester Polytechnic Institute, May 2000. Advisor: Mark Claypool.

[3] Jae Chung and Mark Claypool. Better-Behaved, Better-Performing Multimedia Networking. In *Proceedings of SCS Euromedia*, May 8-10, 2000.

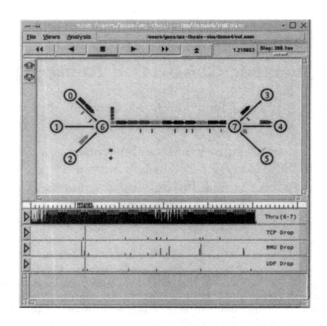

Figure 1: **Depiction of D-CBT in NS using NAM.** There are three flows going through the bottleneck router (6). The red packets are being dropped due to congestion. The bars at the bottom of the window indicate the drops in each class of flow and the throughput on link 6-7.

[4] Jae Chung and Mark Claypool. Demonstration of Dynamic Class-Based Router Queue Managemen. In *Proceedings of the ACM Multimedia Conference*, November 2000.

[5] Jae Chung and Mark Claypool. Dynamic-CBT - Better Performing Active Queue Management for Multimedia Networking. In *International Workshop on Network and Operating System Support for Digital Audio and Video (NOSSDAV)*, June 26-28, 2000.

[6] Mark Claypool and Jonathan Tanner. The Effects of Jitter on the Perceptual Quality of Video. In *Proceedings of the ACM Multimedia Conference*, volume 2, November 1999.

[7] S. Floyd and V. Jacobson. Random Early Detection Gateways for Congestion Avoidance. *IEEE/ACM Transactions on Networking*, August 1993.

[8] S. Floyd and V. Jacobson. Link-sharing and Resource Management Models for Packet Networks. *IEEE/ACM Transactions on Networking*, August 1995.

[9] D. Lin and R. Morris. Dynamics of Random Early Detection. In *Proceedings of ACM SIGCOMM Conference*, September 1997.

[10] Universiy of California Berkeley. Network Simulator 2 (NS). Interent site
http://www-mash.cs.berkeley.edu/ns/.

[11] Mark Parris, Kevin Jeffay, and F. Smith. Lightweight Active Router-Queue Management for Multimedia Networking. In *Proceedings of Multimedia Computing and Networking (MMCN), SPIE Proceedings Series*, January 1999.

Rapid Modeling of Animated Faces From Video Images

[DEMO SUMMARY] *

Zicheng Liu, Zhengyou Zhang, Chuck Jacobs, Michael Cohen
Microsoft Research, One Microsoft Way, Redmond, WA 98052, USA
zliu@microsoft.com, zhang@microsoft.com

ABSTRACT

Generating realistic 3D human face models and facial animations has been a persistent challenge in computer graphics. We have developed a system that constructs textured 3D face models from videos with minimal user interaction. Our system takes images and video sequences of a face with an ordinary video camera. After five manual clicks on two images to tell the system where the eye corners, nose top and mouth corners are, the system automatically generates a realistic looking 3D human head model and the constructed model can be animated immediately. A user, with a PC and an ordinary camera, can use our system to generate his/her face model in a few minutes. We will demonstrate the system at the conference.

Keywords

facial animation, geometric modeling, computer vision

1. INTRODUCTION

One of the most interesting and difficult problems in computer graphics is the effortless generation of realistic looking, animated human face models. Animated face models are essential to computer games, film making, online chat, virtual presence, video conferencing, etc. So far, the most popular commercially available tools have utilized laser scanners. Not only are these scanners expensive, the data are usually quite noisy, requiring hand touchup and manual registration prior to animating the model. Because inexpensive computers and cameras are widely available, there is great interest in producing face models directly from images. In spite of progress toward this goal, the available techniques are either manually intensive or computationally expensive.

The goal of our system is to allow an untrained user with a PC and an ordinary camera to create and instantly animate

---

*A full version of this paper is available as *Microsoft Research Report* MSR-TR-2000-11 at `www.research.microsoft.com/~zhang/Papers/TR00-11.pdf`

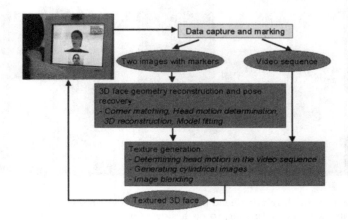

Figure 1: System overview

his/her face model in no more than a few minutes. The user interface for the process comprises three simple steps. First, the user is instructed to pose for two still images. The user is then instructed to turn his/her head horizontally, first in one direction and then in the other. Third, the user is instructed to identify a few key points in the images. Then the system computes the 3D face geometry from the two images, and tracks the video sequences to create a complete facial texture map by blending frames of the sequence. The key observation is that even though it is difficult to extract dense 3D facial geometry from two images, it is possible to match a sparse set of corners and use them to compute head motion and the 3D locations of these corner points. We can then fit a linear class of human face geometries to this sparse set of reconstructed corners to generate the complete face geometry. In this paper, we show that linear classes of face geometries can be used to effectively fit/interpolate a sparse set of 3D reconstructed points. This novel technique is the key to quickly generating photorealistic 3D face models with minimal user intervention.

2. SYSTEM OVERVIEW

Figure 1 outlines the components of our system. The equipment include a computer and a video camera. We assume the intrinsic camera parameters have been calibrated, a reasonable assumption given the simplicity of calibration procedures [1].

The first stage is data capture. The user takes two images

Figure 2: Side by side comparison of the original images with the reconstructed models of various people.

with a small relative head motion, and two video sequences: one with head turning to each side. Or alternatively, the user can simply turn his/her head from left all the way to the right, or vice versa. In that case, the user needs to select two approximately frontal views with head motion of 5 to 10 degrees, and edit the video into two sequences. In the sequel, we call the two images the *base images*.

The user then locates 5 markers in each of the two base images. The 5 markers correspond to the two inner eye corners, nose top, and two mouth corners.

The next processing stage computes the face mesh geometry and the head pose with respect to the camera frame using the two base images and markers as input. This is done through the following steps:

- Preprocessing: compute automatically a mask image to locate the approximate area of head motion.
- Feature matching and motion determination: a robust technique based on least-median-squares is used to match points of interest and simultaneously determine the head motion across images [2].
- 3D reconstruction: Matched points are reconstructed in 3D space.
- Fitting: the so-called *metrics*, i.e., the parameters which define the face mesh geometry, are estimated through fitting face mesh to 3D reconstructed points and also silhouettes.

The final stage determines the head motions in the video sequences, and blends the images to generate a facial texture map.

3. RESULTS

We have used our system to construct face models for various people. Figure 2 shows side-by-side comparisons of

seven reconstructed models with the real images. The accompanying video shows the animations of these models. In all these examples, the video sequences were taken using ordinary video camera in people's offices. No special lighting equipment or background was used. After data-capture and marking, the computations take between 1 and 2 minutes to generate the synthetic textured head. Most of this time is spent tracking the video sequences.

For people with hair on the sides or the front of the face, our system will sometimes pick up corner points on the hair and treat them as points on the face. The reconstructed model may be affected by them. For example, the female in Figure ?? has hair on her forehead above her eyebrows. Our system treats the points on the hair as normal points on the face, thus the forehead of the reconstructed model is higher than the real forehead.

In the animations shown in the accompanying video[1], we have automatically cut out the eye regions and inserted separate geometries for the eye balls. We scale and translate a generic eyeball model. In some cases, the eye textures are modified manually by scaling the color channels of a real eye image to match the face skin colors. We plan to automate this last step shortly.

4. REFERENCES

[1] Z. Zhang. Flexible camera calibration by viewing a plane from unknown orientations. In *ICCV'99*, pp.666–673, 1999.
[2] Z. Zhang, R. Deriche, O. Faugeras, and Q.-T. Luong. A robust technique for matching two uncalibrated images through the recovery of the unknown epipolar geometry. *Artificial Intelligence Journal*, 78:87–119, Oct. 1995.

---

[1]A 5-minutes video is available at ftp://ftp.research.microsoft.com/Users/zhang/FaceModeling.mpg

476

iFind—A System for Semantics and Feature Based Image Retrieval over Internet

Hongjiang Zhang, Liu Wenyin, Chunhui Hu
Microsoft Research China
49 Zhichun Road
Beijing 100080, China
{hjzhang, wyliu, i-chhu }@microsoft.com

iFind© (v1.0) is a web based image retrieval system developed at Microsoft Research China. It provides the functionalities of keyword based image search, query by image example, category based image browsing, relevance feedback, and semi-automatic image annotation. The key technology in the system is the integrated semantics and feature based image retrieval and relevance feedback approach, which will be presented in our paper in the ACM Multimedia 2000 Proceedings [1]. When the user provides feedback images, the system can refine the retrieval result based on the user's feedback. In the meantime, the system updates the annotation of feedback images by increasing the linkage to the positive examples' annotation and decreasing the linkage to the negative examples' annotation. The updated annotation can further help to improve image retrieval results of the system in later use.

Traditional image retrieval methods are either based on low-level visual features only, which fail to address the images' semantic content, or based on manually annotated keywords only, which fail to utilize the images' visual properties. By forming a semantics network on top of the keyword association with images in the database, we are able to accurately deduce and utilize images' semantic content for retrieval purposes. Hence, it can further improve the feature-based image retrieval method. In our demo, we show that the combined semantics- and feature-based image retrieval and relevance feedback approach outperform both the keyword-based and the feature-based image retrieval methods. The accuracy and effectiveness of our method is demonstrated with experimental results on real-world image collections.

The main user interface is shown in Figure 1 and typical scenarios are as follows.

If a user wants to use keyword-based search for, for instance, pictures of girls, he/she can type "girl" in the text search box on the up-left corner of the window and hit the return bar or click the button "GO!". The user will see some images displayed in several pages in the browsing page. The user can use "<<prev" and "next>>" to switch among these pages. Occasionally, the user may see many irrelevant images. In this case, the user can confirm some of those relevant images by clicking on the "√" symbol and those irrelevant images by clicking on the "×" symbol below each image, and then click on the button "Feedback" on the bottom of the page. The user is promised to get much better result after a few iterations of such feedbacks.

In the browsing page, the user can use the hyperlink "View" below each image to see the image in full size. The user can also use the hyperlink "Similar" below each image to find those images that are visually similar to this one. The user can also click on the hyperlink "Query by Example" and follow the instructions to submit the query example image from the local machine to find those images that are visually similar to the query image.

The user may want to find the intended image by browsing in a category or browsing randomly all images in the database. In these cases, he can do so by selecting the "Browse by Categories" or "Browse Randomly" hyperlinks, respectively.

The middle two hyperlinks on the menu are for system test. The system can improve its intelligence (the semantics network of the database) on image retrieval in daily practice. If the user wants to save what the system has recently learnt, the user can click the "save" hyperlink. Otherwise, the user may click "load" to discard it.

We have performed a set of solid experimental evaluations of *iFind* performance in term of retrieval accuracy and learning speed. The ground truth dataset is composed of 122 categories, each consisting of 100 images. Therefore, there are totally 12200 images in the database, most from Corel image databases. The experiments show that our system not only outperforms both the keyword-based and the feature-based image retrieval methods in retrieval accuracy, but is also a fast learner: the combination of semantic annotation and feature-based retrieval makes the system learn and memorize from user's feedback and continuously improve the retrieval performance. Figure 2 shows the retrieval performance and the learning curve of the *iFind* system.

The system is implemented on Microsoft Internet Information Server (IIS). The retrieval algorithm is implemented in an ISAPI extension DLL and the user interface is written in DHTML. We use Microsoft Access as our database scheme and ODBC as the database interface.

REFERENCES

[1] Lu Y et al. (2000) A Unified Framework for Semantics and Feature Based Relevance Feedback in Image Retrieval Systems. *To appear in Proc. ACM MM2000.*

Figure 1. A typical interface page of the *iFind* system.

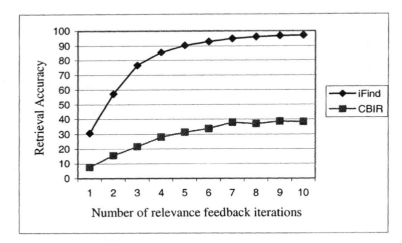

Figure 2: Performance comparison and learning curve.

MiAlbum—A System for Home Photo Management Using the Semi-Automatic Image Annotation Approach

Liu Wenyin, Yanfeng Sun, Hongjiang Zhang
Microsoft Research China
49 Zhichun Road
Beijing 100080, China
{wyliu, i-yfsun, hjzhang}@microsoft.com

MiAlbum© (v1.0) is a system developed at Microsoft Research China for managing family photos with the help of a semi-automatic image annotation approach. It provides functionalities to import (from scanner, digital camera, disks, PC, CD, web, etc.), label (keywords, name, place, etc.), index, browse, and search (by several means), categorize (by automatic classification into some predefined classes), manipulate (in some ways), and export (send or print) family photo images. In this demo, we show the efficiency of the semi-automatic image annotation method and its help in improving the image retrieval accuracy.

As a large number of family photos and other images of personal use have been accumulated, management tasks, including search, browse, and classification of these images are severe problems encountered by the users. Home photo images, which mainly come from scanners or digital cameras, are considered as having no initial annotation at all. Efficient image search requires the help of image annotation. Annotated images can be found using keyword-based search, whilst un-annotated image cannot. Since content-based image retrieval is still at a low performance level, keyword-based image search is more preferable and image annotation is therefore unavoidable.

The system utilizes the semi-automatic image annotation method we proposed [1] to avoid the labor-intensive and tedious manual annotation and the uncertainty of automatic annotation. The semi-automatic image annotation process is embedded in the image retrieval and relevance feedback process based on the integrated semantics and feature based image retrieval and relevance feedback approach, to be presented in our paper in the ACM Multimedia 2000 Proceedings [2]. When the user submits a query of a set of keywords intending to search those images that are semantically relevant and provides relevance feedback while browsing the search result, the association of these keywords and the feedback images are updated. The coverage and quality of image annotation in such a database system is improved progressively as the practice of search and feedback increases.

As we demonstrated, the semi-automatic image annotation method

is effective to annotate images with names, places, objects, events, and other descriptive keywords for different concepts and make future image search more efficient.

The main user interface is shown in Figure 1 and typical scenarios are presented as follows.

When the user imports some images from peripheral devices, the system can automatically search from the album for those visually similar images using the traditional content-based image retrieval. The keywords of high frequency in these similar images can be used as annotation of the imported images. However, the automatic image annotation is not confirmed by the user until in the future retrieval-feedback process, in which they could be either confirmed or rejected. Another important function of the system is to automatically classify the input images into a number (could be specified by the user) of categories using the algorithm proposed by Platt (2000). The user is able to modify the classification later.

If a user wants to use keyword-based search for, for instance, Kaifu's pictures, he/she can type "Kaifu" in the textbox on the bottom-left of the UI page and hit the return bar or click the button "Go". The user will see some images displayed in the browser on the right hand side of the UI page. The user can scroll the browser to see more images. In many cases, especially when the system is used for the first few times, the user may see many irrelevant images. In this case, the user can confirm some of those relevant images by clicking on the "up thumb" button and those irrelevant images by clicking on the "down thumb" button below each image, and then click on the button "Refine" on the bottom-left of the page. The user will then get much better result after several iterations of feedback. Whenever the user provides feedback images, the system automatically updates the association between the keywords and each image based on these feedbacks, e.g., those positive images are annotated as the person's name "Kaifu" and the Kaifu's name is removed from those irrelevant images (if they were previously annotated as "Kaifu"). The annotation process is accomplished in a hidden/implicit fashion, without the user's notice. The user can use the same procedure to annotate places, date, time, event, and other semantic concepts. The image annotation can help improve the retrieval accuracy in the future.

The system also support query by example. They user can only drag an image in the browser to the bottom-left pane and press "Go" and similar images are ranked in the browser. The user may also use the feedback interface to find more similar images. The query image example can also be one outside the album. This can be done by pressing the button "Image" and following the instructions to get the query image.

The system supports both physical folder organization and logical category organization. Both organization schemes can be easily modified using the user interface. The image retrieval process can be specified within each sub-folder or sub-category. Images can also be browsed randomly within each sub-folder or sub-category.

Manual annotation interface is also provided in case some user wants to use it to do some initial annotation, which can help expedite further semi-automatic annotation.

MiAlbum is implemented using Microsoft Visual C++ on Windows 2000. We use Microsoft Access as our database scheme and ODBC as the database interface.

REFERENCES

[1] Liu et al. (2000) A Semi-Automatic Image Annotation Strategy and Its Performance Evaluation. *Microsoft Technical Report.*

[2] Lu Y et al. (2000) A Unified Framework for Semantics and Feature Based Relevance Feedback in Image Retrieval Systems. *To appear in Proc. ACM Multimedia2000.*

[3] Platt J (2000) AutoAlbum: Clustering Digital Photographs Using Probabilistic Model Merging. In: *Proc. IEEE Workshop on Content-Based Access of Image and Video Libraries*, pp. 96-100.

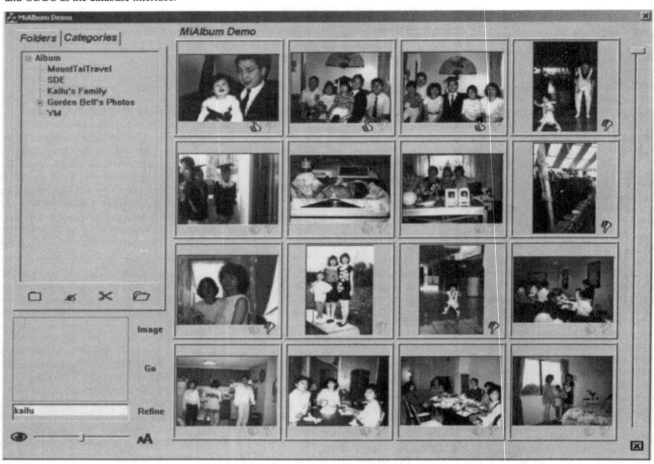

Figure 1. A typical interface page of the *MiAlbum* system.

Diogenes: A Web Search Agent for Person Images

Yuksel Alp Aslandogan
Navigation Technologies Corporation
10400 W. Higgins Rd.
Rosemont, IL 60018 USA
yaslando@chi.navtech.com

Clement T. Yu
Department of EECS
University of Illinois at Chicago
Chicago IL 60607
yu@eecs.uic.edu

ABSTRACT

Diogenes is a web image search agent that retrieves web pages and associates a person name with each facial image on those pages. To accomplish its goal, Diogenes relies on two types of evidence: Visual and textual. A face detection module examines the images on the web page for human faces. A face recognition module identifies the face by using a database of known person images. A text/HTML analysis module analyzes the body of the text with the aim of finding clues about who appears in each image. The outputs of the face detection, text/HTML analysis and face recognition modules are merged using different evidence combination mechanisms to classify each image. Diogenes have been successfully used to retrieve person images from the web with an average precision surpassing those of some commercial image search engines.

1. INTRODUCTION

Diogenes is a web-based, automated image search agent designed specifically for finding person images. It travels the web off-line and builds an indexed image database. In response to a query it searches its index and prepares a page containing the desired images. Diogenes works with the web pages that contain a facial image accompanied by a body of text. The approach is to take advantage of the full text and the HTML tags on the web pages in addition to the visual analysis of the images themselves and to combine the two pieces of information. The first step in this process is to retrieve pages from the World Wide Web. This is done by first obtaining a set of target URLs and then visiting those sites. Text search engines such as Google, AltaVista, and Snap are used to retrieve the initial target set. The lists returned from different search engines are merged and each URL in the merged list is visited to retrieve HTML pages along with the accompanying images. A face detector analyzes each image to detect faces. The output of this module is input to two other modules: A text/HTML module and a face recognition module. The text and HTML structure of the page is analyzed to locate person names and determine their degree

of association with each image. The face in each image is input to the face recognition module. Based on the outputs of these modules and depending on the combination mechanism, Diogenes associates each image containing a face with a person name. We describe the search mechanism and the features used by Diogenes further below.

2. SEARCH MECHANISM

Diogenes starts the search process by submitting queries to text search engines. The URLs obtained from these search engines form the target set of web sites to visit. When Diogenes visits a URL, it looks for pages with images. Diogenes uses both visual and textual features to index these images. The visual features consists of the outputs of face detection and face recognition modules. The neural network-based face detection module [3] examines an image to find a human face. If a face is found, the location is indicated to an intermediate module which crops the facial portion and submits it to both text/HTML analysis and face recognition modules. Diogenes uses a face recognition module which implements the eigen-face method [6, 4]. This module uses a set of known facial images for training. Each of these training images has an associated person name with it. At recognition time, a set of distance values between the input image and those of the training set are reported. These distances indicate how dissimilar the input image is to the training images. In addition, a global distance value called "Distance From Face Space" or DFFS is also reported. This is the global distance of the input image from the facial image space spanned by the training images. Diogenes uses this latter value to determine the uncertainty of the recognition.

The text/HTML analysis module of Diogenes determines a degree of association between each person name on a web page and each facial image on that page. This degree of association is based on two factors: Page-level statistics and local (or structural) statistics. Page-level statistics such as frequency of occurrence and location-within-the-page (title, keyword, body text etc.) are independent of any particular image. Local/structural statistics are those factors that relate a name to an image. Diogenes takes advantage of the HTML structure of a web page in determining the degree of association between a person name and an image. The factors of interest include whether the name occurs in proximity of the image, whether they are enclosed in the same HTML tag, whether the name is part of the image URL/path.

3. EVIDENCE COMBINATION

Once the visual and text/HTML features are computed for a particular web page, they can be combined in a number of ways.

The *simple combination* effectively uses the face detector to screen pages before submitting them to the text/HTML analysis module. When a page is retrieved together with any images on it, each image is analyzed by a face detector. If a face is found in one of the images on the page then the text of the page is submitted to the text/HTML analysis (TA) module.

A basic *linear combination* is a weighted sum of normalized individual features. Diogenes implements a feature-value combination scheme:

$$Score_{combined} = \omega_1 * Score_{FR} + \omega_2 * Score_{TA}$$

Where $Score_{FR}$ and $Score_{TA}$ are the numeric "degree of association" scores assigned to each pair of person name and facial image on a web page by the face recognition and text/HTML analysis modules respectively.

The third combination strategy used by Diogenes is the Dempster-Shafer combination [5]. Dempster-Shafer theory is a generalization of the Bayesian probability theory to account for uncertainty. The important part of this theory for the purpose of image classification is the Dempster's evidence combination formula. If we designate the evidence due to face recognition as m_{FR} and the evidence due to text/HTML analysis as m_{TA}, and apply Dempster's Rule for combination of evidence we get the following:

$$m_{FR,TA}(C) = \frac{\sum_{A,B \subseteq \Theta, A \cap B = C} m_{FR}(A)m_{TA}(B)}{\sum_{A,B \subseteq \Theta, A \cap B \neq \emptyset} m_{FR}(A)m_{TA}(B)}$$

In this formula, the numerator accumulates the evidence which supports a particular hypothesis (C in this case) and the denominator conditions it on the total evidence for those hypotheses supported by both sources. Our face recognition and text/HTML analysis modules give us information about individual images and the uncertainty of the recognition/analysis. This means we have only beliefs for singleton classes (persons) and the body of evidence itself ($m(\Theta)$). With this information, the Dempster combination formula can be simplified as follows:

$$rank(P_C) \quad \propto \quad m_{FR}(P_C)m_{TA}(P_C) + m_{FR}(\Theta)m_{TA}(P_C)$$
$$+m_{FR}(P_C)m_{TA}(\Theta) \qquad (1)$$

Here $\propto$ represents 'is proportional to" relationship. $m_{FR}(P_C)$ and $m_{TA}(P_C)$ are the beliefs assigned to person P_C by the face recognition and text/HTML analysis modules respectively. $m_{FR}(\Theta)$ and $m_{TA}(\Theta)$ represent the uncertainty in the bodies of evidence m_{FR} and m_{TA} respectively. The derivation with examples can be found in [1] and [2]. Both face recognition and text analysis uncertainties are obtained locally, i.e. for each retrieval and automatically without user interaction. This feature enables Diogenes to determine the correct coefficients in emphasizing one feature or the other without input from the user. Since the reliability of any feature may change from retrieval to retrieval, this approach has advantages over relying on the user for confidence values.

4. DEMONSTRATION

In this demonstration the users will be able browse the person image database built by Diogenes and review search results obtained by using different evidence combination mechanisms. We will also demonstrate the relevance feedback mechanism where the user can indicate whether a retrieved image was relevant or not, and see the effect of this feedback on the retrieval. Finally, the user will be able to change certain search parameters used by Diogenes, such as the weights of text/HTML features, and observe the effect on the results. A web-based interface will be used.

5. CONCLUSION

The world wide web offers an enormous, loosely structured collection of multimedia content. On the web, a significant amount of this multimedia content is accompanied by textual context. This enables search agents such as Diogenes to take advantage of both textual and visual clues in indexing this content. This is not as easy as it first appears, however, because the textual descriptions are far from being structured and the quality of multimedia may be very low. To address these challenges different evidence combination mechanisms were implemented by Diogenes, a person-image search agent. The strategies include using face detection as screening and combining text, face detection and face recognition via different mechanisms. Diogenes have been successfully used to retrieve person images from the web with an average precision surpassing a number of commercial image search engines.

Acknowledgments

We would like to thank Matthew Turk (work done at MIT), Alex Pentland (MIT), Takeo Kanade (CMU) and Henry A. Rowley(CMU) for making software available for this project.

6. REFERENCES

[1] Y. Alp Aslandogan and Clement Yu. Multiple Evidence Combination in Image retrieval: Diogenes Searches for People on the Web. Technical Report UIC-EECS-00-1, Department of EECS, University of Illinois at Chicago, January 2000.

[2] Joemon M. Jose, Jonathan Furner, and David J. Harper. Spatial Querying for Image Retrieval: A User Oriented Evaluation. In *ACM SIGIR*, pages 232–240, 1998.

[3] Henry A. Rowley, Shumeet Baluja, and Takeo Kanade. Neural Network-Based Face Detection. *IEEE Transactions on Pattern Analysis and Machine Intelligence*, 20(1):23–38, Jan 1998.

[4] A. Samal and P. A. Iyengar. Automatic Recognition and Analysis of Human Faces and Facial Expressions. *Pattern Recognition*, 25(1):65–77, February 1992.

[5] Glenn Shafer. *A Mathematical Theory of Evidence*. Princeton University Press, 1976.

[6] M. Turk and A. Pentland. Eigenfaces for Recognition. *Cognitive Neuroscience*, 3(1):71–86, 1991.

SIMPLIcity: A Region-based Image Retrieval System for Picture Libraries and Biomedical Image Databases[*]

James Z. Wang
Computer Science and Biomedical Informatics
Stanford University, Stanford, CA 94305
wangz@cs.stanford.edu

ABSTRACT

In this demonstration, we present SIMPLIcity, an image retrieval system for picture libraries and biomedical image databases. The system uses a wavelet-based approach for feature extraction, real-time region segmentation, the Integrated Region Matching (IRM) metric, and image classification methods. Tested on large-scale picture libraries and a database of pathology images, the system has demonstrated accurate and fast retrieval. It is also exceptionally robust to image alterations.

1. INTRODUCTION

The need for efficient content-based image database retrieval has increased tremendously in many application areas such as biomedicine, military, commercial, education, and Web image classification and searching. In the biomedical domain, content-based image retrieval can be used in patient digital libraries, clinical diagnosis, searching of 2-D electrophoresis gels, and pathology slides. In this demonstration, we present a wavelet-based approach for feature extraction, combined with the Integrated Region Matching (IRM) metric [2] and image classification methods.

2. THE SYSTEM

An image in a general-purpose picture library, or a portion of an image in a biomedical image database, is represented by a set of regions, roughly corresponding to objects, which are characterized by color, wavelet-based features, shape, and location. A measure for the overall similarity between images is developed by a region-matching scheme that integrates properties of all the regions in the images. The advantage of using such a "soft matching" is that it makes the metric robust to poor segmentation, an important property that previous work has not solved. High-level image classification methods [3, 6] have been developed and used

---

[*]The demonstration URL is:
http://www-db.stanford.edu/IMAGE/

to categorize images so that semantically-adaptive searching methods can be applied to each category. Figure 1 shows the architecture of the feature indexing process.

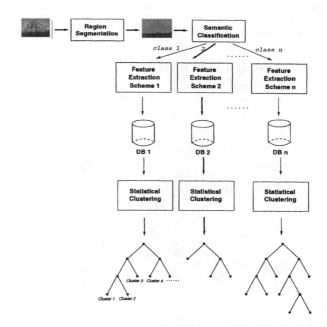

Figure 1: The architecture of feature indexing process. The heavy lines show a sample indexing path of an image.

In this demonstration, we show an experimental image retrieval system, SIMPLIcity (Semantics-sensitive Integrated Matching for Picture LIbraries), built to validate these methods on various image databases, including a database of about 200,000 general-purpose images and a database of more than 70,000 pathology image fragments. We demonstrate that our methods perform much better and much faster than existing methods such as the EMD-based color histogram matching [4] and the WBIIS system based on the Daubechies' wavelets [5]. The system has a friendly user interface which is capable of processing a query based on an outside image or a hand-drawn sketch in real-time.

3. QUERY INTERFACE

Region-based retrieval systems typically have complicated user interfaces [1]. The IRM metric enables us to design *sim-*

ple but capable query interfaces for region-based systems. The current implementation of the SIMPLIcity system provides several query interfaces: a CGI-based Web access interface, a JAVA-based drawing interface, a CGI-based Web interface for submitting a query image of any format anywhere on the Internet.

3.1 Web access interface

This interface is written in CGI and is designed for accessing images in the database with a query image from the database. The user may select a random set of images from the database to start with and click on an image in the window to form a query. Or, the user may enter the ID of an image as the query.

If the user moves the mouse on top of a thumbnail shown in the window, the thumbnail will be automatically changed to its region segmentation and each region is painted with its representing color. This feature is important for partial region matching. For example, the user may choose a subset of the regions of an image to form a query, rather than using all the regions in the query image.

3.2 JAVA drawing interface

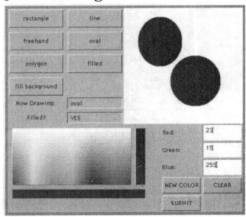

Figure 2: The JAVA drawing query interface allows users to draw sketch queries.

We have developed a JAVA-based drawing interface (Figure 2) for users to make free hand sketch queries. We allow users to draw sketches, straight lines, polygons, rectangles, and eclipses. A 24-bit color palette is provided on the interface for users to choose a representing color for each region or line drawn. We are exploring ways to specify desired textures.

3.3 Outside query interface

We allow the user to submit any images on the Internet as a query image to the system by entering the URL of an image (Figure 3). Our system is capable of handling any image format from anywhere on the Internet and reachable by our server via the HTTP protocol. The image is downloaded and processed by our system on-the-fly. The high efficiency of our image segmentation and matching algorithms made this feature possible.

Figure 3: The outside query interface. The best 17 matched images are presented for a query image selected by the user from the Stanford front Web page. The user enters the URL of the query image (shown in the upper-left corner) to establish a query. Database size: 200,000 images.

4. ACKNOWLEDGMENTS

This work was supported in part by the National Science Foundation Grant No. IIS-9817511. It is a joint work with Jia Li and Gio Wiederhold. The author would like to thank the generous help of Desmond Chan, Oscar Firschein, Donald Regula, and Xin Wang.

5. REFERENCES

[1] C. Carson, M. Thomas, S. Belongie, J. M. Hellerstein, J. Malik, "Blobworld: a system for region-based image indexing and retrieval," *Third Int. Conf. on Visual Information Systems*, D. P. Huijsmans, A. W.M. Smeulders (eds.), Springer, Amsterdam, The Netherlands,

[2] J. Li, J. Z. Wang, G. Wiederhold, "Integrated Region Matching for Image Retrieval," *Proc. of the 2000 ACM Multimedia Conf.*, Los Angeles, October, 2000.

[3] J. Li, J. Z. Wang, G. Wiederhold, "Classification of textured and non-textured images using region segmentation," *Proc. of the Seventh International Conference on Image Processing*, Vancouver, BC, Canada, September, 2000.

[4] Y. Rubner, *Perceptual Metrics for Image Database Navigation*, Ph.D. Dissertation, Computer Science Department, Stanford University, May 1999.

[5] J. Z. Wang, G. Wiederhold, O. Firschein, X.-W. Sha, "Content-based Image Indexing and Searching Using Daubechies' Wavelets," *Int'l J. of Digital Libraries (IJODL)*, 1(4):311-328, Springer-Verlag, 1998.

[6] J. Z. Wang, J. Li, G. Wiederhold, O. Firschein, "System for Screening Objectionable Images," *Computer Communications Journal*, 21(15):1355 -1360, Elsevier Science, 1998.

mediacaptain – a demo

Florian Mueller
FX Palo Alto Laboratory
3400 Hillview Avenue, Bldg. 4
Palo Alto, CA 94304, USA

floyd@mediacaptain.com

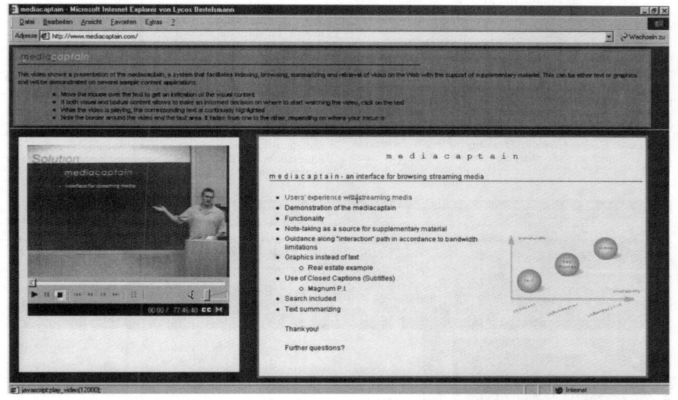

Screenshot 1. The user moves the mouse over the text: the corresponding keyframe is displayed overlaying the video area

ABSTRACT

The mediacaptain is a system that facilitates indexing, browsing, summarizing and retrieval of video on the Web with the support of supplementary material.
The demo is available over the Web at http://www.mediacaptain.com. It is a presentation about the mediacaptain using the features of the mediacaptain.

In order to experience all the possibilities of the mediacaptain, it is advisable to watch the video at the given URL and make use of the provided functionality.

Keywords

Streaming media, streaming video, buffering, supplementary text, supplementary graphics, video on the Web, video and text, user interface. demo.

1. FUNCTIONALITY

The demo presents the mediacaptain, explains its functionality and presents graphical and textual sample applications. Before you play the video, browse through the text to find the point of interest to you. Then move the mouse over the text to see a keyframe taken at that particular point from the movie. If this visual aid confirms your decision to start watching from there, click on the text to start playing the video.

While the video is playing, notice the continuos highlighting of the text. Depending on whether the user's attention should be on the text or on the video, the appropriate area is emphasized.

1.1 mouseOver

Every screen consists of two main parts. On the left, the video window is embedded, on the right is the supplementary material, mostly text, positioned in an extra frame.

In order to get an indication of the visual content, the user can move the mouse over the text, as shown in Screenshot 1.

Please note the cursor cross over the line "User's experience with streaming media". The user moved the mouse over the text in order to get the visual information of what happened in the video at this point. The corresponding JPEG is displayed overlaying the video. Every line of text incorporates this functionality, even the graphic.

If the mouse is moved along while reading the text, it can become like a slideshow of changing images. The user can

basically play the video, with a very small frame rate and no audio, at any speed.

1.2 mouse click

If both visual and textual content allows to make an informed decision on where to start watching the video, the user clicks on the text. The video starts playing at that particular point. While it is playing, the active text segment is highlighted and scrolls into view, which can be seen in Screenshot 2. The video controls the text and text shows where you are in the video, a bi-directional connection, which means interaction on one side triggers action on the other side, and vice versa.

The border around the video and the text area fades from one to the other, depending on where the user's focus is. Once the video is playing, the video border gets highlighted, and the box around the text looses contrast, and vice versa. With this, the focus shifts towards the video and the user gets directed to the other medium. Once the video stops, the initial contrast is restored.

In case of text as supplementary material, the user can also easily retrieve the desired index point by simply utilizing the search functionality of the web browser.

2. DEMO

The demo is available at http://www.mediacaptain.com. Its conceptual foundations, based on user studies, questionnaires and observations, are described in a paper in the short paper/poster section of the ACM Multimedia 2000 proceedings.

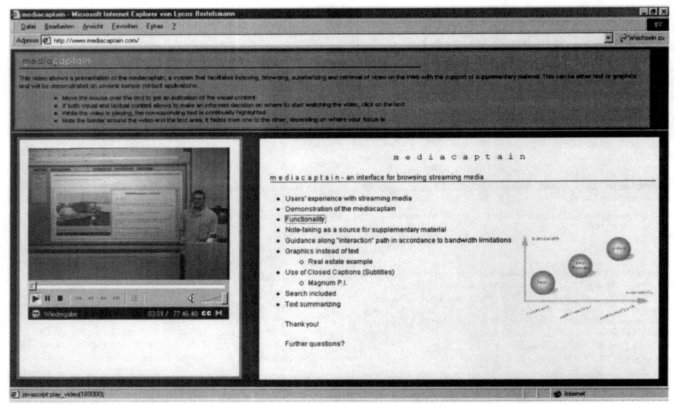

Screenshot 2. The user clicks on the text: the video starts, the text is (continually) highlighted, and the border fades from the text area to the video area

FlyCam: Practical Panoramic Video

Jonathan Foote, Don Kimber

FX Palo Alto Laboratory, Inc.
3400 Hillview Avenue
Palo Alto, CA 94304
{foote, kimber}@pal.xerox.com

ABSTRACT

This demonstration presents a computationally and materially inexpensive system for panoramic video imaging. Digitally combining images from an array of inexpensive video cameras results in a wide-field panoramic camera, from inexpensive off-the-shelf hardware. Digital processing both corrects lens distortion and seamlessly merges images into a panoramic video image. Electronically selecting a region of this results in a rapidly steerable "virtual camera."

Keywords: Panoramic immersive video, image warping, stitching, webcam.

1. OVERVIEW

Teleconferencing and video capture of events such as lectures and meetings require a human operator to orient, zoom, and focus the video or motion picture camera. Automating this task would have many applications in business, education, and entertainment. This paper presents FlyCam, a system that generates a seamless panoramic video images from multiple adjacent cameras. The name alludes to the compound eyes of insects that form sophisticated images from an array of cheap sensors. FlyCam component cameras are mounted on a rigid substrate such that each camera's field of view overlaps that of its neighbor. The resulting images are aligned and corrected using digital warping, and combined to form a large composite image. The result is a seamless high-resolution video image that combines the views of all cameras. Because cameras are mounted in fixed positions relative to each other, the same composition function can be used for all frames. Thus the image composition parameters need only be calculated once, and the actual image composition can be done quickly and efficiently, even at video rates.

Because a FlyCam is fixed with respect to the background, straightforward motion analysis can detect the location of people in the image. This can be used to electronically "pan" and "zoom" a "virtual camera" by cropping the panoramic image. In this system, an appropriate camera view can be automatically determined by finding motion of human images. Thus the system can serve as an automatic camera operator, by steering a real or virtual camera at the most likely subjects. For example, in a teleconference, the

Figure 1. FlyCam videocamera array. Height =4 cm

camera can be automatically steered to capture the person speaking. Also, it is possible for remote viewers to control their own virtual cameras; for example, someone interested in a particular feature or image on a projected slide could zoom in on that feature while others see the entire slide.

2. FLYCAM CONSTRUCTION

The philosophy behind FlyCam was to achieve computationally reasonable panoramic imaging with a minimum of expensive or special-purpose equipment. To this end, a FlyCam is composed of inexpensive (< $120) miniature color video board cameras. Figure 1 shows a FlyCam prototype constructed from four video cameras. It is not necessary to mechanically align the cameras in any way, as long as their fields of view overlap slightly. Small focal length lenses result in substantial radial distortion, however they also yield a large depth-of-field and thus all objects are in focus from a distance of a few centimeters to infinity.

3. PIECEWISE IMAGE STITCHING

We use a piecewise perspective warping of quadrilateral regions to both correct for lens distortion and to map images from adjacent cameras onto a common image plane so they can be merged. In practice, we image a grid of squares, and use the corners as registration points. The four corners of each square form a quadrilateral "patch" in the image of each camera. Every image patch is then corrected back to a square using bilinear warping and tiled with its neighbors to form the panoramic image. Because the necessary warping is never extreme for this application, there is no need for additional interpolation or filtering to reduce aliasing effects. Though this is straightforward to implement, we use the Intel Performance Library subroutines as they are tuned for high throughput on MMX processors.

The luminance across cameras will not be even, primarily because the component cameras have "auto-iris" functions that adapt their gain to match the available light. Thus even when the

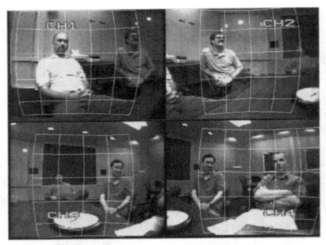

Figure 1. Raw camera images, showing "patches"

Figure 2. Composite panoramic video frame

panoramic image is geometrically correct, seams will be apparent from the brightness differences across cameras [2]. We minimize this problem by the simple measure of cross-fading edge patches. Because these patches are then corrected to a square of known geometry, they can be combined by cross-fading them. The pixel value in a patch is given by a linear combination of the component patches, such that pixels on the left come from the left camera, pixels on the right come from the right camera, and pixels in the middle are a linear mixture of the two.

4. FLYCAM WEB SERVER

.An immediate application of the panoramic image is to select a normal-aspect "virtual" view by cropping the large image. We have built a FlyCam server application that functions as a virtual webcam, allowing each client to request an individual view from the panoramic image. Figure 3 shows the client; a new virtual camera is steered by clicking on the panoramic image. Unlike other webcams that use a steerable camera, every client can choose their own unique combination of pan, tilt, and zoom.

5. RELATED WORK

There has been considerable prior work on combining multiple images into a panoramic scenes; enough that limited space precludes a fuller set of references. Many approaches have been to compose existing still images into a panorama that can be dynamically viewed [3], or by compositing successive video frames into a still panorama [4]. Other approaches create an omnidirectional digital camera using curved mirrors [5,6]. The drawback of this

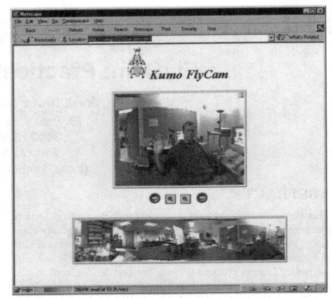

Figure 3. FlyCam webcam application

approach is that subimages extracted from a hemispherical image will be limited in resolution to a small fraction of the single camera, and the necessary image warping will be extreme to regenerate unwarped images. A group at UNC uses 12 video cameras arranged in two hexagons, along with a mirror apparatus to form a common COP. The UNC group devised a similar approach to panoramic image composition, though using the texture mapping hardware of a SGI O2 [2]. Another group at Columbia has taken a similar approach using an array of board cameras. Instead of piecewise image warping, a table lookup system directly warps each image pixel into the composite panorama [7].

6. REFERENCES

[1] G. Wolberg, *Digital Image Warping*, IEEE Computer Society, Press, 1992

[2] A. Majumder, et al., "Immersive teleconferencing: a new algorithm to generate seamless panoramic video imagery," in *Proc. ACM Multimedia 99*, Orlando, FL, pp. 169-178, 1999.

[3] S. Chen and L. Williams, "View interpolation for image synthesis," in *Computer Graphics (SIGGRAPH'93)*, pp.279-288, August 1993.

[4] L. Teodosio and W. Bender, "Salient Video Stills: content and context preserved," in *Proc. ACM Multimedia 93*, Anaheim, CA, pp.39-46, 1993.

[5] Nayar, S., "Catadioptric omnidirectional camera." In Proc. of *IEEE Conference on Computer Vision and Pattern Recognition (CVPR)*, Peurto Rico, June 1997

[6] Huang, Q., Cui., Y., and Samarasekera, S., "Content based active video data acquisition via automated cameramen," in *Proc. IEEE International Conference on Image Processing (ICIP) '98*

[7] R. Swaminathan and S. Nayar, "Non-metric calibration of wide-angle lenses and polycameras," in *Proc. Computer Vision and Pattern Recognition*, June 1999

A Video-Based Augmented Reality Golf Simulator

Alok Govil
Research Assistant

Suya You
Research Associate
Computer Science Department
Integrated Media Systems Center
University of Southern California
001-213-740-4489

Ulrich Neumann
Director, CGIT

govil@usc.edu

suyay@graphics.usc.edu

uneumann@graphics.usc.edu

ABSTRACT

Recent advances in augmented reality technology (AR) have opened a tremendous scope of applications. We describe a use of the technology in virtual golf gaming that exemplifies how the technology can be made to suit the specific needs of distinct applications. Various challenges involved, proposed solutions, and the results obtained are described.

Keywords

Augmented reality, virtual golf, fiducials, camera pose, graphics.

1. INTRODUCTION

With recent advances in computer video processing capabilities, augmented reality has become an important area of research.

We propose use of AR in virtual golf gaming. Virtual reality has also been used for this sport [1-2]. However, the proposed method is much more economical than the systems cited above. Additionally, augmented reality provides a higher fidelity *feel* of the game.

One of the major issues in AR is the accurate merging of the virtual world with the real world. It entails knowledge of the orientation of the camera (or the user's head) in the real world. Several approaches have been used to compute camera pose. We start with the self-tracking system of [3] and adapt it to our application by improving its real-time performance and making it more robust to imaging conditions.

In the golf application, another important issue is tracking of the golf ball in the video images. We developed a method for tracking the fast moving ball in video frames.

2. SYSTEM OVERVIEW

A camera mounted on the user's head grabs images of the real environment that includes the fiducial board [Fig. 2b] and the

golf ball lying on the floor. The system processes these images in real-time to estimate the camera pose, track the golf ball, and display the augmented environment to the user via the head-mounted display (HMD) [Fig. 1].

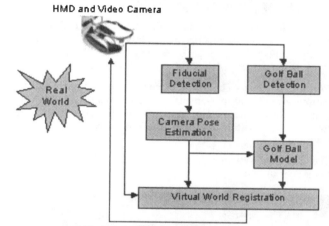

Figure 1. System block diagram.

3. IMPLEMENTATION DETAILS

3.1 Fiducials Detection

Fiducial detection is the first step in camera pose estimation and it is a computationally-expensive process. Carefully designed fiducials are placed on the ground. After evaluating different types of fiducials, we designed a square-shaped fiducial with some unique characters inside (Fig. 2a). The detection and recognition of the landmark are very robust.

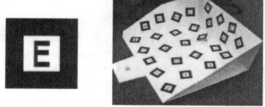

Figure 2. (a) Fiducial, (b) board with calibrated fiducials.

3.2 Camera Pose Estimation

Once the fiducials are detected and identified, the system uses their screen positions to calculate the camera pose. In this work, we adapted a recursive filter motion estimator, namely the iterative Extended Kalman Filter (iEKF), to perform 3D-motion and 6D-pose estimation [5].

3.3 Golf Ball Detection

Golf ball detection is an added requirement for this application of augmented reality. Thus, the computational requirements are further constrained. Additionally, the ball appears diffused even for a nominal putting stroke, so the boundaries cannot be traced reliably. We developed a variant of our technique [6] for ball detection.

3.4 Modeling and Graphics Rendering

Camera pose is used to obtain the 3D position of the golf ball in world coordinates. The z coordinate for the point where the ball is placed just before being hit is assumed to be zero. When the ball is hit, it remains in view for about three to ten frames. The speed and direction of the real ball is computed from these frames and the virtual ball is introduced into a virtual golf course with those same parameters.

4. SIMULATION RESULTS

Our system comprises a Toshiba video camera with F15mm lens, Sony Glasstron head-mounted display, a dual Pentium II machine (2x500Hz, 512MB RAM) with Windows NT Workstation 4.0, and Meteor II frame grabber card.

Playing the game-- The ball is placed on the side of the virtual putting green. The player hits the ball aiming it towards the virtual hole on the putting green. While the actual ball may follow any path, the motion of the virtual ball is computer-controlled.

The described system achieves a frame refresh rate of 12-13 frames per second.

5. DISCUSSION

The application of augmented reality to virtual gaming has been demonstrated. We learned that the image segmentation process is effective in reducing the overall computational requirements of the system, and thus appears to be the key to achieving real-time augmented reality.

6. ACKNOWLEDGMENTS

This research has been funded in part by the Integrated Media Systems Center, a National Science Foundation Engineering Research Center, Cooperative Agreement No. EEC-9529152. Our thanks also go to Bolan Jiang, Jun Park and Jong Weon Lee for their constant technical inputs and support during the duration of the project.

7. REFERENCES

[1] http://www.virtugolf.com

[2] http://www.spokaneindoorgolf.com

[3] Ulrich Neumann and Youngkwan Cho, "A Self-Tracking Augmented Reality System," Proceedings of the ACM Symposium on Virtual Reality Software and Technology, pp. 109-115, July 1996.

[4] G. Welch, G. Bishop, "SCAAT: Incremental Tracking with Incomplete Information," Proceedings of Siggraph97, Computer Graphics, pp. 333-344.

[5] Jun Park, Bolan Jiang, Ulrich Neumann, "Vision-based Pose Computation: Robust and Accurate Augmented Reality Tracking," Proceedings of the 2nd IWAR'99, IEEE Computer Society.

[6] Youngkwan Cho, Jun Park, Ulrich Neumann, "Fast Color Fiducial Detection and Dynamic Workspace Extension in Video See-through Self-Tracking Augmented Reality," Proceedings of the Fifth Pacific Conference on Computer Graphics and Applications, pp. 168-177, Oct. 1997.

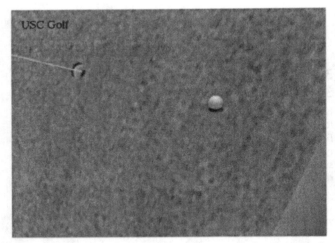

Figure 3. The virtual golf ball moving towards the virtual hole, just after putt. Real ball is occluded by putting green.

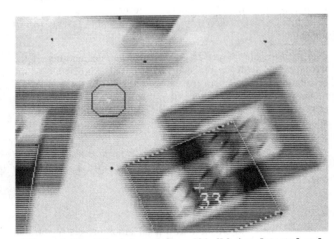

Figure 4. The fiducials and the golf ball being detected and tracked under fast camera motion.

Finding Semantically Related Images in the WWW

Heng Tao Shen   Beng Chin Ooi   Kian-Lee Tan
Department of Computer Science
National University of Singapore

1. INTRODUCTION

In this demonstration, we present a system designed to find semantically relevant images that are embedded in HTML documents in the WWW. The system has been implemented in Java on a Sun Sparc machine, and our experimental study showed the effectiveness of the system [1].

2. IMAGE REPRESENTATION MODEL

The main observation that we made is that an embedded image's semantics are typically captured by its surrounding text in the document. We have identified four parts of the textual content that are well related to the embedded image. These are the *image title, image ALT (alternate text), image caption* and *page title.*

To represent the image semantics more adequately, we propose the Weight ChainNet model that is based on the concept of *lexical chain*. A lexical chain (LC) is a sequence of semantically related words in a text. Here, we define it as one sentence that carries certain semantics by its words. As an image title is just a single word, we say it's a trivial lexical chain - *Title Lexical Chain (TLC)*. The text obtained from the ALT tag is referred to as the *Alt Lexical Chain (ALC)*. The page title is represented as a LC too - *Page Lexical Chain (PLC)*. Finally, since a caption comprises multiple sentences, we represent it as three types of lexical chains. Type one is called *sentence lexical chain (SLC)*, which represents one single sentence in an image caption. Type two is called *reconstructed sentence lexical chain (RSLC)*, and it represents one new sentence reconstructed from related sentences. Two sentences are *related* if both share one or more words. One common word in two SLCs splits each SLC into two. Based on the first common word, the second SLC's second half is connected to the first SLC's first half to form a RSLC. The last type is called *caption lexical chain (CLC)*, which represents the whole image caption. A CLC is formed by connecting SLC one after another.

The ChainNet model is built with these 6 types of lexical chains. To capture the relative importance of the various types of LCs, we assign weights to the various LCs such that LCs that are deem to be more representative of the image content are assigned larger weight values.

For a user query, it's usually a free sentence that describes the image content. Naturally, we represent it as a *Query Lexical Chain - QLC.*

The similarity measure used to determine the degree of similarity between QLC and the various types of LCs of a database image essentially matches each type of LCs against the QLC using the list-space model. However, there are several novel features. First, as mentioned, LCs that are more critical are given higher weights. Second, we capture the closeness of two LCs from the view of match order. For example, one LC is " *US president Clinton and wife visited China in 1997*", and the other one is: " *China president Jiang Zemin welcomed Clinton and wife in Tian'an square*". For these two LCs, there are four matching words. For the first LC, the matched words are in order of *"president Clinton wife China"*, and in the other, they are *"china president Clinton wife"*. We treat each one as a child LC of its original LC. Therefore, the orders of matched words in the two original LCs are not the same. Obviously, the closer the matched order of two children LCs are, the closer the semantics of the original two LCs are. Third, to ensure that an LC and the QLC are *semantically related*, we require the pair shares a certain minimum number of *distinct* matched words.

3. RELEVANCE FEEDBACK

Because of the large image collection and the impreciseness of a query, it is important to provide mechanisms to help users to specify their queries more accurately. For this purpose, we have also developed two feedback techniques:

Semantic Accumulation. In *semantic accumulation*, the user picks one *most relevant* image (from the user's subjective judgement) from the results of previous retrieval as the feedback image. The method accumulates all the previous feedback images' semantics to construct a new query for the next retrieval. The resultant query is represented as a kind of ChainNet called Weight F/Q ChainNet (Feedback/Query ChainNet) since it is constructed by the query and the feedback image's ChainNet.

Semantic Integration and Differentiation. In this method, users can select several relevant and irrelevant images simultaneously. By relevant, we mean images that are semantically related to the query as judged by the user and hence should be retrieved. On the other hand, irrelevant images are those that the user considers to be unrelated and should not have been retrieved. The system *integrates* the related semantics obtained from the relevant feedback images to construct a new query for the next try. After that, the system combines the semantics from irrelevant images to *differentiate* the irrelevant images from the returned results.

4. SYSTEM DESIGN

Figure 1 shows the architecture of the system. The system consists of five basic components: a *Web Crawler*, a *QLC Generator*, an *Image ChainNet Generator*, an *Image Search*

Engine, and a *F/Q ChainNet Generator*. The database consists of three parts: WordNet, Query Profile, and Image Database.

The Web Crawler that operates in the background automatically searches the WWW for documents with embedded images. The crawler also extracts the image title, image ALT, page URL, page title and image caption from the HTML documents as the images' semantic content. It also loads the meaningful images (or their URLs) with their representation into the database. For purpose of testing the model, we "centralized" the image collection (instead of simply extracting the image at runtime from the various Web sites/pages in the form of a search engine). The QLC Generator transforms a user query (free text description) to a *query lexical chain* (QLC). The Image ChainNet Generator constructs image content semantic representation: image weight ChainNet. It retrieves image content from database and creates ChainNet object. The Image Search Engine compares the QLC against the ChainNet of the images, and returns all semantically related images. The images are displayed in order of decreasing degree of similarity. Finally, the F/Q ChainNet Generator is used to generate extended query from the user query and the feedback images. Given the selected images from users, the F/Q ChainNet Generator creates a new weight ChainNet by combining the selected image's ChainNet, and the QLC. Depending on the feedback mechanisms adopted, different new weight ChainNet may be obtained. Finally, the Image Search Engine will perform the next round of retrieval based on the output of F/Q ChainNet Generator.

5. STRUCTURE OF THE DEMO

In this demonstration, we shall illustrate the effectiveness of the proposed system in the following ways:

1. **Semantic extraction**. Given a document with an embedded image, we shall extract its ChainNet. This allows us to have a feel of the exactness of the semantic representation.
2. **Image retrieval**. Given a query (i.e., a set of keywords), we find images that are semantically related to the query. To demonstrate the effectiveness of the proposed system, we shall examine two different systems: traditional approach that is based purely on keyword matching and proposed approach that is based on the Weight ChainNet model.
3. **Feedback Mechanisms**. Given a query, we shall retrieve its semantically relevant images. In addition, the two feedback mechanisms will be employed to facilitate more precise retrieval. This demonstration will also show the relative differences (pros and cons) of the two proposed methods. In the process, we will also show the revised query as a result of the feedback.
4. **Effects of Weights**. The effectiveness of the system is dependent on values assigned to the weights. For the purpose of the demo, the system has been designed so that the tuning parameters can be set "externally". This demonstration will allow us to "tune" the weights, and observe their effects. In fact, we shall see that the default picked by us (obtained after extensive experimental study) is indeed reasonably optimal. Setting the weights externally also has the advantage of allowing different emphasis on different lexical chains.

References

[1] H.T. Shen, B.C. Ooi, K.L. Tan, *Giving Meanings to WWW Images*. MM'00 (to appear).

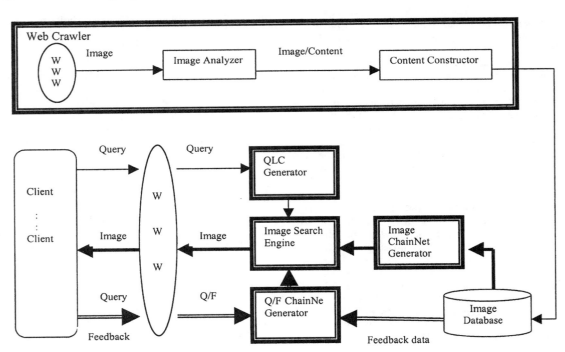

Figure1: Overall system structure in client-server form.

Immersive Panoramic Video

Ulrich Neumann
Integrated Media Systems Center
University of Southern California
Los Angeles CA 90089
213-740-4489

uneumann@usc.edu

Thomas Pintaric
Integrated Media Systems Center
University of Southern California
Los Angeles CA 90089
323-309-1117

tpintari@usc.edu

Albert Rizzo
Integrated Media Systems Center
University of Southern California
Los Angeles CA 90089
213-740-9819

arizzo@usc.edu

ABSTRACT

The acquisition and presentation of high-resolution panoramic video presents a number of technical difficulties. We demonstrate a system that acquires high-resolution (>3Kx480) panoramic images. These images are recorded at 30Hz frame rates and played back for later viewing. During playback users wear a head-mounted display (HMD) and a head-tracking device that allows them to turn their heads freely to observe the desired portions of the panoramic scene. User impressions initially indicate that the experience produces a strong sense of immersion and this new form of media offers new options for creating immersive simulations.

Keywords

Immersion, Panoramic, Virtual Reality.

1. INTRODUCTION

Television and video images pervade the environment we live in. For over fifty years video images have provided a "virtual eye" into distant times and locations. Over the same period, video technology has matured from gray-scale images to big-screen color and digitally processed imagery. One aspect of both the delivery technology and the content creation has remained unchanged however — *the view is controlled at the source and identical for all observers*. Panoramic video overcomes the passive and structured limitations of how video imagery is presented and perceived. The recent convergence of camera, processing, and display technologies make it possible to consider providing each viewer with individual control of their viewing direction. Viewers of panoramic video become virtual participants immersed in the observed scene, creating a new dimension in the way people perceive video imagery. To describe this new media experience, we coin a new term *Immersivision*.

Panoramic image acquisition is based on mosaic approaches developed in the context of still imagery [1]. Mosaics are created from multiple overlapping subimages pieced together to form a high resolution, panoramic, wide field-of-view image. Viewers often dynamically select subsets of the complete panorama for viewing.

Several panoramic video systems use single camera images [2], however, the resolution limits of a single image sensor reduce the quality of the imagery presented to a user.

2. SYSTEM OVERVIEW

We capture high-resolution panoramic video by employing an array of five video cameras viewing the scene over a combined 360-degrees of horizontal arc. The cameras are arrayed to look at a five-facet pyramid mirror. The images from neighboring cameras overlap slightly to facilitate their merger. The camera controllers are each accessible through a serial port so that a host computer can save and restore camera settings as needed. The complete camera system (Fig. 1) is available from Panoram Technologies [3].

Figure 1 – The FullView camera has five cameras and a five-sided pyramid mirror to gather 360-degree view of a scene.

The five camera video streams feed into a digital recording, and playback system that we designed and constructed for maintaining precise frame synchronization. All recording and playback is performed at full video (30Hz) frame rates.

The five live or recorded video streams are digitized and processed in real time by a computer system. The camera lens distortions and colormetric variations are corrected by the software application and a complete panoramic image is constructed in memory. With five cameras, this image has over 3000x480 pixels. From the complete image, one or more scaled subimages are extracted for real-time display in one or

Figure 2 – A 360° image and a selected 120° portion.

more frame buffers and display channels. Figure 2 shows an example screen output containing a full 360° image on the bottom and a selected 120° portion displayed above.

The camera system was designed for viewing the images on a desktop monitor. With a software modification provided by FullView.com [4] we were able to create an immersive viewing interface with a head-mounted display and head tracker. A single window with a resolution of 800x600 is output to the HMD worn by a user. A real-time (inertial-magnetic) orientation tracker [5] is fixed to the HMD to sense the user's head orientation. The orientation is reported to the viewing application through an IP socket, and the output display window is positioned (to mimic pan and tilt) within the full panoramic image in response to the user's head orientation. View control by head motion is a major

Panoramic Camera
5 Panasonic CCD cameras, each looking off an individual planar mirror, controller allows communication via serial port.

↓

Recording System
5 Sony DVCam (DRS-70) recorders, Grassvalley VPE 351 (SuperEdit), VideoTek STG-6000.

↓

Workstation
Dell Precision 220 Workstation (Pentium III 866 MHz, 128 MB RAM), 5 Imagenation PXC 200 frame grabbers, Matrox G400 graphics card.

↓

HMD
Sony PLM-S700 (Glasstron), Intersense IS300 tracker.

Figure 3 – Immersivision system components

contributor to the sense of immersion experienced by the user. It provides the natural viewing control we are accustomed to without any intervening devices or translations. Figure 3 presents a summary of the major system components.

3. Panoramic Recording

The system is "reasonably" portable when packaged into two short racks (Fig. 4). We arranged recording sessions with the assistance of Peter Inova (of Metavision) and Chris Riggins (of Panoram Technologies). We selected recording conditions for a variety of experiments to help us assess the cognitive and perception aspects of Immersivision. Five test environments were chosen for assessment across a range of lighting, external activity, and camera movement conditions. These included:

Figure 4 – Camera system mounted in two short racks and loaded on truck with Thomas (right) and Chris (left).

1. An outdoor mall with the camera in a static position in daytime lighting with background structures and moderate human foot traffic, both close-up and at a distance.

2. A static outdoor setting with extreme direct late afternoon sunlight with high reflectance off of the ocean. The scene includes both distant activity on a beach and close-up activity of human foot traffic and structures.

3. An outside facing elevator with the camera and elevator smoothly rising 15 floors from a low light (street-level shielded) position to intense light as the elevator ascends.

4. The camera mounted at the front of a truck bed near the cab and traveling on a canyon road at speeds between 0-40 mph under ranges of low shaded light to direct sun.

5. Same as #4, except at night on a busy well-lit street and freeway traveling from 0-60 mph.

4. Future Applications

This system present opportunities to capture environments that are difficult and/or labor intensive to produce using traditional computer graphic (CG) modeling methods. While interaction with objects are not possible, a number of application areas could benefit from realistic scene capture and presentation.

Navigation through unfamiliar environments could be readily trained or studied with this system. Entertainment applications would allow safe experience of dangerous or bizarre events. Virtual travel could allow exploration of the streets of Paris or flying near an active volcano from the comfort of home.

Another application domain can be seen in the area of exposure-based habituation therapy for persons with phobias and other forms of anxiety disorders. These types of applications have shown success with CG based VR for fear of heights, flying, spiders, and public speaking [6]. Addressing social anxiety disorder in this manner could be especially advantageous. Flythroughs of in interesting compelling environments could serve as distraction scenarios for persons experiencing intense acute pain. Traditional CG VR has demonstrated the effectiveness of this approach with burn victims receiving wound care and physical therapy [7]. These applications are well suited to Immersivision technology and could serve to advance human welfare.

5. References

[1] S. E. Chen, "QuickTime VR: An Image-Based Approach to Virtual Environment Navigation", Computer Graphics (SIGGRAPH 95), pp 29-38, August 1995.

[2] Nayar, S. K. "Catadioptric Omnidirectional Camera," *Proc. of IEEE Computer Vision and Pattern Recognition (CVPR),* June 1997.

[3] Panoram Technologies Inc. www.panoramtech.com

[4] FullView.com Inc. www.fullview.com

[5] Intersense Inc. www.isense.com

[6] Rothbaum, B.O., & Hodges, L.F. "The use of Virtual Reality Exposure in the Treatment of Anxiety Disorders." *Behavior Modification*, 23(4), 507-525 (1999).

[7] Hoffman HG, et.al.. "Use of virtual reality for adjunctive treatment of adolescent burn pain during wound care." *Pain.* 85:305-309 (2000)

The SMOOTH Video DB - Demonstration of an Integrated Generic Indexing Approach

Technical Demonstration

Alexander Bachlechner, László Böszörményi, Bernhard Dörflinger, Christian Hofbauer, Harald Kosch, Carmen Riedler, Roland Tusch
Institute of Information Technology, University Klagenfurt
9020 Klagenfurt, Austria
harald.kosch@itec.uni-klu.ac.at

ABSTRACT
The SMOOTH Video DB is a distributed system proposing an integral query, browsing, and annotation software framework in common with an index database for video media material.

Categories and Subject Descriptors
H.3.1 [**Information Storage and Retrieval**]: Content Analysis and Indexing—*Indexing Methods, Search Process*

1. THE SMOOTH VIDEO DB
The increased volume of multimedia data available in our everyday lives are related to important social and economic issues and are imperative in various cases of professional and consumer applications, e.g. entertainment, cultural services and tourist information [2]. Such needs require integral multimedia systems which make it possible to effectively *search, access, interact with,* and *present* complex and inhomogeneous information.
The SMOOTH Video DB of the Institute of Information Technology at the University Klagenfurt focuses on developing an integral query, browsing, and annotation framework for video media material driven by the content of an index database (based on the VIDEX model [5]). The framework is generic and integral; integral because it integrates a low-level characteristics (e.g. color histograms) and high-level objects (e.g. name, address of a person) in a common model. It is generic, because it defines basic classes for video segmentation and location and a superclass for content-based information. Specifying an application means thus the definition of content subclasses. It provides thus a more generic system than related ones e.g [4, 1].
Fig. 1 indicates how the proposed SMOOTH Video DB integrates in a distributed multimedia system scenario.

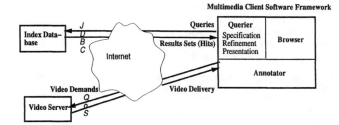

Figure 1: Distributed multimedia system scenario

The first component is the video server providing selective access to the physical video streams. A parallel video server running on the top of PM_2 has been designed to fulfill this task [3]. The supported protocol types are UDP and RTP. We are currently evaluating Quality of Service (QoS) aware network protocols.
The second component is the index database capturing the segment and high-level indexing part of the videos, as semantic information about the stored video streams. It contains the basic set of high-level content classes that are 'events', 'objects', 'persons' and 'locations'. These classes are subclasses of a general 'ContentObject' which may refer to a low-level motion object describing its spatio-temporal characteristics. The model provides means for segmenting video streams in different granularities, such as: 'shot', 'scene' and 'sequence'. A detailed description of the index model VIDEX can be found in [5]. This demonstration presents a soccer-based implementation where the high-level indexing part of the VIDEX model was extended with a rich set of soccer-specific classes.
The third component, the JAVA-based client provides means to annotate, query and browse video material using the graphical library Swing. The core components of the client include the annotator, querier and browser interfaces. The annotator allows the specification of video segments and high-level content objects. The querier follows a text-based, structured query specification technique. It enables the definition of video queries by specifying conditions on content objects and the specification of semantic and temporal relations to other content objects. The browser allows the navigation through the contents of the index database. The database connection is implemented using the JDBC API 2.0.

The interfaces work as follows :

Querier The user is able to submit query conditions through a combination of fill-in forms, menu selections and text fields. Furthermore query refinement, query storage and replay mechanism are provided.

The layout of the initial window follows the pre-categorization of the content in the base classes 'events', 'objects', 'persons' and 'locations' (left window of fig. 2). Conditions of the base classes have to be declared by choosing the query target panel for the class and selecting the 'New' button. Afterwards a dialog containing a list of all types of the base classes appears (i.e. for the type 'person' all subclasses of the class 'person' are retrieved from the index databases ; here 'referee' and 'player' would be found). Finally, the list field 'Concatenation' enables us to connect the different conditions either with 'AND' or 'OR'.
The client implementation contains an abstract class which defines all methods a database manager has to provide for the requirements of the client. Some of the methods are already implemented, as they are valid for all kinds of databases, many others have to be implemented by a special database manager. We provide at time implementation for the *PostgreSQL* and the *Oracle8i* DBMS.

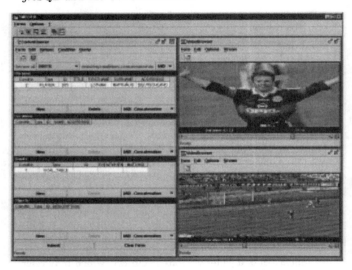

Figure 2: Specifying a query.

Example: Let us consider the following query :
'Find all video shots, where the player Lothar Matthäus scores a goal after a pass over 30 meters'
The query can be specified by using two conditions ('AND' concatenated), the first one on the type 'person' and the second one on 'event' (left window of fig. 2). The videos are displayed in the right window after being selected from the result set in a separate dialog window (not shown).

The default presentation of video units in the prototype implementation is a parallel one, meaning that all retrieved video units are requested at once and received in a parallel fashion. The server addresses, ports, stream identifiers and time intervals of the requested video units are kept by the result sets of the content-based video queries. We are currently developing a presentation composition interface to enable the definition of structural and temporal constraints on the delivery of the videos.

Annotator The Query Annotator provides two basic functions: insert videos into the database and define events for the structural components of the videos.

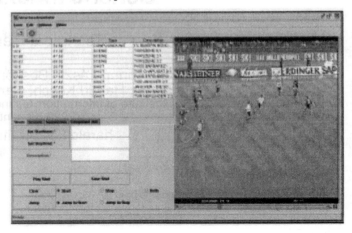

Figure 3: Annotating a video.

Fig. 3 shows a typical annotation situation. In the left window, the already annotated segments are displayed allowing the definition of larger segments (i.e. a 'scene' is built from two 'shots'). Moreover, text fields and menu selections are provided to enter the content information for the events. The interfaces are built dynamically from the class definitions in the index database (i.e. if the selected event type is 'Goal', then the user has to enter (or to reuse) at least the values of all non-NULL attributes of the class 'Goal' from the index database).

Related Links The SMOOTH homepage is located at : http://www.itec.uni-klu.ac.at/~harald/demo/main_start.html

2. REFERENCES

[1] Y. Deng and B.S. Manjunath, *NeTra-V: Toward an object based video representation*, IEEE Transactions on Circuits and Systems for Video Technology **8** (1998), no. 5, 616–627.

[2] R. J. Flynn and W. H. Tetzlaff, *Multimedia-An introduction*, IBM Journal of Research and Development **42** (1998), no. 2, 165–176.

[3] H. Kosch, K. Breidler, and L. Böszörményi, *The Parallel Video Server SESAME-KB*, Peter Kacsuk and Gabriele Kotsis:Distributed and Parallel Systems : From Concepts to Architectures (Balaton, Hungary), Kluwer Press, September 2000.

[4] V. Oria, M.T. Özsu, P. Iglinski, S. Lin, and B. Ya, *DISIMA: A distributed and interoperable image database system*, Proceedings of the ACM SIGMOD International Conference of Management of Data (Dallas, Texas, USA), May 2000, p. 600.

[5] R. Tusch, H. Kosch, and L. Böszörményi, *VIDEX: An integrated generic video indexing approach*, Proceedings of the ACM Multimedia Conference (Los Angeles, California, USA), October-November 2000, long version appeared as Technical Report TR/ITEC/00/2.02 of the Institute of Information Technology, University Klagenfurt, May 2000.

Interactive Tools for Constructing and Browsing Structures for Movie Films * †

Riad Hammoud and Roger Mohr
INRIA Rhône-Alpes and GRAVIR-CNRS
655 avenue de l'Europe,
38330 Montbonnot Saint Martin, FRANCE
riad.hammoud@inrialpes.fr

ABSTRACT

This paper presents a prototype for constructing, browsing and using structures for movie films based on content image analysis only. The goal of the structuring is to facilitate the user's access to the video content (non-linear navigation, etc.). Our prototype provides for the "editor user" advanced tools for structuring the video at its low-level (e.g. shots, key-frames) and high-level structures (e.g. groups of objects, scenes). Also, it provides for the "end user" flexible interfaces for browsing and using constructed video structures.

Against the previous version of this prototype [1], we mainly improved the matching and the clustering of segmented objects. Also, constructing and browsing the high-level scene structure are now available.

Keywords

Interactive videos, Video structuring, Groups/Scenes

1. CONSTRUCTING STRUCTURES

Figure 1 illustrates the system designed for building shots, clusters and scenes structures. It is developed in C++/Ilog-Views and portable under Unix and Linux. In the following, we briefly list its main functionalities. Some modules which implement these functionalities are not completely integrated in the system.

▶ **Basic segmentation.** The partitioning into shots is done firstly using the dominant motion approach. The estimated motion is then used to localize and track mobile objects within shots [2]. The static objects are manually segmented and tracked.

▶ **Characterizing and matching individual objects.** Individual occurrences of tracked objects are characterized

---

*This work is supported by Alcatel CRC

†Demos of this work are available at http://www.inrialpes.fr/movi/people/Hammoud/

by three different features: global color histograms, color correlograms and local differential invariants. The matching process of individual objects is performed on each descriptor separately. A *linear fusion* of the matching results is adopted when multiple descriptors are used. The weight of each descriptor is fixed by the "editor user" which decides the importance of each descriptor (for example, for this sequence colors are more discriminant than geometric informations).

▶ **Characterizing of tracked objects.** Due to the variable appearance of objects during tracking and the acquisition in poorly constrained dynamic scenes, the matching of individual objects using classical features gives poor results. In order to increase the robustness of existing features, we use the Gaussian mixture densities to model the intra-shot variability of each tracked object [6].

Figure 1: System for constructing video structures

▶ **Clustering of objects.** Both supervised and unsupervised clustering of objects are implemented. (1) The user selects by the mouse some tracked objects, considers them as "models" or classes, and then assigns to them all other objects. Currently, this technique is applicable only on modeled tracked objects in the color histogram feature space where the mixture classifier is used to identify classes of individual objects. (2) To avoid a manual selection of "object models", the Ascendant Hierarchical Classification algorithm is used to automatically identify clusters of objects based on different implemented descriptors. The unsupervised classification based on estimated Gaussian mixtures for tracked objects gives good results [5]. The module of this method is not yet integrated in the system.

▶ **User in the loop.** Practically, it is very difficult to perform a perfect clustering of this kind of noisy data (occlusions, illumination changes, etc). The system provides some interactive tools to correct the results of the automatic clustering: (1) *select/browse* clusters at different levels of the hierarchy, (2) *Drag* a badly classified object and *Drop* it into another cluster or a new one.

▶ **key-frames extraction.** A Key-frame is an existing frame which can represent the whole set or a subset of frames of the shot. Usually each shot is represented by only the first frame. In general shots are dynamic, so a single key-frame is not sufficient to represent effectively the content. The modeling of appearances of a tracked object consists in grouping similar views together. An efficient technique is to select from each group of similar views the median image as a key-frame (see [5]).

▶ **Scenes extraction.** A video scene is defined as a collection of semantically related and temporally adjacent shots, depicting and conveying a high-level concept or story. Our approach to extract scenes is an extension of the method of [3]. The method consists firstly in grouping similar shots, of the same predefined temporal window and the same "narrative sequence", into clusters, then exploring the temporal graph of clusters to extract scenes. The temporal relations of Allen (meets, before, ...) are used to connect the nodes of the graph. A scene is formed by merging nodes (clusters) of a sub-graph, which does not contain a temporal relation of type "meets" that can disconnect it into two other sub-graphs. The extension of this method is done at the clustering stage. Three descriptors are used to match similar shots represented by key-frames: histograms, correlograms and the number of similar objects in two compared shots. On each descriptor the hierarchical classification algorithm is performed where the number of clusters is determined using a predefined threshold. Each one of these descriptors summarizes differently the content of a shot. So, the obtained clusters by different descriptors are not necessarily similar. A distance that measures the intersection between two clusters of two different descriptors is computed. Here the goal is to deduce from the three sets of clusters only one set. Based on this, we construct the temporal graph of clusters from which the scenes are extracted as explained previously. The experimental results depict in [4] shown the performance of this extended method against its original form. The related modules to this functionality are in the course of being integrated into this system.

2. BROWSING AND USING STRUCTURES

Once the constructing structures for a movie film is achieved, the "end-user" has the ability to explore the content of the film in a new way. The cluster structure defines in the movie film links between objects. At this level, the end-user clicks an object of interest (actor, car, ...), jumps to its next or previous occurrence in the film, plays the corresponding shot, plays the corresponding action, discovers a related WWW link, etc. The scene structure allows the end user to access the video document as a book (with a table of contents). Each scene describes a story or action of the film.

Figure 2 illustrates the end-user interface for browsing and navigation in the different structure level of the movie film. This interface is developed in **Java** in order to be used on

Figure 2: System for browsing video structures

different user platforms. The next version of this application will be accessible on the World Wide Web.

3. ACKNOWLEDGMENTS

We would like to acknowledge **Alcatel** CRC for its support of this work, and the "Institut National de l'Audiovisuel en France", department of Innovation, for providing the video used in this paper.

4. REFERENCES

[1] S. Benayoun, H. Bernard, P. Bertolino, M. Gelgon, C. Schmid, and F. Spindler. Structuration de vidéos pour des interfaces de consultation avancées. In *CORESA 98 – Journées d'études et d'échanges COmpression et REprésentation des Signaux Audiovisuels.*, June 1998.

[2] M. Gelgon and P. Bouthemy. A region-level graph labeling approch to motion-based segmentation. In *CVPR*, pages 514–519, Puerto Rico, June 17-19 1997.

[3] R. Hammoud, L. Chen, and F. Fontaine. An extensible spatial-temporal model for semantic video segmentation. In *First Int. Forum on Multimedia and Image Processing, Anchorage, Alaska*, 1998.

[4] R. Hammoud and D. G. Kouam. A mixed classification approach of shots for constructing scene structure for movie films. In *Irish Machine Vision and Image Precessing Conference*, The Queen's University of Belfast, Northern Ireland, 31 August-2 Septembre 2000.

[5] R. Hammoud and R. Mohr. Building and browsing hyper-videos: a content variation modeling solution. *Pattern Analysis and Applications*, 2000. Special Issue on Image Indexation, Submitted. In *Irish Machine Vision and Image Precessing Conference*, Belfast, Northern Ireland, 31 August-2 Septembre 2000.

[6] R. Hammoud and R. Mohr. Mixture densities for video objects recognition. In *International Conference on Pattern Recognition*, Barcelona, Spain, 3-8 September 2000. Technical report, INRIA, March 2000. http://www.inria.fr/RRRT/RR-3905.html.

Video Scouting Demonstration: Smart Content Selection and Recording

Nevenka Dimitrova
Lalitha Agnihotri

Radu Jasinschi
John Zimmerman
George Marmaropoulos
Philips Research, 345 Scarborough
Briarcliff Manor, NY 10510, USA

Thomas McGee
Serhan Dagtas

Phone +1 914 945-6059

nevenka.dimitrova@philips.com

ABSTRACT

Smart video content selection and recording is the best selling feature of the current personal TV receivers like TiVo. These devices operate at the TV program level in that they use electronic program guides and user's program personal preferences to help consumers record and watch programs that match their interests. In this Video Scouting demonstration, we present a system that allows for the filtering and retrieving of TV sub-programs based on user's content preferences. The filtering process is realized via real-time video, audio, and transcript analysis. The demonstrator personalizes the TV experience in the areas of celebrity and financial information. The technology can translate into differentiating storage and set-top box product features for finding your favorite actors, most interesting personalized financial news of the day, commercial compaction and enhancement, and content augmentation with other sources of information such as Web pages and encyclopedia. The demonstrator also reflects our active involvement in the MPEG-7 standard (Content Description Interface).

Keywords

Video access, content-based retrieval, multimodal integration.

1. INTRODUCTION

Home entertainment is bound to change due to the introduction of personal TV receivers [1][2] in hard disc recorders. Currently, these devices offer personalization at the TV program level mainly using electronic program guides (EPG). The EPG uses the generic form of metadata consisting of program name, cast, direction, etc. However, audio and visual information can be described in terms of its contents, this at different levels of granularity and levels of abstraction. Therefore audio and video content has potentially higher levels of semantic interpretation that can be exploited by more advanced content analysis methods that operates at the TV program segment level, specially when integrated with textual, e.g., close captioning (CC) information

This would allow consumers to access recorded programs or their segments more effectively. For example, multiple interviews in a TV talk show are automatically separated and guests are identified. In the financial area, segments that are related to the investment portfolio of the user are selected (e.g. "IPO," "market capitalization," "Philips," "IBM," "Oracle" etc.). The identified segments matching the viewer's interests can then be presented.

In this demonstration, we present an architecture for content-based video analysis, filtering, and retrieval. Video Scouting personalizes the TV experience at the program segment level, which is a level deeper than program level selection using only EPG. This is broadly shown in Figure 1.

In Figure 1, there are two inputs to the Video Scouting system: the video stream and the EPG/personal profile. The video stream is demuxed. The resulting audio, video (visual) and CC (textual) stream and the user preferences are input to the TV Program Content Selection module. This module is explained next.

2. TV CONTENT SELECTION : MULTI-MODAL CONTENT ANALYSIS

The TV Program Content Selection module consists of the following layers: (i) feature extraction, (ii) tools, (iii) semantic processes, and (iv) user applications. The *feature extraction layer* performs the segmentation of low-level content from the audio, visual, and textual domain. For example, in the audio domain we have the cepstral coefficients, in the video domain we have color, shape, and edges, and in the textual domain we have words. At the *tools layer*, we have extraction of intermediate-level content. For example, in the audio domain we have audio categories, e.g., speech, music, silence, in the video domain we have scene cuts, color histograms, visual text, or (detected) faces, and finally in the textual domain we have keywords. In the next layer – *the semantic processing layer* -- information across different domains is integrated. For example, TV commercials are segmented based on audio, scene cut rates or CC information. Also, TV program segments are generated. The top layer – *the user application layer* – generates a final segmentation of specific TV programs by combining the program segments obtained at the previous layer into a single unit that unifies them according to the user's profile specifications.

Each of these layers contains a set of elements describing operations on multimedia information. These elements have probabilistic variables associated with them. Taken together, this processing is abstracted by a directed acyclic graph (DAG) for which the nodes represent the individual elements in each layer and the directed arrows represent conditional probabilities. In this demo, the user application layer deals with the representation of two topics: (i) financial, and (ii) celebrities. One of the outputs of this top layer is a probability of occurrence of a specific topic given all dependent information. Initially the multimedia information is processed at the frame level for layers (i) and (ii). At layer (iii) the information is processed at the program segment level. This means that in going from layers (i) and (ii) to layer (iii) all the related multi-modal information is integrated and indexed.

The system runs on a PC-based platform with a Philips Tri-Media multimedia processing board. The input is MPEG-2 video. The extraction of visual features is performed on Tri-Media while audio and textual processing are performed on the PC.

3. RETRIEVAL

For the consumer, the experience is delivered through a simple user interface called the "raindrop model" that removes the difference between live TV and stored content (see Figure 2.) The users will be given the power to design their own "magnets" for desirable or undesirable content. The search power tools include "money seeker" and "celebrity seeker".

4. APPLICATIONS

The applications "inside" the box include personal video content selection and recording, searchable TV, live alerts, commercial detection and enhancement, content augmentation [3], parental control, personalized news retrieval [1], video editing, and content manipulation.

5. SUMMARY

In this demonstration we present an integrated system for audio, visual, and transcript analysis of video content. The function is to provide personalized content selection and recording for TV programs at the subprogram level.

6. REFERENCES

[1] N. Dimitrova, H. Elenbaas, T. McGee, "PNRS - Personal News Retrieval System," *Proc. SPIE Conference on Multimedia Storage and Archiving Systems*, Boston, (September 1999)

[2] N. Dimitrova, T. McGee, L. Agnihotri, S. Dagtas, R. Jasinschi, "On Selective Video Content Analysis and Filtering," *Proc. SPIE on Image and Video Databases*, San Jose, (January 2000).

[3] N. Dimitrova, Y. Chen, L. Nikolovska, "Visual Associations in DejaVideo," *Proc. Asian Conference on Computer Vision*, Taipei, (January 2000).

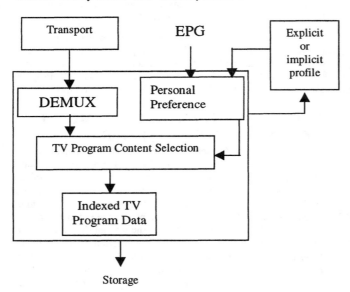

Figure 1. Overall Video Scouting system elements.

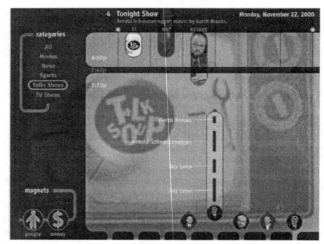

Figure 2. Screen dump of the video scouting system.

A Virtual Media (Vmedia) JPEG 2000 Interactive Image Browser

Jin Li   and   Hong-Hui Sun
Microsoft Research China
5F Research Beijing Sigma Center, 49 Zhichun Road, Haidian, Beijing 100080, P. R. China
Tel. + 86 10 6261 7711 – 5793, Email: jinl@microsoft.com

ABSTRACT

A Vmedia JPEG 2000 interactive image browser is developed. Two key technologies make our system unique: it is the first to implement the decoder ROI access functionality of JPEG 2000, and it uses virtual media (Vmedia) protocol to manage and deliver the ROI bitstream in an efficient fashion. The user browses the image by specifying a region of interest (ROI) with spatial and resolution restriction. Only the portion of the compressed bitstream covering the current ROI is streamed. Moreover, the streaming is performed in a progressive fashion so that a coarse view of the ROI can be rendered very quickly and then gradually refined as more and more bits arrive. Vmedia greatly improves the browsing experience of large images over the slow network.

Keywords: virtual media (Vmedia), JPEG 2000, media access, interactive browsing, streaming, progressive coding, cache

DESCRIPTION

As the Internet becomes popular, more and more high-resolution images are brought online. NASA is putting its collection of space photos online. The Microsoft terra server provides access to high-resolution satellite/aero photographs over the Internet. Museums are digitizing and moving their collectibles online. Even individuals are sharing their personal photos over the web. It is very enjoyable to watch a high-resolution image on the screen; but it is equally painful to download the huge image over the slow Internet. Although the backbone of the Internet keeps improving, the content and the number of users also grow. Efficient delivery of large image is thus crucial to provide enjoyable image browsing experiences on the Internet.

In the early days, compressed images are downloaded entirely from the network before its content is rendered. Delay is inevitable in such a first download and then render model. Newer version of the browser supports progressive JPEG streaming, where views are rendered repeatedly as more and more bitstream arrives. Progressive streaming improves the experience of image browsing. However, for a large image, the size of the compressed bitstream is still too big to be streamed efficiently.

A better way to browse a large image is to use the interactive browsing. Besides reducing the bandwidth requirement, the interactive browsing is also ideal in case the image resolution is higher than the display resolution, such as the handheld device. In interactive browsing, the user interacts with the browser and specifies

the interested region and resolution, which is called a region of interest (ROI). The user may change ROI by panning around (changing the spatial access region), and/or zooming in and out of the image (changing the access resolution). The Live picture viewer [1] has implemented interactive browsing with a multi-resolution JPEG image format called Flashpix. Though enabling better response, Flashpix adds a 33% overhead because multi-resolution compressed bitstreams are stored. In addition, the Live picture browser does not cache the downloaded bitstream. When the ROI is changed, a different compressed bitstream is accessed, which increases the network traffic.

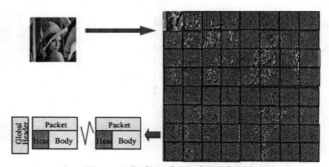

Figure 1 Coding flow of JPEG 2000.

In this work, a network efficient interactive image browser is developed. There are two key technologies that make our system unique. First, we use JPEG 2000, which not only offers a superior compression performance, but also generates a highly structured scalable bitstream that enables ROI access. Second, a virtual media (Vmedia) protocol is developed to efficiently deliver and manage pieces of bitstream related to ROI.

The coding flow of JPEG 2000 is shown in Figure 1. It first transforms an image into the wavelet domain. Each resolution subband is then segmented into fixed size blocks, each of which is encoded by an embedded bitplane coder. The embedded coded block bitstream is chopped into several SNR layers. All chopped bitstreams are then assembled to form the compressed bitstream of JPEG 2000. Such bitstream syntax enables access by region, spatial resolution and quality level.

To access a ROI, we do not need to access the entire JPEG 2000 bitstream. Shown in Figure 2(a), a ROI of size 128x128, with its upper left corner located at (256,256) is accessed. It is easily calculated that a total of 10 wavelet coefficient blocks need to be accessed to decode the ROI[1]. At first not all bitstream segments arrive. But we still can decode a coarse quality view of the ROI. We use the Vmedia protocol, a protocol developed by the

---

[1] Considering the boundary of the wavelet filter, the accessed region is actually a little larger. Though ignored in the discussion for simplicity, the boundary adjustment is implemented in the actual Vmedia interactive image browser.

author, to manage the delivered bitstream segments and priortize the delivery task. As more and more bitstream segments arrive, the quality of the ROI improves.

The browsing experience is very pleasing. We show a picture of the running scene in Figure 3. The image is an aerial photography with size 8192x8192. It is compressed to 1.0 bit per pixel, i.e., 8MB, and is put on the server. It is then interactively browsed through a window of size 600x380 with a simulated modem link at 33.6 kbps. If the image is downloaded and then browsed, it will take more than half an hour. Streaming is also too slow for such large images. However, with the Vmedia interactive image browser, the user can freely wander in the image: zoom in/out or pan around. A coarse quality ROI shows up immediately in response to the selection of the user. The quality of the ROI then gradually improves, and a visually lossless ROI is usually shown within 10 seconds.

ACKNOWLEDGEMENT

The author would like to acknowledge the following individuals: Dr. Xiaoning Lin, for his contribution in initializing the Vmedia project, Dr. Ya-Qin Zhang, for his managerial support and naming of Vmedia, Hu Li, for codes of the Vmedia client, Dr. Qian Zhang, for helping to program the network interface of the Vmedia client and server, Jianping Zhou, for packaging the Vmedia image browser.

BIBLIOGRAPHY

[1] Live picture, www.livepicture.com.
[2] VM adhoc, "JPEG 2000 verification model 5.2 (technical description)", ISO/IEC JTC1/SC29/WG1N1422, Vancouver, BC, Jul. 1999.

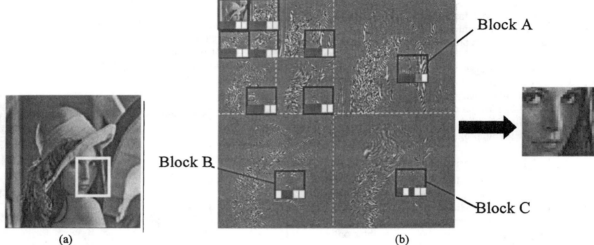

(a)   (b)

Figure 2 (a) A sample of Vmedia image browsing. The Lena image is of size 512x512. The ROI is at (256,256) with size (128,128). (b) The accessed bitstream segments. The black box identifies the coefficient blocks accessed by the Vmedia. A shaded bar identifies an available bitstream segment, and a white bar identifies an unavailable bitstream segment.

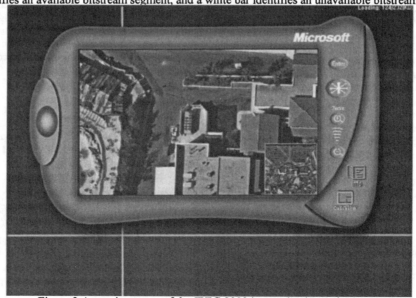

Figure 3 A running scene of the JPEG 2000 interactive image browser.

502

SmartWatch:
An Automated Video Event Finder

Serhan Dagtas, Tom McGee and
Mohamed Abdel-Mottaleb
Philips Research – USA
Briarcliff Manor NY 10510
serhan.dagtas@philips.com

ABSTRACT
In this paper, we present an automated video event detection system that combines textual and aural analysis techniques.

Keywords
Video events, audio, textual search, content based analysis.

SMARTWATCH: DetectingVideo Events

Detecting events in video allows users to view the recorded material in a time saving mode if they do not wish to spend the time to view the whole video. An example scenario is a football fan watching the highlighted touchdowns that may take a few minutes instead of a several hour-long game. While this selection may be straightforward for humans, detecting truly "interesting" events automatically is a tricky task requiring sophisticated analysis tools. In the literature, this has been approached from keyword-based [1] or audio content-based [2] methods. In this application, we combine the two modalities for improved accuracy.

Event detection analysis can take place either at the consumer's end or the broadcaster's end. In our case, we assume the first scenario, which also requires a fair degree of automation.

This demo presents an automatic method for identifying segments in a video where a given event occurs. We combine the use of textual (closed captions or transcripts) and aural analysis for effective and efficient retrieval. Accordingly, users specify their preferences with a list of

keywords that represent interesting events (e.g. goals) and these are first searched in the textual database. We then use audio properties to verify the results of the textual search and create a final list, which is typically more accurate than text-only search results. For this purpose, we detect segments of programs that possess certain audio characteristics such as the announcer shouting "goal". We have performed experiments on eight hours of video where keyword-only search resulted in 20% precision. Combining text and audio improved the precision to 80%. Recall rate was 100% in both cases.

In our demo setup, relevant programs are recorded by a personalized video recording device simulated by a PC. The event detection process is carried out offline in an interactive mode that allows users to pick interesting events of choice (such as a corner kick or the move of a favorite player). The user interface then returns the final list of segments for playback. The segments that are played back are 10 seconds long and the user can opt to continue to watch the rest or skip to the next "interesting" segment. This appears to be more effective then fastforwarding/rewinding in traditional ways although exact user response would be subject to further user studies.

While content-based retrieval of video has been studied extensively in different modalities (visual, textual, aural etc.) our work represents a novel combination of two very important and effective content sources: text and audio. We use a very efficient method for audio processing with minimal processing and storage requirements. Future extensions may include incorporating visual features for a broader query formulation and more precise processing.

REFERENCES
[1] "**Informedia** Digital Video Library Project" www.informedia.cs.cmu.edu

[2] "**MoCA**: Movie Content Analysis" www.informatik.uni-mannheim.de/informatik/pi4/projects/MoCA

MP7TV: A system for Content based Querying and Retrieval of Digital Video

Youngchoon Park & Antonio Pizzarello

*roz **Software Systems, Inc.***

4417 N. Saddlebag Trail, #3

Scottsdale, AZ 85251, USA

{ypark,pizzarello}@rozsoftware.com

The video content retrieval system MP7TV is designed to capture, store, and visually present the information contained in a video sequence. M⌐7TV uses multi-sensory data fusion techniques and machine learning based on domain and user subjectivity modeling to extract the relevant visual information from compressed video streams, such as MPEG.   MP7TV uses advanced spatio-temporal video analysis techniques for spatio-temporal properties such as motion, of video object and highly efficient content based image management environments called **PicDB**™ for frame based video management. PicDB is an image repository with many sophisticated tools for management and retrieval of pictures. In addition to the treatment of color through proprietary techniques, it combines image processing capabilities with database technologies to provide a powerful system for content based retrieval of visual information. Users of PicDB can create, index, modify, store, query, search, retrieve and edit pictures and synthetic images. All these capabilities are built into MP7TV.

With its extensive library of routines for automated analysis and extraction of the contents of all multimedia objects, in particular, images, audio and video, *roz Software Systems* provides a comprehensive solution along with a mark-up language for content based video indexing, classification, comparison and retrieval of distributed multimedia data. More importantly, it provides a mechanism for the generation of panoramic stills for video segments that embody both spatial features (e.g., visible objects) and temporal features (e.g. the trajectories of objects) in the form of video icon. The system enables users to formulate complex queries (say retrieve all images and video segments containing a Jeep with two passengers off road). Such a query may be expressed by making references to a number

of visual, textual, motion, or sound attributes simultaneously. In addition, the user may sketch a shape and draw a desired trajectory and ask the system to retrieve images or video clips that contain objects with such behavior.

MP7TV has six components, namely domain management module, feature extraction module, visual query module, delivery module, multi-similarity based retrieval module and indexing module. See Figure 1. Domain management module is responsible for the acquisition, and management of domain knowledge. MP7TV selects the appropriate methods for spatio-temporal and visual feature extraction based on the domain knowledge with advanced feature selection methods. In addition, the determination of the feature dimensions and the extraction of the various visual features from compressed video streams in the feature extraction module are based on the domain knowledge. The visual query module of MP7TV provides a number of querying modes, including query by concept, example (image and/or video), query by projected object motion, and query by sketch, among others. Delivery module has an interactive content-based video object rendering mechanism. Multi-similarity based retrieval module responsible for measurement of dissimilarities when multiple search criteria are presented.

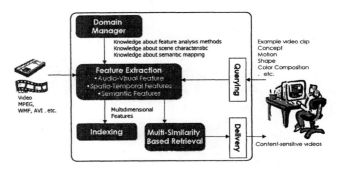

Figure 1: MP7TV main modules

MP7TV, may be customized for specific applications. An example is video conferencing sessions in law firms, used to conduct inquiries or take depositions. Applications such as this accumulate a large video library quickly. Functions provided by MP7TV are very diverse and cater to desktop or high-quality video conferencing archives as well as ordinary video streams. MP7TV can analyze video frames on the basis of color, texture, shape, spatial arrangements, and other visual contents. Skin and face detection is a simple example applicable to video acquired during conferencing sessions. For this type of application, the accompanying audio is of greater importance for search and retrieval. Speech recognition and indexing, together with ontological structures embedded in MP7TV allow search of video archives by keyword, concept, or context.

MP7TV's significant features include:
- Extends the capabilities of **PicDB** for image processing, analysis and retrieval
- A variety of routines for scene cut, dissolve, and morphing detection
- A comprehensive set of routines for content analysis of individual video frames
- Unique techniques and algorithms for motion analysis, extraction and representation
- Automated indexing of sound track
- Interactive semantic annotation of video object, action and event

and retrieval.

- Ontological search on the indexed speech
- A markup language for modeling of the extracted features
- Automatic indexing of audio-visual objects and their features
- Sorting and searching by video contents, both visual appearances and audio features
- Full integration with web-based applications

MP7TV can be used in a variety of applications, particularly, those requiring:
- ✓ Integration with database applications, Oracle, Sybase, MS Access, Jasmine, or any ODBC
- ✓ Video mail, video editing, video search and retrieval
- ✓ Specialized feature extraction, such as skin and face detection
- ✓ Conceptual search on the basis of ontological structures.

MP7TV is customizable to specific needs of the user, and as such is suitable for diverse application domains. As such it provides ease of evolution due to changing application requirements.

The demo highlights MP7TV's capabilities in extracting visual features, audio indexing and conceptual search

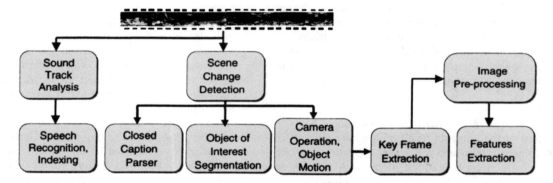

Figure 2: Video content extraction in MP7TV

Doctoral Symposium

Exploring Multimedia Applications Locality to Improve Cache Performance

Andrea Prati
Dipartimento di Scienze dell'Ingegneria
Università di Modena e Reggio Emilia
Via Campi, 213/b - Modena - Italy
prati@dsi.unimo.it

ABSTRACT

This research aims to explore possible solutions to improvement of performance in *multimedia processor* [1]. In this context, cache memory performance plays a more and more critical role in computer systems, since the gap between processor speed and main memory speed tends to increase rather than the contrary. The integration inside the computational units of some SIMD improvements (such as Pentium MMX, HP MAX2 or UltraSparc VIS) for improving the parallel computation on image pixels is the main answer to the heavy workloads of multimedia applications [2]. Moreover, the workload of multimedia applications [3] has a strong impact on cache memory performance, since the locality of memory references embedded in multimedia programs differs from that of traditional programs. In fact, as widely known, programs exhibit two main kind of locality: spatial and temporal. Nevertheless, as stated in [1], multimedia applications seem to present a new kind of locality, called *2D-spatial locality* (i.e. there is an high probability that accessing to an address, future accesses will be in a bidimensional neighborhood of it). For this reason, standard cache memory organization achieves poorer performance when used for multimedia. To achieve an overall performance improvement on specialized multimedia processors, further architectural modification on memory hierarchy and on its management should be fulfilled. This could be coupled with the recent idea of associating programmable components with memory separated from the main processor, such as IRAM [4].

First goal of this research is to prove that common multimedia applications exhibit a 2D-spatial locality. To do this, we developed a benchmark including the most common multimedia and image processing applications. Many trace-driven simulations confirm the hypothesis [5][6].

After this, we try to explore techniques able to exploit this

locality to improve cache performance. Among the various techniques used to improve cache memory performance, prefetching has been one of the most studied and apparently promising (see [7][8], where, however, no assumption on 2D spatial locality is highlighted). Prefetching techniques can be mainly classified according to their potential software or hardware implementation, although some techniques may take advantage of a combined software/hardware implementation [9]. A widely explored approach to improve cache performance is hardware prefetching that allows the pre-loading of data in the cache before they are referenced. However, existing hardware prefetching approaches partially miss the potential performance improvement, since they are not tailored to multimedia locality. In this research we are proposing novel effective approaches to hardware prefetching to be used in image processing programs for multimedia. In particular, we have addressed multimedia image processing, where we have included algorithms like the widespread MPEG-2 decoding used for decompression of audio/video streams and typical image processing operations like convolution for image filtering and edge chain coding, used as a pre-processing step in many image analysis tasks. We have omitted evaluation on sound data (like MP3 decompression or speech recognition), since they exhibit typical array spatial locality and standard prefetching techniques perform well enough. Algorithms have been selected according to their spread and their different data addressing schemes: while convolution is dominated by a regular data addressing scheme which can be predicted a priori, edge chain coding is heavily *data dependent*, in the sense that the address sequence of data references depends on the image and cannot be statically predicted: for example, in this case software prefetching techniques (based on compile-time prediction of future accesses) are not suitable. MPEG-2 exhibits a combination of regular address scheme and data dependency.

Typical hardware prefetching techniques are not suitable in this context: techniques based on one-block-lookahead [10] exploit only 1D spatial locality, while adaptive techniques do not match data dependency of some image processing algorithms.

For this reason, we present novel hardware prefetching techniques oriented to multimedia image processing matching the 2D spatial locality. We called it "**neighbor prefetching technique**" since it tries to pre-fetch all the blocks belonging to the neighborhood of the actual one. We compare their performance with that of other existing hardware prefetching techniques in terms of avoided cache misses and total number of prefetches introduced. Our experimental results prove that cache misses reduction is heavily improved w.r.t. the other techniques. The only drawbacks are the high lookup pressure generated and the increase of the data bandwidth needed for the pre-fetching. For the last, we demonstrate [6] that the average increase is negligible, and for the former we developed many improved version aimed to reduced overall time performance of the proposed approach. We are working to analyze the temporal simulation (with a detailed model of the memory hierarchy) in order to prove the efficiency (besides the efficacy) of the neighbor technique.

In conclusion, the neighbor approach seems promising: multimedia processor should take benefit from the introduction of a cache tailored with multimedia applications and exploiting the proposed approach. In fact, even if the overall temporal performance of this technique should result worst than the others, the benefit gained with the cache misses reduction w.r.t. the cost introduced by the increase of number of prefetches issued is high, since misses are more expensive than prefetches, because the lasts are maskable. This new architectural approach should not tend towards the "specialization" of processors, but towards the integration into general-purpose ones of specialized features, combining generalization with improvements for specialized applications, such as multimedia.

1. REFERENCES

[1] I. Kuroda and T. Niscitani, "Multimedia processors," *Proceedings of the IEEE*, vol. 86, no. 6, pp. 1203–1221, 1998.

[2] K. Diefendoff and P.K. Dubey, "How multimedia workloads will change processor design," *IEEE Computer*, Sept. 1997.

[3] L. Chiariglione, "Impact of multimedia standards on multimedia industry," *Proceedings of the IEEE*, vol. 86, no. 16, pp. 1222–1227, 1998.

[4] D. et al. Patterson, "Intelligent ram (iram): the industrial setting, applications and architectures," in *Proc. of ICCD (Int'l Conf. on Computer Design)*, 1997.

[5] R. Cucchiara and M. Piccardi, "Exploiting image processing locality in cache pre-fetching," in *Proc. of the 5th Intl. Conf. on High Performance Computing (HiPC)*, Dec. 1998.

[6] R. Cucchiara, M. Piccardi, and A. Prati, "Exploiting cache in multimedia," in *Proc. of IEEE Intl. Conf. on Multimedia Computing and Systems (ICMCS)*, 1999, vol. 1.

[7] D. Zucker, M.J. Flynn, and R. Lee, "A comparison of hardware prefetching techniques for multimedia benchmark," in *Proc. of IEEE Multimedia 96*, 1996, pp. 236–244.

[8] P. Soderquist and M. Lesser, "Memory traffic and data cache behavior of an mpeg-2 software decoder," *preprint for ICCD '97*, 1997.

[9] T.F. Chen and J.L. Baer, "A performance study of hardware and software data prefetching schemes," in *Proc. of the 21th Intl. Symp. on Computer Architecture (ISCA)*, 1996, pp. 223–232.

[10] A.J. Smith, "Cache memories," *ACM Computing Surveys*, vol. 14, no. 3, pp. 473–530, 1982.

Region-based Retrieval of Biomedical Images*

James Z. Wang†
Biomedical Informatics and Computer Science
Stanford University
wangz@cs.stanford.edu

ABSTRACT
Searching digital biomedical images is a challenging problem. Prevalent retrieval techniques involve human-supplied text annotations to describe image contents. Biomedical images, such as pathology slides, usually have higher resolution than general-purpose pictures, making it additionally difficult to index. Precise object segmentation is also extremely difficult and is still an open problem. We are developing a multiresolution region-based retrieval system for high-resolution biomedical image databases. The system, based on wavelets, the IRM (Integrated Region Matching) distance, and image classification, is highly robust to inaccurate image segmentation and various visual alterations. Tested on a database of more than 70,000 pathology image fragments, the system has demonstrated high accuracy and fast speed.

1. INTRODUCTION

In biomedicine, content-based image retrieval is critically important in patient digital libraries, clinical diagnosis, clinical trials, searching of 2-D electrophoresis gels, and pathology slides. Most existing content-based image retrieval systems [2, 3, 5, 6, 7, 9] are designed for general-purpose picture libraries such as photos and graphs. In this doctoral dissertation, we present a retrieval system for high-resolution biomedical image databases [10] using wavelet-based [1] multi-scale feature extraction and the Integrated Region Matching (IRM) distance [4].

2. THE SYSTEM
2.1 Semantics-sensitive Retrieval
The capability of existing CBIR systems is essentially limited by the way they function, i.e., they rely on only primitive features of the image. Moreover, the same low-level image features and image similarity measures are typically used for images of all semantic types. However, different image features are sensitive to different semantic types. For example, an OCR (optical character recognition) method may be good for graphs commonly found in biomedical educational materials while a region-based indexing approach is much better for pathology and radiology images.

We propose a *semantics-sensitive* approach to the problem of searching image databases. Semantic classification methods are used to categorize images so that semantically-adaptive searching methods applicable to each category can be applied. At the same time, the system can narrow down the searching range to a subset of the original database to facilitate fast retrieval. A biomedical image database may be categorized into "X-ray", "MRI", "pathology", "graphs", "micro-arrays", etc. We then apply a suitable feature extraction method and a corresponding matching metric to each of the semantic classes.

2.2 Feature Indexing
The purpose of content-based indexing and searching for biomedical image databases is very different from that for picture libraries. Users of a general-purpose picture library are typically interested in images with similar object and color configurations at a global scale, while users of a biomedical image database are often interested in images with similar objects at the finest scale.

The feature extraction in our system is performed on multiresolution image blocks (or fragments) of the original images, rather than the original images. In fact, we first partition the images and lower resolution versions of the same image into overlapping blocks. A user may submit an image patch or a sketch of a desired object to form a query. The system attempts to find image fragments within the database to match with the object specified by the user.

A portion of a high-resolution biomedical image is represented by a set of regions, roughly corresponding to objects, which are characterized by color, wavelet-based features, shape, and location. We used the k-means statistical clustering algorithm to obtain fast segmentation. A measure for the overall similarity between images is developed by a region-matching scheme that integrates properties of all the regions in the images. The advantage of using such a "soft matching" is that it makes the metric robust to inaccurate segmentation, an important property that previous work has not solved.

*Project URL: http://WWW-DB.Stanford.EDU/IMAGE/
†Principal Advisor: Gio Wiederhold

2.3 Matching

Based on the region representations of the image fragments, the Integrated Region Matching (IRM) distance [4] is used to compute the distance between two image fragments. That is, IRM is a similarity measure between images fragments based on region representations. It incorporates the properties of all the segmented regions so that information about a fragment can be fully used. Region-based matching is a difficult problem because of the problems of inaccurate segmentation. Semantically-precise image segmentation is an extremely difficult process and is still an open problem.

Traditionally, region-based matching is performed on individual regions [5]. The IRM metric we have developed has the following major advantages:

1. Compared with retrieval based on individual regions, the overall "soft similarity" approach in IRM reduces the influence of inaccurate segmentation.

2. In many cases, knowing that one object usually appears with another object helps to clarify the semantics of a particular region.

3. By defining an overall image-to-image similarity measure, the SIMPLIcity system provides users with a *simple* querying interface.

Mathematically, defining a similarity measure is equivalent to defining a distance between sets of points in a high-dimensional space, i.e., the feature space. Every point in the space corresponds to the feature vector, or the descriptor, of a region. Although distance between two points in feature space can be easily defined by various measures such as the Euclidean distance, it is not obvious how to define a distance between two sets of feature points. The distance must correspond to a person's concept of semantic "closeness" of two images.

We argue that a similarity measure based on region segmentation of images can be tolerant of inaccurate image segmentation if it takes all the regions in an image into consideration. To define the similarity measure, we first attempt to match regions in two images. Being aware that segmentation process cannot be perfect, we "soften" the matching by allowing one region of an image to be matched to several regions of another image. Here, a region-to-region *match* is obtained when the regions are significantly similar to each other in terms of the features extracted.

The principle of matching is that the most similar region pair is matched first. We call this matching scheme *integrated region matching* (IRM) to stress the incorporation of regions in the retrieval process. After regions are matched, the similarity measure is computed as a weighted sum of the similarity between region pairs, with weights determined by the matching scheme.

3. EXPERIMENTS

We are developing an experimental image retrieval system, SIMPLIcity (Semantics-sensitive Integrated Matching for Picture LIbraries) [8], to validate these methods on both biomedical and general-purpose image databases. We show that our methods perform much better and much faster than existing methods such as the EMD-based color histogram matching [6] and the WBIIS system based on the Daubechies' wavelets [9]. The system is exceptionally robust to image alterations such as intensity variation, sharpness variation, intentional distortions, cropping, shifting, and rotation. These features are important to biomedical image databases because visual features in the query image are not exactly the same as the visual features in the images in the database. The system has a friendly user interface which is capable of processing a query based on an outside image or a hand-drawn sketch in real-time.

4. ACKNOWLEDGMENTS

I would like to thank my principal advisor, Professor Gio Wiederhold, and my committee members Professors Russ B. Altman, Hector Garcia-Molina, Mu-Tao Wang, and Stephen T.C. Wong, for their guidances on this work. This work was supported in part by the National Science Foundation Grant No. IIS-9817511. I would like to thank the help of Oscar Firschein, Jia Li, Donald Regula and anonymous reviewers.

5. REFERENCES

[1] I.Daubechies, *Ten Lectures on Wavelets*, Capital City Press, 1992.

[2] M. Flickner, H. Sawhney, W. Niblack, J. Ashley, Q. Huang, B. Dom, M. Gorkani, J. Hafner, D. Lee, D. Petkovic, D. Steele, P. Yanker, "Query by image and video content: the QBIC system," *Computer*, vol. 28, no. 9, pp. 23-32, Sept. 1995.

[3] A. Gupta, R. Jain, "Visual information retrieval," *Comm. Assoc. Comp. Mach.*, vol. 40, no. 5, pp. 70-79, May 1997.

[4] J. Li, J. Z. Wang, G. Wiederhold, "IRM: Integrated Region Matching for Image Retrieval," *Proc. of the 2000 ACM Multimedia Conf.*, Los Angeles, October, 2000.

[5] W. Y. Ma, B. Manjunath, "NaTra: A toolbox for navigating large image databases," *Proc. IEEE Int. Conf. Image Processing*, pp. 568-71, 1997.

[6] Y. Rubner, *Perceptual Metrics for Image Database Navigation*, Ph.D. Dissertation, Computer Science Department, Stanford University, May 1999.

[7] J. R. Smith, S.-F. Chang, "An image and video search engine for the World-Wide Web," *Storage and Retrieval for Image and Video Databases V (Sethi, I K and Jain, R C, eds), Proc SPIE 3022*, pp. 84-95, 1997.

[8] J. Z. Wang, J. Li, D. Chan, G. Wiederhold, "Semantics-sensitive Retrieval for Digital Picture Libraries," *D-LIB Magazine*, 5(11), November 1999. http://www.dlib.org

[9] J. Z. Wang, G. Wiederhold, O. Firschein, X.-W. Sha, "Content-based Image Indexing and Searching Using Daubechies' Wavelets," *Int'l J. of Digital Libraries (IJODL)*, 1(4):311-328, Springer-Verlag, 1998.

[10] S.T.C. Wong (ed.), *Medical Image Databases*, Kluwer Academic, Boston, 1998.

Query Model-Based Content-Based Image Retrieval:
Similarity Definition, Application and Automation - ABSTRACT

Horst Eidenberger

Vienna University of Technology, Institute of Software Technology, Austria

Favoritenstraße 9-11/188, A-1040 Vienna, Austria

Phone: +43 1 4035158 14

eMail: hme@bibvb.ac.at

Advisor: Prof. Dr. Christian Breiteneder, Vienna University of Technology, Austria

1. Introduction

This abstract describes my doctoral thesis in the field of multimedia / content-based image retrieval (CBIR). CBIR aims at searching image libraries for specific image features (e.g., colors, textures, shapes). Querying is performed by comparing feature vectors (e.g., color histograms) of a search image with the feature vectors of all images in the database. To start a query the user selects search image, features and weights in order to indicate the importance of the selected features. This method is called the computer centric approach (CCA). Currently, the computer centric approach in CBIR suffers from several disadvantages:

- Bad results due to the semantic gap and the subjectivity of human perception: The first point stands for the difference between the high-level CBIR concepts usually presented to users and the low-level features actually employed. The latter addresses the fact that different persons (recipients) or the same person in different situations may judge visual content differently.

- Bad querying performance: Using (computational often very complex) distance functions for the comparison of feature vectors leads to bad, sometimes unacceptable response times.

- Complex interfaces: CBIR is very different from traditional text retrieval. CBIR interfaces tend to be complex and difficult to use. Additionally, average users are overtaxed by the requirement to select features and weights for a specific querying process.

Our work aims at reducing these problems. We developed a system with several simple, but robust features and use them in groups. These groups are called query models and will be discussed in Section 2. We further developed algorithms for the automatic generation of queries from search images and use iterative refinement to improve results. In order to improve the querying performance we developed an algorithm for the performance-optimized ordering of query features.

The remainder of this abstract is organized as follows: Section 2 describes the concepts of our approach to CBIR. Section 3 is dedicated to the implemented algorithms. Finally, in Section 4 we describe the results achieved by the various methods.

2. Our approach to CBIR

The basic idea of our approach is to use several simple features in combination instead of just a few, but more complex ones (e.g., color histogram, etc.) [3]. The features selected for a specific query are grouped into query models. A query model [1] consists of a set of layers. Each layer identifies a feature, its distance function, weight and threshold value. The threshold describes the maximum distance between an image and the search image. During our work we found that controlling the result set by thresholds instead of a number identifying the size of the result set increases the quality of results significantly ([1]).

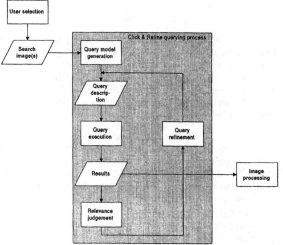

Figure 1. Click & Refine model.

Features utilized in a query model are dynamically chosen and usually cover only a subset of the features available. The query process is based on query models and follows our click & refine model (see Figure 1). In this model the user has to choose one or more search images to initiate a query. From the information in the search image(s) and expert knowledge the system derives a first query model and retrieves a first result. Then, in an iterative refinement process the result can be improved by relevance feedback provided by the user. The click & refine model has two major advantages: First, employing iterative refinement helps reducing the semantic gap. Second, the interface for our system becomes much easier than in traditional CBIR systems. All the user has to do is selecting examples for her/his query and rating results by her/his relevance judgement.

3. Implementation

We implemented our models in a CBIR system for a specific application domain, the retrieval of coats of arms. We implemented altogether 19 features, including a color histogram, symmetry features, etc. (see [1], [3], [4]). All distance functions (including Euclidean distance, city block distance, etc.) are standardized on the interval [0, 1]. For these features four algorithms were implemented to overcome the disadvantages of the computer centered approach:

1. A *weighting algorithm* for the automatic derivation of weights for all features in a query model [4]—For this purpose we clustered the global feature vectors (all feature vectors merged) of images in the test database. The weight of a feature for a specific search image is defined as the contribution of this feature to build the cluster of the search image.

2. An *ordering algorithm* for the performance-optimized ordering of features [5]—The ordering algorithm maintains a prognosis database and sorts query models before their execution according to their predicted number of returned images and the performance of the distance functions. This is a tricky task but allows an enormous increase of performance.

3. Two *generation algorithms* for the automatic generation of query models out of a search image or out of a group of search images and expert knowledge [2] to make the application of the click & refine model possible. The task of these two algorithms is to select features and suitable thresholds for one or more query models. Weighting and ordering is done by the algorithms above.

    The algorithm for the generation of a query model from one search image offers three methods for feature selection and three for threshold definition, which can be arbitrarily combined. Features may be selected by weight (importance), by properties or by a combination. Thresholds can be derived from the weight of a feature, the probable number of returned images or any linear combination of both methods [2].

    The second algorithm for the generation of query models (from a group of search images) performs an even more difficult task. By selecting a group of images the user may define similarity subjectively and asks to retrieve all images that are similar to this search group. Our algorithm solves this task by clustering the presented group of images and calculating a query model for each cluster of search images. If a cluster consists of only one image the algorithm described above is applied. Otherwise, the centroid of the cluster is utilized as the search image and the feature and thresholds are derived from mean and variance of the distances between every element of the cluster and all other elements [2].

These algorithms are implemented in our test environment as C-libraries. The CBIR system is based on IBM's QBIC (version 2; [6]). The features are implemented as QBIC feature classes. The QBIC query engine was replaced by our own query engine, which can handle query models and supports the click & refine model.

The whole system is installed on a Linux-PC [3]. The test environment consists of 888 images of coats of arms.

4. Results

We tested all components of our system except the iterative refinement process. The components of the generation algorithms were evaluated by recall and precision and the ordering algorithm was tested by its performance. The best algorithm for query model derivation from one image has a precision of 68% and a recall of 94%. A human expert in our tests could increase this result to a precision of 91% with a recall of at least 83%. The algorithm for query generation from a group of search images achieves a recall of about 80% with a precision of at least 60%. During the tests we learned that results do not improve with the number of search images but depend rather on the search images chosen [2]. We conclude that the problem of generating queries out of groups of images is difficult to solve, even for coats of arms. However, we think that our algorithm provides a good entry point into an iterative retrieval process.

After these tests we investigated how the quality of our algorithms changes when a certain percentage (n%) of new images is added to the test database. We found out that our algorithms do not depend too much on which images were used to calculate the image clusters and the algorithm parameters.

The weighting algorithm was tested on its own. The testing process and the results cannot be displayed here due to lack of space. The derived weights lead to an ordering of the result set that was at least judged suitable in more than 80% of the cases [4]. The ordering algorithm was tested with more than 1 000 generated query models. We found that our ordering algorithm reduces the average response time in our CBIR system from 190.7 ms by 66% to 64.6 ms [5].

5. ACKNOWLEDGMENTS

I would like to thank my supervisor Prof. Dr. Christian Breiteneder (Vienna University of Technology, Austria) for his conscientious and patient guidance.

6. References

[1] Breiteneder, C., and Eidenberger, H., A Retrieval System for Coats of Arms, *Proc. of ISIMADE'99*, 1999.

[2] Breiteneder, C., and Eidenberger, H., Automatic Query Generation for Content-based Image Retrieval, *Proc. of IEEE Multimedia Conference*, 2000.

[3] Breiteneder, C., and Eidenberger, H., Content-based Image Retrieval of Coats of Arms, *Proc. of the 1999 International Workshop on Multimedia Signal Processing*, Helsingör, 1999.

[4] Breiteneder, C., Merkl, D., and Eidenberger, H., Merging Image Features by Self-organizing Maps in Content-based Image Retrieval, *Proc. of European Conference on Electronic Imaging and the Visual Arts*, Berlin, 1999.

[5] Breiteneder, C., and Eidenberger, H., Performance-optimized feature ordering for Content-based Image Retrieval, *X European Signal Processing Conference*, Tampere, 2000.

[6] Flickner, M., and et al., Query by Image and Video Content: The QBIC System, *IEEE Computer*, 1995.

Multimedia Presentation Database System

Binjia Jiao
National University of Singapore
Department of Computer Science
Email: jiaobinj@comp.nus.edu.sg

1 Abstract

Multimedia presentations are increasingly being used in most spheres of life. Viewing these multimedia presentation as databases help in querying as well as re-using parts of existing presentations to create new ones. This dissertation proposes an object-oriented model for managing multimedia presentations as (temporal) databases based on the web. And the dissertation also discusses the representation of the proposed object-oriented model in Extensible Markup Language (XML). This representation opens up the possibility of employing standard XML products to commit multimedia presentation application over Internet, using the object-oriented model. Most major features such as run-time query arousing, unknown-duration objects control and interdatabase links are captured by the XML representation in the dissertation.

1.1 Keywords

Multimedia Presentation, Authoring, Querying, XML

2 Introduction

With multimedia presentation extensively being used, querying and authoring systems for presentations are strongly needed. And if viewing the presentations as databases will solve the needs better. However, there are few works conducted to explore presentation databases on the web systematically. This dissertation proposes an object-oriented model to view multimedia presentation as temporal databases. This data model has a class hierarchy that captures the temporal relationships governing multimedia data presentations. For this purpose, temporal relationships in a presentation are modelled as a temporal interval tree [1].

Both algebraic operations (such as Insert, Delete, Join, Project,etc) and user interface operations (such as Fast Forward/Rewind, Skip,Link to other presentation databases) have been developed for this data model. In order to carry out multimedia presentation on the web, a web-base structure is introduced into the system. Web-base means considering the web as a database, and users can query their preferable objects using spatial and temporal query operators(such as Above,After,Start,etc). The web-base in the dissertation is an object-based relational database of meta data. As we know, Extensible Markup Language (XML) is emerging as a promising technology for standardizing efforts [2]. Querying and re-using of multimedia presentation will be more effective since

- Presentation resources and information on worldwide web can be represented by standard markup language.

- The object-oriented model can be represented in XML, and the features of the model can be captured by its XML representation. For instance, querying procedures are recorded in XML representation, and invoked only when necessary. Another example is that the XML representation can manage duration-unknown objects as well.

- By XPointers and XLink provided in XML, Link operation can be fully realised in XML representation, thus facilitates the inter-database switching mechanism.

3 Related Work

An object-oriented model for multimedia information based on Petri nets approach for synchronization has been described in [3]. However, no database operations are described for authoring purposes. Another object-oriented multimedia database model for news-on-demand applications is presented in [7]. Another model that is compliant with SGML is described in [8]. Constraints-based techniques were used in [4] for multimedia authoring. Temporal relationships in presentations were modelled as constraints. Nested Context Model in [9] introduces a class hierarchy based on contexts,version etc.

Database aspects of multimedia presentations were first explored in [10, 6]. Here, a multimedia presentation is modelled as a graph where a node in the graph represents a media object and the edges in the graph represent temporal constraints specifying the order in which objects must be shown. Ozsoyoglu, Lee et al describe a graphical query calculus and a graphical query language for this graph based multimedia presentation model. [6] also presents an approach for assembling or authoring a presentation. However, this approach does not consider dynamic interactions during a presentation. Interactive nature of multimedia presentations are considered in [5].

My work is different from other database approaches in the sense that the underlying data model is different, those works are more suitable for querying purposes rather than authoring. This dissertation, with the object-oriented data model built on the interval tree hierarchy of multimedia presentations on the web, authoring and querying are both elegantly handled.

4 Implementation Experiences and Future Work

We have used JDK1.2 on Solaris system to realize the proposed object-oriented model and to implement the database, user interface,and link operations. JMF2.0 is employed to enable the control operations on media data. Java Project X is used to process the XML representation of the object-oriented model. Visualised creation of a multimedia presentation and presentation browser are shown in Figure 1 and Figure 2 respectively.

In the future, shared access to presentation databases as well as support for multicasting delivery of multimedia presentation will be incoporated into the work.

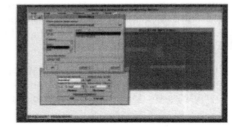

Figure 1: **Visualised Creation of A Multimedia Presentation**

References

[1] Hanan Samet, 'The Design and Analysis of Spatial Data Structures' , Addison-Wesley Publishing Company, INC. 1989.

[2] W3C Recommendation, Extensible Markup Language

Figure 2: **Delivery of A Multimedia Presentation**

XML 1.0, http://www.w3.org/TR/1998/REC-xml-19980210,February 1998.

[3] Mitsutoshi Iino, Young Francis Day, and Arif Ghafoor "An Object-Oriented Model for Spatio-Temporal Synchronization of Multimedia Information", Proc. of IEEE Int. Conf. on Multimedia Computing and Systems, May 1994, Boston, MA

[4] K.S. Candan, B. Prabhakaran and V.S. Subrahmanian -'CHIMP : A Framework for Supporting Multimedia Document Authoring and Presentation', Proceedings of ACM Multimedia '96 Conference, Boston, November 1996.

[5] Sibel Adali, Maria-Luisa Sapino and V.S. Subrahmanian "A Multimedia Presentation Algebra", Proc. of the Sigmod'99 Conference on Management of Data, 1999.

[6] G. Ozsoyoglu, V. Hakkoymaz, and J.D. Kraft, "Automating the Assembly of Presentations from Multimedia Database", Twelfth Int. Conf. On Data Engineering, pp. 593-601, New Orleans, February 1996.

[7] M.T. Ozsu, D. Szafron, G. El-Medani, and C. Vittal, "An Object-oriented Multimedia Database System for News-on-demand Application", ACM/Springer-Verlag Multimedia Systems, Vol.3, No.5/6,1995,pp.182-203.

[8] M.T. Ozsu, P. Iglinski, D. Szafron, S. El-Medani, M. Junghanns. "An Object-Oriented SGML/HYTIME Compliant Multimedia Database Management System", ACM Multimedia '97, Seattle, WA, November 1997, pages 239-249.

[9] L.F.G. Soares, M.A. Casanova, and N.L.R. Rodriguez, "Nested Composite Nodes and Version Control in an Open Hypermedia System", Intl. Journal on Information Systems, Sep 1995, pp. 501-519.

[10] T. Lee, L. Sheng, T. Bozkaya, N.H. Balkir, Z. M. Ozsoyoglu, and G. Ozsoyoglu, "Quering Multimedia Presentation Based on Content", IEEE Transactions on Knowledge and Data Engineering, Vol. 11, No. 3, June 1999.

Rich Interaction in Networked Virtual Environments

Tony Manninen
Department of Information Processing Science, University of Oulu
P.O. Box 3000
90014 Oulun Yliopisto, Finland
Tel. +358-8-5531899
tony.manninen@oulu.fi

Keywords

Communication, behaviour, actions, virtual worlds.

1. INTRODUCTION

The aim of this research is to provide a definition, taxonomy and hierarchical model of interaction in the context of Networked Virtual Environments (Net-VE).[i] This author believes that the theories and use of virtual environments would be expanded and enhanced if researchers and practitioners were to target their focus towards interactions occurring inside the computerised environments.

According to NRC [1] the meaning of word interactivity is not yet fully explored, thus, suggesting further and deeper studies of multidisciplinary approach. Furthermore, the report states that research should also concentrate on understanding interaction in terms of how it is defined and perceived, what is expected and needed, and what are the analogues, for example, in theatre, storytelling, improvisation, and the entertainment industry.

The interaction, interactivity, and interactive applications have been widely studied by many disciplines. Still, it seems that the whole area is not yet covered. Or, if it is covered, it is not explored in the sense of Net-VE theories and applications. Researchers representing various sciences have worked within their own domains, thus leaving a large gap in between technology and human behaviour. The purpose of this work is to suggest a new research approach that would contribute in bridging this gap. The emphasis is on combining the expertise and targeting the focus of various areas, such as the entertainment industry, cognitive and behavioural sciences, information processing sciences, and technology.

1.1 Interaction

The definition of interaction differs according to research domain. Behavioural and educational sciences use the word interaction quite differently than engineering and information processing sciences. The definition of interaction in the context of this research can be considered to follow the lines of natural interaction occurring in real life environments.

The main focus of this interaction study is *inside* the virtual environment, which means that most of the issues are related to content matters not necessarily tied to any input/output device or interaction technique.

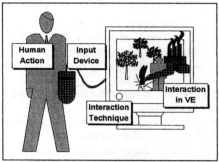

Figure 1. Various components of human-computer interaction.

Figure 1 illustrates the components of human-computer interaction. The interaction sequence starts from human action (in user-launched activities), which is taken by means of input device (e.g., the mouse). Interaction techniques are used to map the user input from the device to the computer application. Finally, there is the executed interaction that occurs within the virtual environment. This task can, for example, be acted out by the avatar of the user.

1.2 Networked Virtual Environments

Net-VEs raise challenging research questions concerning how users interact with objects, applications, and other users. Virtual Environments (VEs) provide another means of simulating real world places and activities. A VE is computer-generated simulated space with which an individual interacts [4]. Further definition and expansion of the term is provided by Singhal and Zyda (1999): Networked Virtual Environment is a software system in which multiple users interact with each other in real-time, even though those users may be located around the world. According to Singhal and Zyda (1999), a Net-VE is distinguished by the following five common features:

1. A shared sense of space (illusion of being located in the same place)
2. A shared sense of presence (avatars of participants)
3. A shared sense of time (real-time interaction possible)
4. A way to communicate (various interaction methods)
5. A way to share (dynamic environment that can be interacted with)

Wann et. al. (1996) propose that virtual environments are a subset of computer simulation and may include the use of multimedia technology. Although this taxonomy is relatively limited for the purposes of this research, it will ground the area of interest from one corner. The other important aspects, or sub-fields, include the ones required to fulfil the aforementioned five common features of Net-VE.

2. MOTIVATION

Higher level interaction (e.g., cognitive, motivational, tacit) is difficult to model & pre-program in computer-mediated communication applications due to the complexity, quantity, and fuzziness of the matter. Partially because of this, the natural ways of interacting are still missing in Net-VEs, thus, resulting in cumbersome and difficult to use VE's and training applications.

Traditional team training usually requires more 'natural' ways to interact with other users and with the environment (physical and situational interaction). One interesting question in relation to this is that whether it is possible to achieve more natural interaction by creating rich interaction support for the lower levels of interaction? In order to find answer to this question, the basic concepts of interaction have to be analysed.

Benefits of the research are as follows:
- More effective applications by using rich interaction (teamwork, training, communication)
- Much-needed tacit knowledge and messages can be conveyed interpersonally
- Rich interaction on lower levels enables more natural forms of interacting
- Terminal independent use of rich interaction (adaptive, autonomous, AI-guided actions)
- General platform for communication and interaction centric tasks (meetings, team training, business, games and entertainment)

Significance of the research relates to:
- Global organisations and virtual enterprises (geographically dispersed teams)
- VR increasingly important area and more time will be spent in various VR environments (virtual communities, entertainment, 3rd sector work)
- Impact on areas such as distance training, virtual enterprises, simulations, entertainment
- Generic tool for numerous human-centred applications
- Generalisation to low-end terminals and less advanced applications by using hierarchical interaction model and autonomous control

3. RESEARCH OBJECTIVES

The underlying approach selected for this research is to utilise entertainment industry solutions (e.g., games domain) in other application areas by using the platforms and existing software architectures in conceptualisation and prototyping work. Based on this approach, the theoretical part of the work concentrates on networked multi-player games. The focus of this research is on the interaction occurring inside and within the Net-VEs.

The *research problems* to be answered are as follows:
- What is the definition of interaction in the context of Net-VEs and what are the major differences to other schools? What is the taxonomy of interaction (what components and categories can be explicitly presented)?

- Is the support of lower level interaction a solution that allows behaviour-based higher level interactions?
- Is high-level interaction a necessary requirement in achieving adequate training and working in VE (will the support for rich interaction enable natural ways of interaction)?

The answers to the research questions will be searched through conceptual analysis and constructivistic approaches. The research methods are qualitative. The end-users will be interviewed using semi-structured interviews and game-playing sessions will be observed using ethnographical approach. The main objective of these interviews and observations is to formulate a tentative taxonomies and categories of interaction. Furthermore, heuristic evaluation will be applied to a limited set of games and corresponding interaction sets. The results will be used as a basis and design guideline for constructing a set of Net-VE applications that include various levels of interaction.

4. EXPECTED RESULTS

Interaction being one of the most important factors in computer mediated communication makes it possible to exploit the results of this work in various application domains. Furthermore, the expected results will serve both practitioners and researchers. The main contribution for practitioners include:
- Interaction model to utilise in designing for interaction
- Practical solutions for various applications and business areas
- Rich interaction enables computer-supported variations of the traditional activities (training, treatment, entertainment, work, etc.)

The main results for researchers are as follows:
- Deeper understanding of the concepts (interaction, behaviour, needs and requirements)
- Environment/application to experiment with (virtual environment)
- Numerous research problems based on this work

5. REFERENCES

[1] NRC, U. S. N. R. C. (1997). More Than Screen Deep - Toward Every-Citizen Interfaces to the Nation's Information Infrastructure, National Academy Press, Washington, DC.

[2] Singhal, S., and Zyda, M. (1999). Networked Virtual Environments: Design and Implementation, ACM Press.

[3] Wann, J., and Mon-Williams, M. (1996). "What does virtual reality NEED?: human factors issues in the design of three-dimensional computer environments." International Journal of Human-Computer Studies, 44, 829-847.

[4] Witmer, B. G., Bailey, J. H., and Knerr, B. W. (1996). "Virtual spaces and real world places: transfer of route knowledge." International Journal of Human-Computer Studies, 45, 413-428.

---

[i] Unabridged version of the paper with full references available at http://www.tol.oulu.fi/~tmannine/ACM_interaction.pdf

Novel Components for supporting Adaptivity in Education Systems – Model-based Integration Approach

Owen Conlan
Trinity College, Dublin,
Ireland.
+35316081335

Supervisor: Vincent P. Wade

Owen.Conlan@cs.tcd.ie

ABSTRACT

The goal of this research is to provide an adaptive learning engine driven by a model based integration approach. The Adaptive Engine should produce a cohesive course adapted to the users individual preferences.

Keywords

Education, adaptivity, hypermedia, model integration, learner, content, narrative.

1. INTRODUCTION

Adaptive Hypermedia Systems (AHS) can be regarded as the integration of intelligent tutoring systems and hypermedia systems. A Hypermedia System is a collection of linked nodes (hyperdocuments), that have links through which the student can traverse to other nodes [2], [3]. Intelligent Tutoring Systems (ITS) incorporate artificial intelligence techniques so that the instruction is adaptable to the learners needs and styles [1]. The main criticism in the past has been that ITSs are based on the premise that for learning to occur, it is sufficient to embed an experts knowledge in the structure of the content and apply an appropriate instructional design model.

Highly structured hypermedia systems do not support the different learning styles and learning rates of students. AHSs bridge the gap between the computer driven tutoring systems and student driven educational environments. An AHS may infer student objectives and help the student to discover the scope of information available or delineate a relevant path to get to the information required [4]. There is considerable evidence that different people learn in different ways, and at different rates [6]. Good educational material should take a particular students background into account so that the instruction can be tailored to their specific capabilities and past history. However, it should not confine them to a restrictive road-map through the content.

For an adaptive hypermedia system to adapt to these differences it must use several information sources such as the learner model and the content model to influence the educational experience. However, AHS tend to have very specific proprietary learner and content models built into them. Frequently these developments have been separate to emergent educational WWW models and standards such as IEEE Learning Object Model and IMS specifications. Such standards bodies are defining frameworks for

various aspects of "Open" education systems with which AHS need to integrate, e.g. learner model, content model, Content API, Question and Test Interoperability etc.

This paper suggests a model-based integration framework for the development of AHS. An important aspect of this is that the AHS framework allows the intelligent integration of different (some external) models, e.g. based on IEEE standards. The paper also outlines adaptive hypermedia developments and techniques as well as emergent educational models and standards. This paper proposes an architecture to support the generic integration of diverse learner and content models to produce coherent, focused and effective adaptive hypermedia.

2. ADAPTIVE HYPERMEDIA IN EDUCATION

Much of the focus in adaptive hypermedia for educational courseware has attempted to alleviate the difficulties of content comprehension (cognitive overload) and orientation (so-called 'lost in hyperspace'). Adaptive presentation techniques which effect changes to both the selection of different media depending on a users preferences and adaptation of the content based on an individual's user model are beginning to show success.

To achieve the maximum effectiveness from the use of non-adaptive Hypermedia in an educational context there are some features of learners that are particularly significant. These include preknowledge, cognitive style, maturity, general ability, confidence and motivation. These features influence the ability of students to accept effectively the additional mental load caused by the need to monitor and self-evaluate as well as learn [7].

Although increasing learner control is thought to increase the learner's motivation and engagement, results in performance using adaptively controlled environments have been superior to systems within which the user is left to their own devices [7]. Studies have shown that users of educational Adaptive Hypermedia systems are faster, more goal-orientated and take fewer steps to complete the course.

3. ADAPTIVE TECHNIQUES

There are several adaptive techniques that may be usefully employed in an educational environment. Adaptive Navigation attempts to guide the student through the system by customising the link structure or format according to a user model. Structural Adaptivity attempts to give the student a spatial representation of the Hyperspace environment. Historical Adaptation may provide history trails, footprints which are made by the system, landmarks, which are made by the student and progression cues.

Adaptive Presentation is the primary adaptive technique to be employed as part of this research. Adaptive Presentation is the customisation of course content to match learning characteristics specified by the user model. This form of adaptivity may be implemented by fragmenting the constituent content components into discrete paragraphs. These components or pagelets constitute a discrete unit of information about a concept. The pagelet is displayed if the user model conforms to required conditions for the display of that pagelet.

4. MODEL-BASED INTEGRATION

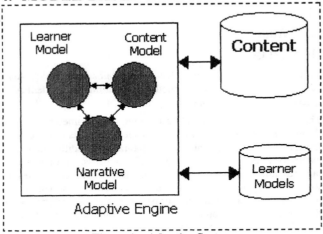

Figure 1 – Adaptive System

The approach to implementing an adaptive education system undertaken as part of this research is to provide a generic architecture for integrating the learner model (which describes the pertinent learner characteristics), content model (which describes the pedagogical qualities of the content) and the narrative model (which describes a mechanism for combining the content to produce a coherent educational courseware component).

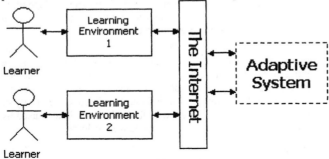

Figure 2 – Learners the Adaptive System

Figure 1 shows the different models interacting in the Adaptive Engine to produce coherent, personalised courseware for the learner. Figure 2 (below) shows that this content may be displayed to the learners using different learning environments (LE). To achieve a high level of adaptivity the models require a high level of detail. As such any models which are used as the basis for the Learner or Content models will need to be augmented to support the level of adaptivity hoped to be achieved.

4.1 Adding to the Models

The principle metadata which needs to be added to all the Content, Learner and Narrative models are more focused pedagogical elements. These should be pertinent to how the Adaptive Engine can combine the models to provide effective and coherent course material to the learner. Elements containing information about the learners preferences, e.g. some learners like to learn by example, should be reflected in all the models, i.e. if the Learner Model specifies that the learner likes examples then the Narrative Model should attempt to deliver content whose metadata says it is an example. The models contain the metadata and rules for the decisions made by the system, but it is the responsibility of the Adaptive Engine to integrate the knowledge within the models to produce the content displayed to the learner.

4.2 Adaptive Engine

The adaptive engine provides the facilities for reconciling the Content, Learner and Narrative models to produce individualised content. It is important that this be achieved in a fashion which is independent of the content or the specific properties of the learner. This generic interpretation of how the Adaptive Engine interprets the models is central to its ability to integrate into different Learning Environments. XML will be the key technology used to describe the models. It is the association and reconciliation of different XML elements in the models that is the responsibility of the Adaptive Engine. How the Adaptive Engine achieves this reconciliation between the models is the core element of the research. A prototype of the adaptive system is currently being developed based on enhanced educational metadata standards. The system will be trailed later this year.

5. ACKNOWLEDGMENTS

This research is partially funded by the European Commission under the auspices of the EASEL (Educator Access to Services in the Electronic Landscape) [5] project.

6. REFERENCES

[1] Boyd, G., "A Theory of Distance Education for the Cyperspace Era" in Theoretical Principles of Distance Learning, edited by Keegan, D., 1993.

[2] Brusilovsky, P., "Methods and Techniques of Adaptive Hypermedia" in User Modeling and User Adapted Interaction, 1996, v6, n2-3.

[3] de Bra, P., "Definition of hypertext and hypermedia", 1998.

[4] de La Passardiere, B., Dufresne, A., "Adaptive Navigational Tools for Educational Hypermedia" in Computer Assisted Learning, I. Tomek (Ed.), 1992.

[5] EASEL, Educator Access to Services in the Electronic Landscape, IST Project 10051.

[6] Patterson, J., "Learning and Computers: A Paradigm Shift for Education" in Scottish Council of Educational Technology, 1994.

[7] Specht, M., "Empirical Evaluation of Adaptive Annotation in Hypermedia" in Proceedings of Edmedia, 1998.

AUTHOR INDEX

NOTES

NOTES

NOTES